"Mr. Blackbourn [has a] commendable passion for evenhandedness. . . . The research is magnificent, with 80 pages of endnotes. . . . [*Germany in the World*] is superbly written, and even Germany buffs will find a surfeit of riches." —Josef Joffe, *Wall Street Journal*

"During the Second World War and the decades that followed, historians of modern Germany focused on one question: how did Nazism . . . take hold in Germany but not elsewhere in Europe? They sought an answer by delving deep into German history, as far back as Martin Luther, or even to the tribes analysed in Tacitus' ethnography *Germania*. . . . David Blackbourn took the lead in dismantling this paradigm. . . . [This book] buries beyond doubt the idea that German history proceeded in isolation, treading a 'special path' culminating in the Third Reich and the Holocaust. In this sense *Germany in the World* is the final step in the process of re-evaluation that Blackbourn began in the 1980s." —Richard J. Evans, *London Review of Books*

"In this detailed and original study, David Blackbourn argues that Germany's influence stretches around the world and has done so since long before there was a unified German geopolitical entity." —*New European*

"David Blackbourn's impressive *Germany in the World*, with its admirable breadth of knowledge and clean prose style, expands his 1997 work *The Long Nineteenth Century*." —Iain Bamforth, *Literary Review*

"David Blackbourn, a preeminent historian of Europe, has always invited us to understand the variety of German experiences beyond Bismarck and Hitler. In this original, exuberant, and fantastically learned panorama spanning five centuries, he reveals how Germans venturing across the globe as adventurers, merchants, settlers, scientists, and soldiers reflected the nation whence they came and added to its energies at home. *Germany in the World* provides a stunning transnational perspective that dissolves the borders of German history." —Charles S. Maier

"Justly renowned for his skill at depicting the local, regional, and national quirks of German history, David Blackbourn's greatest strength as a scholar has always been his ability to put Germany in perspective. . . . Now he shows how the German path was always intertwined with those of other lands, both near and far. From the Welser conquest of Venezuela to the Esperanto rappers of Stuttgart, the reader will find a novel insight on nearly every page." —Niall Ferguson

"Ambitiou[s]. . . . [T]here's no getting around Germany's pivotal place in the world, and Blackbourn ably demonstrates how and why that position has been maintained, for better and worse. A compelling exploration of 'German history viewed through a global lens.'" —*Kirkus Reviews*

"Blackbourn's elegant writing and intriguing insights make for an insightful and stimulating take on German history." —*Publishers Weekly*

GERMANY IN THE WORLD

ALSO BY DAVID BLACKBOURN

Class, Religion and Local Politics in Wilhelmine Germany:
The Centre Party in Württemberg before 1914

The Peculiarities of German History: Bourgeois Society and
Politics in Nineteenth-Century Germany (with Geoff Eley)

Populists and Patricians: Essays in Modern German History

Marpingen: Apparitions of the Virgin
Mary in Bismarckian Germany

The Long Nineteenth Century: A History of Germany, 1780–1918

The Conquest of Nature:
Water, Landscape, and the Making
of Modern Germany

GERMANY
IN THE WORLD

A GLOBAL HISTORY
1500–2000

DAVID BLACKBOURN

LIVERIGHT PUBLISHING CORPORATION

A Division of W. W. Norton & Company

INDEPENDENT PUBLISHERS SINCE 1923

For Celia

For information about permission to reproduce selections from this book,
write to Permissions, Liveright Publishing Corporation, a division of
W. W. Norton & Company, Inc., 500 Fifth Avenue, New York, NY 10110

For information about special discounts for bulk purchases, please contact
W. W. Norton Special Sales at specialsales@wwnorton.com or 800-233-4830

Manufacturing by Lakeside Book Company
Book design by Barbara M. Bachman
Production manager: Anna Oler

ISBN 978-1-324-09512-5 pbk.

Liveright Publishing Corporation, 500 Fifth Avenue, New York, N.Y. 10110
www.wwnorton.com

W. W. Norton & Company Ltd., 15 Carlisle Street, London W1D 3BS

10 9 8 7 6 5 4 3 2 1

CONTENTS

—

PART FOUR

THE "GERMAN CENTURY" CONFOUNDED

LIST OF MAPS

—

INTRODUCTION

—

THE HEADLINES TELL US CONSTANTLY ABOUT GERMANY'S PLACE in the world: "Germany Admits 1 Million Syrian Refugees," "German Publisher Axel Springer to Buy Politico," "Turkish-German Director Wins Golden Globe Award," "Berlin Club Attracts International Youth," and—of course—"Germany Steps Up over Ukraine." After Donald J. Trump was elected president of the United States, German chancellor Angela Merkel was often referred to as "the leader of the free world." If we accept the idea, distasteful though it is, that nations are also brands, then the German brand has been flying high. According to the Anholt Ipsos Nation Brands Index, Germany was number one in 2021, for the seventh time.

But there is a darker side. Headlines tell that story, too. "Germany's China Problem" points our attention to the difficult terrain where commerce, geopolitics, and morality clash. So do headlines about the scandal that engulfed one of Germany's blue-chip companies ("U.S. Indicts Six as Volkswagen Agrees to $4.3 Billion Settlement"). Volkswagen, founded in the Third Reich, also has a compromised history. It is not alone. We regularly read stories about the Nazi past coming back to haunt the present. In 2019 we learned how "Germany's Second-Richest Clan Discovers Dark Nazi Past," referring to the Reimann family, whose billions come today from the sale of Krispy Kreme doughnuts, Jimmy Choo shoes, and Calvin Klein perfume. But it is only right to point out that the Reimanns, like Volkswagen before them, commissioned historians to examine what their predecessors did. That willingness is a recognizable, even defining feature of Germany today, one that has been held up by many as an example of how to come to terms with the past.

My book looks at Germany's past from a global perspective. Think of it as a new German history for a global age, a history that we very much need. It is novel because the multifarious connections between the German-speaking lands of Central Europe and a wider world are my central focus, not an add-on or an afterthought. This is a book about the movement of people, goods, and ideas over the last five hundred years. I show how Germans have been actors in a wider world, for better and worse, and explore the effects this had at home. I also look at the mirror image of this, the non-Germans who came into the German lands, to conquer, to work, or to study, and the cultural practices they brought with them. The pages that follow contain a colorful cast of characters: merchants and missionaries, musicians and mining engineers, students and scientists, explorers and soldiers, emigrants and exiles. There are some nonhuman characters, too, the plants and animals intentionally introduced into Germany from abroad, in botanical gardens and zoos, as well as the invasive species and epidemics that came as stowaways.

I first thought about writing a book like this early in the twenty-first century. Back then, the idea of stepping outside a national framework seemed more daring than it does today, when "global" is a cliché and "transnational" has become an academic buzzword, an adjective sprinkled into a grant application to lend it spice. Among the early advocates of a supranational history, the feeling of challenging the common sense of the time was powerful and the language correspondingly fierce. There was talk of "rescuing history from the nation."[1] Contemporary events have obviously helped to drive this turn away from more narrowly defined national histories. Globalization underlined the importance of cross-border movements, flows, exchanges, and networks—all the terms that have become familiar in our lives. To this we can add the present postcolonial reckoning with empire and race. Debates about the return of museum holdings like the Benin Bronzes, including the hundreds in the Berlin Ethnological Museum, have had their effect on how we think about European history; so has the fact that major European cities have large populations of color, often marginalized and alienated, who are there as a result of imperialism. That has redirected British, French, and Dutch history into promising new channels. And Germany? Its formal colonial empire was short-lived (1884–1918), but it lasted long enough to feature two genocidal African wars that some historians have linked to the Holocaust.[2] Colonies also had a place in the German imagination long before they existed in reality and long after they disappeared. The colonial dimension of German history deserves the attention it is now receiving and receives in my book.

When I first thought about writing the book I was responding, in part, to issues like these, for all history is contemporary history. But history also moves to its own rhythms. What really drew me was trying to think through what it would mean to write a history that did not take the nation for granted as the unquestioned framework. I have long been intrigued by the idea of "playing with scales."[3] Turn the magnification up on a place or an event, and you see things previously invisible. But turn your gaze in the other direction, to look at very large processes, and you also notice patterns previously invisible. These two alternatives to the national frame, the micro and the macro, are not mutually exclusive. "The worldwide does not abolish the local," said the French philosopher Henri Lefebvre.[4] The two often come together in this book, the historian's version of what businesspeople call "glocalization."

Let me give an example. I am interested in the fine-grained detail of how commodities moved across borders, because their movements are so eloquent. Think of the mercury that was mined in sixteenth-century Spain under the auspices of a German merchant house, shipped across the Atlantic on special boats, and carried on mule trains up mountains trails to the mines of Potosí, where it was used to separate silver from rock. The silver was then shipped back to Europe, where it lubricated local trade, or was sent on "Manila galleons" to the Philippines, thereby linking European, American, and Asian trade circuits. This book is filled with commodities— from pepper, spices, diamonds, pearls, coffee, sugar, tobacco, and so on through the "colonial goods" of the nineteenth century and the cornucopia of cars, washing machines, and the other advertisers' dream products of the twentieth. Traced from place of origin to point of consumption, they reveal a lot about status, power, gender, and much else, from science to fashion. The resistance to commodities also has a lot to say to us. Long before the Nazis' notorious policies of economic self-sufficiency, we encounter hostility to pepper and spices in the sixteenth century, coffee in the eighteenth century, and imported grain and meat in the nineteenth century. This book will tell you why.

People crossed borders, too. Five and a half million people left the German lands in the nineteenth century, creating a global diaspora. I have tried to reconstruct what it meant to experience this, to live in one of the "Little Germanys" in the United States, South Australia, or Rio Grande do Sul in Brazil. "Mass emigration" was the sum of thousands of separate decisions to leave. It was not random, but determined by economic cycles and shaped by chain migration, meaning that people from a particular place in Germany went to a particular place abroad and others followed. That is why many Germans in the English city of Liverpool came from Württemberg in southwest Germany, creating what must have been a spectacular fusion of two pungent dialects. As more people left, nationalists at home began to lament their "loss" to the fatherland and label them "Germans abroad" rather than "emigrants." Did they retain their "Germanness"? That depended—on where they came from, whether they settled in town or country, whether they belonged to a close-knit religious community, whether they were young or middle-aged, married or single. What emerged from the experience was often hard to pin down. To take an example from Germans who settled in Australia: what kind of language was "*seinen Foot downputten*"?

The answer is: a hybrid language. Hybridity is one of the most useful ways to think about the cultural contacts you will find in one form or another in every chapter of this book.[5] They extended across large areas of life: language, literature, music, dance, art, philosophical ideas, science and technology, pedagogy, architecture and design, and sport. Sometimes it is Germans absorbing the practices of others, sometimes the reverse. To label this give-and-take "influence" is too vague, but to call it "transfer" suggests the wholesale adoption of a style, an ideology, or an institution. That rarely captures what happened. Even when we are talking about something as seemingly straightforward as the German adoption of English sports, or of dances like the tango and the cakewalk that came from the Americas, local context made a difference to the reception. When it comes to more complex questions (for example: Was the German university a "model" for Americans?), we need a larger vocabulary. One historian has offered up a long list of terms to describe these exchanges. Here are a few: transfer, imitation, appropriation, translation, acculturation, and cross-fertilization.[6] In practice, the movement of ideas and practices was often the work of individuals: cultural brokers or go-betweens. For some (scholars, booksellers, translators, missionaries) it went with the job; for others (emigrants, merchants) it was usually more unconscious or inadvertent. Readers will quickly come to recognize many Germans of both kinds in this book, transnational men and women leading transnational lives.

Diplomats had a professional interest in taking stock of what was happening in other countries. Many also doubled as cultural brokers, especially in earlier centuries when diplomacy was a less specialized occupation. One of them was responsible for a quip that still holds its place in dictionaries of quotations. A diplomat was "a gentleman sent to lie abroad for the good of his country." That was Sir Henry Wotton, in 1604. His bon mot was written in the album of a German friend, for Wotton was a student in Germany before he became a diplomat. He provided his government with intelligence on events in the Holy Roman Empire; he was also a link between the scholarly and scientific worlds of Britain and the Continent, a go-between in "the republic of letters," as contemporaries called it.[7] In the following pages, readers will encounter many Germans who belonged to the republic of letters, before it was transformed in the nineteenth century, largely by Germans, into the university-based scholarly networks of our own time.

Readers will sometimes encounter diplomats going about their professional business. International relations have a place in the book, although not as its main focus. But war inevitably looms large. How could it not? Just as the German lands were a European crossroads for goods and ideas, so they occupied a key position geopolitically. "Germany is the battlefield on which the struggle for mastery in Europe is fought," said the polymath Gottfried Wilhelm Leibniz in 1670.[8] He was writing a generation after the Thirty Years War (1618–1648), which devastated parts of Germany, and just twenty years before the French king Louis XIV's War of the Grand Alliance ravaged the Rhineland in the 1690s. A century later the French Revolutionary and Napoleonic wars reshaped the German lands by destroying the Holy Roman Empire and removing hundreds of tiny principalities from the map. The unification of Germany that followed in the nineteenth century was then made possible by the success of Prussian armies in three wars fought within seven years.

The arrival of a German nation-state made this a crucial turning point. It was also a turning point in another way. For three and a half centuries, European wars had been fought on German soil. These wars in 1864–1871 were not, nor were the colonial wars and the two global conflicts of the twentieth century, at least not until the closing stages of World War Two. Something else changed, too. From the Spanish armies of the sixteenth century to Napoleon's Grand Army, Germans were enlisted to fight on behalf of others. That would no longer be the case. It was German military expertise that was now in demand, from Japan to Latin America. Carl von Clausewitz's famous book, *On War*, was published in 1832 but widely translated into other languages only in the late nineteenth century. This had its unhappy aspect, of course. The association between "German" and "militarism" became increasingly close, until the world wars of the twentieth century made the two adjectives inseparable. It took decades to lay that reputation to rest.

Let me turn to some questions. Is this global history viewed through a German lens? No, it is German history viewed through a global lens.[9] I hope people interested in global history will read it, but my book is an effort (already immodest enough) to rewrite German history. Does "global" include "European"? Here the answer is a resounding yes. While this book spends more time than conventional histories of Germany in the Americas, Africa, Asia, and Australasia, it devotes even more attention to Germany and the Germans within the Eurasian landmass. That reflects where the greatest movements of people, objects, and ideas occurred. Then, a question that I have often been asked (and asked myself): Were these *Germans*, rather than, say, Prussians, Bavarians, or Thuringians? It is not enough to say (although it is true) that English people in the Atlantic world, asked where they came from, might have said "Bristol," and Spanish people "Extremadura."[10] In the end, the existence or nonexistence of a nation-state did make a difference, which is one of the themes pursued in this book.

I want to suggest two further answers. One is pragmatic. The library shelves are filled with series devoted to "German" history. Many stretch far back into the past. Of the twenty-four volumes that make up the standard German history handbook ("Gebhardt"), fifteen are devoted to the years before a German nation-state was established in 1871. A work that promotes the virtues of a different, more global approach has to meet existing accounts on their own ground. There is little point in claiming that we should think about German history in a new way, but only after the age of Bismarck. Why not begin, then, with the Alemanni, or in the Middle Ages? That is where my second answer comes in. There are many good reasons to begin a German history in 1500. It was when people began to refer routinely to the Holy Roman Empire of the *German* Nation. It was when a common form of the language, Early New High German, emerged. Developed in the south and adopted by the Imperial and Saxon chanceries, it was quickly taken up by others. *Muttersprache*, mother-tongue, was one of the words that entered High German soon after. It was a time, not least, when humanists such as Conradus Celtis and Johannes Cochlaeus began to write about a place called "Germany" inhabited by people called "Germans."[11]

Let me turn to the biggest question readers are likely to have: What is *new*, what *difference* does it make, when we view German history through a global lens? The answer to that also falls into two parts. There are important things that become visible only through that lens; then there are familiar landmarks of German history that appear in a different light. One example of the things that become newly visible has already been mentioned: the tradition, extending over centuries, of Germans who fought on behalf of others—Portuguese, Spanish, Dutch, and British. But that is just one part of a larger pattern, I suggest. The early chapters of the book challenge the persistent idea that landlocked Germany was wrapped up in its own affairs while others transformed relations between Europe and the non-European world. The "non-seafaring, German-speaking world" was, we are told, hardly touched by the great European voyages.[12] The philosopher Peter Sloterdijk puts it bluntly: there is "a world history of Spain, a world history of England, a world history of France, a world history of Portugal, and perhaps also a world history of the Netherlands. As far as the world history of the Germans is concerned, the historian's courtesy means that it is better passed over in silence for now."[13] This is simply not true. Germans were ubiquitous in the expanding worlds of the Portuguese, Spanish, Dutch, French, and British, as soldiers, ships' gunners, merchants, surgeons, scientific travelers, missionaries, and settlers. They not only helped to make those empires what they were (for better or worse), they also connected "landlocked" Central Europe to those worlds in numerous ways that are explored in the following pages. I argue, for example, that we need to recognize the existence of a "German Atlantic" in the three centuries after 1500, the years on which Atlantic historians focus their attention. Germans were there in numbers and helped to shape the Atlantic world. That means, on the negative side of the historical ledger, that we need to acknowledge the German role in the slave trade.

Why did this remain largely invisible for so long? One reason is that Germans were often chameleons, or shape-shifters, as they passed through or settled in the empires of others. More than other nationalities, they merged into the local background. Even their names changed: an Ehinger became an Eynguer or an Alfinger in New Spain. Sometimes the new name was a literal translation: Zweig (branch) turned into LaBranche, Blümel (flowers) into Flores. Linguists call this a calque. But the fact that Germans often became invisible points to something important. They disappeared into the empires of others because there was no German empire. That was why they were conquistadores for Spain and Hessian auxiliaries for the British, why they conducted trade with Asia through Antwerp and Lisbon, and became colonists in French Guiana, Dutch Surinam, and British North America. The absence of a flag mattered; state power made a difference.

All this had long-term implications for how Germans saw themselves. On the one hand, it fed a belief that they were above the grubby business of conquest and exploitation, that they inhabited a purer realm. And it is true that German scientific travelers often displayed an exceptional degree of sympathy for Indigenous peoples and were critical of how they were treated in the British, Spanish, and Russian empires. Concern about the threats to other species, including the specter of extinction, was another by-product of this critical distance. A belief that German sensibilities were finer, less crude, was also widespread in the golden age of German culture in the decades on either side of 1800. When Johann Gottfried Herder wrote the preface to a German translation of the Sanskrit work *Sakuntala*, he found space for an anticolonial critique. It was, suggested Herder, lamentable that this "cultural and spiritual treasure of the most peace-loving nations of our earth" had been entrusted to the English, "the most commerce-driven nation of the globe."[14] Self-righteousness like this fed a striking, long-term German identification with colonial subject peoples. This assumed toxic form in the twentieth century, when many Germans after World War One and the Treaty of Versailles liked to see themselves as another colonial victim of the French and Anglo-Saxons. The self-pitying resentment was fully exploited by the National Socialists. Here we have a cluster of themes that span the centuries.

The persistence of political emigration is another pattern that becomes visible when we look at German history through a longer, global lens. Over the centuries, many people left the German lands because they feared for their lives, their liberty, or their livelihoods. The hundreds of thousands who became émigrés from Hitler's Germany are the best known. Most were Jews, joined by non-Jews who left Germany because they were Communists, Social Democrats, or writers, artists, and others whose work was rejected. The émigrés spread themselves around the globe, from Allahabad to Shanghai, Moscow to Istanbul, Sydney to Southern California. Were they not also a part of German history, whether or not they eventually returned? Most people would probably say yes, if they considered the question. This book asks readers to consider it. But we could ask the same question of earlier émigrés, like two who made their names abroad after fleeing the violence of the Thirty Years War. Calvinist Samuel Hartlib ("the Great Intelligencer of Europe") went to London, Catholic priest Athanasius Kircher ("the last man who knew everything") to Rome. Both were remarkable figures who sat at the center of important information networks in Europe and beyond. Like the talented émigrés of the 1930s ("Hitler's gift"), they were an intellectual boon to others from the war-torn German lands. Two waves of nineteenth-century political émigrés fall into the same category. One occurred after passage of the repressive Karlsbad Decrees in 1819, which sent radicals into exile in Switzerland, France, Britain, and the United States; the other commenced after the revolution of 1848, when disappointed radicals fled once again, most to the same places, but some farther afield, to countries such as Australia where the '48ers had an outsized impact on the host society. This is one of the ways my book invites readers to ask themselves: *Where* did modern German history take place?

Turning to the second part of my question about a global perspective: Do we see familiar landmarks in a different light, and if so, how? The Reformation offers a very good example. My focus here is not on the German nation and Martin Luther, or the Reformation in the cities, or the Reformation of the German princes and the process of state building. There are already many excellent accounts of these.[15] Readers of this book will encounter something different, the Reformation as an explosive movement out of Germany (and Switzerland), with a transformative impact on politics, society, and culture in Europe and then globally. It also set off waves of emigration, of which Samuel Hartlib and Athanasius Kircher were just a part, followed later by a wave of immigration by Huguenot refugees entering Germany from France. The Reformation was answered by the Catholic Counter Reformation. This took German Jesuits to China and Latin America and was reimported to Germany in the form of missions, new devotional practices, and the architectural landmarks of the baroque.

Those staples of modern German history, nationalism and unification, also look different in the following pages. German nationalism is often thought to be different from other nationalisms, less civic and more ethnic, rooted in blood and soil. From this perspective, the Nazis' racially based "people's community" seems like a natural end point. I suggest that we see something more complex, more discontinuous, and less self-absorbed when viewed through a wider lens. What did German nationalists want in the 1820s, '30s, and '40s? They wanted a German nation that would transcend the petty interests of local princes. That was the meaning of Hoffmann von Fallersleben's "Deutschland, Deutschland, über Alles" (1841): placing the nation above selfish interests, not placing the nation above other nations. Hoffmann was a progressive, deprived of his academic post and forced into exile. Most German nationalists of the period were liberals or progressives, who embraced national aspirations elsewhere (Latin America, Greece, Poland) as part of a common cause. Whether radical firebrands or sober liberals, German nationalists through the 1848 revolution took their political models from abroad, France and Switzerland for republicans, Britain and the United States for moderates. The defeat of the revolution was a watershed. German nationalism became notably harsher in the 1850s and '60s, as most historians today agree, although it was only in the late nineteenth century that nationalism in Germany (as elsewhere) acquired a still harsher, racially tinged edge to it, such that even the liberal nationalists who had come of age in the 1860s no longer recognized the language of the young pan-Germans.

German unification under Otto von Bismarck also looks different from a global perspective. It took place in the 1860s, a decisive decade of nation building or rebuilding worldwide, in Italy, Russia, Japan, Canada, Mexico, and, not least, in the United States, where the Civil War remade the nation, however imperfectly. It was a civil war in Germany between Prussia and Austria (and contemporaries called it that, a *Bruderkrieg*) that really decided the future of Germany in 1866. This, too, was a civil war between north and south, although in this case the north—Prussia—was the secessionist. German unification, in short, was part of a larger shift that reset the global order in the 1860s. The recast German nation remained internally divided. Efforts to overcome those divisions, insofar as they were attempted, faced one of the same obstacles they faced elsewhere: they were being attempted at exactly the same time that Germany was becoming part of a more interconnected, networked world. The subnational, the national, and the supra-national represented three moving parts that were moving at different speeds. The outcome was friction. The years around 1900 saw a "great acceleration" in trade, communications, new cultural movements, even the sense of time itself.[16] In many ways this era resembled the globalization of our own time. Then, as now, the nature and the pace of change met with strong resistance from those who felt victimized or left behind. Germany was in the thick of all this.

And so we come to the twentieth century, where one question more than any other is likely to be asked: Is there a global or transnational history of Nazi Germany that helps us to see the regime and its crimes differently? Yes. But it is important to be clear that no matter how many non-German models, influences, and parallels we can identify, and no matter how many non-German allies, collaborators, and fellow perpetrators we can point to, this was a genocidal *German* regime. To compare it with others is not to assert identity or equivalence; to trace commonalties and impulses from outside is not to relativize, let alone exculpate. National Socialism was, however, a creature of its time as well as a product of German history. Hitler admired nationalist "strong men" like Chiang Kai-shek and Atatürk; a life-size bust of Mussolini was prominently displayed in Nazi Party headquarters and a signed photo of Henry Ford hung in Hitler's study. National Socialism drew on a wide range of ideas: the antisemitic conspiracy theories of White Russian émigrés, eugenics from Britain and Scandinavia, American race laws. Above all, Nazism was part of a larger fascist movement, first imitating the Italian original, then replacing it as the international leader. This happened only in the course of the 1930s. When Hitler and Mussolini first met in 1934 in Venice, the Duce was still the dominant partner. The German Brownshirts took their place among the fascist Blackshirts, Greyshirts, Greenshirts and Blueshirts all across Europe—every color shirt but red, because the Reds were the enemy, everywhere. That was one of the things fascisms had in common. There were many others, in both style and substance. These were hypernationalist movements but, paradoxical as it may sound, it also makes sense to talk about fascism without borders.[17] Once again, though, it is important to emphasize that even where National Socialism borrowed or adapted (and little in its ideology or policies was truly original), the resulting compound was distinctive. The German variant was a uniquely radical and destructive form of fascism.

The most terrible symbol of that was the Holocaust. A large and impressive body of work, especially in the last thirty-five years, has done much to clarify the process of German decision making and to recover the voices of the victims. Research has also underscored how the genocide was a German-directed undertaking, but one in which large numbers of non-Germans participated. They did so as the leaders of allied or satellite states like Romania and Croatia, as members of paramilitary units and later German-controlled police forces in the Baltic, Ukraine, and elsewhere. Non-Germans killed Jews in large numbers. They identified Jews to the Germans and used their local knowledge in the hunting down of those who fled into the forests or marshes; they cleared ghettos and labor camps, loaded Jews onto trains from transit points across the Continent, and served as guards during round-ups and in camps. And, just as the complicity of

Germans extends far beyond the Nazi and SS leadership to many "ordinary Germans," so the complicity of non-Germans extends beyond local fascist paramilitaries and police forces to business owners, officials, insurance companies, and others who benefited when Jews were shipped to the death camps. The more we learn, the more the old tripartite division into perpetrators, victims, and bystanders breaks down, because so many of the bystanders were actively complicit in one way or another. But there were bystanders, including the Vatican, the International Committee of the Red Cross, Hollywood studios, and Allied decision makers, whose inaction warrants scrutiny as part of a global history of the Holocaust.

The final part of this book is called "The 'German Century' Confounded." Many observers in 1900 thought the twentieth century would be the German century because of the country's economic dynamism and reputation as an educational, scientific, and cultural powerhouse. Instead, it became the German century for the worst of reasons. Germany's shame became the world's civic lesson. But the larger significance of twentieth-century German history is not exhausted by the Third Reich and its legacy, central though they must be in any historical account. Other signature events of the German twentieth century have left their traces on the popular imagination: World War One battlefields, the hyperinflation of the early 1920s, the cultural and sexual modernism of the Weimar Republic, the post–World War Two era with its iconic images of "rubble women" amid the ruins and the Berlin Airlift, then the divided Germany of the Cold War, for which the Berlin Wall served as the ultimate symbol. All of these show how Germany was connected to the larger currents of global history. Other snapshot moments have also become part of how people with no special interest in Germany see the country. Depending on their age, some readers may remember John F. Kennedy's "*Ich bin ein Berliner*" speech in 1963 or Willy Brandt falling to his knees in 1970 at the memorial to the Warsaw ghetto; they will certainly remember global coverage of Angela Merkel's words in 2015, "We can do it," when she talked about the Federal Republic admitting Syrian refugees. But there are other emblems of Germany in the world—Oktoberfest, Volkswagen, the Berlin Philharmonic, and Kraftwerk—that are also part of its modern history.

German history in the twentieth century became even more global, more interconnected. The cast of characters is larger than it is in earlier chapters. We still encounter merchants, soldiers, scholars, and émigrés. But they are joined by other women and men who belong to the border-crossing world-in-motion of the twentieth century: aid workers, exchange students, tourists, cultural diplomats, au pairs, Olympic athletes, human rights campaigners, human traffickers, youth hostelers, antinuclear demonstrators, members of twin city delegations, urban terrorists, spies, touring orchestras, jazz bands, and rap artists, guest workers, and refugees. All testify to the fact that German history does not stop at Germany's borders. Some of them also remind us that the contacts and movements of people in an interconnected world are not always benign. Like the ideas and practices that crossed borders, they were not synonymous with cosmopolitanism or with nice-minded efforts by nice-minded people to break down barriers to mutual understanding.[18]

A last question: What kind of a history is this? As the previous paragraph suggests, I have cast my net wide. Politics, war and peace, economics, culture, gender, education, science, the environment, race, religion—all have a place. My aim has also been to strike a balance between the stories without which history has no life and the arguments without which it has no point. I have tried most of all to capture what the historian E. P. Thompson, in a wonderful phrase, called "the fluency of social life."[19] Let me add one last point about the scope of the book. I have tried to extend German history in one dimension (space) without narrowing it in another dimension (time). *Germany in the World* covers five centuries. I gave some reasons earlier why a starting point around 1500 makes sense from the perspective of German history. There are wider historical changes that justify the choice. That was when a new European state system came into being, when the new print culture made itself felt, when the "unification of the globe by disease" began, and when the Portuguese with their German gunners followed the Venetians and Genoese in reaching out to join an emerging world economy.[20] These were all good reasons to begin in 1500. I wrote a piece a few years ago called "Honey, I Shrunk German History!," lamenting the fact that three-quarters of the books, articles, and conference papers on German history are now concerned with the period since World War One.[21] No one is likely to feel that the twentieth century receives short measure in this book, but I hope readers will agree that a longer time frame brings new perspectives.

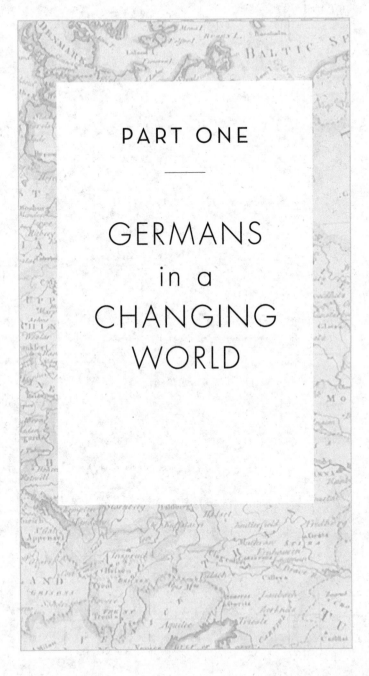

PART ONE

GERMANS in a CHANGING WORLD

CHAPTER I

NEW WORLDS

*Sailors, Conquistadores,
and Legends*

WHERE BETTER TO BEGIN THAN NUREMBERG? THE CITY HAD A population of 30,000 in 1500, making it one of the largest in the German lands and three times the size of Berlin. Nuremberg was at the center of many things. Politically powerful, it twice played host in the early 1520s to the Imperial Diet of the Holy Roman Empire. Nuremberg was home to some of Germany's wealthiest merchant houses and the place where east–west and north–south trade routes met. Its celebrated residents included the artist Albrecht Dürer and leading humanist scholars such as Johannes Cochlaeus. As a center of printing and publishing well supplied with wealthy patrons, it also gathered in the fruits of learning from far and wide. Conradus Celtis, another German humanist, said that its citizens were "like bees in the flowers looking everywhere for treasures and riches to bring back to their city."[1] No city better illustrates how the German-speaking lands formed a crossroads in Europe, a contact zone where peoples and cultures met.

Hieronymus Münzer was one of the Nuremberg citizens who went out into the world. A physician and humanist with a strong interest in cartography, Münzer settled in the city and helped to produce the famous *Nuremberg Chronicle* of 1493, to which he contributed the first printed map of Germany. Münzer set off in 1494 on a grand tour of the Iberian peninsula that lasted a year. He later wrote in great detail about everything he had seen: altarpieces and libraries, hot springs and vineyards. Münzer also noted the many Germans he met—merchants, craftsmen, printers, and artists. They came from all parts of the Holy Roman Empire, from Danzig and Stettin in the north to Kempten and Ulm in the south. He even met people from a village near his own birthplace in the small town of Feldkirch. Everywhere he went, there seemed to be Germans who could show him around.[2]

The Holy Roman Empire was a world in motion. Germans had taken part in the Crusades and in more recent times there were clashes with the Ottoman Turks on the eastern margins of the Empire, a contact zone that was sometimes a war zone. Ottoman forces besieged Vienna in 1529. Sporadic fighting on this frontier continued for the next 150 years. In the Late Middle Ages, Germans had migrated east in large numbers, fanning out in a great arc from the Baltic to the Lower Danube. Around 1500, Germans of every sort traveled across the borders of the Empire. There were members of peripatetic "dishonorable occupations" such as knife grinders, troupes of traveling musicians, players, and tumblers. Wandering journeymen were among the long-distance travelers. First recorded in the German lands after the Black Death in the fourteenth century, their practice soon became highly organized. Then there were soldiers, the swaggering German *Landsknechte,* sought across Europe for their prowess as fighters but feared because of their reputation as thieves, sexual predators, and spreaders of plague.[3]

Artists and the learned were inveterate travelers. Dürer spent two lengthy periods of his life in Italy. He also lived in the Low Countries during his apprentice years and again in 1520–21, in his late forties, spending time in Ghent, Bruges, Brussels, and Antwerp, where he "bought a red beret for my god-child for 18 stuiver" but "lost 12 stuiver at card play."[4] Conradus Celtis studied in Italy; he then traveled through Croatia and Hungary to Cracow, where he arrived at Easter 1489 and stayed a year. He went on a bison hunt, visited a salt mine, and explored the Carpathian Mountains, before returning to Nuremberg.[5] Virtually every German humanist spent time in Venice, Florence, Bologna, or Padua. Members of the religious elite and pious aristocrats also went to Italy, as pilgrims for whom all roads led to Rome. Others joined in the European-wide pilgrimage to the shrine of Santiago de Compostela in Spain. By the 1520s, however, advocates of Martin Luther's message were already zealously at work in Scandinavia, Britain, and eastern Europe.

Merchants had their own networks. The Hanseatic League owned compounds in Novgorod, Bergen, and Bruges, as well as the celebrated

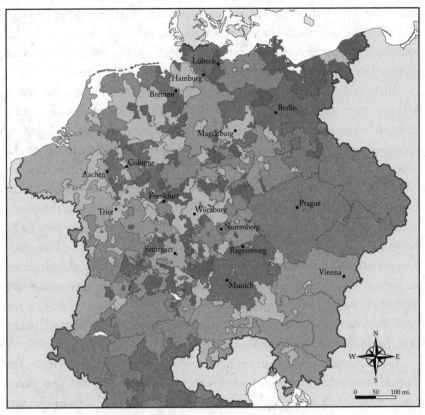

*The Holy Roman Empire in 1500, showing the numerous tiny
principalities that made it resemble, in the words of the writer
Simon Winder, "an explosion in a jigsaw factory."*

Steelyard on the north bank of the Thames, where London's Cannon Street
Station stands today. The best days of the Hansa lay behind it in 1500. The
closing of the Novgorod compound by Tsar Ivan III in 1494 was a sign
of the political pressures the organization faced, just as it faced economic
competition from the Merchant Adventurers, an English trading company,
and the Dutch. But much of the lost northern trade was captured by other
German merchants who exploited overland routes instead. The Fuggers
of Augsburg were the most famous of them, a firm that traded in every
product imaginable and bankrolled princes on the side. Its agents could be
seen all across Europe, carrying their soft, pale, heart-shaped leather bags.
One route took them over the Alps to Venice and Genoa. Agents from
the other great merchant houses of Augsburg and Nuremberg traveled the

same way. When they reached Venice, they made their way to the Fondaco dei Tedeschi near the Rialto, part warehouse, or "staple house," part residential quarters for German merchants. Back in Augsburg the Venetian connection was apparent in the traces of Italianate architecture.[6]

There is a watercolor painting of Augsburg's Jakob Fugger, known as Jakob Fugger the Rich, which shows the great man in 1516 giving instructions to his accountant. The setting is Fugger's luxurious "golden" writing chamber and file boxes in the background bear names that testify to the reach of his mercantile empire: Innsbruck, Venice, Rome, Milan, Cracow, "Anntorff" (Antwerp), Lisbon.[7] It is significant that Lisbon was one of the names, as it would not have been thirty years earlier. The Fuggers opened a warehouse and office there, a *Faktorei*, in 1503. A few years later they had a network of agents in Spain as well. Like the slow decline of the Hanseatic League and the growth of Antwerp in the sixteenth century, the increased activity of Upper German merchant houses in the Iberian peninsula was a sign of changing times. It pointed to the way that Germans seized on the new opportunities that opened up after the voyages of Christopher Columbus, Bartholomeu Dias, and Vasco da Gama.

German economic historians have written about the role played by the Fuggers and other merchant houses such as the Welsers in the new global trade routes, just as art historians have shown how motifs from the new worlds in the east and west found their way into Dürer's work—his woodcut of a rhinoceros, his charcoal drawing of an African's head.[8] Yet the wider German role in the European exploration, conquest, and exploitation of those worlds is only now beginning to receive the attention it deserves.[9] Most works of German history barely mention it. The idea persists that "landlocked" Germany was marginal to all this. What drives German history and provides the narrative momentum in standard accounts of the sixteenth century? The Reformation. While Spain and Portugal were carving up the world, German princes and German cities were—so it usually seems—engaged in the inward-looking struggles that led from Luther's dramatic appearance at the Diet of Worms in 1521 via the Imperial military crackdown against Protestantism in the 1540s to the compromise Peace of Augsburg in 1555.

Yet the religious disputes that shook the sixteenth-century Empire took place in a global setting. What was said and done in Germany was interwoven with events that were happening across the Indian Ocean and the Atlantic. Take the Diet of Worms, where Luther famously refused to recant his works and was condemned by the Emperor Charles V as a heretic. The same meeting issued a series of ordinances against mercantile monopolies and abuses, which was a response to the German trade in eastern spices, an issue that the Diet took up again when it met in 1522, just as news reached Germany of Ferdinand Magellan's circumnavigation of the world. Luther himself thundered against "foreign commerce, which brings goods from Calicut and India and like places, such as expensive silk and articles of gold and spices, which serve magnificence rather than a useful purpose, and which sucks our money from the land and the people." His ally Ulrich von Hutten praised an imagined German golden age of virtuous self-sufficiency supposedly being undermined by imports like "that damned pepper, ginger, cinnamon, saffron, cloves."[10]

Charles V, the emperor who condemned Luther, had been elected to the title just two years earlier, in 1519, helped by generous bribes to the electors with loans provided by the Fuggers and Welsers. He was king of Spain before he became Holy Roman Emperor in Germany. In fact, when the conquistador Hernán Cortés brought down Montezuma's Aztec empire, in the same year, 1519, he wrote to his monarch that Charles could now call himself the Emperor of New Spain as well as Germany: he was on the way to becoming "monarch of the world."[11] Charles adopted *"Plus ultra"* ("Farther beyond") as his personal motto, a nod to the Spanish acquisition of a New World empire, and it was he who organized Spain's transatlantic shipping into regular fleets that ran each year between Seville and Havana, Cartagena, and Veracruz.[12] Charles V's relative neglect of Germany was one reason Lutheranism grew at the expense of the Imperial cause after 1521. But it is no less true that until the abdication of Charles V in 1556, when the Spanish and Austrian parts of the Habsburg patrimony were divided, Charles V's German subjects were part of a "kingdom on which the sun never sets."[13]

Habsburg claims to global dominance were celebrated in some of the finest work the Nuremberg goldsmiths could produce. But a more humble commodity, wood, is a better starting point for exploring how the German lands participated in the celebrated European voyages. When we think of the Germans and their forests around 1500, we are likely to think of how humanists like Conradus Celtis rediscovered Tacitus's *Germania*, the work that first fixed the clichéd image of the Germans as the hairy people of the forest.[14] But what Germans were mostly doing with their forests in 1500, when they were not chopping them down for themselves, was chopping them down to send as timber to Iberian shipbuilders. Northern European timber was highly valued. The large Portuguese pine forest, the Pinhal de Leiria, did not produce enough to meet the demand. Hanseatic shippers carried German as well as Scandinavian timber to Portugal in large quantities. German wood destined for shipbuilding was granted custom-free status in 1494.[15] Timber and other shipbuilding materials also went from Germany to Spain. In 1523 Charles V informed the towns of Lübeck and Danzig that Jakob Fugger had been charged with securing enough copper, masts, pitch, and hemp rope to outfit eight Spanish ships, and asked that they support Fugger by sending these materials to La Coruña.[16]

The German contribution to the construction of oceangoing vessels in Spain and Portugal went well beyond providing timber and pitch. Some of the Portuguese ships that explored the West African coast in the 1480s and '90s and often carried off slaves were either German-built or German in design. Germans had, after all, created in the Hanseatic League a "sea state" that ranked alongside those of Venice, Genoa, and Portugal.[17] There was cross-fertilization between shipbuilding in northern and southern Europe during the fifteenth century, an important part of what made the voyages of exploration possible. The Iberian *reconquista* of the Late Middle Ages, in which German vessels participated, opened the Strait of Gibraltar to non-Islamic shipping and inaugurated closer contact between the inland seas of the Mediterranean and the North and Baltic seas. One maritime historian refers to a "dialogue between the North and the South," a "maritime symbiosis."[18] Genoese and Venetian ships sailed to Flanders, Hanseatic ships headed south. German ships went to the Iberian peninsula partly to deliver their precious cargoes of timber. They also went because the huge expansion of the cod and herring fishing grounds in the north brought a demand for salt that was satisfied in Portugal. The "salt fleets" furthered hybrid shipbuilding. The result—in the hulls and rigging of the ships that the Iberian nations sent to sea—was vessels that were sturdy, fast, and maneuverable and that could sail anywhere and carry heavy armaments in the form of cannon.[19]

Those ships also had German crew members, along with Italians, Flemings, and English. We know that at least one German sailed with Magellan on his last voyage, for Hans of Aachen (Juan Aleman de Aquisgran) was among those who returned to Seville on the *Vittoria* in September 1522, one of 18 survivors of the 270 men who had set out three years earlier. More than 700 vessels left Lisbon as part of the India fleet between 1497 and 1590, with a death rate for those on board close to 10 percent (lower for ship captains and Jesuits).[20] That was why foreign sailors were essential. Germans were most likely to be found on Portuguese ships as gunners, or artillerymen—the *bombardeiros alemaes*. Hans of Aachen was a gunner; so was another German whose name we do not know, a crew member on Vasco da Gama's second voyage to India in 1502 who kept a diary about his experiences.[21] By far the best-known German gunner was Hans Staden, a young man from Hessen. A former soldier, he ran away to sea, found his way to Portugal on a German vessel that was part of the salt fleet, and signed on as a gunner in 1547 with a Portuguese ship headed to Brazil. Staden arrived safely back in Lisbon from this voyage. Two years later he was less lucky on a Spanish ship out of Seville, bound for the Río de la Plata but shipwrecked off the Brazilian coast. After serving in a Portuguese coastal fort, Staden was captured by local Tupinamba Indians. His subsequent captivity narrative, *True History and Description of a Land Belonging to a Wild, Naked, Savage, and Man-Eating People, Situated in the New World* (1557), became a bestseller.[22]

German gunnery enjoyed a high reputation in Spain and Portugal. Germans controlled the supply of metals in this period and their gun foundries were considered the best in Europe. The Spanish military writer Luis Collado thought that German and Flemish castings were "the best available."[23] In the last decades of the fifteenth century the Spanish and Portuguese crowns imported German cannon in large numbers. They also lured German gun founders and ancillary businesses to the Iberian peninsula. A German-owned gunpowder mill was established in Lisbon some time before 1466. The gunners followed, joining what was already a substantial German community of merchants, craftsmen, and printers in the Portuguese capital. Some, like Hans Staden, found their way there alone. Others were recruited as a group in Antwerp, the end point of the Portuguese spice trade. We get some idea of the numbers involved from various pieces of evidence. When Hieronymus Münzer traveled through the Iberian peninsula in 1494 and 1495, he found a warship in Lisbon harbor that had thirty German gunners under German command. We can also point to a request the Portuguese crown received from the Indian town of Cochin in 1525 to send a hundred gunners urgently, half of whom had to be German.[24]

No one believes any more that the Portuguese simply blasted their way into Asia (or Africa). Exploiting local rivalries and striking deals were essential in establishing their trading posts. Nor were they always successful in military encounters with non-Europeans.[25] But Portuguese naval prowess was not entirely a myth, either, and naval artillery was a big part of it. Portuguese vessels were heavily armed; some carried dozens of guns.[26] The German *bombardeiros* were valued accordingly. They enjoyed a status one step up from an ordinary seaman, on a par with the ship's barber or purser, and were granted special privileges. German gunners in Portugal were provided with housing, permitted to carry weapons on their person, and received pensions. By the late fifteenth century, the gunners were so numerous in Lisbon that they began to dominate the St. Bartholomew Brotherhood, the major organization of the German community, which grew out of a chapel originally founded by Hanseatic merchants. The German gunners carried their institutions with them to India, where they established chapels in Cochin and Goa. By the 1540s many of them had changed profession and begun to engage in trade. Some married South Asian women. A few appear to have hired themselves out to native rulers on the basis of their expertise in gunnery, a grassroots example of technology transfer from west to east. But by then the *bombardeiros alemaes* had already played a decisive part in Portuguese expansion, both across the Atlantic to Brazil, and down the West African coast into the Indian Ocean.[27]

German musketeers as well as naval gunners served the Portuguese crown, but they were fewer in number—the Portuguese empire rested overwhelmingly on naval power and the control of strategic coastal bases. German soldiers were more likely to be found in the Spanish army. That was true under Charles V and remained true under Philip II, whose far-flung empire in Spain, Italy, Flanders, and the Americas strained Spanish manpower resources. Despite a reputation for being quarrelsome and violent, German *Landsknechte* were greatly prized. In 1572, at least 20,000 German foot soldiers and a further 11,000 mounted men were fighting for the king of Spain in various (mostly European) theaters.[28] The role of German soldiers in the Spanish American empire was at its greatest during the reign of Charles V. One soldier we know about because he later wrote an account of his experiences. Ulrich Schmidel came from a Bavarian merchant family. In 1534, in his midtwenties, he signed on in Cadiz with a fourteen-ship Spanish expedition to the Río de la Plata, the expedition that led to the founding of Buenos Aires. According to Schmidel's later account, the 2500 Spaniards who took part in the expedition were accompanied by "150 High Germans, Netherlanders and Saxons."[29] It is possible that these soldiers from different parts of the Holy Roman Empire even acquired some kind of common German identity from being together in a foreign land.[30] Schmidel remained in South America for almost twenty years, taking part in expeditions of conquest up the Paraguay River and as far away as present-day Bolivia.

Schmidel and his comrades were German conquistadores between 1520 and 1550, in the years that have been called "the age of the *conquistador*."[31] The most controversial German contribution to this violent era of exploration, conquest, and plunder took place in Venezuela ("Little Venice") under the aegis of the Welsers of Augsburg. They had helped to pay for Charles V's election as Holy Roman Emperor and extended other loans to the permanently cash-strapped Charles in the 1520s, loans even greater than those he owed to the Fuggers. In March 1528 Charles granted an *asiento*, a contract of privileges, to Welser agents. Two years earlier the Welsers had opened a branch in Santo Domingo, on the island of Hispaniola. They exported sugar, pearls, and gold back to Spain and imported food, luxury goods, and the means to make further conquests on the American mainland: weapons and horses. Their resources made the firm attractive to the Spanish crown because it could bear the initial costs of opening up hitherto unexploited land. Under the terms of the 1528 contract the Welsers were to "conquer and settle" Venezuela. They were expected to build two settlements of at least three hundred colonists each within two years and to construct fortifications as needed. They were to bear the costs associated with these and to pay the "royal fifth" on all their income.[32]

The Welser era in Venezuela began in late February 1529, when the first of its governors, Ambrosius Ehinger, arrived on the mainland with three hundred men and established himself in the coastal town of Coro, which was inhabited at the time by a few dozen Europeans who had been drawn there by the nearby pearl banks. Then, only six months after his arrival, Ehinger and most of the new arrivals set off on the first of the *entradas*, or expeditions, which set the pattern of Welser rule in Venezuela and resembled conquistador practice elsewhere. Ehinger spent only a quarter of his time as governor resident in the capital. The same was true of his successors Nikolaus Federmann, Georg Hohermuth, and Philipp von Hutten (cousin of the humanist and ally of Luther, Ulrich von Hutten), all of whom took the first opportunity to leave Coro behind and set off on expeditions. Hohermuth arrived in 1535 with the largest group ever to reach Venezuela during the Welser years. He had never before been out of Europe, but three months after his arrival embarked on an *entrada* with almost five hundred men. Hutten was in Venezuela for more than five years and spent just six months in the capital. While the would-be colonists and their leaders were taking part in expeditions that sometimes lasted years, the settlements suffered—both Coro, and a second settlement at Maraca-ibo. There was little commercial development and exports were negligible. There was no attempt to develop the potential of the pearl banks or—more surprisingly—of Venezuela's mineral resources.

You could call Venezuela a "failed colony," like the French colony in Canada in the 1540s or the later English colony in Roanoke, Virginia—a colony that failed when difficulties of climate were compounded by misdi-rected labor resources and the neglect of long-term prosperity.[33] But Ven-ezuela was never really a colony at all. Although run by the agents of a merchant house, it was a base for exploration and conquest—a conquista-dor undertaking like any other, in which most of the ordinary ranks were Spaniards, recruited in Seville or the Canary Islands, while their leaders happened to be German. The men who went to Venezuela first (and they were virtually all men) joined the *entradas*; so did most of those who came after them, in 1530 and 1535. Many had taken part in expeditions elsewhere in the Americas or fought in the Italian wars. The 1535 contingent had a notably military character. The new arrivals who disembarked in Coro were armed with crossbows and arquebuses, lances and rapiers, determined to "conquer" Indians and make Christians of them while profiting hand-somely at the same time. How the colony was financed also pushed people to join *entradas*. Colonists were extended credit by the Welsers, to be repaid with interest, but they also had to pay the high prices charged for the goods and provisions imported through Santo Domingo. For indebted colonists who were effectively indentured servants in the struggling towns of Coro and Maracaibo, it made sense to gamble by drawing on the Welser credits to equip themselves for an expedition into the interior.

There were six expeditions during the years of Welser rule in Vene-zuela. They became longer over time and covered an impressive amount of ground, some twelve thousand miles in all, a greater distance than any other conquistador undertaking. From Coro, the *entradas* went west to the Colombian Andes and the valley of the Río Magdalena beyond. They also went south, through the flatlands to the east of the Andes that were part of the Orinoco River basin, as far as the site of present-day Bogotá, which Federmann's second expedition reached in 1538 at the same time as two Spanish conquistadores. Hutten's last *entrada* pushed deep into the Amazon basin, to areas not seen again by Europeans until Alexander von

Humboldt's scientific expedition more than 250 years later. The expeditions led by Welser governors or captains-general were classic conquistador journeys of exploration and conquest undertaken by armed men on horseback and on foot. One objective was to find a passage west to Asia. But above all the expeditions went in search of treasure—the kind of treasure seized by Francisco Pizarro after the sacking of the Inca empire in Peru, or the gold supposedly to be found in the mythical kingdom of El Dorado. The *entradas* took a heavy toll on their participants. Ehinger and Hutten both lost their lives; Hohermuth died in Santo Domingo two years after returning from a long expedition that ruined his health. The survival rate on these expeditions was no better than 40 percent, representing hundreds of lives lost.

The results, as it turned out, were modest. The expeditions plundered but the pickings were slim. Ehinger's second *entrada* in the early 1530s was the most successful, but the booty was lost by the party returning to Coro. Everywhere, the Venezuelan conquistadores found some objects to seize— gold earrings and the like, which could be melted down. But they never found the hoard of riches they were seeking. That would have changed if Federmann had been able to establish the primacy of his claim to the riches of the Muisca kingdom in Cundinamarca, but the Spanish crown awarded this area—it became New Granada—to a Spanish claimant. No doubt the Welsers understated what they extracted from the province to reduce the taxes owed to the crown, but Venezuela was clearly much less profitable than other Spanish American provinces, whether Peru, Mexico, or New Granada. Most expeditions failed even to meet their own costs. They eventually became desperate attempts to rescue at least something from the failed Venezuelan enterprise before the Spanish crown canceled the contract.

That seemed increasingly likely, given the disputes over Venezuela inside the company and repeated conflicts that arose in Coro while the governors were away. Tension between the mainly Spanish colonists and the Germans made things worse. Not least, there was the issue of how Indigenous peoples were treated. The Spanish Council of the Indies (as the Americas were called) was already complaining in 1535 about native depopulation because of Welser policy. In 1538 a judicial inquiry was mounted by the Spanish court in Santo Domingo, which dispatched Dr. Antonio Navarro to Venezuela to investigate charges that the German rulers had behaved brutally toward Indians, treated Spanish colonists unfairly, and engaged in administrative irregularities. A further inquiry was commissioned in 1544. By then, the Welsers were proceeding legally against their own former employee, Federmann, on grounds of insubordination and embezzlement. Welser rule in Venezuela was effectively over by the mid-1540s and ended formally in 1554.

Some allegations against the Welser administration were unfair, a by-product of the resentment felt by Spanish colonists. At several critical junctures the Spanish authorities also discriminated against German-run Venezuela in favor of its Spanish-run neighbor, Santa Marta. And when the crown revoked the Welser contract, this was not primarily because the company's agents had abused their power or treated Indigenous peoples brutally, but because in Venezuela—as elsewhere in Spanish America—the age of conquistador marauding was over and the era of settled Spanish administration had begun. The defeat of the Muisca people in Cundina-marca and the founding of Bogotá marked a turning point. After decades of *entradas* into the interior, three expeditions from different directions had met up and New Granada was the result. It was the geographical piece that linked together the Spanish lands in Central America and the Caribbean coast with those in Peru. Figures like Ehinger and Federmann were no more needed now than Cortés or Pizarro, and that would have been true whatever their conduct toward the Indigenes.[34]

The conduct of Welser agents in Venezuela was appalling, nonetheless. The expeditions engaged in systematic pillaging and violence. The Indige-nous were treated with contempt—"a bare, naked, bestial people," Hutten called them.[35] They were coerced into serving as porters, chained together; they were captured and sold into slavery on Hispaniola. Even an author who defends the conduct of the *entradas* against the worst accusations paints a damning picture. During Ehinger's second expedition, argues Jörg Denzer, the conquistadores behaved no worse than others before them. In the Valley of the Pacabueyes, when the native peoples resisted "friendly" overtures, Denzer concedes that there were "terrible excesses" but argues that, however violent the pillage was, it remained a matter of rational cal-culation and did not cross the line into "senseless cruelty." No doubt. But the "rational" violence meted out by Ehinger's men to induce Indigenous peoples to disclose where gold was to be found included torture and hos-tage taking, which in turn included depriving hostages of food and their eventual death.[36]

The reality, certainly dark enough, was the basis on which Spanish contemporaries and later Latin American writers constructed a horror story of uniquely German violence. Some modern versions, which feature concentration camps and genocide, are obvious retrospective projections of twentieth-century history.[37] But the line of argument, familiar in the Latin American world but unfamiliar to most German scholars, has a long history. The most famous contemporary denunciation came from the Dominican friar Bartolomé de Las Casas, a deservedly renowned defender of the rights of the Indigenous against predatory Europeans. Las Casas claimed that "those bestial tyrants, the Germans," had "murdered and strangled" more than four to five million Amerindians. Who would be surprised at such brutal excesses, he asked, for the "tyrannical German governor" in Venezuela was "a heretic . . . who moreover showed clear evidence of Lutheranism."[38] His account, written in 1542 and published ten years later, showed how firmly the Reformation battles over religious faith were being fought on new terrain. Even though most participants in the violent Venezuelan *entradas* were Spanish, it was their German "Lutheran" leaders who were singled out for obloquy. This line of attack was the Catholic counterpart to the *leyenda negra*, or black legend, which Dutch, British, and German Protestant commentators spread about the Spanish, suggesting that their treatment of Amerindians was of a piece with the Inquisition—a symbol of everything oppressively Catholic.

In the nineteenth century and through the first half of the twentieth, German mythologizers had their own version of events. The Welser era in Venezuela became an early example of bold German deeds in the world—"a piece of German vigor, an example of German daring," as one writer put it.[39] But anyone who wanted to build a legend on Welser deeds had to get around the problem of Welser violence. A much more promising symbol of what Germans supposedly contributed to European expansion was someone who came, not from Augsburg, but from Nuremberg. That was Martin Behaim.[40] He remains best known for a globe he commissioned at the beginning of the 1490s, the oldest surviving example of its kind. But that does not explain why this near contemporary of Dürer was celebrated in Nuremberg as one of the city's greatest sons, with a monument in his honor and a school, a street, and a locomotive named after him. A legend was created and passed down through the generations that credited Behaim with remarkable deeds as astronomer, navigator, and bold seafarer—in short, as a great German hero of the age of discovery. Numerous myths about Behaim were circulating by the nineteenth century. Alexander von Humboldt gave credence to some of them; local patriotism and German-national sentiment contributed more to the mythology. For the National Socialists, Behaim was the great German *Raum-Eroberer*, the "conqueror of space." Well into the twentieth century, his accomplishments continued to be "almost grotesquely" exaggerated.[41] Behaim had purportedly reached America before Columbus, or at least suggested to his good friend Columbus the idea of sailing west to the Indies; he had reached Brazil before discovering the passage that came to bear Magellan's name; he had invented the compass. No one today would defend such claims. The problem is that the cleaned-up account of Behaim's deeds is hardly more plausible. A residue of less obviously implausible nonsense remains, and writers who share no local or nationalist political baggage (often they are not German) continue to recycle old legends.

So who was Behaim, what did he actually achieve, and why does it matter? He was born in 1459, into a Nuremberg family of merchant patricians. His father died when he was fifteen, and young Martin was sent by his uncle, a linen dealer, to Flanders. There he worked in trade, had some money troubles (this would be a recurring issue), and in 1484 did what growing numbers of merchants from Flanders and Germany were doing— he moved to Lisbon. In the Portuguese capital he did well for himself, marrying the daughter of Jobst van Huerter, the Flemish-born governor of two islands in the Portuguese Azores. Behaim and his wife, Joanna, had one son, also called Martin, in 1489. That much is clear. Most of the legends about Behaim concern what he did in the 1480s. He had supposedly studied in Nuremberg, at least informally, with the celebrated mathematician Johannes Müller (Regiomontanus), and was therefore welcomed in Portugal because he took with him astronomical tables compiled by his mentor, together with an improved version of a nautical astrolabe (or perhaps it was the Jacob's cross), which proved crucial to Portuguese expansion. Invited almost immediately after his arrival in Lisbon to join the crown's advisory council on questions of navigation, the Junta dos Mathematicos, he subsequently accompanied Diogo Cão on exploratory voyages down the west coast of Africa during which they discovered the mouth of the Congo. As a reward, Behaim was made a knight of the prestigious Order of Christ created by Henry the Navigator.

Every one of these claims is either false or highly speculative. Behaim almost certainly did not study with Regiomontanus (although it is possible he claimed to have done so), and in any event the latter created no tables that were used in Portuguese navigation. The Portuguese already had nautical tables, which they used in combination with the detailed portolan charts made by pilots and sailors. Both nautical astrolabe and Jacob's cross were used by Portuguese mariners long before Behaim arrived in Lisbon. There is no evidence except for a brief entry in a Portuguese chronicle compiled fifty years after the event that Behaim was ever a member of the Junta dos Mathematicos. It is unlikely that Behaim sailed with Diogo Cão, and even more unlikely that he was elevated to the Order of Christ. It is true that he was knighted in 1485, but this was most likely a result of representations by his future father-in-law, who was well connected at court. Knighthoods were anyway bestowed very liberally by João II. The German Anton Herwart was knighted as a courtesy in the 1490s, and he was simply a traveler in Portugal.

We are left with a few other possibilities. Behaim may have taken part in a later (1485–86) expedition to the Gulf of Guinea. One modern writer has also suggested that he could have been a middleman for the import of Nuremberg quality instruments that aided navigation—and certainly these were well regarded in Portugal, just like German ordnance.[42] But there is no evidence for this, and it does not fit the profile of the commodities in which Behaim had traded in Flanders. The larger conclusion is that, with the exception of some accurate maps of the Lower Guinea coast and solar tables produced in Lisbon by the German printer Valentim Fernandes, neither Behaim nor other Germans contributed significant scientific expertise or navigational aids to Portuguese explorers as they struck out for the Atlantic islands and then worked their way down the African coast in the fifteenth century.[43] Behaim's famous globe would be no exception to this, as we shall see.

Behaim returned to Nuremberg in 1490, after his mother's death. He claimed his inheritance and cleared his outstanding debts. He would remain in Nuremberg for three years. The odor of the slightly raffish man of affairs still attached to him, even after the debts were settled. Behaim stayed with his cousin Michael, who wrote Behaim's brother Wolf, living in Lyons at the time, that Martin was "behaving oddly." This produced a heartfelt response from Wolf that "I would be very happy if we were all finally done with him."[44] That was in November 1491. A year later Michael was still reporting that Behaim did little but putter around the garden. But Behaim was actually far from inactive. He provided information about exploration along the African coast to the Nuremberg humanist Hartmann Schedel, whose major cosmographical work, the *Nuremberg Chronicle*, was completed in

1493. And it was during these years that the globe was constructed under Behaim's supervision. It was commissioned by three of Nuremberg's city fathers, probably at Behaim's own urging and with the strong support of an intermediary, financier Georg Holzschuher. The globe, two years in the making, was a thing of beauty. The product of some of the city's leading craftsmen, its surface contained intricately painted maps with detailed written legends.[45] The globe did not, as the Behaim legend claimed, advance scientific knowledge or present a new view of the world. In fact, it lagged behind the geographical knowledge of the time.[46] The likely purpose of the globe was demonstrative—to show Nuremberg's merchants the commercial opportunities that existed in an expanding world, from the gold of the West African coast to the spices of the east. The globe was a gorgeous mercantile gazetteer. No fewer than eleven hundred individual places were marked and blocks of text presented a cornucopia of commodities from precious metals to spices—gold, rubies, pearls, sapphire, emerald, sandalwood, aloe, nutmeg, cinnamon, pepper—all carefully listed, sometimes with added detail about existing trade routes. Behaim was a businessman, his globe an attempt at commercial consciousness-raising.

The globe may well have had a particular purpose: to make the case that the wealth of the Indies could be reached in just a few days by sailing

Martin Behaim shows off his globe in Nuremberg.

west, a proposition that looks more seductive on a globe than on a two-dimensional map. There is circumstantial evidence supporting this. In July 1493, Hieronymus Münzer, a friend of Behaim, wrote a letter to King João II. In it he claimed to speak on behalf of the Emperor Maximilian (João's brother-in-law) in appealing to the Portuguese king to mount just such a voyage west to "Cathay" and commending Martin Behaim as a most suitable person to take part in the journey. The circumstances in which the letter was written are suggestive, however one interprets it. Columbus had returned from his first voyage in March 1493, briefing both the Portuguese and Spanish crowns on what he had found. Two months later, in May, Pope Alexander VI issued the bull *Inter caetera*, which drew a line in the Atlantic dividing Spanish and Portuguese spheres. Assuming that the Münzer letter was not (as some have argued) a Portuguese forgery designed to boost its own case, the likelihood is that Behaim himself carried this letter with him when he returned to Lisbon. Whether Münzer and Behaim were aware when the letter was written of Columbus's return four months earlier is unclear—Columbus is not mentioned, and it is possible the news had not reached Nuremberg. Certainly they were aware of the Spanish-Portuguese rivalry, and it was reasonable to think that João might be receptive to the idea of a westward expedition.[47]

The episode had a strange coda and a murkily inconclusive end, like so much associated with Behaim. The following year, 1494, Münzer set off with three young merchants from Nuremberg and Augsburg on his grand tour of the Iberian peninsula. He had several audiences with King João at the Portuguese court, just as he had audiences with Ferdinand and Isabella in Spain. He spoke to others as well, including two figures intimately connected with Columbus's expeditions. Münzer's journey looks rather like a fact-finding mission following up on the previous year's letter to João II and designed to gather information about voyages to the west. The proposed route of the journey mentioned in Münzer's letter of 1493 is unclear. So are the interests that stood behind Münzer and Behaim. Were they Nurembergers? What role, if any, did Behaim's in-laws in the Azores play, with their friends in mercantile and plantation circles? We know that the proposed journey was never approved by João, but not what happened to Behaim. He and Münzer were still on close terms in 1494 and Münzer lodged with Behaim's in-laws when he was in Lisbon. Then, after 1494, Behaim drops out of the record until we learn of his death as a virtual pauper in Lisbon in July 1507. There have been suggestions that he ran through his inheritance in an effort to win a fortune sailing to the west.[48] There is no evidence that he did, but modern speculation about Behaim as a merchant-chancer gets closer to this shadowy figure than the former legend of the bold scientist-navigator-seafarer.

The Age of the Fuggers

BEHAIM WAS ONE RELATIVELY SMALL FIGURE WITHIN A LARGER network. Upper German merchants were major players in the expanding commercial empires of Portugal and Spain. They were involved directly in the spice trade and the developing sugar plantation economy, with its dependence on slavery, in mining European metals that bought enslaved people and paid for the spices, and in mining American silver that lubricated the sixteenth-century European economy. They also extended loans and bought up government contracts. The powerful German merchant houses formed the Central Europe hinterland of Iberian expansion, as essential to its workings as Genoese capital. Consider Lisbon in the middle of the sixteenth century, a booming city with a population approaching 100,000. The German colony was larger than it had been a hundred years earlier, or even in Martin Behaim's time, although its composition was similar. There were tradesmen, printers, sailors, gunners (of course), and merchants, who were concentrated in the business district behind the docks on the Tagus. The leading merchants had their staple houses there. The ships that docked in Lisbon came from every part of the Portuguese commercial empire—the Atlantic islands, West and East Africa, Brazil, India, and the Spice Islands. German merchants had a hand in all of them.

It was the spice trade that first drew foreign merchants to the Portuguese capital. Until the end of the fifteenth century, Venice was the place to be, the end point of the Levantine overland route that ran from India to Alexandria and on through the Mediterranean. That was where merchants from Central Europe obtained their ginger, cloves, cardamom, nutmeg, and pepper.[49] It was because of the spice trade that the Nuremberg and Augsburg commercial houses maintained their presence in the Fondaco dei Tedeschi. But Ottoman advances made the overland route more vulnerable and costly, which prompted the Portuguese to round the Cape of Good Hope seeking cheaper access.[50] Vasco da Gama's return from his first voyage to India in 1499 was a pivotal moment; it alerted the well-organized information networks of the German merchant houses that something new was afoot. They began to close up shop in Venice and descend on Lisbon even before da Gama's return from a second voyage in 1503 bearing 35,000 hundredweight of pepper and spices. Welser agents asked for the same access to the annual Portuguese fleets that some Italian merchants enjoyed. An agreement with the crown was made in February 1503. Brokered by Valentim Fernandes, the printer who was close to the Welsers and well connected at court, it extended a number of concessions to German merchants, including the right to participate in the spice fleet. This paid off in a small way when agents from two Nuremberg houses traveled with the Albuquerque fleet in 1503 on a fact-finding mission. One of them was Peter Holzschuher, a member of same family that had served as a go-between in the construction of Behaim's globe, for this was a small world. He did not return, but his report on the pepper and spice markets in Cochin and Kozhikode did make it back, along with the other German agent. A further agreement in 1504 permitted six Upper German merchant houses to participate in the fleet that sailed the following year. All owned shares in the German-Italian syndicate that financed the undertaking and three of their own ships were part of the fleet. A trio of young German merchants also went along, with permission to purchase spices directly.[51] One of them, Welser agent Balthasar Sprenger, published a book about his travels a few years later, the first account of India written by a German.[52]

The return of the fleet in 1506 led to a lawsuit between the merchants and the Portuguese crown. It turned on the right of the merchants to dispose freely of their share of the spices after they had paid the necessary duties. The German merchants in the syndicate eventually achieved a return of more than 150 percent on their investment. But the root issue remained the attempt by the crown, after a brief period of free trade, to impose a monopoly on the spice trade. This policy was largely upheld until 1570. But the crown still needed private merchants to buy and distribute spices. Germans continued to do that, in Lisbon and the secondary market of Antwerp, to which the Portuguese increasingly directed spice sales. We are told that in 1509–1511, Germans bought more pepper and spices at Lisbon's India House than any group after the Portuguese. There were many ups and downs in relations between German merchants and successive Portuguese monarchs. In the early years, there was German resentment that Florentines seemed to receive favored treatment. The frustrated Fugger agent Cristobal de Haro dramatically left Lisbon for Seville in 1516, a prelude to his masters' helping to bankroll the Spanish-sponsored voyages of Magellan and others in search of a westward route to the spices of the east, a back door to the Moluccas that turned out not to be economically worthwhile. In 1549, struggling with the high cost of monitoring the sale of spices in Antwerp, King João III closed down crown business there and forced merchants to buy everything in Lisbon. In the following decade, as the overland and Mediterranean route revived, the Fuggers—nimble as ever—temporarily abandoned Lisbon and bought their pepper at Alexandria.[53]

Through these vicissitudes, German merchants remained heavily involved in the syndicates that bought up the rights to distribute Portuguese pepper and spices. They were worth having, despite the frustrations of the monopoly, and despite the moral backlash at home from Luther, Hutten, and other critics.[54] For the Portuguese crown the great advantage of doing business with the Germans was their control of the Central European mines that produced the metals in demand in India for everything from coins to household utensils. The crown reckoned to need 300,000 kilos of copper for India each year. The Fuggers had a big part in this copper-for-pepper exchange.[55] Dramatic evidence of their role came to light in 2008, when the wreck of a Portuguese Indiaman was discovered in the beach sands near the mouth of the Orange River in Namibia. It turned out to be the remains of the *Bom Jesus*, which left Lisbon in 1533 and foundered as it made the turn around the Cape of Good Hope. Among the cannon, muskets, astrolabes, gold coins—and some human toe bones in a shoe pinned beneath a pile of timber—were more than 20 tons of copper ingots bearing the trident marking of the Fuggers.[56]

By 1570 the Portuguese trade monopoly had been undermined by local merchants, who took the profits and left the crown with the costs. The crown abandoned the monopoly and introduced a contract system. Merchants were now invited to bid for the exclusive right to purchase and distribute pepper and spices. A merchant house in Augsburg received the first contract in 1575. That was no surprise; the surprise was the identity of the successful bidder, Konrad Rott, who was not a leading German merchant. The decision was clearly political: to keep the contract out of the hands of the usual suspects because they were too powerful. Rott found Italian partners, the Rovellascas of Milan, and struck a deal with the Elector of Saxony that made Leipzig a key part of the German distribution system. But the terms of the contract and the loans he had undertaken to make to the crown, coupled with a downturn in the volatile pepper market, reduced Rott to bankruptcy in 1580. His Italian partners picked up the slack, retaining the network of German agents that Rott had sent out to India. By the time the next pepper contract came up, it was familiar names, Fuggers and Welsers, who joined the Rovellascas in the successful consortium.[57]

With the end of the monopoly, German agents fanned out through Asia, from western India to Macao. The Fuggers and Welsers built a network along the Malabar Coast of India, headed by an agent named Ferdinand Cron in Cochin. His was one of the more dramatic instances of a German merchant flourishing abroad. The Augsburg-born Cron served his apprenticeship in Lisbon during the 1580s and was in his late twenties when he disembarked at Cochin in 1587. Dispirited by the journey out and the local climate, he wrote to the Welsers: "God knows how I have regretted a thousand times travelling with this ship. If I had known what I know now, I would not have undertaken such a journey for anything in the world."[58] But he eventually spent thirty-seven highly successful years in India. Cron worked for six years as an agent for the Fuggers and Welsers before branching out on his own. He settled in Goa and became fluent in Portuguese, married a Portuguese woman from a noble family, acquired an estate, and married both his daughters well. He cultivated his connections to the court and was a favorite of successive viceroys, but managed to avoid guilt by association when one of them was caught with his fingers in the till and shipped back to Europe in disgrace. He traded judiciously, advanced credit strategically, and was a prime source of information that passed through his courier network. Cron was connected through his marriage to influential *fidalgo* families in Portuguese Asia, but also had close ties to the networks of New Christians (Jewish converts) that linked together different trade routes in the Portuguese empire. Ferdinand Cron's was, in short, a success story. Eventually, however, he became a victim of growing Portuguese suspicion of "spies" who were supposedly aiding the Dutch. Arrested on flimsy evidence along with his son-in-law in 1619, but released after ninety days, he was arrested again in 1624 and deported to Lisbon. But even in old age Cron was a survivor. Kept under loose house arrest, he was consulted as an expert on the possible establishment of a Portuguese East India Company, acquitted by a tribunal of inquiry, and died peacefully in Madrid in 1637.[59]

Like Florentine and Flemish merchants in Goa, Cron exploited every opportunity the Portuguese empire offered. He worked inside the state apparatus and outside it. He speculated in government bonds and traded information. And he dealt in many commodities. As an agent for the Welsers and Fuggers, Cron was responsible for buying and shipping both pepper, the "black gold" that made up two-thirds of the annual "India Run," and spices—ginger, cloves, nutmeg, cardamom, tamarind. Later he was active on his own account in the Asia-Europe textile trade. In 1613 we find him shipping bales of cloth to a Ferdinand Hellemans in Antwerp. The Goan merchant Francisco da Gama was buying textiles on Cron's behalf from Brahmin merchants to ship to Europe. Cron was probably taking advantage of "liberty chests" on the India Run, which allowed merchants to ship textiles and other goods to the Low Countries via Lisbon.[60] The manifest of one shipment by Cron from Goa to Lisbon notes that it contained semiprecious stones.[61] For jewels were another of Cron's business interests, diamonds among them, and in this he was following a practice already well established by German merchants in Portuguese India.

In the years between 1520 and the 1550s, when German merchants were not officially allowed to engage in the spice trade, dealing in precious stones *was* permitted. A roster of German agents traded on behalf of Upper German merchant houses like the Hirschvogels and Herwarts. They were active along the Malabar Coast, purchasing diamonds, rubies, and emeralds. Sometimes they bought directly in one of the prime sites of precious stones, the kingdom of Vijayanagara. It was a lucrative trade—the choicest items went to emperors, kings, and popes—and some German houses specialized in it. The Herwarts established a workshop in Lisbon for cutting and polishing gems. India was also a rich source of pearls. German merchants were active in this trade as well, in India and the European markets of Lisbon and Antwerp. The dimensions of the trade are apparent from the records of the Herwarts' Lisbon agent, who bought up more than 1300 pounds of pearls in 1527.[62]

Sixteenth-century Lisbon was a clearinghouse not only for pepper and spices but for textiles, indigo, and luxury goods of every kind. There were precious stones and pearls, amber, silks, and porcelain from China, sandalwood from Timor, and chests and caskets inlaid with ivory from India, for Vijayanagara was also rich in elephants, many of them sacrificed to satisfy the European taste for ivory. Ships docked in Lisbon carrying goods from west as well as east: boxes of sugar from Madeira, São Tomé, and Brazil, gold from the West African trading port of São Jorge de Mina, and enslaved Africans destined for the plantations. More than five thousand enslaved people arrived in Lisbon every year during the first half of the sixteenth century. In 1550 some ten thousand were living in the city prior to transshipment, making up a tenth of the population.[63]

Germans had a large role in the economy of the Portuguese Atlantic world, especially the sugar plantation system. Sugar was a capital-intensive business that attracted German money. The Welsers already had an agent managing a Madeira plantation in the early sixteenth century; there were also German interests on the sugar island of São Tomé. But the real prize was Brazil, where the sugar economy took off after the 1530s. Examples abound of German investors in the Pernambuco district.[64] The Fuggers were among them. They also engaged in the slave trade that made the expansion of sugar production possible (there were 33,000 slaves in Brazil by 1580, and 120,000 by 1600). Thanks to their control of European copper supplies, the Fuggers supplied goods that were traded for enslaved people along the West African coast. In 1548 the company signed a contract with the Portuguese crown. It undertook over the following four years to supply 400 tons of brass rings, 24,000 pots, 1800 wide-rimmed bowls, 4500 barbers' bowls and 10,500 kettles, brassware expressly destined for trade in Guinea.[65]

By the later sixteenth century Portugal faced mounting Dutch competition in Asia and the larger problem of balancing conflicting demands on its sparse resources—India and the Spice Islands, North Africa, West Africa, and Brazil. Portuguese priorities changed. This was the beginning of an "Atlantic turn" that became more pronounced in the seventeenth century.[66] German merchants, who had flocked to Lisbon around 1500, made an Atlantic turn of their own. Seville, not Lisbon, became the hub of German mercantile activity on the Iberian peninsula. When the Fugger agent Cristobal de Haro left Lisbon for Seville in 1516, he turned out to be the first of many. Some of the most important German commercial agents active in first half of the century would later make the same journey. Their moves marked a larger shift of emphasis among German merchant houses.

German merchants in the "great Babylon of Spain" found themselves in a city that tripled in population between 1480 and the 1580s, to almost 130,000. Seville had once sent its own merchants out; now Italian, German, Flemish, and English merchants came there to do business. Seville was where the trade networks of northern Europe, the Mediterranean, and the Atlantic met, a place where goods were transshipped, and a financial hub. Officials and nobles from everywhere in Spain as well as merchants and commercial agents congregated in Seville, along with travelers and missionaries, people going out to or returning from the New World. Visitors who had business of any kind in the Indies might have to spend weeks in the city, waiting for a decision from the body that controlled Spanish trade with the New World, the Casa de la Contratación (House of Trade).[67]

The American trade eventually became central to German merchants in Seville, but two other reasons drew them there in the first place. One was the promise of the "Moluccan expeditions" in the 1520s. This search for an Atlantic back door to the Spice Islands captured their interest (as it had captured Behaim's). Whereas Germans played little part in financing Columbus's voyages or the ones that immediately followed, they invested heavily in the fleets that pursued the Moluccan prize. It was a Welser agent named Heinrich Ehinger who bought up much of the spice brought back by the one vessel that returned from Magellan's circumnavigation. Subsequent trips proved a costly misadventure for the German investors because the westward route turned out to be uneconomic. That episode came to a close with the Treaty of Saragossa in 1529, when Charles V ceded to Portugal his rights to the Moluccas in exchange for 350,000 ducats.[68] By then the Germans were securely entrenched in Spain for a second reason: because of the large loans they extended to ensure Charles V's election as Holy Roman Emperor in 1519. Their influence continued with the financing of Charles V's ambitious foreign policy. Starting in the 1520s and continuing for decades, the large German merchant and banking houses extended loans to the Spanish crown. Sometimes they did this by buying up state bonds. Another form of repayment granted the Germans a share of crown revenues from its Spanish estates. For decades the Fuggers enjoyed the income from their lease on the rich Maestrazgo lands, interrupted only for a short time in the early 1530s, when it was the Welsers who were beneficiaries of the lease.[69]

The loans brought leverage. As Jakob Fugger pointedly reminded Charles V in 1523: "It is as clear as day that had it not been for me, you would not have been able to obtain the Roman Crown."[70] The same Heinrich Ehinger who bought up the spice cargo had been a cosignatory on the Welser loan to Charles V at the time of his election, and he was one of the agents who negotiated the Welsers' Venezuela contract in 1528.[71] The Atlantic trade soon became the main prize for the German merchants in Seville. The records of the Casa de la Contratación show how the Germans were permitted, stage by stage, to engage in business on the Spanish sugar islands, then to invest in transatlantic trade, and finally to maintain agents in Santo Domingo and on the American mainland.

We can see how this unfolded by following the career of one German merchant in Seville, Lazarus Nürnberger.[72] He is a perfect example of someone who began his commercial life beyond Germany in Lisbon, then moved to Seville. Nürnberger was born in 1499 in a small town not far from Nuremberg. He was apprenticed to the Hirschvogel firm and in 1515 was already working for them in Lisbon. By the age of nineteen, he had been to India and back. He was one of the agents who acted for the Hirschvogels on the Malabar Coast, dealing in pepper and ginger, precious stones and pearls. Nürnberger returned to Lisbon in 1518. He went briefly to Seville, then back to Germany. In 1519 he was at the Frankfurt trade fair and in Nuremberg, where he impressed his employers with his precocious knowledge of Asia (and served as translator for Martin Behaim's nephew, who spoke only Portuguese). By the end of that year, Nürnberger was back in Lisbon, but not for long. The Hirschvogels wanted him in Seville, where the commercial opportunities seemed greater, and that was where he settled in 1520.

The notarial records of the city reveal someone with a finger in every pie. Nürnberger was a go-between, always carrying out third-party commissions—arranging property sales, standing surety, assuming powers of attorney, extending loans, and calling in debts. He went to Seville as an agent of the Hirschvogels but later acted for many other German merchant houses. Nürnberger represented Welser interests until 1528 and remained loosely connected to the company thereafter. He also acted for the Fuggers and often collaborated with Christoph Raiser, the Fugger agent in Seville. (The strength of these links is suggested by the fact that one of his sons became a Fugger agent, while one daughter married another Fugger agent.) Beyond that, Nürnberger enjoyed close business relations with several Upper German merchant houses, with the Antwerp-based German Hans Ort, and with many Flemish and Spanish merchants. He also did business on his own account together with his brother-in-law, Juan Cromberger. As early as the 1520s Nürnberger owned two ships he used in trade with the Americas. The Welser connections to the crown undoubtedly helped Nürnberger during that decade, when he and Cromberger received several concessions from Charles V, including the right to send an agent to America, which resulted in the establishment of an office on Santo Domingo. Nürnberger's commercial activity eventually made him very wealthy. He owned houses in Seville, a vineyard and a mill elsewhere in Andalusia, property in his German hometown, and a valuable collection of jewels.

Nürnberger was engaged in an extraordinary range of business activities.

Early in his Seville career, in 1522, we find him supplying muskets to a Spanish armada sailing to the Azores to protect inbound ships from French privateers. The following year he was shipping "goods" to Mexico—most likely the metal goods and textiles that were the staples of his export business. The next year he and his partner were dealing in American hides (not very successfully). The year after that, 1525, Nürnberger was recorded dealing in pearls from the island of Cubagua. And so it went. A ship would come in laden with sugar, another would go out filled with axes, horseshoes, and nails. Nürnberger worked with partners in Santo Domingo, Mexico, and Peru, trading in many commodities—gold, silver, copper, emeralds, pearls, metalwares, textiles, books, and New World "drugs" such as sarsaparilla, sugar, and enslaved people.

Lazarus Nürnberger did what many German merchants were doing in the Spanish empire. The Welsers also traded in sugar, as well as in enslaved people to work the sugar plantations. Licenses to deal in slaves were transferable, and Nürnberger sometimes sold them on, like sarsaparilla. The Augsburg-based Herwarts, with whom Nürnberger often collaborated, were active in the pearl and emerald trade. And while Nürnberger imported sarsaparilla, other German merchants brought back guaiacum, prized (too optimistically) as a remedy for syphilis. Provisioning the Spanish colonies with grain, textiles, household goods, equipment, and specialist items like books and musical instruments became a staple of the larger German merchants. Viewed in this context, the Welsers' misbegotten venture in Venezuela was an aberration. It ended, as we saw, when the phase of naked conquest was over and New World societies became more settled. That process was one from which the German commercial interests in Seville could benefit, as importers and exporters. The Welsers themselves were among those who did benefit.[73]

There was one central aspect of economic activity in Spanish America in which Germans played a uniquely important role. That was the mining of copper, gold, and, above all, silver. In the early modern centuries, the New World produced 85 percent of the world's silver and 70 percent of its gold. In the years between 1540 and 1700 alone, American mines provided 50,000 tons of silver.[74] It arrived at a time when Europe was experiencing a silver shortage and it doubled the European stock. Shipped back to Spain, it found its way across Europe, to the countinghouses of Upper Germany and the Low Countries, where it greased the wheels of commerce—to the north, where it bought grain, timber, and furs; to the Ottoman Empire;

and to India, where the Portuguese and then the Dutch exchanged it for pepper and spices. Some of the silver found its way directly to the east, shipped to the Philippines by Spain on the "Manila galleons."[75] Silver was the great lubricant of commerce. The American and Asian branches of the new European trade networks were joined together by a "stream of silver."[76]

It was Germans who made this possible. They provided, in the first place, essential expertise. German mining techniques helped to identify and secure the silver. New Spain eventually produced its own body of knowledge, but before that the standard work was *De re metallica*, the posthumous work by the German Georgius Agricola, the "father of mineralogy." His generously illustrated work was an essential handbook on mining, dealing with everything from prospecting and surveying to extraction. The Mexican mining town of Zacatecas had a carefully annotated first edition from 1556.[77] Along with the book learning came German miners with practical skills. Central Europe was the heartland of European mining, from the Harz and the Iron mountains to the Tyrol and Hungary. German miners already had extensive experience with silver—it was not until the 1550s that New World silver production outstripped Europe's. Highly prized and mobile, German miners fanned out in the sixteenth century across Europe, from Scandinavia to Spain.[78] From Galicia and the Asturias to Spanish America was a logical leap. German miners were in the Caribbean at the beginning of the sixteenth century, in Mexico and Peru by the late 1520s.[79] But something else was needed for silver mining, beyond the expertise and the muscle power of German and native miners. That was mercury, or quicksilver, which was used to separate the silver from the rock by the process known as mercury amalgamation. There was a local Peruvian mercury mine, but its output was never sufficient. It was the Fuggers, who controlled the mercury mines of Almadén in Castile, who also controlled the supply of mercury to Mexico and Peru, and hence the continuing flow of silver. Almadén mercury, mined under appalling conditions by forced labor (much of it provided by *Moriscos*, or Arab converts), was shipped to New Spain on the annual fleet to Veracruz, and occasionally in special mercury boats. It arrived packed in wooden boxes or casks, in each of which were two or three leather bags made with three layers of hides, each holding fifty pounds of mercury. It was then transported to the mining towns, still in boxes or casks, by mule train.[80]

The role played by Germans in mining the riches of America and the resulting global flows of metal illustrate perhaps better than anything else the links between the hinterland of Central Europe and the new empires established by the Iberian powers in the sixteenth century. The Welsers' Venezuela contract specified that they arrange the transportation of miners to the New World. The ones who landed in Venezuela itself were not used, but others did work on Santo Domingo and the mainland. The indefatigable Lazarus Nürnberger had mining interests all over Spanish America. He imported gold from Santo Domingo, was involved in mining Cuban copper, owned a share of two mines in Mexico purchased by an agent (one had to be sold, complete with ninety enslaved workers, when the agent encountered liquidity problems), and was active in Peru—one shipment of silver and gold from Peru was shipwrecked off Madeira, but the cargo was landed even though the ship went down. Other German merchants dabbled in metals.[81] But it was the Fuggers who stand as the symbol of German mining interests in the Americas, shipping mercury in, gold and silver out.

The Fugger commercial empire in the sixteenth century linked Europe, America, and Asia. The company conducted trades in florins, gold gulden, and guilders; it was as familiar with the ducats and crusadoes used in Lisbon and Portuguese Asia as it was with the ducats and maravadies used in Seville and Spanish America.[82] The Fuggers' elaborate network of offices, agents, and news-gathering operations extended beyond their original European base. They had offices in the Yucatán peninsula and Brazil, and their trade with the Americas extended from precious metals and pearls to sugar, hides, and medicaments such as guaiacum and canafistula. They financed commercial undertakings in India, sending out large quantities of the metals sought in Asia, importing precious stones, pepper, and spices. They traded in both commodities and enslaved people along Africa's Guinea coast.[83] And they were wealthy—"rico como un Fucar," as rich as a Fugger, said the Spaniards.[84]

The German historian Richard Ehrenberg wrote a book in 1895 called *The Age of the Fuggers*.[85] His title captures the dominance of the firm, especially in the years up to the mid-sixteenth century.[86] For two or three generations the Fuggers enjoyed the kind of financial power and political influence associated in the preceding period with the Medici of Florence, before their era of dominance gave way in turn to what the historian Fernand Braudel called the "age of the Genoese."[87] The end of the 1550s marked a caesura. The patriarch Anton Fugger died in 1560, just one year before

his Welser counterpart, Bartholomäus, and two years after the death of
Charles V, to whom Fugger fortunes had been so closely tied since his election as Holy Roman Emperor. There was no abrupt decline. The company
continued to have an impressive, and widely resented, portfolio of interests:
no straight line leads from the 1550s to the bankruptcy that the Fuggers
(like the Welsers) experienced in the seventeenth century.

In retrospect, though, some of the underlying problems are clear.
Sixteenth-century business was intrinsically risky, but the risks involved
in far-flung trade across the oceans were greater than they were within
Europe. Shipwreck and piracy were obvious hazards. The long lines of
communication also made it harder to monitor the actions of agents on
the spot. The double-dealing factor who conspired with a rival company
was a constant problem for the Upper German merchant houses. It was
hard enough to be sure in Augsburg or Nuremberg about what was happening in Ghent or Valencia. It was much harder when the agents were
on another continent. The problem the Welsers had with their agent in
Venezuela, Nikolaus Federmann, is just one example. In another contemporary case, this time in Asia, the boot was on the other foot. Georg Herwart filed suit in the 1540s against his fellow Augsburger Hans Welser,
arguing that Welser and his Lisbon agent had conspired with Herwart's
agent, Jörg Imhoff, to divert profits from the Indian jewel trade into
Welser pockets.[88]

German merchants also had to navigate an often difficult relationship
with the Portuguese and Spanish monarchs who set the terms of trade.
They chafed in Lisbon over the frequent shifts in Portuguese policy on
the pepper and spice trade. Things were even worse in Seville. If political
influence often gave German merchants the opportunity to make money,
political maneuvering also thwarted them, as the Welsers discovered in
Venezuela. The Fuggers represent a classic case of the dangers that came
with tying oneself too closely to princely power. They traded in almost
everything, but their period of dominance was built on finance and mining.
The two went together from the start. Their influence in Lisbon was based
on their control of European metals that could be used as trade goods in
Asian markets, and that control began with their earliest forays into the
business of extending loans to cash-strapped princes in exchange for mineral rights. This started with loans to the Archduke Sigismund of Tyrol
(known as "the Ore Duke"). By the end of the 1480s the Fuggers received
the entire output of the Tyrolean silver mines as repayment.[89] More loans

followed to the Emperor Maximilian I and his grandson Charles V. These provided the Fuggers with their entry ticket into Spanish transatlantic trade. The loans also gave them control of the all-important mercury mines in Almadén, and with it control of the trade in silver, from which they could expect repayment of their loans. But this locked creditor and debtor into an increasingly difficult relationship. That was the trouble with "political finance."[90] The Welsers faced the same problem. One of their agents wrote to Bartholomäus Welser in 1547, reporting his conversation with an Imperial official about repayment of an outstanding loan, which met with disturbingly insistent requests for a further loan.[91] The Fuggers were much more exposed. The mines at Almadén faced many problems. The Spanish crown complained about shortfalls in the mercury supply; the Fuggers responded that crown payments for the mercury received were chronically in arrears. A vicious circle arose as the sixteenth century gave way to the seventeenth: inadequate supplies of mercury meant an uncertain flow of silver, and the uncertain flow of silver meant that the Fuggers were not paid for the mercury they produced.[92] Almadén was not, in Jakob Fugger's felicitous phrase, a "metallic blessing."[93]

Behind all this was the increasingly parlous state of Spanish state finances. The debt owed to the Fuggers was already enormous under Charles V. Official state bankruptcy was declared in 1557. The debt continued to rise under Philip II, who borrowed to finance his military response to the Dutch revolt. It stood at 50 million ducats in 1573, and at 85 million twenty-five years later, which represented eight or nine years of state revenue. The silver that might have been used to pay off the Fugger debts went instead to sending troops along the "Spanish Road" to the Low Countries.[94] The default of 1557 was followed by further defaults in 1575 and 1596. The merchant and banking houses of Augsburg and Nuremberg were all hit hard. The Fuggers had some leverage and bargained to exclude their own debts from these bankruptcies, but only by agreeing to lower the interest rates on existing loans and accept dubious state paper rather than silver as repayment. The impact on their economic position was disastrous. After the defaults of 1557 and 1575, Fugger agents were desperately trying to call in loans and even selling off stocks to raise cash, with repercussions felt throughout Europe. By the third decade of the seventeenth century the Spanish debt exceeded ten years' revenue.[95] The Fuggers, shackled to the crown by a business model of mining plus "political finance" that had once proved so lucrative, were among the most spectacular victims.

Writers, Artists, and Mapmakers

"RAISE YOUR SPIRITS . . . HEAR ABOUT THE NEW DISCOVERY!" SO
wrote the Italian-born Spanish humanist Pietro Martire d'Anghiera in September 1493, six months after the return of Columbus from his first voyage.
The Portuguese mathematician and cosmographer Pedro Nunes exulted in
1537 about "new islands, new lands, new seas, new peoples."[96] It was not easy
for contemporaries to assimilate all this novelty and many preferred not to
try. As Nuremberg humanist Johannes Cochlaeus remarked a little testily
in 1512 about the reported "discovery" of America: "Whether it is true or a
lie has nothing to do with cosmography or the study of history"—for these
were a matter of textual scrutiny.[97] The authority of the ancients remained
powerful, including the authority of Ptolemaic geography. But even where
they created doubt or uncertainty, the encounters with new worlds had a
powerful impact on European patterns of thought. And Germany, with its
extensive merchant networks, humanist circles, and vigorous publishing
industry, was especially well placed to disseminate knowledge of these new
worlds. Its writers, artists, and mapmakers all played a major part in shaping the European response.

Word about the Spanish and Portuguese voyages found its way to the
German lands in many different ways, including word of mouth. Travelers
to the Iberian peninsula, such as Hieronymus Münzer and the Augsburg
merchant Lukas Rem, were already reporting in the middle of the 1490s
on things they had seen and heard.[98] Permanent residents there were even
better placed, especially if they had good contacts. Martin Behaim is an
example; so is one of his friends, the German-Bohemian printer Valentim
Fernandes, who lived for some time in Seville before settling in Lisbon,
where he was a frequent intermediary between the Portuguese regime and
German merchants. Fernandes was a lively source of information, writing
regularly to his Augsburg friend Konrad Peutinger, a humanist related to
the Welser family. Fernandes also had correspondents in Nuremberg. It
was through him that news first reached Germany of Pedro Cabral's "discovery" of Brazil in 1500.[99] Lisbon and Seville were not the only sources of
information. Antwerp was a clearinghouse of news as well as goods. It was
there that the Augsburg humanists Johannes Kollauer and Matthäus Lang
had a chance encounter in 1503 which caused Kollauer to write excitedly
to his friend Conradus Celtis: "You would see here, among many other

noteworthy things, Portuguese sailors who relate astounding tales. You would see here another kind of map for navigating to the Antarctic pole and men who would relate to you marvelous and unheard of things. . . . Another world has been found unknown to the ancients!"[100]

The messengers and couriers of the great merchant houses, always hungry for information, were another conduit. Merchant networks provided news in another form. These years saw the spread of a form of proto-newspaper, newsletters that merchants (like ambassadors) forwarded to their correspondents. Typically three or four pages in length, they were compiled by professional scribes on the basis of reports. We know of one Fugger factor in Spain who also doubled as a compiler. Mostly the Fuggers and other merchant houses were consumers, and through them information reached a widening circle. The recipients included not only merchants but other urban patricians as well as princes, clergy, and humanists.[101]

Many newsletters were handwritten, and it is easy to overlook how important that medium of communication remained. But newsletters also came in printed form. Print was crucial in spreading news about the European voyages. Contemporaries already made a connection between them. The Paduan philosopher Lazzaro Buonamico insisted in 1538: "Do not believe that there exists anything more honorable to our or the preceding age than the invention of the printing press and the discovery of the new world."[102] Linking the two things had already become something of a cliché in European letters, and a doubly Eurocentric cliché into the bargain, as we would now see it, given that the New World existed before Europeans discovered it and the Chinese were using movable type centuries earlier.[103] But the Italian humanist's comment also suggests another cliché we shall encounter frequently in the following pages: that while others acted, Germans merely wrote about things—or, in this case, provided the print medium through which the deeds of others were recorded.

There is no doubt that German printers played a decisive role in disseminating knowledge about the newly discovered lands. Some were ensconced right in the heartland of the Iberian empires, although that was not necessarily the best place to be if you were looking to publish works on the "discoveries." The Portuguese were very sensitive about potentially valuable information finding its way into rival hands. Valentim Fernandes satisfied the demand for travel reports while playing it safe by publishing a compendium of writings by earlier travelers such as Marco Polo, but at the same time sending up-to-date information privately to his friends in

Germany.[104] Seville was more easygoing. The largest publisher there, the
Cromberger family, was also German (Juan Cromberger, Lazarus Nürnberger's business partner, was the founder's son). The Crombergers published more than 550 books between 1503 and 1557, a great number for one
press at that time. Among them were important works on the Spanish
"discoveries" and colonization in the Americas by scholars such as Pietro
Martire d'Anghiera.[105]

   Most writings on the "discoveries" were published outside the Iberian
peninsula, though, and Germany was rivaled only by Italy as a center of
their production. Around 2200 printed works on the Americas appeared in
Europe during the sixteenth century, between 1 and 2 percent of all titles.
Of these, fully a third (760) were published in just four German-speaking
cities: Augsburg, Basel, Cologne, and Frankfurt.[106] The role played by German publishers was quickly apparent. Columbus's letter describing his first
voyage was immediately published in Basel in a Latin edition; a German
edition appeared in Strasbourg four years later, in 1497. Within a decade,
compilation volumes were coming off the German presses. In 1508, for
example, a book called *New Unknown Lands* was published in Nuremberg.
A German translation of a book that appeared in Italy the previous year, it
included first-person and third-person accounts of Portuguese and Spanish voyages. The entries took in India, Africa, and the Americas. Among
the accounts was a letter attributed to Amerigo Vespucci (and now considered a forgery), editions of which had already appeared by 1508 in Strasbourg, Nuremberg, Augsburg, Rostock, Cologne, Leipzig, Munich, Basel,
and Magdeburg.[107] *New Unknown Lands* appeared in updated editions as
new accounts became available; so did many similar works put together
by enterprising publishers or printers. Some tried to cover all points of the
compass, others concentrated on a particular part of the globe. One example, part of the widening circle of European knowledge of Asia, was a 1532
compilation published in Basel: *Novus orbis regionum ac insularum veteribus
incognitarum*.[108] This collection of early travel narratives, including accounts
of the first five Portuguese journeys to the east, contained nothing original
and was designed to make money. Still, it had an intellectually respectable
pedigree. Gathered together by Johann Huttich of Mainz and the well-
known cosmographer Sebastian Münster, the *Novus orbis* had a preface by
Simon Grynaeus, a Reformation theologian and friend of Erasmus. Two
years later a German edition of the same compendium was published in
Strasbourg.

By the 1530s a new genre of descriptive world geographies appeared in German-speaking Europe, works that included the humanist Sebastian Franck's *Book of the World* (1534) and—the most celebrated of them—Sebastian Münster's *Cosmographia* (1544). All incorporated material about newly discovered lands—in Franck's case, despite his own sardonic view that Germans wanted to know about everything in "the whole wide world" except the German fatherland ("many a German can hardly tell an island in India from the valley of his next-door neighbor").[109] These works were also absorbed into the business of packaged compendium volumes. In 1567 Frankfurt publisher Sigmund Feyerabend brought out a two-volume *Truthful Description of All Parts of the World*, which drew heavily on Franck's book and on that serviceable old standby, the *Novus orbis.*[110]

What can we say about the purpose and tone of these accounts? They were written by a medley of soldiers, navigators, clergy, and officials who had widely varying purposes and perspectives. Some observed closely the flora and fauna (including the human fauna) of the lands they encountered. Others were less attentive to what they saw, or more single-mindedly concerned with the possibilities of trade, conquest, or the winning of souls. German editors, for their part, selected and shaped this raw material. One obvious distinction was between works that passed through the filter of humanist curiosity with the aim of edifying, and others, shorter and more liberally illustrated with woodcuts (sometimes woodcuts illustrating quite different places from those referred to in the text), which played up the sensational, the marvelous, and the exotic. Scholars have contrasted the more scholarly and scientific compendia produced in Italy by writers such as the Venetian Giovanni Battista Ramusio with the more eye-catching and popular equivalents produced in German by commercially minded publishers like Feyerabend.[111] But the distinction is not straightforward. After all, it was the descriptions he heard from Portuguese sailors about "marvelous" things that initially excited the humanist Johannes Kollauer.

Europeans navigated between two possibilities in trying to come to terms with what was novel in these encounters. They could assimilate the unfamiliar to the familiar, or emphasize difference. After all, it was not easy to describe something to someone who had not seen it, and the familiar was an aid. Thus, Cortés likened the Aztec temple to a mosque and compared the marketplace of Tenochtitlán with Salamanca.[112] Even difference often meant invoking familiar and long established categories—"civilized" and "barbarian," for example. Were the reports that Germans now read about strange people, animals, and vegetation in unfamiliar climes really so different from the late medieval descriptions (with which they were sometimes packaged) of encounters with Tatars in Crimea or Muslims in the Holy Land? And when these descriptions of the Americas and their inhabitants underscored the "wondrous" or "marvelous," could these stark differences of appearance and behavior not be brought within a view of the world that emphasized the diversity of humankind and a belief that every part of it somehow served God's purpose? The historian Christine Johnson has persuasively argued for this reading of Sebastian Franck's *Book of the World* and Sebastian Münster's *Cosmographia.*[113]

These questions are worth raising because they complicate the view that the assimilation of European encounters in Asia and the Americas was simply a matter of labeling an exotic "other." It is not hard to find instances where intellectual curiosity and a willingness to look closely at something previously unknown and unseen produced the very opposite of crude or demeaning stereotypes. Albrecht Dürer comes to mind. His interest in the unfamiliar was matched by his capacity for enthusiasm. Both were engaged during his time in Antwerp, where he witnessed close up things from the Americas that thrilled him—clothing, costumes, armory. "I have not seen anything in my whole life which pleased my heart as much. Because I saw in them wonderful artificial things and I have been amazed by the subtle ingenuity of people in foreign lands."[114] He brought the same respectful attitude to people. In 1521 he produced the first European drawing of an enslaved Black woman. She had been given the name Katherina and was the servant of a Portuguese merchant's agent. The portrait shows very close attention to both physiognomy and Indigenous dress. As the historian Ulinka Rublack has argued, perhaps the most remarkable aspect of the drawing is that Dürer did not use his authority to compel a young servant to pose upright or look at him, but produced a dignified, moving drawing of the enslaved woman that respected her evident discomfort at meeting his gaze.[115] Thirteen years earlier, Dürer drew *Head of an African* in black chalk. It is possible he saw the man in Nuremberg, more likely in Venice. The work itself is compelling and marked by warmth and empathy. Dürer broke with stock images of "Moors," seen in countless representations of the Adoration of the Magi, to depict a young, curly-haired, sad-looking Black man.[116]

The same respect is evident in Christoph Weiditz's *Book of Costumes*, published in 1529. This series of more than 150 watercolor and pen drawings by the young Augsburg-trained artist illustrated people he had seen during his travels in Spain, including *Moriscos*, enslaved Black people, and Indigenous Americans brought back to Iberia by Cortés. Weiditz was fascinated by varieties of clothing and seems to have had a special interest in the physical movements involved in both work and play. Some of his most striking images depict Indigenous ball games and dice games; in a three-drawing sequence, an Aztec juggles a wooden block. Another drawing depicts enslaved Black people loading freshwater on board a ship in Barcelona. Weiditz places images of European work and play alongside images of non-European work and play. In each case, he is clearly interested in the effects on the body. In the image from Barcelona the physical toll exacted by the work is clear enough and the artist makes his subjects' status clear by showing the slave anklets they wore.[117] Weiditz shows us how non-Europeans were assimilated and subject to European power in the Spain of Charles V, and in doing so unwittingly creates an ethnographic document.[118] We are a long way removed here from works like Feyerabend's compilations. Of course, those popular works were numerous. In them we can see a process at work in which the new and strange became the "marvelous" and the marvelous became the titillating, the dangerous, and the exotic, especially when it presented itself in the form of naked men and women or cannibalism. These created an unease among Europeans that is often palpable, even as they asserted their own superiority. Then we can refer with good reason to the "colonization of the marvelous."[119]

Where do first-person accounts of new worlds by German writers fit into the picture? Published autobiographical accounts by Germans who had traveled to Asia or the Americas were few in number, just a handful—literally—to set against the numerous non-German works in translation. The earliest was by Balthasar Sprenger, who sailed as a Welser agent to India with the Portuguese fleet in 1505 and kept a diary. His *Sea Voyage and Experiences* was published in 1509. The young Tyrolean is a careful observer of people and places. He has a merchant's eye for good harbors and local tax regimes, but also for commodities, plants, and livestock. Sprenger admiringly records the use of elephants as draft animals in India. He also observes closely the appearance and mores of the Africans, Arabs, and South Asians he meets. He records "wild people," it is true, but writes with neither censure nor salaciousness about the "wonderfully unprudish people of both sexes."[120] Sprenger distinguishes carefully between different non-European peoples, describing skin color, hair, and dress. His prose is supplemented by the tinted woodcuts of the Augsburg engraver Hans Burgkmair, which portray a wide variety of human types in domestic and public settings with close attention to variations in clothing, footwear, and jewelry.

Forty years passed before another German account appeared in print. Some of the many letters Philipp von Hutten wrote from Venezuela were published in 1550.[121] Two more accounts by German conquistadores followed: Nikolaus Federmann's *Indian Histories* in 1557, and Ulrich Schmidel's *New World* ten years later.[122] Like Sprenger, Hutten and Federmann were Welser agents, but their accounts could hardly have been more different from his. They wrote as conquistadores and much of what they describe reads like dispatches from a campaign, filled with attacks and skirmishes, strung on a narrative of endless marches through mountain passes and across fast-flowing rivers as they searched for El Dorado. Problems with horses abound, and one of the most frequent words is *Proviant*—provisions, usually in reference to their scarcity. These are accounts of deeds and actions, but even more of privation and suffering—"hardship and distress, hunger, thirst, trouble and exertions," in Hutten's words.[123] Both were trying to justify themselves, Federmann to his Welser masters, Hutten to a father and brothers to whom he insisted (perhaps too much) that his failures were not of his own making or tinged by any loss of honor. Both brought the conventions of the Old World to their descriptions of the New. They framed their accounts as a series of trials, or tests of character, echoing the genre of chivalric literature. Indeed, they often sound like Crusaders. Divine providence is constantly invoked and Europeans, whether Spaniards or Germans, are always simply "Christians."

Neither shows much curiosity about Indigenous peoples. Federmann often promises to talk about "the peoples, their morals and customs," but never quite gets around to it. Hutten's account is similarly blank. Federmann baptizes Indians at one point as he marches through the land, hopeful that the young will turn away from the "seductive and devilish ceremonies" of their elders, without specifying what these might be. Another people are simply "refractory, wicked and false."[124] Schmidel shows more interest in native peoples, describing many aspects of their physical appearance, food, and cultural practices. Impressed by the Guarayos and their hospitality, he calls their leader a "king." German standards provide the yardstick here, as they do when Schmidel compares a nomadic tribe to "Gypsies" and criticizes another for behaving "just like our highwaymen or street-robbers at home."[125]

There are two subjects on which Hutten, Federmann, and Schmidel all pass comment. The first is Indian nakedness, something that attracted intense European interest going back to the earliest accounts that Germans read in translation. Even before that, the very first mention of the "discoveries" in a German-language text was Sebastian Brant's great moralizing poem, *The Ship of Fools*, which refers to "gold islands and naked people."[126] Female nakedness was especially fascinating to all our trio. Schmidel is the most prurient, noting of one tribe that the women "go about as naked as the day they were born and are beautiful after their fashion, [they] commit indecent acts in the dark without doubt." They were, he added, "very beautiful and carnal, very friendly and very hot in the body, as it seems to me."[127] The view that Indigenous women were exceptionally—perhaps threateningly—erotic seems to have become a cliché back in Germany even before the middle of the sixteenth century, to judge by a remark of Hutten's when writing to his brother: "We laughed not a little when you wrote how news had come that we had all supposedly been captured by Indians and forced to take wives."[128]

The second issue mentioned by all three Germans was cannibalism, or anthropophagy. The references to it are occasional in Hutten and Federmann, more frequent in Schmidel. "These Carios eat man's flesh if they can get it," he writes at one point, "for when they make prisoners in war, male or female, they fatten them as we do swine in Germany. But if the woman be somewhat young and good-looking, they keep her for a year or so, and if during that time she does not live after their desires, they put her to death and eat her, making a solemn banquet of it."[129] Passages like this had become commonplace since the earliest European accounts of the Americas by Columbus and Vespucci. A few scholars have argued that cannibalism was a purely European projection, a view contradicted by abundant evidence.[130] The real issue is how the subject was framed and why it obsessed European writers. Cannibalism was a "powerful cultural fantasy," an expression of real, or stylized, fear.[131] It clearly reinforced a European sense of superiority, serving as a marker of native savagery and "barbarism." Cannibalism thus became a justification for enslavement. But what if it was practiced by Europeans themselves? Hutten describes how Christians on one expedition, reduced by hunger to eating roots, mice, snakes, and other "vermin," also resorted "against nature" to eating human flesh. In fact, his troubled description of how part of a young boy was hacked off and cooked up with herbs has a level of detail lacking in accounts of native cannibalism.[132] If episodes of this kind complicated the conventional contrast between heathen and Christian, German accounts of cannibalism also suggested a division between Catholics and Protestants. Schmidel converted to Lutheranism before he wrote *New World*, the first edition of which was published by an ardent Anabaptist. His text is framed in Protestant terms and includes graphic accounts of Spanish cruelty. He describes one incident in Buenos Aires when three Spaniards were hanged for stealing and eating a horse; on the same night, other Spaniards apparently went to the gallows, where they hacked off the flesh from their fellows and ate it. It has been plausibly suggested that Schmidel's account was a veiled attack on the Catholic Eucharist and the doctrine of transubstantiation, a doctrine many Protestants viewed as no better than cannibalism.[133]

Its Protestant framing is one feature of the most famous and successful sixteenth-century German account of the Americas: Hans Staden's 1557 description of his captivity among the Tupinamba Indians in Brazil. His *True History* is really two books in one, the first detailing Staden's own experiences, the second—its structure almost certainly shaped by his editor, the humanist Johannes Dryander—offering a series of ethnographic descriptions of the customs and culture of his captors. The narrative is organized as a tale of suffering and trials eventually overcome through faith and God's grace—a salvation story, in short. As the references in its title to wild, naked, savage cannibals suggest, *True History* had popular appeal. Nikolaus Federmann's *Indian Histories* may have been described when his son-in-law published it as "very enjoyable to read," and Ulrich Schmidel's account was certainly spiced with scenes that were prurient or made the reader shudder, but it was Staden's work that sold in large numbers and went through four editions in a year. Its resonance with German readers must have owed something to the gruesome illustrations the book contained, beginning with the woodcut on the title page, which depicted a naked man lying in a hammock holding a human foot to his mouth while other feet roasted on a spit. By the 1550s certain stock images of cannibalism had become established from the illustrations that accompanied the accounts of Columbus, Vespucci, and others. Body parts roasting on the spit was one such image.[134] Yet just as Staden's descriptions of the Tupinamba had a singular quality, so the images that accompanied the first edition of *True History* departed from standard representations, woodcuts made especially for the book and a result of close cooperation between Staden and his printer. Text and illustrations together formed a highly original account within the burgeoning sixteenth-century literature on Brazil. In later pirated editions, it is true, publishers eager to cash in on the book's popularity simply employed images drawn from stock. Illustrations were recycled from a decades-old Italian travel book about Asia, with the result that a text about Brazilian Indians was accompanied by pictures of Javanese Muslims.[135]

What made these illustrations possible was the fifteenth-century European invention of printing from woodcuts and engraving from metal plates. Printed maps were a product of the same technical advances. Map design was transformed in the late fifteenth and sixteenth centuries, and Germans were central to this "little scientific revolution." Mapmaking, like the printing of books, flourished at the crossroads where commercial information networks, humanist learning, and technology reinforced one another. That meant Italy, and the usual German suspects: Augsburg,

One of the images depicting cannibalism in
Hans Staden's True History.

Nuremberg, Ulm, Basel, and Strasbourg. The first printed *mappa mundi* of the medieval kind appeared in Augsburg in 1472. Other printed maps soon came out of Germany, including a world map loosely based on Ptolemy in the *Nuremberg Chronicle*—it was designed in the workshop where Dürer served his apprenticeship. Reduced-scale versions followed during the 1490s and beyond.[136] It was a sign of the preeminence enjoyed by German cartographers that it was they who regularly produced new editions of Ptolemy. They were also better placed than others to incorporate the knowledge of the "discoveries." New information from Portuguese and Spanish voyages brought about a revolution in map designs and projections. These maps, in turn, created a powerful visual means of assimilating and representing new worlds.

Renaissance Germany had two major cartographical schools, in Nuremberg and Alsace-Lorraine.[137] It was the second that produced one of the most famous maps of all time, now in the Library of Congress. In 1901 a trove of old documents was discovered in Castle Wolfegg in southwest Germany. It included a series of twelve sheets that formed a world map, or *Universalis cosmographia*, printed in Strasbourg and created by the Lorraine cartographer Martin Waldseemüller and his collaborator Matthias Ringmann. The Waldseemüller world map of 1507 is a hybrid of Ptolemaic geography and information gleaned from the voyages. The two figures at the head of the map, Ptolemy and Vespucci, signify this double debt. While the west coast of Africa is drawn in great detail, almost no use has been made of Portuguese journeys to Asia. The representation of the Americas is more original. The Caribbean islands are shown, along with separate continental landmasses to the north and south that are clearly surrounded by water and not linked to Asia. What makes the map historic is that Waldseemüller gave a new name to what had previously been referred to as the "Indies" or "New World." He called it America, after Amerigo Vespucci. The map uncovered in 1901 is the only surviving copy from an edition of one thousand. Contemporaries immediately recognized Waldseemüller's wall map as an extraordinary cartographical achievement and it continued to be drawn on for another quarter century.[138]

The same bound volume in Castle Wolfegg contained another large-scale work by Waldseemüller, his *Carta marina* (Navigators' Chart) of 1516. This has been called "an even more astonishing tour-de-force" than the world map, and with good reason.[139] In the *Carta marina* Waldseemüller boldly jettisoned much of what had gone into his world map just nine years earlier. Both Vespucci and Ptolemy have been dethroned. Neither appears at the head of the chart, as they had in 1507. A list of sources in the bottom left-hand corner includes Columbus, but not Vespucci, and the name "America" has been tacitly dropped. Ptolemy has been even more clearly put in his place. Whereas the 1507 map was a recognizable modification of a Ptolemaic world, the 1516 chart has a quite different template—a portolan chart made by Nicolo de Caverio—and the full title states explicitly that it is based on information provided by modern voyagers, including information unknown to the ancients. Compared with the 1507 world map, Waldseemüller's *Carta marina* is more original, more up-to-date, more detailed, and more breathtakingly rich in iconography. Areas of coastline have been redrawn. A substantial amount of text refers to contemporary politics and trade, such as a table that lists Asian spices and the prices they command. Two dozen small pictures indicate local rulers around the globe, seated on thrones or posed in front of tents. Miniature illustrations show regionally distinctive animals or human practices. Waldseemüller depicts a South American opossum, the first marsupial to be shown in any European publication, a reindeer, an elephant, and a rhinoceros, one of the first of many German rhinoceros representations. Perhaps inevitably, there are scenes of cannibalism in South America and Java. Less predictably, Waldseemüller depicts a scene of suttee, or widow burning, in South Asia. It is clearly drawn from one of Burgkmair's illustrations to Balthasar Sprenger's book, published just a few years earlier and one of many signs of the research that went into the *Carta marina*.[140]

The iconographical riches raise the question: What purpose was served by a chart or map of this kind? It was not practical or utilitarian. Waldseemüller's was not the kind of navigators' chart you would take to sea. One need only compare his great work with the model on which it was based to see the difference. Nicolo de Caverio's portolan chart is designed for navigation; it has minimal text or illustrations, no ornamentation, and presents mostly bare space when it comes to the interiors that lie behind the coastlines. The *Carta marina* shares its shape with Caverio and includes the extensive, crisscross rhumb lines that were a feature of all portolan charts; however, the highly ornamented borders, cartouches, and festoons, as well as the elaborate illustrations, lend the work a quite different appearance. Like many other German maps and charts of the period, it was to be displayed and admired, a demonstration of knowledge and command. Consider the image at the bottom of Waldseemüller's *Carta*, copied in Lorenz

Fries's *Carta marina universalis* of 1530, which shows King Manuel I riding a harnessed sea monster—an image of mastery carefully placed by the Cape of Good Hope to signify Portuguese discovery of the sea route to India.[141] The ships we find in contemporary maps also served as symbolic devices. If travel narratives pointed out the perils of journeying across the ocean, with its sickness, shipwreck, and piracy, mapmakers' ships under full sail, which were artfully placed along trade routes well away from stray whales, suggested the European dominance of space through technical mastery.[142] In short, these were maps and charts in which to take pleasure and pride. They were sought after by princes, merchants, physicians, scholars, and other members of the urban elite. The print runs indicate that this map-buying public was extensive.

Globes like Martin Behaim's and the many that followed served a similar purpose. Gemma Frisius, a geographer as well as personal physician to Charles V, said that using a globe "delights astronomers, leads geographers, confirms historians, enriches and improves jurists, is admired by grammarians, guides pilots."[143] He was too delicate to add that a globe instructed merchants and flattered the pride of princes. Germany was a central site of their production. There are extant gores (printed ellipses used to create a globe) made in Strasbourg, Nuremberg, Ingolstadt, and Cologne. A set of them was among the finds at Castle Wolfegg. They were made by Waldseemüller and—like the maps in the Wolfegg collection—had once belonged to Johannes Schöner, a mathematician, cartographer, and scientific instrument maker who studied with Waldseemüller. Schöner himself constructed a series of globes between 1515 and 1533, two of which survive, and enjoyed a European-wide reputation.[144] It is hard to think of a better symbol of how Europeans imagined and celebrated their mastery of the world in the first half of the sixteenth century than the globe. Consider *The Ambassadors* (1533), a work painted by the Augsburg-born Hans Holbein the Younger shortly after he moved permanently to London. Displayed between the two eponymous figures, Holbein's picture shows us a distorted skull, or memento mori, and a carefully arranged set of objects that allude to the new world of global exploration: an oriental carpet, Peter Apian's handbook of commercial arithmetic, a quadrant, an equinoctial dial, an astronomical instrument, and two globes, one terrestrial, one celestial.[145]

Members of the elite might collect a globe, or an oriental rug, as a sign of status. The new worlds offered many attractive prestige objects for those who had the means, starting with pepper, cinnamon, and ginger. There were new fabrics and precious stones, new luxury materials such as mother-of-pearl and ivory. The Fuggers imported many objects of conspicuous consumption like this, including ivory, pearls, gemstones, and leopard skins, as well as prize botanical specimens like orange and almond trees. Some were intended as gifts; others were sold or became part of their own collection. Sometimes the sales were to rulers such as the Emperor Rudolf II in Prague and Albrecht V of Bavaria in Munich, whose so-called cabinets of curiosities housed the largest collections of exotica from around the globe.[146] The typical cabinet of curiosities was divided into *naturalia*, such as ivory and ostrich eggs, camel bezoars, birds, and featherwork from the New World, and *artificialia*, or objects that resulted from human craftsmanship, which might include Indian rugs, carved African ivory, and South or Central American gold and silverware. The Elector Augustus of Saxony specialized in collecting materials from India and others parts of Asia. These included textiles, seashells, plants, and animals, as well as maps of the Subcontinent.[147] But the habit of collecting exotic specimens spread beyond princes. By the early seventeenth century, the Augsburg merchant Philipp Hainhofer set himself up as an agent who purchased luxury goods and "marvels" like these; he also bought objects on his account at the Frankfurt fairs, using them to construct cabinets of curiosities, which he then sold. [148]

Ivory and leopard skins reached Europe only when their wearers were dead. Other animals came over alive, although they did not always stay alive for very long. Manuel I of Portugal brought an elephant from India in 1511. Two years later he shipped it as a gift, together with two leopards and a cheetah, to Pope Leo X.[149] Manuel was less fortunate when he brought an Indian rhinoceros to Lisbon. This animal was also sent to Leo, but it died in a shipwreck off the coast of Italy. The image of the rhinoceros became famous, however, because likenesses of it were produced by two of Renaissance Germany's most prominent printmakers. One was Hans Burgkmair, the illustrator of Balthasar Sprenger's travel book; the other was Albrecht Dürer.[150] Both works are woodcuts and both are based on sketches and descriptions, for neither artist saw the rhinoceros. Burgkmair's depiction was more accurate, but it was Dürer's extraordinarily powerful work that became the definitive image of the rhinoceros until well into the eighteenth century and remains familiar today. The literature on this single work is huge, and art historians have speculated at length on the reasons for the inaccuracies, or embellishments, in Dürer's image. Was the armorlike hide an allusion to the artist's youthful work designing armor in his father's workshop? Was the dorsal horn that Dürer gave the animal a calculated gesture designed to establish that this was a work of art and draw the reader's eye to the name of its maker?[151]

Dürer's rhinoceros shows how indelibly the megafauna of distant worlds could enter the European imagination. That may be even truer of the elephant than the rhinoceros. Once a European had seen an elephant, he or she could believe in the existence of almost anything—that was reportedly the view of the American historian Donald Lach, who devoted a scholarly lifetime to teasing out the impact of Asia on Europe.[152] King Manuel's elephant caused a sensation in Lisbon. Forty years later another elephant crossed the Alps and met with a similar response. When the Habsburg Archduke Maximilian visited his uncle in Lisbon, João III of Portugal, he was fascinated by the royal menagerie. João therefore gave him some Bengali dogs, a pack of monkeys, and a collection of parrots. He also arranged for an elephant to be sent to Austria, suggesting that Maximilian name it Sultan Suleiman, after the Ottoman enemy ("In this way he will become

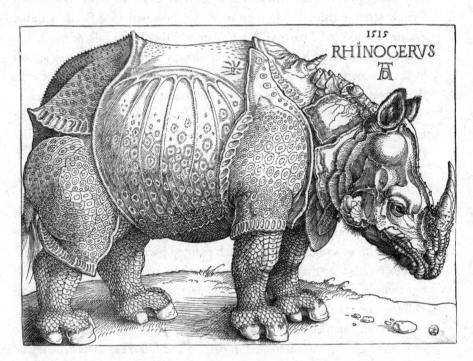

Albrecht Dürer's enigmatic woodcut of a rhinoceros (1515).

your slave and will be properly humiliated"). The animal was shipped to Genoa before traveling with a large escort of horses and men across the snowy Brenner Pass in January 1552 on its way to Vienna. Everywhere it went the elephant caused crowds to turn out. Local versifiers penned doggerel in its praise; innkeepers renamed their hostelries "The Elephant." These were forms of immortality, to be sure, but the animal died the following year of exhaustion and malnutrition.[153]

These were the individual gifts of rulers, but there was a larger European trade in animals. The Fuggers brought over monkeys, wildcats, and parrots in large numbers—to the point that in 1560 Hans Fugger received an indignant letter from the firm's Antwerp agent complaining that the agency was not there to arrange the shipping of wildlife. Parrots had a special fascination for Europeans. They were already to be found in Spain and Italy by the late 1490s. The Nurembergers Anton Tetzel and Willibald Pirckheimer imported parrots in 1505, but the messenger bringing them from Antwerp was robbed. Two years later, the humanist Michael Behaim, another of Martin's younger brothers, received a letter from their brother Wolf in Lisbon that included mention of "a parrot and other strange things they bring from India." Michael reminded Wolf in his reply "how much I enjoy strange things." He then wrote to the agent Jörg Pock in India, asking him to send a parrot ("I don't care whether it can talk or not"). The Augsburg humanist Konrad Peutinger already possessed a talking parrot by then, which he boasted about to fellow humanist Sebastian Brant.[154] In the sixteenth century the parrot was the quintessential exotic marker of wealth and status, favored by princes and patricians. Lucas Cranach the Elder began what became a fashion when his 1502 portrait of Anna Cuspinian, the wife of a Habsburg diplomat, featured a red parrot in the background.[155] Soon, craftsmen producing luxury goods like clocks also took up the parrot as a motif.

Asia and the Americas had a great impact on German art and craft objects. That was true of new materials, like pearl and ivory, and it was true in the realm of iconography. Cranach painted parrots, Waldseemüller put parrots on his 1507 map, and both found a host of imitators. Much of this represented the lure of the exotic. It is particularly notable in the case of Dürer—one scholar has referred to his "quest for the exotic."[156] He sought out materials such as bamboo and coral when on his travels in Antwerp or in Venice, and he was interested in parrots and monkeys, which he incorporated into his work. But how far did non-European art have an impact on European artists, as it clearly did in later centuries? The historian John Elliott has suggested that, however much Dürer might have "gazed in wonder at Montezuma's treasures," the artistic creations of the Indigenous peoples of the Americas exercised "virtually no influence on sixteenth-century European art." They were simply consigned to cabinets of curiosities, "mute witness to the alien customs of non-European man."[157]

Exotic animals, rich fabrics, precious stones, globes—these were the currency of patricians, even of princes and popes. It is therefore worth asking: What impact did the newly discovered worlds have on the everyday life, the material culture or mental universe, of nonelite Germans? Below the elites there was a broader group of the educated. They formed the potential market for Dürer's woodcuts and for popular travel accounts like Feyerabend's compilations or Hans Staden's tale of captivity. In some instances the new worlds found their way right to the heart of popular culture. Playing cards, popular with burghers and common people alike, are an example. The bottom half of playing cards often depicted burlesque scenes of a world turned upside down—a deer roasts a hunter, a wife beats a husband. In one deck, the king of bells card depicted a "Mexican-Indian" king with a savage attendant, and a ship and an elephant in the background. In another set of cards, by the Nuremberg card maker Virgil Solis, the usual suits— acorns, hearts, bells, and leaves—were replaced by lions, monkeys, parrots, and peacocks.[158] Parrots also featured in some popular festivals.[159] There were echoes of new worlds in popular religious culture, too. The Nuremberg carnival procession on Shrove Tuesday, the *Schembartlauf*, featured a ship as one of its floats for the first time in 1506. But there is a larger point to be made here. Looking beyond Protestant Nuremberg and looking ahead to the seventeenth century, it is hard to imagine the richly ornate baroque art of the German Counter Reformation without the gold and silver that flowed into Spain and from there spread through Europe.

CHAPTER 2

COMBUSTIONS

—

*Germany and the
Seventeenth-Century Crisis*

THE SEVENTEENTH CENTURY WAS A TIME OF SOCIAL AND POLITI-
cal upheaval. Rebellions broke out around the world. War, famine, and disease caused prophets to warn that the end-times had come. Witch-hunting
gathered pace. Sitting in his Oxford University study, Robert Burton
recorded this tumult in the baggy masterpiece he published in 1621. In one
of the great, tumbling lists that make *The Anatomy of Melancholy* such com-
pulsive reading, Burton wrote that news came every day of "wars, plagues,
fires, inundations, thefts, murders, massacres, meteors, comets, spectrums,
prodigies, apparitions; of towns taken, cities besieged in France, Germany,
Turky, Persia, Poland, etc., daily musters and preparations, and such-like,
which these tempestuous times afford, battles fought, so many men slain,
monomachies, shipwrecks, piracies, and sea-fights, peace, leagues, strata-
gems, and fresh alarums."[1] His contemporaries painted a no less dramatic
picture of crisis in fewer words. "The world was aflame," said one; these
were the "days of shaking," observed another.[2]

In 1628, the year *The Anatomy of Melancholy* went into its third edition,
a German émigré fled to England from the warfare consuming his native
land. Samuel Hartlib was the son of a German father and an English
mother, a merchant's daughter. He soon established himself in London
with the help of some influential patrons, continued the family tradition by
marrying an Englishwoman, and never returned to Germany. Hartlib was
a Calvinist. He personified the explosive growth of Protestantism over the
previous hundred years, spread by princes and the printed word but also by

émigrés like himself. The Puritan writer John Milton welcomed him as "a person sent hither by some good providence from a farre country." Hartlib was a polymath with a seemingly inexhaustible range of interests. He became an influential figure in his adoptive country and beyond, a cultural broker who sat at the center of a great letter-writing network that stretched across Europe and as far as the American colonies. From his English exile he followed what was happening "in France, Spaine, Germanie, and other Christian Countreys," and he came up with a word for it: "combustions."[3]

The crisis of the seventeenth century, the "combustions," had many causes. Tensions had been building across Europe between rulers and their subjects, especially powerful subjects such as nobles and local estates. Call it a crisis of authority, or legitimacy. The new economic patterns and social relations that emerged in the sixteenth century, partly as a result of overseas expansion into new markets, created a sense of dislocation. Then there was the impact of climate change. The Little Ice Age began to make itself felt severely from the 1590s. Global temperatures dropped sharply, a result of lower levels of sunspot activity and higher levels of volcanic eruptions. An intense version of the El Niño effects with which we have become familiar also played a part. So, in northwestern Europe, did a cycle of the North Atlantic Oscillation that brought colder winters, wetter summers, and more storms.[4] The results were catastrophic. "There is no real constant sunshine," lamented the pastor of Stendal in Prussia; "the earth's crops and produce do not ripen, are no longer as healthy as they were in bygone years. The fruitfulness of all creatures and of the world as a whole is receding."[5] Colder weather shortened the growing season and reduced the cultivable land. That was most spectacularly evident in upland parts of the Holy Roman Empire, like the Alps, where the glaciers that have been shrinking in modern times began a steady advance in the sixteenth century that lasted for three hundred years. In catastrophic years like 1617 and 1618, harvests were ruined, causing chronic food shortages. Malnourished and distressed populations were more vulnerable to the great killers: smallpox, bubonic plague, typhoid, dysentery, and measles. In the case of smallpox, European contacts with Africa and the Americas seem to have introduced more virulent strains that affected people encountering the disease for the first time with special severity.

Epidemic disease was also spread by warfare, as it always has been—it is no accident that typhoid was called "camp fever." War loomed large in the seventeenth-century crisis. "This is the century of the soldiers," said the

Italian diplomat and poet Fulvio Testi in 1641.[6] Those who have counted
these things suggest that more wars were fought around the globe in the
seventeenth century than at any time before the 1940s.[7] The Chinese and
Mughal empires were constantly at war. In Europe, the Ottomans faced
periodic campaigns mounted by the Holy Roman Empire, Hungary, the
Poland-Lithuanian Commonwealth, Russia, and Spain. The Christian
nations also fought among themselves: Sweden went to war against Poland
and Poland against Russia; France fought Spain, Spain fought the Dutch,
and the Dutch fought the English. Just three years in the seventeenth century were entirely free of war in Europe.

Nowhere did war leave a greater or more terrible imprint than in the
German lands. The Thirty Years War (1618–1648) remained "the great war"
in German memory into the twentieth century.[8] Peasants faced marauding armies who lived off the land and committed atrocities on local populations in their search for food, horses, and money. The rural population
was subjected, said a Swabian pastor, to the "enslavement of their villages,
wicked threats from hostile military bands and violent men, plundered,
empty, unplowed fields, bands of robbers, bloodletting, pillaging, arson,
rape, wickedness and disorder."[9] We have around 250 eyewitness accounts
from the Thirty Years War. They paint a consistent picture of the horrors
faced by the peasantry. One resort was to flee to the nearest fortified towns,
but epidemic diseases followed.[10] Almost 10,000 died in Augsburg in the
plague year of 1627.[11] In the worst case, a major town might be sacked. The
sack of Magdeburg in May 1631 by Imperial forces was accompanied by
mass rape and fires that burned down much of the city. Horrified monks
watched six soldiers gang-rape a twelve-year-old girl, who died in the
courtyard of their monastery.[12] As many as 20,000 died in Magdeburg,
which became the supreme example in German collective memory of the
unbridled fury unleashed by the war. It also provided the benchmark for
atrocities elsewhere, like Oliver Cromwell's in Irish Drogheda.[13]

The population loss in the Empire was at least five million, probably
closer to seven million. That meant somewhere between 25 and 45 percent
of the total, greater than in the world wars of the twentieth century. The
worst-hit regions, a diagonal band that ran from Mecklenburg and Pomerania in the northeast to Württemberg and the Upper Rhine in the southwest, lost more than half their population. It took three full generations
for population to return to prewar levels. The balance between people and
animals was altered, too. While people died or abandoned their villages,

The sack of Magdeburg in May 1631, as depicted in 1698
by Pieter van der Aa, a Dutch illustrator.

the wolves moved closer to human settlements. Small wonder, then, that the catastrophic impact of the war lived on in memory. It was passed down in chronicles, given powerful literary form by Hans Jakob Christoffel von Grimmelshausen's perennial bestseller, *Simplicissimus* (1668), and revived for a new nineteenth-century audience by the popular histories of novelist Gustav Freytag.

By the time Freytag published his *Pictures from the German Past* between 1859 and 1867, a narrative of German victimhood was firmly in place. Nationalists deplored the intervention of foreign powers in the Empire's domestic problems and the atrocities that Germans suffered at the hands of non-Germans in consequence. There was some truth in both parts of the story. The army that sacked Magdeburg included Hungarians, Croatians, Poles, Italians, Spaniards, and French, and other powers did make the war longer and more destructive by entering the fray. Unfortunately for Germans, the Empire was the place where the strategic and ideological interests of the major powers intersected. As Sweden's King Gustavus Adolphus said, in Germany "all the wars of Europe are now blended into one."[14] The conflict highlighted the vulnerability of the German lands, as a

conflict that began when Emperor Ferdinand II tried to put down a revolt
of the Bohemian estates, turned into a "European civil war."[15] It is not hard
to see why later nationalist historians chose to frame things as they did,
casting Germans as passive victims caught between tragic political division
at home and predatory foreigners.

Viewed from a different angle, however, the conflict was a domestic
German crisis that spilled over into the rest of Europe, drawing in other
powers that felt that they could not afford to remain uninvolved—Spain
and the papacy joining in on the Habsburg-Imperial side, while Denmark,
Sweden, France, and the United Provinces resisted them. The war also sent
the notorious German soldiery spilling out across Europe—for example,
to Italy. Alessandro Manzoni's great historical novel, *The Betrothed* (1827),
is set in northern Italy in 1630, where Imperial soldiers under Italian command run amok. They are associated with spreading the plague and with
laying waste to everything they encounter. They are "fiends" who threaten,
steal, sack, and burn. The priest's servant Perpetua suggests to her cow-
ardly master, Don Abbondio, that perhaps there is safety in numbers. "In
numbers?" said Don Abbondio. "In numbers? My poor Perpetua, don't
you realize that one German soldier can eat a hundred of these people for
breakfast?"[16] And what if it was the "German" war that helped to cause the
"general crisis." At least one scholar has made that case. Whether European
powers were enticed into intervening in German affairs, or felt compelled
to do so, the effect was the same. It spread instability. Events in Germany
exported disorder across Europe. War caused participants to try to extract
greater resources from their populations. And those efforts triggered the
spate of rebellions that marked the whole period.[17]

The ingredients that produced political instability were many—
economic distress, epidemic disease, the strains of war. But there was an
additional explosive element in the mix and it was made in Germany. The
European crisis was also a result of new religious divisions. The violence of
the period was fueled by new forms of religious zeal. We see it in large-scale
bloodlettings such as the St. Bartholomew's Day Massacre of Protestants in
France (1572), and in the burning of individual martyrs on a scale unequaled
before or since.[18] The same is true of the organized violence we call war.
From the French Wars of Religion (1562–1598) and the Dutch Revolt of the
late sixteenth century to the Thirty Years War, religious conviction and
religious hatred were prime movers. The Thirty Years War has been called
"the greatest of Europe's religious wars."[19] And while the conflict raged on

German soil, foreign observers had no doubt about the stakes. "The Palatinate is on fire; religion is on fire; and all other countries are on fire"—that was how Sir John Davies saw it from the English House of Commons in 1620.[20] Farther away, John Winthrop of Massachusetts told friends in London of his hopes that God would make "the King of Sweden an instrument for the fall of the Antichrist," by which he meant the pope.[21]

Religious Division

THE REFORMATION WAS AN EXPLOSIVE MOVEMENT OUT OF GERmany and Switzerland, which shaped European and world history. Perhaps it would be better to say "Reformations," for the movements in question included not only Martin Luther's challenge, with which it all began, but the so-called Second Reformation associated with John Calvin, the radical sects that surfaced almost from the start, and the Catholic Reformation (or Counter Reformation) that answered them all. The shock waves were widely felt. In 1770 Raymond Revoir, the abbott of Sainte-Geneviève in Paris, linked the New World and the new faith when he proclaimed, "Luther and Columbus appeared, the whole universe trembled, and all Europe was in commotion."[22] Closer to our own time, and our own sensibility, the great nineteenth-century Swiss historian Jacob Burckhardt developed a theory of crises, moments when the course of history accelerated and "ruptures" created an "absolutely new form of life." He believed the Reformation was such a crisis, for it not only brought major change to Germany but marked a "transformation of the world."[23]

The world-historical can often be seen in the local, the world in a grain of sand. Turn up the magnification, for example, and you can see how the Reformation transformed universities like Wittenberg (Lutheran) and Heidelberg (Calvinist) into international destinations. The same is true of Vienna and Ingolstadt, their Catholic counterparts. Other places are important because they were "crossroads cities." Strasbourg and Zürich were two of them, in the south. So, in the north, were Emden and the Baltic ports of Danzig and Lübeck. All were places from which the word, and those who carried the word, moved across borders. The same was true later of Frankfurt am Main, which became a staging post in the routes of Calvinist refugees and a haunt of William Penn's agents in Europe.[24]

Let us look more closely, then, at some of the people and places, the conduits and institutions, through which the Reformation spread beyond

Germany, as well as the reasons it did so. Scandinavia is a good place to start because the introduction of the Reformation there suggests the whole range of ways in which the new faith spread. The pattern in Scandinavia resembled what happened within the Empire: there was a princely Reformation that suited the needs of rulers, but there was also a more popular Reformation. It was least powerful in Sweden, where Gustav Vasa became king in 1523 after a series of wars that broke up the Danish-dominated Kalmar Union of Scandinavian kingdoms. Years of fighting had left many unfilled bishoprics. Filling them became a source of conflict between the new king and Rome. Gustav Vasa was familiar with Lutheran ideas, probably through his chancellor, a Lutheran convert. He encouraged and protected its advocates, such as Olaus Petri, a theologian educated at Rostock, Leipzig, and Wittenberg who wrote Lutheran pastoral works and preached in Stockholm's main church. But the wealth of the church was also a motive behind the Swedish Reformation. Gustav Vasa was looking for a source of funds to repay his Hanseatic financiers in the wars to free Sweden from Danish control. The Catholic Church owned 40 percent of the land in Scandinavia and a third of urban properties, all of it exempt from taxation: a plump target.[25] At a meeting in 1527 Gustav used both carrot and stick to persuade the Swedish estates to end the independence of the church and permit the new faith to be preached. Church property was confiscated and passed to the crown and nobility. That was the key: secularization preceded Reformation.[26]

Religious reform moved slowly at first, because Gustav faced peasant rebellions in which resentment over taxes was joined by opposition to the new faith. Then he picked up the pace. The king made it clear that he wanted to establish royal authority over the Lutheran Church, which he achieved by bringing in German councilors such as Wittenberg-trained Georg Norman. The church reorganization that followed was a thoroughly princely undertaking. Beyond Stockholm, which had a resident German merchant community and where there was popular support for the evangelical cause, the Reformation in Sweden was a top-down affair. It also bore a German stamp. From the first generation of theologians who enjoyed the protection of Gustav Vasa, through to Norman and his reforms, the Wittenberg connection was strong. It would continue: the Lutheran who introduced the Reformation into the Swedish dependency of Finland was Wittenberg-educated; so was Axel Oxenstierna, who served as Sweden's high chancellor to Gustavus Adolphus and his successor, Queen Christina, during the Thirty Years War.

The Wittenberg connection was important in Denmark, too. The most famous examples are Prince Hamlet, his friend Horatio, and his "two schoolfellows," Rosencrantz and Guildenstern—Wittenberg alumni all. But they had their real-life counterparts. The three rulers who presided over the Danish Reformation all brought Wittenberg-educated theologians into the country. The first of them was Christian II, a complex figure who combined cultivation with cruelty. He was related by marriage to the Holy Roman Emperor, visiting Charles V in the Netherlands in 1521, where he discussed the Reformation with the humanist scholar Erasmus of Rotterdam. Christian quarreled with Rome and invited Wittenberg Lutherans into his kingdom in the early 1520s to preach and advise on church reforms. The most daring invitation went to Andreas Karlstadt, Luther's more radical colleague, but his stay in Copenhagen proved brief. Correctly spotting the unstable political situation, Karlstadt scurried back to Wittenberg.[27] Shortly afterward, Christian II was deposed by Danish elites and replaced by his uncle, who ruled as Frederik I. Christian himself became a rather unwelcome émigré in Wittenberg, where he lodged with the artist Lucas Cranach, before moving on to exile in the Netherlands.[28]

Frederik I was more tactful than his predecessor but, like Gustav Vasa in Sweden, eyed church property greedily. In 1527 Frederik broke with Rome, creating a national church and enriching both crown and noble coffers via secularization. But he was also genuinely sympathetic to evangelical reform, with privy councillors around him who tried to advance the Lutheran cause. The Danish Reformation had a broader popular base than in Sweden. Denmark was more urbanized and German merchant communities had established themselves in the large towns that faced each other across the Øresund, Copenhagen, and Malmö. Itinerant German preachers went there to preach the new faith.[29] Malmö soon had a Lutheran printing press and went over to the new faith by the end of the 1520s.[30] To the north, in Viborg, Lutheranism was also preached by two Wittenberg-trained clergy. They were opposed by the local bishop but supported by the magistracy and the more outspoken of the two was placed under royal protection by Frederik. The message was preached even earlier in Schleswig, in the far south of the kingdom. Hermann Tast, yet another Wittenberg-trained clergyman, was in Husum by 1522, preaching the evangelical message in Low German. The "gray town by the sea" proved receptive.

Schleswig helped to spearhead the Danish Reformation. It was the home base of Duke Christian of Schleswig-Holstein, the king's son and the future Christian III. A devoted supporter of the evangelical cause who had attended the Diet of Worms in 1521 and witnessed Luther at first hand, Duke Christian surrounded himself with Lutheran councilors and brought in two German theologians to introduce the new faith. They drafted the Lutheran articles of faith known as the Haderslev Church Order, the first church order of the new kind in Scandinavia (and one of the first anywhere). Evangelical preachers were appointed to urban parishes and longer-serving clergy admonished to preach the gospel and follow Luther's Bible commentaries in their sermons.

When Frederik I died in 1533, Denmark's Catholic bishops, backed by their supporters among the nobility, tried to block Christian's succession. Two years of civil war ensued when Malmö and other cities resisted. Christian emerged as the winner. Entering Copenhagen in 1536 as Christian III, he arrested the bishops who had opposed him, abolished ecclesiastical property, and arranged for the consecration of new bishops who would approve these measures. Their consecration was performed by Johannes Bugenhagen, part of the inner circle at Wittenberg and the minister who had married Martin Luther to Katharina von Bora twelve years earlier. While in Copenhagen, Bugenhagen also crowned Christian III and his queen. But that was not all. A Pomeranian who spoke Low German and could make himself (more or less) understood from the Dutch border to the Polish-Lithuanian Commonwealth, Bugenhagen became a one-man engine of Lutheran reform across the north, in Hamburg, Danzig, and in his native Pomerania.[31] In Denmark he introduced the new Danish Church Order of 1537, much of it drafted by a phalanx of Wittenberg alumni. In 1538 Christian III tied himself more closely to Lutheranism by adopting the Augsburg Confession, a statement of allegiance to the new faith, and joining the Schmalkaldic League of German Protestant princes.[32] In the following decades the reformers tried to spread the new faith from the towns into the countryside. They sent in new clergy, opened schools, and established a system of poor relief. At the same time, the Reformation was imposed on the Danish dependency of Norway. This proved to be a slow process except in Bergen, where the Hanseatic League had a staple house.

In Scandinavia, then, a decisive role was played by princes who were committed to the new faith, or at least could see its uses; but their actions went with the grain of evangelical preaching and the power of print to disseminate the word, whether through the Bible, sermons, or popular works like Luther's *Small Catechism* of 1529. Where new church orders were introduced, music played its part as well. An example is the distinctive hymnody developed in Rostock by the reformer Joachim Slüter, which was influential in Denmark and Sweden.[33] The physical presence of Germans, both permanent residents and incomers, was also important for the Scandinavian Reformation. The same was true in northeastern and Central Europe. Lutheran ideas spread rapidly along the Baltic coast and in the trading cities of the interior, with their German populations, but outside preachers and organizers also played a part. In the 1520s and '30s, two reformers preached and built a Lutheran church in the Baltic, with its center in Riga. Königsberg was another base; it had a Lutheran university established in 1544, the Albertina, led by a Lithuanian who had studied with the scholar and reformer Philipp Melanchthon in Wittenberg. It also became a hub for printing evangelical literature. These publications were not always in German. The very first book printed in Lithuanian was an edition of Luther's *Small Catechism* published in Königsberg, a reminder that the new faith appealed to the Lithuanian-speaking population.[34] Lutheranism also made inroads among the lesser Polish nobility, even as the Polish Jagiellonian kings saw advantages in playing off urban Protestants against noble magnates. The complex politics of Poland-Lithuania, the largest state in sixteenth-century Europe, provided a host of reasons that drew people to the evangelical movement, whether they were Germans, Lithuanians, or Poles, townsmen or nobles.

Lutheranism also won converts in Bohemia among the lesser Czech nobility, but found its strongest support among the German population of the towns. There, just as in heavily German towns in Poland-Lithuania, the pattern resembled what happened in the Empire when cities went over to Protestantism. Joachimsthal in the Bohemian Erzgebirge was a special instance of evangelical ideas establishing themselves in an urban setting. The town sprang up quickly when silver deposits were discovered, drawing Saxon miners who took their Lutheranism with them. The mine owners, too, were Lutherans. The mineral wealth of the town funded a Latin school, a girls' school, and a hospital. Joachimsthal became famous within the Lutheran tradition for two reasons. One was the career of Johann Matthesius, rector of the local Latin school and long-serving church pastor. Matthesius had studied with Luther and became his first biographer. The other source of Joachimthal's celebrity was music. Nikolaus Herman, who was the church organist, cantor and teacher in the Latin school, trained choirs of extraordinary quality. He also composed more than two hundred hymns, many incorporating both folk elements and pre-Reformation plainchant. Some remain in the standard Lutheran hymn repertory, like "Erschienen Ist der Herrlich Tag." Town magistrates supported Herman's work by hiring professional musicians. In Joachimsthal, even more than elsewhere, hymnody became central to the new faith.[35]

Often, a single person carried the new faith. In Hungary, it was Leonhard Stöckel, who had studied with Luther in Wittenberg, worked as a private tutor in Luther's birthplace, Eisleben, then returned to his hometown of Bartfeld in 1539 to become rector of a Latin school there. Bartfeld was one of five German "free cities" in northern Hungary. These Germans were mainly Saxons, as they were in Joachimsthal, but Saxons who had arrived in the twelfth century to farm, not on the eve of the Reformation to dig silver. By the 1540s they had gone over to Lutheranism. Stöckel, twenty-nine when he returned home, was a pedagogue and proselytizer. He was also a playwright who put the drama of spiritual struggle on the stage. His *History of Susanna* (1559) was a tragedy in which virtuous Susanna represented the Lutheran church threatened by the pope and by Ottoman Turks.[36]

Stöckel had a counterpart among the Saxon Germans of the Transylvanian Siebenbürgen (Seven Cities). Johannes Honterus was born in one of those cities, Kronstadt, which was perched in a narrow valley in the Carpathians. He picked up Protestant ideas during his student years in the Empire, then lived for a time in Basel, where he worked as a wood-carver and publisher's reader. Honterus was thirty-five when he returned in 1533 to his hometown, where he was appointed town minister and became rector of the Latin school. (The Latin school, or *Gymnasium*, was a key institution for religious reform across eastern Europe.) In the sixteen years before his death in 1549, Honterus left Kronstadt just once—to visit Luther in Wittenberg. Honterus established a printing press, the first in the region, later a paper mill and library as well. He continued to write, publishing a work of cosmography and a history of the world in verse and maps.[37]

German speakers were the earliest converts to evangelical ideas, but Lutheranism also found supporters in the Hungarian population. Sometimes Hungarian speakers of German descent worked to convert the local population, like Gaspar Heltai, who studied in Wittenberg and returned to Klausenburg in his Transylvanian homeland. There he set up the first printshop in town, as well as a paper mill, a brewery, and public baths. Among the sixteenth-century reformers who followed Heltai, two men who had been classmates at Wittenberg stand out from the rest: the preacher and writer Matyas Devai Biro (known as "the Hungarian Luther"), and the teacher and printer Johannes Sylvester, who published a Hungarian New Testament. On the fringes of Hungary, German evangelical ideas also spread to converts among other ethnic groups like Slovakians and Croats.

Lutheran ideas had made some inroads at court in the early 1520s, but it was the catastrophic Hungarian defeat by the Turks at the Battle of Mohács in 1526 that opened the way to evangelical reform. Twenty-year-old King Lajos II and many of the country's Catholic bishops were killed, along with much of the nobility, as the Ottomans sacked the royal capital in Buda. The authority of church and state was weakened and the disaster heightened the belief that a rotten system was in need of purification. This made the idea of reform more appealing. The effective partitioning of the kingdom that followed made it harder to enforce religious orthodoxy, creating space for the reformers. It also strengthened the hand of large landowners who had gone over to Lutheranism and were able to provide protection for those whose evangelical preaching got them into trouble with local bishops.

Crown and bishops, towns and nobles—they made up the parallelogram of forces within which the Reformation unfolded everywhere in Europe. "Everywhere" includes England. For all the distinctiveness of the Anglican Church eventually established there, it is easy to exaggerate English exceptionalism. The political motives that drove Henry VIII to break with Rome were particular to his marital circumstances, but the trajectory of the English Reformation was similar to the course of events in Scandinavia, especially Sweden. The English Reformation, like its Continental counterparts, was shaped at every turn by the ideas that came out of Germany. England enjoyed close material and cultural ties to the Continent. Evangelical ideas were carried across the Channel by merchants and scholars; circles of supporters discussed the reformers' books and pamphlets. They formed in London, and in Oxford, where the bookseller Thomas Garrett was a central figure. But the most celebrated of these Protestant cells met at the White Horse Inn at Cambridge. Its members included William Tyndale, Hugh Latimer, Thomas Cranmer, Myles Coverdale, John Bale, Nicholas Ridley, Thomas Bilney, and Robert Barnes. Their shared interest in Lutheran ideas made them a "Little Germany."[38] They furnished both leading actors and bit players in the English Reformation, as well as some of England's most celebrated Protestant martyrs.

Henry VIII made himself familiar at an early stage with Luther's ideas and detested them. Named a defender of the faith by Pope Leo X,

Henry threw himself into persecuting Protestant thought. Its followers recanted, lay low, or went into exile on the Continent. Robert Barnes went to Germany, where he met Luther (the two men shared a background as Augustinians) and returned a full convert to the new faith. Myles Coverdale, another Augustinian and author of what would be the first complete English translation of the Bible, also went into exile in 1528, the first of three periods of exile on the Continent. William Tyndale left England in 1524. He went, like others before him, to Wittenberg; then he moved around, trying to find a publisher for his translation of the New Testament, the first in English. Printing began in Cologne in 1525, was interrupted by opposition, and completed the following year in another Rhenish town, Worms, which was in the process of going over to the evangelical cause. Additional copies were printed in Antwerp. All had to be smuggled across the Channel. By 1536, when Tyndale was arrested, strangled, and burned at the stake in Vilvoorde on the orders of the Emperor, it is estimated that some 16,000 copies of his New Testament were circulating in England.[39] In a population of no more than 2.5 million, that is the equivalent of 350,000 copies today.

A more cautious member of the White Horse tavern group, Thomas Cranmer, forged his own Continental connection in 1532 when he married the niece of Andreas Osiander, Nuremberg's most prominent Lutheran theologian.[40] But this was no desperate exile's marriage; it was a sign of changing times in England. What precipitated change was "the king's great matter." Henry VIII had been trying since 1527 to annul his marriage to Catherine of Aragon, arguing that it had been sinful to marry his deceased brother's widow. In 1529, Catherine appealed to Rome. Between 1529 and 1533 Henry's search for an annulment led to schism with Rome. Cranmer was a central figure in this shift. He had been in Germany in 1532 as part of Henry's team of tame theologians charged with canvassing learned opinion on the Continent and finding arguments that supported the king. The next year, Cranmer was appointed archbishop of Canterbury. In that role he declared Henry's marriage annulled, opening the way for the king's second marriage, to Anne Boleyn, to be officially acknowledged.

Cranmer was one of the two key figures responsible for pushing through the Henrician Reformation. The other was Thomas Cromwell, once known to the world (insofar as he was known at all) as the bureaucrat who instituted a "Tudor revolution in government," now much more widely familiar as the surprisingly sympathetic and strikingly modern protagonist of

Hilary Mantel's *Wolf Hall* trilogy of historical novels.[41] The humbly born Cromwell first came to notice politically in the service of someone from a similar background, Cardinal Thomas Wolsey. Ruthless but a consummate tactician, Cromwell survived Wolsey's fall and later became Henry's right-hand man, dissolving the monasteries and friaries and enforcing royal supremacy over the church. He was himself a discreet but convinced Protestant, with links to other evangelicals at home and abroad.[42] One trusted go-between was Stephen Vaughan, a Protestant merchant and occasional royal emissary (he negotiated royal loans from the Fuggers, among other tasks), who entered Cromwell's service in 1523 and had connections to émigré networks on the Continent. Another of Cromwell's close acquaintances during his years of success in the 1530s was Hans Holbein, the German artist who painted *The Ambassadors*. Holbein first visited England in 1526, then returned for a longer stay in 1532 and became the court painter. His flattering portrait of Henry VIII (1536–37) remains one of the most famous likenesses of an English monarch. Anne Boleyn, herself a Protestant convert, was a powerful patron of Holbein, as she was of Cromwell and Cranmer.

By the time Holbein finished his portrait, however, the queen was dead, executed in 1536 after being brought down by a plot that Cromwell engineered. Four years later Cromwell himself was executed on trumped-up charges, the victim of a noble faction of religious conservatives. (The same thing nearly happened to Cranmer a few years later.) The Reformation in England was a drawn-out, discontinuous affair, marked by struggles at court between evangelicals and conservatives, neither of whom were entirely open about their convictions, and challenged by popular revolts like the Pilgrimage of Grace in 1536–37, in which hostility to religious reforms was reinforced by major economic grievances. Henry tacked between different positions, and his death in 1547 introduced a new form of instability. England had three new monarchs in the next twelve years: first the young Edward VI, under whom the Reformation was pursued more wholeheartedly; then his Catholic half sister Mary Tudor, under whom it went into reverse; and finally, Henry's daughter Elizabeth, who came to the throne in 1558 and introduced a kind of stability.

This syncopated rhythm created waves of emigration and immigration that kept England closely connected to the Continent. Many of the original émigrés of the 1520s returned in the following decade, but Henry's bloodletting in 1540, when Robert Barnes and two other evangelicals were executed (along with three Catholics), caused renewed emigration among radical reformers. Myles Coverdale, who returned from his first exile only in 1535, now had to flee again. He worked as a translator in Strasbourg, then earned a theological degree in Tübingen and became a minister in Germany. Not all the émigrés of 1540 were clergy. Merchant Richard Hilles, the later founder of the Merchant Taylors School, also went into exile and ended up in Strasbourg. Migration ran in the opposite direction after Edward VI's accession in 1547. Archbishop Cranmer, finally free of Henry's prevarications, now charted a much firmer Protestant course. His intellectual horizons were European, and he took advantage of the persecution that Protestants on the Continent faced from the Emperor Charles V to attract leading intellectuals to England. Cranmer's European imports filled the Regius professorships at Oxford and Cambridge. There were even unsuccessful attempts to lure Philipp Melanchthon from Wittenberg. The academic theologians who came to England during Edward's reign left their mark on the Anglican Church. Cranmer's second Prayer Book in English showed the influence of Martin Bucer. The doctrinal statement known as the Forty-Two Articles incorporated south German Protestant views. But Continental influences left their trace beyond formal doctrine. Protestant printers in Antwerp fleeing Charles V's crackdown in the Netherlands brought their skills to England. The result was a greatly increased circulation of popular evangelical tracts.

When Mary I ascended to the throne in 1553 upon her half brother's death, the directional arrow of emigration swung round once again. As Mary began to undo the work of the Reformation, some eight hundred clergy, scholars, students, gentry, merchants, and others with means fled with their households to the Continent. They escaped the persecution that cost around three hundred Protestant lives by 1558, Cranmer's among them. A dozen former or future bishops were among the émigrés. Another churchman who left was the historian and dramatist John Bale, part of the original White Horse group, who had fled England after Thomas Cromwell's fall in 1540, returned when Edward VI became king, then fled again in 1553. He went via the Low Countries, to Frankfurt, then Basel. It was the same route followed by Bale's close friend, the young scholar and clergyman John Foxe, who took ship with his pregnant wife just ahead of officers sent to arrest him. It was in Strasbourg and Basel that the earliest versions of his famous work appeared: *Actes and Monuments of These Latter and Perilous Days*, better known as "Foxe's Book of Martyrs." These two early versions were both written in Latin. The more substantial of the two, the

Basel edition of 1559, occupied a modest 600 pages. It was only after Foxe returned to England in the reign of Elizabeth that a longer English version of some 1800 pages came out, incorporating greater and more gruesome detail about the victims of "Bloody Mary." The prototype of the book that served, like few others, to bolster English Protestant identity against the Catholic other was a product of exile "in the far parts of Germany."[43]

The places where the English settled tell us a lot about the developing character of the Reformation. Most exiles sailed first to the Low Countries, usually Antwerp, then they fanned out across Germany, from Emden in the north, Wesel, Duisburg, and Worms in the west, to Frankfurt and points south—Strasbourg, Basel, Aarau, Zurich, or Geneva. These represented a cross-section of non-Lutheran, or Reformed, Protestantism. From an early stage Strasbourg was the great laboratory or incubator of different versions of Reformation. We know from the correspondence of the Swiss reformer Heinrich Bullinger that he was in contact with no fewer than ten of the many English exiles in Strasbourg in the 1550s.[44] Bullinger, who continued Huldrych Zwingli's version of Reformed Protestantism, also welcomed English exiles who sought a haven in Zürich, Aarau, or Basel. Then there was the brand of Reformed Protestantism that increasingly became synonymous with the term, namely Calvinism, the creation of a convert—John Calvin—who fled France and spent time in both Basel and Strasbourg before he settled in Geneva in 1541. Some English exiles went to more northerly Calvinist towns, such as Emden or Wesel; but the largest Marian exile community was in Geneva itself, numbering around 140 households. Its members adopted the presbyterian form of worship, which was later carried back to Britain. Geneva was also the setting for two other landmarks in British Protestantism: the Geneva Bible, overseen by William Whittingham (Calvin's brother-in-law) and Myles Coverdale, and John Knox's notorious *First Blast of the Trumpet Against the Monstrous Regiment of Women*, published in the spring of 1558.

These were practices or works, forged (like Foxe's Book of Martyrs) in a brief but intense period of Central European exile, which had lasting influence back home. So did the divisions that emerged among the exiles. They were most conspicuous within the English community in Frankfurt, where differences between mainstream Anglicans and Reformed radicals led to open conflict between those who sided with Richard Cox, a key figure in the Church of England during Edward VI's reign, and supporters of the Reformed John Knox—a clash of "Coxites" and "Knoxites." It ended when the latter were expelled from the exile church and moved on to Geneva, but the conflicts in Frankfurt established the terms of future differences in Elizabethan England between supporters of moderate Anglicanism and the theological radicals who called themselves the "Godly" and are usually known as Puritans.[45] This conflict, sharpened in exile, eventually assumed even greater importance when Puritans crossed the Atlantic.

From its original base in Switzerland and southern Germany, Calvinism spread across Europe, to England and (especially) Scotland, the Low Countries, France, where its adherents called themselves Huguenots, and to Poland and Hungary, where the Reformed message resonated powerfully in eastern areas of the Hungarian plain, closest to where Turkish successes had discredited old clerical elites. Reformed Protestantism crossed borders more easily than Lutheranism, because it was much less of a princely Reformation from above. But rulers also helped the movement along. Take the case of the cosmopolitan Polish noble and scholar Jan Laski. His peregrinations in the years after 1540 took him from Poland to Basel, Emden, London, Copenhagen, Brandenburg, Lithuania, and back to Poland, a remarkable series of border crossings that would have been impossible without patrons such as the Countess Anna in Emden and influential figures around Edward VI in England. Or think of the university that princely patronage turned into the academic jewel of Calvinism: thanks to Frederick III, the Reformed Elector of the Palatinate, Heidelberg after 1560 eclipsed the Geneva Academy and was rivaled only by the Dutch University of Leiden. It drew students and refugee scholars from across Europe.[46] If the original, Lutheran Reformation was made in Germany, the Second Reformation also bore a strongly German imprint. Its learning came increasingly from Heidelberg, while the metrical hymn-singing that was the "secret weapon" of Reformed congregations came from Strasbourg.[47]

Reformed Protestantism was militant in temper and international in outlook. The two things went together. Not only was there international Calvinism. There was, said critics, also a Calvinist International.[48] It is worth thinking about the implicit modern analogy, although we should be careful not to overdo the parallels with disciplined, ideologically motivated movements of the twentieth century. It is certainly true that the Reformed faith exploded as a popular movement in various parts of Europe after 1560, most notably France and the Low Countries. This led to a backlash, and to waves of emigration that further underscored the international character of the movement. Calvinism was the Reformation of the refugees, at a time when the number of religious émigrés had never been higher.[49] During the Dutch Revolt against Spanish rule, around 100,000 people left the Low Countries for Britain or Germany at the end of the 1560s; more followed in the 1570s, after events like the sack of Antwerp in 1576. The German lands absorbed roughly twice as many of these Dutch exiles as Britain. The town of Wesel doubled in population with the arrival of refugees. Emden, just across the Ems Bay from the Netherlands, was another border town that became a favored destination of religious exiles. It had already served as a refuge for English evangelicals fleeing Queen Mary in the 1550s; now it was transformed. The influx of Dutch mercantile wealth meant that by the time Emden built a grand new town hall in 1573, its 530 ships counted as one of the largest merchant fleets in Europe. Printers came, too, turning Emden into a center for the production of evangelical literature.[50] Like the political émigrés of the twentieth century, those fleeing the "Spanish fury" enriched their host countries, whether as merchants, craftsmen, printers, or publishers. Theodor de Bry and Levinus Hulsius, for example, fled from Liège and Ghent, respectively. They settled in Frankfurt, where both became major publishers of travel books. By 1600 Frankfurt was home to 3000 middle-class émigrés from the Low Countries. They outnumbered the city's Jewish community (around 2500), one of Germany's largest.[51]

The waves of emigration continued into the seventeenth century. Hundreds of thousands fled after the crushing of the Bohemian uprising by Imperial forces in 1620, and the departure of Protestant exiles from the parts of Germany threatened by the forcible reimposition of Catholicism became a familiar by-product of the Thirty Years War.[52] This was the background of turmoil and uncertainty that caused Samuel Hartlib's move to England in 1628. Then, at the end of the century, it was once again German lands that played host to a new generation of exiles. Some 200,000 Huguenots left France after the revocation of the Edict of Nantes in 1685 initiated a period of persecution; 40,000 ended up in Germany. They were actively courted by the Great Elector of Brandenburg, whose agents in the major stop-over cities—Amsterdam, Cologne, Hamburg, Frankfurt—approached newly arrived Huguenots with money and passes. Almost 20,000 Huguenots settled in the Great Elector's territory. In Berlin they formed a fifth of the city's population. These were not the wealthiest émigrés (those people went to England or the Netherlands), but they brought skilled crafts with them. The state of Hessen-Kassel also wooed them, establishing "Huguenot towns" where the newcomers lived among themselves. That made sense: the migrants injected economic dynamism into their host societies, but met with initial hostility because of the special concessions they received, their success in business, the fact that they spoke a different language, and—not least—their distinctive and militant form of faith, which was disliked by many of the Lutherans among whom they now settled almost as much as it had been by the Catholic persecutors from whom they fled.[53]

Reformed Protestants crossed borders more readily than Lutherans partly out of necessity. Survival sometimes meant moving on. How much more true that was for those—Luther called them *Schwärmer*, or fanatics— who were followers of one or another branch of the Radical Reformation. These, mainly Anabaptists and their offshoots, included an array of denominations: South German Anabaptists, Dutch Mennonites, the Moravian Church (or Unity of Brethren), Silesian Schwenkfelder. Some were activist, others quietist. Most harbored millenarian hopes of a new heaven on earth. And the seemingly fixed geographical identities inscribed in the names of these sects belie the fact that they were made up of people who had often had to keep moving on to somewhere else as a matter of self-preservation.[54] Another of these denominations, the Hutterites, first fled the Tyrol and moved in turn to Moravia, Transylvania, and Ukraine. We find such groups spread across Europe, from southern Russia to England, carrying ideas that periodically resurfaced at moments of political crisis.

The historian John Bossy, after pondering how these doctrines seem to have reached seventeenth-century England as "spores secreted in a Christian culture," concluded: "In any case, no one who turns from the history of radical Christianity in the Germany of the 1520s and 1530s to the England of the 1640s and 1650s can fail to get the feeling that he has been there before."[55] The spores reached beyond Europe. Just as English Puritans looked across the Atlantic and French Huguenots tried to establish a colony in Florida, so the more radical Reformation sects—Hutterites, Mennonites, and others—also settled in the New World.[56] Some of them became key intermediaries between the Old World and the New. A remnant of the Hussite Bohemian Brethren, who had been scattered across Europe after the crushing of the Bohemian revolt in 1620, was refounded in Saxony on the estate of a sympathetic German nobleman as the Moravian Church, or Herrnhuter. Their missionary network would be one of the forces that helped to knit together the Atlantic world of the eighteenth century.[57]

Before the 1700s, however, Protestantism was carried beyond Europe's

shores by individuals or small groups of settlers, not by systematic missionary activity.[58] The situation was very different in the case of the Catholic
Church, which in the sixteenth century increasingly made claims to be
global as well as universal. The vigorous response of the Catholic Church
to the Protestant challenge within Europe was accompanied by a series
of missionary initiatives that took the Catholic faith to the Americas, the
Philippines, Japan, China, and India. Many orders were engaged in this
work. Some are well-known, such as the Franciscans, Dominicans, Bene-
dictines, and Augustinians; others are less familiar. In New Spain alone,
we encounter orders like the Mercedarians, Hieronymites, and Antonins.
There were undoubtedly Germans among these missionaries, although the
details are often murky.[59] But the order most closely identified with the
overseas missions, and more broadly with "global mobility," is the Jesuits.[60]
Their activities have attracted enormous interest partly because they kept
much better records than any other order, and from those records we know
that Germans played a remarkably large role in the American and Asian
Jesuit missions.

It was a role that was delayed until the beginning of the seventeenth
century. Before then, German Jesuits were prohibited from going to the
Americas or Asia because their place was supposed to be at home, helping
the church recover from its crisis. When, in 1561, the principal architect of
the Counter Reformation in the Empire, Peter Canisius, proposed four
German fellow Jesuits for the overseas mission, he was rebuffed on the
grounds that all available priests were needed in Central Europe. The following year, German Jesuits were formally banned from participating in
overseas missions.[61] In the half century that followed, more Jesuits entered
the Empire than left it, as Canisius and his colleagues, along with some
other orders like the Capuchins, treated the German lands as a virgin field
for missionary work. They were strongly backed by territorial princes like
the Wittelsbachs in Bavaria and (usually) by the Habsburgs.

The results were dramatic, measured against the dire situation the
church initially faced in Germany, where most Imperial cities and many
territorial rulers had gone over to the new faith and there was widespread
Catholic demoralization. In the second half of the sixteenth century, a
still expanding Reformation controlled half of Europe; a century later that
figure had been rolled back to about a fifth. The greatest changes were
in Central and southeastern Europe: in Austria, Bohemia, Moravia, and
Poland-Lithuania.[62] Within the core German lands, the structures of the

church had been rebuilt and Catholic worship reformed in line with the standardized liturgy and practices that emerged from the Council of Trent (1545–1563). This work of renewal, resented and resisted in parts of the German hierarchy, owed a huge debt to the foreign Jesuits gathered around Canisius (who was himself Dutch, although educated in Cologne). It was a program that included church building; the founding of educational institutions, including universities such as Ingolstadt and Dillingen to train future leaders; establishing printing presses; encouraging lay confraternities; and holding popular missions complete with outdoor altars, music, processions, and gun salutes. One distinctively contemporary aspect of this Catholic renewal was how the "struggle" against the Ottoman Turks was dramatized as a Catholic defense of Christendom. (A few German Jesuits belonged to missions that ministered to German, Hungarian, and Slav Catholics in areas occupied by the Ottomans.)[63] At the same time, the cult of martyrs and saints was revived and extended to new martyrs like Francis Xavier, while pilgrimages like Altötting and Mariazell were heavily promoted.[64] Many practices we associate with "traditional" German (especially Bavarian) Catholicism, such as the cult of saints and relics, Marian devotions, shrines and pilgrimages, were first fully established in these years.

Were the institutions and practices of the Counter Reformation in Germany "southern" imports? That is certainly what some German Catholics thought at the time, grumbling about the influence of Jesuits or Italian styles. The charge is not entirely fair. While some of the new, standardized practices did come from Italy, like the confessional box pioneered by Carlo Borromeo in Milan, others were "northern" in origin, such as emphasizing the rosary and funeral masses.[65] Nor should we forget that the Catholic revival in Central Europe was by no means a top-down-only affair, but something that the Catholic laity had a part in shaping.[66] But when all that has been said, there are two major ways in which Central European Catholicism was pointed in new directions from outside. The first was the emphasis on a new kind of discipline demanded of Catholics, which ran very much in parallel with developments occurring within Lutheranism and Calvinism. This was a central feature of Tridentine Catholicism, symbolized not only by the introduction of new liturgical practices (like the Latin Mass) that had to be followed, but by the confessional box and more frequent confession as instruments of Christian discipline. Whereas penance was something you did, discipline was something you learned.[67]

The Jesuits, inexhaustible catechizers and confessors, were closely associated with this development. But they were also, rightly, identified with a second aspect of German Catholic revival that was "southern" in a different sense. By that I mean the emotional, "Italian" methods the Jesuits favored in spreading the faith. These were on display in the theatrical style of their missions in the German lands, which did not always go down well with the locals, and in more permanent form in the "sensuous worship" embodied in the great Jesuit baroque churches. St. Michael's in Munich, which borrows several features from the Jesuit mother church in Rome, is a good example; so is Mariä Himmelfahrt in Cologne.[68]

Three years before the foundation stone of Mariä Himmelfahrt was laid in 1618, the formal ban on German Jesuits joining the overseas mission was lifted. The Counter Reformation was by now well advanced and the number of priests in the Jesuit order had grown tremendously.[69] When news reached Ingolstadt in January 1616 that four of its students were to be allowed to go to "the Indies," there was an outpouring of joy. The instructor Father Johann Irling wrote to Jesuit General Vitelleschi: "It is unbelievable how much jubilation this special news created . . . in the entire college. O eternally memorable day! The teachers felt obliged to turn a blind eye to the rule of silence so that the overwhelming heartfelt feelings could be expresse. No one could any longer touch a book, no one could go about normal business, no one could stay calm." One of the four who had been chosen, Kaspar Rues, wrote in terms that confirm the rapturous mood: "I have no idea where to begin. I am so filled with jubilation and beside myself with joy. . . . I cannot think of anything on earth that I would have heard more gladly. Yes, I shall go, I shall fly wherever the Good Lord, wherever Holy obedience calls me."[70]

Rapturous zeal, expressions of obedience, hopes for salvation, the attraction of the "exotic," the embrace of a possible martyrdom—these were what animated young German Jesuits of the seventeenth century. Kaspar Rues was not unusual. Nicolas Trigault, a Belgian-born procurator of the Jesuit mission in China, visited Ingolstadt and found that "everyone there is burning with longing for our mission."[71] The Jesuit archive in Rome contains thousands of letters from members of the order written between 1615 and 1728, asking to be accepted for the overseas mission. These *"indipetae"* came in large numbers from all across the German lands. They enumerated the writers' philosophical, linguistic, and mathematical talents, emphasized their robust constitutions as well as their spiritual obedience, and often referred to the vows they had taken to become missionaries when they first joined the order. One sent a copy of his oath, written in blood.[72]

Most of the letter writers would be disappointed. Although the ban had been lifted, the argument was still made that the German provinces needed priests. Even as the first Jesuits in Ingolstadt prepared to leave in 1616, the rector of the college asked ruefully: "But why do they travel to the distant parts of the world? The time is near when we in Germany ourselves will have an Indies, where the number of all the workers now in the province will not suffice."[73] Only 11 percent of those who sought to join the overseas missions were accepted. Some tried again and again. Philipp Jeningen, who conducted dozens of domestic missions in Bavaria, was turned down twenty-one times in the last three decades of the seventeenth century.[74] Jeningen came from the Upper German province from which the number of acceptances was in fact the highest—almost one in four. The number for the Lower Rhine province was only one in six, and for the Upper Rhine province just one in eleven.[75]

Between 1610 and the 1730s, 760 Jesuits from the three core German provinces joined overseas missions, with another 250 or so from Austria and Bohemia, taking the total to more than 1000.[76] The numbers remained small during the Thirty Years War but rose quickly in the second half of the seventeenth century as the number of available German Jesuits became very much larger (it more than doubled between 1650 and 1670). Their destinations were global. A few took part in the mission to the "Orient"—Egypt, Syria, Persia, Armenia, and Greece—and an even smaller number found themselves in Portuguese outposts in Africa (Angola and Mozambique).[77] But the overwhelming majority went to Latin America or Asia.

Those bound for Latin America made their way to Lisbon or Seville (after 1720, Cadiz), before embarking on the months-long journey across the Atlantic. Around 15 percent never made it, the victims of disease, shipwreck, or pirate attacks. Those who reached their destination were widely dispersed. There were German Jesuits in each of the six Latin American Jesuit provinces and in Mexico. They numbered almost 500 priests in all, plus more than 250 "brothers" (mainly craftsmen). They came overwhelmingly from Upper Germany.[78] Bohemian Jesuits were the second-largest group, the contingents from the Lower and Upper Rhine the smallest.

In other words, if the Counter Reformation brought a "southern" quality to Catholicism in Upper German areas like Bavaria, Jesuit missionary activities in turn represented a globalization of Bavarian piety. Before they left, boards of inspectors recorded the name, nationality, and physical description of every departing missionary ("no butcher eyes a calf as these men eyed us," wrote one), and German Jesuits often remained figures of suspicion to Spanish and Portuguese authorities.[79] Only after the middle of the seventeenth century were they permitted in significant numbers as the quota of foreign priests was raised, then raised again. Still, questions of loyalty could cause problems. In Amazonia, the Bohemian Samuel Fritz was subjected to lengthy house arrest by the Portuguese, who accused him of spying for Spain.[80] German Jesuits also had a reputation for looking down on their Spanish fellow religious. Certainly there was more than a touch of condescension in the suggestion made by the author of a guide for German missionaries that they be wary of sharing confidences, because "German sincerity goes poorly with the Iberian mentality."[81]

Because German Jesuits usually arrived later than their Spanish, Portuguese, or Italian counterparts, they were often heavily engaged outside the established urban mission centers. They were active in many missions to convert Indigenous peoples, to whom they offered themselves as priests, teachers, doctors, pharmacists—and, often, as middlemen with Spanish or Portuguese authorities. They also drew maps, recorded local languages, compiled dictionaries, made inventories of local flora and fauna, and wrote comprehensive ethnographies. Arrogant assumptions often colored these activities, of course. Mission fathers wanted to establish settlements and had little sympathy for hunter-gatherer ways of life. They often brought with them highly stereotyped ideas about "savages" and "barbarians," and found the task of catechizing native peoples challenging. Writing to his old philosophy teacher in Graz, a missionary named Franz Xavier Zephyris confessed that, however true it might be that all God's creatures were the sons of Adam, "I have had the melancholy experience that it is easier to teach a parrot a few words than an Indian boy to make the sign of the cross."[82] Attitudes like this softened or changed over time, however—and many Jesuits lived for decades among the people they converted. The South Tyrolean Anton Sepp came to view the Guarani tribe with loving admiration: "I am entirely of the opinion that nowhere under the sun is there a people that departs this life with such decency and calm as these poor, artless Indians who have been held in contempt and abandoned by the whole world."[83]

There was a double-sided quality to everything that German and other Jesuits undertook in the Americas. Cartography made the land legible through European eyes and eventually served state makers; yet it rested on respect for local knowledge as well as observation, and it might be undertaken in the interests of the Indigenous. Samuel Fritz's unprecedentedly detailed and accurate maps of the Amazon region, which he worked on for fifteen years, were designed to show that the Indians among whom he had created thirty-eight mission settlements lived on Spanish soil and that efforts by Brazilian slave hunters to abduct them were therefore unjust.[84] This was measuring the world with a very practical purpose in mind. To take another example, the great pharmaceutical network the Jesuits built up in Latin America was designed to extend the benefits of western medicine to native peoples, but there was also great respect for Indigenous medicaments and healing practices. It was the Jesuits who introduced cinchona to Europe as an antimalarial medicine. Their colleges in Latin America contained many German fathers who were interested in a synthesis of European and native medicine. When the Bavarian Joseph Zeitler drew up an inventory of the pharmacy in Santiago de Chile, he counted nine hundred medicines, both European and Indigenous.[85]

The *reducciones*, or settlements, were at the heart of the Jesuit mission during the roughly 150 years in which the order was active in Latin America, before its expulsion in the mid-eighteenth century. By that date, as many as 300,000 converted, Christianized Indians lived in some form of settlement. The largest, and the ones that have attracted the greatest amount of attention, formed what is often called the "Jesuit state," which extended over parts of present-day Paraguay, Argentina, Bolivia, Uruguay, and Brazil. Established in 1606, the province of Paracuaria contained 120,000 Indigenous peoples in fifty settlements a century later. More Jesuits were engaged here than in any other part of Latin America except Mexico. By the time of the expulsion, 564 members of the order were active in the province, nearly 400 of them priests. The Germans arrived late but then came in numbers—eventually there were more than 100. The settlements were usually built around a central square with a church on one side and long houses on the other three. They were organized on the basis of communal production and their output included cotton, hides, rope, boats, tools, musical instruments, and yerba maté. The economy of the settlements thus combined European and Indigenous elements. Their religious practice also mixed Christian signs and symbols with Indigenous rituals into a syncretic blend. [86]

The *reducciones* formed an autonomous Christian-Indio nation, a buffer zone. They protected Indigenous converts from Portuguese slave hunters on one side and Spanish colonists on the other. But they were vulnerable and ultimately dependent on the political goodwill of those two empires. A Spanish-Portuguese treaty in 1750 forced one group of Guarani to evacuate their land or risk becoming slaves; it led to resistance and the two powers cracked down on both Indios and their Jesuit defenders. The expulsion of the Jesuits then removed the institutions and people that stood between the Indigenous and their predators. The *reducciones* collapsed and many of the Indigenous retreated into the forests from which they had come. Rain forest gradually covered the Jesuit-built churches. There is pathos and drama in what happened, as witness the German bestseller *Paracuaria*, published in 1982, on the lost "artistic treasures of the Jesuit state."[87] There is moral drama, too. Jesuits had to ask themselves whether or not they had a moral obligation to fight on behalf of their charges, an issue dramatized in the 1986 film *The Mission*.[88] But the questions go beyond that moment of decision and get to the heart of encounters between Europeans and Indigenous peoples. The Jesuit state in Paraguay provides almost a laboratory test case of the ambiguities that defined the encounter. Was it a "paradise," a "benevolent European-led dictatorship," a "Christian alternative to colonialism and Marxism," or an example of "cultural imperialism"? One author sees "confrontation and interaction"; another sees "acculturation."[89] Tears were certainly shed on both sides when the Jesuit fathers were forced to leave their "children." There can be no doubting the affective bonds that developed between them. The Jesuits were self-sacrificing and caring; they provided much, just as they learned much and recorded it in ways that had lasting value. The Guarani certainly faced more malevolent Europeans and would probably have been unable to preserve their way of life in the long run. But it was the Jesuits who encouraged their charges to desert that way of life, treated them as children, and left them appallingly vulnerable.

When we look at the Jesuits in Paraguay, it is not the Spanish members of the order but the Germans, Austrians, and Bohemians who stand out, alongside Flemings and Italians. At first glance, things look the same in China. One writer talks about the "triumvirate of great seventeenth-century missionaries": an Italian (Matteo Ricci), a Fleming (Ferdinand Verbiest), and a German (Adam Schall von Bell).[90] Judging by the hostility they attracted, you might think the German Jesuits were numerous. Franciscans and non-German Jesuits alike complained that they monopolized the China mission and would have done better to remain in Europe.[91] It therefore comes as a surprise how small the German presence in the China mission really was. The total number of Jesuits who had arrived in China from Germany, Austria, Bohemia, and Switzerland combined remained below thirty at least until 1730.[92] Central European Jesuits were heavily outnumbered by the Portuguese, Italians, and French.

Most Jesuit priests in China lived in the provinces. By 1631 there were eleven residences spread across more than half of the empire's provinces, and by 1661 only two of those fifteen provinces did not have a residence. Here the work of proselytizing and conversion went on, slowly, in the Lower Yangtze Valley, the Yellow River basin in Shaanxi, coastal areas of Fujian, and elsewhere.[93] German Jesuits were a part of this fairly thin scattering of priests, and we catch an occasional glimpse of them in accounts of the mission.[94] But the residence that has attracted most historical attention by far was in Beijing, where Matteo Ricci's original policy of "accommodationism" was continued by his successors, with Germans—and one German in particular—very much to the fore. The policy had a powerful underlying logic. Unlike conquered Latin America, China remained an intact empire and Jesuits had to work with the grain of local power. They blamed zealous Franciscan and Dominican friars for the anti-Christian backlash and persecution that had occurred in Japan, and they were suspicious when members of the same orders arrived in China eager to make converts. The Jesuit strategy was to learn Chinese, respect local sensibilities, emphasize that Christianity had much in common with Confucianism, and work to win over emperor and civil servants by demonstrating what European learning (especially science) had to offer. That was why the party that arrived at Macao in 1619 brought books and scientific instruments.

The figure most strongly associated with this strategy during the middle decades of the seventeenth century was Adam Schall von Bell. Born into a noble family in Cologne in 1591, Schall had studied at the Jesuit German College in Rome and then at Gregorian University.[95] In 1616 he expressed his desire to join the mission: "I, Adam Schall, albeit most unworthy, . . . here set forth my desire: namely, to go to the East Indies, and especially China, which I have wanted to do most earnestly for a long time."[96] Two years later, he was one of a small group of priests who sailed from Lisbon, arriving in Macao in 1619. After he and his fellow priests were forced to wait a long time in this gateway to mainland China, Schall traveled to Beijing, in 1622. Apart from a brief interlude in the Jesuit residence at Xi'an in Shaanxi province in the southeast, he spent the rest of his life in the

This print from Athanasius Kircher's China Illustrata *(1667) shows Adam Schall von Bell in mandarin robes surrounded by the astronomical and mathematical tools that gained the Jesuits influence at the Chinese court.*

Chinese capital. Schall was in many respects a remarkable figure. Pious and learned in many fields, he had a library of three thousand books by the 1640s and became fluent in Chinese. He was a highly skilled mathematician and astronomer with a practical touch, who could draw up plans for fortifications, cast cannon, and make astronomical instruments.[97]

The strategy of Schall and his colleagues in Beijing was to win converts among reform-minded literati in the closing decades of the Ming dynasty, to attempt the same among the ladies of the court via the influential eunuchs, and to work their way into the confidence of the throne. A key issue here was calendrical reform. Jesuit expertise in mathematics and astronomy had been decisive in the calendar reform of Pope Gregory XIII in 1582. In Beijing the Jesuits brought their instruments, trigonometrical tables, and state-of-the-art star maps to bear on reform of the imperial calendar, which was important because it was considered impossible for the emperor (the ruler of time and space) to rule in the right way without a correct lunar calendar, yet the calendar had become riddled with errors. The Jesuits were pleased to display their European methods to the emperor. The lead role in the 1620s was played by a German Jesuit named Johann Terrenz Schreck, who had once studied alongside Galileo and arrived in Macao on the same boat as Schall. When Terrenz died in 1630, it was Schall who took over the task of steering calendar reform, cleaning up errors, correctly predicting eclipses, and winning imperial support. Even as the Beijing Jesuits established their position at court, however, the dynasty itself came increasingly under attack in China's version of the seventeenth-century crisis, assailed by peasant revolts and Manchu raiders. Schall and his colleagues successfully rode out the violent transition from the Ming to the Qing dynasty, not without charges of opportunism. In fact, they did better than simply ride out the crisis. Schall became director of the Astronomical Bureau in 1645, a post that remained in Jesuit hands for most of the following 130 years.[98] More than that, Schall became a close confidant of the young Emperor Shunzi, almost a de facto regent. The boy monarch called the German Jesuit "*mafa*," the Manchu word for grandfather. He and Schall spent hours talking in the palace and its wooded gardens. Sometimes the young emperor visited Schall's rooms.

Closeness to power like this invites a backlash. That was true especially in the case of Schall, who was always at the palace and had twenty silk robes to choose from when he attended receptions. It is easy to see how this might have been viewed as playing courtier, an exercise in vanity. Schall's personality did not make things easier. Even his defenders acknowledge that he was sarcastic, irascible, and quick to criticize, a man unable to suffer fools gladly.[99] There was criticism of Schall both from Franciscan friars, always quick to find fault with worldly Jesuits, and from disaffected members of his own order, who felt they had been let down by Schall during the political turmoil that marked the overthrow of the Ming dynasty. Two sets of charges were leveled. Schall was accused of conceding too much to Chinese "superstition" in drawing up a calendar that advised the emperor about days on which it was auspicious or inauspicious to act—that was the "calendar dispute."[100] Then there was the personal dimension: it was suggested that Schall was too fond of food and drink as well as other creature comforts, that he had acquired dubious pictures from a member of the Dutch embassy, arranged performances of a bawdy play, and behaved in a manner that mocked his vows of chastity. When, on the urging of Emperor Shunzi, Schall formally adopted the son of his houseboy, tales spread that this was his natural son. These rumors, almost certainly baseless, made the rounds of Beijing and found their way to Macao and Rome. The unpleasantness rumbled on through the 1650s, even while Schall was strongly supported by his superiors.[101]

Not until 1664 did Rome finally decide the calendar dispute in Schall's favor, and it is unlikely that the news reached Beijing before his death. In the same year, there was a strange echo of the intra-Catholic dispute on the part of Chinese critics at the imperial court who also took aim at Schall because of his work at the Astronomical Bureau. Shunzi had died suddenly in 1661 at the age of twenty-three, and in the early days of his successor, Emperor K'ang-hsi, there was an anti-Christian backlash in China. Schall was accused of choosing an inauspicious day for the burial of a child from the imperial household. His main critic, a courtier named Yang Guangxian, was a friend of a Muslim astronomer who had been sacked on Schall's recommendation, and behind the accusation was resentment of the influence Schall and other Jesuits enjoyed. The Jesuits were persecuted as a threat to the Qing state; a trial in Beijing sentenced Schall and his Chinese assistants to death and other foreign missionaries to forty lashes and exile. However, an earthquake soon after the verdict was taken as a sign, and the Jesuits (but not the Chinese assistants) were amnestied. Schall himself died in 1666.

The remaining Jesuits sat out several years of internal exile in Canton, where they regrouped, then returned to their residences in the early 1670s as imperial favor was once more renewed. The Jesuits in Beijing resumed the position that Adam Schall, following Matteo Ricci, had carved out. During the long reign of Emperor K'ang-hsi, through the early 1720s, they served the court not only as astronomers (a field that Germans continued to dominate) but as scientists, the makers of precision instruments, musicians, and—not least—advisers who had the advantage of being outsiders who were not part of the system. In 1724, however, Yongzheng, the new emperor, proscribed Christianity and exiled its priests. Ignaz Kögler, one of Schall's German successors as director of the Astronomical Bureau, was told by the emperor that the Jesuits were lucky to escape with their lives.[102] The mission as a whole was crippled, reduced to a few elderly or undercover priests; but the Beijing Jesuits stayed on, continuing to serve the emperor. Twenty-two years later, when the Bavarian Kögler died, he was peacefully succeeded at the Astronomical Bureau by the Austrian August von Hallerstein.[103]

What did these Jesuit mandarins in silk robes achieve? One answer is that they used their indispensability at court to create an atmosphere in which the task of conversion could continue in the provinces as well as the capital, something that could not have been taken for granted in the early seventeenth century, when Terrenz and Schall first arrived in Macao. At the high point of Schall's influence, in the 1650s and early '60s, there were perhaps 10,000 new converts every year. By 1700, following the emperor's edict of toleration in 1692, there may have been as many as 250,000 Christians in China.[104] But these gains remained vulnerable and were partly reversed later. Meanwhile, the great Jesuit illusion was the belief that they could convert the emperor. In the words of the historian Charles Boxer, the "Fathers had as much hope of converting the emperor as they had of converting the Man in the Moon."[105] Beyond the conversions of individual Chinese, the Jesuit legacy included the rich cultural exchange they helped to institute. Jesuits took European literature and science to China, and they were valued at court for what they offered as mathematicians and astronomers (even if it is true that, after the 1660s, the Jesuits were no longer at the cutting edge of the new science as they had been at the time of Gregorian calendar reform). In some cases, they coauthored works with local scholars, like the 1627 book *Qi qi tu shuo* (Illustrations and Explanations of Wonderful Machines).[106] They also learned Chinese and were able to translate Chinese works and introduce them to European audiences. This translation project was arguably the lasting Jesuit achievement.[107]

The German Jesuits active in China and the Americas were part of a global mission that had a major impact on the non-European societies it touched. What was its impact back in Germany? We know from the heart-felt petitions of would-be missionaries just how earnestly they imagined themselves into these distant parts of the world. The Jesuit mission touched the Holy Roman Empire from top to bottom. It engaged the interest of German princes, especially the Wittelsbachs, who provided the largest and most stable source of funding for the China mission.[108] It had a broader impact among the Catholic elite, the primary recruiting ground of the Jesuits. For example, an Austrian tax official in Freiburg im Breisgau, a Cologne city councilor, a judge in Mainz, a Hungarian count, a baker from Aichach near Augsburg, the mayor of Olpe, a city architect in Luxem-bourg, and a city councilor in Amberg—all had sons who were Jesuit mis-sionaries in Brazil, a reminder that this wider world reached even into what sound almost like a caricature of closed-off backwaters of the Empire.[109]

How many of these Jesuit fathers ever went back to Germany we do not know. Most probably died in Brazil, just as most of the German Jesuits who went to China died there—Terrenz and Schall, Kögler and Haller-stein, as well as others who achieved some modest fame, like Kilian Stumpf and Bernhard Diestel. But there were surely many, and not just among their families and former schoolmates, who remembered who they were and where they went. Some were martyrs, whose memory was cultivated in popular literature. Poetry and theater also brought the global playground of Catholic missionary ambition back to the German lands. Allegorical depictions of the four continents and the religious mission became com-mon in Counter Reformation churches, on their altars, pulpits, and ceil-ing frescoes. They contained stereotyped representations of these lands and cultures—elephant, feathered headdress, turban, spear—and often included the "divine light" that the missionaries carried to them. This aes-thetic was especially prominent in Bavaria, something we can see in the rich iconography of the Jesuit church in Landshut or Georg Asam's fresco ceiling in Tegernsee.[110] The iconography of the Jesuits' global reach also found its way into print. One medium in which it did so was the *Thesen-blatt*, the single-sheet illustration that accompanied a thesis defense and became common in the sixteenth century. A *Thesenblatt* engraving by Bar-tholomäus Kilian, *The World Mission of the Society of Jesus*, was used by stu-dents at several Catholic universities. Its complex imagery depicts Christ, a group of saints posed by a globe, and the light of the faith going out into the world, whose people are represented by an Amerindian, a South Asian from Goa, and an African prince. A heart-shaped map of the world at the center of the engraving shows all the Jesuit missions under the motto "Love of God and neighbor."[111]

Networks of Learning

ONE PARTICULARLY ARRESTING VISUAL REPRESENTATION OF the global mission was produced by the German Jesuit Athanasius Kircher. An image from his book *The Great Art of Light and Shadow* shows the Jesuit mission as a luxuriant tree whose branches and leaves are formed by residences around the world. In elaborate quadrants in each corner we read the phrase "From east to west praiseworthy is the name of our Lord," in thirty-four different languages. The image also served as a global clock, which allowed the correct time in any given Jesuit mission to be read off.[112] Kircher was born in Fulda but spent most of his life in Rome. There he operated a kind of clearinghouse for Jesuits around the world, who sent him, or reported on, astronomical, geographical, ethnographic, botanical, and zoological discoveries. Many of the artifacts went into an institution he created, the Museum Kircherianum, a *Theatrum mundi* or theater of the world. Kircher, whose stock has recently risen to remarkable heights in the academic world, has been described as the last man who knew everything and the first scholar with a global reputation.[113] A polymath who has been compared with Leonardo da Vinci, Kircher embraced such interests as mathematics, physics, astronomy, biology, medicine, geology, ethnography, linguistics, music theory, Sinology, and Egyptology. He created a scientific reconstruction of Noah's Ark that included a means of sanitation for its inhabitants, measured the volcanic craters of Mounts Etna and Stromboli, and showed an interest in mechanical devices such as automata. Admired as a mathematician by Leibniz, he included leading scientists like Pierre Gassendi among his hundreds of scholarly correspondents.

Kircher's interests, activities, and networks make him an exemplary, although unusually colorful member of the republic of letters.[114] The term, which can be traced back to Cicero, was popularized by Erasmus of Rotterdam at the end of the fifteenth century. It denotes the clergy, officials, professors, archivists, scientists, and physicians who together formed networks of the learned that stretched across Europe and beyond. The republic of letters was marked by movement. It was a "kaleidoscope of people, books and objects in motion," whose members "crossed nations, borders and sometimes whole worlds."[115] Travel itself became an object of study in the sixteenth century, as the genre of handbooks and guides for the traveler emerged, and an infrastructure of improved roads, better maps, carriage services, and guesthouses made travel easier.[116] Letter-writing networks were lubricated, at least within Europe, by new postal services like the one operated in Central Europe by the Thurn und Taxis family. The republic of letters also benefited from the lines of communication established by merchants.[117] We see that in the close links between early German humanists and merchants in a city like Nuremberg.

The early German humanists, peripatetic scholars like Conradus Celtis, all spend time in Italy, where they fed from the intellectual revolution of the Renaissance. The same is true of a figure like the Basel physician and humanist scholar Theodor Zwinger in the late sixteenth century. When we think of them, or of Erasmus, it makes the republic of letters seem like an essentially humanistic enterprise, the opposite of the religious strife of the era, even an antidote to it. The historian Friedrich Heer, writing with one eye on the Cold War in his own time, described humanism as a "third force" "between the confessional fronts."[118] But the republic of letters was not so simple. It also derived intellectual energy from the clash of religious views. Kircher's formidable information and correspondence network is a good example. As scientists, scholars, and teachers, Jesuits contributed greatly to the republic of letters. Their missionary writings from Asia and the Americas on natural science, ethnography, languages, and much else were published in all the great Catholic cultural centers of Germany.[119] On the Protestant side, too, confessional identity could foster support for scholarship and learning. It was, after all, the Lutheran Ulrich von Hutten who called Nuremberg "the first city to open its doors to good learning," and Luther's collaborator Philipp Melanchthon who dubbed it "another Athens."[120] The cross-fertilization between late humanism and Lutheranism in Silesia produced a flourishing of the literary arts, natural sciences, and medicine. It was also here that Germany's first agricultural manuals were written, by humanist-trained Lutheran clergy.[121] It is not hard to identify similar Calvinist networks.[122]

Education was a critical area of activity as the dynamics of the confessional divide enhanced its importance. This was a part of what the historian Andrew Pettegree, writing about the Reformation, has called the "culture of persuasion."[123] Lutherans, Calvinists, and Catholics all perceived a need to establish new schools and academies. They also recognized the importance of tertiary education. It is even possible to think about this as an educational arms race.[124] Confessional division and competition helped to establish some of the leading university institutions of the time—Wittenberg and Heidelberg, Ingolstadt and Vienna. All had been founded before Luther posted his theses, part of a cluster of new universities established in the second half of the fifteenth century. But it was the intellectual disputes set in train by the Reformation and Counter Reformation that put them on the map and showed that universities could be "explosive places."[125] An example of how religious disputation could energize intellectual life and foster transnational contacts is to compare what happened to the University of Rostock with Wittenberg. Around 1500, Rostock drew students from the entire North Sea and Baltic regions; but when the local rulers in Mecklenburg reacted slowly to the Reformation, it was Wittenberg (founded only in 1502) that reaped the rewards in student enrollments, including non-German students.[126]

In other words, many activities of the republic of letters went on within religiously defined communities. Each erected its own obstacles and limits to disinterested inquiry—to the work of teaching, learning, interpreting, debating, imagining, remembering, collecting. Faith was a constraint, even if not a straitjacket. As the confessional lines hardened, crossing those lines also created difficulties. A case in point is the Flemish scholar Justus Lipsius (after whom the EU headquarters in Brussels is named). He was educated at the Jesuit College in Cologne, then at the University of Louvain. But conformity to Lutheranism was required when he accepted a position in Jena, so Lipsius retreated to Catholic Cologne and Louvain, before the upheaval of the Dutch Revolt led him to take a position at Leiden in the northern Netherlands in 1578. Lipsius was eventually reconciled to the Catholic Church, and spent his last years back in Louvain. This odyssey understandably made one scholar who has written on Lipsius skeptical about the "communicative community" of the learned.[127]

Lipsius's experiences underscore the existential threat posed by religious warfare in the sixteenth and seventeenth centuries. The impact of the Thirty Years War was felt especially hard in the German lands. Universities on both sides of the religious divide were affected. Tübingen was occupied by soldiers, Leipzig repeatedly fought over, Giessen closed down. Heidelberg was occupied, ransacked, closed in 1626, and reopened as a Catholic institution. Faculty and students fled to Switzerland or the Low Countries. The Bibliotheca Palatina, one of the great collections in Germany, was packed into two hundred boxes and shipped off to the Vatican Library in Rome. When King Gustavus Adolphus of Sweden recaptured the Palatinate, there were plans to reopen Heidelberg as a Protestant university—until the Battle of Nördlingen in 1634, when Imperial troops recaptured the city and subjected it to "re-Catholicization." The university was "completely ruined" for decades.[128] Catholic institutions suffered similar indignities. Thousands of works from the university library in Würzburg were shipped to Stockholm after Swedish troops occupied the city. The Swedish haul from the capture of Olmütz, in Moravia, included ten thousand books along with rings taken from bodies buried in a crypt, and in one of the last campaigns of the war a Swedish commander plundered Prague, sending the remains of the Emperor Rudolf II's art collection to Queen Christina.[129]

People as well as collections were scattered. Like the forced emigrations of the twentieth century, these flights were damaging and destructive to careers, even life-threatening. Yet, like the scholarly diasporas of more recent times, they could have profoundly fruitful effects—unintended benign consequences. Consider what happened to two of the figures we have already met, Athanasius Kircher and Samuel Hartlib. The first of them was caught up three times in the turmoil of the Thirty Years War. Kircher was a novice in Paderborn when the city was captured by Protestant forces in 1622. Fleeing with two fellow students, he managed to evade the hostile soldiery but was nearly drowned in the Rhine. The following year, traveling from Cologne to teach at the Jesuit school in Heiligenstadt, he was captured and narrowly escaped hanging. Kircher established himself in a teaching position at Würzburg but was again forced to flee when that city was captured by Swedish forces. Brief sojourns in the Rhineland were followed by slightly longer stays in France (he would have preferred China), before Kircher was called to Rome. He might well have lost his life during these turbulent ten years; but he survived, and his remarkable network of contacts owed something to the experience.[130]

Hartlib was another émigré from war-torn Germany. He settled in England at the end of the 1620s and became a major intellectual broker of his time.[131] Hartlib has in common with Kircher, his almost exact contemporary, that his life and work have recently attracted renewed interest on a major scale. Perhaps one reason is that Hartlib was another engaging polymath whose interests seemed to have no limits: mathematics, physics, optics, chemistry, botany, natural history, landscape gardens, pearls, beehives, public health, the mechanical arts, and communication in all its forms—languages, cryptography, even the very practical matter of "an Inke

that would give a dozen Copies, moist Sheetes of Paper being pressed on it."
To the diarist John Evelyn he was "Master of Innumerable Curiosities."[132]
If there is an air of condescension in his description, this also recalls how
people reacted to Kircher. The natural philosopher Sir Robert Moray, writing to a fellow scholar about Kircher, suggested that "though there wants
not chaff in his heap of stuff composted in his severall peaces, yet there
is wheat to be found."[133] That suggests another reason for the rising academic stock of Kircher and Hartlib. Those aspects of their work that once
seemed idiosyncratic, occasionally bizarre, and always strongly undergirded
by religious passion—Catholic in the one case, Calvinist in the other—now
receive much more respectful attention from historians of science who have
abandoned the belief that the "scientific revolution" was a straightforward
march of progress, a strictly linear and tough-mindedly secular affair.

The "Hartlib circle" in mid-seventeenth-century England was wide.
At its center were two other figures who shared Hartlib's religious views,
became very close friends, and together with him made up the so-called
Three Strangers. They were the Moravian émigré Jan Comenius and John
Dury, a Scottish Calvinist minister and intellectual who had been educated
in Leiden and spent years living in Europe. Beyond this trio Hartlib had
countless contacts in scientific, theological, political, and literary circles.
They included John Milton and the scientist Robert Boyle among them. A
striking number of Germans belonged to Hartlib's circle of close friends.
Some had come to England to study because of the difficulties at home
and never returned; others had come to England after 1618 to raise support for the Protestant cause, eventually staying. One of them was the poet
Georg Weckherlin. The Stuttgart-born Weckherlin lived in England from
1620 on, first in the service of the beleaguered Elector Palatine, then as an
English government employee whose skills in languages and cryptography were highly valued. A supporter of Parliament in the Civil War, like
all members of the Hartlib group, he was appointed secretary for foreign
tongues in 1644. Another was Theodore Haak, a scholar of independent
means who organized the Calvinist relief effort in England, then decided
to stay. Haak was the first to translate Milton's *Paradise Lost* into German;
he was also (because of his excellent French) the link between the Hartlib
circle and a remarkable group of intellectuals in France that included Blaise
Pascal, René Descartes, and the English exile Thomas Hobbes.[134]

Thus were transnational publics created out of lives lived in exile. The
individual experience was often terribly painful. Comenius suffered the death

of his young family and the destruction of his library before he came to rest in England.[135] Yet these were people driven into creativity even as they were driven into exile.[136] Hartlib, Dury, Comenius, Haak, and the others were animated by a providentialist, millenarian, and humanly generous vision of a world made whole again. Education would be the key. Central to their hopes was Comenius's "pansophical" idea of universal knowledge and education. In adversity, they constructed this idealized vision of truly universal learning, just as three hundred years later émigrés from Nazi Germany constructed an idealized version of the Renaissance as a supra-national community of scholars—in their case, an idealized version of the past, not the future.

Politics shaped the hopes of Hartlib and friends. They were optimistic during the Civil War, especially under the Commonwealth, then disheartened after the Restoration in 1660. By that time many of them were elderly or close to death. Hartlib himself died in 1662.The larger pansophical project failed, but the Hartlib circle and those it fostered left behind accomplishments in fields that ranged from technology to education. Perhaps the best-known achievement of the circle was its contribution to the establishment of the Royal Society in England.[137] The key figure here was a younger member of the group. Bremen-born theologian and natural philosopher Henry Oldenburg settled in England at the beginning of the 1650s after working there as a tutor. He became an inner member of the Hartlib circle and married John Dury's daughter. Oldenburg, who was especially close to Robert Boyle, was one of the founding fellows of the Royal Society and its first secretary. He became an important Anglo-German knowledge broker in his own right and, when Hartlib died, took over his correspondence network.[138]

That communications web may have been Hartlib's single greatest contribution to seventeenth-century intellectual life. His papers, which were lost until 1933, contain more than 4250 letters with some four hundred correspondents. The network extended from England, Scotland, Ireland, and the North American colonies to every part of Europe. Governor John Winthrop of Connecticut called Hartlib "the Great Intelligencer of Europe."[139] Zooming in, we can see why. Take the botanical field as just one example. John Evelyn's celebrated *Sylva, or a Discourse of Forest-Trees and the Propagation of Timber* (1664) owed a debt to correspondence between Hartlib and the Herefordshire minister John Beale. Four years earlier, the first book by the young naturalist John Ray, a catalogue of Cambridge plants, incorporated the ideas on plant morphology of the German scholar Joachim Jungius, thanks to a copy of his work that Hartlib obtained and sent to Ray.[140]

But this only scratches the surface of how Hartlib spread knowledge. A typical Hartlib letter would touch on twenty or thirty different books, papers, scholarly movements: "the mathematical paper sent by Mr. Petreus," "Mr. Evelyn's book concerning Gardens," "the 'Anatomical Excellencies' of Yonker de Bill'ss," "Grotius's book," and so on.[141] This was how ideas spread. The network had a powerful multiplier effect, especially because many of Hartlib's correspondents were themselves people on the move—scholars, merchants, diplomats and so-called projectors with bright ideas.

The republic of letters was a mobile culture. That is why Central Europeans had a large part in shaping a set of institutions that first emerged in the late fifteenth century as an outcrop of Italian humanism.[142] Three of the practices that sustained the republic of letters were travel, writing, and university study. Germans were prominent in all three. They traveled more than most (not always voluntarily, as we have seen) and even established themselves as the leading writers of books on the art of travel. Then there was letter writing. It is hard to miss how many of the great correspondence networks were based in Germany or orchestrated by Germans abroad. That was true in the sixteenth century, when reformers such as the Lutheran Philipp Melanchthon and the Zwinglian Heinrich Bullinger sat at the center of epistolary webs that were the largest of their time. It remained true when Kircher and Hartlib were active. And it continued to be true in the decades on either side of 1700, when the polymath Gottfried Wilhelm Leibniz conducted a correspondence from his Hanoverian base with more than a thousand individuals across Europe and in Goa, Canton, and Beijing, the largest network of its time.[143] German universities added their own contribution to this mobile culture, even if their role did not begin to equal what it would be in the nineteenth century. The Reformation and Counter Reformation made institutions like Wittenberg, Heidelberg, and Ingolstadt magnets for students across Europe, as we have seen. The disasters of the Thirty Years War then scattered talented young Germans abroad, an ordeal for them, a boon for others. German universities recovered after the war, however, contrary to older accounts that they became moribund. New ones were founded, too, above all Halle (1694) and Göttingen (1734), both places where enlightened ideas could be fought over. German universities contributed at least as much as their counterparts in England, France, or Italy, and probably more, to the continuing reception of new learning.[144]

Other institutions gave structure to the republic of letters. One was the learned society; more than twenty-five hundred of these were established in Europe between 1500 and 1800.[145] In Central Europe the nature of these associations shifted over time, as it did elsewhere, from the sodalities created by German humanists like Conradus Celtis to the later literary circles and philosophical societies, then the scientific academies that appeared in the late seventeenth century. Another characteristic practice within the early modern republic of letters was collecting, which included the creation of collections that brought together things that seem to us remarkably disparate. Antiquities, paintings, and coins sat alongside ivory objects, minerals, and precious stones; coral and stuffed mammals or birds, some of them "curiosa" shipped over from Asia or the Americas, shared space with scientific instruments and automata. Athanasius Kircher's Museum Kircherianum in Rome was one such collection. These proto-museums could be found across Europe and were called *Kunstkammer* in the German lands.[146] One of the most celebrated was built up by the Holy Roman Emperor Rudolf II in Prague and housed in the Hradschin Palace.

The princely court was one of the institutions where the German lands played an especially important role in nurturing a pan-European republic of letters.[147] The court of Rudolf II is an unusually good example. Think of the astronomer Johannes Kepler, a Swabian of humble origins and Lutheran faith whose life was repeatedly upended by religious strife and war. In between moments of extraordinary drama—the early experience of being forced out of a teaching post in Graz when he refused to convert to Catholicism; later having to defend his mother from accusations of witchcraft; finding himself in Linz in a town under siege, his library sealed and threatened—Kepler enjoyed a long, peaceful, and productive decade at Rudolf's court, before the religious-political tensions that preceded the Thirty Years War undermined his future there.[148] In the cosmopolitan Prague of Rudolf II, Kepler was successor to the Dane Tycho Brahe, corresponded with Galileo in Padua, exchanged views with thirty different scholars across the Holy Roman Empire (Catholic, Lutheran, and Calvinist) on his favorite subject, chronology, and was surrounded by a motley group of Bohemian and Hungarian courtiers, Italian humanists, Dutch inventors of *perpetuum mobile* machines, and alchemists from every part of Europe.[149] Rudolf's court was undoubtedly an exceptional place, but it was far from the only instance where the republic of letters benefited from princely patronage. Before he went to Prague, Tycho Brahe had been supported by another German prince with a keen interest in astronomy, Landgrave William IV of Hessen-Kassel. Many early modern German rulers were boorish, interested mainly in hunting and soldiers, but the Empire was rich in courts and there were always some where art, science, literature, or music were prized. A Leibniz or a Bach also came cheaper than an army.

The German contribution to learning was indispensable, finally, in everything to do with print culture and books. Rabelais's Gargantua tells his son Pantagruel that times have changed for the better since his youth because of "the elegant and accurate art of printing," as a result of which the whole world was "full of learned men, of very erudite tutors, and of most extensive libraries."[150] It was a common opinion. The printing press altered the very nature of intellectual authority. After Kepler's Rudolphine Tables were published in 1627, their accuracy changed everything (Adam Schall used the tables to good effect in China). The printed version of an argument, unlike a lecture, could be scribbled on in the margin and answered with another argument in print. Print changed how ideas were stored and retrieved, transforming the communication networks of the learned. The proliferation of books caused problems (too much knowledge), but it also stimulated creative solutions—catalogues, reference works, bibliographies,

This copper engraving by Matthäus Merian the Elder from 1632 depicts a printing workshop. Merian is best known for his townscapes, but here it is the interior world of books that receives his attention.

indexes.[151] The printed word "changed the appearance and state of the whole world," said Francis Bacon.[152] The scale of the change was stunning. Not much more than half a century after Gutenberg's Bible, around 1500, there were already 20 million books in the world. By the second half of the seventeenth century, about 6 or 7 million new books were published every year, making a total of around 330 million in the years 1650–1700.[153]

Printing was the German art and it was Germans who introduced it almost everywhere. The first printshop in Italy was established by Germans in Subiaco, outside Rome, and the earliest printers in Rome itself came from Ingolstadt, Würzburg, and Passau. Germans also brought printing to Venice and Modena. In northern Europe, the first printer in Stockholm was from Lübeck and other Germans followed, while printing in early-sixteenth-century Denmark was an appendage of north Germany.[154] The first book produced in France was printed in the basement of the Sorbonne by three Germans (Ulrich Gering, Martin Crantz, and Michael Friburger) who had been invited to Paris by the rector of the university. Germans opened the first printing businesses in Barcelona, Valencia, Saragossa, Lisbon, and Seville. It was through the Cromberger family and other Germans in Seville that print then reached the Americas.[155]

In 1500, when the firm's founder, Jakob Cromberger, arrived in Seville, there were printshops in around sixty cities in the Holy Roman Empire, more than anywhere else in Europe except Italy. This large German technological lead disappeared over time as the "pioneer" was caught and overtaken by others. France emerged as a major book producer; so did England and the Netherlands.[156] That same process of technological transfer out of Germany was evident in specialist fields like printing high-quality visual images—maps, celestial charts, anatomical and botanical drawings. The clear German superiority in the age of Dürer was no longer so clear by the late sixteenth century vis-à-vis, say, the Dutch. But Germany remained a major publishing center. It also became the most important venue for book marketing, and the symbol of that was the Frankfurt Book Fair.

The fair began in the late fifteenth century, when printers, publishers, booksellers, and promoters gathered as part of a long established trade fair. The busy commercial city of Frankfurt had the advantage of a location on the north–south and east–west European trade routes. In the sixteenth century the "books" were still usually unbound sheets, stored in barrels and transported there by cart or on the river, and the fair itself was held in a small street that ran north from the Leonhard Church to a corn market—

the Buchgasse (Book Lane). By the early sixteenth century, Frankfurt was already an event. Printers—and writers—worked flat-out in the months and weeks before the fair to have their works ready. By 1532, the first part of Rabelais's *Pantagruel* ended: "You will have the rest of the story at subsequent Frankfurt Fairs."[157] Ten years later, Erasmus apologized to a friend for being unable to send a copy of his newly published commentary on the Lord's Prayer—it had sold out in three hours after "the book came out at the Frankfurt Fair this spring."[158] Erasmus liked the fair (although not the smoky and uncomfortable German inns at which he had to lodge along the way), and many of his books were first presented there. It was to Frankfurt that Dürer's widow, Agnes, went in 1540 to sell his work; seventeen years later Hans Staden wanted to finish his memoir in time for the spring fair of 1557.[159] Others came, too. Jesuits looked for works that they could take to China as gifts for the emperor.[160] Above all, librarians came looking to scoop up quantity as well as quality. The Elector Palatine had books bought at Frankfurt for his university in Heidelberg; Sir Thomas Bodley acquired books there that became part of the Bodleian Library at Oxford. Published catalogues (the first was in 1564) made things easier for buyers. Galileo used to look at the Frankfurt Fair catalogue to find out what he needed to read.

Fast-forward to the 1620s, when another great astronomer, Johannes Kepler, was selling his work at Frankfurt. By then, the fair was already being affected by the Thirty Years War. Its decline was not sudden. It was in the seventeenth century that the English truly discovered the fair, and that was when English-language catalogues were first printed. Robert Burton mentioned "our Frankfort marts" in 1621, although the gloomy Burton characteristically saw the fair as part of a "vast chaos and confusion" of books that no one had time to read.[161] The effects of war and the longer-term challenge mounted by its rival, the Leipzig Book Fair, did cause the eclipse of Frankfurt, until the twentieth-century revival. But for much of the early modern period the Frankfurt Book Fair signified how central the German lands were to the production and dissemination of the printed word. Robert Burton might grumble, but Frankfurt was a reminder of a distinctive German contribution to the republic of letters, and to what the English Jacobean poet Samuel Daniel, in a wonderful phrase, called "th'intertraffic of the mind."[162]

The art of making books is also a craft. Printing and publishing brought the two together, the author, editor, and indexer with the typesetter. Some early printshops were, in fact, run by "craftsman-scholars."[163] The republic of letters consisted of "worlds made of words," to use the historian Anthony

Grafton's elegant formulation. But those literary and scientific worlds also needed printers, instrument makers, and lens grinders. Germans had a reputation for being gifted at these practical skills. We encountered them in the previous chapter as gunners, mining engineers, and instrument makers, and in this chapter as printers. It is interesting to look at the occupations we find among the Germans in Elizabethan London: crossbow maker, mineral expert and mining engineer, "metallurgist," instrument maker.[164] In the seventeenth century, one contribution made by Samuel Hartlib to science in his adoptive country was to further technological transfer from Germany to England in branches such as metalworking and instrument making. It was through Hartlib that advanced telescopes and microscopes made in Augsburg were brought to England, with long-term benefits for the design of English optical instruments.[165] Given the prevalence of later stereotypes about abstract and cloudy German thought, it is worth emphasizing this reputation for practicality. Leibniz, mathematician and philosopher, also had an eminently practical streak as the inventor of a water-driven propeller, a water pump, and a mining machine, even a proto-steam engine. The picture he painted of the German contribution to knowledge was a striking one. Arguing in 1671 for the establishment of an academy of arts and sciences in Germany, Leibniz suggested that Italians produced "purely aesthetic things." Germans, on the other hand, were always "busy producing moveable works that . . . performed a task, subordinating nature to art and able to make human work easier." He concluded: "Thus I can justifiably tell the truth that Germany, and in particular Augsburg and Nuremberg, is the mother of invention."[166]

The tradition of instrument making continued into the next century. One of Leibniz's many correspondents was a young Danzig merchant's son living in the Netherlands. Both his parents died of mushroom poisoning in 1701, when he was fifteen, and he repeatedly ran away from home to frustrate his guardians' attempts to apprentice him to a prominent merchant (at one point they had a warrant issued for his arrest). Young Daniel Fahrenheit wanted to make instruments, not work in a countinghouse. He traveled, eventually settling in Amsterdam, where he spent the final eighteen years of his life, making a living from selling barometers, thermometers, and aerometers and using his earnings to buy new materials and work on new prototypes. He died at fifty with a net worth of just five hundred Dutch guilders, but with the satisfaction of having been elected eleven years earlier to the Royal Society, which a previous generation of Germans had done so much to create.[167]

CHAPTER 3

EMPIRES

Germans and Imperial Rivalry

IT WAS GOTTFRIED LEIBNIZ WHO FIRST ADVISED PETER THE GREAT of Russia to send a scientific expedition to the North Pacific. The first Kamchatka expedition eventually set off in 1725, the year of the tsar's death. It achieved little. A second proved more successful. Germans would inevitably have an important part in it because Germans dominated the St. Petersburg Academy of Sciences established by Peter. The German naturalist Daniel Gottlieb Messerschmidt had already undertaken a pioneering expedition to Siberia in 1719. It is therefore unsurprising that the historian Gerhard Friedrich Müller and the botanist Johann Georg Gmelin were in the party that set off east in 1733 on the Second Kamchatka expedition, accompanied by sleds carrying bottles of fine Rhine wine that the two Germans drank all the way to Siberia. Gmelin collected plants around the Lake Baikal area and produced a pathbreaking *Flora sibirica*. When he and Müller fell ill and were unable to proceed, it was another German—the Halle-educated Georg Steller—who replaced Gmelin as the expedition's natural scientist. Steller reached the Kamchatka peninsula on the Pacific and survived shipwreck on what was later named Bering Island, but died in Siberia as he returned west in 1746. The notes of his fieldwork in Kamchatka and his book *On the Beasts of the Sea*, which described marine mammals like the sea cow and sea lion that bear his name, appeared over the next thirty years.[1]

Gmelin and Steller stood near the beginning of a long line of German botanists and zoologists who served the Russian empire in the eighteenth century. They retraced the footsteps of Daniel Gottlieb Messerschmidt, who reached Lake Baikal and collected Siberian plants previously unknown to Europeans.[2] (He died in 1735 and Steller married his widow.) They were followed in turn by a later generation of Germans. One was Gmelin's nephew, Samuel Georg, who became professor of botany at St. Petersburg in 1766 and was sent on expeditions to the Don and Volga rivers and the Caspian Sea; he was taken hostage in the Caucasus and died in captivity in 1774 at the age of thirty. His travel writings and work on marine biology were also published posthumously. One of his editors also helped to publish Steller's works. That was the botanist and zoologist Peter Simon Pallas, the most celebrated of all the German naturalist-explorers in the eighteenth-century Russian empire. Invited by Catherine the Great to join the St. Petersburg Academy in 1767, he led expeditions to western Siberia, the Urals, and the upper Amur River and later to the Crimea and Black Sea.[3]

In the second half of the eighteenth century the rulers of Europe's empires sponsored a remarkable number of ambitious expeditions to inventory the natural world and collect samples of things that might prove "useful" in the animal, vegetable, and mineral kingdoms.[4] Some were seaborne, others went overland. They had in common that they were conceived as a way to take stock of resources that might be developed, in line with the dominant mercantilist economic theory of the time. Germans played a central role in these undertakings, sometimes moving from one foreign empire to another. In the same year that Samuel Georg Gmelin arrived in St. Petersburg, Catherine the Great invited another German to Russia. Johann Reinhold Forster traveled with his son Georg to the Volga in 1765, where they investigated the flora and fauna in an area recently settled by Germans and named several new species. Dissatisfied by their treatment in Russia—Johann Reinhold Forster was notoriously choleric in temper—father and son moved to England, where they lived uneasily on the income from teaching, translations, scientific publications, and a loan (never repaid) from the coming man of British imperial botany, Joseph Banks, whose patronage Johann Reinhold eagerly pursued. By a stroke of irony, it was Banks's withdrawal after a quarrel that led the British Admiralty to appoint the Forsters as the naturalists on Captain James Cook's second voyage to the Pacific. A 1780 painting by Francis Rigaud depicts father and son botanizing in Tahiti. Georg Forster, still in his early twenties, became famous when he published the first account of this journey in *A Voyage Around the World in His Britannic Majesty's Sloop Resolution*, a bestseller both in its original English edition of 1777 and the German translation that followed.[5] Joseph Banks, meanwhile, who by 1787 was both director of the Royal Botanical Gardens at Kew and president of the Royal Society, remained (despite his experience with the older Forster) an admirer of Central European scientific expertise and a great spotter of German talent for enterprises that served the botanical interests of the British empire.[6]

The Russian and British cases did not stand alone. German scientific explorers were also employed by the Danish crown. The best-known example is Carsten Niebuhr, who served as mathematician and cartographer on the Danish Arabia expedition of the 1760s, from which he returned as the sole survivor.[7] Less prominent but more directly comparable to the Gmelins or Forsters was the Prussian naturalist Julius von Rohr, another figure within the large correspondence network of Joseph Banks. Rohr fled Germany for Denmark during the Seven Years War and was appointed land surveyor and building inspector of the Danish West Indies in 1757. Commissioned to study the natural history of the islands, he established a botanical garden in Christiansted on St. Croix. Rohr sent plants back to Europe from the Caribbean islands and the South American mainland, investigated the conditions for cotton cultivation in the Antilles, and died on a voyage to the West African coast designed to investigate the potential for plantation agriculture.[8]

German naturalists could also be found scattered across the Dutch empire. Two of them achieved lasting fame. Engelbert Kaempfer traveled to Nagasaki in 1690 as a physician with the Dutch East India Company. There he pursued his passion for botany and later wrote a history of Japanese plants that went far beyond anything previously recorded by Europeans.[9] An almost exact contemporary was the remarkable Maria Sibylla Merian, the independent-minded daughter of a celebrated clan. She was already a skilled naturalist and illustrator when she spent two years in Dutch Surinam and subsequently produced a book on the *Metamorphosis of the Insects of Surinam*, a landmark work of entomology on the insect life cycle. Merian had no interest in the commercial utility of the natural world and complained that the planters in Surinam were interested in nothing but sugar. Unlike most Europeans, who rendered the role of Indigenous peoples invisible when they described their findings, Merian also credited them for their help in finding specimens.[10]

The Spanish empire had been relatively inhospitable to non-Spanish naturalists, but that changed after the 1760s, when successive Spanish kings dispatched dozens of expeditions to explore the flora of their colonies.[11]

Alexander von Humboldt's *Personal Narrative of a Journey to the Equinoctial Regions of the New Continent*, recounting an expedition that began in 1799, is by far the most celebrated example of this opening up, but one of his predecessors anticipated Humboldt in doing for the Spanish what others were doing for the Russians and British. Thaddäus Haenke, sometimes called "the Bohemian Humboldt," joined the Malaspina expedition to the Americas and the Pacific. One of the things he carried with him (it is now in the archives of the Royal Botanical Gardens in Madrid) was a sixteen-page color chart containing hundreds of small delicately painted watercolor panels, all numbered. The idea was that the botanists had to work so quickly with such an overwhelming number of new plants that they drew a specimen and simply wrote in a number, or numbers, so that the correct paint could be added later.[12]

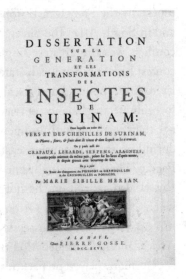

The title page of the third edition, and the first in French, of Maria Sibylla Merian's landmark work of natural history on the insects of Surinam.

Haenke carried his chart as he botanized energetically in the South American interior, up the west coast of the Americas from Chile to Alaska, in Guam and the Philippines. The European discoverer of the redwood tree, Haenke was a classic example of the Linnean naturalist who pursued science and identified potentially useful species for his sponsors.[13]

The drawings, maps, charts, specimens, and field notes the naturalists brought back with them represented a way in which Europeans exerted a form of control over the natural world.[14] Central Europeans were ubiquitous on these expeditions because the German states produced so many well-educated scientists but had no empires of their own.[15] Their contribution to exploration and imperial botany was just one aspect of the distinctive part that Germans played in the eighteenth-century world of European empires, at once central but largely hidden from view. This was a period of intensified imperial competition, both geopolitical and commercial, dominated by the rivalry between the British and the Spanish, Dutch, and especially the French in Europe and the Mediterranean, in the Americas, and in South Asia. The Seven Years War (1756–1763), the first truly global conflict, was the greatest single set piece in this struggle.[16] The imperial contest between European states raised major questions about their capacity to build political and fiscal regimes adequate to their ambitions, how to calibrate the balance between hard and soft power, and how to manage their relations with Indigenous peoples. Similar issues arose for Russia during its rapid expansion eastward beyond the Urals and Siberia to the Pacific, where it eventually encountered the Chinese empire moving west.[17] Russia also arrived on the northern shores of the Black Sea in the 1770s, where it challenged the Ottoman Empire. Even Denmark had a share in this activity, with its possessions in the Caribbean, on the west coast of Africa, and in Tranquebar on the Coromandel coast of India.

Germany played no part in this imperial competition, though there had been moments when it looked as if it might. Johann Joachim Becher, a Rhineland-born physician and scholar, hawked his ideas about colonies and trading companies around the German courts in the 1660s and '70s. While the Dutch were seizing Surinam from the British (1667) and the Danes establishing a Caribbean colony in St. Thomas (1671), Becher was trying to persuade the Bavarians to purchase land in Guiana from the Dutch West India Company. When that failed, he tried to interest the Count of Hanau-Münzenberg in establishing a colony on the "mosquito coast" of South America between the Amazon and the Orinoco, a scheme that eventually foundered and caused the count to be deposed. He promoted similar projects in Vienna in the 1670s, with no more success.[18] A decade later the Great Elector of Brandenburg established the trading post of Grossfriedrichsburg on the African Gold Coast (present-day Ghana) and chartered the Brandenburg-Africa Company. But the commercial results were meager. The competition was too great, the ships were too few and poorly equipped, and the skepticism of the court camarilla ranged against the Great Elector was too great. His grandson, Frederick William I, hostile to "this trading nonsense," sold the post to the Dutch in 1720.[19] There was an even more short-lived Brandenburg lease on Danish St. Thomas.

Another moment of possibility arose in 1750 when Frederick the Great, Frederick William's son, set up the Prussian Asiatic Trading Company. He did so after Prussia acquired the North Sea port of Emden, once a great center for religious exiles, now a possible springboard for commercial ambitions. There was alarm in Amsterdam and London about a potential interloper. But despite modest economic success and even a small dividend for shareholders, the enterprise ended during the Seven Years War, when the French seized Emden. The company also found that its ships were subject to search and seizure by the Royal Navy—the same fate that befell the Ostend Company established in the Austrian Netherlands in the 1720s, which collapsed under pressure from the British and Dutch East India companies.[20] Other German trading companies, like the Prussian Bengal Company chartered in Emden in 1753, were no more successful.[21]

Frederick the Great has a reputation as an inflexible landlubber—"land animals like us are not accustomed to live among whales, dolphins, turbot and codfish," he memorably remarked.[22] But Frederick acquired his opinions the hard way, by experience. Given the reaction of the British, Dutch, and French to his efforts, by the time of his second *Political Testament* (1768) he came to believe that "grand commerce" was not within Prussia's grasp: the absence of a navy meant that the state was unable to protect its merchant vessels and Prussia must be a *"puissance de terre firme."*[23] The well-traveled Prussian seaman Joachim Nettelbeck noted with resignation in his memoirs that "during this time of the Seven Years War Prussian ships and sailors who wanted to go about their business hardly had any other option than to fly under the neutral flag of Danzig."[24] In the eighteenth century the great European empires were amphibious: they projected power on land and sea.[25] That was true of Britain and France, it remained true of Spain and the Netherlands, and after the reign of Peter the Great it became true of Russia. But the German powers were land-bound.

Germans (and indirectly the German states) were nonetheless major actors in the European empires of the eighteenth century. That was true at many different levels. Not to be overlooked is the fact that many of those empires had German rulers. Catherine the Great was a German princess, which is one reason she filled the academy in St. Petersburg with Germans. Denmark's rulers came from the north German house of Oldenburg, a connection reinforced when Frederik IV married a German princess. Then there was the personal union between the crowns of Britain and Hanover, with effects on the shaping of British identity in a formative period that historians have only recently begun to explore.[26] While German naturalists and scientists gravitated toward Russia, German cultural luminaries were drawn to Britain by a sympathetic court, from composer George Frideric Handel in the first half of the eighteenth century to painter Johann Zoffany in the second half. Where there was a shared Protestant identity, Germans sometimes served as missionaries in other empires. Frederik IV recruited German Pietist missionaries to work in Tranquebar, an enterprise protected by the Danish crown and funded by the Society for the Propagation of Christian Knowledge in London. The Pietists had to learn Danish, then Tamil from Portuguese translations, and they enjoyed limited success trying to convert Indian Hindus. Frequently at odds with the Catholics they encountered and with non-German Protestants in the trading post, they wrote many letters back to Germany calling for more support.[27]

The most visible contribution made by Germans to the imperial projects of others continued a pattern already set in the heyday of the Portuguese and Spanish empires. Germans served, in large numbers, as soldiers and sailors—as an imperial fighting force. They fought especially on behalf of three empires, the British, Dutch, and French. The best-known instance is that of the auxiliaries known as "Hessian mercenaries," the thirty-two thousand German contract soldiers who fought for the British in the American War of Independence between 1776 and 1783. They took their popular name from the largest single contingent, supplied by the Landgrave of Hessen-Kassel, but the auxiliaries included units from five other small German principalities.[28] The soldiers were shipped down the Rhine to the Dutch port of Nijmegen, where they mustered for the eight-week Atlantic crossing. There they fought in every major engagement of the conflict and regularly made up as much a third of British forces, sometimes even a half. The "Hessians" were a product of two complementary needs. Britain needed troops but was reluctant for political reasons to maintain a standing army. A Hessian auxiliary not only was a soldier, but released a Briton to pursue gainful economic activity, and was at the same time someone who could not be hired to fight against the British—"three men in one."[29] On the other side of the soldier trade, many small German principalities had oversize armies for reasons of prestige, but needed money and were unwilling to pay the political price of going to their estates to ask for revenue. Establishing a lottery was one resort, but a more lucrative one was to provide soldiers for the British in exchange for cash. What happened after 1776 was only the latest in series of agreements. As early as the first decade of the eighteenth century, Britain had treaties with a dozen European states to provide troops, including Trier, Saxony, Prussia, and the Palatinate as well as Hessen-Kassel. Hessian soldiers assisted in the internal consolidation of the British empire when they helped to put down the Jacobite rebellion in 1715; they fought for the British during the Wars of the Spanish and the Austrian Successions and again in the Seven Years War.[30]

The German auxiliaries who served in America after 1776 were recruited by various means, some as mercenaries, others through a form of conscription. They also varied in quality, at least in the eyes of British officers. Colonel Charles Rainsford, the British commissary in charge of sending them off from Holland, greatly admired a contingent from Ansbach-Bayreuth ("two of the finest Battalions of foreign Troops I ever saw, young, tall, well appointed, and in excellent Condition"). He was less impressed by a troop of reinforcements from Hessen-Kassel, a "very unequal body of men."[31] The German auxiliaries were overwhelmingly Protestant. They included a core of professional soldiers, but most were young and lower class. This is unsurprising. German rulers wanted to establish units quickly and cheaply, so most recruits came from the ranks of the dispensable—the sons of land-poor peasants, the urban unemployed, itinerants, and other marginal groups. This had another advantage for the ruler of a "mercenary state," for it removed those who might otherwise become a burden on poor relief or a source of discontent. Thus it was that young men from villages in Hessen-Kassel and Franconia found their way to America, where thousands of Germans died and thousands more became prisoners of war. But thousands also settled eventually in the country where they had gone to fight, finding brides among the colonial population (even, in some cases, when they already had one at home) and unwittingly doing their bit to vindicate the hostile member of parliament in London who had argued that sending Hessians to fight in the colonies would lead to "peopling America with Germans."[32]

A second contingent of Germans also provided military support for the British empire. They were officers and men of the Hanoverian army.[33] The personal union between the British monarchy and the Electorate of Hanover placed them in a unique position. Hanoverians fought alongside the British in every major conflict of the eighteenth century, often outnumbering British forces, and were stationed in England during the French invasion scare of 1756. This created political friction on both sides. There was suspicion in Britain that the arrangement served to enrich Hanover, as well as fears of a standing army that was foreign to boot; Hanoverians were allergic to the danger of being exploited, serving colonial interests that were not their own. The Hanoverian minister in London warned in 1724 that "Hanover will soon be a province of Great Britain much as Ireland is now."[34]

Tensions ran high during the Seven Years War, but Hanoverian soldiers continued to defend outposts of the British empire. They were deployed in Gibraltar and Minorca in the 1770s and then in India, where two regiments arrived on the Coromandel coast in 1782 as auxiliary troops of the British East India Company in the Second Anglo-Mysore War. Later reinforcements brought the total number of men who made the seven-month journey to twenty-eight hundred, the largest group of Germans ever to set foot on the Subcontinent. Because Hanoverian recruiters cast their net beyond the Electorate, they included Hessians, Thuringians, and many others.[35]

German manpower was even more crucial to the Dutch and the number of men involved much greater. The underlying reasons so many Germans served the Dutch empire as soldiers or sailors were the same reasons that led others to fight for the British empire, but with some important differences. On the one hand, no German state acted as an intermediary—no Hessen-Kassel or Hanover put men into uniform on behalf of the Dutch. On the other hand, the close economic relations between northwest Germany and the Low Countries created a much larger pool of potential German recruits to the Dutch seaborne empire. A small European nation with a far-flung empire, the Dutch were in constant need of manpower. They sent a million people overseas, mostly to Asia, in the years 1600–1800, two-thirds of them in the eighteenth century. The Dutch East India Company (Vereenigte Ostindische Compagnie, or VOC), the motor of Amsterdam's rise and the largest commercial enterprise in the world, employed forty thousand people at its peak. The appetite of the VOC for soldiers and sailors was voracious, especially given the high death rates on board ship (typically one-third of the crew) during the seven-month voyage to Batavia in the East Indies.[36] In the 1760s, as many as 9000 new seamen and soldiers were being recruited every year. Half were foreigners, most of them Germans.[37] In the eighteenth century as many as 150,000 German soldiers were employed by the VOC. In Batavia, we are told, "the entire garrison, both officers and soldiers, is composed mostly of Germans." The numbers in the shrinking Dutch West Indies were much smaller, but the dependence on foreigners—especially Germans—was the same.[38]

Who were these Germans and how did they come to sign on? Some went to the Netherlands intending to do so, attracted by Dutch recruiters, or enlisted as professional soldiers. Others ended up in the employ of the VOC or West India Company for reasons similar to those that caused poor Hessians to fight for the British. They were fished from the large pool of

Germans already working in the Netherlands. Some of the sailors may have been drawn to the Dutch Republic to hire on with whaling boats after the eighteenth-century decline of the industry in areas like Friesland, but the movement was a more general one.[39] In the seventeenth century, six out of ten sailors and seamen in Amsterdam were already foreign, the largest contingent among them German. Marriage registers show that almost a fifth of seamen who married in the city were Germans.[40] They were part of a much larger pattern of labor migration that led poor Germans to seek work in a much more prosperous country where wage levels were higher. These *Hollandgänger*, or Holland migrants, were seasonal laborers, numbering as many as thirty thousand a year by the eighteenth century. They came from heavily populated areas in northwestern Germany where land was scarce and proto-industrialization had not yet developed—the East Friesland peninsula, Westphalia, Lower Saxony. Most worked as agricultural laborers on dairy farms or in peat digging, others in canal construction, dock work, and brickmaking. Female domestic servants were also part of this flow of Germans to the Netherlands. There were even child chimney sweeps from the poor valleys of Westphalia.[41] Germans from the northwest were joined in the eighteenth century by immigrants from the Rhineland, who followed the same route on the Rhine as the timber that was rafted downriver to build Dutch ships. All strengthened the domestic infrastructure of the Dutch empire; some ended up working for it directly in the VOC or the West India Company. A good deal has been written about the notorious *zielverkopers* (literally, "sellers of souls"), unscrupulous brokers acting as recruiters or crimps who inveigled impoverished young men into the arms of the company by offering board and lodging, advancing money, and then selling them into service. This system undoubtedly did operate in the major port cities—Amsterdam, Rotterdam, Delft, and Middelburg.[42] But it could be seen simply as an extreme example of the material circumstances (and exaggerated hopes) that compelled all young Germans who shipped out to Batavia or Surinam.

When another Anglo-Dutch war broke out in 1780, the fourth since 1652, there were Germans on both sides. It was a situation that had long existed in the eighteenth-century colonial conflict between Britain and France. The English East India Company depended on German troops; so did its French opposite number. The British used Germans as colonial garrison troops; so did the French. This strange symmetry continued during the American War of Independence, when the French sent forces contain-

ing large numbers of Germans to support the American colonists against
a British army that relied on "Hessians." German-Americans were also
among the insurrectionary colonists, of course. As a result, there were military engagements with large German contingents in all three of the major
armies in the field—the British, the French, and George Washington's
Continental Army. The decisive Battle of Yorktown in 1781 was dubbed
"the German battle" for that reason.[43]

German soldiers and sometimes sailors provided essential support to
the British, Dutch, and French empires. They even provided modest military support to the Spanish and Danish—the first contracts by Hessen-
Kassel to provide troops were signed with those two powers.[44] Wherever
there were colonial interests at stake in the eighteenth century we find Germans enlisted to defend them. Fighting forces are the most obvious props of
empires, but not the only ones. German naturalists, as we have seen, served
the cause of imperial botany around the globe on expeditions that were typically military in organization. In a broader sense they contributed to the
stock of knowledge and information, about Indigenous peoples as well as
the natural world, which was now becoming a prerequisite of colonial rule.[45]
The same was true of missionaries (often avid botanists and ethnographers
themselves), although—as in the case of the naturalists—the relationship
with the host empire was not always comfortable. These Germans scattered
throughout the empires of others helped to join the German lands to an
increasingly interconnected globe. Pietist missionaries communicated what
they found to their headquarters in Halle in famously voluminous reports.
The scientists had their own networks, so that the information gathered by
Germans in St. Petersburg or points east eventually found its way back to
German centers of learning, as well as to London, Paris, and Carl Linnaeus's Uppsala. Meanwhile, Niebuhr and Georg Forster were celebrated at
home as well as abroad for their travels. More quietly, a number of German
officers who returned from America or India published works that engaged
seriously with those countries and helped to form German attitudes.

Trade played a central part in an increasingly connected world, and German merchants were now spread out in greater numbers than in earlier centuries along the thickening global arteries of communication, playing their
part in what the philosopher Johann Gottlieb Fichte called "the animation
of universal commerce."[46] Settlers from the German lands also contributed
to the peopling of non-European parts of the globe by Europeans. Add
them all together, the soldiers and sailors, scientists and missionaries, com-

posers like Handel and artists like Zoffany, the merchants and colonists, and the resulting mosaic gives us a picture of the part played by Germans— vicariously, through the back door—in the transnational exchanges of goods, botanical specimens, people and ideas in the eighteenth-century era of imperial rivalry. They played those parts in places around the globe, from the Russian Pacific to the Malabar Coast of India, from the Spanish Phil- ippines to the Dutch East Indies. But nowhere was their role greater than in the Atlantic world.

The Atlantic World

ATLANTIC HISTORY, THE HISTORY OF THE GREAT INTERAC- tions that took place between Europe, Africa, and the Americas, has emerged in the last decades as a dynamic field that has generated its own programs, textbooks, essay collections, and book prizes. It has been crit- icized for trying to retrofit old-style imperial history with a new name to make it more acceptable and faulted also for lacking coherence—the Atlantic, after all, was not a bounded inland sea like the Mediterranean written about with such dazzling originality by French historian Fernand Braudel.[47] Yet Atlantic history is a useful frame because it encourages us to pay attention to encounters of various kinds, between Europeans and Indigenous peoples, between Europeans of different nationalities, and not least between humans and the natural world, including the world of disease. For the "Columbian exchange" brought syphilis (along with the potato and the turkey) to Europe, while it carried smallpox, chicken- pox, measles, whooping cough, scarlet fever, typhus, diphtheria, cholera, and bubonic plague to the Americas, where it killed nine-tenths of the population.[48]

There were many different Atlantics. There was the Atlantic of cod and whaling, which stretched from Iceland to New England, just as there was the Atlantic of slavery-based sugar and coffee plantations.[49] There was a Black Atlantic and a Catholic Atlantic.[50] The multitude of transnational connections and interactions across the Atlantic are obvious enough, but the momentum of nationally defined history remains powerful. One excel- lent essay collection begins with a section called "New Atlantic Worlds," which contains five essays that deal, in turn, with the Spanish, Portuguese, British, French, and Dutch.[51] Missing, of course, are the Germans. The obvious reason is that there was no "German Atlantic" in the sense of areas subject to the formal sovereignty of a German state. But the Germans were there, and in numbers. They remain invisible because they were present in the interstices of the Atlantic empires constructed by other Europeans. We need to know where to look for them to recover this invisible history.

Imagine a snapshot of the people who were sailing across the Atlantic at a given moment in the middle of the eighteenth century. It would include sailors, soldiers, supercargoes, merchants, officials, colonists, immigration agents, plantation managers, missionaries, naturalists, mining engineers, surgeons, and couriers.[52] There is hardly an occupational category in which Germans were not represented. But this is only a still picture of what the historian Bernard Bailyn called "worlds in motion."[53] So let us set it in motion, and see where it leads. A good place to start would be the Netherlands. Germans were resident there in large numbers, as we have seen, either permanently or seasonally. They dug the peat that provided the energy for the refineries that processed the sugar that was brought back from the Dutch plantations. It was carried on ships that were constructed from German timber, equipped with German guns, and crewed by German sailors.[54] We can follow one of those ships across the ocean, thanks to the memoirs of the Prussian sailor Joachim Nettelbeck, who made the journey often in the middle of the eighteenth century. The Dutch Atlantic he sailed was smaller than it had been a century earlier in the golden age. New Holland on the coast of Brazil was ceded to the Portuguese in 1654, New Netherland on the eastern seaboard of North America lost to the British ten years later. Dutch possessions now consisted of some trading ports along the African Gold Coast, together with the Antilles islands in the Caribbean and a string of colonies along the South American coast between the Amazon and the Orinoco—Essequibo, Demerara, Berbice, and Surinam.[55]

It was Surinam to which Nettelbeck sailed in 1758, a very quick trip from the Dutch port of Texel that took just twenty days thanks to favorable Passat trade winds. He stayed for eight months, delivering European goods and collecting coffee and sugar in a flat-bottomed boat, like a covered punt, while enjoying the hospitality of fellow countrymen—the "happiest days of my life," so he claimed. Nettelbeck had first been in Surinam four years earlier, when he signed on as a gunner with a Dutch ship captained by one of his relatives. When the helmsman fell overboard Nettelbeck became deputy helmsman, the beginning of a career that led to his eventually captaining his own ship. It was on this earlier trip to Surinam that he first became familiar with the capital Paramaribo and outlying districts.[56] Nettelbeck subsequently visited the Dutch colony many times, often as part of the triangular trade that brought African slaves to work on the sugar plantations. He was impressed enough that he wrote to Frederick the Great urging him to acquire some unclaimed land between Berbice and Surinam as a Prussian colony. Frederick never replied.

In Nettelbeck's account, Surinam itself was German in all but name: "You could have called Surinam then more a German than a Dutch colony, for on the plantations as in Paramaribo perhaps ninety-nine out of every hundred whites you met were people who had found their way here from every region of Germany."[57] Later writers took their lead from him.[58] Surinam did in fact have a strong German presence, although Nettelbeck exaggerated it. Like Berbice, Demerara, and the Dutch Antilles, the colony was a cosmopolitan place where the Dutch jostled alongside Germans, Swiss, French, Spanish, Portuguese, and smaller numbers of English and Scandinavians among a European population no higher than 3400 (out of 50,000) in the 1780s. Germans were spread socially through the population. They could be found in the ranks of craftsmen and the commercial middle class. Many plantation managers or overseers were German, a group that became larger after 1770 as the number of absentee owners rose.[59] Some Germans owned plantations. Nettelbeck's account is colored by his admiration for upwardly mobile German success stories, like the two brothers from Pomerania and a homesick Viennese whom Nettelbeck met on a return voyage, all of whom had gone out to Surinam penniless and become rich through "good fortune, hard work and honesty."[60] Such cases were what made colonies attractive to younger sons, marginal types, and "chancers," or to parents who despaired of their good-for-nothing children. The only son of Hamburg's well-regarded Johann Berenberg was shipped off to Surinam in 1767, the Senate even sending a guard to ensure he reached his destination.[61] A respectable example of upward mobility was the coffee plantation owner Johann Heinrich Schäfer, the German-born son of a carpenter who immigrated to Surinam in 1714. The son established himself in the 1740s on 250 acres along the Commewijne River, gave himself the Dutch-sounding name Schaap, and called his property Schaapstede (Sheepfold). His estate was worth millions when he died in 1765.[62]

But there were also prominent German merchants in Surinam, like the Amsinck family, which engaged in trade and owned a sugar plantation. Originally Dutch patricians, they fled the Low Countries and established themselves in Hamburg in the late sixteenth century, becoming part of the city's merchant elite. The Amsincks straddled the Atlantic world, with branches of the family in Lisbon (the wine business) and London (tobacco) as well as Surinam.[63] Two members of another family that went to Hamburg as refugees, the Huguenot Godeffroys, also did business in Surinam. One married into an English plantation-owning family. The names of other well-known German merchant houses turn up, too. Caspar Voght boasted that he was the first Hamburg merchant to ship coffee from Mocha, tobacco from Baltimore, rubber from Africa, and coffee from Surinam.[64]

This mix of new wealth and old among German plantation owners, managers, and merchants was also typical of one particular subset of them: German Jews. Jews were a major presence in Surinam from the earliest days. In the 1730s they owned more than four out of ten plantations in the colony. However, accusations that Jews were somehow responsible for allowing too many slaves to escape caused many of them to sell up and move to Paramaribo, where they worked as merchants. That was why, in the late 1780s, Jews made up around a third of the small white population in Surinam as a whole but more than a half in the capital. The German Jews in Surinam, mostly Ashkenazi, were a small community and generally less wealthy or educated than their Portuguese Sephardic coreligionists, who came by way of Brazil. They could nonetheless be found among plantation owners, managers, merchants, and the middle class of Paramaribo, although many "impoverished German Jews" also arrived in the late eighteenth century.[65]

They were not alone. Poor Germans arrived in Surinam throughout the eighteenth century. Governor Jan Jacob Mauricius encouraged small landowners to settle the colony, to break the dominance of the sugar barons and serve as a buffer zone against escaped slaves. One group of would-be colonists came from land-hungry southwest Germany. A Surinam commissioner, Cologne-born Philipp Hack, went personally to Rotterdam to talk them into making the Dutch colony, not British Georgia, their destination.[66] They received free land, tools, and cattle, but—in the words of the German explorer and naturalist Albert von Sack, writing in 1805—"fell a sacrifice to the climate."[67] The same happened to German settlers in other parts of the inhospitable Dutch Atlantic.[68] Poor Germans also arrived on a regular basis as soldiers and sailors. Germans made up three-fourths of the garrison strength.[69] Accounts of expeditions to capture escaped slaves always feature names like Creutz, Dorig, and Frick. Some of the soldiers looked to stay on after their period of service ended by finding work on an estate, but others moved on, as many settlers also did, whether to another Dutch colony, to Barbados, or to one of the North American colonies. Merchants were not the only ones who moved around within the Atlantic world.[70]

Other Germans in Surinam were situated socially between plantation owners or merchants and soldiers. They included craftsmen, small traders, and physicians.[71] In 1772 Governor Nepveu asked for a dozen medical works in German to be shipped over, a reflection of the fact that most of the surgeons in Paramaribo and outlying areas were Germans.[72] Two other groups of Germans also came to the colony but enjoyed little success. One of them—no surprise, this—was made up of mining engineers and miners. Four different eighteenth-century expeditions set off inland to investigate the prospects for mining, all of them unproductive.[73] The other group consisted of members of the Moravian Church, commonly known as the Moravian Brethren, who also suffered a series of false starts, although more tragic than those faced by the mining engineers. The first Moravian mission to Surinam arrived in 1735, just three people. One fell ill and died almost immediately; the other two returned to Europe. Another trio followed in 1738: Michael Tannenberger and a married couple, Georg and Rosina Berwig. Georg worked on the plantation of Dutchman Jan Pieter Visser as overseer of field slaves, his wife ran the household. Less than a year after their arrival, Rosina Berwig was violently raped by Visser and died. Efforts by her spouse to bring the well-connected planter to justice having failed, Georg Berwig and Michael Tannenberger left the colony in disgust. A third, somewhat larger mission arrived in 1740 and lasted for five years, until it, too, was shut down as a result of internal rifts and widespread hostility. It was not until a fourth mission that the Moravians finally managed to establish themselves and pursue their goal of winning converts.[74]

They worked among the Indigenous Caribs and Arawaks and among Black slaves or former slaves with some success, although they never had more than six hundred followers in the eighteenth century. Reactions to their work broke along the lines of economic, political, and national divisions. The plantation owners were predictably hostile; so were the Dutch Reformed clergy. The local Jewish community, including Jewish plantation owners, was much more sympathetic. Successive Dutch governors blew hot and cold. As the Visser case showed, they were reluctant to act against a powerful individual; they were also suspicious of Moravian intentions while the long-running conflict went on with the independent Maroon communities of Blacks who controlled upriver areas. But after a truce in the early 1760s, the Moravians were viewed by some governors as a potential ally in converting otherwise hostile Maroons. They could also be used by governors looking to counter the power of the sugar barons. The Moravians aroused strong feelings. The naturalist Albert von Sack, writing later, warmly praised their "good work" among the Indians. But the Englishman John Gabriel Stedman, a soldier in Surinam during the 1770s who wrote a classic account of the colony, heaped scorn on "thy canting Moravians."[75] Stedman's view may reflect the moral ambiguities of his own position: he was a stern critic of slavery but his account of its violence (illustrated by William Blake) passed over or romanticized Stedman's frequent sexual relations with native women.[76] Sack's admiration, on the other hand, may well have been colored by his sympathy for the Moravians as inveterate botanizers who collected plants, established botanical gardens, and shipped specimens back to Europe.[77]

In Surinam we see in miniature some of the many ways that Germans helped to construct the Atlantic world. Zoom out, and we see the same pattern repeating itself, albeit with variations. There are three sets of Germans that we find again and again beyond Surinam—missionaries, colonists, and merchants. Other groups were largely absent from this small, mosquito-ridden, cosmopolitan but racially violent colony. There were no German printers, publishers, and booksellers, such as we find in a city like Philadelphia, and in smaller numbers in the Spanish American empire. Nor, of course, was there much trace of the German cultural diaspora we encounter in a major imperial hub like London, home to German-born scientists, scholars, artists, and musicians. The English music historian Charles Burney wrote in 1773, "It is hardly too much to say, that the best German musicians of the present age, with few exceptions, are to be found out of the country."[78] London was home to hundreds of German musicians— composers, performers, music publishers, and teachers.[79] The German contribution to the "scholarly Atlantic" was represented in Surinam mainly by a few bookish physicians and by the Moravians.[80] But that is an ungenerous a way to put it, for the Moravians were missionaries and much more besides. The network they established was one of the important circuits of knowledge that joined the Atlantic world.

Founded in the 1720s by Count Nikolaus Ludwig von Zinzendorf, the Moravian Church (or Unity of Brethren) was a spectacular instance of the renewal of Protestant evangelicalism in the eighteenth century. The original Moravian base was Herrnhut in Saxony, but expulsion in 1738 led them to establish two new settlements in the hill country north of Frankfurt, long an area hospitable to radical religious refugees. Later they returned to Herrnhut—being able to pick up and move quickly was central to Moravian life. Even before the original move from Herrnhut, Moravian missionaries had fanned out around the Atlantic world. There would eventually be missions in Europe, Africa, the Caribbean, and the North American colonies. A couple named Johannes and Johannette Maria Kimbel Ettwein give us an idea of what this meant in human terms. Each joined the Moravians when young and went to the Netherlands. Married and ordained as deacons in 1746 (Moravians believed in the spiritual equality of men and women), over the next twenty years they established a new Dutch congregation, were sent to London, shuttled back and forth between London and Germany with a growing family, were dispatched to Bethlehem, Pennsylvania, the Moravians' American headquarters, then to another new settlement in the North Carolina backcountry, before returning to Bethlehem.[81]

Moravians not only represented the German wing of the Anglo-American Great Awakening of these years; they played some part in setting it in motion. Future Methodist leader John Wesley first encountered Moravians mid-Atlantic when he crossed to America in 1735, and was so impressed that he started learning German. During the seemingly endless days on board ship he sometimes talked to them for hours.[82] Wesley got to know Moravians better when, while preaching in Georgia, he began translating Moravian hymns into English. Back in England, three years later, Wesley, his brother Charles, and George Whitefield were all members (along with William Blake's parents) at the Fetter Lane Society established by Moravians in London as a place of prayer and fellowship. Peter Böhler of the London Brethren can take some credit for Wesley's conversion soon afterward.[83]

The Moravians took their message to Amerindian peoples and Black slaves throughout the sugar islands and North America, often (as in Surinam) inciting the ire of local planters when they taught the enslaved to read and write. Friedrich Martin was told by one planter on St. Thomas: "Don't teach my Negroes to be Pietists, or you'll know what I will do."[84] As a result of these efforts, and despite threats to both missionaries and slaves, the majority of Black Protestants in the late-eighteenth-century world were Moravians. The belief of Brethren that all souls were equally worthy of salvation brought them to the cusp of a radically egalitarian view of race.

Yet they did not make that final leap, unable to break with convictions about "heathen" nature and the purported biblical justifications for slavery, a stance that was also convenient when they found themselves issued with periodic reminders from imperial power holders about where lines had to be drawn.[85] However, like the Jesuits before them, Moravians paid close attention to the appearance, language, and culture of the non-Europeans they sought to convert, as they did to the flora and fauna of the places where they established missions. They recorded everything and shipped voluminous reports, diaries, and letters back to Germany, where they were filed and extracts published in the Moravian newsletter, the *Gemein Nachrichten*.[86]

The Moravians represented just one part of the unruly Protestant evangelical revival that spilled out of Europe and across the Atlantic in the eighteenth century. A colorful array of German groups established communities in North America—Dunkers, Mennonites, Schwenkfelders, Pietists. Despite their differences, all would have agreed with Zinzendorf that theirs was a "religion of the heart," emotionally intense and very personal. That drove them to share their experiences of salvation with others of like mind and heart, in letters and personal testimony, with the result that they became part of a transatlantic network that linked the American colonies, especially Pennsylvania, to Germany and sometimes to England and the Netherlands as well.[87] The evangelical awakening should be seen, not as the "influence" of a European center on a colonial periphery, but as a circulation of ideas within the Atlantic Protestant world.

A very good example of this can be found in the correspondence between the early Lutheran Pietists in Prussia with like-minded interlocutors in London and Boston. The back-and-forth among the Pietist August Hermann Francke, the New England Puritan Cotton Mather, and others most resembled "a kind of transatlantic echo chamber" of ideas and practices. Mather contemplated this expanding world of communications joyously: "O wide Atlantick, Thou shalt not stand in the way as any Hindrance of those Communications."[88] His enthusiasm was testimony from New England to the remarkable network established by the Pietists, the tradition out of which many Moravians (including Zinzendorf himself) came. The Pietist web radiated out from Halle, where they established educational institutions, a printing press, and the Halle Orphanage. Their missionaries sought converts from Siberia to Malabar and across the Atlantic. Pietists operated an extensive courier system and brought both pharmaceuticals and Bibles to the New World. They shared with the Moravians a keen interest in botany. The key figure in North American Pietism of the mid-eighteenth century was Henry Melchior Mühlenberg, a botanist with a Göttingen degree before a conversion experience led him to Halle and theological training.[89] Like the Moravians, Pietists were active in the intensified Atlantic exchange of books, copper plates, and botanical and agricultural specimens in the late eighteenth century.[90]

That exchange included people. The Moravians decided in 1742 to acquire their own vessel to carry Brethren across the Atlantic, circumventing the profane trade in migrants. This allowed congregations to travel as organized groups with Moravian pastors and crew, maintaining the practice of daily worship on board and excluding the dangers posed by irreligious fellow passengers. Over time, Moravian ships were used mainly for trade purposes, "a commerce that the Lord could sanctify and bless" as one of them called it.[91] A different pattern developed from similar beginnings among a closely connected group of Quaker, Mennonite, and Pietist merchants in Britain, Germany, Switzerland, and the Netherlands. They began to cooperate in the late seventeenth century, organizing relief efforts to assist persecuted members of their faiths, which included shipping them to a place of safety. This network included Benjamin Furly, William Penn's agent in Europe. Out of these efforts emerged the shipping of Germans and Swiss across the Atlantic.[92] Germantown in Pennsylvania, established by the lawyer Daniel Pastorius as the first solidly German settlement in the North American colonies, was one of its early fruits.[93] Soon something more permanent developed, as a service to coreligionists became a specialized trade in the hands of Dutch and English merchants in Rotterdam, who funneled immigrants down the Rhine corridor to the Netherlands and on to the Quaker city of Philadelphia. It was the "prototype of a transatlantic mass migration," a movement of people that took as many as 120,000 German-speaking immigrants to North America between 1683 and 1775, with a peak in the years from 1730 to the outbreak of the Seven Years War in 1756.[94]

These were not trivial numbers. The German flow across the Atlantic was comparable in scale with British and Irish immigration to the American colonies in the eighteenth century. It was also a new destination for a population that had long been willing to leave their homes and done so in large numbers since the late seventeenth century. Inhabitants of the Holy Roman Empire were highly mobile, contrary to the image of a "static" pre-industrial society. As many as one in three adults changed their place of residence during their lifetimes.[95] Most traveled short distances, but not all.

Between the 1680s and the late eighteenth century, around 300,000 people settled in Prussia from other parts of the Holy Roman Empire and Switzerland. Some of these new settlements, many of them on reclaimed former wetlands, were given names like Florida, Saratoga, and Philadelphia—nods to an imagined America.[96] Hundreds of thousands more went farther afield than Prussia, to settle in Russia, Poland, or the southern Hungarian Banat, where land-hungry German peasants were encouraged by the Habsburg monarchy to become colonists who would secure the southeastern "frontier" against the Ottoman Empire.[97] Eight hundred German villages were founded in the Banat between 1711 and 1750. Then there were the Germans who immigrated to the European fringes of the Atlantic world—to the Netherlands, as we have seen, or to Britain. Of the 13,500 German refugees who passed through England in 1709 hoping to be shipped to South Carolina, some 3000 ended up in Ireland as a Protestant bulwark securing a different imperial "frontier." Thousands more from southwest Germany settled in Spain, when the enterprising former soldier Johann Kaspar Thürriegel convinced King Carlos III that they would further the inner colonization of his country.[98]

Some prospective German colonists crossed the Atlantic for destinations in the Caribbean or the nearby South American mainland. Some, as we saw, went to Surinam, unsuccessfully. A more tragic case occurred just along the coast, in what turned out to be one of the great humanitarian disasters of the eighteenth century. In 1763 the French crown was looking to achieve something bold after the humiliations of the Seven Years War. It planned to establish a colony at Kourou, in French Guiana. Germans, thought to be good colonist material, were heavily targeted. A prospectus was drawn up, translated into German, and distributed along with a map of the future colony. Emigrants from Germany were promised food, board, and clothing for themselves and their families for two and a half years; they would pay no taxes and be cared for if they fell ill. They would also have the cost of their journey to Rochefort on the French Atlantic coast covered, as well as their subsistence there and their transport to Guiana. Germans made up three-fourths of the 14,000 hopefuls who turned up in Rochefort. Even the musicians who accompanied the colonists were German: a horn player from Swabia, a guitar player from Baden-Baden, and an eight-year-old harpist from Koblenz. But this was a French fantasy of settlement, undermined by malnutrition and epidemic disease. The would-be colonists recruited in Germany had been fed "illusory hope," Louis XVI's foreign minister later wrote. More than 13,000 people eventually went out to Kourou. At least two-thirds of them died. There was a settlement on the Approuague River where 300 Germans arrived in September and all but 3 were dead by November.[99]

What motivated would-be colonists to follow the pied pipers of the French crown to Kourou, or throw themselves on the mercy of the British crown? What made people willing to confront the obstacles the German states placed in their way when they wanted to emigrate—bans, fines, payments, at the very least having to seek permission and produce paperwork?[100] Why were so many wanderers between worlds prepared to take the risk of crossing the ocean on a daunting two-month journey despite the advice of their social betters that doing so was dangerous and irresponsible? There is no simple answer. Some emigration was relatively low risk, a form of social betterment, if the emigrants had sought-after skills. The Siegerland miners recruited to settle in Virginia, or the German glassblowers brought over by ambitious German-speaking entrepreneurs, had jobs waiting for them.[101] But most emigrants were peasants or craftsmen. Some were undoubtedly desperate, driven by dire material circumstances, but many were responding to perceived opportunities that were new. Their decisions, in other words, were based on "pull" as much as "push." Emigrants were younger and more literate than non-emigrants from the same place.[102]

Those who crossed the Atlantic came disproportionately from certain parts of the Holy Roman Empire. The German emigrants in Britain were dubbed "the poor Palatines," and Benjamin Franklin referred unkindly to the Germans who landed in Pennsylvania as "Palatine boors." The name identified a place on the left bank of the Rhine. It was a shorthand term (like "Hessians") but correctly pinpointed a region that included not only the Palatinate but adjacent areas in the southwest corner of the Empire. "Push" factors were especially strong here: properties were heavily subdivided, taxes were rising, and feudal obligations were growing more burdensome. These were areas from which people had long migrated to Prussia or the Banat. America represented an extension of this historical pattern, once it became possible to imagine.

That is where the "pull" comes in. It mattered that these territories lay along or close to the Rhine. The river became a communications corridor for Germans (and Swiss) traveling to Prussia; it was also a means to transport people to Rotterdam, the port of embarkation for America. From there, a trial-and-error system of transports had generated its own momentum by the 1720s, and merchants carried Germans to the colonies on a regular basis. A good three-fourths of them went to Pennsylvania, but they could also be found in New York, Virginia, the Carolinas, and Georgia. A further mechanism that eased the flow of people was a system of credit that allowed emigrants with few assets to pay their way. This was the "redemptioner" system, whereby the shipping merchants paid for the passage, then sold their passengers into a form of indentured servitude that allowed them to pay off the debt. About half of all Germans entered servitude for a period of two to five years.[103]

America became a more imaginable destination as information about it spread. In the early eighteenth century, many Germans still thought Pennsylvania and Carolina were islands; not many did so after 1730.[104] Literature about the fabled opportunities in America reached into the villages; there were even local songs about it.[105] Of course, what people read about America were often enthusiastic accounts circulated by recruiting agents for Dutch shippers, American landowners, or other advocates of colonization projects. The German states tried hard to keep these promoters out of their territories, with limited success. Word of the opportunities that awaited emigrants across the Atlantic was also spread by "newlanders," peasants, artisans, or traders who had already emigrated, then returned to collect property and settle their affairs. For most, returning was a one-time or occasional event, but some became professional go-betweens, shuttling back and forth across the Atlantic on behalf of others, delivering letters, collecting debts, and perhaps earning a premium from a shipping agent by recruiting new emigrants. By the middle of the eighteenth century this had become (like the shipping of emigrants) an established business. There were hundreds of these go-betweens, who advertised in colonial newspapers and operated with the power of attorney from third parties. Like the letters they carried, the newlanders were also a prime source of information about America as well as advice about such basic matters as when to leave—spring was best, in order to arrive before the winter storms in the Atlantic.[106]

Promoters, agents, and newlanders all helped to channel the flow of emigrants, who mostly sought (and often found) material betterment. But emigration was sometimes organized through religious networks. That was true of the settlement in Germantown led by Daniel Pastorius, an enterprise dedicated to leaving behind sinful Babylon and finding a "new Canaan." It was also true of the settlements established by Moravians and other sectarian Protestants. Pietists recruited entire congregations as emi-

grants. But most emigrants were Lutheran or Reformed, not Pietist or sectarian radicals—the number of the latter has been estimated as no more
than four thousand in all the American colonies, a tiny percentage of the
total German emigration.[107] Given the resistance to emigration by German
rulers, promoters often referred to the benefits of religious freedom and
would-be emigrants learned to use the language of religious persecution.[108]
Sometimes, though, the religious persecution was real, as it was for the
twenty thousand Protestants expelled from the Archbishopric of Salzburg
in 1731. Most went to Prussia, but several hundred accepted the invitation
of the Georgia trustees to immigrate to that new American colony, where
they founded the settlement of Ebenezer.[109] Material and religious motives
can be hard to separate. Moravian ships combined trade and the transport of souls. The Philadelphia merchant Caspar Wistar, who established a
glassworks in New Jersey and brought over German workers as manpower,
was an entrepreneur and a dedicated Quaker well connected with Quaker
and Mennonite merchant networks in the Palatinate, Krefeld, and Amsterdam as well as the American colonies.[110]

We encounter thousands of German merchants like Wistar in the
Atlantic world, including scattered around the Caribbean, in Dutch Surinam, French Saint-Domingue, and the Danish free port of St. Thomas, a
major relay station for ships on their way to or from Hamburg and Bremen.[111] Above all, we find German merchants in the great hubs of Atlantic
trade—London, Amsterdam, Lisbon, Bordeaux, and Cadiz. There were
some 225 German merchants in Bordeaux in 1777; a slightly larger number
were active in Cadiz at some point during the years 1764–1791.[112] The underlying reason for this commercial diaspora was that German merchants
could not trade directly with the colonies of these European powers, at least
not legally: they required a foothold in the country concerned. The English
Navigation Acts and their Continental equivalents made that necessary.

German merchants could be remarkably mobile. Take the case of
Peter Hasenclever, who was born in 1716 on the Lower Rhine. The eldest
of twelve sons of a Remscheid manufacturer, he first worked for a cousin
in Burscheid, near Aachen, traveling widely through Europe as a textile
dealer and building up contacts. Hasenclever went to Lisbon in 1745 with
borrowed French capital to become a partner in his uncle's firm, but found
that his uncle had died and instead went into business with two distant
cousins. Five years later he moved to Cadiz, where he established a commercial firm with two partners, one of them a Londoner. After the partners

fell out, he went into business with two Germans and did well by selling textiles to the Spanish colonies. Hasenclever, who had married an Englishwoman in Lisbon, established himself in London in the late 1750s. By then he had business connections all across Europe. In what turned out to be a venture too far, he went to New York in 1764, set up a company that produced flax and hemp, and established an ironworks on ten thousand acres of rocky land in northern New Jersey, using German miners and ironworkers sent across the Atlantic by yet another cousin.[113]

Hasenclever's efforts ended in failure, a result of overambition and unreliable partners, which ruined his businesses in London and North America. He ended his life in Silesia, still engaged in business, seeking (with eventual success) to restore his British reputation. His activities point to a number of things that are true more generally of Germans engaged in Atlantic trade. One is their sheer mobility and disregard of national borders. Hasenclever's career also underscores the importance of family and the networks (and capital) they provided. Hanseatic commercial houses had a long history of strategic family intermarriages. The merchant elites raised this to an art form. The Amsinck family of Hamburg, whom we encountered briefly in Surinam, had businesses in London, Lisbon, and the Caribbean. Many German merchants who settled in eighteenth-century London had family members spread across the great commercial hubs of Europe. Marrying a non-German, as Hasenclever did, was also commonplace. One in five of the German merchants in Bordeaux married a Frenchwoman.[114] We are not surprised to learn about William de Drusina of Hamburg, who was related to the Amsincks, marrying into the family of a Maryland tobacco merchant in London.[115] That is how networks were built and sustained.

There was a pattern to German participation in Atlantic trade. Textiles and manufactured goods went out, "colonial goods" came back. The basis of Peter Hasenclever's early wealth was typical, for it came from selling textiles in the Spanish empire. Others profited from the same trade. The British empire was even more important as a market. Two-thirds of all British textiles exported across the Atlantic in the eighteenth century were of German origin. This trade linked interior parts of Central Europe to the Atlantic economy and gave these proto-industrial regions a major economic boost. Silesian and Hessian linens are prime examples.[116] A host of other goods made their way from the Central European interior across the ocean—kitchenware, mirrors, clocks, and weapons. That was how ironware from the Bergisch Land and rifles from the Thuringian Forest became part of the Atlantic economy. A stubborn cliché that has been overturned in recent years is the one that sets a thin stratum of Hanseatic merchants engaged in the "world economy" against a mass of German entrepreneurs leading "modest inland existences" that were closed off from that world.[117] The Atlantic economy did not stop at the coasts of Europe. But German trade did run through the coastal ports, especially Hamburg. Linens or metal goods were shipped from Hamburg to London, Bordeaux, or Cadiz for transshipment. What came back were coffee, tobacco, and, above all, sugar, products of the Atlantic plantation economy. In 1791, thirty thousand tons of sugar arrived in Hamburg, most of it shipped from French Saint-Domingue, Martinique, or Guadeloupe via Bordeaux.[118]

That points, of course, to a further crucial element in this Atlantic economy—the shipping of enslaved Africans to the Americas, where they provided labor for the plantations. That was the third side of the notorious triangular trade between Europe, Africa, and the Americas. More than six million Africans were shipped to America in the eighteenth century. Three-fourths of those who crossed the Atlantic in those years were slaves, making the New World demographically much more an extension of Africa than of Europe.[119] Germans had a role in every aspect of the slave trade, direct or indirect, something that is only now being recognized. The Brandenburg-Africa Company traded in slaves who were shipped from West Africa through Arguin, an island off the coast of Mauritania, to the Caribbean. In the words of Frederick William I: "His Electoral Highness intends, because the African Company cannot develop without the trade of slaves to America, that one should establish the slave trade on the island of St. Thomas."[120] Most were then transferred to French possessions; others were re-exported to work on the British sugar islands or sold on to Dutch merchants on Curacao and St. Eustatius. During its relatively brief existence, the Brandenburg-Africa Company sent anywhere from 20,000 to 30,000 enslaved Africans to the Americas.

The direct German role in the slave trade continued after the company was wound up. German merchants owned and equipped slave ships; German bankers insured them. Others owned plantations around the Caribbean. Some were engaged on more than one front. The German firm Romberg, Bapst & Cie, based in Bordeaux, outfitted fourteen ships for the slave trade between 1783 and 1791, undertakings responsible for more than 4000 Africans being sent across the Atlantic. Another branch of the firm in Ghent specialized in the slave trade to Cuba and Saint-Domingue, and the company had a further stake in the trade through the provision of maritime insurance. During the 1780s, when the cost of slaves was rising and the price of colonial goods falling, Romberg, Bapst & Cie also took the opportunity to buy up financially distressed plantations.[121]

Ordinary Germans participated in the slave trade when they signed on as sailors with ships engaged in it, like the men from Föhr who crewed Dutch vessels.[122] Sailors from Schleswig-Holstein, Hamburg, and Lübeck are known to have crewed on slave ships.[123] There must have been thousands of these members of ships' crews, all told. We know a good deal about two of them because they wrote memoirs. The ship's surgeon Johann Peter Oettinger, who came from Franconia, traveled around the Atlantic from Emden to the Gold Coast to Curaçao and St. Thomas during the years when the Brandenburg-Africa Company was still in business. He describes his own and other crew members' small personal stake in the slave trade—the sugar, tobacco, cotton, and medicines crated up for him in St. Thomas. He also describes the everyday barbarities of the slave trade, like the physical inspection of enslaved Africans in which he had an important part and their branding with the company mark, without moral censure. They weigh less in the scales, for him, than instances when his property was stolen.[124]

The Pomeranian sailor Joachim Nettelbeck was in a different position. Born seventy years after Oettinger, he lived long enough to see European attitudes toward the slave trade change. In 1771, Nettelbeck was the helmsman on a Dutch ship out of Amsterdam that went to the Guinea coast, transported slaves to Surinam, and carried sugar back to the Netherlands. A few years later he was engaged in the same trade on an English vessel. In old age Nettelbeck wrote a very defensive account of his involvement. He imagines a reader in 1820 asking: "What? Nettelbeck a slave trader? How can we square an honest Pomeranian heart with such a disreputable business?" Nettelbeck answers his hypothetical reader by arguing that attitudes had changed: "Fifty years ago this evil trade in humans was regarded as a business like any other, without people chewing over its justice or injustice." Nettelbeck expresses himself "heartily glad" to see it disappear—or, as he puts it, at least practiced "in a milder form." As he dances away from the dark heart of the slave trade, Nettelbeck then offers the opinion that "barbaric cruelties" were inflicted on enslaved people "only in isolated cases," and he had personally never taken part in any such thing. He ends with the comforting platitude that brutality and cruelty are, alas, all too familiar in the life of a sailor.[125]

Stepping back to look at the big picture, Germans played a central part in the system of slavery that went beyond the role of individuals, whether sailors, shipowners, merchants, or even plantation owners. Central Europe provided many of the trade goods that were exchanged in Africa for enslaved people, and that were worn or used by them when they reached the Americas. As the demand for Asian cottons in Europe and the European empires exceeded supply, it was German linens that supplanted them. French ships arrived on the Guinea coast loaded with "Hamburg linens." Textiles were not the only German trade goods that ended up in Africa. The nineteenth-century explorer Heinrich Barth encountered German razors, sewing needles, and mirrors in the interior of what is now Nigeria.[126] On the other side of the Atlantic, the English writer William Beckford reported that in Jamaica "all the Negroes and poor white people" wore German linens, or "Osnabrughs." There were similar reports from Barbados and Saint-Domingue.[127] Most of the very rare occasions that Central Europe is mentioned in Adam Smith's *Wealth of Nations* (1776) concern "linen from Germany" or "linen and other goods from Germany."[128] These passing references now seem less innocent.

That was one side of the slave trade system: trade goods. The German contribution was no less important on the other side: handling and processing the commodities produced by plantation slavery. Sugar, coffee, and tobacco came into Germany in mounting quantities during the eighteenth century, passing through London or Bordeaux into Hamburg. London–Hamburg was a main trade route for tobacco from the colonies, turning the city and its hinterland into major centers of tobacco processing. The same became increasingly true of Bremen in the late eighteenth century. Re-exports from the French Caribbean went mainly through Bordeaux to Hamburg. The value of French foreign trade accelerated in the course of the century. Three-fourths of Bordeaux's exports went to the "northern trade" by the 1770s, making France the principal supplier of the Hanseatic cities. Half of that trade was in sugar, another fifth in coffee.[129] As a result, Hamburg also became a major player in sugar refining, assuming the position once held by Amsterdam. There were already 200 refineries in the city by 1727; by midcentury it was 300 (more than twice as many as Amsterdam and Rotterdam combined), by the end of the century 400.[130] The main competition came from London, and there it was Germans who had a large part in establishing the British capital as a major center of refining. Some contemporaries complained that Germans dominated the business. There were certainly many German merchants in London who operated or had a share in refineries, with Hamburg families very much to the fore. The "sugar boilers" and laborers brought over from Germany to do the physical work also came mainly from the Elbe-Weser triangle around Hamburg and Bremen. Not all, however: some came from the German hinterland, especially from Hanover and Hessen. There is a certain symmetry to the fact that, while some Hessians were fighting for the British empire in North America, others were helping to feed the sweet tooth of the imperial capital.[131]

The New Consumer Culture

THE SO-CALLED HESSIANS WERE A SAFETY VALVE FOR THEIR ruler, a way to export rural poverty. Emigration had the same effect, although most territorial rulers still tried to stem it. Emigrants were not the poorest of the poor. It is nonetheless true that there was chronic land hunger among the peasantry in the Palatinate, Württemberg, and other parts of the Upper Rhine corridor, and periodic harvest failures like the ones that affected Saxony, Bohemia, and southern Germany in the 1770s led to widespread starvation. No more than one child in four survived their first year; half died by the age of ten. When epidemic diseases struck, the numbers were even worse. While sugar and coffee (and French wine) from Bordeaux were being landed in Hamburg in record quantities, the Swedish botanist Linnaeus likened the city to an open sewer. And while Bremen prospered from the trade in commodities like tobacco, deaths exceeded live births in the city in every decade from 1740 to 1799.[132]

And yet: a new world of consumption and consumer goods undeniably took shape in eighteenth-century Central Europe. The new stimulants were its most obvious marker, but not the only one. Books, furniture, carpets, clocks, porcelain, musical instruments, childen's toys—all were much more numerous and, in many cases, more widely owned at the end of the century than they were at the beginning. They were most in evidence at court and among officials, merchant elites, professionals, and the educated, but they had started spreading to the "middling sorts."[133] This world of elite and middle-class consumption took in whole areas of dress, domestic life, and leisure, providing individuals and families a means to express their identities. It was subject to fashion at a time when fashion itself emerged as a powerful cultural reflex. It was a form of self-representation on display at court, in clubs, at newly popular gathering places like theaters, spa towns, and coffeehouses, as well as in private homes. When Friedrich Justin Bertuch founded a new publication in 1786, the *Journal of Luxury and Fashion*, he spoke to this public and referred in the first issue to the importance of "material pleasure and the joy of living."[134] The journal had just fifteen hundred subscribers and it is likely many Germans imbibed their luxury and fashion vicariously, by reading about it in magazines and novels or seeing it on the stage.[135] But emulation and aspiration also drove consumption.

Many consumer articles came from other parts of Germany, or Europe. The German addiction to French fashion had long been satirized.[136] In the eighteenth century both the addiction and the satirical attacks grew. But other objects of consumption—not just sugar, coffee, and tobacco—came from farther away. For in the eighteenth century it was not only the Atlantic world that became a zone of exchange, it was the whole world. That is why scholars have referred to an economic "world system," or more recently to an era of "archaic globalization" or proto-globalization.[137] There was a strong element of exoticism in the fashions for "calicoes," chinoiserie in porcelain, Mexican silver teapots, "oriental" rugs and ceramics.[138] The vogue for "exotic" acquisitions extended, as it had done since the sixteenth century, to products of the natural world. That world was now truly global for Europeans, whose knowledge of it extended as far as the South Pacific that Captain Cook had recently sailed and Georg Forster described in his bestseller. When the mathematician and astronomer Johann Bernoulli set off from Berlin in 1777 to spend time at the St. Petersburg Academy of Sciences, he stopped off on the way to visit his friend Count Otto Christoph von Podewils at the family estate in the Oderbruch. He first admired the count's library and collection of scientific instruments. He then inspected the countess's natural history collection. It contained rocks, minerals, seeds, pickled animals, and the two star exhibits: the largest collection of butterflies to be found under glass in Germany, and a set of shells and conches that included South Sea conches just acquired in London.[139] Rare and "exotic" shells were especially prized by collectors.[140]

Exotic peoples were also an object of consumption, things to be gazed at. Sometimes these were stage representations. The pantalooned pashas of eighteenth-century operas are an example of that, although we have to be careful not to assume that these always embodied negative stereotypes. Turkish characters were drawn in a way that suggested a mixture of sentiments on the part of composers and librettists, including curiosity, sympathy, and even identification. The "generous Turk" was a common motif, most famously in Mozart's *The Abduction from the Seraglio*.[141] Janissary music was also taken seriously in the German lands. Its strains found their way into operas and its instruments into German military music-making. While the "Turcomania" of the period was not always slighting and disrespectful, it did represent, at least in part, the appropriation of a rival culture after the Ottoman challenge to the Holy Roman Empire had been successfully repelled. The fascination with all things Turkish also had obviously trivializing, exoticizing elements at times, like the "Turkish gardens" constructed by several German rulers and the Turkish-themed festivities that provided the entertainment for a princely wedding at the Saxon court in Dresden.[142]

The exotic Ottoman also featured in another form of diversion that became an eighteenth-century craze: automata. Devices like the flute player and mechanical duck created by Jacques Vaucanson earned their inventor an invitation to court by Frederick the Great; other automata of the era included figures like the hookah-smoking Turk. Sensuality and self-indulgence, in the harem or at the hookah pipe, were central ingredients in the stereotype of Ottoman culture. Perhaps the most celebrated example of an eighteenth-century automaton was the chess-playing Turk, a more cerebral image, it is true, even if his turbaned garb still suggested oriental exoticism (however, this turned out to be a fake automaton, operated from inside the cabinet by a small, non-Turkish, chess-playing man).[143] Turks also figured among the porcelain figurines that were such a hallmark of the eighteenth-century world of luxury goods. Again, some caution is necessary. Most porcelain figures depicted gods and goddesses, putti, animals, and a wide range of European types, often heavily stylized, like the "haughty Hussar" or the "boorish Russian." Turks and other exotics remained very much in the minority.[144] That said, the figures created in the middle decades of the century by the prolific and gifted Meissen modeler Johann Joachim Kändler did include a young Turkish boy, a Turkish horse tamer, a Turkish woman, and a Turk with a mandolin slung over his shoulder. There were many other exotic figures—a Malabar woman, a Chinese mandarin, a Japanese lady with a parasol.

One of Kändler's figurines, made in 1745, was a "Blackamoor page boy." There were hundreds of images of Black Africans in eighteenth-century Germany, depicted in porcelain and on clocks, in paintings, novels, and plays, and in silhouette on coats of arms.[145] That was similar to the exotic representations of Asians. The difference is that, in the slave trade era, Africans were also property, people who had been bought and sold.[146] Some former slaves were brought to Germany by Moravian missionaries and given a European education, or by merchants who wanted to teach them a trade. Most became domestic servants in princely, aristocratic, military, or wealthy bourgeois households. If not already Christian, they were baptized, their sponsors serving as godparents. Substantial numbers of them moved around between different courts and aristocratic households; some married German women, which appears to have encountered no opposition, certainly compared with marriages between social unequals. They were highly esteemed (the "noble Moor") and kindly treated. Yet, dressed up in fine costumes that were markedly "oriental" (turbans very prominent), they were also displayed as examples of their employers' wealth and taste. Inescapably exotic, mere mascots, they lived in a condition that has been called "privileged dependency."[147]

It was at German courts that Blacks were especially prized for their exotic qualities. Most became servants, musicians, or soldiers (usually in military bands), invariably dressed in elaborate and colorful costumes. There are examples from several German courts, including Württemberg, Bayreuth, and Aurich.[148] They were most numerous in two principalities that had close links to America because they sold their soldiers there as auxiliaries, Braunschweig-Wolfenbüttel and Hessen-Kassel.[149] There are two especially well-known cases from these territories, very different except for the fact that they shared an unhappy ending. The earlier instance is that of a boy from the Gold Coast brought to Amsterdam by the Dutch West India Company and presented to the Duke of Braunschweig-Wolfenbüttel as a "gift." Freed after a baptism, when he was given the name Anton Wilhelm Amo in honor of the duke and his son, he became a servant of the duke (a "chamber Moor") and was educated at the Universities of Halle and Wittenberg, where he received his doctorate in 1734. Amo went on to teach at Halle, then at Jena. He encountered hostility, however, and was the object of a public lampoon in a theater. He returned to West Africa in 1746.[150]

The trajectory of Amo's life in Germany was less brutal than the experience of the Africans brought to Germany by Frederick II of Hessen-Kassel. Frederick built a village called Mulang on the grounds of his palace, a "Moor colony" for Africans. Its buildings were constructed in a pseudo-Chinese style and the Africans were expected to till the soil, a perfect doubling down on racist stereotypes. Because of the exotic buildings and the skin color of those who worked there, Mulang drew spectators from Kassel.

Predictably, the settlement failed to flourish. The local climate and diseases were unfamiliar to the Africans and they were harshly treated; some committed suicide. A number of the dead were then autopsied in the name of science.[151] A third case has echoes of both Amo's experience and the fate of the Africans at Mulang. The former West African Angelo Soliman was a soldier in Austria, served as chamberlain to a number of princes resident in Vienna, and ended his career as a tutor in the household of Prince Franz Joseph von Liechtenstein. Soliman had friends among the Viennese aristocracy and educated elite, and he was active in the same masonic lodge as Mozart. Unlike Amo, Soliman never went back to Africa, dying in Vienna. There, however, for ten years after his death in 1796, his body—stuffed with feathers—was displayed in the Imperial Natural History Collection. The evidence suggests that he dedicated his body in advance to this purpose, which does not make the image any less disturbing.[152]

Most Africans in Germany were beautifully outfitted objects of display in court and other elite settings. The employment of Black household servants never spread beyond these narrow circles. That was also true of other high-status luxuries, whether furniture, glassware, or clothing. In these cases, however, cheaper versions could be produced for a broader middle-class public. That was how the mechanism of emulation worked and it was the reason eighteenth-century German rulers spent time trying to enforce sumptuary codes that dictated what kind of clothing was appropriate to different social ranks, on the principle that it should never be possible for the servant girl to be mistaken for her mistress. The efforts ran up against the reality that legal prescriptions and proscriptions of this kind were becoming harder to enforce. At the same time, the disparities in material circumstances between Germans of different "estates" (as they were usually called) were huge. These differences were obvious in what people wore, what they sat in or gazed at, what they ate and drank, and the plates, cups, and glasses from which they ate and drank.

Johann Joachim Becher, the ardent but unsuccessful advocate for German colonies in the Caribbean, had something to say about this. In his *Political Discourse* of 1668 he wrote about what he saw as the socially virtuous cycle of production and consumption: "Consumption sustains these three estates [peasants, artisans, merchants]. Consumption is their soul. Consumption is the sole bond that binds and fastens the estates to one another."[153] New patterns of consumption were a hallmark of the eighteenth-century world of goods, and most German rulers were a good deal less enthusiastic than Becher about the effects. It is worth looking at the celebrated new commodities that appeared then—tobacco, sugar, coffee—and asking some questions about the ways in which these products of global exchange were consumed. Who used them, when, how, and with what effects?

Consider, first, tobacco. In 1627 the Palatine ambassador in the Netherlands reported on a "new, astonishing fashion that came over to our Europe some years ago from America." He then described how "dissolute persons have taken to imbibing and noisily drinking into their bodies the smoke of a plant they call nicotiana or tobacco, with incredible avidity and an inextinguishable zeal."[154] The ambassador is clearly describing something strikingly novel, and that comes as no surprise. The first tobacco importing firm was not established in Bremen until 1642, by a prominent merchant and later senator, Johannes Lange.[155] It was only later in the century that tobacco was imported on a major scale, to the point that members of ships' crews engaged in it as a side trade. Johann Peter Oettinger was angry when, in 1693, the crates of tobacco he had bought on St. Thomas for resale back in Emden were seized by French privateers on the voyage home.[156] In some German lands the tobacco trade was originally in the hands of minorities, Huguenots or Jews. But as imports grew in the eighteenth century, prominent Hanseatic merchants in London entered the trade; some married into rich Anglo-American tobacco families. By then, 85 percent of the tobacco that reached Britain from the American colonies was re-exported to Europe, where Germany was second only to France as a market.[157]

The social life of tobacco in Germany did not exactly follow the script associated with New World stimulants—that they began as luxury goods, then became products of mass consumption. The first Germans who acquired a taste for tobacco were sailors, who chewed it. Soldiers also used it, establishing a close connection between soldiering and smoking that lasted well into the twentieth century.[158] The Wallraf-Richartz Museum in Cologne has a 1652 painting by Gerard ter Borch II, *The Sleeping Soldier*; it shows a soldier blowing smoke into the face of a sleeping comrade to wake him up. Soldiers spread tobacco use to the civilian population during the Thirty Years War. Tobacco did have its "elite" phase, though, marked by the extraordinary fashion for taking snuff that seized upper-class society in the eighteenth century. Like chocolate, snuff originated in the Americas, came to Europe via Spain, jumped over to the French court, and from there spread to polite society across Europe, including the German courts and aristocracy.[159] Snuff lent itself to ceremonial ritual. Even more important, it required a snuffbox. Few objects of the time were more perfect symbols of conspicuous consumption. The influential Saxon minister and diplomat Heinrich von Brühl was a dedicated follower of fashion, so it is no surprise that Johann Joachim Kändler created a special "swan service" for him. When Brühl died in 1763, he left behind not only the world's largest collection of Meissen porcelain and a vast number of ceremonial wigs and hats, but six hundred suits of clothing with six hundred matching snuffboxes.[160]

The craze for snuff reached its apogee in the 1750s, although the fashion lingered on. Tobacco made the transition to an article of mass consumption. Germans who used tobacco in the eighteenth century, from burghers and students to craftsmen and peasants, mostly smoked it in a pipe. We see these clay pipes in artworks of the time, with those puffing on them typically shown as relaxed. By the end of the eighteenth century, however, a new means of delivering nicotine was developing: the cigar. Manufactories to process tobacco into cigars as well as snuff were established in Spanish Mexico. The largest employed three thousand people. Similar industrialized processing places for tobacco arose in Spain, the first in Seville dating to 1717. The institution of the cigar manufactory spread through the century, following the same route as chocolate and snuff, over the Pyrenees to France and northwestern Europe. Although London and Amsterdam were major centers of tobacco processing in the eighteenth century, soon the German lands had one of their own. Imports to Germany spiked after American independence, but the tobacco was now shipped direct from Baltimore to Bremen. That Hanseatic port became the German tobacco hub, and increasingly the tobacco processed there was rolled into cigars.[161] Whether taken through pipe or cigar, tobacco developed new social rituals when used by middle- and lower-class Germans, just as snuff did when taken by members of the elite.

The tobacco manufactory developed later than the sugar refinery but they served parallel needs. Both arose to process the products of the plantation. Tobacco and sugar had many things in common. They were the fruits of global exchange. Tobacco originated in the Americas, was shipped to Europe, and eventually became a universal drug. Sugar was first domesticated in India and spread to China, Japan, and the Middle East before it reached Europeans, who planted it around the Atlantic world. Sugar was an Asian plant grown by African labor on American soil using European capital.[162] Both tobacco and sugar were long regarded as having medicinal qualities. Under the theory of the four humors, tobacco removed excessive fluid from the body; it was good against mucus and phlegm.[163] Sugar, meanwhile, was treated by early modern Europeans as a super-drug, a staple in every apothecary's shop. Sugar cleaned the blood, strengthened body and mind, and was good for clearing chest and lungs, but also good for bladder, stomach, and eyes; sugar was a specific against the common cold, against coughs and fevers; it even healed wounds.[164] Johann Joachim Becher, wearing his physician's hat, called sugar "the noblest and sweetest juice of the earth."[165] But Becher knew that sugar was also a means of upper-class display, in the form of gigantic sugar sculptures in the shape of palaces and temples as well as elaborate confectionaries served at court and in aristocratic households.[166] In that sense, too, sugar resembled tobacco. Just as the craze for snuff gave way to the mass consumption of tobacco in other forms, so sugar as a marker of privilege and special occasions gave way to its everyday consumption on a huge scale. This was "the spread of sugar downward and outward."[167]

The tens of thousands of tons of colonial sugar that reached Hamburg annually by the late eighteenth century fed the city's sugar refineries, and they in turn fed the rest of the Holy Roman Empire. Hamburg was "the emporium of all Germany."[168] The tributaries of the Elbe and their intersecting canals made possible the transportation of goods to a hinterland that extended from Brandenburg, Saxony, and Thuringia to Bohemia.[169] Sugar was just one of the "colonial goods" that were now beginning (at least in larger towns and cities) to be sold in shops bearing that name. But it was especially important because of the calorific energy it provided. Much has been made, rightly, of how important colonial sugar was to feeding the nascent English working class during the Industrial Revolution. It was "King Sugar."[170] In Germany, too, sugar helped to sustain a growing population and fostered proto-industrialization in rural areas where textile production was increasing.[171] Sugar was not alone. A more unsung product of American origins, the potato, spread from western areas like Alsace and the Palatinate to the rest of the Empire during the eighteenth century. Promoted by princes and clergy but often resisted by peasants, the potato made its breakthrough after the famines of the early 1770s.[172] The calorific value of potatoes from a given acreage was around two and a half times greater than the calorific value of grain.[173] But sugar, imported cane sugar anyway, meant that no one had to choose. Sugar from the Caribbean was paid for by

German trade goods like linens; the sugar in turn provided cheap (although empty) calories for the peasant-workers in proto-industrial areas.

Sugar was more than just a commodity that delivered calories, of course, just as tobacco was more than just a nicotine delivery system. Sugar made its way into everyday life; social rituals accrued around its use. It was extraordinarily versatile. Sugar was both powder and liquid. It could be sculpted, poured, colored, spooned, and dusted; it was a preservative, an additive in everything from blood sausage to cabbage dishes, and an ingredient in the "sugarloaf." Sugar went into confectioneries such as gingerbread and *Stollen* that were eaten even in modest households on special occasions like feast days. These often contained condiments such as cardamom, cinnamon, and cloves as a grace note, examples of a kind of reverse exoticism whereby once rare spices were domesticated and came to be thought of as typical regional fare, as "Dresden" or "Aachen" confectionery.[174] The rise in sugar consumption went hand in hand with the spread of new kitchen utensils, like saucepans, and of new objects for the table, such as sugar bowls and spoons. The bowl might be made of silver or finest porcelain; it might be very simple earthenware. Spoons came in many varieties, too. They had in common only that they allowed the sugar to be added as a sweetener to a variety of beverages, including coffee.

Coffee was the last of the trio, a commodity often used in tandem with the other two. Originally grown only on the Arabian peninsula, in Yemen, coffee spread through the Ottoman Empire. The Augsburg physician Leonhart Rauwulf reported in his *Journey to the Lands of the Orient* (1582) about the Turks and Arabs having "a good drink which they greatly esteem. They call it 'chaube.'" Coffee, too, was initially regarded as a form of drug. Dr. Rauwulf told his readers that the drink was "nearly as black as ink and helpful against stomach complaints."[175] Coffee also purified the blood, so it was believed, and was good against dropsy, gout, colic, and sore eyes. This was a medicinal versatility that rivaled the apothecary's favorite, sugar. But coffee was also likened to tobacco because, according to the humoral theory, it dried out excessive phlegm and mucus. Coffee beans reached western Europe by different routes. Venetian merchants brought it, as they brought so many commodities from the east; Yemen was also a stopping place for Dutch East India Company ships. The Ottomans carried coffee with them as they advanced into the Habsburg Empire in the seventeenth century, and famously left bags of it behind when they retreated after the failed siege of Vienna in 1683. Europeans then planted the crop, the Dutch in Java and Surinam, the French in the Antilles. Saint-Domingue, best known as a sugar island, also produced sixty thousand pounds of coffee in 1789. Coffee was shipped back to Bordeaux, then re-exported to Amsterdam or Hamburg. Coffee drinking became well established in the German lands in the eighteenth century, although it was not the thick, "Turkish" coffee of the Ottomans, but a lighter drink from which the sediment had been removed and to which both milk and sugar were sometimes added.[176]

Probate records give some indication of who drank coffee. In 1775 the estate inventory of Margaretha Barbara Tanner, a Frankfurt physician's widow, included a heavy silver coffee kettle, two coffeepots, a cream jug, two sugar bowls and spoons in silver, as well as a number of porcelain coffeepots, bowls, and coffee cups in a floral design. The widow Tanner also had elaborate equipment for making and drinking tea and chocolate. She lived in a thirteen-room house in the Pferdemarkt and was unusually wealthy, but inventories of eighteenth-century merchants, lawyers, officials, and professors also indicate regular coffee drinking. For his part, the Frankfurt blacksmith Augustin Geißemer might have possessed no silver pot from which to pour his coffee and no expensive porcelain from which to drink it, but he did own a brass coffee kettle, pewter and copper coffeepots, and some cups.[177] There is evidence that in areas such as Westphalia and Saxony, coffee drinking had become a daily practice even among farm servants by the late eighteenth century. It is hardly coincidental that these were areas where proto-industrialization was beginning. The same is true of the Austrian Vorarlberg, where cotton weavers were reportedly drinking coffee by the 1780s. Coffee appears to have made serious inroads into the consumption patterns of the middling and even the lower ranks of Central European society. There, as in England, the American colonies, and the Netherlands, the spread of coffee, sugar, and a wider range of household goods were the consumer payoff of what has been called an "industrious revolution."[178] There is indirect evidence of how widespread coffee drinking had become in the efforts made by German princes to curb the practice because sugar, like tea and sugar, was imported and was therefore in the prevailing mercantilist view a drain on domestic specie. An edict issued by Frederick the Great in 1768 condemned "the excessive drinking of coffee and tea among common citizens, tradesmen, day laborers and servants as well as farmers, tenants, cotters, millers and the like."[179] Ordinances were passed across northern and western German territories, where coffee drinking was most widespread, and excise duties were imposed on coffee imports. These measures may have slowed down the growth in coffee consumption but they did not stop it, let alone reverse it.

The relationship of the Jewish minority to this new commodity was complex. There was a good deal of rabbinical head scratching over coffee drinking because there was no prior experience with the practice. Some rabbis consulted their counterparts in Islamic countries where coffee had a longer history, or made inquiries of merchants. Generally, the outcome was that rabbis approved coffee drinking, even on the Sabbath, and by midcentury coffee and cakes had become an important part of Jewish marriage rituals. What made the Jewish relationship to coffee distinctive was the significant part that both poor Jews and Jewish widows played in the coffee trade, peddling the product to sustain themselves. There were parallels with the role of Jews as small traders of tobacco. Coffee was sold to fellow Jews, including those in rural areas who would otherwise have lacked any access to it, and to Christians. In both Frankfurt and Prussia, other merchants used long-standing stereotypes of dishonest Jewish business practices in complaints to the authorities that were designed to exclude Jews from the coffee trade.[180] Here, arguments about coffee reflected larger antagonisms between Gentiles and Jews.

The same was true when it came to men and women. Men and women consumed coffee together at home, although not in public. But what about women who created all-female occasions for gathering around the coffee cups? The *Kaffeekränzchen*, the weekly or even daily act of socializing over coffee, emerged in the eighteenth century and was often satirized on the stage. Playwrights who did so include such major figures as Gotthold Ephraim Lessing and Christian Friedrich Henrici, who wrote under the Latin name Picander.[181] Henrici, the librettist for Johann Sebastian Bach's *St. Matthew Passion*, was also librettist for a shorter, secular work, "Schweigt Stille, Plaudert Nicht" (Be Quiet and Do Not Chatter), usually known as the Coffee Cantata. This work from 1734–35 is actually a small-scale drama, which revolves around the domestic struggle between Herr Schlendrian and his daughter Liesgen. The daughter is a passionate coffee drinker:

> *Ah! How sweet coffee tastes,*
> *more delicious than a thousand kisses,*
> *milder than muscatel wine.*

Coffee, I have to have coffee,
and, if someone wants to pamper me,
ah, then bring me coffee as a gift!

Herr Schlendrian sees Liesgen's desire for coffee as an unseemly self-indulgence, and her refusal to obey his wishes as the mark of a refractory daughter. Liesgen eventually relents when her father says that she will never marry unless she gives up coffee; but the daughter has the last laugh, because she has secretly ensured that no suitor will ever cross the threshold without first promising to write into the marriage contract Liesgen's right to brew coffee whenever she pleases.[182]

Bach was a regular at Zimmermanns coffeehouse in Leipzig for two decades, and the Coffee Cantata itself was written for the coffeehouse. Music was one of the diversions of the institution, like cards and billiards. The coffeehouse was a male bastion. It was where serious men of affairs

A view of Zimmermanns coffeehouse in 1732. Zimmermanns,
in Leipzig's fashionable Katherinenstrasse, was where the
Collegium Musicum associated with Johann Sebastian Bach
held weekly chamber music concerts.

gathered to drink coffee (sometimes tea or chocolate, although they were more expensive), smoke their pipes, do business, exchange "intelligence," and discuss the state of the world. The coffeehouse arrived in Vienna in the late seventeenth century as a result of Ottoman influence, and in northern Germany in emulation of the Dutch and English. In smaller German towns and in towns with a resident court, there was often one centralized coffeehouse, as in Braunschweig. Major commercial hubs had many more. Still, the numbers were much smaller than they were in Amsterdam or London. Vienna had 37 coffeehouses in 1737; London had 550. Hamburg and Leipzig stood out for the liveliness of their coffeehouse culture, yet Hamburg still had just 6 coffeehouses at the beginning of the eighteenth century and only 32 at the end.[183] The interiors of German coffeehouses also looked more subtly "domestic" than their counterparts in Britain or the Low Countries. At least one scholar has taken these signs and read into them a kind of backward provincialism that resulted from Germany's "non-participation in world history, that is, world economy."[184]

That premise is wrong, and the judgment about German coffeehouses is wrong as well. They were fewer in number, but they were not tame. Just as elsewhere, the flow of commodities that sent German linens across the Atlantic and brought back sugar, tobacco, and coffee was part of a larger expansion of communications and mental universes. The coffeehouse was one of those institutions, alongside the masonic lodge, the reading club, the theater, and the salon, where a "public" began to form.[185] It was a gathering place that stimulated social and political discourse even as its principal beverage stimulated the brain. That was another reason German rulers were suspicious of coffeehouses in the 1770s and '80s, just as Charles II had been in Britain in the previous century, and Muslim rulers of coffeehouses in Cairo or Damascus centuries earlier. At a time when everything from princely rule to slavery was coming to be questioned and a new world was being born, the coffeehouse had at least the potential to be subversive, even in Germany.[186]

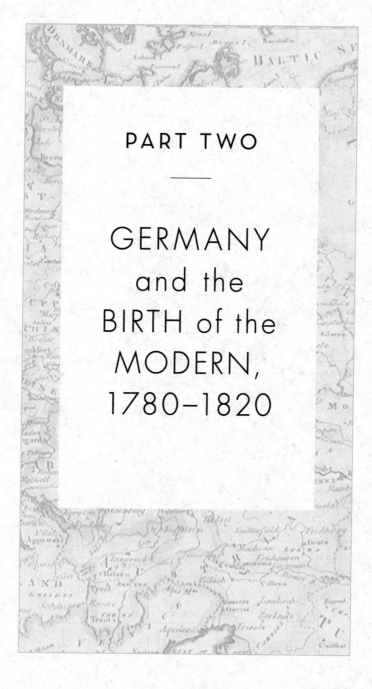

PART TWO

—

GERMANY
and the
BIRTH of the
MODERN,
1780–1820

CHAPTER 4

REVOLUTIONS

"The Noblest Deed of the Century"

THE MEN WHO GATHERED IN THE COFFEEHOUSES OF LEIPZIG AND Hamburg had plenty to discuss in the decades on either side of 1800, for these years marked the birth of the modern world. The French Revolution rightly commands attention as the beginning of something new, but it was not alone. A period of upheaval generated by warfare shook all the major empires, a "geopolitical earthquake" that brought revolution not only to Europe but to the North American colonies, the Caribbean, and Latin America.[1] It resulted in the creation of a new political language of rights and constitutions, sovereignty and nation. Both slavery and serfdom were increasingly questioned as institutions, and in some places were abolished. Political unrest extended to Bengal, Tokugawa Japan, and Qing China, for this was a true "world crisis."[2] One reason for its global character was the growing interconnectedness between different parts of the world. The years between the 1770s and the 1820s formed an era of "archaic globalization," or "soft globalization."[3] It is no coincidence that the English philosopher Jeremy Bentham coined the term "international" in the 1790s.[4]

Contemporaries were aware that this was an era of exceptional upheaval. Christoph Heinrich Korn, a former law student in Tübingen, had been an officer with the Dutch before returning home to make his living as a writer. Fascinated by the American colonists' revolt, Korn asked, "Are we now at the beginning of an epoch in history that will forever remain remarkable to posterity?"[5] Korn died in 1783, too soon to witness the outbreak of the French Revolution six years later. Events in France prompted many more people to wonder whether they were living through something unprecedented. Even how time was experienced seemed to be changing. Wilhelm von Humboldt, the more sedentary of two famous brothers, wrote in 1797: "Our age appears to carry us out of one period, which is just passing by, and into a new, quite different one." The pace of change in the previous fifteen or twenty years had, thought Humboldt, been much faster than it was at the beginning of the eighteenth century.[6] This was not only a time of revolution, it brought with it a revolutionary new experience of time.[7]

How exactly did Germans fit into this picture of transformation? There is one familiar answer: that Germans were onlookers and commentators, but little more. It was during these years that Germany came to be widely described as the land of *"Dichter und Denker,"* writers and thinkers.[8] The poet Friedrich Hölderlin added an extra, negative twist to the idea. Germans, he suggested, were "rich in thoughts but weak in deeds."[9] A little later another poet, Heinrich Heine, added his voice to the choir: Germans had merely thought while others acted. The historian Rolf Engelsing summed this up when he suggested that while the British had an industrial revolution and the French a political revolution, Germany had a reading revolution.[10] This is intuitively plausible but hardly survives closer scrutiny. It is surely dubious to be so dismissive about the written word just as the "century of words" was dawning, or to shrug off the ideas in books at the very moment when a world was being forged in which education, culture, and specialist knowledge would enjoy such huge authority.[11] Little more than a decade after Wilhelm von Humboldt wrote about the arrival of a different age, his proposals underlay the foundation of a new university in Berlin that would be imitated around the world. Should we simply disregard the advent of the modern research university, or the Kindergarten, both of them made in Germany during this era of transition? The same question could be asked of many bodies of knowledge or practices that had their origins in Germany during these decades and would later have a global impact, including the modern discipline of history. Another cliché from these years points to a distinctly German lack of worldliness, or *Innerlichkeit.* This quality of "inwardness" in German culture is easy to recognize. But perhaps it is worth considering what it might have contributed to one more of the far-reaching historical shifts of these years: the "invention of the modern self."[12] And what of "world literature," first named—indeed, invented as an idea—by a German? In all of these ways, as we shall see, German writers and thinkers were co-creators of the modern era that was made in the decades on either side of 1800.

The world continued to become a smaller place in these years. Space shrank even as time accelerated. This was not yet our world, whose unprecedented globalization we celebrate (and exaggerate). It was not yet even the world of the mid-nineteenth century, joined together by steamship and telegraph. But networks of communication were becoming more tightly meshed through travel and exchange, as well as the movement of commodities, people, and ideas. When Wilhelm von Humboldt sat at his desk writing about world languages, he was connected with hundreds of correspondents on five continents: scholars, diplomats, soldiers, merchants, and missionaries. Many of them wrote in the native tongue they shared with Humboldt, for as we saw in the previous chapter Germans had established themselves around the world by the last decades of the eighteenth century, either as permanent settlers or as sojourners. In essence, they formed a kind of "global Germany."

The Holy Roman Empire, however, still had hundreds upon hundreds of examples of the opposite, an intensely local and inward-looking Germany—tiny principalities and lordships, mere flecks on the map, or ecclesiastical enclaves that numbered just a few hundred souls and Imperial "cities" that were more like villages. These could be desperately airless, suffocating places, as those who escaped them often complained. But the larger world often intruded even here, via a returning soldier, missionary, or newlander, just as the putting-out system, with its emphasis on the home-based production of goods, turned many areas of the interior into links in the chain of Atlantic trade. Some territorial states within the Empire had also embarked on the path of enlightened reform "from above," as princes tried to make their populations more productive, to rationalize administration, and to create a more direct bond between subject and ruler. The German lands that experienced the upheaval of these years were a patchwork quilt, and, as we shall see, the shock waves set off many different responses.

The American colonists called their enterprise a revolution and Germans took them at their word. One writer referred matter-of-factly in 1782 to "the present revolution in America"; another spoke more passionately about "the great revolution" undertaken by George Washington's countrymen.[13] This interest in American events extended back to the years before 1775, and continued during the years of military conflict. According to the *Leipziger Zeitung*, "England's dispute with its colonies is at present undoubtedly the most important public topic. Everyone participates in it." That was in February 1776. In September of the same year Joseph Heinrich von Beckers zu Westerstetten, the Palatine minister, wrote to a Bavarian colleague that "everywhere one speaks only of American affairs."[14] It is not clear just how attentive to detail German observers were: when, in 1781, the same *Leipziger Zeitung* published a "Register of the Most Important Events in America since the Beginning of the Unrest," it managed to omit both the Declaration of Independence and the Articles of Confederation.[15] But newspapers, periodicals, and private letters all point to a keen interest in American events, at least among the educated public, even if the understanding of those events was sometimes muddy and invariably viewed through a German lens.

Opinion was divided, but not evenly. There was broad sympathy for the cause of the American colonists and the "free state" (as many Germans called it) that emerged from their efforts.[16] The main exceptions were in conservative ministerial and aristocratic circles, where any kind of upheaval was viewed as alarming in principle, and in parts of Germany where there was especially strong pro-British sentiment. Lack of sympathy for the American cause in Württemberg was the result of Anglophilia that owed something to local pride that the state's parliament (established in 1457) was the closest thing Germany had to the Parliament in Westminster. The English connection in Hanover also shaped responses there, causing divided opinions among Göttingen professors. In Hamburg, too, generations of contact between the mercantile elite and London created sympathy for Britain. But in all these places there were also strong supporters of the American Revolution. That was especially true of enlightened society in Hamburg, where the literary lion Friedrich Gottlieb Klopstock became a prominent advocate of the colonists' cause. A "declared Bostonian," Klopstock penned political odes that celebrated American liberty. "You are the dawn / Of a great day to come!" he wrote in his 1781 ode "The Contemporary War."[17]

The idea of liberty resonated powerfully in the German lands, becoming something of a cult word in the 1770s and '80s. What many enlightened Germans saw as a struggle against the arbitrariness of princes and the restrictions of corporate society struck a chord, the more so as Americans advanced their cause temperately and in the name of reason. The figure who embodied these virtues for many was Benjamin Franklin, already known before the revolution as a scientist and enlightened intellectual—he had toured Germany and been well received in courts, universities, and learned societies. Franklin received close to two hundred letters from German correspondents in the years 1777–1785, almost all in support of the American cause. The letters give some sense of who in the German lands supported it. The writers were young rather than old, bourgeois rather than aristocratic, and there were notable geographical clusters—Prussia and northern Germany, Franconia, the Rhineland, Switzerland, and Vienna.[18]

Germans were not the only foreigners who praised the American success. "Let those who doubt the prodigious effects of liberty on man and his industry come to America!" That was the Frenchman Jacques-Pierre Brissot, reporting on a visit in 1788.[19] By the time his travel account was published in 1791, France had become the new focus of political attention and Brissot himself a leading player in the early stages of the revolution, before he became one of its victims. Germans reacted in many different ways to the welter of events in France, as the revolution passed from moderate constitutionalism, to radicalism and terror, stabilization under the Directory, and finally the imperial rule of Napoleon. The responses in Germany ranged from would-be imitation to outright rejection, and included—one of many lasting legacies—reforms from above aimed at heading off threats from below. From 1792 onward, reactions in Germany took place against a background of war that lasted a generation and transformed the lands of Central Europe. The Holy Roman Empire disappeared after a thousand years, the territorial states of 1815 were unrecognizable versions of their earlier selves, and the vocabulary of German politics was permanently rewritten.

The outbreak of revolution in France elicited a wave of enthusiasm among German writers, from established figures like Christoph Martin Wieland, who was fifty-five when the Bastille was stormed, to young enthusiasts still in their teens whose reputations were not yet made—Ludwig Tieck and Wilhelm Heinrich Wackenroder, both born in 1773, and Friedrich Hölderlin, just three years older and a theology student in Tübingen. He and fellow students planted a liberty tree in the market square of that university town. They were the German counterparts of the English Romantic poets William Wordsworth and Samuel Taylor Coleridge, their exact contemporaries, who rhapsodized in similar terms about the revolution. Among the older generation, Klopstock, former bard of the American Revolution, now praised the French for accomplishing "the noblest deed of the century" in odes such as "Sie, und nicht Wir" (They, and Not We).[20] The philosophers joined the writers in their enthusiasm, the established Immanuel Kant and Johann Gottfried Herder as well as the young Johann Gottlieb Fichte and Georg Wilhelm Friedrich Hegel (Hölderlin's roommate in Tübingen). The French Revolution, said Hegel, was a "glorious sunrise."[21] That was exactly the optic through which enlightened, cosmopolitan Germany initially viewed events in France. In reading clubs and masonic lodges, the early stages of revolution were celebrated as a "dawn" or "sunrise," the triumph of light over dark, reason over unreason, liberty over despotism. The fall of the Bastille stuck an especially powerful chord. The large French literature on the event was eagerly translated, with its highly dramatic narrative of emancipation from tyranny.[22] The sixteen-year-old Tieck, later a leading figure in German Romanticism, wrote a theatrical fragment on the fall of the Bastille called "The Prisoner."[23]

This was admiration from a distance. Some saw the revolution from closer up. Thousands of Germans were resident in France when the revolution broke out, around eight thousand in Paris alone.[24] Most were craftsmen and workers. Some are known to have taken part in the storming of

An undated engraving by the Augsburg artist Paul Jakob Laminit showing the storming of the Bastille in Paris on July 14, 1789, a symbol of tyranny overthrown that was a popular subject with German artists and writers in the early stages of the French Revolution.

the Bastille, which stood near the entrance to the working-class district of Saint-Antoine.[25] But there were also higher-born Germans who welcomed the revolution. An especially colorful example is Jean-Baptiste (later "Anacharsis") Cloots, the son of a Prussian privy councillor in Cleves who had settled in Paris and become a supporter of the radical Enlightenment. After 1789 he joined the Jacobin Club and took to calling himself a "messenger of the human race." Then there was Peter Alexander Wille, the son of Johann Georg Wille, engraver to the French king. The father was ruined and embittered by the revolution, but the son identified with it. He made drawings of sansculotte radicals and commanded a battalion of the National Guard. His story resembled that of Johann Jakob Hauer, an artistically gifted master tailor's son from a small town near Mainz, who went to Paris in 1769 to get an art education, trained with Jacques-Louis David, and stayed to practice his profession. Hauer became a sansculotte and a painter of revolution. Like Wille, he commanded a National Guard unit, which explains how he was able to paint a portrait of Jean-Paul Marat's assassin, Charlotte Corday, shortly before her execution.[26] Every revolution has its "red prince." In this case, Germany provided two. One was Prince Frederick of Salm-Kyrburg, a zealous Jacobin whose elegant palace became a gathering place for the left. The other, Prince Karl-Konstantin of Hessen-Rheinfels-Rothenburg, entered his name in the Jacobin Club as "Charles Hessen."[27]

These were, of course, exceptions among the Germans resident in France in 1789. Others kept their heads down or joined the emigration. But some Germans moved in the opposite direction, traveling to Paris as "pilgrims of revolution." They went to see for themselves, to serve as "eyewitnesses" to the great events (as one of them, the young Silesian Konrad Engelbert Oelsner put it), and to report on what they saw in letters that were often published later as books. Some were high-born or established figures, like Oelsner's friend and fellow Silesian Gustav von Schlabrendorf. Other pilgrims of revolution were more marginal figures, still making their way. Oelsner himself was one such; another was the composer Johann Friedrich Reichardt.[28] Figures like this, enlightened in politics, talented, educated but underplaced or underappreciated (at least in their own eyes), were drawn to events in France and its promise of a new kind of society.

There were certain things every visitor wanted to see, starting with the site of the Bastille. Visitors would often gather up a handful of stones or chip out a piece of the masonry as a talisman of freedom. A visit to the Jaco-

bin Club was also in order; some even joined. One very effusive visitor was
Joachim Heinrich Campe, by then in his forties, an enlightened writer and
pedagogue, and (like Schlabrendorf) a freemason. In his youth Campe had
spent five years as private tutor to the Humboldt brothers, and he arrived in
Paris in the summer of 1789 together with his former pupil Wilhelm. It was
the older Campe who was the enthusiast. Humboldt was bored, and seems
to have noticed only that Paris was "dirty" and overcrowded. Campe was
entranced. Overwhelmed by the "mass of ideas and sensations," he wanted
to "shout with joy"; this was a "great world event," something "never before
heard of in the whole of history." The idea that despotism had been overthrown and given way to liberty runs through Campe's *Letters from Paris*,
written in August 1789. There is plenty of grandiloquent language about the
noble and virtuous in Campe's account. For him the revolution was a "spectacle," or "drama," a metaphor that turns up in many German accounts.[29]
It suggests mere spectators. As Reichardt revealingly put it, "I am not . . .
eager to experience the effects of the revolution on my own body."[30]

Some of these pilgrims of revolution became more than onlookers and
did experience the effects of the revolution on their bodies. So did other
German political radicals who went to France to take part in events. The
border city of Strasbourg became a particularly powerful magnet. By 1791
there were scores of radical Germans resident there, active in the local
Jacobin Club and writing tracts or translating French ones aimed at the
German public.[31] One cluster consisted of radical clergy from the southwest and the ecclesiastical territories. Perhaps the most prominent was the
former Franciscan monk Eulogius Schneider, a firebrand ("the Marat of
Strasbourg") who had formerly taught at the University of Bonn, where the
young Beethoven was one of his auditors. Others were educators, lawyers,
or officials by training, almost all young. Some had barely finished university, like Georg Kerner, who headed to Strasbourg in 1791, threw himself into the activities of the Jacobin Club, and announced, "I have left my
fatherland to find a fatherland in France."[32]

Kerner went voluntarily to France; others (like Schneider, removed
from his chair in Bonn) were fleeing Germany after a conservative crackdown in the 1790s. Political repression was not immediate. Some German
rulers even welcomed the French Revolution in its first, moderate phase,
seeing only a French catching-up with the kinds of enlightened reform they
were already undertaking. Others remained relaxed about events to the
west, taking comfort—false comfort, as it turned out—in the likelihood

that revolution would preoccupy the French. But even before the radicalization of the revolution, the German lands experienced major eruptions of
social unrest. In 1789 and 1790 there were urban riots and rural disturbances
in western areas closest to France, like the Rhineland, the Palatinate, and
the Mosel Valley. In the east, too, there were rural revolts against landlords
in Mecklenburg and Silesia. Then in 1793 came a revolt by journeymen in
Breslau and a weavers' rebellion in the Erzgebirge. The most serious challenge occurred in Saxony. Following successive harvest failures, peasants
angry about seigneurial dues and hunting privileges began to protest in the
spring of 1790. By August an insurrection was underway by ten thousand
armed peasants who burned records and threatened agents and officials,
causing landlords to flee. The Elector of Saxony used armed force to suppress the revolt, but it took until October to do so and renewed rural discontent broke out in the following years. There were occasional outbreaks
of unrest across Germany throughout the 1790s, from Hamburg and Rostock in the north to Munich and Augsburg in the south.[33]

German territorial rulers responded with repression. A "Decree Against
Tumult and Insurrection" was issued in Saxony in 1791. The young Emperor
Francis II, who came to the Imperial throne in 1792, followed the advice
of fearful conservatives after the uncovering of a so-called Jacobin conspiracy in Vienna. These were overreactions. It is true that radical propaganda poured into the German lands via border cities like Strasbourg
and Altona. Jacobin clubs were formed, revolutionary ballads and broadsheets circulated widely, and journeymen who had picked up French ideas
on their travels were behind some of the urban unrest. Even in obscure
corners of Germany, like the Black Forest town of Nagold, local Jacobins
sympathized with the revolution and were emboldened in making political
demands.[34] Peasants, too, used the new language of rights in resisting their
seigneurial lords.[35]

Yet Germany never came close to revolution in the 1790s. The German
lands did not face the deep-seated problems that confronted the French
monarchy, the burden of feudalism on the peasantry was less crushing,
and the armies of the individual states remained loyal when called upon.
The major unrest in Silesia and Saxony remained exceptions; there was
no instance in Germany where popular discontent and political opposition joined hands as they had in France. The Viennese "Jacobin" conspirators (like their counterparts in Bavaria) were really old-style reformers,
masonic "Illuminati" looking for a return to the kind of enlightened reform

from above they had welcomed under an earlier emperor, Joseph II. The one instance of Jacobin rule came in Mainz, after war had broken out and France had occupied the Rhineland. It was both brief and increasingly unpopular locally, thanks to the heavy-handedness of its leaders. Established in October 1792, it ended nine months later, almost to the day, when Prussian troops occupied the city. Those of its leaders who survived the repression that followed fled to France.[36]

For the new German arrivals and the radical sympathizers already there, these were difficult times to be in France as the radical Jacobins of the "Mountain" came to power and the terror began under the Committee of Public Safety. Foreigners, including the sympathetic variety, came under intense scrutiny even before the "law of suspects" was passed in September 1793. Oelsner recorded in August 1792 that the mistrust everywhere made staying in Paris "extremely unpleasant"—no one dared to speak their opinion and executions provided the "daily entertainment of the people." Another German "friend of the revolution" expressed himself even more forcefully at the beginning of 1793: "The hatred of foreigners breaks out ever more maliciously and scurrilously."[37] Those were the words of Georg Forster, the celebrated naturalist and travel writer. Forster had welcomed the revolution, convinced it was part of a general "fermentation among the people," in Germany as well as France—exactly the same metaphor the French revolutionary Camille Desmoulins used when he exulted that "the fermentation is universal.[38] Forster was employed as a librarian at the University of Mainz when the French captured that city and the Mainz Republic was established. For him, this was a moment of decision: "the crisis is here and one must take a side."[39] He became a leading political figure in the republic, much to the chagrin of his more moderate liberal father and like-minded commentators who found it hard to accept that Forster of all people, "the enlightened, warm friend and defender of the rights of humanity," should find himself in a position where he "threatened and coerced" recalcitrant villagers in the area around Mainz.[40]

Forster and a fellow member of the Mainz Jacobin Club, Adam Lux, avoided the repression that marked the end of the Mainz Republic because they had gone to Paris in March 1793 to request that the republic be incorporated into France. Instead, they were caught up in the Terror. Forster was spared its worst because he died of pneumonia at the beginning of the next year. Adam Lux, not so fortunate, was guillotined for his Girondin sympathies; so was the Prince of Salm-Kyrburg. Those radical gadflies Eulogius

Schneider and Anacharsis Cloots were also executed as ultra-leftists, the latter even though he had been one of four Germans (along with Klopstock, Campe, and a writer named in the document as "Gille," but actually Friedrich Schiller) who were granted honorary French citizenship by the National Assembly in August 1792 for serving "the cause of liberty."[41] Others escaped the guillotine by good fortune (Schlabrendorf was arrested but not executed), or by fleeing to Switzerland, like Oelsner and Kerner.[42]

After the overthrow of Maximilien Robespierre and the installation of the Directory, a second wave of German visitors descended on Paris. As in 1789–90, they were of two different kinds: the merely curious and the seriously radical. Wilhelm von Humboldt was a prime instance of the former. He moved to Paris with his family and established himself in the fashionable Faubourg Saint-Germain, where he entertained on a major scale. His visitors included the painter David, Madame Germaine de Staël, and the daughter of the enlightened philosopher Denis Diderot. German visitors also dropped by—Rahel Levin (the later Rahel Varnhagen), who organized an important salon in Berlin, the sculptor Friedrich Tieck, younger brother of the writer—and so did permanent German residents like Schlabrendorf. Another occasional visitor was Oelsner, now (like Kerner) back from Switzerland. Members of the radical contingent, they were joined by a crop of new German political émigrés dismissed from their posts or fleeing from arrest. They came from every corner of the Holy Roman Empire.

One of the most engaging was Georg Friedrich Rebmann, who has been described as "the most perspicacious and intelligent German political journalist of the 1790s."[43] The son of an ambitious father who was treasurer of a small knightly territory in Franconia, Rebmann studied law at Erlangen and Jena, graduating in 1789.[44] After acquiring a reputation as an unruly, seditious student, he returned briefly to the family home to use his legal skills but left to pursue a career as a writer. He first made a name for himself by publishing hostile descriptions (in epistolary form) of the professors and student life at his former universities. At the beginning of *Letters from Erlangen* (1792), Rebmann expressed his conviction that "frankness is never damaging but is always a virtue."[45] This might have been his motto. Travel writing and political satires followed in profusion, including *Hans Kiekindiewelt's Travels to All Four Corners of the Globe and the Moon* (1795), a sharp and delightful satire that holds up a mirror to German institutions and is much funnier than its presumed model, Voltaire's *Candide*. (Rebmann often addresses the reader directly, and with sly wit, as he does in an epilogue that makes fun of any reader foolish enough to expect the book to include travel to the moon just because it appeared in the title.) Rebmann moved in 1794 to Erfurt, where he established a small press with a book dealer named Dietrich Vollmer. They published a political journal, *The New Gray Monster*, in which Rebmann wrote to defend a Robespierre speech criticizing war.[46] Dubbed a Jacobin, Rebmann was forced to flee to Danish Altona and then to Paris to escape political persecution.

Even though the life of Germans in Paris picked up again after 1795, the Terror was a watershed. There were efforts by some Germans to justify, or at least explain it, with arguments that anticipated the anguished responses of twentieth-century revolutionaries faced with a similar dilemma. Forster, for example, wrote of the revolution as historically necessary, and the Terror as something that followed from the crimes of the despotism the revolutionaries had overthrown. The bloody violence was a source of "shame," but history would overlook it because of the benign results of economic and religious policies that were being pursued at the same time. The Terror was a response, moreover, to a counterrevolutionary challenge. Forster came close at times to viewing the radical revolution in providential terms—as a natural event, a "hurricane." Others also emphasized the responsibility of the counterrevolution for revolutionary violence. Although generally less willing than Forster to invoke historical necessity, Oelsner and Rebmann did offer additional arguments that have a familiar ring—the Terror was an aberration from the true revolution, its leaders power-mad "demagogues" who merely hid behind the "mask" of furthering the people's interests. It is striking how often of those who denounced Jacobin Terror mimicked the conspiratorial language of those they were denouncing.[47]

Radical German supporters of the French Revolution needed to find a way to explain the Terror and thereby redeem what they viewed as the "true" revolution from the bloodshed. But none of them saw radical revolution, let alone Terror, as a desirable course for Germany. As early as 1791 Forster wrote that "we are not at the point where a violent revolution could help us in the least or be useful, even if it were possible, which it is not."[48] The danger, he thought, was that violent revolution would occur in Germany—as it had in France—in the absence of reforms. That was common ground among the radicals, who argued along two converging lines. On the one hand, Germany was simply not "mature" enough for a republic; on the other hand, there was a strong and benign tradition of reform from above among German rulers, and it was important to keep them up to the mark (or return them to that path) so that counterrevolution did not scuttle reform and make violent upheaval more likely.[49] Scratch the political views of those grouped together as the "German Jacobins," and it turns out that many of them were (like Rebmann) actually more moderate, or Girondin, in their sympathies.[50]

We therefore find a surprising degree of overlap between the views of the purported Jacobins and those of more moderate liberals, who supported the early stages of the revolution but peeled away in disgust after the September massacres of 1792, the execution of Louis XVI at the beginning of 1793, and the onset of the Terror. "They have betrayed our ideals and dragged them in the mud, these evil, stupid and base people who no longer know what they are doing," lamented the Romantic writer Caroline Schlegel.[51] Klopstock wrote in late 1794 that "there is perhaps no one alive who has shared so inwardly in the revolution and . . . has suffered as much as I."[52] This sounds very self-absorbed, but Klopstock did lose friends to the guillotine (or the "g——,"as he called it in one letter, apparently unable to write out the word), including La Rochefoucauld, the dedicatee in happier days of "They, and Not We."[53] He now displayed a bust of Charlotte Corday, Marat's assassin, in his study. Klopstock continued to write political odes up until his death in 1803—they were a major part of his output in these last years—but they were dark and bitter. Their titles tell the story—"My Error," "The Ruins," "My Sorrow"—and they are filled with images of blood and violence. Language itself is strained to the limit. In the elegy "The New" ("Das Neue," December 1793), Klopstock invents a long and extraordinary compound noun, the *Klubbergmunizipalgüllotinoligkra-/Tierrepublik* to express his contempt for the radical clubs in Paris, the politically ascendant "Mountain" associated with Robespierre, the executions and the "animal" quality of the republic. He makes up nonsense words, practically grunting noises, to put in the mouths of Marat's devotees.[54] Klopstock was not the only poet driven to an almost incoherent fury by the Terror. The gentle lyricist Johann Wilhelm Gleim wrote a series of "poems for the times," in which the Jacobins are excoriated as bloodstained tyrants, despots, murderers, devils, tigers, cannibals, and monsters. In one of them, anticipating Francisco Goya's great etching of the same name by several years, Gleim writes about "the sleep of reason."[55]

Disillusion with the Terror reinforced a German preference for the Girondins' more moderate version of the French Revolution. The translated texts that circulated in the 1790s reflected that. German readers preferred the Count of Mirabeau to Robespierre. The Terror strengthened the identification of German intellectuals with its Girondin victims. The idolization of Charlotte Corday was one sign of this; so was the German cult of Jean-Baptiste Louvet, one of the first parliamentarians to attack Robespierre.[56] There was an elective affinity between most German sympathizers with the French Revolution and the Girondins: a common attachment to the values of the Enlightenment, respect for law and fear of "anarchy," and enthusiasm for the cause of humanity in the abstract coupled with distrust of popular passions. The Girondins also stood for a federal rather than a centralized political system. This, too, recommended them to observers east of the Rhine, a reminder that Germans necessarily viewed events in France (as they did events in America) through German eyes. Even in 1789 and 1790, alongside admiration for France as the leader of "humanity" there had been responses that placed events firmly within a German context. Many German writers suggested that the French Revolution was completing an emancipation of human energies the Reformation had begun.[57] The violent course of the French Revolution also reinforced pride in German "moderation" and a past history of incremental princely reform from above.

The Impact of War

IT WAS NOT THE FRENCH REVOLUTION, BUT A GENERATION OF WARfare, that transformed the German lands. War broke out in 1792 between France and the two major German powers, Austria and Prussia. It is tempting to see this as an ideological conflict between revolution and ancien régime, as many German radicals did. Even a moderate like Klopstock was still sympathetic to the French cause in 1792, and condemned the German powers. They were not wrong to detect a "clash of two worlds."[58] Perfect symbols of the old world were the German princes who, overnight, lost their feudal dues from territories in Alsace and Lorraine when the French National Assembly abolished feudalism in August 1789. Then there were the thousands of French aristocratic émigrés who fled to Vienna, Munich, Hamburg, and, above all, Koblenz, which they turned into a mini-Versailles. They put money in the pockets of the German craftsmen and shopkeepers with whom they ran up bills, but caused widespread offense with their womanizing, gambling, and superior airs. The émigrés intrigued constantly at the German courts, urging a military campaign to restore the status quo ante France.[59] But just as no one was willing to go to war over the lost feudal dues of a few minor German princes, so German rulers discouraged the émigrés' hopes. The Emperor of Austria and the Elector of Cologne rejected their overtures (even though both were brothers of Marie Antoinette, the French queen); the Elector of Trier asked the Prince Condé to stand down the ragtag army he had been drilling in Koblenz. The two largest German powers also had issues other than events in France to consider. When war did come, declared by the French on April 20, 1792, ideology, political calculation, and contingency all played a part.[60]

The revolutionary era brought a new kind of warfare: the people in arms. Johann Wolfgang von Goethe, the all-purpose genius of German letters, gave dramatic expression to this element of novelty. Almost forty years old when the French Revolution broke out, Goethe differed from most of the younger German writers in remaining aloof from the tumultuous events that followed. But he recognized their importance, and not just for France. Goethe accompanied the Duke of Braunschweig-Wolfenbüttel and his Prussian military forces in the campaign against the French Revolutionary army. Sitting around the campfire after the Battle of Valmy in September 1792, Goethe said to the disconsolate officers (or claimed thirty years later that he had said): "From this place and from this day a new epoch in world history begins and you can say you were there to see it."[61] Carl von Clausewitz, who wrote one of the most influential of all works on the soldier's art, On War, was equally forthright: "A force appeared that beggared all imagination. . . . The people became a participant in war; instead of governments and armies as heretofore, the full weight of the nation was thrown into the balance."[62] French forces, which relied on conscription, moved fast and struck quickly, exposed the lumbering "clockwork armies" of the ancien régime. Prussia was forced to sue for peace in 1795. Austria continued the conflict but suffered a string of reverses at the hands of the French Revolutionary and Napoleonic armies, which culminated in the enforced Treaty of Pressburg in 1805. Prussia, resuming hostilities, was humiliated by crushing defeats at the twin battles of Jena and Auerstedt in October 1806—"ruined more completely than any army has ever been ruined on the battlefield," said Clausewitz, one of 140,000 Prussians taken as prisoners of war by the French.[63] Two weeks later Napoleon marched into Berlin.

French victories redrew the map of Central Europe and transformed it politically. France disposed of territories, imposed indemnities, and forced German princes into alliances. The Rhineland, occupied in the 1790s, was incorporated into France in 1802. The Holy Roman Empire, destroyed in all but name in 1803, disappeared entirely in 1806. The numerous tiny entities that had nested within it—Imperial cities, knightly and ecclesiastical territories, some eighteen hundred in all—were incorporated into midsized territorial states like Bavaria and Württemberg. Those states signed treaties with France and sixteen of them (eventually thirty) were organized into the Confederation of the Rhine, which stretched from Mecklenburg to the Tyrol. Two members of the Confederation were entirely novel French creations. Napoleon, having turned the Prince of Anhalt-Köthen into a duke, the Margrave of Baden into a grand duke, and the Duke of Württemberg into a king, had no difficulty conjuring two new sovereign states into existence. The Kingdom of Westphalia and the Grand Duchy of Berg were established as buffer states against Prussia, with members of the extended Bonaparte family installed as rulers. The Confederation of the Rhine was intended to create a compliant "third Germany" as a counterweight against the two leading powers, Austria and Prussia. Both had been humbled in the climactic years 1805–06. Francis II was forced to abdicate as Holy Roman Emperor, and Napoleon reminded the Habsburgs who was master of Europe by marrying Francis's eldest daughter. Vienna was occupied and Austria stripped of its territories in southern Germany, Italy, and the Low Countries. Prussia, like Austria, had to pay a huge indemnity and was reduced to a sorry rump of four provinces, its territory and population halved. The German lands experienced the full range of Napoleon's political repertoire. In these decisive years, territories were annexed, old states built up as French satellites, new states created as French puppets, and large states cut down to size.

All this turned Germany into a political and constitutional laboratory. That was most obviously true in the Rhineland, whose incorporation into France produced the sharpest break with the old order anywhere in Germany. Previous secular and ecclesiastical rulers were overthrown; feudalism was ended, the tithe abolished, guilds eliminated, monopolies overturned, church land secularized, and the Jews emancipated. Here was a crash course in institutional modernization under French auspices. Similar reforms were enacted in the Kingdom of Westphalia and the Grand Duchy of Berg, created partly to show off the superiority of French institutions.[64] The constitution promulgated in Westphalia was the first in German history. But this was very much reform from above. As Napoleon wrote to his younger brother Jerôme, who was king in Westphalia: "If you listen to popular opinion, you will achieve nothing. If the people refuses its own happiness, the people is guilty of anarchy and deserves to be punished."[65] Institutional change and administrative centralization were also driven by something beyond the wish to make "moral conquests." The rationalizing symmetry of French reforms was designed to make it easier to siphon off local wealth. This was, in one way or another, part of the background music to what happened in every German state in the decade before 1815. Whether they were formal allies in the Confederation of the Rhine such as Baden and Bavaria, or defeated and occupied powers like Austria and Prussia, all faced heavy French exactions and material demands. These lent greater urgency to the task of extracting resources from their own populations. Rulers developed and refined the little instruments of power that made this possible (maps, censuses, inventories, law codes), while everywhere they eyed the same kinds of institutional reform.

Reform inside the Confederation of the Rhine was associated especially with those states actually located on or near the Rhine: Baden, Württemberg, Bavaria, and Hessen-Darmstadt. Not coincidentally, all four had adopted constitutions by 1820. Geography made them particularly susceptible to French influence. They also had both motive and opportunity to pursue major reforms. The opportunity came from the territorial transformation that accompanied the end of the Holy Roman Empire, which made these states much larger; the motive was trying to find ways to integrate their new lands while at the same time meeting French demands. These states in the southwest corner of Germany all grew large as they swallowed up formerly independent Imperial cities, secularized ecclesiastical territories, and "mediatized" knights' estates. Württemberg doubled in size, Baden quadrupled.

Dealing with the administrative, religious, and legal diversity of these new possessions and trying to create some kind of unity out of the patchwork drove the reform process. As one of the leading Badenese reformers, Sigismund von Reitzenstein, was about to return home in 1803 after five years as a diplomat in Paris, he wrote that the main task confronting his much enlarged state was "to give an entirely new shape to lands made up of a mass of heterogeneous elements."[66] The most important means of doing this was asserting state sovereignty through administrative centralization, and its main agent was an enlarged body of officials who were better trained and better paid. A retooled machinery of government expanded the reach of the state. This meant cutting back the privileged powers of intermediate corporate institutions like guilds, municipalities, and religious entities—an echo of what had happened in France. It also meant more efficient tax collection, improved educational institutions, and novel infrastructure projects. A plan like the one developed by Badenese military engineer Johann Tulla to make wholesale "corrections" to the course of the Rhine, straightening bends and removing islands, would have been unthinkable without the simplification of the map of Germany brought about by Napoleon and the ambitions of Baden's grand duke and administrative elite, who wanted a new river to serve as the axis of a new state.[67]

The great Rhine project, first set out in an 1809 memorandum, illustrates in microcosm what German state building in these years owed (and did not owe) to the French. Tulla himself, partly trained as an engineer in France, believed strongly in the superiority of free rather than feudal labor for projects like this, a sign of what he owed to the ideas of 1789. It was also easier after French military successes dismantled the Holy Roman Empire to conduct the necessary treaty work with neighboring states that made the river corrections possible, because there were no longer hundreds of tiny principalities on the opposite bank, any one of which could obstruct the process. But the project was also homegrown, at least in part. What outside ideas and changed circumstances did was make it possible to imagine, on a large scale, something that had frequently occupied the attention of Baden's officials on a smaller scale before 1789, when plenty of piecemeal river corrections had been undertaken. Other reforms followed the same pattern. French ideas and military dominance reinforced or reanimated an existing German tradition of enlightened reform from above. That tradition, cautiously progressive, suspicious of vested interests, impatient with anything that smacked of the backward-looking, was perfectly embodied in a figure like Reitzenstein, as well as Maximilian von Montgelas, his Bavarian counterpart.[68]

Baden and Bavaria enacted reforms because they had grown and needed to absorb new populations. Reform in Prussia resulted from the opposite problem: crushing defeat had reduced the state to a torso. There were other differences, too. In the southwestern states reform was most far-reaching in the area of constitutionalism and legal rights; it stopped halfway when it came to the emancipation of the peasantry and the status of the guilds. Prussia was the mirror image. A constitution was twice promised by the monarch, and twice failed to materialize. (It was eventually granted only after another revolution, in 1848.) But Prussian

economic and social reform cut deeper. Peasant emancipation, eviscer-
ated guild privileges, the abolition of other corporate restrictions—all
removed barriers to the ownership and disposability of land and property.
Educational reform was also more radical. From the elementary school to
the university, nothing was left untouched. Prussian reformers were committed to the idea that the energies of the population had to be tapped,
and Prussia was a more dynamic and mobile society after the reform era
than either Baden or Bavaria.

The reforms also had common features, although they proceeded from
different starting points. The German states were all trying to establish
new forms of legitimacy in a world where the old territorial structure of
the German lands had been pulled apart and put back together in an unfamiliar shape. That was why improving the machinery of government was
central to reform. If we step back to look at the big picture, another common feature of reform everywhere (except the Kingdom of Westphalia and
the Grand Duchy of Berg, where it was a French imposition) is that it represented some compound of indigenous German political traditions and
foreign borrowings or adaptations. The elements in the compound varied.
When the Prussian minister Carl August von Struensee told the French
chargé d'affaires in 1799 that the revolution the French had made "from
below" would be completed "gradually, from above" in Prussia, he was
alluding to a pattern of reform from above that had existed prior to the
death of Frederick the Great in 1786.[69] Enlightened reform of this kind was
common across the German lands before 1789, not least in Austria under
Joseph II; however, it was resisted everywhere by vested interests and subject to reversal when a new monarch came to the throne or conservatives
gained ascendancy at court. It flamed out again when circumstances permitted, or seemed to demand it. That is why reform was more muted in
Austria, which after the critical years 1803–1806 neither had to deal (as did
Baden and Bavaria) with digesting a host of new territories, nor confronted
(as did Prussia) an existential crisis. And that was what gave Prussian
reformers a wind at their backs. There were plenty of frustrated would-be
reformers in Berlin in the late 1790s. Some of the younger ones moved in
the same enlightened, cosmopolitan circles as Struensee.[70] The disaster of
1806 gave them their opportunity, as it did senior and better-known figures
like the Baron vom Stein and Karl August von Hardenberg. When Hardenberg in his "Riga memorandum" of 1807 used language similar to Struensee's eight years earlier, calling for "revolution in a positive sense," he was

no longer voicing a pious hope but setting out a reform program he would himself oversee.[71]

Hardenberg wanted that "positive" revolution to come not "through violent impulses from below or outside, but through the wisdom of government." There were plenty of nonviolent impulses "from outside," however. Some came from Denmark, with its unbroken tradition of enlightened reform from above; others came from Britain. Many of the leading Prussian reformers had studied at Anglophile Göttingen. There, or in Königsberg, they encountered Adam Smith's work—"the divine Smith," as one of them called the economist.[72] Smith's ideas about the market and releasing the energies of civil society were widely discussed in enlightened East Prussian circles and found their way into the Prussian reforms. When it came to economic policy, the French physiocrats also had their influence. Above all, however, it was French military ideas that Prussian reformers took to heart. The leading military reformers recognized that resisting Napoleonic forces would require changes in the composition and training of the army. The officer corps became less aristocratic as officers were cashiered or pensioned off, and professional competence replaced social pedigree as an essential requirement for obtaining a commission. The manuals used in the newly established training schools now emphasized the importance of light infantry, skirmishing, and the other elements that underlay French success, and the reformers kept themselves sufficiently up to date that the training manuals even drew on a case where French forces encountered difficulty, the guerrilla attacks of the Peninsular War in Spain. The one aspect of the new-style French armies that was stubbornly resisted by Frederick William III was conscription. The reformers wanted to forge a "nation in arms"; the king thought this sounded too revolutionary. By the beginning of 1813, however, with Prussia reentering the field against France, conscription was decreed. That was what made it possible for Prussia to put 90,000 men into the field at the decisive Battle of the Nations in Leipzig in October 1813.

The numbers engaged in the great battles of the Napoleonic years were unprecedented: 300,000 at Wagram, 550,000 at Leipzig. The toll of casualties would not be seen again in Europe until 1914. It took months to bury the dead from Leipzig. Total deaths during the period from 1792 to 1815 approached five million.[73] There were German casualties on both sides because many Central Europeans were pressed into French service. The Revolutionary army began as the French nation in arms, but the foreign element in Napoleon's Grand Army increased sharply as Frenchmen avoided conscription or deserted. The German element spiked after 1805. Some 375,000 men from the German lands served in Napoleon's army between 1805 and 1813. Even at the Battle of the Nations, 40,000 of the 250,000 Germans in the field in Leipzig were fighting with the French. Napoleon's south German allies were forced to provide tens of thousands of soldiers. Germans fought in Spain. Above all, they fought in the Russian campaign of 1812. Fully a third of the 600,000 men in the Grand Army that went to Russia were German speakers.[74]

The losses were terrible. Only one in ten of the Bavarian soldiers came home. It was just one in thirty of those conscripted from Westphalia and Württemberg.[75] In his memoirs, one surviving Swabian officer, a twenty-seven-year-old captain called Karl Kurz, appended a list of fallen Württemberg officers. It contains 176 names, from Aarhloff to Zschok.[76] Officers and other ranks alike died on the battlefield, from their wounds, and in chaotic incidents like the retreat across the Berezina under fire, when as many as 20,000 died, crushed under foot and hoof or drowned in the icy river.[77]

They died in much larger numbers from exposure, starvation, dysentery, and typhus. Field hospitals became "death chambers." As many as 150 a day died in one set of four field hospitals, their bodies tossed into

A dramatic painting from 1844 by Peter von Hess of Napoleon's Grand Army crossing the Berezina River in November 1812.

the River Duna.[78] Another lucky Swabian survivor, twenty-one-year-old Lieutenant Heinrich Vossler from Tuttlingen, described frostbitten men who lost hands, feet, noses, and ears, some so desperately cold that when they found a fire they "put their limbs right into the embers and perished, half roasted and half frozen to death." Hunger, meanwhile, led them to eat dogs, cats, carrion, and the corpses of the dead.[79]

It is unsurprising that a significant number of survivors wanted to write about their experiences—they *had*, after all, survived, and experienced many things that were remarkable and dramatic. That is surely one reason for the cult of Napoleon among German veterans. These personal accounts formed part of a larger flowering of autobiographical works in these years, one sign of a burgeoning new sense of self. They also reflected the new worlds that were opened up to hundreds of thousands of Germans who marched and fought across Europe. Some, it is true, might have ventured beyond German borders before, even though still young, perhaps as journeymen "on the tramp" or (in the case of educated officers) on study trips. But most were seeing what they saw for the first time and their accounts often resemble a travelogue: descriptions of landscape and people, a pencil sketch of the Kremlin. The descriptions of people run along stereotypical lines—the "savagery" of the Spanish (Germans fighting on both sides of the Peninsular War hated its guerrilla aspect), the "dirty" Poles and Jews, "backward" Russians, "sinister" Bashkirs—but in other cases were offset by gratitude for acts of kindness that almost certainly saved lives, like being taken in and fed by a Russian peasant woman.[80]

Soldiers wrote home to their wives expressing homesickness and offering advice from a distance. Bavarian Corporal Josef Layrer in Russia poured his heart out to his wife, Rosina, and their younger daughter: "Much beloved, best and most wonderful wife! . . . All my memories of you, and especially of my little Wusserl make nights and days filled with torment and painful, and many is the time I eat my bread coated with bitter tears."[81]

But what was life back home like for the Rosinas and Wusserls, for the German civilian population, during two decades of warfare? These were years of violence and insecurity for them, too. It is surely telling that the words "militarism" and "civilian" (in the sense of noncombatant) both appeared in the 1790s.[82] Across Central Europe, areas changed hands as armies marched and countermarched. Saxony, the Rhineland, and southern Germany experienced the worst. Some places changed hands repeatedly, like the unfortunate wine-growing town of Oppenheim on the Rhine, which shuttled back and forth between French and Austrian occupiers. French Revolutionary armies lived off the land—that was how they were able to move so fast. Sulpiz Boisserée, a young art collector who saw the French soldiers march into Cologne in October 1794, recorded that they still had bread and meat hanging from their bayonets and were wrapped in recently plundered rugs and carpets.[83]

The politics of plunder went beyond opportunist individuals. One French general, looking down in 1794 on the "rich and abundant country" along the Rhine and Mosel, saw a "true milk cow for the French republic." Two years later, a fellow general surveyed a nearby area that had been stripped of horses, cattle, grain, forage, tools, household utensils, firewood, clothes, and shoes, reporting back to Paris on the "hideous desert" that surrounded him.[84] Harsh French procurement and requisitioning practices went together with forced loans and the conscription of local manpower for military service and to build fortifications and roads. Punitive billeting and hostage taking were instruments of persuasion where communities showed signs of resistance. Some of the brutality of the war was captured in three plays by one of Germany's leading writers, Friedrich Schiller. His Wallenstein trilogy was set in the Thirty Years War but clearly alluded to the contemporary conflict. The plays were written at the end of the 1790s. Reading them ten years later, as the war still went on, the writer and salon hostess Rahel Levin was impressed by "how every word fits."[85]

Three ugly specters stalk every modern war: sexual violence, epidemic disease, and desperate deserters. Germans experienced all three in these decades. Sexual violence by soldiers against women was commonplace. Male commentators referred to it euphemistically when they mentioned it at all ("no woman was safe"; "women were especially mistreated"), for rape challenged the domestic gender order and underscored the inability of German men to protect their wives and daughters. In some cases, attempts were made to direct occupying soldiers' attention to socially inferior or marginal women, or—in the case of the Austrian village of Villingen—to the houses of unmarried women.[86] The spread of sexually transmitted diseases was one result. Epidemic diseases were also carried by armies and struck populations already weakened by privation. The movement of soldiers, sailors, and refugees between different theaters of war brought yellow fever from the Caribbean to Europe in the early years of the nineteenth century, especially to Spain, but also to Italy, the Low Countries, and Central Europe.[87] Germans soldiers who came back from Russia brought typhus with them.

The disease flared up again in 1813 and 1814 after the Battle of Leipzig. As many as one in ten Germans fell sick as the combatants returned home.[88] Livestock diseases were another menace of armies on the move. Then there were the deserters. Desertion rates were high: 10 percent in the French Grand Army. Deserters banded together and preyed on communities. They also swelled the ranks of bandit gangs, which enjoyed their last hurrah in Central Europe at the beginning of the nineteenth century.[89]

Topsy-turvy

FLIGHT, OR DISPLACEMENT, WAS A COMMON DENOMINATOR OF THE revolutionary era. Loyalists fled the United States and émigrés fled revolutionary France. German supporters of the French Revolution went to Paris, then had to flee the Terror, or they arrived after the Terror fleeing from German authorities. Reluctant soldiers were displaced from home; some fled their army and became deserters. Meanwhile, civilians fled in the face of occupying armies, whether to a neighboring town or into the woods. Those are dramatic instances of displacement.

But the experience was actually much more widespread, even routine. Think of the monks and nuns turned out of religious institutions that were secularized, or the faculty and students at Catholic universities that suffered the same fate.[90] Catholic institutions were also prominent victims of French cultural looting. More than six thousand drawings and nearly twenty-seven thousand prints from the Jesuits' collection in Cologne were carted off to the Louvre or the Bibliothèque Nationale in Paris.[91] Then there were the chamberlains, bureaucrats, and diplomats trained for a life of service in an Imperial knightly territory or another of the many tiny micro-states of the Holy Roman Empire that simply disappeared overnight, cruel instances of how "a worldview loses its world."[92] Examples can be multiplied across the venerable patchwork of institutions that defined ancien régime Germany—guild masters who lost their guilds, placeholders who lost their places, beneficiaries of religious charity who lost their benefactors.[93] More than half the population of Central Europe were displaced in a very basic sense, for they became subject to a new ruler as territories changed hands and new borders were drawn.

There were winners as well as losers in this topsy-turvy world. Those who served new regimes were among them. Georg Friedrich Rebmann, the erstwhile revolutionary in Paris, returned to his occupation of lawyer when he went back to the Rhineland, now a part of France, to serve as a magistrate. As if his life in the 1790s had not been colorful enough, Rebmann presided over the trial in Mainz of the most famous bandit of the era, "Schinderhannes," whose execution in 1803 drew thirty thousand spectators. Officials were usually beneficiaries of change, because state building meant better salaries, pensions, and social standing—for those, at least, who survived the more rigorous procedures for appointments and promotions. Merchants and manufacturers also benefited (like their counterparts in France) from institutional changes that removed restrictions on their business activity.[94] They were also well represented among those who purchased former ecclesiastical property. Instances abound of monasteries that suddenly became warehouses or coal depots. The protracted, step-by-step process of Jewish emancipation in the German lands also began in these years.[95] The German version of the French "career open to talents" was likely, in fact, to benefit anyone who was able to rise on merit but lacked the birth or connections to prosper in the ancien régime. That did not necessarily mean just the business or educated classes. It might apply to a craftsman held back in the guild system because his great-grandfather had been a shepherd, pursuing a "dishonorable" occupation.[96]

Unsurprisingly, then, there was no singular "German" experience of the revolutionary era, and no singular response. So much depended on who you were, where you lived, and exactly when we are talking about. Take the case of Hamburg. There was initial enthusiasm for the French Revolution among merchants and members of the educated elite. Hamburg patricians planted liberty trees and celebrated the first anniversary of the Bastille's fall. But disgust at the Terror, which claimed the lives of their Girondin friends, and social unrest at home brought a change of view. Widen the frame, and we see how the city experienced wild ups and downs during the revolutionary era. The revolt of the American colonies was a boon, which opened up American ports to direct trade by Hanseatic merchants. The British blockade of French ports and Napoleon's embargo on British trade in response then closed it down again. Hamburg's most negative direct experiences of French events came only after 1806, but it was traumatic when it did. French occupation was brief, but the *Franzosenzeit* left long and bitter memories.[97] The experience of the Rhineland was the exact mirror image. It felt the full force of French exactions in the 1790s. Life then became easier after incorporation into France.

In all periods of revolutionary upheaval, the balance sheet varies according to the timescale we use. The French dragooning of Germans to work on construction projects bore down hard on those who did the work, but the benefits of improved roads were lasting. Some German regions were economically harmed in the short term by Napoleon's trade embargo, but many infant industries benefited in the long term from the removal of English competition. Sometimes necessity was the mother of invention: disruption in the imports of sugarcane gave a major fillip to the sugar beet industry. The dismantling of much of the old social order, whether by the French or by German reformers, brought great immediate hardship but also released social energies that had previously been suppressed.

The political legacy of the revolutionary era was equally mixed. The French Revolution bequeathed a potent political vocabulary of nation, rights, and liberty, as well as a new set of political symbols—the tricolor flag, the liberty tree. These played an important part in German politics after 1815. So did the cult of Napoleon, which persisted in the form of broadsheets, toasts to the former emperor in taverns, and songs.[98] But the French Revolution was also responsible for creating a modern conservatism that had its own reference points, the "historical" and "organic," and its own vocabulary: hierarchy, order, faith. Nostalgia was one of its characteristic registers.[99] One counterintuitive effect of the revolution was to strengthen religious institutions, especially the Roman Catholic Church. Radical revolution discredited moderate church reformers and strengthened traditionalists. Meanwhile, secularization deprived the Catholic Church of land and property but simultaneously made it a less privileged institution with a more plausible claim to be close to the people. Some apostates of revolution also became political advocates of the Catholic cause, all the more fierce from having passed themselves through a Jacobin phase (like ex-Communists in a later age). The Rhinelander Joseph Görres is a good example of the type.[100]

The lessons learned from France often floated free of their original source. That is notably true of nationalism as an adopted German cause. Later nationalists admittedly created many myths about the "war of national liberation" against Napoleon in 1813, which was a much more conventional set of engagements than they depicted. But references to "nation" did multiply in these years. The Prussian reformers referred to national spirit and national consciousness, and although by "nation" they typically meant Prussia rather than Germany, there was ambiguity and overlap between the two meanings.[101] Some younger German intellectuals embraced a more belligerent, anti-French nationalism. Nationalist sentiment was conditioned by the disappearance of the Holy Roman Empire, fed by the growing interest in German language and folkways, and sharpened by the French occupation.[102] In some cases it amounted almost to a spasm of rage: "I hate all the French without exception in the name of God and my people," proclaimed the historian and writer Ernst Moritz Arndt. He nonetheless argued that it would be a mark of ingratitude and hypocrisy not to acknowledge what Germans owed to this "wild and raging revolution," which had "ignited a great sea of fire in the mind."[103]

One French lesson had a long afterlife: the lesson of the Terror. But Germans understood the lesson in different ways. Liberals, heirs of those who sympathized with the Girondins in the 1790, argued that reform was necessary, because reform denied led to revolution. Conservatives took exactly the opposite view, that reform undermined order and opened the way to violence. Some passed from one camp to another, like the mercurial writer and later diplomat Friedrich von Gentz. Twenty-five years old when the French Revolution broke out, Gentz was initially enthusiastic but followed a familiar path of disillusionment. He translated Edmund Burke's critical *Reflections on the Revolution in France* into German in 1794 and became an advocate of British liberal "gradualism." After 1815, however, he became increasingly conservative and served as the right-hand man of Austrian chancellor Klemens von Metternich. It was during his liberal phase that Gentz wrote a book comparing the American and French revolutions.[104] In praising one for its moderation while condemning the other for its violence, Gentz was broadly in line with German opinion after 1800.

Events across the Atlantic served, but only in retrospect from the 1790s onward, as a foil to the German reception of the revolution in France. The American Revolution had, it was argued, been less bloody and more practical than the French—less "metaphysical," said one admiring writer.[105] That was a recurring theme after 1815, when the volume of writing about the United States grew, including articles in journals dedicated to the New World such as *Columbus* and *Atlantis*. The United States especially interested German liberals because of the emphasis placed there on constitutionalism, individual rights, religious toleration, and the rule of law—in other words, for the same reasons that Britain interested them as a potential model. But it also offered the example of a new state's being built from scratch, as the post-1815 German states were being built. However, the signature aspect of the American Revolution—"we, the people," or popular sovereignty—was largely bracketed out of German liberal discourse, although not out of debates among radicals and democrats. Despite their sympathy for the American experiment, postrevolutionary German liberals largely agreed with conservatives that its institutions could not simply be "transplanted" into Germany. What was suitable for a rudely vigorous people in a wide-open land without history was not necessarily right for an old society. Liberals drew the same conclusion from the Latin American struggles for independence.[106]

Radicals disagreed. These "world-historical events" (the term was much bandied about in the early nineteenth century) represented "the seeds of a better future," according to an 1815 article in the *Politisches Journal*. The great revolt in South America would "perhaps sooner than some would like to think pull the European motherland into its powerful vortex."[107] Some wanted to speed the course of world history along. South America became a site of German radicalism. In the years after 1815, hundreds of Germans fought in Simón Bolívar's legions, others in the Uruguayan war of independence and in two republican uprisings in southern Brazil. The Germans who fought alongside Giuseppe Garibaldi in the second of these, the Guerra dos Farrapos (the Ragamuffin War), flew the German red-black-gold tricolor. These "displaced" radical German nationalists are much less familiar than the revolutionary "pilgrims" to Paris in 1789 and 1790, or the Germans who in recoiled from the Terror in disgust, but they also form part of the political legacy of the revolutionary era and make up one strand of German nineteenth-century nationalism.

CHAPTER 5

KNOWLEDGE

Scientific Travelers

ONE GERMAN WHO STRUCK UP A FRIENDSHIP WITH SIMÓN Bolívar before he became "the Liberator" was Alexander von Humboldt. They met in Paris sometime in 1804, and later in Rome. Some writers suggest that it was Humboldt who encouraged Bolívar to challenge Spanish dominance in South America, which probably overstates his role, but their later correspondence indicates that they did talk politics in those early days. Humboldt, writing to Bolívar in 1821 to recommend a French scientific colleague who was traveling to Colombia, recalled their first friendship "in an epoch when we made vows for the liberty and independence of the New Continent." Two years later, Bolívar wrote to a colleague in Paraguay about how honored he had been in youth by his friendship with "Baron de Humboldt, whose learning has done America more good than all of the conquistadores."[1] What did Bolívar mean by this, and why did the German nineteenth-century geographer Carl Ritter call Humboldt the "scholarly rediscoverer of America"?[2] The answer, in both cases, refers to Humboldt's five-year journey to the equinoctial regions, undertaken with the French botanist Aimé Bonpland.[3] The journey made his name. Humboldt returned in 1804 a celebrity—"our conqueror of the world," in Goethe's words.[4] The English social theorist Harriet Martineau would call him "the Monarch of science," Lord Byron put him into his poem *Don Juan*.[5]

Humboldt's father was a member of the minor nobility and a royal chamberlain. Alexander was born in 1769. He and his older brother Wilhelm grew up just outside Berlin in the family home at Tegel (Alexander called it "Castle Boredom"), where they were privately tutored. Wilhelm was considered the prodigy; his younger brother was the dreamy one, happiest collecting plants and insects. Alexander studied at the Viadrina University in Frankfurt an der Oder, then followed Wilhelm to Göttingen. He befriended Georg Forster during a visit to Mainz. In 1790 they traveled to England, where Humboldt looked at caves in Derbyshire, visited Kew Gardens, and met Sir Joseph Banks, the great impresario of British imperial science. On the way back they stayed briefly in Paris (Humboldt later called those days "the most instructive and unforgettable" of his life). After enrolling at the School of Mines in Freiberg, where he devoured the three-year curriculum in eight months, Humboldt entered Prussian state service and rose quickly through the ranks, but continued to work on his own scientific projects. His first book, on the basalt rock of the Rhine Valley, was published in 1790. Other works followed, as he traveled Europe in pursuit of his geological and botanical interests.

When his mother died in 1799, Humboldt came into money and resigned his position, contemplating a more ambitious journey like the one that had made the name of his friend Forster. He hoped to be part of Napoleon's Egyptian expedition, but that fell through; instead, he and Bonpland traveled to the Americas. The two scientists left the Spanish port of La Coruña that June, stopping briefly in Tenerife before sailing on to Venezuela. There they explored the Orinoco and established its connection with the Amazon river system. Humboldt and Bonpland navigated the Orinoco in a forty-foot boat laden with guides, scientific instruments, plant samples, cages of monkeys and birds (among them seven parrots), and an adopted dog that was eventually eaten by a jaguar. They then visited Cuba, of which Humboldt wrote the first detailed physical description, returned to the American mainland, went up the Magdalena River to Bogotá, then on to Quito and Lima, before taking ship to Mexico. Then it was back to Cuba, followed by a brief stay in the United States, where Thomas Jefferson welcomed Humboldt at the White House, before returning to Bordeaux. In the course of his journey Humboldt scaled volcanoes, descended mines, collected rock samples, and handled electric eels; he studied flora and fauna and sent specimens back to Europe. He examined everything from the properties of guano to the prospects for sugar plantations, and everywhere he went he measured things—heights, distances, temperatures.[6]

Humboldt did not do everything by himself. Like all European scientific travelers, he and Bonpland depended on porters and guides, people on the spot with local knowledge to transport them and point them in the

*This portrait of Alexander von Humboldt was
painted by Friedrich Georg Weitsch in 1806, after the
scientist's return from his American journey. The
Orinoco River is in the background.*

right direction. Humboldt also had the benefit of work done by Creole
naturalists. They learned from him, but it was a two-way exchange.[7] Strip
away the heroic tone that can still be found in some writing on Humboldt,
though, and it remains clear that he was an exceptional figure for many
different reasons, starting with the degree of celebrity he garnered at an
early age and retained through a long life (he died four months short of his
ninetieth birthday).[8] He was also exceptional as a scientist. That was partly

because of his preoccupation with measurement and instrumentation, a key element in "Humboldtian science" and the quality affectionately satirized in Daniel Kehlmann's bestselling novel of 2005 about Humboldt and the German mathematician Carl Friedrich Gauss, *Measuring the World*.[9] But there was also the matter of Humboldt's sheer range. His publications extended across geography, geology, mineralogy, botany, zoology, climatology, chemistry, and astronomy, as well as ethnography and political economy. While the insistence on measurement was satirized even by some contemporaries, it went hand in hand with Humboldt's passionate attachment to the idea of the unity of knowledge, something he expressed as early as 1794 in a letter to Friedrich Schiller, a breathless, tumbling plea for a dynamic rather than narrowly descriptive account of the natural world, not like "our miserable archivists of nature," a letter that Humboldt concluded apologetically with the words "I find that I have expressed myself as one demented."[10] His commitment to the unity of scientific knowledge was increasingly challenged in an age of specialization, not least as it developed in nineteenth-century German universities.

Humboldt was undoubtedly exceptional when it came to reputation, quality of mind, and range, but in other respects he resembled the many other German scientific travelers. With the exception of a few Habsburg expeditions, all continued to work for non-German masters. In those same years on either side of 1800, other Germans followed in the footsteps of Johann Georg Gmelin, Samuel Georg Gmelin, and Peter Pallas by taking part in Russian journeys of exploration. Carl Heinrich Merck served as naturalist on the Billings expedition to eastern Siberia and Alaska in 1785–1794.[11] The first Russian circumnavigation of the globe (1803–1806) was led by a Baltic German, Adam Johann von Krusenstern, and had another Baltic German as cartographer and two German physician-naturalists. An ambitious Russian voyage to explore Oceania in 1815–1818 on the ship the *Rurik* had a similar cast of characters. Its leader was the Baltic German Otto von Kotzebue and its two naturalists were the Baltic German entomologist Johann Friedrich Eschscholtz and Adelbert von Chamisso, a German writer famous for his story about Peter Schlemihl, the man who sold his shadow. The expedition artist was once again an ethnic German, the Ukrainian-born Ludwig Choris.[12]

It is worth stopping for a moment to look in more detail at two of the people taken on board the *Rurik* who became very important to Chamisso, one in 1816, the second the following year. Both illustrate the cross-cultural swirl of people, cultures, and languages in the early-nineteenth-century Pacific. When the *Rurik* left San Francisco at the beginning of November 1816, bound for Hawaii, it had several new passengers. One of them was named John Elliot de Castro. A man of British-Portuguese background, he had previously worked as a commercial agent aboard a Russian-American Company ship until arrested in California by the Spaniards for illegal trading. Before that had spent two years trying to make his fortune fishing for pearls in Hawaii, where he became personal physician to King Kamehameha I and a member of the court. During the three weeks' journey from San Francisco to Honolulu, de Castro taught some elements of the Hawaiian language to Chamisso, himself a French émigré. De Castro stayed in Hawaii when the Russian expedition left for Micronesia.

A few months later, in February 1817, the *Rurik* encountered some native boats near the Ratak island group of the Marshall Islands. Several of the boatmen came aboard and one of them stayed. Kadu was from Ulea, one of the Caroline Islands, and found himself on the Ratak chain because he had been blown off course in a storm while on a mission for his ruler. He would stay on the *Rurik* for eight and a half months. He became close to many of the crew, including Choris, who drew him and whose own ethnographic vision was partly shaped by Kadu's influence. Chamisso described him as "one of the finest characters I have met in my life, one of the people I have loved most." Kadu was immensely valuable to the expedition because of his navigational knowledge and his quick, alert intelligence. He and Chamisso found ways to communicate (as Georg Forster had forty-four years earlier with a Polynesian called Mahine), building up a common language that began with some Polynesian and Oceanic words that both knew. It turned out that Kadu also had some previous contact with Europeans, mostly Spaniards, an instance of how the Pacific had become a contact zone for Europeans and non-Europeans.[13]

In 1823 a further Russian expedition headed to the Pacific, led once again by Otto von Kotzebue, its complement of naturalists once again filled with Germans. One of them was Eschscholtz, who had been on the *Rurik*; another was the Silesian ornithologist Friedrich Wilhelm Heinrich von Kittlitz.[14] And so a pattern of German naturalists serving the Russian empire begun a century earlier persisted into the 1820s. Humboldt himself made one more great journey, an eight-month expedition to the Urals and Siberia funded by the tsarist government. But whereas the thirty-year-old had traveled rough with Bonpland as company, the sixty-year-old went

*A drawing by Ludwig Choris of the remarkable Kadu, who spent eight
and a half months aboard the* Rurik. *It is shown here printed opposite
the title page of Adalbert von Chamisso's memoirs of the voyage.*

across the steppe in a horse-drawn carriage accompanied by two German
scientists, a cook, a valet, and a changing retinue of Russian minders.

The Russian minders point to how patronage shaped the production of
knowledge. Humboldt's patrons for his two great journeys were Spain and
Russia. For other German naturalist-travelers, it was Denmark or Britain.
A common thread that linked many of them was the University of Göttingen.[15] Humboldt had studied there; so had Carsten Niebuhr, Peter Pallas,
and others who followed him. Georg Forster established close connections
with scholars there. One of Göttingen's most prominent professors of natural history, Johann Friedrich Blumenbach, had close links with Sir Joseph
Banks in London. When Banks was looking for promising talent to send
to Africa in the early nineteenth century, it was in Blumenbach's Göttingen
pool that he once again went fishing. Four graduates of the university, Friedrich Hornemann, Ulrich Seetzen, Heinrich Röntgen, and Johann Ludwig Burckhardt, went off in turn to North Africa. Every one of them died

there between 1801 and 1817, four civilian casualties at a time of war—a reminder of the ultimate peril of patronage.[16] Mostly, however, the problem for scientific travelers was how to get around irksome restrictions, especially on reporting their discoveries. It was possible to finesse this, however. The powers that commissioned expeditions wanted exclusive access to the results, but naturalists often reported their findings to colleagues even while they were still in the field. Afterward, they typically wrote up their part of the official report, then published further accounts under their own names. After all, they had an international audience in universities, academies, and learned societies, among fellow naturalists with whom they had personal connections. Humboldt is the classic case, although not alone in this kind of scientific-literary self-fashioning. He paid very close attention to the form and style of his publications, and his correspondence network was such that he was writing two thousand letters a year even in old age.[17] One scholar has called Humboldt a "broker" or "intermediary" between different cultures; another has gone even further and argued that his position at the center of a global republic of letters makes him an exemplary figure who stands at the beginning of a modern networked world of scholars: Alexander von Humboldt, our contemporary.[18]

Who, then, benefited from this flood of new information? The expeditions were intended to produce useful knowledge, and the observations, tabulations, maps, measurements, drawings, and samples delivered by the naturalists certainly fitted the bill. That was most obviously true of information about mineral wealth, one of Humboldt's charges in South America and in Siberia.[19] The work of Humboldt, the former mine official, overlapped with what Germans had long been doing around the world as mining experts. Expedition sponsors also wanted information about climate, flora, and fauna because they were interested in the possibilities for cultivation and settlement. Once again, the scientists obliged. The Göttingen-trained naturalist and explorer Georg von Langsdorff recommended more intensive potato planting and reindeer breeding for Kamchatka; Humboldt advised on sugar cultivation.

There was no obvious use to many of these naturalist-explorers' findings, however. Sometimes they were even subversive, especially when it came to the degradation of nature. It is important not to get this out of proportion. Through the end of the eighteenth century, the language of most naturalists still reflected the instrumental, Enlightenment view that the natural world was something to be "conquered" in the interests of humankind—the view that led the prominent French naturalist Georges-Louis Leclerc, the Comte de Buffon, to say that "wild nature is hideous," and Georg Forster, observing a settlement in New Zealand, to reflect on the "superiority of a state of civilization over that of barbarism."[20] But views about nature were shifting, and German writers played a major part in shifting them. In the most general terms, Forster helped to set a new tone with his "panoramic" descriptions, aesthetic judgments about natural beauty and emotional responses to what he saw. Humboldt wrote in the same idiom, in *Journey to the Equinoctial Regions* and in the short book *Views of Nature* that preceded it (and remained a personal favorite). He also epitomized a more holistic view of nature that can already be seen emerging in the 1780s. That is when we find a cluster of writers referring to "the whole of nature" (Forster), or proposing that nature was "one continued web of life" (the Dutch naturalist John Bruckner) and "everywhere a living whole" (Johann Gottfried Herder).[21] This approach came to be infused with the spirit of Romanticism around 1800 and acquired greater purchase, not least because it was clear that the transformation of the natural world was accelerating.

Nature as an interconnected, living whole was more than a philosophical or literary trope. It was underpinned by observation. One reason that Humboldt has been hailed as a forerunner of modern environmental thinking is his demonstration that individual plant species had their place within larger plant communities, their distribution determined by temperature, elevation, and type of soil.[22] Building on the work of others, including the Colombian naturalist Francisco José de Caldas, as well as his own measurements during the American journey, Humboldt's *Essay on the Geography of Plants*, published in French in 1805, was a "milestone in ecological thought linking climate and botany in systemic fashion."[23] Many of the phenomena he and other naturalists observed also raised troubling questions. Was deforestation causing climate change? What about soil erosion? Was "nature's economy" (Linnaeus's term) invariably self-correcting, or could human overfishing and overhunting have dire consequences? The pressure being placed on certain species loomed as a new issue.

Take the German scientists in the Russian North Pacific as an example. On the Billings expedition of the 1790s, even the not very perceptive Carl Heinrich Merck remarked that stocks of sea otters and fur seals were not inexhaustible. A decade later Georg von Langsdorff was more sharply critical—although he was, at the same time, an advocate of whaling, and believed that the rate of killing of other species (such as puffins) could be increased. Another ten years on, and Chamisso continued to sound the alarm about sea otters and fur seals.[24] Of the three, Chamisso was the one who seems to have developed the closest affective relationship with the creatures in question. On a beach in the Pribilof Islands he "observed and stroked a . . . new-born [fur seal]" until the seal pup's father charged him angrily.[25] (It is not recorded whether Chamisso was smoking the pipe that hardly ever left his mouth.) Langsdorff, however, is the one who thought hardest about the problem of extinction. Few were fully persuaded of the concept at the end of the eighteenth century. Perhaps a species that had disappeared from one place had simply migrated to another; perhaps it had "transmuted" (evolved, as we would say). It was thought that a dodo might still turn up, while some of the signature extinctions of modern times (like the passenger pigeon) still lay in the future. But fossil evidence newly uncovered by geologists pointed to past extinctions. The pioneering French geologist Georges Cuvier published an article to that effect in 1796.[26] Sir Joseph Banks was among those edging toward the idea. Langsdorff played a part in this history. After returning from the Krusenstern voyage, he reported that he was now sure Steller's sea cow had joined the "dudu," the mammoth, and the carnivorous elephant whose bones had been found in Ohio "among the list of beings lost from the animal kingdom."[27] Even before returning, Langsdorff had written about this to Blumenbach, his Göttingen mentor, a key conduit for scientific ideas and one of the naturalists willing to entertain the idea of extinction.

Were German naturalists more likely than others to raise difficult questions because of their "outsider" status?[28] They were certainly a strikingly mobile, even "displaced" bunch. Humboldt spent twenty-five years living in Paris before returning reluctantly to Berlin, Georg Forster died in Paris as a disillusioned revolutionary, while Chamisso went in the opposite direction as the young son of French aristocratic émigrés who settled in Germany. Many German natural scientists in Russia returned home only at the end of their lives after spending their most productive years outside Germany. Then there was the ethnic German Ludwig Choris, who lived in Paris after returning from Kotzebue's circumnavigation, where he established himself as a scientific illustrator before being killed by bandits in Mexico, where he had gone to draw plants for the Musée des Jardins des Plantes. These peregrinations may have honed a critical distance in some cases. But patronage could also inhibit outspokenness, as it did in Peter Pallas's case. All belonged, anyway, to an international network of naturalists. Questions about the unwelcome effects of the human domination of nature were also being raised in these years by Lord Kames in Britain, by the Finn Pehr Kalm, and by the French botanist Philibert Commerson. The German naturalists were citizens of this wider world. At the same time, it is hard to overlook the fact that criticism about the poor stewardship of natural resources was being leveled by German naturalists against the empires of others that they saw as harsh and predatory, something we shall also encounter in German responses to the treatment of Indigenous peoples.

The great voyages and overland expeditions of the period were intended to describe humans as well as plants and nonhuman animals, information that would help to construct the "great map of mankind."[29] The instructions for Captain Cook's second voyage in 1772 included the following: "You are likewise to observe the Genius, Temper, Disposition and Number of the Natives or Inhabitants, if there be any & endeavour by all proper means to cultivate a Friendship and Alliance with them."[30] This is what we would today call ethnography, a discipline that German travelers had an outsized role in developing. Georg Forster and his father, Johann Reinhold, who accompanied Cook on his second voyage, were arguably the outstanding ethnographers of the Pacific in the late eighteenth century, a reputation that Chamisso enjoyed in the early nineteenth. Ethnography was indeed a German invention. It was one of the Germans who took part in a second Kamchatka expedition that set off in 1733 (Gerhard Friedrich Müller) who first systematized the practice of what he called "description of peoples" (*Völker-Beschreibung*), another German (Johann Friedrich Schöpperlin) who coined the term *ethnographia*.[31] There were underlying strategic and material motives at play here, no less than in the drawing up of inventories of flora and fauna. Whether they arrived on a ship or a sled, the representatives of empire were dependent on local supplies and local knowledge. At the same time, the travelers (like their predecessors during earlier encounters) saw things they had never seen before, whether these were social organizations, notions of honor and value, body markings, or forms of sexuality. And what they saw prompted comparisons with their own civilizations. Sometimes the comparison made them complacent, at other times critical.

Germans, once again, leaned toward the critical. An issue that exercised many of them was the existential threat faced by Indigenous peoples who came into contact with expanding European empires. This was a motif in German naturalists' reports from the Russian North Pacific. Merck, Langsdorff, and Chamisso all pointed to the declining numbers of Aleuts, Alutiits, and Kamchadals.[32] They suggested a connection with threatened nonhuman species, which in turn pointed to the danger of extinction. From a different part of the world, Alexander von Humboldt alluded directly to this issue with his poignant anecdote about the parrot of Atures, the sole living creature that could speak the language of a lost tribe, a story that impressed itself on the mind of Charles Darwin.[33] The Forsters were constantly critical of what was being done to the peoples of the Pacific, concerned they were being debased, debauched, and drawn into one of the least attractive European habits, the taste for luxury.[34] Both father and son deplored one particular form of exchange: the sexual relations between Europeans and Indigenous peoples. Johann Reinhold thundered about the long-term effects, the "general devastation," that would result from sexually transmitted diseases.[35] Georg reflected sadly "that hitherto our intercourse has been wholly disadvantageous to the nations of the South Seas"; those who had kept their distance from the "spirit of debauchery" had been the "least injured."[36] One episode that appalled him, of sexual relations between the crew on one of Cook's ships, the *Resolution*, and Maori women, took place in May 1773 at a site in New Zealand that Cook named Queen Charlotte Sound. Forster denounced the mariners as well as the Indigenous males who pimped out their female relations: "Whether the members of a civilized society, who could act such a brutal part, or the barbarians who could force their own women to submit to such an indignity, deserve the greater abhorrence, is a question not easily to be decided."[37]

There is no doubting the genuineness of the outrage, but we need to dig a little deeper. At Queen Charlotte Sound, Forster was doing more than issuing a plague on both houses, deploring sailors and Maori males alike. There was also an aesthetic judgment at work in his remark that it was "astounding that persons could be found, who could gratify an animal appetite with such loathsome objects." (He and his father made similar slighting observations about Tahitian women.)[38] Would the satisfying of those appetites have been less "astounding," then, if the women had been less "loathsome"?[39] It is not clear here exactly where Forster stands. He also moved back and forth on the "innocence" of the Indigenes. Sometimes he gives us the "noble savage"; at other times, his Enlightenment conviction that European forms of material consumption and exchange were the necessary prerequisite for a critical civil society.[40] Like his father, Georg was shocked when he found Indigenous peoples "seemingly without the smallest degree of curiosity."[41] Not least, there was a reflex we have seen before: to blame evils on the empires of others, while standing above it all as Germans. This was a familiar argument among German naturalists in Russia and in German commentary on colonization in Central and South America.[42] This stance of moral superiority, the supposedly disinterested pursuit of "curiosity" rather than "vulgar" commerce or "animal" appetites, was surely one reason, although certainly not the only one, that "the foreign gentleman" Johann Reinhold Forster was so heartily detested by the British officers and crew of the *Resolution*.[43] Moral superiority and his good-hearted, enlightened belief in "humanity" come together in one of Georg Forster's comments in *Voyage Around the World*. "Perhaps in future ages, when the maritime powers of Europe lose their American colonies," he wrote presciently (this was 1777), "they may think of making new establishments in more distant regions; and if it were ever possible for Europeans to have humanity enough to acknowledge the indigenous tribes of the South Seas as their brethren, we might have settlements which would not be defiled with the blood of innocent nations."[44]

The Invention of Race

LURKING BEHIND THE ETHNOGRAPHY—DESCRIBING AND CLASSIfying peoples newly encountered by Europeans—was the element of race. What name should be given to these subdivisions within humanity: were they tribes, nations, kinds, classes, orders, varieties, families, or races? The idea of race and racial difference had been around at least since the late seventeenth century, but the concept began to be defined in the closing decades of the eighteenth and it was Germans who defined it. This originary moment is filled with paradoxes, starting with the fact that the "concept of race bears Kant's signature"—that its prime mover, in other words, was Immanuel Kant, embodiment of Enlightenment rationality.[45] He was contributing in the most general sense to contemporary European debates about classifying humans, but responding in particular to the revival of arguments in favor of polygenesis, which held that the variety of humankind was such that it was impossible all had descended from Adam and Eve. Polygenesis was proposed as a thesis by scholars like Lord Kames; it was also taken up as an argument by defenders of slavery (who argued that Blacks were a different, inferior species), as well as by fierce opponents of slavery like Georg Forster. Kant objected because it upended the biblical narrative, and because he thought its advocates frivolous. The "scientific"

theory of race therefore began as a defense of German professorial seriousness and the Book of Genesis, against arguments used by contemporary
British slaveholders. In a 1775 essay, "Of the Different Human Races," Kant
made the case for the singular origins of humankind (monogenesis), defining race as a "class distinction between animals of one and the same line
of descent, which is unfailingly transmitted by inheritance."[46] "Seeds," he
argued, latent in all humans, were activated by climate and environment;
but once these had produced their effects, the results were irreversible and
visible in the four or five human races marked by differences of color.[47]

Kant was criticized by major figures, including Georg Forster and one
of his own former pupils, the philosopher Johann Gottfried Herder. Both
denied that race was a reality, let alone a permanently fixed quality, and
argued for a broader understanding of human diversity and a continuum
of skin colors. "The colors do run into each other," wrote Herder.[48] But
Kant's most important interlocutor was Johann Friedrich Blumenbach, the
rising young Göttingen natural scientist whose dissertation *On the Natural
Variety of Mankind* appeared in the same year as Kant's essay. The Blumenbach we encountered earlier, puzzling over the question of extinctions
with Georg von Langsdorff in the early years of the nineteenth century,
had by then become a powerful figure in Göttingen.[49] In 1775 he was just
twenty-three years old, although he would become a full professor three
years later. Much better versed in natural history and anatomy than Kant,
he also had access to the university's unrivaled collection of travel books
and narratives. Blumenbach was equally firm in dismissing the supporters
of polygenesis but differed in many points of detail from Kant. He was
skeptical about skin color as the clearest marker of racial difference and
came close to the arguments advanced by Herder and Forster in acknowl-
edging the great variety within humankind: "When the matter is thoroughly considered, you see that all do run into one another, and that one
variety of mankind does so sensibly pass into the other, that you cannot
mark out the limits between them."[50] On the other hand, he saw variations in the shape of skulls as a more promising avenue of research, and
that comparative-morphological approach would become dominant in the
nineteenth century. Kant and Blumenbach each conceded ground to and
borrowed from the other. Kant had a more sharply defined concept of race,
but Blumenbach gave the concept a wider purchase among scientists. Both
changed their minds and respected evidence; one scholar has called their
key texts "tentative, exploratory, and even equivocal."[51]

Neither ever made the argument that there were "superior" and "inferior" races. Blumenbach, in fact, insisted on the equality of the races and called color "an adventitious and changeable thing." "The least racist and most genial of all Enlightenment thinkers," as the modern American writer Stephen Jay Gould has called him, Blumenbach had a special section of his private library devoted to Black authors and singled out the writing of the enslaved Bostonian poet Phillis Wheatley for special praise. Yet, in the 1795 third edition of *On the Natural Variety of Mankind*, Blumenbach assigned "primeval" quality to the "Caucasian" (a term he coined) and suggested that this race had "that kind of appearance which, according to our opinion of symmetry, we consider the most handsome and becoming."[52] The "we" refers, of course, to white Europeans, and it would be wrong to overlook the tremendous impact in these years that the art history writings of Johannes Joachim Winckelmann had in establishing the whiteness of Greek statues as a yardstick of aesthetic beauty, outer form supposedly reflecting inner quality.[53] That white or light skin was more beautiful became an implicit value judgment even in many, such as Herder and Georg Forster, who were explicit advocates of human equality, just as stereotypes about the "childishness" of Amerindian peoples or the "sensuality" of Blacks nestled within texts that bore a different overt message.

Other Germans went much further, however, in making claims for a hierarchy of races that placed whites explicitly on top. Samuel Thomas Soemmering was a Göttingen-trained anatomist who dissected the bodies of Africans who had died or taken their own lives at Mulang. He compared them with the bodies of orangutans and mandrills he had dissected, and published a work in 1784 *On the Physical Differences of the Moor from the European* in which he claimed that "the conclusion is neither unfair nor unfounded that in general, on average, the African Moor is closer to the apes than the European."[54] He was sharply attacked by Blumenbach, but Soemmering had made his overtly racist argument using tools Blumenbach himself had created. Moreover, Soemmering was quoted in turn by Kant.[55] An even more notorious figure than Soemmering was Christoph Meiners. Another Göttingen professor (he was appointed in the same year that Blumenbach, five years younger, finished his dissertation), Meiners had his modus operandi, piecing together bits and pieces of other scholars' findings and presenting them in popular, oversimplified form but with the seemingly scholarly trappings of arguments and footnotes. His writings on race took evidence about skulls, hair, and skin color, mixed it up together with aesthetic judgments about beauty, and came to triumphantly racist conclusions. That was the case, for example, in his 1790 article "On the Nature of African Negroes (and the Emancipation or Containment of Blacks that Follows from It)," which appeared in a magazine that Meiners coedited.[56] The article argued strongly that Blacks were inferior and undeserving of emancipation, with side arguments about Jews that reached the same conclusion. More pieces followed along the same lines, such as "On the Growth of Hair and Beards Among Ugly and Dark-Skinned People" (1792). Meiners had a following but was held in contempt and strongly criticized by other Göttingen professors, Blumenbach prominent among them.[57]

As the subtitle of Meiners's 1790 article indicates, debates about slavery formed the backdrop to arguments about race. These pan-European debates intensified in the closing decades of the eighteenth century, even as the volume of slaves trafficked across the Atlantic grew. Two broadsides give a sense of how strong German antislavery sentiment could be. The cameralist writer Johann Heinrich Justi delivered a blistering rebuke in 1762. He criticized European greed and lust for land, then continued: "The misery that Europeans caused by such behavior in all three parts of the world cannot be contemplated without causing human nature to tremble. We depopulated the whole of America. . . . We shall soon depopulate Africa as well, without repopulating America."[58] Ten years later, while translating the explorer Louis de Bougainville into English, Johann Reinhold Forster encountered the Frenchman's claim that one saw "sentiments of honour combined with slavery" in the Isle de France. He responded with a furious translator's note: "Slavery endeavours to extirpate and to smother all sentiments of honour, which can only operate in the breast of a really free man; true honour, therefore, and slavery, are in direct opposition, and can be combined as little as fire and water." Bougainville had, thought Forster, been led into error either by the desire to make slavery appear less intolerable or (even worse) been "carried away by the itch to say something extraordinary and paradoxical."[59] Georg Forster was just as fierce in his opposition to slavery; so was his brother-in-law, Matthias Christian Sprengel, whose Göttingen inaugural lecture in 1779 denounced the slave trade.[60] Leading intellectuals were critical of slavery; so were most enlightened, educated Germans who gathered in masonic lodges, reading clubs, or coffeehouses.

The French Revolution then changed everything because it sharpened questions about rights and about who (in Hannah Arendt's later formulation) had "the right to have rights."[61] Did women enjoy the universal "rights of man and citizen" promulgated by the French National Assembly in August 1789? What about Black people? France abolished slavery in 1794 (Napoleon reintroduced it eight years later), although only after it had already been abolished on Saint-Domingue following a successful slave revolt in 1791. Denmark abolished the slave trade in 1792. Britain and the United States followed in 1807, although slavery itself continued in the United States and elsewhere. Slavery became a kind of cynosure of European philosophical, legal, and anthropological debates at this key historical juncture, a focus of many concerns, some of which—concerning gender and sexuality, for example—remained implicit or just below the surface. That was especially true of events in Saint-Domingue, the future Haiti. "The eyes of the world are now on St. Domingo," began an 1804 article in the journal *Minerva*, which had begun reporting on the slave uprising thirteen years earlier and made the names Toussaint-Louverture and Jean-Jacques Dessalines familiar to a German public.[62] Events in Haiti alone gave rise to hundreds of works by German writers, ranging from journalistic commentary and histories to dramas and historical novels, as well as many translations from English and French.[63]

Germans came to debates over slavery from an angle of their own. Consider the drama *The Negro Slaves*, first produced in 1796. Its author was August von Kotzebue, the father of the Baltic German circumnavigator, who was prolific both in children (eighteen) and literary output (forty-four volumes). His play was immediately translated into English, and the translator dedicated it to the leading English abolitionist of the time, in the hope that he would recognize "that the Germans have a just veneration for the name of WILBERFORCE." Kotzebue himself urged playgoers and readers "not to consider his piece merely as a drama. It is intended to represent at one view all the horrible cruelties which are practiced towards our black brethren."[64] On the surface this was a straightforwardly abolitionist work, like other works of literature written by Germans in these years, and a continuation of enlightened ways of thought. And that is certainly true, up to a point. Even the erotic charge delivered by the theme of the sexual attraction of a cruel white slave owner for a Black slave was a familiar enough motif. But two important subtexts are worth noting. One is that Kotzebue, a Baltic German landowner by background, was probably using the theme of slavery in the Caribbean as an indirect means of criticizing harsh forms of personal servitude in Central Europe. This was a common tactic in contemporary German works on slavery, whether set in the Atlantic or the ancient world.[65] The second point is that Kotzebue, like other German writers, was taking aim at a trade that was in the hands of non-Germans.* More than that, his play raises the question, at least tentatively, of whether Germans might not have been kinder, more responsible masters, if they had colonies themselves.[66]

This theme is more fully developed in another contemporary drama, Friedrich Döhner's *The Terrible Consequences of the Rebellion; or, the Negroes.* Döhner's 1792 play has a more transgressive erotic relationship at its center between Marie, the daughter of a French slaveholder, and a noble slave, Omar. They marry, but Omar is executed defending his father against white violence and Marie kills herself. Although the premise of the play is enlightened and cosmopolitan, the resolution is paternalistic. The ideal is represented by a second slaveholder, the kind German Fleri. As Omar says to his fellow slaves, seeking to quell indiscriminate antiwhite sentiment: "It is not the white color that outrages you—our forefathers deemed it at one time the color of the gods—but the harsh, cruel treatment some of them mete out to the likes of us. Not all of them do, to be sure; is there among you a slave of the honest Fleri, the German planter? Not one!"[67]

What happened in Saint-Domingue became a kind of script that allowed Germans to rehearse their own responses to a world in upheaval. Casting off the shackles of slavery even became, by analogy, a way for Germans to dramatize their own resistance to "enslavement" by Napoleon. This attachment to the idea of German victimhood would recur in the twentieth century. In the hands of Hegel, meanwhile, the slave revolt was transmuted into something just as explosive: a tenet of political philosophy that echoed down the next two centuries. It has long been recognized that Hegel's first major work, *The Phenomenology of Spirit,* completed in Jena in 1806 just as Napoleon and his French troops entered the city, was written against the double background of the French Revolution and the new division of labor described by Adam Smith in *The Wealth of Nations*—that it engaged, in other words, with the great political and social issues of the day. The historian Susan Buck-Morss has suggested that the slave revolt in Saint-Domingue inspired Hegel's celebrated passages about "master-slave" relations, in which he set out the relationship between the two and the necessity of slaves' coming to their own awareness of being oppressed.[68] In later works Hegel would exclude Africans from "world history" on Euro-

---

* Although German merchants did not have clean hands (as discussed in chapter 3).

centric grounds ("in this largest part of Africa no real history can take place"), but the process he described in the *Phenomenology* of a class becoming conscious of itself was intellectually revolutionary. It became crucial for the later theories of Karl Marx.[69]

Forms of Knowledge, Places of Knowledge

DIFFICULT, CONVOLUTED, AND WRITTEN AT GREAT SPEED, *The Phenomenology of Spirit* was described by Hegel as his "voyage of discovery."[70] A book that examines the many shapes and forms of human consciousness, it has been interpreted as the origin of theories about everything from the death of God to the end of history. What is not in doubt is the confidence of its claims. The *Phenomenology* addresses the challenges of the "modern world" and traverses a huge range of human experience—social, cultural, historical, political, and religious—in addressing the dilemmas of modern life. The preface contains a ringing declaration: "The spirit of man has broken with the old order of things."[71] Later, there is a key passage where Hegel remarks that the revolution has passed from France to Germany, so that the Germans would complete "in thought" what the French had begun and partly accomplished in practice. The "novel" of the revolution would be completed, as philosophy took over where politics left off.[72] There could hardly be a bolder assertion from one of those famous "writers and thinkers," a direct challenge to those who have argued that the Germans have merely thought what others did. *Merely?* Did ideas themselves not change the world? Hegel was not alone in believing so.

Like many German contemporaries he traced a modern revolution in thought to one source: Immanuel Kant. In 1793, fresh out of the Protestant seminary in Tübingen, Hegel himself had written that "from the Kantian philosophy and its highest completion I expect a revolution in Germany."[73] Two years earlier Johann Gottlieb Fichte—although, like Hegel, a supporter of the French Revolution—called the Kantian revolution "incomparably more important" than what had happened in France. The young Joseph Görres was only slightly more modest: "In the last ten years," he wrote in 1797, "there has occurred in Germany the revolution by which this country has in the realm of theory contributed almost as much to humanity as has France in the realm of practice, I mean our immortal Kant."[74] The comparison became commonplace. The most brilliant (although unfair) variation on the theme came three decades later from the pen of poet and essayist Heinrich Heine, who found points of comparison between Robespierre and Kant. Both, argued Heine, had the same rigid sense of integrity and innate distrust; both were perfectly cast by temperament to be narrow-minded provincial grocers who "weigh out sugar and coffee"; instead, Kant became a "great destroyer in the realm of ideas," who "far exceeded Robespierre in terrorism."[75]

A leading present-day philosopher has described the appearance of Kant's first major work, the 1781 *Critique of Pure Reason*, as a "lightning bolt." It overthrew the old metaphysics and introduced a new term into the vocabulary that modern Europeans used to speak about their lives: self-determination.[76] This concept, *Selbstbestimmung* in the original German, was central to Kant's understanding of the rational individual who chose to be free of external tutelage. Self-determination meant that the individual "constitutes himself through the attainment of knowledge, and thereby becomes self-knowing and capable of emancipation."[77] That is why Kant welcomed the French Revolution as a sign of humanity's ability to emancipate itself. The evidence of this, for him, was to be found not in the political actions of the revolutionaries, but in the fact that their actions kindled sympathy in the hearts and minds of foreign observers, whose disinterested enthusiasm could be understood only as the result of a "moral disposition within the human race," an inner capacity for freedom.[78] Kant therefore emphasized moral autonomy as central to humanity. But self-determination also emphasized the role of the subject in apprehending, or "knowing," the physical world.

There is no easy summary of Kant's achievements. He contributed in important ways to what we would today consider widely different disciplines (philosophy, geography, anthropology, international relations); he addressed fundamental questions (how do we perceive? on what basis do we make judgments?); he argued for the ethical precept that humans should be treated as ends, not means; and he invented the idea of a critical philosophy willing to inquire into its own limits. As his work was absorbed in the course of the 1780s and beyond, contemporaries came to agree with Kant's own view that he had brought about a "Copernican revolution" in philosophy.[79]

Kant died in 1804. His last words were "it is good." Those who followed were engaged in working through his legacy: clarifying, elaborating, challenging. As in Hegel's case, they did so in awareness that a new material and political world was simultaneously in the making. It is impossible to talk about Germany and the birth of the modern world without noting the extraordinary flowering of German philosophy and humanistic learning that occurred in these years alongside German expertise in zoology, botany, and other scientific fields. Consider just the celebrated names. There were the established figures—Herder, Blumenbach, Kant, Fichte—to whom we can add the two dominant literary figures of Goethe and Schiller, who also made scholarly contributions to aesthetic theory, history, and much else besides. Then there was the generation defined by the upheavals of the late eighteenth century, whose members (all born between 1767 and 1775) included Hegel, the philosopher Friedrich Schelling, the theologian Friedrich Schleiermacher, the literary critics and writers August and Friedrich Schlegel, and another pair of brothers, Alexander and Wilhelm von Humboldt. They stand proxy for many others. In the years around 1800, German writers changed the way we think about ethics, religion, history, music, art and aesthetics, work and vocation, and the place of humans in the natural world.

It was working through the implications of Kant's revolution in philosophy that produced this explosion of thought. Philology, the study of language, was central to it all, the key to pathbreaking German achievements in everything from biblical criticism to the study of folklore.[80] If Alexander von Humboldt deciphered the language of nature, Wilhelm deciphered the nature of language.[81] Together with the grammarian Jacob Grimm (of fairy tale fame) and the comparative philologist Franz Bopp, Wilhelm von Humboldt helped to revolutionize language study.[82] This is just one instance of how, in field after field, leadership was passing to Germans. An infallible sign of this was that foreign scholars found they had to learn German, like the innovative United States scholar of Amerindian languages, Daniel Pickering—or, at the very least, announce self-consciously that they were not going to, like the English philologist Richard Porson ("life is too short to learn German").[83] Others began to satirize the fact that German scholarship (like German scholars) now seemed to be everywhere. And scholars from the German lands were everywhere because Central Europe produced more scholars than it could consume.

There was an institutional dimension to this, and its name was the German research university. The rise and rise of the German university is often traced back to the founding of a new institution in Berlin in 1811 (today the Humboldt University); the reality is less dramatic, a more incremental story of growing eminence. It is true that in the eighteenth century there were many torpid universities across the German lands. But there were important exceptions even then. They included the major "new" university of the time, Göttingen, founded in 1737 and quite unbearably self-satisfied within half a century ("drunk with the proud sense of their merits," was one of many similar comments about the faculty by a visiting Prussian education official).[84] But Göttingen had much to be satisfied about, from its star professors and the quality of instruction in seminars to an outstanding library with a modern systematic catalogue. Nor was it the only sign of intellectual life in the late-eighteenth-century university landscape. One scholar has identified an "academic fertile crescent" in northwest Germany that contained Göttingen, Halle (another "new" university), Jena, and Leipzig.[85] Meanwhile, in Berlin, the late 1780s saw a sudden burst of reforms. A new Prussian Ministry for Higher Education was founded and began to recruit professors aggressively. A new (and lasting) university entrance exam also made its appearance in these years: the *Abitur*.[86]

What, then, was new about the university founded in Berlin in 1811? Why did its founding come to be celebrated as a milestone? The answer is partly timing: the university came out of the Prussian reform era, which was the response to crushing defeat by France in 1806. It became a symbol of self-assertion, as encrusted with myth as the myth of "national liberation" on the battlefield.[87] But more than myth was at work. For all the Prussian and Hanoverian antecedents, it was Berlin that exemplified the idea of the modern university. That is to say, it brought together the task of training state officials with other purposes: the advancement of learning, combining research and teaching in one institution, and the pursuit of general education. This was novel. Wilhelm von Humboldt is usually credited with setting down the major principles in a celebrated 1809 memorandum (not published until decades later), so that people refer as a shorthand to the "Humboldtian idea" of the university, although other prominent intellectuals argued for the same ideas.[88] Berlin then became famous even more quickly than Göttingen because of the celebrated professors it hired: Fichte and Schleiermacher, Hegel and Schelling, and later both Grimm brothers. But it was not the only new, or effectively new, institution of higher education in Central Europe. In the early nineteenth century, twenty-two German universities either disappeared, moved, or merged. The post-Napoleonic universities were of much higher quality. That includes some famous names: Leipzig, Marburg, Heidelberg, and Tübingen were all founded, refounded, or reformed.[89] Berlin may have been the object of special admiration abroad, but the German university system that became a global model in the nineteenth century was a competitive, decentered system. Foreign students flocked to Göttingen, Heidelberg, and Leipzig as well as Berlin.

It was in German-speaking Europe during the decades on either side of 1800 that new educational patterns were also set down for learners in a different age group: children. For if the English invented childhood as a consumer category in the eighteenth century, and Jean-Jacques Rousseau's *Émile* (1762) was the first modern treatise on childhood education, it was Germans and Swiss-Germans who gave institutional shape to the new pedagogy. They did so in both words and physical spaces. Christian Felix Weisse, for example, was one of the founders of German children's literature and publisher of *The Children's Friend*, which appeared between 1775 and 1782, the first magazine of its kind. His writing for children overlapped with that of someone we have already met, the Humboldts' tutor and French Revolution enthusiast Joachim Heinrich Campe. The author of pioneering children's fiction and travel books, he also founded a successful schoolbook publishing house and wrote on educational theory.[90] Campe taught for a year at the Philanthropinum, a progressive school established in Dessau by the reformist pedagogue Johann Bernhard Basedow, leaving after he fell out with some younger teachers.[91] Basedow was one of those "friends of humanity" who find it hard to get on with people. He resigned as director of the Philanthropinum in 1778 and the institution hardly outlasted his own lifetime. Christian Gotthilf Salzmann's Schnepfenthal School near Gotha was more successful. Like Basedow, Salzmann drew inspiration from Rousseau and was influential in turn beyond Germany. One of his books was translated into English by the feminist Mary Wollstonecraft.

Johann Heinrich Pestalozzi, a Zurich pedagogue and reformer, had an even greater impact. Born in the same year as Campe (1746), Pestalozzi owed more to Romanticism than did the German reformers, but like them he emphasized the need to develop the child's imagination. All agreed, too, that physical exercise and crafts were important. Basedow and Salzmann would not have quarreled with Pestalozzi's motto: "Learning by head, heart and hand." This was the rich soil of pedagogical reform in which perhaps the most influential of all German educational models was rooted. One of Pestalozzi's students was Friedrich Fröbel, the son of a Thuringian pastor.

Fröbel taught at the Pestalozzi school at Frankfurt in 1805, wrote works on childhood education, and opened a series of educational institutions in Germany and Switzerland. They included a "play and activity center" for preschool children in Bad Blankenburg, which Fröbel later renamed a "Kindergarten." The outcrop of a remarkable Swiss-German axis of pedagogical reform in the late eighteenth century, the Kindergarten had its origins in Thuringia in the years after 1816 and achieved a global impact in the century that followed.

The Kindergarten and the new university, products of the same era, sat awkwardly with the new age of state building—and with the imperatives of commerce. The Kindergarten was denounced for its supposedly atheistic tendencies; universities, at least before 1848, were centers of political opposition. Both were concerned with knowledge, and one idea they had in common was the value they placed on the interior self—the development of the child in one case, adult self-cultivation, or *Bildung*, in the other. In fact, an important part of how scholars came to understand what they were doing in the post-Humboldt era was the emphasis (it came from Romanticism) placed on the inner qualities of the scholar rather than the external markers of material success that were prized at the "academic factory" of Göttingen, that "great merchant house of scholarship."[92] Kindergarten and Humboldtian university alike point to a particular form of knowledge that commanded growing attention in these years—knowledge acquired, not by travel, examining the natural world, or scrutinizing a text, but by looking inside the self. Germans were not alone in this pursuit, but they played a particularly important role in providing a conceptual vocabulary with which to think about selfhood and subjectivity.

The idea of the self was not invented in the late eighteenth century, but it reached a new level of interest then. Among many indicators of this is a sharp increase in forms of self-presentation like letter writing, diaries, and autobiographies. Germans were a part of this, but hardly leaders—the British were the great diarists, and Jean-Jacques Rousseau's *Confessions* had a much wider impact than any German autobiography of the time.[93] While there were also German works that aimed "to depict the inner history of a person," as Karl Philipp Moritz said of his autobiographical novel *Anton Reiser*, there was only one that had a major impact: Goethe's epistolary novel about the interior emotional life of its protagonist, *The Sorrows of Young Werther* (1774), a wild success that made its youthful author a celebrity and incited "Werther fever" across Europe.[94] This outlier aside, there were three areas where Germans contributed influentially to ways of thinking about the inner self. The first was "physiognomy," an observational technique that (supposedly) allowed inner emotions to be read off from outward appearance. It was closely associated in the late eighteenth century with the Zurich-born poet and mystic Johann Kaspar Lavater, although there were German forerunners. Lavater called physiognomy a method for the "advancement of knowledge of human nature" and laid out the techniques necessary to master this "science of the signs of the passions" in his four-volume *Physiognomic Fragments*. There was much that was dubious and faddish about this, but a physiognomical mania spread to England and France as well as Germany in the 1770s and '80s and physiognomy remained influential well into the nineteenth century as an attempt to penetrate and understand human character.[95]

Physiognomy was one strand within a larger, often messy process: the emerging science of psychology at the end of the eighteenth century and the beginning of the nineteenth. This was the second area in which Germans made a major contribution to thinking about the self. One distinctively German strand in the making of psychology came from the Pietist tradition of examining the conscience, or soul, through methods such as the interpretation of dreams.[96] Karl Philipp Moritz, the author of *Anton Reiser*, was the key link in the chain. Born in a poor Pietist family, Moritz escaped an apprenticeship to a brutal hatmaker to acquire an education and become an academic teacher, writer, and freemason, a classic Enlightenment figure. His interest in psychology drew on his social experience and Pietist background. Moritz edited the widely read *Magazin zur Erfahrungsseelenkunde*, a term translated by dictionaries today as "empirical psychology" or "experiential psychology," but better captured by an awkward but accurate phrase like "science of the experience of the soul." The magazine, which ran from 1783 to 1793, dealt in individual "cases" and was concerned with a spectrum of emotions and actions: madness, what it meant to be born deaf or dumb, premonitions of death, and histories of individual suicides and infanticides. Dreams were an important source; sometimes the magazine read like a secularized version of the Pietist interpretation of dreams. Moritz has been called the "initiator of clinical psychological journalism in Germany" and his magazine opened the way for others published in the 1790s.[97]

Moritz inhabited a gray zone between journalism and popular philosophy. The academic philosophers also created new ways of understanding the self in these years. This was the third distinctively German contribution to thinking about the self. Friedrich Schelling was the most important figure when it came to psychology. His interest in subjectivity led him to pursue the psyche and invent a new vocabulary for talking about it, in the course of which he coined the term "unconscious." In the long run, Schelling's approach, including his discussion of how individuals remember (and forget) the past, would be taken up by Sigmund Freud and his followers.[98] In the shorter term, Schelling's ideas passed quickly across the Channel, thanks to Samuel Taylor Coleridge, who traveled to Germany with his fellow poet William Wordsworth in 1798, stayed there to study (in Göttingen he listened to Blumenbach's lectures), and filled his head with German Idealist philosophy.[99] Back home, Coleridge put his newfound knowledge to use, introducing German philosophical and literary thought into England, often without attribution. His introduction of Schelling's "unconscious" into English is one example among many.

In the decades on either side of 1800, Germans took a leading role in recasting knowledge. That meant knowledge of both the world and the individual—"the starry heavens above me and the moral law within me," to quote Kant's own words. Kant led the way in tackling fundamental questions of subjectivity and selfhood philosophically, and the younger generation worked through his legacy. The self was, in one sense, everywhere in Kant—"thinking the self," "self-education," "self-determination," "self-realization." This was the agenda of the Enlightenment, pointedly expressed. The thinking being came first and it was, Kant believed, necessary and useful to observe our own mental powers. But he was suspicious of efforts to "eavesdrop on ourselves," as he called it, and warned against "occupying ourselves with spying out the involuntary course of our thoughts and feelings."[100] Fichte, for whom the first-person singular was never far away, disagreed. Schelling also took a different view. Both were typical of the Romantics, who turned eavesdropping on themselves into a way of life. We can call this the cultivation of "inwardness." We can also see it, for better or worse, as a foundational moment in modern notions of selfhood and authenticity.

CHAPTER 6

WORLD LITERATURE

Encounters

F THERE WAS A REVOLUTION IN LEARNING THAT CAME OUT OF THE German lands in these years, there was also a literary revolution that spanned the era from the Sturm und Drang writers of the 1770s to the early nineteenth century. In fact, there were two. One usually goes by the name Weimar classicism, after the small town where a remarkable quartet of writers, led by Goethe, created an influential model of what literature should be. The other was Romanticism. Both movements cast a spell beyond Germany. During those same decades, German readers also absorbed an unprecedented number of works in translation. This was the era when the professional translator first appeared.[1] It was also when the growth in literary traffic gave rise to a new idea, for which Goethe had a name: world literature.

Weimar was a town of six thousand people in 1800, the capital of the Duchy of Saxe-Weimar-Eisenach. The Reformation painter Lucas Cranach had lived there briefly, and Bach served even more briefly as court musician, but Weimar was otherwise remarkably free of cultural associations when the ambitious Duchess Anna Amalia began to gather writers at her court. Christoph Martin Wieland was hired in 1772 to serve as tutor to the crown prince, the classic occupation of the late-eighteenth-century man of letters. Goethe came three years later, fresh from the European success of *The Sorrows of Young Werther*. He recommended another polymath, Johann Gottfried Herder, who arrived in Weimar to become general superintendent of churches and oversee the school system in 1776. These central figures at the so-called Muses' Court were joined in 1787 by the young Friedrich Schiller, whose play *The Robbers* had been a sensation five years earlier. Together, these luminaries turned Weimar into "Athens on the Ilm." Their achievements were partly individual. Wieland was a major poet who founded and edited Germany's leading literary journal, *Der Teutsche Merkur*, Herder the author of important works on history and aesthetics whose collections of folk poetry were hugely influential, Schiller a poet as well as the leading playwright of his time, Goethe the writer who could turn his hand to anything. Wieland has been credited with writing the first *Bildungsroman*, or coming-of-age novel, with his work *The History of Agathon* (1766–67), before Goethe's vastly more influential *Wilhelm Meister's Apprenticeship* (1795–96) became the model for the genre across Europe.[2] There were collaborative ventures, too, although not without friction. Wieland was vain, Herder a depressive hypochondriac, Goethe effortlessly superior. Schiller arrived during Goethe's absence in Italy; then he was snubbed by the older man. It took six years before they established their fruitful partnership at the Weimar court theater, in the journal *Die Horen*, and in works like the *Xenien*.

Weimar's golden age ended in the early nineteenth century. Herder died in 1803, Schiller in 1805, Wieland in 1813. Goethe lived on until 1832. Weimar classicism was both the sum of the works that came out of it and an idea. The underlying aesthetic aspiration was to create a harmonious synthesis between the emotionally charged sensibility of the Sturm und Drang movement (to which Goethe and Schiller had both belonged) and the values of the Enlightenment. Weimar exported its texts and its philosophical ideas globally. It also created myths about itself, especially in Goethe's final years, when Weimar became a place of literary pilgrimage for visitors from Britain, France, and America as well as Germany.[3]

Romanticism represented a different kind of literary revolution. Romantic writers preferred the darkly mysterious to the enlightened and went with the heart rather than the head. Above all, they valued feeling and the inner emotions of the individual. Romantic writers were not alone, of course, in this preoccupation with the self. The "I" was everywhere in German writing during these years, as we have seen, not least in the new kind of travel writing. The first paragraph of Alexander von Humboldt's *Journey to the Equinoctial Regions* contains fourteen instances of "I," "my," and "mine."[4] And what else is *Wilhelm Meister's Apprenticeship* than a novel about a young man's personal progress through the world? At first glance, contemporary Romantic works of fiction share the same characteristics.

Jean Paul's *Siebenkäs* (1796–97), Ludwig Tieck's *Franz Sternbalds Wan-*
derungen (1798), Friedrich Schlegel's *Lucinde* (1799), Novalis's *Heinrich von*
Ofterdingen (1802)—all are autobiographical novels whose protagonists are
constantly on the move. But they are also very different in texture and
subject matter from Humboldt, or Goethe. They have a more dreamlike
quality and thinly realized social settings, and they devote more space to
discussing the nature of art and creativity. The real journey in these books
is the journey inward, to the self. In the words of Novalis (the pen name
of Friedrich von Hardenberg), "The most mysterious path leads inward."⁵
His friend Friedrich Schlegel, dismissing the minute social observation in
English novels, claimed that "the best part of the best novels is nothing
other than the more or less concealed self-awareness of the author."⁶

These were textbook expressions of the Romantic sensibility, on perfect
display in the circle that gathered in Jena between 1797 and 1804. Its members included Friedrich Schlegel and his wife Dorothea, August Schlegel
and his wife Caroline, Schelling (who later married Caroline Schlegel),
Johann Gottlieb Fichte, Novalis, and Ludwig Tieck. It was an intellectually glittering group, overwhelmingly youthful (Fichte was the exception),
and self-conscious about forming a cultural avant-garde.⁷ Its collective voice
was the journal *Athenaeum*, edited by the Schlegel brothers, which was the
most important expression of early Romanticism while it lasted—although
its run was just six issues between 1798 and 1800. When the Jena circle
broke up soon afterward, its members scattered across Europe. That was
the context of a letter written by Jean Paul in 1805 and addressed, magnifi-
cently, to "Ludwig Tieck in space and time."⁸

As the members of the circle dispersed, their ideas went with them.
Sometimes we can even track their movements. One important intermediary was Germaine de Staël, the daughter of Louis XVI's Swiss finance
minister Jacques Necker, who did more than anyone else to spread the idea
of Germany as the land of "writers and thinkers." While Napoleon was
in power in France she used the family home in Coppet, on the shores of
Lake Geneva, as a base from which she traveled extensively in Germany,
Italy, England, Scandinavia, and Russia. In Berlin she met August Schlegel, who became the tutor of her children, a frequent traveling companion, and a guest at Coppet. Together with the writers she met on visits
to Weimar and other cultural pilgrimage sites, they helped to shaped her
view of Germany and what she termed its "intellectual riches amidst the
ravages of war," views that were set out in her 1813 book *De l'Allemagne*.

The book had a mixed reception. Madame de Staël's German was not very good, her thumbnail sketches often smacked of the quick survey, she scattered the word "genius" around rather freely (eight times in seven pages on Goethe), and her central distinction between the literatures of "North" and "South" (which drew heavily on ideas about the influence of climate) was more bold than nuanced. Schlegel felt that she underplayed German medievalism, which was important to the Romantics. But these shortcomings were beside the point. The German writers who talked with de Staël believed that she would become a herald for their culture, and so it proved. *De l'Allemagne* and its translations helped to foster appreciation for German culture in France, Britain, and elsewhere.[9]

Samuel Taylor Coleridge was also a key cultural broker. We have already seen how he introduced Schelling's idea of the unconscious to the English, but he did much more than that. Coleridge encountered German writing early and was bowled over. As an undergraduate at Cambridge, he devoured an English translation of *The Robbers* with "chill and trembling" into the early hours of the morning, then wrote to his friend Robert Southey: *"Who is this Schiller? This convulser of the heart?"*[10] That was in 1792. Eight years later, after his year of study in Göttingen, Coleridge would himself translate another of Schiller's plays, *Wallenstein*. Coleridge did not encounter German ideas only in England and Germany. He first met Ludwig Tieck in Italy, at the house Wilhelm von Humboldt was renting in Rome. Tieck and Coleridge, contemporaries who shared a passion for folk diction and Shakespeare, struck up a close friendship.[11] Coleridge translated other German literary works and worked many ideas of the German Romantics into his *Biographia Literaria* (1817).[12] He was a central figure in the British reception of German culture that began in the Romantic period with Shelley, Byron, Thomas Carlyle, and Walter Scott and continued through the nineteenth century.[13] In the 1820s alone, Thomas Carlyle managed to translate *Wilhelm Meister's Apprenticeship* and other works by Goethe, Tieck, Jean Paul, and E. T. A. Hoffmann, as well as publish critical essays on the major German writers and a biography of Schiller. A few years on, and we find Emily Brontë sitting at the kitchen table in the Haworth parsonage teaching herself German so that she could read works in the original—although the line that runs "from Werther to Wuthering Heights" remains speculative.[14]

We can therefore follow how German literature and the claims of German culture spread from Lake Geneva to the Yorkshire Dales. It did so through the efforts of intermediaries like de Staël and Coleridge, and thanks to translators such as Carlyle and the French-Swiss writer Benjamin Constant, a member of de Stael's Coppet circle, as well as individuals who are no longer known for their own writings and are remembered (if at all) only as translators. Others carried the German literary revolution to Scandinavia.[15]

This kind of cultural transfer and appropriation went in both directions. Tieck and Coleridge shared a passion for Shakespeare, but Tieck was not just an admirer. In 1789 he and August Schlegel began to translate the Bard's works, creating what became the standard German version, the one that established Shakespeare as an essentially German writer who just happened to be English—"*ganz unser*," entirely ours, as Schlegel called him. (The most famous of Hamlet's soliloquies sounds distinctly Hegelian in German: *Sein oder nicht sein, das ist hier die Frage.*) Miguel de Cervantes's *Don Quixote* also received its fullest German translation near the end of the eighteenth century, in a 1777 version by Friedrich Justin Bertuch, the magazine publisher who also lived in Weimar.[16] Both writers were admired for their broad humanity and rich, natural, everyday vocabulary, a language and an emotional register completely different from the refined, formalized style of French literature. This made Shakespeare and Cervantes attractive to Germans reacting against the tyranny of French taste.

Since the 1760s, Herder and others had insisted that folk language was the "mirror of the people." This search for an "authentic" popular culture took different forms. One example is the "shadow-play" performed by cutout puppets, a popular entertainment that reached Germany from the Ottoman Empire via Italy, then in the late eighteenth century moved out of the market square into the drawing rooms of the educated, taken up by Romantic writers like Christian Brentano and Ludwig Tieck.[17] The pursuit of an elusive popular culture reached its culmination at the beginning of the nineteenth century in the compilations of the Heidelberg Romantics Achim von Arnim and Clemens Brentano, Christian's brother, who brought together folk poetry, songs, and tales in *Des Knaben Wunderhorn*, and most famously in the tales of murder, mutilation, infanticide, and incest collected (and sanitized) by the Brothers Grimm.[18]

German writers and intellectuals were animated by a truly pan-European mania for the real or imagined literature of the "people." The best-known instance is the cycle of epic poems supposedly narrated by Gaelic bard Ossian and edited (although in fact authored) by the Scottish poet James Macpherson. Received with enthusiasm by Thomas Jefferson and by educated publics across Europe, Ossian found translators and many admirers in Germany—Goethe, Schiller, Jean Paul, Novalis. Friedrich Gottlieb Klopstock even argued that Ossian was of German origin. The Romantic writer Wilhelm Heinse, a skeptic, noted sourly that "what we wish, we easily believe," but only a minority (it included August Schlegel) shared his view that the poems were a sentimental fabrication.[19] Devotees regarded Ossian as the "Homer of the North," their enthusiasm just the most spectacular expression of a larger Nordic turn at the end of the eighteenth century that created a fashion for Icelandic, Lapp, and other Scandinavian literatures.[20]

German writers sometimes made foreign genres their own, adapting them to their own purposes. There is no more striking example than Daniel Defoe's famous novel *The Life and Strange Surprizing Adventures of Robinson Crusoe of York, Mariner*, published in 1719. It is worth noting that the English original was itself a hybrid, owing something to German sources.[21] But it is what happened in the decades after the novel was published that is really remarkable. The story of the solitary man on his island became fashionable and inspired imitations across Europe. By 1800 there had been 9 published in English, 10 in Dutch, 6 in French, and 128 in German.[22] What are we to make of this cornucopia? In the first place, it allowed for German regional identities to assert themselves. Soon there was a Saxon Robinson, then a Silesian Robinson, and so on through the Thuringian, East Frisian, and many others.[23] But we are also dealing with a particular instance of the larger German tendency to devour works on travel. By 1800 Germans were the leading consumers of the genre in Europe. The output of travel books quintupled in the three decades before the turn of the century.[24] There was surely an element of compensation or wish fulfillment at work here, as there was in the plethora of German Robinsons, which allowed non-seafaring Central Europeans to imagine themselves into the ocean world that the English, Dutch, and French took for granted. Young Adam Henss, the son of a lowly groom in Mainz, later traveled all across Europe and made *Wanderungen* the key word in the title of his autobiography. But his first journeys were made in the imagination. He sailed the Atlantic with Columbus, he was with Cortés in Mexico, and of course he "lived with Robinson on his island."[25]

Two of these "Robinsonades," in particular, suggest other ways in which Germans took the original and put it to their own uses. That, after all, is how literary reception works—as Novalis put it, in a hardheaded moment, "the transformation of the foreign into one's own, appropriation, is the never-ending business of the mind."[26] The first is a 1731 novel by Johann Gottfried Schnabel that has come to be known by its abridged title, *Felsenburg Island*. The book tells how, following a shipwreck in the South Atlantic, two men who represent corrupt old Europe die as a result of their violence, leaving virtuous Albertus Julius and Concordia to marry and found a just, fruitful, and god-fearing society. Their island is part Eden, part Utopia: a "green Utopia."[27] The other especially interesting adaptation is Joachim Heinrich Campe's *Robinson the Younger*, written for children. It appeared in 1779–80, when the cult of Goethe's Young Werther was at its peak, and aimed to be a corrective to "unhealthy" emotion. Narrated by a father to his children, it is didactic, emphasizing good sense and practicality. But Campe has "green" elements, too. One message of his Robinson is that Europeans must learn about the flora and fauna of their island. In his book, unlike Defoe's original, Robinson has no access to tools from the start: he must make do, adapting to his surroundings. There are echoes here of German naturalists from Georg Forster to Adalbert von Chamisso. The same is true of Robinson's relationship with "Friday." In Campe's telling, this is close and filled with mutual affection. "Freitag" eventually returns with Robinson to Hamburg, learns a craft, and the two men remain lifelong friends. There is nonetheless an element of European paternalism in all this, and also something specifically German. Campe presents us with the ideal of the "kindly German," the colonist sensitive to his environment who treats non-Europeans well. It is the same theme that we saw in the contemporary dramas of August von Kotzebue and Friedrich Döhner.[28]

The nineteenth-century French historian Jules Michelet compared the miracle of German creativity in the years on either side of 1800 to water pouring out of rock or sterile sand, the outcrop of a powerful underground stream.[29] There is insight in his metaphor, but it is important to add that the underground stream was fed from many sources. In an age when German literature flowered as never before or since, it was also never more open to multiple influences spread across time and space. There was enthusiasm for Ossian and the Norse Edda, for the shadow-play and the mystique of Robinson Crusoe's island, but these coexisted alongside other intellectual enthusiasms. The most obvious was a powerfully renewed engagement with the culture of the ancient world, especially Greece, once described rather floridly as the "tyranny of Greece over Germany."[30] Greek art became a measure of beauty and proportion. But Greek literature from the sunny south also met with acclaim in Germany for the same reason that Scandinavian literature from the icy north did—because it spoke, supposedly, with the voice of "the people." That was what, in the eyes of Germans who had read their Herder, Homer, and Icelandic sagas had in common.[31] Nor did the newfound German kinship with Shakespeare and Cervantes preclude appreciation for the literature of Enlightenment France. Goethe staged Voltaire's dramas *Mahomet* and *Tancrede* in Weimar, and in 1805 translated the cleverest, most "modern" fictional product of the French Enlightenment, *Rameau's Nephew* by Denis Diderot, having heard about the work from his friend Schiller, who had heard about it from a Russian.[32] Translators, most of them much less famous than Goethe, were decisively important in this era. Their work underscores what American poet and translator Ezra Pound said a century later: "A great age of literature is perhaps always a great age of translation; or follows it."[33]

"Oriental Renaissance"

THIS WAS NOWHERE MORE OBVIOUS THAN IN THE IMPACT OF MIDdle Eastern, Arabic, and South Asian literature in Germany around 1800. Friedrich Schlegel called it an "Oriental renaissance."[34] Sanskrit literature came into special vogue in Germany in these years. Take the case of the Romantic writer E. T. A. Hoffmann, author of The "Tales" of Hoffmann and the original novella of *The Nutcracker*. Obsessed, like many Romantics, by music as the ultimately "deep," mysterious, and ineffable art form, he came up with a literary comparison. Music was, he decided, "Sanskrit . . . translated into sound!"[35] The Romantic poet Karoline von Günderode paid the language an even greater and no less melodramatic compliment. Deserted by her lover, she took her own life on the banks of the Rhine and left a suicide note in Sanskrit.[36] Most Germans came by Sanskrit literature in translation, and the translations came sometimes from the French but above all from the British. It was via a group of scholars working under the aegis of the East India Company that knowledge of Sanskrit and its literature reached Europe; one such translator was William Jones—widely referred to as "Oriental Jones," dubbed by an admiring Goethe "the incomparable Jones."[37]

The British role as go-betweens is nicely illustrated by the case of Friedrich Schlegel, who learned Sanskrit in Paris. He was taught by another of the East India Company linguists, a naval officer stranded in Paris when war resumed in 1802 and put to work by the French cataloguing Sanskrit manuscripts. The officer's name was Alexander Hamilton and he was first cousin to the American founding father of the same name.[38] Schlegel was smitten as he learned the language. "Everything, everything, without exception, has its origins in India," he wrote to Tieck.[39] In 1808 he published a key text of the German Oriental renaissance, *On the Language and Wisdom of the Indians*. It was an important book, for better and worse. Schlegel's starting point was William Jones's descriptions of the similarities between Sanskrit, ancient Greek and Latin, and most modern European languages. In developing the insight of Jones and others, Schlegel looked closely at the structural similarities of the languages, not just the similarities of individual words, and in doing so made a fundamental contribution to linguistics. Schlegel's methods, in turn, inspired the German scholar Franz Bopp to learn Sanskrit and then to develop the morphological principles that provide the foundation of comparative linguistics. The problem is that Schlegel's "Indian" account of German linguistic and religious origins had an anti-Hebraic element that provided the basis of the crudely racist "Aryan" theory in the late nineteenth century.[40]

One Sanskrit text above all others captured the imagination of German readers: the drama *Sakuntala*, written by the classical Sanskrit writer Kālidāsa who lived in the fourth and fifth centuries CE.[41] It was translated by William Jones, first into Latin (which he considered closer to the Sanskrit original), then into English, and published in Calcutta in 1789, the following year in London. A German translation from the English followed immediately. It was done by none other than Georg Forster, appeared in May 1791, and set off a wave of enthusiasm.[42] The "Indian Shakespeare" had followers everywhere in Europe, but the German reception was especially rapturous. Forster's translation inaugurated the "Sakuntala era."[43] "Do you want heaven and earth comprehended in a single name?" asked Goethe. "I name you, *Sakuntala*, and thus all is said."[44]

Herder and Schlegel were entranced, seeing in the drama an image of innocence, sacred wisdom and wholeness. We can follow its influence in the case of Novalis. Even before he met Schlegel and became a part of the Jena circle, we find Novalis referring to his youthful fiancée, Sophie von Kühn, as "Sakuntala." That was in 1795. His novel *Heinrich von Ofterdingen* was unfinished when Novalis died of tuberculosis in 1801, but his notes for the unwritten part use "Sakuntala" as a shorthand for the achievement of harmony through poetry at the end of the quest for self-realization and a new golden age. Novalis also borrows from the Sanskrit drama the most famous image in the book, and a central image of German Romanticism as a whole: the blue flower.[45]

In his classic account of "Orientalism," Edward Said focused attention on Britain and France, whose intellectual and literary engagement with India, Persia, and the Ottoman Empire was inseparable from the assertion of economic and political power over those areas.[46] There, Orientalism could not be innocent, no matter how much William Jones might have won the confidence of local *pandits*. The German case was more complicated, for Germans stood off to the side of colonial enterprises, except where they served the empires of others, as scientists or soldiers. One of the latter was Karl Schlegel, older brother of Friedrich and August, a British East India Company soldier who died in Madras in 1789 while the world's attention was elsewhere, a death that some have argued shaped his brothers' fascination with India.[47] German outsider status, as we have seen in other contexts, often produced a tone of self-righteousness. This carried over into the literary realm. When Herder wrote the preface to a new edition of Forster's translation of *Sakuntala* in 1803, he combined literary criticism with anti-colonial critique: "English rhyme schemes suit Indian poetry as searing-hot water acts on the sweet blooms of the [mango tree], which singe and destroy them (as the English do the Hindus themselves)." He lamented that "this cultural and spiritual treasure of the most peace-loving nations of our earth" had been consigned to "the most commerce-driven nation of the globe."[48]

Herder may have been right, but his claim was also self-serving because it bolstered the view that Germans were more sensitive to other cultures than the arrogant French or the moneygrubbing British. It was precisely in the years on either side of 1800 that such a view took shape. Novalis, for example, in his book *Christianity or Europe*, published in 1799, looked forward to the time in the near future when the (malign) effects of the first Reformation would be reversed by a second, in which Germany would once again lead the way. "In Germany," he wrote, "one can with certainty already point out traces of a new world. Germany is taking a slow but steady path ahead of the other European countries. While the others are busy with war, speculation, and partisan spirit, the German is diligently educating himself to take part in a higher cultural epoch, and this advance must give him a superiority over the others in course of time."[49] This self-satisfied view of things was helped on its way by non-German commentators. It was Michelet, once again, following in the footsteps of Germaine de Staël and her land of "writers and thinkers," who described Germany as the "India of Europe," the western country that had most successfully preserved a child-like innocence and simplicity.[50]

How, then, did German writers use the literature of India, Persia, and the Ottoman world in their own writing? Sometimes it served as exotic garnish, but often it was more than that. Any encounter with another literature will leave traces that betray a range of possibilities—quotation, selective borrowing, appropriation, reworking. *Heinrich von Ofterdingen*, for example, has an increasingly magical, fairy-tale structure populated by characters like the Arab girl Zulima, a Persian princess, the female guide Cyane, a Greek lyre player, and the mysterious Ginnistan, whose name clearly derives from the Jinn, or genie.[51] That makes it sound like a well-stocked toy shop of Orientalist clichés. But these served Novalis's purpose. He was looking for a literary form that would represent searching for "the great Orient within us," as he put it, meaning religion. The Grail narrative became one means of doing that; the conventions of Indian, Persian, and Arabic literature provided others. As many writers have pointed out, Orientalism can take more than one form, including a genuine openness and respect for another culture, where "knowledge as understanding can also lead to appreciation, dialogue, self-critique, perspectival orientation, and personal and cultural enrichment."[52]

Perhaps the best example of openness and respect is the *West-Eastern Divan*, the collection (or "divan") of lyric poems composed by Goethe between 1814 and 1819. The poems draw on both verse structure and imagery of Arabic and Persian poetry, while incorporating rhythms from the indigenous popular forms that had found their way into German (as into other European) verse since the late eighteenth century—ballads, tales, lullabies, and serenades.[53] Goethe had studied Arabic, enough to write some poems in Arabic script; he had also studied the Qur'an closely. The immediate stimulus for the *West-Eastern Divan* was the work of the fourteenth-century Persian poet Hāfez, translated in 1812–13 by the Viennese Orientalist Joseph von Hammer-Purgstall, founder of a journal called *Treasure Troves of the Orient* that published articles on poetry, history, and travel.[54] Almost everyone recognized that his translation was poor, but it nonetheless inspired Goethe to try to write in the style of someone he called his "twin spirit."[55] There were parallels. Hāfez lived in Shīrāz after Tamerlane's invasion,

Goethe in Napoleonic Germany. In one sequence of the collection, "The Book of Displeasure," Goethe follows Hāfez with bitter observations on the politics of the time. Mostly, though, the poetry celebrates the sensual pleasures of life: roses and nightingales, wine and women. The format of the *West-Eastern Divan* allows Goethe to inhabit a different persona, or series of personas, while the content of the verse provides a counterimage of playfulness and erotic desire to set against what Goethe viewed as stifling Christian morality. The West-Eastern Divan Orchestra is the name Edward Said and the pianist and conductor Daniel Barenboim decided on when, in 1999, they had the idea of creating a musical ensemble that would bring together young Arab and Israeli musicians. The seriousness with which Goethe performed his act of identification with Persian and Arabic literary forms, and his demonstration of the power of poetry to create the possibility of an alternative identity—these are what made Said a devotee of the work. In conversation with Barenboim, Said lavished praise on "this extraordinary set of poems about the 'other' really, *West-östlicher Divan* (*The West-Eastern Divan*), which is, I think, unique in the history of European culture." Why? Because Goethe was concerned not with affirming his own identity (Said was skeptical of "identity" and the "need for roots"), but with the "articulation of other selves."[56]

Cosmopolitanism and Nation

GOETHE WAS A CELEBRATED POLYMATH, AT ONCE POET, DRA-matist, novelist, critic, theater director, statesman, inspector of mines, color theorist, and botanist. His literary interests alone were all-embracing. A Grecophile before he was an Indophile, Goethe followed the literatures of Italy, Spain, Russia, and the Americas as well as Britain and France. When visitors from abroad paid him a visit, as hundreds did, he always had questions about the literature of their home countries; and the catalogue of his private library in Weimar includes the titles of literary works in twenty languages, some in the original, others in translation.[57] There is no record of any book translated from Chinese, but there must have been such works in the Grand Ducal Library because in a documented conversations with Johann Peter Eckermann, his longtime assistant, on January 31, 1827, Goethe remarked that he was reading a "Chinese novel." This was the occasion when he said to Eckermann: "National literature is now a rather meaningless term; the epoch of world literature is at hand, and everyone must strive to hasten its approach."[58] Later the same year Goethe used the term in print. Writing in the journal *On Art and Antiquity* about discussions of his work in France, he cited a review of his drama *Torquato Tasso* in a Parisian newspaper and commented that he was "convinced a universal world literature is in the process of being constituted, in which an honorable role is reserved for us Germans."[59]

*A part of Johann Wolfgang von Goethe's
library in Weimar.*

World literature—*Weltliteratur*! It is a resonant term that has had a long afterlife and meant many different things to different people. It formed the basis for the study of comparative literature when this emerged as a discipline later in the nineteenth century (just as Friedrich Schlegel's research helped to pave the way for comparative linguistics). In the United States, it often became the rather fuzzy justification for undergraduate "great books" courses, much to the distress of those who were serious about comparative literature. Then, starting in the closing decades of the twentieth century, lively discussions took place about world literature as a literature of exile and displacement, while others floated alternative terms that might signal something more inclusive (global lit, transnational literary studies, comparative postcolonial and diaspora studies).[60] Like many of the concepts and ideas that came out of Germany in the years between 1780 and 1830, world literature is still worth arguing about.

The term was invoked just twenty years after Goethe used it by Karl Marx and Friedrich Engels in *The Communist Manifesto*, where they proclaimed: "National one-sidedness and narrow-mindedness become more and more impossible, and from the many national and local literatures, a world literature arises."[61] It was not too much of a stretch to link the term, as Marx and Engels did, to the development of markets. After all, many of Goethe's contemporaries did so. Fichte talked about "workshops of culture" and the theologian Friedrich Schleiermacher believed that global markets went hand in hand with cultural exchange, "for the ideal communication necessary for progress cannot be separated from material communication."[62] Goethe himself did the same on many different occasions when he talked about "world literature."[63] He used words like "products," "traffic," and "trade"; he talked about the "commerce of ideas among people" and a "universal world market of exchange." Translators, he once said, performed "one of the most essential tasks and one of the worthiest of esteem in the universal market of world trade."[64]

"World literature" therefore pointed in two different directions. It was cosmopolitan (against "narrow-mindedness"), but it was also competitive (the "market of world trade"). The two meanings were in tension with each other, and both can be found in Goethe. They can be found earlier, as well, for the term "world literature" actually predated Goethe by several decades and was closely tied to translation. Ludwig Schlözer, a professor at Göttingen, used the word when writing in 1773 about Icelandic literature for German readers.[65] Another academic, the poet and critic Christoph Martin

Wieland, used the term around the same time, in a letter of dedication to Duke Carl August of Saxony that enclosed his translation of Horace's letters. The urbanity of Rome, he wrote, had been marked by "this fine tincture of knowledge of the world and world literature."[66] Wieland did more than use the term in passing: as a prolific early translator of Shakespeare and of classical writers, and as editor of *Der Teutsche Merkur*, he made foreign literatures familiar to German readers on a huge scale. In its thirty-eight-year run, the *Merkur* reviewed works in French, English, Spanish, Italian, Portuguese, Swedish, Hungarian, Turkish, Arabic, and Chinese.[67] "World literature," in this sense, meant making the literatures of the world available through reviews and translations, whether ancient or modern, Shakespeare or Sakuntala. Foreign literatures and cultures deserved to be known because they were authentic mirrors of the peoples who created them—that was the influential argument of Herder, and what Schlözer, Wieland, and countless others did was put it into practice. [68]

"World literature" in this sense is a part of what Goethe was talking about. But he also believed that it served other cosmopolitan purposes. It was a benign check on a national literature becoming too inward-looking and desiccated, a source of "reinvigoration." If the Germans did not embrace world literature, they might slip into "pedantic arrogance."[69] Goethe also saw world literature, meaning especially the literature of European nations, as a cultural bridge, a means of achieving mutual understanding in a post-war era.[70] So it is unsurprising that in 1946, in the immediate aftermath of the Third Reich, as Goethe Societies were formed amid the rubble as symbols of a different and better Germany, the scholar Fritz Strich wrote the first major work on Goethe and world literature, making the case for its cosmopolitan message.[71]

World literature also pointed toward competition, however, and to German assertiveness in the burgeoning literary marketplace. Herder's argument about the authenticity of every national literature had been aimed at the dominance of French culture, an argument that gained force in the period of French political occupation. The German view of French literature as superficial and insincere became familiar in the closing decades of the eighteenth century and took firm hold at the beginning of the nineteenth.[72] The advocacy of world literature, from Schlözer and Wieland to Goethe, was therefore a natural continuation of Herder's ideas about national literature. Both were a by-product of German resistance to French cultural universalism. That was one of the points being made whenever a German author translated a Shakespeare play, an Icelandic saga, or a work of Sanskrit literature. We can view translation itself as a strategic intellectual move, a cultural weapon.[73] Often, that subtext peeped through. Friedrich Schlegel's *On the Language and Wisdom of the Indians* refers numerous times to "our" prehistory, meaning the history of the Germanic tribes.[74] Schlegel, in fact, was very firmly of the view that the Germans translated not only more than others, but better. Better, especially, than the French, who appropriated when they translated, whereas the Germans ("true and honest as in all things") were "trusty translators."[75] During the era of Romanticism it became widely believed that German, a "later" language, less inflected by stilted court culture, was more flexible, more adaptable to the idioms of others, less arrogant, and therefore more suited to translation. Here was something that puts one in mind of Forster: taking pride in German modesty and unobtrusiveness. The spirit of openness to other literatures encompassed by the term "world literature" had the same double quality. The feeling of generosity brought its own satisfactions, so that Germans could experience national pride in their cosmopolitanism.

PART THREE

GERMANS and the GERMAN NATION in a GLOBALIZING WORLD: THE NINETEENTH CENTURY

CHAPTER 7

A NATION AMONG OTHERS

Imagining the Nation

"PART OF OUR NATIONALITY CONSISTS IN DENYING THE NATIONAL," complains Friederich, who considers it a sign that something is seriously wrong in Germany when people argue about whether the nation even exists. His friend Wilhelm agrees. The "heresy of cosmopolitanism" has deep roots among Germans. They gladly raise their voices on behalf of Poles, Greeks, and Belgians, but are too modest and passive on their own behalf.[1] Friederich and Wilhelm are two fictitious friends created by Paul Pfizer in his 1831 book *The Correspondence of Two Germans*.* Pfizer was twenty-nine at the time, a talented young legal official in Stuttgart and a deeply frustrated German nationalist. His book became a Germany-wide sensation. Pfizer proposed that Prussia should take the lead in creating a unified nation. This proved to be prophetic, but it was an unusual suggestion in 1831, especially coming from a south German. Pfizer felt the backlash locally. When he was elected to the Württemberg state parliament a year later, the king stayed away from the official opening rather than administer the oath in person to such an apostate. The book derailed a promising career by making it difficult for Pfizer to continue serving as an official. He went on to fill a succession of posts that were clearly beneath him, and his later life was plagued by physical and mental afflictions. Pfizer lived just long enough to witness the decisive moment in German unification, when Prussian victory on the battlefield in 1866 excluded Austria from German affairs and laid the foundation for a "Lesser Germany" of the kind he himself had

---

* The book came out of an actual exchange of letters between Pfizer and a friend.

called for thirty-five years earlier. Although in a state of advanced mental derangement, he was reportedly gratified.[2]

The Correspondence touches on all the main themes we think of when we think of German nationalism, but it also holds some surprises. Written by a philosophically trained and highly cultivated young man who was also a devout Protestant, the book approaches its subject from a high altitude. The early letters range over freedom and necessity, death and immortality. Then the book narrows in on Germany. The friends discuss many of the things you would expect them to discuss—the rivalry between Austria and Prussia, the Reformation (the last time when Germany was at the forefront of history, or so both of them believe), German culture, and (much more sparingly) "German blood." Running through the letters is a fierce critique of bookish passivity. Like any good educated German of his time, Pfizer invokes Shakespeare. Germany was Hamlet: too much thinking, too little action. But something else stands out. Germany is constantly being placed into a wider framework of "world history" and measured against other nations. Sometimes the comparison is historical, to ancient Athens or to Venice at the height of its power. More often, it is to a major European power, like Britain or France. And sometimes the glance is sideways, at other aspiring nations. "The great struggle of the present, which is now shaking and rocking the European world to its foundations, is being fought over the rights of nations," writes Wilhelm. "In this struggle Poland has three times been defeated, but Greece, Belgium and Ireland have been partly victorious; soon Italy will follow. Shall Germany alone remain behind?"[3]

This concern with other nations was common among German nationalists of the nineteenth century. Nothing was more international than the formation of national identities.[4] Pfizer was also singing an old song when he deplored the lack of German national sentiment. Sixty-six years earlier, another Stuttgart-born official made exactly the same complaint. Friedrich Karl Moser's *On the German National Spirit* was published anonymously in 1765. Moser suggested that despite their shared language and culture, Germans lacked a "national way of thinking" by comparison with "the British, Swiss, Dutch or Swedish."[5] His widely read tract was one instance of a slowly gathering sense of national identity in the late eighteenth century. We saw how the German love affair with Shakespeare and the folk literature of Scots and Icelanders often carried an anti-French charge. Justus Möser also had France in mind when he urged educated Germans not to be "apes of foreign fashion." This was directed at witty, superficial French ways of thinking and the highly refined objects of French material culture. Moser was interested in the idea of a simple German "national dress," an idea also taken up by others.[6] The nation became an object of identification in literary works and in late-eighteenth-century literature on "patriotism." Attachment to the nation was often intertwined with attachment to the Holy Roman Empire, or to an individual state like Prussia, but it was there. Even the xenophobic tones associated with a later era made an occasional appearance in this "patriotic" literature.[7] German nationalism had a longer incubation period than we used to think.[8]

Napoleonic occupation nonetheless created something qualitatively different. The poems of Theodor Körner, the speeches of Johann Gottlieb Fichte, and the writings of Ernst Moritz Arndt are familiar markers of this new nationalist sentiment. Anti-French rage was unconfined, at least for the moment. Heinrich von Kleist wrote these bitter lines:[9]

> *Bleach every space, field and town*
> *White with their bones;*
> *Spurned by crow and fox,*
> *Deliver them unto the fishes;*
> *Dam the Rhine with their bodies[.]*

National sentiment was fostered in poetry and song. The German language itself felt the effects, in the form of a "purification" movement. Joachim Heinrich Campe, that gentle child of the Enlightenment, was one of its leaders. His *Dictionary of the German Language* published between 1807 and 1811 created three thousand new words, three hundred of which established themselves and remain standard. Campe saw himself working within an Enlightenment tradition, but what he was doing inevitably meant "Germanization," creating new German words to replace (mostly) French ones.[10]

Nationalism found expression in other ways, too. While poets discovered a violent new register with which to lacerate the French, the painter Caspar David Friedrich produced canvases on the national theme. A painting from 1812 shows two French chasseurs gazing at a sarcophagus with an inscription in praise of Arminius, or Hermann, leader of the Germanic Cherusci tribe, who won a victory over the Roman Empire at the Battle of the Teutoburg Forest in 9 CE. The message was clear: the French would be defeated, like the Romans, for the heroic German spirit of Hermann was alive and well. The French chasseurs are tiny figures who are dwarfed, almost swallowed up by the landscape. A French chasseur, solitary this time, appears in another Friedrich painting from this period, one of his most famous. *The French Chasseur in the Forest* depicts a disconsolate figure entirely surrounded by evergreens.[11] In these years, when Germans imagined the nation even in nature, no aspect of nature seemed more German than the forest. Had Tacitus's *Germania* not described the warlike Germanic tribes as forest peoples? Had the decisive victory against the "Gallic" Romans not taken place in the Teutoburg Forest?[12] The idea of the "German forest," the antithesis of the "unnatural" formal garden of the French, became part of the mental furniture of German nationalists—of some nationalists, at any rate.

Nationalists also organized themselves in these years. The gymnastics movement founded by Friedrich Ludwig Jahn was a prime example. A pastor's son from Brandenburg, Jahn had a decidedly checkered career before achieving fame as the "father of gymnastics." He attended many universities between 1796 and 1806 without ever graduating and served several stints as a private tutor. But when he settled in Berlin in December 1809 as a thirty-one-year-old, he had (by his own admission) "long years of missteps and wanderings" behind him and no secure job prospects in front of him.[13] Eighteen months later, in June 1811, Jahn established the first gymnastic exercise place in Germany. In doing so he blended two distinct sets of ideas. Jahn learned about gymnastics at Christian Gotthilf Salzmann's school in Schnepfenthal, which was a product of Swiss-German pedagogical reformers. Jahn mixed this cosmopolitan, healthy-mind-in-a-healthy-body reform tradition with hypernationalism. He was consumed by the issue of language purity, a major theme in an early publication that got him into trouble with the Prussian authorities and in his 1810 work, *German Folkdom*. There, he identified the dominance of the French language as a source of German subjugation:[14] "Unhappy Germany! Contempt for your mother tongue has taken a terrible revenge on you. For a long time you have unwittingly been conquered by a foreign language, rendered powerless by addiction to the alien, degraded by idolatry of the foreign. . . . This language has bewitched your men, seduced your youth, dishonored your women." Masculine pathos colored the early, quasi-paramilitary gymnastic movement. A gymnast pledged "to become and remain a German man, in order to work vigorously for people and fatherland." Embracing "foreignness" meant expulsion.[15]

The student fraternity movement also mobilized youth. It was created in June 1815 by students in Jena who had fought in a volunteer unit of the

Prussian army during the "war of liberation," where they met students from other parts of Germany, then returned to university life disappointed that the postwar settlement had left the princes in place and established no unified Germany. Jahn was one of the figures who inspired the founders. The fraternity adopted the red-black-gold colors of the wartime volunteer unit and its members addressed one another with the informal "*du*." The watchwords of the movement were "honor, freedom, fatherland." Its members talked a lot about awakening the national spirit, fostering German manners and morals and especially the German language. Like the gymnasts, fraternity brothers were self-consciously masculine. Both organizations emphasized the importance of keeping the body chaste. The fraternity movement also borrowed some outward symbols from the gymnastic movement (among them, simple dress, flag flying, patriotic songs, and torchlit processions), but added elements of their own, such as masquerades. Like the gymnasts, they held gatherings that brought people together from different German regions.[16]

The nation was therefore imagined in many forms—in art, nature, history, and, above all, in language, thanks to writers, dictionary makers, folktale compilers, and language purifiers. Identification with the nation was also, for the first time, starting to be performed at processions and gatherings, and through the collective rituals of fraternities and gymnastic and choral societies. The nationally minded still consisted mainly of professors, students, writers, officials, and others who had attended university—in other words, sections of the educated middle classes who, together with elementary school teachers and the occasional craftsman or shopkeeper, formed the core social group of nationalists everywhere in Europe. These Germans were learning to think and speak nationally.

But what did it *mean* to think "nationally"? That is much harder to say, because nationalism was compatible with many different political beliefs. The most important new idea in nineteenth-century Europe, nationalism caught fire in Germany during (and because of) a monumental political upheaval, but one that gave no answer to the question of what form "Germany" might take or where its borders should be.

The Congress of Vienna established a German Confederation of thirty-nine states, to replace the Holy Roman Empire and Napoleon's Confederation of the Rhine. This was an entirely new creation. It resembled a constitutional laboratory for trying out different ways of binding subjects to the state, which was both necessary but elusive, given that half of all Germans had new rulers

The German Confederation of 1815.

after 1815. Critics attacked the lack of legitimacy in these states, the absence of constitutions in most of them (even where, as in Prussia, they had been promised), and the widespread censorship. German rulers were also accused of *Kleinstaaterei*, or petty localism, a term of abuse largely invented in the nineteenth century. Nationalism soaked up these criticisms like a sponge.[17] The idea of the nation could be filled with so many different kinds of political content: liberal, radical-democratic, but also conservative. It was the "ideal vehicle for every kind of anti-establishment creative idea." Or, in the contemptuous words of Friedrich von Gentz, now an adviser to the Austrian chancellor Metternich, who hated and feared it, nationalism was a "blank slate on which anyone can write and sketch anything."[18]

Every strand of nationalism was represented at the famous fraternity gathering that took place at Wartburg Castle outside Eisenach in October 1817, on the fourth anniversary of the Battle of the Nations, where Napoleon had been defeated, and the tercentenary of Luther nailing up (if he did) his ninety-five theses. Some 450 people attended the Wartburg events, temporarily united in a single cause. Many remained active in politics, so they represent a cross-section of the different kinds of nationalism Germans espoused in the nineteenth century.[19] The Wartburg gathering had a main act, a notorious sideshow, and two sequels, one of them deadly. In the main act, students from fourteen different universities, representing one in twenty of all German students, went in procession up the hillside to the castle where Luther had taken refuge in 1521. They went in the name of "honor, freedom, fatherland," dressed in simple "German" garb. Some carried branches of trusty "German" oak, others the red-black-gold flag. Toasts were offered to Luther and fallen heroes of the "war of liberation," before the assembled students sang the Lutheran hymn "Nun Danket Alle Gott" ["Now Thank We All Our God"] (associated since the Battle of Leuthen of 1757 with Prussian military prowess) and dispersed after a blessing. The sideshow took place some distance away, where about three dozen spectators who had little idea what was going on watched a student called Hans Ferdinand Massmann, assisted by a small group of initiates, consign a series of "reactionary" books to the flames. The books were in fact bundles of papers made up to resemble books and this self-important little ceremony orchestrated by Friedrich Jahn was the notorious "Wartburg book-burning."[20]

The student procession up the hill at the Wartburg festival
in October 1817. Engraving by an unknown artist.

The first of the sequels was peaceful. Two students, advised by a Jena history professor named Heinrich Luden, arranged the ideas aired during the gathering into a program of principles and resolutions. These called for a unified German empire made up of constitutional monarchies, equality before the law, freedom of the press, and the replacement of standing armies with a militia. It was also resolved, more dubiously, that "dry scholarship" be replaced by work that served people and nation, and that every fraternity brother eschew local loyalties and "foreignness." The violent sequel occurred seventeen months later, when Karl Sand, a former Wartburg participant, called on the writer August von Kotzebue at his home in Mannheim and stabbed him to death in the drawing room. Kotzebue had long been a critic of "Teutomania." One of his books was among those symbolically burned in 1817, which led him to heap more scorn on the student nationalists. The rigidly moralistic Sand, whose views had been radicalized by Karl Follen, a student leader at the University of Giessen, concluded that Kotzebue was a "seducer of our youth, the desecrator of our national history," and deserved to die.[21]

Wartburg and its sequels present a cocktail of political ingredients. Given what happened to German nationalism in the late nineteenth century and especially in the twentieth, it is tempting to focus on the primordial, Romantic, myth-laden aspects—the celebration of Arminius and his heroic exploits, the talk of Luther as bearer of "German" values against a corrupt papacy, the defense of German linguistic purity, and the obsession with the "seductive power" of foreign (i.e., French) culture. That was only one side of the story, however. Heinrich Luden was indeed the author of a twelve-volume history of the German people that incorporated many strands of Teutomania. But his statement of Wartburg principles largely reflected the demands of the liberal phase of the French Revolution, with a few radical elements mixed in. The red-black-gold flag flown by the students denoted what became the German national colors, but the model of the tricolor was French. So was the very idea of an open-air gathering— Wartburg was the French *fête* become *Fest*.[22] There are other French parallels. The students emphasized male purity and self-sacrifice and were deeply suspicion of the "feminine," whether this came in the guise of Catholicism, French coquettishness, or the supposedly woman-pleasing plays of Kotzebue. (When Karl Sand was asked why he had not attacked Kotzebue in print, he replied that this was impossible "because all the females in Germany would have cried with him and worshipped him.")[23] But this was not so different from the radical French revolutionaries, the Jacobins and sans-culottes, ascetics who fashioned themselves as virtuous male citizens and regarded women with suspicion. Follen's group did, in fact, seek contact with foreign revolutionaries.[24] When Metternich used Kotzebue's murder to crack down on nationalists with the Karlsbad Decrees in September 1819, it was obviously convenient to invoke the "Jacobin" threat, but it was not entirely disingenuous.

The radical upsurge during 1815–1819 brought radicals, liberals, and Romantic conservatives temporarily together in the name of German nationalism. Then these very different groups went their separate ways. The later careers of those who took part in the Wartburg festivities offer dramatic evidence of this.[25] Some former participants became nationalists of a church-and-king "Germanic" kind. Unsurprisingly, this was true of many who became theologians.[26] But we find the same thing among other former fraternity brothers. Friedrich Frommann, who became a well-known figure in the German book trade, also followed the Protestant-conservative path.[27] A more dramatic case is that of Heinrich Leo, a medieval historian who had carried the red-black-gold flag from Jena to the Wartburg Castle in 1817. He became a polemical defender of Prussian throne-and-altar conservatism and an opponent of Jewish emancipation.[28]

But perhaps the true embodiment of the conservative, "Germanic" aspect of the fraternity movement was the Wartburg book-burner-in-chief, Hans Ferdinand Massmann. He became a philologist, moved to Munich, and continued to write and speak for the rest of his life as if the calendar had never moved on from 1817. He still wore his hair long and affected simple "German" garb, praised gymnastics, and idealized the culture of the folk. Massmann lived to the age of seventy-six, long enough to become a widely mocked figure.[29]

His longtime guide and inspiration, Friedrich Jahn, suffered the same fate. Heinrich von Treitschke, a professor of history whose nationalist credentials could hardly be questioned, disliked the old Teutomaniac Jahn and ridiculed the idea of a future French attack being crushed by a gymnastic "wave of bellies."[30] Similar mockery was directed at another Wartburg figure. The liberal writer Friedrich Buchholz demolished the claims of his fellow historian Luden to have found "Germans" in late antiquity and in the tenth century. How could the early Germanic tribes have been attached to the soil of the fatherland when they were nomads? How could the Otto-nians have been opposed to everything non-German when Otto II, the

Holy Roman Emperor, married a Greek princess? Luden and his followers should stop talking about "a unity that isn't one and a collective spirit
that doesn't exist," said Buchholz.[31] The Teutomaniacs were mocked in
urbane journals like *Europa* and by liberal nationalists. But the harshest
criticism came from radical democrats. Heinrich Heine was a merciless
critic of Massmann.[32] Wilhelm Schulz, a democrat from Darmstadt, likewise distanced himself from the "errors and childishness" of the fraternity
students, criticizing their "fantasy" of "super-German national pride" that
caused them to express "contempt for other peoples."[33]

Born in 1797, Schulz belonged to the Wartburg generation but did not
go. He was a student at the time in Giessen, a member of the radical group
around Karl Follen. Conservatives later condemned radicals like them for
"poisoning the poetic innocence" of Wartburg and introducing alien "revolutionary" ideas.[34] But some of those who went to Wartburg shared the radical ideas in question. Their later lives offer a striking contrast with those of
Massmann and the rest who construed German nationalism as Protestant-
Teutonic renewal.

Here are thumbnail sketches of eight lives that stand as representative
for many others. Karl Völker, who came from Eisenach, fled to Switzerland after the Kotzebue assassination, moved to London, where he was a
teacher, established a boys' school in Liverpool, and transferred the establishment to Switzerland in 1839, where he spent the rest of his long life. The
Thuringian Daniel Elster also ended up in Swiss exile, but only after traveling to England and France in hopes of fighting for Simón Bolívar in South
America, and actually fighting for Greece in its war of independence. Karl
Gustav Jung (grandfather of the psychiatrist) had a simpler journey into
Swiss exile, moving to Paris in 1821 and Basel the following year, where
he became a professor of medicine. None of these three men returned to
Germany, except temporarily. Nor did the Dresden-born Heinrich Linstedt, who died fighting in Greece in 1821. Others went into exile, then
returned. Christian Samuel Schier fled to New York City in 1817, but came
back three years later. Ludwig von Mühlenfels faced a more difficult situation. A student at Heidelberg, he was caught up in the police investi-
gations that followed Kotzebue's murder and served almost two years in
detention awaiting trial before breaking out of jail and fleeing to Sweden.
On the verge of going to the United States, he accepted the offer of a pro-
fessorship in London; he returned to Germany in 1829 and rehabilitated
himself. Others served their sentences, then left. Robert Wesselhöft, a Jena

fraternity leader and Wartburg organizer, went underground in 1819 but was captured and served seven years in prison before heading to America, where he worked as a doctor in Cambridge, Massachusetts. Christian Sartorius, a Giessen theology student who was arrested and jailed in 1819, went to Mexico in 1824 and became rich from sugar cultivation.[35]

These stories of lives in motion illustrate the variety of ways in which German nationalism assumed a global character. Most obviously, repression scattered nationalists beyond German borders, a paradoxical outcome. Often the journey into political exile involved more than one resting place before the final one, as it did for Karl Jung and Karl Völker, and for one of the most celebrated of all post-1817 political émigrés, Karl Follen, who went first to France, then Switzerland, and finally to the United States, where he changed his first name to Charles, married well (his wife was a Boston Cabot), and became Harvard's first professor of German.[36] Within Europe, the emigration created communities of radical nationalists in France, Switzerland, and England who were in touch with others inside Germany, something that would be repeated after uprisings in 1830 and on a larger scale after the revolutions of 1848.

German nationalists who fought for the liberation of other nations, like Daniel Elster and Heinrich Linstedt, were rare. But identifying with the cause of others was not. It was expressed in vivid terms by Heinrich Heine, himself an émigré in Paris: "What, then, is the great mission of our times? . . . It is emancipation. Not only the Irish, Greeks, Frankfurt Jews, West Indian Blacks and such oppressed peoples, rather it is the emancipation of the world, Europe in particular, which has come of age and is now tearing itself loose from the leading strings of privilege, of aristocracy."[37] German identification with pan-European nationalism began in 1820 with the response to that year's revolutions in Spain and Italy. The Central Committee to Investigate Treasonous Activity, established in Mainz the previous year to monitor political radicalism, took note of the impact that events beyond the Pyrenees had in Germany. There were toasts to the Spanish in Munich coffeehouses; students on Unter den Linden in Berlin shouted, "Long live the Spanish constitution."[38] The Italian revolutions, which began in Sicily and spread to the north, aroused similar sentiments. Nationalists hoped, and the authorities feared, that unrest would spill over into Germany. When Austria marched into Italy to put down the unrest and France did the same in Spain, Germans collected money. Some went off to fight for the cause. Among the German enthusiasts who went to Spain was Victor Aimé Huber, the son of Georg Forster's former wife, Therese, and the writer Ludwig Ferdinand Huber. He was there for more than eighteen months and briefly a member of the Madrid civil guard, although in deference to his mother's wishes Huber remained a sympathetic onlooker.[39] The Spanish cause was a rallying point for radical and liberal opinion in Germany. Despite censorship, it left an imprint on German public life in newspaper reports, literary works, and songs.[40]

The struggles for national independence in Latin America also attracted attention in Germany. Conservatives were critical while the left was enthusiastic. The Hamburg-based journal *Columbus* was very pro-Bolívar and writers painted a rosy picture of what the struggles for national independence had achieved. The most radical saw the birth of a new world.[41] The fight for independence in Latin America also drew German participants, some three hundred in all, admittedly a modest number set against the total of six thousand foreign legionaries who fought with Bolívar and his comrades.[42] Little is known about them, in most cases not even their names, but they probably included the same mix of people we find among the insurgents of other nationalities who fought in Latin America—would-be revolutionaries, officers at a loose end, plus adventurers.[43] The one about whom most has been written is Otto Philipp Braun, the son of a court carriage builder from Kassel: he fought in campaigns in Venezuela, Ecuador, and Peru, became a confidant of Bolívar, and eventually, in 1838, was appointed a grand marshal of Bolivia. Braun was a rolling stone. He joined Bolívar only after failing to make a career, first in Philadelphia, then in Haiti, as a veterinarian and riding master.[44] Born in 1799 and a youthful veteran of the war against Napoleon, he resembles some older German foreign legionaries who were restless after peace broke out in Europe. But restlessness does not preclude political convictions. As he lay dying in 1824 in Peru after the Battle of Junín, Jacob Carl Sowersby, the Bremen-born son of English parents, reportedly said that he had given his life for a "glorious cause."[45]

Among the Germans who fought in South America was the remarkable Harro Harring. Persona non grata in most German states, expelled from Switzerland, deported twice by the British from Heligoland, Harring was an indefatigable activist at large, always ready to support the nationalist cause wherever that might take him.[46] He was one of the Germans who fought for Greek independence from the Ottoman Empire. A sizable number of German volunteers died there: the memorial monument in the town of Nafplio to the foreigners who lost their lives lists 274 names, 100 of them German, the largest single national group.[47] Emotional identification with Greece ran high among German nationalists. The cause went with the grain of long-standing anti-Turkish sentiment and admiration for all things Greek. Demonstrations of support took place across Germany as soon as the rising began in 1821. Solidarity committees were established to assist Greek émigrés and support volunteers who went to fight. These support groups were especially numerous in the south. By the time Greek independence was achieved in 1830, the organization Friends of Greece had six hundred members in southwest Germany alone, as well as almost thirteen hundred financial supporters. This was the first public political organization in the German Confederation with a broad social basis, and it built a communication network that extended to German émigrés. Professors, students, clergy, booksellers, and publishers were the most prominent Philhellenes, but this projection of German national sentiment onto Greece also had a popular dimension. The *Bänkelsänger*, or itinerant balladeers who sang in the streets and at markets and fairs, included songs about Greece in their repertory during the revolt, praising heroes and celebrating final victory.[48]

The Polish insurrection of 1830–31 against tsarist Russia generated even more popular songs, such as "No, Poland May Not Perish." The "Polish mania" of those years created a fashion for Polish tunics. Tin soldiers of Polish "freedom fighters" were snapped up; so were snuff boxes, plates, and handkerchiefs bearing the portraits of Polish patriots. They "captivated every heart," wrote a sympathetic newspaper editor.[49] There were toasts at banquets organized by newly formed Poland Associations. Once again, some Germans became combatants. Seventy physicians also went to assist the insurgents. But contact with the Polish cause came mainly on German soil, as the defeated insurgents made their way to France in 1831–32. More than thirty-five hundred Polish émigrés passed through Germany. Frédéric Chopin composed his great "Revolutionary Étude" in Stuttgart. Even more than Greece, Poland became a proxy for German national aspirations.[50]

The two causes became virtually fused together at the democratic-nationalist Hambach festival, which took place at the end of May 1832. Thirty thousand people gathered at the ruins of a hilltop castle in the Palatinate for a demonstration organized by the newly formed German Press and Fatherland Association. Four of the thirteen songs on the program were about Poland; the head of the Polish National Committee in Paris offered a toast to "our German brothers," and one of the principal organizers, Johann Wirth, made a passionate speech arguing that the Polish and German causes were one. Just as German princes had aided the "Russian despot" in suppressing the "noble nation," so the successful restoration of Poland would follow from the "emancipation and reunification of Germany." Henceforth, said Wirth, "the Polish cause and the German cause are indivisible."[51]

That was the spirit of Hambach. German unity was the "magic word," the "electrical spark," but the German cause was rhetorically linked by speaker after speaker with the causes of other nations—Poland and Greece, Italy and Belgium. In that sense, it could hardly have been more different from Wartburg. In both cases, people carried flags up a hill to take part in a political demonstration disguised for political reasons as a festival. But there the resemblances ended. Hambach was much larger and more socially inclusive. It included peasants and craftsmen. The organizers also wanted women to be represented, and they were, whereas the fraternity brothers at Wartburg took the view of their mentor Jacob Friedrich Fries that "woman should be silent in all public affairs."[52] Above all, German nationalism at Hambach was conceived as part of a European cause. It belonged to an historical moment, 1830–1832, that was very different from the moment that gave rise to Wartburg in 1817. Wartburg followed a much vaunted "war of liberation" against France; Hambach followed the 1830 revolution in France, which detonated revolutions or national uprisings in Belgium, Italy, Poland, and in several German states.

France was central to the rhetoric of Hambach, as a positive model for the Germans. The assembled patriots heard the fraternal greetings of the Friends of the People in the border city of Strasbourg. They also considered the sentiments of a "graybeard" from Lake Constance who recalled the excitement of 1789 and the promise of emancipation for the whole of Europe that this "great world event" held out. Alas, said the graybeard, the bravery of the French had not been matched elsewhere because of ignorance and a slave mentality among the populace. The French and German causes were the same cause, he went on, and the German people should not let itself be duped and robbed of its chance of freedom by the specter of a French war of conquest.[53] We should not underestimate how much France, which had provided a choreography of revolution and a host of revolutionary symbols (open-air festivities, cockades, liberty trees, popular songs), still served as a beacon for democratic nationalists. Even a liberal nationalist such as Paul Pfizer was still, in 1832, urging the establishment of a German nation-state based on popular sovereignty and explicitly modeled on France.[54] Paris remained "the Mecca of devout liberals," said one of them.[55] France was also where the more radical nationalists associated with Hambach fled when the German authorities cracked down. There they joined members of the Young Germany literary movement in exile. Both main organizers of Hambach, Philipp Siebenpfeiffer and Johann Wirth, fled to France. Strasbourg became, once again, a crossing point to safety, as it had been in the 1790s.

Siebenpfeiffer's speech at Hambach contained an extended metaphor contrasting the verdant Rhine Valley, where nature had "spread an abundance of blessings" and German industriousness had produced fruit, wine, and corn, with the barren soil of the fatherland that had only thistles and thorns thanks to political reactionaries.[56] It was a classic instance of imagining the nation through nature. But his comrade Wirth sounded a more discordant note when talking about the Rhine. If France supported the German cause, he said, it might demand the left bank as its reward, and that would be too high a price to pay. Wirth worried that most people in France, other than a few "far-sighted cosmopolitans," saw the left bank as self-evidently French. His warning sounded a jarring, unwelcome note. A French participant immediately jumped up to deny any such designs.[57]

But Wirth's comments anticipated the Rhine crisis of 1840, precipitated by Prime Minister Adolphe Thiers's renewed claims on the left bank. Troops were mobilized and the French press rallied behind the cause. The diplomatic response in Germany was measured, but the popular response was heated. The patriotic verse "Die Wacht am Rhein" (The Watch on the Rhine) was a by-product of the Rhine crisis. So, above all, was the "Rhine Song" composed by an obscure Cologne courthouse clerk named Nikolaus Becker, which began "They shall not have it / Our free German Rhine." First published in a Trier newspaper, it was reprinted across Germany, set to two hundred different tunes, and prompted hundreds of imitations, an outpouring so large that newspapers had to stop accepting unsolicited verse from readers.[58]

The Rhine crisis is often described as a turning point, the moment when German nationalism reverted to a more visceral, anti-French expression of German identity—more Wartburg than Hambach.[59] The chauvinist spasm was real enough, and nowhere more obvious than in the extraordinary burst of popularity that Becker's song enjoyed. It was not only widely sung but turned up as a text on postcards, plates, and playing cards; it was even embroidered on woolen nightcaps. But the episode was short-lived, a panic that quickly ebbed after Thiers was dismissed from office at the end of October. By January 1841 it had run its course. The public response to the "Rhine Song" was also mixed. Many condemned the song as "nauseating" (Heinrich von Gagern, a liberal nationalist who would play a prominent role in later debates about German unification) or suggested that its efforts to tap chauvinist sentiment were "empty and vulgar" (the philosopher Arnold Ruge).[60] In a Frankfurt theater, audiences hissed the Becker song and demanded the "Marseillaise." There was a backlash against Becker's simplistic verse in numerous lampoons and satires. A few radical nationalists briefly embraced the chauvinistic moment of late 1840, but most condemned the upsurge of anti-French warmongering. So did left-leaning nationalist intellectuals, and moderate liberal nationalists.

The 1840 crisis left behind no widespread or lasting Francophobia. Pro-French songs (even toasts to Napoleon) could still be heard in taverns and from balladeers and hurdy-gurdy men; pro-French motifs still featured strongly during the highly political carnival celebrations in Cologne and Mainz.[61] These carnival centers were both Rhineland cities and it is not really paradoxical that anti-French sentiment was least likely to resonate there. The Rhineland was a border zone of shared economic activity, shared religious faith, and a shared legal code, this last a legacy of earlier French occupation that was prized by most Rhinelanders. Still, in the German lands as a whole, the heady "European"-oriented German nationalism of earlier years had ebbed by the 1840s. It still had its followers, especially on the left, but it existed alongside other, more conservative kinds of nationalism. We see this in the emergence of a new generation of historians who still called themselves liberal but were more German-nationalist in tone.[62] We see it also in the movement to construct national monuments, such as the Valhalla Hall of Fame near Regensburg, and to complete the construction of Cologne Cathedral in "German" Gothic style. In both cases, German princes tried to identify themselves with the cause.[63]

The view that German identity was defined by blood and culture, wrongly seen by some scholars as the dominant form of German nationalism, probably gained ground in the 1840s, although it also drew scathing criticism. The Hanoverian politician Gustav Zimmermann scorned those who "test the blood of the inhabitants and want to count none as German who are not full-blooded descendants of the flaxen-haired, blue-eyed *Germanen* described by Tacitus." These zealots should be treated as "the idiots of the age," suggested Zimmermann.[64] We should be wary, anyway, of taking this kind of "Germanic" language at face value. After all, cosmopolitan nationalists often talked about German "tribes," then raised their glasses to the French revolutionary tradition. Some of the nonsense spouted by nationalists about ancient "Germanic liberties" was also tactical, designed to make foreign ideas about rights and constitutions more acceptable.[65]

As political prohibitions eased in the 1840s, what kind of nationalism was espoused in gymnastic clubs, choral societies, and embryonic political organizations? We certainly find "Germanic" attitudes. But more typical of the nationalist public was a broadly liberal identification with "western" kinds of rights and constitutional arrangements as the basis of a future German nation. There was agreement that "freedom" and "unity" were the joint goals, perceived as two sides of the same coin. Civil rights and national independence were, in the striking words of one liberal nationalist, a "cosmopolitan common heritage."[66] The arguments took place over matters of emphasis, and especially over the role of the German princes. France was not the only potential model. Britain was admired for its constitutional monarchy, absence of censorship, and legal system. But the attraction was complicated by the fact that Britain was coming to be seen by some nationalists, especially those influenced by the economist Friedrich List, a supporter of protective tariffs, as a country that used its material might to keep down up-and-coming nations such as Germany. Admiration was therefore mixed with resentment.[67]

List developed his idea of an economic "national system" partly as a result of exposure to the ideas of Alexander Hamilton during years of exile in the United States. Economic developments in the German states prompted others to think optimistically about possible American parallels. One member of the Bremen Senate expressed the hope that the German Customs Union would lead to a "United States of Germany."[68] There were other reasons, too, that Germans became close observers of America, especially as immigration to the country grew. The United States interested German liberal nationalists for the same reasons that drew them to the British example, with the added attraction that the United States was a federal system. Perhaps the central body of the German Confederation, the Bundestag, could be turned into something resembling Congress? One of the German academics who knew its political history best, Robert von Mohl, wrote that America was the state "which has taken up and represented in purest form the ideas that have so violently turned our time upside down."[69] But Mohl was no firebrand, and in that he was typical. It was not the revolutionary origins of the American experiment that attracted most German commentators, but the idea of "ordered freedom."[70] Moderate reformers like Mohl were looking for incremental changes. Like reformers in other times and places, however, they were not free to choose their own historical circumstances, and in 1848 the world was once again turned violently upside down.

Germany and the Revolution of 1848

ISTORY SPEEDS UP DURING REVOLUTIONS. GERMANY LEARNED that truth again during the revolution of 1848. German nationalism, which waxed and waned through the nineteenth century, entered another intense phase. The revolution began in March 1848 and affected every part of the Confederation. It was caused by social distress in town and country and by a crisis of confidence in Germany's princely rulers. Although not driven by nationalism, the revolution created a political opportunity for nationalist demands. The political opposition called for liberal (and in some cases radical) reforms; it also called for a German nation-state. A "Pre-Parliament" convened at St. Paul's Church in Frankfurt at the end of March. Its members agreed that all adult males should vote in nationwide elections to be held on May 1. The deputies who were elected then gathered in Frankfurt on May 18 as the members of Germany's first national assembly, with the task of constructing a new nation-state (the term itself, Nationalstaat, was used in 1848, although rarely.)[71] Like the revolution as a whole, this enterprise failed, but it brought key issues to the fore. "We must answer the question of what 'a German' actually is," said the liberal nationalist Georg Beseler.[72] As Germans debated this and related questions at Frankfurt, in state parliaments with newly installed "March ministries," in the new political clubs that sprang up, and sometimes in the streets, the world beyond Germany was ever present. The German revolution was intertwined at every stage with larger European and international issues.

That was true, in the first place, of its revolutionary origins. France once again provided the spark for political upheaval. Revolution had broken out in January in Palermo, but it was the news from Paris the following month that the regime of King Louis-Philippe had been overthrown that seemed to signal the old regime was ready to collapse. This was the first revolution in which word was spread by the railway and telegraph, the new means of communication of the era. Trains bringing newspapers and letters with the latest reports from France were met by excited crowds. Even in isolated, politically reactionary Oldenburg, a gathering on February 28 toasted the "world-shaking news from Paris."[73] The conservative Scot William Aytoun, describing Cologne for the readers of *Blackwood's Magazine*, expressed himself "right sorry" that "quiet Germany had lighted her revolutionary pipe from the French insurrectionary fires."[74] For the third (and last) time, France triggered revolution across Europe. Not everywhere in Europe, though, for—with the obvious exception of France itself, where the revolutionary tradition provided its own momentum—1848 affected neither advanced western areas such Britain and Belgium, nor backward Russia. It was most strongly felt in areas that were, in more than just a geographical sense, in between, by regimes that were neither liberal-constitutional nor simply repressive, in societies that were no longer predominantly agricultural and craft-based but in which commerce and industry were still establishing themselves. The parts of Europe that were in transition proved most explosive in 1848. The Prussian liberal Victor von Unruh put his finger on this: "We live in transitional times. The old has not yet been overcome, the new is still being born."[75] That meant the epicenter of revolution was the German Confederation and the non-German lands of the Habsburgs, in Italy, Bohemia, and Hungary. It followed that the future of Germany was bound up with the fate of other aspiring European nations.

Debates about the form a future Germany should take were also marked by constant references to other nations as possible models. The constitution makers in St. Paul's Church cast their net wide. Article 101, dealing with how parliament could override a suspensive veto, was borrowed from Norway.[76] *Which* nations became models depended partly on the experiences that former émigrés brought back with them. Those who had spent time in France and Switzerland were likely to be more radical nationalists in the first place, and for that reason they often called for a German republic. France was attractive to democratic nationalists more generally. Their meetings included exuberant singing of the "Marseillaise" and routine invocations of "liberty, equality, fraternity."[77] A minority of the left in Frankfurt, members of the Donnersberg faction, supported a French-style republic for Germany, but most deputies recoiled from the idea and the initial wave of sentimental enthusiasm for France in March even among moderates soon gave way to a darker view.[78] Other members of the left in Frankfurt called for a republic, but a republic perched atop individual

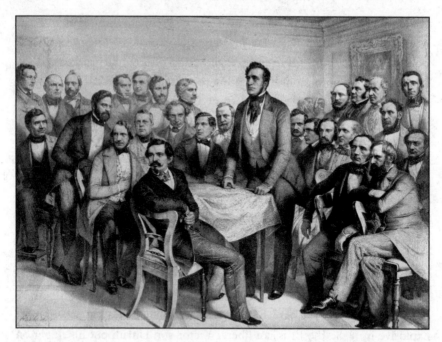

Members of the Casino Faction, made up of moderate liberal nationalists. An 1849 lithograph by Friedrich Pecht, one of his series of group portraits of Frankfurt parliamentarians.

German states that retained their princely rulers.[79] The French (and Swiss) example of the civil guard commanded widespread support at local level. As a state model, however, moderate liberals and centrists looked more to Britain.

But it was the United States that received more attention than any other country. At least ten German translations of the U.S. Constitution were published in 1848–49; some went through multiple editions. Even the constitutions of individual states were translated.[80] A list of the politicians, academics and journalists who wrote or spoke on the American constitution as a model reads like an A to Z of German public life at midcentury. The first draft of the German Constitution produced by the so-called Committee of Seventeen hewed closely to the U.S. Constitution; so did the March 1849 constitution, which followed its American predecessor, sometimes word for word, in setting out the responsibilities of the federal government and establishing the basic principle that the individual states enjoyed any rights not expressly transferred to the center.

The U.S. model was important for the politicians in Frankfurt because its federal structure seemed most suited to the German situation. True, the different factions picked what they liked best from the American example. The left seized on the democratic aspect and called for a republic with a president and a vice president popularly elected for four years. That is why the Stars and Stripes hung alongside the French tricolor at democratic gatherings. Moderates and center-left liberals saw the possibility of grafting a federal united states onto a monarchical system. For them, one great advantage of the American political model was precisely that it was not French, or "Jacobin," but instead could serve as the vehicle for a "defensive revolution."[81] The eventual constitution was more centralized than its American counterpart, which was predictably identified as a weakness by John C. Calhoun, the South Carolina senator and preeminent champion of "states' rights," when his opinion was sought by the Prussian envoy in Washington.[82] But this remained moot because (as Calhoun also predicted) the constitution, like the larger process of nation-making, fell victim to the growing authority wielded by the major German powers, Prussia and Austria, and the irreconcilable conflict between them over who held political primacy in the German lands.

Who belonged within the proposed new Germany? The thorny question of who, exactly, was "a German"—Beseler's question—was another way in which the putative German nation was bound up with the issue of where non-Germans fitted in. There are many different ways to define who belongs within a nation-state—by territory, law, language, culture, custom, or ethnic descent. Contrary to a commonly held view, as we have seen, it is not the case that early-nineteenth-century Germans were irresistibly drawn to the last of these. The nation makers in Frankfurt, and public opinion, largely continued to reject ethnic definitions. There were many non-Germans who inhabited the German lands—the Poles in eastern parts of Prussia, and the many non-German peoples within the Habsburg Empire. Constitution makers were agreed that they should be considered full citizens, with the same civil and political rights as other members of the Germany-to-be. At the suggestion of a representative from Vienna, the Pre-Parliament had replaced the phrase "every German" with "every citizen" in the proposal about elections to the National Assembly. This was accepted without a vote. In October, the Constitutional Committee, which succeeded the Committee of Seventeen, similarly inserted a new introductory paragraph on basic rights: "Since the quality of being German, through which Reich citizenship is conditioned, is not determined by nationality as tribal relationship, it can only be founded thereupon, that someone is either subject to the Reich government, or to the government of an individual German state, by virtue of permanent residence within Reich territory alone or within a particular state territory."[83] This was an explicitly political or civic definition of citizenship, designed to exclude Germans (by language or descent) living on the Volga or in America but to include non-Germans living within the nation's borders. There was a practical motive here, a desire not to repel non-Germans. At the same time, the German state makers in Frankfurt did not want to compromise the unity of the new nation, so at key moments they played down this inclusive approach. That is why they chose not to set out a formal naturalization procedure.

Even where their arguments were palpably humane, things were not entirely straightforward. When, for example, the Catholic left liberal Johann Peter Werner asked, "Why should not the child who was born on German soil and has grown up among Germans, and has formed manifold ties with the German—why should not this child too have the expectation of German citizenship?," he conveyed the largely unquestioned belief that becoming German was a kind of gift.[84] While non-Germans were accepted as citizens, it was assumed that German would become the language of state and non-Germans would assimilate. There was broad agreement— shared by many on the left, with their dismissive talk of "little nations"— that German culture and civilization were superior, and that they would play the dominant role within the new nation-state.[85] But Poles, Czechs, and Italians had their own ideas about building a nation-state and bridled at suggestions of German superiority.

The generous and romantic impulse to view 1848 as the "springtime of peoples" initially held sway on the German left. When the Polish revolutionary Ludwik Mierosławski was released from jail in Berlin, he was triumphantly escorted by a procession led by someone carrying the German red-black-gold tricolor. A radical Prussian officer named Wilhelm Rüstow captured this moment when he described himself as a "friend of humanity" and referred loftily to a "European humanity" whose common interests were thwarted by rulers and their standing armies. Democratic speakers at mass meetings in the Rhineland routinely linked the German cause to the national aspirations of Italians, Poles, and Hungarians. In Frankfurt, too, radicals like Arnold Ruge and Gustav Struve, a republican democrat who had renounced his aristocratic title, thought about convening a "congress of nations." Even moderate liberals harbored hopes that, freed from old-style dynastic power plays, the nations of Europe would live in mutual harmony.[86] This optimism was still apparent when the National Assembly convened. It melted away between spring and fall, as a result of one dispute after another, with Denmark over Schleswig-Holstein, with Italians over the Tyrol, with the Poles of Posen, and with other Slav peoples who met at a Slav congress in Prague and made their voices felt through the summer and fall.

The question of where to draw borders proved especially contentious. It led to heated demands by Germans and non-Germans alike. Czechs, Poles, and Hungarians all asserted national claims in 1848 that were territorially extensive and cut across the claims of others. A Czech national state would have included Slovaks, Hungarians, and Germans. Poles dreamed of a resurrected nation that would have incorporated Lithuanians, Belorussians, and Ukrainians within its borders. Greater Hungary would have taken in Romanians and Croats.[87] Then there was Italy. Even Giuseppe Mazzini, the gentle Italian apostle of the nationality principle, viewed Italy as one of the small number of true nations in Europe. His rhetoric invoked "history, genealogy, blood, land, and the nation's honour."[88]

Rival national claims in 1848 involved more than words. In May there was a Polish uprising against the Germans in Posen. Then came talk of expelling Germans from Bohemia, followed by a Prague uprising in June, which came in response to heavy-handed Habsburg repression of the Czechs. The earliest and perhaps greatest provocation of all was the announcement on March 21, 1848, by King Frederik VII that he intended to annex the entire majority-German province of Schleswig to Denmark in deference to the Danish nationalist movement. There is a case to be made for seeing German nationalism in 1848–49 as largely reactive, just as it is possible to maintain that the hopeful nation builders in Frankfurt stuck largely to the borders of the 1815 German Confederation when deciding where to draw lines.

But the would-be nation builders in Frankfurt also displayed both inconsistency and arrogance in staking German claims. While the borders of the Confederation served as the basis of deliberations, there were instances where it was proposed to push beyond those borders. The arguments for doing so were often contradictory. The Frankfurt debaters pointed to legal and historical grounds and emphasized territorial integrity when it came to Schleswig and the Tyrol, but switched to arguments based on German nationality when proposing to partition majority-Polish Posen. Members of the left at Frankfurt pointed to the contradiction.[89] Sometimes the German arguments about borders were frankly strategic, as they were in disputing Italian claims. That was also true in the east, where creating a strong frontier against Russia was one German motive in overriding Polish interests. But the assertion of German over Polish claims went well beyond that. The notorious speech of the young writer and journalist Wilhelm Jordan in July 1848, with its harsh comments about the "superiority of the German people over most of the Slavic peoples" and unsparing stereotypes of backward Poles, may have been exceptional in its verbal brutality but not in its broad prejudices. Jordan's colleagues also spoke about Polish backwardness and superior German civilization. Julius Ostendorf used what was becoming a familiar figure of speech that likened Germans to American settlers on the western frontier and Poles on the eastern frontier to Native Americans.[90] This marked a full-scale retreat from the pro-Polish sentiment of the years since 1830, still evident just a few months earlier. Some on the left clung to their views, but it is worth noting (and was noted by contemporaries) that Jordan himself was a member of the left.

His was not the only speech at Frankfurt marked by a full-throated insistence on German civilizational superiority. Heinrich von Gagern, the moderate liberal who was the first president of the National Assembly, was equally uninhibited when referring to the ethnically mixed Danubian provinces of the Habsburg monarchy. In arguing for including these mainly non-German-speaking areas within the new state, he called upon Germany to assume the Habsburg "mission to spread the German culture, language and way of life that follow the Danube to the Black Sea, into those lands sparsely populated by various peoples, but lands full of hope, the entire civilization of which is used to leaning on the German one, which is longing for Austrian-German protection and increased influence." It would, he suggested, be "irresponsible" to abandon Germany's "calling to play a world-commanding role."[91] Similar arguments were made about the "German springs" of culture among non-German peoples in Bohemia and Moravia. The moderate press applauded this civilizing mission in liberal-nationalist dress.[92] Some speakers in Frankfurt foresaw a future Central Europe, or *Mitteleuropa*, dominated by German influence. A few were even more ambitious and imagined the German state as a "magnet" that might eventually attract others of "the German tongue" who already had states of their own. The shorthand term for this was "Germanic populations on the Upper and Lower Rhine"—that is to say, the Swiss and Dutch (even, perhaps, the Alsatians). But that was for the future. For the moment, the majority at Frankfurt were content to vote in July 1848 to incorporate the Duchy of Limburg, a member of the German Confederation but also a province of the Kingdom of the Netherlands, into Germany.[93]

In April 1848, the future British prime minister Benjamin Disraeli referred to "that dreary and dangerous nonsense called 'German nationality.'"[94] It was the Schleswig-Holstein conflict, closely followed in London, that caused his remark. German and Danish nationalists had been rehearsing their respective grievances for two decades before 1848. The Danish decision in March to annex Schleswig prompted an uprising by German nationalists. The National Assembly supported the German claim on both duchies, and Prussia intervened against Danish forces on behalf of the Provisional Central Power (as the government was called) in Frankfurt. The cause of Schleswig-Holstein aroused national passions across Germany. Volunteers went north to join the fight. When, therefore, under pressure from Britain and Russia, Prussia signed an armistice on September 5 and withdrew, against the wishes of the Frankfurt parliament, that became both a symbol of national shame and a rallying cry—"a world-historical day," in the words of a Stuttgart newspaper.[95] The climbdown intensified demands for a German navy. "Naval fever" burned in 1848. A nation without a fleet, wrote one radical, was like a bird without wings.[96] Pamphlets were published, collections made and petitions sent to the National Assembly urging the establishment of a German navy, a demand that fell on willing ears. Only one vote was cast in Frankfurt against the establishment of a national navy, by a member of the left-wing Donnersberg faction.[97]

The war with Denmark provided the immediate spur to build a fleet, because the Danish seizure of German merchant shipping was an embarrassing reminder of German naval weakness. But the naval ambitions of German nationalists went beyond coastal defense. A Memorandum on the Construction of a German Fleet commissioned by the Frankfurt parliament, written by the Hohenzollern admiral and naval theorist Prince Adalbert of Prussia, presented defense of the north German coast as the minimum requirement of any navy; a larger program would permit the navy to defend German citizens and German commerce beyond home waters, while an even more ambitious program would establish the nation in the front rank of naval powers. Prince Adalbert made it clear that he favored the third option. So did many speakers in the National Assembly. They referred to German material interests overseas and linked these to cultural progress by means of a set of arguments that were characteristic of mid-century liberal nationalism and often went by the name "Manchesterism" because of what they owed to English free-trade liberalism. But what ran through the arguments in Frankfurt calling for a German fleet, whether geopolitical, material, or cultural, was the constant background noise of references to German pride—to be somebody on the seas and to count for something, to be recognized, to be in possession of one's honor and dignity, above all not to be (in Georg Beseler's words) "a laughing stock abroad."[98]

This did not preclude seeking help from sympathetic nations, above all Britain and the United States. The Provisional Central Power in Frankfurt was looking for assistance at many levels—with acquiring ships, crews, officers, and organizational expertise. It was America that proved most amenable. Many members of the National Assembly had personal connections there and official channels of communication were established with President James K. Polk and Secretary of State James Buchanan through Andrew Jackson Donelson, the American envoy to Frankfurt. Two secret American missions went to Frankfurt to discuss how the United States might help. The leader of the second mission, Commodore Foxhall Alexander Parker, was offered the post of commander in chief of the German navy, but he declined and wrote a largely negative report for his superiors in Washington. In the end, what Germany received (mainly ships) came too late to be useful in the war against Denmark or for the Central Power in Frankfurt. But there is a question of the chicken and the egg here. Parker's gloomy report—his warning, for example, that it would do little for the honor of American officers to be seconded to the German navy—was based partly on his negative views about what Germany could achieve in the short run against Danish superiority, and even more on the concerns passed on to him by Donelson that the Central Power itself was in a vulnerable position vis-à-vis Prussia, so that it would be an embarrassment to the United States to give full backing to a body with such a short life expectancy.[99]

The Tennessean Donelson turned out to have a surer grasp on political realities than many German liberals in Frankfurt. Revolutions are dynamic events. What happened in 1848–49 was especially tangled in Germany because the revolution had domestic political and social as well as national strands, and played out simultaneously in the National Assembly, in the parliaments of the constituent states, in the clubs, and in the streets. The Prussian decision to disengage from war with Denmark in September 1848 was in part a by-product of the recovery of the German dynasties after the shock of the March events and their loss of nerve. Donelson arrived as U.S. envoy that September, just when the tide was clearly turning against the Central Power. Creeping counterrevolution was underway in most German states. In the Habsburg monarchy, where the court had fled from Vienna to Innsbruck, nationalist opposition in Bohemia, Italy, and Hungary was militarily crushed between June and October, the month in which Vienna was recaptured from radical revolutionaries. During the same summer and fall, military hard-liners increasingly set the tone in Prussia. The appointment in September of the hawkish General Friedrich Heinrich von Wrangel as supreme commander in Berlin was the prelude to a coup two months later, when parliament was prorogued and the gains of March rolled back.

Counterrevolution in the two largest German states left the would-be nation builders in Frankfurt increasingly isolated. A measure of their weakness was the execution of one of them, Robert Blum. Sent in October 1848 by fellow left-wing members of the assembly to deliver greetings to the revolutionaries then in charge in Vienna, he was seized when General Alfred Windischgrätz recaptured the city, accused of taking part in an insurrection, and executed in November despite his parliamentary immunity. None of this marked the final end of the revolution. The military crackdown in Prussia and Austria showed where ultimate authority lay, but the army shared power with more flexible, postrevolutionary conservatives. Prussia received a new constitution in December; in Austria, key liberal ministers were retained, and Prince Felix zu Schwarzenberg, the prime minister, persuaded Emperor Ferdinand to step down in favor of his eighteen-year-old nephew, Franz Joseph. It was recognized in both Berlin and Vienna that the "German question" remained open until the National Assembly had completed its work.

The Frankfurt parliament had voted overwhelmingly in October 1848 to establish a Greater Germany, which incorporated the German but not the non-German lands of the Habsburg monarchy into the new nation. This encountered predictably strong resistance in Vienna because it challenged the integrity of the empire. While the Central Power was entertaining Commodore Parker in January 1849 and hoping for help with building a navy to defeat Denmark, efforts continued to meet Austrian objections. Heinrich von Gagern, the great architect of compromise, put together a plan for a Prussian-led Germany that had some form of association with Austria. But his proposal proved to be a hard sell among the Frankfurt parliamentarians. Then Vienna slammed the door on remaining hopes of a Greater Germany in early March by signaling that the Habsburg Empire would not be broken up. That left only the Lesser German option. The National Assembly finally produced a constitution for Germany on March 28. Five days later, on April 2, Frederick William IV of Prussia refused the imperial crown of Germany offered to him by a delegation from Frankfurt, politely in public, contemptuously in private.

The revolution then entered its final phase. Moderates drifted away from the National Assembly and other elected members were (unlawfully) recalled by Prussia and Austria. A rump parliament dominated by the left retreated to Stuttgart, where it was dissolved by Württemberg soldiers in June. There was a final burst of radical action in the spring of 1849, ostensibly in defense of the constitution, but in fact the outcrop of accumulated frustration with the rightward shift of the revolution. Fighting took place in the southwest, on the Lower Rhine, and in Saxony, where a young Richard Wagner famously manned the barricades. This last gasp of the revolution, put down by Prussian troops, was fought mostly by radical Germans in the provinces, but enjoyed some support from foreign revolutionaries, a last, faint echo of the hopes placed in "European humanity" and the "springtime of peoples" just one year earlier.[100]

The revolution failed, in the sense that the princes retained their thrones (although rulers in Vienna and Munich abdicated) and no United States of Germany was created. The failure to create a unified Germany was more effect than cause of the larger failure. Disputes between Greater German and Lesser German advocates over the contours of the hoped-for nation certainly divided and weakened the politicians at Frankfurt and elsewhere. But it was only one of the political fault lines in 1848, and these anyway were not the main reason the revolution ended as it did. The principal reasons were the gap that opened up between the political and social revolutions, and the sheer firepower in the hands of dynastic rulers, especially in Berlin and Vienna, once they recovered their nerve. In the Habsburg case, the non-Germans who served in its army showed how adept the dynasty proved to be at using some subject peoples within a multinational empire to suppress other subject peoples, as well as to crush the revolutionary German nationalists in Vienna.

German nationalism itself had changed since March 1848. The revolution inflamed national antagonisms and resentments that were not easily extinguished. There had been excited talk of German honor, pride, and standing in the world. The need for a strong navy became a central feature of nationalist thinking, and dreams of a German-dominated *Mitteleuropa* were voiced. The wing of German nationalism that emphasized "European humanity" and linked the German cause to the cause of others was seriously weakened.[101]

Radical-democratic nationalism was also most affected by the great wave of political emigration that followed the final crushing of the revolution. Among members of the Frankfurt parliament alone, half of those (around 235 in all) who belonged to one of the left or center-left factions were tried after the revolution, mostly in absentia. Some were sentenced to death. The overall number of political émigrés ran into the tens of thousands. Their destinations included Belgium, South America, and Australia, but most went—like the emigrants from earlier cycles of postrevolutionary repression—to one of a small number of countries. France was not an option this time because of a conservative crackdown there under Napoleon III, which meant that refugees were turned away and those already there expelled. That left Switzerland, Britain, and the United States. By July 1849 there were more than ten thousand German émigrés on Swiss soil alone. The cost of supporting them led Swiss authorities to negotiate with the German states to urge leniency. When this failed, they pressed émigrés who faced only light sentences to return. Others took the hint and left: by 1852 the numbers in Switzerland were in the hundreds, not the thousands.[102] Britain continued to be favored as a political haven and the German colony grew much larger after 1849.[103]

America was an even more popular destination. The German states, especially those in the southwest, were relieved when political émigrés just across the border in Switzerland moved on to the distant United States. There was much less danger that they would try to slip back into Germany, so money and effort no longer had to be expended on finding former '48ers who could be persuaded to spy on their fellows, or on other forms of surveillance on foreign soil. In fact, some states offered amnesty to political prisoners if they agreed to cross the Atlantic and never be heard from again.[104] This was a variation on the policy of shipping criminals to the Americas.[105] Whether these "voluntary" political émigrés were as likely to engage in political activity in their new home is an open question. Certainly many of the original '48ers did become active in American politics. Carl Schurz is just the best known of the many who threw themselves into American radical movements such as abolitionism, or into trade union and socialist organizing in big cities like New York, Cincinnati, and St. Louis and in small ones like Hoboken, New Jersey.[106] In the 1850s, some displaced nationalists from the failed uprisings, especially radical officers, also attached themselves to groupings of irregulars like General William Walker's "filibusters" in Nicaragua.[107] They represented a debased, almost comic-opera rerun of the German radical nationalists who had fought thirty years earlier for the cause of Spain or Greece, a perfect illustration of Karl Marx's post-1848 dictum that history repeats itself, the first time as tragedy, the second time as farce.

Making the Nation

WE KNOW HOW THE STORY ENDED, WITH THE CREATION OF A Lesser Germany under Otto von Bismarck's leadership. But let us look for a moment at how the disappointed and dejected of 1848 saw the possibilities while the future remained open. Many émigrés hoped to return, so they followed German politics closely. An important part of the public debate about how to achieve a German nation-state therefore took place outside Germany's borders, in exile colonies and in letters that flew back and forth between Switzerland, Britain, and the United States. Émigré life was often difficult. The historian Carl Nauwerck became a cigar dealer in Zurich, while the journalist Carl Mayer sold watches and jewelry in Neuchâtel (his correspondents were sometimes invited to purchase items from a catalogue included with his letters). The radical Hegelian philosopher Arnold Ruge established a daguerreotype business in Brighton on the south coast of England, earning the enmity of the Englishman who ran the only previous business of its kind in town.[108] Émigrés fretted and feuded and were homesick. "I would as soon leave the country today as tomorrow," the exiled politician Friedrich Kapp wrote from New York City to his friend Moritz Hartmann, whose emigration was spent in France, Britain, and Switzerland.[109] It was a "hard school," observed the veteran democrat Wilhelm Schulz in 1851.[110]

Ludwig Bamberger, the son of a wealthy Jewish family who became a democratic journalist during the revolution, and his fellow radical Gustav Struve composed a long circular to members of the left at the beginning of 1850, a clear-eyed survey of political life. German democrats had long had reason to be grateful to France, they wrote, but no one should now expect liberation to come from there; nor was this the moment to emphasize solidarity with other European nations. Better for Germany to establish itself as a democracy, then face neighboring peoples on a basis of equality, not just in political principles but in the external force they were able to muster: *that* was when to extend the hand of brotherhood. Germans, they continued, were not bound by the narrow ties of nationhood like Poles or Italians, but were bearers of a "higher, more general nationality," and democrats should be mindful of the "world-historical position and role of Germany."[111] These immodest sentiments were widely shared.

Bamberger and Struve went into exile; others stayed. There were obvious differences between the camps. Most émigrés stood further to the left and were inclined to suspect those who stayed home of "opportunism," while the latter considered émigrés "utopian" or "unrealistic." But the groups also had much in common. While émigré life had its trials, liberal nationalists at home also faced a ramped-up system of surveillance greater than anything Metternich commanded before 1848: counterinsurgency with a modern face.[112] Writing became a form of therapy for those at home as well as abroad. Both groups placed their faith in "progress," that great buzzword of the time, symbolized by the railroad and the telegraph. While émigrés fled physically, those who stayed fled in a different way, at least temporarily, from formal politics into railway committees and the like.[113] Even more important, a new kind of pragmatic "realism" became evident among both stayers and leavers, liberals and democrats.

Ludwig August von Rochau gave them their slogan. An émigré in France during the 1830s, forced into emigration again after 1848 (this time to Italy), Rochau returned, settled in Heidelberg, and in 1853 published the book that made his name: *The Principles of Realpolitik.*[114] Part of the new tough-mindedness concerned foreign affairs and military issues. Fewer hopes were placed in help from other nations, while the military lesson of 1848–49 (standing armies were strong, the people in arms were no match for them) led to renewed emphasis on the importance of a civilian militia and paramilitary gymnastics programs to support it. In this hardheaded postrevolutionary mood, many liberal nationalists even hoped for a "good war" that would bring about a German nation-state.[115]

The tempo of German political life quickened in the late 1850s as censorship and police surveillance were relaxed. When William I replaced his brother Frederick William IV as regent in Prussia, it marked the beginning of a "new era"—one that had counterparts throughout the Confederation. Liberal and democratic politician reemerged in public or made their way cautiously back from abroad. They held meetings and were elected in large numbers to parliaments all across Germany. Now, as in 1848, the domestic issues they cared about—constitutionalism, parliamentary power, freedom of speech and assembly, the rule of law—were coupled with calls for a unified Germany. Liberals and democrats wanted both "freedom" and "unity," although their emphases varied, and both were more likely than they had been before 1848 to underline the "power" of the future nation as a third element in the equation.[116] A harsh tone was also injected into liberal nationalist discourse by a growing Protestant anticlericalism that often tipped over into anti-Catholicism. This was driven partly by dislike of the reactionary political role played by the Catholic Church in the 1850s, and by the willingness of some southern states to sign concordats with Rome. Above all, German liberal nationalists loathed the double papal provocation of supranational claims and hostility to the creed of progress.[117]

The Catholic-Protestant divide had an obvious bearing on the struggle between Catholic Austria and Protestant Prussia over the "German question," which was unresolved in 1848–49. The two sparred in the 1850s over customs unions, reform of the Confederation, and countless smaller procedural issues. The conflict was conducted over the heads of the smaller states ("middle Germany," or the "third Germany"), but at the same time in front of a nationalist popular opinion that proved to be sizable when allowed to be public. The Crimean War of 1854–1856 had a delayed but major effect on German politics because it underscored Austrian weakness and isolated it on the international stage.[118] The dramatic events of 1859 in Italy had a more direct impact in Germany. The Kingdom of Piedmont-Sardinia, with French backing, successfully went to war over Habsburg possessions in northern Italy and forced Vienna to cede Lombardy. This was not just an Austrian military disaster. Nationalists viewed it as a German humiliation. It strengthened the view that a powerful, unified Germany could come only through Prussian leadership.[119] That same year, the National Association was founded, a pressure group that favored a Lesser German, or "Greater Prussian," solution; at its peak in 1862–63, the association had as many as 25,000 members (600 were émigrés), mainly among the propertied and educated Protestant middle class.[120] Many festivals were also held in 1859 to mark the centenary of Friedrich Schiller's birth, occasions that mirrored the views of this influential segment of opinion—liberal, nationalist, tinged with Protestantism, and increasingly sympathetic to Prussia as the trustee of German culture.[121]

It seems obvious in hindsight that Prussia would win the struggle for Germany. Unlike Austria, it was not distracted by the need to manage a host of subject nationalities, and it was much more dynamic economically and in all the categories by which "progress" was measured, from universities to steam-powered engines. Prussia also had a more demanding nationalist public at its back. If the membership of the National Association seems quite modest at 25,000, it dwarfed the membership of its pro-Austrian rival, just 1500. But contemporaries were no better than we are at predicting the future. The fighting in Italy, for example, elicited some wildly inaccurate forecasts. The zoologist and scientific popularizer Carl Vogt wrote from his Swiss exile to German newspapers with his prediction that the conflict would last at least two years and cost the French 200,000 men (it lasted ten weeks and cost 7000 French lives).[122] It was not obvious at the time, therefore, that Austria would be pushed out of Germany, or even that it should be. Plenty of nationalists hoped, until the last moment (which turned out to be 1866) that their German-speaking Austrian brothers would be part of the future nation, and many were disturbed that Prussia had done nothing to help Austria in Italy and instead allowed Napoleon III to score a success. (France took the opportunity in 1859 to acquire Savoy, a step that the liberal Karl Biedermann regarded as a *casus belli*.)[123] In the words of one famous left-wing émigré, Friedrich Engels, it was necessary "to defend the Rhine on the Po."[124] There was a broader and growing "militarization" of German nationalism in the years after 1859.[125]

In the early 1860s Austria renewed its challenge to Prussia, backing a Saxon plan to reform the German Confederation and gathering support for a Central European Customs Union that would dilute Prussian dominance. Both were efforts to court smaller German states fearful of an overmighty Prussia. After the debacle of 1859, Vienna also embarked on some modest constitutional reforms designed to improve its reputation within the Confederation. In the early 1860s it looked, in fact, as if constitutionalism was working better in Austria than in Prussia, given the conflict between crown and parliament that had developed in Berlin. In 1860 Albrecht von Roon, the Prussian minister of war, introduced a bill that strengthened the standing army and weakened the militia—the "sole truly popular institution in Prussia," in the words of an outraged Heinrich Simon, a veteran of 1848 living in Swiss exile. The bill was a slap in the face for liberals and democrats, who wanted to strengthen military preparedness (they were no pacifists), but not in a way that reinforced the military caste at the expense of civilian soldiers and taxpayers.

When William I dug his heels in, the opposition in the Prussian parliament did the same. A new party, the Progressive Party, was founded in January 1861, the same month that William became king on the death of Frederick William IV. Elections that December produced a left-wing majority. William stubbornly appointed more reactionary ministers and dissolved parliament, only to face an even larger opposition majority after elections in May 1862. The Progressive Party and its allies then mounted a campaign of resistance: boycotts of official receptions, political banquets, mass meetings. This had echoes of 1848. A liberal newspaper in Frankfurt claimed that Prussia would soon be "ripe for revolution."[126] British foreign secretary Lord John Russell offered (only partly in jest) to reserve rooms at the Claridge Hotel in London for the soon-to-be-exiled monarch.[127] In this crisis atmosphere William rejected giving in to the opposition, dismissed the idea of mounting a coup, and had to be talked out of abdicating by Crown Prince Frederick. Instead, in September 1862, he decided on a desperate throw of the dice and appointed Bismarck, someone with a reputation for being clever but untrustworthy and regarded with suspicion on both left and right, as prime minister.

Fast-forward nine years and a unified nation, the German empire of 1871, had been created under Prussian auspices. William I was now emperor of Germany as well as king of Prussia, Bismarck German chancellor as well as Prussian prime minister. Unification came as the result of three wars. In the first of these, in 1864, Prussian and Austrian troops combined to occupy the duchies of Schleswig and Holstein after the Danish king died and a succession dispute reignited conflict there. Bismarck then cultivated points of friction between the two German powers, before proposing a Prussian plan to reshape the Confederation in ways that marginalized Austria. This (as intended) provoked war with Austria, which was backed by most of the states in "middle Germany" and by every one of its other monarchies. In the short conflict that followed, Prussia was victorious at the Battle of König-grätz in July 1866. This was the decisive moment in unification. It excluded Austria from German affairs and led to the establishment the following year of the North German Confederation. This Prussian success also ended the constitutional conflict, when supporters of Bismarck in the Progressive Party split off to form the National Liberal Party and the Prussian parliament agreed to "indemnify" the regime retroactively for its breach of the constitution. Finally, in 1870, Napoleon III allowed himself to be provoked into hostilities and the south German states joined with the Prussian-led forces of the North German Confederation in a successful war with France.

Unified Germany, 1871.

This was the military prelude to their becoming part of unified Germany.

German unification was an event of global significance. It was made possible by the remarkable success of Prussian arms and by Prussia's underlying economic dynamism, for as the English economist John Maynard Keynes later said (varying a notorious phrase of Bismarck's) the German empire was "built more truly on coal and iron than on blood and iron."[128] The military road to unification meant that this was also, emphatically, the creation of the nation "from above" and not, as democratic nationalists had always hoped, "from below."[129] That hardly made Germany unusual. New nations in nineteenth-century Europe mostly came into being, as they had

A photograph showing some of the artillery and transport
wagons that were a key to German success against the French
at the Battle of Sedan in September 1870.

in Latin America, as a result of war—witness Greece in the 1820s, Germany and Italy in the 1860s, Romania and Serbia in the late 1870s.[130]

But the creation of a powerful new state in the center of Europe still raises the question: Why did the other great powers allow it to happen? There were many reasons. Russia, humiliated in the Crimean War, was preoccupied with a series of internal reforms under Tsar Alexander II. Bismarck had also cultivated Russia by assuring it of Prussian support after a second Polish uprising in 1863. Britain had pressing colonial problems. It was suspicious of French ambitions on the Continent and viewed Germany as a power that did not threaten major British interests. There was also broad sympathy in Britain for German self-determination, as well as a fund of goodwill that had accrued as a result of admiration for German culture. Benjamin Disraeli warned that the "German revolution" of 1871 had created "a new world, new influences at work, new and unknown dangers," but this still—for now—weighed less heavily in the balance.[131] As for Austria and France, the other major powers, the first was struggling with dissatisfied subject peoples in its far-flung empire and was diplomatically isolated after the Crimean War. It also faced the intractable problem that its main ally, Prussia, was also its greatest rival. As for France, the recklessly adventurist foreign policy of Napoleon III had made the country an object of universal suspicion.

German unification actually owed a curious double debt to France. By 1871, France served the unwitting purpose of uniting most Germans in opposition to it, even Bavarians and other south Germans who still distrusted Prussia. This marked a real shift of views since the 1820s or 1830s. The French writer Ernst Renan had an interesting gloss on German anti-French sentiment. Just as France had once come to define its own identity against English dominance, suggested Renan, so Germany had now done the same against France: the French "archenemy" was the "midwife" of the German nation.[132]

The other German debt to France was owed by Bismarck to Napoleon III. The French emperor fascinated Germans. Even a democrat like Heinrich Simon, who loathed him, conceded that Napoleon III was a clever man who absorbed the ideas of his time.[133] Like other intelligent conservatives, Bismarck paid close attention to the hybrid style of Napoleon III's regime, its mixture of authoritarian and populist elements. One of the things that divided Bismarck from former conservative allies was his belief that revolutionary means could be used to preserve the inherited social order—a view abhorrent to orthodox conservatives. But Bismarck was bolder, a "white revolutionary" willing to experiment.[134] He was prepared to use foreign policy for domestic purposes and even to wager politically (like the French emperor) on the conservatism of the peasantry. That is why he was criticized by liberals for "Bonapartism," or "Caesarism."[135] Bismarck's flexible political repertoire, like his gambler's instincts, made him a perfect fit for a moment when the rules of the political game were changing.

The international rules of the game were changing, too. After 1815 the so-called Concert of Europe prevailed, a system based on dynastic legitimacy and the status quo. That broke down with the Crimean War, but a new set of ground rules based on the primacy of nation-states did not immediately replace it. German unification was both cause and effect of this difficult transition from one kind of international system to another. Prussian-Austrian rivalry over the "German question" was one reason that the old system broke down. At the same time Bismarck clearly benefited from this period of uncertainty. After 1871, Germany then became part of the new order.

Viewed through an even wider-angled lens, the 1860s were a pivotal decade of nation building or rebuilding globally.[136] Russia, as we have seen,

embarked on a crash program of domestic reform that included emancipation of the serfs. In Japan, the Meiji Restoration of 1867–68 paralleled
events in Germany, as the former Tokugawa regime, like the German
Confederation, was overthrown "from above" and a new, more powerful
nation-state came into being. In the Americas, these were also times of
change, as Canada became unified and independent as a result of confederation in 1867.

An even closer parallel to events in Germany can be seen in the United
States, where a civil war was fought between north and south over where
sovereignty lay within a federal system. In America, as in Germany, the war
might have come earlier, but for agreements that postponed the reckoning:
first the Missouri Compromise of 1820 between free and slave states in the
United States, and then the Treaty of Olmütz in 1850 between Prussia and
Austria, which temporarily fudged their differences.[137] In America, as in
Germany, it was the economically dynamic north that won, with the all-
important difference that in Germany the north—Prussia—was the secessionist. There is another strong connection between these two momentous
events. German-born officers and men played a large role in the Union
army. Fully 10 percent of Union soldiers were German-born, the largest
single group of those born outside the United States. They included prominent émigrés. Leading figures in the revolutionary uprisings of 1848–49
became Union generals, among them Carl Schurz and Gustav Struve. Karl
Marx's close friend Joseph Weydemeyer was a colonel. For all of them, the
Civil War offered a second chance to fight for their values.[138] German '48ers
from the gymnastic movement likewise took their democratic nationalist
convictions with them to America and later celebrated being among "Germania's sons" who were part of the Union army in the "great struggle for
freedom against the slave aristocracy."[139]

And then, much closer to home, there was Italy. The roads to unification in the two countries not only resembled each other; at key points
they intersected. The Italian war of 1859 weakened Austria and brought
German nationalism back to the boil; Piedmont was Prussia's ally in 1866,
so Austria's defeat excluded it from Italy as well as Germany; and France's
defeat in 1871 by German forces meant that Rome, previously occupied by
French troops, finally became part of Italy. The parallels are not just evident
with the benefit of hindsight. Contemporaries in both countries were aware
of what they had in common. That was why the Italian Society wrote to its
newly founded German equivalent in December 1859, proposing that the

two organizations combine their efforts to achieve "a German fatherland and an Italian fatherland." It received a cool response, a result both of genuine concern that close cooperation would run afoul of the German laws of association, and of hardheaded recognition that German and Italian interests were not identical.[140] But events in Italy remained a major reference point for German nationalists of all stripes.

Giuseppe Garibaldi was a magnetic figure for nationalists of the left. While in Zurich, the German émigré Fritz Anneke came close to joining Garibaldi's "Thousand" in 1859, before crossing the Atlantic and later accepting a commission in the Union army. Wilhelm Rüstow, the radical Prussian officer who was court-martialed in 1850 for sedition, escaped from jail and did join Garibaldi, serving as chief of general staff of the Army of the South. This was perfect for Rüstow, whose twin passions were popular militias and "European humanity."[141] Democratic German nationalists found Garibaldi especially inspirational. Some moderate liberals admired Garibaldi, too—the novelist Gustav Freytag was one. But they were more likely to be drawn to Count Cavour in Piedmont, the Italian political figure who most resembled Bismarck, just as Piedmont most resembled Prussia. The parallels were not lost on German observers. Arnold Ruge, from his English exile, saw the impact of Cavour's policies in 1859 on other Italian states like Tuscany, and concluded: "Our German case is very similar; unity would be ours if only we could throw the Austrians out of the Confederation and build a strong [north]."[142] That turned out to be close to what eventually happened in 1866–67. The liberal nationalist Karl Twesten proved farsighted when he remarked in 1862 that if a Prussian Cavour brought about German unity by violating international law and tearing up treaties, he would have monuments erected in his honor.[143] Bismarck himself, to whom a great many monuments were later erected, was aware of the strange symmetries between German and Italian unification. He expressed this in typically brutal fashion when (in 1869) he likened the "stubborn, heavy, backward race" of south Germans to the southern Italians: "We do not want another Calabria attached to us."[144]

In his memoirs, the Piedmontese politician Massimo d'Azeglio said of his country's unification: "We have made Italy; it remains to make Italians."[145] Was the same true of Germany and Germans? Not really. To take an obvious difference, most inhabitants of newly unified Germany spoke German. Prussians and Bavarians, for all their mutual dislike, could insult one another in a common language. Standard German actually became more standardized in the decades after 1871. No single sectional divide in Germany, whether north–south or east–west, came close to the division between the north and south in Italy. Neither brigandage nor a boycott of politics by a major part of the population cast a shadow over politics in Germany as each did in Italy. All this is true. Yet the German empire of 1871 was by no means the natural culmination of German history, even if pro-Prussian historians described it that way. Its creation did violence to many historical continuities and was as much a beginning as an end. Bismarck's Germany contained numerous divisions and fault lines. What is more, overcoming these—insofar as they were overcome—took place at the same time that Germany was also becoming part of an increasingly dense network of international agreements. The process of unification meant recalibrating relations between the nation and its parts as well as the nation and a wider world. The subnational, the national, and the supra-national represented three delicate moving parts that were moving at the same time, although not necessarily at the same speed.

There were three major divisions in the German empire, in addition to the fault lines of social class. In the first place, around 4 million of its 65 million inhabitants were Alsatians, Danes, or Poles.* Restrictions on the use of their language caused friction with all three groups. The French speakers in the west were treated best in this respect, but Alsace and Lorraine remained sensitive border regions, directly administered for almost the entire lifetime of the empire as a special territory with its own governor, like a colonial dependency. The Poles, meanwhile, labored under a growing sense of German cultural superiority and periodic bouts of "Germanization." Like Poles and Alsatians, the Danes of Schleswig-Holstein were also subject to harsh forms of treatment that extended to mass expulsions.[146] All three minorities established separatist parties, which won 10 percent of the vote in 1874. This was alienation expressed through the ballot box, not banditry, it is true. That was different from Italy. But Polish frustration also exploded in direct action like a series of school strikes that began in 1901 and lasted for three years.[147]

Support for the separatist parties declined over time. Catholic Alsatians and Poles mostly transferred their support to the Catholic Center Party. The large Catholic minority, just over one-third of the population, represented the second major fault line within the German empire. Cath-

---

* There were also 100,000 Czechs, 100,000 Lithuanians, and 90,000 Serbs.

olics, too, were alienated, especially in the early years. There were riots when Catholic Austria was defeated by Protestant Prussia in 1866.[148] Catholics understandably felt disrespected or worse by the arrogant, aggressively Protestant tenor of German nationalist language, which was riddled with contempt for "backward," "superstitious" Catholics who supposedly owed allegiance to Rome, not Germany. Then, shortly after unification, came an all-out attack against the Catholic Church known as the *Kulturkampf*, or what we might today call a "culture war."[149] This was a pan-European phenomenon, something that made German Catholics very conscious of what they shared with coreligionists across Germany's borders in Belgium and Switzerland.

The *Kulturkampf* was far from the dull church-state dispute that used to be depicted in textbooks. It was marked by violence: the expulsion and imprisonment of clergy, seizures of church property, even sending in the army with fixed bayonets against Catholic gatherings.[150] By the time the conflict ended in the late 1870s, more than 1800 priests had been jailed or exiled and 16 million marks' worth of property impounded. The Cologne lawyer and writer Julius Bachem referred to a period of "Diocletian persecution."[151] The many instances of violence against Catholic populations and their clergy were perpetrated by gendarmes and soldiers who sometimes behaved as if they were in an occupied land, or a colonial territory. In Polish Prussia, as in Alsace-Lorraine, the denominational divide overlapped with the ethnic divide, accentuating the problem of a marginalized minority. People often think of "German Catholics" as synonymous with "Bavarians." In fact, Catholics formed a kind of "Celtic fringe" around the German empire to the east, west, and south. The *Kulturkampf* hit hardest in Prussia and Baden. But even where its direct effects were not felt, Catholics everywhere were made to feel like pariahs.

The third kind of division within the new Germany could not have been more basic. It was territorial and was marked, literally, by the borders around each of its three dozen constituent parts. This was a composite state that assembled under one roof a conglomeration of monarchies, grand duchies, duchies, minor principalities, and free cities.[152] The larger ones continued to exchange ambassadors with one another. Many were accustomed to thinking of themselves as "nations," "fatherlands," and "countries." For decades, going back to 1815 and with redoubled effort after 1848, German rulers in the kingdoms of Württemberg, Saxony, Hanover, and Bavaria had worked hard to create monuments, schoolbooks, festivities, and other symbols that would attach citizens more closely to their "nations."[153] The rulers of smaller states did the same. All of this took place in parallel with, and potentially as a rival to, the construction of all-German symbols and identities in the same years. That, after all, was the meaning of "Deutschland, Deutschland über Alles" in Hoffmann von Fallersleben's song—the "über alles" was a plea that Germany take priority over Saxony or Württemberg. But that did not always happen. Sometimes belief in the local fatherland went hand in hand with German nationalism.[154] Resentful inhabitants of an area assigned in 1815 to a state they viewed as alien might embrace a German identity more strongly as a result, like people in the Palatinate, who were happy to be more German in order to be less Bavarian.[155] It all depended. Those classic midcentury forms of communication, railroad and telegraph, often seen as the instruments of widening horizons, might work to integrate different parts of Germany; but they might also work in ways that strengthened one kingdom or grand duchy within Germany's borders.[156]

Many institutions had the potential to knit the empire together—railroad, post office, a common currency, conscription, legal codes, parliamentary elections. But even while relations in the German empire between the whole and the parts were still being defined, Germany was becoming more heavily engaged in a globalizing world. These accommodations, internal and external, were going on simultaneously. Here is an example. It was agreed at an early stage that Germany should have a supreme court, and further decided by a narrow vote that it should sit in Leipzig. By the time that the justices began their work on the first day of October 1879, the German empire had not only posted ambassadors and consular officials around the globe and hosted the international Congress of Berlin in 1878, but made a series of international commitments. It became part of the London-based gold-standard system, joined the International Telegraph Union and the Universal Postal Union, and signed the treaty in Paris that established the International Bureau of Weights and Measures. That all took place in the 1870s, the decade when the new German parliament was busy creating a common code of criminal and commercial law. There was still no uniform German civil law until passage of the civil code, which came into effect on January 1, 1900. By then, Germany had acquired colonies, signed a series of bilateral trade treaties, joined the International Statistical Institute, signed the Berne Convention on copyright, and accepted many further international commitments. One of the most momentous was the decision at the International Meridian Conference in Washington, D.C., to adopt Greenwich Mean Time as a global baseline.

By 1893 (just within the ten-year grace period agreed upon in Washington) Germany had adopted standardized international time for both official business and everyday purposes, overriding the array of local times used in Berlin, Munich, Frankfurt, Karlsruhe, Ludwigshafen, Stuttgart, and elsewhere, not without misgivings about the effects this might have on local arrangements made with matters like daylight saving in mind.[157] This was one very concrete way in which global forces turned Prussians and Bavarians in Germans.

Unification in 1871 answered one question (Where is Germany?), only to open others. The most basic of these was the one the constitution makers had grappled with in 1848: Who is German? The answer in 1871 was "someone who is already a Prussian or a Bavarian." German nationality was still defined through citizenship in one of the constituent states of the empire. But that hardly ended debate. Were Austrians really not Germans? Many Catholics inside Prussian-dominated Germany wished they were. So did many non-Catholic nationalists. Those inveterate nationalists, the gymnasts, were among them; so, after the 1890s, were the Pan-German League and other radical nationalists, who were intellectually the bastard heirs (and sometimes the biological children) of the democratic nationalist '48ers.[158] Looking beyond Austria, how was one to regard Baltic Germans? And what about German emigrants to the Americas? The category of the *Auslandsdeutscher*, or German abroad, was created in the years of unification, even as realistic hopes ebbed that solidly German settler communities could be established in the United States or Brazil. That was one of the things that drove the demand for colonies, as places of truly *German* settlement. And the importance of this global dimension to how Germans in Germany saw themselves is brought home by the debates over the 1913 German citizenship law, which for the first time established a category of citizenship not derived from one of the constituent states. The new law was an attempt to deal with the rights of Germans abroad, even while issues arising in the German colonies—not least, mixed-race marriages—became a part of the debates.

CHAPTER 8

ON THE MOVE

The German Diaspora

THE WORLD WAS ON THE MOVE IN THE NINETEENTH CENTURY. People and goods traveled around an increasingly interconnected globe on a scale never seen before, or perhaps since, for the movement of people was probably greater as a proportion of population than in our own globalized times. All this was shaped by some of the same forces as now: a global labor market, faster and cheaper means of transportation and communication, and free-trade ideology. Along with tens of millions of South Asian and Chinese migrants, around 60 million Europeans emigrated in the nineteenth century, a true "exit revolution."[1] Among them were 5.5 million Germans. There was a first, fairly small spike in numbers in 1817, after a series of harvest failures. A gentle upward movement from the 1830s was then followed by a huge wave of emigrants between 1846 and 1857, around 1.3 million people in all. A second wave came in 1864–1873 and an even larger third one in 1880–1893, when 2 million left. In the peak nineteenth-century years the number of emigrants approached a quarter of a million annually.[2]

Some had religious motives, like the Swabian Pietists who went to Russia, or the Old Lutherans from Prussia who settled in Australia, Canada, and the United States. There were also emigrants from the small German Mennonite communities. On the Catholic side, the charismatic Ambros Oschwald led more than a hundred members of his Black Forest congregation to Wisconsin, where they established a religious community.[3] There were secular counterparts of these often utopian undertakings. In spring 1834, nearly five hundred Germans traveled in two ships across the Atlantic, members of the Giessen Emigration Society hoping to establish a community dedicated to democracy and freedom. They were led by two men with links to the radical fraternity movement. Their dreams were not realized, but they played an important role in the abolitionist movement as well as enriching Missouri with their winemaking skills.[4] One celebrated instance is the radical freethinker Ottilie Assing, who worked closely with Frederick Douglass and became his lover.[5]

It is not always easy to draw a clear line between those who left for political and religious reasons, and the much larger number whose motives were mainly economic. Political and religious émigrés faced material challenges, after all, while "economic migrants" took their religious identities and folkways with them. The picture is further complicated by the fact that a small minority of economically motived migrants were business or professional people, merchants, engineers, and scholars, either squeezed out of a tightening market at home or hoping to parlay their specialist skills into greater success abroad. But most emigrants were driven by more basic material concerns. The syncopated rhythms of mass emigration closely followed the economic cycle. Most of those who left in the first two waves were peasants and craftsmen from overpopulated areas in the southwest and west. In these areas, inheritance customs meant that properties had been repeatedly subdivided until they became "dwarf holdings." Sons stood to inherit land too meager to farm, the dowry for daughters had shrunk to almost nothing.[6] Emigration seemed like the only way out. Most left a few years after a major crisis, as families took the opportunity to pay off debt and sell land as the market improved. Later emigrants came increasingly from the east and northeast, where there were fewer small family farms. They were more likely to be agricultural laborers and servants, or factory hands affected by the economic downturn that began in 1873 when a post-unification economic bubble burst.

Where did emigrants go? During the first two-thirds of the nineteenth century, many still went to affluent parts of northwestern Europe. This continued a long tradition of seasonal migration that sometimes turned into permanent emigration. The Netherlands remained a common destination. A few emigrants practiced highly prized occupations, like the German pastry chefs in Amsterdam; most still did the dirty jobs they had done in an earlier century. It was the same story in France. The Germans in Paris included professionals and others with special expertise (among them the expert in satire and lyric verse Heinrich Heine), but most came from the rural poor of Hessen and the Palatinate and worked in construction, factories, street cleaning, and domestic service. Around 1850 there were as many as 100,000 Germans in Paris, making it the sixth-largest "German" city in the world.[7] The numbers remained high even through the war of 1870–71 and seriously declined only in the 1880s.

The German community in Britain was smaller, just under 60,000 at the end of the nineteenth century, although this still made it the largest (non-Irish) immigrant group in Britain until the arrival of East European Jews around that time. Half lived in London, with smaller groups in Glasgow and northern provincial cities. Some were business people and professionals. In London, they formed little colonies in districts such as Camberwell and Sydenham in the southeast. But most Germans in Britain came from the lower or lower-middle class. They could be found in crafts like tailoring and shoemaking, in the dye industry, and especially as "sugar bakers" and "sugar boilers" in the refining industry. There was also a clustering of Germans in the service sector, not only domestic servants, but butchers, bakers, waiters, and hairdressers.[8] In 1900 there were also around 2000 German commercial clerks in England. English clerks responded to the influx with hostility. *The Clerks' Journal* referred resentfully in 1888 to the "incredible number of Germans employed in London," who—it claimed—grabbed the best positions in an "over-glutted market." The London *Telegraph* agreed that English clerks were "being pushed off their stools" by the interlopers; a clerk in Liverpool complained about "the obsequious German clerk, Max von Sauerkraut."[9]

There was plenty of turnover in Britain's German community. Some went back, others arrived to take their places. That was especially true of groups such as waiters and commercial clerks, for whom the time spent in England (and in the case of waiters, often in France, too) was a form of overseas apprenticeship that preceded permanent employment in a German hotel or merchant house. Some manual workers also moved back and forth. For Germans in Britain, France, or the Netherlands, the prospect of eventually returning was real. The shorter the distance, the easier it was to contemplate. In other words, this was still a form of seasonal migration for many, even if it lasted for years. Going farther afield, especially leaving Europe altogether, was a different matter. Returning was less likely, although more common than we used to think.[10]

Mass emigration overseas was the novel aspect of German nineteenth-century migration. It began before the new steam-based technologies became widespread. Early emigrants made their way to the ports of embarkation by covered wagon or in small boats. Once in Bremen or Hamburg, they were as likely in the 1840s or '50s to leave on a sailing ship as a steamship. Even in 1866, when the second great wave of emigration was already underway, two-thirds of the passengers who left Bremen did so aboard sailing ships. These were considered safer; they were also cheaper.[11] But things changed dramatically over the next few years. By 1871, less than one emigrant in six left under sail. Most now took advantage of the growing capacity, greater speed, and falling cost of steamships, just as they traveled by train to the north German ports. Shipping companies, emigration agents, and boosters did their bit to advance this business; so did popular pamphlets that sang the praises of distant lands where the milk and honey flowed; and so, more indirectly, did the organizations that aided emigrants, such as the Catholic St. Raphael Association. Another aspect of the "great acceleration" in the nineteenth century was the speed with which letters and financial remissions made their way back to Germany.[12] These encouraged the recipients to follow. The prepaid ticket to friends and relations underpinned chain migration.

Mass emigration can easily seem like an abstract affair. One way to counter that is to zoom in on one place. Australia was described by a German writer in 1851 as "the end of the earth."[13] Those were the words of Rudolf Reimer, in a little booklet written on behalf of the German Immigration Association of Adelaide. Its aim was to dispel misinformation about land and climate while offering practical advice to prospective immigrants. By the time he wrote, there were already more than 8000 Germans in South Australia, enough to sustain a surprising number of German-language newspapers, such as the *Adelaide Deutsche Zeitung* and the *Süd-Australische Zeitung*. The earliest arrivals were Old Lutherans escaping persecution in Prussia. They sailed from Hamburg. The first group on board the *Zebra* passed Kangaroo Island and docked in Holdfast Bay near Adelaide just after Christmas 1838, their original numbers thinned out by those who died of typhus and were buried at sea. Three more ships followed, landing a party of close to 500 all told. They had been financially supported by the Scottish proprietor of the South Australia Company, a sympathetic Baptist.[14] The Lutherans often named new settlements after their former Silesian villages, like Klemzig in the Torrens Valley outside Adelaide. They were soon joined by economic migrants from the same regions.[15]

Firstcomers and aftercomers alike fanned out into the Adelaide Hills and then into the Barossa Valley northeast of the city, where the soil supported the growing of wheat, barley, fruit, vegetables, and vines. German immigrants opened the first wineries there (as they did elsewhere in Australia). The chain migration that began in the 1840s continued until late in the century. But high birthrates and increasing land prices led German families to move on. Some went to Victoria, others to the Riverina district of New South Wales. These communities fitted the image cultivated by German-Australians that they represented "sturdy German farming stock." It was always misleading, to the extent that it ignored laborers and the poor. The idealized image also excluded the German immigrants who stayed in towns and cities. There were 2500 Germans in Adelaide by the early 1850s.[16] Most were craftsmen or laborers. One of the places they met was the Süd-Australischer Allgemeiner Deutscher Verein, or South Australian General German Club, which had a working-class clientele with a reputation for radicalism.[17] Perhaps these were the "infidel and dissolute Germans that were now scattered through our population" described contemptuously by an English clergyman.[18] There were also German craftsmen who built themselves houses and rented out rooms as a source of income. In other words, the lines between "rough" and "respectable" working classes in Germany, as defined by clergy and bourgeois observers like Reimer, were reproduced in Australia.

The rich Australian mineral deposits also attracted that eminently mobile group, German miners. As many as 1300 German miners went to the newly opened Burra copper mines in South Australia in the decade after 1845, where they worked alongside miners from Cornwall, Wales, South America, and China. Many came from the Harz Mountains in northern Germany, encouraged to emigrate by the Hanoverian state, which advanced their fares against future earnings because this was a way to export social problems when domestic lead mining declined.[19] The gold rushes of the 1850s then attracted large numbers to Victoria. By 1861, 10,000 of the 30,000 Germans who had gone to Australia were in Victoria, 6000 of them in the goldfields of Ballarat and Castlemaine.[20] Most, unsuccessful there or in the goldfields of New South Wales, joined the steady stream of Germans who continued to arrive to settle in those states and, after 1860, in Queensland, where Germans played a big part in the development of sugarcane cultivation.[21]

German migrants included the comfortably off. Rudolf Reimer's circle was made up of merchants and professionals, figures like the Bremen-born merchant Henry (or Heinrich) Noltenius, whom an English-language newspaper described as "an Anglo-German in whom all may find / The virtues of both countries well combined."[22] This was the other German Adelaide, the men (and they were all men) from the propertied and educated bourgeoisie who gathered at the German Club on Pirie Street or at the Hamburgh Hotel, the former Suffolk Inn until it was taken over and renamed by a German proprietor. Merchants and physicians, drapers and pharmacists, journalists and senior clergy of various denominations, these Germans formed singing groups, supported the theater, and engaged in philanthropic work. They could hardly have been more different from the lower-class German immigrants. Yet the lives of the two groups were interlinked. The gentlemen of the German Club employed other Germans (mostly women) as servants in their homes. Their philanthropic ventures, like a proposed German Hospital in Adelaide, were aimed at fellow Germans. They also encouraged German immigration through publications like Reimer's and sometimes furthered it directly, like the miners brought over by Noltenius.

Among the supporters listed at the front of Rudolf Reimer's booklet was the name Otto Schomburgk. He had a very different background. A former medical student who had fallen foul of the Saxon authorities as a radical fraternity member, he owed his release from the Magdeburg citadel in 1837 to the intervention of Alexander von Humboldt. Humboldt knew the family, having recommended two of Otto's brothers, Robert and Richard, as members of an expedition to British Guiana. Otto and Richard Schomburgk were active in the 1848 revolution. The following year, disillusioned and apprehensive, they formed the South Australia Colonization Society with like-minded friends. With the financial assistance of a geologist friend of Humboldt, they chartered a sailing ship. The *Prinzessin Luise* reached Adelaide in early August 1849, after a four-month journey, with a remarkable collection of talent among its 162 passengers. They became known as the '49ers and included both artisans and professionals who placed their imprint on the culture of South Australia during the following decades.[23]

Mass emigration therefore turns out to be the sum of many micromigrations. We find Germans of every kind in Australia, although the numbers were skewed toward the lower and lower-middle classes. Around 70,000 German-speaking emigrants went to Australia in the fifty years after 1840. By 1891, Germans and their descendants made up one in every twenty Australians, with the highest proportions in South Australia and

Queensland.[24] That made them the largest immigrant group after the Anglo-Scots and Irish. The same was true in New Zealand, which took in 20,000 German immigrants between 1840 and 1914.[25] Germans also emigrated to the English Cape Colony in South Africa and to Canada, where there were 150,000 Germans when the country became independent in 1867.[26]

To what degree did Germans who went to non-German-speaking countries retain, or wish to retain, the language and culture they brought with them? That is a question about identity, and the first thing to say is that the people we call German-Australian or German-Canadian were in fact neither wholly one thing nor the other. They did not simply transplant German culture to the host country, as strident nationalists at home liked to believe; but nor did they simply assimilate within a "nation of immigrants," as state builders in Australia and Canada preferred to say. Instead, the incomers lived their lives, often independently of nationalist politics, in a variety of ways that lay along a spectrum from separation to integration. Much depended on the particulars of gender, class, and region of origin.

Take the case of the proposed "German Hospital" in Adelaide in the 1850s (never actually built). The committee that proposed it initially referred to a German Hospital, but in later documents it was variously called the German and British Hospital, the Deutsch und Britisch Hospital, the Deutsch British Hospital, the German and English Hospital, and the English and German Hospital.[27] There was an obvious desire among these bourgeois German worthies not to appear clannish, and especially not to seem "disloyal," but the confusion of terms also points to the larger reality that men of this class lived transnational lives, which is why it was sometimes hard to tell the Anglo-Germans apart from the German-Anglos—to differentiate between the English merchant who came to Australia after years in Hamburg and the German who came after years in London. Adelaide and Melbourne were homes to both types—temporary homes, anyway, for those were mobile people.

The Lutherans in the Barossa Valley were located at the other end of the social spectrum. They check all the boxes that define communities likely to retain language and culture. They were rural, relatively isolated, and homogeneous; there was a high degree of marriage within the community, and German was used in church, Sunday school, and Lutheran day schools. People celebrated a "*Heimat* abroad" through their dress, music, and cuisine, and they created classic immigrant "frontier stories," like the "great trek" in wagons along the Murray River from the Barossa Valley to the Albury district in New South Wales. The powerful collective memory they constructed was closely tied to Lutheran identity and the region in Germany from which they came. But even in these communities there were influences that worked against an unchanging, singular identity. The public schools taught in English (with German sometimes used for religious instruction, as a concession), and in any case the German they spoke was subject to lexical transference. New words came in, and syntax changed; a "compromise dialect" emerged. What language was "*if der Vater hat keine Farm,*" or "*seinen Foot downputten*"?[28] The real paradox is that, even when the language did remain the same, it inevitably diverged from the changing German being spoken in Germany, for it was filled with unconscious archaisms.

Even closed-off Lutheran communities had to navigate between two cultures in matters ranging from the material (jobs, trade) to the emotional (marriage partners). This happened even more in urban settings. Single young men who did not come over as part of a group were much likelier to marry a non-German. (They were also the most likely to be in touch with trade union or Social Democratic friends at home, a reminder that bourgeois Germans were not alone in leading transnational lives.)[29] Young urban German immigrants were especially subject to the crosscurrents of popular culture, in sports, reading matter and music, notwithstanding the German brass bands and shooting and gymnastic clubs. Even before 1914 divided time into a "before" and "after," Germans in Australia were living their lives across cultures. They were bicultural as well as bilingual, able to switch. Like the Australian vineyards, which were usually German in origin but grew largely non-German grapes, they were hybrids.

Most German immigrants to non-English-speaking countries were to be found in Latin America. A few thousand went there in the early nineteenth century. At least 150,000 followed them between the 1840s and 1914. More than half went to Brazil, the rest to the Spanish-speaking countries, with Argentina and Chile the two most common destinations.[30] The more modest in size the community, the likelier it was to consist of the socially well established, or at least young men of good family looking to make their way in the world. A classic example of the type was Rudolf Ludwig, the eldest son of a Württemberg clergyman, who went out to Bolivia at the age of twenty-one to represent an import-export firm. In letters to his parents and his brothers (one of whom, also footloose, settled in Shanghai), Ludwig offered an upbeat account of life in Latin America, "the land of my fortune." He described the pleasures of being his own boss, the material opportunities, the good food and wine, the riding, and the Indigenous servant girl that came with wealth, as well as the balls at which "Don Rodolfo" was much sought after. "Here, I am the big shot," as he wrote his mother. We can see the element of self-fashioning in all this, the determination to prove that he had made it. Even when the letters adopt a querulous tone, Ludwig makes it quite clear what kind of life he has chosen. He complains that a zither has not yet arrived, and asks that his family send him German illustrated magazines, not religious tracts. He also complains about the rain, mosquitoes, and occasional bouts of homesickness. Ludwig nonetheless expected not to return to Germany, but to stay in South America, or perhaps seek a position in China, Japan, or Australia.[31]

There were many German merchants in Latin America. Mexico City is a good example of a German community built around a mercantile core. Just fifty strong in 1820, the German colony had grown to more than twelve hundred people by 1914. The once predominantly male population included many more women and children. Sojourners had become permanent residents, the loose German diaspora an ethnic enclave. The last twenty years before World War One saw the founding of a German newspaper, sports clubs devoted to rowing, riding, swimming, and gymnastics, masonic lodges, a women's organization, and a German school. In this self-sufficient world, intermarriage was rare and German continued to be spoken in the home, except for the minimal Spanish needed to instruct servants.[32] There were German communities like this across Latin America. They had merchants or financiers at their center, and included engineers, scientists, academics, diplomats, and the occasional army officer. Where there were also German miners or settlers in the country, there would be virtually no contact between them and the well-heeled urban Germans. They lived in separate worlds.

The two largest German communities were in Brazil and Argentina, although in both cases it is probably misleading to use the term "community" for such diverse groups. Take the booming nineteenth-century city of Buenos Aires. It had a German merchant colony, which by midcentury had established its own social organizations and a Protestant church. But the bankers and merchants were soon surrounded by a broader swathe of professionals and scholars, printers, restaurateurs, and the entrepreneurs who established breweries just outside the city. All helped to sustain German sports clubs, theater, and newspapers (the conservative *Deutsche La Plata Zeitung* and the liberal *Argentinisches Tageblatt*). The immigrants' children attended the many German schools in the city, which were supported by parental contributions and generous subsidies from the German Foreign Office, tens of thousands of marks a year by 1914. The teachers themselves, typically volunteers who filled short-term positions abroad before returning to Germany, were another link with the homeland. This conscious cultivation of German language and culture did not preclude intermarriage with social equals among the local population. Buenos Aires was home to Belgrano-Deutsch, a hybrid mixture of German and Spanish that took its name from a wealthy suburb of the capital.[33] It was in Belgrano that the later Nazi "blood and soil" food minister Walther Darré (full name Ricardo Walther Oscar Darré) was born in 1895, the son of a German merchant of Huguenot origins and a mother who was of mixed Swedish, German, and Spanish ethnicity.

Less salubrious parts of the city had many more Germans. The port of Buenos Aires became a great entrepôt for shipping out wheat and beef from the pampas. Thousands of German sailors passed through the city. Some of them stayed. A rough measure of their numbers is suggested by the twelve hundred merchant seamen from Hamburg alone who jumped ship in Buenos Aires between 1890 and 1910—a good place to do so, because Argentina had refused to sign an extradition treaty with Germany. As for the German sailors who did return to their ships, the moral perils they supposedly faced led the Protestant "inner mission" to establish a German sailors' home in the waterfront district of La Boca.[34] The cheap board, showers, mail service, and picnics (beer included) were popular. Whether they were entirely successful in preventing sailors from visiting brothels or in "hindering the growth of a useless seafaring proletariat" is less certain.[35] What is certain is that large-scale German immigration in the decades before 1914 created a proletariat on dry land. In Buenos Aires, as in Adelaide, German craftsmen and laborers arrived with socialist ideas in their baggage. In 1882 they founded a socialist organization with a newspaper, *Vorwärts*, and applied German-style class analysis to the stockyards and factories of the booming capital. Buenos Aires was part of an exploitative global market, they argued, advising German workers to learn Spanish and join the Argentinian labor movement.[36] The contrast with the way that bourgeois Germans saw the world could hardly have been greater.

Ethnic Germans from Russia also moved to Argentina. They were a distinctive group, rather like the Lutherans of South Australia. Some were Mennonites. These German immigrants to Argentina in the 1880s were descendants of those who emigrated from southwest Germany a century earlier in search of land, encouraged by Catherine the Great. Having left the Rhine for the Volga, they now left the Volga for the Río Plata. Having abandoned Russia because their separate schools and exemption from military conscription were under attack, they were welcomed in Argentina and offered special concessions as settlers in areas recently "pacified" by a murderous military campaign against the Indigenous population, the Argentinian version of the U.S. Indian Wars, known as the *conquista del desierto*. The "clearing" of the pampas put into practice what Domingo Faustino Sarmiento, Argentina's Germanophile president, called the triumph of civilization over barbarism. It opened up vast new territories for stock raising and grain cultivation. The Volga Germans who built colonies in the former frontier provinces of La Pampa and Río Negro were as much a part of that process as the German merchants and workers in Buenos Aires.[37]

The Germans in Brazil also helped to open up the South American hinterland. Germans had been active in the business of sugar cultivation since the sixteenth century. In *Nine Generations*, his history of a Hamburg merchant dynasty based on family papers, Percy Ernst Schramm describes the three decades one of his forebears spent in Brazil during the mid-nineteenth century. Ernst Schramm went there with his wife and child to run a sugar export business founded by his brother in a town on the Sergipe River. Steamship service had been established just a few years earlier when, in 1858, he wrote home about the "huge resources" of Brazil and the wonderful things that might be achieved by the "cultivated European hand of man." Alas, he added, everything was still neglected and undeveloped, for it was the "curse" of the lands most favored by nature that their human inhabitants were the most "careless and indolent." It was a typical European view. So was the attitude to slavery recorded by his wife, Adolphine, in a letter: "We are reasonably happy with our slaves; they all steal and lie, naturally. But we never beat them; the greatest punishment is when we threaten to sell them, for they love us and the good life enough to make them shrink from any change." She hastened to assure her friend in Germany that the Schramms would dearly have liked to free their slaves, but— so she argued—slavery was a "necessary evil" and emancipation "a more complicated question" than sentimentalists believed.[38]

That was how things looked in sugar country. But everywhere in Brazil we find clusters of German merchants, professionals, and scholars in the towns and cities, as in other South American countries. And, of course, wherever there were mines there were German mining engineers. But most Germans in Brazil lived rural lives. They settled in the three southern states of Rio Grande do Sul, Paraná, and Santa Catarina, which absorbed a majority of the roughly 100,000 German immigrants between the 1820s and World War One. Their birthrates were exceptionally high. Families with ten children were common, so the numbers of second- and third-generation German-Brazilians rose quickly. Rio Grande do Sul alone had 150,000 inhabitants of German descent by 1914. German immigrants established three hundred settlements in all, many formed by clearing the interior rain forest of the south and establishing stock-raising or growing cash crops—wheat, maize, tobacco, and cassava. Rural businesses like mills, tanneries, and stores developed to service these *colonias*, as well as heavily German towns like Pôrto Alegre. There was much pioneer myth-making about the arduous labor and sacrifice involved in conquering "wild nature," a story line amplified by German travelers to Brazil and writers back home who praised the order that had been created by "German" hard work. Commentators passed over the slash-and-burn agriculture, just as their gaze passed over the Indigenous peoples who stood in the way of commercial development.[39]

The late-nineteenth-century Brazilian government policy of encouraging European immigration had a racial as well as economic motive. It was intended to be part of the process of *embranquecimento*, or "whitening" the population.[40] The Germans were, in that sense, a racial tool, like the more numerous Italians, Spanish, and Portuguese. But Germans kept to themselves more than other European immigrant groups, a self-segregation that went hand in hand with their relatively isolated rural settlements. They established their own German-language schools in which Portuguese was not taught, the only Brazilian schools of which that was true. This led to complaints about German arrogance and unwillingness to assimilate. The schools were Protestant, something else that set Germans apart.

Some German Protestants belonged to nonmainstream sects. This was the milieu that spawned a violently messianic movement in the rural district of Rio Grande do Sul in the early 1870s. Jakobine Mentz was the daughter of Anabaptists who had fled Germany as religious émigrés in 1824. She married the settler Georg Maurer, who had a reputation for performing miraculous cures, and in 1872 Jakobine Maurer began to call herself a "female Christ" who communed directly with Jesus and the Almighty. She quickly acquired a cult following, like many European female prophets of the nineteenth century, proclaiming that the end-times were near and only those who followed her would be saved. The movement took on increasingly darker tones as Jakobine encouraged violence against opponents and apostates, culminating in the night of June 25, 1874, when scores of German colonists were killed by her loyal disciples in shootings and arson attacks on more than a dozen homesteads. The first detachment of soldiers sent to put down what was now considered an uprising were ambushed and forced to withdraw, with thirty-five officers and men killed or seriously injured. A second contingent, this one five hundred strong, then moved against the well-provisioned tabernacle-cum-fortress that cult members had built. A bloody shoot-out ensued, first at the fortress, then in the surrounding forest. The death toll among sectarians and soldiers almost certainly ran to more than one hundred. The violence perpetrated by cult members was then repaid postmortem by outraged colonists who dismembered their dead bodies. The event completely upended the usual settler narrative. Karl von Koseritz, the liberal Protestant editor of *Die Deutsche Zeitung* in nearby Pôrto Alegre, wrote an account of events for readers of a German weekly magazine. It was filled with a sense of outrage that this kind of "fanaticism"—and from Protestants, no less!—should have erupted in the age of progress and overshadowed what hardworking German colonists had achieved.[41]

The experiences of Germans in Australia, Brazil, and Argentina were remarkably diverse. They showcase a wide range of German and hybrid identities. Yet these communities were relatively small. The place where we find every possible variation of the German diasporic experience was the place to which, by a wide margin, they went in the largest numbers: the United States. The great majority of Germans who migrated overseas in the nineteenth century went to America, around 5 million out of 5.5 million. That is to say, nine out of ten Germans went to the United States, a higher proportion than we find among other European emigrants.[42] They went in waves, with peaks resembling those to other destinations in the 1850s and '60s, and especially the 1880s. Two million German men, women, and children arrived in the United States between 1878 and 1893.[43] The peak period of German mass migration coincided with the movement of other north Europeans across the Atlantic (Anglo-

Scots, Irish, Scandinavians), and it overlapped at the end with the growing numbers reaching America from Italy and eastern Europe.

*An undated photograph of German emigrants taking a meal in
Hamburg before boarding their ship to cross the Atlantic.*

Where did they go? Almost everywhere. The original eighteenth-
century German settlements were on the eastern seaboard. The newcomers moved into the Ohio River Valley and the midwest. After the Civil
War those seeking land fanned out into Michigan, Wisconsin, Iowa, and
Minnesota, then farther west. For a long time, accounts of the "German
element" in the United States emphasized sturdy farmers on the western
frontier.[44] And is true that the arrival of early German immigrants during
a period of westward expansion and white settlement meant that many
peasant families exchanged the land hunger of Baden or Württemberg for
a farm in Indiana or Wisconsin. A generation after the Homestead Act
of 1862, about one-third of the German-born population in America was
engaged in agriculture.

But the typical German experience in the United States was urban, and
increasingly so as the century went on. German-born immigrants and their

children helped to fill growing American cities from the Atlantic coast, through upstate New York and the industrial towns of Pennsylvania and Ohio, to the "German triangle" in the midwest between Cincinnati, St. Louis, and Milwaukee.[45] One measure of the spread of Germans into urban areas was the decision of major U.S. cities to introduce German-language instruction into public schools. Eight did so between 1864 and 1874.[46] Milwaukee was the most German city of all. More than half of its inhabitants in 1910 were first- or second-generation Germans and it was said that "a visit to Milwaukee is almost like a visit to one of the cities of the Rhine."[47] But just to the south, along the shore of Lake Michigan, the numerical presence of Germans in Chicago was even greater. They made up between a quarter and a third of the masses who fueled the astonishing growth of the city, from 300,000 in 1870 to 1 million twenty years later. Chicago in 1900 was one of the leading "German" cities in the world, as Paris had been fifty years earlier.

Germans created distinctive urban neighborhoods: Klein Deutschland in New York City, the Swillburg in Rochester, New York, Over-the-Rhine in Cincinnati, Deutschtown in Pittsburgh, Little Saxony in New Orleans. In Tennessee, both Memphis and Nashville boasted a Germantown. The larger cities had German newspapers and periodicals, theaters, choral societies, gymnastic and shooting clubs, associations of every kind, and of course beer gardens. The sheer density of these institutions was astounding. In the early twentieth century there were more German-language periodicals published in the United States than all other non-English periodicals combined.[48] So pervasive was German-American theater that we have studies of it in twenty cities and states.[49] Eating and drinking, singing and playgoing—the outgoing conviviality of German-American life was often remarked on by others. It appeared "more public and more sensuous" than the surrounding culture.[50] These thousands of institutions helped to create a German-American world. They marked out the "invention of ethnicity" by German migrants.[51]

That does not mean the German neighborhoods were homogeneous. In the cities, unlike many rural settlements, the Germans came from different areas back home. They were also divided in their religious observances. Among the beer gardens, stores, and clubs in German neighborhoods were churches serving both Protestants and Catholics. German urban communities were also socially diverse. The people emphasized by the heritage industry, alongside the highly visible '48ers, are the captains of industry, the famous success stories. They have been the subject of a major study on German "immigrant entrepreneurs."[52] It has 128 entries on individuals, many of them household names: Pfizer (pharmaceuticals), Singer (sewing machines), Levi Strauss (jeans), Steinway (pianos), Wurlitzer (musical instruments), Berlitz (language schools), Kroger (grocery stores), Filenes (department stores), the Goldman of Goldman Sachs (finance), the Ridder of Knight Ridder (newspapers), both halves of Anheuser-Busch, as well as Pabst and Yuengling (beer). It might well have included the founder of the H. J. Heinz Company, born shortly after his parents left the Palatinate for Pittsburgh in the 1840s. There were others, too, who were not household names but helped to define American life. Claus Spreckels, the "Sugar King of the West," introduced both granulated sugar and the sugar cube to the United States and became one of the ten richest men in the country while doing so.[53] Some of the successful entrepreneurs were German-Jewish immigrants, who (like the much larger number of their fellow Jews who did not became rich) remained invisible in many earlier accounts of Germans in America.[54] Stepping back, though, the single most striking aspect of this entrepreneurial roll call is how many businesses were in the service sector—food, drink, retail, apparel, leisure. This points to a broader characteristic of German-Americans, which is the size of the lower-middle class of small businesses and service workers.

But the largest single group of Germans in the United States consisted of workers. That became increasingly true because later German immigrants were no longer small farmers but factory hands and laborers. Germans were very active in supporting and sometimes founding trade unions, socialist parties, and left-wing newspapers. This politically conscious proletarian milieu, female as well as male, helped to support the Social Democratic Party (SPD) in Germany during the period of political persecution, between 1878 and 1890. German socialism in America even reproduced some of the same divisions that existed within the German SPD between radical and pragmatic or reformist elements. A classic embodiment of the latter was the Milwaukee socialist leader Victor Berger, who became an "evolutionary moderate."[55] The same divisions ran through the trade union movement. In Milwaukee, German-Americans led both the radical Central Labor Union and the more moderate Knights of Labor.[56]

Then there were the German anarchists. They are probably best known because of the Haymarket affair in May 1886, when a peaceful demonstration in Chicago in favor of the eight-hour day ended when an unknown person threw a bomb that killed seven police officers and four others. Eight anarchists were subsequently tried for conspiracy. The trial, which took place against the background of a "red scare," was seriously flawed and ended with seven death sentences and one sentence of fifteen years, despite the absence of evidence that the accused had any role in the bombing. Two of the sentences were later commuted by the governor of Illinois, one defendant committed suicide in his cell, and the remaining four were executed. Like the Sacco and Vanzetti case thirty-four years later, the Haymarket trial became an international cause célèbre. Five of the eight defendants were German-born immigrants and a sixth was American-born with German parents.[57]

From immigrant entrepreneurs to immigrant radicals, Germans left their imprint. The architecture of entire city neighborhoods, like the ornate brick vernacular of Over-the-Rhine in Cincinnati, bore the stamp of the Germans who built them. Downtown Milwaukee had its Pfister Hotel, Pabst Theater, and Schlitz Palm Garden, as well as the city's first skyscraper, the thirteen-story Pabst Building completed in 1892.[58] It was a second-generation German who gave America the Louisville Slugger, Germans who gave America its pretzels, brats, and beer—the last-named a major source of friction with nativist temperance supporters.[59] It was the Germans Rudolph Dirks and Harold Knerr who gave America one of its first and most enduring comic strips, *The Katzenjammer Kids*, based on the children's stories of Wilhelm Busch about the mischievous Max and Moritz.[60] All this belonged to one side of a double-sided process, for in numerous ways America left its imprint on German immigrants. There were changes in reproductive patterns, as families became smaller in the second generation. Modifications in names marked a further shift. Consider just one German-American baby born in Manhattan in 1891 and brought up in Brooklyn. He became the celebrated but controversial writer Henry Miller. The son of Heinrich Miller and the grandson of Heinrich Müller, he was the perfect example of a three-generation name shift.

Both of Henry Miller's parents were German, but "marrying out" was another way German-Americans became acculturated. There were many others. German-American women's organizations show how this happened in everyday life. At social events mounted by the women's sections of clubs, the American flag was displayed alongside club banners. Women formed themselves into female branches of masonic lodges, copying an American practice that remained unknown in Germany before 1914. Even a traditionalist Catholic organization like the Christian Mothers Association borrowed American methods that were unfamiliar at home, such as door-to-door collections.[61] In the labor market, workers mingled with workers of other ethnicities—male workers, at any rate, for the proportion of German women who worked outside the home was lower than in any immigrant group other than Italians.[62] The fact that Germans were disproportionately engaged in the service sector, earning a living as brewers, tailors, tobac-conists, and sellers of musical instruments, inevitably brought them into contact with non-German customers. They might even be seen as brokers between communities. As for the thousands of German newspapers and periodicals, they served the purpose of "translating" America to German speakers and showing how it worked, even if the guardians of "institu-tional" German-American culture wanted them to shore up German iden-tity.[63] The heated discussions among self-appointed guardians of German culture about the "Americanization" of youth suggest just how widespread the phenomenon was.

Language was the key. German-American teachers noticed how the children of German families spoke English among themselves. English was spoken in German gymnastic societies and even by the typesetters on German-American newspapers.[64] But this was not a straightforward mat-ter of German language and identity being "lost" in an American melt-ing pot. Many German-Americans spoke a mixture of mother tongue and foreign language, moving between German as a domestic language, or *Tischgespräch*, and English as a public language.[65] In a larger sense, they cre-ated a hybrid culture with hazy boundaries. They lived across and between cultures. As in Australia, this happened more quickly in cities than in rural areas, and it accelerated as the flow of new arrivals dried up and earlier generations died off. The cycle began early in a city such as New Orleans, where the inflow of new immigrants was shut off unusually early.[66] In most places, the 1890s marked a high point in the size and influence of the Ger-man press and theater that was never reached again.

What impact did the German immigration to America have on soci-ety at home? Many emigrants returned, especially when the journey by steamship was reduced to a mere nine or ten days. They went back in larger numbers than the Irish, although in smaller numbers than the Italians, and the pace picked up in the late nineteenth century. The precise numbers are hard to pin down because returners have to be disentangled from business travelers and visitors, but we are talking about hundreds of thousands. The reasons were many. Some were disappointed in their hopes. One disillusioned upholsterer and decorator who went to upstate New York wrote to a friend complaining that the positions available in America were worse than those in Germany. He had become thoroughly miserable after just nine months: "Life in Buffalo is a real dog's life." He begged his friend to go to his mother and tell her he would shoot himself unless she sent money for the return journey.[67] But the disappointed "failures" were probably a minority of returners. Most had greater assets when they returned than when they left. They came back to pursue their old craft with more capital behind them, to buy a plot of land, or to retire on their American earnings. Johann Albert Diercks went to the United States as a sixteen-year-old in 1872, working as a commercial clerk in New York and in Savannah, where he opened a grocery store and then a bar. In 1903, he returned as a forty-seven-year-old to Bremen, where he lived comfortably off the income from his business and properties in Georgia.[68] Another type of returner was the entrepreneur looking to apply techniques learned in America to the German market. Most who re-migrated were surely not pursuing comparative advantage in this way. But all, in one way or another, were leading transnational lives. And so were the political returners: the '48ers who eventually went back to Germany (some after twenty years), and the Social Democrats who fled to the United States in 1878 and stayed until Bismarck's antisocialist law was lifted in 1890. They carried their American experiences back to Germany with them, just as they had carried their German experiences with them to America.

The American impact on Germany went beyond the physical presence of those who returned. The uncle in America became a clichéd figure in German society by the late nineteenth century; a picture of America formed in the minds of everyone who read letters from friends and relations.[69] An imagined America was also created by the voluminous German travel literature and fiction about the United States.[70] Friedrich Gerstäcker contributed to both genres. The Hamburg-born son of an actress and an operatic tenor, young Gerstäcker was destined for a life in commerce after his father died, but rebelled. Having devoured both *Robinson Crusoe* and the Leatherstocking tales of James Fenimore Cooper, he told his mother that he wanted to emigrate to America. He did so in 1837, just short of his twenty-first birthday. His mother persuaded Gerstäcker to acquire some training in agriculture before he left, so he could succeed as a farmer, but he lived a picaresque existence in the United States, earning his living variously as a farmer, hunter, lumberjack, deckhand, riverboat stoker, chocolate maker, silversmith, trader, and hotelkeeper. He returned after six years. His novel *The Arkansas Regulators* appeared in 1845, *The River Pirates of the Mississippi* three years later. Both were bestsellers, allowing Gerstäcker to devote himself full-time to writing. Other novels followed; so did dramas, poetry, and essays. Gerstäcker made two further visits to America. Out of his experiences he fashioned lively works of reportage for German readers—*In the Arkansas Backwoods*, *Rambles Through America*, *Scenes of Life in California*, and many more. He also wrote about German emigrants to America, together with a book—*To America!*—that encouraged others to follow.[71]

There were other prolific nineteenth-century German writers on America. Charles Sealsfield, the pseudonym of Moravian-born Carl Anton Postl, was one. Like Gerstäcker, he had lived in the United States and knew the country well. Neither was true of Karl May, the most famous German writer on America (and Hitler's favorite), whose many works about Winnetou, Old Shatterhand, and the American west were untouched by personal experience. May did not visit the United States until 1908, when he spent six weeks far removed from the west in New York and Massachusetts.[72] America also turned up in Gustav Freytag's bestseller *Soll und Haben* (*Credit and Debit*). The character Fritz von Fink first truly finds himself on the American frontier, before returning to help his friend and the hero of the novel, Anton Wohlfahrt, to defend a German settlement against Polish rebels on another "frontier," this one in the German east rather than the American west.

As the German love affair with the Polish cause faded after 1848, it is remarkable how often the clash between white settlement and Native American resistance suggested itself to German writers as a parallel to ethnic conflict closer to home. Germans routinely wrote about the Poles, dismissively, as "Indians" or "redskins," something the Polish writer Ludwik Powidaj noted as early as 1864, in an article called "Poles and Indians."[73] Germans were clearly cast as the hardy, fearless settlers, a view that also found its way into historical and fictional works about German medieval settlement in the east that appeared in large numbers in the late nineteenth century. In these, Germans were always "pioneers" who brought farming, trade, and the rule of law, while the indigenous Slavs were nomadic peoples who tried to resist the march of civilization. This was a form of German self-image, expressed in the language of the frontier, which would gain even greater purchase in the first half of the twentieth century. But it was at odds with another form of self-image that became increasingly popular toward the end of the nineteenth century, not least because of Karl May—the honest, upright German and the "noble" Native American as kindred spirits.[74] Could Germans really be both sturdy frontiersmen and noble Native Americans? In the twentieth century they would be forced to choose. In the nineteenth century America remained for Germans in Germany a mirror—actually, a large distorting mirror—in which they saw their own society reflected.

Colonies

GOVERNMENTS, WORRIED ABOUT LOSING PRODUCTIVE CITIzens, had often tried to restrict emigration. But they also saw the value of exporting potential unrest. This "safety-valve" view commanded widespread support in the nineteenth century, going back to the disastrous year of postwar famine and rural distress in 1817, when the diplomat and politician Hans von Gagern wrote that mass emigration was "without doubt desirable and hugely beneficial to internal order."[75] Later commentators agreed that, in light of German "overpopulation" (the term was routinely used), emigration should be encouraged to head off the threat of pauperism and social unrest.

But there was another side to the question. Paul Pfizer was already worrying in the early 1830s in his book *The Correspondence* about Germans being assimilated by their host societies and losing their "Germanness." Many contemporaries wrote in similar vein. Friedrich List was one of the most influential. He knew the United States well because he had lived there in the 1820s before returning to Europe. He had also seen at first hand as a Württemberg official in the crisis year 1817 how government indifference and incompetence drove people to leave. He loathed the consequences. "How does it help the German nation," asked List, "no matter how happy the emigrants to North America become, if their persons are lost to German nationality for all time?"[76] The same question was posed by the Frankfurt parliamentarians in 1848.[77] The "loss" of *Volkskraft*, or national energy, exercised many German minds in the era of mass emigration after the midcentury. The fact that Prussia and other states ceased to recognize the continued citizenship of emigrants who had lived abroad uninterruptedly for ten years heightened the concern. It was in response to fears about "lost"

Germans that the 1870 citizenship law of the North German Confederation, which became German law the following year, modified the ten-year
rule. Germans abroad could now retain their citizenship if they reported
to consular officials every ten years—not a very high bar, although it did
require emigrants to be thinking about returning home, or at least keeping
their options open.[78]

What to call those who departed Germany—"emigrants" or "Germans
abroad," *Auswanderer* or *Auslandsdeutche*? The second term began to replace
the first after midcentury. It conveyed the consoling message that those
who had left were not really "lost" to the homeland, but remained a part of
the imagined nation, spreading the values of German culture, hard work,
and discipline around the globe.[79] The invention of "Germans abroad" as a
label was how nationalists reassured themselves, like the Italian elites who
referred in the same way to Italians abroad—the *Italiani al estero*.[80] The idea
that a global Germany existed beyond the confines of Bismarck's nation-
state was an article of faith for radical nationalists. An organization was
founded in 1881 to support the German diaspora. It lobbied the Foreign
Office successfully to subsidize German schools overseas. The tens of thousands of marks that went to German schools in Buenos Aires were among
the millions of marks that flowed around the world by 1914 to fund German
teachers, books, maps, and gymnastic equipment.[81]

Maps and vaulting horses no doubt served to tend the flame of German identity, but nationalists wanted stronger responses to the "loss" of
Germandom abroad. The one they favored was the establishment of German settler colonies. For much of the nineteenth century, German colonial advocates looked to the United States as the most suitable place for
them. In 1817, Hans von Gagern sent his cousin on a fact-finding mission
to explore the feasibility of a German colony in the American west, but
concluded regretfully that such a colony would be politically impossible to
establish.[82] That did not deter other enthusiasts. The *Augsburger Allgemeine
Zeitung* pushed for the establishment of German colonies in North America as a matter of urgency. "Germany could spill her heart's blood for centuries if she does not found a new Germany on another continent," wrote
the paper in 1843.[83] As German emigration soared in the 1840s, so did the
number of newspaper articles linking emigration with colonization. Well-
known America experts like Friedrich List and Robert von Mohl were
among those who weighed in.

The writers differed on where exactly these German colonies should be. Sometimes they pointed to the American midwest, sometimes to the southwest, sometimes to the far west. The democratic nationalist Franz Löher, hedging his bets, proposed that the German Confederation purchase land for German settlement from either Canada or Mexico.[84] The liberal nationalists Hermann Blumenau and Ernst Ludwig Brauns both pointed to the west as the ideal place for German settlers. Brauns made the case forcefully, even belligerently. Instead of allowing German nationality to seep away in scattered settlements, he wrote, a consolidated colony should be established west of the Mississippi. Germany was not San Marino, and Germans should not be treated as an "appendage" of the Yankees, a "helot" people. The German population should not "allow itself to be disparaged like a Negro from the African coast."[85] Let Germans purchase land from Mexico or from the "bold Comanchees and Apaches," establish a New Germany in the west, and proudly fly the German flag.[86]

There had, in fact, been an attempt to create a German colony in the southwest just a few years earlier. It was undertaken by the Mainzer Adelsverein, popularly known as the Texas Association, a company formed in 1842 by Rhineland aristocrats to establish a German colony in Texas through organized mass emigration. It eventually settled just seven thousand Germans in Texas, more than half of whom died. The enterprise was a fiasco. The company had clearly failed in its main objective by 1845 and went bankrupt in 1853.[87] But it is impossible, anyway, to imagine that a New Germany of the kind Blumenau and Brauns envisioned could have established itself in Texas or California. This was the era of American "manifest destiny" (the phrase was coined by newspaper editor John O'Sullivan in 1845). The United States annexed Texas in 1845, and fought a war with Mexico the following year to retain it. In the same campaign, Commodore John Sloat sailed into Monterey Bay and the American government secured military control of California.[88] In those same years Americans harbored dark suspicions about British designs on Oregon. There is no chance whatsoever that U.S. leaders would have tolerated a sovereign colony that flew the flag of the German Confederation.

The revolutionary year 1848 nonetheless brought renewed enthusiasm for German colonies in the United States. Politicians in Frankfurt argued that the creation of a new German nation-state would be the springboard. Unified Germany would have the leverage that individuals or small states lacked, and Washington would welcome this because it would strengthen the "natural friendship between us."[89] The enthusiasm for establishing German colonies in North America was most pronounced on the left, although it existed across the political spectrum. The revolution energized politics and gave the issue new life. Twenty-two new organizations concerned with emigration and colonization in America were founded in 1848–49. Dozens of plans, petitions, and memoranda on the subject poured into Frankfurt.[90]

It remained illusory, however, to believe that the Germans already in the United States or later arrivals who went as a part of directed settlement plans could become the raw material of German colonies—that it would be possible, somehow, to convert the qualities associated with German settlers into a form of sovereignty. These dreams were being pursued at the very moment when the lands singled out by the dreamers were, one by one, joining the Union as states—Texas in 1845, Iowa in 1846, Wisconsin in 1848, California in 1850. The radical democrat Wilhelm Schulz urged Germans to "make haste," but in fact it was already too late. By the 1850s colonial fantasies had been quietly laid to rest. There was still discussion of German settlers in America, in popular journals and specialist publications, but these now emphasized the German contribution to American westward expansion, a flattering self-image of the role the "German race" supposedly played in the opening up of American continental space by white settlers.

Many German colonial enthusiasts shifted their sights after midcentury from North America to South and Central America, where allegedly "soft" Hispanic inhabitants were expected to exert less pressure to assimilate.[91] The case for South America was already being made in the 1840s and the plans kept coming. Baron Alexander von Bülow founded the Berlin Colonization Association, which settled a hundred German families in Nicaragua in 1853. Despite many examples of misbegotten settlements in the recent past, the "mosquito coast" continued to exert its allure.[92] Karl Gaillard, a writer and music critic (he was an early Wagner enthusiast), was one voice in the chorus. He foresaw Germans spreading out from Nicaragua to Guatemala, and beyond. "Spanish America—that is our Canaan," he suggested grandly.[93] Gaillard also proposed a German colony in Brazil, the darling of many colonial advocates as a place where Germandom could flourish.

By the 1870s, there were few places in the world that had not been identified at one time or another as the ideal site for a German colony. Friedrich List, tireless in coming up with places where Germans might settle, had eyed Australia, New Zealand, and the South Sea islands. The Lower Danube Valley, Bermuda, Abyssinia, Borneo—all had their advocates.[94] In

1847, a pamphlet on Prussia's future as a naval, colonial, and world power identified Africa as "the key to the world," and proposed that the continent receive 10 to 20 million Prussians who would Germanize "100 million Blacks." The three great German empires (in Africa, Europe, and America) would then allow "German blood" to rule the world with "humanity, virtue and justice."[95] Thirty-two years later, in his widely read book *Does Germany Need Colonies?*, Friedrich Fabri, a former missionary and colonial advocate, was more sober in tone but no less confident about the "tasks" facing the German race and no less global in his ambitions. He identified two main kinds of colony, for settlement and trade, while noting briefly a third kind—penal colonies to which a variety of political "subversives" could be packed off in the age of anarchist plots. Fabri offered no suggestions on where Germany might find its version of Russian Siberia or France's Devil's Island. His ideas about where Germany should look to fulfill its other colonial "needs" had, by the late 1870s, become familiar. Fabri pointed to Asia Minor, Australia, and New Zealand, but above all South America as places to which organized German emigration should be directed. As for trade colonies, he saw opportunities everywhere, from the Samoan islands to Central Africa.[96]

It was a series of German territorial acquisitions in Africa, in the mid-1880s, that propelled Germany into the ranks of European imperial powers. Within the space of just two years there were German colonies in Southwest Africa, Togo, Cameroon, and East Africa. A second flurry of new colonies followed in the late 1890s, with the province of Kiaochow in northern China and its hinterland on the Shandong peninsula, then the Pacific territories of eastern New Guinea, Samoa, and some smaller island chains. By the end of the century, Germany presided over the fourth-largest European empire.[97] How do we explain this quite sudden move to acquire colonies, and what were the effects at home?

The causes were, to borrow a term from Sigmund Freud, "overdetermined"—that is, we have more reasons than we need to explain why Germany became a colonial power when it did.[98] One driving force was the pressure exerted by public opinion and lobby groups. Books like Fabri's, and Wilhelm Hübbe-Schleiden's *German Colonization*, represented a new, more aggressive advocacy.[99] They amplified the message coming from such organizations as the German Colonial Association and the Society for German Colonization. The writers and pressure groups voiced a number of concerns. One was the long-standing nationalist complaint that emigration meant a loss of "national energy." The last and largest wave of emigration in the 1870s and '80s raised this anxiety to a new pitch and brought urgent appeals to preserve German culture through settlements.[100] The same years brought the "Great Depression," the global economic downturn that began in 1873 and triggered a move toward tariff protection and a new kind of imperialism. The so-called scramble for Africa was the classic expression of this. Businesses, colonial pressure groups, and other advocates argued that colonies offered the triple advantage of raw materials, markets, and a place where capital could be profitably invested. That was the case made by Fabri, who presented colonies as a solution to the problems of where to export people, goods, and capital. His landmark work offered "a comprehensive crisis therapy."[101]

These arguments for colonies were not just economic, and the noneconomic arguments were not just rationalizations of material interests. They were signs of the global imagination evident among members of the reading public by the 1880s. Germans had become familiar with reports about distant parts of the world. Some were produced by missionaries; others came from scientific travelers or explorers and were published in the major geographical journal of the day, *Petermann's Geographical Transactions*, but also in popular weeklies. Captain Karl Koldewey's second North Pole expedition of 1869–70 became a source of national pride when its crew, having wintered over in pack ice, arrived back in Bremen while the Franco-Prussian War was underway to find themselves toasted as having "gloriously demonstrated German nautical proficiency, German persistence and German striving for the enrichment of science."[102]

The cold, white Arctic was a place to plant a flag or name a sound. Africa, "hot" and "dark" in the German imagination, held a greater exotic, racially suffused fascination. Heinrich Barth, the geographer and explorer, had published his five-volume *Travels and Discoveries in North and Central Africa in 1857–58*, but it was mainly scholars who were interested. Gerhard Rohlfs was a more popular public figure. A youthful volunteer with the nationalist Schleswig-Holstein campaign in 1848 and a former physician with the French Foreign Legion, he was more adventurer than scholar. Rohlfs crossed the Sahara Desert in the mid-1860s from Tripoli to the Gulf of Guinea.[103] He was just one of a string of German Africa explorers who enjoyed a heyday as celebrities in the 1860s and '70s. Gerhard Rohlfs, Georg Schweinfurth, Karl Mauch, Gustav Nachtigal, Eduard Mohr—the list is long. Their travels took in the west and east coasts and the interior, although most ventured at some point into the Sahara. All fed a thirst for knowledge about Africa they had themselves helped to create.[104] They fostered a sense of European superiority and a belief that Germans had a civilizing mission—in Africa, and other parts of the world—by virtue of their supposedly greater energy and more developed culture.[105]

German colonial acquisition also had a tangled political background. The shift that occurred in the mid-1880s was partly a result of facts on the ground created by African adventurers like Carl Peters and Adolf Lüderitz. Peters, a clergyman's son who earned a doctorate in history, had spent time in Britain and saw himself as the German Cecil Rhodes. He founded the Society for German Colonization in 1884. At the end of that year Peters mounted an East African expedition in present-day Tanzania during which he signed a series of unscrupulously one-sided "treaties" with local chiefs granting him rights to commercial exploitation of the land.[106] Sixteen hundred miles away to the southwest, on the opposite coast of Africa, Adolf Lüderitz was up to the same tricks. Lüderitz came from a Bremen merchant family that dealt in tobacco. After working in the tobacco exchanges of the United States and trying his hand unsuccessfully as a rancher in Mexico, the twenty-five-year-old Lüderitz returned to Bremen bankrupt, but married into money and took over the family tobacco business when his father died. In 1882 he acquired a trading company on the Gold Coast, but that business failed. The following year he bought the Bay of Angra Pequena, in present-day Namibia, then conducted a series of dishonest negotiations with Africans chieftains that led to his owning a private empire of 225,000 square miles.

Bismarck agreed to make these territories German protectorates. That was what marked the beginning of Germany's formal empire. Rather like the sovereign entity established on Borneo by James Brooke, the self-styled Raja of Sarawak (the model for Rudyard Kipling's *The Man Who Would Be King*), Peters and Lüderitz carved out private states—"rogue empires." That was one of the things that recommended these territories to Bismarck, well-known as a colonial skeptic, especially after Peters threatened to cede his holdings to King Leopold of Belgium. German Foreign Office officials kept Bismarck carefully briefed on the Sarawak precedent. In theory, German East Africa and German Southwest Africa would not be a drain on public revenue even after Bismarck designated them formal protectorates (he avoided the word "colony"), and his decision to do so marked no major change of direction for the German chancellor. However, the decision to

establish protectorates had the effect of sucking the state into greater colonial engagement (and eventually military engagement), in a pattern that
was common to other European empires.[107]

Bismarck was also thinking about domestic politics. He saw the colonial issue as an opportunity to rally the parties of the center-right behind
him with a Reichstag election coming up, and perhaps even to counter-
act the appeal of the Social Democrats to German workers by waving the
national flag.[108] Both conservatives and liberals made this argument. Friedrich Fabri's book presented the conservative variant.[109] Liberal nationalists
had their own version of "social imperialism," the idea that workers could
be weaned from socialism if given reasons to identify more strongly with
the nation. Not all German liberals took this view. There was always a
stubbornly anticolonial strand among progressives. But in the 1880s, as in
1848, many liberals of different shades argued that in an increasingly competitive world a nation needed colonies, just as it needed a navy to protect
them, and this outward projection of German power would have an edu-
cative effect at home on the lower classes.[110] There was one more powerful
sentiment that helps to explain the widespread support for colonies. It was
the belief that Germany, finally united, needed to make up for lost time.
Call it a new assertiveness within the "belated nation," a desire to cut a figure in the world, often accompanied by sideways glances at Britain, which
was both admired and envied. That was a view widely held in conservative
and liberal circles, among business elites and the educated middle classes,
although it encountered opposition from Social Democrats, Catholics, and
some progressives.

Supporters advanced the same mix of economic arguments to justify the
colonial acquisitions of the late 1890s, although the downturn in German
emigration meant that settlement colonies received less emphasis, while a
rapidly globalizing economy meant that naval bases and coaling stations
received much more. Social imperialist arguments about the domestic use-
fulness of an aggressive foreign policy became even more central. They were
made by ministers like Navy Secretary Alfred von Tirpitz, the admiral who
was the architect of the German battle fleet and who saw great national
tasks as "a strong palliative against educated and uneducated Social-
democrats."[111] But they also came from liberal imperialists like the sociologist Max Weber, one of many "naval professors" who joined the Navy
League, a mass-membership civic organization. The case for colonies based
on prestige, or Germany's proper place in the world, had a sharper edge in

the 1890s, with Britain still serving as an admired but often resented point of reference.

The tone was set by Kaiser William II, who came to the throne in 1888 and voiced his desire for an assertive "world policy." One of his chosen instruments was the suave and self-confident Bernhard von Bülow, William's foreign minister from 1897 to 1900, then German chancellor until a great falling-out with the kaiser in 1909. Bülow's first speech as foreign minister contained two phrases that quickly found their way into the dictionaries of quotations. One was "place in the sun" ("we do not want to put anyone in our shadow, but we also demand our place in the sun"); the other was a sharply worded rejection of the idea that Germany was the contemplative "land of writers and thinkers." As Bülow put it, "The days when Germans granted one neighbor the earth, the other the sea, and reserved for themselves the sky, where pure doctrine reigns . . . those days are over."[112] It was while he was foreign minister that Germany acquired its second major tranche of colonies, the ones in China and the Pacific.

The German colonies lasted for just thirty years. The Dutch were in Java eleven times as long, the British in India six times as long. But during those thirty years Germans exercised every form of rule in the imperial repertoire—direct, indirect, "scientific" and developmental, paternalist, and brutally violent. This diversity was a result partly of the differences in size, environment, population, and function of the German colonies—whether they were seen as places where trade, plantations, or settlers had primacy. How power was exercised also depended on the nature of pre-existing political structures, on the reactions of Indigenous peoples to colonial authority, and on what Germans learned or adapted from other colonial nations during an era when one-fourth of the globe fell under the control of western powers. As in other empires, authority was often exercised by men on the ground, mostly few in number—just four hundred German officers and administrators ruled German East Africa in 1900. There were nonetheless major shifts over time in the policy handed down from Berlin. In the earliest, experimental stage, informal authority was exercised by a few individuals, primarily merchants and adventurers, under the protectorate system of royal charters. The resulting mismanagement and crass abuses, requiring interventions from Berlin, led to a more centralized system after 1890 (and Bismarck's fall from power) under a new colonial department within the German Foreign Office. This second phase of colonial rule ended when German policies provoked resistance, above all in East and Southwest Africa. It was answered by military violence, which reached genocidal proportions. The eventual result, after the colonial crisis ignited domestic political criticism, was a relatively less draconian exercise of colonial power after 1907 under Bernhard Dernburg, the liberal head of a newly created Colonial Office.[113]

German rule was most tolerant and paternalist in the Pacific: in New Guinea, which became a formal colony in 1898, after the German New Guinea Company failed, and in Samoa, acquired by international agreement the same year, following an equally inauspicious period of indirect rule by a German trading company. There was a reason for the tolerance, and it went beyond a desire to live down the earlier exploitation by German companies and planters. Going back to the time of the Forsters' and Chamisso's travels in the Pacific, Germans had read about the romantic "paradise" of the South Seas and the "noble savages" who lived there. That inveterate world traveler Friedrich Gerstäcker wrote in a similar vein during the 1860s. And at the end of the nineteenth century, as Germany took possession of its Pacific colonies, sentimental fascination with these (in jaded European eyes) simple, innocent peoples enjoyed new resurgence in an era when an affected distaste for materialism became fashionable once again.[114]

The governors who ruled after 1899 showed a notable sensitivity to local culture. Albert Hahl, the governor of New Guinea and a Bavarian lawyer by background, set out to limit the German planters' influence and supported native cultivation of the land. He used local officials to mediate between the German administration and the Indigenous population; traditional power structures were turned to German advantage rather than overturned. While governor, Hahl learned the Tolai language and maintained a relationship with a Tolai woman, with whom he had a child. In Samoa, Wilhelm Solf became governor in 1900. A philologist with a PhD in Sanskrit, Solf gave his children Samoan names, used Samoan terms and rituals when he met with local leaders, and happily performed the role of native king when it suited his purposes. These symbolic acts were a way of appropriating Samoan forms in order to exercise German authority noncoercively. There were no German military or police force in Samoa. But there was no doubting ultimate German authority. When it came to local culture, Solf permitted but regulated both long-standing customs and newer enthusiasms like cricket; he also challenged missionary zeal in protecting the local practice of *avaga*, a form of elopement. His chief justice, Erich Schultz, agreed to the imprisonment of Samoans who insulted local chiefs, part of a larger German design of working through traditional power structures. Schultz, who succeeded Solf as governor in 1911, even had himself tattooed.[115]

Solf, Schulz, and Hahl all faced down the German planters, relatively few in number, to try to prevent the exploitation of Indigenous peoples. But all was not sweetness and light. A report of the Rhenish Mission from New Guinea in 1903, five years after the New Guinea Company had relinquished control, claimed that missionaries still had to act as "advocates of the natives against many an unscrupulous European." Their meditation had prevented "injustice and baseness," possibly "bloodbaths."[116] Even the successes of German governors in protecting the Indigenes of New Guinea and Samoa rested on dubious foundations, for one way they prevented the exploitation of "noble" native peoples of the Pacific was by importing cheap Chinese "coolie" labor to work the cotton, coffee, and cocoa plantations. Some thirty-five hundred Chinese and two hundred Malays worked in the two German colonies by 1914. Their treatment caused Chinese ambassadors in Berlin to submit a series of diplomatic protests.[117]

In China itself, German rule differed fundamentally from the pattern in the Pacific. Kiaochow became a German colony after the murder of two Catholic missionaries in 1897. The ninety-nine-year leasehold (like the one the British enjoyed in Hong Kong) was part of the settlement with the Qing court over the missionaries' death. But the murders were really a convenient pretext to take control of an area long identified as a potentially valuable naval base and coaling station. Ferdinand von Richthofen, a German geographer and traveler in China who had been passing on his local knowledge to Bismarck since the 1860s, described Kiaochow Bay in 1882 as "the biggest and best ocean harbor in all of northern China." Admiral von Tirpitz visited the site and called for its occupation; in 1896 William II instructed the Imperial Navy Office to draw up plans. The killing of the missionaries the following year then provided the opportunity for Germany to pounce.[118]

The province and its main town, Qingdao, were directly run by the Navy Office, which made it singular among German colonies. Kiaochow was intended to be a naval base and a foothold for trade interests; it was also supposed to be a "model" colony, a showcase for German culture and scientific know-how. Exactly what this meant in practice changed over time. It always included the ostentatious display of German technological prowess. New harbor facilities were built in Qingdao and a new town laid out on the basis of a master plan. Rivers were regulated, railways constructed to link the port with the coal-rich interior, and specialists brought in to oversee the German-owned coal mines. German engineers were everywhere. In the early years of the colony, this hyperactivity by the "foreign devils" led to Chinese resistance by the Boxer rebels, which in turn was met by a brutal "pacification" campaign after the murder of a German envoy in 1900. The kaiser notoriously urged the departing soldiers to behave like "Huns," and the soldiers under the command of Alfred von Waldersee were guilty of massacres, violence that was loudly criticized by anticolonial opinion at home.

Most German administrators and residents of Qingdao showed racist contempt toward the Chinese. The colony was designed on a racially segregated basis as it grew in just fifteen years from a fishing village to a port and trading center with more than 55,000 inhabitants, mostly Chinese. Around 1904, however, the emphasis shifted and the "model" aspect of the colony acquired a different meaning. A combination of things—greater pushback by the Chinese state, the desire to accommodate Chinese business interests, the influence of more liberal Foreign Office factions—led to a change of course. Sinophile officials, translators, and missionaries went to Kiaochow and made their voices heard in the formulation of "native policy," drawing on a prior tradition of respect for Chinese culture that was now resurrected. The Seminar for Oriental Languages in Berlin fed sympathetic newcomers into the colony, and new institutions came into being. A German-Chinese college was established in 1909, the only university-level institution in the German colonies. Where once German residents had used whips on Chinese who failed to move off the sidewalk quickly enough, some Chinese were now permitted to play tennis at the Tsingtau Club. Whereas the earliest German architecture in Qingdao was designed to be authoritatively European, later buildings incorporated elements of the Chinese vernacular. None of this overturned the fundamentals of racial segregation, but it was a sign of cultural rapprochement and exchange, superimposed on the original system—an outcrop of what might be called benign Orientalism. Having shown northern China the mailed fist, Germany drew on the velvet glove.[119]

In Africa, the direction and severity of German rule varied greatly across the different colonies, but physical force was never far from the surface. The episodes of extreme violence against the African population occurred a generation after the Germans arrived, when military power was used to crush full-scale rebellions. Resistance was a response to policies that undermined and in some cases destroyed the existing way of life. That process began with the drawing of arbitrary boundary lines on the map, which casually divided African peoples between German and other colonial powers. Even the "tribal" units they took as the defining feature of local peoples were to a significant degree a European construct, a projection onto Africans of the conquerors' own understanding of ethnicity and identity.[120] While German administrators made some use of local ceremonial forms (like the *shauri* in East Africa, a kind of negotiation procedure), local power holders were constantly undercut and sometimes deposed by district officers wielding huge authority on the ground. This was especially true during military expeditions into the interior, from the coastal regions where the German rulers felt most secure. What administrators and missionaries arrogantly presented as a "civilizing mission" also weakened Indigenous cultural practices, religious rites, gender relations, and inheritance customs. Most subversive of all were the economic arrangements Germans imposed on unwilling Africans. Everywhere, land was expropriated, sometimes to make large plantations growing cotton, cocoa, sisal, or other single-crop monocultures, as in Cameroon and East Africa, sometimes to provide farms for German settlers, as in Southwest Africa.

Three-quarters of their land was confiscated from the Herero and Nama peoples in Southwest Africa, and much of their livestock with it. Governor Theodor Leutwein said in 1894, "The entire future of the colony lies in the gradual transfer of land from the hands of the work-shy natives to the Europeans."[121] Land and livestock seizures, taxation policies, and education designed to inculcate European "work-discipline"—all were intended to turn seminomadic African cattle herders into a pliant labor force living on reservations. An outbreak of rinderpest, a cattle disease, in 1897 ravaged the Hereros' remaining cattle and heightened the distress. The backlash came in the form of attacks on German settlers, a revolt led by Samuel Maherero, who had earlier cooperated with Governor Leutwein in order to slow the pace of land seizures. The uprising of the Herero began in 1904 and lasted for three years. It was eventually crushed by military force under the command of General Lothar von Trotha, a veteran of earlier pacification campaigns in East Africa and China. Trotha, who was appointed governor in place of the more conciliatory Leutwein, was frank about his policy. Africans were "all alike insofar as they only yield to violence. My policy was, and is, to exercise this violence with blatant terrorism and even cruelty." He promised to finish off the rebels with "rivers of blood."[122]

Trotha was as good as his word. After his forces failed to achieve total victory over the Herero at the Battle of Waterberg, which "enraged" Trotha, he followed a policy of "annihilation." German troops shot men, women, and children, then pursued the remaining Herero into the Omaheke Desert, a western extension of the Kalahari, where they were trapped and denied access to water. Those who tried to escape were shot. Other Herero were imprisoned in concentration camps with grossly inadequate food supplies. The Nama also rose in 1904, conducting a guerrilla war that was met with equal brutality. They too were imprisoned in poorly provisioned camps, including the notorious Shark Island. As many as 65,000 out of 80,000 Herero lost their lives as a result of these genocidal campaigns, and around half of the 20,000 Nama did.[123]

The death toll from the nearly contemporary Maji-Maji risings in German East Africa was even higher. The revolt was caused by similar anger about administrative high-handedness, interference with local cultural practices, and a new economic regime that meant land seizures and plantations on which Africans were reduced to forced labor. It was the last of these that triggered revolt in 1905. The uprising was fueled, like the Boxer Rebellion in China, by millenarian religious sentiment, and was crushed with equal ferocity. Captured rebels were summarily executed, often fifty or one hundred at a time, on the grounds that they did not deserve the treatment afforded in warfare among "civilized" Europeans. As many as 80,000 Africans lost their lives in the fighting, another 200,000 in the famine that followed.[124]

It was in East Africa and in Southwest Africa (the "colonial grotesque")[125] that the breech-loading gun and machine gun were wielded most conspicuously by German troops as "tools of empire."[126] But in Cameroon, too, there were punitive although less deadly campaigns to snuff out resistance to land seizures and forced labor on the new cocoa and cotton plantations. The governor there was a career diplomat, Jesko von Puttkamer. He was a friend of the British diplomat and Irish nationalist Roger Casement, who played a large part in exposing colonial abuses in the Belgian Congo. But Puttkamer proved to be an autocrat, a governor who promoted military expeditions into the interior and tolerated widespread violence against Africans on the plantations, a policy condemned by missionaries. Critics eventually forced his early retirement, although he was brought down over minor peccadilloes, not his autocratic ways.[127] Even in the so-called model colony of Togo, a coastal trading post where merchants and missionaries together prevented large-scale land seizures for plantations, military campaigns were conducted into the interior. During the "Tove war" of 1895, collective reprisals were undertaken against insurgent villages, farms and houses were torched, and prisoners of war were used to perform forced labor. Local crafts were vindictively destroyed, like the pottery industry, mainly in the hands of women, whose artifacts were smashed into shards that still littered the roadside years later.[128] Even in Togo then, the state deployed violence, even if intermittently. There, as in every German colony in Africa, ostentatious public executions and the display of bodies were intended as reminders of the power that the colonial authority held in reserve. Everywhere, too, Africans experienced the "soft" violence of residential segregation and curfews, as well as routine beatings on plantations and in private households.

Overt violence had a place in the German colonies, especially in Africa, that it did not have at home. Racism and cultural contempt made colonial subjects into dehumanized objects, while Berlin was willing to give wide discretion to the men on the spot and not ask too many questions unless a missionary or member of the Reichstag made a case of abuse too public to ignore (and the missionaries often kept quiet, because this gave them a hold over the colonial administration that increased their own freedom of action).[129] Violence was also the other side of the coin of weak everyday control: the "islands of rule" in East Africa, the uncertain state power in Southwest Africa outside the designated "police zone." In other words, German rule never achieved the kind of reach or established the level of legitimacy that it did within the borders of the 1871 nation-state.[130] That alone hardly set Germany apart from other European powers, all of whom sanctioned or tolerated high levels of violence against their colonial subjects, and for similar reasons. If there was something that made Germany distinctive, it was the size of the gap between the socially and bureaucratically disciplined society at home and the violent practices that marked German rule in Africa. Compulsory school attendance enforced in some German cities by gendarmes, the factory whistle and time clock, the presence of uniformed government officials in every walk of life, the workhouse—these exerted their own kind of disciplinary power. They made public executions and violent whippings, quotidian events in Cameroon and Southwest Africa, unheard of in Württemberg or Saxony.

Conscription was another of those disciplining agencies within metropolitan Germany. There *were* high levels of violence in the army, including the whipping of conscripts. Social Democrat Karl Liebknecht exposed these in his 1907 polemic against militarism.[131] But Liebknecht also noted that the German army intervened less to break up strikes than in most European countries. He might have added that the same reserve was generally true of the army's relations with minority communities on Germany's borderlands. The most notorious instance of the German army's domestic misbehavior was in the Alsatian town of Zabern in 1913, when insults by a junior officer directed against the local population led to protests, which in turn led to wholesale arrests. Twenty-six people were locked up in a coal cellar overnight; martial law was briefly declared. Zabern became a cause célèbre, the subject of a full-scale parliamentary debate about militarism. But no one died or was seriously injured.[132] By comparison with what happened in Southwest or East Africa, the scandal seems almost laughable, just as the actions of prewar antisemitic students who let mice loose in Jewish-owned department stores seem merely obnoxious in light of what was to follow thirty years later.

That prompts a big question. The colonies were sites of violence. Were they also breeding grounds of genocidal violence? Anyone who wants to argue for a line that runs from German atrocities in Southwest Africa to Nazi crimes in eastern Europe ("from Windhoek to Auschwitz") can point to continuities of people and ideas, there is no doubt about that.[133] But the lines of continuity are complicated. It is as plausible to argue that the Germans applied in Africa the lessons of their brutal responses to French franc-tireurs during the war of 1870–71 as it is to pin the "barbarism" of German military culture after 1914 on earlier colonial episodes.[134] The violence of the German colonial experience may loom larger in hindsight than it did to contemporaries. It is instructive to look at this through the eyes of Major Charles Edward Callwell, a pioneering British writer on colonial counterinsurgency. His book *Small Wars: Their Principles and Practice*, published in 1896, was concerned with irregular, guerrilla conflicts in European empires—the French, Dutch, Belgian, Portuguese, and Italian as well as the British. Callwell has a few comments, too, on the United States and Japan. On Germany, however, there is nothing. Only in the third edition, in 1906, does Germany enter the picture, and then only barely.[135]

Were the German colonies "laboratories of modernity" in a larger sense— places where it was possible to try out things that could not be tried out at home?[136] In some ways, they were. Consider agriculture. In East Africa the German state established a two-million-mark agricultural research station, the Amani Institute. New crops like cotton, sisal, cocoa, and tobacco were introduced on a major scale, especially in Africa. In one case, Booker T. Washington's Tuskegee Institute in Alabama was invited to send an expedition to Togo, in the hope that a cotton economy like that of the American south could be established in West Africa, a striking episode of three-way transfer.[137] Many of these experiments failed, as has often happened when monocultures are established. The German colonizers ignored the virtues of African interplanting, a practice well adapted to the local climate that conserved the soil but looked messy and asymmetrical to European eyes.[138] There were also sustained German efforts at town planning not only in Qingdao but in Douala, in Cameroon, in both cases based on the ruthless appropriation of land, the destruction of existing street plans, and the objective of creating racially segregated communities.[139] Hong Kong may have had some impact on the master plan for Qingdao. In the end, though, German urban planning in the colonies did not rival the scale of French efforts in Morocco, Indochina, and Madagascar, or similar projects in British India.[140]

Often, policies that look as if they owed their existence to the greater opportunities (read: lack of resistance) in a colonial setting turn out to be no bolder than policies enacted at home. Were the blueprints for Qingdao or Douala really any more daring than James Hobrecht's 1860s strategic plan for the development of Berlin, with its fifty-year time frame?[141] To take another example, German colonial authorities assumed major powers in policing the movement of Indigenous people, but it is not obvious that these efforts went beyond the increasingly strict controls imposed within Germany itself, especially on non-German groups such as Poles, Sinti, and Roma. Even the relative ease with which it was possible to deport Europeans from the German colonies has to be set against the history of deportation of Europeans—Alsatians, Poles, Danes, and German Jesuits—from metropolitan Germany.[142] Nor did these policing and deportation practices at home have colonial dress rehearsals, for they mostly came before, not after. The same is true in the realm of medicine. The inoculation of soldiers against typhoid may have been tried out first in Southwest Africa; however, compulsory immunization against smallpox had already been introduced in Germany in 1874, just three years after unification.

Germans nonetheless flaunted their technological accomplishments in the colonies. These went by the name "progress," a domestic keyword of liberal nationalists in the third quarter of the nineteenth century, now transferred to a global stage. That is what made colonies a liberal project as much as a conservative one, especially after 1907, when the "civilizing mission" took a progressive turn. One aspect of this was the huge railway-building program undertaken during the later years of German colonialism, especially in Africa. Rail lines were strategic battering rams into the interior, and a means of transporting German products in and raw materials and precious metals out. They were also demonstrative, a form of braggadocio. The Germans were, of course, watching other colonial powers (above all the British), and there was some gnashing of teeth over what the British had achieved in matters of infrastructure. The Aswan Low Dam in Egypt was widely envied.

Germans took pride in their tropical medicine, immunology, and veterinary science. The colonies provided a showcase for all of them, but many instances of "success" had a dark side. German scientists developed a vaccination against rinderpest, but the vaccine was used to preserve European rather than African cattle stocks. The differential rate at which the two herds died made a critical difference in destroying the basis of the Heros' existence in Southwest Africa. Colonial medicine was shot through with eugenicist assumptions based on racial thinking. Hans Ziemann, who headed the medical administration in Cameroon, made a study of malaria

Africans laboring on the East African railroad.
A photograph from December 1909.

and came to the conclusion that the incidence of the disease in the African population justified strict residential racial segregation in Douala on hygienic grounds.[143] It is tempting to project this forward to the racist eugenics of the Nazi regime. But German conduct in this sphere differed little before 1914 from what other colonial powers were doing. Colonies gave a boost to European institutes of hygiene and tropical medicine. In Germany, as elsewhere, the effect of colonies was felt in many disciplines— medicine, zoology, anthropology. The self-conscious application of science was probably more pronounced in the German colonies. Even those with no liking for the Germans acknowledged this grudgingly.

Many also saw the colonies as a potential source of German "renewal," a place where virtuous settlers could live out the ideals of Germandom. That had been an important part of Friedrich Fabri's case for colonies. It was very much the view of a younger figure from the same milieu, Ernst Fabarius, a military chaplain in Koblenz and secretary of the Rhineland branch of the Protestant Africa Association. In 1899 Fabarius founded a German colonial school at Witzenhausen in the Werra Valley. The school trained young men as farmer-settlers and "cultural pioneers."[144] The Women's League of the German Colonial Society* also founded a colonial school for women to train would-be female colonists in maternity care, cooking, darning, and the other skills of the loyal helpmeet on the frontier. The numbers of those who passed through these schools was small, but the modest numbers were in line with the dimensions of German settlements. Southwest Africa, the only true settler colony, never had more than 14,000 German residents. That was the same number of people who moved to Greater Berlin every four months—every four months for forty years.

Settler colonialism enjoyed the mystique it did partly because it embodied the white family, as opposed to the racially mixed marriages—or other sexual liaisons—between German men and Indigenous women that were common, especially in the early years of German colonial rule. These raised the specter of white men "going native" or indulging in behavior that undermined Europeans' supposed racial superiority. In 1905 marriage between German men and African women was forbidden by administrative decree in Southwest Africa and made retroactive, so that already existing marriages were annulled.[145] The same prohibition was later extended to

---

* The German Colonial Society was formed in 1887 via the merger of the German Colonial Association and the Society for German Colonization.

East Africa and Samoa. Similar concerns prompted Governor Leutwein's 1898 proposal to pay the passage of single German women to Southwest Africa—sending "suitable female breeding material from the Reich," as the feminist Gertrud Bülow von Dennewitz contemptuously called it.[146] But many German women, in the colonies and at home, supported these policies. Grete Ziemann, who went to Cameroon to keep house for her brother Hans, the medical officer, left no doubt where she stood: "In my opinion, race pride—naturally only in the best and noblest sense—cannot be exercised strictly enough. *If Germany wants to conquer Africa, in no circumstances may a mixed race arise.*"[147] Even a feminist like Minna Cauer saw a case for encouraging women to go to the colonies because (in the classic argument of contemporary feminism) they would "civilize" the "uncivilized" conduct to which men were always prey.[148]

When the Women's League of the German Colonial Society placed an advertisement inviting women to apply for assistance in traveling to the colonies, it was surprised by the large response. In addition to the "undemanding, simple girls" who were most easily placed, there were educated women—housekeepers, Kindergarten teachers, companions—who wanted the opportunity to fashion a more independent life for themselves than they enjoyed in Germany. They were rejected by Margarete Schnitzler, one of those vetting the applications, because there was no demand for such women in the colonies. These educated young women she turned down with regret. Other applicants wanted to get away from their husbands, "had gotten into distressing situations, usually because the father had died," or "just wanted to get out a bit" or "had lust for adventure of all kinds written plainly all over their face."[149] Schnitzler turned these women down straight away, with no regrets.

Yes, at the same time, many men in the German colonies conducted themselves in ways that not only mocked the idea of a "civilizing mission" but exceeded what was acceptable under the double standards that governed male and female behavior. What could get you into trouble with the government, even deported? Indigence, for one—failing as a settler and taking to drink (not necessarily in that order), becoming a disreputable hanger-on. That was letting down the white race. So were homosexual acts, especially if performed with African men.[150] Then there were crimes that went beyond the tacitly accepted everyday violence, including sexual violence. German missionaries in Southwest Africa complained repeatedly about the rape of African women. Some took to calling the *Schutztruppe* ("protective force") the *Schmutztruppe* ("dirty troops").[151] But this had little effect and it required something out of the ordinary to create a scandal. A man named Heinrich Odelwald was jailed, then deported from Southwest Africa in 1912, for raping an African child.[152] The misuse of alcohol featured in many cases that became scandals. A settler called Kurt Berner was recommended for deportation from Southwest Africa after he shot one of his African workers in an alcohol-fueled rage.[153] An incident involving alcohol and sexual assault occurs in one of the African novels written by Frieda von Bülow, a distant cousin of Gertrud and herself a feminist as well as a radical nationalist who sought personal freedom in East Africa in the late 1880s, where she founded and ran German nursing facilities. In *Tropic Rage*, the heroine's brother and his friends drunkenly break into African homes and attempt to rape the women.[154] It is worth noting that while in East Africa Bülow had an unhappy love affair with the colonial adventurer Carl Peters, who was forced to leave the colony after having two Africans hanged, his concubine and her purported lover.[155] Franz Giesebrecht, a left-leaning cultural critic, wrote a study of Peters in 1897 in which he called him, sarcastically, a "German colonial hero." It is a psychological portrait of a monster, but Giesebrecht suggests that the monstrosity—the "colonial abominations"—were somehow released by Africa: "Out there, in the wild land . . . culture and civilization went to the devil." That was where the evil, previously hidden, emerged and triumphed—"the beast inside the human."[156] It was as if Giesebrecht could imagine the horror being released only in an African setting. Here was a *Heart of Darkness* script several years before Joseph Conrad's famous book.

The colonies assumed an outsized importance in the German imagination. One aspect of that, not to be overlooked, is the criticism that some Germans leveled against the brutality of colonial exploitation. This reached a high point in 1906–07, while two wars were being fought in Africa, and was triggered by criticism of the colonial administration in the Reichstag by members of the Catholic Center Party who had been briefed by missionaries. The Social Democrats, long-standing critics of colonialism, added harsh strictures of their own. The upshot was a parliamentary election in 1907 called by Chancellor Bülow, the so-called Hottentot elections, designed to isolate Catholic and Social Democratic critics. The policy worked, although what followed was a reform-minded new colonial regime under Bernhard Dernburg. The lineup of parties that backed Bülow in the election—Conservatives, right-wing National Liberals, and Progressives—

indicates the broad support for the colonial project. But its greatest support came from branches of the Veterans' Association and the radical right: the Colonial Society, Pan-German League, and Navy League. They were the organizations that produced wall charts and maps for schools and doctors' waiting rooms, and sponsored lectures and slide shows where famous figures like Gerhard Rohlfs and other "experts" held forth on Germany's colonial mission. These drew packed crowds, as many as seven hundred for an evening lecture even in a midsized town like Osnabrück. That was where, in February 1913, the "Africa adventurer" Albert Spring spoke about East Africa. Before the Germans arrived, he explained, it had been in "an almost completely primeval state. The Negroes squatted idly into front of their filthy huts." Then came the transformation: "Now there are clean villages in which the electricity shines at night. The steam-powered steed traverses the fruitful land. Well-clothed Negroes and Negresses go to the station, just as we do in provincial places, to wait for the train."[157] This was the disdainful racism of the "civilizing mission."

Was it likely that a German would encounter Africans in Germany? Possible, certainly, although not likely. Africans from the German colonies did travel to Germany, mainly from Togo, Cameroon, and East Africa. Some were the children of social elites, whose families wanted them to have a German education. Others went as translators and language instructors, as the personal servants of colonial officials, or as part of training programs run by one of the German missions. A few were sailors, or apprentices learning a trade their German instructors expected them to practice when they returned to Africa. They were, in other words, a very disparate group of individuals. Those who came from Cameroon included both Christians and Muslims and speakers of four different languages.[158] The experiences of Africans in Germany varied as well. Two children from elite families in Cameroon, placed in a Protestant school in the small Württemberg town of Aalen, were greeted by a brass band when they arrived and were apparently very popular. But unwanted curiosity or abuse were more frequent.[159] What Africans in Germany had in common was that they expected (and were expected) to return, which explains the high turnover in Germany's Black African population. Several thousand probably passed through in the three decades before 1914, but the population at any given time numbered less than a thousand.[160] That was around 1 in 70,000 of the overall population on the eve of war.

Germans were more likely to encounter representations of Africans, generally caricatured and demeaning. The slides that accompanied talks like Albert Spring's in Osnabrück were part of a society suffused with exotic images from the colonies. Mass-circulation illustrated newspapers jostled alongside posters, placards, and advertisements. Navigating the growing big cities of the kaiser's Germany meant learning to read these visual cues, while those who wanted to advertise a show or a product tried to catch the attention of hurrying city dwellers with spectacular images.[161] Many advertisements played up the exotic. Stylized, often grotesquely caricatured images of Black people appeared in ads selling a wide range of products: chocolate, ready-made cake mix, margarine, cigars and cigarettes, alcohol ("Herero Liquor"), bicycle tires, sodium bicarbonate, soap, toothpaste, metal polish, and boot and shoe polish. Products that claimed to clean things and images that showed cleaning in some form were especially prominent, like the white soap being applied to a child's Black face in a Mohr's soap advertisement.[162] Similar images adorned trading cards and posters advertising wax museums, exhibitions, and shows.

Some of the shows featured live exhibits of colonial peoples and others from around the world deemed to be "exotic" or "primitive." These were the notorious "people shows," in which non-Europeans from the tropics to the Arctic Circle—Africans, Inuit, Native Americans, Pacific Islanders, Singhalese—were placed on display for European audiences.[163] These exhibits began as carnival sideshows several decades before Germany acquired colonies, but they soared in popularity and became more mainstream in the 1880s. That was when prominent scholars gave the shows their seal of approval as scientific, and therefore edifying. The scientists studied those being displayed, vouched for their "authenticity," and provided a cover for the impresarios. This amounted to a kind of "commercial ethnography," the joining together of moneymaking entertainment with scholarship.[164] More than a hundred large-scale people shows and countless minor ones toured German and other European cities in the thirty years before the war. For Carl Hagenbeck, the best-known German organizer, the people shows grew naturally out of his previous business, which was importing wild animals for zoos.[165] Zoological gardens were among the respectable, middle-class places where people shows were mounted.

A variant was the minutely choreographed "native village," complete with huts, tools, and animals, which became a standard part of major exhibitions. The Berlin Trade Exhibition of 1896 boasted such a display. So, the following year, did the Saxon and Thuringian Trade Exhibition in Leipzig, which included forty-seven Africans expressly brought over for the purpose and handpicked to represent "inner-African tribes" unfamiliar to Europeans. The veneer of seriousness and public edification that was always a part of these staged displays was undercut in this instance by the trade fair newspaper, which shamelessly played up the element of spectacle by suggesting that members of the Wadoe tribe practiced cannibalism and might have been responsible for eating three German sailors who had gone missing in 1888.[166] Ethnographic displays also took place at large popular festivals, such as the Oktoberfest in Munich. Bavarian Prince Regent Luitpold visited the Samoa Show there in 1910.[167]

The original "sideshow" form of display meanwhile enjoyed new life in the wax museums, or Panoptiken, that sprang up in German cities in the late nineteenth century with Madame Tussaud's in London as their model. Castan's Panoptikum in Berlin was the first, in 1871, with four provincial branches opening later. Rivals and imitators followed in St. Pauli, neighboring Hamburg, and Frankfurt. Carl Gabriel, a circus director's son who was already mounting shows every year at the Oktoberfest, then opened his International Panoptikum in Munich.[168] These businesses usually had a theater attached to the wax museum, which is where the people shows were held. All emphasized the exotic and sensational.

Berlin, Hamburg, and Munich were big cities. But images and accounts of a wider, "exotic" world also made their way into smaller towns. In 1905, an "African village" was on display in Oldenburg, in the north German fens.[169] Weimar, the small but famous town whose residents during its late-nineteenth-century silver age included musicians (Franz Liszt, Richard Strauss), art connoisseurs (Count Harry Kessler), and a mad philosopher (Friedrich Nietzsche), was also a hotbed of colonialism, thanks in no small part to Grand Duke Carl Alexander. He funded Carl Peters lavishly, maintained a close personal relationship with Adolf Lüderitz, and gave land to Gerhard Rohlfs, who built a villa in the town. Weimar's newspaper carried extensive material on Africa and the local chapter of the Colonial Society was very active. The local regiment also participated in the Boxer Rebellion and the Herero war, another link to the colonies.[170] There were many conduits through which that wider world reached into provincial life. Street names and commemorative plaques were an everyday reminder of the colonial. So were those colorful advertisements, and the "colonial goods" shops that sold the commodities they advertised. Illustrated magazines carried colonial stories. Germans could buy cheap editions of colonial adventure stories or the *"Farmersfrau"* style of memoir pioneered by Frieda von Bülow.[171] Nor should we forget the literature, games, and toys produced for children and young people. Just as the model train set domesticated that great symbol of nineteenth-century progress, so board games like Die Kolonisten and models like the miniature African village domesticated the distant colonial world. They allowed children to "play empire."[172]

These influences were pervasive.[173] But did they necessarily encourage people to identify with the German colonial empire? Some obviously did—a local regiment that had fought there, street names honoring German "colonial heroes," wall maps of the German empire, colonial literature set in Southwest Africa. But the elements of the "exotic" were often quite unrelated to German overseas possessions. The African village in Oldenburg called itself a "Somali village." Any claims it might have had to authenticity concerned a part of Africa divided between Britain and Italy. That was no accident. The Herero displayed at the Berlin Exhibition of 1896 were the last Africans from the German empire to be part of any people show or display. The missionaries in Southwest Africa had objected at the time.[174] Four years later the German government caught up with them. Chancellor Chlodwig von Hohenlohe-Schillingsfürst and the Colonial Council (a group that advised the Colonial Office) banned the export of native peoples from the German colonies for display in Europe, on the grounds that these moneymaking ventures possessed no educational value and had adverse effects on the health of the individuals concerned and on colonial relations.[175]

The often spuriously labeled peoples who appeared in later shows came from all over the world. They were Nubians, Burmese, Zulus, and North American "wild Indians" and "Eskimos." Advertisements, board games, and popular literature also included a much wider range of peoples than were to be found in the German colonies. The racist sentiment that was fed by these cruel displays and grotesque caricatures belonged to a wider racialized European imagination.

World Economy

CONTEMPORARIES KNEW THAT THE WORLD WAS GROWING smaller. They were also aware how economic exchanges were helping to drive that process and create a "world horizon" (in the words of the theologian Ernst Troeltsch).[176] A truly global economy took shape toward the end of the nineteenth century, marked by the extraordinary multiplication of trade links and tied together by the rapid growth in shipping, undersea cables, and the activity of merchants and bankers whose frame of reference was international. Almost nowhere on earth remained untouched by the ability of a dynamic capitalist system to commandeer new resources and open new markets. That is why the period before 1914 is now widely regarded as the first age of globalization, its interconnections and linkages unequaled until the closing years of the twentieth century.[177]

German observers were especially quick to spot the trend. The economist Adolph Wagner was already writing in 1879 that "current conditions have allowed commerce to unite the national economies into a single globe-spanning world economic organism."[178] The term *Weltwirtschaft*— world economy—was widely used from the 1880s, decades before it became familiar in English.[179] One reason is that, since the time of Friedrich List earlier in the century, economics was typically viewed in Germany through a national lens. German economists therefore saw the globalizing trend as just the latest stage of a development from domestic, to urban, to national, to global economy. More than that, however, Germany's increasingly active role in global trade became a contentious issue in domestic politics. The economic strength of the new nation was a source of widespread pride, especially when—in some areas, at least—it began to overtake Britain, which was at once model and rival. But Germany's expanding role in the global economy followed from the fact that it had, in the jargon of the time, made the transition from "agrarian" to "industrial" state. That shift encountered resistance from conservative intellectuals, and from those—a minority by the 1890s, but a large one—who lived in the countryside and small towns, felt left behind, and saw world trade as a threat, not an opportunity. Germany's place in the global economy often caused antagonism to flare up between town and country, industry and agriculture, when political battle was joined over trade treaties, tariffs, and seemingly innocent matters like veterinary border controls.

That Germany had become an economic leader on the world stage is beyond question. A few statistics will show how intimately the German economy was enmeshed in the global movement of commodities. The value of German imports increased from 2.8 to 10.8 billion marks between 1880 and 1913. Exports followed a similar trajectory, rising from 2.9 billion to 10.1 billion marks over the same period. In both cases, the curve rose most steeply in the last prewar decade. Germany was the world's most dynamic capitalist nation, rivaled only by the United States, when it came to the growth of external trade. Even as it imported more foodstuffs from overseas to feed a growing urban-industrial population, the share of GNP accounted for by exports almost doubled. In 1880 the German share of the global export of manufactured goods lagged a little behind France and was less than half that of Britain. Fast-forward to 1913, and the German share was twice the French and closing in rapidly on the British.[180]

Steel tells the story dramatically. In 1880 Britain produced twice as much of it as Germany; by 1913 the positions were reversed.[181] The example of steel is potentially misleading, though. It is true that German output in the "heavy metal" branches of iron and steel, like the related production of coal, increased dramatically in these years. But the real secret of German export success lay in more sophisticated goods. Some were the products of engineering companies, like the armaments made by Alfred Krupp and marketed around the world, the turbines made by the J. M. Voith Company in Heidenheim that were installed at Niagara Falls, and the spark plugs patented by Robert Bosch in Stuttgart, a company that earned 90 percent of its income from exports by 1913. Other German global successes came from companies in quintessentially modern branches of the economy that came into their own in the late nineteenth century: Siemens and its electrical products; Carl Zeiss of Jena, maker of precision optical instruments; and companies such as Bayer and BASF, which had global markets for their chemicals, dyestuffs, and pharmaceuticals. It was in Germany that methamphetamine was first synthesized (in 1887) and the drug we know as aspirin synthesized and marketed by Bayer (in 1897–1899). By 1914 Germany was the European leader in chemicals and pharmaceuticals, the world leader in electrical goods. Germany was king when it came to the products of the so-called Second Industrial Revolution.

These were the goods marked "Made in Germany." It is ironic that the label originated with the British Merchandizing Marks Act of 1887, which aimed to protect British consumers by identifying "cheap and shoddy" German products. Fear of German competition drove this British attempt to stigmatize foreign imports, but the association of German products with low quality was not entirely cynical or wrongheaded at the time. The German exhibits at the 1876 Centennial Exposition in Philadelphia were denounced for their poor quality by German journalists. It was only later that the designation "Made in Germany" became a marker of quality, and the nature of British concern started to shift. Between 1886 and 1900, the six largest German firms filed almost a thousand patents in Britain, while the six largest British firms filed fewer than a hundred. By the beginning of the twentieth century, some British firms were slapping a "Made in Germany" label on their products as a way of passing them off as higher quality.[182]

During the decades when Germany become a dominant economic power, the value of imported food and raw materials was slightly higher in most years than the value of exports. This negative trade balance was one of the trends that disturbed conservatives, already alarmed by the speed of Germany's transition to an urban-industrial society. The trade gap was filled, as it was in the case of Britain, the industrial pioneer, by "invisible earnings." They included repatriated profits from German businesses that established plants outside the country, either to circumvent tariffs or to take advantage of lower labor costs. There were also earnings from services, such as the German contribution to international construction projects (the rail tunnel through the Gotthard Pass, the Berlin–Baghdad railway), for these were years when German engineers and architects started to enjoy a higher profile in the world. In the late 1880s, before he achieved fame in Germany for his advocacy of the English arts and crafts movement, the architect Hermann Muthesius worked as a construction supervisor in the Japanese office of the German firm invited by the Meiji government to develop a plan for rebuilding Tokyo as a modern city.

German capital was also invested overseas on a growing scale. By 1914 Germany had become the world's third-largest creditor nation, thanks to direct investments by companies and the purchase of foreign government bonds. Germany still exported much less capital than Britain or France; its overseas investments were just a third of Britain's.[183] Germany also offered no competition to the City of London when it came to the arcane world of underwriting and reinsurance. But in another sphere where Britain had long been dominant, Germany was catching up quickly. That was merchant shipping. In 1880 Germany still had less steam tonnage than Spain; thirty years later German steam tonnage was three times greater than the French, four times greater than the American. Only the British merchant marine was larger. It was a remarkable transformation, helped by subsidies to shipbuilders in Hamburg and Bremen and a dizzying tempo of investment in new harbor facilities. By 1914 the value of the trade passing through the port of Hamburg was exceeded only by New York and Antwerp. German shipping lines such as the Hamburg-Amerika and the Nord-Deutscher

Lloyd had a worldwide presence, supported by a global network of agents and coaling stations.

The first German steamship lines reached the coast of Africa in the 1880s and Germany's transformation into a global economic powerhouse coincided with its acquisition of colonies. Was it just a coincidence? How important were German colonies to its dramatic growth spurt? One of the main arguments on behalf of colonies was economic, after all. It was merchant adventurers such as Adolf Lüderitz who often drew Germany into imperial entanglements, and hardheaded organizations like chambers of commerce, banks, and manufacturers' associations all expressed keen interest in what colonies had to offer. The membership of the German Colonial Association read like a who's who of the business world: Krupp, Stumm, Siemens, Kirdorf. Individual firms certainly benefited. The colonies provide a market for capital goods like railroad track, electrical equipment, and dynamite for mining. Copper mining was a lucrative enterprise for the companies that undertook it in Southwest Africa and so, even more, was diamond mining after the precious stones were discovered there in 1908.[184] The colonies also turned a profit for companies that traded in raw materials such as palm oil, peanuts, cocoa, rubber, and ivory from Cameroon. Hanseatic merchants were very much to the fore. Hamburg handled a third of all West African trade by the end of the nineteenth century.[185] German East Africa, meanwhile, was a valuable source of raw cotton for the domestic textile industry at a time when world supplies were uncertain. It was, in the words of one German economist, a way to break "the economic rule of America over the European cotton industry."[186] Yet, in the end, even if some companies benefited, most colonies needed subsidies and their overall contribution to the economy was negligible. Just 2 percent of German capital investment went to the colonies, which accounted for less than 1 percent of German exports and only one-half of 1 percent of imports.[187] Africa was "irrelevant" in terms of trade, said economist Adolph Wagner.[188]

He was not quite right. It was colonial borders that were really irrelevant. German economic success in Africa was greatest in areas not under German jurisdiction—Egypt, the Congo, and above all South Africa, where Deutsche Bank had a major presence and German companies exported steel, machinery, chemicals, and household goods, held the local dynamite monopoly, and supplied the water. This was the opposite of the situation in Qingdao, where Germany invested heavily in infrastructure but most of the imports came from Japan and the German share of the trade pass-

ing through the port was just 8 percent.[189] On balance, Germany came out
ahead. It did good business in other people's empires and in parts of the
world where it lacked any formal political influence. South America is the
classic case: the biggest political influences were British and American, but
Latin America became an important market for German manufactures, an
essential source of food, and a place where 3.8 billion marks were invested
by 1914.

Germany became a global economic power, but its most important
trade by far was with other European countries. Its eight top trading partners in 1913, ranked by the value of German exports, were Britain, Austria,
the United States (the sole non-European country), Russia, France, the
Netherlands, Belgium, and Switzerland.[190] But the economic importance
of Europe went beyond these core countries. German exports penetrated
Scandinavian markets to the north and Italian markets to the south. The
primacy of Europe was evident when industrialists warned about antagonizing Spain during a dispute over the Caroline Islands, because Germany
stood to lose much more in trade with Spain than it could ever gain in the
Pacific.[191] In the early 1890s Leo von Caprivi, Bismarck's successor as chancellor, negotiated a series of trade treaties with other European countries.
Four of them—with Austria-Hungary, Russia, Serbia, and Romania—
indicate the expansion of German trade to the east and southeast. Tsarist Russia, industrializing in a hurry in the decades before 1914, borrowed
French money and spent it on German goods. German economic tentacles
were meanwhile reaching into *Mitteleuropa* and along the Lower Danube
into the Balkans and the Ottoman Empire. These areas purchased German
railroad track and manufactured goods, supplying food and (in the last
prewar years) oil in return. In 1913, German exports to Romania were three
times more valuable than exports to all the German colonies combined.[192]

Economic power brought global prestige. The major powers and those
looking to join their ranks compared themselves constantly, almost obses-
sively, against one another. The harsh, pseudo-Darwinian language of the
"survival of the fittest" ran thorough contemporary discussions of economic
trends, with the suggestion that competition was a zero-sum game.[193]
Attachment to an older liberal economic order did not entirely disappear. It
was still passionately advocated by leading economists like Lujo Brentano
(a nephew of Clemens Brentano), who looked to Britain as a model.[194] In
the emotive language of another liberal economist, Heinrich Dietzel, free
trade was like the human body—"to sever the sinews of trade is to slice into

one's own flesh."[195] But by the time Dietzel said this, in 1900, his view was more likely than would have been the case twenty years earlier to be dismissed as outdated Manchesterism, the derisive label attached to English-style free trade. To conservative economists, free trade was dangerous. It made Germany vulnerable to the vagaries of a global economic order, they argued, including manipulative ventures like the attempt by a Chicago dealer named Joseph Leiter to corner the world wheat market in 1897–98. Above all, it threatened national security and Germany's ability to feed itself in the event of war by making the population dependent on imported food.[196] Capital recognized "no fatherland," in Wagner's ominous phrase.

The gathering interest in imperialism and the calls for protective tariffs to insulate Germany from world markets were both reactions against economic globalization. They were signs of what the political scientist Karl Polanyi described seventy-five years ago as "the new crustacean kind of nation."[197] Antiglobalization was a global phenomenon. The McKinley tariff in the United States (1890), the Mendeleev tariff in Russia (1891), and the Méline tariff in France (1892) were outcrops of the same instinct. Protectionism was more the norm than the exception in these years. That is why, although one German historian has referred to Germany's "tariff isolation," it would be more accurate to talk about Britain's free-trade isolation.[198] But Germany does illustrate as well as anywhere the crustacean reflex of the era, which meant being unavoidably part of a globalizing world, yet putting up defenses against it. The economists argued over these issues; so did the political parties and Germany's well-organized economic interest groups. Questions about trade and tariffs, or how to position the nation within the global economy, were a red thread that ran through imperial German political debates.

Tariffs were introduced by Bismarck in 1879, in response to the Great Depression that began six years earlier, although there was also political calculation in play, as there usually was with Bismarck.[199] Other countries retaliated, with negative effects on German exports. The trade treaties that Chancellor Caprivi negotiated with other European countries in the early 1890s aroused violent political opposition and led eventually to his downfall. A decade later, in 1902, tariffs were raised again by Chancellor Bülow. *Cui bono*—who benefited? The conventional answer is: heavy industry and agriculture. Tariffs sealed the "marriage of iron and rye," an alliance of industrial barons like Krupp with the Junkers, the aristocratic Prussian estate owners, directed against the interests of finance, export industries, and consumers. There is a pleasing symmetry to this idea, which puts two of German history's bad boys in the stocks together. Nor is it entirely wrong. These were the main beneficiaries of the 1879 tariffs. The 1902 tariffs then granted agriculture higher levels of protection, while heavy industry benefited from the steel-devouring new battle fleet. But if this was a marriage, it was one in which the two partners were constantly at odds. As in a bad marriage, each thought the other partner unreasonable. Heavy industrialists shared with more liberal, export-oriented branches of industry the view that the agrarians went too far with their tariff demands. Representatives of agriculture, for their part, did everything possible to slow down Germany's transition to an industrial economy tied to world markets, and if possible to reverse it.[200]

It was German agrarian interests that demanded protection most loudly, because agriculture was hardest hit by the impact of a globalizing economy. The prices of primary commodities tumbled in the 1870s as freight rates fell and cheap grain came in from Russia and the North American prairies, as well as cheap meat from Argentina, a business that was transformed by refrigeration. Falling prices exacerbated other problems like labor shortages (the so-called flight from the land) and the costs of fertilizer. Primary producers also faced new challenges that arose from industrialization, like the competition the dairy industry faced from the chemical product margarine. That would have existed whether or not Germany was tied to global markets, but it was still one of many symbols (like cheap overseas grain) of life-and-death decisions being made in distant centers of power. The margarine factories on the Lower Rhine had a similar place in the agrarian demonology to the giant commercial mills on the Upper Rhine that processed American wheat. More than one-third of the German labor force in the early twentieth century was still employed in agriculture, where there were big increases in productivity during the prewar decades. But that did not stop primary producers from feeling that they were being taken for granted and exploited.

There was a major rural revolt in the early 1890s. It followed another downturn in world prices, which coincided with feedstuff shortages, outbreaks of foot-and-mouth disease, and—the final straw—Caprivi's trade treaties. The Bavarian Peasant League and the Central German Peasants Association founded by the folklorist and archivist Otto Böckel represented an eruption of populist rage, directed against urban consumers and anyone associated with "internationalism": liberal politicians, financiers,

"Jewish" speculators. More disturbing to established elites, these populist movements also attacked them—"against the Junkers and the Jews" was the rallying cry of Böckel, "the peasant king of Hessen," who also demanded a progressive income tax. The Prussian political maverick Hermann Ahlwardt used the same populist and antisemitic rhetoric when winning a Reichstag seat from the Conservatives in 1892. The Bavarian Peasant League took on nobility, clergy, and other elites with its 1893 election slogan "No aristocrats, no priests, no doctors, no professors, only peasants for the representation of peasant interests."[201]

The elites were alarmed but responded quickly. Catholic peasant leagues kept their members within the ambit of the church and the Catholic Center Party. Leaders of the party were willing to tolerate a good deal of antisemitic rabble-rousing at the local level to appease angry rural constituents. The Conservative Party traveled even further down the same road, mindful that (as one of its leaders put it) "we could not avoid the Jewish question unless we wanted to leave the demagogic antisemites a full wind in their sails with which they would have sailed right past us."[202] The "demagogic antisemites" were men like Ahlwardt, but the Conservatives themselves became consummate demagogues, setting up the Agrarian League and enrolling some 330,000 members in it by 1914, mainly peasants and craftsmen whom they pointed politically against their putative "cosmopolitan" enemies. In the process, the Conservatives were effectively taken over by the economic interests of the Junker landowners who dominated the party. Conservative and Catholic Center Party politics was meanwhile filled with rhetoric about the peasant and craftsman as the hardworking core of a healthy society, the wholesome elements that would keep Germany fed and defend it in the event of war.

Protective tariffs certainly helped Prussian Junkers and other large landowners, but they also benefited small and midsized peasant farmers.[203] So did other pieces of legislation, such as a measure designed to support dairy farmers by requiring margarine to be dyed an obnoxious color to differentiate it from butter, laughably presented as a bill to protect the consumer, which passed with backing from the parties of the center right and far right.[204] But many demands were rejected, especially the ones that challenged the basic direction of German economic policy. Agrarians received a no to bimetallism (the favorite solution of agrarian populists everywhere), which would have taken Germany off the gold standard, a no to nationalized grain imports at a fixed price, a no to changes to the bulk mailing

A membership card of the Agrarian League, with its idealized imagery of a common rural front and the slogan "Unity is strength." This card was issued in 1893 to a peasant farmer named A. Haupt in Berlstedt, Thuringia.

rates that (agrarians argued) favored business, a no to scrapping the special workers' trains that (they also argued) encouraged the growth of an industrial proletariat, and a no to cancellation of the Mittelland Canal, a symbol of industrial development against which they raged. But it was not just that these demands failed. Beyond the dramas of agrarian windmill tilting, countless pieces of everyday legislation were enacted, by conservative-leaning administrations, on patents, the credit system, company law, trade descriptions, the bankruptcy code, accounting procedures, and a hundred other subjects, measures that confirmed Germany's emergence as a sophisticated industrial and commercial economy absolutely dependent on trade with the rest of the world. That was also the lesson of a new round of trade treaties that came into effect in 1906.

Even the tariffs of 1902 were lower than agrarians had asked for. But they still kept prices higher than they would otherwise have been, and thus harmed consumers. Tariffs made Germany more self-sufficient in foodstuffs and led to an effective redistribution of income from town to country. For that was the double-sided coin of low commodity prices on the world market. They triggered violent opposition from agrarians but represented a cheap supply of calories that permitted German cities to grow at a fantastic pace by feeding those now laboring in the factory and not on the farm. For the workers themselves, they allowed living standards to edge up even as wages remained flat. Tariffs, even at modest levels, cut into that improvement. It is no surprise that the Social Democratic Party (SPD), easily the world's largest socialist or labor party in the early twentieth century, made "cheap food" the centerpiece of its campaign in the Reichstag election of 1903, which immediately followed the noisy, contentious reintroduction of tariffs.[205] In attacking the "hunger tariff," the SPD was part of a global movement, for the protectionist turn of the 1890s was followed by a pro-consumer backlash from Vienna to Santiago.[206]

One set of agrarian protectionist measures in Germany consisted of veterinary laws that kept out cheap foreign meat. A "pork war" rumbled on through the 1880s. The *New-York Tribune* declared dramatically that "Bismarck's war against the American pig" was the greatest German conflict since the time of Frederick the Great.[207] Measures were also taken against the import of other live animals and of meat. The German Meat Inspection Law of 1900 then virtually excluded American products. The political lineup was a familiar one: Conservatives and Catholic Center voted in favor, Social Democrats and liberals against. There is no question that veterinary concerns were used as a protectionist weapon. But the health arguments were not entirely spurious. There was reason for alarm about the threat posed by trichinosis in pigs, tuberculosis and pleuropneumonia (so-called Texas fever) in cattle, and foot-and-mouth disease in livestock of every kind. These were international concerns, and they were mounting in an era when animals and meat were being shipped across borders on an unprecedented scale.[208]

Animal diseases, or epizootics, were just one sign of a larger problem closely linked to global economic exchanges. Call it the problem of stowaways. Trichonosis and cattle tuberculosis accompanied their animal hosts, uninvited. So did the vine disease phylloxera and the Colorado beetle, which attacked potatoes. This mattered in a country that produced 40 million tons of potatoes a year by the early twentieth century.[209] Adolf Wermuth, a government official charged with addressing these threats to German agriculture, wrote a lightly ironic account many years later about the "war of extermination" waged against these and other harmful insects, but humor was in short supply at the time.[210] The problem of invasive species was felt on water as well as on land. The zebra mussel and other molluscs were carried into international waterways like the Rhine, where they established themselves in already damaged ecosystems. So did the common water hyacinth, native to the Amazon basin and a tenacious invasive species elsewhere, which began to infest German rivers in the nineteenth century. These problems became more acute when the ballast tank came into general use around 1880, intensifying the "ecological roulette" of aquatic invasions.[211]

The language of zoological threats and invasive species started to be applied to people in the late nineteenth century, a disturbing portent of what was to come. During the *Kulturkampf* in the 1870s we find a nationalist writer lumping phylloxera and Colorado beetle together with the Jesuits and "other enemies of the Reich."[212] Language that elided the distinction between human and nonhuman species served a purpose. Catholics were dehumanized as a prelude to persecution, just as Jews were described as a "bacillus" or "vermin" by followers of the pseudoscientific antisemitism that emerged at the end of the 1870s.[213] A generation later, proposals that Germany recruit cheap Chinese labor were greeted by one newspaper with the response that the United States, Australia, and South Africa had all learned to fear "the yellow plague."[214] The link between a class of humans and the biological "threat" of "invasion" and "infection" was perhaps most broadly applied by Germans of the late nineteenth century to seasonal migrant workers.

Nationalists had complained in the past about mass emigration as a threat to Germandom. Then, around 1890, Germany changed from an exporter to an importer of people. As a result, nationalists complained instead about the threat supposedly posed by foreigners inside German borders. By 1914 there were around 1.2 million foreign laborers in Germany. Most were Polish, others Italian and Dutch.[215] The rise in seasonal migration was driven by the shortage of agricultural labor, especially on the estates of Prussia's eastern provinces, as Germans moved to better-paying jobs in the cities. A network of agents, middlemen, and village mayors was established in Habsburg Galicia to recruit Polish laborers for Germany. Others came from Polish areas of Russia. On the large farms in the south, rural labor was brought in from Italy. In Catholic Upper Swabia a distinct form of seasonal migration quickened in tempo in the late nineteenth century, namely the use of child laborers—the so-called Swabian children—who crossed the Alps from Austria and Switzerland to be auctioned off as farm servants and cowherds at markets held every spring in Württemberg.[216] Foreign laborers also worked in factories and especially in "dirty jobs" like street cleaning and construction. The giant dams that were built in the early 1900s could not have been built without them. These construction projects employed as many as a thousand men at a time. Bosnians, Croats, Poles, and Czechs were among the army of workers who were excavating, stone-breaking, dynamiting, or operating the steam-driven winches. Italians were invariably present as skilled masons as well as laborers. On the biggest sites temporary townships of barracks were constructed, larger than the villages scheduled to be drowned behind the new dam walls. However, it was where the laborers were not separated from the locals that antiforeigner feeling was strongest.[217]

Fears about "invasions" by non-German peoples were amplified by ultra-nationalist organizations like the Pan-German League and German Society for the Eastern Marches. Chauvinist sentiments were fed from many sources, including the tacit message sent by German governments. Between 1880 and 1914, for example, some 2 million Russian Jews passed through Germany on the way to ports that would take them to the United States. They were permitted to do so (a Conservative Reichstag motion to ban their entry was defeated), but subject to strict transit controls to prevent them from remaining on German soil, and almost none did.[218] In effect, a cordon sanitaire was placed around them. Something similar happened in the case of Poles. Bismarck had expelled Poles from eastern areas of Prussia in 1884–85, but urgent labor needs made Polish workers indispensable. They were therefore allowed into Germany, but strictly as seasonal migrant laborers, without their families, and required to leave the country during the winter "waiting period." Their coming and going was regulated and monitored; registration was mandatory. There were hygiene checks and disinfection stations at border posts, which could handle up to ten thousand people a day, and the laborers carried ID cards that bore the name of their employer as well as their own. These procedures, and what they implied, were as eloquent in their way as the openly racist sentiments espoused by members of the Society for the Eastern Marches or the crude representations of the "Slav flood" that became common in literary and historical works during the prewar years.[219]

These movements of people generated hostility. The Jews who passed through Germany on their way to America, the Poles who stayed in Germany (but only from spring through fall), and the Chinese sailors on German vessels who created a "Chinese quarter" in Hamburg (but one that numbered in the hundreds only) all aroused antipathy. Sometimes it came from unexpected quarters. The prominent liberal academic Max Weber had notoriously critical things to say about the cultural and civilizational "backwardness" of Polish laborers in his Freiburg inaugural address of 1895.[220] Weber wanted to expose the landowning Junkers' hypocrisy for arguing, on the one hand, that agriculture needed special protection because it served the national interest and, on the other hand, calling for the import of cheap Polish labor.[221] His rhetoric was harsh, but Weber was, and remained, a fierce critic of what he contemptuously called "zoological nationalism." Members of the Sailors' Union opposed the hiring of Chinese crew by German owners and were supported in this by the Social Democrats. They did so on good trade union grounds, arguing that the owners were interested in cost cutting and oblivious to safety—but they also made odious comparisons between the "yellow peril" and "yellow unions," i.e., the company unions set up by shipping lines.[222] Overall, however, the trade union movement and the SPD played a much underrated role in inoculating German workers against racism, or at least making the open expression of racist views unacceptable in the labor movement.

The picture looked very different on the political right. Hostility to any kind of cross-border movement by non-Germans was strong among the peasants and craftsmen. Like hostility to free trade, it was part of the backlash against the global economy in its many forms. Populist demagogues played on these resentments, and established conservative politicians were happy to steal the demagogues' slogans. Many in the growing white-collar class also proved susceptible to arguments about the threat supposedly posed by racially defined outsiders. But material security and education conferred no immunity when it came to racist attitudes. The colonial societies and nationalist organizations like the Pan-German League had solidly bourgeois memberships. A fourth of the Pan-German League's local chapter leaders held PhDs. At the beginning of the twentieth century it was here, as much as anywhere else in German society, that we encounter a noisy, racially imbued kind of hypernationalism emerging more aggressively in response to a globalizing world.

CHAPTER 9

GLOBAL TRAFFIC AND THE CLAIMS OF GERMAN CULTURE

Transnational Lives

IT IS A PARADOX THAT THE AGE OF NATIONALISM SAW AN UNPRECE-
dented volume of travel between countries. The philosopher Georg Sim-
mel, writing in 1900, identified the "mania for traveling" as one symptom
of a restless, nervous age.[1] Railroad and steamship made possible a "global
society on the move," especially in the last decades before World War One.[2]
Germans were well represented in these crowds, driven to travel by a variety
of motives, professional and recreational. A few even made "world journeys,"
now much easier to accomplish than in the days of Georg Forster.[3] Jules
Verne's character Phileas Fogg went around the world in eighty days. The
Austrian archduke Franz Ferdinand's journey round the world in 1892–93
took ten months, but that was because of his many stops for socializing, collecting objects (17,000 were eventually sent back home), and above all hunting—tigers, panthers, elephants, all part of the archduke's lifetime bag of
275,000 creatures shot.[4] Some upper-class Germans found spouses abroad.
The mother of the famous literary brothers Thomas and Heinrich Mann was
Brazilian (their father owned a plantation there). Bismarck's son, Herbert,
married the daughter of an Austro-Hungarian diplomat and an English
mother. One of Bismarck's successors, Bernhard von Bülow, married an
Italian princess after the annulment of her first marriage, also to a German.

These were people who led transnational lives. Sometimes they seem
to be very trivial lives, like Franz Ferdinand's jaunts or the peregrinations

of the rich to international destinations marked out by the "season." German spa towns became global destinations of the wealthy during the Belle Époque. In the spa towns of Wiesbaden and Baden-Baden one heard "the clatter of a thousand tongues in a dozen different languages." These were fashionable meeting places where the croupiers were always French and the femmes fatales Russian, the architecture a mixture of pseudo-Japanese and pseudo-Moorish.[5] The Germans who frequented them merged imperceptibly with other members of a global elite that was mainly European but included Americans and others like the Aga Khan and Emperor Dom Pedro of Brazil.

It would be hard to find a sharper contrast than the Germans who gathered with people from other nations to pursue internationalist political ends. Five of the twenty "core women," as the historian Bonnie Anderson describes them, in the first generation of European and American feminists were Germans. Louise Otto was one of them. She wrote in the wake of the 1848 revolution about "the great World Liberation" and welcomed a new journal edited by fellow German Louise Dittmar as part of a "great all-encompassing World-Movement."[6] Both belonged to a network of women who corresponded, read, and translated one another's work. Ideas and institutions moved easily across borders. The arrival of feminist '48ers from Germany brought new energy to the U.S. women's movement. Conversely, the English Society for Promoting the Employment of Women was quickly imitated in the *Frauenerwerbsverein* in Berlin, then across Central Europe.[7] The women's movement of the late nineteenth century retained its internationalist character, even as it split into moderate and radical wings. Germans were prominent in both; so was the German language. It was in German that Dutch feminist Martina Kramers wrote to Hungarian feminist Rosika Schwimmer about translating one of her articles into English for the sake of "the poor monolingual Americans."[8]

German was also one of the languages of international socialism—rather too much so, in the eyes of some. The socialist Second International founded in 1889 had its share of disagreements. The disputes usually turned, as they did in the women's movement, on doctrinal rather than national differences. But the sheer size of German social democracy compared with socialist parties elsewhere did cause complaints about arrogant and schoolmasterly Germans. There was a particularly strong undercurrent of Franco-German tension. The Second International remained a symbol of resistance to the hypernationalism of the era—until the moment, in

1914, when it failed the ultimate test.[9] War also laid waste to the hopes of the international pacifist movement. In this case, it is the weakness of German pacifism relative to the strength of the movement elsewhere that tells the story.[10]

Attempts to create an international language were part of the same "international turn" at the end of the nineteenth century.[11] The most familiar of these is Esperanto, the brainchild of Polish-Jewish eye doctor Ludwik Zamenhof, who published his first book on the language in 1887. But Esperanto was preceded a few years earlier by Volapük, created by a south German Catholic priest. Father Johann Martin Schleyer believed that God had told him in a dream to invent an international language. Volapük spread quickly. Conventions were held in Friedrichshafen (1884), Munich (1887), and Paris (1889), the first two in German, the third in Volapük. By the end of the 1880s there were almost three hundred Volapük clubs and up to a million adherents, across Europe and as far away as San Francisco and Melbourne. Even more than feminism and socialism, the Volapük movement was riven by doctrinal disputes. Some followers attached themselves to a rival language, Idiom Neutral. Many more turned to Esperanto, which after 1890 carried the hopes for an international language. The journal of that movement, *La Esperantisto*, was published in Germany by the president of the Nuremberg International Language Club, which became the world's first Esperanto Club after switching its allegiance from Volapük in 1888.[12]

These were serious people bent on serious purposes. That was one reason for the many disputes and schisms. The same earnestness was characteristic of another group of men (they were virtually all men) that was also decidedly international in outlook. Social reformers grew rapidly in numbers and influence after the mid-nineteenth century. Trained in the law, medicine, and the new social sciences, they were interested in a set of interlinked issues—criminology and penal reform, public health and hygiene, housing and poor relief. Their network was European-wide and extended across the Atlantic. These social reformers corresponded with one another, read the same periodicals, went to the same congresses, and spread their ideas vigorously from one country to another. Ernst Engel, a Saxon-born statistician, was at the heart of this network. A cofounder of the International Congress of Statisticians, Engel had studied in Paris, spent time in Brussels, and had close contacts in Britain. The social reformers blurred at the edges into another group for whom social reform meant moral reform, the campaigners against "white slavery," prostitution, and alcohol, dubbed by one writer the "forces of organized virtue."[13] Their horizons were often international, too, although they were more likely to be propelled by religious motives and more likely to include women. These morality campaigns often resembled the mobilization of opinion against foreign "atrocities," another hallmark of the era.

Every one of these movements was novel to the nineteenth century, often its last decades. But most Germans who led transnational lives were members of groups that had long been mobile, even if never before in such large numbers. German merchants resided across Europe, from Seville to St. Petersburg. They were (like commercial consuls) thickest on the ground in the places where Germany did most of its business, in western Europe. But commercial families could be part of astonishingly wide networks. Auguste Michaelis was born in 1831, the daughter of a Hamburg merchant. By the time she was in her twenties, Michaelis had two sisters who worked in England and a brother who worked for a French company in Saigon. Forty years later, by then a widow living in a small north German town, she had relations who had emigrated to South Africa as well as acquaintances (through family, neighbors, or friends) in a dozen countries around the world, from Peru to China.[14]

It is probably easier to name the places where there was *no* German merchant colony. There were German merchants in Haifa, but not in other great port cities of the Middle East, like Alexandria and Beirut.[15] There were relatively few German merchants in India. Elsewhere in Asia they had more of a presence. German merchants in Japan lived (like other foreign merchants) mainly in Yokohama. In China they were resident in the colony of Qingdao, in treaty ports like Canton, and above all in Shanghai. There were about eight hundred Germans in the city by 1905, enough to support a German-language newspaper, although still accounting for just one in fourteen foreign residents.[16] Saigon was another hub, a bustling port where Germans owned rice mills and wrote marine insurance.[17] Merchants in these global outposts could travel back and forth to Germany much more often than in the past, thanks to the great steamship lines. The German-American sugar magnate Claus Spreckels crossed the Atlantic more than two dozen times.[18]

If there was a more mobile, networked group of nineteenth-century Germans than merchants, then missionaries have a better claim to the title than most. German missionaries from different denominations were active in every part of the world. They had a huge effect on the global expansion of Christianity in the nineteenth century. The lateness of German colonial acquisitions meant that most were active in the empires of others, a familiar story. Karl Gützlaff was the most famous (or infamous) German missionary of the nineteenth century. A tailor's son from a small town in Pomerania, the intellectually gifted Gützlaff was taken up and educated by Pietists in Berlin. He had a talent for foreign languages. At the age of twenty, Gützlaff went to the Dutch Missionary Society in Rotterdam, where he studied theology and languages, a three-year period of training that included short stays in England and France. In 1827, the Dutch sent this former apprentice saddler to Batavia, where he added Chinese to his stock of languages. But Gützlaff left the Dutch society after a year and went to Singapore, then to Thailand, with Jacob Tomlin of the London Missionary Society. In Singapore he married a British missionary, Mary Newell, and after her death in childbirth he married a second Englishwoman, Mary Wanstall. When she died, he married yet a third English missionary wife, Dora Gabriel. His preference in spouses reflected the sphere of Gützlaff's missionary activities. From the time he arrived in Singapore, he worked within the British empire.

It was in Hong Kong that he became one of the most controversial China missionaries of the century. Gützlaff evangelized in the Chinese interior, using his proficiency in different dialects and wearing Chinese clothing, the first Protestant missionary to do so and follow in the footsteps of the Jesuit Adam Schall von Bell two centuries earlier (although Gützlaff thought the Jesuits had conceded too much to Chinese culture). He distributed tracts and Chinese versions of the Bible he had himself helped to translate, and established a mission school. The Chinese Union he founded rested on the support of local converts. Gützlaff stood clearly on the "pro" side of perennial missionary debates about the "indigenization" of the Christian church. Only after his death in 1851 did it become apparent that (as earlier critics suggested) he had been defrauded by many supposed converts, opium users in need of funds, who took his Bibles and sold them to the printer, who then sold them back to Gützlaff. He was also connected indirectly with the bloody Taiping Rebellion, which broke out in 1850. Gützlaff had financially supported the American Southern Baptist missionary Issachar Jacox Roberts, who schooled the Taiping leader Hong Xiquan and initially sympathized with the rebels.

Gützlaff was controversial in another, more worldly way. His talent and ambition, coupled with the permanent need for backing from the dominant imperial power, led him to serve the British as an intermediary with the Chinese, first as an interpreter, later as a magistrate and as Chinese secretary to the governor in Hong Kong. He anglicized his name to "Charles" and tutored leading British officials in Chinese language and culture. Gützlaff believed in opening China to European trade, because he saw this as the way to open the country to missionary work. Christianity and commerce went together, in Gützlaff's view, so it is no surprise that his writings influenced the Scottish missionary-explorer David Livingstone. But he became seriously compromised as a result, serving as an interpreter for the opium traders Jardine, Matheson & Co. and providing the British with intelligence during the Opium Wars, some of it from Chinese informers he had recruited.[19]

It was not every missionary who found himself implicated in both sides of the opium trade, nor every missionary whose writings were drawn on by both David Livingstone and Karl Marx. In some respects, though, Gützlaff was not so unusual. Like other missionaries, he was plucked out of provincial obscurity and cast in a global role. And, like all German missionaries, he had to work within terms set by the major colonial powers. German Catholic missionaries found that, wherever they went, others had got there before them: French White Fathers, or some Belgian or Portuguese order. In China, the French protectorate established by a Sino-French treaty in 1858 meant that for decades all Catholic missionaries who wanted to enter the country, whatever their nationality, had to apply for French passports.[20] Their Protestant counterparts found themselves in a position similar to Danish or Norwegian mission societies, filling the need for missionaries in parts of the globe dominated by Protestant colonial powers. That usually meant Britain. The three main Protestant organizations, the Basel, Berlin, and Rhenish missionary societies, all sent trainees to Britain. Most went to the college run by the Anglican Church Mission Society in London, others to the nondenominational London Missionary Society. These two organizations trained more than 130 German missionaries in the first half of the nineteenth century, before sending them off to Africa or India. It was not just Lutherans and Pietists who passed through Britain. There were German members of the Baptist Missionary Society. The equation was simple. German missionaries lacked an empire; British mission societies lacked warm bodies.[21]

The secretary of the London Missionary Society, William Jowett, noted cheerfully that British and Germans were "fellow-labourers in the same vineyard."[22] Anglo-German cooperation was part of an international exchange of ideas, as missionaries debated whether convert communities could become "self-governing" and tried to develop a common "missionary alphabet."[23] But there was tension as well as cooperation. One Berlin missionary trained in London and sent to Sierra Leone complained that local Anglicans criticized his sermons as "mean, vulgar and Methodistical."[24] German Protestants chafed under Anglo-Saxon tutelage they often found arrogant and supercilious. Dissatisfaction and self-assertion grew after unification. Gustav Warneck, a missionary theologian, denounced British and American missionaries as theologically jejune and self-righteous; the nationalist, pro-colonial views of Rhenish Missionary Society leader Friedrich Fabri (the author, years later, of *Does Germany Need Colonies?*) signaled how things were changing.[25]

German missionary activity had many repercussions at home. Some were ephemeral, like the "China fever" sparked by Karl Gützlaff on his travels through Germany in the late 1840s to gain support for his work, which included an audience with the king and queen of Prussia.[26] More lasting were the missionary societies. The first were founded in the historically "awakened" Protestant parts of the country, but most German towns had one by 1900. They were among the largest civic associations in a country famous for them. The societies raised money, hosted talks, organized festivities, and gave their members in the most provincial backwaters a sense of being engaged in a worldwide undertaking.[27]

Missionaries usually went back to Germany when they retired. The life cycle of a missionary might take him from Württemberg to London, on to Africa, then back to Korntal just outside Stuttgart, which became a well-known retired missionary community. Sometimes missionaries were accompanied home by African assistants. African mission school students were also brought to Europe to be trained.[28] Some were the children of local African aristocrats, others orphans or former slaves. After training, the "Black brothers" returned to Africa as missionaries, sometimes after spending time at a school and orphanage in Jerusalem with which the south German Pietists had close connections. Their experiences in Germany provided them with agency and resources they could use.[29] But not all of these young Africans survived their experience in Central Europe. Tuberculosis, especially, took its toll. In 1871, it claimed the life of Samuel Galla, described by the German missionary Johann Ludwig Krapf as a

"dear Negro lad."[30] There was both genuine emotion and enormous condescension in a description like that. A photo from 1869 or 1870 shows
Krapf's colleague in Korntal, Martin Flad, and his family with Flad's African assistant, the Ethiopian Mikael Aregawi. All are formally dressed in
European clothes. Aregawi strikes a confident pose—he stands next to
Friedrich Flad, his foster brother (and later biographer), while he and his
foster father, Martin, clasp hands.[31] It recalls another photograph from the
same era that depicts the Catholic Center Party leader Ludwig Windthorst
with his Black godchildren.[32] There is paternalism on display in both pho-
tos, to be sure, but this was far removed from the people shows, or the cruel
buffoonery that saw "Prince Dido" of Cameroon dressed up as a *Hosennig-
ger*" in top hat and tails to make German audiences chortle.[33]

Perhaps the most important domestic effect of global missionary activity was that, in Germany as elsewhere, it gave rise to the idea of an "inner
mission." If the "heathens" abroad were to be targeted, why not the "godless" masses in the great cities at home? That was something both Protestant and Catholic clergy took up. The inner mission emphasized the
same virtues as the overseas mission—sobriety, cleanliness, regular work, a
well-ordered family life. Even the distinctive cult of the missionary "hero,"
struggling against savage, potentially dangerous natives to save souls, was
the same. When the young Protestant clergyman Paul Göhre spent three
months among urban workers, he found them to be "wild, heathen Social
Democracy."[34] The German variant of the inner mission bore many non-
German influences. The organizing center for Catholic orders devoted to
the inner mission was France. Protestant initiatives were also fed from foreign, mostly Anglo-Saxon, sources. The founding figure of this Protestant
inner mission, Johann Hinrich Wichern, was one of many German clergy
who made a tour of London's East End and its "city mission"; the English
social reformer Elizabeth Fry also inspired German clergy interested in
social work on her travels through Central Europe in the 1840s.[35]

German-American exchanges were embodied in the zealous transnational life of Friedrich von Schlümbach, who was born in the small Württemberg town of Öhringen in 1842 and died in Cleveland, Ohio, in 1901.
Schlümbach came from a military family, entered the army himself in 1859,
fell into debt, and then (against his father's wishes) emigrated to the United
States. He fought in the Civil War before being swept up in the Third
Great Awakening in the 1860s. A series of wartime escapes from death
apparently prepared the way for a "miraculous conversion." In Schlüm-

bach's own account this occurred in 1868, putting an end to a "terrible life of atheism and debauchery," by which he meant consorting with radical German gymnasts. He became a key intermediary between Protestants in Germany and America, first as a preacher to German immigrants in Baltimore, then as secretary of the German-speaking branch of the YMCA, an institution he introduced into Germany. Schlümbach traveled back and forth across the Atlantic during the 1880s, joining the American preacher Dwight L. Moody for an evangelizing mission in Chicago, then doing the same thing back home in German cities.[36]

This was not the first injection of Anglo-Saxon-style evangelizing in Germany. The Methodist Church established itself in Germany during the nineteenth century, carried there by returning emigrants from Britain or the United States. Given how much Methodism owed to the doctrines of German Pietism, it is no surprise that Pietist Württemberg was one area where it took root. Hamburg, with its historic ties to England, and Bremen, the principal port for America, were also centers. It was near Bremen, in the north German flatlands of East Friesland (which resembled John Wesley's native Lincolnshire), that the Methodist preacher Franz Klüsner was active in the late nineteenth century.[37] By then the Salvation Army, founded in London by the former Methodist William Booth, was also making inroads in Germany. With the help of Booth's deputy, dispatched from London to help with recruitment, the Heilsarmee expanded from its first foothold in Stuttgart; by 1914, it had corps in 150 towns. Methodists and Salvation Army carried the emotional drama of religious conversion onto a German stage. Preachers in Britain and Germany joined forces in an effort to replicate the Welsh great awakening of 1905–06, setting up a tent mission in the Ruhr that attracted thousands who traveled from all over the extensive coal-mining area in their "Hallelujah trains."[38]

Mounting revivalist missions in Europe and evangelizing "heathens" in the colonies were activities that crossed national borders. Germans mostly deferred to others in these matters, at least until 1871. But there were other areas of expertise in which Germans were considered global leaders. Some were of long standing. German geologists and mining engineers continued to be sought after from the Andes to the Urals. Alexander von Humboldt's second great journey was an eight-month trip in 1829 through the eastern Russian empire to examine mineral deposits. He bore the title of an official in the tsarist Department of Mines. German geologists and surveyors turned up everywhere.[39]

*The Salvation Army, or Heilsarmee, arrived in Stuttgart
in 1886 and soon established itself across Germany.*

There was global demand for German scientists of every kind. The Southern Hemisphere offers two striking examples. One is Latin America, thanks partly to Humboldt's legacy. There were hundreds of German scientists in Argentina alone by the early twentieth century, and many others in Chile, Peru, and elsewhere.[40] German scientists also played an equally outsized role in Australia. We have already seen the impact made by the botanist Richard Schomburgk and his circle of '49ers in South Australia. Among the many German scientists who arrived after midcentury and shaped Australia's scientific landscape were several who were well connected internationally. The geophysicist Georg von Neumayer is a perfect specimen of the type. Neumayer enjoyed support in British scientific circles and was a disciple of the American astronomer and oceanographer Matthew Maury, who had himself been inspired by Humboldt. In Australia Neumayer established an observatory in Melbourne, before returning to Germany, where he chaired the International Polar Commission in 1879.[41]

Neumayer is a reminder that Germans remained, as they had been in the era of Forster and Pallas, inveterate scientific travelers. Some became famous through their travels. Ferdinand von Richthofen was one. Celebrated at the time for his writings on China, he has enjoyed a long afterlife thanks to his felicitous coining of the term "silk road" in 1877. Ludwig Leichhardt was another German explorer with a long afterlife. A Prussian-born naturalist who left Germany in his early twenties, Leichhardt spent five years in England and France training himself in botany before shipping out in 1842 to Australia. There he undertook two major expeditions, one to the north, a second to the west, into areas previously unknown to Europeans. On a third expedition into the interior, he and the rest of his party (four other Europeans and two Aboriginal guides) went missing, in April 1848. Their bodies were never discovered, a disappearance that has been called "the greatest mystery in Australian history."[42]

Leichhardt and Richthofen, both larger-than-life figures, also raise two large questions about German scientific travelers: Who supported them and where did their loyalties lie? Born twenty years apart, Leichhardt in 1813, Richthofen in 1833, their careers illustrate a shift over time. Leichhardt's journeys were funded partly by Australian government, partly by private subscription. His relationship to his Prussian homeland was fractured. He left partly to avoid military service and later wrote to his brother-in-law back home that he had wanted "to serve my country and to serve science . . . by traveling to faraway corners of the globe," not drilling on a parade ground. In his last letter, on February 22, 1848, he noted proudly the honors he had received from English and French scientific societies, and then—referring to his collections of dried plants and seeds—added, "You might perhaps wonder why I did not send these collections to one of our German museums. The answer is that I conducted my studies of natural history primarily in English and French museums, and that I did not cultivate friendly relations with any of my compatriots during my youth."[43] Leichhardt, who died during the "springtime of peoples," still exudes the innocent, cosmopolitan spirit of that time. This is still the world of Forster and the young Humboldt.

Richthofen's life resembled Leichhardt's in some respects, but their trajectories diverged. Richthofen also went off to an English-speaking country at the age of twenty-nine—in his case the United States. After the gold rush he reported on mines in California and Nevada for six years and did geological research. When he went to China in 1868, it was with the financial support of the Bank of California and the San Francisco Chamber of Commerce. But Richthofen's position differed greatly from Leichhardt's. He had finished his degree, for one thing, and was careful to stay in touch

with the German academic world while away. Thanks to good family connections, he had also taken part in an 1860 Prussian expedition to China.
When Richthofen returned in 1872 from his first solo journey to China, he
was therefore welcomed in newly unified Germany and became an important organizer of German scientific expeditions from his lofty position in
the Berlin Geographical Society.[44]

Leichhardt and Richthofen personify a larger shift. Most scientific
expeditions undertaken by Germans before the 1870s were supported or
sponsored by an imperial power like tsarist Russia or Britain. That was
true of many journeys made by German explorer-scientists in Africa, a tradition that went back to the days of Sir Joseph Banks's talent spotting in
Germany.[45] It was also true of many expeditions in British India, like the
remarkable one undertaken by three Bavarian brothers, Hermann, Adolf,
and Robert Schlagintweit, who came recommended by Humboldt and
were commissioned by the East India Company to engage in geographical
and botanical research through the Deccan plateau and up into the Hima-
layas. Their journey began in 1854, lasted almost four years, and cost the
life of the youngest brother, Adolf, a botanist who was executed without
trial in Kashgar as a suspected Chinese spy.[46] Scientific travel after 1871 was
different, acquiring a more nationalist coloring. That was partly because of
the institutional change brought about by the advent of a unified Germany,
which could sponsor more ambitious undertakings. Like the missionaries,
scientific travelers also became more nationalist in the changed world of the
late nineteenth century.

There were new areas of German expertise that came to be globally
acknowledged in the nineteenth century. Three, in particular, were markers of Germany's growing prestige in the world: forestry, military knowledge, and medicine. Germany became famous as the modern "fatherland
of forestry," the place where so-called scientific forestry emerged at the end
of the eighteenth century and became the gold standard for conservationist thinking. Probably the most celebrated instance of the global influence
achieved by German forestry came in British India, where dozens of Germans shaped the Imperial Forestry Service. The dominant figure in every
sense was Dietrich—later Sir Dietrich—Brandis, "the giant German," as
Rudyard Kipling called him.[47] A philosopher's son who studied in Germany, Denmark, and France, then taught briefly at Bonn, Brandis went
out to the Indian empire after marrying a well-connected Englishwoman.
He was recommended by Humboldt (who else?) and initially appointed

superintendent of a teak forest in Burma. Rising through the ranks, he was appointed at the age of forty as the first superintendent of Indian forests in 1864. Brandis established conservationist norms and built up a cadre of German foresters around him who institutionalized those practices. The experience gained by Brandis and his followers shaped forestry practices in the German colonies acquired shortly after his own return to Germany.[48]

Other Germans went to preach forest conservation in the English-speaking world, but Brandis was the figure with global influence. His impact was powerfully felt in the United States. It came directly through pioneering German-born foresters like Bernhard Fernow (the "father of professional forestry" in America) and Carl Schenk. Fernow became the first chief of the U.S. Department of Agriculture's Division of Forestry in 1886, leaving to serve as dean of the first four-year forestry school in the country, the New York State College of Forestry at Cornell. Schenk was brought over from Germany to run the first forestry school of any kind in the United States, the Biltmore Forest School. The American-born blue blood Gifford Pinchot also drew heavily on the advice of Brandis when he succeeded Fernow as head of the Division of Forestry, soon to become the U.S. Forest Service. Pinchot became a key American conservationist in the age of Theodore Roosevelt. The influence of Brandis in the United States was ubiquitous. Mira Lloyd Dock was a progressive-era conservationist who wrote and lectured widely on forest management. In 1901 she joined the Pennsylvania Forestry Commission, the first woman appointed by the governor to any commission in the state. Dock, who had undertaken a study tour of German forests, liked to tell her students at the forest academy where she lectured about the things she had learned from Dietrich Brandis in Germany.[49]

German military know-how spread even more widely around the globe. There was, as we have seen, a tradition of German irregulars fighting in national struggles of the nineteenth century, and an even longer tradition of Germans fighting on behalf of colonial powers. This pattern persisted in the nineteenth-century French Foreign Legion, where the hard-bitten German non-commissioned officer was a cliché.[50] But what was completely new was the global prestige of German military organization after the three successful wars between 1864 and 1871. German military advisers were invited everywhere in the following decades. German instructors trained the armies of Argentina, Bolivia, and Chile and German military ideas were dominant everywhere in Latin America except Peru.[51] Wherever states looked to strengthen their armies, thoughts turned to Germany. Wilhelm von der Goltz was invited by Sultan Abdül Hamid II to reform the Ottoman army after its defeat in the Russo-Turkish War of 1877–78. "Goltz Pasha" arrived in 1883 and stayed until 1895, training a generation of "Goltz officers." In the same years, reformers in Qing China brought in German military advisers to staff the new Tianjin Military Academy and sent Chinese officers to train in Germany. After the Meiji Restoration, Japanese leaders did the same. A measure of German prestige in military affairs is the translation history of the most famous modern book on warfare. Carl von Clausewitz's *On War*, first published posthumously in 1832, was translated into English in 1873, Russian in 1905, Japanese in 1903, and Chinese in 1910.[52]

No single work by a German physician, not even by an internationally renowned figure like Robert Koch, who won the Nobel Prize in 1905 for his work on infectious diseases, rivaled the fame of Clausewitz's book. But the reputation enjoyed by German medicine by the late nineteenth century could hardly have been higher. Germany boasted a growing share of medical discoveries and German medical training was in demand everywhere. The same reformers who invited German military advisers to Japan and sent Japanese students to Germany followed suit in the field of medicine. Dozens of leading German physicians were brought to Japan, where they founded medical schools and established medical education on a new footing. Around twelve hundred Japanese students went in the other direction, studying medicine in Berlin and Munich. We know a good deal about their lives, including their sometimes puzzled encounters with German landladies and student culture, and the fondness for beer drinking that they took back with them to Japan along with their medical degrees.[53] One by-product of the exchange was therefore the impressive volume of beer consumed by Japanese members of the Berlin Beer Association when they reconvened in Tokyo, and the introduction of a German-style beverage known as Kaiser Beer to meet this demand from physicians and professors who had trained in Germany.[54] Less innocently, some of the medical science and practices the Japanese acquired from the Germans, such as military hygiene and bacteriology, were later put to use in imperialist undertakings in Korea and China.

For an American example of German medical expertise at work, there was no better place to look than the medical faculty of the new Johns Hopkins University, sometimes called "Göttingen in Baltimore" because of its heavily German flavor.[55] The Johns Hopkins Hospital opened in 1889, the medical school four years later. Daniel Coit Gilman, the first president of the university, hired its faculty. His choices immediately established the medical school as the gold standard in the United States. A John Singer Sargent portrait, *The Four Doctors*, shows the most prominent original teachers at the medical school.

It was quite a group. There was the portly William Welch, "Popsy" to his students, the consummate "medical politician," now regarded as the

John Singer Sargent's 1906 portrait The Four Doctors. *They are (from left) William Welch, William Halsted, William Osler, and Howard Atwood Kelly.*

"father of modern medicine in America"; William Halsted, a brilliant chief surgeon and lifelong cocaine addict; the Canadian William Osler, an inveterate practical joker who invented the medical residency system; and, not least, the remarkable Howard Atwood Kelly, another outstanding surgeon, who had recovered from a youthful breakdown by heading out west to work as a cowboy and Pony Express mail carrier in Colorado, where he became a serious snake collector. Kelly, a fundamentalist Christian convinced of the literal truth of the Bible, poured some of his remarkable energy into temperance and morality campaigns. His sparring partner in Baltimore, H. L. Mencken, once wrote, "Before cock-crow in the morning he has got out of bed, held a song of praise service, read two or three chapters in his Greek Old Testament, cut off six or eight legs, pulled out a pint of tonsils and eyeballs, relieved a dozen patients of their appendices, pronounced the benediction, washed up, filled his pockets with tracts, got into a high-speed automobile . . . and started off at 50 miles an hour to raid a gambling house and close the red light district."[56] What all four doctors had in common was training in Germany. Kelly even married the daughter of a Danzig physician. And these four individuals were not alone in having German training. An estimated fifteen thousand American medical students and practitioners, almost exclusively male, studied in Germany between 1870 and 1914.[57]

The Americans in Germany were eventually outnumbered by Russians. It is a remarkable coincidence that the American William Welch and the Russian Ivan Pavlov, who later became Welch's counterpart as a founding father of medical education in the USSR, both studied at the same university, Leipzig. At another institution, Halle, the foreign contingent accounted for more than one in four medical students, prompting a student strike on the grounds that domestic students were being squeezed out.[58] German institutions were training a global medical elite, scores of thousands of physicians of many different nationalities. But the true impact of German educational institutions and practices was far wider.

Educating the World

THE ASCENDANCY ENJOYED BY GERMAN EDUCATIONAL MODELS started with small children and Friedrich Fröbel's Kindergarten. The Kindergarten embodied progressive, anti-authoritarian values, so it is no surprise that it spread first through radicals, especially radical woman. Two sisters, Bertha and Margarethe Meyer, daughters of a wealthy Hamburg family, played a very large role. Bertha was born in 1818 and married at sixteen to the thirty-year-old Christian Traun, the private secretary to the Duchess of Cambridge, with whom she had six children. She became active in women's and educational issues, and in 1849 established a pioneering School for Women in Hamburg designed to prepare its students for Kindergarten teaching. She fell in love with the cofounder of the school, Johannes Ronge, received a divorce from Traun, and moved with Ronge to England, where they were married in 1850 and opened the first English Kindergarten the following year in the London suburb of Hampstead. Other schools followed, before Bertha Meyer Ronge moved back to Germany in 1861. Her sister Margarethe married the '48er Carl Schurz and was one of those radical feminists who carried their ideas across the Atlantic. She established the first German-language Kindergarten in the United States in 1856, in Watertown, Wisconsin. It became a model for the first English-language Kindergarten, founded four years later in Boston by the educational reformer Elizabeth Peabody.[59]

Women moving within a transatlantic network of freethinkers played a decisive role in the spread of the Kindergarten in America. Maria Boelte, a wealthy young German woman from Mecklenburg, became interested in the Kindergarten idea and trained with Fröbel's widow before going off to teach in one of Bertha Ronge's schools in England. She returned to Germany and established a Kindergarten in Lübeck. The second time Boelte was invited to the United States by Elizabeth Peabody, she accepted. She moved in 1872 to New York City, where she established a Kindergarten and a training program. She ran these with an educationalist named John Kraus, whom she married. Hundreds of future teachers passed through the program. They including Susan Blow, later dubbed "the Mother of the Kindergarten," a freethinking woman from a wealthy liberal family in St. Louis, who first encountered Fröbel's ideas during a visit to Germany and later opened the first publicly funded Kindergarten in the United States in her hometown.

The initial impulse for a Kindergarten anywhere typically came from wealthy young women from progressive-minded families, interested in German culture (Susan Blow was in Germany to study Hegelian philosophy), and often able to draw on international networks for support. Julie Salis-Schwabe, the young German-Jewish woman who established the first Kindergarten in Naples, was part of Anglo-German reformist circles and well connected culturally. The famous soprano Jenny Lind ("the Swedish Nightingale") sang to raise money for the Neapolitan enterprise. The Kindergarten movement spread rapidly in the closing decades of the century, and not just in Europe and North America. The first Kindergarten in Tokyo was opened in 1876; by 1900 there were two hundred in Japan.

The Kindergarten stood for freedom and creativity. That was why German governments regarded it with suspicion. What, then, did the celebrated "Prussian ideas" of education stand for? Surely, one might think, for the *absence* of freedom and creativity? Yet the Prussian model was widely admired by reformers because it was public, free, comprehensive (from primary to tertiary), rigorous, and nonsectarian. The moment when Prussian educational ideas began their heady ascent can be precisely dated. In 1831, Victor Cousin, a French philosopher deeply influenced by German thought, presented the first of several reports to the Ministry of Public Instruction in France on education in Prussia and Saxony. Cousin considered the Prussian model exemplary. His recommendations were taken up in France and his report was quickly translated into English. By midcentury, enthusiasm for German educational practices was almost universal in Britain. Royal commissions, parliamentary select committees, reports by educationists such as Matthew Arnold—all took German practice as the yardstick.[60]

The same happened in the United States, where Horace Mann was a pioneering reformer. Mann was appointed secretary in 1837 to the newly established Board of Education in Massachusetts, the first of its kind in the country. He had made a series of speeches in the State Senate during the 1830s advocating the "Prussian ideas" of free, universal, nonsectarian education. In 1838 he founded *The Common School Journal*, and five years later went on a tour of institutions in Europe. He traveled with his second wife, Mary Tyler Peabody (sister of the Kindergarten founder Elizabeth Peabody), combining fact-finding and honeymoon. (Together with another American couple, they also visited prisons and insane asylums: these were serious people.) As Mary wrote self-effacingly in her later *Life and Works of Horace Mann*, "On May 1, 1843, Mr. Mann again married and sailed to Europe to visit European schools, especially in Germany, where he expected to derive most benefit."[61] Following his celebrated Seventh Annual Report, Mann persuaded Massachusetts to adopt the Prussian system in 1852. New York quickly followed, then other states.[62]

There is irony in the course of school reform in America, and it comes back to the question of what we mean by "Prussian ideals." Horace Mann and his allies saw themselves fighting the good fight against obscurantism, and it is true that they had to face down vigorous criticism from religious conservatives. But if this suggests a victory of "progressive" over "reactionary" ideals, the situation is complicated by the fact that the reforms were highly centralized, were imposed from above on often reluctant constituencies, and succeeded because of what one modern writer has called "an almost brutal exercise of power"—that they were, in short, "Prussian" in a more familiar sense of the term.[63]

Germany continued to influence American ideas about secondary education through the progressive era. But in the United States, as elsewhere, it was the university that became the most potent German educational model of the nineteenth century, rivaled only by the Kindergarten. Foreigners flocked to German universities, accounting for one in eleven students at Prussian universities in 1905–06, more than one in five at polytechnics. The Pan-German League and right-wing student organizations reacted with hostility, especially when the foreign students were Russian Jews. Ministers and educational administrators responded with the argument that foreign students increased German influence and standing in the world.[64]

Around nine thousand British students attended German universities between 1849 and 1914. Some had even been to school in Germany, like the novelist George Meredith and Henry Morley, Charles Dickens's collaborator.[65] As a youth, the politician Richard Haldane went off in 1874 to study at Göttingen, partly because his Scottish Presbyterian parents believed it would be less harmful to his soul than Anglican Oxford. He returned thinner and long-haired, smitten by the air of serious academic inquiry despite the beer-swilling atmosphere of German student life. Haldane described the lecture room of Hermann Lotze, a philosophy professor, as his "spiritual home."[66] Many motives drove these students, or their parents. Admiration for German culture was one, recognition of German scientific excellence another. The German laboratory was a magnet. Virtually every professor of chemistry in a British university before 1914 held a German doctorate. It was no different in physics or the life sciences. Even in a field such as plant ecology, where the British were at the cutting edge and some of newest ideas were coming from Scandinavia or the United States, British plant ecologists still wanted to identify themselves with German botanical traditions, such was the prestige enjoyed by German science.[67]

Americans were equally in thrall. Some ten thousand Americans were enrolled at German universities during the nineteenth century. Ralph

Waldo Emerson's older brother, William, was one; so was George Bancroft, the distinguished historian and later U.S. ambassador to Germany. There were scientists, too, such as Benjamin Apthorp Gould, who founded the *Astronomical Journal* after he returned from studying with the celebrated Carl Friedrich Gauss. The men just named all went in the first half of the century and all, as it happens, were Harvard graduates who studied at Göttingen. That was typical of the period, when Göttingen was a favored destination and graduates of Harvard and other northeastern colleges claimed a disproportionate share of the still modest number of American students. The numbers rose in midcentury and again in the 1870s. American students came from all parts of the Union, although northeasterners remained the largest single group. They also studied all over Germany, at Bonn and Freiburg, even more at Berlin and Heidelberg, and after the 1870s increasingly at Leipzig.

We know a good deal about these men (once again, they were overwhelmingly male): their ages, where they came from, their social pastimes, and what they brought back with them—degrees, books (sometimes entire libraries), journals, and ideas.[68] Of course, they brought their own preconceptions to what they heard. The historian Michael O'Brien writes about the young southern gentleman George Calvert listening to the elderly natural history teacher Johann Friedrich Blumenbach and others in Göttingen, and comments (quite unfairly), "From these professors Calvert got a steady dose of Göttingen's characteristic racialist social theory, ideas not puzzling to a Marylander."[69] But sometimes the ideas were puzzling, or inspiring; and sometimes the German experience suggested things that might improve education at home. These students also came back with mentors and contacts—with networks.

What they came back to was a system of higher education widely perceived to be in need of reform. The antebellum American college was a "marginal institution."[70] Contemporary critics were harsh. Andrew Dickson White, later the first president of Cornell, called the curriculum of the eastern colleges "narrow" and the methods of instruction "outworn." "Each of them," he wrote later, "was as stagnant as a Spanish convent, and as self-satisfied as a Bourbon duchy," the most damning comparisons an anticlerical like him could imagine. White was a graduate of Yale, which "substituted gerund-grinding for ancient literature" and "recitals from textbooks for instruction in history."[71] This description would have fitted Brown or Amherst equally well, and it certainly applied to Harvard, generally regarded as the best of a bad bunch. Henry Adams (Harvard class of 1858) memorably said of his alma mater that "it taught little, and that little ill." He added—a typical Adams touch—"but it left the mind open, free from bias, ignorant of facts, but docile . . . , ready to receive knowledge."[72] Harvard still had a required curriculum of thirty-three courses that students had to take in sequence, which meant reading the set books and reciting them to professors.

The surprise is that reform did not come sooner. After all, the Russian university system of the nineteenth century was built on German lines; so was the newly founded University of Athens.[73] In fact, nods to the German system could be found in university reforms across Europe from Scandinavia to Spain, as well as in the Ottoman Empire, China, and Japan.[74] The models were Göttingen and, even more, Wilhelm von Humboldt's Berlin. University College London (that "godless institution in Gower Street") had been established in 1826 as an explicit counter to Oxford and Cambridge, supported by reformers and inspired once again by Berlin.[75] There was no shortage of admiration in America for Berlin, and no shortage of voices there calling for reform.

They were especially loud at Harvard. George Bancroft went to Europe with three traveling companions: the classicist Edward Everett, the geologist Joseph Cogswell, and the modern linguist George Ticknor.[76] All were at Göttingen, all held chairs at Harvard by the early 1820s, all were appalled by the "provincialism" of the curriculum, all were determined to reform the system and believed they had the support of the university's president, John Thornton Kirkland. Their hand was strengthened by a Board of Overseers report that followed a student riot in 1823. The report called for changes in the system of college discipline and administration; it also called for curricular and pedagogical reforms: the organization of instruction by departments, fewer recitations, and more lectures that put the faculty's learning to use. The administrative reforms went through, the pedagogical reforms did not. Kirkland, facing resistance from faculty and parents, dragged his feet. Three of the four German-educated reformers left (Cogswell and Bancroft initially to run a school based on best "German principles"); only Ticknor remained, and he eventually departed, too, in 1835.[77] Reform at Harvard would wait another forty years. The episode no doubt reinforced the caution of would-be reformers elsewhere, like Francis Wayland at Brown, and makes it more understandable that other proposals for change (like a critical Yale report of 1828) achieved little.

The American university was eventually remade by selective appropriation of the German model, but this happened later, after the 1860s. Why not before? After all, the prestige of the German university was already high when Ticknor and friends studied there. Humboldt's Berlin was widely admired for raising the philosophical faculty to the status enjoyed by theology, law, and medicine, allowing specialist disciplines, the lecture, and the seminar system to develop. These laid the foundations of the research university. One reason reform along German lines came only after midcentury is momentum. The sheer numbers returning from Germany, the thickening of their networks, meant that reformers were less isolated. The leading American college presidents of the reform era had either studied in Germany, or gone to observe its universities at first hand, and that generation was there during the 1840s and '50s. A second reason is how well the natural sciences flourished under the German system. That, as much as broader humanistic values, became an increasingly attractive aspect of the German university in American eyes. U.S. reformers sought a greater role for science in the university because of its perceived social utility and as a counter to religious obscurantism. That argument acquired more force in the 1860s and '70s during an era of national reconstruction.

One of the great state universities shows what it meant to appropriate the German idea of the university. The University of Michigan was chartered in 1836 and moved to its Ann Arbor site the following year. But the real foundation of the modern university dates to 1850, when a new state constitution established the office of university president, a position filled in 1852 by Henry Philip Tappan. Born in Rhinebeck, New York, of German and Dutch parents, Tappan was educated as a theologian before joining the faculty of the University of the City of New York (now NYU) as a professor of philosophy. In 1849 he undertook a two-year tour of Europe, and on his return published a book called *University Education*. It has been described as "an exposition of the German system."[78] Tappan saw an opportunity to implement that system in Michigan, because the state constitution made possible a Prussian-style integrated system of public education. As president, Tappan tried to shape the university along German lines, increasing the size of the faculty and the number of electives and higher-level lectures. He introduced graduate study and put money into the library and scientific equipment. He also broke with the previous principle that chairs were appointed on a system that balanced the representation of Presbyterians, Baptists, Methodists, and Episcopalians.

Tappan has been called "the John the Baptist of the age of the American university." Of course, things did not end well for John the Baptist, nor did they for Tappan, a victim of what the editor of the *American Journal of Education* called "an act of savage, unmitigated barbarism"—by which he meant Tappan's dismissal in 1863.[79] The role of Salome was played by a member of the board of regents, a strict teetotaler who objected to Tappan's practice of having wine at table. But the larger objections, which came from faculty and regents, were that Tappan did not encourage daily prayers and was arrogant, which was certainly true. Tappan retreated with his family to Europe, where he lived in Germany and France and died in Switzerland.

Tappan was dismissed during the Civil War. It was in the postbellum years that the new American university took shape. The first major new institution was authorized less than three weeks after the Battle of Appomattox that ended the war, when the New York legislature authorized Cornell as a private land grant university in April 1865. The money came from Ezra Cornell, a New York state senator who had done well out of the telegraph, but it was a fellow senator, Andrew Dickson White, who shaped the institution as its first president. A graduate of Yale, White spent nearly three years in Europe in the mid-1850s, two of them studying in Berlin, where he heard the celebrated historian Leopold von Ranke and others.[80] Henry Adams was there just two years later, but what a difference! Adams heard one lecture in Berlin, and that was enough. White, on the other hand, loved Berlin. It is true that he found Ranke impossible to understand ("He had the habit of becoming so absorbed in his subject, as to slide down in his chair, hold his finger up to the ceiling, and then, with his eye fastened on the tip of it, to go mumbling through a kind of rhapsody").[81] But his German fellow students could not understand Ranke either. Everything else in Berlin inspired White: the theater, the music, but especially the university. He wrote later: "There I saw my ideal of a university not only realized, but extended and glorified—with renowned professors, with ample lecture halls, with everything possible in the way of illustrative materials, with laboratories, museums, and a concourse of youth from all parts of the world."[82]

Cornell had many models. There were traces of Oxford and Cambridge, even of Yale, in White's determination that Cornell be "beautiful and dignified."[83] The university's nonsectarianism, modern curriculum, and system of lectures were by then as much "European" as specifically German. It was nonetheless German institutions above all that White had in mind, and it was mostly in Germany that he used Ezra Cornell's money to buy books and equipment—physical and chemical apparatus from Berlin and Heidelberg, model plows from Hohenheim, botanical models from Breslau. These often just lay around the site at Ithaca during the construction phase. A large Holtz electrical machine disappeared for weeks, before it was found behind pots and pans in a storage cellar.[84]

White often felt tied down by Cornell. He wrote to a friend in 1874, "Europe still seems far off. I long for a run on the other side."[85] His correspondent was Daniel Coit Gilman, who occupies a special place in the history of German-American educational exchanges as the architect of the first true American research university. Classmates at Yale, White and Gilman went to Europe together in the 1850s; they even heard some of the same lecturers in Berlin. When White went off to Michigan, Gilman returned to Yale, where he became a librarian and professor of geography.[86] Passed over for the presidency at Yale, although the favorite of younger faculty, he served for three years as president of the recently founded University of California. Then, in 1875, he was appointed president of a new university to be named after its donor, the Baltimore financier Johns Hopkins. Andrew White was among the college presidents who recommended Gilman for the job.

Did Johns Hopkins University deserve its reputation as a "Göttingen in Baltimore"? Gilman himself was at pains to emphasize that he set out to create, not a German or English, but an American university. But he would say that, of course, mindful at the beginning of the need to win over trustees and a local press skeptical of too much "abstract" knowledge that would not serve the local community, and mindful later that his legacy rested on the creation of something distinctive, not a mere copy. Gilman did praise the German university on many occasions. After all, praising German precedents, up to a point, garnered respect in advance for an institution that had to be built from nothing. When Gilman went off on a fact-finding tour of Europe in July 1875, it was a matter of politeness to old friends in Germany and made for good publicity when Gilman expressed admiration for the German system while there. And if his long letters back to the trustees expressed similar sentiments, that was partly because he wanted to "educate" them. Not everything he said or wrote can be taken at face value. But if he was trying to "educate" the trustees, this suggests his own strong attraction to the German model.[87]

Gilman's admiration was evident in what he did as much as what he said. His hiring policy showed a marked preference for German-trained scholars: chemist Ira Remsen, physicist Henry Rowland, Sanskrit scholar Charles Lanman, and—one of Gilman's prize acquisitions—classicist Basil Gildersleeve. Curriculum and pedagogy were also German-inspired. True, Gilman's original emphasis on research and graduate education was modified, while other German elements were (as one historian of the university put it) no longer "hardy immigrants" but had been "Americanized."[88] Still, the use of the seminar, the awarding of PhDs, and the heavy emphasis placed on research by the faculty—all were innovative, and German. So was Gilman's encouragement of faculty to found journals in their fields. It was professors at Johns Hopkins who founded *The American Journal of Mathematics*, *The American Chemical Journal*, and *The American Journal of Philology*.[89]

Back in 1871, one of the young Yale faculty members who wanted Gilman to be made president had said, "He would be the ideal man for the place and would do for Yale what President Eliot was doing for Harvard."[90] Charles W. Eliot was a well-connected Bostonian. He held a BA from Harvard College, where he taught as an instructor and assistant professor, not much liked by students, first in mathematics, then in chemistry. After being rightly passed over for a chair in chemistry, he left Harvard, went on a tour of Europe, and became a professor at the newly founded MIT. He was appointed president of Harvard in 1869, at the age of thirty-five.[91] Eliot remained president for forty years. The German philosopher Eugen Kühnemann, who was twice an exchange professor at Harvard, said that Eliot inherited the best-known college in the land and transformed it into the leading university in America.[92]

Eliot was a revolutionary. He introduced a system of pure electives—no more prescribed curriculum. This was the ultimate form of German *Lernfreiheit*, "freedom to learn." From that, everything else followed—lectures and seminars rather than recitations, an honors system, faculty organized by departments, the incorporation of new fields of knowledge into the curriculum, and new faculty to teach them. (The growth of faculty was astounding: including the professional schools, the number of instructors rose from sixty to six hundred during Eliot's term of office.)[93] Within fifteen years of Eliot's arrival, Harvard resembled a German university more than the New England college it had been (and that Yale remained). Eliot even abolished compulsory chapel. The growing faculty bore a decidedly German stamp—actual Germans, like the scholar of art and culture Kuno

Francke and the psychologist Hugo Münsterberg, and German-trained Americans. That was true in both sciences and humanities. Harvard, like Johns Hopkins, Cornell, and Michigan, had its German-trained historian. Not Henry Adams—he hardly counts as German-trained. The dominant Harvard figure in this first generation of professionally trained historians was Albert Bushnell Hart, educated in Berlin and Freiburg, later president of the American Historical Association and editor of the *American Historical Review* (he was also the dissertation adviser of the African-American scholar W. E. B. Du Bois, who himself spent years studying in Berlin before returning to take his Harvard PhD in 1895). But it was the Harvard philosophy department in its late-nineteenth-century golden age that best illustrates the complex ways that German scholarship colored what Americans were doing. It was in Germany that William James realized that his true interests lay in philosophy and psychology, not medicine. His colleague Josiah Royce was a Johns Hopkins PhD but had studied in Göttingen with Hermann Lotze. A third member of the department was George Santayana, who was in Berlin before returning to write his Harvard dissertation on . . . Hermann Lotze! Finally, there was George Herbert Palmer, the least of the quartet intellectually, although the most popular teacher, an alumnus of Tübingen.

Palmer's case illustrates how complicated it was to "Germanize" the American university. If someone remarked that Palmer "taught Greek," he would reply, "No, I teach boys; Greek is where I start."[94] This schoolmasterly sentiment would have fitted well into an earlier Harvard College that was, by European standards, an institution of secondary rather than higher education (many of the students were just sixteen). Yet Palmer often referred to the excellence of the German model, and never doubted that ending the system of recitations was a good thing. As he wrote drily in 1908: "Lectures have been introduced, and the time formerly spent by a professor in hearing boys is now spent by boys in hearing professors."[95] Palmer was critical of lectures, but not because he wanted the return of recitations. He wanted more independent work by students, more critical engagement with books and ideas: "Learning . . . is criticism, it is attack, it is doing."[96] This all sounds very modern; but Palmer still had that older, schoolmasterly quality. In other words, he made his own accommodation between Harvard and Tübingen, America and Germany.

What was true of Palmer was true more broadly. Even where the German influence was strongest, even when entirely new institutions were created, the borrowing was selective. This was no transplanting, but a grafting of the foreign onto native stock to create a distinct American hybrid. University reforms occurred first at Michigan, Cornell, Johns Hopkins, and Harvard. They were then widely imitated, at Chicago and Stanford, and in the south, not least at Vanderbilt, where James Kirkland, who became president in 1893, surrounded himself with Leipzig-educated faculty and broke with the Methodist Church, which originally had oversight of the university. But this was no simple story of the triumph of progress over obscurantism, even if some—like Andrew Dickson White—presented it that way. Reform answered a perceived need for national reconstruction after the Civil War and during a time of large-scale immigration, circumstances that led a generation of university presidents to emphasize the training of a new, meritocratic elite. The German model provided weapons to support that task. It also lent new prestige to university instructors in the process of making themselves, via the PhD as entry ticket and peer review, into a profession distinct from others, especially the clergy.

The reformed American university adapted German precedents to its own purposes.[97] The superstructure of the German research university was placed atop the original, more "English" collegiate base. The college part was retained because the American system of secondary education produced no classical grammar school, no *Gymnasium* or *lycée*, so more basic undergraduate instruction continued in U.S. universities, especially in the freshman and sophomore years, even though the students were now older than they had been. That was one compromise Gilman made with his original idea that Johns Hopkins would be a graduate-only institution. The methods of undergraduate instruction changed (more lectures, more electives), but the "research" part of the American university was sharply differentiated from undergraduate instruction.

University governance also differed from the German model. The individual professor was less important, the department more important. Above all, the American university president was more powerful than the German *Rektor*, inside the university and outside.[98] Max Weber, who had seen both systems and clashed publicly with the powerful Prussian education official Friedrich Althoff, told a German academic audience in 1911 that there was an Althoff at every American university: its president. Weber told the same audience that "nothing in the world interested [American students] as much as learning about a German student duel" and described how he was invited at Columbia to "a proper German drinking bout, with sabers and all that goes with them. . . . It was staged by the German department of the university as part of an introduction to German culture."[99] Here is another reminder that the "Prussian ideas" celebrated by foreign educators sometimes went hand in hand with Prussian values of a different kind—that what many saw as the triumph of German culture had its darker side.

The Triumph of German Culture?

THOSE WHO ADMIRED GERMAN CULTURE USUALLY GRANTED MUSIC a prominent place. Germany was "the land of music *par excellence*," according to the *Musical Times* of London.[100] The same sentiment echoed down the nineteenth century, often expressed in highly emotional terms. The American writer Margaret Fuller knew Europe well and had traveled in England, France, and Italy, but she confided to her journal that Beethoven (by then dead some fifteen years) was "my only friend."[101] Henry Adams, ever the contrarian, claimed that he did not share the enjoyment his fellow Americans found in German music ("Adams replied simply that he loathed Beethoven; and felt a slight surprise when Mr Apthorp and the others laughed as though they thought it humor. He saw no humor in it. He supposed that, except musicians, everyone thought Beethoven a bore, as everyone except mathematicians thought mathematics a bore"). But even Adams, who liked to be the exception to every rule, came around to Beethoven as part of his "accidental education."[102]

It was the decades on either side of 1800 that first established a tight fit between music and the Germans. An important part of that was a flourishing new musical public in the German-speaking lands, alongside the appearance of new musical journals and sheet music publishers.[103] But the main reason, of course, was the extraordinary cohort of composers active in those decades. They included Johann Sebastian Bach, who died in 1750 but was "rediscovered" later, Joseph Haydn, Wolfgang Amadeus Mozart, Ludwig van Beethoven, Franz Schubert, Robert Schumann, and Felix Mendelssohn. They created the canon of what we call classical and Romantic music, which became truly global in the dawning age of the concert hall.[104] Johannes Brahms, Richard Wagner, and others in a familiar roll call followed.

The dominance of the German repertoire would be hard to exaggerate. At the 1884 Italian Exposition in Turin, intended as a showcase of the nation, the musical program included works by Mozart, Beethoven, Mendelssohn, Schumann, and Wagner, but not Verdi. The symphonic works of German and Austrian composers dominated English concert programs and accounted for 60 percent of the music played by American symphony orchestras between 1890 and 1915.[105] Beyond the concert hall and opera house, the work of Central European composers found a larger audience as part of the musical programs at spa towns and at the world's fairs that began in London in 1851. The music also entered middle-class homes in the form of chamber music and piano transcriptions of symphonic and operatic works. Claude Debussy, who would eventually become the anti-Wagner with his impressionist tone poems, came of age as *Parsifal* was being premiered in 1882. He played transcriptions of the major Wagner operas on the piano, and as an impecunious young composer in the 1880s made a modest living lecturing on the Ring Cycle to amateur listeners, with musical examples on the keyboard.[106]

We know a lot about the impact of these composers' works—the reception of Mozart in France, Beethoven in Italy, Brahms in the United States, and Wagner everywhere.[107] The case of Japan stands on its own, because of the remarkable way in which "the Japanese made western classical music their own in only a few decades" during the 1870s and '80s.[108] That music was, overwhelmingly, German. Of course, audiences outside Germany absorbed and appropriated composers in ways that made sense to them, often shaped by key intermediaries. Schubert, for example, who died in 1828, did not become generally known and appreciated in Britain until the 1850s and '60s, when admirers such as George Grove and the German-born conductor August Manns conjured up a figure consistent with Victorian expectations.[109] Often, the reception did not take the form we might expect. The Wagner who enthused Italian audiences was the apostle of modernity, not the Wagner of German myth or Nuremberg mastersingers. His was the "music of the future," embraced by progressives who wanted to shake the peninsula out of its provincial lethargy.[110] The attraction of the "modern" was central to the Wagner reception everywhere. This went beyond music. Vincent van Gogh wrote to his brother Theo, "What an artist! A man like him in painting would be quite something, and *one will come.*"[111] Perhaps more surprising is that Brahms, too, who was dismissed (quite unfairly) by advocates of Wagner, Liszt, and the "new music" as a dull traditionalist, also sounded to some ears like a difficult and cerebral modernist. When his long awaited Symphony No. 1 of 1876 was first played in New York and Boston, critics called it "dry," "hard," "mathematical music." It is hard to believe that this almost unbearably intense outpouring of passion could have been so received, but so it was. Brahms remained controversial in Boston. Many walked out of the first performance of his Symphony No. 3 (1883) and stories went the rounds that the management considered installing red emergency lights in the Music Hall marked "This Way Out in Case of Brahms."[112]

If Boston concertgoers were told that plenty of strong coffee was in order before listening to Brahms, the underlying point remained that the music was serious and German—two adjectives that were inextricably joined. If American audiences found Brahms heavy going, just as they would later find Arnold Schönberg heavy going, then that only underlines how the German-Austrian repertoire represented the yardstick. At least within the western, classical tradition, it was taken by its devotees to be universal. If music was, as the American composer and scholar Daniel Gregory Mason suggested, an "international language," its grammar and vocabulary were unmistakably German.[113] That is why, when musicologists wrote about the emergence of "national" styles of music in the second half of the nineteenth century, it was never German music they meant, but the attempts elsewhere—in Scandinavia and Central Europe, especially—to create a national musical idiom that broke free from German influence.[114]

That influence was a product not only of the composers, but of how the music was performed, and how it was heard. It was German audiences who led the way in listening attentively, and above all quietly. Listening to music was, for them, a kind of secularized religious practice. The British, on the other hand, treated musical events as social occasions until well into the second half of the nineteenth century, dressing up for the evening, then hailing their friends and chattering during the performance. It was the heavy weight of disapproval from German musicians and critics that eventually taught them to listen quietly.[115] The orchestras they listened to also became more disciplined, thanks to the German model. That was the work of the conductor Hans von Bülow. His importance has been overshadowed by the fact that the one thing everyone who has heard of him knows is that he was cuckolded by Wagner. But it was Bülow, while serving as musical director in the small principality of Saxe-Meiningen in the 1880s, who established the modern practice of long, painstaking rehearsals, the "Meiningen principle."[116]

The heavy German imprint on classical music therefore derived from the canon, plus the practices of those who performed, conducted, and taught it, and more broadly still, of the music companies that published it and even the instruments on which it was played. Publisher and instrument maker were sometimes combined in one, such as Musikverlag Zimmermann, a company founded in 1876 by the young German Julius Heinrich Zimmermann in St. Petersburg. He later opened branches in Moscow, Riga, Leipzig, and London. Zimmermanns published music; they also manufactured and sold brass, string and wind instruments.[117] Then there were pianos. People sometimes refer to a "big four" of piano manufacturers: Bösendorfer, Bechstein, Blüthner, and—the best known of all—Steinway. The Viennese Börsendorfer company was founded in 1828. The others, by happy chance, all came into being in the same year, 1853, although in different places. Carl Bechstein built his pianos in Berlin, Julius Blüthner in Leipzig. Henry Steinway established his business nearly four thousand miles away in Manhattan; but he had been in the United States for only three years when he did so, arriving as a fifty-three-year-old who had built his first piano thirty years earlier and marketed them under his original family name for years. That is why the first piano made by Steinway & Sons was given the number 483, because Heinrich Steinweg had already manufactured 482 instruments in Germany. The business came full circle in 1880, when Steinway opened a branch in Hamburg to handle European and global sales.[118]

Those who played and taught the instruments formed the key link in the chain. Germans were keenly sought after abroad as musicians and music tutors. Some, as émigrés, made a lasting impact on the musical scene of their host societies. Two such were the '48ers Carl Linger and Karl Halle. Linger, an engraver's son, was born in Berlin in 1810. He had already composed operas and symphonies before deciding, after the 1848 revolution, to join other radicals seeking a new life in Australia. He was one of the talented group that arrived in Adelaide in the summer of 1849 on board the *Prinzessin Luise,* in his case together with his wife and a daughter born during the voyage. Linger established himself in Adelaide, first as a piano tuner, music tutor, and pianist at dances, then as a successful musician and composer. It was he who wrote the melody to Caroline Carleton's patriotic "Song of Australia" in 1859, one of four finalists in a 1977 plebiscite to choose the country's national anthem (it came in last, however, behind "God Save the Queen," "Waltzing Matilda," and the winner, "Advance Australia Fair"). Linger founded the first symphony orchestra and a celebrated male voice choir in his adopted city. That was in 1858, the same year Charles Hallé founded an orchestra in Manchester that became one of the best in

England. Karl Halle was born in the town of Hagen and studied music in Darmstadt. He went to Paris in 1836, at the age of seventeen, where his circle included another émigré and pianist, Chopin. Fleeing France after 1848, Halle settled in England as Charles Hallé, where he made his name in London as a pianist—he was the first person in England to play the compete cycle of Beethoven piano sonatas—before forming the orchestra that bore his name. Hallé was a cosmopolitan German who became a British establishment figure and was knighted in 1888 for services to music.

Germans also had a dominant role in creating the classical music infrastructure in the United States. Most major American symphony orchestras were conducted by Germans or Austrians. Of the eight conductors who led the New York Philharmonic in the second half of the nineteenth century, six were German or German-born, one was Austrian, and one was a German-trained Hungarian. The same pattern was evident at the Boston Symphony Orchestra, established in 1881 by Henry Lee Higginson, who had studied music in Germany in his twenties, hoped to become a classical pianist, and later, as a successful businessman, dreamed of creating an orchestra that would "reach the playing of the great German orchestras."[119] The first six conductors of the BSO were Central Europeans, before the Frenchman Henri Rabaud broke the pattern in 1918. Germans or Austrians led most of the fledgling ensembles during the foundational period of American symphony orchestras in the years around 1900. Germanic dominance was satirized in a piece of doggerel from St. Louis:

> Der feller vot schtands on the blatform dair
> Unt fools der barber by vearing long hair
> Unt shakes a schtick all round in der air
> Dot is der leader. . . .

The anonymous writer goes on to talk humorously about "der brombone blayer," "der concertmeister," and "der drummer," a reminder that the players who followed the lead of the "schtick" were mostly Germans, too. Leopold Damrosch and Emil Paur usually spoke to their New York orchestras in German, and even where (as in Boston) the musicians had a dozen different nationalities, the non-Germans were likely to be German-trained.[120]

Germany's music schools and conservatories were a magnet for ambitious composers and musicians everywhere. Take the Leipzig Conservatory, founded in 1843 by Felix Mendelssohn and widely regarded as the best in the world. Its alumni among the cohort of those born around midcentury included the Englishmen Arthur Sullivan and Frederick Delius, the Norwegian Edvard Grieg, the Czech Leoš Janáček, and the Frenchman Émile Sauret.[121] All but one of these went on to have careers as major composers. The exception was Sauret, who became better known for his virtuoso skills as a violinist than for his difficult compositions. But Sauret also demonstrates how a German musical education could reverberate around the globe. After teaching in Berlin, Sauret became professor of violin at the Royal Academy of Music in London, then a faculty member at the Chicago Musical College. But these figures, the ones whose names have lasted, represent just the tip of the iceberg. All told, German conservatories, music schools, and academies taught around fifteen thousand students a year by the 1890s, many of them foreigners. Almost a third of students enrolled in Prussian music schools in 1914 came from outside Germany. The Berlin Conservatory had students from more than twenty countries.

Why did the foreign students enroll in Germany's conservatories and music schools? Partly for the same reason that so many enrolled in German medical schools—because of Germany's global reputation in the field. Amy Fay, an American concert pianist who studied there from 1869 to 1875, urged all aspiring young musicians to go to "that marvelous and only real home of music—GERMANY."[122] But there was more to it than that. The idea of Germany as the land of music was inseparable from the aura that attached to Germany as the nation of poets and thinkers, going back to the early nineteenth century. Amy Fay's tremulous enthusiasm echoed that expressed a generation earlier by Margaret Fuller, who belonged to a circle where the reverence for German culture was close to idolatrous. In fact, learning German and translating German works into English proved to be Fuller's entry ticket into the circle of New England transcendentalists, the world of Ralph Waldo Emerson, Henry David Thoreau, Orestes Brownson, Nathaniel Hawthorne, and his sister-in-law Elizabeth Peabody.[123] The atmosphere is captured by the story of the young Thoreau, still a student at Harvard, lodging with Brownson, a Unitarian minister, in the summer of 1835, learning German and talking German culture as the two of them walked along the banks of the Neponset River. Thoreau, trying out his new language skills, exulted that this was the "morning of a new *Lebenstag*."[124] Southerners were equally in thrall. And so were prominent members of the same generations in Britain, from Thomas Carlyle, who was slightly older than Emerson, to Thoreau's contemporaries George Eliot, John Ruskin, and Matthew Arnold. In the sardonic words of Henry Adams: "The literary world then agreed that truth survived in Germany alone."[125]

The respect among the educated for German culture embraced music, philosophy, and literature. German culture became the measure of "seriousness." This extended far beyond the Anglo-Saxon world. Ernest Renan, the nineteenth-century French scholar whom we met earlier, was a pious young Catholic when he encountered Kant and Hegel. It turned his mental world upside down. The prestige of German culture held sway across much of Scandinavia. Russian "westernizers" like the novelist Ivan Turgenev, who studied in Berlin from 1838 to 1841, also looked to Germany for lessons on how to live. He told the Slavophile Fyodor Dostoyevsky, "You should know that I consider myself a German, not a Russian, and I'm proud of it."[126] This kind of attachment to German culture could also be found in South America and parts of Asia.

It would be too simple to say that this attachment disappeared in the late nineteenth century. The sentiment lived on in Goethe societies and in editions of German writers. Richard Haldane, the British Liberal, may have fallen more heavily than most under the spell of German literature and philosophy (he claimed to have read Hegel's *The Phenomenology of Spirit* nineteen times), but his contemporary the Conservative Party leader Andrew Bonar Law was also sufficiently attached to German culture that in early 1914 he took one of his sons to Germany to learn its language and literature.[127] On the other side of the Atlantic, it was in 1913 that Harvard professor Kuno Francke began publishing his twenty-volume edition of *The German Classics*.[128] And in Japan, admiration for German culture grew in the wake of the academic exchanges in the 1870s and '80s. Mori Ogai, a military surgeon who had studied in Germany during the 1880s, was a crucial intermediary, translating works by Goethe, Schiller, and many others.[129] Thanks to Kuno Francke and Mori Ogai, members of the educated middle classes in New York and Tokyo had ready access to the German classics in translation, just as they could listen to Beethoven in their concert halls.

And yet, German culture did not cast the same spell in 1900 that it had between the 1830s and 1860s. Respect for German excellence in classical music and for German universities was unbroken, it is true—likewise, the respect for German science and medicine. It was the larger, more nebulous reputation of the land of "writers and thinkers" that had changed. There were many reasons for this. One was the course of political events, which clearly affected how others saw Germany. For the French philosopher Émile Caro, writing one year after the humiliation of 1871, there were now "two Germanys," the Germany of Kant and Beethoven and the Germany of Prussian "barbarism," and the second had pushed the first aside.[130] The idea of the two Germanys would persist through the middle of the twentieth century.

There was a further problem for Germany's cultural reputation and it had nothing to do with Prussian spiked helmets. Unification brought with it a new national pride in German culture, which undermined its claims to universality. That reinforced the backlash against German culture, not only in France but among the Slavophiles in Russia and in Scandinavia. The Danish literary critic Georg Brandes was eager to break German cultural dominance in Europe and consciously wielded French modernist ideas as a weapon against German influence.[131] There was even a backlash in the area where Germany remained the undisputed yardstick of excellence: music. "National" schools emerged, in Scandinavia, once again, in the Slavic lands, and even in the United States and Britain.[132] The Australian Percy Grainger, who attended the Hoch Academy in Frankfurt at the end of the nineteenth century, belonged to the "Frankfurt group" of foreign students there who hoped to rescue British and Scandinavian music from German dominance. A writer in the *Morning Post* of London a few years later referred to Germans as "the imperialists of music." This came in a review of Arnold Schönberg. Everyone knew, said the writer, that Schönberg was one of those "imperialists" who were opening up new country, some of it "seemingly uninhabitable."[133] This was a very English quip, which went with the grain of a common English response to German "complexity," never entirely absent even when coupled with respect. When an English book called *The Secret of Hegel* was published in 1865, a witty reviewer said that its author had succeeded in keeping the secret.[134] But the Schönberg review fifty years later was harsher, and rounded off with a piece of violent scorn. The English, said the reviewer, were "not yet so degenerated as to accept his 'music.'"

"Degeneration" was the language of the 1890s and beyond. An 1892 book of that name by the physician-writer Max Nordau made it a catchphrase. Denunciations like this filled the book. Given the later Nazi use of the term in their notorious attacks on "degenerate art," it may come as a surprise to learn that *Degeneration* was the work of a liberal, secular German Jew deeply attached to the culture of Goethe and Schiller, Shakespeare and Cervantes.[135] His book allows us to see how the fin de siècle differed from the midcentury years when German culture still carried all before it. If German culture ceased to cast the same spell, that was a result, not least, of the fact that the idea of culture itself was shifting in fundamental ways.

Three of those shifting ideas were central to Nordau's concerns. The first was the advent of avant-garde, modernist movements, the second the growing fashion for various forms of "alternative" culture, the third the emergence of popular or "mass" culture. All three cast doubt on inherited notions of culture as "the best that has been thought and said," to use the formulation of that eminent Victorian Germanophile, Matthew Arnold.[136] The changes that occurred in the meaning of culture at the end of the nineteenth century were basic and lasting. Germany was in the middle of these global shifts. Sometimes it was a major staging post, at other times a battleground.

The modernist avant-garde came into its own and set off a great explosion of creativity in the years around 1900. Its hallmarks were impatience with stuffy elders ("youth" figured prominently in its "manifestos"), radically reworking the formal rules of the different art forms, and a head-spinning succession of new movements or "isms": realism, naturalism, impressionism, symbolism, expressionism. Avant-garde writers, dramatists, painters, and composers had their own cliques, patrons, and critical supporters. They had their own haunts as well, bars and cafés that marked out the bohemian quarter, as captured in Giacomo Puccini's 1896 opera *La Bohème*.

Puccini's opera was set in Paris, still the undisputed cultural capital of the world in 1900, including the world of the avant-garde. But there were bohemian quarters in other major cities, from London to Milan. Fin de siècle modernist culture was mainly a European big-city affair, for these metropolises had closer links with one another, and even with New York or Buenos Aires, than they did with their own hinterlands.[137] Germany had two undisputed centers of the avant-garde, Berlin and Munich, three if we include Vienna, which blazed with extraordinary cultural intensity before 1914.[138] The Austrian capital gathered artists and writers from the entire Habsburg Empire and beyond. Munich also became home to many writers, who congregated in the bohemian quarter of Schwabing. But it was the artists, many of them foreign, who gave the Munich avant-garde its international stamp. They were there as stage designers and caricaturists for the satirical magazine *Simplicissimus*. Three Russians and an American were part of the city's most famous school of modernist painters, the expressionist Der Blaue Reiter (The Blue Rider). In the matter of artists, at least, Munich outdid Berlin, with three times as many in proportion to population.[139]

But it was Berlin that, quite suddenly at the end of the nineteenth century, became the world city it had never managed to be before, a pulsating metropolis that typified "modern times." This was captured in the wonderful photographs of Waldemar Titzenthaler, many of which depict the perpetual motion created by train, streetcar, carriage, and automobile. According to the writer Anselm Heine, 416 streetcars crossed the Potsdamer Platz every hour.[140] The city was a magnet for cutting-edge artists, writers, and performers. The German expressionist movement that called itself Die Brücke (The Bridge) began life in Dresden but moved to Berlin in 1910. The city had numerous theaters, journals, and publishers, alongside galleries and private patrons of avant-garde art, especially among the wealthy Jewish bourgeoisie. It also had a vigorous café culture that attracted both the successful and the aspiring, venues like the Café des Westens in Charlottenburg (unofficially called the Café Delusions of Grandeur) and the Café Josty on the Potsdamer Platz, immortalized in a 1912 poem by the expressionist writer Paul Boldt that tried to capture the rhythms of urban life. A more modest haunt that became fashionable in bohemian circles was a small wine tavern on the corner of Unter den Linden and Wilhelmstrasse, first discovered by the Swedish playwright August Strindberg and dubbed by him At the Black Piglet, because of the shape of the Persian wineskin that hung outside. This particular group had a strongly Scandinavian cast. Its writer and artist regulars included Baltic Germans as well Poles, Swedes, Danes, and Norwegians, one of whom, the painter Edvard Munch, made a lasting name for himself.[141]

Berlin's geographical location meant that its cultural scene included more foreigners from northern and eastern Europe than the west. But the nationality of the city's creative residents is a poor measure of what made Berlin a center of cultural experimentation in these years, a crossroads where ideas and practices from Europe and around the world were taken up or reworked. It was mostly German (and Austrian) artists, writers, and dramatists who did that. Their efforts were pushed forward by the stimulus of an exceptional group of critics, sympathetic gallerists, and theater directors, and by new publications that sprang up on a regular basis: the art journal *Pan* in the 1890s, later the literary-artistic journals *Die Aktion* and *Sturm* (both 1910), even their titles signifying restless expressionist energy. Two individuals, born within ten months of each other, encapsulate what

Waldemar Titzenthaler's 1907 photograph of
Blücherplatz, Belle-Alliance Bridge and the Hallesches
Tor station captures the sense of movement and energy
in early-twentieth-century Berlin.

was happening in these years. One was a prolific writer now all but forgotten, the other a cultural go-between on a heroic scale who remains famous for nurturing the avant-garde. Each, from a different direction, illuminates the role that Germans played within an increasingly global cultural world that was being electrified by the shock of the new.[142]

The less familiar figure is Max Dauthendey. Born in 1867, the eighth child (and the first born in Germany) of a photographer father and a mother whose German family had settled in Russia, Dauthendey spent much of his life trying to escape the shadow of his authoritarian father. He contemplated joining the Dutch colonial forces in Indonesia, ran away from home repeatedly, had a breakdown in 1891, then found his way into bohemian circles, first in Berlin, later in Munich. In Berlin he wrote a classic novel of bohemia, *Maja* (1911), based on the triangular relationship among three members of the Black Piglet crowd. Dauthendey's own emotional life was inseparable from his *Wanderlust*. While traveling in Sweden, he met Annie Johanson, the just divorced wife of a writer friend. They married in Paris and set off straight away for Mexico, where they hoped to establish an artists' colony with an American couple, both actors, Dauthendey had met in London. Its predictable failure did not deter Dauthendey from traveling, sometimes with his wife, sometimes without, across Europe and then in 1905 around the world.

Dauthendey lived in permanently straitened circumstances. He ran through his inheritance traveling and made do on the occasional advance and money borrowed from friends. His sometime lover, a painter named Gretraud Rostosky, sold works to keep him in funds. Dauthendey longed for distant worlds, but was homesick for Germany when he reached them. In the story "Himalayan Darkness," he remarks that the curse and the ecstasy of travel is how the infinite and unattainable becomes finite and attainable as soon as you set foot in it; then you find yourself in "the prison of reality."[143] Dauthendey's writing drew heavily on the "exotic." He has been called the "poet of colors" and the "Gauguin of literature." He was immensely productive, although not commercially successful. Dauthendey was praised by contemporaries whose names have lasted. Rainer Maria Rilke called him "our most sensuous poet in an almost Eastern sense"; Stefan George said that his was "a singular art that can be more richly enjoyed than music or painting because it is both."[144] But the reality is that Dauthendey's carefully staged life was more interesting than his writing. The unwitting chronicler of a certain moment, he is valuable because he absorbed the tendencies of a restless age.

Harry Kessler is better known, a tireless intermediary in a cultural world that transcended borders. He bought an apartment in Berlin in 1893 and kept it, returning regularly to the city even during the years when he tried to restore Weimar to its former glory. Kessler had money and traveled regularly between Berlin, Paris, and London, as well as more widely across Europe and in the Americas and Asia. One of the leading backers of *Pan*, he was friends with the French sculptor Auguste Rodin and with the Belgian Henry van de Velde, the leading figure in art nouveau. Kessler brought van de Velde to Berlin to advise on the furnishing of his apartment, and then to Weimar to run a school of design; he bought works by Cézanne and Van Gogh, dined with Degas, and had his portrait painted by Munch. And that was just the art. Kessler was no less interested in the revolutionary developments in theater and stage design around 1900, to which he made his own contribution. He was also a balletomane and a great supporter of modern dance in its founding period, working on one of his own projects with the Ballets Russes and closely following the performances of the American and Japanese dancers who made such an impact in Europe in the early twentieth century.

Art, theater, dance—these were the three branches of the arts in which

Harry Kessler served as a go-between in the world of the avant-garde. They were also where Germany played a decisive role as a cultural crossroads. The history of art, remarked the French critic Georges Lafenestre in 1890, was a history of "intermittent exchanges, reciprocal examples, and stimulation between the different nations."[145] He was commenting on the world's fair held the previous year in Paris, when four dozen German artists defied Bismarck's wishes and exhibited their work. "Art knows no fatherland" was Lafenestre's rallying cry. This noble sentiment also served a domestic purpose. It was, after all, from France that these German artists had largely learned, so exhibiting their work underscored the importance of French cultural leadership. But there was an added layer of complexity. Some of those same German artists, like Max Liebermann, were also praised by French critics for painting naturalist scenes of rural life that contrasted favorably with the "chaos of the French school" (i.e., impressionism). If the Germans had learned from the French, wrote Lafenestre, they had also brought "a certain health and vitality in return."[146] Here were critics who wanted to use the work of German painters both as a form of French self-affirmation and as a warning against domestic decadence. Their intellectual moves provide a perfect French lesson on how tricky it can be to examine reception and influence.

The impact of the new French art in Germany was equally complex. At first glance, it seems obvious enough. The "secessions" from establishment arts institutions that began in Munich in 1892 followed a pattern laid down in Paris. Forward-looking gallery owners like Paul Cassirer stocked works by the great French modernists, while Harry Kessler and a few other bold patrons proudly showed off their acquisitions. Kessler's main aim in starting up *Pan* was to publicize the new work coming from France. Liebermann, the leading light in the Berlin secession of 1898, was also a tireless advocate of the French school.[147] But all were, in a sense, using the French connection. Just as French critics made use of German painters to score points in domestic arguments, so German advocates of avant-garde art wielded French painters as a weapon against opposition at home.

Liebermann was initially hostile to the expressionist artists who came to define the modern German school.[148] Does German expressionism deserve its defining national adjective? Yes, in the sense that the two schools associated with the movement, the Bridge and the Blue Rider, created in Germany something distinctive and recognizable that eventually spread across Europe. But expressionism was not solely German in its origins. When the

English artist and critic Roger Fry organized an exhibition called "Manet and the Post-Impressionists" at the Grafton Gallery in London, he still associated expressionism with French artists. Two years earlier, in 1908, Henri Matisse had written in a well-known essay: "What I am after, above all, is expression."[149] There was, in other words, "a transnational fluidity" to the term.[150] How the German expressionist artists arrived at their styles was a result of many influences. They include Vincent van Gogh, French artists like Matisse, and Kessler's friend Munch.

The "exotic" was also powerfully present in the work of the German expressionists. Some of that came indirectly, via the work of an artist like Paul Gauguin, some of it from direct observation. German museums had large collections of non-European objects on display by the late nineteenth century. When the Berlin Museum for Ethnology opened in 1886, it had almost ten thousand African objects. Sometime between 1903 and 1905, Ernst Ludwig Kirchner saw a decorated roof beam from the Pacific island of Palau in the Dresden Ethnographic Museum and admired its apparently spontaneous, uninhibited qualities. Like fellow artists Erich Heckel and Max Pechstein he also enthused about African work he saw, such as bronzes from Benin and wood carvings from Cameroon. Kirchner's work developed away from the original influence of Matisse as a result. African wood carvings found their way into many of these artists' works, such as Pechstein's *Somali Dance* (1910). All used Black models, too. They are depicted in positive ways that reflect the artists' admiration for African culture, by contrast with a painting like Max Slevogt's *Victor* (1912), with its sexually charged image of a dominating African male figure and three naked white women.[151] The extraordinary 1912 Blue Rider *Almanac* included reproductions of pieces from Africa and Oceania, Japanese drawings, Egyptian puppets, and Russian folk art, as well as Renaissance woodcuts and works by major modernist painters.[152]

Drama was a second major area, after art, in which Germany became a great crossroads of modernism. European theater around 1900 was revolutionized from the periphery, by playwrights from Scandinavia, Russia, and Ireland. The dominating figure in this golden age of drama was the Norwegian Henrik Ibsen. He was performed everywhere in Germany: in Munich, a hub of theatrical modernism; in Berlin, where his *Ghosts* was the first production staged at the avant-garde Free Stage established in 1889; and in provincial cities, too. The widow of the expressionist painter August Macke later remarked, sourly, that perpetual Ibsen productions had "spoiled" the Düsseldorf theater because they encouraged a stylized kind of acting.[153]

Ibsen had an enormous impact in Germany, but not in any one obvious direction. There were many Ibsens. The literary critic Pascale Casanova has drawn a contrast between Ibsen's reception in England, where he was treated as a dramatist of the "social question," and his slightly later reception in France, where he was regarded as a symbolist.[154] In Germany, arguably, he was both. Gerhart Hauptmann's *Before Daybreak*, mounted at the Berlin Free Stage in 1889, bore an obvious debt to the "social" side of the Norwegian playwright. It was, in fact, "the consummation of Ibsen," in the opinion of the novelist and theater critic Theodor Fontane.[155] But there was another Ibsen, concerned with individuals crushed by conventional morality in their emotional and sexual lives, who found a different echo. Frank Wedekind's remarkable *Spring Awakening* owed something to that other Ibsen, with its harsh demonstration of the tragedy to which sexual repression could lead, although in staging and language as well as content it represented a more radically modern step, so radical that it took fifteen years before it was staged in 1906 in Berlin, another two years before it could be performed in Munich.[156]

Wedekind lived most of his adult life in Munich, starting as a law student in the mid-1880s, when he spent most of his time going to the theater—six or seven times a week, according to his account.[157] That was during the sixteen years (1875–1891) when Ibsen himself, finding Norway too narrow, lived in Munich and wrote some of his best works. Germany attracted major theatrical talents. The English stage designer Edward Gordon Craig also went to Berlin at the invitation of Harry Kessler, who had met him in London. Craig was a true revolutionary. He replaced fussy, naturalistic stage sets with spare and abstract ones, used new forms of overhead lighting to create atmosphere on stage, and integrated design elements with the work of the actors. During his time in Berlin, Craig's stage designs inspired some of Max Reinhardt's great successes as a pioneering director.[158] An English-born designer, brought to Berlin by a Francophile Anglo-German aristocrat and working with an Austrian-born Jew: here was a perfect vignette of the German stage in the early twentieth century. It attracted talent and greedily sucked up influences from everywhere. At a time when the stage was enjoying new triumphs in many different parts of Europe, it was in Germany that the great Russians (Leo Tolstoy, Anton

Chekhov, Maxim Gorky) and Scandinavians (Ibsen, Strindberg) achieved their greatest *international* fame.[159]

Germany proved to be a key staging post, too, in the creation of modern dance. New dance movements came into the country from every direction. The Japanese dancer Sada Yacco went on an acclaimed tour of German cities between November 1901 and March 1902. An even greater stir was created by the Ballets Russes, the Paris-based company directed by Sergey Diaghilev. Their performances generated great excitement in Germany, as they did everywhere. Harry Kessler, an avid devotee of dance, called the Ballets Russes "the most remarkable and valuable artistic phenomenon of our time." He became close friends with Diaghilev and later worked hard to bring Richard Strauss and Hugo von Hofmannsthal together to create a ballet (*The Legend of Joseph*) that was premiered by the company in Paris in May 1914, with Strauss conducting, the first time since 1870 that a German work had been premiered at the Paris Grand Opera.[160]

Innovation came from the New World as well. It not only came, but stayed, making Germany its temporary home. Isadora Duncan established a dance school in Berlin-Grunewald, which espoused the principle of natural bodily movements. It was during her decade in the German capital that her young protégées, the "Isadorables," received their training. Kessler had been disappointed when he first saw Duncan dance in France, but visited her school with his friends Reinhardt and Hofmannsthal and found there "great freshness and grace."[161] Then there was Ruth St. Denis (her mother added the "St." when she went to Europe), a modern dance pioneer who later trained Martha Graham. Kessler was smitten when he saw St. Denis during a European tour, in dances that featured "eastern" motifs. He introduced her to his friends, Berlin's cultural luminaries. St. Denis believed that "something in me began to open up and respond to this new country, which was to give me so much joy and satisfaction." She saw "the wonders of modern artistic Berlin," she later said, and was "never so happy as in those early days in Germany." St. Denis thought Germany was responsive to modern dance "because it was a vital thing that might have far-reaching effects upon their culture."[162]

As it turned out, the reverse was also true: German innovations in modern dance would have far-reaching effects elsewhere, above all in the United States. The figure who did most to spread them was a young bicycle dealer's daughter from Hanover called Marie Wiegmann. She trained at the dance school established in Hellerau, Germany's first garden city, by the Swiss music theorist Emile Jaques-Dalcroze. It was dedicated to the idea of eurhythmics, or experiencing music through movement. Later she learned "expressionist dance" from another boldface name in the history of modern dance, Rudolf Laban. It was Laban who persuaded her to change her name to Mary Wigman. In her later tours of the United States, and through her many protégés, Wigman disseminated a distinctly German form of modern dance, derived not from classical ballet but from the idea that emotional states were best expressed through pure, unmediated physicality—the dancer as a kind of gymnast.[163]

Laban, a Habsburg senior administrator's son, embraced a footloose, artistic life. During his two sojourns in Munich, he lived in the bohemian district of Schwabing and tried to make ends meet by drawing cartoons for *Simplicissimus*. In 1913 he began teaching summer courses in dance at Monte Verità in Switzerland. The "mountain of truth," founded as an artistic-utopian retreat in 1900, soon became famous because of those it attracted and the prurient gossip about their behavior. Isadora Duncan and Mary Wigman both went. Even a very partial list of others who found their way there reads like a roll call of German cultural modernism. Writers Stefan George and Hermann Hesse went. So did Hugo Ball, later the creator of Dadaism, the painter Paul Klee, and Harry Kessler's friend Henry van de Velde. The psychoanalyst Carl Jung was a regular. Then there were the remarkable Richthofen sisters. Else, a PhD in economics, married the sociologist Edgar Jaffé, later had a child by the psychoanalyst Otto Gross, and conducted affairs with both Max Weber and his brother Alfred. Frieda, who was married to an English professor, eloped to Germany in 1912 with D. H. Lawrence.[164]

Monte Verità represented an alternative culture. That was the second major challenge in these years to inherited meanings of culture. Alternative culture was not just a German phenomenon, of course. But it was strongly associated with Germany. The term was shorthand for a cluster of enthusiasms and fashions. Some were spiritual or religious, like the Theosophical movement and its German breakaway, Anthroposophy, the fascination with the paranormal, the enthusiasm for Tolstoy as a "prophet of the unmodern," and the growing interest in Buddhism and yoga.[165] In the realm of education, the reform school movement rejected conventional hierarchical models. One of its most prominent supporters coined the term "youth culture." Youth began to organize in the 1890s, with the formation of the "Wandervogel," who sought to escape the city with hiking trips into the countryside. When the organizations making up Free German Youth gathered in the Hessian hills in 1913, they took their cue from the Wartburg festival nearly a hundred years earlier, offering guidelines for German youth groups designed to further a "plain and simple" way of living.

That was another sign of the times, not only among the young. Plenty of adults urged the simple life, the little hut by the lake, alternative medicine, abstaining from alcohol and tobacco, drinking only water, practicing vegetarianism, and wearing sandals and loose clothing, or no clothing at all. Most of these movements can be grouped under the heading of what contemporaries called *Lebensreform*, or life reform, and they were a type of cultural revolt.[166] Life reformers were the by-product of a "nervous" age, when a burst of technological changes caused life to speed up and talk of "neurasthenia" was as common as the talk of "stress" in our own time.[167] There are some obvious similarities with today's alternative or new age culture.

Freedom of the body was a central concern of many alternative movements, whether freedom from regimentation and corporal punishment, freedom from "unnatural" food, drink, and stimulants, or freedom from restrictive clothing.[168] One issue that inevitably emerged as soon as freedom of the body came under discussion was sexuality. These years saw a revolt against sexual repression that included debates among progressive pedagogues about sex education in schools and discussion among feminists about the role of sexual satisfaction in marriage.[169] Germans eagerly read the Swedish feminist Ellen Key, whose books on love and marriage emphasized "the erotic happiness of the individual."[170] Paragraph 175 of the penal code, which criminalized sexual acts between men, also became an issue. A campaign against it was mounted by a committee established in Berlin in 1897 and led by a physician named Magnus Hirschfeld. This was a field in which Germans were pioneers. It was the lawyer Karl Heinrich Ulrichs who had argued, back in the 1860s, that criminalizing gay men (he called them "Urnings") was a "violation of human rights"; it was psychiatrists like Richard von Krafft-Ebing and Albert Moll who first made the medical case that they should not be persecuted. It was therefore appropriate that the term "homosexuality" was also coined in Germany. No wonder that one scholar has talked about the "German invention of homosexuality" and identified Berlin as the "birthplace of a modern identity."[171]

Germany around 1900 sometimes seems like a laboratory for testing reactions to the culture of "modern times," whether that meant new technology and fast-paced city streets, the specter of bureaucratic regimentation, or new questions about sexuality and the relations between men and women. Those markers of modernity were the context in which two of the most original German-speaking thinkers of the early twentieth century began to create bodies of work that would have a global impact. Sigmund Freud and Max Weber both emerged as major figures in the same decade. In 1895 Freud had published *Studies on Hysteria*, with Josef Breuer, the breakthrough work in which major themes of psychoanalysis were already aired: the existence of the unconscious mind, the strength of the sexual instinct, the unwitting resistance of the patient, and the problem of transference.[172] Freud developed his ideas further in *The Interpretation of Dreams* (1900), *The Psychopathology of Everyday Life* (1901), *Jokes and Their Relation to the Unconscious*, and *Three Essays on the Theory of Sexuality* (both 1905). It was an extraordinary burst of creativity. By 1906 Freud had pupils in Vienna and several Swiss psychiatrists, Carl Jung among them, had adopted his views. In 1908 an international conference of psychoanalysts was held in Salzburg. The following year Freud was invited to lecture in the United States.

The same ten years also propelled Weber to academic celebrity, even though they featured a major breakdown in the middle. In 1904, ten years after delivering his celebrated and controversial inaugural lecture in Freiburg, Weber went to St. Louis as part of the German academic delegation at the world's fair and returned to publish in 1905 *The Protestant Ethic and the Spirit of Capitalism*, a text that closed with metaphors of the "iron cage" and the "machine" that threatened to confine humanity.[173] Weber continued to confront what he called the "disenchantment of the world" (the idea goes back to Schiller) and the ambiguities of modernity. While he saw no alternative to capitalism, and recognized the human gains from science and instrumental reason, he warned about the forces of regimentation. The issue, for Weber, was "what we can oppose to this machinery, in order to keep a portion of humanity free from this parceling out of the soul, from this total dominance of the bureaucratic ideal of life."[174]

Freud and Weber differed significantly in their attitudes toward alternative culture and the avant-garde. Freud kept his distance from both. He expressly wanted to substitute "neurosis" (with its sexual origins) for the vague diagnosis of "neurasthenia" and grew estranged from his former assistant, Carl Jung, who belonged to the Monte Verità group. As for culture, Freud found it a valuable subject for his reflections, but the range of reference in his writings did not extend beyond the established canon of high culture: Greek tragedy, Shakespeare, Michelangelo, Leonardo da

Vinci.[175] Weber's case is more complicated. He, too, was rooted in classic high culture, but his musical tastes ran to Wagner and the modernist works of Richard Strauss like *Salome*, as well as Beethoven, and he was interested in the literary avant-garde, despite misgivings.[176] Ambivalent fascination also characterized Weber's attitude toward countercultural ideas and practices. He showed scant sympathy for simple-minded back-to-the-land notions or any other fad he considered a sign of mental laziness. Yet Weber and his wife, Marianne, experimented with vegetarianism and Weber, a person of great but mostly suppressed passion, also went twice to Monte Verità, where he was intrigued by the uninhibited displays of eros. Else von Richthofen Jaffé, his onetime lover, was part of Weber's Heidelberg circle; so was the writer Ernst Toller, another regular at Monte Verità, and so were several Neo-Romantic intellectuals who later made names for themselves, including Ernst Bloch and the Hungarian György Lukács.[177]

Weber found attractive aspects to both avant-garde and alternative culture. At Monte Verità the two presented themselves in tandem. That was true in many other cases. Again and again, we find an elective affinity between life reform, or counterculture, and avant-garde. Modern dance owed a large debt to physical culture. Among the playwrights, a work like Wedekind's *Spring Awakening* dramatized the cry for an end to sexual repression and hypocrisy, a theme that ran through expressionist theater. As for the painters, their work and lives display many strands of alternative culture. Expressionist works were charged with sexuality. Both the Bridge and Blue Rider artists incorporated "eastern" motifs in their work. The mystical dimension was formative for Wassily Kandinsky, a Theosophist. The Munich artists also exemplify the back-to-the-land aspect of alternative culture. In 1908 they discovered the village of Murnau on the Staffelsee, then spent every summer there. Another, permanent artists' colony became celebrated in these years, the moorland settlement in Worpswede, outside Bremen.

Berlin was the site of the largest colony of this kind, the Friedrichshagen writers' circle on the Müggelsee. It was important as a center of avant-garde writers and critics. Members of the circle helped to create the Free Stage. Through their many networks Friedrichshagen was also linked to bohemians in the Black Piglet crowd, to Harry Kessler and his foreign friends, and to writers like Wedekind, who completed *Spring Awakening* there. Founded originally by two political radicals, this writers' colony by the lake was also connected to reform networks of every kind. One of its members abandoned a writing career to become the most vocal advocate of land reform in Germany. Others helped to begin the garden city movement and the Orchard Eden Colony (1893), a vegetarian cooperative near the Berlin suburb of Oranienburg. Magnus Hirschfeld, the homosexual law reformer, also joined the community. Through its members, visitors, and friends, the Friedrichshagen colony was linked to the youth movement, feminism, pacifism, and a host of life reform causes.[178]

Inherited notions of culture were challenged, finally, by new forms of commercialized mass or popular culture—vaudeville, dance halls, cinema, and sports. All emerged at the end of the nineteenth century. Vaudeville, known in German as *Variétés* or *Tingel-Tangel*, meant a variety show that had juggling, wrestling, or trapeze acts combined with singing, dancing, comedy skits, and some striptease. By 1901 Munich had ten major venues.[179] The dance hall was another by-product of the rise in urban population after the 1880s. The dances themselves were also novel, often imported from the Americas. The dance that has mostly captured the historical imagination was the tango, which reached Germany and other parts of Europe via Paris, where Argentinian musicians had gone to make records (another new technology). The music set off a "tango-craze," and German composers of popular songs jumped on the bandwagon with numbers like Richard Eilenberg's "The Beauties of Santa Fe." But the tango, for all its lower-class origins in Buenos Aires, became fashionable in Germany among well-off young people in dance cafés. The dances that achieved mass prewar popularity were imports from the United States, like the cakewalk, then the more simplified two-step and one-step.[180] New fashions in clothing and makeup developed alongside these dance crazes, while the dances themselves celebrated modern times with their frequent references to cars and films.

The cinema, which grew out of earlier bioscopes and dioramas, established itself in the 1890s. Films were first shown in vaudeville theaters, at fairs or in mobile, tentlike structures, but fixed cinemas proliferated quickly after 1905. By 1914 there were three hundred cinemas in Berlin and around twenty-five hundred in Germany.[181] The spread of spectator sports followed a similar upward trajectory. Soccer began its advance in the 1880s; the German Football Association was established in 1900, and the first national championship contested three years later. Like horse racing and tennis, soccer came originally from England. The story of bicycle racing was more complex.[182] The sport began in Paris in the 1860s, then spread to Britain and the United States. It was in Boston that the engineer Heinrich Kleyer saw a race in 1879 and later introduced the sport into Germany.[183] The first velodrome was built in 1880, but the real uptick in numbers came after 1900.

There was less of a two-way relationship between avant-garde and mass culture than there was between avant-garde and alternative culture. You might almost say that how avant-garde and popular culture dealt with contemporary questions represented a division of labor, one tending toward abstraction, the other toward the dramatic and spectacular.[184] Yet there were also commonalities. Avant-garde and mass culture both made a fetish of the new and fashionable. The mass communications industry entered in these years on what would become a familiar feature of modern times, selectively pilfering and domesticating elements of the avant-garde that could be turned to profitable use. From the other direction, parts of the avant-garde put popular culture to use. That was especially true among the playwrights and theater directors. Max Reinhardt's modernist theater productions used elements of popular song and dance. Theatrical modernism in Munich borrowed heavily from vaudeville, circus, and fairground as a way to inject vitality into a "retheatricalized" theater. It was very apparent in the staging of plays by Frank Wedekind and Oskar Panizza.[185] The energy of mass culture was what attracted the avant-garde. The icons of Americana were especially seductive. The expressionist poet Walter Hasenclever praised the cinema for its American qualities. The young artist Georg Grosz was among those captivated by western movies.[186] The embrace of American popular culture—jazz, cinema, boxing—by intellectuals in the 1920s was anticipated before the war. Perhaps in the end, what avant-garde and popular culture had most in common with each other, and with alternative culture, too, was that all of them challenged established forms of culture they viewed as dull and lifeless.

It comes as no surprise that these new cultural forms had something else in common—all encountered a powerful backlash. The case of Max Nordau should be a reminder that these broadsides did not always come from the expected conservative direction. The politics of the culture wars were not straightforward. Formal innovators were sometimes very rightwing (like the theatrical designer Georg Fuchs), while appalled liberals denounced the avant-garde for meretriciousness and the purveyors of mass culture for moneygrubbing cynicism (in both cases with some justice). And yet: most of the attacks did come from conservatives and religious morality campaigners. That was most obviously the case in attacks on "filth and trash," as it came to be called: pulp literature, vaudeville, and cinema. But avant-garde and alternative culture were also vulnerable to charges that they were trading in blasphemy, sensuality, and immorality.

There was no single "traditional" culture that conservatives claimed to be defending. In his notorious attack on modern art for its "excess, licentiousness, and presumption," the kaiser invoked the ancients and the Renaissance in praising "beauty" and "harmony," but the only artist he named was Reinhold Begas, the sculptor responsible for the hideous monuments on Berlin's Siegesallee that were being honored in William's speech.[187] Sometimes, Goethe, or the Greeks, might be invoked against the "decadence" of contemporary literature and drama. Yet many of these critics, especially the Catholic morality campaigners, came from a cultural tradition that had long been suspicious of Goethe as a sensualist and (like the Greeks) a "pagan." Only in the 1870s was Goethe truly canonized as *the* German writer.[188] It is telling that when, in 1900, a group was founded that adopted his name, the Goethe League, it was an impressive alliance of artists, writers, and critics who mobilized to defeat efforts in the Reichstag to extend the laws against obscenity. They succeeded, thanks to support from left liberals and Social Democrats.[189] The critics of modernist "excesses" were even less likely to invoke Heinrich Heine as an exemplar of "German culture," and more likely to see him as representative of a certain kind of "un-German" and "Jewish" form of writing.[190] No, the critics of avant-garde modernism and popular culture might invoke the "German classics," but what they were really defending were various forms of more insipid culture—salon art, the celebratory work of the court painter Anton von Werner, the conventional contemporary dramas of the court theaters, middlebrow literature of the kind that was serialized in family magazines, or bucolic *Heimat* literature with its cherry-picking maidens.

Those who denounced avant-garde, popular, and alternative culture often clothed their criticism in national terms. They were defending not only culture against immorality, but German culture against harmful foreign influences. Morality campaigners in Munich, always very vocal, complained about the "heredity-theories of Mr. Ibsen."[191] Criticizing foreign dramatists was common because they were so prominent. But the same thing happened in the field of art. When Harry Kessler was director of the Grand Ducal Museum of Arts and Crafts in Weimar, he arranged an exhibition of drawings and watercolors by his friend Auguste Rodin, who had donated them with a dedication to the grand duke. The works included sketches of female nudes, however, some showing genitalia. During the

ensuing scandal, a conservative warned that "what is displayed is so revolt-
ing that we must warn our wives and daughters not to visit the museum,"
then thundered that "it is an impudence of the foreigner to offer such
things."[192]

France was always a favorite target. A hive of modernism, it also had
a stagnant birthrate and was routinely associated in the conservative mind
with decadence and immorality. The other country that drew condemnation was the United States. Unlike its French sister republic, America was
clearly dynamic, but for conservatives it was dynamic in the wrong ways—
materialist, vulgar, and violent. American big-city architecture was reviled,
like the culture it symbolized. It was the United States that conservatives
pointed to when they wanted a symbol for modern mechanized soulless-
ness. The world was becoming "more hateful, more artificial, more Americanized every day," lamented Ernst Rudorff, a professor of music who
founded Germany's main *Heimat* protection movement.[193] American dance
music was widely deplored; so was the medium of mass entertainment that
was starting to become associated with the United States. The "cinema
addiction," said one critic, threatened "the strength of the nation."[194]

In culture, as in economics, conservatives were protectionists, anxious
about "imports." And they had much to be anxious about. It was harder to
stop Argentinian music getting into the country than Argentinian beef,
harder to exclude American dances than American pork. The life reformers
borrowed eclectically from every kind of foreign model. And when it came
to the modernist avant-garde, the painters took their cue from France, the
dramatists from Scandinavia, the architects from Britain and America. The
institutional borrowings were many. The Berlin Free Stage was modeled
on the Théâtre-Libre in Paris, Albert Langen's Munich-based magazine
Simplicissimus on the French *Gil Blas*, and Herwarth Walden's *Sturm* on
the Italian magazine *La Voce*. There is no mistaking the element of cosmopolitan cultural exchange here, or in the case of key intermediaries such as
Harry Kessler and gallery owner Paul Cassirer.

But things were not quite so simple. It is not only, as we have seen
many times, that foreign models were adapted and changed in the course
of being selectively appropriated. The ideas that were exchanged were not
always benignly cosmopolitan. Dubious notions of "hygiene" had a place in
the discourse of some reformers, just as the "self-expression" of youth that
Wedekind and others preached took antisemitic form in parts of the youth
movement. Nor did the internationalism of the modern preclude chauvin-

ism. The secessionist painter Lovis Corinth admired Manet and Cézanne, but lectured on the need to protect German art from the danger of contamination by Gallic fashion.[195] (Cézanne himself was an "anti-Dreyfusard" on the great issue that divided France, a reminder that greatness as an artist does not always go hand in hand with agreeably liberal views.) Corinth was not alone. The contemporary understanding of German expressionism had nationalist undertones.

There is something else, too: even as cultural exchanges across national borders proceeded at an unprecedented pace in the years before 1914, culture became a site of competition among nations. Here was another parallel between culture and economy. Or, shall we say, the two were often intertwined. Modern design is a good example. Germany was where global innovations in design met. The English arts and crafts movement found its way to Germany via Hermann Muthesius, who served as an attaché in the German embassy in London from 1896 to 1903. He returned an enthusiast for English design and vernacular architecture and helped to set up the Deutscher Werkbund, the celebrated German industrial design body, in 1907. But modernist design also entered Germany via the art nouveau movement (Germans called it Jugendstil) associated with Kessler's friend van de Velde. Advocates of the two movements, rival forms of modernism in design, ended up locked in conflict. The Werkbund is where that conflict played out. The outcome was paradoxical. Judged by purely aesthetic criteria, and with the benefit of hindsight, van de Velde's faction won the day, because it clearly anticipated the Bauhaus, the famous German design school of the 1920s. Van de Velde himself directed the design school in Weimar that was the forerunner of the Bauhaus. But it was the formally less adventurous Muthesius faction in the Werkbund that came out on top in the short run, because (to the horror of van de Velde) it called for greater use of standardized design and mechanical production to capture world markets.[196] That strategy enabled Germany to overtake France in the field of applied art and design in the years before 1914.

Cultural competition was joined in many different places. World's fairs were one, an opportunity for cultural as well as economic self-presentation. Universities were another. Once, it had been self-evident that Germany was where foreign students would head. But the numbers leveled off at the beginning of the twentieth century, partly because of resistance at home, while France and the United States made successful efforts to attract foreign students. Paul von Salvisberg, a higher education expert, pointed this out in a 1913 article intended to sound the alarm. Foreign students were, he argued, a way to spread "German ideas in the world."[197] The phrase was one that Paul Rohrbach, a former colonial official and writer on colonial affairs, had made popular the previous year in a book of that title.[198] It is a limited book in many ways, mostly concerned with material things and highly bombastic in tone. Rohrbach uses phrases like "German ideas" and "cultural influences" without mentioning the name of a single German writer, philosopher, or artist. His view of culture is entirely transactional. What he cared about was German influence, or "moral conquests," and he complained that the British and French had a better press among foreign nations. His solution was "cultural policy."

That was something Germany's rulers began to practice in the years before 1914, although haltingly, partly in imitation of France, for whom the "civilizing mission" served (like colonialism) as a form of compensation for defeat in 1870–71. The kaiser was especially keen on cultural diplomacy if it came in the form of grand gestures. A notable instance was the founding of a Germanic Museum at Harvard. The idea was first mooted by Kuno Francke, the same Harvard professor who would later publish his twenty-volume series *The German Classics* and now wanted to show the American public German artistic accomplishments. He discussed it with the German ambassador in Washington, who raised it with the Foreign Office. The kaiser enthusiastically threw himself into arranging the shipment of plaster casts of statues, cathedral doors, and other artifacts. Prince Henry, the kaiser's brother, received an honorary doctorate from Harvard; the university received an art museum, dedicated in 1903 and initially housed in an old gymnasium until money from the St. Louis brewing company Anheuser-Busch funded the construction of a dedicated building.[199] This remained a one-off, however. There were some in the administration who advocated doing more: Chancellor Theobald Bethmann Hollweg was very taken in 1913 by what the French nationalist Edmond Rostand had just christened the "imperialism of the idea." But no systematic practice of cultural diplomacy emerged in prewar Germany.[200]

In 1905, Harry Kessler and his English artist friend William Rothenstein undertook some cultural diplomacy of their own, independent of their governments. They gathered the signatures of German and English artistic luminaries on open letters that expressed admiration for the culture of the other country and regretted the rising hostility between them during a diplomatic crisis that had arisen over Morocco. The letters eventually appeared in *The Times* of London and in German newspapers, in January 1906. The signatories were impressive. But Kessler and Rothenstein also had difficulties with people they approached. Some refused altogether, others equivocated or demanded changes in wording (Gerhart Hauptmann was successful in having "deeply regret" amended to "regret" where the letter mentioned hostile German press coverage of the Boer War).[201] Even in 1906, and among cultural figures who rejected the arguments of their own crass chauvinists, there was suspicion about the intentions of the other that had not been present earlier.

Familiarity with the other culture did not necessarily change that. There were plenty of Englishmen in Heidelberg and Germans at Oxford in the years after 1900.[202] Some of the leading anti-German voices in British public life knew the German language and were steeped in German culture. The *Times* journalists Wickham Steed and George Saunders had both been students in Germany. Eyre Crowe, author of a famous Foreign Office memorandum warning about German great power aspirations, had a German mother, was brought up in Germany, and married a German cousin.[203] On the German side, too, there was widespread familiarity with English culture in high places. Just as the British had their Goethe Society, Germans embraced Shakespeare as one of their own. German chancellor Bethmann Hollweg sent his eldest son, Friedrich, to Oxford. The former governor of Heligoland, the island ceded by Britain to Germany in 1890, wrote shortly before the war about the "countless threads which intersect the intellectual life of Germany and England in science, in art, in literature."[204] But what did it all add up to? If, on the one hand, the growing political antagonism between the two countries did not prevent continuing cultural exchanges, neither did the cultural affinities prevent the growing antagonism.[205] Even Harry Kessler, half British by birth and upbringing, and perhaps the most Francophile German of his day, shared the widespread German suspicion of British intentions and worried about rising nationalism in France.

After the third London performance of the ballet *The Legend of Joseph*, which Kessler had masterminded, he wrote to his sister, "All the royalty were to be there but of course under the circumstances (the assassination of the Austrian Gr. Duke), they cannot." Kessler was not too concerned at the time about the assassination of the "Gr. Duke," but by the end of July 1914 he was making arrangements for his mother and sister to hole up in England, and worrying about his brother-in-law, who was about to don a

French uniform, before himself joining the German artillery munitions unit he commanded.[206]

Kessler survived the war. Many who belonged to his world were less lucky. Max Dauthendey, interned by the Dutch in Java, died of malaria. Frank Wedekind, weakened by wartime food shortages, died from a routine operation. Expressionist painter August Macke was killed in France in September 1914. His friend and fellow artist Franz Marc was killed in France two years later. Peter, the younger son of Käthe Kollwitz, was killed in October 1914, a loss to which the grief-stricken artist returned again and again in her wartime diaries.[207] The expressionist poet Ernst Stadler was killed at the Battle of Ypres in the same month. As another expressionist poet, August Stramm, wrote in February 1915, "There is horror in me, there is horror around me, bubbling, surging around, throttling, ensnaring. There is no way out."[208] He was killed on the eastern front later that year. Friedrich Bethmann Hollweg, the chancellor's son, was killed on the eastern front in December 1914. Two years later, Raymond Asquith, the eldest son of British prime minister Herbert Asquith, was killed on the Somme. Both had been students at Balliol College, Oxford. Another young man in England, the aspiring composer Edward Brittain, left school in July 1914 with a place at Oxford and dreams of studying later at a German conservatory, in Leipzig or Dresden. He was killed on the Italian front, as his older sister Vera recorded with sorrow in one of the great books to come out of World War One, *Testament of Youth*, her harrowing "indictment of a civilisation." The war took her brother, her fiancé, and two of her closest friends. When it was over, "a new age was beginning; but the dead were dead and would never return."[209]

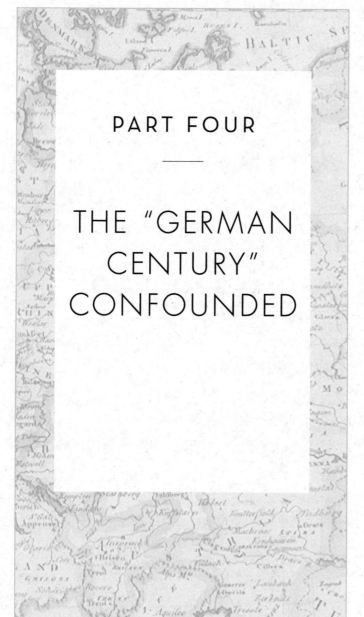

PART FOUR

———

THE "GERMAN
CENTURY"
CONFOUNDED

CHAPTER 10

WAR, REPUBLIC, THIRD REICH: GERMANY, 1914–1939

War

NOT LONG BEFORE HIS DEATH IN 1983, THE FRENCH POLITICAL philosopher Raymond Aron remarked that the twentieth century "could have been the German century."[1] He was talking to his friend Fritz Stern, a historian and Jewish exile from the Third Reich. Aron was surely thinking about German accomplishments in science and medicine, its globally admired universities and cultural standing. His backward glance was very much in tune with the sentiments of Germans themselves in 1900, as they looked forward to the new century with pride and optimism.[2] It turned out differently, of course. The German century became synonymous instead with military aggression and Nazi dictatorship, above all with the Holocaust. In the words of novelist Thomas Mann, another exile, speaking in May 1945 from Washington, D.C., Germany had become "a thorn in the flesh of the world."[3]

Then came the slow climb back to acceptance and respect. The trajectory of German history in the twentieth century is a textbook case for those who like their history to come with a moral: the descent into barbarism and moral catastrophe, followed by a prolonged "atonement" (division) and eventual "redemption" (reunification).[4] That is one way of telling the story. But there are other ways to place Germany inside the tumultuous history of the twentieth century. Take Berlin as an example and think about what it stood for decade by decade. The dynamic world metropolis of the years before 1914 was transformed into the desperate, starving city of World War One, before it became a major site of revolution during the turbulent postwar era. Then Berlin, the pulsating symbol of modernity that we associate with Weimar culture and the Roaring Twenties, turned into the capital of Adolf Hitler's murderous Third Reich. After 1945, reduced to rubble and divided, the city enjoyed a new kind of celebrity as the capital of the Cold War, becoming the classic playground of spies and providing photo opportunities from the time of the Airlift (1948–49) to the era of the Wall (1961–1989). It was in Berlin that each half-Germany set out its stall, one economic system against another, one version of culture against another. Meanwhile, on either side of the Wall, a world in motion made itself felt as Turkish workers established themselves in Kreuzberg (West) and Vietnamese workers in Mitte (East). Then, in 1989, the city was once again the center of global media attention as the Wall fell and signaled the unofficial end of the Cold War. Ten years on, as the century came to a close, Berlin became once more the capital of a now reunited country as well as a favored destination for Jews from the former Soviet Union and a global magnet for young creatives. These vignettes from Berlin suggest some of the ways in which twentieth-century Germany was part of a larger global history. They are among the many themes that will be explored in the final three chapters of this book.

But let me go back to the beginning. When did it all start to go wrong? According to the American diplomat and historian George Kennan, it was with World War One, the "great seminal catastrophe" of the century.[5] This war is the most studied event in history. A Google search produces 4.1 billion hits, outstripping even World War Two (3.1 billion hits). More than 13 million Germans put on uniforms, meaning that almost nine in ten of the male population between the ages of eighteen and fifty were in the armed forces at some point. More than 2 million Germans died and more than 5.5 million were wounded. That death toll was proportionately the heaviest among the major combatants, amounting to 1300 deaths every day for more than four years. The French death rate, terrible enough, was 850 a day. The fighting claimed 10 million lives altogether. Civilian casualties came to another 7 to 10 million, a figure that rises sharply if we include the effects of the influenza pandemic that began in January 1918 and which the conflict helped to spread. This was the "people's war" that Helmuth Karl von Moltke, the longtime chief of the Prussian and German General Staff, had predicted in 1890, and the "total war" that General Erich Ludendorff later called it.[6]

The war placed unprecedented strains on society, affecting relations between workers and the better-off, town and country, men and women. The conflict was indeed the great watershed that Thomas Mann suggested when he told readers of his 1924 novel *The Magic Mountain* that it was set "in the long ago, in the old days, the days of the world before the Great War."[7] It was also a truly global conflict. This both determined its outcome and led in the long run to the reduced place of Europe in the world. In the short term the war brought down four multiethnic empires, including Germany and Austria-Hungary; it created millions of refugees, and spawned both bolshevism and fascism. Small wonder that the conflict has been described as a "global revolution."[8]

It was triggered by an act of violence in the Balkans, already the site of two dangerous local conflicts in the recent past. Archduke Franz Ferdinand, the heir to the Habsburg throne, and his wife, Sophie, were assassinated in Sarajevo, the Bosnian capital, on June 28, 1914. The nineteen-year-old who fired the gun, Gavrilo Princip, was a Bosnian Serb nationalist with links to the terrorist Black Hand organization, which was supported by leading figures in Serbian army intelligence. His act was a protest against the Austrian annexation of Bosnia-Hercegovina six years earlier. The assassination set in motion the "July crisis" that confronted decision makers and eventually led to war.

How and why war came has been vigorously debated ever since. German actions received special scrutiny from the start, because the Treaty of Versailles in 1919 ascribed "responsibility" to Germany. Trying to reconstruct the steps that led to the outbreak of war is like working through the moves in a particularly complex version of three-dimensional chess—something like the *Raumschach*, or space chess, invented in 1907 by the German physician Ferdinand Maack. The three dimensions in this case were, first, the larger forces that shaped international relations before 1914—imperialist rivalry, the alliance system, the arms race, and the role of domestic issues in determining foreign policy. The second dimension consists of German actions, although its policy choices are impossible to separate cleanly from the shifting policies pursued by others, both allies and adversaries—it is, in other words, often difficult to distinguish between action and reaction. The third dimension is the July crisis itself, with all its hazards and opportunities. Were German decision makers leading or following during the cascade of events that ended with mobilizations and declarations of war? My overall outbreak-of-war verdict is that Germany bore a substantial share of responsibility for the war but was by no means solely responsible.

Two armed blocs faced each other in Europe on the eve of war. On one side was the Triple Alliance of Germany and Austria-Hungary, with its notional ally, Italy; on the other, the Triple Entente of France, Russia, and Britain. Italy was a notional ally because neither of the partners confidently expected its support in the event of war, and in fact Italy remained neutral in 1914, then joined the war on the other side the next year. A joke made the rounds in Germany: "What is the difference between a modern marriage and the Triple Alliance? In a modern marriage you can depend on there being a third party somewhere, but in the Triple Alliance you can safely depend on there being only two."[9] The unreliability of the Italian ally is one answer to the charge made by contemporary critics that the alliance system created rigidity and was destabilizing by itself. The alliances changed their character over time, and the allies could—and did—hold their partners back as well as urge them on. In the pre-1914 Balkan imbroglio, Britain usually held back the Russians, while Germany did the same with Austria-Hungary. Of course, that is another way of saying that a system of armed blocs can serve to keep the peace—until it fails. Even before the July crisis the alliance system undeniably gave shape to growing international tension, and arguably gave it momentum as well.

The true diplomatic revolution of the prewar years was the Triple Entente, which resulted from agreements between France and Russia (1894), Britain and France (1904), and Britain and Russia (1907). In German eyes, this was "encirclement," for what else could have led democratic Britain and France to make common cause with autocratic Russia; and why otherwise would Britain ally with France, when the two had clashed repeatedly in Africa, and with Russia, while disputes over Afghanistan still simmered? Germans saw anti-German animus at work—in France, the desire to "revenge" the defeat of 1870–71; in Russia, a Slav backlash against all things German; and in Britain, "trade envy" and resentment of a vigorous newcomer. None of these suspicions was groundless. But Germany misread the thinking behind these agreements, which were motivated by a sense of vulnerability. Britain, the "weary Titan," faced the challenge of Russian rivalry in Asia, French rivalry in Africa, and the rise of the United States and Japan as naval powers.[10] In response, it ceded primacy in the Western Hemisphere to America, signed a naval treaty with Japan, and came to agreements with France and Russia that settled outstanding colonial disputes. France and Russia had concerns of their own. The final act of this treaty work, the Anglo-Russian agreement of 1907, came after the Russo-Japanese War brought home to St. Petersburg its own vulnerability. In other words, the Triple Entente altered the dynamics of international relations, but it was brought about by a series of defensive alliances that Germans chose to perceive as aggressive.

However, Germany also contributed to its own isolation through miscalculation and arrogance. The attempt to maintain a "free hand" between Britain and Russia antagonized both nations. So did a host of decisions made in Berlin. German tariff policies and a growing presence in southeast Europe created friction with tsarist Russia, making Russia more susceptible to British overtures. Meanwhile, the German challenge to British naval power set off alarm bells in London. The expansion of German influence in the Ottoman Empire, symbolized by the German-financed Berlin–Baghdad railway, had the same effect. German policy toward Britain was sometimes menacing, sometimes accommodating. German statesmen behaved like abusive suitors who alternated between whispered endearments and threats. By 1907, German policy had helped to bring about its own isolation. Attempts after that to undermine the Triple Entente proved counterproductive. When the French created international tension over Morocco by occupying Fez in 1911, Germany tried to use the incident to drive a wedge between Britain and France. Instead, this heavy-handed response drew them only closer together.

Colonial rivalry did not necessarily make war more likely. Overseas conquests might even serve as a lightning rod to deflect tensions from Europe, as they did for France after its humiliation in 1870–71. International capitalists frequently cooperated, just as their governments did when they worked together to protect European interests in Egypt or China. European white settler solidarity vis-à-vis native peoples prevailed from Algeria to South Africa. But imperialist rivalry did create new tensions. As the acquisition (or retention) of colonies became a key marker of prestige, their function as a lightning rod disappeared and colonial conflicts were instead conducted back to Europe, as happened over Morocco. While other new players such as the United States, Japan, and Italy joined the imperial rivalry around 1900, Germany's role was especially disruptive. A restless "latecomer" nation looking for its "place in the sun," Germany would have been seen under any circumstances as a challenger to established colonial powers like Britain and France. The hyperactive, petulant style in which

the kaiser conducted "world policy" only made the frequent German interventions more offensive (although not more successful). But there was
something else that made German aspirations potentially more disruptive
than great-power conflict over Morocco or Samoa. Germany's true "colonial" sphere was arguably in southeastern Europe, where it was extending
its influence in the declining Ottoman Empire while tied to an Austrian
ally that felt threatened by a combative Serbia. Austrian fears and German
ambitions met in the Balkans, the most volatile region in the world in 1914.

The prewar arms buildup injected further volatility into the interna-
tional system. German strategic choices made a difference here as well.
After the Franco-Russian agreement of 1894, Germany faced the threat
of a war on two fronts. Hence the Schlieffen Plan, devised by Alfred von
Schlieffen, the chief of the General Staff, which proposed a quick strike on
France before turning to face Russia.[11] It is hardly surprising that German
army planners addressed the war they might have to fight; the French Plan
XVII and Russian Plan 19A did the same. But Schlieffen built into his
plan a violation of Belgian neutrality that would make it harder to ensure
British neutrality in the event of war. Any military planning geared to a
future war against France and Russia should also have been accompanied
by attempts to win British support. Yet in 1898 Germany began to build a
battle fleet that challenged the Royal Navy. Why? Naval enthusiasm was
the German version of a global obsession among contemporaries with the
importance of sea power, created partly by the writings of the American
admiral Alfred Thayer Mahan. Other reasons were specific to Germany.
The battle fleet was a favored child of the kaiser, while popular with heavy
industrialists, pan-Germans, and liberal nationalists. It was, like colonies,
proof that Germany had arrived as a major power—and it is hard to dispute the view in Berlin that Germany would be taken more seriously if it
possessed a fleet. Some, including Admiral Tirpitz, its chief architect, also
saw it as a means of rallying working-class support behind the monarchy.[12]

The results of German battleship building were uniformly negative.
Around 1900, Britain was worried by French and Russian naval strength—
it was in response to the French that the Admiralty came up with the
"Dreadnought," even if many Germans believed (as some historians still
do) that it was directed at them.[13] After 1904, though, it was increasingly the
German threat that London perceived, and understandably so. The Tirpitz Plan challenged the Royal Navy in home waters. The battle fleet was
supposed to be the lever that would force Britain to accept Germany as an

equal and come to terms. The plan failed: Germany found itself with an unwinnable naval race and a potential ally alienated. The return to a "Continental strategy" after 1909, followed by belated efforts to reach out to Britain, was a tacit acknowledgment of the failure. Like German "world policy" as a whole, this was a case of sound and fury signifying nothing—nothing, at least, in the way of practical results.

The combination of noisy demands and minimal results created dissatisfaction at home. The fact that Germany was being outspent in the arms race only made things worse. There were many reasons for being outspent: the federal tax structure, the reluctance of the landed elite to pay its share of taxes, competing demands for spending on social programs, opposition to military expenditure on the left, and mounting public debt. The outcome was clear. Even after an army expansion in 1912–13, Germany was still spending just 3.5 percent of GNP on defense (and its Austrian ally 2.8 percent), compared with 4.6 percent in Russia and 3.9 percent in France.[14] French and Russian military reforms already in the pipeline on the eve of war would only widen the gap between Triple Alliance and Triple Entente.

None of this was received well by German nationalists. Not that their edgy, dissaffected mood was unique to Germany. A sense of crisis was becoming unmistakable among European publics in the prewar years, fed by the yellow press, popular jingoism, and "invasion scare" novels. Stereotypes about the "enemy" hardened everywhere, making periodic panics more likely. In Britain, wild rumors about German spies prompted the establishment in 1909 of the Secret Service Bureau, forerunner of MI5 and MI6.[15] A newly belligerent mood, even a "nationalist revival," was evident among young educated bourgeois in France after the second Moroccan crisis in 1911.[16] Whether similar sentiments were more widespread or intense in Germany is hard to say. The social Darwinist view that the struggle for power was inevitable and war toughened the racial stock probably gained special traction among German radical nationalists because it fitted so neatly their belief in a vigorous newcomer taking on effete established powers. *Germany and the Next War*, a 1912 bestseller by a retired cavalry offer named Friedrich von Bernhardi, captured this mind-set perfectly. The repeated cycles of expectation and disappointment created an especially toxic mood among German nationalists, made up of anger, anxiety, and resentment over having seemingly been outwitted and left empty-handed by malign adversaries—and perhaps by bungling on the part of German decision makers.

Some of those decision makers shared the pan-Germans' impatience. Kaiser William had bouts of bellicosity, alternating with panic when the prospect of conflict hove into view. There was impatience and pessimism in military circles. Schlieffen's successor, Helmuth Johannes von Moltke, the nephew of Helmuth Karl, was paranoid about Germany's position. It was he who declared, at a meeting of German military leaders with the kaiser on December 8, 1912, that war was unavoidable and "the sooner the better." Some have seen this Sunday morning gathering as the moment when the German elite decided on a preventive war. Few still try to make that case because so much speaks against it. The meeting was called at short notice to address a series of aggressive Russian moves against Austria. Tirpitz warned against war and Moltke failed to follow up his provocative comments. The Chief of Navy Cabinet Admiral Alexander von Müller wrote in his diary that the outcome was "pretty much zero." Chancellor Theobald von Bethmann Hollweg, who was not present, subsequently took the kaiser in hand and calmed his nerves.[17]

There was no German decision in 1912 in favor of a preemptive strike (for which 1905, 1908–09, and 1911 had all presented better opportunities). This was not a point of no return, in Berlin or elsewhere. The international system was still capable of crisis management. But the repeated standoffs since 1905 had made decision makers everywhere jittery and prepared Europeans psychologically for war. Each crisis left behind resentment. In St. Petersburg and Vienna at least as much as in Berlin, rulers and military and civilian leaders fretted that *they* had been the ones to back down. Radical nationalists everywhere amplified the resentment, making it harder for political leaders to pull back during the next crisis. Backing down meant losing face. Decision makers talked constantly in these years about the importance of "honor," "resolve," "firmness" of will, and other manly qualities.[18] There was also widespread fatalism about the inevitability of war. Yet the fact that so many crises had been weathered induced a certain complacency when Archduke Franz Ferdinand was assassinated.

The short version of the ensuing July crisis goes as follows. Austria, after consulting its German ally, delivered a strongly worded ultimatum to Serbia. The note was not sent until July 23, partly because of the need to win over a more skeptical Hungarian partner, partly because it was thought better that the ultimatum not arrive in Belgrade until after a scheduled visit by the French president to Russia. Serbia, after consulting its Russian ally, agreed to accept most but not all of the Austrian demands. That was the point at which the final stage of the crisis began. Despite British efforts to mediate, the movement to war gathered momentum and the sequence of mobilizations and countermobilizations then made it inevitable. The dice were tumbling, as Bethmann put it; the "tragic game of poker had begun," in the words of Louis de Robien, a young French diplomat who had just arrived in St. Petersburg.

The origins of the war have provided a classic test case for competing historical interpretations ever since. The recent tendency has been to play down underlying structural forces—the alliance system, imperialism, chauvinist opinion—and emphasize instead the contingent elements involved in the choices made by a score or so men. Did it matter that during the July crisis both Austria and Russia had foreign ministers who were less decisive than their predecessors? Would it have made a difference if Austria's chief of staff, Conrad von Hötzendorf, had been less bellicose or Bethmann less of a Hamlet figure? What if the peace-minded French prime minister René Viviani had not felt unwell (possibly even suffered a nervous collapse) and therefore left most of the talking to President Raymond Poincaré, a more belligerent nationalist, during the crucial French visit to St. Petersburg in July? There are many more questions of this kind. To which one answer is to quote the Russian proverb: If my grandmother had a beard, my grandmother would be my grandfather. But in our poststructuralist age, the importance of individuals and the decision-making process has returned to center stage, along with counterfactual (or what-if?) questions. That has meant paying more attention to how war came about, rather than why, and spending less time asking who started it.

But the question of responsibility cannot be avoided. That means the long-term policies that made war more likely, but also how the powers behaved in July 1914. There is plenty of responsibility to spread around when we look at the final summer crisis: Serbian irresponsibility, Russian intransigence, the strong backing they received from the French, the mixed signals that emanated from London, and—not least—the Austrian desire to teach the "Serbian scallywag" a lesson that would send a message to subject peoples in its multiethnic empire.

When it comes to Germany there are really three questions. The first and most easily answered is whether intolerable domestic pressures led German decision makers to embark on an "escape forward" into war. The evidence for this is not compelling. There was no German political crisis in 1914. Chancellor Bethmann Hollweg's pragmatic "politics of the diagonal," tacking between left and right, had actually been working rather well. It was war itself that represented the greatest threat of future revolution, as Bethmann himself recognized. It is true that civilian decision makers in Berlin faced both impatient soldiers and a nationalist public opinion that demanded firmness. But both of those things were also true elsewhere, above all in Vienna and St. Petersburg.

That raises the second question, about German support for its Austrian ally during the July crisis. Count Alexander Hoyos, Austrian foreign minister Leopold Berchtold's *chef de cabinet*, arrived by night train in Berlin on the morning of July 5. He came to receive a formal answer to the question of German support for Austria as it responded to the assassination. He left with the so-called blank check ("whatever our decision turned out to be, we could be confident that Germany as our ally and a friend of the Monarchy would stand behind us").[19] The kaiser, the generals, and Bethmann were agreed on this. So why did Germany not restrain its ally, as it had during the Balkan Wars in 1912–13? The answer lies partly on the Austrian side. Vienna had expressly sought reassurances of German support. Anything less would have created difficulties for Berlin. Leaving aside the unreliable Italians, Germany was "one of two in a world of five," with Austria its only real ally. As Bethmann mused to his private secretary, Kurt Riezler, on the verandah of his country estate on the evening of July 6: "It's our old dilemma with every Austrian action in the Balkans. If we encourage them, they will say we pushed them into it. If we counsel against it, they will say we left them in the lurch."[20] So there was pull as well as push. But the Germans did push. One reason Bethmann continued to press Austria to take a hard line was concern for Germany's own position. He feared that "the future belongs to Russia, which grows and grows and becomes an even greater nightmare to us."[21]

Here we come to the third and final question. Surely Germany risked a wider conflict by backing Austria so strongly through the middle weeks of July? Admittedly, any offer of support for Austria conditional on Russian nonintervention would rightly have been viewed in Vienna as worthless— the offer of an umbrella, but only until it rained. Russian intervention could not be excluded as a possibility. Bethmann believed that a quick Austrian knockout blow against Serbia could be achieved without Russia intervening; perhaps the French would hold them back, and surely the tsar would be unwilling to fight in defense of a rogue state that encouraged regicides. The delayed Austrian ultimatum undermined one part of this calculation;

the rest of it included plenty of wishful thinking. Berlin knew that Russia was essentially being asked to back down once again, enraging domestic critics. Bethmann later conceded that the blank check to Austria had been a "policy of utmost risk."[22] It has been ingeniously argued that German policy was guided by the conviction that if Russia *did* choose to enter the fray, it could only be because of a prior determination to go to war with Germany, which would prove that war was bound to come anyway, and therefore—following Moltke's dictum—the sooner, the better. This has been described as "testing for threats," but might more accurately be called what most historians have called it: risk taking.[23]

Berlin was also willing to roll the dice when it came to Britain's likely behavior. In the final stages of the July crisis, when it was clear that the optimistic view of Russian and French reactions had been proved wrong, German hopes were pinned on Britain not intervening, or at least not entering the war immediately. How realistic was this? It is true that Britain had held Russia back during the Balkan Wars. Sir Edward Grey, the British foreign minister, was making desperate efforts in late July to prevent a European war, so there is some reason to talk of mixed signals coming from London. The seriousness of the crisis in Ireland also held out hope that Britain would be reluctant to commit troops to a Continental war. But German decision makers knew that trying to drive a wedge between Britain and its partners had proved counterproductive during the second Moroccan crisis, and all the efforts after 1912 to extract a promise of British neutrality had proved fruitless. Grey was privately disgusted by Serbian behavior and dismayed at the idea that the great powers might be dragged into war because of it, but he believed that it would be morally wrong and ruin the country's reputation if Britain failed to honor its commitments. Bethmann instructed the German ambassador in London, Prince Lichnowsky, to do everything possible to avoid giving the impression that "we are egging the Austrians on to war," which suggests that the German chancellor still hoped Britain might stay neutral. But Lichnowsky was reporting that this was not the case. So this, too, was a gamble. When Bethmann referred to Germany's "leap in the dark," he captured the ominous combination of risk taking and fatalism.[24]

Austria rejected Belgrade's response to its ultimatum and declared war on Serbia on July 28. Russia issued the order for general mobilization on July 30, which prompted a German ultimatum calling on Russia to cease preparations for war. Receiving no answer, Germany declared war on Russia on

August 1 and on France two days after that. The kaiser signed the August 1 mobilization order at his writing table, which was made of wood from Admiral Horatio Nelson's ship *Victory*. Three days later Britain declared war on Germany.

The Schlieffen Plan called for an offensive first in the west. In early August five hundred trains a day rolled across the Rhine carrying German soldiers. The wagons were inscribed with upbeat, cheerful slogans: "Excursion to Paris," "*Auf Wiedersehen* on the boulevards!" The expressionist writer Hermann Bahr described the mobilization as a German miracle, which he compared to a Wagner opera: "complete rapture together with complete precision."[25] The resistance in Belgium was greater than expected but German forces still advanced quickly at the beginning. They crossed the Marne in early September, causing panic in Paris. The government fled to Bordeaux. It was in this period of elation that the notorious "September program" was formulated, a maximalist statement of German war aims that has often been read back, wrongly, into German objectives at the outbreak of war. It was actually the by-product of a moment of intoxication, although the ambitions remained outsized even as the military situation changed. The German advance was repelled at the Battle of the Marne. What followed was stalemate. The two sides dug themselves into fixed positions, along a front that by November stretched from the coast of Flanders to the Vosges. Elaborate trenches were a response to the lethal artillery fire that mocked initial hopes for a quick, decisive war of movement. In late November *The Times* in London allowed itself a cry of pain: "Day after day the butchery of the unknown by the unseen. . . . War has become stupid."[26]

That remains the classic image of World War One in most people's minds, the war of attrition depicted in Erich Maria Remarque's 1929 novel *All Quiet on the Western Front* and in countless photographs—trenches and barbed wire, deafening big guns and mortars, mud everywhere, a blasted landscape, then the periodic bloodletting as soldiers were ordered "over the top" in the great battles of the western front: Verdun, the Somme, Ypres, Passchendaele. Schlieffen had foreseen the use of modern communications technology at command level, in the form of telegraph, wireless, telephone, and motorcycle dispatch riders, but not the industrialized carnage that mocked every notion of chivalric war. Efforts to break through the stalemate led to the use of terrible new weapons. The flamethrower was invented by the Germans, just as it was they who first built trenches and used barbed wire to top them off, trenches greatly admired by Marshal Ferdinand Foch, who wanted the French to copy them.[27] This was technological transfer in time of war. The French were the first to use gas, but this was "merely" tear gas. It was the German chemist Fritz Haber (by 1918, a Nobel Prize winner), working in leafy Berlin-Dahlem, who came up with chlorine gas.[28]

The dreadful sights, sounds, and smells of the western front have understandably secured its place in the modern memory of the war. So has the much more developed modern culture of commemoration. This was also the front where the largest numbers were engaged: 4.35 million in 1915. But it was not the only theater of war. From the start there was fighting in eastern and southeastern Europe, where the fronts were more mobile. Then the war spread as other powers came in. The Ottoman Empire and Bulgaria joined the Central Powers (as the German-Austrian alliance became known), Italy and Romania attached themselves to the Triple Entente (soon to be known as the Allies), all of them hoping to make territorial gains. The entry of the Ottomans turned the whole Middle East into a potential war zone. Japan's early entry on the side of the Entente was aimed at making gains from Germany in the Pacific and the China coast, which duly occurred. Two naval battles in late 1914 underscore the truly global character of the war, one off the coast of Chile (won by the Germans), the second near the Falkland Islands (won by the British). What is remarkable is that the German vessels belonged to an East Asian Squadron commanded by Admiral Graf Maximilian von Spee; it had steamed fifteen thousand miles across the Pacific when the Japanese blockaded its base in Qingdao, in search of neutral Latin American waters and a possible shot at Royal Navy vessels.[29] Spee's death off the Falklands made him a martyred hero at home.

There was German provocation in taking on the Royal Navy like this, as there was when attacks were mounted against oil depots in Madras and against Allied ships in British Malaya. These were glancing blows. But Germany had plans to undermine the British empire on many fronts. India was an early target. Berlin made repeated attempts in 1914–15 to ship arms to India through the Hindu anticolonial network in the United States, which had some prewar contact with the German Foreign Office. Three separate expeditions set out to revolutionize the Raj from Afghanistan. One of them even named a Provisional Government of India in Kabul. Constantinople became the center of efforts to undermine British imperial power by using Indian nationalists. "Eastern experts" in the German Foreign Office, obsessed with the "Muslim mind," believed that Islam was the key to success. That is why Germany funded a pan-Islamic magazine called *Jihad-Islam* and asked nationalist Hindus working on their behalf to assume Muslim names, so that B. N. Dasgupta became "Ali Haidar."[30]

The German fixation on Islamic revolt ran deep. Kaiser William wrote in July 1914 that "our consuls in Turkey and India . . . must inflame the whole Mohammedan world to wild revolt." A witty U.S. ambassador dubbed the wartime pursuit of this policy "Deutschland über Allah."[31] Wilhelm Wassmuss was just one of several claimants to the title the "German Lawrence of Arabia," figures active from Mesopotamia to Libya.[32] The British were anxious, but German efforts achieved little. The arms shipments were intercepted and the Emir of Afghanistan declined to enter the war on the German side. Efforts to subvert the Raj were largely given up in 1915. The "German Lawrences" were no more successful. Germany played no role in the main uprising against the Allies in Central Asia, the revolt of Uzbeks, Kirghiz, and Kazakhs against the tsar.[33]

The Half-Moon Camp in Wünsdorf, south of Berlin, was an initiative on German soil to mobilize colonial peoples against the Entente. The camp housed mainly Islamic prisoners of war who had fought for Britain or France. They were relatively well treated and could worship at a mosque built within the camp, the first in Germany. Some three thousand of them eventually fought with German armies in the Middle East, but morale was low and there were mutinies.[34] It is easy to see why there were few converts to the German cause, given the racist comments about the "wild hordes" in his charge made by the deputy commandant of the camp. The "jihad experiment" was another venture that failed to bear fruit, except for the scholarly materials compiled by the ethnologists, linguists, and musicologists who poured into the camp to examine the bodies, photograph, and record the words and music of these "exotic" specimens, who included Indians, North Africans, and at least one Australian Aboriginal whose name we happen to know, Douglas Grant.[35] To the scholars the camp offered a captive population, like the participants in Carl Hagenbeck's earlier people shows.

The POWs at Wünsdorf also included several Irishmen. Ireland was another part of the British empire Germany hoped to subvert. Sir Roger Casement, the prominent Ulster-born humanitarian and former British consular official, played a tragic role in this episode. He had become an Irish nationalist before 1914 and took a sympathetic view of Germany when the conflict broke out because it fought against "the hordes of Russian barbarism, the sword of French hatred and the long purse of British greed."[36] Casement spent much of the war in Berlin trying to raise an Irish brigade and secure German support for an uprising. By 1916 the Germans were fed up with him and he with them (they were "cads," that was why they were "hated by the world").[37] Disillusioned, unwell, and out of touch with both Irish-American nationalists and the conspirators in Ireland, Casement found out about the planned insurrection of Easter 1916 and was landed on the west coast of Ireland by a German submarine in hopes of postponing an uprising he considered doomed. He was arrested and later executed for treason. A German arms shipment (much smaller than the one requested) was also intercepted. The British feared and the Irish rebels hoped for major German support, but it never came.

While Germany hoped to undermine the British empire, the British were looking to do the same against Germany's allies. They attempted to raise an Arab revolt against the Ottoman Empire, and placed their hopes in discontented subject peoples of the Austro-Hungarian Empire. These were not notably more successful than German efforts. It was conventional forces that defeated the Ottomans: T. E. Lawrence's self-dramatizing exploits were militarily unimportant. As for Austria-Hungary, the Habsburg army, symbol of the Empire's multiethnic composition, remained intact almost until the end. There were few desertions or downed weapons among the Czechs, for example, even though Austrian-German nationalists and some army leaders complained that there were, probably to deflect attention from military incompetence. Later Czech nationalists happily perpetuated these myths to help their own cause.[38]

What happened in Germany's overseas colonies was more clear-cut. They were simply seized or conquered. Qingdao and the German Pacific possessions were lost by the end of 1914. In Africa, too, vulnerable Togo was overrun within a month. German Southwest Africa was defeated by a combination of British naval power and South African ground forces. Its governor signed an armistice in July 1915. In Cameroon, a joint campaign by British, French, and Belgian troops was successful by early 1916. It was German East Africa that the British and their South African, Belgian, and Portuguese allies failed to subdue. German troops under Paul von Lettow-Vorbeck succeeded in doing what German forces elsewhere had tried to do—retreat into the interior and refuse to engage in fixed battles, fighting the same kind of guerrilla war the Boers had fought earlier against the British. Lettow-Vorbeck did not surrender his small troop until November 1918.[39]

He was hailed back home as "the Lion of Africa" and greatly respected as a commander by adversaries such as the South African Jan Smuts. That, at any rate, was the way the war in Africa was remembered—as a white man's war. The relatively small number of European casualties, compared with the western front, may also be why it has been seen as a sideshow—an "ice-cream war" (because everyone would melt in the sun) in the words of a British soldier in William Boyd's 1982 novel.[40] This ignores the importance of Africans, who were mustered by every European army. When the Germans surrendered in Togo, they consisted of 300 Europeans and 1200 Africans. The ratio when Lettow-Vorbeck surrendered was even greater: 155 Germans, 1168 "askaris," or Indigenous soldiers. He also had 3500 African porters with him. Far more Africans were engaged in these campaigns as porters than in any other capacity. The British mobilized hundreds of thousands, the Belgians in the Congo 250,000 (to service fewer than 20,000 Belgian soldiers). Their mortality rates were appallingly high. Deaths also followed in the wake of the scorched-earth policy pursued by European commanders, not least Lettow-Vorbeck, a veteran of the Boxer Rebellion and the genocidal war against the Herero. An estimated 650,000 African porters and civilians lost their lives in East Africa because of the war.[41]

The colonial theater of war underscores the asymmetry in the global resources available to the two sides. Britain and France could mobilize soldiers, workers, and economic resources in ways that the Central Powers simply could not. More than a million Indians fought for Britain, mainly in the Middle East. It was Nigerians, Kenyans, and South Africans (Black and white) who bore arms in Africa. British forces also included 450,000 Canadians and 330,000 Australians. France mobilized hundreds of thousands of soldiers from French West and Equatorial Africa, whose casualty rates in the last years of the war were two to three times higher than they were in French regiments. Britain and France also depended on colonial labor power to support the war effort, and exacted a financial contribution as well. India contributed 100 million pounds in 1917 to assist with paying Britain's war debt, as well as 20 to 30 million pounds a year in war expenses. This dragooning of the colonies exacerbated prewar unrest. In the long run it fueled liberation movements from India and Cochin China to Algeria. In the short term it reinforced the advantage the Entente powers enjoyed. They could import strategic goods like tin, rubber, and the jute used to make sandbags for the trenches, and in everything from horses to phosphates the world market remained at their disposal. That rested on control of global shipping lanes.[42]

One consequence, decisive for the outcome of the war, was the British blockade, which cut Germany off from the global markets on which it had come to depend. Prewar Germany imported a quarter of its food. These supplies stopped abruptly and efforts to import Argentinian grain and meat through neutral Scandinavia were blocked. Animal fodder imports also collapsed. So did the supply of Chilean nitrates that provided the base for fertilizer. This further reduced domestic agricultural output, already harmed by so many peasants and laborers joining the army. Things were made worse by policy blunders like the wholesale slaughter of pigs in 1915 (designed to release grain onto the market), and by organizational problems with requisitioning and rationing. But the Allied blockade of Germany was at the root of the crisis. A week after Britain declared war, future British prime minister David Lloyd George said to his wife: "Beat the Junkers, but no war on the German people."[43] The blockade amounted to exactly that, however. We have descriptions of what this meant in practice. Thomas Mann's children in Munich were reduced to eating garden snails. "Our hunger got the better of our disgust," wrote Golo Mann later.[44] Ethel Cooper, an Australian who spent the war in Leipzig, returned again and again in her letters to food shortages, likening the obsession to Antarctic explorers who "talked and dreamed of food." She and others in her circle tried crow and raven, walrus and rat. All of them scavenged in the countryside.[45]

These are middle-class accounts. The deprivation was not felt equally. The army and navy were favored in food supplies; so were large companies with their own canteens, such as engineering and munitions works. The countryside and small towns did relatively well in provisioning themselves, even while complaining about government requisitioning and midnight raids by city dwellers. The black market, which accounted for around a quarter of all food available by war's end, was the resort of urban bourgeois families that could afford it, although the wartime squeeze on middle- and lower-middle-class incomes meant that many could not. Resentment of both "Jewish black marketeers" and well-paid factory workers was commonplace. Urban workers in general fared poorly, although a comparative study of London, Paris, and Berlin suggests that the rising mortality rates in Berlin after 1916 were worse than those in the other cities mainly because more of the middle class fell into poverty.[46] The worst-off were those in institutions—the inmates of mental asylums, hospital patients, and prisoners. They had the highest death rates. Elsewhere, a combination of self-provisioning, black market, theft, and "stretching" rations meant that few starved to death, but persistent hunger took its toll. Deaths from tuberculosis rose significantly; so did deaths in childbirth.[47] In the cities, mortality rates were 65 percent higher during the war. According to German life insurance companies, the death rate of the civilian population in 1918 was approaching the death rate on the battlefield.[48]

The Committee of Imperial Defence in London discussed in advance "how Britain would isolate Germany from the world" if war came.[49] A first step was ruthlessly cutting German submarine cables, but the isolation of Germany and its allies meant cutting off the supply of food, raw materials, and industrial goods as well. German global assets were also forfeited. Overseas investments were confiscated, German merchant banks with branches on British imperial territory were expropriated, and close to a half of the prewar merchant fleet was seized or sunk.[50] The Germans responded to this constraining "ring of steel" in a variety of ways. All their responses ended up doing great damage to Germany's reputation in the world, and one of them—the turn to unrestricted submarine warfare—helped to confirm the outcome of the war.

Allied control of global resources forced the Central Powers back onto the exploitation of those areas of the Continent they occupied. Until the last days of the war, Germany was fighting beyond its own borders. Together with its Austrian ally, Germany occupied vast tracts of Europe east and west, lands that offered a supply of resources no longer available elsewhere. These were ransacked. Romania provided nearly 2 million tons of grain in 1916–1918, plus half a million head of sheep and goats. The 350,000 pigs in occupied France when war broke out had become just 25,000 at war's end.[51] It was the same story everywhere, and not just with food. The occupiers shipped back horses, fodder, metals, and fuel. A million tons of oil came from Romania and over 7 million tons of timber from Poland, as the hardwoods of the Białowieża forest were harvested by forestry officials who had learned about resource extraction in prewar Cameroon.[52]

German labor regimes varied greatly from place to place. The harshest was in the area of Lithuania and the Baltic known as Ober-Ost (for Supreme Command-East) where General Erich Ludendorff ran his fiefdom as a technocratic military dictatorship. Investments in infrastructure were designed to project German cultural superiority, while the lives of the local population were controlled through a system of checkpoints and identity cards. Forced labor became routine. If the occupation anywhere prefigured German World War Two policies in the occupied east, then it was in the Ober-Ost, although it still fell short of later Nazi brutality. The unconstrained exercise of military power stood in contrast to the relatively more benign military-civilian hybrid regime in the neighboring General Government Warsaw, where the use of local labor built on the tradition of Polish seasonal workers in Germany.[53] But there, too, the exploitation of resources was accompanied by severe reprisals against those who flouted German orders or tore down official notices. "Lead us not into temptation but deliver us from the Germans," prayed the Poles.[54] When, in December 1916, Germany decided to install an independent Kingdom of Poland, it came too late and was too compromised by prior behavior to be persuasive—although whether it was more compromised than the Allied encouragement of Arab independence from the Ottomans is an open question.

In the west, German treatment of civilians was especially harsh behind the lines on the French front. This was a regime of curfews, deportations, and large-scale requisitions. Entire factories were dismantled in the name of military security. The mixed military-civilian administration in Belgium was less draconian. The governor general of Belgium in 1914–1917, General Moritz von Bissing, was unflatteringly described by an American diplomat as "the only German general who could strut sitting down." But he was seen in military circles as too soft on civilians—"always too much concerned with sparing the Belgians," according to General Karl Wilhelm von Einem.[55] Things came to a head in 1916, when the German Supreme Command under Generals Paul von Hindenburg and Erich Ludendorff called for the use of Belgian forced labor. Bissing rebuffed them three times before, in October, reluctantly falling into line. "I am of the opinion that a pressed lemon has no value, and that a dead cow gives no more milk," as he put it.[56] His pessimism was vindicated by the fiasco that followed, when sixty thousand Belgians were transported to camps in Germany, where many sickened and at least one in twenty died from overwork, malnutrition, or inadequate shelter. The program was called off in February 1917, but not before it caused public outrage among neutrals and in the Entente countries.

Anything that involved Belgium was especially sensitive because of what had happened there in the early weeks of the war. As the advancing German army was held up by unexpectedly stiff Belgian resistance, it committed a series of war crimes. Some six thousand civilians were killed by summary execution, hostages taken and used as human shields, buildings and whole towns destroyed.[57] Dinant was razed and 674 of its inhabitants were killed. The destruction in Louvain included the university library. The "Belgian atrocities," as they quickly came to be called, were mainly concentrated in the second half of August. They had many causes—frustration about the slow advance and a feeling of being pressed for time, inexperience and jittery nerves, anti-Catholic stereotypes about a "priest-ridden" country, and a fixed belief that German soldiers were being fired on by irregulars, or franc-tireurs, as they had been in the war with France in 1870. (There were in fact no shots from irregulars in 1914, unlike 1870.) That German soldiers genuinely believed there were, as diaries show, does not excuse their conduct. Harry Kessler, who saw some of this firsthand, likened it to the Thirty Years War. Kessler still thought the Belgians had brought it on themselves. International opinion thought differently. The Germans were condemned as barbarian "Huns." In the Entente countries, minds were also changed. British academics who had initially been dubious about allying with tsarist Russia against Germany, whose culture they admired, now condemned German actions. Many French intellectuals decided that they had been guilty of an "optical illusion" in respecting German culture too much, and now took to writing the word as "*Kultur*" to denote Germany's lack of civilized values.[58] In their turn, ninety-three prominent German scholars, scientists, and writers, many of them impeccable liberals such as Max Liebermann and Gerhart Hauptmann, responded indignantly with their October 4 "Appeal to the World of Culture!," which denied the accusations against the German army and accused British and French intellectuals of hypocrisy. Thomas Mann's *Reflections of a Nonpolitical Man* (1918) later reclaimed *Kultur* as something that denoted true, deep German culture, the opposite of British materialism and French frivolity.[59]

But Germany lost the propaganda war with the neutrals. The Belgian atrocities in August 1914 fixed the German reputation for barbarism. Their bombardment of the great Gothic Rheims Cathedral the following month under ambiguous circumstances (French artillery batteries may have been located behind the cathedral) only seemed to confirm an established fact. *The New York Times* called it "the Great Crime of Rheims."[60] German actions in France and Belgium caused much greater outrage than comparable events in eastern or southeastern Europe, to say nothing of Africa or Asia. For example, the "Belgian atrocities" attracted far more attention than the brutal Austrian conduct in Serbia, where thousands of civilians were executed and ill treatment and epidemic disease caused the death of

The destruction of Louvain in August 1914 was one of the "Belgian atrocities" that outraged Allied opinion and damaged Germany's reputation in neutral countries.

three hundred thousand people, a tenth of the population.[61] Neutrals and Allied commentators also wasted no words on the maltreatment of German POWs in the tsarist empire, where the death rate was one in five, much higher than that of Russians in German captivity. They also passed over the deportation of hundreds of thousands of ethnic Germans and Jews from Russian border regions as part of a "complete cleansing." By the end of 1915, more than 3 million people had been displaced; by the beginning of 1917, almost 6 million.[62]

The Russians cited military security. It was the same justification offered by the German army in northern France, and the same reason given by Turkish authorities when they began systematically deporting the Armenian population in May 1915. Eastern Anatolia was too close to the Caucasus front, they argued, and the Armenians were aiding the Russian enemy. There was murderous intent behind these claims. Some Armenians were killed on the spot. Most were deported, a few in cattle trucks, the remainder on death marches that led them round in circles or deposited their victims in the Syrian desert. There had been massacres of Armenians in the Ottoman Empire in 1894–1896 and again in 1909, but this was different in scale. Contemporaries called it a "massacre to end all massacres." It would later be called genocide, a systematic Turkish undertaking that caused the death from exhaustion, hunger, disease, or execution of at least two-thirds of the 1.5 million Armenians in the Ottoman Empire.[63]

What responsibility, if any, did Germany bear for the actions of its Turkish ally?[64] Some have suggested that Germany was a joint perpetrator, or even gave the orders, but there is no evidence for this. It was leading figures in the Young Turk government who planned the genocide, and paramilitary units controlled by their CUP Party that mainly carried it out. Some very pro-Turkish members of the German military mission went along enthusiastically. Lieutenant Commander Hans Humann wrote to Berlin in June 1915, "Because of their conspiracy with the Russians, the Armenians are being more or less annihilated. That is hard, but useful."[65] But even this harsh judgment suggests that he believed, or chose to believe, the Turkish version of Armenian treachery and the military threat it posed. Almost no German had any direct part in the genocide, although some advised on the logistics of deportation and most accepted the official line. Even when they recognized that the deportations went far beyond anything justified by military necessity, they chose to see this as an internal Turkish affair. When the scale of the deaths became clear, they blamed it on mismanagement.

Plenty of German voices were raised against what was happening—some soldiers, many more diplomats, teachers, and missionaries. German consuls bombarded their ambassador, Hans Wangenheim, with detailed evidence; German private citizens reported on the horrors they had seen. Many called it "extermination."[66] Wangenheim began to question the official version. He reported along those lines to Berlin and lodged protests in Constantinople. After he returned to Germany on sick leave, his temporary replacement continued the protests. So did his permanent successor, Paul Wolff-Metternich. Within Germany, the "massacres" and "atrocities" were an open secret among the elite by 1916. Arthur von Gwinner of the Deutsche Bank, which funded the Berlin–Baghdad railway, heard from his deputy director on the spot about the Turkish regime's determination to "eradicate" the Armenians; leading parliamentarians found similar evidence during a fact-finding visit; missionaries and scholars provided details that a Protestant pastor named Johannes Lepsius wrote up into a damning *Report on the Situation of the Armenian People in Turkey*. But their concern never sparked a wider public debate, thanks to the censorship. Lepsius mailed out twenty thousand copies of his account, but many were impounded. The press muzzled itself. The German Foreign Office soft-pedaled its criticism of Turkish policy and Wolff-Metternich became an isolated figure.

The main reason for this muted and inadequate response was the value of Germany's Ottoman ally in military and geopolitical terms. The unfolding of the Armenian genocide coincided exactly with the successful Turkish campaign against British and ANZAC forces on the Gallipoli peninsula. Turkish forces pinned down a million Entente troops all told. It is not hard to see why the beleaguered Central Powers would be unwilling to place this support at risk. Decision makers in Berlin also knew that Germany had little leverage: Constantinople brushed off the protests that were made. It should be said that neither Britain nor France protested about the large-scale and violent (although not genocidal) Russian deportations from rear areas. When London inquired anxiously of its ambassador in St. Petersburg what was going on, he assured them that the measures were justified by the treasonous conduct of those deported.[67] Nonetheless, even on the most generous reading, Germany was tarred with the brush of Turkish actions, and deservedly so. Four German missionaries wrote to the Foreign Office from Aleppo warning that German honor was "in danger of being smirched forever" by the treatment of the Armenians. "The fact of our living abroad," they added, "enables us to see more clearly the immense danger by which the German name is threatened here."[68] Two and a half months earlier, in July 1915, *The New York Times* reported the words of British peer Lord Crewe, as he denounced the German influence in the Ottoman Empire as "an absolute and unmitigated curse."[69]

Even more damage was done to Germany's reputation by the policy of unrestricted submarine warfare. It has been called "the worst decision of the war" and a "turning point in world history."[70] German submarines, known as U-boats, few in number in 1914, became a key weapon as the war went on. If Britain controlled the world's sea lanes, Germany dominated the ocean depths. The German use of U-boats was an indirect response to the British blockade. Both infringed on the rights of neutral and merchant shipping. The Declaration of London in 1909, designed to offer protection to merchant shipping, had been signed by all the participants at the conference that gave rise to it, including Britain and Germany, but no nation ratified the declaration and it never came into force. Both British and German naval forces harassed neutral shipping during the war. The difference lay in the anomalous position of submarines. The international rules governing vessels suspected of carrying munitions called for a warning to be given and crews evacuated before a vessel was sunk, if munitions were found. This was much harder for a submarine, which was uniquely vulnerable when it surfaced and had scant space to accommodate evacuated crews. Germany had previously changed the rules of engagement to allow its U-boats to sink vessels without warning. This happened for the first time in March 1915. Two months later came the sinking of the *Lusitania*, a passenger ship that was also carrying munitions to Britain. It went down with the loss of 1200 lives, including 128 U.S. citizens, prompting an exchange of diplomatic notes between Washington and Berlin. The practice of sinking without warning was ended, but became another symbol of German cruelty. The rage extended to the British and French trenches, where letters and diaries indicate that soldiers killed German prisoners in cold blood after learning about the *Lusitania*.[71]

The resumption of unrestricted submarine warfare in 1917 followed intense pressure on a reluctant Chancellor Bethmann Hollweg from both the German Admiralty and the Supreme Command. The Admiralty presented statistics based on a heady mix of miscalculation and wishful thinking, purporting to prove that unrestricted U-boat warfare, by answering the Allied blockade with a German blockade, could starve Britain into submission within six months. Submarine crews became national heroes, celebrated in cheap novels rushed out by publishers. The policy succeeded at first, partly by keeping the U-boats at sea longer, but the high point in tonnage sunk was reached in April. Then the Allied convoy system turned the tide. Meanwhile, what Bethmann had feared came to pass. The United States broke off diplomatic relations with Germany on February 3. Sixteen days later, the British passed on to the Americans the contents of a telegram they had intercepted and decoded. It came from German foreign secretary Arthur Zimmermann and promised to help Mexico "reconquer" the territory of three southwestern states lost in the nineteenth century, if it declared war on the United States.[72] This piece of folly, undertaken in anticipation of American entry into the war, continued Zimmermann's enthusiastic embrace of efforts to stir up "subject peoples," following earlier efforts in Ireland, India, and the Middle East. In this instance the results were disastrous. American anti-German sentiment hardened when President Woodrow Wilson released the text of the telegram. The United States had only recently ended a three-year military intervention in Mexico following a 1913 coup there. Germany's challenge to the Monroe Doctrine compounded the greater provocation of unrestricted submarine warfare. On April 6, America declared war on Germany.

Try, for a moment, to view the resumption of unrestricted submarine warfare through German eyes. There was ambiguity in international law and the so-called prize rules governing how U-boats were supposed to conduct themselves. The rules were written with surface vessels in mind, which meant that a submarine had to surface to issue a warning to a merchant ship. But what if the merchant ship was armed, or was an auxiliary cruiser disguised as a merchant ship? The larger moral issue is that the quick and singular cruelty of sinking a vessel without warning, drowning innocents in the process, was no different in its effects from the slow starvation to which the blockade subjected German civilians. That was exactly what Germans argued. Some in the United States agreed. Before he resigned as Woodrow Wilson's secretary of state, William Jennings Bryan urged the president to balance his condemnation of the sinking of the *Lusitania* with condemnation of the Allied blockade. Wilson refused.[73] He offered occasional criticism of the blockade, but his sympathies lay with the Allies. That was true of most Americans. The United States also had a growing financial stake in Allied victory, given the scale of the loans that had been made. For all these reasons, American "neutrality" prior to April 1917 was something of a misnomer.

But American entry into the war still made a huge difference. One irreversible long-term effect was felt by German-Americans. A spasm of anti-German hostility vented itself, as it had earlier in Britain, Canada, Australia, and New Zealand, and as it would in Brazil after that country declared war on Germany in November 1917.[74] The backlash in the United States took many forms. German culture—or, with a snarl, *Kultur*—was one target. Earlier resentment of German "superiority" was often evident. German orchestral conductors and hundreds of musicians lost their jobs or were deported; some had their lives threatened. A writer in the *Chicago Post* thundered that "the Teutonization of our music in America began with the establishment of the symphony orchestra."[75] German composers were banned from the repertoire, German books burned, German language instructors sacked. At Harvard, Adolphus Busch Hall, built to house an art collection gifted by the German government before the war, was completed in 1917 but not opened until 1921 because of anti-German sentiment.[76] Beethoven was banned in Pittsburgh, the pretzel in Boston. The German language was at the center of the storm. Sauerkraut ("Liberty

Cabbage"), hamburger ("Liberty Steak"), and dachshunds ("Liberty Pups") were given more acceptable names. Towns, streets, and parks were permanently renamed to remove the Teutonic stain. Berlin Avenue in St. Louis became Pershing Avenue. The German language was banned in schools and even churches. One Iowa politician suggested that "ninety percent of all the men and women who teach the German language are traitors."[77] This was the atmosphere in which mobs attacked and lynched German-Americans. The onslaught continued in postwar campaigns against the German language and "hyphenated Americans" whose loyalty was suspect. This delivered a deathblow to a German-American culture that had begun to fray around the edges before the war, but now fell victim with terrible suddenness to external assault.

The biggest immediate impact of American entry was felt, of course, in its contribution to the outcome of the war. The U.S. Navy supported the British blockade of Germany and joined the convoys that warded off U-boat attacks. The American army, smaller than Belgium's in 1914, grew quickly with conscription. General John J. Pershing arrived in France with the first contingent of 14,000 men in June 1917. The American Expeditionary Forces numbered 175,000 by January 1918 and over 1 million by May. By then, a quarter of a million soldiers were arriving every month, many crossing the Atlantic in German ships that had been impounded. U.S. material and financial support for the Allied cause was also critical. American economic output overtook that of Britain and its empire in 1916. It was during the war, and partly because of it, that the United States flexed its muscles as a global economic power and creditor nation for the first time. After America entered the conflict, munitions, civilian goods, and credits poured into Britain and France. From the middle of 1917, the United States spent almost $43 million a day on the war, more than any other combatant.[78]

U.S. entry into the war was one of the two reasons that 1917 turned out to be a pivotal year—a watershed in global as well as European history.[79] The other reason was the double revolution in Russia. In February the tsar became the first European ruler to lose his throne during the war. That created the potential opening for a separate peace in the east. Chancellor Bethmann Hollweg had always tried to keep German war aims vague (although by no means modest) because of just such a possibility of detaching one partner from the Allied coalition. Informal talks in Stockholm between two envoys, Matthias Erzberger and Josef Kolyschko, during March and April mapped out conditions for an armistice and peace, although this was possible only because neither of the two officially represented his government. Kolyschko was regarded by some members of the Russian cabinet as too pro-German. On the other side, Erzberger went to Stockholm with Bethmann's blessing but had been instructed to listen, not talk, something that never proved easy for the locquacious Erzberger.[80]

These talks came to nothing, just as nothing came of other peace feelers in 1917, like those from Austria-Hungary and Pope Benedict XV, and for the same reason. Neither side was willing, in the end, to budge, given how much had already been sacrificed. Would-be peace offers from combatants always turned out to contain unacceptable conditions. Russia in 1917 may have been more willing than Germany (in fact, more willing than Britain or France) to agree to a peace that restored the prewar status quo. But even the Russians would not compromise on Poland or control of the Dardanelles. Despite steady criticism on the left from the Bolsheviks, the government of Prime Minister Prince Georgy Lvov in the spring and summer of 1917 wanted to pursue the war more effectively than the tsar, not to end it. That was why Russia began a new offensive in June.

The German side was equally intransigent. At the time of the Erzberger-Kolyschko talks there was clear daylight between the moderate Bethmann and the hawks in the Supreme Command. But Erzberger's overreach in discussing an armistice with his Russian opposite number gave Ludendorff his chance. He let it be known to Kolyschko that the German Supreme Command would never agree to the moderate terms discussed in Stockholm. The talks were scuppered. The Supreme Command, backed by the kaiser, business groups, and conservative annexationists, forced Bethmann to accept a minimum program of German gains from the war. These amounted to a dictated peace of conquest on the eastern front. Bethmann called the demands "fantasies," but had no room for maneuver.[81] Any opportunity for a separate peace was now gone. Instead, the German government sent Vladimir Lenin back to Russia in the famous sealed train to undermine the Provisional Government (he was working on his "April theses" calling for a second revolution while the train rolled through Frankfurt), and the Supreme Command began a campaign to subvert the Russian army through a blizzard of propaganda leaflets.

War weariness and antiwar sentiment were felt everywhere in 1917. That was most obviously true in Russia, where a second revolution in October brought Lenin and the Bolsheviks to power. But it was true in France as well, where the huge losses sustained in the Nivelle offensive that year sparked mutinies, followed by strikes. The bloodletting of Ypres and Passchendaele, coupled with the absence of any clear-cut victory, had their effects on morale in Britain. In Italy there were antiwar riots; then came humiliation at Caporetto, where a military collapse resulted in 30,000 dead or wounded and 370,000 prisoners taken. Everywhere that the censors allowed it, liberal and socialist voices called for an end to war and a peace without annexations.

Germany was no closer to collapse in 1917 than France or Italy, never mind Russia. But social tensions were growing. Despite the no-strike pledge made by trade union leaders when war broke out, there were five hundred strikes in 1917 involving 1.5 million people. Many were organized by a radical movement of factory shop stewards. They resulted from worsening shop floor conditions, plus dissatisfaction with food shortages and the growing difficulty of finding basics like matches and soap. Political polarization increased. In early 1917 the Independent Social Democratic Party broke away from the Social Democratic Party, calling for peace without annexations and domestic reform. That fall, a new right-wing political organization was founded. The Fatherland Party supported a maximum program of German annexations and denounced critics who allegedly undermined the war effort. Its founders were former Admiral Tirpitz and Wolfgang Kapp, who later led an unsuccessful coup against the Weimar Republic. The party's uncompromising views, like its violent antisemitism, marked the appearance of a new right in German politics. It attracted 1.25 million members in less than a year. One of them was the Bavarian Anton Drexler, who later founded the Nazi Party.

Germany's political leadership changed decisively in 1917. Bethmann, mindful that what had happened in Russia might happen in Germany in the absence of reform, drafted proposals for a democratic franchise in Prussia. But these were watered down by conservatives into vague promises. At the end of June, as the failure of unrestricted submarine warfare to knock Britain out of the war became obvious and any prospect of a separate peace with Russia disappeared, Social Democrats urged the chancellor to reject annexationist demands and introduce domestic reforms. Soon thereafter, opposition parties in the Reichstag formed the Interparty Committee, a step on the way to a future parliamentary form of government, and Matthias Erzberger gave notice that he would introduce a peace resolution. Germany's second "July crisis" had a paradoxical outcome. The peace resolution passed in the Reichstag but was ignored. Bethmann had been dismissed six days earlier, discarded by Kaiser William because the Supreme Command and Prussian conservatives had no further use for him. They rejected his conversion to domestic reform and could dispense with his "diplomatic" qualities now that the United States was in the war anyway.

If 1917 was the year of decision in Russia, the same was true in Germany, but the outcome was—for the moment—very different. It is even more revealing to compare what happened in Germany with what happened in the three west European Allies when they faced their moments of wartime crisis. David Lloyd George in Britain, Georges Clemenceau in France, and Vittorio Emanuele Orlando in Italy all emerged as powerful, charismatic civilian war leaders. They are evidence for political scientist Max Weber's contention that one advantage of a parliamentary system was its ability to select effective leaders, which he set out in a series of trenchant newspaper articles in 1917.[82] The German parliament flexed its muscles with the peace resolution, but Bethmann fell because he lost the confidence of the army. The identity of his successors was largely irrelevant. Power lay with the Supreme Command and its right-wing backers. Even the kaiser slipped increasingly into the shadows. This brought into the open what had been latent since the beginning of the war.

The "silent dictatorship" of Hindenburg and Ludendorff became increasingly apparent after July 1917. At home, state-of-siege laws were used against domestic protests. Wilhelm Groener, one of the few generals convinced that the war could not be won by "fighting against the workers," was dismissed because he was considered too hard on profiteers and too soft on trade unions.[83] Some of the eugenicist fantasies that flourished in the occupied Ober-Ost were also brought back home. The Supreme Command called for a ban on contraception and the punitive taxation of unmarried men, who were failing in their "natural duties" to the nation. The military leadership continued to pursue aggressive war aims. It called for annexations or control of territory to secure supplies of food, raw materials, and oil, especially in the east, where cease-fires with Russia and Romania were followed by the harsh peace treaties of Brest Litovsk and Bucharest.

The military position still looked favorable for the Central Powers as 1917 ended, even though the Allies enjoyed a huge superiority in economic resources. Italy had been routed at Caporetto, Russia and Romania were out of the war, and American troops were still arriving in Europe. The Balfour Declaration in November 1917, designed to win world Jewry for the Allied cause, was partly an attempt to regain the initiative. It was born of an awareness that, as the Zionist leader Chaim Weizmann liked to suggest, if the Entente did not offer the Jews their own homeland the Germans surely would.[84] Later the same month Lord Lansdowne, a member of Britain's wartime coalition as recently as the year before, published a letter in the *Daily Telegraph* calling for a negotiated peace.[85] After Allied forces captured Jerusalem in December, Britain could transfer soldiers to the western front; but Germany could do the same after victory over Russia. Strengthened by forty-four divisions pulled from the east, the German army in the spring of 1918 enjoyed numerical superiority on the western front for the first time since 1914.

In March the German Supreme Command launched Operation Michael, its spring offensive, which began with a lengthy artillery bombardment and an infantry assault across a fifty-mile front—"the greatest onslaught in the history of the world," said Winston Churchill, who witnessed it.[86] There were five waves of German attacks between March 21 and July 15. They advanced the German lines as much as forty miles, within artillery range of Paris. But this was another gamble by German military commanders, another roll of the dice. The advances stretched the supply lines and exhausted the troops. While more and more Americans were now available to the Allies, Germany lacked reserves to replace the huge losses of this spring offensive—240,000 dead or severely wounded in the initial offensive as many as 700,000 casualties in all. Some of the soldiers still preserving German victory in the east might have been better used in the west. From June onward the numbers increasingly favored the Allies. Like the advance of August–September 1914 and the first months of unrestricted submarine warfare in 1917, the intoxicating initial success of the spring offensive was unsustainable. The Allies counterattacked in July, Ludendorff ordered a retreat from the Marne on the twenty-second, and just over two weeks later the German lines were broken. German resistance was hampered by the spread of the influenza epidemic, to which German soldiers proved especially susceptible because of their meager diet and weariness. By summer a crisis of morale led to growing rates of desertion and a great increase in mass surrenders. "No war can be won with men who give themselves up," complained General von Einem.[87] For ordinary soldiers, the elation of spring, with its promise of quick victory and war's end, gave way to the despondency of summer and fall.

The architect of the spring offensive, Ludendorff, remained impervious to growing concerns about the military situation among officers in the

Supreme Command. After a crushing defeat on the Somme, he cast about for scapegoats. In mid-August he was still assuring the kaiser that victory was possible. Ludendorff's nervous exhaustion and erratic decision making led to the appointment of a new chief of operations and the intervention of a psychologist. That doctor ordered his patient to sleep more, take exercise, and (less conventionally) sing German folk songs when he woke up in the morning. Ludendorff, remarkably, did what he was told. The Supreme Command was divided in August and September on whether Ludendorff should be replaced, whether Germany should seek an armistice, and if so, who should seek it and on what terms. A better time to have asked for an armistice would have been April. Even in July, an orderly withdrawal behind the Rhine, coupled with a willingness to give up Belgium and make other concessions, would have made things difficult for the Allies militarily and politically. By late September, the Bulgarian army had been defeated, the Ottomans were on the losing end of an Allied offensive in Palestine, and the Austrian army was falling apart. Even then, Allied military commanders still believed that the Germans could have held out for a long time. So did Lloyd George. Instead, suddenly, shockingly, Ludendorff told Kaiser William at the end of September that the war was lost and an immediate cease-fire was necessary—it was cease-fire or catastrophe. This all-or-nothing quality was characteristic of Ludendorff, making him in some ways a perfect embodiment of the German military.

Ludendorff and the Supreme Command now made a brazen attempt to blame the civilian population for German defeat and foist responsibility onto the politicians they had always treated with contempt. This was the beginning of the pernicious "stab in the back" legend about an "undefeated army," which gained credibility from the fact that Ludendorff threw up his hands while German forces were still fighting on French soil five hundred miles from Berlin. Ludendorff told his section chiefs that he had advised the kaiser to bring into the government the people "largely responsible that things have turned out as they have. . . . They must now eat the soup which they have served us!"[88] Ludendorff's soup was served in the poisoned chalice of the imperial chancellorship, which now passed to its fourth and final wartime bearer, Prince Max of Baden. It says something about the kaiser's Germany that its most reformist chancellor was a prince, albeit a liberal-minded one who brought Social Democrats into the government for the first time alongside representatives of the other parties that supported the peace resolution.

Prince Max rightly believed that an immediate call for an armistice was tantamount to an admission of defeat and tried to persuade Ludendorff and Hindenburg to delay. They refused. The new chancellor therefore sent a note to Woodrow Wilson in the early hours of October 4 to ask the Allies for an armistice. The role of the Supreme Command in insisting that the note be sent, and sent immediately, was not made public. For a month, everything remained open-ended, as decisions were made against a background of military collapse and popular discontent. At home, a series of reforms sailed through after being blocked for years. They included abolition of the notorious three-class Prussian franchise. Meanwhile, Prince Max's government responded to a series of notes from the American president that made an armistice conditional on very harsh terms. Ludendorff, keen as ever not to be associated with the defeat, proposed resuming the war, but succeeded finally in straining the patience of the kaiser and was sacked. German negotiators led by Matthias Erzberger traveled to France on November 8 and reluctantly attached their signatures to an armistice agreements that laid down severe terms. It came into effect on November 11.

By then the political landscape had changed utterly. Domestic reform and the search for an armistice took place while the power of the army was broken, at least temporarily, although it seemed possible that a military putsch might occur in Germany similar to the one attempted against the Provisional Government in Russia in September 1917. Instead, Germany had its version of the Bolshevik Revolution. It was sparked by sailors' mutinies in the north, in Kiel and Wilhelmshaven, after the Naval Command—angered at the armistice talks, and concerned to salvage its reputation after the wartime inactivity of Tirpitz's much vaunted battleships—ordered the fleet to set sail in a futile gesture of defiance. There had been mutinous outbreaks the previous year, but these were more serious. The sailors addressed one another as "comrade Bolsheviks." The mutiny became a revolt, and the revolt a revolution as unrest spread inland. Nineteen eighteen had been a year of growing unrest. In the first week of November, workers' and soldiers' councils—or "Soviets"; the German word *Räte* can be translated as either—were established across Germany. The kaiser fled across the Dutch border and revolutionary crowds filled the streets of Berlin. The War Ministry was occupied by a soldiers' council. At noon on November 9, Prince Max announced that William had abdicated and named Social Democrat Friedrich Ebert his own successor as chancellor. Two hours later Philipp

Scheidemann, another Social Democrat who had served in Prince Max's government, went out onto the balcony of the Reichstag building and proclaimed the German republic.

The Weimar Republic

GERMANY WAS NAMED A REPUBLIC ON NOVEMBER 9, 1918. IT became the Weimar Republic the following year, after a National Assembly elected in January 1919 convened in the Thuringian town and produced a constitution that came into effect in August. That January election had been the first in Germany history that enfranchised women. But why Weimar? One reason was a desire to associate the new Germany with the "good" Germany of Goethe and Schiller. That was in the minds of the center-left parties who dominated the assembly, because they were aware that the victorious Allies were meeting in Versailles during the same months to decide Germany's fate. Choosing a city other than Berlin was also a nod to other parts of Germany leery of what the Prussian capital denoted, which is why cities like Frankfurt and Nuremberg were also considered. There was another reason to avoid Berlin. The capital was the scene of continuing revolutionary unrest, during which the interior of the Reichstag had been seriously damaged. Weimar could be protected by a military cordon. Passes were needed to enter the town; 4000 militia members established machine-gun posts in windows and on rooftops. That was the setting for the 423 delegates who deliberated in the Weimar State Theater and the 1000 members of the press corps who covered them.[89] Not until August 1919 did the government move back permanently to Berlin.

The Weimar Republic began, as it ended, in violence. The violence of its beginning was intertwined with a wider postwar upheaval across Europe, generated by territorial disputes, by revolutionary and counterrevolutionary violence, and in the movement of millions of people across contested borders. All three created turmoil that lasted well into the 1920s.

The politics of peacemaking was a prime source of continuing conflict. Representatives of more than two dozen Allies, dominated by the big three of Britain, France, and the United States, convened in Paris in January 1919. They hammered out terms that were presented in early May to members of a shocked German delegation, whose wishful thinking had led them to expect a milder settlement. The treaty was signed, reluctantly, by members of the Social Democratic government on June 28, five years to the day after the assassination of Archduke Franz Ferdinand. Its terms were punitive. Germany lost one-tenth of its population, one-seventh of its territory, one-fourth of its coal, and half of its iron. In the east, Posen, and parts of West Prussia and Upper Silesia were ceded to Poland, while an area of East Prussia was carved out to create a "Polish corridor" to the sea. Danzig became a "free city." Memel passed into Allied hands and eventually became Lithuanian. In the west, Alsace and Lorraine reverted to France, Eupen and Malmedy became Belgian. The Saarland was to be administered by the League of Nations, with the French granted rights to mine its coal, and a strip of land along the Rhine border was "demilitarized." North Schleswig was ceded to Denmark. Germany lost its colonies, had the size of its army restricted to 100,000, and was denied tanks, submarines, or planes. It was forbidden to sign any treaty allying it with Austria or to join the League of Nations. Germany was required, finally, to pay scores of billions of marks in reparations, and to accept "responsibility" for the war as set out in article 231 of the treaty.

President Woodrow Wilson had warned the European powers in January 1917 what the alternative to "peace without victory" would look like. It would, he said, "mean peace forced upon the loser. . . . It would be accepted in humiliation, under duress, as an intolerable sacrifice and would leave a sting, a resentment, a bitter memory."[90] That was how Germans perceived the Treaty of Versailles, as a vindictive victors' peace. It was a sentiment shared across the political spectrum, although voiced most violently and unceasingly on the right, where the denial of defeat was most intense and the legend that Germany had been stabbed in the back by traitors at home became an article of faith.[91] There were also non-Germans who thought that Versailles was a foolishly harsh, "Carthaginian" peace. The most famous of them was a member of the British delegation at Versailles, the economist John Maynard Keynes.

Were they right? Only in part. The fact is that the Allies disagreed among themselves, the French invariably taking a tougher view than the Anglo-Saxons, and the Germans benefited from that. The French, for example, had pressed for Danzig to be awarded outright to Poland, and for the whole of Upper Silesia to become Polish without a plebiscite. France had also wanted to annex the Saarland and occupy the left bank of the Rhine. The Versailles Treaty is notable in other ways for what it did *not* contain. A preamble that would have underscored German guilt was dropped. The Allies rejected the idea of exacting tribute, instead going the legal route of asking for itemized "reparations" that reflected heavy real losses (especially for France and Belgium) and were anyway repeatedly scaled back.[92] The loss of colonies was, like so much else in the treaty, a blow to German pride, but might be considered a blessing given the prewar balance sheet and the costs in imperial policing that Germany no longer had to bear. As the pacifist Carl von Ossietzky noted, "Germans can sleep peacefully when the guns start firing in China or Morocco."[93] German territorial losses on the Continent were hardly unreasonable, moreover, given the historical identity and ethnic composition of the country's contested borderlands. Three million of the 6.5 million people living on the "lost" lands were non-German speakers. The new borders in the east were actually drawn with great care. The "Polish corridor," for example, was kept as thin as possible and every effort made to minimize the severing of transportation routes. In the end, despite its losses, Germany remained both intact and a major power in Europe—more like France after Napoleon than Germany after Hitler.

German losses were also modest compared with those sustained by its Central European allies Austria, Hungary, and Bulgaria. Widening the lens to include these settlements reminds us that the German-speaking lands were part of a much larger postwar recasting of former empires, sometimes by treaty, often by violence. Four multinational empires broke apart as a result of the war: the Romanov, Habsburg, and Ottoman as well as the Hohenzollern. The "shatter zones" they left behind were sites of violent conflict for years after the war ended, fueled by the legacy of militarism, the bitterness of defeat, and efforts to construct new nation-states in ethnically mixed areas. The violence flared up across east-central Europe.[94] Ethnic Germans did not play a particularly large role in this, with some important exceptions. In Latvia, German paramilitary Freikorps forces numbering as many as forty thousand men fought brutally, first against the Bolsheviks at the invitation of local authorities, then against Latvians to secure a German presence.[95] In the new Czechoslovakian state, ultra-nationalists among the German-speaking population established "German provinces." They dreamed about becoming part of an Austrian or Greater German homeland, until the Czech army marched in and quickly quelled the upstart movement, setting off wild rumors across the German border about a threatened "Czech invasion."[96] Above all, there was the German-Polish border. A Silesian plebiscite was held under Allied auspices in March 1921, which led to a short-lived Polish revolt and answering violence from

German paramilitary Freikorps units. As many as two thousand people were killed.[97]

The final postwar settlement of German borders was mostly less violent elsewhere. Plebiscites in Schleswig passed off peacefully, and there was nothing in Alsace-Lorraine or the Saarland that came close to the bloodletting in the Baltic and the German-Polish borderlands. But there was violence along the Rhine corridor. One notorious instance of it remained largely rhetorical. The stationing of around twenty-five thousand French soldiers from North Africa, Senegal, and Madagascar in the occupied Rhineland gave rise to an ugly racist campaign against the "black horror on the Rhine" in word and image, including Carl Boese's 1921 film *Die schwarze Schmach*.[98] Graphic cartoons depicted the rape of German women and girls by semianimal "barbarians." This campaign reached its peak in 1920–21. It was orchestrated by the government in Berlin and played on domestic resentment that Germany's own colonies had just been lost, but the intended audience was also international. The purpose was to discredit the French occupation and the provisions of the Versailles Treaty with it. The politics of the campaign were far from straightforward. The government worked with organizations like the Rhenish Women's League, which spread "black horror" propaganda internationally and found support from women's organizations in Britain and the United States. The British Labour politician E. D. Morel, a fierce critic of earlier Belgian violence in the Congo, wrote a 1920 pamphlet, *The Horror on the Rhine*, which attacked France as an imperialist power that exploited subject peoples far from home while exposing German women to their supposedly uncontrolled sexual appetites.[99] This racism of the left also had a right-wing German counterpart, represented by ultra-nationalist organizations like the German Emergency League Against the Black Horror, whose president, Heinrich Distler, wrote the screenplay for Boese's film. The vicious campaign of 1920–21 left a residue of hatred and fed the longer-term stigmatization of the so-called Rhineland bastards.

There was also more physical violence along the Rhine border in the years 1918–1923 than is sometimes recognized. The region's future was unresolved and a variety of colorful adventurers advocated the cause of Rhenish separatism—the creation of some kind of republic that would be neutral (although effectively pro-French), perhaps under League of Nations protection. A separatist putsch was attempted in 1919 in Speyer. Some leading French figures, including the head of the French Army on the Rhine, still favored dismemberment of Germany's westernmost limb, however much the British and (while they were still there) the Americans made it clear that this was unacceptable.

Hanging over all this were questions about the size of German reparations, still being haggled over, and the delivery of reparations in kind. The Ruhr, in the northern Rhineland, was the great prize here because it provided most of Germany's remaining coal, iron, and steel. French planning for a possible occupation of the Ruhr went back to 1918, initially conceived as a measure of military security, but increasingly viewed as a way to secure reparations. The Ruhr ports of Düsseldorf, Duisburg, and Ruhrort were occupied in 1921 in response to German stubbornness, and French plans for full-scale occupation were well advanced. "It will come—sooner or later," said a fatalistic Lord Curzon, the British foreign minister.[100]

It came in January 1923, when France finally lost patience with German negotiators and used a shortfall in timber deliveries as justification to occupy the Ruhr. For good measure, they also occupied the right-bank territory between the French military bridgeheads. The German government called for noncooperation and passive resistance. That expressed the feelings of most Ruhr dwellers but was almost certainly the wrong policy choice. Germany could have acquiesced, expressed moral indignation, and insisted on an immediate conference. Given British and American attitudes, this would probably have delivered in 1923 the kind of compromise actually achieved in 1924, but without the intervening pain.[101] In the event, France responded to passive resistance by expelling thousands of German officials, bringing in French personnel, and trying "saboteurs" in military courts. The Berlin government acceded to French demands in the fall, but not before its policy of printing money to keep the economy going during the crisis caused serious inflation (with its origins in the war) to become dramatically worse. This ended in the notorious hyperinflation in November 1923, when a dollar was worth 4.2 trillion marks. The political cost of this "world turned upside down" would be paid later.[102]

The Ruhr crisis prompted a final separatist spasm. There had been French back-channel support for Rhenish separatists since the end of the war, but in 1923 it was the separatists who acted, causing Paris to scramble in response. There was a comic-opera element to some of the putsches and seizures of town halls. The separatists were relatively few and disorganized. Often, their actions bordered on brigandage. But by the first week of November 1923, the Rhenish red-white-green tricolor flew over many towns in the

Rhineland. This final postwar effort to alter Germany's western border by violence was answered with violence. Eight months earlier, in March, a separatist named Josef Smeets had been shot and injured by German nationalists in Cologne and his brother-in-law killed. Six months later, there was a shoot-out between separatists and nationalists in Düsseldorf, which became known as Bloody Sunday. Two months after that, another skirmish outside Bonn left more than a hundred dead. The end of the so-called revolver republic in the Palatinate was equally brutal. Franz-Josef Heinz, self-styled head of the Palatine Republic, was assassinated by nationalists in early January 1924, together with his main advisers, while enjoying afterdinner drinks in a Speyer hotel. Weeks later, a nationalist mob in the town of Pirmasens trapped the remnants of the Palatine separatist movement in the town hall, which they set alight, shooting those who tried to escape. Fifteen bodies were recovered from the ashes the next morning.[103]

This bloodletting was the German version of the borderland violence that exploded across postwar Europe. The revolutionary and counterrevolutionary violence that raged from 1918 through 1923 was felt with equal force. Reds and Whites fought each other as viciously in Central Europe as they did in Russia, and with the same slogans. This was a pan-European conflict, which stretched from Russia to Spain and northern Italy. But events in Germany assumed special importance, for what happened there was seen by supporters and opponents of revolution alike as critical for the future.

"The common people are furious, but what is the use of furious sheep." That was the scornful diary entry of Australian Ethel Cooper, who had spent the war years in Leipzig, after the government raided a radical newspaper.[104] It is a familiar gibe: Lenin once scoffed that German comrades told to storm a railroad station would buy platform tickets first.[105] But the cliché is quite wrong. After the initial events that brought down the monarchy in 1918, moderate Social Democrats tried to lead the revolution into safely parliamentary channels. They were challenged not only by attempts on the right to overthrow the new republic, like the putsch in 1920 led by right-wing civil servant Wolfgang Kapp but instigated by elements of the army and Hitler's Beer Hall putsch in 1923, but by repeated efforts on the left to establish a revolutionary or Bolshevik-style regime in Germany. These began with the Spartacist Uprising of January 1919 and the Bavarian Soviet Republic in April of that year, continued with the Red Army of the Ruhr uprising in the spring of 1920 and the so-called March action of 1921, and ended with the October uprising in 1923. All were put down.

Friedrich Ebert and his fellow Social Democrats have been heavily criticized for their conduct, especially for their willingness to use both Freikorps paramilitaries and army to suppress the Spartacist Uprising, in the course of which the radical leaders Rosa Luxemburg and Karl Lieb-knecht were murdered. Accused by contemporary conservatives of stabbing the old regime in the back, the Social Democrats are now more likely to be accused by historians of not stabbing it hard enough. The critics have a point. The SPD's indecently rapid willingness to embrace the forces of "order" against social revolution emboldened conservatives and left many antirepublicans in place because of the failure to do more housecleaning of the old elite. The judiciary was just one example, with its remarkable leniency in sentencing conservatives who committed political assassina-tions, which took the lives of prominent figures like Matthias Erzberger and Walther Rathenau. Social Democratic sins of omission and commis-sion undoubtedly contributed to the division and bitterness on the left that proved so disastrous in the last years of Weimar.

But the balance sheet of the SPD's role has entries in both columns. At the head of the Weimar coalition (with the Catholic Center and Democratic parties) the Social Democrats presided over the creation of Germany's first parliamentary democracy, while instituting advanced welfare provisions (hated by much of industry) without resort to the dictatorial methods used by the Bolsheviks in Russia. And they achieved this while constrained by the politics of peacemaking, for the Allied blockade remained in place until the Versailles Treaty was signed in June 1919. Critics might reply that Ebert ("I hate the social revolution like sin") was only doing what he wanted to do anyway, which is true, and that he could and should have harnessed the grassroots radicalism of the councils and shop stewards' movement against the old elite, which is a more dubious proposition. The radical forces unleashed by the revolution were hard for any political party to control, not just Social Democrats, but those to the left of them, too. The revolu-tion was desperate, chaotic, and anarchic. Its ferocious energy came from war weariness and the indignities that workers faced during the war: labor "mobilization," hectoring by the military, dangerously speeded-up produc-tion lines, hunger. The sudden collapse of the old regime in November 1918 propelled previously unorganized groups into the streets. For workers of every kind, and especially for the young, the revolution was an opportunity to settle accounts with authority and "them up there." The estimated two million rifles unlawfully in circulation hardly made things more sedate.[106]

Even Rosa Luxemburg, who probably had more faith in the spontaneous good sense of the "masses" than any revolutionary in Europe, referred to the problem of the many "little revolutions," local, splintered, disparate— the *Revolutiönchen*—that defined events in Germany.[107]

An "unscripted" revolution, then?[108] In many ways, yes. But no revolution completely lacks a script, even a choreography. Both moderates and radicals were heirs to a wide repertoire of pre-1918 activism, both practical and performative. Social Democrats could invoke the world of workers' libraries and cycling clubs, "respectable" trade unionism, well-organized May Day rallies, and election campaigns; radicals could point to the mass strike, street protests, and a more distant history of building barricades and exercising power directly. When the revolution fell into their hands in 1918, the SPD wanted to tame it; they rejected the "Russian madness" (in the words of Philipp Scheidemann) offered by Lenin and his comrades.[109] The left, meanwhile, drew its inspiration from far and wide. Karl Artelt, a leading figure in the Kiel naval mutiny and later a Communist Party member, had witnessed the 1911 revolution in China as a sailor in the German Pacific squadron stationed in Qingdao. Then, in 1917, he grew close to French and Belgian radicals while imprisoned with them after his arrest for distributing strike material in the Kiel navy yard. Ireland also played its part. When Lieutenant Colonel William Roddie arrived in Berlin during the Spartacist Uprising to report to the British War Office on conditions in Germany, he was disconcerted to be told by a taxi driver that the man firing a machine gun from the top of the Brandenburg Gate was one of "Roger Casement's Irishmen."[110] Revolutionaries were mobile; sometimes they had to be. After Béla Kun's Hungarian Soviet Republic was overthrown at the beginning of August 1919, many supporters joined him in Austrian exile or went on to Germany, where they created a "Budapest-Berlin axis."[111] One of them was the Hungarian Communist Alexander Rado, who fled Budapest for Austria in 1919, moved to Germany in 1922, and played a leading in the Communists' central German uprising in October the following year.[112]

The Russian Revolution that inspired Béla Kun and Alexander Rado had the same effect in Germany, enlarging the sense of what was possible. Leading German radicals had intimate ties to Russia. Rosa Luxemburg was born in the tsarist empire and had been politically active as a student in Warsaw before fleeing as an eighteen-year-old to Zurich and moving to Berlin ten years later. Her close friend Sophie Ryss, from Kharkov, went to Germany to study and married Karl Liebknecht.[113] The hopes Luxemburg placed in Russia run through the many letters she wrote to Sophie, as they do in a letter to Clara Zetkin, a fellow radical, which called the February Revolution an "overture" and predicted "an echo in the whole world."[114] Russian events also had a powerful impact on Ernst Däumig, a spokesman for the workers' council movement and sometime chairman of the Independent Social Democrats, who briefly joined the Communists. After the October Revolution, he proclaimed: "We are not mere spectators of events in Russia, we participate in them with full fervor. We mean to learn from what happens there and then apply the lessons fruitfully to the struggles for the salvation of humanity from the claws of capitalism."[115]

Russia also inspired Germans of a younger generation. Ernst Reuter, later the high-profile Social Democratic mayor of West Berlin during the Cold War, but an unknown radical thirty years earlier, learned his Communist politics as a Russian POW.[116] Max Hoelz, who became notorious for his left-wing political banditry in the German Vogtland, was an apolitical young man, more Christian than socialist, when he served on the eastern front and learned about the Russian Revolution. This "made a great impression even on those of us who were not socialists," he wrote. None of the German soldiers believed that the revolution would be confined to Russia.[117]

The Red Army was another Russian institution adopted in Germany. Self-styled Red armies formed in several regions where attempts were made to bring about a more radical revolution. The first was created during the tragic sequence of events that transpired in Bavaria. A Bavarian Soviet Republic was established in Munich in April 1919, led by playwright Ernst Toller. Well-meaning and ineffectual, a socialist republic run by bohemian intellectuals, it was overthrown after a week and replaced by a more obviously Soviet-style regime whose leaders were the Russian-born Eugen Leviné and Max Levien. They built a Red army thirty thousand strong. Their attempt to apply uncompromising Soviet methods in Germany ended in violence, with the killing of hostages, which was followed by a bout of "white terror" from the right. Toller, who tried hard to save the hostages, later described how children in Munich played Red army, locking their enemies up in outbuildings or cellars and shouting "Up the Reds" or "Down with the Whites." It was dreadful to hear these games, he said; but the reality was more dreadful.[118] Toller disliked his successors' version of class warfare and criticized how the "magical glow" of the Bolshevik Revolution and the words "we do things differently in Russia" silenced all debate.[119] But Toller as well as Leviné and Levien had plenty to answer for. During a year, 1919, when social privation was greater than ever, when Germany's political future was still open, the revolutionary playacting by Munich's salon radicals and the ideological rigidity of the Soviet republic that replaced it combined to do great damage to the left-wing cause. They also turned Munich, overnight, into a bastion of the authoritarian right.

The second Red army in Germany during these turbulent years was mustered in the Ruhr, in response to the Kapp putsch. It numbered at least 50,000. The insurrection it mounted in March 1920 was the largest workers' uprising anywhere in Germany. The Red Army of the Ruhr controlled cities large and small. As many as 300,000 miners followed the call for a general strike during negotiations between the insurgents and the newly restored government in Berlin. The broad support enjoyed in the Ruhr by this Red army made it very different from its namesake in Munich. The driving force of working-class radicalism was different, too—it was, above all, a by-product of fierce antimilitarism reawakened by the Kapp putsch. But the ending was horribly similar. Military forces and Freikorps units suppressed the uprising. More than one thousand members of the Red army died, many shot while already in captivity or "seeking to escape." It was another white terror.[120]

The radical left was united in the belief that events in Germany formed part of a larger struggle. This was also the view in Moscow. Grigory Zinoviev, head of the new Communist International (Comintern), founded in March 1919, proclaimed the following month that Munich was "where the immediate fate of the proletarian revolution throughout Europe will be decided."[121] The failures that year in Bavaria, Hungary, and in the equally short-lived Slovakian Soviet Republic did not dampen hopes. A west European secretariat of Comintern was opened in Berlin. That was where agents received new identities and papers before going off to the Balkans or Spain. Berlin was the "waiting room of the world revolution."[122] Even in 1920, as the Red Army advanced on Warsaw in the Polish-Soviet War and the prospects still seemed open for Red revolution in Spain and Italy, Germany remained the great prize for Lenin and the Bolsheviks. It was the most industrially advanced country with the largest organized working class. But 1920 marked the high point of realistic Soviet hopes. What happened in the Ruhr was matched by similar defeats in Italy and Spain. Farther east, the Red Army was turned back from Warsaw.

The prospects for revolution in the west were never what Moscow thought they were. The most radical movements of the left in Germany (as in Italy and Spain) were regional or workplace forms of activism not easily assimilable to a Leninist view of revolution.[123] They were closer to what Lenin denounced in *Left-Wing Communism: An Infantile Disorder*, written in 1920. Twice in three years, however, the German Communist Party itself tried to hurry history along with failed uprisings. The catastrophic March action of 1921, with its "theory of the offensive" (begin the uprising, and the workers will join it) and attempts at provocation with staged attacks on Communist buildings, was a piece of desperate political adventurism, pressed on the German Communists by Zinoviev and Comintern envoys like Béla Kun. The final disaster was an attempt to seize power in the October uprising of 1923, to take advantage of the Ruhr crisis. The decision came from Moscow, which sent Soviet advisers to help set up "Red hundreds," or paramilitary detachments, in Germany. The uprising was called off before it began when the hopelessness of its prospects became obvious. It went ahead only in Hamburg, where one hundred insurgents died on the barricades. This failed "German October" strengthened the reactionary right and further poisoned relations between different parts of the left, for the Communists had recently joined coalition governments with the left-leaning Social Democrats in central Germany, who now understandably felt betrayed.[124]

The radical left crossed borders with ease. Alexander Rado, the Hungarian who headed Leipzig's Communist military units in the October uprising, moved on to Moscow the following year. Ruth Fischer, later a leader of the German Communist Party, passed back and forth frequently between Berlin and Moscow before October 1923. Another inveterate border crosser was the revolutionary-at-large Karl Radek. Born in the Habsburg Empire, he had fought during the 1905 Russian revolution in Warsaw, then settled in Germany as a Social Democratic journalist, before going to Switzerland during the war, where he boarded the "sealed train" as one of Lenin's companions. As the Comintern's German expert, Radek practically commuted between Berlin and Moscow in the early 1920s.[125]

The ultra-nationalist right crossed borders, too. Paramilitary groups in Germany, Austria, and Hungary cooperated closely. Erich Ludendorff, now an embittered enemy of the republic, and Admiral Miklós Horthy of Hungary were in contact with each other, two military men born in the second half of the 1860s and profoundly hostile to the postwar world. Clandestine meetings took place in the summer of 1920 in Budapest and Bavaria, to coordinate plans for suppressing revolution and installing authoritarian regimes in Germany and Austria. The members of European paramilitary groups had much in common. The young men in their twenties who filled the ranks of the German Freikorps had experiences that resembled those of young men of similar age and nonproletarian background elsewhere, even in countries that were neutral in the war (like Spain) or nominal victors (like Italy), but especially in the Central European shatter zones of empire. There, paramilitaries were forged by the same encounters with war, defeat, territorial loss, and revolutionary upheaval. Their bedrock mentality was similar. They were violent, ultra-nationalist, anti-Bolshevik, antisemitic, hypermasculine, and antifeminist.[126]

The postwar political turmoil caused another, more large-scale, and often desperate kind of border crossing. No previous conflict produced so many refugees. Ten million people left their country of origin at the end of the war. Sometimes these had become new countries in which people felt, and often were, unwelcome. Some citizens became stateless; revolution or civil war set others on the road to somewhere else. In the case of Germany, large numbers moved in both directions across the country's new borders. Baltic Germans who had been recently dispossessed went to Germany, like Russian Germans whose involuntary displacement had begun in 1914. Then there were Germans from the "lost territories" in the east and from Alsace-Lorraine, 1.3 million in total. One-fifth of all the ethnic Germans living in territory ceded to other powers migrated to Germany. But it was not just Germans who poured into Germany. So did as many as 100,000 Jews, escaping pogroms in Ukraine and Galicia, on the borderlands of the collapsed tsarist and Habsburg empires. Some 40,000 of these *Ostjuden* (Eastern Jews) traveled on to the Netherlands, the United States, or Palestine. The majority settled in Germany, especially Berlin, where their precarious existence was brilliantly described by another Galician-born Jew, the journalist and writer Joseph Roth.[127] Berlin was also the preferred destination for another group from eastern Europe, Russians fleeing from revolution and civil war. Half a million of them went to Germany. In Berlin they settled in Charlottenburg (which was nicknamed Charlottengrad) and in Schöneberg (St. Petersburg on the Wittenbergplatz).[128] Large numbers of Russians moved simultaneously in the opposite direction, former POWs in Germany (approaching two million, all told) who returned home in stages, the last leaving in 1921. More than 100,000 "enemy aliens" who had been interned also left Germany—Britons, other Europeans, Australians, and

New Zealanders.[129] So did large numbers of Poles, among them longtime residents. They moved east into the newly established Polish state while Germans moved west out of the "lost territories," a relatively peaceful exchange of populations, certainly by comparison with the fate of Greeks and Turks in the same years.

Ethel Cooper, the Australian diarist, spoke in 1916 with a Leipzig chimney sweep who assured her bitterly that when the war was over, everyone who wasn't dead would emigrate.[130] Germans did, in fact, emigrate after 1918, but the numbers were smaller than expected and most emigrants had left by 1924. The most unconventional group of them consisted of the 150 Communists who went to the Soviet Union in 1920 to become pioneers in an "Eastern Settlement," helping to build socialism. They belonged to an organization founded by a Leipzig Communist, Alfons Goldschmidt, who was confident that the example of "German work" would be welcomed in the new regime. But when the pioneers arrived in Kolomna, south of Moscow, their "factory in the forest" turned out to be decrepit and filled with hostile Russians. Living conditions were intolerable and most of the Germans returned home.[131]

Latin America was a more common destination for German emigrants, strongly favored by the Foreign Office and newly created Office of Migration, which encouraged emigrants to choose places of existing German settlement and thus "preserve Germandom abroad." A flurry of emigrants left after 1919, 140,000 people, almost equaling the numbers who had left for Latin America in the whole of the previous seventy years. But most went to major cities like São Paolo and Buenos Aires, not to rural "German" settlements. Their exodus was a blip, anyway. After the first postwar years, emigration from the Weimar Republic never approached nineteenth-century levels. The numbers not only lagged far behind emigration levels from Britain and Italy, they trailed those of Portugal and Poland.[132]

The year 1924 marked a change, in this as in so many other respects. It was when the Ruhr crisis ended, and the postwar cycle of attempted insurrections also came to an end. It was when hyperinflation gave way to economic stability, and the Dawes Plan rescheduled German reparations payments. It was when the architect of those policies, Gustav Stresemann, initiated the policy of cooperation with the western Allies that culminated in the Locarno Treaty of 1925. In one of those rare instances when cultural change moved to the same rhythm as political and socioeconomic change, it was also when the edgy, expressionist art, literature, and cinema of the immediate postwar years was replaced by something more cool, so-called Neue Sachlichkeit, the "new sobriety." The years 1924–1929 are usually thought of as the golden years, between the crises of the early and late years of the Weimar Republic. Were they? And how did Germany recalibrate its relations with the wider world after the animosities and broken relations of the war and postwar years had receded?

The German economy was thoroughly deglobalized during the war and its immediate aftermath because of the Allied blockade and the seizure of German overseas assets. The country's prewar capital investments were reduced by more than 90 percent.[133] One positive aspect of the inflationary era, at least until the final hyperinflationary phase, was that German goods were much cheaper on world markets. That produced an export boom, which created full employment and allowed the government to finance its social programs. In the short run, at least, Germany could ride out the world economic crisis of 1920–21 better than its competitors. It is even possible that Germany's export-led boom helped to lift other countries out of the postwar slump.[134]

Longer-term efforts to restore Germany's global economic links had mixed results. In Latin America, for example, German trade grew through the 1920s and German firms were involved in construction and electrification projects, including a large-scale electrification program in Colombia. German banks also issued a loan that helped to finance this undertaking.[135] Everything was not rosy, however. Issuing loans to other countries caused the Foreign Office to worry that this would undermine German claims about its inability to pay reparations. But the larger problems were twofold: the "nationalizing" economic policies that took hold in Latin America and the growing regional dominance of the United States, which made it impossible to restore the prewar status quo. And this was before the world depression after 1929 wiped out three-quarters of German trade with the region.[136]

Latin America encapsulated Germany's problems, which were partly the problems faced by all the established European economies. The German share of world exports fell by almost a third between 1913 and the late 1920s, as global production and trade between non-European countries grew. The United States, Canada, and Japan were the big winners in the postwar economy. World trade also grew more sluggishly than it had in the heady prewar years because of uncertainties in the global financial system and the tariffs imposed almost everywhere. German economic output finally returned to prewar levels by the late 1920s, but the economy faced two serious underlying problems, both of them connected in one way or another with the United States.

One was the process of "rationalization," which increased productivity but at the cost of unemployment. In the Ruhr, the mechanization of coal mining led to a drastic reduction in the number of miners, from 550,000 to 350,000.[137] This shakeout meant that jobless rates, so low in the early 1920s, rose steadily during the so-called golden years. Unemployment stood at nearly 3 million in the spring of 1929, six months before the Wall Street crash. Rationalization did not just cost jobs; it led to speeded-up work conditions, in mines, factories, and offices.[138] This process was closely associated with two Americans. One was Frederick Taylor, whose time-and-motion, "scientific management" approach to efficiency on the factory floor (known as Taylorism) provided the underlying philosophy of the rationalization movement. The other was Henry Ford, who gave his name to an "ism" in Germany, *Fordismus*. Germans bought 200,000 copies of Ford's *My Life and Work* in translation, and more than fifty books were written about him in the 1920s. Ford represented different things to different people, and arguments about Fordism were really arguments about how to use American economic models in Germany. Industrialists argued that American success was based on the fast pace of work, high productivity, and lack of protective labor legislation. Trade unionists and Social Democrats countered that it was advanced technology coupled with high wages and the resulting mass consumption which underlay American success. These were proxy debates for the fierce class struggles that animated Weimar politics.[139]

Excessive dependence on foreign capital was the other economic problem that lurked beneath the German economic recovery. This was an American question, too, because the United States was Germany's major creditor. Germany borrowed 28 billion marks between 1924 and 1930. About two-thirds was invested, the rest went to reparation payments.[140] These created a perfect triangular system: the United States lent the Germans money, which they sent as reparations to the British and French, who used it to repay their huge war debts to America. German dependence on foreign capital was partly a result of the inflation, which first wiped out domestic savings that might have been invested at home, then caused flights of capital by nervous would-be investors worried about another inflation. So Germany came to depend on foreign capital—which was forthcoming, but at relatively high rates of interest, and left the country exposed when short-term loans were called home in 1929.

Despite the loss of Saarland and Upper Silesian coalfields, the "heavy metal" branches of coal-iron-steel remained a formidable part of the German economy. This was still the "century of steel," as a French minister remarked during the Ruhr occupation.[141] That was why France took the Ruhr so seriously—can one imagine the occupation of a region that produced shirts or typewriters? Heavy industry represented the sinews of war in a future conflict as well as the hard currency of reparations. German heavy industrialists formed notorious combines and cartels. But so did companies in chemicals, optics, and electrics, the industries that had made Germany a global economic heavyweight. The chemical combine IG-Farben was the classic instance. Both old and new branches faced more difficult conditions than before the war, but the problems facing the agricultural sector were still greater. Like primary producers everywhere, estates owners and peasant farmers alike faced low commodity prices with less tariff protection than they had previously enjoyed. That would have political repercussions.

What captured the imagination of contemporaries was the economy of mass consumption. We are talking here about dance halls and bars, phonographs, the cinema and radio, fashionable clothes and makeup, and sports of every kind, together with new magazines devoted to these activities. The 1930 film *Menschen am Sonntag* (*People on Sunday*) portrays this world, which is above all the world of young people, with affection but also a satirical edge. Directed by Robert Siodmak and Edgar G. Ulmer, with a screenplay by the young Billy Wilder and camerawork by Fred Zinnemann, all of them later successful in Hollywood, the film follows a group of young people as they argue and flirt, go on an outing, and enjoy themselves by the lake at the weekend before work begins again on Monday morning. The amateur actors who play themselves have characteristically "modern" occupations—record seller, taxi driver, fashion model, film extra, wine salesman. Annie has pictures of film actors on the wall, Erwin pictures of actresses, and they quarrel over whether Annie should wear the brim of her hat up or down. Debonair Wolfgang takes Christl to eat ice cream at the beginning of the film, when they meet after her date fails to turn up. Later, Wolfgang and Erwin drink beer and talk about going to a soccer game. As the couples relax by the lake they listen to a portable phonograph.[142]

This culture had prewar origins but came into its own in the postwar years. City dwellers reportedly rushed past gunfire and barricades even during the Spartacist Uprising to reach cinemas and dance halls.[143] Tennis clubs, dance music, and fashionably dressed girls turn up in the memoirs of young men who grew up in the 1920s and later achieved fame as émigrés, historian and journalist Sebastian Haffner.[144] The culture of entertainment, which came in upper-middle-class and lower-middle-class versions, attracted the attention of some of Weimar Germany's sharpest social observers. Siegfried Kracauer pinned down one version in his article "The Little Shopgirls Go to the Movies," a trenchant account of how capitalist mass culture offered an emptied-out, escapist experience.[145] Joseph Roth ranged widely over upper- and lower-class pleasure haunts in journalistic pieces devoted to a movie theater, amusement parks, Berlin's six-day cycle race, and drinking joints where he managed "to take malicious pleasure at the phenomenon of so much industrialized merriment.[146] In another piece he muses on the imminent arrival of the skyscraper in Germany, adding a typically barbed tailpiece: "Oh—and already you hear that the first skyscraper in Berlin is to have a great entertainment palace, with cinemas, dance hall, bar, Negro bands, vaudeville, jazz."[147] Roth was alluding to new dances like the shimmy and Charleston that took German cities by storm, and to the jazz bands that played them, including the Chocolate Kiddies (with young Duke Ellington) and the great saxophonist Sidney Bechet.[148]

The Tiller Girls on the stage of a Berlin vaudeville theater in 1926. Popular with audiences, they interested critics like Siegfried Kracauer as an example of "assembly-line" entertainment.

Germans referred to *die verrückten Zwanziger Jahre*, their version of the Roaring Twenties. Movies, skyscrapers, cocktails, and jazz were all shorthand for "American." The supposed "Americanization" of society was something Germans argued about vigorously in the Weimar Republic. There was undeniably a growing U.S. influence on patterns of getting and spending. It could be seen on the silver screen, where over 40 percent of films shown in Germany by the mid-1920s were made in Hollywood. The Ford Motor Company opened a factory in Cologne. Coca-Cola opened a bottling plant. And when, in its campaign to make "modern" Europeans as clean shaven as their American counterparts, the Boston razor blade company Gillette encountered its chief competition in Germany, it responded by buying a controlling interest in the local company.[149] Coca-Cola and Gillette were two U.S. brands whose advertising in Germany was handled, after January 1927, by the newly opened Berlin office of American advertising behemoth J. Walter Thompson, whose other clients included Kodak, Kellogg's cereals, and Wrigley chewing gum.[150] Even the modern office, like JWT's in Berlin, smacked of America, with its typing pool and messages zooming around in pneumatic tubes. The office and the white-collar workers in it also attracted the attention of critical social observers (including, once again, Kracauer).[151] Then there were those retail emporiums, the department store and chain store. The department store reached Germany before the war. Conservatives criticized it as a "Jewish" institution that supposedly harmed the small shopkeeper, engaged in sharp business practices, and encouraged kleptomania, charges first leveled in the 1880s and repeated almost unchanged into the 1920s.[152] The chain store (the "five-and-dime") did not arrive in Germany until 1927, when the first branch of Woolworth's opened its doors in Bremen. Twenty-three more branches followed in 1928. It was, ironically, the often reviled department stores like Tietz and Karstadt that responded to this American retail "invasion" by establishing German chain stores to compete with Woolworth's.[153]

The turnover of department and chain stores was much lower in Germany than in the United States or Britain. But the arguments about them were highly charged because they raised questions about identity and the future of society, not just what one bought and where one bought it. Like debates over cinemas and dance halls, they exposed generational fault lines. They were also closely tied up with questions of gender. Department stores had been criticized even before the war for their largely female sales staffs and for the unfettered purchase of "luxury" goods by the well-off women who shopped there. In, the 1920s, a distinct type of female consumer emerged—the "modern girl" (the English term was used interchangeably with the *neue Frau*, or "new woman"). Like her counterparts in other countries, the flapper (U.S.), *garçonne* (France), *modan garu* (Japan), and *modeng xiaojie* (China), the modern girl in Germany used lipstick, nail polish, face cream, fancy soaps, and deodorant; she smoked cigarettes, wore high heels, and favored cloche hats. She was chic, cosmopolitan, sexually adventurous, and nobody's fool.[154] This was not a version of womanhood that went down well among conservative Germans. In fact, many German men were concerned about the "feminization" of German society and the accompanying erosion of "manly" virtues. The critique of "Americanization" was often a proxy for "feminization" in this negative sense.

The scrambling of gender identities is something we associate with "Weimar culture." When the actresses Carola Neher and Marlene Dietrich laced up their gloves and joined the novelist Vicki Baum in Sabri Mahir's Studio for Boxing and Physical Culture on the Kurfürstendamm, they were self-consciously rejecting the image of pliant femininity and proclaiming their own muscularity and power.[155] In Dietrich's case, this androgynous look was very different from the persona of the stocking-clad cabaret siren Lola Lola she would play in the film *The Blue Angel* (1930), the iconic embodiment of "dangerous" female sexuality.[156] Dietrich herself was bisexual. An openness and willingness to experiment with living out different kinds of sexual identity was another characteristic associated with Weimar culture, above all with Berlin. In the 1920s it was "heaven on earth in the German metropolis," recalled Charlotte Wolff, an enthusiastic participant in the lesbian scene. The city had numerous bars and private clubs for gay women, ranging socially from the tony Club Montbijou West (by invitation only from one of its members) to loud, sometimes violent lower-class haunts like Taverne. Newspapers like *Die Freundin*, which featured nudes on the cover, were readily available at news kiosks. Small wonder that a letter from Brooklyn published in *Die Freundin* lamented the relative lack of freedom enjoyed by American lesbians, even in New York City, and proclaimed that "America is fifty years behind Germany."[157] Berlin became the "international center of female homosexuality" in the 1920s.[158]

Male homosexuality, too. Not every gay visitor was enchanted, it is true. Brian Howard, a former Oxford dandy and the probable model for Anthony Blanche in Evelyn Waugh's *Brideshead Revisited*, found Berlin "unbearably ugly and quite quite awful"; the American composer Paul Bowles thought the city "the least amusing place I have ever seen."[159] But that was a minority view (and even Howard made an exception for the music and the embroideries in the Kaiser Friedrich Museum).[160] Probably the best-known foreign enthusiasts were the young English writers W. H. Auden and Christopher Isherwood, the latter because in his *Berlin Stories* and in the character Sally Bowles, part femme fatale, part camp figure, he gave us a lasting picture of a time and place. (A case can be made that, for English speakers, Isherwood "invented" Weimar Berlin, the modern Babylon, rather as Charles Dickens "invented" Victorian London.) Auden and "Herr Issywoo" introduced many English friends such as the poet Stephen Spender to gay Berlin. Others from Oxford and Cambridge also found their way there, including several who moved in the circle around the Oxford classicist Maurice Bowra, the leader of what the writer Jocelyn Brooke dubbed the Homintern.[161]

They were drawn by the hundred or more gay locales and the much greater ease of finding sexual partners than at home. It was the same with young American homosexuals, like the painter Marsden Hartley and the architect Philip Johnson. The American lesbian writer Djuna Barnes found Berlin "full of buggers from America who bought boys cheap," and that was no doubt part of the appeal.[162] Following Auden's example, Isherwood carefully recorded his sexual partners, most of them at least occasional prostitutes, a disconcerting parade of Bertholds, Ottos, Heinzes, Piepses, Frantzes, and so on. But Berlin offered more than rent boys: it could be key to accepting one's real identity. Isherwood later said the city had been a revelation because there he was "brought face to face with his tribe," something he had previously denied.[163] He also said that if he had been asked the purpose of his visit when returning to Berlin in 1929, he could have truthfully replied: "I'm looking for my homeland and I've come to find out if this is it."[164] Auden, meanwhile, came out while there, breaking off his engagement with a young woman in England. There is something else. Auden's German was not especially good, but he did learn the word *schwul*. Originally derived from Berlin dialect, the word, still used today, was in circulation in Germany for decades before the equivalent English term, "gay," came into use. Auden was forced to refer to himself in English with the only words available, all of which (like "queer" and "pansy") carried pejorative connotations.[165] But in Germany he could be *schwul*.

Berlin had more than two million visitors a year by 1930. It was exciting and a cheap place to live. Practicing or aspiring writers and artists were not the only ones drawn by the explosion of creative talent and formal experimentation in virtually every branch of the arts. Often the innovation came precisely from mixing and recombining cultural forms. Alfred Döblin's pyrotechnic novel *Berlin Alexanderplatz* (1929) derives its extraordinary energy from juxtaposing the story of Franz Biberkopf with popular songs, sound effects, lists of advertisements, and reports of events like the Tunney–Dempsey fight in 1927. The novel's jump cuts and syncopated rhythm, borrowed from contemporary cinema and jazz, mimic the street life of the era even as carefully placed episodes from the Book of Job and Greek tragedy offer moral commentary on the action.[166] The novel, in turn, quickly became a radio play, then a film.[167]

Or consider Bertolt Brecht, a poet and dramatist whose sharp political dialogues borrowed from popular culture and cabaret, who used American settings, wrote screenplays, and employed the novel medium of the radio for a new kind of didactic radio play, the *Lehrstück* (the first, in 1929, was called *Lindbergh's Flight*). He also subverted an established form of musical drama in the internationally successful *Threepenny Opera* (1928), for which Kurt Weill wrote the jazz-inflected music. Weill was preceded by Ernst Krenek's jazz opera *Jonny spielt auf* ("Jonny Strikes Up"), based on a seductive African-American character, a figure found in cabaret and popular songs going back to Friedrich Hollaender's 1920 hit song "Jonny."[168] Weimar high culture plundered popular forms. Jazz was a prominent example. German critics wrote again and again about "jazz as deliverance" or "jazz as point of departure."[169] The poet Yvan Goll argued for Black jazz as a rejuvenating force, ending with the provocative question: "Do the Negroes need us? Or are we not sooner in need of them?"[170]

Goll was born in Lorraine—as he put it, a Jew by fate, French by accident of birth, labeled German by an official stamp. He lived in Paris but frequently visited Berlin, where he had a lover and artistic collaborators. It sometimes seems as if everyone ended up in Berlin. Brecht, born in the Bavarian provincial town of Augsburg, moved first to Munich, then to Berlin. That was fairly typical. Weimar Berlin became the preeminent cultural gathering place, even more than before the war because conservative Munich was now less welcoming. Berlin was home to Germans and Austrians from the provinces, including some (like Joseph Roth and the playwright Carl Zuckmayer) who thought the city cold, even hateful, but found it impossible to leave. It also attracted Poles, Czechs, Scandinavians, and Turks, as well as hundreds of Indian students and intellectuals who turned the area around Kantstrasse into "Little Asia."[171] Charlottenburg was also where Russian émigrés settled. Conservatives fleeing revolution came first, Vladimir Nabokov among them; they were followed in the years 1921–22 by writers and artists who had initially supported the revolution. Berlin was the intellectual center of the Russian diaspora in the 1920s, with forty Russian publishing houses, cafés, bookstores, newspapers, and magazines. It was home to Marc Chagall, Marina Tsvetayeva, and Boris Pasternak.[172]

If there is a single word that summons up how people thought about Berlin in the 1920s, its sights and sounds, sexual openness, cultural experimentation, and sheer energy, it is "modernity." Foreigners remarked on this all the time. Emily Pollard, a young American and the niece of the governor of Virginia, was impressed from the moment she stepped off the plane at Tempelhof Airport: "Germany is very ahead of us in its adoption of the modern," she wrote in her diary. The French writer Roger Martin du Gard thought that "the new man, the man of the future" was being created there.[173] One of the greatest achievements of Weimar Berlin was gaining acceptance for the idea that it was the incarnation of the modern.[174] The city has come to be seen as the temporary resting place of the baton of modernity, as it passed from Paris in the nineteenth century to New York City in the 1940s.

There was another iconic site of modernity in Weimar Germany. The Bauhaus began life in the town of Weimar, moved to Dessau in 1925, and ended its short but brilliant career in Berlin. Its tubular steel chairs, designed by Marcel Breuer, are as emblematic of Weimar culture as Marlene Dietrich's stockinged legs in *The Blue Angel* or the song "Mack the Knife" from *The Threepenny Opera*. The Bauhaus brought art and design together under one roof (a flat roof, of course), combining fine arts, crafts, and technology, and subordinating ornament to function—or, better, insisting that form follow function, so that everything from teapots to typography could dispense with unnecessary curlicues. The Belgian Henry van de Velde had run the prewar forerunner of the Bauhaus, and the 1919 version was self-consciously international in personnel and ideas. Among the Bauhaus teachers were Paul Klee and Johannes Itten (Swiss), Wassily Kandinsky (Russian), László Moholy-Nagy (Hungarian), and Lyonel Feininger (German-American). Guest lecturers included a Czech artist and a Dutch designer. The Russian constructivist El Lissitzky was a visitor. Russia was an important point of reference from the start. There were many parallels between the Bauhaus and the Vkhutemas, the Moscow art and technical school established in 1920. They shared underlying principles, were torn by many of the same internal debates, and engaged in exchanges of various kinds.

Cultural exchanges were a problem for Weimar Germany. The country was deglobalized culturally as well as economically by the war. That was especially true in the early postwar years. Germany was not only prevented from joining the League of Nations, but banned from cultural and academic gatherings, sports, and even the Rotary Club—when the organization expanded into Europe, the French insisted on the Germans being excluded.[175] Germans and Austrians were barred when the International Research Council (for the natural sciences) and the International Academic Union (for the humanities) were founded in 1919. Germans were unwelcome at academic conferences, and German was no longer a recognized language at those gatherings.[176] French and Belgian scholars proved especially unforgiving. In the field of history, some of the great figures condemned the wholesale rejection of German scholarship. Marc Bloch called the chauvinism of Alsatian historian Jacques Flach "vulgar and absurd"; the Belgian Henri Pirenne warned of a "fashionable crusade" against German scholarship. But run-of-the-mill historians argued that instead of "learning from the Germans" it was now time to "unlearn."[177] There was also a backlash in Britain, especially against those who had signed the wartime declaration in defense of German culture. Ernst Troeltsch had been sought after as a lecturer before the war, but invitations from Oxford and Cambridge in the early 1920s were withdrawn because of vocal opposition.[178] German scholars made things worse by retreating into petulant self-pity, failing to recognize their own wartime chauvinism or why there was so much postwar bitterness.

In the early years of the Weimar Republic, there were efforts to end the isolation by cultural bureaucrats of a new kind who recognized the importance of soft power and saw culture was a means of restoring Germany's standing in the world. Johannes Sievers is an example of the type, a trained art historian before he joined the Prussian Ministry of Education. One of his successes was making it possible for German artists to be shown at the Venice Biennale in 1922. But there were limits to what could be achieved. Even in the mid-1920s the French rejected German arts and crafts. At an international exhibition in Paris of the decorative and industrial arts in 1925, the Bauhaus went unrepresented and even the pavilion of the Swiss Le Corbusier was attacked for representing the *"style boche."*[179] Music was an easier sell. By the early 1920s the Berlin Philharmonic had already returned to play in Paris as well as London, although in France—as in the United States—there were still reservations about the German repertoire. Some French critics, taking their cue from Debussy, made the case against German music on aesthetic grounds. The arguments resembled those of French historians: German music was "heavy" and pompous, at odds with the Gallic spirit, and therefore to be rejected as a model. This was the exact mirror image of the long-standing German view that their own music was "deep" and French music was superficial.

Weimar cultural diplomacy had successes to its name. Lecture tours by Albert Einstein successfully presented the "other" Germany, untainted by militarism. The Foreign Office worked behind the scenes to cultivate good relations with wartime neutrals, such as Spain. Some familiar instruments of cultural diplomacy date from the mid-1920s, like the German Academic Exchange Service and the Alexander von Humboldt Foundation, which arranged exchanges of students and scholars. But there was a built-in conflict inside the cultural department of the German Foreign Office between fostering this kind of cultural outreach and supporting Germans abroad, the *Auslandsdeutsche*. Much of the budget ultimately went to support Germans abroad through subsidies to German libraries and schools. In Poland and Czechoslovakia, the support was clandestine.[180]

Many cultural exchanges resulted from individual contacts. A spectacular example of what individuals could achieve, with the right networks, was a German-Indian artistic exchange in 1922–23. It sent 175 pieces of Bauhaus art to Calcutta, while 113 artworks by Bengal modernists were shown in Berlin.[181] The idea for the exchange began with a young Moravian-born expert on Indian art, Stella Kramrisch, who believed that German and Indian artistic modernisms had many common features. She first pitched the idea of a Bauhaus exhibition in Calcutta to the Bengal intellectual Rabindranath Tagore, whom she met in England. The project also needed someone at the Bauhaus who could make it happen. That person was Johannes Itten, who was teaching at the University of Vienna when Kramrisch wrote her dissertation there, and had since joined the Bauhaus. A Zoroastrian with eastern spiritual leanings, Itten was a perfect partner for Kramrisch. The central figure in organizing the exhibition of Indian artworks that traveled in the opposite direction was Benoy Kumar Sarkar. An anticolonial intellectual and art historian in Calcutta, Sarkar had married an Austrian woman and moved to Berlin in 1921. He gained the support of Carl Heinrich Becker, who was Prussian minister of culture in the early 1920s and one of the intellectual architects of German cultural diplomacy. Becker then recommended the idea to the director of the National Museum. The two exhibitions inaugurated a decade-long artistic exchange between Germany and Bengal.

Mending the broken links with the western Allies was harder. The Foreign Office worked on this through the League of Nations' International Committee on Intellectual Cooperation.[182] Cultural relations with France improved after Germany signed the Treaty of Locarno, the key to Stresemann's policy of getting on the right side of the Allies by accepting the western border in the hope of gaining support for eventual revisions of the eastern border. The "spirit of Locarno" brought change, but not all German diplomats were persuaded that cultural diplomacy was important. Nongovernmental organizations were bolder. The pacifist German League for Human Rights organized a one-day conference in the Reichstag in June 1922, with participation by its French sister organization. It also held events to foster understanding on both sides of the French-German border. French speakers regularly lectured in Germany, and vice versa, braving hecklers. The leading figures in the league were the usual suspects—Harry Kessler, the ultimate cultured cosmopolitan, the veteran pacifist Ludwig Quidde, and that perpetual thorn in the side of militarists everywhere, Albert Einstein. The league successfully promoted school exchanges and supported initiatives like the one dreamed up by the Catholic pacifist Marc Sangnier in France to hold a "Locarno of youth."[183] Richard Schirrmann, the founder of the German Youth Hostel Association, sought to build "bridges for peace" through the International Youth Hosteling Association.[184] These efforts all inclined politically to the center-left.

Culture bore a different kind of internationalist stamp on the far left. German agitprop groups like the Red Rockets and Red Megaphone, which performed in streets, factories, and workers' clubs, took their inspiration from the Soviet model.[185] In the 1920s, Berlin also became a hub for anticolonial intellectuals who were drawn to the capital of a no longer colonial power. The young Jawaharlal Nehru commented on the strategic importance of Berlin, where Indian nationalists mingled with their Chinese, Indonesian, and North African counterparts. Their writings and lectures at discussion evenings lent a truly global quality to cultural debates on the Communist and fellow-traveling left. The culture of the left was also modern in form. A new kind of travel journalism reported in nonpatronizing ways on non-European worlds. Arthur Koestler and

Egon Erwin Kisch were two stars of this genre; another, still making her name, was the American Agnes Smedley, who lived in Berlin in the 1920s with an Indian Communist. Photography was another key medium of communication. Willi Münzenberg, an indefatigable Communist organizer, founded a photo magazine in 1921 called *Soviet Russia in Pictures*. It became a huge success when renamed the *Arbeiter Illustrierte Zeitung*, or *AIZ* (Workers' Illustrated Paper), and sold 500,000 copies a week by 1930, making it the second-best-selling magazine in Germany. *AIZ* gave visual form to the class struggle at home and the anticolonial struggle abroad. "Red Orientalism" found cinematic expression, too, as German Communist film production units created works like *The Struggle for the Earth* and *Gandhi*.[186]

Urban, self-consciously modern, experimental, internationalist, left-leaning—these are the terms we associate with "Weimar culture," and rightly so. But if we look beyond "Weimar culture" to Weimar cultures, plural, then it is a very different story. The huge, pompous memorial to the Battle of Tannenberg dedicated in 1927 was also a product of Weimar culture. It represented the culture of militarism that still flourished in the republic, fed by postwar resentment. The hero of Tannenberg, Paul von Hindenburg, already almost eighty years old, spoke at the dedication in typically nationalist vein.[187] In German cities, monuments went up to commemorate the country's lost colonies. Publishers released a stream of memoirs, novels, and adventure stories about the colonies, which retained a powerful place in the German imagination. Hans Grimm's colonial novel, *People Without Space*, became a bestseller that fed German self-pity and coined a slogan with ominous undertones.[188] Germany's university towns like Marburg and Göttingen were as deeply conservative then as they are left-leaning now. Professors defended "traditional German culture" out of mandarin disdain for both mass culture and modernist experimentation, while students favored the nationalist right. Fear and loathing of the left was common to both.[189] Even the town that gave its name to the republic and initially housed the Bauhaus became a bastion of culturally conservative antirepublican sentiment. Weimar expelled the Bauhaus in 1924, after the right won a majority in Thuringia. Goethe was harnessed to the nationalist cause, just as Nuremberg harnessed Albrecht Dürer.[190]

The energy and visibility of the "modern" invited a backlash, especially in matters that touched on morality or national identity. Religious morality campaigners redoubled their efforts to stamp out "smut and filth" in the new republic, their efforts rewarded with a 1926 law designed to protect young people from "immorality." In the countryside, where cinema and radio barely penetrated, local cultural activities often remained in clerical hands and the preferred reading was sentimental *Heimat* literature. Rural Germany retained a rooted dislike of the "decadent" big city, a hostility reinforced by the conservative press. Culture was unmistakably politicized in the last years of the Weimar Republic, after the Wall Street crash of October 1929 triggered a global depression that hit Germany especially hard. How could culture not be affected by a crisis of such magnitude, and how could the political response not be mediated in part through culture? Two films released in 1930 indicate what polarization meant. *The Flute Concert of Sans-Souci,* one of the first "talkies" seen by many Germans, was a conservative celebration of Frederick the Great with an anti-French message. *All Quiet on the Western Front* was the Hollywood version of Erich Maria Remarque's antiwar novel. Its Berlin premiere was interrupted by violent demonstrations from Nazi storm troopers, causing the film to be banned after just a week.[191]

"Whenever I hear the word culture, I release the safety catch of my Browning." This line, often misquoted as "reach for my gun" and attributed to Hermann Göring or Joseph Goebbels, comes in fact from *Schlageter,* a play by Nazi playwright Hanns Johst about a Freikorps soldier executed by the French. The sneering brutality is what we expect from the Nazis, a denunciation of everything associated with Weimar culture. It is not wrong to regard the National Socialists as the party of negation, starting with their rejection of the revolution and the republic to which it gave birth. Anything that was, or seemed to be, international, or cosmopolitan, or "un-German," they rejected. They rejected the Treaty of Versailles, rejected Stresemann's Locarno Treaty and the "spirit of Locarno," rejected the Dawes Plan and its successor, the Young Plan, both drawn up by American bankers, rejected the presence of *Ostjuden,* rejected "Jewish" department stores, rejected modernist art and architecture as foreign and alien, rejected modernist literature and theater for the same reason, rejected jazz as American "mongrel" music, rejected homosexuality and contraception, rejected long-haired men and short-haired women, rejected pacifism, and rejected socialism and communism because they rejected class struggle as an un-German outcrop of "Judeo-Bolshevik" Marxism.

These views had broad appeal among the Germans who propelled the Nazi Party from a mere 2.6 percent of the vote in the 1928 elections to 37.3

percent in July 1932, as the number of seats it held in the Reichstag rose from 12 to 230, making it the largest single party. This remained well short of a majority, but was still an impressive tally in a multiparty system that featured not only six other major parties, but another eight or nine smaller ones. Nazi voters came from every class and region, but not in equal numbers. It is often said that the party owed its success to propaganda, but that hardly explains why its message was so much more successful with some parts of the population than others. The party did poorly at the polls with Catholics and workers. German Catholics mostly stayed with the Center Party; many workers moved from the Social Democrats over to the Communists but the total vote for the two left-wing parties remained the same. It was the conservative and liberal parties that shed votes in large numbers, and the small single-interest protest parties whose supporters deserted them for the National Socialists. To put it another way, the Nazis did exceptionally well among non-working-class Protestants.

National Socialism played adroitly on a host of fears and resentments among these groups. For teachers and for the "little man" who had risen into the white-collar ranks, that meant the threat or reality of unemployment and the accompanying humiliation, for business owners the power of labor and Weimar's generous social welfare, for doctors the expansion of the state insurance system and the problems of an "overcrowded" profession, for shopkeepers the competition of "Jewish" department stores and socialist consumer cooperatives. In the countryside where they did best of all, the Nazis exploited new problems and old hatreds. Mass unemployment meant a collapse in demand for the grain and milk that peasant farmers produced; it also led to raiding parties of urban workers who stripped the crops from the fields. The Nazis blamed the peasant's dilemma on the world economic crisis, and they blamed the world economic crisis on "Jewish finance" on Wall Street. At the same time, there were political rallying cries that resonated with all these groups. The Nazis relentlessly denounced the Versailles Treaty, called for a return to "traditional morality," and attacked the left. They also appealed for "law and order," which may seem counterintuitive, given the notoriously violent storm troopers of the SA (Sturmabteilung). But their violence was selective, directed against those perceived by Nazi voters as a threat, especially Communists. Photographs show well-dressed bourgeois looking on indulgently as thugs in Brownshirt uniforms march past.

How did the Nazis come out on top against conventional parties on the right, which shared many of the same goals and policies? The answer takes us back to propaganda. The Nazis generated a much greater sense of dynamism with their parades and rallies. Before the 1930 election, the party held thirty-four thousand meetings in just six months. Their motorized columns of cars, motorbikes, and trucks with loudspeakers had a powerful impact in rural areas. An activist in Württemberg described how in small towns and villages "the people, who had never seen a *Motorsturm*, were wide-eyed."[192] Dramatizing politics like this was the Nazi version of agitprop. It underscored the party's contention that it was not part of "the system," unlike the conservatives. But something else was at work, too, and it concerned substance as well as style. When the Depression hit rural Germany, traditional conservatives were quick to help themselves, through the assistance to large estates called Eastern Aid, while talking about a common rural front. But the strategy, successful in the past, failed to work this time. Peasant farmers voted for Hitler. Conservative elites, who had practiced the politics of demagogy in rural Germany for decades, were out-demagogued by a populist party that had perfected the art.

Many elements combined to bring the National Socialists into power. The Depression polarized politics and narrowed the room for maneuver in the Reichstag. With the Communists and the Nazis increasing their vote and unwilling to take part in government, the parliamentary arithmetic pointed to only one possibility—a succession of chancellors who, after March 1930, resorted to rule by emergency decree, without a reliable parliamentary majority. This undermined the legitimacy of Weimar democracy and lent plausibility to Nazi claims about a dysfunctional system. The parties of the left bear some responsibility for bringing Hitler to power. Communist hostility to the republic, and their willingness even to accept support from a Nazi organization during the Berlin transport strike in 1932, followed from their view that the Depression signaled the death throes of capitalism and would bring about a Communist Germany. Hence their disastrous policy that the Social Democrats were the real enemy. The SPD, for its part, was too wedded to a wait-and-see policy, too slow to appreciate the threat. The two parties, divided by ideology and memories of the postwar revolution, were further divided by the Depression. The Social Democrats were the party of older workers more likely to be employed, the Communists of younger workers who were mostly unemployed (a remarkable 85 percent of party members by 1932). One minor tragedy of the late Weimar Republic was the sight of unemployed Communists attacking

Social Democratic welfare clerks as mass unemployment undermined the social security system.

Without question, the right bore much greater direct responsibility for bringing down democracy. Conservatives undermined the republic by their constant criticism and made the Nazis look respectable because they advocated so many of the same policies. Landowning Junkers, army officers, Protestant church and business leaders—all came to believe that their goals and the Nazis' goals overlapped, even if they were not identical. Locally, prominent community figures also lent Hitler respectability. When a village mayor or someone of similar standing backed the Nazi Party, a veterinarian or auctioneer here, a forestry official or estate manager there, others followed. In university towns, the party made inroads among professors and other members of the educated in their social clubs. The Nazis benefited from presenting themselves as outsiders untainted by the system, but they also benefited from insider support.

On the national stage it was the elites that helped Hitler into power. After the failed Beer Hall putsch, he avoided any attempt to seize power by force. Violence remained a weapon to be used on the streets, not against the state. Hitler's opportunity came in 1933. Germany had three chancellors who ruled by decree between March 1930 and January 1933. By the time General Kurt von Schleicher, the last of this trio, took office in December 1932 the Nazi Party had lost some momentum. Its share of the vote and number of Reichstag seats had fallen in elections the previous month, although it remained the largest party. Then, on January 30, President Hindenburg offered the chancellorship to Hitler, who accepted and became the fifteenth and final chancellor of the republic. The former field marshal was a perfect embodiment of the German elites who helped Hitler into power, hoping that he could be tamed and made to do their bidding.

National Socialism

NATIONAL SOCIALISTS PROCLAIMED THAT THEY WERE PURSUing the only legitimate kind of revolution, a "national revolution." Germany withdrew from the League of Nations. Nazi leaders repeatedly denounced internationalism, emphasizing again and again the centrality of the German *Volk* and the *Volksgemeinschaft*, the "people's community." The regime promoted pseudo-Germanic cults, trumpeted the virtue of "authentically German" culture over "degenerate art," and denounced "cosmopolitan" values. And yet: the regime was influenced by ideas and political movements beyond Germany, just as it exerted influence on others. Even the term "National Socialism" was invented by a Frenchman, the nationalist Maurice Barrès.[193] National Socialism can be compared (and has been compared) to other regimes of the 1930s, on both right and left. That is what I want to explore here, looking mainly at the regime and its domestic policies in the years before World War Two.

Where better to start than with the self-styled Führer? Hitler was like the brooding central figure of Joseph Conrad's *Heart of Darkness*. "All Europe contributed to the making of Kurtz," says Marlow, the narrator of that novella.[194] All Europe contributed to the making of the German dictator. He likened himself and was likened by others to Italian Fascist leader Benito Mussolini. The Beer Hall putsch of 1923 was Hitler's attempt to imitate Mussolini's March on Rome a year earlier. Hitler admired Kemal Atatürk as a ruthless, antireligious leader who had restored Turkish fortunes.[195] In writing *Mein Kampf*, Hitler borrowed ideas, vocabulary, and whole passages from *Foundations of the Nineteenth Century*, a violently antisemitic work by Houston Stewart Chamberlain, the British-born writer who became Richard Wagner's son-in-law.[196] Hitler also absorbed the message of the notorious antisemitic forgery *The Protocols of the Elders of Zion*, which circulated widely in Germany through right-wing Russian émigrés.[197] But it was not just "all Europe" that contributed to the making of Hitler. He admired Chiang Kai-shek, as he did Atatürk, for promoting a strong state. He also admired Henry Ford, a large picture of whom adorned the wall of his study. Hitler told a journalist who asked about it: "I regard Ford as my inspiration." He owned a German translation of Ford's book *The International Jew*, which argued that Germany was, with the possible exception of the United States, "the most Jew-controlled country in the world."[198] Hitler admired the work of another American, too: Madison Grant, eugenicist author of *The Passing of the Great Race* (1916), which lauded the historical achievements of a "Nordic" race now under threat. Hitler read the book in the German translation of 1925, wrote the author a fan letter, and described the book as "my Bible."[199]

National Socialism as a movement, for all its hypernationalist qualities, also had many non-German genealogies and affinities. So how does it fit into the political landscape of the time? A first way of thinking about that is to draw two lines. One is a straight line, with communism on the left and National Socialism on the right. That puts German fascism with other

European fascisms, on the extreme right. The other line is a horseshoe, with communism on the left and National Socialism on the right, close together, almost touching. Here, Communist and Nazi regimes had more in common than separated them. The straight-line version seems much more persuasive to me, although there are elements of the horseshoe version that make sense. I want to follow each of these lines in turn, because both offer up revealing comparisons and uncover some of the non-German ideas and practices that found their way into the Third Reich.

Italy gave fascism its name. It was home to the first fascist movement, and the place where a fascist movement first came to power. Germans followed events in Italy closely. For the left, the coming of fascism was a warning, for many on the right a source of hope. Sympathetic German writers and publicists sought an audience with the Duce.[200] It is not too much to say that the fascist experiment served as a kind of model.[201] Much of what we think of as the external *style* of fascism was invented in Italy and became standard across European fascisms, including the Nazi movement. The basic elements of fascist style were the leader principle, parades and mass rallies, special salutes, the rhetoric of struggle, dramatic logos, and uniforms. Every movement had its logo, or symbol. The Italian prototype was the "fasces," the bundle of rods enclosing an ax. The Hungarians had their arrow cross, the Romanians their iron guard (a metal shield, or grille), while the British Union of Fascists used a lightning bolt in a circle (critics called it a "flash in the pan"). For the Nazis it was, of course, the swastika. As for the uniforms, they featured in all fascist movements and came in every color except red, for the Reds were the enemy. Wherever we look across Europe, we find Blackshirts, Greyshirts, Greenshirts, and Blueshirts. The National Socialists adopted the Brownshirt uniform, although it was not introduced until 1924, three years after the storm troopers were founded.[202]

The outward display of marches, mass meetings, and dramatic symbols points to the performative quality of fascism, the element of "spectacle," which Hitler's movement had in common with its counterparts everywhere.[203] The German literary and cultural critic Walter Benjamin, later a victim of National Socialism, was among the first to draw attention to this when he suggested that fascism was responsible for the "introduction of aesthetics into political life."[204] The annual Nuremberg rally is the quintessential example. As many as seven hundred thousand people attended in 1934, an occasion filmed by the "mountain film" actress and director Leni Riefenstahl and released the following year as *Triumph of the Will*. The

French fascist writer Robert Brasillach called the Nuremberg rallies "the highest artistic creation of our times."[205] This kind of theatrical politics was distinctively fascist. The parading and chanting were largely symbolic, a substitute for decision making that served the dual function of disciplining and diverting the populace.

Fascism may have looked and sounded the same everywhere, but it was not equally successful everywhere. Looking at where it came to power, and where (as well as why) it failed to do so in most of Europe, helps us to understand the German case. Fascist movements did not come close to power anywhere in northwestern Europe, except when installed as puppet regimes during wartime occupation. The British Union of Fascists, Léon Degrelle's Rexists in Belgium, the Croix de Feu in France, Vidkun Quisling's Nasjonal Samling in Norway—all remained out in the cold. Mature parliamentary systems in those countries were able to absorb the shock of the economic crisis, and none faced the additional burden of a lost war and a hated peace treaty that undermined the Weimar Republic. In eastern and southern Europe, on the other hand, parliamentary systems were overthrown in country after country during the interwar years—in Poland, Lithuania, Yugoslavia, Romania, Greece, Spain, and Portugal—but it was old-style conservative authoritarians who did the overthrowing. These regimes represented old elites (aristocracy, army, church, monarchy where it still existed) and spoke the language of hierarchy, order, and obedience, with none of the radical rhetoric or mass mobilization of fascism. Many of them were brutal, and some co-opted fascist parties or ideas, especially General Francisco Franco in Spain and Antonio de Oliveira Salazar in Portugal. There were also cases where authoritarian regimes pushed back against domestic fascist movements, even as they themselves borrowed more than a little fascist political coloring. That was true in Romania and in Austria, where the "Austro-Fascist" governments of Engelbert Dollfuss and Kurt Schuschnigg borrowed the nomenclature of the "Führer-state" and adopted many trappings of fascism, but resisted the demands of local National Socialists, until Schuschnigg was toppled by German forces in March 1938.[206] The line between fascist and authoritarian-fascist hybrid regimes is not easy to draw cleanly.

But Germany and Italy remain the two countries where fascists came to power thanks to their own popular support, even if support from traditional elites was also indispensable. The resemblances between the two go well beyond the Duce and the Führer. Germany and Italy shared intertwined histories in the nineteenth century, two "belated nations" with belated colonial empires. They fought on different sides in World War One, but many Italians were frustrated by their country's modest gains in the peacemaking process. If Germany was a sore loser, Italy was a sore winner. Fascist movements in both countries fused radical hostility to the establishment with hypernationalism and the rejection of Marxist socialism—Mussolini the former socialist, Hitler who joined a party called the German Workers' Party before he took it over and renamed it. Both brought pressure to bear on parliamentary systems in crisis. Paramilitary Italian Blackshirts and German Brownshirts directed their violence against the left, and the image of young men clambering onto trucks and going off to battle Reds in the name of the nation belonged to the mystique of each movement. Mussolini and Hitler both moved away from their early appeal to workers and established a more secure rural base, with the Po Valley and Schleswig-Holstein respectively providing key provincial breakthroughs at an early stage.[207] And both came to power by constitutional means, thanks to elites who opened the door to them. King Victor Emmanuel III was to Mussolini what President Hindenburg was to Hitler—the man who held the keys to power.

The two regimes also pursued similar policies, with some mutual borrowing. The points of comparison are instructive, but so are the places where comparison breaks down. National Socialists and Italian Fascists were both inventive in finding ways to attach people to their cause. They believed in carrots as well as sticks. But the sticks were wielded with a brutality that would have made nineteenth-century autocratic rulers blanch. The open, unashamed celebration of violence was part of what defined fascism. And fascists practiced as well as celebrated it. They threatened, jailed, tortured, and exiled their opponents. In Italy, violence was at its greatest just before the Fascists came to power. Some two thousand anti-Fascists were killed between 1920 and 1922, another thousand in the four years that followed.[208] In Germany, it was after Hitler became chancellor that violence reached new levels, especially following the Reichstag fire on February 27, 1933, which was started by the Nazis themselves.[209] The burning of the Reichstag provided the pretext for passing an Enabling Act the following month that gave Hitler's government sweeping new powers. It also led to a wave of raids on the offices of left-wing opponents. Those seized there were taken to improvised "wild concentration camps" set up in local party headquarters, taverns, and even individual apartments, where they were beaten and sometimes killed. By the end of 1933, the number of those temporarily detained in "protective custody" had probably reached at least 150,000, with many hundreds, perhaps thousands killed. The first formal concentration camp, at Dachau outside Munich, was constructed in March 1933, with maximum publicity, as a warning to opponents of the regime.[210]

Nazi Germany incarcerated many more of its opponents than Fascist Italy. Even before its wartime radicalization, the Third Reich was also incomparably more violent than its Italian counterpart. In fact, the closest European comparison in the 1930s is with the extraordinary bloodletting carried out by Franco's military insurgents in Spain, who killed 200,000 men and women behind the lines during the Civil War and executed at least another 20,000 after their victory, a "Spanish Holocaust."[211] The violence in Spain reminds us that there was a long history of counterrevolutionary white terror stretching back to the French Revolution, the most recent episodes of which occurred after World War One. National Socialism would become uniquely genocidal. Prior to 1939 the violence of the regime, like that of Spanish Francoists, bore at least a family resemblance to that tradition of white terror.

The Communist Third International had its own version of where Nazi violence came from. The Third Reich was, in its words, "the open, terrorist dictatorship of the most reactionary, most chauvinist and most imperialist element of finance capital."[212] The jargon is dismal, but the relationship of fascism to capitalism remains a fundamental question. Even before coming to power, Mussolini reassured Confindustria, the federation of Italian employers and chambers of commerce, that fascism would not challenge its members' interests. Ten years later, at a comparable moment, Hitler (dressed in suit and tie, not in Nazi uniform) delivered the same message to the Industry Club in Düsseldorf. Those reassurances were mostly honored by both regimes.

Italian business would have preferred an authoritarian but non-Fascist regime. It was large landowners, not industrialists, who first called on the Blackshirt *squadristi* to put down labor activism. But capitalists came around when Mussolini sidelined more radical elements in the party, banned strikes, and replaced trade unions with tame state organizations. Business leaders ran the so-called corporatist economic system. Most German capitalists would also have preferred a non-Nazi solution to the crisis of 1929–1933—if they could have found one. As it was, the Nazis still enjoyed more support from big businesses (especially heavy industry) when they came to power than Italian Fascists did at a comparable point, although not as much as they received from small business, and not as much as you might think from looking at John Heartfield's brilliant but misleading photomontage *The Meaning of the Hitler Salute* (1932), which showed a figure representing big capital putting a sheaf of money into the Führer's back-stretched hands, above the slogan "Millions are behind me." After 1933 the new regime pushed aside the "socialist" wing of the party, represented by figures like Otto Wagener and Gottfried Feder. Strikes were banned, as in Italy, and independent trade unions replaced by the German Labor Front, headed by Robert Ley, a party loyalist who came from IG-Farben. Application of the "leadership" principle on the factory floor strengthened the authority of bosses over workers, while the system of "co-determination" through factory councils inherited from Weimar was first watered down, then abolished. "Honor courts" that supposedly provided a means of redress against badly behaved employers were a typically paternalist piece of window dressing.

Private capital certainly did not have free rein. Nazi foreign-exchange controls imposed restrictions on all businesses, especially in the financial sector. Industries or firms that showed signs of noncooperation faced retaliation. Among the Ruhr steel barons, those who adapted themselves to what was asked, like Friedrich Flick, flourished, while others like Paul Reusch did not.[213] Chemical companies generally complied and were rewarded. Private companies played an essential part in the regime's never-ending pursuit of *Ersatz* or substitute materials, which was closely tied to the achievement of wartime self-sufficiency. IG-Farben invested heavily in synthetic fuel, producing nearly 900,000 tons in 1938. The Four-Year Plan announced in 1936 and headed by Hermann Göring, marked a new phase of central direction, even a "command economy," although one that operated by incorporating leading industrial managers into the state apparatus, not replacing them. In the end, it was the owners and managers of large businesses that did best, because they were free to accumulate and reinvest profits, not stockholders (because dividends were controlled), not workers (who benefited from the return to full employment, but whose real wages rose little), and not small businesses, either, for their problems became even worse.

There is something especially poignant about the fate of small businesses, craftsmen, and shopkeepers, the so-called *Mittelstand*, one of Hitler's electoral mainstays. The economic preparations for war led to Nazi complaints that small businesses were "hoarding" labor, and they were brutally culled. The number of independent businesses in Berlin fell by a quarter during the peacetime years of the Third Reich. Small businesses had always been flattered by the Nazis (like conservatives before them) as the "healthy backbone of the nation." Now the "little man" was squeezed out of both traditional and modern branches.[214] In a mordant underground joke of the era, Hitler rages to Göring about a criminal, complaining that mere execution was too good for him, he deserved to die a horribly slow, painful death. "Why don't you buy him a small shop?" replies Göring.[215] Peasant farmers, who had also been loyal Nazi voters, fared no better. Agricultural producers did benefit from more stable prices, and those with larger farms were allowed (like Junker aristocrats) to entail their properties. But farm incomes did not keep up with economic growth after 1935, debt mounted, and the "flight from the land"—so loudly deplored by the Nazis when they were campaigning—reached new levels after 1933.

This faster pace of urbanization points to the modern, technocratic aspect of the regime, another parallel with Italy. Motorization was the obvious symbol of technocracy in the Third Reich. One thing everyone knows about the regime is that Hitler built the first *Autobahnen*. These did not have primarily military objectives, as used to be believed, but served many purposes.[216] Like other public works programs, they were designed to reduce unemployment and speed economic recovery. Hitler himself was an enthusiast for motor vehicles, and this was a classic propaganda project intended to represent the dynamism of the regime.

Was there anything novel or especially "National Socialist" about these highways? The Italian *autostrada* got there first, and plans for a network of highways across Europe had been widely discussed in the 1920s by engineers and planning officials.[217] The idea touted by the Nazis that driving the *Autobahnen* provided perfect "vistas" of nature was equally a feature of the U.S. parkways under construction in the 1920s and '30s. What was distinctive in Germany was the ideological framing of the project. The Nazis took ideas that had long circulated among European technocrats and dressed them up in nationalist clothing: German drivers would drive through German nature. "Indigenous species" were carefully planted alongside the *Autobahnen*, an undertaking overseen by the "landscape advocate" Alwin Seifert. A proto-environmentalist voice mainly preoccupied with the threat of "desertification," Seifert found himself designing aesthetic add-ons to the ribbons of concrete that cut through the countryside, a characteristically Nazi emphasis on appearances.[218]

It is impossible to talk about motorization without talking about the *Volkswagen*. German car ownership lagged behind that of the United States, Britain, and France, and Hitler was enthused by the idea of a "people's car." There was an Italian precedent for this, too. Giovanni Agnelli, the owner of Fiat, had visited America, seen what Ford had done, and proceeded to build his own giant plant in Turin. The Lingotto opened in 1923. Mussolini wanted Agnelli to build a car for under five thousand lire, but the Fiat 500A turned out to cost much more. In Germany, neither the German manufacturers nor the U.S.-based producers who owned a large share of the market showed any interest in producing a cheap car. So Hitler asked Ferdinand Porsche, an automotive engineer who had founded his own company, to visit Michigan and design a German equivalent of the Model T. The new *Volkswagen* plant in Wolfsburg was supposed to be a fully integrated, modern production facility like the Ford plant, River Rouge, in Michigan. It was designed by the chief engineer at River Rouge, who had left Germany in the 1920s and returned to work for VW in 1937. In the end, it proved impossible to purchase the former Ford machines as expected. The plant never produced anything other than prototypes because war came and Wolfsburg was converted to the production of military jeeps. But a remarkable 340,000 Germans, mainly middle-class, paid regular installments on a car, expecting to receive their vehicle when they had finished paying—the reverse of the purchasing on credit system that Ford and others used in the United States. Their contributions provided the revenue stream that funded Wolfsburg, while the consumers transferred their material desires to the future.[219]

The *Volkswagen* program was administered by Strength Through Joy, the leisure arm of the German Labor Front. This had an exact Italian equivalent, Dopolavoro (After Work).[220] Both organizations provided leisure-time activities, which replaced (in Germany) or competed with (in Italy) the offerings of the church and other institutions. In Germany these activities ranged from soccer clubs and swimming courses to cheap train outings that took country people to concerts in town. The Nazis boasted about the opportunities for cheap travel provided by Strength Through Joy: day trips to the Black Forest or the Harz Mountains for most, a cruise to Madeira or the Norwegian fjords for a handpicked few. Whether it was the prospect of a cruise, or the immediate opportunity to do something formerly associated with the educated elite, like listening to Wilhelm Furtwängler conducting the Berlin Philharmonic, the National Socialists said that they wanted to break down old hierarchies and class barriers. If there was any kind of Nazi "social revolution," this was it—in the realm of behavior and attitudes. Strength Through Joy, like other auxiliary organizations, claimed to be building a people's community. That there were serious limits to this hardly needs to be emphasized. Most obviously, it did not apply to those who were excluded by race, "asocial" attitudes, or political views. It was also simply not true, whatever Nazi propaganda claimed, that Strength Through Joy transcended class and other divisions. We know there was tension between urban tourists from the Protestant north and rural Catholics, and between Strength Through Joy tourists and fellow Germans they encountered who were vacationing privately and looked down on them.[221]

Strength Through Joy, like Dopolavoro, aimed to depoliticize the population, especially the working class, even if achieving full conformity was beyond reach. It had some success. When workers who had previously been active in socialist sports clubs ventured cautiously into Strength Through Joy venues, because there was nowhere else to go, they were often relieved to find "scarcely any Heil Hitlers" and "nothing National Socialist," at least overtly.[222] But those workers still had to check their politics at the door. Depoliticization was also created by mass consumption, fascist-style: the world of professional sports, glossy magazines, and movies fostered by both German and Italian regimes. Italian film directors imitated Hollywood styles, even if the comedy genre known as white telephone films was distinctly Italian. Most German films made after 1933 were also designed to entertain, whether costume dramas, adventures, comedies, or musicals. Many presented their audience with exotic foreign locales; some were even made there. Between 1933 and 1939, around sixty-five German feature films were set and filmed abroad—in Britain, France, Italy, Hungary, even in the United States. German cinema also had a higher proportion of foreign stars than Hollywood, of whom Zarah Leander from Sweden was probably the most famous. Of course, some Nazi-era feature films (perhaps one in seven) were obvious propaganda vehicles, including odious productions like the antisemitic *Jud Süss* (1934). Others carried a less obvious message (about authority, for example) that was nonetheless still there. But its escapist, "dream machinery" quality was the most salient characteristic of Nazi cinema.[223]

The dreams sold by the cinema had something in common with the dream of owning a *Volkswagen* and traveling, or moving into a new home. A million Germans toured the model homes with their modern conveniences at the *"Schaffendes Volk"* (A Nation at Work) exhibition in 1937.[224] Modern

advertising thrived in Nazi Germany, although stripped like other professions of the Jews who had once worked in it. American-style advertisements,
which relied less on design and had longer text, took off in Nazi Germany
as they never had in the Weimar Republic.[225] Was all this "Americanization"
or mass consumerism with Nazi attitude? It combined elements of both. The
National Socialists liked the text of ads to be written in Gothic-German
script, but this was not required; German words were also preferred to
"international" words, but again, this was left to the companies concerned.
Heinrich Hunke, who headed the Third Reich's Advertising Council, also
declined to follow the wishes of the Nazi Party's public health offices to ban
ads for those immensely popular items of consumption: cigarettes and alcohol. At the same time, when advertisers addressed their appeal to "German
women," the underlying message of who came into that category, and who
did not, was hard to miss.[226] Images of material plenty (and the promise
of more to come) were also used, relentlessly, to bolster the popularity of
the regime. Even when the products were quintessentially American, like
screwball comedies and Busby Berkeley–type musical extravaganzas, they
were presented as thoroughly German. Coca-Cola is a striking instance.
Sales grew substantially under Hitler, but the American origins of the drink
were sufficiently obscured that later German POWs in the United States
were astonished to find that Coke was not in fact German.[227]

The promise of material pleasures, even when wrapped in the language
of a supposedly classless "people's community," sat awkwardly alongside the
pinched, resentful values of provincial Germany to which National Socialism appealed in its rise to power. It also antagonized those elements in the
party who disliked "materialism" and wanted to create a more "wholesome"
society. National Socialism, like other fascisms, was a potentially unstable amalgam of values and impulses. The Nazis promised Germans the
fruits of modernity, but also ran campaigns that satisfied resentful mor-
alists. Cultural decadence was a favorite target. The exhibition of "degenerate art" is a notorious example. This collection of modernist works was
exhibited in Munich in July 1937 as a cautionary tale of everything that was
"un-German" and viewed by adult members of the public (minors were forbidden entry) who were informed by the brochure guide why they should
scorn and hate what they were seeing. The free exhibition was seen by over
two million men and women before it went on the road four months later.[228]
Harsh crackdowns on homosexuality and constant emphasis on "healthy"
German bodies represented the same moralism. These antidecadence cam-

paigns had their Italian counterparts, too. Perhaps the most startling was led by the futurist and Fascist intellectual Filippo Tommaso Marinetti, who targeted spaghetti because it was "no food for fighters."[229]

Marinetti was an intensely masculine figure, scornful of women, eager to attack anything that smacked of "effeminacy" in men.[230] Fascist Italy and Nazi Germany were regimes that emphasized distinct gender roles. Pushing women out of the workforce back into the home was one way to attack the problem of unemployment, but the policy was also ideologically driven. Men were to be virile, women maternal. Both regimes were pro-natalist, offering couples a variety of material incentives to have children. With typical bombast, Mussolini called this the "battle of the birthrate." Each year, starting in 1933, prolific couples (twelve living children or more) were brought together and celebrated in Rome's Palazzo Venezia. Nazi Germany awarded bronze, silver, and gold medals to women with large numbers of children (five, six, and seven, respectively), a practice that had begun in interwar France (where the motherhood bar was set higher, at five, eight, and ten children).[231] Germany took this policy further than any other country. Even in foster parenting, the central role of the mother was now emphasized, rather than that of both foster parents.[232]

These were policies that clerical conservatives welcomed. But fascist and clerical views did not always dovetail so neatly. The family was often the place where tensions came to the surface. Italian fascism talked about the family as sacrosanct, but then insisted on what men, women, and children owed to the Duce and the nation.[233] The clashes with religious conservatives were more serious in Germany. In Italy, after all, the Fascist regime put crucifixes back in the schoolroom; in Germany, the regime tried to take them out, causing one of the most sustained instances of resistance to Nazi authority, as German "fathers of families," backed by Catholic priests, demonstrated their opposition.[234] National Socialists were at odds with conservative family values in other ways, too. The regime's major goal of "purifying the *Volk*" meant that, even as they condemned "unworthy" single mothers, they encouraged "racially valuable" German women to have children outside marriage. The best-known instance is the series of *Lebensborn* homes for unmarried mothers established in 1935 by the SS (the Schutz-staffel, the paramilitary branch of the Nazi Party, which grew into a state-within-a-state).[235] The other side of the same coin was the Janus-faced Nazi policy on abortion. The left-leaning sex reformers of the Weimar Republic were persecuted and exiled, while the possibilities that the existing law allowed for women to terminate a pregnancy on specified medical grounds were closed off. Heinrich Himmler, the head of the SS, set up a Bureau to Combat Homosexuality and Abortion in 1936. Yet abortion was encouraged in those cases where the pregnancy was the result of "racial mixing" or where the mother was considered to be "hereditarily defective."[236]

All this points to the centrality of eugenics and "racial hygiene" in Nazi policy. Italian Fascists might talk about *la razza,* but the word "race" carried a more cultural than biological meaning and race did not drive policy. The Third Reich was a racial state: race became the determinant of citizenship, the ability to work, access to welfare, the choice of marriage partner, and the right to reproduce. Ultimately, of course, it determined whether you lived or died. In the words of Interior Minister Wilhelm Frick in 1933: "We must once more have the courage to classify our *Volk* according to their hereditary value."[237] That meant separating out members of the *Volk* community who were racially sound, healthy, productive, and orderly from the rest—those who were, in Nazi terms, racially alien, unhealthy, unproductive, or asocial. National Socialist policy on welfare, health, and family was geared to redistributing resources from the second group to the first, and unabashedly so. The director of the party's welfare department laid this out clearly: welfare would be based on the science of "hereditary biology and racial hygiene. The principle of the equality of all citizens is no longer valid because we have recognized that heredity insures that individuals are of different value for the welfare of the whole."[238] Posters in doctors' waiting rooms and slide series like "Blood and Soil" drove the message home. One such slide juxtaposed a picture of a "hereditarily diseased man" and a smiling family group, pointedly noting that each cost the state 5.50 marks a day.

This was the ugly language of eugenics, a language spoken by many in the 1930s. Invented in England by Francis Galton, Darwin's cousin, eugenics had supporters everywhere by the early twentieth century. It was no disreputable pseudoscience but a "wellborn science," inextricably linked to the emerging discipline of genetics.[239] It found its earliest advocates in Britain, Scandinavia, and the United States but soon established a presence elsewhere in Europe, as well as in Latin America and Japan. The First International Eugenics Congress was held in 1912, in London, and the basic ideas of eugenics could be found in schoolbooks around the world by the 1930s. The keywords were "racial hygiene," "improving the race," "good and bad blood," "the healthy" and "the defective," "degeneration" and "regeneration." Even Wilhelm Frick's suggestion that classifying people by "hereditary value" required courage was standard fare. Major Leonard Darwin, the scientist's son, said the same thing at the First International Eugenics Conference.

The eugenicist ideas espoused by the Nazis were not unusual in themselves. They were widely shared internationally. But they did not take the same form everywhere. Often, they were a subsidiary element in progressive (and feminist) programs, or the more coercive aspects were rejected. The commonplaceness of the ideas, in other words, should not blind us to the fact that the Nazi application of them was uniquely radical. Almost none of their ideas and practices were original; it was the brutal energy and uncompromising force with which they pursued them, as well as their scale, that stands out.

Sterilization is a cogent example. Voluntary sterilization was widely practiced globally. Involuntary sterilization also predated Nazism by a generation, in Scandinavia, Japan, and the United States.[240] The American example was especially important because of the intense exchanges of views between German and U.S. eugenicists. The Rockefeller Foundation funded research on "racial hygiene" conducted in Munich by the Swiss-born psychiatrist and eugenicist Ernst Rüdin. In America, the first law permitting compulsory sterilization was passed in Indiana in 1907; it was followed by laws in twenty-nine other states. In a 1927 Supreme Court decision upholding the Virginia statute, Justice Oliver Wendell Holmes made his frequently quoted remark: "Three generations of imbeciles are enough."[241] Articles in the *Journal of the American Medical Association* and the *New England Journal of Medicine* referred routinely to the "unfit" and "defectives." When the Law for the Prevention of Offspring with Hereditary Diseases was passed in Germany in 1933, with Ernst Rüdin as one of its principal authors, it built on the work of American eugenicists as well as homegrown figures.

However, American eugenicists looked enviously at the German legislation.[242] It went further than sterilization laws elsewhere. The law included those targeted by eugenicists everywhere—the "congenitally feeble-minded," those suffering from schizophrenia and manic depression, epilepsy, Huntington's chorea, the deaf, those with severe hereditary physical deformity, and "asocials" such as alcoholics.[243] But it also included the blind, which American eugenicists such as Harry Laughlin had tried, without success, to include in U.S. legislation. Why did the Third Reich include blind people? Probably because, relatively small though the numbers of the blind were, their inclusion reinforced the supposedly "scientific" validity of the measure.[244] That was exceptionally cold-blooded. So was the scale on which the Nazis conducted involuntary sterilization. The American laws covered mainly those who were in psychiatric hospitals or prisons; the German law applied to the general population and there was pressure on doctors to report everyone who qualified. As a result, while there were around 30,000 cases in the United States between 1907 and the early 1940s, 400,000 Germans were condemned to compulsory sterilizations by Genetic Health Courts in just eleven years.

These were Germans deemed "alien to the community" because they were supposedly "damaged" or "deviant." Other Germans offended National Socialists because they were people of "alien blood." Three groups defined in racial terms faced persecution in the Third Reich. One was the small but highly differentiated Black population. It included Black Germans from the former colonies of Cameroon, Togo, and East Africa, as well as Liberians and South Africans, African-Americans and West Indians. Those who carried German papers had these replaced by "alien passes." All became the targets of antimiscegenation laws. Many also lost their jobs and found themselves banned from public places (although not everywhere). A subgroup of the Black population, 385 of the so-called Rhineland bastards, was forcibly sterilized in 1937; so were others of "mixed race," perceived to pose a special threat to racial purity.[245] As an afterthought of Nazi policy, their treatment varied locally and arbitrarily. Most (but not all) were kept out of the German Labor Front, and most (but not all) were denied membership of the Hitler Youth and League of German Girls. The strongest pressure was brought to bear on mixed-race couples to separate.[246] It is a perfect instance of the cruel absurdity of "race" as a category, when we see photographs of Mandenga Ngando in Reich Labor Service uniform and Ekwe Ngando in Reichswehr uniform, both surrounded by comrades, then learn that their parents in Hanover, a Cameroonian man and his German wife, were forced to separate.[247]

The second racially defined group consisted of Sinti and Roma ("Gypsies"), who numbered about thirty thousand in Germany and Austria in 1939. Already marginalized in the kaiser's Germany and the Weimar Republic, their position deteriorated sharply after 1933. Like Blacks in Germany, they became subject to the law prohibiting marriage or sexual relations with "Aryans." They were also targeted because the Nazis were obsessed with "half-caste" races and with the "asocial" or "work-shy," and

Gypsies were placed in both categories. In the words of Dr. Robert Ritter, the neurologist who headed the Racial Hygiene and Population Biology unit of the criminal police, the "problem" they presented "can be considered solved only when the majority of the asocial and unproductive Gypsies are placed in large work camps and the further reproduction of this half-caste population is terminated. Only then will future generations of the German people be freed from this burden."[248] An improvised internment camp was set up in 1934 on the outskirts of Cologne. Other cities followed suit. One of the most notorious camps was established on the eve of the 1936 Olympic Games in the eastern Berlin suburb of Marzahn, next to a sewage works, where outbreaks of diphtheria and tuberculosis became commonplace. Ritter's assistants were active in the camps, measuring, photographing, and taking blood as they worked to "classify" the different "racial types." Several hundred Sinti and Roma also became victims of involuntary sterilization. After Heinrich Himmler had classified them as an "alien and inferior race," further large-scale round-ups occurred in 1937 and 1938.[249] "Like the Jews, we had homes there, businesses," recalled a Sinti named Katja H. "We Sinti were upstanding Germans; we didn't think anything could happen to us. We were reared in Germany; it was our home."[250]

"Like the Jews. . . ." What was done to the Jews has become the defining feature of Hitler's regime, and what was done had no precedent. That was true of the persecution faced by Jews in Germany even before 1939 and the wartime genocide. The combination of brutality and bureaucracy, old-style prejudice and pseudoscience made Nazi policy unique. The persecution, exclusion, isolation, and humiliation experienced by German Jews proceeded unevenly during the prewar years, with a marked radicalization in 1938–39. But the coupling of physical violence and legal discrimination was a pattern from the start. Storm troopers and party radicals assaulted Jews in the street and attacked Jewish businesses immediately after the Nazis came to power, until these activities were channeled into the "Jewish boycott" of April 1, 1933, out of fear that the army and foreign opinion would react negatively to continuing "disorder." Away from the eyes of the foreign press, however, attacks on Jewish businesses continued. That same month, the blandly named Law for the Restoration of the Professional Civil Service excluded non-Aryans (except, for the moment, Jewish war veterans) from a wide range of public positions. Other legislation drove Jews out of orchestras and theaters and limited the number of Jewish school and university students. The Aryanization of Jewish businesses also began in 1933.

Violence and legal discrimination came together again in 1935. Gau-leiters such as Joseph Goebbels in Berlin and Julius Streicher in Franconia picked up and amplified dissatisfaction among Brownshirts and young party members that the campaign against the Jews was not proceeding energetically enough. The spring of 1935 saw a mounting number of physical attacks on Jews, which led more conservative members of the political elite such as Interior Minster Frick and Economics Minister Hjalmar Schacht to urge Hitler to "regularize" things through legislation. The Nuremberg Laws were the result, a milestone in "Jewish policy." The Reich Citizenship Law deprived Jews of their civil rights by removing their German citizen-ship and reducing them to mere subjects. The Law for the Protection of German Blood and German Honor prohibited new marriages or sexual relations between Aryans and non-Aryans. As in the case of marriages between Germans and Africans, pressure was also brought to bear on cou-ples in existing mixed marriages to separate or divorce, intruding intoler-able strains into the most intimate sphere of life and eliciting both craven behavior and courage. One man, told that it would be easy to divorce his Jewish wife by claiming "insurmountable aversion," replied that this would not be possible because of an "insurmountable attraction."[251] Jewish children were forced to sit apart from their classmates at school and forbidden to participate in school events. They had to listen to teachers dressed ostenta-tiously in SA or SS uniform teaching about Jewish iniquities during lessons on "racial science."

The step-by-step exclusion of Jews from German society occurred in every area of life. Jews found that customers and clients disappeared. They were refused loans and credit, turned away in shops, and denied accommo-dation at hotels. They were insulted in the streets and had to watch the pro-liferation of "Jews Not Wanted" signs by the roadside and in public places like cinemas and parks. All of this isolated Jews, forcing them out of public view and into the home. The screw tightened even during the ostensibly quiet years of 1936–37, when the regime avoided major antisemitic displays or new measures. A principal reason was the desire to use the 1936 Olym-pics as a propaganda showcase, and therefore to prevent foreign visitors being confronted with "unpleasantness." The run-up to the Olympics also created the possibility of a U.S. boycott if Jewish athletes were not allowed on the German team. On this issue, German sports leaders and Hitler made promises they subsequently broke, although it should be said that they gave those assurances to International Olympic Committee members who were highly sympathetic to their cause and looking for reasons to reject a boycott. One of them was an influential Swede, Sigfrid Edström, who wrote to his American IOC colleague Avery Brundage that although he was "not at all in favor" of the persecution of Jews in Germany, he fully understood that things had to change because "a great part of the German nation was led by the Jews and not by the Germans themselves." He added, "Even in the USA the day may come when you have to stop the activities of the Jews." Brundage himself thought that day had already come. He wrote to Edström about the "anti-Nazi bias" of the "Jewish-controlled press of New York City" and told his hosts during a visit to Germany in 1934 that his own men's club in Chicago barred Jews.[252]

The Olympics were a propaganda success. But even after the stage set designed for international visitors had been packed away, there were no major developments in Nazi Jewish policy at first. In early 1937 Hitler celebrated four years in power and boasted that he had made Germany great again, but he made no further moves for the moment against Germany's Jews. Around one-third of them had emigrated by then. Those who remained were isolated and increasingly impoverished. By that point a variety of views on the "Jewish question" circulated in the Nazi Party, SA, SS, and Foreign Office, as well as among the "experts" in "racial science." Hitler held back, concerned about foreign opinion and advised by Schacht not to jeopardize the economic recovery by radical moves, even as he reiterated his "final objective" to remove all Jews from Germany.

The violent reversal that came in 1938 was linked to a radicalization of foreign policy. Hitler shocked military leaders in November 1937 with his talk of future war for "living space" in the east. The following February the conservative military men Werner von Blomberg, the war minister and commander in chief of the armed forces, and Werner von Fritsch, the commander in chief of the army, were sacked; so were Economics Minister Schacht and Foreign Minister Konstantin von Neurath. This removed the cautious voices and was the prelude to a renewed onslaught against German Jews. The annexation of Austria in March 1938 (the *Anschluss*) was accompanied by physical violence against Jews reminiscent of what had happened in Germany five years earlier. In Germany, the forced Aryanization of businesses intensified and would be nearly complete by the end of the year. The legal and property rights of Jewish communities were removed, and the remaining Jewish physicians and lawyers had their professional licenses and titles revoked, with just a few hundred permitted to continue serving other Jews as "carers" and "legal advisers." In a so-called June action, fif-teen hundred "asocial" Jewish men were sent to concentration camps (many guilty of minor offenses such as traffic violations). All Jews were compelled to add "Israel" or "Sarah" to their existing names, and to have a "J" for *Jude* stamped in their passports (and, from January 1939, in their identity papers). At the same time, annexing to the "greater Reich" a country that contained almost 200,000 Jews also made a mockery of the proclaimed Nazi aim to make Germany "free of Jews." As Hitler upped the aggressive tempo of German foreign policy, leading to the fall crisis over Czechoslovakia, his convictions about the Jewish "enemy within" were translated into actions.

It was one such action, the proposal to expel all non-German Jews from the country, that triggered the most notorious eruption of antisemitic vio-lence in prewar Germany. At the end of October 1938, 18,000 Polish Jews were rounded up and taken to the border with Poland. The Poles refused to accept them; the desperate victims were left in the border zone without food or shelter. Herschel Grynszpan had family members among them. The seventeen-year-old, brought up in Germany, had tried unsuccessfully to emigrate to Palestine and had been living illegally in France with an aunt and uncle since 1936. On November 7, he walked into the German embassy in Paris and shot the young third secretary Ernst vom Rath, who died two days later. This became the pretext for an unleashing of violence and destruction against the Jewish community in Germany, a pogrom that became known euphemistically as the *Reichskristallnacht*, or Night of Bro-ken Glass. Approved by Hitler and choreographed by Goebbels, always one of the party's antisemitic radicals, these supposedly "spontaneous" attacks on the night of November 9–10 were in fact led by party activ-ists and Brownshirts in civilian clothes. They destroyed hundreds of syn-agogues and damaged thousands more. Jewish businesses were destroyed, Jewish homes invaded and looted, and their inhabitants assaulted. Along with the broken glass, victims remembered the feathers flying everywhere as the mobs systematically ripped open and destroyed bedding.[253] Almost 100 Jews are known to have died, but the true number is certainly higher and should also include more than 600 suicides and the deaths that fol-lowed in concentration camps after some 35,000 Jewish men were rounded up. Even Germans who supported "moderate" measures against the Jews were reportedly shocked at the violence and destruction of property. In the aftermath, German insurance companies were instructed not to reimburse Jews for their losses. Instead, the state received the insurance payments that were made as "damages." A fine of one billion Reichsmarks was also levied collectively on German Jews as "punishment" for the assassination of vom Rath. The screw was progressively tightened on Jews later in 1938 and in 1939 and the pace of emigration increased, even as the deliberate impoverishment of the would-be emigrants made leaving more difficult.

Was there anything unique about Nazi antisemitism in the years 1933–39? Pogroms had, of course, disfigured Europe for centuries. In the modern era they had been much less common in Germany than in Russia and eastern Europe. Attacks on Sinti and Roma were distressingly common in rural Germany before 1914, but physical violence against Jews was rare between the 1848 revolution and the 1920s. When prewar antisemitic mob violence threatened in the wake of ritual murder allegations, as it did in Xanten (1891) and Konitz (1900), the Prussian authorities quickly stepped in.[254] The impact of World War One and the all-important fact that the Nazis now wielded state power made the physical violence of 1933 and 1938 conceivable. Antisemitism was, of course, commonplace in fascist and right-wing authoritarian movements across Europe, where the Jews as the "murderers of Christ" and the "blood libel" canard represented an older, religious tradition of Jew-hatred. Like nineteenth-century conservatives before them, fascists also muttered about the Jews as anticlericals, often tracing the supposedly malign role of the Jews back to the French Revolution, and there was a ready audience for *The Protocol of the Elders of Zion*, the right-wing Russian forgery that had claimed there was a Jewish plot to establish world domination. After the Bolshevik Revolution, the idea of a "Judeo-Bolshevik" conspiracy then found willing listeners. Cardinal Michael von Faulhaber, the archbishop of Munich, visiting Hitler at Berchtesgaden in November 1936, complimented the Führer on a speech two months earlier about Judeo-Bolshevism in which Hitler had referred to "subhumans" who had "created havoc in Spain like beasts."[255] General Franco's supporters would have added their compliments.

Their bigotry overlapped, but hatred of the Jew was not a defining article of faith for Spanish fascists as it was for Hitler and committed National Socialists. One reason is that National Socialist antisemitism was race-based and pseudoscientific, like other policies based on the eugenics that came out of Protestant northern Europe—but without any of the political constraints that limited the damage eugenic doctrines could inflict in Britain or Scandinavia. Politics mattered as well as ideology: the Nazis did what they did to the Jews because they could. But the ideology was distinctive, too. National Socialism fused together different kinds of antisemitism into an amalgam that had no equivalent elsewhere. "The Jew" as composite enemy was assailed on every one of the grounds that antisemites had dreamed up over the years: as criminal, sexual predator and master manipulator, as someone with no loyalty to the nation, as decadent cultural modernist, as parasitical finance capitalist but also as revolutionary, as dirty, unassimilable *Ostjude* but also as sleek, all-too-assimilated doctor or lawyer. Nazi antisemitism brought together old and new forms of hatred in uniquely toxic form.

National Socialist methods were likewise eclectic, in part because of the tension between the movement's populist and bureaucratic wings. Anti-Jewish policies between 1933 and 1939 ran the gamut from outright violence to surveillance, bans, boycotts, expulsion, incarceration, and discriminatory legislation. Some of these measures had a prehistory in Germany. Racially defined groups had been carefully monitored and policed before 1914: Gypsies and Polish seasonal laborers as well as Russian Jews passing through Germany on their way to the United States. Many hotels had operated de facto bans on Jewish guests, while antisemitic writers urged Christian boycotts of Jewish businesses. At different points between 1871 and 1914, French, Danish, and Polish citizens were also expelled from Germany.

What did not have a direct German prewar precedent was the concentration camp, originally set up to house political opponents of the regime but filled with increasing numbers of Jews as the war approached—and, of course, an institution that in its genocidal wartime mutation has come to define the Nazi regime. The concentration camp had a complicated lineage. The Germans borrowed it from the British, who borrowed it from the Spanish. General Valeriano Weyler, the "Spanish butcher," became known during the Spanish-Cuban War of 1895–1898 for the tactic of herding civilians into Spanish-held towns, a practice he had developed earlier in the Philippines. This policy of *reconcentración* was taken over by the British during the Boer War, when Lord Kitchener "concentrated" civilians into camps to separate them from guerrillas. The Germans then borrowed the practice in Southwest Africa.[256] These were all colonial locations, but by 1914 the term "concentration camp" had become standard usage among English and French speakers. Ruhleben, where the Germans interned Allies during World War One, was "the Berlin concentration camp."[257]

Another central aspect of Jewish policy in the Third Reich had a colonial lineage. That was the opposition to racially mixed marriages. In fact, no single policy was applied uniformly across Germany's prewar colonies. In 1905 there was an outright ban on racially mixed marriages in Southwest Africa, which was made retroactive. No such ban was imposed until 1912 in Samoa, where somewhere between a quarter and a third of German officials were married to "half-caste" women and Governor Wilhelm Solf himself insisted that the children of such marriages "took the legal status of the father and were whites, despite their dark skin color."[258] In Qingdao, several wealthy Chinese residents had German wives and no law banning racial intermarriage was seriously considered.[259] Race, in short, was an unstable category very much subject to local dynamics. There is no straight line that runs from the pre-1914 German colonies to the racial politics of the Third Reich, from Windhoek to Nuremberg.[260] But the colonies did put the question of racial intermarriage on the agenda and led to a flurry of eugenicist writing by figures such as Eugen Fischer, who helped to shape thinking about race laws in the 1930s.

The Nuremberg Laws drew more direct inspiration from another source: the United States. National Socialists took great interest in the United States, closely following and reporting on treatment of the African-American population. This was partly tactical. Whenever Americans criticized German policy toward the Jews, a Nazi politician or newspaper would remind Americans pointedly about lynchings (Goebbels's Propaganda Ministry kept detailed files on the subject).[261] But the Nazi interest in the U.S. racial regime went beyond exposing American hypocrisy. The United States was a direct source of inspiration on matters of race. National Socialists admired the Jim Crow laws, but it was above all American citizenship and antimiscegenation laws that lawyers combed through when framing the two main Nuremberg Laws, on Citizenship and the Protection of German Blood and Honor. Both were formulated using American precedents. However, the "one-drop" rule adopted in Virginia and other southern states was considered too radical for Germany, where Jews were much more integrated than Blacks were in America and a category such as the "octoroon" would, from the Nazi perspective, have meant jettisoning a person who was seven-eighths Aryan.[262]

The parallels were nonetheless evident to people in both countries. They also went beyond the Nuremberg Laws. When Charles Sherrill, an International Olympic Committee member and a former American diplomat, traveled to Germany just before the 1935 Nuremberg Rally to urge Nazi authorities to name at least one Jew to the German Olympic squad, he described this helpfully to his hosts as a symbolic gesture like the American tradition of the "token Negro."[263] Germans, meanwhile, were not the only ones alert to American hypocrisy. Black publications such as the *Philadelphia Tribune*, the *Chicago Defender*, and *The Crisis*, the NAACP magazine, ran articles and cartoons that pointed up the parallels between Ku Klux Klan atrocities and what storm troopers were doing to Jews in Germany.[264] Still, there were differences. The African-American intellectual W. E. B. Du Bois, who never forgot that in the 1890s he had faced more racial animosity in Harvard Yard than he did at the University of Berlin and retained his admiration for Germany, was in no doubt about what he witnessed during five months spent in Germany in 1936. "The campaign against the Jews," he wrote in the *Pittsburgh Courier*, "surpasses in vindictive cruelty and public insult anything I have ever seen; and I have seen much."[265]

While it is important to look at the non-German ideas and practices that influenced Nazi policies, it is no less important to look at the reverse process: the magnetic attraction that National Socialism exerted on others. It may seem odd to talk about "fascism without borders," given the intense nationalism that all fascisms had in common. But fascist movements were tied together by many links.[266] Some were spontaneous. Intellectuals and young people, especially the bourgeois young, were drawn to the idea of fascism, through study or travel abroad, or simply because of what they read. Then fascist parties developed. In the 1920s it was Italy and Mussolini that had the glow of novelty. Italy subsidized fascists in Belgium and Austria; it even helped train the Croatian Ustasha and the Ukrainian OUN. But after 1933 Nazi Germany became increasingly the beacon. In the 1920s, the British Union of Fascists had highlighted the Italian corporate state in its program and spent little time on race. Financial support came via the Italian ambassador in London. After 1936, though, the party added the words "and National Socialists" to its name, mentions of the corporate state disappeared, and antisemitism took center stage. Modest subsidies now came from Berlin. Across Europe the German influence on local fascists grew. One effect everywhere was to "racialize" fascist programs. Even in eastern European countries that were authoritarian but not (yet) fascist, the Nuremberg Laws broke taboos, influencing the Romanian citizenship law of 1938 and the Hungarian racial laws of 1938–39.[267] The most remarkable instance of this came in Italy. Mussolini had Jewish industrialist backers and associates. Around two hundred Jews took part in the 1922 March on Rome. American Jewish publishers even listed Mussolini in 1933 as one of the "twelve greatest Christian champions" of the Jews.[268] Then, in 1938, Italy introduced laws that imitated German racial legislation, a result of diplomatic alignment rather than any authentic or powerful domestic sentiment.

Italy and Germany were simultaneously partners and rivals in forging an international fascist front. Both regimes encouraged the formation of branches abroad, whether Italians in London or Germans in Buenos Aires.[269] Both staked out positions as guardians of European culture against

Hitler and Mussolini on the cover of Italy's La Tribuna Illustrata *in May 1938, at the time of the dictators' second meeting, in Rome.*

liberal-internationalist and Communist challenges. Italy was first in the field, establishing the Action Committees for the Universality of Rome in 1933. But the Italian version of fascist "renewal" in Europe was challenged by the Nazi Party ideologist Alfred Rosenberg, with his more racially inflected vision of the "crisis and rebirth of Europe."[270] Germany then set up its own institutions designed to reshape the European cultural landscape: the Union of National Writers and the Permanent Council for International Cooperation Among Composers (both 1934) and the International Film Chamber (1935). These were cultural umbrella organizations designed to be inter-nationalist, not internationalist in the cosmopolitan sense of existing League of Nations bodies. Italy was very much junior partner, as it was in the diplomatic Rome–Berlin axis announced in 1936. A cultural accord between the two countries signed in 1938 was a counterpart to the Italian adoption of German racial laws. It signified the primacy of the *völkisch* German vision of culture in a so-called New European Order of the future.[271] The Third Reich also signed a cultural exchange agreement with Japan in 1938, two years after the Anti-Comintern Pact was signed, another example of "transnational Nazism" in the cultural sphere.[272]

Fascism has been called a "traveling political universe," and it is now clear just how extensive the exchanges were between different fascist movements.[273] These cast new light on the Third Reich. But what if we look at National Socialism from the opposite direction: as one of the two "evil twins" of modern history, along with Soviet communism?[274] Were these not two totalitarian regimes extremes of right and left that touched? Totalitarianism has an interesting history. Coined by Mussolini to describe his regime in Italy, the term was applied to the Italian, German, and Soviet regimes in the 1930s. But it really took off and was widely used by journalists and the general public during the Cold War to denote the equivalence of Nazi Germany and Soviet Russia.[275] Totalitarianism as a concept has often met with skepticism because it was so obviously used as a political weapon. But political baggage does not by itself invalidate a way of seeing things ("fascism," after all, has often been misused as a political label). To compare, anyway, does not mean an assertion of similarity, let alone identity. Looking at National Socialism and Soviet communism side by side actually produces a revealing picture of similarity and dissimilarity, parallels and divergences.[276]

First, how not to do it. The West German historian Ernst Nolte ignited the great "historians' debate" of the 1980s when he suggested that National Socialism was a response to the "class genocide" and "Asiatic barbarism" of the Bolsheviks: their very existence, and their later crimes, should therefore be viewed as reactive, even preemptive. This argument was almost universally rejected by historians.[277] But it is still worth asking what, if anything, the Nazis inherited, or learned, from the left. Some fascist leaders had backgrounds in the socialist movement. That was true of Mussolini, Oswald Mosley in Britain, and Marcel Déat in France. Another French fascist, Jacques Doriot, was a former member of the French Communist Party. In Germany, no major figure on the left went over to National Socialism, nor did any prominent National Socialist have a left-wing background. Hitler did, however, become leader of a party that had both "socialist" and "worker" in its name. Like fascists elsewhere, the Nazis also borrowed techniques of mass mobilization developed on the left, while putting them to very different uses. This was an updated version of something that went back to unorthodox nineteenth-century leaders who used populist language to win mass support for authoritarian regimes. Emperor Napoleon III of France was one of them, which explains why a few heterodox Communists of the time, Leon Trotsky among them, pondered whether fascism was a form of "Bonapartism."[278]

Nowadays most people would agree that fascism was itself a kind of revolutionary movement, although what it revolutionized was politics, culture, and attitudes, not the economic basis of society, its property relations. That remains a fundamental difference between National Socialist Germany and the Soviet Union. There is another major difficulty in comparing the two dictatorships. It is the question of longevity. One regime endured for seventy-four years, the other for just twelve. One proved capable of change and reproduced itself politically under Lenin, Stalin, Malenkov, Khrushchev, Brezhnev, Andropov, Chernenko, and Gorbachev, the unwitting gravedigger of the system; the other knew only Hitler, unwitting gravedigger of the Third Reich in a quite different sense. Any worthwhile comparison should therefore restrict itself to the regimes presided over by Hitler and Stalin.

Nazi Germany and Stalinist Russia were both dictatorial one-party states. Both drew strength from their conviction that liberal democracy was a weak, outdated political system that lacked the energy to tackle the problems of the day. Both believed that they were creating a new kind of society, even a "new man." Both kept close control of the media and piped out propaganda relentlessly. Both produced conformists and opportunists: Soviet citizens learned to "speak Bolshevik," their German counterparts learned the jargon of "*Volksgemeinschaft.*" All true. Yet is there a single one of these common features that does not apply to Mussolini's Italy, too? A more promising comparison is that Nazi Germany and Stalinist Russia both emphasized youth, creating cults around martyrs such as Herbert Norkus (whose story was quickly memorialized in the book *Hitler Youth Quex* and a film version) and Pavel Morozov, who denounced his own father.[279] Nazi and Soviet propaganda both praised youthful informants (although these were actually very rare).[280] The fact that cults were developed around "martyrs" like these raises the question of whether Nazism and communism were "secular religions," with their own faiths and rituals. Perhaps. But the content of the rituals was very different. Nazi martyrs were always "blood witnesses," the flag always the "blood flag." This simply had no counterpart in Soviet rituals. There is another important difference: the case for a "secular religion" makes some sense when applied to the Soviet Union, a ruthlessly secularizing regime, but can it be plausibly applied to Nazi Germany, where much of the mythmaking and celebration of martyrs came with benefit of clergy? It was Protestant churchmen who celebrated Hitler as a "savior," a "political Luther"; and it was a Protestant pastor named Gerhard Meyer who described murdered storm troopers as modern martyrs who would follow in the footsteps of Jesus.[281]

Surely we can, at least, find points of comparison between Hitler and Stalin? There were obvious similarities between the two, the Führer (the leader) and the *Vozhd* (the guide). A cult of charismatic leadership was created around both. They were painted as heroic figures, yet ordinary men who came from the people. Both caused subordinates to try to divine their wishes so that they could comply, what one German official called "working towards the Führer."[282] Both were histrionic, arbitrary, and subject to bouts of rage, creating paranoia among all around them. Both ignored unwelcome truths and tried to distance themselves from the effects of unpopular policies. And both were murderous dictators. But there were also huge differences in their personal styles and forms of rule. Stalin was a committee man, a creature of the machine who had risen through the party secretariat, while Hitler hated bureaucracy, seeing it as a constraint. While Stalin stayed up until the early hours, reading policy papers and signing death warrants, Hitler stayed up until the early hours talking and talking, driving those present mad with the effort needed to keep their eyes propped open. ("He can be Führer as much as he likes, but he always repeats himself and bores his guests," complained Magda Goebbels.)[283] In short, Hitler's form of rule was more truly charismatic, Stalin's more bureaucratic. Stalin intervened more actively in decision making, Hitler remained more aloof. Stalin created a greater sense of insecurity among his entourage; Hitler cultivated quasi-feudal bonds of loyalty.

The two brutal dictators were unalike even in their brutality. The same goes for the regimes over which they presided. Both were terror states, which rested on coercion (although not on coercion alone), meaning a system of surveillance, repression, extrajudicial punishment, and an extensive system of camps to which opponents were consigned. The similarities extend to the singling out of so-called asocials and ethnic minorities for persecution.[284] Yet there were also big differences, even in the ways that terror and violence operated. (I am talking here about the years up to 1939.) Two major differences stand out.

The first is the scale of direct police surveillance. The NKVD in the

USSR employed twenty times more people than the Gestapo in proportion to overall population. The success of the Gestapo rested on the numerous denunciations it received from ordinary citizens. Nazi Germany was a much more self-policing society than the Soviet Union of the 1930s.[285] The second major difference is that it was much less dangerous to live in Hitler's Germany than in Stalin's Russia *if* you were an Aryan who kept your head down and caused no trouble. That applied with special force to party members in the two states. The Russian Revolution, like the French Revolution before it, devoured its own children. Bolsheviks found themselves accused of deviations, heresies, and plotting with the enemy. The victims included leaders like Lev Kamenev, Grigory Zinoviev, and Nikolai Bukharin. National Socialist Germany had nothing resembling this. There was no such thing as ideological orthodoxy; party members did not engage in self-criticism. There was just one purge in the Third Reich. It came in the Night of the Long Knives, which began in the early hours June 30, 1934, when SS and police interrupted a gathering of prominent storm troopers, arresting and later killing their leader, Ernst Röhm, and two hundred others in a series of extrajudicial executions. The victims included Gregor Strasser, a Nazi leader who had crossed Hitler in 1932, and former conservative opponents Gustav von Kahr and Kurt von Schleicher. This was a case of Hitler settling old scores, while doing what the army wanted by cutting the paramilitary SA down to size. It was a violent and cynical episode, but remained a singular brutal outlier. Leading Nazis such as Hans Frank allowed themselves a striking degree of freedom to argue with the Führer. A midlevel figure like environmentalist Alwin Seifert was often outspoken in his criticisms of official policy, but suffered no penalty.

None of this indulgence, it hardly needs to be said, was extended to those deemed to be outside the "people's community" by reason of ethnic identity or political behavior. They were persecuted purely on the basis of who they were. Germans who attempted resistance by forming underground cells, distributing oppositional newspapers printed abroad, or writing up graffiti were relatively quickly caught and severely punished. Those who survived and were released from prison or camp then had the choice of resuming resistance, keeping their heads down, or following those Social Democrats and Communists who left Germany when Hitler came to power. Around five thousand Social Democrats emigrated. Almost all of them stayed in Europe, "with their faces turned towards Germany," in the sorrowful words of Otto Wels, who had made the only speech in the Reichstag against Hitler's Enabling Act of March 1933. Wels went to Prague, the headquarters of the SPD in exile, then to Paris, where he died in 1939. Czechoslovakia was a favored destination of Social Democratic émigrés. Others found their way to France, Britain, the Netherlands, and Scandinavia. Twenty-year-old Herbert Frahm went to Norway, where he adopted the pseudonym under which he would later become famous: Willy Brandt. In 1937 he spent time as a journalist in Spain, covering the Civil War.

Spain became a gathering place for Germans from different parts of the left. Around five thousand Germans fought in the International Brigades to defend the Republic. Three-quarters of them were Communists. Communists left Germany in greater numbers than Social Democrats, some to the west, others to the USSR. Around four thousand German Communists went to the Soviet Union before the doors were closed at the end of 1935, because of suspicion about non-Russian immigrants. Most of them were victimized twice over, first by Hitler, then by Stalin. Caught up in the paranoia of the time, they were accused of Trotskyism, sabotage, and desertion from the battlefield of class struggle. Five of the sixteen defendants at the first Moscow show trial in August 1936 were German-Jewish émigrés. In all, 70 percent of German Communists in the USSR were arrested during the great purges. Most died as a result.[286] This closed a dark circle. Ultra-conservative Russians fleeing the revolution settled in Germany and helped to shape the far right there; later, German Communists fleeing the Nazi "national revolution" lost their lives at the hands of Stalin.

Social Democrats and Communists represented a tiny minority, no more than one in twenty-five, of the hundreds of thousands of people who fled from Hitler's Germany. The great majority of the émigrés were Jewish. Half a million Central European Jews escaped Hitler, 320,000 from Germany, another 180,000 from Austria and occupied Czechoslovakia. That meant three-fifths of German Jews got away, a somewhat higher proportion than from Austria, although a much lower one than from Bohemia and Moravia. They left in three waves: in 1933–34, after the Nuremberg Laws of 1935, and in 1938–39. The process of leaving and finding a place willing to accept you was never easy. The National Socialists wanted the Jews out of Germany but Jews were not allowed to take their assets with them. By 1938–39, desperate would-be émigrés had been reduced to destitution. That is one reason for the reluctance shown by liberal democracies like Britain, France, Denmark, and Switzerland to take in significant numbers. Opponents in those countries argued that Jewish competitors would "swamp" the professions, a fear reinforced by elite antisemitism. Widespread popular prejudice also discouraged political leaders from taking up the cause of Jewish refugees. These were all barriers to their acceptance. So was the belief in the democracies, not without foundation, that if they opened their doors wider it would only encourage right-wing regimes in Poland and Romania to enact harsher antisemitic legislation to drive out their own Jews.[287] Small wonder that Chaim Weizmann, president of the World Zionist Organization, said bitterly in 1936 that Jews faced a world "divided into places where they cannot live and places where they cannot enter."[288]

The Evian Conference of July 1938, convened by U.S. president Franklin D. Roosevelt to discuss the fate of European Jews, had few positive results. Some European democracies even tightened their rules in 1938 and 1939, just when Jews most needed a haven. In Britain, it is true, 50,000 of the 70,000 Jews admitted overall came in 1939. They included the 10,000 unaccompanied children of the *Kindertransport*. But Britain was adamant about keeping down the number of Jews allowed into the Palestine Mandate. The British dominions also proved exceptionally ungenerous. Just 754 Germans and 1100 European refugees in all were accepted in New Zealand in 1939 and not all were Jews—although applications had run to more than ten times that level.[289] Some 5000 German and Austrian émigrés went to British India. Professional and business networks led some refugees to receive offers from the Subcontinent, where their expertise, whether in medicine, science, or textile production, was valued. Sometimes nonprofessional qualities tipped the scales. Frederick Gordon Pearce, the British principal of a school in India, vouched for an Austrian dentist named Alfred Holloszytz and his family. He had known them for years through the Theosophical Society and had stayed at their home: "I can unhesitatingly testify to the fact that they are persons of good character and balanced views, who will not take part in any movement likely to cause embarrassment to the Government. They are not interested in politics."[290]

Shanghai was another destination for Central European Jews that might have seemed improbable a decade earlier; small communities of Jews from Baghdad and Russia were joined there after 1933 by 17,000 refugees.[291] Then there was Bolivia, one of the few Latin American countries that welcomed Jews in the 1930s and took in 20,000 refugees. The long-standing German tradition of mining played an indirect part in this, in the person of Moritz (Mauricio) Hochschild. A 1905 graduate of the Freiberg Mining Academy, Hochschild worked as a mining engineer and metals speculator around the world before setting up a company in Bolivia that established him as one of the country's tin barons. A foreign Jew himself, he identified with the refugees and personally brought several thousand to Bolivia. The government issued visas in the expectation that it would receive farmers, but the émigrés were urban bourgeois and most stayed in the cities. Efforts by Hochschild to fund a rural settlement failed. The "Hotel Bolivia," as it came to be called, was a largely urban affair.[292] That was not true in the Dominican Republic, one of the more remarkable instances of a Jewish safe haven. After the Evian Conference, Dominican dictator Rafael Trujillo offered to accept 100,000 refugees. He was looking to mend his reputation, especially with the United States, after the recent massacre of thousands of Haitians by the Dominican army. He also wanted to attract settlers and to "whiten" the country's population, the same motive that led earlier South American rulers to seek non-Jewish German immigrants. A Dominican settlement organization was established, nearly 500 Jews arrived, and a dairy and cattle-farming settlement was established, not without tensions between traumatized refugees and hosts. The project ended abruptly when the Americans began denying refugees the necessary transit visas.[293]

Cuba was an important staging post for Jews traveling to the United States. What this meant is vividly described in a memoir by the young Berliner Peter Fröhlich, who eventually joined relatives in America, where he anglicized his name and became a celebrated history professor at Yale. Peter Gay describes the painful uncertainties of the wait in Cuba and the suicides among some Jewish émigrés who were so close, but then denied entry. Washington placed many obstacles in the way of refugees. President Roosevelt's options were limited by the system of immigration quotas and by opposition within his own administration and from the Republican Party, where some referred to the New Deal as a "Jew Deal." Given the constraints, FDR achieved a great deal. In all, 120,000 German and Austrian Jews found refuge in the United States, plus another 100,000 from elsewhere in Europe.[294]

Many of the Jews who escaped from Central Europe would have been at risk for reasons other than their Jewishness—because of their political convictions or their identification with an intellectual tendency the Nazis deplored as "un-German." Albert Einstein is a good example. The non-Jews who became émigrés were also at risk for a variety of reasons. Some were prominent or active on the political left; others had reason to fear for their livelihoods, even if not their lives, because of their music, art, writing or filmmaking. Many had, in fact, lost their positions and means of earning a living before they emigrated. All had the course of their lives violently upended by Hitler. Leaving was never easy, which is why so many Jews delayed, sometimes for good, and fatally. It meant leaving family, friends, neighborhood, cultural habits of a lifetime, and not least the German language. Giving up speaking German, except at home or in the company of fellow émigrés, was painful. Professionally, moving to a place where people spoke a language other than German was probably least hard for those who had obviously transferable skills, like that blamelessly apolitical dentist in India, although even then there were issues of accreditation and acceptance. "What would a neurologist from Berlin do in Australia, what a lawyer from Frankfurt in Guatemala?" asked Thomas Mann's son Klaus.[295] Émigrés who created things in an international language, whether that language was architecture, theoretical physics, or music, still faced problems. Many Jewish émigré composers in Britain struggled mightily, not helped by a BBC blacklist of their work pressed on the broadcaster by the composer Ralph Vaughan Williams and others.[296]

Working in a foreign language and losing everyday touch with your own was especially hard on actors and writers, for whom language was everything. It is true that the "alchemy of exile"—learning to engage with another culture, to negotiate a new identity—could be a source of creativity. The philologist and literary critic Erich Auerbach, a Jewish war veteran forced out of his position at the University of Marburg, moved in 1936 to Istanbul. There he wrote one of the great works of twentieth-century literary criticism, *Mimesis*. Could Auerbach have developed his ideas on language and culture without his exile experience?[297] But a counterexample would be Heinrich Mann, the older brother of Thomas and a literary figure in his own right, who fled Germany for Czechoslovakia before eventually joining Thomas in Southern California, where his poor command of English made his stint as a Hollywood scriptwriter unsuccessful and deeply unhappy, not helped by his wife Nelly's suicide.[298]

Both sides of exile, the chutes and ladders, are apparent in the experiences of Bertolt Brecht. He left Germany in February 1933, moved to Denmark, and suffered the common problems of émigré writers—loss of books and papers, difficulty in getting published, frozen or irregular royalties. As a playwright he lost something else. The Nazi regime, he said, had proletarianized him: "Not only have they robbed me of my house, my fishpond and my car, but they've also stolen my stage and my audience."[299] He was stripped of his citizenship, had problems getting his plays mounted, and watched from a distance as friends died in the Moscow purges. Yet he wrote his greatest plays in these years (*Life of Galileo, Mother Courage and Her Children, The Good Person of Szechuan*) and some of his greatest verse. Then, forced to flee Denmark, he went as Heinrich Mann had done to Los Angeles, where he hated everything from the food and the gaudiness to the "shithouse" of Hollywood, which he blamed among other things for the drug addiction of his actor friend Peter Lorre.[300]

Southern California was the setting for much émigré unhappiness. There was drinking and despair, sometimes suicide, in the upscale neighborhoods where the luminaries lived: Santa Monica, Brentwood, Beverly Hills, Pacific Palisades. Yet what an extraordinary contribution the Germans and Austrians in Southern California made to American culture. They re-created a "Weimar on the Pacific."[301] The Frankfurt School philosophers Max Horkheimer and Theodor Adorno were there; so were the writers, not just Thomas Mann, but Lion Feuchtwanger, Franz Werfel, and Alfred Döblin, too. Life was difficult for many, however. Brecht visited Döblin and found him unemployed ("He has nothing and has nowhere to go").[302] Theater director Max Reinhardt had a big villa by the ocean, but the actors' academy he opened on Sunset Boulevard went bankrupt. The émigré film directors had a better time of it. G. W. Pabst, Fritz Lang, Otto Preminger, the Siodmak brothers, and Billy Wilder—all were there, an extraordinary influx of talent. The film industry drew Friedrich Hollaender, late of the Berlin cabaret scene, who wrote the music for several Wilder films, and Erich Korngold, who became the most accomplished classical composer to turn his hand to writing film scores. Los Angeles also became home to the composer Arnold Schönberg, the leading theorist of the Second Viennese School, and the conductor Otto Klemperer, who became musical director of the L.A. Philharmonic.[303]

Given past history, it is no surprise that music was an aspect of American life especially enriched by Central European émigrés. It was perhaps less predictable how great their influence would be beyond classical music. The writers of Hollywood film scores are just one example. Brecht's former collaborator, Kurt Weill, reinvented himself in the United States, writing more popular music that was long regarded as second-rate compared with his earlier work but has now been reevaluated. Then there was the huge contribution made to American jazz by two German-Jewish émigrés who had grown up together in Berlin. Alfred Lion (born Löw) left Germany for South America in 1933 and moved to New York City in 1938. There he encountered his old childhood friend Jacob Franz (Francis) Wolff. Both were devotees of jazz. In 1939, still in their early thirties, they founded Blue Note Records, which became one of the most important of all jazz labels. German musical culture passed into American life in another way: through teaching. Schoenberg, as he called himself after moving to the United States, taught at the University of Southern California and UCLA. His students and fellow émigrés taught at Vassar College and the New School for Social Research in New York and at Black Mountain College in North Carolina.

The New School (founded in 1919) and Black Mountain College (founded 1933) were self-consciously experimental. Black Mountain College was partly modeled on the Bauhaus. The New School established a "University in Exile" in 1933, renamed the Graduate Faculty of Political and Social Science the following year, in response to events in Germany. Both institutions benefited from the inflow of Central European émigrés for whom they provided a haven. The same was true of the Institute for Advanced Study (founded 1930) in Princeton, which became closely identified with its most famous member, Einstein, and other German physicists, as well as émigré historians. These were just three exceptional places of research and learning. But the impact of the refugees was felt across the country in every field, in the sciences (especially mathematics and physics), and in art history, literary criticism, history, philosophy, psychology, and social science. Major Bauhaus figures went to the United States and helped to shape architecture and design in their adoptive homeland. Josef and Anni Albers taught at Black Mountain College before Josef joined the Yale faculty in 1950. Walter Gropius became head of the Harvard Graduate School of Design, where he and ex-Bauhaus colleague Marcel Breuer taught an influential generation of postwar architects, including Philip Johnson and I. M. Pei. The creative and scholarly talent that crossed the Atlantic after 1933 was the largest, most concentrated example of cultural and intellectual transfer the world has ever seen.[304]

The United States took in the largest number of refugees, and benefited accordingly, but "Hitler's gift" was distributed around the globe. German émigrés added a new seriousness to the intellectual life of British universities, especially Oxford and Cambridge. They also needed it most, although it was surely disconcerting for undergraduates when the philosopher Ernst Cassirer delivered his earliest lectures at Oxford in German.[305] The much younger Tübingen-born brothers Ludwig and Gottfried Ehrenberg spoke perfect English by the time they made their mark on British academic life, one as a physicist and expert on higher education, under the anglicized name Lewis Elton, the other as the historian who transformed the study of Tudor history, Geoffrey Elton. No area of British cultural life was untouched.[306] André Deutsch, George Weidenfeld, and Tom Maschler challenged the gentlemanly family publishing houses. The German musical director Fritz Busch and the stage director Carl Ebert were the creative founders of the Glyndebourne Festival, which transformed the staging of opera in Britain; the Viennese musical impresario Rudolf Bing cofounded the Edinburgh Festival. Three-fourths of the Amadeus Quartet were Viennese Jews, who came as young men of sixteen after the *Anschluss* and met in internment camps. London provided a home for much of the Freud family. Lucian, grandson of Sigmund, later became a leading member of the "School of London" figurative painters together with Frank Auerbach, who arrived in Britain unaccompanied on the *Kindertransport*. Both were members of the so-called second generation, children or teenagers when they left Central Europe.[307] Hitler's was the gift that kept on giving.

The bounty was truly global. The Viennese philosopher Karl Popper was teaching in New Zealand when his most famous book, *The Open Society and Its Enemies*, appeared. Across the Tasman Sea, Felix Werder and George Dreyfus, Australia's leading modern composers, were German émigrés and Sydney's Musica Viva Society was founded by a refugee from Vienna.[308] Fritz Busch and Carl Ebert spread their talents beyond Glyndebourne. They had worked together in Buenos Aires; Busch later served as musical director with the Danish Radio Symphony Orchestra and the Stockholm Symphony, while Ebert, who lived in Turkey from 1940 to 1947, established the Ankara Conservatory. Several German cultural émigrés made their way to Majorca, Harry Kessler among them, although for most that Spanish island was a way station to somewhere else.[309] A cluster of political and cultural émigrés fetched up in Mexico.[310] The writer, photographer, and leftist at large Franz Pfemfert was one of them, a venturesome spirit who had nurtured the prewar work of expressionist artists and writers as editor of *Die Aktion* and was in his midfifties when Hitler came to power. He and his Russian wife fled to Czechoslovakia, then to France. They were interned, escaped, and managed to reach Lisbon, from where they traveled via New York to Mexico City. There they eked out a living with help from Trotsky's widow, because Pfemfert's wife had been Trotsky's translator. Despite the best efforts of Einstein, the Pfemferts were never allowed into the United States.[311]

Not all of the émigrés were successful, not all of them were innovators, not all of them were grateful to their host countries, and not all of them stayed when it became possible to return in 1945. As in the seventeenth century, however, and again after 1848—although this time on a vastly greater scale—émigrés from German-speaking Europe left a large imprint on the world. But their flight proved to be merely a prelude to the recasting of global history that occurred after 1939. The emigration was Hitler's unwitting gift. World War Two was something he willed, a conflict that became the most destructive in human history.

CHAPTER II

THE PIVOTAL DECADE: GERMANY AND GLOBAL HISTORY, 1939–1949

War and the Nazi New Order

ON THE MORNING OF SEPTEMBER 1, 1939, GERMAN TROOPS invaded Poland from north, south, and west. The previous day, Germans dressed in Polish uniforms had seized control of a border radio station and broadcast anti-German messages, a false-flag operation designed to provide a justification for war. Concentration camp inmates, killed by lethal injection and dressed in German uniforms, provided the "evidence" of Polish misdeeds. Hitler announced that Polish aggression left no other choice than to meet force with force. Those were the opening shots of the deadliest conflict in human history, which killed at least 70 million people. Among them were the victims of the Holocaust and a German occupation policy in eastern Europe that rested on the systematic starvation of civilian populations. The shifting fortunes of war then brought suffering home to German civilians, with saturation bombing and the flight or expulsion of millions of ethnic Germans from the east, who became part of a great army of refugees in a world of so-called displaced persons. The occupied and rubble-strewn Germany to which they fled was the outcome of Hitler's hubris. Instead of a Europe united under German control, he left a Germany divided under Allied control. In a moment of clarity shortly before his suicide in April 1945, Hitler recognized that Germany's defeat would leave just two great powers confronting each other.[1] His own policies brought that about.

In the late summer of 1939, Britain and France had given Poland guarantees of support. They declared war on Germany two days later, on September 3, but neither intervened militarily, still hoping that a compromise peace could be arranged. The Polish army was crushed by superior German force and the population subjugated by terror bombing. From Washington, President Roosevelt urged the combatants "under no circumstances to undertake the bombardment from the air of civilian populations or unfortified cities," to no avail.[2] On the tenth, Warsaw suffered seventeen raids in one day. Poland was effectively defeated before Soviet forces, by prior agreement with Germany, invaded from the east on September 17. Hostilities ended in early October and the smiling face of General Walther von Brauchitsch, the German commander in chief, appeared on the cover of *Time* magazine, above the bland caption "The campaign hung on him." In the course of the campaign, members of the Wehrmacht murdered uniformed POWs, attacked clearly marked first-aid stations, and took brutal reprisals against civilian resistance. German officers, with few exceptions, also turned a blind eye to the actions of SS special operation groups, or *Einsatzgruppen*, that worked behind the lines and deliberately targeted the Polish political and intellectual elite. They murdered as many as sixty thousand civilians, seven thousand Polish Jews among them. These killings were the shape of things to come.

The outbreak of war marked the end of a "twenty years' crisis" stretching back to the 1919 peace treaties.[3] Putting it like that underscores how one war grew out of the other. The first global conflict and its aftermath created more than enough combustible material to provoke a second. Before 1914 it was Austria-Hungary and Germany that contained unhappy minorities; after 1919 it was the new "successor states" in Central and eastern Europe that faced this problem. All contained sizable ethnic minorities, and they argued among themselves about where borders should be drawn. The Romanians were at odds with the Hungarians, the Hungarians with the Czechs, the Czechs with the Poles. Then there were the Germans, the largest of all the minority groups in interwar Europe. After the Treaty of Versailles, 13 million Germans in Europe lived outside Germany, half of them in Austria, the other half scattered across Italy, Poland, the Baltics, Romania, Czechoslovakia (where ethnic Germans outnumbered Slovaks), and the Yugoslav Kingdom.[4] By 1930, Germans made up close to a fourth of all the minority populations living in Central Europe, although they did not necessarily identify closely with one another—Germans in western Poland looked down on fellow Germans in eastern areas like Galicia as backward and "denationalized."[5] In theory, all enjoyed the protections offered to minorities by the League of Nations. In practice, they were treated better in some places than others—better in Latvia and Estonia than in Czechoslovakia, better in Czechoslovakia than Poland. It was their grievances, real and imagined, that Hitler used as a wedge issue in trying to undo Versailles.

The postwar settlements were potentially destabilizing in other ways. Despite its territorial losses, Germany was not divided and (thanks to the collapse of the empires to its east) actually loomed larger as a power across Central Europe than it did in 1871. At the same time, hostility to the Versailles Treaty helped put Hitler into power and his promise to revise its terms was widely popular. There was also sympathy for German claims in Britain. That was just one of the circumstances that favored Hitler's increasingly aggressive policies. The United States retreated into isolation. Britain and France were economically weakened by the war. They were preoccupied with preserving their overseas empires and faced public opposition to military expenditure. Both were willing to concede almost anything to avoid another conflict. The specter of aerial bombing was a novel source of dread. One British military strategist predicted 250,000 civilian deaths from bombing in the first week of war (in fact, there would be 40,000 British deaths during the entire Blitz). Anti-Bolshevism was crucial, too, all but excluding a favorable British and French response to Soviet diplomatic overtures. Stalin's purges of the Red Army made decision makers in the west believe, in any event, that the Soviets would bring little to the table. All this fueled their appeasement of Hitler.

Hitler exploited these weaknesses. He also benefited from the inability of the League of Nations to find an answer to the larger pattern of aggression in the 1930s by powers that eventually became Germany's allies—by Italy in Ethiopia, Japan in Manchuria—even as his own actions underscored the league's impotence. Germany withdrew from the league in October 1933. Two years later, Hitler publicly announced large-scale German rearmament—which was in fact already underway in direct breach of the Versailles Treaty. German plans caused the hasty formation of the so-called Stresa Front of Britain, France, and Italy. It lasted all of six months: in June 1935 the British signed a naval agreement with Germany, which infuriated France and Italy, and in October, Mussolini invaded Ethiopia, which infuriated Britain and France. That put an end to the Stresa Front. When Germany occupied the Rhineland the following spring there was no reaction. What unfolded next are among the most grimly familiar events in modern history. In March 1938, German soldiers marched into Austria, which became part of the Greater German Reich. Austrian apologists later pointed to this moment when they described their country as "the first victim of National Socialism," although the festive reception given to German soldiers suggests otherwise. Hitler turned his attention then to Czechoslovakia, playing up the grievances of the German minority. The pressure brought to bear on the regime in Prague, directly by Germany and indirectly by Britain and France, led to the notorious Munich agreement of September 1938, when the Czechs were browbeaten into giving up one-third of their territory and population and two-fifths of their industrial plant. The policy of using the western allies to help Germany revise the terms of Versailles was hardly novel—it had been Gustav Stresemann's policy at Locarno and would have been the policy of any German regime in the 1930s. But Hitler pursued it with singularly brazen aggression and, characteristically, was even disappointed when the British and French capitulated because this cheated him of the successful short war he craved.[6]

"Attractive new trips to the Ostmark and the Sudetengau," announced the *Berliner Illustrirte*, referring to the recently acquired Austrian and Czech lands. "Your travel agent will tell you everything you need to know."[7] The rolling hills of the Sudetenland were strategically significant as well as picturesque. Among the assets the Czechs were forced to concede at Munich were defensible borders. That mattered, because six months later Hitler took advantage of an internal conflict between Czechs and Slovaks to invade Czechoslovakia and destroy it as an independent state, establishing a German "protectorate" of Bohemia and Moravia and installing a satellite Slovak regime. Poland and Hungary jumped in to seize territory for themselves. The League of Nations characteristically did nothing. Britain and France also did nothing. Well, they did do something: alarmed by this evidence of Hitler's seemingly unlimited appetite, they issued formal guarantees of Polish and Romanian independence—although not of territorial integrity, which potentially opened the door to another "Munich." Stalin, concerned about German intentions and suspicious of the western democracies, proposed a Franco-British-Russian alliance to guarantee the territorial status quo in eastern Europe. The talks dragged on, with reluctance in the west and concern in Warsaw that any agreement would permit Soviet troops to cross Polish territory. Then came the bombshell that the two dictators had made common cause in the Nazi-Soviet Nonaggression

Pact of August 23, 1939. After communism and Nazism contracted their marriage of convenience, a British Foreign Office official remarked that all the "isms" had become "wasms."[8] You could rely on the Foreign Office for a piece of well-turned wit, although not necessarily for much else, as the Czechs and Poles would have been the first to agree. Nine days after the pact was signed, Germany invaded Poland.

Hitler was a gambler. His actions often horrified senior Wehrmacht officers, who shared his aims of rearming Germany and revising Versailles, but believed he was moving too quickly. There were also instances of tactical finesse on Hitler's part, moves that wrong-footed his adversaries, like a nonaggression pact with Poland in 1934 and the Anglo-German naval agreement. There was no *Stufenplan* ("stages plan"), no timetable for war. Most of the economic and armaments-related planning for a future war assumed that it would come in the early 1940s, not in 1939. But that there would be war, and that Germany would start it, was as close to a certainty as anything can be in history. The Third Reich was a regime geared toward war, especially after 1936. The share of public expenditure going to the armed forces rose from 4 percent in 1933 to 50 percent in 1938. By then a remarkable quarter of German national income was devoted to armaments.[9] Nazi economic policy also demonstrated aggressive intent: refusing to make foreign debt payments, imposing strict foreign-exchange controls, and ramping up production of *Ersatz* products like synthetic rubber and artificial petroleum, a policy designed to make Germany more self-sufficient. But even the country's powerful chemical industry could not make Germany close to self-sufficient in these strategically crucial products. At the same time, running a huge rearmament program while maintaining living standards, on top of the autarkic economic policy, created difficulties: mounting debt, shortage of foreign currency, and inflation. These were problems caused by an economy increasingly organized for war, and war itself was seen as the solution to them.

What kind of war? In an early scene in the 1980 film *Germany, Pale Mother* set in a newspaper office, a skeptical editor (a former socialist) puts his hands on a globe and says ruminatively: "There is Germany. I can cover it with my thumb." A contemptuous young Nazi in the office barks back: "We shall rule the world."[10] The Nazis talked a lot about "the world"—the philologist Victor Klemperer thought that it should be one of the entries in his great book on Nazi jargon.[11] German aims in 1939 were large. Hitler was not just a Versailles "revisionist," a hyperaggressive version of Stresemann.

Nazi Germany resembled Japan as a "system-defying" regime that challenged the international status quo. And Hitler was no mere *Grenzpolitiker*, concerned mainly with border revisions, but a *Raumpolitiker*, someone who thought in large-scale geopolitical terms about space—*Raum*.[12] Race and space went together in National Socialist war aims. Central and eastern Europe were to provide "living space," a place of settlement for the German "people without space," as well as food and raw materials. All of these were mentioned by the Führer in the two-hour monologue to which he subjected Germany's top military leaders on November 5, 1937. Hitler's military adjutant took minutes at the meeting and these have come to be named after him as the Hossbach memorandum. Historians have argued about whether or not Hitler's words were a specific war plan, a blueprint for aggression, but two things are certain. One is that his listeners were shocked by the wideranging Continental ambition, as Hitler knew they would be; the second is the emphasis he placed on the economic necessity of German dominance in Europe.[13] Hitler saw Germany competing in the world with the British empire and the increasingly powerful United States.[14] His speeches and private talks are littered with hostile and envious comparisons to both. A dominant position in the Eurasian landmass would allow Germany to pursue a truly global politics. The Z-Plan of January 1939 called for an eighthundred-vessel battle fleet. The Ministry of Aviation was already thinking about the construction of long-range bombers that could reach the United States.[15] But all of this would follow eventual victory over Russia.

The subjugation of Poland in 1939 was the first of what became an unbroken series of German military successes at the beginning of the war. But there was no immediate follow-up that fall. Instead, there was a period of military inactivity dubbed the "bore war" (by the British), the "funny war" (by the French), and the "phony war" (by the Americans). Hitler hoped that the British and French would abandon Poland and come to the negotiating table, his generals were cautious about the strength of the opposition in the west, and Germany was still building up its armaments. Several times Hitler came close to launching an offensive in the west, then called it off. The audacious plan eventually used was not even adopted until February 1940. The first German move came elsewhere, in April, a preemptive strike against Denmark and Norway designed to stop the Allies from mining northern waters to cut off German ore supplies from Scandinavia. It was followed by the shockingly quick success of German forces in May as they rolled over the Netherlands, Belgium, and France. The collapse of France within a few weeks was not foreseen by anyone, including Hitler. It made a mockery of the 20 billion francs spent on rearmament and building the Maginot Line.

Helmuth James von Moltke, grandnephew of the World War One Chief of General Staff and later a prominent figure in the resistance, was a German intelligence official at the time. In letters to his wife, Freya, during the winter of 1939–40 he wrote about "disaster postponed" and "disaster called off" each time Hitler changed his mind. Expecting German defeat and shocked by the French capitulation, Moltke blamed Commander in Chief Maurice Gamelin, although the rot and division in France went deeper. Whatever the causes, Moltke now had to contemplate the "triumph of evil" and the ugliness of civilian officials "drunk with victory."[16] Many of the 1.5 million French POWs were transported to Germany. Like the captured British soldiers who had been unable to evacuate from the beaches of Dunkirk, they were mostly treated correctly, under the 1929 Geneva Convention. The exception, and in some respects the missing link between German behavior in Poland and what was to come on the eastern front, was the massacre of between 1500 and 3000 West African French soldiers in May and June 1940. Remembered stories about the "Black horror on the Rhine" may have played a part in this, although there were more recent tirades from Joseph Goebbels about the "Black animals" in uniform ready to leap from the trees to attack German soldiers with their machetes.[17]

The speed and completeness of German success in the west was a propaganda triumph for Hitler, who proclaimed it "the most glorious victory of all time."[18] In Dresden Victor Klemperer, writing his diary as the world closed in on the Jews still living in Germany, recorded dolefully, "I fear Hitler's halo of invincibility."[19] German forces continued to carry all before them. After Mussolini launched a poorly conceived attack on Greece in October 1940, Germany took over when its Italian ally faltered; a Balkan campaign the following April subjugated Yugoslavia, where a blitzkrieg attack virtually destroyed Belgrade, then Greece. The sole fly in the ointment was the German failure to achieve air superiority during the Battle of Britain the previous summer, which meant no invasion and no knockout blow. But Germany did mount a threat to Britain with victories in Libya in the spring of 1941. Hitler planned to build on these successes and secure the entire Middle East. But first he turned to a campaign that had seemed inevitable ever since the Nazi-Soviet Pact was signed.

That June Hitler launched Operation Barbarossa against the Soviet

Union, still the principal ideological enemy of National Socialist Germany. This was the most important decision of the war, and arguably the pivotal moment in twentieth-century history. Hitler expected a quick victory. It would be a *Sandkastenspiel*, child's play. London and Washington also expected a German victory, given its overwhelming success in the west and the purge-weakened Red Army. At first, German forces swept triumphantly east, taking as many as three million POWs, but they became overstretched as summer turned to autumn. Motorized units could move so much more quickly than infantry divisions or the 625,000 horses that were used by Germany in the invasion (although they never appeared in newsreels that lingered on the mechanized and "modern").[20] Unexpectedly strong Soviet resistance, large German losses, and breakdowns of tanks and motorized vehicles blunted the initial onslaught, even as supply line problems mounted and the weather turned. By November 1941 the joke was making the rounds among the highly placed: "Eastern campaign extended by a month owing to its great success."[21] In the final months of the year, the Germans failed to take Moscow and the Red Army counterattacked. This marked the end of the first phase of unbroken German successes.[22] While German forces were trying unsuccessfully to capture Moscow, the attack on Pearl Harbor by Germany's ally Japan brought the Americans into the war. Hitler took this as an opportunity to declare war on the United States, in line with his repeatedly expressed view that Roosevelt was the "chosen one" of world Jewry and therefore an archenemy of the German *Volk*.[23] U.S. entry was another decisive moment in the Second World War, as it had been in the First, because of its unparalleled resources.

In 1942, however, Germany still enjoyed a dominant position across the European Continent, commanding a landmass larger than the United States. Even the neutrals bent toward Germany. Only General Franco's Spain wanted a German victory, but Portugal, Switzerland, Sweden, and Turkey all established mutually beneficial economic arrangements with the Nazis. Other countries fitted in different ways into what Hitler in 1941 called the German "New Order" in Europe. It was quite a patchwork quilt. In western Europe alone, we find a "model protectorate" (Denmark), civil administration by Reich commissioners (the Netherlands, Norway), military governments (northern France, Belgium), and a notionally independent satellite regime (Vichy France). Northern France and Belgium later came under Nazi civilian administration, while the Vichy regime ceased to enjoy even the title of a "free zone" after November 1942. Eastern Europe was likewise a patchwork, with its juxtaposition of satellite states, the Protectorate of Bohemia and Moravia, civilian-run Reich commissariats like Ukraine, and direct military occupation in Russia. Poland was a special case because its western territory was annexed by Germany and the rest placed under civilian administration as the General Government for the Occupied Polish Territories. These variations point to some of the different, often competing German agencies that exercised some responsibility for annexed, occupied, and Allied territory—the army, the Foreign Office, uniformed police (the "green battalions"), the myriad branches of the SS, and a host of other civilian administrators who included the gauleiters of annexed areas and officials working for Göring's Office for the Four-Year Plan, the Ministry for the Occupied Eastern Territories, and the Todt Organization, which undertook construction projects across Europe.

What to make of all this variety? One safe generalization is that the

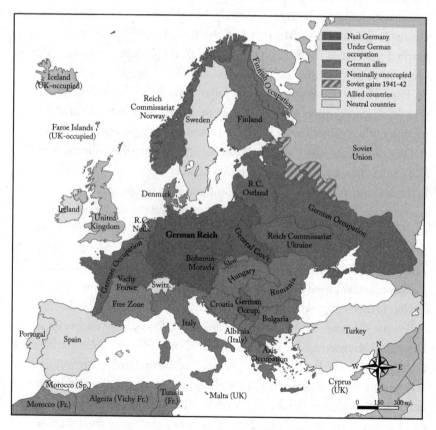

German-occupied Europe in 1941–42.

weight of German dominance was felt much more heavily in the east than in the west. That was true of those under both military and civilian administration, and it was true throughout the war. Another safe generalization is that German occupiers exercised a lighter touch when dealing with European populations that they considered more "Germanic" and therefore like themselves. German actions also depended on the degree of resistance they encountered. But perhaps the most useful way to view the larger pattern of variations is to imagine the New Order in Europe as a Nazi empire that faced the same set of choices faced by other empires. This idea has been around for a long time: it was proposed in Hannah Arendt's *The Origins of Totalitarianism* (1951). Anticolonial Black intellectuals such as Frantz Fanon and Aimé Césaire made the same point, arguing as Césaire did in his *Discourse on Colonialism* (1955) that the Germans had done to other Europeans what Europeans had previously done only to Arabs, Africans, and Indians. German-occupied Europe as empire has now become a standard view.[24] It accords with what German actors themselves said. Goebbels talked (although not for public consumption) about using "colonial methods." Governor-General Hans Frank referred to his fiefdom in German-occupied Poland as a "colony" and a "protectorate, a kind of Tunis."[25] Hitler often used analogies with the British empire. When high-ranking SA leaders met in Posen in 1944 for a workshop on the problems of the day, the lectures they listened to included "The Form of Rule in the Roman Empire" and "The Foundations of the British Empire."[26]

Empires come in many shapes and sizes, but all have four things in common. They look for local collaborators, they exploit resources, they harbor a sense of racial superiority over those they govern, and they are willing to use violence. The balance between these elements varies greatly from empire to empire. In the German New Order in Europe they were very much out of balance. The occupiers had more opportunities than most empires to rule through collaborators, but wasted them. Exploitation, racism, and violence were dominant.

There was no shortage of collaborators. Vidkun Quisling is the person whose name has become synonymous with collaboration, the local fascist who led Norway from 1942 to 1945, but he was hardly alone. Western European political elites, civil servants, and professionals cooperated with the occupying forces. That is why there were just two hundred Germans in occupied Paris and why the ratio of Germans occupiers to natives in Denmark was 1:43,000. Business owners also collaborated, sometimes enthusiastically.[27] In eastern Europe, local elites saw the opportunity to acquire more territory for the nation (as in Hungary and Bulgaria), even to acquire their own state (like the Slovaks and Croats) on the back of German victories. The reasons for collaboration were many. In 1939–1941 the Germans seemed unstoppable. What was the point of trying to resist, especially when there were benefits for not doing so? Why not jump on an express train? Call that opportunism, whether economic or political. But there was also an ideological dimension to collaboration. From France and Scandinavia to the Balkans, Europeans had their own homegrown fascisms. German military success gave figures such as Marcel Déat (Vichy France), Léon Degrelle (Belgium), and Ion Antonescu (Romania) positions of political influence they would never otherwise have enjoyed. For them, this was the payoff of transnational fascist networks. But ideological support for the Germans extended beyond the ranks of full-blown fascists. Just as the Nazis had found support in Germany from conservatives and authoritarians whose views overlapped with theirs, although not identical, so they now benefited from a European-wide disillusionment with liberal democracy, which many viewed as toothless in the face of the Great Depression and communism. After all, the slogan among French right wingers, who hated the 1930s Popular Front government of socialist Léon Blum, was "Better Hitler than Blum." That Blum was a Jew reinforced conservative hatred. Antisemitism was pervasive throughout the European right.

Efforts to present Germany as the cultural leader of a "new Europe" intensified during the war. In June 1940, Hitler gave an interview to an American journalist in which he talked about "Europe for the Europeans." The German Office of Information made this into the title of a booklet, seeing it as a winning slogan in trying to wrest the mantle of "cultural internationalism" from French hands.[28] At almost the same time, a chance find provided an institutional means of doing so. When German forces occupied Brussels in 1940 they seized all the records of the Union of International Associations, including membership material, file cards, punch cards, and documents about conferences. This material was shipped back to Germany (an official in the Ministry of Propaganda complained that it included "an excessive quantity of typewriters and office furniture"), where the German Cultural Conference Office, once responsible for obtaining foreign currency for German conference-goers, took over these networks and ran them on Germany's behalf.[29] In the same heady days of 1940–41, largely on Goebbels's initiative, a Union of National Journalists Organizations and a European Writers Union were established. After Operation Barbarossa, a European Youth Federation and a European Chess Federation were set up. Preparations were made to organize professional groups like lawyers. It was all part of an effort to win hearts and minds for Germany as the defender of "European" civilization against "Jewish" and "Asiatic" bolshevism. This found an audience.[30]

Anticommunism had a more immediate and visceral appeal in eastern Europe among peoples who had suffered under the Soviet regime, in Lithuania and Latvia, Belarus, and Ukraine. All were among the nationalities who fought with the Germans against Stalin. They were joined by allied field armies of Romanians, Hungarians, Italians, and Finns, as well as volunteer legions from occupied France, Belgium, and the Netherlands. These contingents were by no means token. Three million German soldiers were engaged in Operation Barbarossa; so were one million non-Germans. In later fighting on the eastern front, the non-German contingent often reached two million.[31] Germans had fought in the past for the Spanish and British empires, then in Napoleon's Grand Army; now others fought on behalf of the German empire.

Muslims formed one subgroup of them. We have long known about the links between Nazi Germany and Muslims in the Middle East who wanted to expel the British and French: politically minded junior army officers like the young Anwar el-Sadat in Egypt, politicians such as Iraqi Rashid Ali al-Gaylani who mounted an anti-British coup in April 1941, and religious leaders like the notorious Amin al-Husseini, Grand Mufti of Jerusalem.[32] But only recently have we learned the full picture of how Germany mobilized Muslims on the eastern front. There were as many as 285,000 in all, most of them Soviet citizens who resented their treatment and the treatment of Islam, like other religions, by Stalin. These soldiers were Turkestanis (the largest single group), Azerbaijanis, Tatars, Kalmyks, Georgians, and Ukrainians. The Germans respected their prayer times and dietary restrictions, distributed copies of the Qur'an, and posted Wehrmacht- and SS-trained mullahs to Muslim military units.[33]

Given the widespread hatred of the Soviet Union and the no less widespread antisemitism, and given the depth and breadth of the desire to collaborate with Germany, why did things go wrong? Why was there so much friction and tension, even with allies like Quisling and French collaborators like Pierre Laval, why the failure to secure the support of such an obvious anti-Soviet ally as Ukraine, why so much resistance to

German policies? One answer, true as far as it goes, is that the changing fortunes of war influenced how people behaved. If Germany looked unbeatable in 1939–1941, that became less true in the years that followed. Despite successes in North Africa and some advances in southern Russia, 1942 saw important German reverses. Its submarines started to lose the battle against the Atlantic convoys that kept Britain supplied. This mattered because of the increasing amount of American war matériel. By the end of 1942 the United States was producing three times more military goods than Germany. The Ford Motor Company produced a new B-24 bomber every sixty minutes. The air war started to come home to Germany with the British and U.S. bombing raids on German industries and cities, which intensified after February 1942. That June, the United States defeated Japan in the Battle of Midway, a pivotal moment in the war in the Pacific. For Germany itself, the late-1942 disaster of the Second Battle of El Alamein in North Africa was soon followed by the much greater disaster of Stalingrad, which ended in early February 1943 with a catastrophic defeat. The German Sixth Army was destroyed. Total losses on the Axis side—the dead, wounded, missing, and captured—amounted to 800,000. Shifting military fortunes made a real difference in the Middle East, where anti-imperialists in Egypt, Syria, Lebanon, and Iraq who had regarded the Germans as a lever with which to dislodge the British backed away as the United Kingdom reasserted control. In Europe, too, allies such as Hungary, Bulgaria, and Romania had already made territorial gains as a result of German success; it looked as if their future role was to be bled for soldiers who would die in future Stalingrads.

Beyond the calculus of success and failure, the Germans failed to take full advantage of the opportunities they had to work through collaborators. Successful empires find ways to include local interests and values, at least symbolically. Nazi Germany rarely did. True, it mobilized huge numbers of non-German soldiers into a "European" army, and even paid attention to the religious requirements of the Muslims among them, although foreign troops were generally less well trained and more poorly equipped, and were often looked down on. And, yes, there were cases—the Croats and Slovaks were the two most obvious, the Slovenes another—where the Germans were flexible about "race," partly for tactical reasons, partly because (in the lunatic Nazi world of racial hierarchies) some ethnic groups were deemed closer to the German master race than others.[34] SS leader Heinrich Himmler, for example, believed that in the Baltic the Estonians and

Latvians were more "Germanic" and less "Slavic" than the Lithuanians. In a similar way, German recruitment of Muslims and the alliance with Japan also owed something to ideological conviction that Islam was a "warrior faith" and Japan a martial culture.[35] But none of this negates the fact that the driving force of German imperialism in Europe was a race-based policy of settlement and exploitation of resources, carried through with exceptional violence. It was above all in eastern Europe that this violence was unleashed. That was where most of Europe's Jews lived in 1939 and the principal site of the Holocaust, as we shall see. Nazi violence also fell overwhelmingly on the Slav peoples—Poles, Ukrainians, and Russians—who died in the millions as a result of beatings, shootings, slave labor, medical neglect, and starvation. Violence led to resistance, in western as well as eastern Europe, and resistance led to brutal reprisals.

Hermann Göring called World War Two the "great racial war" and it was during the war that the imperatives of race and settlement came together.[36] Nazi policy aimed to turn eastern Europe into a German living space. Poland was where it all began. Hundreds of thousands of Poles were evicted from their farms on Polish land now incorporated into Germany, to make way for ethnic Germans repatriated to Germany from areas that became Soviet in 1939 under the Nazi-Soviet Pact. The Poles were either deported to the General Government or shipped off to the Reich as laborers. The numbers of those violently removed from their own property reached 80,000 by the end of 1939 and over half a million by 1941.[37] The round-ups and deportations amounted to an ethnic cleansing unlike anything inflicted on the region by German occupiers in World War One.[38] It was carried through with a mixture of bureaucratic obsessiveness and brutality under Himmler, who was entrusted by Hitler in 1939 with the task of "strengthening Germandom." The first group of future settlers who would provide the raw material of "Germanization" came from Estonia and Latvia. They arrived on ships belonging to Strength Through Joy in the main Baltic ports, where they were met by loudspeakers that blared out sentimental folk songs and uniformed members of the League of German Girls who distributed bread rolls. Like the ethnic Germans who followed overland from Lithuania, Bessarabia, and Bukovina, they were transferred to one of the fifteen hundred camps run by Himmler's auxiliary organization, the Ethnic German Liaison Office, where they were screened by physicians and "racial experts" to determine whether they were healthy and German enough to receive the color-coded card marked "O" (for *Ost*, meaning racially suitable for the east) or the one marked "A," which meant they were designated for labor in the "Old Reich." A third of a million were eventually settled in the newly reincorporated areas of the Gau Wartheland and the Gau Danzig–West Prussia. Sometimes they arrived to find unmade beds and the remains of a hurried meal still on the table, evidence of a hasty departure by the Polish owners; sometimes a Polish family was forcibly evicted as the German family arrived, and the same truck that had brought the newcomers carried the legal owners away.[39]

Poland was the testing ground for racially based resettlement policies, as it was to be for the evolution of Jewish policy. It was where the overt violence of the *Einsatzgruppen*, which helped in forcibly dispossessing Polish peasants, joined hands with the institutional violence of the bureaucrats and "experts." The racial screening of ethnic Germans from Lithuania and Bessarabia took place alongside similar efforts to identify "racially valuable" Poles, "human material" that might be salvaged for the master race, the *Herrenvolk*, by Germanization. These were efforts that went on across Europe, from Prague to Odessa.[40] Poland was also where large numbers of Germans not in uniform—or not in Wehrmacht uniform—had their first experience of what came to be called the *Ostrausch*, the "intoxication" or "rush" of the east. There were unmistakable elements of a colonial mind-set in this. The intoxication flowed from a sense of belonging to a master race, engaged in a "civilizing mission" that involved sacrifice but brought rewards. That was the promise of the east.[41] Deployment there was an adventure; it also caused a frisson of fear, because this was, after all, the "wild east."[42] Eventually some thirty thousand German civilians went to the east. Most were men, often young men—administrative officials, planners, engineers, demographers, physicians—promoted (like colonial officials everywhere) to positions of responsibility beyond what they could have expected at home. But thousands of them were women, again mostly young, and again often able to exercise a degree of authority that contrasts sharply with our idea of women in the Third Reich. They were leaders from the League of German Girls, student volunteers, teachers and school assistants, members of the National Socialist People's Welfare Organization and the Women's Labor Service. Among their tasks was helping to "resettle" ethnic German families on former Polish property and teach them the "German way of housekeeping," meaning "order culture, hygiene—the elements of Germandom."[43]

German ambitions to create living space in the east expanded in scope, driven in part by competition among different organizations. Hans Frank pushed back against SS plans to use his domain as a dumping ground for "racially undesirable" elements. After the German victories in the west, he obtained Hitler's permission to develop the General Government (which now lost the phrase "for the Occupied Polish Territories" from its title) as German settlement land. It would no longer be "a dung hill into which you could sweep and shove all the filth of the Reich."[44] The Vistula Valley would one day be as German as the Rhine Valley—more so, in fact, because won by heroic settler deeds. Frank told members of the Hitler Youth and League of German Girls in June 1942 that they would one day form the "strong roots of a new German living space."[45] Frank then turned his attention to an eastward expansion of the General Government into the Pripet marshes of southern Belarus and northern Ukraine. Hansjulius Schepers, the director of the Office of Regional Planning at age thirty-two, prepared the grandiose plans for reclamation and German settlement. He was joined by another young tyro who had just arrived in Cracow. Helmut Meinhold was twenty-eight, already a senior economic planner, and enthusiastic about contributing to something "extraordinarily exciting."[46]

The east became a dreamland, a space onto which utopian fantasies of Germanization were projected.[47] The very idea of "space" became a talisman. Walter Christaller, a German geographer but an outsider in his discipline, wrote harshly about the seductive power of the "fashionable" word *Raum*: "People have become too easily satisfied with slogans about the power that is to be found in a space, or that emanates from it, about the narrowness of space, the domination of space, the magic of space."[48] German designs on the east always bore traces of that magical thinking. They also carried the implicit assumption that these were empty spaces. Helmut Meinhold referred to the east as a "tabula rasa." So did a young landscape planner named Erhard Mäding. Another of his colleagues, the village planner Herbert Frank, wrote about "virgin land."[49] The Slav peoples who actually lived in these "empty spaces" were routinely dismissed by German observers of every kind as incompetent tillers of the soil, or else as primitive hunter-gatherers. The attitude is familiar from other empires, where Indigenous peoples were simply thought out of the picture, leaving the land there for the taking: *terra nullius*. It was an attitude that always boded ill for the Indigenous.

Germans sometimes compared their dreams of eastward expansion with American westward expansion. This started at the top. Hitler was a critic of pre-1914 German overseas imperialism and emphasized instead the importance of Continental expansion, American-style. In his unpublished *Second Book* of 1928, he expressed admiration for the sturdy white settlers of good racial stock (often "Nordic" stock) subjugating the Indigenous population and settling the land. Here and elsewhere he made it plain that the east was to be Germany's frontier. The American example was a recurring theme of his speeches and table talk. "The Volga must be our Mississippi," he said in the autumn of 1941. Europe, not America, would become the land of unlimited opportunities, he said on another occasion. Then there was the time when, after ranting about the "mongrelized" culture of the United States, he observed: "But the Americans have one thing that is becoming lost to us, a feeling for the wide open spaces. Hence our longing to extend our space."[50]

More darkly, Hitler referred to those who would pay the price of the moving frontier, telling a small circle at his headquarters that he had never heard of a German eating a loaf of bread and worrying about whether the land that grew the grain had been conquered by force: "We also eat Canadian wheat and don't think about the Indians." Then he spelled out the message more directly: "There is only one task: To set about the Germanization of the land by bringing in Germans and to regard the indigenous inhabitants as Indians."[51] Hitler was using a language that went back at least to the eighteenth century, when Frederick the Great likened the "slovenly Polish trash" of newly acquired West Prussia to Iroquois. It became a favorite theme of German writers. One of them argued that the Poles, like the "American redskins," were doomed to extinction as they yielded to a superior civilization.[52] But Hitler was not the only one who invoked these comparisons with the American west. Hans Frank did the same. Heinrich Himmler wrote rhapsodically about a future time when German settlers had turned the arid lands of the east into "a paradise, a European California."[53]

The project of Germanizing the east was filled with talk of hardy pioneers. Goebbels filmed the Volhynian Germans returning to the Reich in their horse-drawn wagons to settle former Polish land. But the words and images were deceptive. Most ethnic Germans returned by train, not wagon, and they hardly resembled sturdy settlers as they were shuttled through the reception camps wearing numbered tags, examined, sorted, and (if approved) handed the blue-colored documents marked "O" assigning them to the east, where they were shipped to their newly assigned farms by truck, provided with equipment (plus a picture of the Führer and a copy of *Mein Kampf*) by the SS, then found their housekeeping and child-rearing monitored by young women from the Settlement Research Unit. They were treated more like laboratory rats, deprived at every step of the one quality that was central to what both the frontier myth and traditional advocates of "inner colonization" had always claimed was essential: self-reliance.[54] In fact, Nazi rhetoric about the east was strongly flavored with technocratic language. That is nowhere more evident than in the General Plan for the East, drawn up under the auspices of the Reich Security Head Office by Konrad Meyer, a former professor of regional planning in Berlin.[55] First drafted in mid-1940, the plan went through several versions before the fourth and final one in October 1942. After the summer of 1941, Jews no longer featured in it because a separate policy emerged for a "Final Solution" to the "Jewish question."

Deputy leader of the Nazi Party Rudolf Hess and Heinrich Himmler examine a model of future German settlements in the east. The display in March 1941, mounted by the SS Ethnic German Liaison Office, was part of the General Plan for the East. Hess is at the far end; Himmler, wearing glasses, is immediately to his left.

The General Plan for the East envisioned a future Germanized eastern Europe that stretched all the way to the Urals and the Crimea, settled by different groups: returning ethnic Germans, Germans from the Old Reich, and "Germanic" peoples from Scandinavia and the Netherlands. The number of settlers was expected to approach 3.5 million over a thirty-year period—the total was listed as a maniacally precise 3,345,805. They would settle land from which most of the original inhabitants had been deported. The planners foresaw the expulsion of two-thirds or more of Poles, Belorussians, and Ukrainians. Himmler called this *Platzschaffung*, "making room," a rare break with the usual euphemisms. The General Plan was littered with jargon words favored by Nazi technocrats, like *Aufbau* (construction) and *Gestaltung* (shaping).[56] The repeated emphasis on "total planning" points to the scale of German ambitions.[57] The proposals foresaw a series of futuristic geometrical settlements, surrounded by concentric rings of villages and all linked by new rail networks and *Autobahnen*. That was the macro-level planning, which included large-scale maps covered with the dynamic-looking arrows the Nazis loved. The planners also dwelled on the details. The main settlements would be fortified but include leisure centers and cinemas. The blueprints covered everything from the layout of villages and the angles at which tree were to be planted to the labor-saving style of farmhouse kitchens and the design of teapots.[58] An SS "settlement expert" named Friedrich Kann suggested that the expansion of German "living space" in the east presented opportunities "of a magnitude never before seen in history."[59]

This is the language of twentieth-century empire. If the violence of the German east recalls what had been done to Nama and Herero in Southwest Africa, the futuristic planning zeal resembles what German colonizers had begun in Qingdao and Douala. Nazi planners in the east were mindful of what other nations were doing. They were inclined to see the British and French as too beholden to old-style liberal economics. Japanese imperialism in Korea was more attractive. But there was another, more recent imperial model that attracted German planners. That was the Italian colonization in Libya during the 1930s. One German settlement expert wrote admiringly about Italy's "experiments" as a likely model for "the enormous colonization tasks facing us in the Eastern territories, and perhaps one day in the African colonies."[60] Just as Italian success in draining the Pontine marshes southeast of Rome was cited by German engineers who promoted reclamation projects in eastern Europe, Italian colonization and settlement policies in Libya attracted keen German interest.[61] Himmler went on a fact-finding tour of *Africa italiana* and returned home impressed.[62]

Few of the elaborate plans left the drawing board because the era of German control was so short. But it lasted long enough for some familiar characteristics of empire to become visible—long enough for people to be posted around the empire from one place to another, and long enough for the emergence of residential racial segregation in cities like Warsaw and

Minsk, which reflected the German conviction that they were superior to Slav subject peoples.[63] In the racial hierarchy, those Slavs who were not selected to be Germanized were destined to be no more than slaves, or helot peoples, where they had not died of starvation or been deported to some indeterminate point "in the east." Germans were the masters. That brought with it opportunities for misbehavior. That, too, was a classic colonial situation. Just as there were figures like Rudolf Kiepert from the Berlin branch of the Ethnic German Liaison Office, who was relieved of his duties for financial and sexual improprieties, so there were corrupt district administrators in the east who had to be sent home in disgrace.[64] Wehrmacht officers called them "golden pheasants" because of the way they strutted around.[65] The arrogance comes through clearly in the words of SS-*Obersturmführer* Karl Kretschmer, writing to his wife in October 1942 from Kursk about their seven-year-old daughter. Dagi, he wrote, now had to learn to sit properly at table and not put her elbows on it. "When she's grown up she will move around the world a lot as a German girl. Everyone will be watching and learning from her. Foreigners immediately notice any weaknesses and take advantage. That is why we have to make a big effort with ourselves and always take care. *After all, fate permitting we Germans are the people of the future.*"[66]

The table on which Dagi was not supposed to rest her elbows would have a cornucopia of food on it. Germans in occupied Europe and Germans at home managed to eat well through most of the war. One German girl remembered her soldier father returning from Paris on leave with almonds, pears, pâté, and carrots wrapped in ham.[67] Domestic consumption actually rose between 1940 and 1944. Food rationing was introduced early in the war, but rations remained generous until near the end. This was by design. Hitler was determined that food shortages and poor morale on the home front would not, for a second time, undermine German military success. Goebbels boasted about the "fully laden breakfast, lunch and dinner table."[68] But the food available in Germany came from occupied Europe. In 1942, at a time when supplies briefly dwindled, Göring summoned a group of Reich commissars and military commanders to Berlin where he ranted about the occupied territories: "I see people there stuffed full of food while our own people are starving." This ludicrously false account was the prelude to a demand that his listeners extract more from their territories: "I could not care less if you tell me your people are collapsing from hunger. They can do that by all means so long as no German collapses from hunger."[69]

Göring went on to pour abuse on western European countries. These were crucial suppliers of food to Germany.

It was, above all, in eastern Europe that the local population starved so that Germans could eat. Readers of Olivia Manning's *The Balkan Trilogy* about the British couple Guy and Harriet Pringle, who arrive in Bucharest in September 1939, will remember that a recurrent, almost obsessive theme in those books is how food of every kind disappears bit by bit as it is siphoned off to Germany.[70] And Romania was an ally! Some of the richest Polish farmlands were seized and incorporated into Germany. The gauleiter Arthur Greiser said that the task of his newly created Gau Wartheland was to produce "grain, grain, and more grain."[71] In the General Government, where the food ration in early 1940 was 2600 calories for Germans and 609 for Poles, Governor-General Hans Frank made his priorities quite clear: "I shall feed these Poles what is left over and what we can spare."[72] The General Government produced food surpluses by starving the local population. The thirty-eight volumes of Frank's work diaries are littered with boasts about the productive output of his domain—the 600,000 tons of grain and 300 million eggs sent to the Reich in one year, the thousands of tons of fats, vegetables, and other provisions delivered to the Wehrmacht.[73]

With the invasion of the USSR in 1941, deliberately starving people became policy. This was built into German war planning from the time of Operation Barbarossa. The "hunger plan" was devised by Herbert Backe, state secretary for food and agriculture in Göring's Office for the Four-Year-Plan, and by General Georg Thomas in the Economics and Armaments Office of the Wehrmacht. Hitler and army leaders signed off on a plan that foresaw mass starvation of Slav peoples in Belarus, Ukraine, and other parts of the western Soviet Union. Military occupation authorities received instructions stating that "many tens of millions of people in this area will become surplus to requirements and will die or will be forced to emigrate to Siberia." They were not to be saved from starvation, because that food was needed in Germany. It was widely accepted by planners that 20 to 30 million people would die. That was the number used by both Göring and Himmler. Officials from Göring's economic empire, the SS, and Alfred Rosenberg's Ministry for the Occupied Eastern Territories all helped to administer the plan. But the Wehrmacht was chiefly responsible for implementing this human-induced famine. It was achieved by sealing off Soviet cities from their agricultural hinterlands and food supply. The siege of Leningrad, where 100,000 civilians died every month during the winter of 1941–42, is the most notorious example of the hunger plan in operation, but the same effect was produced everywhere. In the Ukrainian city of Kharkov, 80,000 died during the German occupation. As much as half the Soviet population suffered some form of starvation under German occupation. The High Command, generals in the field, and army quartermasters were complicit in this policy of starving civilians, just as the Wehrmacht was responsible for the deaths through starvation, as well as grossly inadequate shelter and medical treatment, of at least three million Soviet POWs.[74]

At the November 1937 meeting recorded in the Hossbach memorandum, Hitler had invoked "the security of our food situation," along with German settlement land, as two objectives of European conquest. He also spoke at length about a third. "Areas producing raw materials," he argued, "can be more usefully sought in Europe, in immediate proximity to the Reich, than overseas.[75] As it turned out, in the Second World War as in the First, Germany was dependent on the resources of Europe because it was cut off from global markets. This became an acute problem in the case of energy, especially oil. If, in Lord Curzon's words, the Allies had "floated to victory on a wave of oil" in 1914–1918, how much more important was oil as the lubricant of military success in the mid-twentieth century.[76] But Hitler's Europe never had enough. The overwhelming victories in 1940 brought a windfall as Germany became temporarily flush with oil and petroleum seized from refineries and storage tanks in France and the Netherlands. In the long run, however, the expansion of the German Continental empire simply added new countries that, like Germany itself, were not self-sufficient in oil. One-sided agreements forced on Romania, then the world's fourth-largest oil producer, gave Germany access to most of what came from the wells there, but energy security remained elusive. Specialized units positioned behind the front moved in quickly to seize control of Poland's Galician oil fields and Estonian shale deposits. Despite all this, and despite the chemical industry's synthetic fuels, oil and gasoline shortfalls continued. They led one general to suggest, remarkably enough, "demotorization" of the Wehrmacht.[77] That was in May 1941, a month before Operation Barbarossa. Oil was one of the reasons for attacking the USSR. The oil fields of the Caucasus were a major prize, and there was hope that military success there could be coupled with seizure of Middle Eastern oil fields under British control. In the event, both objectives failed, but they illustrate the dilemma that drove Hitler's Germany forward: it fought to lay its hands on oil, because it needed oil in order to fight.[78]

Germany also found itself cut off from global markets in raw materials. It compensated by exploiting what it controlled to the maximum. German occupiers plundered Europe on a gargantuan scale. They took livestock like horses, and timber, copper, tin, manganese, bauxite, and refined uranium (this last from Belgium, a product of the Congo). They also seized finished goods—weapons and ammunition, vehicles, locomotives, freight cars, and machine tools. This is not to mention the wholesale looting of artworks, furniture, carpets, fine clothing, jewelry, vintage wines, and the like. By one calculation, Germans took goods to the value of 154 billion francs from France between 1940 and 1944.[79] The German occupiers also struck up agreements with compliant French business leaders, as they did in Belgium and the Netherlands. In Denmark the German hand was lighter. Business went on without a major break and the occupiers contented themselves with skimming off a share of Danish industrial output. It was in eastern Europe, predictably, that the extraction of resources resembled violent plunder. Where there was production or construction in occupied territory, much of it was done by slave labor in camps established by the Wehrmacht, cooperating with the security forces and civilian bodies like the Todt Organization, or within the metastasizing system of SS labor camps.

The SS camps were spread across the occupied east even as they multiplied within the Reich itself. They contained more than 700,000 inmates by early 1945, housed in main camps and an archipelago of satellite camps.[80] Neuengamme in northern Germany alone had eighty-five of these.[81] The slave workers behind barbed wire formed just one part of a huge army of foreign labor in Germany. Others were POWs and civilian workers from across Europe who had volunteered, responding to economic rather than physical coercion. "Europe is at work in Germany," boasted a propaganda booklet in 1943.[82] Before the war began there had been about half a million foreign workers in Germany, mainly Czechs from the protectorate and Polish seasonal laborers, plus a few thousand Italians working in construction. After the fall of Poland in 1939, Polish workers were press-ganged to work in the Reich, mainly in agriculture, 700,000 of them by May 1940. They were required to wear a badge marked "P" (this was before Jews in Germany were forced to wear the yellow star), subject to curfews, and prohibited from using public baths or trains, even from riding bicycles. These were the first instances of eastern workers in Germany being treated as racially marked slaves. Workers from Belgium and France (1.3 million by 1944) were better treated, not just the first wave of volunteers, but those later forced to work in Germany. Worst treated of all were the Russians, Ukrainians, and Belorussians rounded up in the east and shipped off to the Reich as forced laborers, where they had to wear a badge showing that they were from the east. Between April and December 1942, 1.3 million Soviet citizens were deported to Germany, an average of 40,000 a week. Many were housed in specially built camps, of which there were tens of thousands. Others were placed in barracks, schools, farm outbuildings, and private homes. The violent round-ups that plucked them up and dropped them in Germany were orchestrated by a former gauleiter, Fritz Sauckel, appointed by Hitler in March 1942 as general plenipotentiary for labor deployment. Not including the SS concentration camp population, by 1945 there were more than 7.5 million foreign workers in the Reich, three-quarters of them civilians, the other quarter POWs. They made up a fourth of the labor force.[83]

The paradox of wartime Germany is that the racially pure "people's community" rested on the involuntary labor of millions of foreigners, mainly Slavs. They were essential for agriculture and transportation. The wartime slogan of the German railroad was "Wheels must turn for victory." But those wheels would not have turned without nearly 200,000 Russians who serviced the trains (they were issued with illustrated directions with terms like "oil can" translated into Russian).[84] In the modestly sized north German town of Oldenburg, close to the Dutch border, 350 foreign workers were employed by the railroad and its workshop.[85] The involuntary labor force of foreigners worked for some of the leading firms that were crucial to the war effort, such as IG-Farben, Siemens, and Krupp. Four out of ten workers in the armaments industry were foreigners. When the Royal Air Force launched its "dambusters" raid in May 1943, which breached two large dams in the Ruhr and destroyed the industrial plant below them, the floodwaters took 1284 human lives. More than 700 of them were Russian and Ukrainian women who worked as slave labor in local munitions works.[86]

What impact did the presence of millions of foreigners have on the German population? They would have been hard to avoid, these columns of ill-fed, ill-clothed people shuffling from labor camps or barracks to factories. A town like Osnabrück, where few non-Germans lived before the war, now had 12,000 of them speaking nineteen different languages.[87] The evidence suggests that most Germans soon came to take foreign laborers for granted as part of the backdrop of life, without seeing them as fellow humans. Foreigners were the object of resentment, blamed for domestic disruptions and black market activity.[88] But there were also Germans who offered workplace solidarity and assistance: gifts of bread and cigarettes, help with directions or mailing letters home. In some cases foreign workers were unavoidably present in the everyday lives of Germans. That was true of the 100,000 young women, half of them from the USSR, who were assigned as servants and nannies to large German families. Many more foreigners, especially Poles and French, worked in agriculture. Forced laborers assigned to farms in rural areas generally fared better than those who worked anonymously in large factories. Studies of southern areas suggest that local Catholic farmers got on better with their fellow Catholic Polish laborers than they did with German evacuees from the alien north.[89] The enforcement of "racial policy" was more relaxed, and denunciations were fewer in number. The security forces were always complaining about farmers' lack of racial consciousness.

The most charged relationships between Germans and non-Germans were sexual, usually between German women and foreign men, which were regarded by Nazi authorities as a threat to German "blood purity." There may have been a prurient tendency on the part of the security services to exaggerate "the immoral behavior of German women," as a 1944 report called it. Still, many cases did come before the courts, sometimes following denunciations. Between October 1941 and May 1945, the district court in Oldenburg heard seventy-three cases of forbidden relations.[90] The postwar German writer Rolf Hochhuth depicted such a relationship in his book *A German Love Story*. A "documentary novel" based on a true story, it reconstructs the development of a love affair between a south German shopkeeper's wife, Pauline, and her Polish worker, Stani, a POW, which leads eventually to Stani's execution and Pauline's imprisonment.[91]

The affair between Pauline and Stani was the most intimate kind of encounter across national lines. By forcing millions of men and women from all over Europe to work in the Reich, German authorities created myriad opportunities for transnational encounters, good, bad, and ugly. There were obvious differences inside the labor camps between nationalities, generations, and occupational groups. Tensions were inevitable, and heightened by the wide variations between inmates when it came to questions like whether they could go out when free from work, or only at prescribed times, or only under guard, whether they were allowed to travel on public transport, or buy a beer. We rightly see the forced laborers in Germany mainly as victims, because their lives were regulated, often enough ruined, and sometimes ended by German fiat. But there was also violence and predatory behavior in the camps. Alongside the overwork, meager food, poor medical provision, and other indignities of life in the labor camps was the fact that the men and women forced to live there had no choice about their neighbors.

Opportunities to resist the harsh German system of control were limited. One possibility was to work more slowly, the resort of workers everywhere since the beginning of industrial capitalism, including German workers after 1933, when it remained their only resort. But this was potentially dangerous because "sabotage" was a capital offense. A widespread form of nonconformist behavior was engaging in the system of barter and black market exchange that developed in the labor camps, with the help of corrupt guards. This was an important means of supplementing the food rations. Trying to escape was a more active response. The number of escape attempts by foreign workers more than doubled between February and December 1943, to 46,000. It was in the same period, beginning in the winter of 1942–43 and the Battle of Stalingrad, that organized groups began to form in camps, especially among laborers from the Soviet Union, organizing food, helping the sick, and providing escape documents.[92]

Did they form any kind of collectivity? The anti-Nazi journalist Ursula von Kardorff kept a wartime diary. At the end of November 1944, she recorded her impressions of foreign laborers gathered at the Friedrichstrasse Station in Berlin, which reminded her of Shanghai:

> Ragged picturesque figures in ragged jackets with the high cheekbones of the Slavs, among them blond Danes and Norwegians, flirtatiously made-up Frenchwomen, Poles with looks of hatred, pale, freezing Italians—a mix of peoples such as probably never before seen in a German city. It's almost exclusively foreigners down there, you hardly hear German spoken.

Kardorff, whose account has its own stereotypes, notes that they do not look "depressed" but are talking loudly, singing, and bartering, "living by their own laws." They seem to know one another. Then comes the payoff: "There are twelve million foreign laborers in Germany. An army by itself. Some call it the Trojan Horse of the present war."[93]

Kardorff was wrong. The real "army" of foreigners formed back home in the countries from which the slave laborers came. Its name was armed resistance and eastern Europe was its epicenter. The growing resistance and the brutal German response continued the cycle of violence that began in Poland. German brutality acquired a new intensity with Operation Barbarossa. Hitler told a gathering of 250 generals in March 1941 that the impending invasion would unleash a "war of extermination."[94] The Wehrmacht played its full part in making that a reality. Orders that May and June authorized military leaders to kill or hand over to the SS the political commissars attached to the Red Army and to kill guerrillas and exact collective punishment against civilians believed to support them.[95] The maltreatment of Soviet POWs was of a piece with this brutal disregard for human life. Sometimes the German army did not even bother to take prisoners, simply executing them. The war diary of the Thirty-Fifth Infantry Division noted without comment on June 30, 1941, that "regarding the prisoner counts of the last few days, it can be assumed that the enemy body counts far outnumber them, because the troops have mostly taken no prisoners due to their bitterness over their own losses, the butchering of their own wounded, and the insidious tactics of the enemy."[96] In four days of combat the division took exactly seven prisoners.

As Barbarossa stalled, Wehrmacht conduct became even more ruthless. Russians were not alone in feeling its force. Studies of German army conduct have demonstrated a similar pattern across eastern and southeastern Europe, in Belarus, Ukraine, Serbia, and Greece.[97] In response to partisan attacks, an order of October 1941 established that one hundred civilians should be killed for every German soldier. Tens of thousands of hostages were killed in Serbia alone. General Walter Hinghofer, who commanded the 342nd Infantry Division, ordered twenty-three hundred civilians killed as a reprisal for eight German soldiers, an orgy of killing that caused his men to run out of hostages to shoot.[98]

These were colonial levels of violence, even if there is no good reason to argue that there was any direct transfer or carryover from German military operations in prewar Southwest Africa. A more plausible connection between German colonies and the violence of the 1940s is the resentment in the Wehrmacht, as in the nation at large, about the sudden, humiliating decolonization forced on the country at Versailles—plus the fact that the loss deprived Germany of a colonial space beyond the home country where violence could be "discharged."[99] But Germany's true colonial space, anyway, was eastern Europe, and a sufficient reason for the extreme violence of war in the east can be found in long-standing anti-Slav sentiment, sharpened by the National Socialists' relentless emphasis on the "Judeo-Bolshevik" enemy. Wehrmacht officers attended lecture and summer school courses after 1933 that instructed them on subjects like "Eastern Space" and "Racial and Population Policy."[100] The German death toll on the eastern front also brought promotion to a younger generation of more Nazified officers.[101] But senior Wehrmacht figures who did not hold strongly National Socialist views were also complicit. A study of twenty-five generals who commanded an army group or an army, who therefore stood between Hitler and the senior Wehrmacht leadership and field commanders, demonstrated their willingness to carry out criminal orders in the name of "military utility."[102]

Partisans induced a particularly intense soldierly rage. An aversion to irregulars, or franc-tireurs, went back to World War One and even to the Franco-Prussian War. But irregular warfare was precisely what the German occupiers faced because of the changing face of war. Once, countries had been hard to occupy but relatively easy to hold; by the middle of the twentieth century they were relatively easy to occupy but hard to hold. In eastern and southeastern Europe, ideology and circumstances came together to produce extreme German violence: anti-Slav sentiment, hostility to Judeo-Bolshevism and Soviet "bestiality," heavier than expected losses, and then the all-consuming hatred of partisans and those who actually or purportedly helped them.

Helmuth James von Moltke, who was aware of Wehrmacht atrocities, wrote to his wife in November 1941 about a mutual acquaintance who was too shortsighted to recognize that Germany was harming its reputation with criminal behavior like this. The person in question failed to see that "every action takes place in the universe, that all things are interrelated, that a murder in Warsaw has repercussions in Calcutta and Sydney, at the North Pole and in Kurdistan, not political but moral repercussions."[103] But the immediate repercussions were felt in Europe itself, where German conduct cut the legs out from under any possibility of finding and keeping willing collaborators, even where the prospects for that seemed good.

The population of Ukraine harbored powerful anti-Soviet sentiment, because as many as 3 million Ukrainians died as a result of Stalin's 1933 famine policies. The Germans were widely welcomed as liberators; many Ukrainians volunteered for a new Waffen-SS unit. So what did the Germans do? Their starvation policies caused another 4 million Ukrainians to die under German occupation, while 2.3 million more were deported to the Reich as forced laborers. The occupiers disappointed Ukrainian nationalists by appointing ethnic Germans as mayors, village elders, and collective farm leaders. Meanwhile, Himmler's SS began to do what it had done in Poland, settling Germans on land and farms seized from Ukrainian families. The largest of these was Hegewald, a settlement project of twenty-eight townships in western Ukraine. Some voices in the Nazi administration urged a policy of cooperation to win the Ukrainians as allies against Bolshevism. Alfred Rosenberg of the Eastern Occupied Territories Ministry was a strong advocate of this course, with support in the Foreign Office. But Hitler, the SS, and Göring's Four-Year Plan Office favored exploitation.[104] So did Erich Koch, the violently anti-Slav Reich commissioner of Ukraine, who referred to Ukrainians as a *Negervolk* (Negro race) and commented that whenever he met an intelligent Ukrainian he felt called upon to shoot him. Koch's working philosophy was clear: "I will pump every last thing out of this country."[105] The effect of German starvation policies, violent settlements, and forced-labor round-ups was predictable. It fed resistance, especially among the group most heavily targeted as forced laborers, young men. Joining the partisans seemed less risky if the alternative was to be press-ganged and sent to work a thousand miles away in dreadful conditions in which you might die of exhaustion or during a bombing raid. The Ukrainian Insurgent Army, which consisted of as many as twenty thousand partisans in the spring of 1943, launched attacks on German settlements before turning their attention to killing Poles.

From the Ukraine and Belarus in the east to Serbia in the southeast and France in the west, partisans became more numerous, resistance more widespread, and the reprisals that followed more brutal. "Pacification" through terror was the norm. In some cases, whole towns or areas of towns were destroyed. That happened in France to the old port in Marseilles and the village of Oradour-sur-Glane, whose 642 inhabitants were killed (just 6 escaped) and the village burned to the ground. Similar destruction befell Lidice in Bohemia as a reprisal for the assassination of Reinhard Heydrich, head of the Protectorate of Bohemia and Moravia. All the adult males in the town were killed, and all the women and children were sent to concentration camps, except for a few children deemed worthy of Germanization. In the east, hundreds of villages and small towns were burned down as German forces conducted "combing" operations in the hunt for partisans.[106] The largest single death toll from resistance came in Warsaw, where the August 1944 uprising cost the lives of 15,000 Polish fighters and 185,000 civilians as well as the physical devastation of the city.

By then, the war had turned decisively against Germany. The previous year, during the ten days in January 1943 when the Battle of Stalingrad was reaching its disastrous conclusion for the German Sixth Army, Winston Churchill and Franklin D. Roosevelt met in Casablanca, where they agreed on the necessity of Germany's unconditional surrender. This war aim was reiterated by the "Big Three"—Churchill and FDR plus Stalin—at later wartime summits in Teheran in 1943 and Yalta in 1945. At Yalta, the three leaders also agreed to divide postwar Germany into four zones of occupation, with the fourth zone, in the southwest, allocated to France. The Allied invasion of Normandy began on June 6, 1944, the last and most decisive of the breaches in Hitler's "Fortress Europe." By the end of August, Paris had been liberated and the Red Army was in East Prussia. German defeat was only a matter of time. It was from a belief that the war as well as German honor was lost, and in the hope that a compromise peace could be arranged with the western Allies, that a few members of the military and aristocratic elite plotted unsuccessfully to assassinate Hitler in July 1944. The final phase of the war proved exceptionally costly of lives. Germany suffered more than five million military fatalities in all. A quarter of them died in the first four months of 1945, when the war was clearly lost. January 1945 was the single worst month: 450,000 German soldiers lost their lives, more than either British or U.S. losses during the entire conflict. By the time of the final capitulation on May 7, one in three of the male children born in Germany between 1915 and 1924 was dead.[107]

Even before Allied armies reached German soil, the war came home to Germany from the skies. The most damaging attack on a German city was Operation Gomorrah, the series of raids on Hamburg that began on July 24, 1943, and lasted for eight days and seven nights, leaving 58,000 civilians dead, 180,000 injured, and the city virtually destroyed. The raid was carefully planned, the mix of explosives and incendiary devices calculated to achieve the effects it did. The most notorious case was the firebombing of Dresden nearly two years later on February 13–15, 1945, which took 25,000 lives and destroyed 40 percent of the city's dwellings as well as the architectural and cultural treasures that made Dresden the "Florence on the Elbe." Careful scrutiny has led scholars to scale down the death toll at Dresden—Nazi propaganda estimates at the time referred to as many as 200,000 dead. The overall death toll from air raids is also now thought to be in the range of 350,000 to 370,000, rather than the 600,000 or more cited by some.[108] That is still nine times the number of British civilians killed in

the Blitz. And the planned, deliberate destruction of homes reached astonishing levels. A raid on Darmstadt, near Frankfurt, in September 1944, a
so-called Night of Fire designed by the Royal Air Force to test a new system of flares, destroyed more than three-quarters of all the city's structures
and cost 70,000 inhabitants their homes.[109] All told, between seven and
eight million Germans lost their homes. They were, in the ugly new word,
ausgebombt—bombed out.

The "area bombing" practiced by both the British and American air
forces raises two large questions. The first is ethical, an issue that has rever-
berated well beyond Germany. What happened in Hamburg, Dresden, and
elsewhere has engaged the attention of authors as various as the American novelist Kurt Vonnegut, the British Holocaust denier David Irving,
the Swedish writer Sven Lindqvist, and the Israeli philosopher Igor Primoratz.[110] *Slaughterhouse-Five*, Vonnegut's 1969 novel about the event, has
sold more than 800,000 copies in the United States. It has been filmed,
staged, turned into a radio drama, adapted as a graphic novel, and been
adapted into an opera by the Bavarian State Opera. The deliberate target-
ing of German civilian populations has been described as terrorism, a war
crime, even as genocide. One defense of the practice is the old schoolyard
retort: Germany started it. As Sir Arthur "Bomber" Harris of the Royal Air
Force Bomber Command pugnaciously insisted, Göring's Luftwaffe sowed
the wind and Germans reaped the whirlwind. There is a strategic defense,
too. Operationally, the airpower that Germany was forced to divert from
the eastern front certainly helped the Red Army, even if it was not decisive.
In the end, though, views about the morality of the strategy are likely to
turn on whether it worked, causing German morale to collapse and thereby
potentially shortening the war.

That is where the second large question arises: *Did* area bombing lead
to a collapse of German morale? Goebbels certainly regarded the problems
caused by air raids as the most serious domestic concern in the Third Reich.
Disputes arose over housing as bomb damage mounted. Evacuations were
also contentious. Some were reluctant to be evacuated (in the Ruhr city of
Witten, angry women forced the local authorities to end mandatory evac-
uation), and evacuees were unpopular in rural areas. Like growing complaints in the last year of war about inequitable rationing, these conflicts
placed strains on the wartime "community of fate." Even a propaganda film
designed to lift morale, like the romantic drama *The Great Love*, shows
scenes of discord in an air-raid shelter, before the hero (himself an airman

on leave) takes charge.[111] Yet Germans still cleared up after air raids, volunteered for the Red Cross, and joined antiaircraft units. Some 650,000 German boys and older men were mustered into a Home Guard. Industrial output remained surprisingly high almost to the end. There was, it is true, a wave of suicides in the spring of 1945.[112] But the civilian population largely remained resilient.

Some of this is attributable to the radicalization of terror with which the regime threatened its own citizens, especially after February 1945—women and children forced at gunpoint to build barricades, "defeatists" summarily shot, many more arrested. Nazi propaganda also continued to encourage belief that a "wonder weapon" would, even at the final hour, bring victory. Hitler's charisma and Nazi ideology seem to have counted for less in the final stages of the war. Defense of family, friends, and the immediate homeland weighed more heavily. But larger questions were also part of the mix. Most Germans still believed that overturning the Treaty of Versailles was a just cause and saw the final stages of the conflict as a "defensive" war against the Judeo-Bolshevik enemy. Nazi propaganda about the "blind destructive fury" of the "Asiatic hordes" went with the grain of popular sentiment. Then there was the question of what Germans themselves had done, above all "in the east," and what Germans back in the Reich knew about it. What has been called the "shared secret" of the murder of the Jews created a guilt of sorts, but many Germans then persuaded themselves that the Allied bombing raids were a form of punishment. That, in turn, became a tacit belief that there was a moral equivalence between what was being done to them and what they had done to others, even as half-acknowledged guilt fueled a dread of what defeat and occupation might bring.[113]

The Holocaust

A SENSE OF GUILT AND SHAME IS UNMISTAKABLE IN THE LETTERS and diaries of Germans who hated the regime and deplored its crimes. Ursula von Kardorff talked about a "disgraced land." The novelist Fritz von Reck-Malleczewen wrote in his diary that when the end came it would not be heroic but "a dirty end, in shame and degradation." In sonnets written in Berlin's Moabit jail after his arrest in December 1944, Albrecht Haushofer, a geography professor who had also advised on foreign affairs, excoriated himself ("I should have recognized my duty sooner / more sharply named disaster as disaster") and invoked Kant, Bach, and Goethe as witnesses of a better Germany. Helmuth von Moltke, arrested one month later, was a horrified witness of round-ups of Jews in Berlin and learned details in 1942 about the "SS blast-furnace" in the General Government.[114] Their moral outrage was real. It prompted acts of resistance that cost Reck-Malleczewen, Haushofer, and Moltke their lives. But there was also, mixed in with the shame and perhaps inseparable from it, a powerful sense of foreboding about the reckoning Germans would face—"when our turn comes," as Moltke put it, a sentiment expressed in almost identical terms by Haushofer in the sonnet "Downfall."[115] Fear of what would happen when the tables were turned runs through the recorded sentiments of ordinary Germans. "May God grant us victory because if they get their revenge we are in for a hard time," said a driver in a Wehrmacht motorized unit who witnessed Jews being killed in Lithuania. "We all said to one another what on earth would happen if we lost the war and had to pay for all this," according to a fellow driver.[116] The same fear was felt back home. An everyday dispute in a Berlin streetcar led to an argument about the "Jewish war" that caused some passengers to exclaim "we have already weighed ourselves down with enough guilt for our treatment of the Jews and Poles, which will yet be paid back to us."[117]

Germans feared condign punishment. The Jews of Europe feared other things in those years, of course—not only their own persecution and death, but also that what was being done to them would be expunged from memory. The desire to record every last detail for posterity was what led the Dresden Jew Victor Klemperer to keep his diaries in order to "bear witness to the end."[118] The impulse to record took on an even greater urgency, if that were possible, in the ghettos and camps. Chaim Kaplan, a school principal, kept a diary in the Warsaw ghetto, despite the risk, because he was "afraid that the impressions of this terrible era will be lost because they have not been adequately recorded." That was in August 1940. Two years later his fear took grimly practical form: "My utmost concern is for hiding my diary so that it will be preserved for future generations."[119] He gave the diary to a friend to smuggle out of the ghetto, and it was found after the war hidden in a kerosene can.

The Warsaw ghetto produced the most remarkable record of Jewish life under Nazi rule. It was the inspiration of Emanuel Ringelblum, who celebrated his fortieth birthday the month the ghetto was created in November 1940. He was a historian who had written a dissertation on the Jews of medieval Warsaw. Ringelblum and his colleagues compiled a clandestine collection that went by the code name Oneg Shabbat (Sabbath Delight), containing diaries, reports, essays, children's accounts, underground newspapers, photographs, artworks, concert programs, food coupons, official decrees, and narratives of deportations. As members of the archive team began to be deported to Treblinka, steps were taken to bury the materials in milk churns and other containers. Two of the three caches were uncovered after the war.[120] Less extensive archives were created in other ghettos. Making any kind of written record was incomparably harder in the camps, but a few were able to do so. Three were members of the Auschwitz-Birkenau *Sonderkommando* (work units of Jews forced to help with the disposal of victims), who wrote accounts of their experiences and buried them near the crematoria at Birkenau, where they were later disinterred.[121] This was documentary evidence, laid down—literally—against the threat of oblivion or disbelief. Camp prisoners were haunted by that twofold threat. Primo Levi, perhaps the most famous survivor to write his memoirs, said that the history of the Third Reich could be read as "a war against memory."[122]

As the Red Army approached the death camps, the perpetrators did try to destroy the evidence of what they had done, but too much remained both there and elsewhere for them to succeed—physical evidence, deportation records, prisoner death registries, orders for Zyklon gas, photographs of victims' clothes and belongings, itemized reports from the *Einsatzgruppen*, diaries of leading Nazis, and minutes of the Wannsee Conference in January 1942, where the details of implementing the Final Solution were discussed. Postwar prosecutors at the International Military Tribunal in Nuremberg added to the mound of evidence, publishing twenty-seven volumes of it to go along with forty-two volumes of trial records. The confessions of the Auschwitz commandant Rudolf Höss and others also became part of the record. And so, more painfully and profoundly, did the contemporary evidence smuggled out of ghettos and camps, or buried and later retrieved, and the accounts of survivors already being collected in postwar displaced person camps.

Far from being forgotten, the Holocaust became the "ultimate core event of 'our' time," the "emblematic memory of the twentieth century," and a symbol of universal evil.[123] The work done by thousands of scholars, with gathering pace since the 1980s, makes this one of the best documented events of a well-documented century. The basic facts about the murder of the Jews are known and undisputed by all except a small number of willful deniers. At least 5.7 million Jews were killed during the war, most of them after June 1941 and especially in the twelve months between January 1942 and January 1943, when 3 million perished. The murdered Jews came disproportionately from one northeastern quadrant of Europe. Around 2.7 million lived in Poland, another 2.1 million were Soviet citizens from the Lithuanian-Belorussian-Ukrainian borderlands. One and a half million of the dead were children. Those murdered represented two-thirds of all the Jews living in Europe at the time, and three-quarters of all those who were within the grasp of Nazi Germany. The distribution of the Jewish population around the globe was fundamentally changed as a result of prewar emigration from Germany and Austria, the Holocaust itself, and the eventual resettlement of survivors in the United States and Israel. According to the Israeli demographer Sergio DellaPergola, almost three in five of the world's Jews still lived in Europe in 1939. By 1945 that figure was down to just over one in three, by 1970 to just one in four.[124]

A broad consensus now exists about the timing and decision-making process that led to the Holocaust. There are four things on which most historians agree, even though they hold differing views on many details. First, notwithstanding the cruel persecution and violent rhetoric of Hitler and other leading Nazis, especially during and after the destruction of November 1938, there was no plan when war broke out to exterminate European Jewry. Secondly, the Final Solution of the Jewish Question was the product of a cumulative radicalization of policy, the result of a series of decisions or green lights rather than one single decision, with 1941 the single most important year when the fate of Europe's Jews was determined. Thirdly, Hitler remains the central figure, even though there was almost certainly no formal "Führer order" calling for the murder of the Jews. His fingerprints were all over the policies that led to the Holocaust, more so in fact than they had been in setting so-called Jewish policy in 1933–1939. Fourth, and last, the Holocaust is inseparable from the war. If it is true that "no Hitler, no Holocaust," then it is also true that "no war, no Holocaust," although it is necessary to add straight away that it is extremely difficult to imagine the Third Reich as a regime that did not end by going to war.

War, especially the war in the east, lowered moral thresholds and made it possible to think the unthinkable. That was immediately apparent in the killing of Polish civilians, Jewish and non-Jewish, in 1939–40. The conflict also meant that there was little need to pay further attention to foreign opinion—with one possible exception. Given the Nazi view that policy in Washington was dictated by Jews on Wall Street and elsewhere, European

Jews served in a sense as collective hostages for as long as the United States remained neutral. But the war also ran counter to the project to rid Germany of its Jews, a bedrock of Nazi policy since the seizure of power. That aim had been pursued before 1939 by increasingly cruel policies of exclusion and persecution that led to emigration financed by Jewish émigrés themselves via "taxes" that amounted to expropriation of property. Emigration was not, in fact, banned until May 1941 and a few thousand Jews were still able to leave Germany. In November 1938, as a new wave of emigration followed the Night of Broken Glass, Reinhard Heydrich, then the head of the Reich Security Head Office, had estimated that it would take another decade to make Germany *judenfrei* (free of Jews).[125] However, just as the Austrian *Anschluss* and the occupation of Czechoslovakia brought many more Jews under German control, so did the war, and on a much greater scale. That happened first in Poland, the largest single home of prewar European Jewry. There were 2.2 million Jews in German-occupied Poland, while the areas of western Poland annexed to the Reich included an additional half a million Jews. The gauleiters of these territories expected that their domains would become *judenfrei*.

Here was the first of several self-created problems faced by the German authorities. The initial solution was to create ghettos as temporary holding areas to house Jews before they were deported. But what was the destination to which Jews would be deported? There were various plans to ship them east, including one proposal to establish a "Jewish reservation" near Lublin on the eastern edge of the General Government. But these plans failed because of friction between different agencies and conflicting Nazi goals. The priority for Himmler's SS in 1939–40 was to find farms on which to resettle ethnic Germans, which meant that more non-Jewish Poles than Polish Jews were deported and the large-scale removal of Jews was temporarily postponed. With the failure of the Lublin settlement proposal, those Jews who were deported from the newly annexed areas were sent to the General Government. Deported Poles and Jews alike were packed into overcrowded railroad cars without adequate food or drink. The transportations were chaotically organized and were sometimes shuttled around for days before reaching their destinations, with predictable results. This led to complaints from Governor-General Hans Frank—but not on humanitarian grounds. In a speech in late 1942 to colleagues, he looked back in self-pitying terms at those months in 1940: "Then there came the fantasies of resettling hundreds of thousands of Jews and Poles in the General

Government. You will remember those terrible months, when freight cars rolled into the General Government day and night, fully laden with people, some wagons full to the top with bodies. That was a dreadful time. . . ." Frank was determined that his fiefdom cease to be a dumping ground, because this was at odds with his vision of turning it into a productive land of German settlement, a view that had support from Göring and with which Hitler came to agree.[126]

Another proposal for deportation enjoyed brief but serious consideration: that European Jews might be shipped off to the French colony of Madagascar, off the coast of East Africa. This was a fantasy entertained by some British, French, and Polish antisemites in the late 1930s. Predictably, it attracted attention from leading Nazis. But the spark that ignited wartime policy discussions came from the German Foreign Office. Joachim von Ribbentrop had learned in a 1938 conversation with his French counterpart, Georges Bonnet, about a French proposal to send ten thousand French Jews to the island. Two years later, in June 1940, with France about to be defeated, the idea formed the subject of a memorandum by Fritz Rademacher, an ambitious young official on the Jewish Desk of the Foreign Office. It quickly met with enthusiasm, from the SS and from Hans Frank, who saw an opportunity to be rid of Jews in the General Government. By June 18 Hitler was talking about the Madagascar plan to Mussolini and Count Ciano, the Italian foreign minister, when they met in Munich to discuss the end of the French empire, and in mid-August Adolf Eichmann of the SS and Theo Dannecker, his assistant, had the printed copy of a plan ready, complete with maps. Earlier feasibility studies, like one undertaken by the Poles, had talked of settling a few thousand Jews; the SS version called for a million Jews a year to be shipped off, four million in four years. This had nothing to do with settlement; it was a plan for murderous mass deportation with a high death rate built into it by design. In the event, the failure to defeat Britain made it impossible to pursue because Germany lacked the shipping fleet or control of the sea lanes they would have needed.[127]

Had the plan been realized, Madagascar would have resembled a giant SS-run ghetto. As it was, the ghettos now constructed across German-occupied territory became another self-created problem for German administrators, because of the appalling conditions in which they forced Jews to live. The site chosen for the ghetto was always in the poorest part of town, because this provided maximum opportunities to expropriate wealthy

Jews and free up good houses for the German occupiers. The meager food rations for Jews (much lower even than those of non-Jewish Poles), together with overcrowded housing, grossly inadequate medical care, and overwork, created a starving and disease-ridden population. Conditions also fostered smuggling and desperate black market barter. All of this Germans blamed on the Jews they had ghettoized.[128] German films and photographs of the ghettos were expressly intended, like the propaganda film *The Eternal Jew*, to paint a picture of "oriental" filth and disease. The entrance to the Cracow ghetto (built to German specifications with Jewish slave labor) had oriental design features; "Asia Has Come to Europe," ran the headline of an SS propaganda piece on the Warsaw ghetto.[129] Visiting parties from Germany were given tours designed to show the menace that Jews purportedly represented. "Seeing this race en masse, which is decaying, decomposing and rotten to the core, will banish any sentimental humanitarianism," wrote Alfred Rosenberg after visiting the Lublin and Warsaw ghettos.[130]

The ghetto managers all knew that concentrating Jews in this way was not a permanent solution. For as long as the ghettos lasted, some managers were "productivists," building relations with the local Jewish Council and valuing the contribution ghetto labor made to the German war effort. Others were open "attritionists," happy to oversee the culling of the Jewish population. Both styles were compatible with greed and corruption on the part of German managers, and morbidity and mortality rates were high in ghettos of every kind. In the largest, Łódź and Warsaw, the death rate was running at 180 a day in the summer of 1941. By then, however, the invasion of the USSR had changed things fundamentally.

Jewish policy evolved in 1941 within the larger hunger plan and the grandiose proposals for racial engineering in the General Plan for the East. Military successes brought into German hands millions more unwanted Jews, the most reviled of all the "unproductive eaters." That Nazi Germany was finally confronting the Judeo-Bolshevik enemy added ideological reinforcement. The association of Jews with the Communist enemy was a powerful fixed idea. *Einsatzgruppen* operating in the rear areas began to kill Jews in much larger numbers than in Poland—adult men at first, but increasingly others, too—because they "sheltered" partisans or represented a "security risk." The Wehrmacht also justified killing Jews as part of "pacification" efforts, citing the need for "ruthlessness" in response to a "sly," "barbaric" enemy. Across the occupied lands of the Baltic, Ukraine, and Belarus, new ghettos were created, bringing with them the same self-created problems and dilemmas, although in these occupied territories—unlike in Poland—mass murders of Jews often preceded ghettoization.

The sheer volume of killing was extraordinary, given that the four *Einsatzgruppen* numbered no more than 3000 men, a total that included drivers, communications specialists, and interpreters. It was possible only because of the assistance of other SS units, army security divisions, the Order Police, and local non-German militias. In July 1941, 5000 Lithuanian male Jews from Vilna were murdered in Ponar under the auspices of *Einsatzgruppe* A, the beginning of a killing spree that went on through the summer and included women and children.[131] At the end of September, a unit of *Einsatzgruppe* C together with a Police Battalion (a unit of the Order Police) shot 34,000 Jews from Kyiv in just two days and threw their bodies into the sandy ravine of Babi Yar. A Ukrainian named Iryna Koroshunova wrote in her diary, "There is something terrible, horrible going on, something inconceivable, which cannot be understood, grasped or explained." Several days later she had heard more. The accounts still seemed "too monstrous to believe. But we are forced to believe them, for the shooting of the Jews is a fact. A fact which is starting to drive us insane."[132]

What drove this murderous behavior? Let us look at *Einsatzgruppe* D, the smallest of the four task forces, with just 600 men, as it followed Army Group South through Romania, Bessarabia, the Crimea, and the Caucasus. It was established in June 1941 and headed by an academic highflyer, Otto Ohlendorf, who had a doctorate in jurisprudence. *Einsatzgruppe* D performed many tasks: supporting the Wehrmacht, conducting intelligence operations, and helping ethnic Germans. But its main task was killing, mainly by shooting (Ohlendorf preferred shots from a distance, not the bullet in the back of the neck). Members of the task force murdered Sinti and Roma, asylum patients, Soviet engineers, and tubercular children. They even murdered in order to make buildings available for their own recreational purposes. But, above all, they murdered Jews, combing through POW camps to find Jews to kill outright. In the Crimea they encountered two groups, the Karaites and the Krimchaki. Uncertain how to deal with them, they referred the question to the racial "experts" in the SS. Ultimately, it was Himmler himself who made the decision that the Karaites were Jewish by religious faith but not by ethnicity, whereas the Kirmchaki were descended from Sephardic Jews but had given up their Judaism. *Einsatzgruppe* D killed the Krimchaki. Their motives for murder were racial-biological—the killing of racial "inferiors" and "lives unworthy of life," "useless eaters." There was also careerism, peer pressure, and professional pride, which included a perverted sense of being part of a "civilizing mission." The leaders of the *Einsatzgruppen*, all highly educated, shared with top SS men like Heinrich Himmler a belief that their behavior was "hard" and "determined," but not "savage" or brutal." It was, in this perverse and inverted worldview, those they killed who represented "barbarism."[133] But underlying everything was a fanatical, ideologically deep-wired antisemitism.[134] Between July 1941 and the end of the year, the *Einsatzgruppen* killed half a million Jews. This was already systematic mass murder, the numbers of the dead carefully tallied, even if it was not yet the Final Solution.

At the beginning of 1941 the long-term goal of German Jewish policy was still deportation, slave labor, and selective killing. But the summer killings meant that any remaining moral thresholds had been crossed. The four *Einsatzgruppen* moved to a policy of mass killings, including women and children, at different times. That was a result of the ambiguity of the instructions from Heydrich and the discretion permitted to task force units on the ground. But the move toward mass murder was sanctioned at every stage by Berlin, with Hitler asking to be kept informed, especially after the beginning of August. In the course of 1941 the violent reality of Nazi policy caught up with the violence of Nazi rhetoric. Hitler and others had used terms such as "destruction" (*Vernichtung*) and "extermination" (*Ausrottung*) for years, Hitler most notoriously in a Reichstag speech in 1939 in which he "prophesied" the "destruction of the Jewish race in Europe" if the Jews were to "cause" another world war. Language like this signified a murderous state of mind and raised expectations among hard-core Nazi supporters, but it remained metaphorical. Even someone like Victor Klemperer, a linguist by training and a man whose very life as a Jew in Germany depended on trying to "read" the meaning of official statements, believed until late in the war that words like "annihilation" pointed to future pogroms of some kind, not to wholesale destruction.

It was in 1941, however, that Germany moved toward a policy of systematic mass murder of the Jews. In January Hitler instructed Heydrich to prepare a "total solution" of the Jewish question. That May German rulers in occupied western Europe were told to suspend any further Jewish emigration pending a "final solution" of the Jewish question that would be forthcoming. In July, Heydrich was again authorized via Göring, nominally in charge of Jewish policy since November 1938, to find an "overall" or "total solution" to the Jewish question. These terms were used increas-

ingly during 1941. In July they came to mean killing all the Jews in the
Soviet Union, and then, at some point between mid-September and late
October, killing all the Jews in Europe. Several developments led to this
decision. The invasion of the USSR marked an even more murderous turn
in policy, but some kind of "territorial solution" remained the long-term
goal. The Jews would be cleared from the reincorporated areas, then from
the General Government, and deported to somewhere unspecified "in the
east"—beyond the Urals, or in the Arctic—after the Soviet Union had
been subjugated. Although the German advance was still on course when
the fateful decisions were taken, there was mounting impatience about
when the "territorial solution" would be implemented. Arthur Greiser in
the Gau Wartheland and Hans Frank in the General Government both
called angrily for action.

Hitler himself was impatient. The U.S. Lend-Lease program in March
1941 and the Atlantic Charter in August, in which President Roosevelt
made clear the joint Anglo-American aims for a democratic postwar world,
removed any last purpose the captive Jews of Europe had served as hostages to influence U.S. policy. Even before the German declaration of war
on America, Hitler saw policy in Washington as the outcome of Jewish
influence, which he had warned about in his "prophecy" of January 1939.
Meanwhile, the Germans' self-created problem of the disease-ridden ghettos had been joined by the self-created problem of the psychological "burden" on the *Einsatzgruppen* and others engaged in mass shootings. Karl
Jäger reported on how demanding this had proved for the unit of *Einsatzgruppe* A he commanded. There was the preparation and reconnaissance,
then assembling the Jews, transporting them to the execution areas, organizing the grave digging; above all, there was the "acutely stressful nature of
the work," the shooting itself, which caused breakdowns and drunkenness.
All these "difficulties" were noted by Jäger even as he reported proudly on
the 133,346 people his men had killed in their efforts "to solve the Jewish
problem for Lithuania."[135]

Mass shootings continued through the end of the year and beyond, but
by October there was already discussion about using some kind of gassing device to speed up the killing process. The technology had already
been used in killing more than 70,000 disabled people in Germany, until
that euthanasia program was suspended in September 1941 after opposition
from church leaders. Both technology and personnel were transferred over
from the so-called T4 program, named after the Tiergartenstrasse address

in Berlin where it was based, to serve a new purpose. Mobile gassing vans were tested on Soviet POWs. At the beginning of November, construction began on two new camps, Chełmno and Bełżec, soon to be staffed by T4 veterans. At the end of the month, Heydrich invited representatives of various ministerial departments to attend a meeting to agree on the "organizational and technical preparations for a comprehensive solution of the Jewish question."[136] Originally scheduled for December 9, the meeting was postponed until January 20 because of the Soviet counterattack near Moscow on December 5 and the bombing of Pearl Harbor two days later. The Wannsee Conference was intended to cross the t's and dot the i's of decisions already made.[137] The day after Hitler declared war on America, he met with party leaders and referred back once again to his "prophecy" in 1939: "The world war is here. The annihilation of the Jews must be the necessary consequence."[138]

The first two death camps, at Chełmno and Bełżec, were followed by four more, at Sobibór, Treblinka, Auschwitz-Birkenau, and Majdanek. All became operational between March and July 1942. They killed those who passed through them at an astounding rate, especially the four camps charged with the "Reinhardt program" to kill the Jews of Europe, which were given that name after the assassination of Heydrich by the Czech resistance that June. Those four (Chełmno, Bełżec, Sobibór, and Treblinka) killed more than 1 million Jews in the six months from July to December 1942. In all, the "Reinhardt camps" murdered at least 1.75 million and as many as 2 million Jews. Up to 1 million more died at Auschwitz, a hybrid death camp and forced-labor camp, and some 60,000 at Majdanek. During the most murderous period, between March 1942 and February 1943, the camps were killing 10,000 Jews every day.[139]

The victims came from all across Europe. At Auschwitz, the first transports came from Polish areas reincorporated into Germany and from the General Government, as the ghettos were cleared starting in the spring of 1942. Then came Jews from Slovakia and western Europe, transported weekly from transit camps in France (Drancy), the Netherlands (Westerbork), and Belgium (Mechelen). They were followed by Jews from Germany itself, Romania, Norway, and Croatia, and later from the Balkans, Hungary, and the southern half of France. The Nazis brought together Jewish humankind from across the Continent, with the intention of killing them either immediately or after extracting the last ounce of labor from them. The official language was German ("camp German," a series of nouns and verbs barked as commands), the unofficial language varied. In Auschwitz, Yiddish and Polish were most common earlier, Hungarian prominent for a time after the Hungarian Jews were deported in 1944, but the overwhelming impression was of a "perpetual Babel," as Primo Levi described it. Tadeusz Borowski, a non-Jewish Pole who survived Auschwitz (but, like Levi, later committed suicide), described French, Russians, Poles, and Greeks communicating in what he called, with dark humor, "crematorium Esperanto."[140]

The death camps were the most notorious part of the Nazi "concentrationary universe," to use a phrase coined in 1946 by a French survivor of Neuengamme and Buchenwald.[141] The sheer volume and speed of the killings has made them the central symbol of the Holocaust. "Auschwitz" serves as shorthand for the larger process. Quite ordinary words like "oven," "chimney," and "hair" take on an intense emotional charge when invoked within the context of the Holocaust.[142] The idea of the death camp carries powerful associations. From the relentless arrival of the transports by train, to the careful bookkeeping, the killing process, and finally the crematorium that burned the dead bodies, most people have in their minds the image of an assembly line in reverse—smooth, industrialized, high-tech killing. There is truth in that, of course, just as it is true that hideous medical experiments were performed in the camps on powerless human subjects. All this points to the "modernity" of the Holocaust, like the eugenics and "racial science" used to justify the killing.

But it is important not to overlook that the death camps were rudimentary, even crude structures, their buildings easily assembled. Built quickly and cheaply, partly with materials looted from ghettos, they looked like POW camps and used basic barracks buildings and barbed wire in the same way. The substantial two-story brick gate tower at the entrance to Birkenau was the only structure of its kind.[143] The first two gas chambers at Birkenau were converted peasant cottages; the ashes from the crematoria were dumped in the Vistula. The killing process resembled the nineteenth-century abattoir more than the sophisticated industrial assembly line of the 1930s.[144] And almost half the killings in the death camps came not in the gas chambers (or the mobile gassing vans at Chełmno) but in a host of other ways, especially at Auschwitz, where the time between prisoners' arrival and their deaths was usually longer. They were killed by overwork, starvation, disease, beatings, the random sadistic shooting, or the spade across the throat.

When the Italian journalist Curzio Malaparte visited Warsaw, having just witnessed a Romanian massacre of Jews, Governor-General Hans Frank assured him over lunch that, as a man and a German, he thoroughly disapproved of pogroms: "Germany is a country that has a higher civilization and abominates barbaric methods." It was guided not by "bestial methods," but by science. Its model was the surgeon, not the butcher.[145] Heinrich Himmler repeatedly used similar terms. The reality undercut the German conceit that their methods were "civilized" and "scientific." The more fine-grained our view has become of what actually happened during the Holocaust, the more attention has been directed to the murders of Jews that took place outside the camps, in thousands of smaller events that cumulatively added up to almost half of all the dead.

As many as 1.5 million were killed by or at the direction of the *Einsatzgruppen*. Then there were the Jews who died of starvation or disease in the ghettos, some half a million. The number was that high because more than 1100 ghettos were established in the east: over 140 in the newly reincorporated territories, 380 in the General Government, around 600 in other occupied territories. Many more Jews were shot when the ghettos were cleared, before they ever reached the death camps. Forced labor under appalling conditions cost tens of thousands more lives. Work on the notorious highway Durchgangsstrasse IV in the Ukraine, which began in September 1941, was performed by Jews and Russian POWs and designed to work the laborers to death. Around 25,000 Jews were killed when the labor camps associated with the highway were liquidated in late 1943 and early 1944.[146] Some forced labor was a death sentence in itself. In the Skarzysko-Kamienna work camp in the General Government, Jewish prisoners were forced to make underwater mines based on a very poisonous mixture of saltpeter and picric acid, working without protective clothing or gloves. Most died soon after coming into contact with the chemicals.

The many different ways in which Jews were murdered emerges from a micro-history of Buczacz, a Galician town that housed Ukrainians, Poles, and Jews. The Germans, with local assistance, killed as many as 60,000 Jews in the district; however, those Jews were killed over a period of three years, not all at once, and not with the surgical precision that Hans Frank invoked. Thousands were shot in periodic "actions" at a site called Fedor Hill, or in the Jewish cemetery, but sometimes more randomly in their homes or on the street. A ghetto was built in December 1942. Jews died there because of starvation, inadequate shelter and disease, including an outbreak of typhus, but some Jews were also shot in the ghetto. An operation in June 1943 to make the town "free of Jews" led to the killing of workers from a local slave-labor camp and members of the Jewish "order police." Some survived the liquidation and were hunted down in the nearby forests. Jews from Buczacz were also taken to a nearby town to be shot or transported to the closest extermination camp, Bełżec, until it closed down at the end of 1942.[147] It was not, therefore, one of the camps from which surviving prisoners were hurriedly evacuated and marched westward as the Red Army approached.

Auschwitz *was* one of those camps. The dismantling of the gas chambers and desperate burning of records began in late 1944. Then, as the Russians approached in January 1945, inmates were sent on what soon became death marches. Other concentration or labor camps were liquidated hurriedly during these weeks. Most of the 700,000 to 800,000 former camp inmates force-marched westward in the closing months of the war were Jews. An estimated quarter million died in the process, of exhaustion, exposure, or shooting. Stragglers were routinely killed. Sometimes an entire group was shot.[148] At the end of January, around 7000 people, mostly Jewish women, were assembled in Königsberg from Stutthof and its six satellite camps. The group, dressed in dirty, threadbare blankets, newspaper and rags, shod in wooden clogs, was marched at gunpoint through ice and snow along the Baltic coast, with those unable to keep up shot, clubbed with rifle butts, or left to die. When they reached the fishing village of Palmnicken, they found their overland route cut off by the Red Army. Collectively, local SS men, the former camp commandant, the gauleiter of East Prussia, and members of the Todt Organization made the decision to shoot the remaining 3000 survivors on the spot. Among the Germans guarding them were members of the Hitler Youth who had been plied with alcohol. Only a few hundred of the women survived.[149]

The Holocaust was not one event, but thousands of events. The more we learn, the wider the circle of perpetrators has grown. It includes middle-ranking SS figures and members of many other organizations whose behavior went beyond mere indifference to active complicity. Palmnicken was not the only place where members of the Todt Organization engaged in mass killings. In Buczacz they took part in the round-up and murder of Jews. A witness saw the head of the local Todt Organization shoot a Jewish woman on the street.[150] In the same town, a driver with the SS Security Police took part in the shootings. German employees of a private construction company that employed Jewish slave labor watched the shootings, looted Jewish homes, and may have used their own weapons.[151] In Lithuania members of the National Socialist Drivers Corps guarded some of the 10,400 Jews who were killed in one "action."[152] Elsewhere, it was German employees of the local savings bank who lent a hand with the clearing of a Polish ghetto.

Just as an army needs its cooks, drivers, and pay clerks, so the Nazi murder of the Jews needed the more or less active contributions of lowly German civilians working in banks and businesses, labor and planning departments, railroads and construction companies. If they did not shoot Jews themselves, then they guarded them, or drew up the paperwork that sent them to their deaths, or gave their fellow countrymen support by watching proceedings. Some took photographs. One of the organizations most directly involved was the green-uniformed Order Police, some 400,000 strong and already bloodied by criminal behavior in the wake of the Austrian *Anschluss* and the prewar invasion of Czechoslovakia. More than twenty Order Police battalions took part in genocidal actions during the war, as an independent force, or attached to one of the Wehrmacht security divisions operating behind the lines or to an *Einsatzgruppe*. The Order Police had some part in the murder of up to a million noncombatants, not all of them Jews. Younger battalion commanders, socialized after 1933 at Nazi officer schools, were especially likely to organize mass killings on their own initiative.[153]

There are parallels with the uniformed personnel of a much larger body: the Wehrmacht. The promotion of younger officers led to a similar Nazification. But the murderous conduct of the Wehrmacht, denied for so long as part of the postwar myth about the army's "clean hands," was not restricted to younger Nazi types. The killing of Jews took place within "the most brutal military occupation regime in history."[154] These crimes were committed in a war that most Wehrmacht soldiers saw as a life-and-death struggle against a uniquely dangerous Judeo-Bolshevik enemy. General Bernhard Ramcke, captured in France in September 1944, told interrogators from a British army intelligence unit that Hitler "was right in recognizing this great Jewish danger threatening all nations and in realizing the Jewish communist threat from the east. At one time it was Genghis Khan and at another Attila. This time it is Jewish Bolshevism spreading over Europe from the Asiatic steppes, a tide we *had* to stem."[155] Ramcke was not regarded by the British as part of the "Nazi clique" among captured German officers, but his was not an atypical view. The army took a particularly direct role in mass murder of Jews in Serbia and Belarus, but everywhere on the eastern front "antipartisan" actions became occasions for killing Jews. After initial mistrust, army commanders developed a good working relationship with the SS, including the *Einsatzgruppen*. The army provided the SS with equipment, ammunition, transport, and housing. Wehrmacht units helped to establish ghettos and guard victims. Sometimes they participated in shootings. Commanders at every level were responsible for killing Jewish and other civilians, and the perpetrators included frontline troops as well as security units operating behind the lines.[156]

If a wider (and more damning) view of German perpetrators has now become standard, then a wider (and more generous) perspective has altered our view of Jewish responses. In the early postwar decades, it was part of the self-understanding of the new state of Israel that the Jews who lived there were a new breed, tough and willing to fight, unlike the "passive" Jews of the European diaspora. Jews in Israel and some European countries strongly criticized members of the Nazi-appointed Jewish Councils for complying too readily with German orders. Two influential books in the early 1960s lent their weight to this view. One was Raul Hilberg's pathbreaking *The Destruction of the European Jews*, the other Hannah Arendt's *Eichmann in Jerusalem*, based on a set of *New Yorker* articles covering Adolf Eichmann's trial.[157] Sixty years on, not much remains of the argument that Jews, abetted by their leaders, went like "sheep to the slaughter."

In the first place, as some earlier writers were keen to emphasize, there *was* physical resistance. The biblical metaphor of sheep to the slaughter can be traced back to Jews who called in 1942 and 1943 for active resistance. "Let us not be led like sheep to the slaughter," read a manifesto by young Zionists in the Vilna ghetto in early 1942. The same call came the following year from the resistance organization in the Warsaw ghetto and in a manifesto published by the Jewish Military Union.[158] Armed underground movements formed in fifty Polish ghettos, including half a dozen of the largest. There were some ghettos, such as Minsk and Białystok, where the Jewish leadership maintained regular contact with the Communist underground in the ghetto and beyond. There were uprisings in several ghettos, most famously in Warsaw, but also in Vilna. Uprisings also took place in three death camps (Treblinka, Sobibór, and Auschwitz) and in other camps. Jewish partisan groups formed, as well, in Lithuania, Poland, and the occupied USSR, with perhaps thirty thousand members in all.[159] One such group was portrayed in Primo Levi's novel, *If Not Now, When?*, which drew on conversations with former partisans he met during his long, circuitous postwar journey back to Italy.[160] The Jewish partisan group was just one of the resistance organizations operating in the Pripet marshes that stretched across eastern Poland and Belarus. In 1941, the year of decision, the metaphor of "driving Jews into the marshes" had been a euphemism that nonetheless betrayed the murderous intent of Nazi leaders. "Express orders from the *Reichsführer*-SS. All Jews must be shot. Drive Jewish women into the marshes," Himmler told *Einsatzgruppe* C in July 31. Three months later, echoing Himmler's words, Hitler raged against this "criminal race": "Don't anyone tell me that we can't send them into the marshes."[161] By 1943, however, the Pripet marshes were a base of operations for Jewish (and non-Jewish) partisans, just as the forests or mountains were in other parts of Europe.

Jews, especially young Jews who had escaped from deportations, ghettos, or slave-labor camps, also joined partisan groups that were not exclusively Jewish.[162] Historians are aware that one of their own gave his life working for the French resistance. A fifty-four-year-old bespectacled medievalist was not the typical resistance profile, but Marc Bloch (code name Narbonne) became an important organizer in the Lyons region, working within the unified non-Communist resistance, running agents, liaising with the Maquis guerrilla bands, and helping to prepare the uprisings that were to accompany the Allied landings. Arrested in March 1944, interrogated, and tortured, he was shot alongside resistance comrades on June 16, ten days after D-Day. His reported last words were *"Vive la France!"* Bloch was a thoroughly assimilated, secular French Jew, a passionate believer in the universal, republican ideal.[163] Like the many Jews who joined resistance movements of the secular left, his identity as a Jew was not the primary motivation of his actions. Rather, joining the resistance was a powerful statement that he denied the right of the Germans or the Vichy regime to treat him differently from other French citizens because he was a Jew.[164]

Organized Jewish resistance, whether in ghettos and camps, marshes or forests, was real. But it should not be the standard against which to measure all Jewish responses. In the ghettos, and even more in the camps, the obstacles to rebellion of any kind were overwhelming. They began with the physical debilitation of people weakened by starvation and illness. Resistance was hard to manage or even to imagine on 200 calories a day. Think, after all, of the Soviet POWs incarcerated during these same years, more than three million of whom died. These were all young men with military training, who could see for themselves—if they survived for any length of time—what the death rate was, and surely had little to lose. Yet they, equally sapped by malnutrition and sickness, did not revolt. Jewish ghetto dwellers did not know their eventual fate and wanted not to believe the worst, hoping that if the ghetto remained economically productive their lives would continue, albeit in limbo. That was an understandable hope, especially in ghettos like Łódź and Kaunas that lasted longest. The Germans also disguised their intentions, spacing out deportations and even issuing new currency to those being "resettled." At the same time, the physical force available to the Germans was overwhelming and the price of resistance high. The death counts after the Warsaw and Vilna ghetto uprisings were horrifying. The same was true of the resistance to the German liquidation of the Białystok ghetto in August 1943. The insurgents had Molotov cocktails but few guns. Their resistance was ruthlessly crushed. A few dozen insurgents escaped to join partisan groups in the nearby forests, but the deportation of ten thousand Białystok Jews to Majdanek, Treblinka, and Auschwitz was barely delayed.[165]

Everywhere there were brutal reprisals against resistance organizers and the families of those who escaped from a ghetto. On April 17, 1942, the Germans got wind of organized political activity in the Warsaw ghetto and shot fifty-one Jews, mostly members of the socialist Bund and others working for the underground press.[166] Jewish Council leaders faced threats. In some places those who seemed reluctant to follow German orders were summarily shot to instill terror. In Warsaw Adam Czerniakow was informed that his wife would be killed if he tried to block deportations.[167] Here, the power relations of the ghetto were laid bare in the starkest possible way. The diligent, well-meaning Czerniakow was engaged on a daily basis, as his diary shows, with trying to mitigate the impact of German commands. He had only minor, short-term successes and eventually committed suicide in July 1942, recognizing that the German objective was genocide. His counterpart in Łódź, Chaim Rumkowski, still believed in the efficacy of bargaining, sacrificing some to preserve others. In his horrifying "Give me your children" speech to fifteen hundred ghetto inhabitants in September 1942, he urged handing over twenty thousand children to meet German demands, knowing that they would almost certainly not survive: "I must amputate limbs in order to save the body."[168]

Nazi overlords at every level passed down to Jews a form of pseudo-decision-making that saddled them with responsibility but no power. They faced what the American Holocaust scholar Lawrence Langer has called "choiceless choices."[169] Czerniakow was an unimaginative but decent man, Rumkowski a vain, dictatorial melagomaniac ("King Chaim"), but in the end this made no difference, just as it made no difference whether Jewish ghetto leaders were willing or not to establish links with underground movements. All the ghettos suffered the same fate. Rumkowski's harsh regime and insistence on maintaining a "productive" ghetto meant that Łódź was the last one to be liquidated, its sixty thousand remaining inhabitants sent to Auschwitz in August 1944, Rumkowski and his family among them. Because of the lateness of its liquidation—or, it could be argued, because of Rumkowski's policy—the ghetto came within three days of being liberated by the Red Army.[170]

Rumkowski was a hated figure at the time, and in subsequent Jewish memory. So were other Jews who, for whatever reasons, agreed to be delegated by the Germans to do their dirty work for them: members of the Jewish police in the ghettos, the *Kapos* and members of the *Sonderkommandos*, the special squads in the camps, whose job was to ferry fellow Jews to their deaths, then cut hair, extract gold teeth, burn bodies, and dispose of the ashes. When it comes to judgment, Primo Levi has written in *The Drowned and the Saved* of a "gray zone" that forbids outright condemnation.[171] An acceptance that these were all, without exception, people placed by German power in an intolerable position has largely replaced lamentations about lack of fighting spirit. Recognize that, and every gesture of defiance has the power to move, like those about to be shot who tore their money into shreds to prevent it being used by the Germans. Jews tried to defy Germans with small acts of nonconformity. That might mean keeping a diary or simply attending a musical performance, or smuggling food and medicine that prolonged life for oneself or others. Under a regime that starved and degraded its victims before it killed them outright, refusing degradation and dehumanization, even staying alive, was a form of resistance.[172]

An increasingly fine-grained understanding of the Holocaust has brought many more historical actors onto the stage. Not all belong to the principal perpetrators and victims, Germans and Jews. The January 2000 Declaration of the Stockholm International Forum on the Holocaust refers to "the horrors that engulfed the Jewish people," then adds: "The terrible suffering of the many other victims of the Nazis has left an indelible scar across Europe as well."[173] Here is a nod to the fact that Jews were not the Nazis' only targeted victims, just as it is a fact that the Germans did not lack collaborators in killing Jews. Both of these truths are incontrovertible, but uncomfortable.

The "universalization" of the Holocaust in the last decades of the twentieth century, its standing as the ultimate exemplar of inhumanity, is one reason that we may and must compare. There is also a word that helps us do so: genocide. The word was itself a by-product of the Holocaust, coined by the Polish Jew Raphael Lemkin in a book published in 1944 after he had escaped Poland, first to Sweden, then to the United States. Genocide partly underlay the prosecution case at the Nuremberg Military Tribunal that met to try the principal surviving perpetrators of German war crimes. Lemkin played an important part, too, in the passage of the 1948 United Nations Convention on Genocide. His own thinking on the subject, and especially on the need to prosecute perpetrators (he was an international lawyer by training), was first aroused by learning in his twenties about the fate of the Armenians.[174]

Hitler admired what the Turks had done to the Armenians in 1915–16 and was aware that Turkey had paid no price internationally for its actions.[175] A week before the invasion of Poland in 1939, he sarcastically asked a group of his military commanders: "Who still talks nowadays about the extermination of the Armenians?"[176] There are also some parallels between the two sets of events. Like the Holocaust, the Armenian genocide was preceded by earlier acts of violence. It was a murderous, government-backed policy against a purported "internal enemy" that unfolded during wartime and was driven forward by an ideology of national regeneration. Yet there were differences, too. One was strategic. Even if Turkish claims of an Armenian uprising were false, Armenians certainly represented more of a potential domestic threat than did Jews in German-controlled Europe. Turkish policy had no basis in biological racism and tens of thousands of Armenians saved themselves by converting to Islam. The killing was also not universal. In addition to the Armenians who escaped Turkish violence by flight, as many as 140,000 survived and lived in the postwar Turkish Republic (although they faced major discrimination). The perpetrators of the genocide apparently did not feel that they had left some of their task undone, nor did they move against Armenians living beyond the Anatolian heartland, in Ottoman Jerusalem, for example.[177] Nonetheless, the Armenian genocide was a precedent in Hitler's mind. Comparing the two events points up similarities, but also differences. Both are important: to compare is not to equate.

The same applies when the Holocaust is set within the larger context of Nazi Germany's policies in World War Two, especially on the eastern front. The destruction of European Jewry was at the core of a murderous program of demographic engineering that claimed millions of non-Jewish civilian lives, mainly the lives of Slavs—Russians, Ukrainians, Poles, Serbs. Then there was the death by deliberate starvation and neglect of three million Soviet POWs. As the historian Christopher Browning has noted, if the Nazi regime had collapsed in spring 1942 those mass deaths would have been considered the greatest of its war crimes.[178] Murderous German policies touched many groups: Jehovah's Witnesses, gay men, disabled people. In Auschwitz the mentally ill, Soviet POWs, and non-Jewish Poles were among those who were gassed; so were twenty thousand Sinti and Roma from the "Gypsy camp." But even where murderous German policies led to millions of civilian victims, as it did in the case of many Slav peoples, there was no intent to kill all Poles or Russians, but rather to reduce them to slave status. The anti-Slav animus of the German occupiers was race-based, but was hardly consistent. Croats, Slovaks, and Bulgarians, no less Slav, were considered "racial allies"; even some Poles were thought to be capable of Germanization.

German policies toward Sinti and Roma reveal, perhaps more than any other case, both the similarities and the crucial differences when it came to the treatment of Jews compared with other victims. Was there a *Porrajmos*, a Romani Holocaust? An SS document dating back to March 1938 refers to a "final solution of the Gypsy question" and there was much discussion during the war, especially in the SS, about whether Gypsies should be grouped together with Jews. The Brazilian-born SS man Pery Broad, who worked in the Political Division at Auschwitz from 1942 to 1945, later testified that "it was the wish of the all-powerful *Reichsführer* [Heinrich Himmler] to have the Gypsies disappear from the face of the earth."[179] But German policy was highly inconsistent in practice. An order to remove Gypsies from the Wehrmacht was not issued until 1941 and some were permitted to remain until 1943. This reflected internal disputes over how to categorize Sinti and Roma. Himmler was convinced that some Roma were "pure-blooded" descendants of an Aryan tribe, which led him to lobby against their deportation from Germany and Austria. In German-occupied Central and eastern Europe Sinti and Roma were, like Jews, killed in mass shootings and sent to death camps, but the uneven patchwork of German policy is apparent from the wildly different death rates from country to country. Few survived in Latvia and Estonia, or in the Crimea, where *Einsatzgruppe* D interpreted its instructions differently from the other task forces and went out of its way to kill all the Sinti and Roma it could find. The death rate was also high in the Protectorate of Bohemia and Moravia. Elsewhere—Serbia and Hungary, for example—the majority survived. The number of those murdered is usually reckoned to be in the range of 200,000 to 500,000, a horrifying enough figure. Some estimates are even higher. There is uncertainty about the size of the Sinti and Roma population before the war, but the proportion of the population killed may have been as high as a quarter. That it was not higher is a result not only of inconsistency and disputed definitions but an underlying decision apparently reached in late 1941, to kill all the itinerant Sinti and Roma but not those who were settled, which also explains why rates of deportation from western Europe were low.[180]

Suffering is indivisible and murder is murder. It is right—essential, in fact—to see how the Holocaust formed one part of a larger, murderous German design. Racial thinking drove Nazi policy when it came to Slav *Untermenschen* and to "half-breed" Gypsies, as indeed it underlay the policy of involuntary euthanasia for disabled Germans. But the Nazis singled out the Jews as a special racial threat, a danger of a unique kind. The Jew checked every box in the Nazi demonology—racial, political, economic, social, and cultural. The Jew was at once enemy within, parasite, black marketer, spreader of disease, speculator, and exploiter, but also fomenter of revolution and degenerate agent of cultural dissolution. And it was only in the case of the Jews that the Nazis reached a decision in 1941 to kill every last man, woman, and child. It was the systematic effort to kill every member of an entire race that sets the murder of Europe's Jews apart. That is reflected in the fact that so high a proportion of the Jews in Germany's grasp were in fact killed. And it is why the paperwork for the Wannsee Conference listed even tiny Jewish communities in Ireland and Portugal that the Germans were unable at the time to lay their hands on.[181]

The Jews who were within their power could not have been rounded up and killed as comprehensively as they were without the collaboration of non-Germans, who assisted with the process everywhere, from Trondheim to Athens, Biarritz to Babi Yar. The Holocaust was a German-directed but pan-European operation, a "supremely transnational" undertaking.[182] The complicity of non-Germans took different forms. There was the cooperation of allies and satellite states such as Italy, Hungary, Romania, Bulgaria,

Slovakia, and Croatia; the part played by nonstate actors, whether spontaneous mobs, paramilitaries, or German-organized police forces, who were instrumental in killing Jews in the Baltic states, Poland, Belarus, and Ukraine; and the indirect, enabling role played by officials, business owners, and others who were complicit in one way or another.

Romania, with the third-largest Jewish population in Europe, killed more Jews than any country other than Germany. Antisemitism ran deep in Romanian politics. The prewar prime minister, Octavian Coga, one of the poet-fascists who flourished in those years, wanted to remove half a million Jews from any role in national life and expatriate them. His deputy, Alexander Cusa, saw himself as the true father of modern antisemitism (and Hitler as no more than a follower). Their government fell after three weeks but antisemitic measures continued. After the war broke out, King Carol II was forced by the strongman of Romanian politics, General Ion Antonescu, to abdicate in favor of his son; the fascist Iron Guard was brought into government, and a policy of "Romanianization" was announced to drive Jews out of business, the professions, schools, and universities. In July 1940 Romania lost territory to the USSR and Hungary, a result of German diplomacy. It was, however, Romanian Jews who were blamed. The army committed massacres as it withdrew. Worse followed. In the wake of an abortive coup attempt in January 1941, the Iron Guard went on a three-day rampage in the Jewish quarter of Bucharest, killing with "quite bestial ferocity," in the words of a witness. Then, after Romanian forces invaded Russia as part of Operation Barbarossa and sustained heavy casualties against the Judeo-Bolshevik enemy, the first mass killing of Jews on Romanian soil took place. It happened in the town of Iasi, birthplace of Alexander Cusa and the original political base of Iron Guard founder Corneliu Codreanu. Soldiers, police, members of the secret service, and Iron Guard legionaries stabbed, beat, and shot thousands of Jews and looted their bodies, before packing thousands more into sealed freight cars, where they suffocated or died of thirst.

It was the Iasi pogrom that the Italian journalist Curzio Malaparte had just witnessed when he flew to Warsaw for his meal with Hans Frank. But the governor-general's expressed surprise at Romanian ferocity was disingenuous, for German army intelligence officers had helped to instigate this alleged suppression of a "Jewish uprising" in late June. Weeks later, the reoccupation of the "lost provinces" of Bukovina and Bessarabia was accompanied by an antisemitic killing spree that lasted for a year, carried out by the Romanian army and police in cooperation with *Einsatzgruppe* D and with the full support of the Antonescu regime, which urged a policy of "ethnic purification." Jews were forcibly deported, ghettoized, driven into labor camps, shot, blown up with explosives, and burned alive. Tens of thousands were killed when Romania occupied Odessa in October 1941. The total number of victims was as high as 380,000.[183]

Romania was an outlier when it came to the sheer volume of killing. Otherwise, its conduct resembled that of other German allies. Romania worked closely with German forces but pursued its own objectives at the same time. Friction arose between Romanian security forces and *Einsatzgruppe* D in the occupied Ukraine because one of the main Romanian aims was the ethnic cleansing of Ukrainians, while the German task force was using Ukrainian collaborators to kill Jews. We see a variation of this in the Balkans. The Ustasha regime in Croatia focused its murderous attention on Serbs, eventually killing as many as 400,000, although it also killed most of the country's 45,000 Jews either directly or by handing them over to its German ally.[184] Many allied states exhibited lethal zeal, in fact, but some things still set them apart from Germany. Romania and Bulgaria behaved with more murderous consistency toward Jews in the territories they occupied during the war than in their core lands. Romania also wound down the persecution of the Jews after 1942, as the prospect of a German victory receded, even as Germany intensified its efforts in the face of defeat, a fanatical determination illustrated by its transporting a small number of Jews in July 1944 from the Aegean islands of Rhodes and Kos to mainland Greece and on to Auschwitz just days before the Majdanek camp was liberated by the Red Army.

A similar dynamic was at work in Hungary, but with a tragic twist. Before the war, the Hungarian regent, Admiral Horthy, a traditional conservative with clerical backing, kept the violently antisemitic fascists of the Arrow Cross movement at bay by passing "moderate" anti-Jewish legislation such as quotas. He followed the same playbook in dealing with Germany during the war. His concessions included 40,000 Jewish men sent as forced laborers to the east and another 18,000 foreign Jews living in Hungary who were handed over to the SS and eventually killed. But news of their fate strengthened Horthy's determination not to hand Hungarian Jews over to Germany. He replaced his prime minister with a less pro-German figure, Miklós Kállay, in March 1942. For the next two years his regime passed further anti-Jewish measures but resisted German pressure to turn over its large population of Jews, or to require Jews to wear the yellow star that would have been the prelude to deportation. Horthy withstood bullying by Hitler in a meeting. Prime Minister Kállay said pointedly in a 1943 speech that Hungary could not relinquish its Jews until it received a satisfactory answer to the question of where they were to be resettled.

The Germans lost patience and assumed direct political control of Hungary in March 1944. Then Hungarian Jews were deported with extraordinary speed, some 435,000 in just fifty-five days in May, June, and July. Most were killed in Auschwitz. A later round of deportations after October 1944 and a series of death marches meant that more than half a million Hungarian Jews lost their lives in the Holocaust. Germans directed all this, but they followed the detailed plan drawn up by right-wing Hungarian generals two years earlier. There were no more than two hundred SS personnel in the country. They could not have done what they did without the support of Hungarian police, bureaucracy, and homegrown fascists. That was true in the summer of 1944, and again after Horthy was deposed in October and an Arrow Cross government installed. The violence of the Jewish round-ups made Hungary resemble Romania three years earlier. But the timing meant that some foreign diplomats and representatives of humanitarian organizations mobilized to help the Jews of Budapest by issuing "protection

Jewish women being rounded up in Budapest by the local Arrow Cross fascists in October 1944.

papers," providing safe houses, and organizing escape lines. The Swedish diplomat Raoul Wallenberg is the best known figure in this group, whose efforts saved thousands of lives.[185]

Another of the diplomats was Giorgio Perlasca, a former Fascist who had fought as a volunteer for Franco in the Spanish Civil War. He is an unlikely hero, but his loathing of Nazism led him to play a role similar to Wallenberg's. As an Italian diplomat in Budapest, Perlasca distanced himself from the Republic of Salò, the puppet state created by the Germans after they occupied Italy in September 1943. He was interned but used a medical pass to present himself along with his Civil War credentials at the embassy of neutral Spain. He adopted the first name Jorge and worked together with the Spanish chargé d'affaires, Ángel Sanz Briz, to protect Jews from deportation by every means possible. Between them they saved more than five thousand Jewish lives.[186]

Perlasca's conduct was hardly typical of Italian reactions in the face of the Holocaust, but it remains striking how little cooperation Germany received, relatively speaking, from its principal diplomatic partner. Antisemitism had never been important in Italian fascism, which explains why more than 10 percent of Italy's Jews became members of the party between 1928 and 1933. The racial laws passed in November 1938 were a concession to Germany and unpopular with many Italians and even some leading Fascists, like the aviator Italo Balbo. The discrimination Jews then faced was real, but their isolation in everyday life was much less complete than in Germany. It is a classic instance of the Italian dance with the devil that Jews could no longer be listed in the phone book—but their numbers were still available from the operator on request. Jews in wartime Italy remained relatively safe until 1943, which is why thousands of foreign Jews chose to enter Italy or Italian-held territory. After Mussolini had been installed in the Republic of Salò puppet regime, Germany tried to deport Italy's Jews to the death camps, with limited success. The puppet regime ordered all Jews to be placed in transit camps. From the end of 1943 to the liberation, many Italian agencies took part in round-ups: the National Guard, the Black Brigade of the Fascist Party, the Italian SS, and Fascist irregulars. Their task was made easier by informers. But there was also substantial resistance. Even before 1943, Italian soldiers and officials in Greece and Croatia had been inventive in stalling German demands to hand over Jews. The same thing happened in German-occupied Italy after 1943. Fascist mayors turned a blind eye to fugitives, carabinieri tipped off those about to be arrested, and many Italians provided Jews with food, shelter, and false papers. Catholic clergy offered refuge in churches and monasteries.[187]

About 85 percent of Italian Jews survived the Holocaust, a percentage equaled only in Denmark. Timing and topography were two of the many reasons. The chaos of the German army moving into Italy gave Jews time to escape into hiding in the Apennines or Alps. The occupation was also relatively short (although longer than the German occupation of Hungary). It mattered that in Italy, as in Denmark, Jews were a small, highly assimilated community not closely associated either with business or with Communist politics. Beyond the fact that the Fascist movement was less antisemitic than its counterparts in Romania or Hungary, Italy as a whole had no strong tradition of antisemitism.

Most victims of the Holocaust lived and died in the old Jewish Pale of Settlement, where the Germans did not work through allied or satellite states but ruled directly. Here, in Poland, Belarus, the Baltics, and Ukraine, Jews mostly lived separate lives. There were few conversions, few intermarriages or shared activities with the non-Jewish majority. Periodic pogroms testified to persistent and visceral anti-Jewish sentiment. Recent politics also made a difference. Before the Germans arrived in June or July 1941, these were areas the USSR had occupied since 1939, sometimes longer, leaving behind bitterness about their brutality and deportations of local people. Jews were all too readily identified with the hated Bolsheviks. Younger Jews were, in fact, strongly represented in local Communist cadres, an understandable response to persecution. The larger truth, that the Soviet occupiers actually dispossessed and deported more Jews than other nationalities, was not going to disturb the certitudes of local antisemites.

The departure of the Russians and the arrival of the Germans in the summer of 1941 ignited outbreaks of murderous violence across the region. Jews were attacked and killed in the thousands. These spasms of violence were often spontaneous, especially those that occurred after the Soviets had left and before the Germans arrived. But some caution is needed here, because the German authorities tried hard to make pogroms they directed look spontaneous, and in some cases recorded their disappointment about the lack of local cooperation. Franz Walter Stahlecker, the head of *Einsatzgruppe* A, reported from Lithuania that within a few hours of their entering Kaunas "local antisemitic elements were induced to engage in pogroms against the Jews." He went on, "The impression had to be created that the local population itself had taken the first steps of its own accord as a natural reaction to decades of oppression by the Jews." But later in the same report he remarked how at first "it was surprisingly difficult to set a fairly large-scale pogrom in motion there."[188]

Lithuanian antisemites nonetheless showed plenty of zeal for the task once they had started. A paramilitary group killed as many as 5000 Jews in and around Kaunas during four days at the end of June. Photographs show the bodies of Jews who had been publicly beaten to death in front of a crowd that includes women and children while German soldiers take photographs. At the notorious Fort VII and Fort IX outside the city, 45,000 to 50,000 Jews were killed in a matter of months. By the end of 1941, 180,000 Lithuanian Jews had been killed, most by Lithuanian paramilitaries working with the Germans.[189] That was the pattern elsewhere in the Baltic.[190] So, too, in Ukraine, where the number of Jewish victims beaten and shot reached Lithuanian levels. Again, the change in political control established the context of the killing. Ukrainian nationalists issued a leaflet calling for the "destruction" of Jewry on July 1, one day after the Germans occupied Lviv. Ukrainian antisemites eventually killed some 200,000 Jews.[191] In Poland as well, the German occupation of formerly Soviet-controlled eastern parts of the country unleashed pogroms. The best-known case occurred in Jedwabne on July 10, 1941, when at least 340 Jewish men, women, and children were locked in a barn that was set on fire.[192] But it was one of two hundred similar incidents at this time in former Soviet-occupied Poland.[193]

The more we learn about the murders committed at hundreds of different sites, the harder it becomes to overlook the role played by non-Germans. There was a spontaneous local element to many of the pogroms in June and July 1941. Germans were invariably present, however, and the murderous violence directed against Jews could not have taken place without their approval and encouragement. After this first wave of killings, the German occupiers also organized the local violence. In a second wave of killings, which took place in 1942–43, Lithuanians, Ukrainians, and others were enrolled in auxiliary police forces under German control. They killed, helped to clear ghettos, guarded Jews during round-ups and in camps, and used their local knowledge, helping Germans to identify the Jews (for these were their former neighbors) and assisting with manhunts where their familiarity with forests and marshes was indispensable.[194]

The motives that drove people to participate were many: hatred or resentment of Jews, anticommunism and nationalist sentiment, a desire to exercise power, a liking for violence, fear, careerism, community pressure, calculation, greed.[195] This last should not be underestimated. There were plenty of spoils to be had. Again and again, we read of houses being looted, bodies stripped of clothes and boots. For those who did this, ideological motives were not necessarily uppermost, just avarice coupled with callous indifference. The looting of bodies happened more systematically in the death camps, largely to the benefit of the Germans who controlled everything that happened there, with the crumbs going to non-German guards. But all across Europe there were people complicit in the fate of the Jews because they benefited materially. At least ten thousand Frenchmen became managers of former Jewish businesses.[196] Others simply plundered. The stolen and quasi-stolen artwork has become notorious. Most of it was shipped back to Germany, but some found its way into the eager hands of other Europeans and all of it generated income for dealers, shippers, and insurers. Art was only one part of the plunder. In Paris forty thousand apartments owned by Jews were cleared, an operation that involved fifteen hundred removal men and many others who knew what was happening and why—landlords and concierges, the police, registrars of property, the tax authorities, banks and insurance companies.

In W. G. Sebald's last novel, a Jew called Jacques Austerlitz who escaped Central Europe as a boy on a *Kindertransport* to England, returns to Europe. He learns from a surviving witness how his mother's apartment in Prague was looted; then, in Paris, another witness describes how the same thing happened there. Louis XVI furniture, Meissen porcelain, Persian rugs, entire libraries, violins, cooking pots, tableware, everything "down to the last saltcellar and pepper mill" was carried off and shipped to Germany. The French individuals and agencies responsible for this knew that the interned Jews would not be coming back.[197] This went on across occupied Europe.[198] There were fascists and nonfascists everywhere who relished the task, and police who rounded up Jews and took them to transit camps for deportation to Auschwitz. But many more were indirectly involved or looked the other way.

Non-Jews living in occupied Europe did not confront the terrible "choiceless choices" faced by Jewish leaders, but they were also not free agents. There were limits to what they could do. On the one occasion when a local population took collective action expressly in response to anti-Jewish policies, the outcome only underscored German power and proved counterproductive. After a German raid on the Jewish quarter in Amsterdam in February 1941, Dutch outrage led to a general strike organized by the underground Communist Party. It began with city streetcar drivers, soon joined by other workers. Eventually 300,000 people joined the strike in Amsterdam and the action spread to Utrecht and Hilversum. The Germans, initially taken by surprise, regained control of the streets within a few days. The repercussions for the Jews of the Netherlands were severe. Deportations were speeded up. One result was the "Dutch paradox," that so many Jews in one of the most tolerant countries of Europe were killed (70 percent, compared with 20 percent in France).[199] The Dutch, who were paid an unintended compliment by Goebbels when he called them "the most insolent and obstreperous people in Europe," were also cowed by a German show of force.[200] Yet in the Netherlands, as elsewhere, despite the risks, there were people willing to hide Jews or bring them food, even to run underground railroads to smuggle Jews to safety and then find ways to remove their names from official records. There were cases like this even in parts of Europe where there was widespread support for German actions against the Jews. Few people realize that the largest national group of those honored at Yad Vashem as the "righteous among the nations" consists of Poles. As many as a thousand Poles were executed for helping Jews.[201]

Perpetrators, victims, and bystanders—that was once the familiar trinity in Holocaust history. The third category has shrunk over time as more of the bystanders turn out to have been perpetrators, or at least complicit in some way. But there still were bystanders in German-occupied Europe, those who neither assisted nor resisted but minded their own business and aimed simply to survive. That also describes the behavior of some institutions, such as the Papacy. Even before the war, Pope Pius XI was reluctant to confront Hitler's policy directly. He signed a concordat with the new regime in July 1933 and the well-known encyclical *Mit brennender Sorge* (With Deep Anxiety) issued four years later criticized racism but failed to mention National Socialism by name. Anticommunism reinforced institutional caution and led the pope to pull his punches. When Pius XI died in February 1939, he was succeeded by the candidate favored in Berlin, Eugenio Pacelli, a former papal nuncio in Germany. A deep-dyed conservative, hostile to democracy as well as communism, Pius XII was even less inclined than his predecessor to expose the church to risk. That, more than the antisemitism or anticommunism rife in leading Vatican circles, was what guided his hypercautious policy. He dropped the more critical encyclical planned by Pius XI and refused to denounce Nazi

policy even when round-ups of Jews began in German-occupied Rome in
1943.[202] Those inclined to pronounce retrospective condemnations have not
always acknowledged the genuine fears that existed in Rome. But the Vatican's lukewarm public criticisms of National Socialism can reasonably be
compared with the scathing language it used against communism or with
the full-blown opposition the Catholic Church demonstrated toward state
"overreach" in the various *Kulturkampf* struggles of the later nineteenth
century, not least in Germany. Yet, even as some Catholic clergy as well
as laypeople lent themselves to the murderous persecution of Jews, from
Poland to Croatia, others conducted themselves very differently. In every
part of Europe, Catholics priests sheltered and fed Jews, ran escape lines,
and sometimes paid with their lives.

Papal nuncios were among the diplomats of neutral powers who did
most to spread news of the Holocaust. Some pleaded with local rulers to
treat Jews humanely and stop deportations, among them Giuseppe Burzio
in Slovakia, Andrea Cassulo in Romania, and Angelo Roncalli, the future
Pope John XXIII, who was nuncio in Turkey. The most energetic and effective in saving Jewish lives was Angelo Rotta, papal nuncio in Budapest,
who played a leading role in establishing the "International Ghetto" over
which the neutral powers (Sweden, Switzerland, Spain, Portugal, and the
Vatican) tried to spread their protection. The elderly Rotta led the protests
of neutral diplomats against deportations and obtained Vatican permission
to issue thousands of protective passes.[203]

In Budapest he worked alongside Friedrich Born, the Swiss-born representative of the International Committee of the Red Cross. Born was
also an exception within the organization he represented. The Red Cross
knew better than most what was happening. Its vice chairman, Carl Burckhardt, even relayed information about the gassing of Jews in death camps
to the State Department in Washington. Like the Vatican, however, the
Red Cross chose public silence. At a key meeting in October 1942 the decision was taken not to expose or condemn the genocide already underway,
details of which had become widely known through reports from the Polish underground, diplomats, and newspaper correspondents from neutral countries. The Red Cross even had its headquarters in the same city,
Geneva, as the World Jewish Congress, which reported in August 1942 that
Germany planned to murder all the Jews of Europe. But the organization
saw the cause of the Jews as a distraction from its mission and judged that
speaking out would threaten its neutrality. It was the same instinct that led

the Red Cross to accept German demands on the eastern front that it not attend to Soviet POWs.[204]

A third global institution also pulled its punches: Hollywood. All the major film studios in Hollywood except for Twentieth Century–Fox were run by Jews and plenty of anti-Nazi German émigrés found their way there, too—many of them also Jews, as we saw earlier. But this situation bred a nervous concern with institutional self-preservation not dissimilar to that shown by the Catholic Church and the Red Cross. The studio heads were right to be nervous, given the potential for antisemitic backlash. Joseph I. Breen, the right-wing Catholic appointed by the Hays Office to enforce the production code, once wrote to a friend that "people whose daily morals would not be tolerated in the toilet of a pest house hold the good jobs out here and wax fat on it. Ninety-five percent of these folks are Jews of an Eastern European lineage. They are, probably, the scum of the scum of the earth."[205] The Nazi German consul in Los Angeles, Georg Gyssling, went to screenings, wrote letters, suggested revisions, and generally made a nuisance of himself until June 1941, when the United States broke off diplomatic relations with Germany.[206] The studios were terrified of appearing to take up the Jewish cause, a stance in which they were joined by the Anti-Defamation League. The result was the virtual absence of any criticism, however oblique, of Nazi Germany. Even in a film about Émile Zola and the Dreyfus affair, antisemitism went unmentioned. When Hollywood went to war after December 1941, the picture it offered of occupied Europe was highly skewed. The Nazis were a few evil men, the German people mostly deluded victims, and the Christian churches both the principal target and the main resistance to "godless" Nazism. Jews were nowhere to be seen.[207] The desperate refugees seeking safe passage from Casablanca were mostly Jews, but the refugees in *Casablanca* were never identified as such.

The Allied powers were much more forthright, at least in their language. On December 17, 1942, a joint declaration was issued on behalf of all the Allies. It was based on a report presented to the British government by the Polish government in exile in London, which drew on information from the Polish underground. The declaration announced plainly that "the German authorities, not content with denying to people of Jewish race in all the territories over which their barbarous rule has been extended, the most elementary human rights, are now carrying into effect Hitler's oft-repeated intention to exterminate the Jewish people in Europe."[208] Foreign Secretary

Anthony Eden read the declaration to the British House of Commons. It was simultaneously released by the Allies and reported in Allied and neutral countries. The gravity of the occasion and the shock of the revelations were apparent in the words of Lord Addison. Referring to the report of the Polish government in exile, he said to fellow peers: "A more awful exposure of horrors, I imagine, has never been issued by any government in the history of the world."[209] In the summer of 1944 Winston Churchill called the genocide "probably the greatest and most horrible crime ever committed in the whole history of the world," a striking statement coming from a politician who liked to think of himself as a historian.[210]

Yet the Allies did little to address the fate of European Jews. Churchill, the most sympathetic of the Big Three, wanted plans drawn up in 1944 to consider how Auschwitz might be attacked, but there was no appetite for this in the British cabinet. Then, as German control weakened and the possibility arose of rescuing (or ransoming) Jews from Romania, Hungary, and elsewhere, Britain remained reluctant to allow Jews to enter its Palestine Mandate, fearing the Arab backlash and resulting political instability. Stalin mentioned the persecution of the Jews just once in the course of the war, in a November 1941 speech about German pogroms. The USSR arguably had the most realistic opportunity to attack Auschwitz, for it had advanced close by the late summer of 1944 and enjoyed air superiority on the eastern front for five months before it liberated the camp the following January. (Bombing Auschwitz might, of course, have been counterproductive in killing Jews or hastening the death marches that eventually killed so many.) Roosevelt proceeded very cautiously, mindful of the widespread antisemitism among the American public (in a 1942 opinion poll, 44 percent thought that Jews had too much power and influence in the United States) and unwilling to spend political capital on the issue.[211] Roosevelt did not formally condemn German policy until March 1944, although two months before that he had—under pressure—established the War Refugee Board, which saved tens of thousands of Jewish lives.

The two western leaders both wanted to avoid playing into the hands of Nazi propaganda by giving the appearance that they were fighting the war "for the Jews." That genuine concern overlapped with another consideration. The best way to help the Jews, so they said and believed, was to end the war as speedily as possible. Like Stalin, Churchill and FDR had developed a rhetoric about what was at stake in the war and it did not include the question, invariably seen as a subordinate issue, of the murder of European

Jews. All three were focused on the immediate war aim of beating Hitler and forcing Germany to surrender unconditionally. That was what they affirmed at Teheran and Yalta, and that was the course they pursued until the German capitulation on May 7, 1945.

From Defeat to Division

A MONTH BEFORE THE GERMAN SURRENDER, TROOPS FROM THE Sixth Armored Division of the U.S. army liberated Buchenwald concentration camp. There they found twenty-one thousand emaciated men, a small group of whom had nonetheless managed to take control of the camp from the remaining German guards just before their liberators arrived. The survivors included long-term political prisoners and Jews who had been marched there in January from Auschwitz and the Gross-Rosen camp in Lower Silesia. They came from all across Europe and beyond, more than thirty different nations. Some had been prominent figures before their confinement in Buchenwald, like the Polish scientist Marian Ciepielowski and the Viennese cabaret artist Hermann Leopoldi. Others were still in their early twenties, such as Jorge Semprún, a Spanish writer and left-wing activist. Semprún survived to write one of the most profound of all books about captivity in a Nazi camp and its aftermath. In *Literature or Life* he talks about people he knew in Buchenwald, like the members of an illicit jazz group led by the Czech poet Jiri Krak (on drums), with a Serbian saxophonist, a Norwegian trumpet player, and arrangements by Semprún's close friend, a Frenchman named Yves Darriet.[212] There were also two young Jews, still just fifteen or sixteen, who became famous years later: the Romanian-born Elie Wiesel, winner of the 1986 Nobel Peace Prize, and Hungarian Imre Kertész, winner of the 2002 Nobel Prize for Literature. A third, only slightly older, was Robert Widerman, who later achieved celebrity of a different kind as actor Robert Clary when he played the part of Corporal LeBeau in *Hogan's Heroes*, the 1960s U.S. sitcom set in a German POW camp.

That was just Buchenwald itself, which had more than a hundred satellite camps. As the Allies advanced into Germany they liberated over a thousand camps, not counting the ones that had recently housed forced foreign laborers or POWs. All these together formed a vast archipelago of camps containing mostly non-Germans that were now emptied out. Tadeusz Borowski, liberated from Dachau, wrote about "the incredible, almost com-ical, melting-pot of peoples and nationalities sizzling dangerously in the very heart of Europe."[213] The historian Karl Schlögel had a different image, a postwar Central Europe of desperate "passengers," living lives in transit.[214]

At war's end there were some eight million so-called displaced persons (DPs) on German territory, in addition to POWs. They were cared for by relief detachments of the Allies and by the new United Nations Relief and Rehabilitation Administration (UNRRA).[215] Most wanted to return to their homes. Well over six million had done so by the end of 1945. But more than a million remained, mainly Poles, Ukrainians, and Baltic citizens unwilling to return to a Soviet-dominated region, and Jews still waiting to travel on to the United States or Palestine. Their numbers were then swollen by as many as a quarter million Jews who fled to the west, or in some cases fled back to the west after they had returned to eastern Europe and found their homes occupied by people who had seized them during the war and refused to give them back. Hostile locals did more than turn a cold shoulder. Several Jews who returned to the southern Polish town of Nowy Targ were murdered by Polish nationalists. They included Ludwig Herz and Salomon Lindenberger, who had been rescued during the war by Oskar Schindler.[216] Physical attacks on Jews were commonplace. They were accused, once more, of having too much sympathy for the Soviet forces of occupation, and sometimes faced violence of a horribly familiar kind. A pogrom in the Polish town of Kielce in July 1946 that followed accusations of ritual murder left forty-two Jews dead.

The DPs in Germany, almost all veterans of Nazi camp life in one form or another, were housed in hundreds of camps set up by UNRRA. The two main groups—anti-Communist, often antisemitic Poles and Ukrainians, and Jews who were often Zionists—lived in separate camps. They organized themselves, formed committees, and made demands.[217] These long-term DPs received education and job training as well as food and shelter. The camps became a kind of laboratory of international welfare and their inhabitants the object of keen attention from social workers, psychologists, and child welfare experts. Almost all were eventually resettled, although not necessarily "repatriated." Of the approximately 1.3 million DPs still under the care of UNRRA or its eventual successor organization in the fall of 1947, 100,000 were settled in Latin America and another 182,000 in Australia. The rest went to the United States or Canada, and in the case of the Jews to Palestine and, after 1948, to the new state of Israel. The postwar moment of the DPs may have been brief but it was truly foundational, and global in impact, for not only did the DPs themselves resettle around the world but their experience helped to establish the modern category of the "refugee" and the concept of political asylum, both enshrined in a 1951 U.N. convention.[218]

While millions of non-Germans returned to their homes or resettled elsewhere, millions of Germans in east-central Europe either fled or were forcibly expelled. They numbered around 12.5 million in all: 7 million from Poland, 3 million from Czechoslovakia, 2.5 million in total from Russia, Ukraine, the Baltic, Romania, Hungary, and Yugoslavia. This was the largest involuntary movement of a people in modern history. Germans fled out of fear of the Red Army or were expelled in episodes of ethnic cleansing that mimicked German conduct in these same areas just a few years earlier. Some found transportation. The dashing Countess Marion Dönhoff rode west on horseback. But for most of these expellees, the journey west meant an arduous trek on foot with as many possessions as possible packed into a handcart, which became an iconic object in later memory and museum displays.[219] As many as a quarter of a million Germans were killed. Another two million died from exposure, malnutrition, sickness, or exhaustion.

Some of the Germans who fled or were expelled from the east after 1944. Note the handcarts, which became iconic symbols of flight and expulsion.

The violence directed against Germans was organized. It helped Communist authorities to rally support among the local population. Camps were set up to intern Germans, often the same camps that the Germans themselves had used (including Auschwitz); they were forced to wear badges marking them as Germans, just as Germans had once forced badge wearing on others, and they were taken on death marches horribly reminiscent of death marches perpetrated earlier by Germans, such as the notorious Brno death march at the end of May 1945, when 30,000 Germans were thrown out of their Czech homes and sent on a forced march to the Austrian border, during which 1700 of them died. Some of the violence shocked Soviet soldiers and officials. During the early, "wild" expulsions, Germans were beaten, humiliated, shot, and burned alive after being doused in gasoline. This was violence from below, driven by a mixture of motives that included, obviously, revenge. But there was also the desire to seize German homes at a time of homelessness and privation, especially when this could be seen as an act of national "purification," something that again echoed earlier German justifications for brutality. The expulsions made a mockery of the "orderly and humane" process called for by the Allies. But the victors, in east and west alike, had geopolitical reasons for wanting to reduce German influence as well as German territory across east-central Europe. The wholesale clearing-out of Germans achieved both objectives. The decisions made during the war legitimized their expulsion, even if the Allies did not anticipate the violence of the ethnic cleansing.[220]

The fate of the Germans was the greatest single instance of the many expulsions that convulsed the Continent at the end of the war. Fighting between Poles and Ukrainians on the eastern Polish borderlands caused 100,000 deaths and 1.4 million expulsions. Combined with the wartime murder of Polish Jews and the ethnic cleansing of Germans from the western areas, they turned Poland, 35 percent non-Polish before 1939, into an ethnically homogeneous Polish state. The same happened elsewhere: 150,000 ethnic Turks were expelled from Bulgaria, 200,000 Italians fled Yugoslav terror campaigns in Dalmatia and Istria. Widen the lens further, and we see these forced movements of population everywhere in this "midcentury maelstrom." The creation of Israel caused the displacement of 700,000 Palestinians; the hurried partition of the Indian Subcontinent in 1947 affected as many as 15 million people who moved from West and East Pakistan to India or the reverse.[221] These were cases where violent movements of population followed the retreat of colonialism. In some ways the departure of Germans from areas of east-central Europe they had colonized, sometimes as long ago as the High Middle Ages, was another case of colonial retreat. And there are some parallels between German expellees and Algerian *pied-noir* settlers fifteen years later.[222]

Germans refugees and expellees passed first through reception camps. The numbers were daunting. In April 1946, 85,000 arrived in Bavaria alone; in June it was 142,000.[223] The camps were designed to be places where new arrivals were processed quickly, given food and a medical examination, sprayed with DDT powder, then sent on their way. But, like refugee camps in our own time, many become semipermanent. By one estimate, 10 percent of families were still living in camps or sim-

ilar emergency accommodation in 1953. Camp Poxdorf in Bavaria, a former Luftwaffe spare-parts storage area that became a reception camp
for Sudeten Germans, was not closed until 1963.[224] Long-term camps
provided a sense of community. They may have helped the refugees to
find their feet. But they also reflected the difficulties many faced. In 1948
there was an uprising at the Dachau reception camp over poor conditions. Contrary to upbeat later accounts of incomers who had quickly
assimilated and thrived, they mostly encountered a "cold homeland"
where they felt unwelcome.[225] That was partly because they were easterners, for whom (despite Nazi propaganda) there was little sympathy in
the rest of Germany. They often represented the intrusion of a different
religious denomination where they settled, the first Catholics or Protestants who had ever been seen there. Camp dwellers were associated with
disease and crime and, especially in the desperate early postwar years,
they represented unwanted competition for scarce necessities of food,
fuel, and shelter.

The rural areas that initially housed many of the refugees, from
Schleswig-Holstein in the north to Württemberg in the south, were also
places where other Germans had taken temporary refuge: wartime evacuees, three million of whom had still not returned in 1946, or people who
had simply fled bombed-out cities to stay with relatives in the country. The
situation in the urban areas was catastrophic. The sustained bombing of
Hamburg in July 1943 had destroyed the homes of a quarter million people, as well as three hundred schools and twenty-five hospitals. In Frankfurt am Main only 44,000 out of 177,000 houses still stood; in Nuremberg
only one dwelling in ten was undamaged; in the industrial Ruhr it was just
one in twenty. Across Germany one-fourth of the housing stock had been
destroyed and at least as much again seriously damaged. Hastily erected
Nissen huts housed a few; others made do in damaged rooms and flooded
cellars. The immediate postwar period is also when the "rubble women"
became iconic figures, forming chain gangs to clear the ruined buildings
brick by brick.

Germany's industrial capacity was much less damaged, but could be put
back to use only when the workers had somewhere to live and the transportation system had been mended. In 1945–46 the rubble and the broken
railroad tracks made it hard for anyone to move around, just as it was hard
to move coal, food, or raw materials. "Only the rivers were whole," says
one of John le Carré's characters, remembering those years.[226] But that was

not true either. The rivers were filled with unexploded ordnance as well as the debris of sunken vessels and bridges blown up by the retreating Wehrmacht, which created—most evocatively in the buckled Hohenzollern Bridge in Cologne—the enduring image of a world turned upside down. The bridges had "dropped to their knees in the water," wrote the Swiss dramatist Max Frisch in his diary.[227]

Frisch was touching on the moral crisis bequeathed by National Socialism. Many foreign observers felt strongly that Germans did not really accept that there *was* a moral crisis. It was inevitable that the occupiers would judge the local population. In fact, they were required to. In the documentary short *Your Job in Germany*, directed by Frank Capra and scripted by Theodor Geisel (better known as Dr. Seuss), American GIs were told, "You'll see ruins. You'll see flowers. You'll see some mighty pretty scenery. Don't let it fool you. You are in enemy country."[228] The regulations about nonfraternization for Allied soldiers reinforced the message, even if they were often flouted. What Allied soldiers saw when they liberated the camps shocked them. In the summer of 1945, posters went up in towns and villages bearing images from Bergen-Belsen and the bold black headline: "This Town Is Guilty! You Are Guilty!" In a 1946 book on the question of guilt, the German philosopher Karl Jaspers (whose anti-Nazi credentials were beyond reproach) pointed out that, in the absence of any authority claiming responsibility for the accusation, this was bound to appear like a bolt from the blue and cause bewilderment.[229] But Germans could hardly fail to be aware of the horror they aroused in the eyes of at least some of the occupiers. We have many descriptions of battle-tested GIs who turned away to cry, or to vomit, when they liberated the camps.

We also have a very striking case of "before" and "after." During the war, the urbane British actor Hugh Williams wrote lightheartedly to his wife, including a whimsical poem in the style of Noël Coward. But after he had witnessed Bergen-Belsen, Williams rejected Coward's famous line ("Don't let's be beastly to the Germans") and wrote his wife a very different letter, filled with rage: "Vengeance, vengeance, vengeance. I loathe every rotten gutted son of a fucking bastard of them. . . . As long as I can get out and about and see . . . the filthy swine either caged or hobbling down the roads I shan't be bored." You can still smell the brimstone three-quarters of a century later.[230] It was the instinct to rub German noses in their own behavior that led to Germans being marched by Allied soldiers to showings of documentaries such as *Todesmühlen* (*Death Mills*).[231]

That Germans seemed wrapped up in their own misery only compounded the offense. Of course, their privations were appallingly real. Even for those who had not fled or been expelled, these were harsh years of homelessness and cellar dwelling, desperate black market dealing, stealing lumps of coal and food. The Allies did not follow Wehrmacht wartime practice. Germans were kept alive by Allied rations, but these were meager: 860 calories a day in the American zone in 1945.[232] One of the greatest uncertainties affected millions of women waiting for husbands and sons to return from the war. The waiting was often based on false hope, for the Wehrmacht had lost count of the dead in the last stages of the war and the number of those still alive as POWs was believed to be 1.5 million larger than it actually was.[233] Many of those women would have suffered rape. That was the fate of 100,000 women in Berlin, another 1.4 million in East Prussia, Silesia, and Pomerania. Rape happened in every zone of occupation, but especially in the Soviet zone, and it continued through the beginning of 1947.[234] This was, for Germans, a violent peace, a "time of the wolves."[235]

Many foreign writers who traveled in Germany in these years were sympathetic to German suffering. One was the precocious Swedish poet, novelist, and literary journalist Stig Dagerman. He was married to the daughter of left-wing Germans who had fought in the Spanish Civil War and eventually fled to Sweden. Dagerman arrived in Germany in the fall of 1946, when he was about to turn twenty-three, and wrote a series of sketches of daily life that became the book *German Autumn*. In one vignette, an old lady at a Hamburg streetcar stop has a sack of potatoes; the string breaks, potatoes roll into the road, and children, men, and women scramble to grab them, while English army cars honk their horns. Fräulein S., who is showing Dagerman around the city, says bitterly: "That's Germany today—risk your life for a potato."[236] Dagerman was scornful of those Allied journalists who settled lazily for calling conditions in Germany "indescribable" and made no effort to describe them. These journalists made a practice of seeking out half-starved people in flooded cellars, asking them if they had been better off under Hitler, then—after getting the expected answer— announcing to their readers that Nazism was alive and well. Dagerman did not doubt that there had been Nazi crimes, but he rejected the doctrine of collective guilt and regarded hunger as a poor educator.

Dorothy Thompson, the celebrated American foreign correspondent, took a similar view. Expelled from Germany in 1934 for her anti-Nazi views, she refused to judge all Germans guilty when she returned after the war and soon encountered criticism that she showed more sympathy for the Nazis than their victims.[237] But Thompson believed that Germany represented only one part of a larger postwar moral crisis. The British writer and publisher Victor Gollancz, a Jew and a socialist, derived his sympathy for the German people from his political convictions. What he saw in postwar Germany was a working class forced to live in inhuman conditions. He was especially moved by the plight of children. Gollancz took note of the children who went to school in damaged shoes, wrong-sized shoes, or no shoes at all. His book *In Darkest Germany* has many pictures of broken shoes. Gollancz's hand is often visible. He explained: "I thought that my visible presence would add verisimilitude, and obviate the charge, for instance, that these were really agency photographs taken in China in 1932."[238]

Stephen Spender was another English writer who traveled in postwar Germany and wrote about it in *European Witness*. A 1930s Communist turned liberal, Spender was also skeptical about collective guilt and uneasy in his official role (he was supposed to report to the Allied Control Commission on the condition of intellectuals and libraries). But Spender talked to Poles still stranded in Germany, who told him that British and American soldiers treated the Germans too well. Another of Spender's countrymen experienced the same thing. Anglo-Irish writer James Stern (like Spender he had a partly Jewish family background) was in Germany with a traveling companion he calls "Mervyn," who was actually W. H. Auden returning to old haunts. Stern and Auden were told by a group of Poles how bewildered they were by the benign treatment of the Germans. They mimed for their English interlocutors ("punctuated by pouncing on our cigarette butts") how German soldiers would have behaved if the roles were reversed.[239] Stern himself was shocked that most Germans showed so little remorse and came to believe that their feelings of guilt were too "colossal" for them to face.[240]

A policy of "de-Nazification" was agreed upon by Stalin, Roosevelt, and Churchill at the Yalta summit, but what that meant in practice was (like much else) left unspecified. Even the question of how to treat the principal Nazi leaders was contentious. The Moscow Declaration of the Big Three on November 1, 1943, announced that the "major criminals" would be "punished by a joint decision of the Governments of the Allies."[241] At the Teheran Conference later that month Stalin was apparently teasing Churchill when he suggested that as many as fifty thousand be summarily executed, but the British leader himself spoke of summary justice and there was strong opposition in Britain to going down the legal path. John

Simon, who as Lord Chancellor held the most senior legal post in Britain, was adamant that this was a political, not a judicial matter. Convening any kind of court would be time-consuming and might well be regarded as victors' justice. And what if the defendants turned the tables and asked awkward questions or made political speeches, as Hitler had done at his trial in 1924? But by the summer of 1945 Hitler was dead, and the British had come around to the Soviet and U.S. preference for a full-scale trial.

The International Military Tribunal convened in Nuremberg in November 1945 with judges from each of the three Allies, plus France. Nuremberg, in the American zone, was chosen because the city's Palace of Justice and adjacent prison had not been bombed, but also because of its importance to National Socialism as the site of the infamous rallies. Indictments were handed down against twenty-four prominent Nazis and twenty-two were brought to trial. After almost a year of proceedings in four languages (an IBM system of simultaneous translation was used for the first time), after four hundred sessions, hundreds of witnesses and hundreds of thousands of affidavits, twelve of the accused were sentenced to death (one of them, Martin Bormann, in absentia), seven to imprisonment, and three acquitted. Ten were hanged on October 16, 1946; Göring had swallowed a cyanide tablet the night before.

The proceedings were widely criticized at the time. The chief justice of the U.S. Supreme Court, Harlan Fiske Stone, described the trial in a private letter as a "high-grade lynching party." There were major problems with at least two of the counts. One was the charge of crimes against the peace, which rested on the dubious premise that international actors were bound to solve their conflicts by legal means. The hypocrisy of this was exposed by the fact that the United States had never joined the League of Nations and the USSR had been expelled from it for attacking Finland. The British government, meanwhile, had accepted every one of Hitler's aggressive actions right up until September 1939, as E. L. Woodward, the historical adviser to the Foreign Office, pointed out during preparations for the trial.[242] Even more awkwardly for the Allies' moral standing, Germany had been allied with the USSR when it attacked Poland. A second indictment, of "conspiracy against the peace," was just as problematic. It was the brainchild of Murray Bernays in the U.S. Department of War. He came from the Securities and Exchange Commission, which used conspiracy charges in pursuing financial crimes.[243] The other Allies were unenthusiastic. It fell to Robert H. Jackson, the chief U.S. prosecutor, to pursue the conspiracy charge by trying to establish a blueprint for aggression on Hitler's part. The tribunal might have been better served by concentrating on the other two counts, war crimes and crimes against humanity, although these presented difficulties of their own. The charges allowed prosecutors to lay out in detail the murder of the Jews as well as atrocities such as the destruction of the towns of Lidice and Oradour-sur-Glane. At the same time, what the Allies had done in firebombing Hamburg and Dresden, and at Hiroshima and Nagasaki, laid them open to charges of hypocrisy. So did the Soviet insistence on laying the Katyn massacre of Polish officers in 1940 at the door of Nazi Germany.

Yet the Nuremberg Military Tribunal was important for both present and future. It helped to establish the concept of crimes against humanity. The U.N. Universal Declaration of Human Rights (1948) was one of its by-products. More direct legal descendants were the International Criminal Tribunal for the Former Yugoslavia (1993), the International Criminal Tribunal for Rwanda (1994), and the International Criminal Court established in 2002. The Nuremberg trial also served its contemporary purpose. Primo Levi later referred to "the symbolic, incomplete, tendentious, modern morality at Nuremberg" but said that he had been "intimately satisfied" with it.[244] The principal Nazi war criminals still alive were brought to account, through a trial, not summary justice. The judgments were calibrated and were rendered against individuals, which ought to have softened German criticisms about the doctrine of "collective guilt," although of course it did not.

Nuremberg was a precedent for the International Military Tribunal for the Far East, which convened in April 1946, and for the many follow-up trials in Germany. Some of the most important of these were also conducted in Nuremberg, but by the United States alone. The first, which began in December 1946, was a trial of Nazi doctors. Another eleven trials followed, of Nazi judges and prosecutors, ministers and diplomats, military leaders, industrialists and financiers, SS officers, and members of the *Einsatzgruppen*. In all, of the 177 defendants who were tried, 144 were found guilty; 25 of those were sentenced to death and the others to prison terms—although none ended up serving a very long term (the last one to be released from prison walked free in 1958).[245] These far-reaching American military tribunals are one reason that the reckoning with Nazi perpetrators after 1945 was more complete than in any other modern genocide.[246] They also had their counterparts in the other occupation zones, where tens of thousands were found guilty after trial, especially in the Soviet zone.[247]

These were still very modest numbers in a country where 8.5 million Germans had been members of the Nazi Party and millions more active in auxiliary organizations. De-Nazification of the general population continued. The most ambitious attempt to screen the entire population was undertaken in the American zone. There, after a first wave of dismissals of officials carried out in April 1945, a new directive in July called for the whole population to fill out questionnaires, the notorious *Fragebogen*, which contained 131 questions. These soon became the object of bitter jokes ("Did you hear about the three U.S. ships that have docked in Hamburg? One has food, the other two questionnaires"). By the end of November, the U.S. Army's Special Branch had evaluated 783,000 *Fragebogen*. It ordered almost 164,000 dismissals and recommended another 59,000.[248] The volume of dismissals threatened to paralyze administration and criticism mounted in Washington. The criteria were relaxed, much of the evaluation was turned over to Germans, and leniency grew. Increasing numbers were

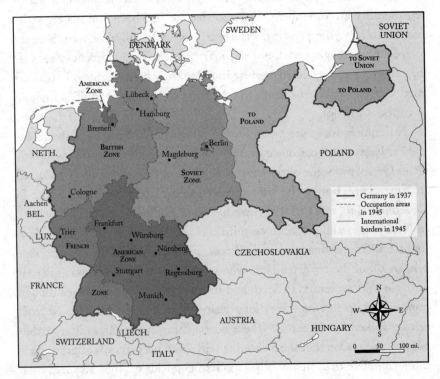

The occupation zones in postwar Germany.

placed in the less severe category of mere followers, or fellow travelers, so that the process came to resemble a *Mitläuferfabrik*, a factory that manufactured fellow travelers.[249] Hearings became occasions when individuals laundered their pasts and walked out cleansed, wielding a "Persil certificate" of de-Nazification, as the sarcastic expression had it.

The British and French zones followed the broad lines set out by U.S. occupation forces, but they were less ambitious in trying to screen everyone. The absence of the compulsory registration that was required in the American zone also made them bolt-holes for heavily compromised former Nazis, especially if they worked in the free professions or took temporary jobs as manual workers, like Goebbels's designated successor at the Ministry of Propaganda, Werner Naumann, who went underground as a construction worker in the British zone. The French and British gave a higher priority than the Americans to administrative efficiency, which made them less willing to purge former Nazis from industry, or at least to purge them on a permanent basis. For example, of the 200 mostly senior people dismissed by the British from Volkswagen, 138 of them were back at their desks by February 1947.[250] The French zone was commonly regarded as the most lax, its occupation forces more susceptible to bribes and more willing to overlook a Nazi past if someone affected separatist sentiments that accorded with the French view of the world. But they labeled many fewer "exonerated" than the British. There was some convergence in the western zones. In all three, those such as judges and senior administrators who had been dismissed from their positions crept back into them. Everywhere, policy became more lax over time, even as Germans complained about arbitrariness and unfairness. There was undoubtedly plenty of both. A common complaint was that too many of the small fry were hauled in while the big fish escaped. There was a lot of truth in this, too, for the vetting process typically began with the easiest cases (because they were the easiest), deferring potentially serious cases until later, by which time the likelihood of being exonerated was much greater.

De-Nazification followed a different pattern in the Soviet zone. More were dismissed and fewer returned to their positions later. Civil service, judiciary, and schools at every level were more thoroughly and permanently purged of former Nazis. So was business, in line with the Marxist view that capitalism was the root cause of Nazi fascism. There were regional variations. Thuringia, a Nazi hotbed compared with other parts of the eastern zone, lagged behind in cleaning house. Walter Ulbricht, the dominant figure in the new Socialist Unity Party (SED), berated the local party chairman in the summer of 1947 for the slow pace of expropriating factories owned by former Nazis.[251] The more structural approach to de-Nazification in the Soviet zone made the process less open to the charge that the big fish got away too easily. But it had its own problems. While party leaders recognized that ordinary Germans, including the working class, had not been innocent victims of the Nazis—that they had, in Marxist terms, "failed the test of history"—the official emphasis on the key role of capitalists, Junkers, and militarists in Hitler's coming to power nonetheless had an exculpatory effect when it came to everyone else. "Minor" ex-Nazis were also welcomed into the ranks of the SED, provided they committed themselves to the building of socialism.

There were other deformations in the everyday practice of de-Nazification in the Soviet zone. When vacant positions in the bureaucracy and universities were filled, the use of rigid ideological and class criteria resulted in many individual injustices. They were also a way to punish political opponents, including former Social Democrats. The same was true of the Soviet policy of internment. All the occupying powers interned Germans, and used Nazi camps to do so, but the treatment of internees in the Soviet zone was more brutal. There were many deaths from overcrowding, malnutrition, and disease in these "special camps." Official Soviet statistics later admitted to 43,000 deaths in internment camps, meaning that one in three of those who passed through them died (western estimates were much higher). As the death rate rose, reaching its peak in 1947, the criticism of Soviet "concentration camps" grew louder in the western zones.[252]

By then the "one world" of the coalition against Hitler had become the two camps of the Cold War.[253] The wartime marriage of convenience entered into by the Allies had irretrievably broken down. Many different flashpoints brought on the conflict. There was Western concern over Stalin's policy in Iran and Poland. The civil war in Greece after 1945 between monarchist and Communist forces was another source of alarm in the West, even though Stalin in fact urged caution on the Greek Communists. It was the British decision to withdraw from Greece that prompted President Harry S. Truman's speech on March 12, 1947, in which he urged Congress to support the Greeks as a "free people." The Truman Doctrine, as it became known, mentions Greece or the Greeks forty-nine times. There are also references to the threat represented by "totalitarianism" to Turkey and the Middle East as well as the Balkans, with Albania, Bulgaria, and

Yugoslavia accused of border violations against Greece. The president also referred to the "coercion and intimidation" that was, he said, occurring in Poland and Romania in violation of the Yalta agreement. Germany is mentioned just twice in Truman's speech, both of them references to Nazi Germany.[254]

Yet Germany was no mere victim of a Cold War that began elsewhere. Disagreements among the Allies over how to deal with their defeated foe contributed substantially to their mounting mutual suspicion. The division of Germany in 1949, like the conflicts that led to it, was doubly linked to the onset of the Cold War, as both cause and effect. Winston Churchill gave his famous Iron Curtain speech in Fulton, Missouri, on March 5, 1946, just one year before Truman's speech to Congress. The curtain had fallen, he said, between Stettin on the Baltic and Trieste on the Adriatic—a German city that that had just become Polish, and the old Habsburg outlet to the sea. Central Europe was at the center of the early Cold War and divided Germany became the powerful symbol of a divided continent and a divided world. But this was not preordained and there are at least two other possible outcomes of the fluid postwar situation that did not come about but are historically plausible.[255]

The first might-have-been was an undivided Germany within a divided Europe—a large neutral state, like a much bigger version of Austria or Finland. This was what the West German left was calling for in the 1980s, when the Cold War heated up again, and it was what some people wanted in the late 1940s—Stalin may even have been one of them.[256] The second hypothetical outcome was a divided Germany within a united Europe. There had, after all, been numerous suggestions emanating from the Allies about breaking up Germany. At the Teheran Conference, Roosevelt talked of dividing the country into five autonomous states, with two industrial areas (the Saar–Ruhr and Hamburg–Kiel Canal) under international administration. Sumner Welles, Roosevelt's influential under secretary of state until ousted by a sex scandal in September 1943, also advocated partition as a curb on future German aggression.[257] The most punitive plan was proposed by Treasury Secretary Henry Morgenthau in 1944, calling for Germany to be broken up and "pastoralized." Most British planners expected some kind of postwar partition;[258] Stalin also entertained the idea. The Yalta Declaration of the Big Three had referred to the possible "dismemberment" of Germany. This was also what France wanted. So did other German neighbors: former Czech president Edvard Beneš wrote in

1942 that Germany should be broken up into a decentralized confederation as it had existed in the early nineteenth century.[259]

As it turned out, Germany was divided, but it was not broken up or dismembered along the lines many had proposed during the war, nor was it divided as a punitive measure. On the contrary, the initiative for creating two Germanys came from the United States, with the aim of speeding up the economic recovery of the western zones. America, followed by its Western allies, began to retreat in 1946 from its initial stance on Germany and took a series of steps that made permanent division increasingly inevitable. Western actions were a response to desperate material conditions and fear that these would open the door to communism, as desperate material conditions had opened the door to Hitler just a dozen years earlier. Brutish Soviet responses at every stage only reinforced Western leaders in the rightness of their view; so did the behavior of Stalin's proxies in Poland and Czechoslovakia, his eastern sphere of influence. In Soviet eyes, the Americans and their allies were hypocrites who were reneging, one by one, on earlier agreements and waving the flag of the "free world" to mask their drive for dominance. In part, then, we are talking about a road to German division paved with mutual misperceptions, or at least two sides that each came increasingly to attribute bad faith to the other. But beyond the level of perceptions there were also inbuilt responses to issues by the United States and the USSR that reflected their wholly different experiences during the war and their wholly different circumstances at the end of it.

For almost a year after the war ended, the mechanisms of Allied cooperation still worked. In Germany the earliest problems over four-power administration were caused largely by the French, not the Russians. U.S. deputy military governor Lucius Clay reported in October 1945 on "the unwillingness of the French authorities to agree to the establishment of central German administrative machinery provided for by the Potsdam agreement." He was supported by the findings of an independent presidential mission dispatched by Truman later that fall, which concluded that attempts to set up common policies on railways and other essential facilities had failed, "due almost entirely to the rigid opposition of the French."[260] Churchill's Iron Curtain speech the following spring, later seen as prophetic, was widely criticized at the time as warmongering.

U.S.-Soviet antagonism grew sharply in May 1946, when Lucius Clay ended the "dismantling" of German industry and stopped the transfers from west to east that had been agreed at Potsdam as a form of German reparations to the USSR. The British and French soon followed. They did so in the wake of the harsh winter of 1945–46, the refugee problem, and the material privation across Germany. Moscow viewed this as a betrayal. In a signature moment of the emerging Cold War in Germany, U.S. secretary of state James Byrnes signaled a new course in September 1946. Addressing an audience in the Stuttgart Opera House that included General Clay, U.S. senators, and prominent Germans, Byrnes spoke in upbeat fashion about German political and economic recovery. Germany was part of Europe, said Byrnes, and the recovery of countries such as Belgium and the Netherlands would suffer if Germany were "turned into a poor-house." Gone were the harsh strictures of April 1945. This was the "speech of hope." Byrnes even dangled the prospect that a future peace treaty might adjust the Oder-Neisse line as Germany's eastern border with Poland.[261]

When do events become unstoppable? At what point was the future division of Germany sealed? The answer is probably during the first six months of 1947, a period defined by three important things that happened and one important thing that did not. The first of these was the decision of the United States and the United Kingdom to merge their zones into a Bizone in January 1947. This made it easier to exchange goods between the heavily industrial British and the more agricultural American zones. It would also lower the costs of occupation for taxpayers at home. The move was presented as a practical response to circumstances that did not preclude future Allied cooperation on a German-wide basis. But it did represent a decision by the two most important Western occupying powers to retreat further from the principles established at Potsdam and to build up German economic capacity. Combining the zones limned the outlines of a future West German state.

A little more than two months after the Bizone was created, the foreign ministers of the four occupying powers met in Moscow: new U.S. secretary of state George Marshall, British foreign minister Ernest Bevin, French foreign minister Georges Bidault, and their Soviet host, Vyacheslav Molotov. It was in Moscow that the important non-event occurred: there was no agreement on a German peace treaty, or on anything else. One week into the conference President Truman enunciated his doctrine to Congress (the second important thing that happened), but that was not what scuttled the Moscow gathering, for just as Truman had carefully avoided mentioning the USSR by name, Molotov avoided mentioning Truman's speech. Germany remained the focus of discussions, and on every issue there was disagreement: control of the Ruhr, levels of industry, reparations, future German disarmament. In preparing for Moscow, the hard-liners in the State Department won out over the wishes of the U.S. military govern- ment to continue seeking common ground with its wartime Soviet ally. Lucius Clay absented himself angrily from the meeting, until summoned to attend. The American delegation was determined to rebuild the German economy, if necessary in the western zones alone, and presented the Soviet side with offers it was bound to refuse. The meeting, originally scheduled to last three months, was abandoned after seven fruitless weeks.[262]

Toward the end, Secretary of State Marshall had a meeting with Joseph Stalin, in the hope that it would expedite proceedings. Stalin urged patience, arguing that an accommodation could still be reached. Mar- shall was frustrated, however, and in a radio broadcast to the American public on April 28 he dramatized the delay as something that jeopardized European recovery: "The patient is sinking while the doctors deliberate."[263] A little more than five weeks later, at the Harvard commencement cere- mony, he announced the European Recovery Program. It set out the issue as U.S. policy makers saw it, placing the German question in the context of a struggling Europe and presenting free-market economic growth as the solution to both, and it became known as the Marshall Plan. "The break- down of the business structure of Europe during the war was complete," said Marshall. "Recovery has been seriously retarded by the fact that two years after the close of hostilities a peace settlement with Germany and Austria has not been agreed upon."[264] The Marshall Plan was the last of the three key events in the first six months of 1947, following the creation of the Bizone and the announcement of the Truman Doctrine. It was arguably the most important of the three in pointing the way to division.

Positions hardened on both sides in the second half of 1947. The Com- munist grip on Eastern Europe tightened, foreign-policy hard-liners in the Kremlin gained in influence, and the Soviet Union announced the estab- lishment of Cominform as a successor to the Communist International. At the same time, the Americans and their British ally were already thinking about the formation of a separate West German state and using harsh Cold War language to frame the German question. When the foreign ministers convened again in London at the end of November, the U.S. delegation was hoping for a display of Soviet bad temper and intransigence. Molotov quickly obliged with a diatribe about broken promises, hypocrisy, and cap- italist self-interest. It was when Molotov then appeared to be more open to compromise that the Americans worried. A top member of the American delegation expressed the concern candidly in a private letter. U.S. ambassador to Moscow Walter Bedell Smith wrote to General Dwight Eisenhower (whose chief of staff he had once been): "The difficulty under which we labor is that despite our announced position, we really do not want nor intend to accept German unification on any terms that the Russians might agree to, even though they seemed to meet most of our requirements."[265] By the end of 1947, both sides were painting the other as the aggressor. Both were also mindful of the commitment they had made to their German political allies, whose wishes were a part of the equation. Konrad Adenauer and his Christian Democratic colleagues in the western zones were no keener to see continuing Soviet influence (and four-power control of the Ruhr) in a unified Germany than Walter Ulbricht and his Stalinist comrades were to see their power in the Soviet zone placed at risk if they had to submit themselves to German-wide elections.

What happened over the next two years followed the logic of division as it had emerged in 1947. In February 1948, a Communist coup in Czechoslovakia was greeted with both genuine and theatrical revulsion in the West. The coup had a major impact in France, where it persuaded key figures like Georges Bidault, who had urged political cooperation with Communists, to see his country's future security within a U.S.-backed alliance.[266] That same month, a six-power conference in London brought together the three Western occupying powers and representatives of the Benelux nations. The Russians were not invited. The issue of currency reform was uppermost at this point. Through March, all four occupying powers negotiated over a new, German-wide currency, but the Western powers had plans for their own currency ready if talks broke down. American Finance Directorate member Jack Bennett told a British colleague that he was hoping for a final report that would feature "disagreements on two or three world convincing points"—propaganda points, that is, to be used against the USSR.[267] When the Soviet side walked out of the Allied Control Commission in March in protest against the London meeting, the path was open for the Western powers to go it alone. In June 1948 the Deutschmark was introduced into the western zones. Currency reform was the harbinger of division, just as currency reform was the harbinger of reunification in 1990. The French had been persuaded to go along with it, and in August 1948 they joined the Bizone to create the Trizone—"Trizonia," as many Germans called it. The name was humorous and ironic, although it had an edge directed against the occupying powers, as in Karl Berbuer's song "We Are the Natives of Trizonia," which became an unofficial German anthem.

Berbuer's song was first presented to the public in November 1948, during the dramatic Berlin Airlift, when the Americans and British flew food and fuel supplies into West Berlin after the Russians cut off road access in retaliation against the introduction of the Deutschmark. The Airlift went on for 323 days, from June 1948 to May 1949. There were 276,926 flights in all. At times the planes were landing every three minutes at Tempelhof Airport. The legend of the Airlift leaves out much—the initial doubts and the shaky start, the bottlenecks and operational disputes, the great good fortune that a mild winter reduced the amount of coal that had to be flown in, and the fact that the West would, if necessary, have been willing to sacrifice West Berlin in the interest of its larger program.[268] The blockade and the Airlift were nonetheless a political and diplomatic disaster for Stalin, pointing up the ugly, coercive aspects of Soviet policy and undermining residual sympathy for the USSR among Europeans, including Germans. On the other side, the episode muted some of the residual suspicion of "brash" Americans among European workers and elites. For Germans, the optics suggested that the Russians wanted to starve them, while the Americans and British wanted to feed them.

The Airlift came with risks. Ambassador Smith was one of those on the U.S. side who became alarmed about the consequences of confrontation. Others wavered for a different reason. George Kennan, a well-known State Department critic of Soviet intentions and advocate of partitioning Germany, became less sure about division after 1948 because it would close off the prospect of future liberalization in Eastern Europe. Even President Truman, one of the strongest advocates of the Airlift, had to be dissuaded from going on a personal last-ditch mission to see Stalin in the fall of 1948, which would have delayed the establishment of the West German state then being planned.[269] In the event, the Federal Republic of Germany was duly founded in May 1949 and the German Democratic Republic five months later. If Truman was in many ways inattentive and poorly informed when it came to Germany, Stalin also vacillated, torn between a partition that consolidated Soviet control in its own zone and continued four-power control within a unified country.

Neither leader aimed consciously for the division that came about in 1949, but the outcome had been prepared by actors on both sides, including German politicians. If Americans took the lead when it came to the step-by-step decisions that led to the breach, which is hard to dispute, they were acting against the background of increasingly harsh political repression in the Soviet sphere of influence in Europe, including Germany. Division came about, in the end, because the two great powers left standing in 1945 both found themselves in Germany and differed fundamentally on what to do with it. De-Nazification, demilitarization, and democratization did not mean the same to them. That was a result of ideological differences and the radically dissimilar postwar circumstances in the two countries—in the words of one historian, "One was almost unscathed and the other was almost ruined."[270] The continental United States had not been occupied and had suffered no physical damage; the country's GDP had almost doubled during the war. By contrast, the Soviet Union had been invaded and laid waste; agriculture and industry had been devastated, and seventeen hundred towns and seventy thousand villages destroyed. The American death toll in the war was 418,000; the Soviet death toll was sixty-five times greater, at 27 million.

Small wonder, then, that the USSR took a different view of German levels of industry, or attached more importance to four-power control of the Ruhr, than the United States. What, in Western eyes, looked like a cynical Communist ploy to keep Germans impoverished in order to exploit their grievances politically was, for Moscow, a question of future security. The policy of "dismantling" and reparations represented, in Soviet eyes, a form of demilitarization. Every Western retreat from the provisions of Yalta and Potsdam looked like a move to resurrect German economic might in the interests of American free-market capitalism at the expense of its former Soviet ally. And so Moscow clung grimly and legalistically to the letter of previous agreements about Germany, even as it snuffed out opposition political voices in its new East European satellites, including breaking agreements it had made, for example to hold free elections in Poland. If Soviet policy was guided by a sense of vulnerability, economically and politically, American policy was an expression of the uniquely powerful circumstances in which the country found itself in 1945 and the years immediately after. At war's end the United States controlled two-thirds of the world's gold supply, half the world's shipping, and more than half of the world's manufacturing production. With every other power prostrate—not only Germany, but its erstwhile allies both east and west—America stood, at this key historical moment, in a singular position. In 1950, a year after the formation of two German states, the United States still had a GDP larger than the Soviet Union, Britain, France, West Germany, Italy, and Japan combined.

The international system after 1945 was bipolar, which is to say it featured two major powers, rather than the five that had typically counted as great powers during the previous three hundred years. But the two powers were not equal. This was "asymmetrical bipolarity." The fact was not lost on Soviet leaders. Some of the statistics on U.S. economic dominance were cited by Molotov in a speech at a Parisian peace conference in October 1946, when he leveled a fierce attack on American demands for "equal opportunity" in Eastern Europe by asking how "equal" the opportunity would really be in Romania or Yugoslavia if these countries, ruined by war, found themselves trying to cope with the penetration of American capital.[271] Molotov had a point. Still, it would have been remarkable if the United States had not taken advantage of the opportunities presented by this singular moment to remake (much of) the world in its own image, the more so as the instruments of American domination—free-market capitalism and convertible currencies, backed by the International Monetary Fund, the World Bank, and the General Agreement on Tariffs and Trade (GATT), the predecessor of the World Trade Organization—were perceived by U.S. decision makers as the natural order of things. For surely, they believed, it was protectionism and autarky that had landed the world with Nazi Germany in the first place, and the USSR offered more of the same medicine, only with a different label on the bottle. There was undoubtedly self-interest at play here, but there was also a strong sense of American mission as well.[272]

Dividing Germany was a "double solution" to the long-standing "German problem."[273] Karl Berbuer's seriocomic song about the natives of Trizonia casts Germans as the playthings of the Allies:

> *A small group of diplomats*
> *Makes politics today*
> *They create zones, alter states*

That was how many Germans saw themselves in the immediate postwar years and it is one way of looking at the postwar outcome: as a condominium agreement of the kind that Western powers in the previous century had imposed on weaker countries, like the 1889 agreement between Britain, Germany, and the United States to divide up Samoa. But looking at it this way leaves German agency out of the picture in two ways. It was, in the first place, Germans' support for Hitler's regime that brought down the catastrophe of 1945 and opened the door to division. Then, after 1945, Germans in both the eastern and western zones did not simply follow along passively as the occupying powers acted. In the Soviet zone, Walter Ulbricht's determination to maintain power for his party, coupled with that party's disappointing election results, made it harder for Stalin to decide clearly on a policy of maintaining a unified Germany. Ulbricht's behavior undermined (some would even say sabotaged) Stalin's preferred policy.[274] In the West, too, Konrad Adenauer was happy, despite lip service, to write off Germans in the eastern zone if it meant the opportunity to shape a Western state in the ways he and his colleagues wanted.

It was not only the occupying powers whose ideological divisions grew in the years 1945–1949. The logic of division extended to German politicians as political life gradually resumed under Allied supervision. This happened much more brutally in the East, where the stifling of political opposition affected Social Democrats as well as Christian Democrats. Others in the Soviet zone capitulated to a narrowing orthodoxy. Anton Ackermann, one of the most prominent of the Communists who returned to Germany from Moscow in 1945, repudiated his advocacy of a "German socialism" in a 1946 article about "giving room to anti-Bolshevism."[275] There was no equivalent narrowing of political views in the West, except insofar as anticommunism was common ground among all parties other than the Communist Party. That was in line with the political purpose of the Marshall Plan, which sought to rally center-right and center-left parties across Western Europe behind anticommunism.

Some German politicians in the western zones were more willing than others to fall in with the views of the occupying powers. Kurt Schumacher, the leader of the Social Democrats and a survivor of the Nazi camps, was strongly anti-Communist but also retained his party's old class-struggle vocabulary and was critical of some American moves. It was his fellow Social Democrat, West Berlin mayor Ernst Reuter, who became the darling of the Americans. A hero of the Berlin Airlift, he joined with other regional Social Democratic leaders in support of American plans for West Germany's Basic Law, its founding constitutional document, which Schumacher rejected. It was Reuter, not Schumacher, whom *Time* magazine described as "one of the few really great men in Western Europe."[276] On the Christian Democratic side, it was even more conspicuous how politicians emerged to support and reinforce the policies of the Western powers. The left wing of the Christian Democrats was marginalized in the process and the dominant figure that emerged was Adenauer, the champion of an "Atlanticist" political course. Anticommunism was central to Adenauer's political repertoire at the founding of the Federal Republic, and beyond. The two Germanys that confronted each other in 1949, embodied in the symbolic figures of Ulbricht and Adenauer, represented political opposites in concentrated form.

Was there no "third way," no opening for an authentically German, left-leaning, but non-Communist solution to the postwar situation? The spontaneous antifascist committees that sprang up at the end of the war might seem like a possible answer to that question. There was, briefly, a controlled experiment in one small part of Germany to test the hypothesis. In the western Iron Mountains, wedged between Saxony and Czechoslovakia, was a triangle of no-man's-land where the U.S. Army and the Red Army both held back in 1945, so that for two months half a million people came temporarily under the political administration of local "antifa" groups. They tried to organize food, transportation, and housing, the departure of slave laborers, and the arrival of refugees. The experiment was a failure. The reason was partly the severity of the challenges. But it was also a result of the behavior of the mostly youthful, male, left-leaning antifascists, who were aware that the area in question had been a Nazi stronghold, distrusted the people, and met each frustration by treating the population with the same brusque high-handedness meted out to inhabitants of the Soviet zone by Ulbricht and his comrades. The fact that this little corner of Germany seemed destined to end in the Soviet zone (as it did) hardly made their task easier.[277] By 1949 antifascism had become a slogan wielded by Ulbricht's Socialist Unity Party, just as anticommunism was a rallying cry for Adenauer's Christian Democrats.

CHAPTER 12

THE GERMAN QUESTION ANSWERED

—

Double Vision: 1949–1973

"WE LOVE GERMANY SO MUCH WE ARE HAPPY TO HAVE TWO of them." These words of the French writer François Mauriac were a clever variation on the widespread view that the "German question" had to be solved. The Allies of Yalta and Potsdam increasingly disagreed on the solution and fell out among themselves. What followed was the division of Germany into two states, an unplanned, provisional solution that lasted for forty years. During that time Germany was occasionally the focus of the world's attention as a flashpoint of international relations, most obviously during the Berlin Crisis of 1958–1961, but the German question in its previous form disappeared. While wars and civil wars cost millions of lives elsewhere, citizens of the two German states lived in a state of uneasy peace. The only German casualties that matched the 3.5 million Koreans killed or injured in the 1950–1953 conflict were the imaginary victims of war games, like the 1955 NATO exercise "Carte Blanche," which dropped 335 hypothetical nuclear bombs on Germany, with a death toll calculated at 1.7 million.[1] Exercises like this are a reminder, however, that the peace was uneasy and the two Germanys were frontline states in the Cold War. The hopes (and fears) of a unified, neutral Germany never bore fruit: the line of division in Europe ran through Germany, not around it. After 1949, Germany in the world meant a divided Germany in a divided world.

In *Divided Heaven*, Christa Wolf's 1963 novel about a pair of East German lovers, one of the characters, a research chemist, says, "These days, everything is done twice in Germany, chemistry as well."² The years after 1949 were a kind of controlled experiment in how to do all manner of things twice.³ Some of them are big and obvious—economics, religion, the family and the place of women, environmental protection, dealing with the Nazi past. Others are less obvious: How did each Germany deal with returning POWs, commemorate World War Two bombing, or tackle the problem of heart disease? Scholars have had their say on all these subjects.⁴ East and West Germans themselves were constantly comparing and contrasting, usually with an eye on the wider world and its judgments. That was part of the process of creating a separate identity, one Germany defining itself against the other.

The brutal simplicity of us-versus-them was never again as stark as it was in the 1950s and early 1960s, perfectly symbolized in the two leaders, Konrad Adenauer and Walter Ulbricht. They were night and day. Adenauer, born in 1876 (when life expectancy for men was less than forty), was seventy-three when he assumed the chancellorship of the Federal Republic of Germany (FRG). Ulbricht, born in 1894, was a generation younger. Adenauer, a son of the Rhineland Catholic bourgeoisie, studied law, became a long-serving mayor of Cologne, and mostly kept his head down during the Third Reich; Ulbricht, the son of an impoverished tailor in Leipzig, was a lapsed Protestant and a young Communist organizer in the last years of Weimar; he spent the Nazi years in Moscow and (unlike so many German Communists) survived Stalin's purges.

Adenauer and Ulbricht represented the uncompromising elements on each side. Adenauer's Christian Democratic Party (the CDU, and its Bavarian sister party, the CSU), which dominated the politics of the early Federal Republic, traded heavily on anticommunism, which went down well with the United States and with émigrés and expellees. Adenauer himself had little regard for "Easterners," but willingly courted their organizations for political reasons. Anticommunism was also a way to discredit the Social Democrats as another Marxist party like the one "over there" in what conservatives liked to call "the Zone." Ulbricht, meanwhile, delivered cascades of Cold War rhetoric about warmongering Americans and revanchist West Germans, playing up the antifascist credentials of the German Democratic Republic (GDR). Ulbricht and the East German press had a plump propaganda target when it came to figures like Hans Globke, under secretary of state and chief of staff in the Federal Chancellery, who had a large part in drafting the Nuremberg Laws. While

Adenauer and CDU colleagues used the threat of communism to discredit the Social Democratic Party, Ulbricht and hard-line allies in his Socialist Unity Party used the threat from the West to stigmatize opposition within the party.

The Cold War adversaries propped each other up, like two wheat sheaves; they were "brother enemies."[5] The two Germanys became reliable members of their respective alliances, NATO and the Warsaw Pact, which they joined in 1955 when each became a formally sovereign state. There was none of the posturing toward an independent foreign policy of the kind associated with France under Charles de Gaulle or Nicolae Ceausescu's Romania. There was just one occasion when East Germany took anything resembling an independent line, leveraging its own vulnerability in 1961 to persuade the USSR to approve building the Berlin Wall—"driving the Soviets up the wall," as one scholar has called it.[6] The larger and more powerful Federal Republic was just as loyal within its bloc. De Gaulle wanted the 1963 Élysée Treaty between France and West Germany to be the start of a diplomatic axis in Europe directed against the United States, but the Christian Democrats (with a nudge from Washington) added a preamble that underscored Bonn's overarching commitment to NATO and the Western alliance. De Gaulle was left frustrated.

A longer-running concern in the United States was that the Federal Republic might strike a deal with the Soviet Union in order to achieve German reunification. Henry Kissinger, President Richard Nixon's national security adviser, worried at first that *Ostpolitik*—the policy of rapprochement with the East conceived by Willy Brandt's adviser Egon Bahr and practiced by Brandt as chancellor after 1969—would turn the Federal Republic into a loose cannon, maneuvering between East and West, undermining Atlantic unity and playing into Russian hands. Others in Washington worried that Brandt was soft on communism. Speaking to Kissinger in late 1970, Secretary of State William Rogers said, "If we decide that they are moving in a direction that we don't like or in a way which is wrong, we probably by our actions can have the government thrown out." (He meant by working on skeptical members of the German parliament.)[7] But Brandt was attentive to American concerns. German *Ostpolitik* eventually dovetailed with the politics of détente being pursued in Washington. In fact, it served as the catalyst of superpower détente.[8] Brandt's opening toward Moscow eventually gave the United States an opportunity to press for Soviet concessions, which it achieved with the 1971 four-power agreement on Berlin that guaranteed access to the city, so that (as Kissinger later wrote) "Berlin disappeared from the list of international crisis spots."[9]

The most controversial issue that followed from German membership in the two alliance systems was rearmament. A newly minted force called the Bundeswehr was created in the FRG, followed soon after by the National People's Army in the GDR. Germany became two heavily armed camps. In 1963 the Federal Republic (number one) and the Democratic Republic (number six) were among the world's leading recipients of arms, accounting together for almost a fifth of the global total. In 1972 they still accounted for a tenth, although West Germany had dropped into third place behind South and North Vietnam.[10] Some of the weapons made headlines, like the F-104 Starfighter that Lockheed sold to the West German Ministry of Defense, soon dubbed "the widow-maker." Four Starfighters crashed during practices in June 1962, before they were even introduced into service. Another 61 had crashed by mid-1966. All told, 292 of the 916 purchased by the Defense Ministry crashed, with 115 pilots killed.[11] Hence this joke: How do you acquire a Starfighter? Buy a plot of land and wait. The Cold War came home to both Germanys more routinely in the requisitioning of land for airfields, firing ranges, training grounds, and barracks. Buildings were requisitioned, too, not only houses and apartments but hotels and restaurants. In 1951 alone, the British Army of the Rhine took possession of twelve hundred hotels and six hundred restaurants in North Rhine–Westphalia.[12]

Requisitioning was just one potential source of friction between Germans and the members of four large armies of occupation. The situation was especially problematic in the East, certainly at the beginning, given the postwar experience of mass rape by Red Army soldiers and the deep bitterness (as well as the 150,000 to 200,000 *Russenkinder*) it left behind.[13] Then, on June 17, 1953, the most serious challenge to the authority of the new state in the form of a workers' uprising was crushed by Russian soldiers and tanks. But the half-million-strong Soviet occupying force generally lived apart, in self-contained "Little Moscows." In the Federal Republic, foreign troops were more likely to interact with the locals. West Germany, like other U.S. outposts, had its share of "GI brides."[14] Members of the British and French forces also married local women. More than eleven hundred British soldiers married German women in 1950 and 1951.[15] Some German women married occupation soldiers from the French colonies, emigrating with their spouses to Algeria or Vietnam. But not all interactions were positive. The occupying troops were young men, away from home, often bored, with access to cheap alcohol. According to one British conscript who served in Braunschweig, a favorite response to boredom among the soldiers was to go down to the local railroad station and start a fight with Germans—they called these "goodwill visits." Sometimes hundreds were involved in the brawls.[16] The record of Canadian troops attached to British units was worse, although not as bad as the behavior of the Americans. In the fourteen months between July 1956 and September 1957, U.S. soldiers in Bavaria committed 714 offenses, including 8 murders, 207 rapes, and 319 aggravated assaults.[17]

American violence on German soil often had its origins in race. White GIs regularly picked bar fights with Africans studying in the Federal Republic. In one case in 1965, they also wrote to Ghanaian student representatives threatening to "lynch" them, forcing the U.S. ambassador to issue an apology.[18] Many white GIs also reacted with hostility when they saw African-Americans with German women. Military police tried to keep Black GIs out of German bars, a policy that many bar owners themselves wanted. So American occupation forces unwittingly acted out for their German audience how the democratic values of the free world were compatible with racial discrimination. Race entered the picture in another way. A small subset of the children born out of relationships between occupation soldiers and German women were so-called *farbige Mischlinge*, "colored half-bloods," who had African-American fathers and German mothers. Since it was virtually impossible for Black GIs to receive permission to marry white German women, even when they wished to, the great majority of these children were classed as illegitimate. They grew up as German citizens, with their mothers looked down on, and they themselves the object of an intense, prurient interest quite out of proportion to their relatively small numbers. Some were placed for adoption with Black families in the United States, but the disadvantages they faced in a segregated country led to a change of course in the late 1950s and growing numbers were adopted instead by Danish parents. In the early 1960s there were more Black-German children being adopted there than in the United States.[19] By then, the children of German mothers and Western occupation soldiers were growing up in the United States, Britain, Canada, France, North Africa, Indochina, and Denmark, as well as Germany.

With the consolidation of two states and armed alliances came other institutions in matching pairs. Two systems of intelligence and espionage were among them. Berlin was the undisputed capital of the Cold War fictional spy world—think of Len Deighton's *Funeral in Berlin*, Joseph Kanon's *Leaving Berlin*, and, not least, *The Spy Who Came in from the Cold* and other books by John le Carré. Plenty of real-life activity in the divided city had the ring of fiction, like scattering leaflets in East Berlin via balloon, building a tunnel to tap into Soviet communications (an enterprise betrayed from the start by the British Soviet agent George Blake), and the putative Soviet defector dubbed "the banana queen" because she always peeled and ate one at key moments in her debriefings. There were ambiguous cases like that of Otto John, head of West Germany's domestic intelligence agency, who disappeared and turned up in East Berlin in July 1954, in what is best described as part-defection, part-abduction, and returned to the Federal Republic the following year.[20] The situation that most resembled a le Carré novel was Operation Panoptikum, mounted by West Germany's foreign intelligence service, the BND, in which the person charged with investigating whether there was a "mole"—Heinz Felfe—was later revealed to have been the "mole."[21]

The case points to the effectiveness of the East German espionage apparatus headed by Markus Wolf. He had as many as three thousand agents in place in West Germany by the late 1950s, in the Federal Chancellery, every major ministry, the intelligence services, and the political parties. The most spectacular success was Günter Guillaume, who rose in the SPD to become secretary to Willy Brandt, precipitating Brandt's resignation as chancellor when Guillaume was uncovered as an agent in 1974. Guillaume and his wife, Christel, entered the Federal Republic in 1956 as supposed émigrés from the East, like many other agents before the Wall was built. Wolf also had agents inside U.S. Forces headquarters in Stuttgart and Heidelberg; others were active at NATO headquarters and in NATO member countries. One of Wolf's trademark strategies was the use of "Romeo spies" or "Red Casanovas," who seduced secretaries with access to classified material. But in this world of mirrors the spying was done by both sides. The only country as thoroughly penetrated by agents as West Germany was East Germany. The West German BND as well as the British, Americans, and French all operated spies there.[22]

This special form of double vision, in which everything German appeared twice, affected all areas of life. West German youth organizations were affiliated with the American-backed World Alliance of Youth, their East German counterparts with the Soviet-sponsored World Federation of Democratic Youth. West Germany joined the European Broadcasting Union, established in Britain in 1950, East Germany the International Radio and Television Network, set up in Czechoslovakia the same year. That was why West Germany had entries every year in the Eurovision Song Contest, which began its brilliant career in 1956, while East Germany was left with Soviet bloc attempts like the Intervision Song Contest to emulate the all-conquering kitsch of the West.[23] The two Germanys had radically different versions of outer space, and even called those who ventured there by different names. In the West they were astronauts, the American term; in the East they were cosmonauts, Soviet style. Even science fiction came in two versions. Perry Rhodan, the West German space hero who made his first appearance in 1961, was American; so was Major Cliff Allister McLane, the daredevil commander in the West German TV program *Raumpatrouille* (Space Patrol), first broadcast in 1966. Both featured later in a book called *Deutsche Helden!* (German Heroes!), alongside the model Claudia Schiffer and tennis star Steffi Graf. East Germans, meanwhile, were told by the party newspaper *Neues Deutschland* that sci-fi allowed readers "to learn to dream like Lenin."[24]

Each Germany developed its own networks of political and professional exchanges. Members of the political elite that built the GDR had mostly spent the Nazi years in Moscow, spoke Russian, and maintained connections there. Up-and-coming politicians, academics, and technocrats had access to networks connecting them with their counterparts in the USSR and Soviet bloc countries. But the networks linking the FRG with the United States and Western Europe were far more extensive. Organizations like the Ford Foundation and the American Council on Germany fostered these links with programs like the annual Young Leaders conference. By the early 1960s nearly a third of the members of the West German parliament had visited America. The academic exchanges so characteristic of the postwar years were also important. Some took place in institutions shaped by German émigrés from the Third Reich, like the Institute for Advanced Study in Princeton, others in institutions that were a product of the early Cold War, like the Free University in Berlin and St. Antony's College, Oxford. The Fulbright program and others like it such as the German Academic Exchange Service played an essential role. By the 1980s, almost ten thousand American and German fellows had passed through the Fulbright program. West Germans were linked in myriad ways with other societies in the West. One practice that fostered exchanges was the system of twin towns, or sister cities. Thousands of these agreements were struck between towns in West Germany and France. There was simply nothing on this scale in East Germany.[25]

If we look at Germans who crossed borders on a permanent basis, we find the same asymmetry. Even before the two German states were founded, most of the millions of Germans who fled or were expelled from Eastern Europe continued on into the western zones. The east–west movement did not end in 1949 but instead became movement from one Germany to the other. There were 675,000 registered refugees from East to West Germany in 1949–1952, and a third of a million in the course of 1953, the year of the workers' uprising. Between 1949 and 1961 there were never fewer than 7000 a month who headed west. In June 1961, 20,000 left, the following month 30,000. That was what prompted the building of the Berlin Wall that August. By then East Germany had lost 3.5 million people, more than a sixth of its population.

West Germans emigrated, too, but mostly not to East Germany. Around half a million did move permanently from West to East before the wall was built, some out of ideological conviction, more for family reasons. But most emigrants from the Federal Republic had other destinations in mind. Starting in 1945 and continuing into the early 1950s, at least 180,000 Germans left the western zones and the FRG to settle permanently in neighboring countries, mostly France or Britain. Until the beginning of the 1960s a larger stream of emigrants went overseas: half a million to the United States, a quarter of a million to Canada, 80,000 to Australia, smaller numbers to Latin America. Given the severe postwar gender imbalance, the West German Labor Office tried without much success to discourage working-age men from emigrating while encouraging women to do so. The evidence from Australia suggests that those who left the Federal Republic in the 1950s had values that were typically petit bourgeois, conservative, and materialistic, not so very different from their domestic counterparts during the "economic miracle" years, except that they cultivated a German club culture of beer, skittles, and oompah music in the suburbs of Melbourne rather than Munich.[26]

Through the 1950s the West German labor force received constant replenishment from the East. But even before that spigot was abruptly turned off in 1961, agreements had been signed that brought in workers from poorer countries on a short-term basis as *Gastarbeiter*, or guest workers. The first of these agreements, with Italy in 1955, provided the model for others with Spain, Greece, Turkey, Morocco, Portugal, South Korea, Tunisia, and Yugoslavia. *Gastarbeiter* worked in construction, mining, heavy industry, and on factory production lines. The earliest were mostly men in their twenties and thirties; later, young women were recruited to work in the textile, clothing, food, and electrical goods branches, and in the case of South Koreans, as nurses. West German employers were perfectly candid about the advantages. As the employers' confederation newspaper noted: "A foreigner in our employ places the best years of his labor power at our disposal."[27] Better yet, older and unfit workers did not have to be kept on the payroll. Conservative governments of the era welcomed the much needed labor and the downward pressure that *Gastarbeiter* exerted on wages. The trade unions hoped that the long overtime hours logged by foreign workers would make possible a shorter working week for their members.

Italian guest workers arriving in West Germany in 1962.

By October 1964 the millionth guest worker had arrived, a Portuguese named Armando Rodrigues, who was presented with a motorcycle to mark the occasion.[28] The number of new arrivals slowed after an economic downturn in 1966–67, then recruitment picked up again with a vengeance. More than 1.5 million foreign workers came to the Federal Republic between

1968 and 1973. By then, they were mainly Turks, who became the largest single ethnic group. In 1973 there were 2.6 million guest workers in West Germany, one in eight of the working population. Most of those who had come in the previous eighteen years had returned home, as originally envisaged, but not all. Employers gradually relaxed the short-stay rules, having invested time and money in training. The workers themselves no longer lived in the crude barracks-like housing to which most were relegated in the early years. They brought their families to Germany and began to move into privately rented apartments. By the time the FRG responded to the economic crisis that followed the first oil-price shock in 1973 by stopping recruitment of new workers, the guest worker program had created an unintended outcome: adults from abroad who were long-term residents and wanted to stay, together with children who had been brought up and increasingly been born in Germany, a sizable minority population that was only slowly and grudgingly recognized as such.[29]

The Federal Republic was not alone in using foreign workers during the boom years. It was the pattern throughout the core countries of Western Europe, which sucked in cheap labor from poorer peripheral regions. The minority population in some cases was proportionally larger—more than twice as large in Switzerland, a third larger in Belgium.[30] But West Germany represented the system in its classic form, both the idea of the temporary "guest" worker, and the reality of what happened behind the backs of the system's architects. Intended and unintended consequences alike stood in sharp contrast to the other Germany, where there were practically no foreign workers at all. After the GDR signed agreements with Poland and Hungary in the 1960s, small numbers of "contract workers" came from those countries, although none yet from the global South, which provided most foreign labor in later decades. The two Germanys addressed their labor needs in radically different ways, which had domestic ramifications. One Germany brought in foreign workers to avoid having women leave their "natural" domestic role to take up paid employment; the other Germany did everything possible to increase female participation in the workforce. By 1970 almost three-quarters of working-age women able to work held jobs in East Germany. The mirror image of that was the difference in numbers of foreign workers, 2.6 million in the West against a mere 15,000 in the East.

The two Germanys belonged to very different economic systems, not just labor markets. West Germany signed on to the U.S.-sponsored Bretton Woods Agreement, with its supporting institutions like the International Monetary Fund. It was part of the global system that, until 1973, regulated the monetary policy followed by the main capitalist countries, whose currencies were convertible and pegged to the dollar, which in turn was pegged to gold. The Federal Republic followed the same path as other West European countries, including its partners in what began in 1951 as the European Coal and Steel Community and became the European Economic Community (EEC) after the Treaty of Rome in 1957. East Germany became part of the Council for Mutual Economic Assistance (usually known as Comecon), established in 1949 and dominated by the USSR. Its currency was not convertible. The GDR suffered major disadvantages as part of Comecon. Under the "Sofia principle" adopted in 1949, intellectual-property rights and patents were weakened in the name of socialist solidarity. This was especially damaging to East Germany and Czechoslovakia. The terms of trade in the Soviet bloc turned the law of comparative advantage on its head, forcing the GDR to trade its undervalued industrial products for overvalued food and raw materials.[31]

There were stark contrasts on the ground, too. One Germany liberalized its economy, the other took industries into public ownership and collectivized agriculture. There is an overdrawn, cartoonish version of this, in which an "Americanized" and a "Sovietized" economy faced off against each other. West Germany witnessed an "economic miracle" by letting consumer spending rip, buying popular prosperity and leisure at the price of "Coca-Colonization," while East Germany announced in 1952 that its economic policy was to "build socialism" and proceeded to build it Soviet-style with new heavy-industrial settlements like the town of Stalinstadt (later renamed Eisenhüttenstadt, or Iron Foundry City). The reality in both cases is more complicated.

The much vaunted "economic miracle" in the West was real. Growth rates of 8 to 10 percent a year made the Federal Republic the engine of postwar economic growth in Western Europe. The boom followed a liberal-capitalist break with the Nazi era, as free-market economists at the end of the war had urged. Friedrich Hayek wanted the Allies to "make Germany a free trade territory . . . as closely as possible economically entangled with the surrounding world." Wilhelm Röpke, in *The Solution of the German Problem*, likewise emphasized the primacy of free trade and exports. Then Germany "would become a sort of enlarged Belgium, and with its extreme dependence on foreign trade would have to abandon any idea of building up an 'autarchic' war industry."[32] These are pretty accurate descriptions of what the West Germany economy looked like in the 1950s and '60s, although there are some persistent myths about these years that need to be cleared away.

Ludwig Erhard, the economic liberal who as minister of economic affairs put his stamp on the "golden years," had to confront an older, protectionist mentality among business leaders, many of whom had thrived in the Third Reich. That did not happen overnight.[33] But even after he succeeded, the economic miracle was not based on the kind of weakest-to-the-wall economic liberalism practiced (often in Hayek's name) by conservatives in the 1980s, but on a form of liberal capitalism that married market and welfare state. That was the basis of Erhard's social market economy. Like some Western European neighbors, West Germany found a model of cooperation between capital, labor, and state that seemed, at least for a generation, to deliver growth. The existence of another Germany may have had some influence—the Christian Democrats were determined not to be outdone in welfare by the Communist East. But the pensions and family support the Federal Republic offered were, in fact, well within West European norms, however un-American those benefits might seem.

Hayek and Röpke were more right than they knew to emphasize trade and exports above all else, for it was these—not mass consumption—that drove the economic miracle. During the 1950s the share of West German GNP taken by exports more than doubled (from 9 to 19 percent). It is symbolically fitting that a "milestone legal judgment" of the European Court of Justice involved German exports, when the court confirmed that member states were bound by European law, upholding an appeal by a Dutch haulage company against the Dutch tax authorities, which had levied import duties on German chemicals.[34] The export boom was led by the industries like chemicals, along with pharmaceuticals, precision engineering, electrics, and optical instruments, which first emerged in the late nineteenth century. The big newcomer in postwar exports was automobiles. This was when BMW, Mercedes, and Audi established their reputations. And so, above all, did Volkswagen. The Beetle became a global brand. "Dulles Is Driving His Second Volkswagen Already," proclaimed the headline of an Augsburg newspaper in 1957, referring to John Foster Dulles, President Eisenhower's secretary of state.[35]

Production, not consumption, was the key to the economic miracle through the 1950s. It was the work of a labor force boosted by expellees and

émigrés, then by refugees from East Germany and the first guest workers. People still worked hard, fifty hours a week, Saturdays included. We
should not antedate the consumer and leisure boom. When Erhard published his *Prosperity for All* in 1957, presenting "free consumer choice" as an
"inalienable right," this was more prescriptive than descriptive. The "golden
fifties" were more austere in reality than the era of plenty fondly remembered later. But the 1950s were filled with images of plenty, in advertisements, and in popular songs that associated love with holidays on Capri
and bottles of chianti in straw baskets. The titles of just a few of the many
hit songs by René Carol (real name: Gerhard Tschierschnitz) make the
point: "In the Tavern in San Remo," "Come with Me to Palermo," "The
Sun over the Adriatic," "The Serenade of Naples," and "Andalusian Wine."
These remained dreams of pleasures to come. Leisure was still hard-won
in the late 1950s. There were also more radios than TVs, more bicycles and
mopeds than cars.[36] In 1950 nine European countries had more cars per
capita than West Germany; in 1960 there were still five, but by 1970 the
number was down to two (France and Sweden).[37] It was only in the late
1950s and even more in the 1960s that the real consumer boom arrived.[38] A
West German referred for the first time in 1959 to "our consumer society."[39]

Did these changes in the Federal Republic mean its Americanization?
In marketing and retailing, the answer is yes, with qualifications. The first
supermarket in Europe was opened by Herbert Eklöh in Cologne in 1957.
He had experimented with self-service in Osnabrück just before the war,
but this two-thousand-square-meter store was something new. In a story
headed "Supermarkt," the weekly newspaper *Die Zeit* explained to readers
that a supermarket was a "large store with complete self-service on the
American model." Eklöh himself was unsure whether this would catch
on with "the housewife," and *Die Zeit* noted the widespread skepticism
and even hostility among traditional retailers to "this American 'import
good.'"[40] A few years later, another American retailing practice crossed the
Atlantic. While traveling in the United States as a wholesaler in electron-
ics, Otto Beisheim noticed how goods were sold to Americans direct from
warehouses. Back in Germany he cofounded the company Metro, which
opened its first cash-and-carry branches in Essen and Mülheim, eventually
becoming one of Europe's largest retailers.[41] Another German retail chain
that later conquered the world was Aldi, founded in Essen in 1946 and
given its familiar present-day name in 1962. Aldi thrived by cutting costs
to the bone, which included not using advertising. Elsewhere, the FRG's

miracle years were saturated with advertising campaigns based on market research with focus groups that tested consumer preferences. We think of this as American-style selling, the methods of those Vance Packard called "hidden persuaders" in his influential 1957 book of that name. The historical irony is that these sales methods were a "reimport" of ideas originally carried to the United States by Germans.[42] Think of them as the profane adman's version of what happened with the ideas of the social scientist Max Weber, reimported to postwar West Germany in altered form after passing though the hands of American scholars such as Talcott Parsons and Edward Shils.[43]

As prosperity advanced, there was some adoption of "American" forms of consumption, but this was always selective. West Germans came to love their cars, but they never gave up their railroads. Nor did the huge postwar housing boom lead to American-style suburbanization. There were no Levittowns in the Federal Republic. Here, West Germany followed a European pattern, as it did in its welfare provision and social market economy. In many everyday matters of consumption and lifestyle choices, evolving tastes meant Europeanization as much as Americanization. That became more evident with the passing years. The domestic interiors of West German homes tell the story. Their kitchens had appliances that were smaller, more efficient, and more stylish than their outsized American counterparts (and less likely to have been bought on credit). When Germans eventually had the money to buy a washing machine, it might be a Bosch or a Zanussi; it would not be a bulky Whirlpool.[44] When the economist Uwe Kitzinger surveyed the so-called New Europeans in 1963, on behalf of *Reader's Digest*, he found that "the homes of the Dutch have much of the same durable goods as the homes of the North West Italians, the homes of the Germans have much the same amenities as those of the Dutch."[45] Even those who criticized the new world of material goods placed Germany against a European backdrop. Franz-Josef Wuermeling, the Christian Democratic minister of family affairs, gave a Mother's Day speech in 1959 warning about the potentially damaging influence of television, car, and phonograph. A "Europe of strong mothers" was better than a "Europe merely of motors and machines," he said, holding up the traditional family as part of a "shared European future." "Europe" and "Europeans" are referred to seven times in this short address.[46] Was there an unspoken criticism of Americanization in this invocation of European values? Perhaps.

It was in the realms of popular culture and leisure that American influence was most obvious. Almost half of all films shown between 1949 and 1963 were Hollywood productions, mainly westerns, detective films, and melodramas. For a while, the domestic film industry enjoyed commercial success with a German genre, the sentimental *Heimat* film, but by the late 1950s it was clear that American imports appealed to a wider audience, although they also attracted criticism.[47] A taste for American popular music spread widely through listening to American Forces Network radio, the Voice of America, West Berlin's Radio in the American Sector (RIAS), and Radio Luxemburg. Sometimes the taste was acquired by those who had spent time on the other side of the Atlantic, especially young people enrolled in exchange programs like Youth for Understanding (which welcomed its first German teenagers to Michigan in July 1951) and the American Field Service. Singers like Bill Haley also toured Germany, eliciting the same decidedly mixed reactions that performances of rock 'n' roll produced elsewhere in Europe. The newsmagazine *Der Spiegel* reported in sour (and racially charged) terms on dancers at an Elvis Presley concert "like haunted medicine men of a jungle tribe governed only by music—rock 'n' roll."[48]

The reception of American popular culture was far from uniform. Hollywood westerns, for example, appealed to the middle-aged because the sheriff who tamed a lawless town was a positive role model with whom they identified, the firm but fair authority figure. Young people, on the other hand, identified with rebels like Marlon Brando and James Dean, just as they seized on rock 'n' roll as a way to fight a generational battle by proxy.[49] "He gave us something to use against our parents," said the German rock star Udo Lindenberg, recalling his reaction as an eleven-year-old to hearing Elvis Presley on the radio.[50] Rock 'n' roll in West Germany began as a working-class subculture but (like the British "beat" music that arrived later) soon attracted middle-class youth.[51] Others were drawn to jazz, which enjoyed new postwar popularity. A jazz festival was established in Frankfurt in 1953 and jazz clubs existed in major cities by 1960.[52] Jazz in the Federal Republic (as in the United States) migrated in the 1950s and '60s from the dance music of the swing era to music that was listened to carefully, on records or in clubs, a more "respectable" genre.[53] One subset of the young—the cool kind, from the urban university and art-school scene—disliked the "crassness" of American culture but identified with cool jazz, which they associated with the fashionable French existentialist culture.[54] After all, Miles Davis, the archetypal exponent of late fifties cool jazz, was known to be the lover of Juliette Gréco and wrote the soundtrack to Louis Malle's noirish French thriller *Elevator to the Gallows*. Older Germans could admire American popular music that was not so different from the German *Schlager*, for not all American music was rock 'n' roll or jazz. It is no surprise that when we look at German entries to the Eurovision Song Contest we find, alongside the banal, ersatz "Europeanism" of "Bonne Nuit, Ma Chérie," the banal, ersatz "Americanism" of "Sing, Sang, Song" and "Johnny Blue."

West Germans took what they wanted from America, they selected, adapted, and made it their own.[55] The result was often a hybrid. In one of the best-known *Heimat* films, *The Girl from the Black Forest*, the heroine, Bärbel, represents rural virtue but is also open to the promise of the modern. She wins a red Ford convertible in a raffle and poses next to the car in her dirndl before driving off.[56] Nowhere is this hybridity more evident than in the reception of Coca-Cola. West Germans drank it avidly, which we might be tempted to take as a marker of how the American pleasure principle had eclipsed older German traditions, until we look at the marketing campaign behind its success. Drinking Coca-Cola was linked to the economic miracle and to Germans' hard work in bringing it about. The advertising slogan that hit the spot was *"Mach mal Pause"* ("Take a break"), which came from the blue-collar Ruhr industrial area and carried the implication that the work went on, even as the cold, refreshing drink provided a well-deserved break.[57]

In the Federal Republic, hard work, the strong Deutschmark and the country's prowess as an export *Weltmeister* became acceptable forms of national pride. The lifestyle that had developed by the beginning of the 1970s was a blend of the European, the American, and the German, in which the emphasis on consumption, comfort, and leisure in some ways created a West German identity that replaced older identities of work, duty, and nation. These material pleasures were also perfectly compatible with a culturally conservative emphasis on home, family, and religion, especially in the foundational period of the economic miracle, between 1949 and 1963.

East German economic and social development was also more complex than simple Sovietization. Many aspects of the Soviet system were introduced, of course, starting with the rapid socialization of industry and collectivization of agriculture. The fixation on coal, iron, and steel output remained something of a fetish. Top-down planning with fixed quotas underlay the approach to production; so did a Soviet-style emphasis on sheer volume and weight of output, quantity over quality, well captured by the German term *Tonnenideologie*, the "ideology of tons." East German planners in many fields were in thrall to Soviet gigantomania. The Plan for Implementing the Transformation of Nature in Germany, drawn up in 1951–1953, was modeled on an almost identically named Soviet plan, with its ambitious proposals for river regulation and attempts to alter local climate. Collectivization would supposedly prove that big was beautiful, as huge fields were tilled by Soviet tractors and sprayed from the air with insecticide.[58] It is true that in West Germany, too, small family farms were disappearing in the 1950s and '60s, but not with the same brute force or such counterproductive results (and politicians were careful to praise the family farm even as it disappeared). On the shop floor as well, the regime introduced the Soviet system of piecework, encouraging work brigades to compete against one another and achieve heroic feats of output. Piecework was never popular. It was the sudden raising of work norms that triggered the 1953 uprising.

Plans, quotas, workplace norms—all concerned production. It was in matters of consumption that East Germany came up short, a common problem in the Soviet bloc. Unwanted and unsaleable goods piled up in warehouses while sought-after items were unavailable. Yet the conventional view of a uniformly gray, drab country whose leaders simply ignored consumer demand is misleading. Although the period of postwar recovery went on longer than in the West (rationing did not end until 1958), the regime made conscious efforts to address consumer needs in the "new course" that began after 1953.[59] The manufacture of clothing and household gadgets picked up speed. Then, under the New Economic System launched in 1963, factory managers received greater discretion and the banks were supposed to channel credit to deserving recipients while denying it to others. Most important, efforts were made to create a distinctly socialist kind of consumption based on needs and the common good, not on what Marx had called commodity fetishism. But this was easier said than done. The East German economy had not been constructed with consumer interests in mind. Prejudices against "decadent" and "American" practices had to be overcome and socialist versions invented, whether it was advertising, packaging, or supermarkets. After 1961 the state advertising agency DEWAG consciously promoted a "socialist way of life" that embraced consumption, although its sober, matter-of-fact product promotion lacked the verve of the ads East Germans could see on West German TV.[60]

The regime paid close attention to interior design, furniture, and every-day objects like eggcups and toys. It hit upon plastic as an all-purpose material for manufacturing a range of household items. The objects in question were certainly not drab: with their bright primary colors, these plastic household goods remain instantly recognizable as East German. The evidence suggests that many consumers thought them modern, fashionable, and therefore preferable to more "old-fashioned" versions in wood or metal, but they did not think of them as particularly socialist. There was also the problem that, like much else, they were not always available.[61] That was certainly true of another plastic wonder, the Trabant car, with its two-stroke engine and duroplast body. The "Trabi" became a byword for the failure of the East German economy, not without reason, but the lightweight plastic body embodied a vision of modernity, however imperfectly realized. That vision and its association with the Sputnik era is evident even in the name. Trabant is the German word for "satellite," and the regime paid valuable foreign currency to the Swiss trademark holder for the right to use it.[62]

The Trabant was only one sign of the fascination of GDR leaders in the late 1950s and 1960s with science, modernity, and technology as the keys to the socialist future. This was partly a matter of dancing, once more, to a Soviet tune. New or rebuilt residential areas in Frankfurt am Oder and Zwickau were called the "cosmonaut district," with streets named after Soviet cosmonauts like Yuri Gagarin and Vladimir Komarov. There was keen interest in the Soviet engineer Sergei Mitrofanov's "group technology." Walter Ulbricht was personally interested to an almost obsessive degree in the possibilities of cybernetics and systems theory. Much of this "messianic" zeal reflected a desperate search for a technological solution that would give East Germany a boost in competing with the West.[63] It also marked an unwitting convergence with a moment in Western Europe when science, technology, and planning achieved almost magical potency, from the French zeal for planning and confidence in nuclear technology to British Labour Party leader Harold Wilson's wager in 1963 on the "white heat of technological change."[64]

Enthusiasm for technology did not preclude a sharp increase in the provision of consumer goods and leisure activities. The number of cars per capita increased fivefold between 1960 and 1975, as East Germany overtook Czechoslovakia as the country with the highest density of car ownership in the Soviet bloc.[65] There was similar growth in the ownership of televisions and refrigerators. Special attention was paid to young people, because the regime was concerned in the 1960s that they looked too much to the West. Motorbikes and mopeds, transistor radios, and camping equipment were produced in greater numbers and by the end of the 1960s jeans, records, and other objects of "youth fashion" became available in department stores.[66]

But it was never enough. The jeans were not Western jeans, the records were not Western records. The attempt to create an East German fashion industry, a socialist challenger to the haute couture of the West, was no more successful, and the fashion shows designed to promote it had been largely discontinued by the end of the 1960s.[67] The boast at the Fifth Party Congress in 1958 that socialist Germany would overtake capitalist Germany (echoing Nikita Khrushchev's "we will bury you" claim in 1956) had clearly been exposed by 1970 as empty. That was the year the New Economic System was ended, largely for political reasons because of the crackdown that followed the crushing of the Prague Spring in August 1968. But the problems went deeper, and it is not clear that the New Economic System could have solved them. The planned economy had too many rigidities and quantity too often triumphed over quality. Where was the gain if more households had a Combi washing machine but, as the Women's Division of the SED complained, it was below international standards, far inferior to the French brand?[68] East German citizens were still being asked to defer their gratification during the era of cybernetics and systems theory. But they wanted oranges and bananas to be available, they wanted fish sticks not to be a luxury commodity, they did not want periodic shortages of basic items like toothbrushes, and they did not want to wait eight years for a car. Managing scarcity became a part of life in the GDR, one that fell disproportionately on women, who (like their counterparts elsewhere in the Eastern bloc) spent the most time standing in line.

East Germany was far more successful at delivering the goods than Poland or Hungary, but those were not the comparisons that East Germans made. West Germany set the standards by which East Germans judged. The GDR regime wanted, above all, to compete with the other Germany. Competition was joined in the matchup between two major trade fairs, the historic one in Leipzig inherited by the German Democratic Republic and the new Hanover Trade Fair established by the Federal Republic as a rival. The Leipzig Fair remained an important point of international contact between East and West for as long as the Cold War lasted. But as far as economic competition was concerned, East Germany had thrown in the towel by the end of the 1960s.[69]

The Leipzig and Hanover trade fairs happened once a year. Another German city provided a stage set for Cold War competition all the year round: Berlin. It began with the blockade, which recast the western part of the city as an outpost of freedom. Hans Hirschfeld, an émigré who had returned from the United States after the war and become speaker of the Berlin Senate, went on an American lecture tour in 1953. He spoke of his city "thriving 100 miles behind the Iron Curtain" and hoped his audiences would be curious enough to visit a place that had been rebuilt from a wasteland of rubble to a "cosmopolitan center of art, fashion, industry and education."[70] The American identification with West Berlin was especially intense. It became an almost mythical place, "the Cold War city on a hill."[71] Then, with the building of the Wall, politicians in the West made understandable use of this potent symbol. It was the backdrop to John F. Kennedy's famous *Ich bin ein Berliner*" speech in 1963.[72] Gazing from the lookout platform at Checkpoint Charlie into the East became a ritual. There were other places where "border tourism" allowed Westerners of different nationalities to feel the frisson of armed East German guards from a safe distance, but Berlin offered the most intense political theater of this kind.[73] In East Berlin, meanwhile, a huge television tower was built near Alexanderplatz in the 1960s, the tallest structure on German soil. Intended as a symbol of socialist science and technology, its style was a hybrid, the basic structure modeled on the Stuttgart TV tower, the sphere at the top designed to resemble the Soviet Sputnik.

Other forms of competition were played out in Berlin, like the early Cold War "battle of the billboards" on Potsdamer Platz. In 1950 construction workers erected a gigantic screen on the western side of the plaza with two thousand lightbulbs that proclaimed "DIE FREIE BERLINER PRESSE MELDET" ("Berlin's free press reports") and underneath it a series of news crawls aimed at the East. East Berlin responded with an illuminated billboard of its own, cheekily urging West Berliners to shop at the HO, East Germany's state-owned retail organization.[74] Competition was then joined over the rival merits of the eight-story Innsbrucker Platz apartments built in West Berlin with aid from the Marshall Plan and the Weberwiese highrise apartments constructed with great fanfare as a model socialist undertaking in the East. The East tried to seize the high ground by denouncing the western apartments as "formalist eggshells," nothing but "ugly, artistically worthless slabs," according to Walter Ulbricht.[75] The problem was that East Germany found itself in the middle of a messy debate about architectural styles in which, unsurprisingly, the Soviet Sixteen Principles of Urbanism won out over modernist international style. The result was a gift to Western anti-Soviet propaganda. It was in West Berlin that African-American jazz stars Louis Armstrong and Ella Fitzgerald performed as a part of U.S. Cold War "cultural diplomacy," while in East Berlin the regime welcomed Paul Robeson, the Black actor, singer, activist, and victim of America's McCarthy era blacklist, who received an honorary doctorate and sang before a crowd of thousands.

The world tended to take note of what happened in Berlin (as it did later events in Belfast and Beirut) because it was a divided city. That was why the battle of billboards and buildings had special importance. But the two Germanys competed before the eyes of the world in many things. This was competition of a very particular kind because each laid claim to be the "real" or "better" Germany. West Germany boasted its credentials as the "democratic miracle," where democracy finally spoke German.[76] These were claims the other side constantly challenged by referring to the former Nazis in prominent positions, each revelation a propaganda coup. Episodes like the so-called *Spiegel* affair did not help, when eleven editors of the newsmagazine were arrested and its offices raided in a hunt for classified material after the publication of an article in October 1962 critical of West Germany's defense capability. However, the subsequent widespread outcry, the fact that it became a major scandal, was its most important aspect. This was a political stress test the Federal Republic passed. One year earlier, by contrast, the building of the Berlin Wall delivered the most damning verdict imaginable on the political legitimacy of the East German regime. Asymmetry was built into German-German politics. The international expression of it was the West German Hallstein Doctrine, which stipulated that the FRG would consider recognition of the GDR an "unfriendly act." It broke off diplomatic relations accordingly with Yugoslavia (1957) and Cuba (1963), and temporarily froze foreign aid to Ceylon (present-day Sri Lanka) in 1964 after Prime Minister Sirimavo Bandaranaike approved the establishment of an East German consulate general in Colombo.

The GDR craved recognition and pursued it in the 1950s and '60s through every possible extradiplomatic channel. Relations with Britain offer an example of what this meant in practice. In 1959 East Germany was permitted to set up a Chamber of Foreign Trade in London, which concluded agreements with the Federation of British Industry, the main employers' organization. The Leipzig Trade Fair was a contact point for visitors, whether businessmen or Labour Party Members of Parliament. British-based organizations such as Berolina Travel encouraged travel to the GDR. East Berlin assiduously cultivated links with trade unions, churches, peace movements, teachers, and town councils. In 1956 Dresden and Coventry, symbols of the horrors inflicted by saturation bombing during World War Two, became twin cities. In 1971 the British Committee for the Recognition of the GDR was set up by a retired UK diplomat.[77]

In every case the GDR faced competition from the West. Sport, cultural diplomacy, and the cultivation of Third World countries were three of the many arenas in which the systems clashed. Sport had become an arena of international competition in the 1930s. Nazi Germany and Fascist Italy used it to boost their standing; the USSR also embraced sporting competition under Stalin.[78] It was predictable that East Germany would do the same, partly because of the historic link between sport and dictatorship, partly because it followed the Soviet lead, but above all because sport was a means of seeking the international recognition the regime craved but was largely denied until the early 1970s. In the 1950s success came mainly on two wheels. In 1952 the GDR became part of the newly established East European Ride for Peace, a two-week cycle race from Warsaw to Prague. East Germany won the race in 1953 and the country had its first sporting hero, Gustav-Adolf Schur, who won again in 1955 and 1959. Germans living abroad wrote letters to "Täve." Ingrid, in London, sent him a provocative photo of herself in a swimsuit.[79]

East Germany saw athletes as "diplomats in tracksuits," and most people associate the country's sporting success with the Olympic Games. But that was part of a tangled international history. No German team competed at the 1948 Olympics in London: Germans were still unwanted. In 1952 a "German" team competed and so did a separate team representing the Saarland, not yet reunited with the Federal Republic; but the Democratic Republic declined to take part. In 1956, 1960, and 1964 a team called "Germany" competed (now referred to in Olympic records as the "United Team of Germany"), drawn from both countries, which used the German tricolor with Olympic rings as its flag and the final movement of Beethoven's Ninth Symphony as its anthem. Not until 1968 did the two Germanys compete as separate teams ("Germany" and "German Democratic Republic"), although they were still required by the IOC to use the same flag and anthem they had used four years earlier.[80] Only thereafter was the "Cold War on the cinder track" really joined, with East German teams routinely taking second or third place in the medal table. The GDR achieved success in track and field and in the Olympic pool partly by following the Soviet model of identifying elite athletes at an early age. Its coaches also used performance-enhancing drugs on a huge scale. The remarkable haul of medals and the global recognition that went with it was bought at the expense of the athletes' long-term health. There was another, less obvious price: the greatly reduced financial support for other sports in East Germany in the 1970s and '80s.[81]

It is ironic that the self-proclaimed socialist Germany made such a poor showing in team sports, most obviously in soccer's World Cup. Other Eastern bloc countries enjoyed at least occasional successes. East Germany qualified for the competition just once in forty years, in 1974, whereas West Germany was consistently successful. The first and most dramatic of those successes came in 1954, when West Germany defeated the favorite, Hungary, in the final played in Switzerland, the so-called miracle of Berne. At the end of Rainer Werner Fassbinder's film *The Marriage of Maria Braun* (1979), we hear the final minutes of the game on the radio and an exultant commentator shouting, "Germany is World Champion!" just as the heroine's house is destroyed by a gas explosion. This piece of melodramatic symbolism is Fassbinder's later commentary on the self-destructive quality of the economic miracle. At the time, however, the victory was taken in the Federal Republic as another sign (like the strong Deutschmark) that "Germany" once again counted for something in the world.

Culture was a major arena where the two Germanys fought for primacy. The GDR accused the West of capitulating to crass American *Unkultur*; the FRG responded that Germans in the East had succumbed to the *Unkultur* of Russian communism. There were, in fact, some obvious commonalities. Both Germanys were trying to step out of the shadow cast by National Socialism, which had made the words "German culture" suspect. Both claimed the moral high ground in doing so, defining that high ground largely in terms of high culture. The two Germanys supported orchestras and theaters with subsidies on a scale unmatched in the United States or Britain. Walter Ulbricht boasted about performance spaces and classical music programs. In West Germany, there were four opera houses within a twenty-five-mile radius of Frankfurt (in Frankfurt itself, Darmstadt, Mainz, and Wiesbaden), two of them destroyed and two seriously damaged by wartime bombing, but all of them up and running in the 1950s. It was in Berlin that the two sets of high cultural offerings played out before a larger audience. West Berlin had charismatic, Austrian-born Herbert von Karajan, musical director of the Berlin Philharmonic, whose recordings sold 200 million copies worldwide. Karajan, with his leonine good looks and playboy lifestyle, was something of an international star. East Berlin had no one in the field of classical music to rival him, although it might have had if efforts to recruit Erich Kleiber permanently as conductor of the celebrated Staatsoper had been successful. Austrian-born like Karajan but a generation older, Kleiber left Germany when Hitler came to power (unlike Karajan) and went to Argentina, before making his name in postwar London. He accepted the Staatsoper position, then changed his mind, under pressure from individuals in the West who felt that this amounted to support for communism, whereas Kleiber saw it as bridge building.[82]

East Berlin had one cultural figure whose international celebrity matched Karajan's. The poet and dramatist Bertolt Brecht was, like Kleiber, a former émigré. With the Berliner Ensemble, Brecht put into practice his dramatic principles, to international acclaim. Delegations of progressive directors and actors made pilgrimages to the Theater am Schiffbauerdamm; Brecht was sought after in London, Paris, and Brussels. Picasso's dove of peace adorned the front curtain of the theater. That was orthodox enough. But Brecht had constant fights with party apparatchiks over his plays. Outside East Germany he enjoyed "pre-eminent international status"; inside he was worn down by running battles.[83] A lesser figure, one less valuable to the regime, would not have been allowed the latitude he did enjoy. Brecht died in August 1956, from a long-term heart condition. Not long before, he told a friend his views about an obituary: "Don't write that you admire me. Write that I was recalcitrant and intend to remain that way after my death."[84] The Berliner Ensemble continued to enjoy high prestige in the West, but there was no longer an obvious successor in East Germany to play the rebel as Brecht had done and get away with it because of his reputation outside the country, except perhaps the young singer-poet Wolf Biermann, a convinced Communist whose independence nonetheless led to his being labeled a "class traitor" in 1965 and banned from publishing or performing.

In the same year Brecht died, there was a design competition for a new home for the Berlin Philharmonic. The new building, by Hans Scharoun, was finished in 1963. The site was at the western end of the Tiergarten near the Soviet zone, part of the cluster of buildings designed to create a Kulturforum around the Potsdamer Platz. By the time the new Philharmonie was completed, it stood close to the recently built Wall. It also stood on the site that Albert Speer, Hitler's architect, had earmarked for a huge Soldiers' Hall to commemorate the World War One dead. The style of the building, as well as its location, made a statement. On the outside, the curvy, tent-like structure could not have been more different from the monumentality favored by Speer, or the unimaginative, blocky structures preferred in East Berlin. Inside, too, the Philharmonic broke with tradition by placing the stage in the middle and the seating all around, with asymmetrical terraces that Scharoun likened to a vineyard. The design, especially the placement of the stage, later served as a model for other prominent concert halls like the Sydney Opera House (1973), Suntory Hall in Tokyo (1986), and Walt Disney Hall in Los Angeles (2003). In the Cold War early 1960s, the place where Karajan and his orchestra performed represented a powerful piece of self-assertion in the modernist mode.

The Federal Republic was carried along on the wave of cultural modernism that swept the West in the 1950s and '60s, especially in art and architecture. The West German embrace of architectural modernism was another instance of reimporting what had left Germany earlier—in this case, Bauhaus ideas. Walter Gropius was invited back to serve as architectural adviser to Lucius Clay. The Ulm School of Design, opened in 1953, functioned as a reincarnation of the Bauhaus. What was by then called "international style" became, in the FRG, a kind of American-German "joint venture of the Cold War."[85] The sophisticated glass buildings that made up the West German pavilion at Expo 58 in Brussels, the first postwar world's fair, were widely regarded as the most stylish and polished on display.[86] Like Scharoun's concert hall, they made a statement.

The break with the Nazi past and the embrace of the contemporary in art was signaled by one institution more than any other: documenta. This was a hundred-day art exhibition held in Kassel, at first every four or five years, after 1972 every five years. The first documenta showcased the art deemed "decadent" in the Third Reich. Later shows embraced contemporary art in its many different forms. There was a place in documenta for installations and the political provocations of the enfant terrible Joseph Beuys. The works were often edgy and sometimes self-indulgent. They made documenta into an international event, attracting 200,000 visitors in 1964.[87] It is striking how often West Germans were at the center of European and even global art movements that challenged convention. Hans Neuendorf, later the founder of Artnet, stumbled into an entirely novel way of selling art in 1967 when he sold works of American pop art in Cologne at the world's first art fair. Beuys helped to found Fluxus, a performance art group whose best-known members were Yoko Ono and the American composer John Cage. The Artists Placement Group, which began in Britain in 1965, also had multiple connections to the Federal Republic; for example, the composer Hugh Davies, closely associated with this group, had been Karlheinz Stockhausen's assistant in Cologne.

Stockhausen stands as the prime example of West Germany's importance in the musical avant-garde of the period. He and the Darmstadt school were at the center of serialism and the composition of electronic music. Stockhausen's work had an impact on composers across Europe, west and east. At the 1970 World's Fair in Osaka, Stockhausen's works were performed for more than five hours each day. By the time the fair ended, an estimated one million people had heard them. The list of those who claim to have been influenced by the German composer stretches from jazz musicians to musically adventurous groups of the 1960s like Frank Zappa's Mothers of Invention and Pink Floyd. Stockhausen's is one of the faces on the cover of the Beatles' *Sgt. Pepper's Lonely Hearts Club Band*.

There was almost nothing in East Germany to compare with this. The two apparent exceptions, cinema and town planning, turn out to be exceptions that prove the rule. East Germany's DEFA film studios produced some outstanding films. Konrad Wolf's *Divided Heaven* (1964), his film version of Christa Wolf's novel, may be the greatest European new wave film made in either Germany. We watch it now and admire how its modernist aesthetic perfectly meets the needs of the plot. But the film was periodically removed from circulation, just as other outstanding DEFA films of this era were banned or withdrawn. Kurt Maetzig's *The Rabbit Is Me* (1965) and Frank Beyer's *Traces of Stone* (1966) both fell victim to the renewed political repression that followed the cultural thaw of the early 1960s.[88]

Modern town planners also had to tread carefully. Proposals for new towns in Schwedt and Hoyerswerda had a utopian quality that drew on Bauhaus traditions and on the work of modern American urban planners, but politics created difficulties. Selman Selmanagić, a Bosnian-born former Bauhaus student with strong antifascist credentials, was replaced as director of new town planning because of his "individualism."[89] In architecture, as in the arts, it was easy to run afoul of orthodoxy. Party functionaries and arbiters of culture disdained modernism and the avant-garde as "formalism" or "cosmopolitanism." The second of these terms, once used by the Nazis against art they disliked, was now being wielded by an "anti-fascist" regime. Two kinds of architecture, art, and music were acceptable in East Germany. There was what had been passed down to the present, "assuming the heritage of the past" in party jargon, which was little different in practice from what was done in the West. Or there was socialist realist art, its production pursued with Stalinist rigor through much of the 1950s, even after Stalin's death. "Our culture-creators must portray life correctly, that is, in its forward development," urged a resolution of the Central Committee of the Socialist Unity Party. There was no place for doubt, or "decadence."

The constraints of socialist realism drove leading artists to leave for the West, including three born in the 1930s who later established international reputations: Gerhard Richter, Georg Baselitz, and A. R. Penck (Ralf Winkler). East Germany likewise walled itself off against musical modernism. Even politically reliable composers were criticized if they showed signs of being drawn to the work of modernists or composed music that was too "pessimistic" and removed from the masses. Two of Brecht's musical collaborators faced this situation. Hanns Eisler had been a politically engaged leftist composer since the late 1920s and wrote the music to the East German anthem, but his attachment to work of his mentor, Arnold Schönberg, caused strained relations with the party right up to his death in 1962. Criticism was also directed against Paul Dessau for music that "overwhelmed listeners with discordance and intellectual sophistries"—and that was music written for Brecht.[90] Much greater pressure was placed on classical composers in the GDR than in neighboring Poland, and it lasted much longer. Polish composers were largely left alone after 1956 to compose as they wished, a freedom that helped Krzysztof Penderecki and Henryk Gorecki achieve international acclaim for their work.[91]

How much did this matter? Few people on either side of the Iron Curtain listened to Penderecki, after all, just as few listened to Stockhausen. Modernist high culture veered even further away from popular taste in the twenty years after the two German states were founded than it had in the past, while traditional high culture carried less weight than it once did. But these forms of culture mattered to opinion-forming elites, on the left as well as the right, and not just in Germany. That is why, to offer a variation on the musical theme, it mattered that East Germany clearly lost the public relations battle over jazz. GDR advocates of the music like Reginald Rudorf faced an uphill struggle in making the case for an "authentic" jazz.

Critics could not be unaware that Comrade Ulbricht had denounced the "'ape culture' of decadent jazz."[92] Rudorf himself was placed under surveillance by the East German intelligence service, the Stasi, arrested in 1957, and jailed for two years. Then he went to the West, like some top jazz musicians. By the 1960s jazz had become more high culture than popular culture, the preserve of the educated, but the ham-fisted way in which the music was handled in East Germany proved, like the response to rock 'n' roll, to be a harbinger of the difficulties that would arise in the future when new forms of popular music emerged.

When Louis Armstrong played in West Berlin and Paul Robeson sang in East Berlin, these were one-off Cold War propaganda moments. But each Germany pursued a longer-term cultural diplomacy. Between 1950 and 1969, the GDR signed cultural agreements with twenty-two countries, inside and outside the Soviet bloc. Reaching out beyond the socialist countries mattered. In 1964, Manfred Feist, a Central Committee member with responsibility for foreign cultural affairs, visited Moscow. There he learned from his opposite number that the USSR had cultural connections through Soviet Friendship Societies with many countries with which it had no diplomatic relations. Cultural diplomacy was even more important for a country that was recognized diplomatically by almost no one.[93]

West Germany had a more sprawling network of institutions. Cultural diplomats referred later to a period of "wild growth" in the 1950s, which saw the founding or refounding of the German Academic Exchange Service, the Goethe Institutes, the Alexander von Humboldt Foundation and the Deutsche Welle. There was certainly the will to mount a Cold War "cultural offensive," to quote an internal memorandum from the Foreign Office's Cultural Division.[94] But Chancellor Konrad Adenauer was not very interested in soft power. The Cultural Division remained the Cinderella branch of the Foreign Office until the 1960s when this, like so many things, changed. Culture became the "third pillar" of the Federal Republic's foreign policy, alongside politics and economics. The Goethe Institutes, largely concerned until then with language training, became the main conduit of cultural outreach and offered the world a broader, less nationalist version of "German culture," Bonn-style. The Goethe Institutes would later provide post-Franco Spain with the model for its Cervantes Institutes.

Here was double vision, once again. German cultural policies came in two versions; local populations had their pick. In Stockholm, neutral Swedes took this in stride and apparently regarded the two cultural institutes as offering interesting versions of the same thing.[95] In Italy, the rival offerings were more obviously part of Cold War competition. Christian Democrats in Bonn were close to their Italian counterparts and shared the same values. The Federal Republic planted its cultural institutions in Rome as a matter of course. But Rome was also chosen by East German leaders as the location of a major cultural center, the Centro Thomas Mann. That owed something to the strength of the Italian Communist Party and the close links it enjoyed (notwithstanding doctrinal differences) with the GDR.[96] It is no coincidence that in the first Cold War decades Leipzig had just one twin city partnership in the West. It was established in 1962 with "Red Bologna," the Italian city governed by the Communist Party.

The competition between the two German states was global, like the Cold War of which it was a version in miniature. They tussled for influence in Asia, Africa, and the Middle East, subject to the constraints imposed by their own political camp and the frictions that arose whenever Europeans arrived (under whichever political banner) to tell non-European peoples what was good for them. The darkest aspect of this competition was the sale of arms, but the range of possible inducements was wide: educational programs, economic aid, medical resources, and engineering, agronomic, and other forms of professional expertise. They can be grouped under two large headings, "development" and "humanitarian aid," both contemporary buzzwords, both offered by Germans in two political flavors.[97]

East Germany pursued a strong anti-imperialist foreign policy in the 1950s and '60s, years when the last desperate attempts at self-preservation against growing liberation movements by colonial powers and white settler societies produced case after case of behavior that mocked the claims of the so-called free world: British brutality in Kenya, Belgian violence in the Congo, French torture in Algeria, the Sharpeville massacre in South Africa. Always acutely aware of its international isolation, the Democratic Republic also had another reason to court newly independent nations and supported liberation movements, from Algeria and Angola to Mozambique. It was especially active in Africa, but also provided medical resources, educational expertise, and intelligence training in Cuba. The spymaster Markus Wolf later wrote in affectionate but rather condescending terms about Cuba's interior minister, Ramon Valdez, who had a "boyish" fascination with Bond-like devices such as poison-spitting pens. "His disappointment in me as a traveling salesman of espionage equipment grew increasingly obvious," Wolf said of their early encounters.[98] But the Cuban intelligence service quickly became very effective, Wolf's relationship with Piñeiro grew closer, and the resources East Germany lavished on Cuba earned the precious reward of diplomatic recognition.

It was to prevent just such a thing that the West Germans chased the East Germans halfway round the world. "From Bogota to Baghdad, from Addis Ababa to Phnom Penh," writes one scholar, "West German diplomats intervened to protest against the smallest gesture of kindness" to the other Germany.[99] As a result, the Federal Republic found itself engaged in parts of the world to which it might not otherwise have paid much attention. It was also drawn into bidding wars with East Germany over assistance to nonaligned nations. There was another unseemly scramble for Africa between the two Germanys, this one conducted not with the Bible and the Gatling gun, but with promises of aid. Between 1960 and 1964, West Germany opened twenty-six new embassies in sub-Saharan Africa.[100] Bonn was very aware of the East German challenge in an influential capital like Cairo, where every industrial exhibition and cultural program, even a closing fireworks display, became a form of competition.[101]

The global dimension of German-German competition presented policy makers in Bonn with some difficult issues. One arose in the 1960s with its most important ally. Ludwig Erhard, Adenauer's successor as chancellor, firmly refused to send troops to Vietnam at the request of President Lyndon Johnson, after Secretary of State Dean Rusk had urged the need to "get some Germans into the field."[102] That turned out not to be a big problem. Britain refused similar requests, after all, and neither country undermined the U.S. position in public. But the Federal Republic also had to tread carefully among its European allies when it came to global entanglements. Britain, France, Belgium, the Netherlands, and Portugal were all beleaguered colonial powers in an era of decolonization. West Germany was palpably not a colonial power and worked hard to turn its development and aid policies to political account in the Third World, especially in blocking East German recognition. Yet the FRG supported its European allies loyally as they responded with greater or lesser degrees of violence to liberation movements. In 1956, when Secretary of State John Foster Dulles telephoned Premier Guy Mollet to tell him that the Anglo-French Suez invasion had to end, Mollet happened to be with Adenauer, who told his French opposite number that the Europeans needed to stick together against the Americans and consoled him with the often quoted words: "Europe will be your revenge."[103]

Bonn viewed the French rearguard action in Algeria as a distraction from the defense of Europe but supported it anyway to maintain good relations with France, even as allegations of torture by the colonial power became hard to deny. The Federal Republic went further, surveilling Algerian National Liberation Front militants resident there and making no protest even when French counterintelligence operatives attacked its members and German arms dealers who supplied them on German soil.[104] West Germany was equally supportive of Belgium. In 1964 it hosted Moise Tshombe, prime minister and former head of the pseudostate of Katanga created by Belgian mining interests, and the man responsible for the death of Congolese prime minister Patrice Lumumba, after he had been overthrown by a CIA coup and delivered to Katanga to be killed. Tshombe was welcomed on a formal state visit to the Federal Republic as an ally against communism and photographed looking thoughtfully across the Berlin Wall.[105] West Germany was also the leading supplier of arms to Portugal as it hung on desperately to its African colonies. An end-user clause in the sales maintained the polite fiction that the weapons could not be used against the Frelimo guerrilla movement fighting for independence in Mozambique.[106]

South Africa presented a special difficulty. West Germany's first ambassador in Pretoria, Rudolf Holzhausen, was a strong critic of the apartheid system. Others in the Foreign Office were more indulgent toward South Africa and so were some leading Christian Democrats. But the world was changing and the Federal Republic tried hard to avoid antagonizing African states being courted by East Germany. Its solution was to separate trade from politics. That made it all the more surprising when Gustav Sonnenhohl was appointed ambassador in 1968, probably because of his close friendship with the chancellor at the time, Kurt Georg Kiesinger. A former SS man, Sonnenhohl accused South Africa's critics of naïveté, defended apartheid, and even talked about military cooperation between the two governments, which exceeded his official instructions. This exposed divisions within the Foreign Office. Ambassador Michael Jovy in Mali, who was unusual among diplomats in having been jailed as an oppositional youth leader in the Third Reich, challenged Sonnenhohl. The Federal Republic faced a choice, argued Jovy, either "to stand on the side of emancipation of the Africans or to become dependent on a policy of racial suppression and exploitation which will ruin our reputation and destroy our influence in Africa and run counter to our interests." The exchange was leaked to the left-wing journal *konkret* and gleefully exploited by East Berlin.[107]

The global sixties brought political and generational differences to the fore in West Germany. Not everyone welcomed the changing times. Some resisted change violently. Rolf Steiner served with the French Foreign Legion in Vietnam and Algeria, then as a mercenary in sub-Saharan Africa; Siegfried "Kongo" Müller led Tshombe's notorious mercenary army in Congo.[108] As we have seen, many Germans in the past had served other empires as soldiers. But Steiner and Müller were a new breed and a dying breed at the same time—postcolonial Germans trying to uphold a soon-to-be-postcolonial world. Nostalgia for the German empire was common among the older generation, especially those with relatives in former German Southwest Africa, which was administered by South Africa until it became independent Namibia in 1990, and the German–South African Society lobbied for close ties with the apartheid nation. There was widespread conservative criticism of development aid as a "squandering" of taxpayers' money, often accompanied by racial stereotypes about African corruption and incompetence.[109]

Nevertheless, West German awareness of the Third World did elicit more generous impulses. The churches raised money for aid and trained field workers. Volunteer bodies proliferated. Organizations were set up to channel humanitarian and developmental aid, such as the German Foundation for Developed Countries (1959), the German Society for Economic Cooperation/German Development Society (1962), and the German Development Service (1963). These programs were naturally open to the charge of European paternalism or, going a step further, of serving as agents of an exploitative developmental regime.[110] Exactly these arguments came from within the system itself, from churches, scholars, and aid workers. Their concerns overlapped with the full-throated denunciations that came from the 1960s New Left, which saw development and aid as tools of Western neoimperialism, perpetuating structures of Third World dependency that rested on the use of violence. The criticism reached its culmination in what is often called by the shorthand "1968," although the elements that went into that movement had been years in the making. One of its characteristics was the coming together of the global and the local.

The second half of the 1960s saw an upsurge of New Left radicalism in West Germany and West Berlin. Much of what propelled it was specific to West Germany. The Grand Coalition formed by the two major parties (the Christian Democrats and the Social Democrats) in 1966, and the effective disappearance of parliamentary opposition, gave the self-styled extra-parliamentary opposition on the left its name and raison d'être. That the new chancellor, Kurt Georg Kiesinger, was a former Nazi highlighted another distinctively German issue that fueled the movement, the alleged amnesia of the older generation about the Third Reich and its crimes. It went hand in hand with the pervasive antiauthoritarianism of the movement, rooted in rebellion against the bourgeois domestic values of the Federal Republic and a hierarchical educational system. That was a central issue for the Socialist German Student League (SDS). There was a generational dimension, too, in New Left critiques of stifling consumer capitalism. There was one more potent local villain, the media magnate Axel Springer, who was to German sixties' radicals what Rupert Murdoch became for later generations. The populist Springer press fanned the flames of hostility against all protesters and demonstrators, whether peaceful or not. These constant attacks goaded an anti-Communist named Josef Bachmann into the attempted assassination of student leader Rudi Dutschke in April 1968.

Radical protest in West Germany was simultaneously very German and very global. It was the German version of a movement challenging authority that was taking place from Berkeley and Paris to Mexico City and Wuhan.[111] The movements shared texts, slogans, and methods. Like other New Left protesters, the West Germans read Frantz Fanon, Herbert Marcuse, and Che Guevara, talked about "cultural revolution," and quickly adopted forms of action that had proved successful elsewhere— street theater, happenings, sit-ins. German demonstrators learned from the Berkeley free speech movement; the French situationists offered ideas on how to subvert the capitalist "spectacle." But the movement of ideas was not all one-way. "It was in Berlin that we learned how to demonstrate in the streets," said one French militant.[112] West Berlin became a magnet for French, British, and American radicals. West Germany and West Berlin were part of a transnational political counterculture. As an SDS member named Claus Offe said in 1968, it was a truism that political forms could not simply be copied from another country, but there was nonetheless an "internationalism of protest."[113]

Radical protesters took up global issues as well. What bound them all together was Third World solidarity, the German version of the Third Worldism that flourished across Western Europe. In the early sixties it was Algeria that engaged New Left intellectuals. "Algeria is everywhere," said the poet and essayist Hans Magnus Enzensberger, editor of the left-wing *Kursbuch*.[114] There were other flashpoints and causes in these years, above all in Africa, such as apartheid and the murder of Patrice Lumumba. Then there were China and Cuba, whose revolutions were welcomed (thanks to generous helpings of self-delusion) as attractive alternatives to the bureaucratic socialism of the Soviet bloc. The U.S. response to the Cuban revolution, especially the Bay of Pigs invasion, brought American imperialism directly into focus. There had been other recent examples of U.S. misbehavior, like the 1954 coup that overthrew the Arbenz government in Guatemala. West Germans and West Berliners were also keenly aware of the American civil rights struggle (Martin Luther King Jr. visited both West and East Berlin in 1964) and the emergence of the Black Panther movement. The new satellite technology of the early 1960s brought American television pictures instantly to Germany. The alliance between the United States and West Germany was now mirrored by a very different kind of alliance between protest movements in the two countries.[115] Above all, the Vietnam War became the focus of radical protest. Germany, said Rudi Dutschke, was the "second front against Vietnam."[116]

Comments like Dutschke's point to a vicarious element in sixties radicalism, the projection of German revolutionary hopes and frustrations onto Third World peoples. At its worst, the movement was both condescending about the sufferings and naïve about the politics of those with whom it identified. Enzensberger, who was nobody's fool, wrote a highly unromantic account of the Cuban revolution before the 1960s were out, followed by a beady-eyed look at "tourists of the revolution." He later went after the hypocritical elements of Third Worldism in the West.[117] It is therefore all the more important to recognize the major role that foreign émigrés and students played in the West German movement. Just as Berlin in the 1920s became home to radical Asian students and intellectuals, so West Germany and West Berlin played host in the 1960s to growing numbers of politically engaged Africans, Asians, and Latin Americans. They came to study at German universities, or they came as dissident intellectuals through the sponsorship of churches, political parties, foundations, and NGOs.[118] In Germany, they became political actors as members of the African Student League and the Latin American Student League. Dutschke saw foreign students protesting against Moise Tshombe and wrote in his diary, "Our friends from the Third World stepped into the breach and the Germans had to follow."[119]

Some of the "friends" came from the Middle East, especially Iran. It was a visit to West Berlin on June 2, 1967, by the Shah of Iran that led to one of the landmark events of the era. The shah had returned to power after the 1953 overthrow, engineered by Britain and the United States, of Mohammad Mosaddeq, the democratically elected prime minister. Ever since then, the shah's politically repressive "developmental" regime had made him a natural target for protesters. Before he arrived for a noon meeting with the mayor, around two to three thousand demonstrators, many of them Iranian, had gathered. Then a bus arrived and the unarmed demonstrators found themselves under attack by members of Iran's secret service, Savak, wielding wooden sticks and metal blackjacks. Police intervened belatedly, before violently dispersing the demonstrators. That evening there was a demonstration of perhaps six thousand people, among them a literature student named Benno Ohnesorg. According to a Chilean friend, Ohnesorg decided to go because of what he had read about conditions in Iran. In the chaotic scenes that unfolded when police tried to disperse the demonstrators, Ohnesorg was shot in the back of the head and killed by Karl-Heinz Kurras, a plainclothes police officer.* Ohnesorg's death became a rallying point for the left and radicalized many in the student movement.[120]

Was there also a global sixties in East Germany? There is, at one level, an obvious resemblance between the official ideology enunciated in East Berlin and the convictions held by radical demonstrators in the West. The GDR identified itself as a socialist state that supported the victims of Western imperialism and encouraged its citizens to see themselves as part of a global struggle. Support for minorities in the United States was an important part of that. African-American plays such as Lorraine Hansberry's *A Raisin in the Sun* and James Baldwin's *Blues for Mister Charlie* were staged as a means of portraying a racist America—this work of Baldwin's from 1964 was considered more consonant with Marxist principles than his earlier novels *Giovanni's Room* and *Another Country*, with their portrayals of gay love.[121] Black GIs serving in West Germany who sought political asylum in the East became symbolic trophies for the antiracism of the regime. So, too, did the African-American radical Angela Davis, who received her PhD at Humboldt University in East Berlin. The GDR organized a campaign against her subsequent imprisonment in the United States and garlanded her in East Berlin after her release.[122] Leaders of the American Indian Movement were equally welcome guests.[123]

---

* It became known in 2009 that Kurras was an East German Stasi officer, although there is no evidence that he was acting that evening on behalf of the Stasi.

Cuba served the East German regime as a symbol of resistance to U.S. imperialism. In the early 1960s, the vulnerability of the socialist experiment in Cuba also proved useful as a lesson to East Germans about their own vulnerability, absent the Wall. In *And Your Love Too* (1962), the first of the so-called Wall films, the main theme is a love triangle between a young, politically immature woman and two brothers, the arrogant Western-oriented Klaus and the good East German Ulli; virtue eventually wins out. But there is an important subplot: Ulli meets his Cuban friend Alfredo because both are radio hams. Alfredo makes a surprise visit to East Berlin during August 1961, when the Wall is being built and Ulli, doing his duty, is defending the GDR, although the two comrades still have time to sing socialist songs together. The message about a common imperialist threat is even more obvious in *Preludio 11* (1963), which dramatizes the Bay of Pigs. Neither film was very popular with East German audiences, however.[124] The legend of Tamara Bunke had more resonance. She met Che Guevara when acting as an East German interpreter, traveled to South America, and was killed in Bolivia a few weeks before him in 1967. Her carefully cultivated story lent itself to propaganda. Schools, brigades, and youth groups were named after Bunke. Markus Wolf later described her as a popular idol among East German teenagers.[125]

East Germans were constantly invited to identify with struggles in faraway and "exotic" socialist places. Sometimes the global context was lightly sketched into works where it was not the main theme. The plot of the 1971 film *Do You Know Urban?* revolves around the relationship between Urban and young Hoffi, who has gone astray and served prison time for violence. Urban is the model citizen, who shows Hoffi how to reform. We learn gradually that Urban worked as a surveyor in Algeria, where a little mirror he always carried, stamped "Made in East Germany," proved to the National Liberation Front that he was not a Western agent. It also emerges that he has spent time in Cuba and Vietnam.

Vietnam was the issue East Berlin used most successfully. Like student radicals in the West, the regime denounced the war, taking the opportunity to attack West Germany as a U.S. ally and to establish connections with the international antiwar movement. Unlike the construction of the Wall or support for the Warsaw Pact invasion of Czechoslovakia in 1968, the official campaign against the Vietnam War enjoyed popular support. A secret opinion survey in 1966 by the U.S. Information Agency conceded as much. "The East German regime's propaganda drumfire and its 'solidarity' meetings on VN doubtless have had some impact, fostering the belief that the US is a colonialist and imperialist power bent on squashing a legitimate national liberation movement," the survey noted. It continued: "While East Germans are constitutionally skeptical of regime propaganda on all issues, the official line may have more credibility on VN than all other issues."[126]

However provincial East Germany may have been in some ways, it was no insular society but played its part in the "socialist sixties" when members of the Soviet bloc crossed borders in the name of solidarity.[127] But these exercises in mutual comradely support had their problems. There had been a foretaste of these in the 1950s, when a team of East German engineers and architects went to help rebuild North Korea's second city, Hamhung, after the Korean War. Russians, Poles, and Czechs were working there to the same end. East Berlin put serious money into the project and there were examples of genuine cross-cultural solidarity and friendship between Germans and Koreans. The East Germans called themselves "Tokils" (Tokil is the Korean word for Germany) and "Hamhunger." But there were problems of alcohol abuse and sexual assaults on Korean women by some Germans, who had to be sent home. There was a broader problem with perceived "arrogance." The East Germans were likened by some Koreans to "Hitler-fascists" and even compared unfavorably with the Japanese occupiers. There were tensions at the planning level, too. The two sides finally decided to call the whole thing off in 1962, still insisting that "fraternal friendship and cooperation" and "proletarian internationalism" would continue.[128]

The East Germans in Hamhung liked to drink Chinese beer and visit Beijing on their way home to Berlin. But the fraying of socialist solidarity in North Korea was, in part, a by-product of the Sino-Soviet split, which was fully in the open by 1961. Kim Il Sung, the North Korean leader, was increasingly drawn to the model of the Chinese Great Leap Forward rather than the Soviet methods represented by East Germany. This division in the socialist "second world" made itself felt throughout the Soviet bloc.[129] But there was also the overarching issue that, in Asia and Africa, the East Germans often looked like the West Germans. They just offered a variation on European modernity, together with the same certainty that they knew best. The limits of socialist solidarity were also evident closer to home. The African students who enrolled in East German universities (although in much smaller numbers than in the West) encountered everyday racism and were widely viewed as a sexual threat.[130] In other cases, the propaganda of the regime ran along implicitly racialized lines even when it held up its antiracism to be admired. An example is how the image of Angela Davis, her so-called *Afrika*-Look, was sexualized and exoticized.[131]

Some of the same contradictions were evident in the West, of course. But a huge divide nonetheless separated the impact of the global sixties in the two Germanys. On one side stood the uncomfortable, oppositional identification of West German students and New Left with the Vietnamese people, Che Guevara, and the American civil rights movement; on the other stood the programmed orthodoxy of those who invoked them in East Berlin. There was an obviously staged quality to the GDR's expressions of solidarity. Figures such as Che also had to be handled carefully because they were implicitly dangerous. Cuba had the capacity to excite hopes of a better, less bureaucratic kind of socialism, which is why literary works that mentioned the Cuban revolution were carefully monitored and in some cases banned.

There were politically aware dissidents in East Germany who followed events in the West, admired Rudi Dutschke, and shared the belief in a better socialist society. Their "1968" was vicarious: it took place in Prague. They identified intensely with the Prague Spring and Communist reformer Alexander Dubček's "socialism with a human face." The Warsaw Pact invasion of August, strongly supported by the regime, was a bitter blow. Those who responded included prominent dissidents like Frank and Florian Havemann, sons of the chemist Robert Havemann, and others in their circle who were the children of party officials and intellectuals. Florian hung a Czech flag from his window. But Stasi records make it clear that the protests did not come only from students and intellectual circles. Across the GDR, nearly two thousand acts of protest were recorded, mainly distributing flyers and writing graffiti like "Long live Dubček" and—more pointedly—"Hands off Red Prague" and "Ho-Chi-Minh-Dubček." There were other forms of protest: refusing to sign official letters of support for the invasion, calls for minutes of silence or sympathy strikes, anonymous telephone calls threatening party functionaries, and acts of sabotage and arson. The flyer distributors and graffiti writers were quickly rounded up and jailed. More than three hundred arrests were made between August and December. The East German '68ers shared much of the style of their Western counterparts and identified with many of the same issues, but political repression excluded the possibility of public debate.[132]

Five years later, in the summer of 1973, the largest expressions of global socialist solidarity in East German history took place—the World Festival of Youth and Students, popularly known as Red Woodstock. By then, several leading dissidents of 1968 had fled to the West, Florian Havemann among them. The festival was carefully planned and controlled. Those entering the country to attend were monitored to keep out "right-wing extremists" (West German conservatives) and "left-wing extremists" (West German Trotskyists and Maoists). Official footage shows seemingly endless parades of well-ordered youth, who had been drilled for months in advance and vetted for political reliability. Yet the organizers were uneasy and kept on their toes by episodes that illustrated the danger (from their point of view) of radical sentiments not fully under control. It might be Wolf Biermann singing a song about Che Guevara, which he was not supposed to do, with words that clearly suggested the possibility of a different kind of socialism, or an Australian activist named Peter Tatchell who came with a delegation from the British National Union of Students and distributed gay rights flyers. The West German left-wing group Floh de Cologne sang a song satirizing capitalism by noting things (like rent increases and unemployment) that were "forbidden" in the GDR. Yet the very act of singing about forbidden things sent a potentially subversive message that would not have been lost on East German youth. Even in a heavily staged event like this, other worlds kept breaking through.[133]

Global Shocks and Global Forces: 1973–1989

AMONG THE TWENTY-FIVE THOUSAND FOREIGN VISITORS TO Red Woodstock was a delegation from Chile. We have a photograph of one group of them, young men and women posing in front of a "Chile" banner, some clapping or waving, two making the clenched-fist salute.[134] The festival ended on August 5. Just over a month later, a military coup in Chile overthrew socialist president Salvador Allende and brought to power a brutal junta. This September 11 coup was the first, bloody "9/11." It had a very personal meaning for Erich Honecker, who had succeeded Walter Ulbricht as leader of the GDR two years earlier, and his wife, Margot, the minister of education: their daughter, Sonja, was living in Chile at the time. But she and her future husband, an engineer named Leonardo Yáñez Betancourt, got out safely and went to live in East Berlin.

There was a large Chilean solidarity campaign in East Germany, which provided a home to more than four thousand émigrés. There was also a major campaign in the Federal Republic, as in other parts of Western

Europe, and by 1979 twenty-seven hundred Chilean refugees had entered West Germany (the junta later allowed some to exchange a prison or camp for foreign exile).[135] The campaigns in the two Germanys raised the question of what exactly was being campaigned about—was "solidarity" with the Chilean victims a form of antifascism, or was it a question of human rights?[136] Here was a foretaste of future clashes around the world between Germans, East and West, in an era when antifascism was proving less effective as an idea to mobilize people and yielding instead to human rights as the political coin of the realm in a globalizing world.[137]

Other events in 1973 pointed to the future. Viewed through a global lens, in fact, this was a pivotal year in postwar German history. One week after the Chilean coup, the two Germanys were admitted together into the United Nations. That was the end point of West German *Ostpolitik*, but only the beginning of a process that eventually undermined East Germany, one that was fundamentally advanced by economic events. The Yom Kippur War in October 1973 and the retaliatory price hike by the Organization of the Petroleum Exporting Countries (OPEC) created the first oil shock for the developed nations. This set in motion major changes in the global economy, with very different impacts east and west. These reinforced what were already different responses to the challenge of postindustrial society. The oil shock of 1973 also led indirectly to a basic difference in how the two Germanys saw themselves. Questions about history and identity assumed renewed prominence in both countries in the 1970s and '80s, but only in West Germany did the issues of "foreign" cultures and assimilation make it necessary to ask "What does it mean to be German?" These debates in the Federal Republic were often mean-spirited and sometimes racist in their assumptions; but they did take place.

Other seemingly isolated events in 1973 can be seen, with the benefit of hindsight, as markers of a widening gap between the two Germanys. That summer, the state parliament of Baden-Württemberg decided to locate a new nuclear power plant at an obscure town called Wyhl. It became the site of a major demonstration against nuclear power, the first of many. It was also in 1973 that the first women's center opened in West Germany, in Frankfurt. These were straws in the wind, signs of the new social movements that became such a feature of the global 1970s and '80s but had no counterparts in the other Germany. There were environmentalists and feminists in East Germany, of course, just as there were gays and pacifists, but they were unable to form independent movements and express their identities publicly. Critique and debate had to be joined obliquely, through literature and art. Heiner Carow's 1973 film, *The Legend of Paul and Paula*, is an example, a work that celebrates female self-expression, including the satisfaction of sexual desire, endorses the pursuit of private pleasure over public duty, and satirizes the bureaucratic, buttoned-up Socialist Unity Party. All this, plus a "chorus" provided by the Puhdys—a rock group, of all things. The film was criticized by West German feminists (Paula dies at the end, just like the female protagonists of so many operas), but overall it is the daring, heterodox elements that stand out.[138] Enormously popular with audiences, *The Legend of Paul and Paula* belongs to the period of cultural thaw in the early Honecker years, soon to be reversed.

In West Germany, 1973 also marked what would turn out to be the onset of an exuberant cultural resurgence in one field after another, led by the generation of war children born between 1939 and 1945. It was the year when Pina Bausch established the pioneering Wuppertal Dance Theater; when half a dozen now classic jazz albums were released on the innovative ECM label, created four years earlier by Manfred Eicher; when Anselm Kiefer was already producing dramatic, neoexpressionist canvasses in the Odenwald; and when early films by Wim Wenders and Rainer Werner Fassbinder announced the arrival of the so-called Young German Cinema, fifteen years later than its French and Italian new wave predecessors but worth the wait. All would acquire worldwide audiences.

Because the 1970s were the best of times, and they were the worst of times, there was something else that soon acquired a worldwide audience: German terrorism. West Germany became a site of terrorism for a billion television viewers in September 1972, when the Palestinian group Black September attacked the Olympic Games in Munich, taking Israeli hostages and demanding the release of prisoners in Israel. The episode ended with the death of ten Israelis, a German police officer, and five members of Black September. One response came from Ulrike Meinhof, a former journalist then in jail in Cologne for taking part in the first wave of violence by the Red Army Faction (RAF), dubbed by police and public the Baader-Meinhof Gang. She wrote a manifesto titled "The Action of Black September at Munich—Toward the Strategy of the Anti-Imperialist Struggle." Meinhof and fellow RAF members had been trained two years earlier at a Palestinian camp in Jordan run by Hassan Salameh, who planned the attack in Munich. Meinhof had also arranged for her twin daughters to be taken to a camp for Palestinian orphans, although the plan fell through.

In 1973 she was still waiting to be transferred to a new maximum-security wing under construction in Stuttgart's Stammheim Prison. In December, Meinhof finally broke off all contact with her twin eleven-year-old girls, returning their letters.[139] The previous month a German militant group called the Revolutionary Cells announced its arrival with attacks on buildings owned by the U.S. conglomerate ITT in Nuremberg and West Berlin. The company was rightly suspected of involvement in the Chilean coup—one of its buildings in New York City had already been bombed by members of the Weather Underground. The Revolutionary Cells went on to claim responsibility for almost two hundred attacks, including the hijacking of a French plane to Uganda in 1976. But in 1973, the largest wave of German terrorism still lay in the future, much of it concerned with efforts to "liberate" those who were imprisoned.

We are talking about a dizzying array of changes that came together in the early 1970s. Many of them were interconnected. All had a major bearing on the place occupied by the two Germanys in an increasingly globalized world. Where to begin? Perhaps the best starting point is with the diplomatic revolution of the early 1970s, from which so much else followed. There is (so far) no opera based on Willy Brandt in Warsaw to set alongside John Adams's *Nixon in China*, but the centrality of the West German role in the great geopolitical transformation of the era is beyond doubt. The entry of both German states into the United Nations in 1973 was the culmination of Brandt's policy, which ran from the Moscow Treaty with the USSR (August 1970) and the Warsaw Treaty with Poland (December 1970) through the Four-Power Agreement on Berlin (September 1971) to the Basic Treaty between the two German states (December 1972) and the Prague Treaty with Czechoslovakia (December 1973).

Ostpolitik "fully Germanizes the German question," wrote the German-born American diplomat Helmut Sonnenfeldt in November 1972 to his boss, Henry Kissinger.[140] But the policy was not just (as Nixon and Kissinger would have preferred) a set of regional responses to regional issues. It introduced a "new tone" into the Cold War and represented a counterpoint to the more limited détente of the superpowers.[141] Brandt himself worried, as a globally minded Social Democrat, that the East European emphasis of his foreign policy might overshadow his government's wider engagement with the world. But the ripple effects of the policy were in fact far-reaching. The treaty work and the mood music that accompanied it not only reset West German relations with the USSR, Poland, and Czechoslovakia, they earned praise from such nonaligned nations as India and Yugoslavia, which moved closer to the Federal Republic. The German-German political motives driving *Ostpolitik* also had an impact on another divided country, although the immediate outcome was different. South Korean president Park Chung-hee took a first step toward engagement with the North in a speech on the twenty-fifth anniversary of the end of Japanese colonial rule in 1970, when he suggested that the two countries could coexist peacefully. This was codified in the North-South Joint Communiqué of July 1972. But mutual bitterness over the Korean War and ideological differences prevented further movement: the "sunshine" policy, anticipated in the short-lived breakthrough of the 1970s, had to wait another thirty years.[142]

German-German relations were fundamentally changed. In the Basic Treaty of 1972 the two states confirmed existing borders and agreed that each represented the population within those borders. The Federal Republic stopped short of full recognition and exchange of ambassadors but agreed to establish a "permanent representation" in East Berlin. The treaty also eased restrictions on travel and telephone communication. On the surface, at least, East Germany got what it wanted. Above all else, it received the formal recognition it had long craved. In September 1974 the United States became the 110th country and the last of the four occupying powers to recognize the GDR diplomatically. The smaller Germany was now free to "demarcate" itself from the larger Germany and develop a separate identity. It continued to project itself outward into the world, especially in the Middle East, East Africa, and the Horn of Africa. It now had access to credits from the West, which continued, as did *Ostpolitik*, when Brandt stepped down as chancellor and the more hard-nosed Helmut Schmidt replaced him, and when the CDU/CSU government of Helmut Kohl came to power in 1982. And the price of all this? Critics at the time argued, and some scholars have agreed, that the architects of *Ostpolitik*, prizing security over human rights, effectively propped up a regime that continued to repress its own population and was not required as part of the German-German agreement to change its ways.[143] In the years after 1972, the Stasi and its network of informers grew and grew.

But if we pull back and widen our angle, East Berlin's success seems less impressive. The GDR was forced to recognize its subordination to Moscow (a different situation from 1961). One result was seriously deteriorating relations with Beijing, a sign of East Germany's limited room for maneuver. East Berlin had to swallow Chinese taunts that it was a "Soviet vassal."[144]

Meanwhile, the nonaligned nations edged closer to Bonn. While this was happening, the Federal Republic grew in global stature as it continued to demonstrate a finely honed talent for spreading its friendship around and signing up for every multilateral opportunity that presented itself. It followed up the historic treaty making in Moscow and Eastern Europe with cultural outreach that saw the opening of six Goethe Institutes across that region. More twin city agreements were struck.[145] But Bonn also proved its reliability to Washington in the era of the Iranian revolution and renewed Cold War after 1979. At the same time, West Germany cultivated even closer relations with France and took a leading role in advancing the European project. Annual summits of the seven economically largest Western countries, which came to be known as the G7 meetings, began as a joint initiative of Helmut Schmidt and French president Valéry Giscard d'Estaing. The European Monetary System of 1979 and the Single European Act of 1986, a revision of the Treaty of Rome, also owed much to Franco-German cooperation. In 1985, Mikhail Gorbachev, the new leader of the Soviet Union, said that West Germany was "a massive weight in the balance of world power and its role in international affairs will grow."[146]

Out in the wider world, the relative weight of the two Germanys changed, too. That was partly the result of an intangible: the fact that the citizens of one Germany seemed to be everywhere and the citizens of the other Germany, almost nowhere. West Germans were not only three-time World Cup winners in soccer, or *Weltmeister*, they were perennial *Reiseweltmeister*—world champions of travel. With growing wealth and leisure, West Germans used the freedom to go wherever their money would take them. By the 1980s, they were by far the largest single group of foreign tourists not only in Austria and Switzerland, but in Italy, France, the Netherlands, Turkey, and Yugoslavia.[147] They were to be found (and often resented) from the Adriatic coast and the Black Sea to Belize and Kenya's Diani Beach. That informal West German presence could be multiplied across many other categories of traveler in a Europe and a world becoming smaller thanks to cheaper communications—business people, academics and exchange students, au pairs and nannies. The severe limits on travel for East German citizens meant that the GDR's global presence was incomparably smaller.

There was asymmetry, too, in the formal presence of the two states. Both maintained aid-and-development programs and cultural institutions, but the Federal Republic was no longer chasing the Democratic Republic around the world to preserve the Hallstein Doctrine. It demonstrated a new confidence after that Cold War ballast had been finally cast off. Especially in the years when Hildegard Hamm-Brücher was a minister in the Foreign Office (1977–1982), an emphasis on a policy of "reciprocity, exchange, partnership" in cultural policy signaled a new international openness in West Germany.[148] Expenditure on foreign aid around the world remained high, under both center-left and conservative administrations.

In East Germany by contrast, the change of course under Erich Honecker led to an emphasis on cultivating a separate East German identity and addressing domestic social issues such as the chronic housing shortage. It was accompanied by diminished global ambition. The GDR had never wielded much soft power through cultural outreach. Now some of its programs of economic, medical, and military aid were also scaled back. The desperate need for recognition was no longer there as a spur. Confidence about contributing to a global socialist future was also in shorter supply. "There was a time in the late 1960s and early 1970s when our alliances with the Third World and our activities there made us feel as though we were winning the Cold War," wrote the spymaster Markus Wolf.[149] That became less true. Wolf describes firsthand the disillusion and frustrations. Local leaders proved less pliant than East Berlin expected. East Germans became targets in civil wars like the one in Mozambique. The Chinese were making their presence felt in Tanzania. Everywhere, the economic cost was rising: the aid to Frelimo and independent Mozambique came to almost 150 million East German DM. Wolf, who was in a position to know, writes that efforts in East Africa were wound down.[150]

He may have painted too negative a picture. Commitments to socialist allies continued. At the direct request of Mozambique's President Samora Machel, East Germany built a "friendship school" in 1981 to train young Mozambicans, although the number of students was only half what had been asked for and the length of the training reduced. Even then, the undertaking caused friction because of East German misgivings about the direction of Mozambican socialism.[151] Fraternal cooperation also continued after 1975 with the victorious Socialist Republic of Vietnam. Alongside aid in the intelligence field, the GDR undertook the manufacture of Vietnamese banknotes and coins, which had previously been the work of the Chinese. These were made in Leipzig and East Berlin, then shipped back to Vietnam in secrecy, disguised (in an unwitting piece of black comedy) as innocent weapons deliveries. Around 120 Vietnamese specialists worked

*Erich Honecker and Fidel Castro at the airport in Havana
during the East German leader's visit in February 1974.*

in East Germany on this delicate business, guarded by members of the
Stasi and its Vietnamese counterpart. There were virtually no other Vietnamese in the country in 1975, when the operation began. But there were
fifty-eight thousand contract workers from Vietnam by the late 1980s, the
largest single foreign group. Like workers from Mozambique, Angola, and
Cuba, their contribution to the East German labor force was intended to
be a form of quid pro quo for the provision of aid. This reflected a shift of
view in the GDR, away from the socialist idealism of the 1960s toward the
idea that aid should pay for itself in some way. While Hanoi still talked
pointedly about the obligations of its rich socialist ally, East Berlin looked
for ways to recoup some of its outlay. One idea, still not fully realized by the
end of the 1980s, was investment in Vietnamese coffee plantations, which
would provide East Germans with coffee and repay Vietnamese debt.[152]

Vietnam and the Vietnamese also had an important place in the West German imagination of the late 1970s because of the boat people. Some eight hundred thousand refugees fled Vietnam after the war ended, many in the boats that came to define them. The peak exodus was in 1978–79. Television pictures in November 1978 of the *Hai Hong*, a barely seaworthy craft carrying two thousand refugees, half of them children, helped establish the fact that a humanitarian disaster was in progress. While Vietnam's neighbors expressed themselves unable to cope with the numbers, opinion was mobilized in developed countries to offer assistance. In the Federal Republic, Ernst Albrecht, the premier of Lower Saxony, announced that his state would take in eight hundred Vietnamese. Half of them, at the request of Foreign Minister Hans-Dietrich Genscher, had been rescued by a German freighter. They duly arrived in Hanover amid massive media coverage. A Cologne radio producer named Rupert Neudeck borrowed an idea from a French campaign ("*un bateau pour le Vietnam*") and began raising money to fund a German rescue boat. Some thirty-five thousand donors helped to launch the *Cap Anamur*. The German Red Cross was active, too, although sometimes at odds with private initiatives like Neudeck's. In all, forty-five thousand Vietnamese refugees were admitted to West Germany.

The campaign had strong support from the right, including German expellee organizations, for it was not hard to paint the parallel between themselves and the boat people as victims of communism. Whereas in France prominent figures on the left such as Jean-Paul Sartre supported the movement to save the boat people, some on the West German left wrote them off unsympathetically as black marketeers and pimps. However, the left-wing writer Heinrich Böll responded that he would save a pimp if he was drowning, adding that he would also rescue a drowning Adolf Eichmann.[53]

The Nazi era was in the minds of many who joined the campaign to save the boat people. Parallels between Vietnamese refugees in the 1970s and German Jews forty years earlier struck home. The crisis coincided with the airing of the American soap opera *Holocaust* on West German TV in January 1979. This did what years of scholarly books, documentaries, and earnest talking heads had failed to do, which was to engage the emotions of the broad population in the fate of the Jews. The late 1970s marked the beginning of an unprecedented new interest in the Holocaust, in West Germany and beyond. Even as the murder of the Jews became firmly established as the world's civics lesson, Germans responded to contemporary events through the prism of their own history. Empathy with the victims of what was happening in Vietnam, or the Cambodian genocide that unfolded after 1975, was a form of belated empathy with earlier Jewish victims, a more or less conscious act of expiation. But it could also be a way to relativize German crimes.[154] Both of those responses, the self-critical and the self-exculpatory, were evident in the great debates over history and identity that played out in the 1980s over museums and in the "historians' debate," which was discussed earlier. But these difficult confrontations with the Nazi past took place only in one Germany. The GDR remained in what the Dutch writer Ian Buruma called its "peculiar state of innocence."[155]

The episode of the Vietnamese boat people highlights two other ways in which East Germany preserved a kind of "innocence" in the face of movements and forces that were reshaping the world. One was the explosive growth of humanitarian and human rights movements in the 1970s. Like the related new social movements of the era (feminism, ecology, pacifism), these were on full-throated display in the Federal Republic but found only a faint, belated echo in the Democratic Republic. The other was the challenge of coming to terms with the presence of non-Germans, whether refugees or former guest workers, which led to painful arguments in West Germany but no public debate at all in the East.

Interest in individual human rights surged in the 1970s. This owed something to disillusionment with socialism. Western politicians were also less reluctant to discuss human rights after decolonization and the passage of American civil rights legislation. Not least, new technology and communications now sent news and pictures quickly around the globe. The emerging activism in the developed world was rooted in identification with "distant suffering."[156] Some of the organizations that emerged out of this new concern with human rights have names that are now familiar, such as Doctors Without Borders; meanwhile, the long established Amnesty International (founded in 1961) mounted an international campaign against torture in the 1970s that led to the U.N. Convention Against Torture in 1975. But there were countless individual campaigns dedicated to refugees or to victims of famine or human rights abuses. Although the highest-profile organizations were founded elsewhere—in Britain, France, or Switzerland—West Germans were active in local chapters of these organizations and founded many smaller ones. Church-based groups had their own place in the human rights upsurge of the 1970s. International humanitarian jurisprudence also developed in the Federal Republic, through figures such as the legal scholar Otto Kimminich, whose lifelong support for the expellee organizations of his Sudeten German homeland made him a powerful advocate for the human rights of refugees and asylum seekers.[157] Human rights drew support from across the political spectrum, and while the Federal Republic actively pressed for intergovernmental agreements, it was organizations in civil society that injected a new note into the humanitarian engagement of the 1970s.

This was in stark contrast to the state-controlled programs in the GDR. Even when solidarity groups formed there, often under the umbrella of Protestant churches, their activities were severely restricted. Nicaragua in the 1980s offers a telling case study, because we know from a recent oral history that Germans from both states traveled there to support the new Sandinista regime and engage in humanitarian efforts after the Somoza dictatorship was overthrown. East Germans went there as representatives of their regime, which attached great symbolic importance to Nicaragua, as it had to Cuba. The resources of the state meant they could play a big part in building the Hospital Carlos Marx and other infrastructure projects, whereas the West Germans had to raise funds to pay their own way. But (as the East Germans noticed) the Westerners, radicals at odds with the pro-U.S., anti-Sandinista policy of their own government, had more freedom to choose their projects, responded more quickly to events on the ground, and even mixed more freely with the local population. Back in East Germany, church-based solidarity organizations sprang up to support Nicaraguans, but their activity was closely monitored and their members were refused permission to travel there or even to send aid.[158]

Those restrictions were typical, it hardly needs saying, of the severe limits on human rights in the GDR. East Berlin had an answer ready for that, arguing that human rights as defined in the West were purely formal and lacked the social substance that would have given them meaning. To critics who cried "no socialism without human rights," they replied "no human rights without socialism."[159] That was certainly a case worth making. The snag was that Alexander Dubček would have agreed about "no human rights without socialism," yet East German citizens who expressed their support for Dubček were jailed.

Human rights became an issue in the Soviet bloc after the Conference on Security and Cooperation in Europe (CSCE), the meetings that took place between 1973 and 1975 in the wake of *Ostpolitik* as part of the wider process of détente. The USSR initially pressed for the CSCE, hoping to marginalize the United States in European affairs, and some in the West saw the guarantees of existing borders in the final agreement, the Helsinki Accords, as a gift to the Soviets. But the sections of the agreement dealing with education, culture, and information opened up other perspectives. The signatories agreed to "respect human rights and fundamental freedoms, including the freedom of thought, conscience, religion or belief." Freedom of movement was expressly included.[160] Henry Kissinger, then the U.S. secretary of state, a skeptic about mixing human rights with diplomacy, said dismissively that this might as well have been written in Swahili, and it is true that everyone could place their own interpretation on this part of the Helsinki Accords. But the British diplomat George Walden rightly saw a chance to "spread the contagion of liberty," and Yuri Andropov, then the head of the KGB, worried about the threat of increased contacts.[161] All signatories were required to publish the Helsinki Accords in their local press. In East Germany, *Neues Deutschland* sold out by 11:00 a.m. The clause about free movement attracted avid interest. An Austrian diplomat named Franz Ceska recorded people saying to one another "Honecker signed, we want to go to West Germany." Applications to leave the country soared into the tens of thousands. Karl-Heinz Nitschke, a physician in a small Saxon town, drew up a petition asking that the freedom to emigrate be honored. It gathered a thousand signatures.[162]

The Helsinki Accords' clause about freedom of movement simply restated the principle embodied in article 13 of the U.N. Declaration of Human Rights: "Everyone has the right to leave any country, including his own, and to return to his country." But restating this principle was important, especially to East Germans, because there was a country next door where people spoke the same language and immediate citizenship was permanently on offer. The issue of emigration cut two ways. For East Germany's rulers, allowing senior citizens to leave saved on pension payments, while the effective "sale" of political offenders earned hard currency and exported troublesome dissent: a win-win. But those (the great majority) refused permission to leave were likely to become more disaffected, while those who left created new networks of communication linking East and West and reinforcing discontent. When, in 1976, the regime stripped dissident Wolf Biermann of his citizenship while the singer-poet was on a concert tour in Cologne, refusing him reentry, this crude act of expatriation led to a rare protest in an open letter published in the West by such leading East German writers as Christa Wolf and Heiner Müller.[163] Biermann did not want to leave the socialist Germany; he wanted to make it a better socialist Germany. In the end, however, Helsinki emboldened those who wanted to emigrate from East Germany and thereby drove a wedge between them and others who wanted to reform the system. There was nothing in East Germany resembling post-Helsinki opposition movements like Charter 77 in Czechoslovakia or KOR (the Center for the Defense of Workers) and later Solidarity in Poland. Not until the 1980s did organized, independent groups of feminists, environmentalists, and peace campaigners emerge.

Those same social movements established themselves in West Germany in the 1970s. That was also, as we have seen, the somber decade of urban terrorism. Both grew out of 1960s radicalism. One was the large, democratically invigorating harvest, the other the small, poisonous fruit. After a campaign of bomb attacks on U.S. military and German targets, the core members of the Red Army Faction (RAF) were arrested in 1972, put on trial in 1975, and sentenced in 1977. There were repeated attempts by members still at large and by "second generation" groups like the 2 June Movement to free them by taking hostages. The most violent episodes occurred at the beginning of the trials in 1975, when the Christian Democratic politician Peter Lorenz was held hostage, and again in a spurt after the guilty verdicts in 1977 that became known as the German Autumn. On the latter occasion Siegfried Buback, the federal prosecutor, and two of his escorts were killed in revenge, Dresdner Bank president Jürgen Ponto was killed during a botched kidnapping, and the head of the German Employers' Association, Hanns Martin Schleyer was successfully kidnapped, and his chauffeur and bodyguards killed. Five weeks later, members of the Popular Front for the Liberation of Palestine hijacked a Lufthansa jet to Mogadishu and demanded the release of eleven RAF members. The Schmidt government refused. Instead, an antiterrorist unit created after the attack at the Munich Olympics was sent. It successfully stormed the plane and released the hostages. RAF leaders committed suicide when they heard the news (Ulrike Meinhof had already done so) and the dead body of Schleyer was found shortly afterward. That was the bitter, melancholy end of the German Autumn. The closing scene of a film with that title shows the burial of the terrorists in Stuttgart's Dornhalden Cemetery, with a huge police presence and mourners who yell "murderers" at them, while we hear the voice of Joan Baez singing "The Ballad of Sacco and Vanzetti" over the shouts and helicopter noise.[164]

The 1970s was an age of global terrorism, when Palestinian groups, Latin American insurgents, the Provisional IRA in Northern Ireland, and the Basque organization ETA were all active. The Red Brigades in Italy were the closest in kind to the German groups, another episode in the parallel histories of the two countries that went back to the nineteenth century. German terrorists had both intellectual affiliations and practical connections with movements elsewhere. Strategically, they believed that they could fight imperialism by creating guerrilla cells, as practiced by the Tupamaros in Uruguay and described by the Brazilian Carlos Marighella in *Minimanual of the Urban Guerrilla* (1969), with its emphasis on establishing safe houses, using speed and surprise, selecting symbolic targets, and learning how to use small arms. Members of the RAF trained in Jordan alongside Palestinians, Irish Republicans, and Basques, although their nude sunbathing, arrogance, and resistance to discipline made them unpopular. The border crossing continued to the end. After the German Autumn, the remnants of the RAF spent time in Iraq, financially supported by Palestinian groups, before many went to East Germany, where the Stasi helped them to establish new identities.[165]

German urban terrorists were fewer in number than their Italian counterparts. They were also less murderous. The RAF are reckoned to have killed twenty-eight people by 1977; seventeen of their own number were killed, and two members of the public were mistakenly shot by police, including a Scottish businessman in Stuttgart.[166] The Red Brigades killed four times as many. It is probably true that the reactions to terrorism were more of a threat than the terrorists themselves. That has a lot to do with the media coverage, especially by the Springer press. While the RAF, like terrorists elsewhere, had absolute need of the media—it was a symbiotic relationship—the coverage by newspapers like *Bild-Zeitung* created a pervasive sense of panic.[167] Those like Heinrich Böll who warned about an overreaction were quickly labeled "sympathizers" and there were ugly instances of people being reported to police because their conversations seemed "suspicious." Böll himself captured the atmosphere, and the damage it could do, in his novella *The Lost Honor of Katharina Blum.*[168]

In West Germany, the terrorist panic led to huge, demonstrative police operations, a permanent increase in security personnel, and passage of the Decree on Radicals, which applied a political test for state employment.[169] Of course, terrorist violence against individuals was designed to elicit violence or repression in return—"tearing away the mask" to reveal the "fascist" reality. But the response was (mostly) measured and the revulsion against RAF killings was felt on the left as well as the right. Joschka Fischer, later a cofounder of the Green Party and later still the foreign minister but in the 1970s still a member of the ultra-left Frankfurt "scene" and a street-fighting man, abandoned his faith in the use of violence after the terrorist bloodletting.[170] A left-wing member of the Social Democratic Party, "Red Jochen" Steffen expressed bitter contempt for the "anarchist" theatricality of the RAF, which—he believed—only invited reaction. Steffen later left the SPD, but because of its rightward drift in social and economic policy, not Helmut Schmidt's handling of terrorism. In the end, the Federal Republic passed the terrorism test, as it had passed the test of the *Spiegel* affair, overcoming the years of panic better than might have been expected given how the Springer press fanned the flames. That owed something to the refusal of Schmidt's coalition government to be pushed into the repressive measures that some on the right demanded—to its forthright defense, in other words, of the democratic constitutional order, not the "strong state." It also owed something to the more vigorous civil society that had grown in the shadow of terrorism.[171]

The new social movements of the 1970s were the institutional expression of that vigor. All were part of larger, global developments. The burgeoning women's movement is a case in point. As West German feminists built a movement through a women's press and bookstores, a record label, and health centers, the experience of other countries pointed the way. Alice Schwarzer's magazine *Emma* (the title was a play on "*emanzipiert*," which means emancipated) took the American magazine *Ms.* as its model. Consciousness-raising groups borrowed from American practice, too, although they also owed something to the intense discussions that took place in the homegrown *Wohngemeinschaft*, a cross between house sharing and a political commune that came out of the 1960s and was ubiquitous in the 1970s. (No one who spent even a brief time living in a "WG" will forget the stern sign on the bathroom door, "*Männer Pissen im Sitzen*," or the communal gatherings where people shared their *Bedürfnisse*, their "needs.") Europeans sometimes provided the blueprint. When 374 prominent West German women proclaimed in 1971 that they had had abortions, their powerful call in *Stern* magazine for abortion law reform was modeled on a similar announcement by 343 French women in *Le Nouvel Observateur*. Some German activists also took note of the Dutch Dolle Minas, radical feminists who staged publicity-seeking events such as blocking men's urinals with pink ribbons to protest the absence of public toilets for women. Again, however, there was already a homegrown tradition (in reality, a transplanted French tradition) of political theater going back to the 1960s.

The inspirations were not all European. Many radical feminists were drawn to the example of women's empowerment they believed they saw in Mao's China. In works translated from French (Claudie Broyelle's *Moitié du Ciel*) and English (Jack Belden's *China Shakes the World*), German women read accounts of women's liberation that formed part of creating a socialist society. Feminists adopted some techniques, like "speaking bitterness" and collectively confronting abusers, from China. Other feminists, Alice Schwarzer among them, were skeptical from the start. A broader disenchantment set in at the end of the 1970s as China opened up more to visitors after the Cultural Revolution, and the idealized picture of women's empowerment became impossible to sustain.[172]

China attracted interest partly because it seemed to present alternative ways of raising children. A renewed embrace of motherhood among some West German feminists formed a part of the "new sensitivity" of the 1970s. It was often linked to an ecofeminist perspective that was hostile to technology, including the new reproductive technologies such as in vitro fertilization. German women were part of a larger international movement, expressing concerns shared with American ecofeminists like Carolyn Merchant and activists in Western Europe. This defense of the body against "unnatural" incursions pointed in several possible directions. Much later, it would provide the rationale for a "Green" antivax movement in unified Germany. In the 1970s it provided the intellectual foundations of an ecofeminist network in which German women were exceptionally active— unsurprisingly perhaps, given the history of Nazi eugenics.[173]

Ecology, environmentalism, saving the earth—like human rights, these became a powerful global cause in the 1970s. The haunting photograph *Earthrise*, taken by Apollo astronaut Bill Anders in 1968, set the tone and the term "spaceship earth," with its undertone of fragility, entered the vocabulary. The Council of Europe designated 1970 as the year of nature conservation and Earth Day was celebrated in the United States for the first time in 1970. David Brower, an American who founded Friends of the Earth in 1969, joined with environmentalists in Britain, France and, Sweden to create Friends of the Earth International in 1971. The following year the Club of Rome published its celebrated warning *The Limits to Growth*. There was nothing specifically German, in other words, when an incoming coalition government of Social Democrats and Free Democrats in Bonn passed a host of laws on everything from airplane noise to leaded gasoline, and established a Federal Office for the Environment. West Germany was moving to the same rhythm as governments in other Western countries, including some (like the United States and United Kingdom) where conservatives were in power. Across the developed world in the early 1970s, and quite suddenly, "the environment" became an issue, the focus of disparate concerns about pollution, nature conservation, and resource depletion. At the beginning of the decade West Germany was not in the global vanguard, but during the 1970s environmental questions were debated there with unusual intensity by politicians, press, and public. Citizens' initiatives were founded to protest against pollution, technocratic projects (like new runways) that swallowed up land, and above all nuclear installations. The first of these antinuclear protests were directed at the proposed reactors at Wyhl, mentioned earlier, and at Brokdorf on the lower Elbe. Demonstrations followed at other locations earmarked for nuclear power, waste disposal, or reprocessing plants, places whose names soon became familiar in headlines.[174]

The protests at Wyhl in 1975 acquired a certain mystique because they were large, festive, and peaceful; they were successful (unlike most demonstrations later), and they brought together students and activists from the university town of Freiburg with local winegrowers.[175] They also drew in French protesters from across the nearby border, for German antinuclear protests included French participants, just as French protests included German participants. These were transnational movements. They translated (and sometimes mistranslated) each other's texts and tried to learn from one another as they debated tactics, and especially the issue of violence versus nonviolence. The utility companies and police also learned from each other, and the main lesson they learned was to respond with maximum force.[176] The result was a series of pitched battles. One of the most violent occurred at Malville, France, in July 1977. Large numbers of Germans crossed the border to protest the building of a nuclear power plant, where they joined with others from Switzerland and Italy. There were twenty thousand protesters in all. The coordination with local organizers was poor, which meant that many Germans misread the "choreography" of local protests and were unfamiliar with French police tactics or equipment—unfamiliar, for example, with the fact that French tear gas grenades explode as well as emit smoke, so that picking one up to throw it back risks loss of an arm, as happened to a nineteen-year-old from Bremen. One protester died, three were maimed, and more than a hundred injured at Malville; five police officers were seriously injured. French police and press blamed the violence on a German "invasion," even a "second occupation." Others linked the violence to the Red Army Faction.[177]

There were German Maoists (French Maoists, too) among the 300 to 400 violent protesters at Malville who wielded iron bars and threw Molotov cocktails.* They were wholly unrepresentative of the West German environmental movement, which leaned clearly to the nonviolent left after the 1970s. The movement still had a conservative wing, which was organized in the Association for the Protection of Nature and the Environment in Germany. A few had no doubt been conservationists in the Third Reich, applauding the 1935 Reich Nature Protection Law. Critics had a name for this, referring to the "avocado syndrome"—those who were green on the outside but had a "brown," or Nazi, kernel.[178] But the 40,000 conservative conservationists were heavily outnumbered by the roughly 500,000 people organized in 950 member organizations under the umbrella of the Federal Association for Environmental Protection.[179] The groups concerned themselves with an array of issues, mostly local—a children's playground here, an industrial polluter there, demanding a cycle path, trying to preserve a building. Politically, the movement gathered up remnants of the student movement and the extra-parliamentary opposition, together with feminists, anarchists, members of the alternative "scene," and anticonsumerist advocates of the simple life.[180]

It sounds very German, and in many ways it was. The environmentalist milieu was reminiscent of the German life reform movement around 1900, with its emphasis on care of the body, vegetarianism, "natural" medicines, and anxiety about technological overreach. But those same concerns made German environmentalists constantly aware of what was happening beyond Germany's borders: the threat posed by imported foodstuffs, the dangers to life that might at any time flow into the country through its waterways or waft into it through the air. Egmont Koch and Fritz Vahrenholt published a book in 1978 called *Seveso Is Everywhere*, referring to the explosion two years earlier at a north Italian chemical plant that released a cloud of dioxin.[181] It came to seem prescient. The Three Mile Island nuclear

---

* These figures are the internal estimates of the French police; the numbers they gave to the public were much higher.

accident at Harrisburg, Pennsylvania, occurred a year after the book was published. It was followed by a series of frightening accidents, some of them close to home for Germans, like the Chernobyl nuclear disaster of 1986 and the Sandoz chemical spill and fire in Basel six months later, which polluted the Rhine.

The pervasive sense of insecurity that underlay environmental activism had a lot in common with the fears that animated the West German peace movement. Fear of nuclear power and fear of nuclear weapons were linked concerns. As the Cold War heated up again, the USSR stationed a new generation of intermediate-range nuclear missiles in Eastern Europe. Prompted by a hawkish Helmut Schmidt, NATO made its Dual-Track Decision in 1979: if arms limitation talks failed, it would deploy its own intermediate-range Pershing and Cruise missiles in Western Europe. That December, the Soviet Union invaded Afghanistan; the following year Ronald Reagan was elected president of the United States. The tension in the early 1980s was greater than anything felt since the Cuban Missile Crisis, when global communications were more primitive. The possibility of nuclear armageddon became a theme within popular culture on both sides of the Atlantic, in Nena's song "99 Luftballons" as much as in a film like *The Day After* (both 1983). In November 1980, West German peace groups issued the Krefeld Appeal, urging the Federal Republic to withdraw support for the Dual-Track Decision. By 1983 more than four million citizens had signed. As many as half a million took part in Easter peace marches.

Petra Kelly was a principal author of the Krefeld Appeal, just as she was a founding member of the Green Party, established in January 1980. Her identity as an ecofeminist who was at the center of the campaign against intermediate-range missiles perfectly captures the close fit between the three social movements that underpinned the Green Party: feminism, environmentalism, and pacifism. Ecofeminism already fused together two of those movements. The language of the peace campaign, meanwhile, was saturated by feminist rhetoric, with hostility to the missiles presented as opposition to "male madness."[182] "Green" and "peace" made another potent pairing. Activists on the West Coast of North America already had the idea in the early 1970s of joining them together in the brilliantly named Greenpeace. That organization established its reputation with imaginative campaigns, especially against whaling, but was riven by disputes between utopians and pragmatists as well as turf battles among its Vancouver, Seattle, and San Francisco chapters. At the end of the 1970s, leadership of

Greenpeace (renamed Greenpeace International) passed from the Pacific Ocean to the North Sea. The new power centers of the organization became London, Amsterdam, and Hamburg.[183]

Petra Kelly exemplifies something else as well: the global nature of the green movement and the Green Party. She was born Petra Lehmann in Bavaria, but her father walked out and her mother married John E. Kelly, an American army officer. In 1959, as a twelve-year-old, she moved to the United States, where she attended high school and studied at American University in Washington, D.C. Kelly admired the civil rights movement but was less impressed by the American student left (too much Frisbee and Timothy Leary, not enough seriousness). Her own talent for serious organization was evident during the presidential primary season in 1968, when she was coordinator of the Students for Kennedy campaign in Washington. After Robert Kennedy's assassination she served in the same role for Hubert Humphrey, the Democratic nominee. Kelly returned to Europe in 1970 and earned an MA in European integration at the University of Amsterdam, then worked for more than a decade at the European Economic Commission in Brussels. While Joschka Fischer was still battling the police in Frankfurt, Kelly was having an affair with Sicco Mansholt, the president of the commission and author of its common agricultural policy, networking with other champions of European integration, and building up a formidable Rolodex of contacts across Europe and the United States. This was a history and a profile very different from that of the typical '68er, and Kelly represented a different kind of postsocialist politics. The massive demonstrations at Wyhl were an "aha" moment, for they brought together her "European" aspirations with her belief in a kind of popular politics that crossed borders. Pointing to the French, Swiss, and German protesters, she invoked a new Europe of the regions and the people. In November 1975 she wrote excitedly about the protest as evidence of a *"transnational consciousness,"* the phrase underlined for emphasis.[184]

When the Green Party was founded, Petra Kelly was its figurehead. Her standing in the party fell abruptly in the following years. In an ironic reversal, the former anarchist Joschka Fischer became the pragmatist who led the Greens into political coalitions, while the former campaign coordinator and fledgling Eurocrat represented the intransigent wing of the party. Kelly had lost much of her influence with the Greens long before the tragedy of the suicide pact that took the lives of her and lover, Gert Bastian, in 1992. But the transnational note she struck remained a hallmark of the

Greens through the 1980s. True, the most compelling issue that propelled the party's first electoral breakthrough at national level in 1983 was intensely German: a warning about the "acid rain" supposedly destroying the German forest. But the Greens still emphasized the global interconnectedness of environmental issues, whether disasters like Chernobyl or the threat of climate change. The party's supporters were examples of "rooted cosmopolitans," transnational activists who talk the language of "global citizenship" but are rooted in local networks.[185] People elsewhere took note of the Greens' ascent. Other environmental parties existed before them, but the German party's success in the 1980s made it the one to imitate even while it helped to establish West Germany's "green" reputation.

The Greens had an impact across the border in East Germany, thanks to TV coverage. But the environmentally aware in the East faced a dire situation. Although a Ministry of Environmental Protection and Water Management was established in 1972, pollution grew steadily worse. A few scientists issued warnings. An East German hydrobiologist named Dietrich Uhlmann wrote a paper in 1977 about the excessive use of pesticides and the problem of acid rain. "For all the progress of science," he warned, "no one at present knows precisely enough the limits of stability of the biosphere, which will have to be preserved on a world-wide scale for the protection of future generations."[186] This was the same language used by scientists in the West. Uhlmann and others were indeed familiar with the work of West German, British, Scandinavian, and American colleagues. But the fact that Uhlmann had to start his paper with a carefully chosen quotation from Engels points to the problem: the East German regime viewed environmental degradation as a by-product of capitalism. Scientists were expected to offer constructive criticism, nothing more.

Those who broke with that understanding were isolated and paid a price. Three East German writers and three books tell the story. In 1975 Wolfgang Harich wrote *Communism Without Growth?*, a response to the Club of Rome Report three years earlier and a socialist critique of Honecker's attachment to Western "norms of consumption." In 1977 Rudolf Bahro's *The Alternative* called in similar terms for the "re-establishment of ecological stability." Then, in 1980, Robert Havemann, the dissident scientist, published *Industrial Society at the Crossroads*, where he referred to an "ecological crisis" that capitalism could not address and "real existing socialism" would not address. All three books appeared in the West, but not in the East. Harich and Havemann were persecuted for their troubles; Bahro went to the West, where he became a cofounder of the Green Party. In many ways these writers were ahead of their counterparts in the Federal Republic, where the "greening" of the intelligentsia did not take place until the 1980s, but their experiences point to the decisive absence of any kind of autonomous opinion in the GDR.[187]

There were party-organized "environmental" initiatives within the official youth movement and at regional level in East Germany, but they were little more than prettification campaigns. The conservationists who belonged to the Culture League had more ambitious goals, but their absence of power was compounded by absence of information. In 1982, all data on environmental damage was abruptly classified, because the facts were so damning. Senior government figures were well aware of the environmental problems, but these could be discussed, if at all, only in the pages of scientific journals. Independent movements that might have put pressure on the regime were officially impossible, although they began to form unofficially in the 1970s under the protective umbrella of the Protestant churches. The church provided a safe haven, where people could meet, hear a lecture, or print something up on an old mimeograph machine, which made *samizdat* publications possible. The authors often depended on West German or U.S. sources for their evidence.[188]

Individual groups did what alternative groups did in the West: practice organic gardening or limit personal consumption. These efforts sometimes acquired a modest public face, like the Ten Commandments rewritten by one group and circulated in its newsletter (the expanded Tenth Commandment read, "We must alter our attitude towards earthly good so that it is consistent with environmental sustainability").[189] But these groups remained small and isolated. Chernobyl registered as a shock, but the implications could not be publicly discussed. Only in the last years of the regime were there signs of change, such as the establishment of the Environmental Library in the basement of the Zion Church in East Berlin. That was in 1986, the year of Chernobyl. The library provided a forum for talks, concerts, and guest lecturers from the West, but its challenge to the state monopoly on debate about the environment led to the harassment of individuals and a raid on the library in 1987.[190]

Independent feminist and peace movements faced the same obstacles. The regime claimed that these were simply unnecessary. The East German Family Code, for example, noted solemnly that the "social and legal degradation of women" was a product of "bourgeois society." Under socialism, relations were based on "comradely interactions, equal rights for women, and educational opportunities for all citizens."[191] If all this was true, then feminism was obviously necessary over there in the West, but not in the East. Plenty of evidence suggests that women in the GDR did in fact enjoy advantages over women in the Federal Republic when it came to employment possibilities. The widespread provision of child care also made this a practical possibility. The high female workforce participation was, at the same time, a pattern forced on East Germany by the hemorrhage of labor before 1961 and the low birthrate after. Unsurprisingly, greater employment opportunities did not prevent gender discrimination in the workplace, or solve the problem of the "double burden" faced by women who worked and bore the larger share of domestic responsibilities. The personal was political in East Germany, too.[192] But the regime did not accept that women, as women, should have a public voice. The party and its organs, the petition system, the dispute commissions—these were the approved conduits for female comrades who wished to raise an issue. That was why, in the official view, a feminist movement was unnecessary and illegitimate. It was a view similar to the one reportedly expressed by Kurt Hager, a member of the SED's Politburo, its principal decision-making body, when responding to gay activism: "Anyone who sees homosexuality in political terms is a fool."[193]

An independent peace movement faced the same problem: that it was regarded as wholly unnecessary. The socialist bloc had always identified itself with the cause of peace; East Germany held "festivals of peace" and built "peace dams." Demonstrations in favor of peace were welcome— provided they were directed against the "militarists" in the capitalist West. This is what the Czech dissident Vaclav Havel meant when he said that every political space was already filled with official Soviet declarations about peace. But independent groups started to form in the GDR, even though the movement was less powerful than its counterparts in Czechoslovakia or Hungary.[194] In 1972 the first "peace seminar" was held by veterans of the civilian service (which had been introduced in 1964 as an alternative to military service). By 1979, there were more than a hundred participants and the seminar moved into larger church premises. The Protestant churches would be important when the peace movement grew after that. The regime wanted demonstrations against the NATO Dual-Track Decision; it did not want questioning of the entire system of armed blocs. In the fall of 1980 a "peace week" was held. Its symbol was a "swords into ploughshares" badge, which artfully depicted the biblical injunction in question (Micah 4:3) alongside a picture of a statue presented to the United Nations by the USSR. But wearing this armband soon became an emblem of protest against militarism everywhere. In the spring of 1982 it was forbidden at a Dresden peace forum and police tore them off people wearing them.[195] Three weeks earlier, Pastor Rainer Eppelmann, whose "blues masses" at the Samaritan Church in Berlin attracted crowds of many hundreds to listen to music and poetry and discuss contemporary issues, was the lead signatory of the Berlin Appeal to "make peace without weapons," along with Robert Havemann and eighty others. Eppelmann was briefly jailed. Havemann was already under house arrest at the time, as he remained until his death that April.

An autonomous peace movement survived, however. Peace week became an annual event. There were regular prayers for peace and peace forums, also under the aegis of the church. Women for Peace was founded in 1983. This stirring revealed some obvious influences from the world of protest beyond the GDR's borders; for example, the Berlin Appeal was modeled on the Krefeld Appeal. In other cases Western influences seemed more like a throwback to the flower power and love-ins of the late 1960s, but within the Christian moral framework of the East German 1980s.[196] News of what was happening in Prague and Budapest also filtered through. Representatives of the European Nuclear Disarmament (END) movement, which was based in the West but wanted to be pan-European, made contact with the artist and peace campaigner Bärbel Bohley and Women for Peace. In May 1983, Petra Kelly, Gert Bastian, and three other members of the Green Party unfurled a banner in East Berlin's Alexanderplatz with the message "The Greens—Swords into Ploughshares." They were briefly detained, before meeting with local peace activists. The sequel to the story is that the Green messengers were invited back in October to meet with Honecker, who welcomed their opposition to the NATO decision although not their support for a homegrown movement. Kelly wore a "Swords into Ploughshares" sweater and asked the East German leader to release imprisoned peace activists.

Bärbel Bohley, like Rainer Eppelmann and others in the peace and environmental movements, spent time in jail. Activists were arrested, events had to be called off, unofficial publications were seized, and groups were subject to both surveillance and infiltration. There was a thickening of activist activity around the middle of the 1980s, and that would be important for the events of 1989. But the obstacles to the creation of independent civic movements in the GDR remained formidable. In the Federal Republic there were almost a thousand movements dedicated to environmental issues alone; in the Democratic Republic it was a step forward when isolated groups began to talk to one another and publish *samizdat* newsletters. The things that were impossible in East Germany were not necessarily "political" in an obvious sense. When Bärbel Bohley spent the summer of 1988 in involuntary exile in Britain, one of her friends there had a severely disabled child. She noticed the difference between the services available in the United Kingdom and what happened to a mother and child judged "ineligible for aid" in East Germany. It was a judgment from which there was no appeal (it reminded her of the Nazis' "life unworthy of life"), and there was no possibility of organizing a citizens' initiative to press for changes in the law.[197]

There was a huge asymmetry between the two Germanys when it came to environmentalism, feminism, pacifism, and the possibility of organizing parents with disabled children. Jürgen Habermas, one of West Germany's leading intellectuals, a philosopher whose global reputation rested on his writings about civil society, communication, and rational debate, argued eloquently that the crucial thing about truly independent and accessible organizations (associations, charities, not-for-profits, NGOs) is that they link what he called the "lifeworld" of people to the public sphere of debate and argument. The absence of such organizations meant an absent link and an impoverished civil society in East Germany, as well as a narrowed range of opinions that reached citizens from outside.

People as well as opinions crossed the borders into both Germanys in the 1970s and '80s, but once again there was a basic asymmetry between the two. East Germany signed agreements with Poland in the 1960s that brought in limited numbers of "contract workers." Similar agreements followed with Mozambique (1979) and Vietnam (1980). Workers from Angola, Cuba, Nicaragua, and Yemen also came to the GDR under a different arrangement, as "trainees." The numbers remained modest. In 1989 there were around 190,000 foreigners in East Germany. Half were contract workers, around two-thirds of them Vietnamese, mostly women; the rest were trainees, together with students and academic or professional visitors. Altogether, then, non-Germans made up something over 1 percent of the population, although their impact was limited by their isolation from the host population. The tasks they performed were mostly routine, work discipline was harsh, and they lived in accommodations resembling those that the first generation of guest workers in the West had endured. These non-Germans were forced to contribute to East German social security but were unable to receive retirement benefits or disability payments. Pregnant workers were immediately deported, which happened to about 1 percent of Vietnamese women each year. When permanent relationships were established between East German citizens and foreign workers, permission to marry was usually denied, even when the female partner was pregnant. Marriage would mean either that the foreign worker (usually male) would be allowed to stay in East Germany, or that the spouse would be allowed to leave, neither a desirable outcome in official eyes. Forced separations created anguish, even suicide.[198]

If the treatment of foreign workers mocked the regime's official embrace of internationalism, the East German population was mostly hostile or indifferent. Kathrin Schmidt's novel *The Gunnar Lennefsen Expedition* paints a picture of the racist stereotypes in circulation: "the Cubans drank a lot," the "dark men from Algeria . . . stalked blonde women, if the teacher was to be believed," while "no city resident had ever seen the Vietnamese women carrying out everyday tasks, nobody even knew where they lived."[199] The foreigners were all too visible, in other words, unless they were suspiciously invisible. Foreigners suffered physical attacks. One study found 725 acts of racist violence in the 1970s and '80s, causing at least 10 deaths.[200]

The non-German population was much larger in the West, in absolute numbers and proportionately. The Federal Republic also had two kinds of foreign residents, although not the same two kinds as in the East. One consisted of asylum seekers. There had been few before the 1970s, mainly Europeans fleeing the crises in Hungary (1956) and Czechoslovakia (1968). But in the 1970s asylum seekers came in growing numbers from Latin America, Asia, and Africa, the Vietnamese boat people constituting just one example. Civil war and violence drove large numbers of political refugees from the global South to Europe, and West Germany was a primary destination. In 1973, applications for asylum were filed on behalf of 5595 people; in 1980 there were applications on behalf of 108,000 people. During the peak years of 1979–1981, more than 200,000 people applied for asylum. The numbers never returned to the level of the early 1970s.[201]

A far greater number of non-German residents were former guest workers who stayed in Germany and brought family members to join them. The halt to new recruitment in November 1973, a result of the oil shock, was supposed to mark the beginning of a return to their countries of origin. If, as expected, 250,000 left each year, then half would have gone within ten years. In fact, just half a million left, while a larger number of family members arrived. There were a million more residents of foreign origin in West Germany in 1980 than there had been in 1972 and the proportion of nonworking family members had risen sharply. The "halt" in 1973 had the unintended consequence that guest workers already in Germany, fearing future restrictions, brought in more family members more quickly. That was especially true of Turks, the largest single ethnic group. They had a double incentive to stay and reunite their families on German soil. First, unlike Italians or Spaniards, they were citizens of a non-EEC country with no automatic right to come and go without a work permit, and they feared that if they left it would be impossible to return. Second, a military coup in Turkey in September 1981 made return there less attractive and gave Turks living in Germany an additional claim to stay. By 1980 there were 2.1 million foreigners working in Germany, but 2.4 million family members living with them. The numbers of children grew and links to the original "homeland" declined. The Federal Republic had become, in effect, a country of immigrants.[202]

It took an unconscionably long time for politicians to accept that fact. Churches and charities were quicker to see the true situation. In 1978, however, Chancellor Helmut Schmidt created a new post, the Federal Commissioner for the Promotion of Integration among Foreign Workers and Their Families. Heinz Kühn, the first incumbent, was a Social Democrat and former premier of North Rhine–Westphalia. In 1979 he released a memorandum that was highly critical of previous neglect and urged a program of integration (not Germanization) through curricular changes in schools, including ethnically mixed classrooms, adult education, the training of new teachers, enhanced legal aid, and local voting. This became the policy of the Social Democrat–Free Democrat coalition, which made integration a prime political issue. The following years saw a chauvinistic backlash fanned by demagogues on the right. The spike in asylum requests in 1979–1981 was run together with the rise in the number of family reunions, especially among Turks, and labeled the "foreigner question," where the word "question" really meant "problem." There were physical attacks on non-Germans. Two Vietnamese refugees were killed by an arson attack on their hostel in Hamburg, there was an arson attack on Ethiopians living near Stuttgart, and a Turkish store was destroyed in Hanover.[203] Ugly metaphors circulated to describe this new "threat"—the refugees were a "flood," they were all "parasites." The more fastidious suggested that there had to be a "limit to the burdens" because "the boat was full." Hostility to asylum seekers spilled over into heightened resentment of Turks and other former guest workers. In 1978, 40 percent of those polled believed that these should "return to their own country"; four years later the number was 70 percent.[204]

Race was central to all this. Racism now found a new target. At a 1979 conference in Stuttgart, Heinz Kühn warned about a new "racial arrogance" and suggested that anti-Turkish sentiment borrowed from Nazi antisemitic stereotypes.[205] The language used about asylum seekers certainly echoed earlier condemnations of the "Slav flood." There was overt racism on the far right, in the form of a new party called the Republicans, founded in 1983, and from the revival of an older far-right party, the NPD. A group of conservative professors published the Heidelberg Declaration in March 1982. While distancing themselves formally from racism, the signatories nonetheless talked of the "need to preserve the German *Volk* and its spiritual identity" while invoking biology.[206] What was arguably more dangerous than these open manifestations of racism, though, was the way that antiforeigner sentiment was taken up by mainstream politicians on the right, like Franz Josef Strauss, the longtime head of the Christian Social Union and the premier of Bavaria, and Alfred Dregger, the leader of the Christian Democrats in the Bundestag.

The CDU under Chancellor Helmut Kohl returned to power in the early 1980s, in a coalition with the CSU and the Free Democrats. The undercurrent of antiforeigner sentiment was one strand within a larger set of arguments that Germans needed to be less "apologetic" about German nationality and identity. There were some obvious parallels here with the changing political climate in Britain, where Margaret Thatcher appropriated the language of the far right when she spoke about immigration in 1978 and said that people were really afraid that the country might be rather "swamped by people of a different culture."[207] In West Germany, as in Britain, the dominant language of the new racism was cultural, not biological. The Turks and the asylum seekers (half of them also Turks in the early 1980s, following the military coup) were supposedly unassimilable, unwilling to "adapt" to the host culture, as it was assumed they must do. During a parliamentary debate in 1982, Dregger invoked "human nature" and the value people place on "preserving their national identity" as he outlined familiar arguments about the putative differentness of Turks, including how they had been shaped by something other than Christian culture.[208]

Ugly elements marked West German "foreigner" debates through the

1980s. That was especially true of the asylum issue, where another spike in the number of applications occurred after 1986, although the majority now came from Eastern Europe, including Poles, Yugoslavs, and Russian Jews, as well as those fleeing Iran and Lebanon. One of the framers of West Germany's constitution, the Basic Law, Social Democrat Carlo Schmid, had said in 1949: "Asylum law is always a question of generosity and if you wish to be generous it is necessary to risk making a mistake sometimes with an individual."[209] The Kohl administration did not err on the side of generosity as Schmid urged, or as a Christian Democratic chancellor would do in the next millennium. The Basic Law guaranteed the right of asylum, but the West German government interpreted the law narrowly to restrict admissions as far as possible and eventually dispatched asylum seekers to refugee camps (or, in one case witnessed by this author, a boat moored along the Rhine in Mainz), where the enforced idleness of the applicants only reinforced the hostile image of "parasites." Then, when large numbers of claims were rejected, it seemingly confirmed that these were not true asylum seekers.

Historically, Germany had not been ethnically homogeneous, but a land of immigration. That fact received new emphasis as West Germans pushed back powerfully against antiforeigner sentiment. The Declaration of the 60, for example, was a reasoned refutation by migration experts, legal scholars, and public intellectuals of the Heidelberg Declaration.[210] The opposition Social Democrats and Greens pressed for a less harsh application of asylum law and for integrating former guest workers and their families in ways that did not require their Germanization. The Christian Democrats, too, ended up pursuing a middle course on integration. Helmut Kohl was no Margaret Thatcher. He also had to be mindful of the CDU's liberal coalition partners, the Free Democrats. That party's leader and the Federal Republic's high-profile foreign minister, Hans-Dietrich Genscher, threatened to resign when Interior Minister Friedrich Zimmermann proposed revising the law and severely curtailing family reunions. Zimmermann wanted to preserve the "homogeneity" of German society and prevent it from becoming "a multinational and multicultural society, which would be permanently plagued by minority problems." But that position no longer represented the mainstream of Christian Democratic thinking and Zimmermann himself resigned under pressure in 1988. Nonetheless, the governing party also rejected the more wholehearted embrace of multiculturalism urged by its general secretary, Heiner Geissler, who also lost his position, one year after Zimmermann.[211]

The Federal Republic hardly embraced multiculturalism with enthusiasm. There was widespread opposition even to local voting by non-Germans. Rates of naturalization of foreign residents remained very low: in the late 1980s just fourteen thousand naturalizations took place each year, a third of them the spouses of Germans. The rate in France was four times as high, in the United States ten times, and in Canada twenty times.[212] Yet there were signs of new thinking by the late 1980s that had not been present when the recruitment of guest workers was halted back in 1973. Early efforts in the schools often focused on ensuring that Turkish children did not grow up educationally deprived in both Turkish and German. Teachers from Turkey taught students Turkish history and geography, with the idea that they would one day return "home." Elsewhere, "bilingual" education (for Turkish students only) was geared to the ultimate goal of assimilation. But, over time, other practices developed where genuine intercultural understanding was built into the curriculum. German teachers learned Turkish, starting with the desire simply to pronounce their students' names correctly, then going further. In some schools bilingual teaching was introduced for all students, not just the "foreign" ones. Thanks to an oral history project in Berlin-Wedding, we have anecdotal evidence of German teachers exchanging invitations with Turkish parents, a German student who taught a Turkish friend to swim, others who helped with homework and learned about Turkish culture at the same time, apprentices who played soccer and drank together. The workplace and the neighborhood bar, the soccer pitch and grocery store, were, like the school, places of encounter and exchange.[213]

We should not idealize any of this. Encounters could be tense, as contests over shared space often are. There were other issues, too. As a Turkish-German literature emerged, the paradox arose that a prize-winning author like Aras Ören remained ineligible to become a German citizen under the still operative nationality law of 1913.[214] The shifting cultural canon did not translate into commensurate legal or political change. Minority authors also found themselves in the position faced by African-American authors in the United States: that—however creative and hybrid their work—they were often called upon, in however well-meaning a way, to "speak for their community." There were tensions, not least, over cultural clashes that had no easy resolution. Was it wrong for West German feminists to urge the emancipation of Turkish women from patriarchal authority if this meant cutting them off from their support systems in Germany? Was the revival of corporal punishment part of the price to be paid for an open-ended journey toward multiculturalism? In the 1980s these questions were asked on the left as well as the right, asked as genuine and difficult questions to which answers were sought, not as populist posturing. Salman Rushdie's novel *The Satanic Verses* (1988) and the *fatwa* against him were widely debated in the Federal Republic, raising some of these questions in sharpened, sometimes uncomfortable form.[215] And yet: these are questions that healthy societies debate vigorously; they are a sign of strength, not weakness. There was, of course, no public debate over any of these issues—rights of asylum, citizenship law, voting rights for noncitizens, multiculturalism in schools—in the German Democratic Republic.

The reason recruitment of guest workers ended in 1973 was the first oil shock and its economic impact. A primary reason for the rising antiforeigner sentiment in 1979 was the second oil shock and *its* economic impact. The 1970s were framed by the shock of the global.[216] OPEC's actions added a final element, an urgent, unanticipated crisis that came on top of a recent shake-up of world financial markets and a painful long-term shift from an industrial to a postindustrial economy among the advanced nations. West Germany weathered this perfect storm, not always comfortably. East Germany was able to sail around it, at least in the short term. Thanks to the access it enjoyed to Western credits as a result of *Ostpolitik*, the GDR inhabited a kind of fool's paradise in the 1970s, until the price became increasingly obvious in the 1980s. The years between the first oil shock of 1973 and the events of 1989 can be seen, through the lens of economics, as a tale of two German states in an increasingly globalized world. One underwent painful structural change; the other largely avoided doing so and ultimately paid for that with its existence.

The years after 1973 belonged to the era "after the boom."[217] The most potent symbol of before-and-after is what happened to the price of oil. When Egypt and Syria led a coalition of states against Israel in the Yom Kippur War of October 1973, Arab oil-producing states in OPEC announced an embargo against supporters of Israel and reductions in production that led to price increases. After Israel's quick victory, frustrated Arab states engineered further price hikes. A barrel of crude, which cost just over $2 in 1971 and $3 in September 1973, reached $12 by the end of the year. Oil provided almost 60 percent of West Germany's energy supply (the figure was even higher in France), so this had effects throughout the economy. Driving was banned on four consecutive Sundays and a temporary speed limit of 62.5 mph imposed on the *Autobahnen*. This was a true crisis signal in a country where the sanctity of the automobile was so great that no one had ever gotten around to translating Ralph Nader's *Unsafe at Any Speed*.[218] The liberal journalist Sebastian Haffner, best known for his reflections on Hitler, pondered energy security and proposed that West Germans wean themselves off oil.[219] He suggested returning to coal, but the politicians looked instead to nuclear power. That led to major conflicts. What the first oil shock did, above all, was bring home to West Germans how vulnerable they were in the face of global economic forces.

The quadrupling of the price of oil was only one sign of that vulnerability. It was preceded by an episode of global financial turbulence, when President Nixon announced in August 1971 that he was suspending the convertibility of American dollars into gold. This undermined the Bretton Woods Agreement, the system of fixed exchange rates that had been in operation since 1944. Nixon's decision was prompted by U.S. economic weakness, one symptom of which was the large trade deficits the United States was running with other countries, including the Federal Republic. The dollar/Deutschmark exchange rate did not reflect underlying economic realities, which put pressure on the dollar and caused speculative capital to flow into West Germany in hope of a revaluation. Nixon's decision forced EEC countries to respond, which they did at a meeting in March 1973—the crucial year, once again—to move to a system of "floating" exchange rates. The strong West German economy meant that the Deutschmark was likely to float up. That is exactly what happened, causing German exports to become more expensive, a serious blow to the quintessential trading nation for which foreign trade made up a third of GNP.[220]

The oil shock and financial uncertainty were superimposed on a third, longer-term problem: the decline of old staple industries like mining, iron and steel, and shipbuilding. This was also a result of globalization, as these industries expanded in less developed countries where production costs were lower. What the American sociologist Daniel Bell described in 1973 as the "coming of post-industrial society" was really a resetting of the international division of labor, as core Western nations were forced to shift their economic focus to high-end products and the service sector.[221] Helmut Schmidt, who became chancellor in May 1974, was very aware of the global economic (and noneconomic) problems the Federal Republic faced. In his first speech as chancellor he spoke about a "time of growing global problems." A year later, during a conversation with U.S. President Gerald Ford and Henry Kissinger, he referred to the "first global business cycle."²²² During his 1976 election campaign, Schmidt brandished the slogan "*Modell Deutschland,*" holding Germany up as the model for how to respond to the global economic shocks of the 1970s. This bold claim was also, of course, a boast about Schmidt's own prowess as a "crisis manager."

The Federal Republic did weather the crisis after 1973, and the renewed crisis after the second oil shock of 1979, more effectively than most of its rivals. The mining and heavy metal branches of the first Industrial Revolution continued to be phased out. Gains in efficiency meant that familiar exports—pharmaceuticals, precision instruments, automobiles—did well despite the strong Deutschmark. The price of this was higher unemployment. But West Germany did not experience the "stagflation" (low growth with high inflation) that occurred elsewhere, such as in the United States and United Kingdom. Inflation remained lower than in other capitalist economies. Helmut Schmidt also positioned the Federal Republic at the center of the Western response to the 1970s crises. It played a leading role, as we saw, in establishing the G7 and the European Monetary System, and was equally instrumental in the creation of the International Energy Agency, set up in 1974 in response to the first oil shock. With its overriding interest as an exporting nation in avoiding a lurch into protectionism, West Germany was also active in the Tokyo Round of GATT multinational trade negotiations (1973–1979). If there was a shadow side to this familiar pattern of busy multilateral engagement, now reaffirmed at a time of crisis, it was the obsession with fiscal rectitude and low inflation as the markers of virtue. West Germany's rigid attachment to these influenced the International Monetary Fund's policy of "conditionality," meaning that borrowers were required to cut public expenditure and rein in costs, what would later be called "austerity."

East Germany was also embroiled in international economic networks but much less able to determine its own fate. It was caught between East and West. Two vignettes from 1973 illustrate the problem. That year Soviet leader Leonid Brezhnev visited the Federal Republic. A highlight of his visit was a helicopter ride over the Ruhr district, whose mines and heavy industry had fueled German economic success since the nineteenth century. But even while Brezhnev admired it, former industrial installations in the Ruhr were already on their way to becoming arts centers and museums. There were also plenty of economic museum pieces in the Soviet economic bloc, including the GDR—unfortunately, they were still in production. Yet, as one of the advanced economies in the bloc, East Germany was expected to take a leading role in catch-up efforts with the West—in information technology, for example. Cue the second vignette. In 1973 East Germany brought its ES-1040 mainframe computer to market (ES stood for the Russian *Edinaja Sistema*, or unified system). The CIA was impressed. A report a few years later stated: "As for East-European producers, East Germany provides the only success story. East Germany developed and produced the ES-1040, a well-made and apparently reliable machine."[223] Not for the first time, though, the CIA had it wrong. East German machines were ten years behind the West; they were also a gigantic money pit.

Money—where to get it and how to spend it—defined the East German dilemma in the 1970s and '80s. If West Germany struggled with an overvalued Deutschmark, East Germany struggled with a shortage of hard Western currency. After *Ostpolitik*, it could always borrow money from an obliging Federal Republic. But where to put that money—in a gamble on the future (computers), on updating plant and infrastructure, or on trying to offer the consumer goods that its citizens wanted because they saw them on Western TV? In the end, it was the last of these that soaked up more and more of the borrowed money, even as the tab grew longer.

In 1973, when the Western industrialized world was hit by the OPEC price hike, East Germany enjoyed the initial advantage that it was shielded from world prices because it had access to cheap Soviet oil. In fact, for a time it even earned hard currency by processing the oil and selling it to the West. But in the mid-1970s, once the Soviet Union itself needed to buy oil on world markets, it raised the price charged to bloc countries. This was the beginning of disputes that lasted through the lifetime of the GDR, as the price it had to pay in industrial goods in exchange for Soviet oil rose steadily. In 1981 the USSR also cut back on oil deliveries. East Berlin complained bitterly that it had West Germany at its front and "counterrevolutionary" Poland at its back—surely Moscow could see why East Germany needed the oil? To which Moscow replied: Should we, then, cut back instead on supplies to Poland, Vietnam, and Yemen?[224] The East German response was to burn increasing amounts of lignite, or "brown coal," which helps to explain the country's appalling environmental record in its last years.

Pollution was also a by-product of aging plants and machinery. Old chemical works, mines, and power stations had not been replaced or updated. Fires, accidents, spills—all slowed down production, threatened lives, and burdened the environment. The story was the same in the construction industry, where only 30 percent of vehicles were in use at a given time and three-quarters of them were antiquated. Almost half of the country's warehouses had leaking roofs. The older housing stock was crumbling, too. The agricultural sector was not spared from this neglect. Declining standards of fodder, hygiene, and veterinary care created a crisis in animal husbandry that became catastrophic in 1982, when three-quarters of a million hogs died in three months.[225] The word critics used in the last days of the regime was *verkommen*—broken-down, dilapidated.[226] This was the East German version of the Brezhnev era: stasis, or slow decay. The shake-out that occurred in the West never happened in the East. On the contrary: as we saw, the New Economic System of the 1960s, with its loosening of top-down planning, ended. There was renewed centralization. East Germany avoided the unemployment of the West, but not underemployment or reduced-hours working, a result of the frequent breakdowns in production. The shortcomings of unreformed state socialism became more apparent: inefficiencies grew, productivity fell. Gone were the days when the GDR could sell goods like optics beyond the Comecon bloc for hard currency. Southern European and Asian producers now beat them for quality and price.[227]

There was one holdover from the space-age utopianism of the Ulbricht era, when cybernetics and systems analysis were going to prove the superiority of socialism. That was the faith in computers. In 1964 Ulbricht boasted in a Politburo meeting that East German information technology would achieve "world standard" by 1970. He was contradicted by an East German computer pioneer named N. Joachim Lehmann, who was present at the meeting as a guest. But hopes persisted.[228] In the Honecker era, the pipe dream was that developing the high-tech sector would produce large gains in productivity and generate hard currency from foreign sales. Scientists and engineers set to work, but breakdowns in production and delivery bottlenecks plagued the project. Deals were struck with Western firms like Toshiba; spies were placed in IBM, Texas Instruments, Siemens, and the West German aerospace company MBB. None of this helped. The "spy-tech" efforts meant that East German computers ended up borrowing a lot from the West, but the machines themselves were slow to arrive, clunky, and very expensive. The gamble wasted a huge amount of money and the investment still brought no success.[229]

The consumer economy swallowed up even more borrowed money. The regime was very aware that popular discontent had led to unrest in neighboring Poland and tried to meet its citizens' demands with the "unity of social and economic policy" that began in the early 1970s. Housing was the centerpiece, for this was the number one complaint at the time. Design and construction of the prefabricated *Plattenbau* high-rise buildings differed little from what urban planners were constructing elsewhere, East and West. In many ways the new East German housing followed Le Corbusier's modernist blueprint for the "city of tomorrow," once deemed "cosmopolitan" and unacceptable, now embraced as socialist modernity. Giant developments like Marzahn, to the east of Berlin, were conspicuously international in pedigree. The chief architect, Roland Korn, had worked for the Allende regime in Chile, the large cement panels came from a Finnish factory, and the construction method (the "Slobin technique") was Soviet. Marzahn and the other developments were ambitious. They included schools, shops, parks, cafés and beer gardens, dance halls, public libraries, bookstores, health care centers, swimming pools—and, of course, party offices.[230] Many citizens were undoubtedly pleased to have modern dwellings after years of cramped quarters, together with the amenities. Few Western housing developments were so well provisioned. But one of the reasons for the alienation felt by high-rise dwellers everywhere was a major problem in East Germany: poor upkeep. In the GDR it was an all too familiar syndrome. Resources went into construction, not maintenance. Cheap subsidized rents made it even harder to find the money for repairs. Deferred maintenance defined the East German economy.

During the 1970s and '80s GDR citizens directed a growing volume of petitions to the Council of Ministers and party organizations. The number more than doubled over those decades. By the late 1980s, East Germans complained less about housing but more about everything else.[231] The shortage and poor quality of consumer goods was a constant source of resentment. The waiting list for cars remained astonishingly long. Shoddy goods abounded—shoes and clothes that fell apart, TVs that had to be repaired almost immediately after purchase. There were periodic, unpredictable shortages of basic goods. Coffee temporarily disappeared in 1976, bananas and oranges in 1979. In 1982 the animal husbandry disaster caused a chronic shortage of pork products. At different times that same year, there was no coffee in Erfurt and no toilet paper in rural Mecklenburg. Potatoes disappeared in Dresden. It was a sign of the failed consumer economy that those with access to Western currency could purchase things that were otherwise unavailable at the so-called Intershops. These capitalist islands within the socialist sea were more responsive to consumer demand; however, they were also criticized for failing to stock spare parts or provide repairs, leaving consumers holding expensive Western goods that had become useless.[232] The outlook for consumers became worse in 1988–89. Shoppers were more likely to find their local branch of the HO, the main retail chain, closed or to encounter empty shelves. The experience of standing in line took its toll and was one reason for East Germany's high levels of worker absenteeism. In 1987 the number of hours lost to absenteeism was already twice as high as in West Germany, four times the level in the United States.

Meanwhile, in trying to buy off discontent by investing in housing and consumer goods, the country borrowed, borrowed, and borrowed again from the West. This became much easier after *Ostpolitik* opened up the lines of credit. East Germany was not alone in pursuing this policy: Poland and Hungary also borrowed very heavily from Western, especially German, banks. The money went largely into consumption, not new investment or maintenance, and when there were efforts to earn a return that would enable debt to be repaid (whether from computers or a deal with Pepsi-Cola) the hopes were unrealized. East German foreign debt stood at 2 billion valuta marks in 1971, the year before the Basic Treaty with the Federal Republic.* Günter Ehrensperger, the party's chief financial expert, later pointed back to 1973, when his projections showed the foreign debt rising to 20 billion marks by 1980. He was summoned to see Honecker, who told him to stop doing the calculations. "That was the beginning," he said.[233] In fact, the debt grew to 25 billion by 1980 and reached 46 billion by 1989. This was the "kiss of debt."[234] As the situation worsened, party leaders laid hands on anything they could turn into cash, selling off 50 million marks' worth of art and antiquities, gold reserves, weapons stockpiles, even selling the blood of East German citizens to the West. They also developed a vigorous East-West trade in political prisoners, "selling" around 34,000 for a return of 3.5 billion marks.[235] But these sums barely dented the rising debt, which eventually reached 60 percent of the country's export earnings. Unlike some Latin American countries, East Germany never defaulted on its debt. Nor did it, like Romania, enter a crash course of austerity to get

* Valuta marks were the currency unit used in the GDR for foreign trade accounting. They were roughly pegged to the West German Deutschmark.

the debt under control—a policy that, in Romania, brought power cuts, rationing, and widespread misery. An austerity program to stabilize the debt in the GDR would probably have meant a cut in living standards of 30 percent, something Honecker and his colleagues were utterly unwilling to contemplate.

By 1989 East Germany was unable to maintain its industrial plant, prevent breakdowns in production, reverse falling productivity, allocate resources effectively, or adjust to a postindustrial society. It was unable to prevent mounting damage to the environment, to allow key statistics to be published because they were so damning, or to satisfy growing consumer demand, even after borrowing billions from the West that it was unable to repay. These many sins of omission were among the reasons that, as its leaders prepared to celebrate the country's fortieth birthday in October 1989, their legitimacy was being seriously questioned and they would soon find themselves thrown out of power.

From the Fall of the Wall
to the Millennium

O N THE EVENING OF NOVEMBER 9, 1989, THE POLITBURO MEMber in charge of media affairs, Günter Schabowski, held a press conference for foreign journalists. The proceedings went along routinely until an Italian journalist asked Schabowski about travel. His reply was vague and stilted until he suddenly remembered the papers he had been handed just before the meeting, which outlined a more liberal policy agreed hurriedly that afternoon at a Central Committee meeting of the ruling SED. Schabowski had not attended the meeting (although he was supposed to), nor had he read the papers. As a result, he failed to notice that the press release was embargoed until the next morning. He also gave a garbled version of the contents, glancing at the press release and picking out phrases as he went along. The new policy permitted East Germans to travel outside the country, but required prior application and an official stamp, whereas Schabowski said that the law went into effect "immediately" and gave the impression that the border was now open. The earlier sleepy atmosphere had gone and the room was now alive. When a British journalist asked what this meant for the Wall, Schabowski switched awkwardly to another topic, leaving the question hanging in the air as he left the room.[236]

A few East Germans who had heard Schabowski's words headed for the border crossings to West Berlin. Their numbers grew as news spread over West German television. Thousands had gathered by the evening at the Bornholmer Strasse crossing. The border guards were unprepared and the Stasi officer in command there, Harald Jäger, made dozens of attempts throughout the evening to receive clear instructions. At 9:00 p.m. he was told to pull aside those with the loudest voices and let them through to the West, stamping their IDs so that (unknown to them) they would not be permitted to return; the rest should be told to disperse. But the crowds were emboldened by those who had been allowed though. The numbers had reached tens of thousands chanting, "Open the gate!" when, at 11:30, Jäger took the decision to open the barrier. His action was the immediate cause of the great flood of people passing through, climbing the Wall, and celebrating, the joyous scenes captured on camera and described by American TV news anchor Tom Brokaw to a prime-time audience in the United States, where it was almost 6:00 p.m. on the East Coast.[237]

The fall of the Wall was a global media event, capping what has been called the "best year in European history."[238] The dramatic scenes showed the German people taking history into their own hands. And that they certainly did. But the German revolution of 1989, like the 1848 revolutions (which it partly resembled), belonged to something pan-European in scale. The events in 1989 and during the previous few years were intricately connected with what was happening beyond East German borders. The rapidly changing political situation in the Eastern bloc made a decisive difference. So did influences from the outside world that galvanized the East German opposition.

Those influences came from East and West. The Czech opposition was a major inspiration. "We are all happy that there is a Havel and a Charter 77 in Prague," wrote Bärbel Bohley in her diary, "for they are a source of hope not only for Czechoslovakia."[239] Charter 77 was likewise a model for the Working Group on Human Rights established in 1986 in Leipzig to monitor human rights abuses. East German environmentalists had connections with their counterparts in Poland and Hungary as well as the West.[240] The foreign contacts multiplied in the 1980s, especially when it came to peace and human rights issues. Petra Kelly and Gert Bastian became important go-betweens. A British leader of European Nuclear Disarmament visited East Berlin. So did activists from the United States, Japan, and France who had been attending a 1983 peace conference in West Berlin. Ulrike Poppe, a cofounder of Women for Peace and the Initiative for Peace and Human

Rights, told an interviewer in 2014: "After that we were networked rather well."[241] The networking proved important when she and fellow dissident Bohley were later arrested. Protest letters to East German leaders poured in from Western Europe.

In the last years before 1989, some East German groups began to step gingerly out of the protective embrace of the Protestant church. The weight of public opinion in the West provided some measure of protection, too. But support from the West supplemented rather than replaced what the church offered. Often, in fact, the two went hand in hand. When the Stasi adopted a new policy in 1988 of temporarily "expatriating" dissidents such as Bohley, it was the church that usually acted as a go-between. In Bohley's case the arrangement was made between an East German bishop who had supported Swords into Ploughshares, and Paul Oestreicher, the dean of Coventry Cathedral in England, a German émigré who headed the British branch of Amnesty International. The six months Bohley spent in 1988 away from East Germany, living first in West Germany, then in the United Kingdom, were a revelation. From Petra Kelly's office in Bonn, Bohley "telephoned with half the world." She sat on a panel with a leader of the French Greens, met one of Jesse Jackson's advisers, and visited the women who camped out at Royal Air Force Greenham Common to protest the stationing of NATO missiles. Being in the West only made her more radical, she told her friend Katja Havemann, the widow of the dissident scientist Robert Havemann and a cofounder of Women for Peace.[242]

Just before her arrest in 1988, Bohley had remarked on yet another politically motivated visit she was making to Gethsemane Church in East Berlin: "My God, how often one has to go to church like this!"[243] Her comment captures the strangeness of the situation. An even stranger alliance was the one that saw East German punks find a haven in the Protestant church. The punk movement was a dramatic instance of transnational influences fostering opposition. Punk music, which established itself in the United States and Britain in 1976–77, reached young East Germans soon after. They listened to it and taped it from Radio Luxemburg, RIAS, or DJ John Peel's show on the British Forces Broadcasting Service. Pictures and articles about punks also appeared in West German youth magazines like *Bravo* and *Blickpunkt* that circulated in the East. Both the music and paraphernalia of punk—fanzines, buttons, jackets—circulated within the Eastern bloc. They were more readily available in Budapest, Warsaw, or Prague than at home. They could also be had in the West, of course, and one channel through which punk music reached East Germany was the elderly who were allowed to travel, the "grandmas" who stood in line at West Berlin record stores buying punk albums from shopping lists provided by their grandchildren. One store became so familiar with this routine that they put the records into Frank Sinatra sleeves to ensure that the border guards ignored them. East Germany also had homegrown punk bands. The names they took were (like the Sex Pistols and the Clash in Britain) a deliberate provocation: Wutanfall (Tantrum) in Leipzig, Schleimkeim (Slime Germ) in Erfurt. Like punk bands in the West, their playing was loud and aggressive, full of "textual shrapnel," a statement of defiant hostility toward norms and regimentation.[244] The wider punk scene—in basements and squats, on the street and in certain parks—projected the same insubordinate, glowering attitude. Punks went in for what the punk-influenced British fashion designer Vivienne Westwood called "confrontation dressing"—usually even more do-it-yourself (and therefore cutting edge) than might have been found in London or Hamburg.[245] That was why Western punks and their sympathizers, in a reversal of the normal East-West roles, expressed envy for the dangerous, unspoiled "authenticity" of their Eastern brethren.[246]

The publicity the East German punk scene received in the West, from the West German and British press, goaded the regime into a counterattack. In theory, punk was a product of capitalist decadence and therefore existed in the East only as a result of Western infiltration. A violent campaign in 1983 called "Hard Against Punk" led to arrests, beatings, drafting punks into the army, and expatriations. The crackdown reduced the size of the movement, but it also politicized it.[247] Many punks found a refuge in the church. That is where they now had a secure place to play, and where visiting punk groups also played, like Die Toten Hosen (Nothing Going On) from West Germany and Karcer (Solitary Confinement) from Poland. As they moved into churches, so the punks were drawn into overtly political oppositional causes like human rights and environmentalism. References to punk also found their way into opposition literature.[248] The Stasi, meanwhile, put informers into the punk movement, as it did with every opposition movement. The regime also tried belatedly to co-opt punk and produce a better-groomed, ideologically sound version, as they had tried to do (more successfully) with rock music in the 1970s.[249]

Rock music nonetheless had the potential to join hands with political dissent in the Eastern bloc. It had, after all, been the arrest of members of the Czech group Plastic People of the Universe that led Havel and others to draft Charter 77. A fixture of Czech underground culture with a devoted youth following, the group was heavily influenced by the American Frank Zappa and his Mothers of Invention, one of whose songs ("Plastic People") provided its name. A different Western rock eminence tapped the reservoir of discontent among young East Germans in June 1987. That was when a three-day Concert for West Berlin was held near the Reichstag, right by the Wall, with seventy thousand people there. David Bowie was the headline act on the second night. Bowie had gone to live in West Berlin in 1976 to get clean from cocaine. He read Brecht, painted, and went to art museums. He also composed. His two-year stay marked a creative rebirth during which he recorded three landmark albums, known as the "Berlin trilogy." One of them, *Heroes*, had a title track that referred to lovers divided by the Wall that Bowie saw outside his apartment in Schöneberg. At this concert ten years later, Bowie returned and sang "Heroes." A crowd gathered in the East sang along, joining in a song about love overcoming an artificial divide. There was an obviously poignant, double-edged quality to this, as the audience behind the Wall imagined themselves out of East Germany. On this evening, however, the crowds did more than imagine getting out. They shouted "down with the Wall." Harshly dispersed, they gathered again the next night, when the police again responded with force and made mass arrests. Like the crackdowns against punk, this overreaction against people listening to popular music was counterproductive. Even Erich Honecker seems to have recognized it as a mistake.[250]

One of the chants from the East Berlin crowds listening by the Wall in June 1987 was "Gorbi, let us out!" Mikhail Gorbachev had a crucial impact on the growing protest movement in East Germany after 1985, the year he came to power in the USSR. He changed the equation in two ways. First, he made it clear that he was unwilling to do what had been done in 1953, 1956, and 1968. There would be no more use of Soviet troops to repress opposition movements. This shift resulted partly from the disastrous occupation of Afghanistan, which weakened the Soviet hold on the Warsaw Pact states and further damaged its economy. The Russian democratic activist Andrei Piontkovsky wrote that it was "the Mujahedin in the hills of Afghanistan who were the real liberators of Eastern Europe.[251] In a 1988 speech at the United Nations, Gorbachev effectively renounced the Brezhnev Doctrine, which held that the USSR had the right to intervene to "protect socialism." Soviet Foreign Ministry spokesman Gennady Gerasimov later offered a livelier version of this when he said on American television that the Brezhnev Doctrine was dead: "We now have the Frank Sinatra doctrine. He had a song, 'I had it my way.' So every country decides, on its own, which way to take."[252] When Gorbachev visited East Berlin during the GDR anniversary celebrations in October 1989, he expressly ruled out the use of Soviet troops to crush opposition and made it clear that he disapproved of East German rulers using force against dissidents.

The end of the Brezhnev Doctrine went together with Gorbachev's policies of *perestroika* (restructuring) and *glasnost* (openness). Like the removal of the threat of armed intervention, these emboldened reformers across the Eastern bloc. East Germany was a notable exception, for the hard-liners remained in power there and would-be local Gorbachev reformers (like the Dresden party boss Hans Modrow) kept their heads down. But the GDR still faced the spillover effect from neighbors, especially Poland and Hungary, where Gorbachev's arrival transformed the political landscape. The changes came to a head in 1989. In February round-table talks began in Poland between the Communist Party and the independent trade union Solidarity. They ended in agreement to hold open elections and legalize non-Communist trade unions. In the free elections that followed in June, Solidarity won an overwhelming victory. Gorbachev made it plain that the election result had to stand and in September Tadeusz Mazowiecki became the first non-Communist prime minister in the history of the people's democracies. In Hungary, reformers inside the Communist Party replaced the seventy-six-year-old János Kádár in 1988 with a Gorbachev-type named Károly Grósz. The modest market reforms already in place were extended. Then it was decided to allow other political parties to operate and permit free assembly. In April 1989, a commission of inquiry was opened into the events of 1956, now described as a "popular uprising against an oligarchic rule that debased the nation." On June 16, the anniversary of the death of Imre Nagy, the uprising's leader, his remains and those of four others were ceremonially reburied in Budapest in front of a crowd of two hundred thousand. That same month, Polish-style round-table talks began and plans were drawn up for Soviet troop withdrawals.[253]

It was another Hungarian event in June that had most effect in East Germany—that was, in fact, one of the principal episodes that led to the fall of the Wall four and a half months later. On June 27, Hungarian foreign minister Gyula Horn and his Austrian counterpart, Alois Mock, posed with wire cutters for the press as they opened a 150-mile stretch of their border. East Germans soon gathered in Hungary, hoping to be allowed to travel to Austria and on to West Germany. By early July there were 25,000 Germans camped out in Hungary. The Hungarian authorities refused to let them through unless they had an exit visa, which is how East Berlin expected them to behave. But neither did they apprehend those who tried to cross, or send them back to East Germany, or even report them. The floating population of East Germans in Hungary grew, creating a summer crisis. The Hungarians estimated their numbers in mid-August at an astonishing 200,000. Caught in a no-man's-land, unable to leave and unwilling to return, thousands sought asylum in the West German embassy in Budapest, turning a part of the city into a surreal stage set of abandoned Trabants.

In an agreement brokered by Chancellor Kohl in late August, the asylum seekers in Budapest were allowed to travel to the West on September 10. The following day Hungary opened its borders fully. Its leaders were relieved of an increasingly onerous refugee problem. They had also been promised assistance from Bonn with their economic problems. The open border triggered a mass exodus. When East Berlin tried to block travel to Hungary, would-be leavers went to Czechoslovakia, seeking refuge in the West German embassy in Prague, before that border, too, was sealed. Others did the same in Warsaw. Eventually, in early October, they were shipped to the West in sealed trains (Lenin style, only in reverse), leaving more East European capitals littered with discarded Trabants.[254] There were violent scenes as the trains passed through East German territory on their way west and others tried to leap aboard. One would-be emigrant was killed and a police car set alight. All this appeared on TV news internationally.

Time speeds up in moments of political crisis. It is extraordinary what a distance there already was between 1987 and 1989. In July 1987, Gorbachev had told West German president Richard von Weizsäcker that German unification was perhaps a hundred years away (when Weizsäcker demurred, the Soviet leader obligingly reduced it to fifty). When Gorbachev visited the Federal Republic in June 1989, with rapturous crowds chanting, "Gorbi, Gorbi!," he said during an unguarded moment that the Wall had been constructed during a "special situation" and "could disappear once the conditions that created the need for it disappeared."[255] The pace of change quickened again in September and October because of the mass exodus. About 340,000 people left East Germany in the course of 1989, 2 percent of the population. Contrary to what is often said (and was alleged at the time by some East German dissidents), most gave the political situation and the lack of civil liberties as their main reason for leaving, rather than material motives, although it is obviously hard to separate the two cleanly.[256] Their departure ignited a full-scale domestic crisis. What had been a safety valve when it happened in a small, controlled way ("expatriation") became an existential threat when it happened as a mass event. The emigrants were skilled workers and professionals from industry, health care, and teaching. More than 80 percent of them were under forty. Their departure was worse than the exodus immediately prior to the building of the Wall, because greater in scale and more sudden. The bumbling response of the regime undermined its credibility. Those who left therefore had a huge impact on those who stayed.

Shortly before his expatriation in 1976, Wolf Biermann wrote a song called "And as We Came to the Riverbank." The second verse turns to the question of what to do:

> *And what about all our friends*
> *And what about you and me?*
> *I most want to get away*
> *I most want to stay right here*

To leave or to stay? Or, in the famous alternatives set out by the economist Albert Hirschman twenty year earlier: "exit" or "voice"?[257] Writing in February 1989, Bärbel Bohley saw the options exactly like that and was clear that she had to stay. After all, the previous year the regime would have been delighted if she had chosen to remain in the West, but she had been determined to return. So were other dissidents who had been temporarily exiled in 1988. In the crisis of the summer and autumn of 1989, they felt that their moment had come, as did a growing number of others. As demonstrators went onto the streets in late September they shouted defiantly, "We're staying here!"[258] Without the mass exodus it is inconceivable that the crisis would have intensified as it did. Hirschman, revisiting his own model and applying it to East Germany, argued in 1993 that "exit" and "voice" were no longer at odds with each other but had become "confederates," a "joint grave-digging act."[259]

In the months before the fall of the Wall on November 9, two other events had special symbolic significance. They occurred, with pleasing symmetry, on September 9 and October 9. The first date marked the founding of a New Forum by Bärbel Bohley, Katja Havemann, and others. Some were prominent figures already active in the peace and human rights movements, but others had previously been "corridor dissidents" like Jens Reich, meeting for years in discussion groups and waiting for some kind of reform from above. Rolf Henrich had still been a member of the ruling party at the beginning of 1989, when he was expelled for publishing (in the West) a book criticizing "real existing socialism" from the left. Bohley went out of her way to invite a broad cross-section of dissidents, but almost all were members of the educated middle class: scientists, clergy, physicians, academics. Thirty people signed the founding appeal, which called for reform and dialogue and expressed the "desire for justice, democracy, peace, and protection of nature."[260] The founders asked for New Forum to be legally recognized as an association under the GDR constitution. It took nearly seven weeks for this to be granted. New Forum existed meanwhile in a gray zone of semilegality. Its importance was that the founders were willing to stick their heads above the parapet. Others followed. Several openly political groups were founded in the following weeks: Democracy Now, Democratic Awakening, an East German version of the Social Democratic Party, as well as others espousing environmentalist and feminist views. Small circles of people found that there were others like them and were emboldened. By the end of 1989, two hundred thousand people had signed the New Forum appeal.[261]

What happened in Leipzig on October 9 was a much more dramatic version of the same truth: success breeds confidence. The march that Monday evening can reasonably be seen as the decisive turning point in the German revolution—an "October revolution" of sorts.[262] Leipzig was a city of multiple discontents. It had a crumbling infrastructure and was heavily polluted even by East German standards. The Saxon cities of Leipzig and Dresden were the epicenter of the mass exodus from the GDR, and local dissident groups had worked closely with those wishing to leave. The most potent symbol of protest in Leipzig was the tradition of Monday evening marches that followed services in St. Nicholas Church. "Prayers for peace" had been said since 1982, but the action of the Protestant church leadership in the fall of 1988 to take the prayers out of the hands of Christoph Wonneberger, St. Nicholas's activist priest, had the unintended consequence that it moved the main focus of the Monday events from inside to outside.

The size of the marches grew in 1989 as the crisis grew. On October 2, the crowd reached ten thousand, the largest demonstration in East German history to that point. Police used water cannon, batons, and dogs on demonstrators. The week that followed was tense. The sealed trains taking East Germans to the West from Czechoslovakia on the fourth led to violent scenes in Saxony. Then, on October 7, the official fortieth anniversary celebrations of the Democratic Republic were disrupted by protests that were brutally handled by the police. There was a mood of fear and apprehension before the ninth. Honecker had signaled that this was to be a day of reckoning. Erich Mielke, the head of the Stasi, call for a "full alert." The army was on standby, along with the police and paramilitary units. The state had armored vehicles, machine guns, and other weapons at its disposal, including tear gas and water cannon. The official rhetoric was uncompromising and the situation had the potential to replicate the massacres at Tian'anmen Square a few months earlier.

People gathered on October 9 from services at St. Nicholas Church and three other churches that had agreed to hold prayers at the same time. Most simply assembled outside at 6:00 p.m. The crowd was seventy thousand strong. But there was no bloodshed. That was a result, not least, of the restraint shown by the marchers. Pastor Wonneberger, the original moving spirit of the Monday evenings, admired Martin Luther King Jr. and the power of nonviolent protest. He and others spent forty hours on an ancient church mimeograph machine turning out thirty thousand leaflets that urged peaceful conduct. Marchers who had been to church heard the same message. Pastor Hans-Jürgen Sievers of the Reformed Church, who had sung in the choir when King visited both parts of divided Berlin, invoked King's 1963 "I have a dream" speech at the Lincoln Memorial when he called on the fifteen hundred people in his church to avoid violence. An appeal for nonviolence was also read out in St. Nicholas Church and later broadcast from loudspeakers. It was jointly signed by Kurt Masur, the well-known musical director of Leipzig's Gewandhaus Orchestra, the cabaret artist Bernd-Lutz Lange, the theologian Peter Zimmermann (later revealed to be a Stasi spy), and three local Party secretaries, two of them reform-minded, the third previously known as a hard-liner. Later in the evening, as the huge crowd moved off, the acting first secretary of the party in Leipzig tried to get confirmation of his instructions from East Berlin to oppose the marchers. By the time he heard back, however, he had decided to order the security forces to stand down. The night ended with a victory for nonviolent protest by a large crowd chanting, "We are the people!" The scenes were captured on camera by two East Germans filming from the tower of the Reformed Church. Smuggled to the West, the film appeared the next day on television, where East Germans could watch it. The following week the Monday crowd in Leipzig reached over one hundred thousand; the week after that, a quarter of a million.

By then, the division in the ranks of the party that were apparent locally on October 9 had become evident at the highest level. Divisions in the ruling class are an indispensable ingredient of revolution, as Lenin knew. The differences of opinion in the GDR leadership were an unmistakable sign of crisis. In a palace coup on October 17–18, Honecker was forced to step down and Egon Krenz, the recognized crown prince, took over. Krenz went to Moscow and received Gorbachev's blessing, but it was too late. After he had fallen from power himself, Krenz told everyone who would listen that he ought to have moved earlier. "I should have done it sooner" became his mantra.[263] But Krenz's hesitation was not just a personal weakness but a problem he shared with the whole leadership. And this was not a psychological issue, a collective Hamlet complex, but a deep-wired resistance to reform. The party that had always urged its citizens to "learn from the Soviet Union" was unwilling to follow its own advice. When Gorbachev visited East Berlin for the fortieth anniversary celebrations, he pointedly warned Honecker that "life punishes those who delay."[264] But the warning was ignored until it was too late. Krenz himself was rightly perceived by critical citizens as a pseudoreformer, desperately trying to shore up the authority of the party rather than engage in dialogue. But morale within the party fell as popular confidence rose. At a mass rally in Alexanderplatz on November 4, with hundreds of thousands present, the speakers from a makeshift podium included not only members of recently legalized New Forum but intellectuals like Christa Wolf and her fellow writer Stefan Heym, who had previously avoided open dissidence, and—most striking of all—prominent party figures including Günter Schabowski and former spymaster Markus Wolf. By this stage, East Germany's panicked rulers were always chasing the game, searching for concessions that would satisfy popular dissatisfaction but only stoking it further. New travel rules announced on November 6 fell a long way short of permitting travel "visa-*frei* to Hawaii," as banners demanded. The Council of Ministers resigned the next day and the Politburo on the eighth, but this failed to inspire popular trust that their successors would be any better. Then came Schabowski's press conference and the fall of the Wall.

The historic events that reached a climax on the night of November 9 became known as *Die Wende*, "the turn." What followed was the "turn within the turn," which has also been described as the "deflected revolution" and the "rush to German unity."[265] In the autumn of 1989 it was a series of outside events—in the USSR, Poland, and above all Hungary—that created a situation in which the people of East Germany took events into their own hands. In the nine or ten months between the Wall coming down and the formal treaty of unification between the two Germanys on August 31, 1990, the people of East Germany once again made it clear what they wanted, which was not to reform the socialist state as prominent dissidents wished, but to join the prosperous West. But that process inevitably involved many other parties, above all the four Allies who occupied postwar Germany. The drama of November 9 initially caught everyone by surprise. It was not clear how the new situation would work itself out. But Gorbachev's foreign policy adviser, Anatoly Chernyaev, immediately saw the event in world-historical terms and wrote in his diary that when the Wall fell "a whole era of the socialist system ended"; for the USSR "now only our 'best friends' Castro, Ceaucescu, Kim Il Sung are left. They hate us passionately."[266]

"I don't understand the world anymore," said one angry border guard who resented the chaotic unfolding of events on November 9.[267] He was not alone. Demoralization within the ruling party ran deep. Its members melted away. Reports came to East Berlin from party branches everywhere reporting disillusion, despair, even "suicidal thoughts."[268] The leadership met in emergency session and added "Party of Democratic Socialism" to its old name. The Politburo resigned *en bloc*, for the second time in a month. Honecker and Krenz were expelled; Hans Modrow, the closest thing to an East German Gorbachev and a personal friend of the Soviet leader, became prime minister. Parliament voted to remove Leninist language about the leading role of the party from the constitution. The vote was 420–0 (old habits die hard). But it became clear that it was not just the party, but the state, that had lost legitimacy. Quite suddenly, what had seemed formidable and frightening just weeks earlier resembled an ancien régime that had been overthrown. Rumors circulated about high living in the compound where party bosses resided in Wandlitz, known derisively as "Volvograd" because of all the chauffeured Swedish cars.[269] Margot Honecker was cast in the role of Marie Antoinette, for every modern revolution needs a female scapegoat as a symbol of corruption. In the streets, meanwhile, the crowds started chanting, "We are *one* people" rather than "We are *the* people." All this cut the ground from under the feet of those like Bärbel Bohley and Christa Wolf who wanted to keep their state and reform it.

The collapse of authority in the GDR outran the response of the politicians, including those in the West. Helmut Kohl had telephoned Egon Krenz on October 26 to wish him success with his difficult task and express the hope that there would be a "calm, sensible development."[270] A month later, three weeks after the Wall fell, Kohl presented the Federal Republic's parliament with a ten-point plan that foresaw growing cooperation between the two German states, leading to the creation of common institutions in some kind of confederation, a "growing together" and an "organic development," all within the larger framework of East-West relations in Europe. Many thought this "too fast" and "premature," but soon it came to seem too cautious. Kohl himself paid a visit to Dresden just before Christmas and witnessed a huge crowd shouting, "Helmut, Helmut!" as they had once called out "Willy, Willy!" in the heady days of Brandt's *Ostpolitik*. The American art critic Peter Schjeldahl was in East Berlin just after Christmas, there to chip pieces off the wall (and finding it harder than he expected). In an article published in the New York magazine *7 Days* he referred to the "weedy acres of the Potsdamer Platz, the bomb-obliterated and Wall-riven former crossroads of Europe that is going to be incredibly expensive real estate when the Germanys reunify, which they will." How did he reach this conclusion? Intuitively: "In Berlin you feel the inevitability not in what people say to you—usually some cagey, befuddling German bullshit—but in the air, with a momentum like the hero and heroine rushing to embrace on the train platform so that the movie can be over."[271]

The momentum all came from one direction, as people in the East rushed to embrace the West. They left behind severe labor shortages in factories, offices, and hospitals. Daily life became harder and loyalty to the East German state even more strained. The mass movement of people also threatened to overwhelm the Federal Republic. That happened first in border towns like Mellrichstadt in Franconia (population: 5000), which played temporary host to hundreds of thousands of East Germans.[272] There were longer-term housing and welfare implications. West German politicians feared that the unrelenting influx and the difficulties it brought would feed the radical right. In January 1990 it was agreed that new East German elections, scheduled for May, would be brought forward to March. But the rush to the West continued. Reporters increasingly laid bare the underlying economic conditions and confirmed East Germans in their profound lack of confidence about the future. The Eastern mark was a symbol of this. People now began to use the Western currency, if they had it, in private transactions. Crowds chanted, "If the D-Mark comes to us, we'll stay here / If not, we'll go to it over there."[273] In February, Kohl reversed his previous stance—it was better to take the Deutschmark to the people than have the people come for the Deutschmark, as he put it. This was also a clever political move in advance of the March elections. The prospect of monetary union therefore became a promise of unification. The Christian Democrats and their allies won the March elections handily. Currency union followed on July 1, creating another historical symmetry: currency reform in 1990 opened the way to unification, just as it had opened the way to division forty-one years earlier. The two Germanys signed a unification treaty on August 31.

Plenty of observers were nervous about the prospect of a united Germany, writers in *The New York Times* and *The New Republic* among them.[274] So were many of Germany's neighbors, East and West. The nervousness extended to Kohl's fellow Christian Democratic heads of government, such as Ruud Lubbers in the Netherlands and Giulio Andreotti in Italy. Potentially more important were the misgivings on the part of two Western leaders who would have some kind of say in approving the process: Prime Minister Margaret Thatcher of Britain and President François Mitterrand of France. Both, at an early stage, tried to work through Gorbachev, whose advisers complained that the pair of Western leaders wanted Gorbachev to "play the heavy" by blocking unification but would not openly support him if he did.[275] Mitterrand was more flexible than his British counterpart. He disliked Kohl's ten-point program and was well aware of widespread French distrust of a newly powerful Germany, but soon became convinced unification was inevitable and continued to play up to Thatcher mainly so that he could later present himself to the Germans as a mediator. Mitterrand's main interest was that unification be accompanied by a more integrated European Community to "contain" Germany, something that went with the grain of Kohl's own thinking.[276] As for Thatcher, not until February 1990 did she reluctantly yield to the view of her own Foreign Office that Britain should unconditionally support the German right to self-determination, when it became clear that neither Mitterrand nor Gorbachev would support her. By the end of January 1990, Gorbachev himself had come to the conclusion that unification was inevitable. He rejected the view of military hard-liners in Moscow who wanted to reestablish the Wall, if necessary by committing a million Soviet troops. The more it became clear that Modrow had failed to reassert authority, or even hold the state together, the wiser it appeared to reach an agreement before East Germany descended into still greater chaos. Earlier, Gorbachev had put out feelers to Kohl in the forlorn hope that the West German chancellor would be interested in Moscow's blessing for unification in exchange for German neutrality. This possibility caused concern in Washington, but was never a starter. In the end, Gorbachev had few cards to play.

The foreign ministers of the NATO and Warsaw Pact powers met in Ottawa on February 13, 1990, and agreed on a formula for German unification: $2 + 4 = 1$. The two Germanys would negotiate first, then the four Allied powers would give their approval. The "2" was really one, a dominant West Germany, and the "4" was really two, with Britain and France on the sidelines. As for the other powers, they had no place in the formula, although the eventual agreement was approved by the Conference on Security and Cooperation in Europe. As one commentator noted tartly, "Everyone in sight was wooed, reassured, sometimes informed and even occasionally consulted," but only the USSR and the United States had the power to impede the process.[277] When Giulio Andreotti asked West German foreign minister Hans-Dietrich Genscher to brief him on the state of play, Genscher replied, "You are not part of the game."[278] It was Genscher who said that $2 + 4$ was "perhaps two and a half."[279] West Germany and the Soviet Union were the two decisive partners, with the United States acting as broker.

Ever since coming to power, Gorbachev had wanted the Soviet Union to move closer to Western Europe and especially to its economic powerhouse, West Germany. That was one reason he had been frustrated by Honecker's stubborn immovability. In 1990, Kohl successfully persuaded Gorbachev that a unified Germany within NATO would not be a threat. The chancellor also made promises of generous economic assistance. The deal was sealed at the Kohl-Gorbachev July 1990 summit in the Caucasus. But the United States was important, too. President George H. W. Bush strongly supported unification. Even before the fall of the Wall, both during a visit to the Federal Republic in May 1989 and in a *New York Times* interview that October, he said, "I don't share the concern that some European countries have about a reunified Germany."[280] The American president and his secretary of state, James Baker, eased the process along at every stage. The diplomatic phase was completed in September and a unification treaty ratified in both German parliaments went into effect on October 3, 1990.

The events of 1989–90 were quickly followed by the collapse of the Soviet Union in 1991 and the end of the Cold War. Together these marked a hard historical break.[281] Some historians talk about a "short twentieth century" beginning in 1914 and coming to an end in 1990. That underscores, perhaps too heavily, the idea of a "German century." For Germany itself, 1990 served as a kind of "reset button."[282] Did the disappearance of the East German state signify the unified country's final "arrival in the West"?[283] In a way, clearly it did. Yet there are also reasons to question that comfortable view of "the West" and the larger narrative of benign globalization in which it is usually framed.

When the Wall fell, Willy Brandt talked about the "growing together of what belongs together." Helmut Kohl's Christian Democrats owed their great electoral success in the East to their promises of "blossoming landscapes." But the German-German history that followed was a difficult one. The West dominated both the formal unification process and unification on the ground. The larger economy swallowed up the smaller one, privatized its assets through the organization established for that purpose, the Treuhandanstalt (Trust Agency), and in the process created widespread unemployment and insecurity. Work, welfare, child care—all changed quickly in the former East. The shock of transition caused bitterness and there was much talk about a Western "takeover." A wave of *Ostalgie*, "Eastern nostalgia," expressed an understandable feeling that forty years of lived experience were being coldly wiped out. Thirty years on, there is clear evidence of economic convergence, as household incomes in the East have reached 80–85 percent of those in the West. But the hostility has not all disappeared. For their part, West Germans often expressed bitterness that they have borne the burden of the environmental cleanup and investment in the East through "solidarity" surtaxes, earning no thanks. In 1989, remembering her brief stay in the West the previous year, Bärbel Bohley had written about the need to "recognize the difference between two different ways of seeing, thinking, working, eating."[284] Mutual resentments persisted. And yet, if we look at the post–Cold War history of Russia, or at the bloodshed in former Yugoslavia, where 300,000 people died in the 1990s, or at many places in the global South that received far less attention once the Cold War was over, then it is hard not to see the process of nation rebuilding in unified Germany as one of the most successful projects of the era.[285]

What about the place of united Germany in the world? It was a larger country, of course, but still geographically small by global standards. You

could have fitted Germany almost twice over into Texas. It was modest in
size compared even with many other European states: smaller than France
and Spain as well as Russia. Demographically, Germany was a European
heavyweight, second only to Russia. At the time of unification its population of 82 million made it number twelve in the world, although that ranking
dropped seven places by 2020 as its population grew slowly. Its flat, aging
population would form part of the background to German debates about
immigration. In the matter of language, unified Germany became by far
the largest of the countries where German was spoken as a first language,
82 million out of 100 million in Europe and perhaps 120 million globally.
But the more important development was the continuing collapse in the
numbers of those who spoke German as a second or third language. By
the end of the twentieth century German was clearly no longer an essential
language of science and humanistic scholarship or a lingua franca for many
Scandinavians and Central Europeans. They now had a different common
language. Just as Germans called their male children Patrick and Robin,
not Friedrich or Jürgen, so the rest of the European (and non-European)
world spoke English. It was in its economic performance that the new Federal Republic, like the old Federal Republic, punched well above its weight.
United Germany ranked fourth globally in GDP and has continued to do
so in the years since, even as the German economy has been transformed
by neoliberal legislation and globalization.

Did unification make a difference to Germany's political role in the
world? The old Federal Republic spent forty years as a large country that
behaved politically like a small country. It tried not to stand out and was
the very incarnation of the committed multilateral actor, a "team player."
This culture of restraint was a reaction to the Nazi past and the means
by which Germany reassured potentially nervous neighbors. Postunifica-
tion, the new Federal Republic preferred to continue throwing itself into
the familiar and congenial task of working multilaterally to create stronger
ties with European neighbors, whether through regional organizations like
the Council of the Baltic Sea States, or the Organization for Security and
Cooperation in Europe. The weightiest European project was the one set
out in the Maastricht Treaty of 1992, when members of the EEC agreed
to create a European Union with a common currency. Over the following years Germany played a central role in shaping what became a union
of twenty-eight nation-states (twenty-seven after Brexit) and 450 million
people. Germany was the most "European" of the large European nations,

and its population identified with the European project more than their counterparts in France or Spain, not to mention Britain. Europe stood for reassuring stability. Germans even accepted the disappearance of the Deutschmark and its replacement by the euro with equanimity.

But it was harder for united Germany to hide itself away in the new world order. The first Gulf War over Kuwait in 1990–91 produced an immediate challenge. Germany declined to join the coalition mobilized by President Bush against Iraqi leader Saddam Hussein, offering financial and logistical backing but no military support. Its decision was supported by three-quarters of the German public but criticized by some Western allies. There were also German critics on both left and right who wanted the country to play a more active role. Conservatives wanted Germany to be less "frightened of power" and more willing to articulate a national interest; critics on the left wanted more openness to the idea of humanitarian interventionism. It was the return of war and ethnic cleansing to Europe in former Yugoslavia that eventually brought about a change of policy. In 1994 the German Constitutional Court in Karlsruhe ruled that German forces were permitted to operate "out of area," if under a U.N. mandate, which removed arguments that any German military engagement would contravene the Basic Law.

The Kosovo crisis then led to the decisive break with the past when, in early 1999, Germany committed troops to the NATO campaign against Serbia. Ground troops went to Macedonia to protect Kosovar refugees, and served as peacekeepers in Kosovo and Bosnia. But the true novelty was the action of the German air force, in operation for the first time since 1945, as German Tornado aircraft took part in the bombing campaign against Serbia. True, they flew very few missions, but a precedent had been set. Helmut Kohl had lost the federal election the previous year and it was the new coalition of Social Democrats and Greens headed by Gerhard Schröder that authorized the air strikes. That it was a government of the left which finally broke the postwar taboo made it easier. It was the mirror image of conservative Charles de Gaulle ending the French war in Algeria or Richard Nixon going to China. The distinctively German aspect of the policy change in 1999 was the justification offered by Foreign Minister Joschka Fischer and Defense Minister Rudolf Scharping that military intervention was necessary to prevent another genocide, another "Auschwitz." The German past was never far away.

In the same year, 1999, the capital of united Germany was moved from

Bonn to Berlin. There was grumbling from western Germans and the vote in parliament was close, but the move excited no alarm around the world. The image of Germany had softened, just as Christo's *Wrapped Reichstag* in 1995 softened the outlines of the once and future German parliament. The German question, as it presented itself for much of the twentieth century, had been laid to rest. When the rest of the world thought of Germany now, the associations were very different, in some ways more like those of earlier years. German technology, like German science, excited admiration. It even featured in a clever advertising campaign for Audi cars, which achieved global success with a German slogan: *"Vorsprung durch Technik."* The reputation of German culture stood equally high and was starting to be more carefully cultivated with the rise of the heritage industry. At the same time, Germany at the end of the twentieth century was rightly viewed as a world leader in conservation and green energy. That image was further reinforced when four members of the Green Party won cabinet posts in Schröder's so-called Red-Green administration in 1998. As for Berlin, the new seat of government, it was not yet the hipster paradise it would become over the following twenty years, but techno clubs that later became a global tourist attraction were already opening their doors in the 1990s and the reunited city was starting to win back a reputation for cultural dynamism and excitement of the kind it had enjoyed around 1900 and even more in the 1920s.

When it came to geopolitics, the world was now more likely to criticize Germany for its excessive restraint and penchant for "checkbook diplomacy," not for aggression. Anti-German sentiment was more likely to be directed at tourists with fat wallets, ubiquitous global symbols of the country's wealth. But behind that object of resentment was something much more serious and potentially disturbing, which was how Germany used its growing economic power to impose its national preferences on others. That would become an explosive issue during the European debt crisis of 2008. At the close of the twentieth century, Germany's role within the global economy raised a second troubling question. Was the Federal Republic's commitment to Western democracy and human rights compromised by its unfettered pursuit of commercial advantage, wherever it was to be found? Growing German economic ties to China and Russia would make this issue increasingly salient in the twenty-first century. In the case of German energy dependence on Russia and its political consequences, the late 1990s marked a crucial turning point. That was when Chancellor Gerhard

Schröder and Vladimir Putin began their close friendship and the sinister Russian corporation Gazprom began to burrow into the German energy market with the help of former Stasi agents on its payroll.[286] In the new millennium, these issues had the potential to become a "German question" of a new kind.

EPILOGUE

—

RUSSIA INVADED UKRAINE ON FEBRUARY 24, 2022. GERMANY'S Social Democratic chancellor, Olaf Scholz, in office for less than three months, responded firmly to this "historic turning point in the history of our continent." His decision to increase German military expenditure and impose tough economic sanctions was widely seen as a "foreign policy turn-around."[1] Critics at home and abroad had long described Germany as a "reluctant hegemon," a major power unwilling to behave like one. Even a Polish foreign minister joined the chorus: Radek Sikorski told the German Council on Foreign Relations in 2011, "I fear German power less than I am beginning to fear German inactivity. You have become Europe's indispensable nation."[2] Germany served four times between 1995 and 2020 as a temporary member of the U.N. Security Council and made it (quietly) clear that it would welcome a permanent seat. But critics saw a country that walked away from the dilemmas of exercising power, preferring to stay on its moral high horse and exercise the right to look the other way because of the Nazi past.

In fact, the twenty-first-century Federal Republic was no longer a total abstainer when it came to the world's conflicts. But Germany picked its fights. After the attacks of 9/11 the Schröder administration sent seven thousand German soldiers to Afghanistan. "The Federal Republic of Germany is being defended in the Hindu Kush, too," said Defense Minister Peter Struck, although he later came to doubt the wisdom of the campaign.[3] The war in Afghanistan was unpopular in Germany. The second Gulf War of 2003 against Iraq was overwhelmingly unpopular, as it was across Western Europe, in countries such as Britain and Spain that participated as well as those like France and Germany that declined to do so. It is hard to disagree with what critics said at the time, that this was a war of choice with ulterior motives justified by dubious intelligence. Germany bore some responsibility for the dubious intelligence, although not the purpose to which it was put, because "Curveball," the Iraqi defector who made false claims about Saddam's biological weapons program, was an asset of the German intelligence service.[4]

In the following years Germany chose whether or not to engage in military missions on a case-by-case basis. It sent military observers to the Sudan in 2005 as part of a U.N. peacekeeping mission: "We must not look away when people . . . are murdered or persecuted," said Defense Minister Struck.[5] The calibrated approach continued in the era of Chancellor Angela Merkel, which began later in 2005. Germany refused to join the Anglo-French intervention against Libya in 2011. "There are no such things as surgical strikes," said Foreign Minister Guido Westerwelle. The German stance was criticized, once again, from both right and left. German public opinion provided no clear mandate: it was in favor of removing Muammar Qaddafi from power, but against the use of force to remove him.[6] But when Vladimir Putin's Russia annexed the Crimean peninsula in 2014 and gave military support to pro-Russian separatists in eastern Ukraine, Merkel worked closely with President Barack Obama and took the lead in securing European support for sanctions. Four years later, Merkel's response to the crisis in Syria and the emergence of the Islamic State was cautious. She condemned Syrian use of chemical weapons but made clear that Germany would not join the U.S., British, and French military strikes, although it did provide reconnaissance aircraft and a refueling plane. Merkel also criticized Putin's support for the Syrian regime, but gingerly. Olaf Scholz's response to the Russian invasion of Ukraine in 2022 did, therefore, mark a shift.

Three years earlier, the liberal German journalist Jochen Bittner, varying a famous comment by Theodore Roosevelt, suggested scornfully that Germany had perfected the ability to speak softly while carrying a big carrot.[7] Yet, as Bittner acknowledged, the Federal Republic had provided leadership, but in a different way. Global governance requires carrots as well as sticks. Germany had diplomatic credibility, not least because it did not deploy military power as frequently as the United States, Britain, or France did, and it had no colonial history in the Middle East or North Africa. Merkel was able to act as mediator between Russia and the West over the Georgia crisis in 2008. Germany was more trusted by both sides in the Middle East. German reluctance to participate in military missions was also balanced by its leadership on nonmilitary, humanitarian endeavors. Its willingness to accept refugees is exhibit A. Here, too, Germany was a large country that behaved like a small country—in the sense that it showed the kind of generosity typically displayed by small Scandinavian countries

rather than the lack of generosity displayed by Britain, France, and the
United States. The history of united Germany is a history of openness to
refugees and asylum seekers. It took in Jews escaping post-Soviet Russia
(more than 200,000 between 1990 and 2010), then hundreds of thousands
of refugees from former Yugoslavia, Iran, and Iraq in the 1990s, and from
Afghanistan after 2002. There were Kurds and Kosovars fleeing regional
conflicts, Ethiopians and Eritreans fleeing wars in Africa.[8] The numbers
involved could be huge. Just one year after unification, in 1991, Germany
accepted 250,000 asylum seekers from Yugoslavia alone (Britain admitted
4000).[9]

There were precedents, in other words, for Angela Merkel's dramatic
decision on Syrian refugees in August 2015. Some 6.5 million Syrians were
driven from their country after 2011 by civil war. Two million went to Lebanon, Jordan, Iraq, and Egypt, another 3.6 million (the largest single group)
to Turkey. Others, spilling out of refugee camps in the Middle East and
moving through Turkey or across the Adriatic, reached the borders of the
EU, where their presence set off fierce arguments and led Croatia and Hungary to build fences. Merkel's decision to accept all Syrian refugees, including those who had already sought asylum elsewhere, was rooted largely in
humanitarian impulses, although long-term calculation no doubt played
a part. Germany eventually accepted more than 573,000 Syrian refugees
in 2015, well over half of those who settled in non-Turkish Europe, and in
the course of 2015–16 the Federal Republic received applications from more
than a million first-time asylum seekers from Syria and elsewhere. Merkel's
unilateral decision encountered strong resistance from other Europeans,
including normal allies like France, who claimed she was placing the entire
Schengen system of open European borders in jeopardy. But her move led
to important changes in the Common European Asylum System, which
aimed to redistribute refugees more equally across the Continent.

By the time of the Syrian refugee crisis, Germany's leadership of
Europe was undisputed. Britain was preoccupied by the debates that led to
Brexit, France becoming less and less an equal partner. A Brussels bureaucrat described how, when the German position changed on an issue, other
countries quickly lined up behind it. That was unprecedented in the EU.[10]
The reason was economic dominance: Germany accounted for a fifth of
EU output and a quarter of its exports. It was the largest trading partner
of most EU member states and the EU's leading paymaster. Germany may
have been reluctant to exercise power with conventional political weapons,

but it pressed its wishes on others as a "geo-economic power."[11] That went back to the Maastricht Treaty in 1992 and the architecture of the future EU. Germany got what it wanted, a European Central Bank modeled on the German Federal Bank and a euro modeled on the Deutschmark. The EU economy was to be built on low inflation, tight money, and low public debt. Regional funds and other transfers were supposed to compensate the "softer" economies of Spain, Portugal, and Greece.

Two years after the euro was introduced in 1999, Germany (like France) fell out of compliance with its own rules on public debt. The rules were politely ignored. Not so during the Great Recession that began in 2008, triggered by the exposure of banks, pensions funds, and other institutions around the globe to the subprime securities they had purchased from American lenders. The situation was made worse by housing bubbles that burst in Ireland and Spain and by rising public debt. The financial crisis devastated the real economy. Output in the EU fell by a fifth from the fall of 2008 to the fall of 2009. The German economy remained on an upward trajectory, despite the losses its banks incurred from bad loans. But the German recipe for recovery, which became the European recipe, damaged the weaker economies. Greece was bailed out on very harsh terms monitored by the "troika"—the EU (led by Germany), the European Central Bank (based in Frankfurt), and the International Monetary Fund. The bailout became the template for austerity regimes elsewhere, causing the rise of populist parties across Europe. Merkel followed up by insisting in 2012 that EU rules be made more stringent through a "fiscal compact" that required all members to have a "debt brake" on public spending. While the German popular press indulged itself with self-congratulatory clichés about "prudent" Germans and "feckless" southern Europeans, caricatures of Merkel in Greece depicted her with a Hitler mustache and her policy as a second German invasion.

Merkel was widely praised, although not in southern Europe, for "steering" the EU through the Great Recession. But the austerity approach was damaging. Merkel's tight-money policy reflected a long-standing German preference based on memories of the 1923 hyperinflation. But Merkel also had less sympathy for Europe as an emotional or historical project than some predecessors. Adenauer and Kohl, both Rhinelanders, wanted to draw a line under a dark past by submerging Germany in Europe. Merkel was less swayed by ideas of solidarity. The German solution to the debt crisis was hypocritical, too. The Germans, after all, had benefited in the twentieth century from debt forgiveness, as the French economist Thomas Piketty pointed out.[12] The economic system that got the Greeks and others into trouble had also worked to Germany's advantage for years. German banks lent money to countries whose consumers bought German products, while the countries repaid the loans, and so the cycle continued until 2008. Germany had built up large trade surpluses with other EU members by extending them credit. To put it provocatively, "Germany blew the bubbles that popped in the rest of Europe."[13] It had come to resemble China, the export juggernaut that was everyone's creditor. Would it not be better, critics wondered, if Germany relaxed the fiscal prudence, eased down its large trade surplus, and directed more of its impressive economic output to domestic consumers?

German domestic consumption was weak because globalization had caused fundamental changes in its economy and how wealth was distributed. The changes were easy to miss because Germany remained the same on the surface: an economic dynamo powered by exports. But much had been transformed beneath the surface. Privatization and deregulation made Germany more like Anglo-Saxon economies, while German firms located their production increasingly in low-cost countries in Europe and beyond. The reforms introduced by the Schröder administration and known as Hartz IV (after the former Volkswagen executive who recommended them) weakened labor protection and lowered unemployment benefits, encouraging low-paid "mini-jobs." A two-tiered job market developed. Skilled and unionized workers still enjoyed high wages, but unemployment remained low only because of the growth in low-wage and part-time jobs. Germany had no minimum wage until 2015. All this exerted downward pressure on living standards. The Federal Republic in 2018 had more working poor than any other EU state. Germans had surprisingly low median household assets, lower than Italians or Spaniards. Some of that was because households were smaller and rates of home ownership lower, but not all. The sociologist Gerhard Bosch described the much vaunted German social model as "a Swiss cheese where the holes are getting larger and larger."[14] Meanwhile, the number of very rich people grew. In 2011 Germany had 400,000 dollar-millionaires (up from 67,000 in 1985) and 839 "super-rich" households worth more than $100 million, second only to the United States (2692) and slightly ahead of Saudi Arabia (826).[15] This was interesting company to keep for a country that had once boasted of its broad middle-class society. The rise of social inequality as a result of what the historian Hans-

Ulrich Wehler called "turbo-capitalism" and "casino capitalism" did not go uncriticized.[16] Neoliberal globalization was targeted by the left and the Greens as well as the right-wing Alternative for Germany (AfD). There were large antiglobalization protests, most dramatically at the G20 summit in Hamburg in July 2017.

German-Chinese economic relations offer a perfect example of the dilemmas created by the new global regime. Trade between the two countries grew phenomenally in the early twenty-first century. German exports to China more than quadrupled between 2000 and 2018, even as exports to the United States fell. The two lines seem sure to cross soon. When it comes to German imports, they already have. By 2018 China provided almost 10 percent of all German imports, becoming the largest non-European supplier and overtaking the United States. Each country also invests heavily in the other. Since 1985, 350 German companies have established themselves in the port city of Taicang, an hour northwest of Shanghai. Most are engaged in manufacturing, although they have created a market for the sausage and sauerkraut served at the local Schindlers Tankstelle restaurant. The German family-owned firm Storopack, a global leader in protective packaging, opened its first manufacturing facility in China in 2000. By 2013 it had ten.[17]

So where is the problem? There are several. German exports to China are impressive, but the long-term outlook is uncertain. Germany's strengths—in machine tools, chemicals, motor vehicles, and specialist products like tunneling equipment—exactly meet current Chinese needs but may not in the future. There is also a risk that German companies train local managers, who then leave to establish competitors, a pattern already visible. When it comes to Chinese inward investment in Germany, security issues are the major concern. When the Chinese sovereign wealth fund bought up German woodlands, it ruffled feathers because of the mythic "German Forest"; but investment in security-related branches—energy, transportation, the digital infrastructure—touched a more sensitive nerve. In December 2018 the federal government tightened the regulations on foreign investment in ways that were clearly aimed at China. This was part of a larger unease about China's global agenda.[18] Germany took the lead in negotiating an EU investment protection deal with China, the Comprehensive Agreement on Investment signed in January 2021. But Germany and its European partners faced two major issues, as did Japan. One was how to balance relations with the United States against its growing trade with China. The other was how to reconcile its trade interests with its commitment to human rights, which were violated every day in the People's Republic.

The human rights issue goes well beyond China, or Russia, where Germany has had a long and uncomfortably cozy relationship with Gazprom. German companies that built factories overseas where labor was cheap and legislation on workplace health and safety scant were always making a Faustian bargain. So were companies that exported hazardous waste to the global South in contravention of the Basel Convention. Greenpeace called Germany the "world champion waste exporter" in the 1990s.[19] Then there was the case of German companies selling chemicals to Syria that could be used to manufacture chemical weapons. Accusations of illegal or borderline-illegal arms sales have been leveled at Germany for decades.[20] The country's habitual stance of moral rectitude makes it understandable that some take pleasure in calling this hypocrisy. The same might be said about elements of the much vaunted *Energiewende,* the "energy transformation," embarked on a decade ago. Germany has been rightly praised for boldness in addressing climate change and investing heavily in renewables. After the Fukushima nuclear disaster of 2011, the German government decided to decommission all its nuclear power plants by 2022, a popular decision although one that sat uneasily with the original thrust of the policy to reduce CO_2 emissions and also increased its dependence on Russia. The hypocrisy? Germany accepts plaudits for phasing out nuclear power, but imports electricity from France and the Czech Republic that is generated by . . . nuclear power.[21] Not every instance of hypocrisy is an ethical violation and not every ethical violation becomes public knowledge. One that did, spectacularly, is the Volkswagen emissions scandal that broke in 2016. It gave "Made in Germany" a new meaning. The scandal pointed up the potential hazards confronting the German economic juggernaut in an age of global trade and a global news cycle.

The news cycle is a reminder that globalization is about much more than capital flows, labor markets, and trade. It encompasses communications networks, the movement of people, the exchange of ideas, and the intermingling of cultures on an unprecedented scale. All create possibilities both good and bad. Reputable German publications and news outlets such as *Die Zeit* have a global online presence thanks to their English editions, but far-right groups in Germany have also exploited the internet to spread their message. The connections among scholars and students promoted by organizations like the German Academic Exchange Service and the EU's

Erasmus Programme promote intellectual encounters that most would consider desirable and blameless, except perhaps for their tendency to leave a heavy carbon footprint. But what about the exchange that transferred soccer hooliganism from its birthplace in 1970s England to Germany and other parts of the Continent? The German groups even adopted English names, like Bayern München's "Munich Service Crew."[22]

A more ambiguous instance of cross-border movement is the case of Germans who took their wealth abroad, whether as vacationers, second-home owners, or retirees. Their presence could be positive (they learned something about a different country, perhaps even its language, and injected money into the local economy); but it could also be negative. German tourists crowding the beaches of Dalmatia were a source of irritation; the colonizing of whole areas of Tuscany and of Kenya's Diani Beach by German homeowners raised more awkward question about the dominance of foreign wealth.[23] Take the case of Germans on the Spanish island of Mallorca. At the end of the twentieth century, 70,000 German citizens owned property there. That meant a fifth of all the land was in German hands. Mass tourism brought another 3.5 million visitors a year. That is why a Bavarian Christian Democrat suggested facetiously that Mallorca become a seventeenth federal state. The arrogance is astounding. Yet the reality was that 35,000 of the Germans on the island lived there permanently, mostly in retirement, and a Spanish niche industry had developed to care for and nurse elderly Germans.

The arrival of asylum seekers is what comes to mind first when we think about Germany and recent cross-border movements of people. Refugees changed the face of the country—they, and the second- and third-generation Turkish-Germans and others born to former guest workers who settled in Germany. Their presence changed how Germany looked and felt—the names and appearance of its people, the stores, the faces on television, the popular music and those who performed it, the writers and filmmakers. A Rip van Winkle who fell asleep in Frankfurt in 1970 and woke up forty years later would have been astonished. Five out of six children under six years of age were non-German by ethnicity, or had "immigrant backgrounds," as the phrase went. This transformation was accompanied by some ugly, xenophobic reactions, as it was elsewhere in Europe, even in bastions of liberal tolerance like Scandinavia. There was physical violence against foreigners. A first cluster of violence followed unification and came at a time when the number of asylum seekers was growing fast, although it was not always they who were targeted. In September 1991 a building occupied by Mozambican and Vietnamese contract workers in the East German town of Hoyerswerda was attacked with Molotov cocktails, bottles, and rocks until the inhabitants were evacuated. Hundreds of onlookers cheered the attackers. The following year a hostel for Vietnamese and asylum-seeking Roma in Rostock, also in the former East, was assaulted with rocks and improvised explosives. Again, the victims were evacuated. More deadly attacks took place in the West. A home occupied by Turks in Mölln was firebombed in November 1992: three died. Six months later another Turkish family was firebombed in Solingen: all five people in the house were killed. It is important to record that in December 1992 and January 1993, after Mölln, almost two million Germans took part in candlelit vigils.[24]

Violence against "foreigners" never disappeared completely. In the case of the self-styled National Socialist Underground, the violence became a deadly terrorist campaign. Its members came from the East German town of Jena and were radicalized as teenagers by the attacks at Hoyerswerda and Rostock. They killed ethnic Turks, Kurds, and Greeks, and they detonated a nail bomb in a Turkish neighborhood of Cologne. The group did not publicize its killings. Only after its existence was uncovered in 2011 were the killings of the previous decade shown to be linked.[25] With the surge of asylum seekers a few years later, Germany witnessed levels of violence against foreign-born people not seen since the early 1990s. Two new political organizations exploited German fears: AfD, founded in 2013, and the anti-Islamic PEGIDA, founded the following year. But there was also an outpouring of welcome for Syrians and other refugees by Germans responding to Merkel's famous assertion that "we can do it!"

Just a few years on, the impact of the most recent arrivals has yet to be seen. The challenge of so many arriving so quickly is real, and concern is not restricted to ultra-nationalist xenophobes or calculating politicians on the right who use coded language.[26] Recent arrivals make up a disproportionate number of those living in poverty in German cities. Large numbers of vulnerable immigrants have also made Germany a major center of human trafficking. The Federal Republic's poor record in combating this has attracted critical attention from the EU, the U.S. State Department, UNICEF, and antitrafficking NGOs.[27] But the architecture of integration exists, in the training and apprenticeship system, in the provision of language and civics courses, and in the overhaul of the legal framework belatedly adapted to the reality of earlier immigrants in Germany, above all former guest workers and their children. Reform was under consideration in the late 1980s, delayed by unification, and eventually arrived with the new millennium. In 2000, the citizenship law of 1913, based on blood, was finally revised and citizenship opened to millions of people who had lived in Germany, many of them for more than twenty years. It was automatically granted to the children of parents with a residence permit or who had lived in Germany for at least eight years. A route to citizenship was also created for non-EU adults. A revised immigration law also came into effect in 2005, tightening controls and giving priority to skilled workers, but also allocating funding to language courses.

New arrivals in Germany in the twenty-first century, whether immigrants or asylum seekers, joined what had become a multicultural society. It was impossible to miss in German city streets and in the most prominent German institutions. Eleven of the twenty-three players in the German 2010 World Cup squad had a foreign background, meaning that they had either been born outside Germany or had a non-German parent.

The German 2010 World Cup squad. The eleven players with foreign backgrounds were Miroslav Klose, Lukas Podolski, and Piotr Trochowski (Polish); Mesut Özil and Serdar Tasci (Turkish); Marco Marin (Bosnian); Mario Gomez (Spanish); Cacau, nicknamed Helmut (Brazilian); and the African trio of Dennis Aogo (Nigerian), Jérôme Boateng (Ghanaian), and Sami Khedira (Tunisian).

In politics, Turkish-German Cem Özdemir was cochair of the Green Party for ten years, a member of parliament, and a member of the European Parliament. Aminata Touré, born in Neumünster of parents who fled Mali after the 1991 coup there, was elected at age twenty-five to the state parliament in Schleswig-Holstein and became its vice president in 2019. The German parliament elected in 2017 contained 58 out of 709 members who were either not themselves born German citizens or had a parent who was not. The numbers were highest for the left (the Greens and the Social Democrats), much lower for the Christian Democrats, but 8 of the 92 AfD representatives also had non-German or partly non-German backgrounds of various kinds.[28] The same multiculturalism could be observed in journalism, cinema, and literature.

The flowering of German-Turkish literature has received especially close attention. It encompasses dozens of major figures writing in diverse styles. One strand was the so-called angry-young-Turkish-man Kanak-literature, which took its name from a derogatory term used about Turks by Germans, although it also owed a debt to American underground and rap culture. German-Turkish literature includes a range of forms, high and low, serious and playful: expressionist poetry, satire, a German-Turkish version of "chick lit," and the genre of the *Katzenkrimi* created by Akif Pirinçci, whose feline detective Francis solves mysteries in the Felidae series of books. These are authors who write in German and they cannot be easily pigeonholed.[29] As the literary scholar Karin Yesilada has said, the Turkish-German cultural scene is both Turkish and German but also many other things besides: Its members are "lyricists and novelists, lovers of Paul Celan, Martin Scorsese fans, auteur filmmakers, theater actors, peace activists, Muslims, CDU members of parliament, vegetarians, smokers, etc."[30]

There is a wonderful moment in Fatih Akin's 2004 film *Head On* when the lead male character goes to Istanbul and takes a taxi. The Hamburg-born Cahit speaks Turkish poorly but quickly discovers that his Turkish cabdriver was brought up in Munich ("oh God, a Bavarian") and the two then carry on talking in German.[31] Akin's films are defined by characters with complex multicultural identities. Like Turkish-German literature, they represent a new departure in German culture. The acclaim that Akin's films garnered beyond Germany demonstrates something else, too. After Young German Cinema directors like Wim Wenders and Rainer Werner Fassbinder established the reputation of German movies in the 1970s, they were succeeded by a generation of directors born in the 1960s or '70s, such as

Christian Petzold (*Barbara*), Tom Tywker (*Run Lola Run*), Maren Ade (*Toni Erdmann*), and Jan-Ole Gerster (*A Coffee in Berlin*). All won international recognition and awards. So did Wenders's near contemporary, the Austrian Michael Haneke, who has made films in French, German, and English.

It is not hard to find other examples of German high culture achieving global recognition. By one measure, the Nobel Prize for Literature, it enjoyed an extraordinary run of success between 1999 and 2019, with four Nobel laureates, although two were Austrians (Elfriede Jelinek and Peter Handke), one was Romanian-German (Herta Müller), and the fourth came from a city that had long been called Gdansk (Günter Grass)—all witnesses to German history beyond the borders of the present nation-state. But it was not only canonical German works of the past that enjoyed success. So did new works, new impulses. That was nowhere more obvious than in modern art. By the late twentieth century, German artists were making waves globally among gallerists, collectors, and museumgoers, admired for their formal innovation and their ambition, scrutinized for what (if anything) they had to say about the state of Germany. American critic Peter Schjeldahl, writing in 1997, recalled meeting one of these artists, Martin Kippenberger, in Madrid. He disliked him but recognized "a leading light in the fourth generation of a German art juggernaut."[32] Germany also retained its reputation as an innovative center of modern dance. That derived in the contemporary era, above all, from the Pina Bausch's dance theater. In 2020, Sadler's Wells in London described her as bringing about "a revolution that was to emancipate, and redefine dance throughout the world."[33] The company continued after her death in 2009, drawing dancers from around the globe. Count them among the numerous world-class performers in different fields who work in Germany and give its culture such a cosmopolitan feel. At present, just eleven of the top forty-one orchestras in Germany have musical directors who are German or Austrian. The other thirty come from eighteen different countries. In the nineteenth century everyone in the world wanted a German conductor; in the twenty-first century the world came to Germany to conduct.

These are among the myriad ways in which German culture features prominently in global culture—global high culture, that is. High culture has, of course, been dethroned as the only culture that matters. Imagine, then, that you have no interest in art-house movies or modern dance, classical music or modern art. Do the styles and sounds and images that define German popular culture also belong to a broader, global culture? They certainly do, and it is nowhere more evident than in the popular music scene, where multiple non-German influences have combined to create syncretic genres. The eleven-member Berlin band Seeed, founded in 1998, mixes hip-hop, dub, and reggae styles and sings in German, English, and Jamaican patois. The three lead singers are a Basque-German and two West African–Germans. The dance-hall and hip-hop group Culcha Candela is another incarnation of multicultural Germany. The group sings in four languages. Its members have Colombian, Ugandan, and Polish backgrounds and the band's DJ is Korean.[34] One of the earliest rap and hip-hop scenes in Germany emerged in Stuttgart, as the city cast off its reputation for provincialism and became a hub of multicultural energy. Massive Töne, founded in 1991, modeled itself on American and French hip-hop groups. It formed part of a hip-hop collective in the city and often collaborated with others like Freundeskreis, surely the only hip-hop artists in the world who sing in Esperanto as well as German, French, and English. A striking aspect of these musical groups is how they combine rich musical genres and multilingual lyrics with an intense but nonconservative local patriotism. Massive Töne were well-known supporters of VfB Stuttgart soccer team and sang affectionately in "Mutterstadt" about the local pleasures of their native city on the Neckar, expressing scorn for the newly rich who jetted off on foreign vacations when they could stay in Stuttgart.

Much of the culture that Germans consume today would seem familiar to people around the world—soccer, of course, world music, K-pop and American popular music, detective series and reality shows on television. The growing presence of American popular culture began in the old Federal Republic, with a sharply increased percentage of Hollywood film on German screens (there was an increase in East Germany, too, but less sharp), and the opening of the airwaves in the 1980s to new, private TV channels like SAT1 and RTL. One aspect of Americanization was the arrival of music TV, in the form of VIVA. Established to provide a German competitor to MTV, VIVA started to falter when MTV-Germany began in 1997 and the company was eventually bought by MTV in 2005. Its history provides an object lesson in how popular culture is part of a world of global takeovers, mergers, and acquisitions.

While it was on the air, VIVA tried to bring politics to a young audience in entertaining ways. In 2002 the channel produced a signature moment in German political discourse. Two years earlier, Free Democratic leader Guido Westerwelle had climbed into the Container on RTL2's *Big Brother* show. In

2002 it was Franz Münterfering's turn to be "on the couch" for an interview with VIVA-Zwei ("the CNN of music television"). Münterfering was the secretary general of the Social Democrats at the time, and had overseen the move of the capital from Bonn to Berlin while a minister in the Schröder administration. When he appeared on the show, the twenty-three-year-old moderator, Sarah Kuttner, welcomed her guest, turned to the camera, and said, *"Der eine oder der andere hat sich vielleicht gefragt,* Who the fuck is Franz Münterfering?"* A stony-faced Münterfering (born in 1940) was no doubt thinking that no one had ever before introduced a German government minister that way and wondering why he had agreed to appear.[35] It was a perfect symbol of the adoption by young Germans of a hip, casual style that was deliberately "un-German" to the degree that it adopted unstuffy American words—although, in this case, a word that could not have been used on American network television.

In the 1830s and '40s, "Young Germany" had denoted a group of writers who, like their counterparts in Italy and France, advocated the cause of liberalism, democracy, and women's rights. Its members were few and its readers limited in number. Young Germany in the early twenty-first century described a much broader, more diffuse, casual, multicultural generation within an aging nation, a generation that nonetheless helped to create Germany's image in the world. Bands like Seeed were the headline acts at foreign music festivals. Berlin drew people to it, especially young people, not because of the symphony or ballet, but because it was the city of hipsters and creatives, techno clubs like Berghain, yoga studios, and artisan bakeries, fashion week and the Love Parade. In 2012 the *New York Times Magazine* reported on an Australian who had to leave Berlin because he was having too much fun to get anything done. The city's English-language website was called Toytown Germany. If the Schröder administration borrowed a lot from Tony Blair's New Labour in its Hartz IV reforms, Klaus Wowereit ("Wowi"), Berlin's gay mayor, appeared to be borrowing Blair's clever branding of "Cool Britannia." In Berlin as much as London, the multicultural energy was real, the cool, hipster image proved to be a compelling brand, but there was a largely invisible underside of poverty, unemployment, and residents who were unable to afford inflated property prices.[36]

Berlin might have pushed its poor out of sight, but the past was still

---

* The first half of Kuttner's introduction means "Some of you may have asked yourselves," before she continued in English.

everywhere around. Occasionally it made its presence dangerously felt from one of the estimated fifteen thousand unexploded bombs in the city.[37] Many traces of the recent Communist past have been removed, both street names and buildings like the Palace of the Republic, but impressive imagination has been devoted to remembering the Nazi past. Daniel Libeskind's Jewish Museum has been justly praised for its startling originality, but it is not alone. At the Bebelplatz memorial to the 1933 book burning, you look through a glass plate set in the cobblestones to empty bookshelves below. The Memorial to the Murdered Jews of Europe has a deliberately uneven floor and differently sized concrete slabs so that visitors walking through it feel a sense of disorientation, while all around the city are *Stolpersteine* ("stumbling stones") embedded in sidewalks, each commemorating a single victim. It is not just in Berlin, though, and not just in its memorials, that the National Socialist era—now more than seventy-five years in the past—remains a reference point, a part of the German past that present-day Germany has accepted as an indelible part of its identity. It is there in history books, novels, films, and music. *"Leg dein Ohr auf die Schiene der Geschichte,"* sing the Stuttgart rappers Freundeskreis: Lay your ear on the railroad track of history.

The German history in question, above all the history of the Holocaust, has also become a part of global history. That was already starting to happen in the 1970s and '80s, but the process speeded up after the Cold War ended. Auschwitz became a "global site of memory" and the Holocaust the "emblematic memory for the twentieth century," a universal symbol of genocide and inhumanity: the world's civic lesson.[38] In the process, something that acute observers like Hans Magnus Enzensberger had long pointed out about debates among Germans, that they risked becoming purely ritual invocations, threatened to become true universally. Thirty years ago, in the early days of the internet, Mike Godwin, an American lawyer and writer, coined Godwin's law, which stipulated that as an online discussion thread becomes longer, the probability of a comparison involving the Nazis or Hitler approaches, at which point the value of the discussion ends. As Holocaust museums and memorials have multiplied in countries around the world, they have sometimes served to deflect attention away from those countries' treatment of Indigenous or colonial peoples. There is one final irony that follows from the phenomenon of the global Holocaust. Some now point to the former perpetrators, note how thoroughly they have come to terms with their dark past, and urge us to "learn from the Germans." In that sense, the twentieth century really was the German century after all.

ACKNOWLEDGMENTS

—

ONE OF THE PLEASURES OF FINISHING A BOOK IS THE OPPORtunity it presents for thanking the people and institutions who helped in its making. I had two academic homes while working on this book, Harvard and Vanderbilt. I want to express my gratitude for the friendship, collegiality, and intellectual stimulation provided by colleagues at both universities. I would particularly like to thank Charles Maier, Patrice Higonnet, Alison Frank Johnson, Niall Ferguson, Mary Lewis, Peter Gordon, and Emma Rothschild at Harvard, and Helmut Walser Smith, Meike Werner, Ari Joskowicz, Jim Epstein, Emily Greble, Michael Bess, Joel Harrington, Catherine Molineux, and Peter Lake at Vanderbilt. Special thanks go to Joel, who very kindly read the first two chapters of the book in draft. A host of talented undergraduate and graduate students in Cambridge and Nashville had questions and interests of their own that kept me thinking anew about history. Those of us privileged to teach and mentor students learn greatly from doing so. I am also grateful to deans at both institutions for sabbatical leaves that allowed me to make progress on the book.

One of those leaves, in 2017–18, was spent at the Institute for Advanced Study in Princeton. It would be hard to imagine a more ideal scholarly setting. My thanks to Glen Bowersock, Jonathan Haslam, Jonathan Israel, Joan Scott, and many others at the institute who helped to make the experience so rewarding, and particular thanks to the group of fellow members whose collegiality made it a memorable year: Timothy Brook, Catherine Clark, Kathleen Coleman, Cynthia Hahn, William Diebold, Alison Games, Jörg Peltzer, Jonathan Unglaub, and Angela Zimmerman.

I used three principal libraries while working on the book: Widener Library at Harvard, the Heard Library at Vanderbilt, and the Firestone Library at Princeton. I am very glad to record here my gratitude to the staff of all three for their unfailing helpfulness. My sincere thanks also to institutions that have made German sources, especially older ones, much more widely available in digitized form than they were when this project began: the Bayerische Landesbibliothek and HathiTrust deserve special mention in this regard.

The material in this book has been delivered in the form of lectures and conference and seminar papers on some four dozen occasions to audiences in the United States, Canada, Germany, Russia, England, Scotland, and Australia. I would like to thank the individuals and institutions that invited me and the audience members for their questions, critical engagement, and encouragement. Special thanks to John Breuilly, Marta Hanson, Peter Holquist, and John McNeill for sending helpful suggestions and comments after they heard my talks. I also want to thank Patrice Dabrowski, Eric Kurlander, Kris Manjapra, Christopher Mapes, and Annette Schlagenhauff for bringing material to my attention that I would otherwise have missed. This is a work of synthesis, which is based on extensive printed sources but also on a very large number of secondary works, many of them highly specialized, all of them instructive. I therefore owe an enormous debt to the thousands of scholars, most of them personally unknown to me, whose work I have read with profit. They form a true global community of scholars of which I am proud to be a part.

I began writing the book in February 2014, completed a first draft in November 2021, and made extensive revisions during the following six months. A final round of corrections and minor revisions took place, after the copyediting process, during the final weeks of summer in 2022. I would like to express my thanks to Robert Weil, my remarkable editor at Liveright/W. W. Norton, for his energy, sharp eye, and commitment to this book. I owe an enormous debt of gratitude to my wonderful copyeditor, Trent Duffy. All authors should be so fortunate. In addition, I should like to thank Haley Bracken at Liveright, as well as Kathleen Karcher for her work in obtaining permissions for the illustrations. I should also like to thank, once again, my New York agent, Robin Straus, and my former London agent, Maggie Hanbury.

My thanks go, finally, to Celia Applegate, my colleague, fellow historian of Germany, and wife. She laid aside her own work to read every word of this manuscript in draft, but that generosity is only a small part of what I owe to her. Through the years when I was working on this book she has been my intellectual companion and closest friend, a true *Lebensgefährtin*, who has enriched my life with her intelligence, wit, and love. The book is dedicated to her.

NOTES

INTRODUCTION

1 Prasenjit Duara, *Rescuing History from the Nation* (Chicago, 1995); Andrew Wimmer and Nina Glick Schiller, "Methodological Nationalism and Beyond," *Global Networks: A Journal of Transnational Affairs* 2, no. 4 (2002): 301–34.

2 Jürgen Zimmerer, *Von Windhuk nach Auschwitz?* (Berlin, 2011).

3 Jacques Revel, *Jeux d'échelles. La micro-analyse à l'expérience* (Paris, 1996).

4 Henri Lefebvre, *The Production of Space* (Cambridge, Mass., 1991), 86.

5 See Homi K. Bhabha, *The Location of Culture* (London, 1994).

6 Peter Burke, *Cultural Hybridity* (Malden, Mass., 2009), 34–65.

7 Gerald Curzon, *Wotton and His Worlds* (Philadelphia, 2004).

8 Brendan Simms, *Europe* (New York, 2013), 42.

9 Jürgen Osterhammel, "Global History in a National Context: The Case of Germany," *Österreichische Zeitschrift fur Geschichtswissenschaft* 20, no. 2 (2009): 40–58.

10 Nicholas Canny, "Atlantic History," in *Atlantic History*, ed. Horst Pietschmann (Göttingen, 2002), 58.

11 Wolfgang Reinhardt, *Gebhardt/Handbuch der deutschen Geschichte*, vol. 9, *Probleme deutscher Geschichte 1495–1806: Reichsreform und Reformation 1495–1555* (Stuttgart, 2004), 55–57, 223–54; Thomas Brady, *German Histories in the Age of Reformations, 1400–1650* (New York, 2009), 12–20; John Watts, *The Making of Politics: Europe, 1300–1500* (New York, 2009), 353–55; Bethany Wiggin, "Monolinguism, World Literature, and the Return of History," *GSR* 41, no. 3 (2018): 491.

12 Karl S. Guthke, *Exploring the Interior* (Cambridge, 2018), 7.

13 Peter Sloterdijk, *Im Weltinnenraum des Kapitals* (Frankfurt/Main, 2005), 263.

14 Suzanne Marchand, *German Orientalism in the Age of Empire* (Princeton, N.J., 2009), 49.

15 A. G. Dickens, *The German Nation and Martin Luther* (London, 1974); Steven Ozment, *The Reformation in the Cities* (New Haven, 1975); Heinz Schilling, *Konfessionskonflikt und Staatsbildung* (Gütersloh, 1981).

16 C. A. Bayly, *The Birth of the Modern World, 1780–1914* (Malden, Mass., 2004), 451–87.

17 See Arnd Bauerkämper and Grzegorz Rossolinski-Liebe, eds., *Fascism Without Borders* (New York, 2017).

18 Patricia Clavin, "Defining Transnationalism," *ConEH* 14, no. 4 (2005): 424.

19 E. P. Thompson, *The Making of the English Working Class* (Harmondsworth, Eng., 1968), 417.

20 Emmanuel Le Roy Ladurie, "A Concept: The Unification of the Globe by Disease," in *The Mind and Method of the Historian* (Chicago, 1981), 28–91.

21 David Blackbourn, "Honey, I Shrunk German History," *German Studies Association Newsletter* 38, no. 2 (2013–2014): 44–53.

CHAPTER ONE: NEW WORLDS

1 Lewis W. Spitz, *Conrad Celtis* (Cambridge, Mass., 1957), 39–40.

2 Albrecht Classen, "Die Ibirische Halbinsel aus der Sicht eines humanistischen Nürnberger Gelehrten," *Mitteilungen des Instituts für Österreichische Geschichtsforschung* 111 (2003): 317–40.

3 Reinhard Baumann, *Landsknechte* (Munich, 1994); Thomas Brady, *German Histories in the Age of Reformations, 1400–1650* (New York, 2009), 351–53.

4 Lisa Jardine, *Worldly Goods* (New York, 1996), 100.

5 Spitz, *Conrad Celtis*, 11–19.

6 Michel Mollat du Jourdin, *Europe and the Sea* (Cambridge, Mass., 1993), 80–81; Fernand Braudel, *The Mediterranean and the Mediterranean World in the Age of Philip II* (London, 1975), 1:209–10.

7 Ulinka Rublack, *Dressing Up* (New York, 2010), 47.

8 Hermann Kellenbenz, *Die Fugger in Spanien und Portugal bis 1560*, vol. 1 (Munich, 1990); Jürgen Pohle, *Deutschland und die überseeische Expansion Portugals im 15. und 16. Jahrhundert* (Munich, 2000); Susan Dackerman, ed., *Prints and the Pursuit of Knowledge in Early Modern Europe* (Cambridge, Mass., 2011), 164–73; Andrew Robison and Klaus Albrecht Schröder, eds., *Albrecht Dürer* (New York, 2013), 284–85.

9 "Forum: Globalizing Early Modern German History," *GH* 31, no. 3 (2013): 366–82.

10 Christine R. Johnson, *The German Discovery of the World* (Charlottesville, Va., 2008), 143; Jerry Brotton, *Trading Territories* (Ithaca, N.Y., 1998), 127.

11 J. H. Elliott, *The Old World and the New, 1492–1650* (Cambridge, 1970), 84.

12 Horst Pietschmann, "Introduction," in *Atlantic History*, ed. Horst Pietschmann (Göttingen, 2002), 15.

13 This saying is attributed to Francisco Ugarte de Hermosa by Henry Kamen, *Golden Age Spain* (New York, 2005), 23, and to Ludovico Ariosto by Brendan Simms, *Europe* (New York, 2013), 34.

14 Christopher B. Krebs, *A Most Dangerous Book* (New York, 2011).

15 Walther Vogel, *Die Deutschen als Seefahrer* (Hamburg, 1949), 104; Pius Malekandathil, *The Germans, the Portuguese and India* (Münster, 1999), 23–25.

16 Hermann Kellenbenz, "Die Finanzierung der spanischen Entdeckungen," *VSWG* 69, no. 2 (1982): 168–69.

17 John Darwin, *After Tamerlane* (New York, 2008), 95–96.

18 Mollat du Jourdin, *Europe and the Sea*, 62, 147.

19 J. R. McNeill and William H. McNeill, *The Human Web* (New York, 2003), 163–64.

20 T. Bentley Duncan, "Navigation Between Portugal and Asia in the Sixteenth and Seventeenth Centuries," in *Asia and the World*, ed. Cyriac K. Pullapilly and Edwin J. Van Kley (Notre Dame, Ind., 1986), 7–11.

21 Malekandathil, *Germans, Portuguese and India*, 32–33.

22 Hans Staden, *True History*, ed. Neil Whitehead and Michael Harbsmeier (Durham, N.C., 2008); Eve Duffy and Alida Metcalf, *The Return of Hans Staden* (Baltimore, 2012).

23 Carlo Cipolla, *European Culture and Overseas Expansion* (Harmondsworth, Eng., 1970), 39–40.

24 Karl Heinz Panhorst, *Deutschland und Amerika* (Munich, 1928), 39; Malekandathil, *Germans, Portuguese and India*, 39.

25 J. C. Sharman, *Empires of the Weak* (Princeton, N.J., 2019), 47–64.

26 Dietmar Rothermund, "Asian Emporia and European Bridgeheads," in *Emporia, Commodities, and Entrepreneurs in Asian Maritime Trade, c. 1400–1750*, ed. Roderich Ptak and Dietmar Rothermund (Stuttgart, 1991), 7.

27 Duffy and Metcalf, *Return of Hans Staden*, 30–32; Malekandathil, *Germans, Portuguese and India*, 35–42.

28 Friedrich Edelmayer, *Söldner und Pensionäre* (Vienna, 2002), 250.

29 Ulrich Schmidel, *Reise nach Süd-Amerika in den Jahren 1534 bis 1554*, ed. Valentin Langmantel (Tübingen, 1889), 21.

30 Gene Rhea Tucker, "The Discovery of Germany in America," *Traversea: Journal of Transatlantic History* 1 (2011): 26–45.

31 J. H. Parry, *The Age of Reconnaissance* (London, 1963), 162.

32 The following discussion draws on Götz Simmer, *Gold und Sklaven* (Berlin, 2000) and Jörg Denzer, *Die Konquista der Augsburger Welser-Gesellschaft in Südamerika 1528–1556* (Munich, 2005).

33 Stefan Lang, "Colonial Failure in the New World in the Sixteenth Century" (MPhil thesis, University of Birmingham [U.K.], 2011).

34 Denzer, *Die Konquista*, 152–56, 191–93.

35 Lang, "Colonial Failure," 66.

36 Denzer, *Die Konquista*, 93.

37 Ibid., 13–16, 218–50.

38 Günter Kahle, "Deutsche Landsknechte, Legionäre und Militärinstrukteure in Lateinamerika," *JbLA* 30 (1983): 355–66; Lawrence Clayton, *Bartolomé de las Casas and the Conquest of the Americas* (Malden, Mass., 2011).

39 Panhorst, *Deutschland und Amerika*, 181.

40 Hermann Kellenbenz, "Portugiesische Forschungen und Quellen zur Behaimfrage," *Mitteilungen des Vereins für Geschichte der Stadt Nürnbergs* 48 (1958): 79–95; Otto Berninger, "Martin Behaim," *Mitteilungen der Fränkischen Geographischen Gesellschaft* 6 (1959): 141–51; Johannes Willers, ed., *Focus Behaim-Globus* (Nuremberg, 1990); Peter J. Bräunlein, *Martin Behaim* (Bamberg, 1992).

41 Bräunlein, *Martin Behaim*, 27.

42 The writer is Theodor Gustav Werner: see ibid., 43–44.

43 Brotton, *Trading Territories*, 54–60; Andrew Massing, "Mapping the Malagueta Coast" and "Valentin Fernandes' Five Maps and the Early History and Geography of São Tomé," *History in Africa* 36 (2009): 331–65 and 367–86.

44 Bräunlein, *Martin Behaim*, 39.

45 https://bayern-online.de/nuernberg/erleben/wissenswertes/der-behaim-globus/.

46 Donald Lach, *Asia in the Making of Europe* (Chicago, 1965), 1:70; Willers, ed., *Focus Behaim-Globus*.

47 Bräunlein, *Martin Behaim*, 84–85.

48 Douglas Hunter, *The Race to the West* (New York, 2011).

49 Jardine, *Worldly Goods*, 53.

50 Malekandathil, *Germans, Portuguese and India*, 1–22.

51 Lach, *Asia in the Making of Europe*, 1:107–10.

52 Beate Borowka-Clausberg, *Balthasar Sprenger und der frühneuzeitliche Reisebericht* (Munich, 1999).

53 Lach, *Asia in the Making of Europe*, 1:110–28.

54 Johnson, *German Discovery of the World*, 123–65.

55 Malekandathil, *Germans, Portuguese and India*, 55–56.

56 Andreas Hauptman et al., "The Shipwreck of the 'Bom Jesus,'" *Journal of African Archaeology* 14, no. 2 (2016): 181–207.

57 Om Prakash, *Bullion for Goods* (New Delhi, 2004), 56–57; Johnson, *German Discovery of the World,* 191–95; Lach, *Asia in the Making of Europe,* 1:133–37.

58 Malekandathil, *Germans, Portuguese and India,* 97.

59 Sanjay Subrahmanyam, "An Augsburger in Asia Portuguesa," in Ptak and Rothermund, eds., *Emporia, Commodities, and Entrepreneurs,* 401–22.

60 Michael N. Pearson, "Markets and Merchant Communities in the Indian Ocean," in *Portuguese Oceanic Expansion, 1400–1800,* ed. Francisco Bethencourt and Diogo Ramada Curto (New York, 2007), 103.

61 Subrahmanyam, "An Augsburger in Asia Portuguesa," 409.

62 Malekandathil, *Germans, Portuguese and India,* 63.

63 Duffy and Metcalf, *Return of Hans Staden,* 25–26.

64 Klaus Weber, "Deutschland, der atlantische Sklavenhandel und die Plantagenwirtschaft der Neuen Welt," *JMEH* 7, no. 1 (2009): 40–41; Eddy Stols, "The Expansion of the Sugar Market in Western Europe," in *Tropical Babylons,* ed. Stuart Schwartz (Chapel Hill, N.C., 2004), 260–65.

65 Weber, "Deutschland, der atlantische Sklavenhandel und die Plantagenwirtschaft," 42.

66 Sanjay Subrahmanyam, *The Portuguese Empire in Asia, 1500–1800* (Malden, Mass., 2012), 120–24.

67 Renate Pieper, *Die Vermittlung einer neuen Welt* (Mainz, 2000), 12.

68 Kellenbenz, "Finanzierung," 153–81.

69 Mark Häberlein, *The Fuggers of Augsburg* (Charlottesville, Va., 2012), 75–80.

70 Jeannette Graulau, "Finance, Industry and Globalisation in the Early Modern Period," *Rivista di Studi Politici Internazionali* 75, no. 4 (2008): 574.

71 Rolf Walter, "Einleitung," in *Oberdeutsche Kaufleute in Sevilla und Cadiz (1525–1560),* ed. Hermann Kellenbenz and Rolf Walter (Stuttgart, 2001), 13.

72 The account of Nürnberger's career is from ibid., 18–29.

73 Ibid., 29–38.

74 Ward Barrett, "World Bullion Flows, 1450–1800," in *The Rise of Merchant Empires,* ed. James D. Tracy (Cambridge, 1990), 224, 236; Kamen, *Golden Age Spain,* 42.

75 Elliott, *Old World and New,* 60–61; McNeill and McNeill, *The Human Web,* 202; Jose L. Gasch-Tomas, *The Atlantic World and the Manila Galleons* (Boston, 2019).

76 James D. Tracy, "Introduction," in Tracy, ed., *Rise of Merchant Empires,* 3.

77 P. J. Bakewell, *Silver Mining and Society in Colonial Mexico* (Cambridge, 1971), 130–39.

78 Dirk Hoerder, *Geschichte der deutschen Migration* (Munich, 2010), 25, 54.

79 Götz Simmer, *Die deutsche Auswanderung nach Mittel- und Südamerika im 16. und frühen 17. Jahrhundert* (Bamberg, 1993), 15; Bakewell, *Silver Mining,* 144.

80 Bakewell, *Silver Mining,* 170–71.

81 Denzer, *Die Konquista,* 58–59, 79–81; Walter, "Einleitung," 28; Johnson, *German Discovery of the World,* 111–12; Enrique Otte, "Träger und Formen der wirtschaftlichen Erschliessung Lateinamerikas im 16. Jahrhundert," *JbLA* 4 (1967): 253–54.

82 Graulau, "Finance, Industry and Globalisation," 597.

83 Kellenbenz, *Die Fugger in Spanien und Portugal;* Häberlein, *Fuggers of Augsburg,* 68–99.

84 Viktor Hantzsch, *Deutsche Reisende des sechzehnten Jahrhunderts* (Leipzig, 1895), 7.

85 Richard Ehrenberg, *Das Zeitalter der Fugger,* 2 vols. (Jena, 1896).

86 For skepticism about whether this truly was the "age of the Fuggers," see Häberlein, *Fuggers of Augsburg,* 95–98.

87 Braudel, *Mediterranean,* 1:500–4.

88 Johnson, *German Discovery of the World,* 182.

89 Graulau, "Finance, Industry and Globalisation," 557.

90 The phrase comes from the German economic historian Götz von Pölnitz.

91 Johnson, *German Discovery of the World,* 166.

92 Bakewell, *Silver Mining,* 167.

93 Graulau, "Finance, Industry and Globalisation," 592.

94 Geoffrey Parker, *The Army of Flanders and the Spanish Road, 1567–1659* (Cambridge, 1972).

95 Walter, "Einleitung," 14; Graulau, "Finance, Industry and Globalisation," 574–95; Häberlein, *Fuggers of Augsburg,* 92–94.

96 Elliott, *Old World and New,* 8, 39–40.

97 Anthony Pagden, *European Encounters with the New World* (New Haven, 1993), 94–95.

98 Pieper, *Vermittlung*, 26–27.

99 Malekandathil, *Germans, Portuguese and India*, 29–30.

100 Spitz, *Conrad Celtis*, 103–4.

101 Pieper, *Vermittlung*, 23–24, 30–31

102 Elliott, *Old World and New*, 9–10.

103 Frank Bösch, *Mass Media and Historical Change* (New York, 2015), 13–18.

104 Justin Stagl, *A History of Curiosity* (Chur, 1995), 55.

105 Clive Griffin, *The Crombergers of Seville* (New York, 1988), 132–36, 162–63.

106 Pieper, *Vermittlung*, 11n28.

107 Johnson, *German Discovery of the World*, 19–20, 289.

108 Lach, *Asia in the Making of Europe*, 1:179–80.

109 Gerald Strauss, *Sixteenth-Century Germany* (Madison, Wisc., 1959), 10.

110 Johnson, *German Discovery of the World*, 32.

111 Lach, *Asia in the Making of Europe*, 1:215; Michiel van Groesen, *The Representations of the Overseas World in the Dr. Bry Collection of Voyages* (Boston, 2008), 37–42.

112 Elliott, *Old World and New*, 14–27. Pagden, *European Encounters*.

113 Johnson, *German Discovery of the World*, 38–40.

114 Rublack, *Dressing Up*, 184.

115 Ibid., 185 (the image is on the following page).

116 Robison and Schröder, eds., *Albrecht Dürer*, 284–85.

117 Rublack, *Dressing Up*, 187–93.

118 Andrea McKenzie Satterfield, "The Assimilation of the Marvelous Other" (MA thesis, University of South Florida, 2007).

119 Stephen Greenblatt, *Marvelous Possessions* (Chicago, 1991), 24–25.

120 Balthasar Sprenger, *Die Merfart vnd erfarung nüwer Schiffung und Wege zu viln oner-kanten Inseln und Künigreichen* ([Oppenheim], 1509), 10. See also Borowka-Clausberg, *Balthasar Sprenger und der frühneuzeitliche Reisebericht*.

121 I consulted an online edition of Hutten's letters: "Zeitung aus India Junckher Philipps von Hutten: Aus seiner zum Theil unleserlich gewordenen Handschrift," *Historisch-literarishes Magazin* (Erster Theil, 1785), 51–117, http://ds.ub.uni-bielefeld.de/viewer/image/1923975_001/68/LOG_0014/.

122 Nikolaus Federmann, *Indianische Historia* (1557; repr., Munich, 1965); Ulrich Schmidel, *Neue Welt: Das ist, warhafftige Beschreibunge aller schönen Historien von Erfindung viler vnbekanten Königreichen, Landschafften, Insulen vnnd Stedten* (Frankfurt/Main, 1567), https://archive.org/details/neueweltdasistwaoounkn. An English-language version of the latter source is available: Ulrich Schmidel, *A True and Agreeable Description of Some Principal Indian Lands* (London, 1891).

123 "Zeitung aus India," 73.

124 Federmann, *Indianische Historia*.

125 Schmidel, *True and Agreeable Description*, 17, 44–45; Tucker, "Discovery," 36, 39.

126 Johnson, *German Discovery of the World*, 38.

127 Schmidel, *True and Agreeable Description*, 20; Tucker, "Discovery," 36.

128 Letter to brother, Jan. 16, 1540: "Zeitung aus India," 89.

129 Schmidel, *True and Agreeable Description*, 20; Tucker, "Discovery," 36.

130 William Arens, *The Man-Eating Myth* (New York, 1979).

131 Greenblatt, *Marvelous Possessions*, 111.

132 "Zeitung aus India," 73, 78.

133 Tucker, "Discovery," 36–37.

134 Franz Obermeier, "Bilder von Kannibalen, Kannibalismus im Bild," *JbLA* 38 (2001): 49–72.

135 Duffy and Metcalf, *Return of Hans Staden*, 93–135.

136 Rodney Shirley, *The Mapping of the World* (London, 1993), 1–19.

137 Lucien Gallois, *Les géographes allemands de la Renaissance* (Paris, 1890), 73–131.

138 John Hessler, *The Naming of America* (London, 2008); Gallois, *Les géographes*, 38–69; Shirley, *Mapping*, 28–31, 51–55; Christine R. Johnson, "Renaissance German Cosmographers and the Naming of America," *PP* 191 (2006): 3–43; Brotton, *Trading Territories*,

154–55; Horst Pietschmann, "Bemerkungen zur 'Jubiläumshistoriographie' am Beispiel '500 Jahre Martin Waldseemüller und der Name Amerika,'" *JbLA* 44 (2007): 367–89.

139 Shirley, *Mapping*, 46.

140 John Hessler and Chet Van Duzer, *Seeing the World Anew* (Delray Beach, Fla., 2012); Chet Van Duzer, *Martin Waldseemüller's "Carta Marina" of 1516*, https://doi.org/10.1007/978-3-030-22703-6.

141 Van Duzer, *Waldseemüller's "Carta Marina*," 19–39.

142 Richard Unger, *Ships on Maps* (New York, 2010).

143 Brotton, *Trading Territories*, 19–20.

144 John Hessler, *A Renaissance Globemaker's Toolbox* (Washington, D.C., 2013).

145 Jardine, *Worldly Goods*, 425–36; Susan Foister et al., *Making and Meaning: Holbein's Ambassadors* (London, 1997).

146 Mark A. Meadow, "Merchants and Marvels," in *Merchants and Marvels*, ed. Pamela H. Smith and Paula Findlen (New York, 2002), 182–95.

147 Malekandathil, *Germans, Portuguese and India*, 115.

148 Paula Findlen, "Inventing Nature," in Smith and Findlen, eds., *Merchants and Marvels*, 300.

149 Silvio A. Bedini, *The Pope's Elephant* (Manchester, Eng., 1997).

150 Susan Dackerman, "Dürer's Indexical Fantasy: The Rhinoceros and Printmaking," in Dackerman, ed., *Prints and the Pursuit of Knowledge*, 164–83.

151 Ibid., 169; Ernst Gombrich, *Art and Illusion* (Princeton, N.J., 1969), 82–83; Neil Mac-Gregor, *A History of the World in 100 Objects* (New York, 2011), 482–89.

152 "Introduction," in Pullapilly and Van Kley, eds., *Asia and the World*, xiv.

153 Karl Saurer and Elena Hinshaw-Fischli, "They Called Him Suleyman," in *Maritime Malabar and the Europeans, 1500–1962*, ed. K. S. Mathew (London, 2003), 153–63.

154 Johnson, *German Discovery of the World*, 34–35; Meadow, "Merchants and Marvels," 183.

155 Pieper, *Vermittlung*, 265.

156 Jean Michel Massing, "The Quest for the Exotic," in *Circa 1492: Art in the Age of Exploration*, ed. Jay A. Levenson (New Haven, 1991), 115–19.

157 Elliott, *Old World and New*, 32.

158 Laura Smoller, "Playing Cards and Popular Culture in Sixteenth-Century Nuremberg," *The Sixteenth Century Journal* 17, no. 2 (1986), 198, 206.

159 Pieper, *Vermittlung*, 257.

CHAPTER TWO: COMBUSTIONS

1 Robert Burton, *The Anatomy of Melancholy* (1521; repr., New York, 2001), 23.

2 Geoffrey Parker, *Global Crisis* (New Haven, 2013), vii; Geoffrey Parker and Lesley M. Smith, eds., *The General Crisis of the Seventeenth Century* (New York, 1997), 1.

3 Charles Webster, ed., *Samuel Hartlib and the Advancement of Learning* (London, 1970), 88.

4 Brian Fagan, *The Little Ice Age* (New York, 2000).

5 Ibid., 90.

6 Parker, *Global Crisis*, 26.

7 Max Roser, "Global Deaths in Conflict Since 1400," https://www.vox.com/2015/6/23/8832311/war-casualties–600-years.

8 The title of Ricarda Huch's 1912 book on the conflict.

9 Thomas Brady, *German Histories in the Age of Reformations, 1400–1650* (New York, 2009), 388.

10 Geoffrey Mortimer, "Individual Experience and Perception of the Thirty Years War in Eyewitness Personal Accounts," *GH* 20, no. 2 (2002): 141–60; Hans Medick, *Der Dreissigjährige Krieg: Zeugnisse vom Leben mit Gewalt* (Göttingen, 2018).

11 R. Po-chia Hsia, "The German Seventeenth Century," *JMH* 66 (1994): 735.

12 Peter H. Wilson, *The Thirty Years War* (Cambridge, Mass., 2009), 469.

13 Kevin Cramer, *The Thirty Years War in German Memory in the Nineteenth Century* (Lincoln, Neb., 2007), 141–77; Wilson, *Thirty Years War*, 470.

14 Theodore K. Rabb, *The Struggle for Stability in Early Modern Europe* (New York, 1975), 76.

15 H. G. Koenigsberger, *The Habsburgs and Europe 1516–1660* (Ithaca, N.Y., 1971), 219.

16 Allessandro Manzoni, *The Betrothed* (1827; repr., Harmondsworth, Eng., 1972), 521–51.

17 Sheilagh Ogilvie, "Germany and the Seventeenth-Century Crisis," in Parker and Smith, eds., *General Crisis*, 57–86.

18 Brad S. Gregory, *Salvation at Stake* (Cambridge, Mass., 1999).

19 Brady, *German Histories*, 6.

20 Brendan Simms, *Europe* (New York, 2013), 24.

21 Nicholas Canny, "Atlantic History, 1492–1700," in *Atlantic History*, ed. Horst Pietschmann (Göttingen, 2002), 60.

22 J. H. Elliott, *The Old World and the New, 1492–1650* (Cambridge, 1970), 58.

23 Alexander Demandt, *Zeit und Unzeit* (Cologne, 2002), 165–80; James R. Martin, "The Theory of Storms: Jacob Burckhardt and the Concept of 'Historical Crisis,'" *Journal of European Studies* 40, no. 4 (2010): 307-27.

24 C. Scott Dixon, *Protestants: A History from Wittenberg to Pennsylvania, 1517–1740* (Malden, Mass., 2010).

25 Ole Peter Grell, "Scandinavia," in *The Reformation World*, ed. Andrew Pettegree (New York, 2000), 260.

26 Euan Cameron, *The European Reformation* (New York, 2012), 277.

27 On Karlstadt and Luther, see Lyndal Roper, *Martin Luther* (New York, 2016), 206–29.

28 Diarmaid MacCulloch, *The Reformation: A History* (New York, 2003), 135.

29 Ole Peter Grell, "The Emergence of Two Cities," in *Die Dänische Reformation vor ihrem internationalen Hintergrund*, ed. Leif Grane and Kai Hørby (Göttingen, 1990), 129–48.

30 Colin Clair, *A History of European Printing* (London, 1976), 225–28.

31 Owen Chadwick, *The Early Reformation on the Continent* (New York, 2001), 140, 218, 226.

32 Martin Schwarz Lausten, "Weltliche Obrigkeit und Kirche bei König Christian III von Dänemark," in Grane and Hørby, eds., *Die Dänische Reformation*, 91–110.

33 Andrew Pettegree, *Reformation and the Culture of Persuasion* (New York, 2005), 46–47.

34 MacCulloch, *The Reformation: A History*, 191.

35 Christopher Boyd Brown, *Singing the Gospel* (Cambridge, Mass., 2005).

36 Johannes Bolte, "Leonhard Stöckel," *ADB* 36 (1893): 282–83.

37 Cameron, *European Reformation*, 281–83.

38 G. R. Elton, *The Tudor Revolution in Government*, 3rd ed. (New York, 2005), 111.

39 Clair, *History of European Printing*, 127–28; Patrick Collinson, *The Reformation* (London, 2003), 38–40; MacCulloch, *The Reformation: A History*, 203.

40 Steven Ozment, *Protestants* (New York, 1992), 105; MacCulloch, *The Reformation: A History*, 199, 649–50.

41 Elton, *Tudor Revolution in Government*. Hilary Mantel's trilogy consists of *Wolf Hall* (2009), *Bring up the Bodies* (2012), and *The Mirror and the Light* (2020).

42 Michael Everett, *The Rise of Thomas Cromwell* (New Haven, 2015).

43 Patrick Collinson, *Archbishop Grindal, 1519–1583* (Berkeley, Calif., 1979), 80.

44 See the Bullinger Correspondence edition at the University of Zurich, Institut für Schweizerische Reformationsgeschichte, https://www.irg.uzh.ch/de/bullinger-edition .html.

45 Patrick Collinson, *The Godly* (London, 2003), 191–211.

46 Eike Wolgast, *Die Universität Heidelberg, 1386–1986* (Berlin, 1986), 40; MacCulloch, *The Reformation: A History*, 307–8, 354–55.

47 Pettegree, *Reformation and the Culture of Persuasion*, 54–75; MacCulloch, *The Reformation: A History*, 307.

48 Alastair Duke, "Perspectives on International Calvinism," in *Calvinism in Europe 1540–1620*, ed. Andrew Pettegree et al. (New York, 1994), 1–20; Ole Peter Grell, *Brethren in Christ* (New York, 2011).

49 Heiko Oberman, *John Calvin and the Reformation of the Refugees* (Geneva, 2009); Nicholas Terpstra, *Religious Refugees in the Early Modern World* (New York, 2015).

50 Andrew Pettegree, *Emden and the Dutch Revolt* (New York, 1992).

51 MacCulloch, *The Reformation: A History*, 310–13; Simms, *Europe*, 14; Wilson, *Thirty*

Years War, 129, 149, 230; Walther Vogel, *Die Deutschen als Seefahrer* (Hamburg, 1949), 112; Dirk Hoerder, *Geschichte der deutschen Migration* (Munich, 2010), 46.

52 Joachim Whaley, *Germany and the Holy Roman Empire* (New York, 2012), 1:641; Wilson, *Thirty Years War*, 360–61.

53 Anne Goldgar, "Singing in a Strange Land," in *Die europäische Gelehrtenrepublik im Zeitalter des Konfessionalismus*, ed. Herbert Jaumann (Wiesbaden, 2001), 112–19; Whaley, *Germany and the Holy Roman Empire*, 2:266; Harald Kleinschmidt, *People on the Move* (Westport, Conn., 2003), 157–58.

54 Collinson, *Reformation*, 70–72; MacCulloch, *The Reformation: A History*, 550–55.

55 John Bossy, *Christianity in the West, 1400–1700* (New York, 1985), 110.

56 On the Florida colony, see Renate Pieper, *Die Vermittlung einer neuen Welt* (Mainz, 2000), 162–77.

57 Michele Gillespie and Robert Beachy, eds., *Pious Pursuits* (New York, 2007).

58 Among the individuals who did so are Hans Staden and a German merchant named Jörg Pock, who wrote from India that he wished to read the "newsletters of the monk of Wittenberg": Pius Malekandethil, *The Germans, the Portuguese and India* (Münster, 1999), 65.

59 Anton Huonder, *Deutsche Jesuitenmissionäre des 17. und 18. Jahrhunderts* (Freiburg i. B., 1899), 2.

60 Johannes Meier, *"Totus mundus nostra fit habitatio": Jesuiten aus dem deutschen Sprachraum im Portugiesisch und Spanisch-Amerika* (Stuttgart, 2007), 7. For a more skeptical viewpoint about the "global," see Liam Matthew Brockey, *The Visitor* (Cambridge, Mass., 2014), 428–29.

61 Luke Clossey, *Salvation and Globalization in the Early Jesuit Missions* (New York, 2008), 136–37; Huonder, *Deutsche Jesuitenmissionäre*, 11–12.

62 MacCulloch, *The Reformation: A History*, 669–70; R. Po-Chia Hsia, *The World of Catholic Renewal, 1540–1740* (New York, 2005), 75–81.

63 Clossey, *Salvation and Globalization*, 137.

64 MacCulloch, *The Reformation: A History*, 442–57; Marc Forster, *Catholic Revival in the Age of the Baroque* (New York, 2001).

65 MacCulloch, *The Reformation: A History*, 329, 422.

66 Forster, *Catholic Revival*.

67 Bossy, *Christianity in the West*, 132; W. David Myers, *"Poor Sinning Folk"* (Ithaca, N.Y., 1996).

68 Jeffrey Chipps Smith, *Sensuous Worship* (Princeton, N.J., 2002); John W. O'Malley and Gavin A. Bailey, eds., *The Jesuits and the Arts, 1540–1773* (Philadelphia, 2005); Evonne Levy, *Propaganda and the Jesuit Baroque* (Berkeley, Calif., 2004).

69 The total number of Jesuits rose steeply, from 1500 in 1556 to 5000 in 1580 and 13,000 in 1615: Meier, *"Totus mundus,"* 8–9.

70 Huonder, *Deutsche Jesuitenmissionäre*, 12–13.

71 Clossey, *Salvation and Globalization*, 138.

72 Christoph Nebgen, *Missionsberufungen nach Übersee in drei deutschen Provinzen der Gesellschaft Jesu im 17. und 18. Jahrhundert* (Regensburg, 2007).

73 Clossey, *Salvation and Globalization*, 117, 140.

74 Ibid., 138; Rudolf Grulich, *Der Beitrag der böhmischen Länder zur Weltmission des 17. und 18. Jahrhunderts* (Königstein, 1981), 38–41.

75 Meier, *"Totus mundus,"* 14, drawing on Nebgen, *Missionsberufungen*.

76 Clossey, *Salvation and Globalization*, 142.

77 Huonder, *Deutsche Jesuitenmissionen*, 197–200 lists the names.

78 Meier, *"Totus mundus,"* 13–17; Nebgen, *Missionsberufungen*; Bernd Hausberger, *Für Gott und König* (Vienna, 2000).

79 Clossey, *Salvation and Globalization*, 148.

80 Jonathan Wright, *The Jesuits* (London, 2004), 70 (Wright wrongly calls Samuel Fritz a "Bavarian"); Meier, *"Totus mundus,"* 22.

81 Clossey, *Salvation and Globalization*, 62.

82 Meier, *"Totus mundus,"* 18–19.

83 Ibid., 20.

84 Wright, *Jesuits*, 70; Meier, *"Totus mundus,"* 22.
85 Meier, *"Totus mundus,"* 22–23.
86 Grulich, *Beitrag der böhmischen Länder*, 82–91; Maria Fassbinder, *Der "Jesuitenstaat" in Paraguay* (Halle, 1926); Peter C. Hartmann, *Der Jesuitenstaat in Südamerika, 1609–1768: Eine christliche Alternative zu Kolonialismus und Marxismus* (Weissenhorn, 1994); Julia J. S. Sarreal, *The Guarani and Their Missions* (Stanford, Calif., 2014).
87 Paul Frings and Josef Übelmesser, eds., *Paracuaria* (Mainz, 1982). Two of the ruins are UNESCO World Heritage Sites.
88 *The Mission*, dir. Roland Joffé (1986).
89 Philip Caraman, *The Lost Paradise* (New York, 1976); Hartmann, *Jesuitenstaat*; Wolfgang Reinhard, "Gelenkter Kulturwandel im siebzehnten Jahrhundert," *HZ* 223 (1976): 529–90; Klaus Koschorke, ed., *"Christen und Gewürze": Konfrontation und Interaktion kolonialer und indigener Christentumsvarianten*, vol. 1 (Göttingen, 1998).
90 Paul A. Rule, "Jesuit Sources," in *Essays on the Sources for Chinese History*, ed. Donald Daniel Leslie (Canberra, 1973), 178.
91 Clossey, *Salvation and Globalization*, 62, 107; Liam Matthew Brockey, *Journey to the East* (Cambridge, Mass., 2007), 126–27.
92 Clossey, *Salvation and Globalization*, 159, says twenty-one "German" Jesuits had arrived by 1690. Franz Übleis, "Deutsche in Indien 1600–1700," *Zeitschrift für Religions- und Geistesgeschichte* 32, no. 2 (1980): 128, suggests that twenty-six Central European Jesuits traveled on Portuguese ships to "the Indies" between 1600 and 1700, most of those after 1675. Grulich, *Beitrag der böhmischen Länder*, 113–20, has numbers on Bohemian Jesuits in China. Joseph Dehergne, *Répertoire des Jésuites de Chine de 1552 à 1800* (Rome, 1973), 397–407, says that thirty-seven German, Austrian, Bohemian, and Swiss Jesuits departed for China before 1723, and twenty-four actually served there.
93 Brockey, *Journey to the East*, 18–19, 88–89.
94 For example, see Dehergne, *Répertoire des Jésuites de Chine*, which has a listing of individual priests.
95 Alfons Väth, *Johann Adam Schall von Bell S.J.: Missionar in China, kaiserlicher Astronom und Ratgeber am Hofe von Peking, 1592–1666* (Nettetal, 1991); Joseph Duhr, *Adam Schall* (Brussels, 1936); Rachel Attwater, *Adam Schall, A Jesuit at the Court of China, 1592–1666* (Milwaukee, 1963).
96 Duhr, *Adam Schall*, 20–21 (with the Latin original); Attwater, *Adam Schall: A Jesuit*, 27.
97 Väth, *Johann Adam Schall von Bell*, 241–43.
98 George H. Dunne, *Generation of Giants* (London, 1962), 211.
99 Attwater, *Adam Schall: A Jesuit*, 45, 128, 134; Dunne, *Generation of Giants*, 250. Väth, *Johann Adam Schall von Bell*, 248, refers delicately to Schall's "Rhenish humor."
100 Väth, *Johann Adam Schall von Bell*, 267–92.
101 Ibid., 241–66; J. S. Cummins, *A Question of Rites* (Brookfield, Vt., 1993), 124–30; Attwater, *Adam Schall: A Jesuit*, 126–34.
102 Brockey, *Journey to the East*, 200.
103 Dehergne, *Répertoire des Jésuites de Chine*, 122–23.
104 MacCulloch, *The Reformation: A History*, 434; Väth, *Johann Adam Schall von Bell*, 224.
105 Cited in Cummins, *A Question of Rites*, 2.
106 Brockey, *Journey to the East*, 80.
107 Benjamin A. Elman, *On Their Own Terms* (Cambridge, Mass., 2006), 104–6.
108 Clossey, *Salvation and Globalization*, 173–86.
109 Meier, *"Totus mundus,"* 17.
110 Clossey, *Salvation and Globalization*, 72–89.
111 Ibid., 83–84, drawing on Sibylle Appuhn-Radtke, *Das Thesenblatt im Hochbarock* (Weissenhorn, 1988).
112 Clossey, *Salvation and Globalization*, 81.
113 Paula Findlen, ed., *Athanasius Kircher: The Last Man Who Knew Everything* (New York, 2004); Paula Findlen, *Possessing Nature* (Berkeley, Calif., 1994).
114 Anne Goldgar, *Impolite Learning* (New Haven, 1995); Jaumann, ed., *europäische Gelehrtenrepublik*; Lorraine Daston, "The Republic of Letters," *Journal of the History of Ideas* 65, no. 3 (2004): 421–31; Ian McNeely with Lisa Wolverton, *Reinventing Knowledge*

(New York, 2008), 119–59; Anthony Grafton, "A Sketch Map of a Lost Continent: The Republic of Letters," in *Worlds Made by Words* (Cambridge, Mass., 2009), 9–34.

115 Grafton, "A Sketch Map of a Lost Continent," 17–18; Justin Stagl, *A History of Curiosity* (Chur, 1995), 97–99.

116 Kleinschmidt, *People on the Move*, 163–64.

117 Lisa Jardine, *Worldly Goods* (New York, 1996), 223–25.

118 Friedrich Heer, *Die dritte Kraft* (Frankfurt/Main, 1959).

119 Clossey, *Salvation and Globalization*, 195–215. For an interesting discussion of "confessionalized knowledge," see Brad S. Gregory, *The Unintended Reformation* (Cambridge, Mass., 2012), 331.

120 Lewis W. Spitz, *Conrad Celtis* (Cambridge, Mass., 1957), 35.

121 Manfred P. Fleischer, *Späthumanismus in Schlesien* (Munich, 1984).

122 Grell, *Brethren in Christ*.

123 Pettegree, *Reformation and the Culture of Persuasion*.

124 Ian Hunter, "The University Philosopher in Early Modern Germany," in *The Philosopher in Early Modern Europe*, ed. Conan Condren et al. (New York, 2004), 37.

125 Gregory, *Unintended Reformation*, 329.

126 R. J. W. Evans, "German Universities After the Thirty Years War," *History of Universities* 1 (1981): 169–88.

127 Markus Völkel, "Das Verhältnis von religio, patriae, confession und erudition bei Marx Welser," in Jaumann, ed., *Die europäische Gelehrtenrepublik*, 127–40, and Herbert Jaumann, "Vorwort," in ibid., 7–8.

128 Wolgast, *Universität Heidelberg*, 51–55; Evans, "German Universities," 169–70; Wilson, *Thirty Years War*, 814.

129 Wilson, *Thirty Years War*, 745, 813–14.

130 Klaus Wittstadt, "Der Enzyklopädist und Polyhistoriker als neuzeitlicher Gelehrtentypus—Athanasius Kircher (1602–1680)," in *Literaten, Kleriker, Gelehrte*, ed. Rudolf Keck et al. (Cologne, 1996), 269–87.

131 Mark Greengrass, Michael Leslie, and Timothy Raylor, "Introduction," in *Samuel Hartlib and Universal Reformation: Studies in Intellectual Communication*, ed. Mark Greengrass, Michael Leslie, and Timothy Raylor (Cambridge, 1994), 2.

132 Ibid., 12–13.

133 Michael John Gorman, "From 'The Eyes of All' to 'Usefull Quarries in philosophy and good literature,'" in O'Malley and Bailey, eds., *The Jesuits and the Arts*, 182.

134 Pamela Barnett, *Theodore Haak* (The Hague, 1962); Grell, *Brethren in Christ*, 186, 210–14.

135 Dagmar Čapková, "Comenius and His Ideals," in Greenglass, Leslie, and Raylor, eds., *Samuel Hartlib and Universal Reformation*, 77.

136 As Ann Goldgar has argued of a later Calvinist émigré group, the Huguenots: "Singing in a Strange Land," 107–9.

137 Michael Hunter, *Science and Society in Restoration England* (New York, 1981); Barnett, *Theodore Haak*, 120–21.

138 Charles Webster, *The Great Instauration* (New York, 1976), 70; Marie Boas Hall, *Henry Oldenburg: Shaping the Royal Society* (New York, 2002).

139 Greengrass, Leslie and Raylor, "Introduction," 16.

140 Webster, *Samuel Hartlib and the Advancement of Learning*, 14, 70.

141 Ibid, 196–99: Hartlib to Lord Worthington, Jan. 30, 1660.

142 Herbert Jaumann, "Respublica litteraria/Republic of Letters," in Jaumann, ed., *Die europäische Gelehrtenrepublik*, 14–15.

143 Richard van Dülmen, "Gespräche, Korrespondenzen, Sozietäten," in *Denkwelten um 1700*, ed. Richard van Dülmen and Sina Rauschenbach (Cologne, 2002), 123–40; Georg Gerber, "Leibniz und seine Korrespondenz," in *Leibniz*, ed. Wilhelm Totok and Carl Haase (Hanover, 1966), 141–71.

144 Whaley, *Germany and the Holy Roman Empire*, 2:88–90.

145 David S. Lux, "The Reorganization of Science, 1450–1700," in *Patronage and Institutions: Science, Technology, and Medicine at the European Court, 1500–1750*, ed. Bruce T. Moran (Woodbridge, Eng., 1991), 189.

146 Stagl, *Curiosity*, 112–16; Julius Schlosser, *Die Kunst- und Wunderkammer der Spätrenais-*

sance (Braunschweig, 1978); Oliver Impey and Arthur MacGregor, eds., *The Origins of Museums* (Oxford, 1985); Dominik Collet, *Die Welt in der Stube* (Göttingen, 2007).

147 Wilhelm Kühlmann, *Gelehrtenrepublik und Fürstenstaat* (Tübingen, 1982).

148 Ulinka Rublack, *The Astronomer and the Witch* (New York, 2015).

149 R. J. W. Evans, *Rudolf II and His World* (New York, 1973); Grafton, *World Made by Words*, 114–36.

150 Quentin Skinner, *The Foundations of Political Thought*, vol. 1, *The Renaissance* (New York, 1978), 193.

151 Ann Blair, *Too Much Knowledge* (New Haven, 2010).

152 Elizabeth L. Eisenstein, *The Printing Press as an Agent of Change* (New York, 1979), 3.

153 J. R. McNeill and William H. McNeill, *The Human Web* (New York, 2003), 180; E. Buringh and J. L. Van Zanden, "Charting the 'Rise of the West': Manuscript and Printed Books in Europe," *JEH*, 69, no. 2 (2009): 409–45, table 2.

154 Jardine, *Worldly Goods*, 129–30; Clair, *History of European Printing*, 37–58, 224–25.

155 Clair, *History of European Printing*, 59, 78, 81; Skinner, *Foundations of Political Thought*, 1:195; Rolf Walter, "Einleitung," in *Oberdeutsche Kaufleute in Sevilla und Cadiz (1525–1560)*, ed. Hermann Kellenbenz and Rolf Walter (Stuttgart, 2001), 18–20, 59; Clive Griffin, *The Crombergers of Seville* (New York, 1988).

156 See Buringh and Van Zanden, "Charting the 'Rise of the West,'" table 4. On technological transfer to England, see Anja Hill-Zenk and Felix Sprang, "Kontinentaleuropäisch-Englischer Wissenstransfer und das gedruckte Buch in der Englischen Renaissance," in *Innovation durch Wissenstransfer in der Frühen Neuzeit*, ed. Johann Anselm Steiger et al. (New York, 2010), 209–47.

157 Peter Weidhaas, *A History of the Frankfurt Book Fair* (Toronto, 2007), 45.

158 Jardine, *Worldly Goods*, 166.

159 Weidhaas, *Frankfurt Book Fair*, 39, 45; Eve Duffy and Alida Metcalf, *The Return of Hans Staden* (Baltimore, 2012), 89.

160 Clossey, *Salvation and Globalization*, 190.

161 Burton, *Anatomy of Melancholy*, 24.

162 David Wootton, "Traffic of the Mind," *Times Literary Supplement*, Oct. 21, 2011.

163 Stagl, *Curiosity*, 98.

164 Deborah E. Harkness, *The Jewel House* (New Haven, 2007), 155–57, 173, 194, 216.

165 Greengrass, Leslie, and Raylor, "Introduction," 22; Inge Keil, "Technology Transfer and Scientific Specialization," in Greengrass, Leslie, and Raylor, eds., *Samuel Hartlib and Universal Reformation*, 268–78.

166 Horst Bredekamp, *The Lure of Antiquity and the Cult of the Machine* (Princeton, N.J., 1995), 81–82.

167 Pieter Van Der Star, ed., *Fahrenheit's Letters to Leibniz and Boerhaave* (Leiden, 1983), 1–17.

CHAPTER THREE: EMPIRES

1 Ryan Tucker Jones, *Empire of Extinction* (New York, 2014), 1–59.

2 Anke te Heesen, "Accounting for the Natural World," in *Colonial Botany*, ed. Londa Schiebinger and Claudia Swan (Philadelphia, 2005), 237–51.

3 Jones, *Empire of Extinction*; Lisbet Koerner, "Daedalus Hyperboreus," in *The Sciences in Enlightened Europe*, ed. William Clark et al. (Chicago, 1999), 389–422; David Moon, *The Plough That Broke the Steppes* (New York, 2013), 25, 46–65, 73–76, 98–100, 148–49.

4 Schiebinger and Swan, eds., *Colonial Botany*; Lisbet Koerner, *Linnaeus: Nature and Nation* (Cambridge, Mass., 1999).

5 Michael E. Hoare, *The Tactless Philosopher* (Melbourne, 1976); Anne Mariss, *Johann Reinhold Forster and the Making of Natural History on Cook's Second Voyage* (Lanham, Md., 2019); Ludwig Uhlig, *Georg Forster* (Göttingen, 2004); Jürgen Goldstein, *Georg Forster* (Chicago, 2019).

6 John Gascoigne, *Science in the Service of Empire* (New York, 1998).

7 Lawrence J. Baack, *Undying Curiosity* (Stuttgart, 2014).

8 Daniel Hopkins, "Julius von Rohr, an Enlightenment Scientist of the Plantation Atlan-

tic," in *Slavery Hinterland: Transatlantic Slavery and Continental Europe, 1680–1850*, ed. Felix Brahm and Eve Rosenhaft (Rochester, N.Y., 2016), 133–60.

9 Detlef Haberland, ed., *Engelbert Kaempfer (1651–1716)* (Wiesbaden, 2005); David Mervat, "A Closed Country in the Open Seas: Engelbert Kaempfer's Japanese Solution for European Modernity's Predicament," *History of European Ideas* 35, no. 3 (2009): 321–29; Benjamin Schmidt, *Inventing Exoticism* (Philadelphia, 2015), 63, 85, 157–59, 173–75.

10 Natalie Zemon Davis, *Women on the Margins* (Cambridge, Mass., 1995), 140–202; Helmut Kaiser, *Maria Sibylla Merian* (Düsseldorf, 2001); Londa Schiebinger, "Prospecting for Drugs," in Schiebinger and Swan, eds., *Colonial Botany*, 126.

11 There were fifty-seven expeditions between 1760 and 1807: Antonio Lafuente and Nuria Valverde, "Linnean Botany and Spanish Imperial Biopolitics," in Schiebinger and Swan, eds., *Colonial Botany*, 136.

12 Daniela Bleichmar, *Visible Empire* (Chicago, 2012), 97–99, reproduces two pages of this beautiful color chart.

13 Josef Kühnel, "Haenke, Thaddaeus," *NDB* 7 (1966): 444–45; Iris H. W. Engstrand, *Spanish Scientists in the New World* (Seattle, 1981), 47–48, 73.

14 Mary Louise Pratt, *Imperial Eyes* (New York, 1992), 38; James Delbourgo and Nicholas Dew, eds., *Science and Empire in the Atlantic World* (New York, 2008).

15 Harry Liebersohn, *The Travelers' World* (Cambridge, Mass., 2006), 123–38.

16 Mark H. Danley and Patrick J. Speelman, eds., *The Seven Years' War* (Boston, 2013).

17 Jane Burbank and Frederick Cooper, *Empires in World History* (Princeton, N.J., 2010), 214–15.

18 Joachim Whaley, *Germany and the Holy Roman Empire* (New York, 2012), 2:80–81; Pamela Smith, "Curing the Body Politic," in *Patronage and Institutions: Science, Technology, and Medicine at the European Court, 1500–1750*, ed. Bruce T. Moran (Woodbridge, Eng., 1991), 195–209.

19 Jürgen Nadel, "Die Brandenburgisch-Africanische Compagnie," *Scripta Mercaturae* 30 (1994): 44–94; Nils Brübach, "'Seefahrt und Handel sind die vornembsten Säulen eines Etats,'" in *Amerikaner wider Willen*, ed. R. Zoller (Frankfurt/Main, 1994), 11–42; Ulrich van der Heyden, *Rote Adler an Afrikas Küste* (Berlin, 2001); Sven Klosa, *Die Brandenburgische-Africanische Compagnie in Emden* (Frankfurt/Main, 2011); Jürgen Overhoff, *Friedrich der Grosse und George Washington* (Stuttgart, 2011), 92–93; Craig Koslofsky and Roberto Zaugg, "Ship's Surgeon Johann Peter Oettinger," in Brahm and Rosenhaft, eds., *Slavery Hinterland*, 25–30.

20 Florian Schui, "Prussia's 'Trans-Oceanic Moment,'" *The Historical Journal* 49, no. 1 (2006): 143–60; Isaac Nakhimovsky, *The Closed Commercial State* (Princeton, N.J., 2011), 95; Christian Koninckz, "Ownership in East India Company Shipping: Prussia, Scandinavia and the Austrian Netherlands in the 18th Century," in *Bijdragen tot de internationale maritieme geschiedenis*, ed. Christian Koninckz (Brussels, 1988), 33–42.

21 Schui, "Prussia's 'Trans-Oceanic Moment,'" 152n32; Om Prakasch, *European Commercial Enterprise in Pre-Colonial India* (Cambridge, 1998), 81. Another unsuccessful company was the Imperial East India Company of Trieste in the 1770s, founded by a former English East India Company employee, an adventurer of German origin named William Bolts.

22 David Blackbourn, *The Conquest of Nature: Water, Landscape, and the Making of Modern Germany* (New York, 2006), 122.

23 Schui, "Prussia's 'Trans-Oceanic Moment,'" 156–58.

24 Joachim Nettelbeck, *Ein Mann: Des Seefahrers und aufrechten Bürgers Joachim Nettelbeck wundersame Lebensgeschichte von ihm selbst erzählt* (1821; repr., Ebenhausen, 1910), 71.

25 C. A. Bayly, *The Birth of the Modern World, 1780–1914* (Malden, Mass., 2004), 62. But not the great non-European land empires of the Ottomans, Safavid, Mughal, and Qing.

26 Stephen Conway, *Britain, Ireland and Continental Europe in the Eighteenth Century* (New York, 2011); Andrew Thompson, *Britain, Hanover and the Protestant Interest, 1688–1756* (Rochester, N.Y., 2006); Nick Harding, *Hanover and the British Empire, 1700–1837* (Woodbridge, Eng., 2007). See also Heinz Duchhardt, ed., *Der Herrscher in der Doppelpflicht* (Mainz, 1997).

27 Andreas Gross et al., eds., *Halle and the Beginning of Protestant Mission in India* (Halle,

2006); Michael Mann, ed., *Europäische Aufklärung und protestantische Mission in Indien* (Heidelberg, 2006); Albert Wu, *From Christ to Confucius* (New Haven, 2016), 24–26; Bernard Bailyn, "Reflections on Some Major Themes," in *Soundings in Atlantic History*, ed. Bernard Bailyn and Patricia Denault (Cambridge, Mass., 2011), 21–22.

28 The other five leading principalities supplying troops to the British were, ordered by size, Braunschweig-Wolfenbüttel (5723), Hessen-Hanau (2400), Ansbach-Bayreuth (2353), Waldeck (1200), and Anhalt-Zerbst (1200). The total number of soldiers supplied by Hessen-Kassel was 18,970: Mark Wishon, *German Forces and the British Army* (Basingstoke, Eng., 2013), 106–7.

29 Ibid., 81, citing Christopher Duffy.

30 Ibid., 104–37; Rodney Atwood, *The Hessians* (New York, 1980); Charles Ingrao, *The Hessian Mercenary State* (New York, 1987); Peter H. Wilson, "The German 'Soldiertrade' of the Seventeenth and Eighteenth Centuries: A Reassessment," *International History Review* 18 (1996): 757–92.

31 Daniel Krebs, *A Generous and Merciful Enemy* (Norman, Okla., 2013), 17.

32 Wishon, *German Forces*, 92, 136 (quotation).

33 Chen Tzoref-Ashkenazi, *British Soldiers in Colonial India* (London, 2014), 21–47.

34 Ibid., 26.

35 Ibid.; Chen Tzoref-Ashkenazi, "Hanoverians, Germans, and Europeans," *CEH* 43, no. 2 (2010): 221–38.

36 Jan Lucassen, "The Netherlands, the Dutch, and Long Distance Migration in the Late Sixteenth to Early Nineteenth Centuries," in *Europeans on the Move*, ed. Nicholas Canny (Oxford, 1994), 165–69.

37 Thirty-five percent of the sailors and 60 percent of the soldiers were foreign (50 and 80 percent, respectively, after 1750).

38 Based on Jaap Bruijn, "Productivity, Profitability, and Costs of Private and Corporate Dutch Ship Owning in the Seventeenth and Eighteenth Centuries," in *The Rise of Merchant Empires*, ed. James D. Tracy (Cambridge, 1990), 174–94; A. C. J. Vermeulen, "The People on Board," in *Dutch Shipping in the 17th and 18th Centuries*, ed. Jaap R. Bruijn et al. (The Hague, 1987), 143–72; James Belich, *Replenishing the Earth* (New York, 2009), 29; Charles R. Boxer, *The Dutch Seaborne Empire, 1600–1800* (London, 1965), 71–83; Klaus J. Bade, *Migration in European History* (Malden, Mass., 2003), 16–17; Claudia Rei, "Careers and Wages in the Dutch East India Company," *Cliometrica* 8, no. 1 (2014): 27–48; Tzoref-Ashkenazi, *British Soldiers*, 14–16 (quotation at 14); Piet Emmer, "The Dutch Atlantic 1600–1800," *JbLA* 38 (2001): 31–48; Roelof van Gelder, *Das ostindische Abenteuer* (Hamburg, 2004).

39 Henry Makowski and Bernhard Buderath, *"Die Natur dem Menschen Untertan"* (Munich, 1983), 246–49.

40 Leslie Page Moch, *Moving Europeans* (Bloomington, Ind., 1992), 29; Catia Antunes, "Amsterdam and Lisbon 1640–1710," in *Rivalry and Conflict*, ed. Ernst van Veen and Leonard Blusse (Leiden, 2005), 317.

41 Lucassen, "The Netherlands, the Dutch, and Long Distance Migration," 153–91; Jan Lucassen, *Migrant Labour in Europe, 1600–1900* (London, 1987); Bade, *Migration in European History*, 12–20; Dirk Hoerder, *Geschichte der deutschen Migration* (Munich, 2010), 53–55; Moch, *Moving Europeans*, 29, 40–43.

42 See William O'Reilly, "Migration, Recruitment and the Law," in *Atlantic History*, ed. Horst Pietschmann (Göttingen, 2002), 126–27; Jaap Bruijn, "Seamen in Dutch Ports: c. 1700–1914," *The Mariner's Mirror* 65 (1979): 327–37; Jaap Jacobs, "Soldiers of the Company," in *Jacob Leisler's Atlantic World in the Later Seventeenth Century*, ed. Hermann Wellenreuther (Piscataway, N.J., 2009), 11–31; Jaap Jacobs, *The Colony of the New Netherlands* (Ithaca, N.Y., 2009), 36–38.

43 Tzoref-Ashkenazi, *British Soldiers*, 17–19.

44 Krebs, *A Generous and Merciful Enemy*, 286n3; Philipp Losch, *Soldatenhandel* (Kassel, 1933), 7.

45 Christopher Bayly, *Empire and Information* (New York, 1996).

46 Nakhimovsky, *Closed Commercial State*, 109.

47 Fernand Braudel, *The Mediterranean and the Mediterranean World in the Age of Philip II*, 2

vols. (1949; repr., London, 1972), is the book against which to measure all other histories of seas and oceans. For comparison of Mediterranean and Atlantic, see Wim Klooster, "Atlantische Geschichte und der Begriff der Frühen Neuzeit," in *Die Frühe Neuzeit als Epoche*, ed. Helmut Neuhaus (Munich, 2009), 472; Alison Games, "Atlantic History: Definitions, Challenges, and Opportunities," *AHR* 111, no. 3 (2006): 741–57.

48 Alfred Crosby, *The Columbian Exchange* (Westport, Conn., 1972).

49 Bernard Bailyn, *Atlantic History* (Cambridge, Mass., 2005); Pietschmann, ed., *Atlantic History*; Jorge Cañizares-Esguerra and Erik R. Seeman, eds., *The Atlantic in Global History, 1500–2000* (Upper Saddle River, N.J., 2006); Thomas Benjamin, *The Atlantic World* (New York, 2009); Joseph C. Miller, ed., *The Princeton Companion to Atlantic History* (Princeton, N.J., 2015).

50 Paul Gilroy, *The Black Atlantic* (Cambridge, Mass., 1993); Allan Greer and Kenneth Mills, "A Catholic Atlantic," in Cañizares-Esguerra and Seeman, eds., *The Atlantic in Global History*, 3–19.

51 Jack P. Greene and Philip D. Morgan, eds., *Atlantic History* (New York, 2009).

52 See Hermann Wellenreuther, "Exploring Misunderstandings," in Pietschmann, ed., *Atlantic History*, 161.

53 Bernard Bailyn, *The Peopling of British North America* (New York, 1986), ix.

54 Violet Barbour, *Capitalism in Amsterdam in the Seventeenth Century* (Ann Arbor, Mich., 1966), 91; Joachim Radkau, *Wood* (Malden, Mass., 2012), 140–46; Carlo M. Cipolla, *European Culture and Overseas Expansion* (Harmondsworth, Eng., 1970), 56; John McNeill, "Empires of Energy 1580–1980," paper given to the MIT Seminar on Agricultural and Environmental History, May 8, 2009.

55 Benjamin Schmidt, "The Dutch Atlantic," in Greene and Morgan, eds., *Atlantic History*, 163–87; Emmer, "The Dutch Atlantic."

56 Nettelbeck, *Ein Mann*, 22, 67.

57 Ibid., 25.

58 Percy Ernst Schramm, *Neun Generationen* (Göttingen, 1963), 1:174, who slightly alters the wording of the original.

59 Nettelbeck, *Ein Mann*, 67; Cornelis Goslinga, *The Dutch in the Caribbean and the Guianas, 1680–1791* (Dover, N.H., 1985), 294, 353, 356; Rudolf Jacob van Lier, *Frontier Society* (The Hague, 1971), 35.

60 Nettelbeck, *Ein Mann*, 25 (quotation), 68.

61 Hermann Kellenbenz, "Deutsche Plantagenbesitzer und Kaufleute in Surinam vom Ende des 18. bis zur Mitte des 19. Jahrhunderts," *JbLA* 3 (1966): 142.

62 Van Lier, *Frontier Society*, 35.

63 Margrit Schulte Beerbühl, "German Merchants and the British Empire During the Eighteenth Century," in *Transnational Networks*, ed. John R. Davis et al. (Boston, 2012), 47–48.

64 Kellenbenz, "Deutsche Plantagenbesitzer und Kaufleute," 143–46.

65 Goslinga, *The Dutch in the Caribbean*, 353–64 (quotation at 363); van Lier, *Frontier Society*, 32–33; David Nassy, *Historical Essay on the Colony of Surinam* (Cincinnati, 1974), 141–42.

66 Karwan Fatah-Black, "Suriname and the Atlantic World, 1650–1800" (PhD diss., University of Leiden, 2013), 153–57.

67 Albert von Sack, *A Narrative of a Journey to Surinam* (London, 1810), 100; Goslinga, *The Dutch*, 291; van Lier, *Frontier Society*, 35.

68 Gert Oostindie and Jessica Roitman, "Introduction," in *Dutch Atlantic Connections*, ed. Gert Oostindie and Jessica Roitman (Boston, 2014), 8–9; Emmer, "The Dutch Atlantic," 31–48.

69 Fatah-Black, "Suriname and the Atlantic World," 145.

70 Ibid., 139–44.

71 Kellenbenz, "Deutsche Plantagenbesitzer und Kaufleute," 162.

72 Van Lier, *Frontier Society*, 35.

73 Fatah-Black, "Suriname and the Atlantic World," 83–84.

74 Aaron Fogelman, *Two Troubled Souls* (Chapel Hill, N.C., 2013), 101–46.

75 Goslinga, *The Dutch*, 370–71; van Lier, *Fronter Society*, 35–36; Nassy, *Historical Essay*,

134–35; Sack, *A Narrative of a Journey*, 92; Ellen Klinkers, "Moravian Missions in Times of Emancipation," in *Pious Pursuits*, ed. Michele Gillespie and Robert Beachy (New York, 2007), 208; Richard Price and Sally Price, eds., *Stedman's Surinam* (Baltimore, 1992), 265.

76 On the ambiguities of Stedman's position, see ibid. Also see Pratt, *Imperial Eyes*, 90–102; Simon Gikandi, *Slavery and the Culture of Taste* (Princeton, N.J., 2011), 183–87.

77 Michael T. Bravo, "Mission Gardens," in Schiebinger and Swan, eds., *Colonial Botany*, 49–65; James R. Troyer, "Early American Moravian Botanists in North Carolina and Elsewhere," *Journal of the North Carolina Academy of Science* 125, no. 1 (2009): 1–6.

78 F. Anne M. R. Jarvis, "German Musicians in London, ca. 1750–1850," in *Migration and Transfer from Germany to Britain, 1660–1914*, ed. Stefan Manz et al. (Malden, Mass., 2009), 37.

79 Ibid., 37–47.

80 Karel Davids, "The Scholarly Atlantic," in Oostindie and Roitman, eds., *Dutch Atlantic Connections*, 224–48.

81 "Introduction," in Gillespie and Beachy, eds., *Pious Pursuits*, 1; Robert Beachy, "Manuscript Missions in the Age of Print," in ibid., 36.

82 Stephen Berry, *A Path in the Mighty Waters* (New Haven, 2015), 176–77.

83 Beachy, "Manuscript Missions," 38–39; Frank Hatje, "Revivalists Abroad," in Manz et al., eds., *Migration and Transfer*, 74–75; Colin Podmore, *The Moravian Church in England, 1728–1760* (New York, 1998).

84 Jon F. Sensbach, "Don't Teach My Negroes to Be Pietists," in *Pietism in Germany and North America, 1680–1820*, ed. Jonathan Strom, Hartmut Lehmann, and James van Horn Melton (Burlington, Vt., 2009), 183.

85 Jon F. Sensbach, "Slavery, Race, and the Global Fellowship," in Gillespie and Beachy, eds., *Pious Pursuits*, 223–43.

86 Gisela Mettele, *Weltbürgertum oder Gottesreich* (Göttingen, 2008); Hatje, "Revivalists Abroad," 75–76.

87 Donald F. Durnbaugh, "Communication Networks as One Aspect of Pietist Definition," in Strom, Lehmann, and Melton, eds., *Pietism in Germany and North America*, 33–49.

88 Mark A. Peterson, "Theopolis Americana," in Bailyn and Denault, eds., *Soundings in Atlantic History*, 359–70.

89 Hermann Wellenreuther, *Heinrich Melchior Mühlenberg und die deutschen Lutheraner in Nordamerika, 1742–1787* (Münster, 2013); Hermann Wellenreuther, "Heinrich Melchior Mühlenberg and the Pietisms in Colonial America," in Strom, Lehmann, and Melton, eds., *Pietism in Germany and North America*, 127–32.

90 Renate Wilson, *Pious Traders in Medicine* (University Park, Pa., 2000), esp. 207.

91 Katherine Carte Engel, "'Commerce That the Lord Could Sanctify and Bless,'" in Gillespie and Beachy, eds., *Pious Pursuits*, 121.

92 Rosalind Beiler, "Dissenting Religious Communication Networks and European Migration, 1660–1710," in Bailyn and Denault, eds., *Soundings in Atlantic History*, 210–36. See also Sünne Juterczenka, *Über Gott und die Welt* (Göttingen, 2008).

93 Stephanie Grauman Wolf, "Hyphenated America," in *America and the Germans*, ed. Frank Trommler and Joseph McVeigh, vol. 1, *Immigration, Language, Ethnicity* (Philadelphia, 1985), 66–84; Margo M. Lambert, "Mediation, Assimilation, and German Foundations in North America," *Pennsylvania History: A Journal of Mid-Atlantic Studies* 84, no. 2 (2017): 141–70.

94 Marianne Wokeck, "Colonial Immigration," in Trommler and McVeigh, eds., *America and the Germans*, 1:3–13; Marianne Wokeck, *Trade in Strangers* (University Park, Pa., 1999), 40–46.

95 Georg Fertig, "Transatlantic Migration from the German-Speaking Parts of Central Europe, 1600–1800," in Canny, ed., *Europeans on the Move*, 195.

96 Blackbourn, *Conquest of Nature*, 303.

97 Mathias Beer and Dittmar Dahlmann, eds., *Migration nach Ost- und Südosteuropa vom 18. bis zum Beginn des 19. Jahrhunderts* (Stuttgart, 1999); Karl Roider and Robert Forrest, "German Colonization in the Banat and Transylvania in the Eighteenth Cen-

tury," in *The Germans and the East*, ed. Charles W. Ingrao and Franz A. J. Szabo (West Lafayette, Ind., 2008), 89–104; Hans Fenske, "International Migration: Germany in the Eighteenth Century," *CEH* 13, no. 4 (1980): 332–47.

98 Alois Schmid, "Johann Kaspar von Thürriegel (1732–1795) und seine Kolonie in der Sierra Morena," in *Bayern mitten in Europa*, ed. Alois Schmid and Katharina Weigand (Munich, 2005), 228–41. I thank Christopher Mapes for bringing Thürriegel to my attention.

99 Emma Rothschild, "A Horrible Tragedy in the French Atlantic," *PP* 192 (2006): 67–108. John McNeill, *Mosquito Empires* (New York, 2010), 123–35, gives a higher death rate for the colony of 85–90 percent.

100 O'Reilly, "Migration, Recruitment and the Law," 119–37.

101 Mark Häberlein, "Migration and Business Ventures," in Davis et al., eds., *Transnational Networks*, 25.

102 Georg Fertig, *Lokales Leben, atlantische Welt* (Osnabrück, 2000); Fertig, "Transatlantic Migration," esp. 231–32.

103 Wokeck, *Trade in Strangers*; Marianne Wokeck, "Promoters and Passengers," in *The World of William Penn*, ed. Richard S. Dunn and Mary Maples Dunn (Philadelphia, 1986), 259–78; Farley Grubb, "The Market Structure of Shipping German Immigrants to Colonial America," *Pennsylvania Magazine of History and Biography* 111 (1987): 27–48; Andreas Brinck, *Die deutsche Auswanderungswelle in die britischen Kolonien um die Mitte des 18. Jahrhunderts* (Stuttgart, 1993); Aaron Fogelman, *Hopeful Journeys* (Philadelphia, 1996).

104 Fertig, "Transatlantic Migration," 212–13.

105 A. G. Roeber, "In German Ways?," *William and Mary Quarterly* 44, no. 4 (1987): 750–74, drawing on Wolf-Heino Struck's work on Hessian villages.

106 Wokeck, *Trade in Strangers*, 32; A. G. Roeber, *Palatines, Liberty, and Property* (Baltimore, 1993), 118–31; Häberlein, "Migration and Business Ventures," 29–32.

107 Fogelman, *Hopeful Journeys*.

108 O'Reilly, "Migration, Recruitment and the Law," 128; Fertig, "Transatlantic Migration," 219–20.

109 Mack Walker, *The Salzburg Transaction* (Ithaca, N.Y., 1992); James van Horn Melton, "From Alpine Miner to Low-Country Yeoman," *PP* 201 (2008): 97–140; James van Horn Melton, *Religion, Community, and Slavery on the Colonial Southern Frontier* (New York, 2015).

110 See Rosalind J. Beiler, *Immigrant and Entrepreneur: The Atlantic World of Caspar Wistar* (University Park, Pa., 2008).

111 Hermann Kellenbenz, "Von den karibischen Inseln," *JbLA* 7 (1970): 382, 400–8; Hermann Kellenbenz, "St. Thomas, Treffpunkt des karibischen Handelns," *Lateinamerika-Studien* 11 (1982): 135–45.

112 Klaus Weber, *Deutsche Kaufleute im Atlantikhandel 1680–1830* (Munich, 2004), 164, 174; Paul Butel, "France, the Antilles, and Europe in the Seventeenth and Eighteenth Centuries," in Tracy, ed., *Rise of Merchant Empires*, 167.

113 Margrit Schulte Beerbühl, "Commercial Networks, Transfer and Innovation," in Manz et al., eds., *Migration and Transfer from Germany to Britain*, 25, 31–34; Häberlein, "Migration and Business Ventures," 27–28; "Peter Hasenclever" (2017), in *Immigrant Entrepreneurship (GHI)*, http://www.immigrantentrepreneurship.org/entry .php?rec=22.

114 Weber, *Deutsche Kaufleute*, 176.

115 Beerbühl, "German Merchants and the British Empire," 47–48.

116 Klooster, "Atlantische Geschichte und der Begriff," 470; Percy Ernst Schramm, *Hamburg: Ein Sonderfall in der Geschichte Deutschlands* (Hamburg, 1964), 5–6; Beerbühl, "German Merchants and the British Empire," 42; Weber, "Deutschland, der atlantische Sklavenhandel und die Plantagenwirtschaft," *JMEH* 7, no. 1 (2009): 54–55; Anke Steffen and Klaus Weber, "Spinning and Weaving for the Slave Trade," in Brahm and Rosenhaft, eds., *Slavery Hinterland*, 87–107.

117 Hans-Ulrich Wehler, "Globalgeschichte ante portas," in *Wozu noch Sozialgeschichte?*, ed. Pascal Maeder et al. (Göttingen, 2012), 192, for "modest inland existences"; Sam

A. Mustafa, "Arnold Delius and the Hanseatic 'Discovery' of America," *GH* 18, no. 1 (2000): 49, on Hanseatic merchants and "inward-looking" merchants elsewhere.

118 Weber, "Deutschland, der atlantische Sklavenhandel und die Plantagenwirtschaft," 60.

119 Philip D. Curtin, *The Atlantic Slave Trade* (Madison, Wisc., 1969), 268; Burbank and Cooper, *Empires in World History*, 178.

120 Cited in Koslofsky and Zaugg, "Ship's Surgeon Johann Peter Oettinger," 28.

121 Weber, "Deutschland, der atlantische Sklavenhandel und die Plantagenwirtschaft," 48–50.

122 Walter Lüden, *Führer Seefahrer und ihre Schiffe* (Heide, 1989), 205.

123 Catharina Lüden, *Sklavenfahrt mit Seeleuten aus Schleswig-Holstein, Hamburg und Lübeck im 18. Jahrhundert* (Heide, 1983).

124 Koslofsky and Zaugg, "Ship's Surgeon Johann Peter Oettinger," 30–43.

125 Joachim Nettelbeck, *Ein Mann*, 168–231, describes acquiring and selling slaves.

126 Weber, "Deutschland, der atlantische Sklavenhandel und die Plantagenwirtschaft," 52, 55.

127 Beerbühl, "German Merchants and the British Empire," 42–43; Thorsten Heese, "Das koloniale Osnabrück," in *Kolonialismus hierzulande: Eine Spurensuche*, ed. Ulrich van der Heyden and Joachim Zeller (Erfurt, 2007), 40; Steffen and Weber, "Spinning and Weaving for the Slave Trade," 90–92; Kellenbenz, "Von den karibischen Inseln," 393.

128 Adam Smith, *The Wealth of Nations* (1776; repr., Harmondsworth, Eng., 1999), bk. IV, 173, 187, 211.

129 Butel, "France, the Antilles, and Europe," 163–68.

130 Eddy Stolls, "The Expansion of the Sugar Market," in *Tropical Babylons*, ed. Stuart B. Schwartz (Chapel Hill, N.C., 2004), 271–72; Weber, "Deutschland, der atlantische Sklavenhandel und die Plantagenwirtschaft," 58–60.

131 Beerbühl, "Commercial Networks, Transfer and Innovation," 30–31; Horst Rössler, "Germans from Hanover in the British Sugar Industry," in Manz et al., eds., *Migration and Transfer from Germany to Britain*, 49–53.

132 David Blackbourn, *The Long Nineteenth Century* (New York, 1998), 2–3.

133 Michael North, *"Material Delight and the Joy of Living"* (Burlington, Vt., 2008), 50.

134 Ibid., 1. The German phrase is *"Genuss und Glück des Lebens."* North renders *Genuss* as "material delight"; I believe "material pleasure" is closer.

135 Ibid., 48.

136 Bethany Wiggin, *Novel Translations* (Ithaca, N.Y., 2011), 24–34, 67.

137 Immanuel Wallerstein, *The Modern World System*, 2 vols. (New York, 1974, 1980); Bayly, *Birth of the Modern World*, 27–48; Jürgen Osterhammel and Niels P. Petersson, *Globalization* (Princeton, N.J., 2005).

138 Schmidt, *Inventing Exoticism*, places the "invention" in the years 1680–1730.

139 Johann Bernoulli, *Reisen durch Brandenburg, Pommern, Preussen, Curland, Russland und Polen in den Jahren 1777 und 1778* (Leipzig, 1779), 1:31–38.

140 Bettina Dietz, "Exotische Naturalien as Statussymbol," in *Exotica*, ed. Hans-Peter Bayerdörfer and Eckhardt Hellmuth (Münster, 2003).

141 Larry Wolff, *The Singing Turk* (Stanford, Calif., 2016).

142 Nina Berman, *German Literature on the Middle East* (Ann Arbor, Mich., 2011), 104–9.

143 Simon Schaffer, "Enlightened Automata," in Clark et al., eds., *The Sciences in Enlightened Europe*, 126–65; Adelheid Voskuhl, *Androids in the Enlightenment* (Chicago, 2013).

144 Suzanne Marchand, *Porcelain* (Princeton, N.J., 2020), 139–44.

145 David Bindman and Henry Louis Gates, eds., *The Image of the Black in Western Art*, vol. 3, pt. 2, *Europe and the World Beyond* (Cambridge, Mass., 2011); Uta Sadji, *Der Mohr auf der deutschen Bühne des 18. Jahrhunderts* (Anif/Salzburg, 1992).

146 Rebekka von Mallinckrodt, "There Are No Slaves in Prussia?," in Brahm and Rosenhaft, eds., *Slavery Hinterland*, 109–31.

147 Vera Lind, "Privileged Dependency on the Edge of the Atlantic World," in *Interpreting Colonialism*, ed. Byron Wells and Philip Stewart (Oxford, 2004), 369–91.

148 Monika Firla, "Afrikanische Pauker und Trompeter am Württembergischen Herzogshof im 17. und 18. Jahrhundert," *Musik in Baden-Württemberg* 3 (1996): 11–42; Monika Firla, "Samuel Urlsperger und zwei 'Mohren' (Anonymus und Wilhelm Samson) am

Württembergischen Herzogshof," *Blätter für württemberische Kirchengschichte* 97 (1997): 83–97; Monika Firla, *Exotisch-höfisch-bürgerlich: Afrikaner in Württemberg vom 15. bis 19. Jahrhundert* (Stuttgart, 2001); Vera Lind, "Africans in Early Modern German Society," *BGHI* 28 (Spring 2001): 74–82; Anne Kuhlmann, "Ambiguous Duty," in *Germany and the Black Diaspora*, ed. Mischa Honeck et al. (New York, 2013), 57–73; Rashid-S. Pegah, "Real and Imagined Africans in Baroque Court Divertissements," in Honeck et al., eds., *Germany and the Black Diaspora*, 74–91.

149 Ingeborg Kittel, "Mohren als Hofbediente und Soldaten im Herzogtum Braunschweig-Wolfenbüttel," *Braunschweigisches Jahrbuch* 46 (1965): 78–103; Wolfgang Schäfer, "Von 'Kammermohren,' 'Mohren'-Tambouren und 'Ost Indianern,'" *Hessische Blätter für Volks- und Kulturforschung* 23 (1988): 35–79.

150 Burchard Brentjes, *Anton Wilhelm Amo* (Leipzig, 1976); Peter Martin, *Schwarze Teufel, edle Mohren* (Hamburg, 1993), 308–27; Jacob Emmanuel Mabe, *Anton Wilhelm Amo interkulturell gelesen* (Nordhausen, 2007).

151 Martin, *Schwarze Teufel, edle Mohren*, 141–42; Kleinschmidt, *People on the Move*, 155.

152 Monika Firla, *"Segen, Segen, Segen auf Dich, guter Mann!"* (Vienna, 2003).

153 Smith, "Curing the Body Politic," 202.

154 Wolfgang Schivelbusch, *Tastes of Paradise* (New York, 1993), 96.

155 Mustafa, "Arnold Delius and the Hanseatic 'Discovery' of America," 47.

156 Koslofsky and Zaugg, "Ship's Surgeon Johann Peter Oettinger," 35.

157 Peer Schmidt, "Les *minorités religieuses européennes* face à l'espace atlantique à l'époque moderne," in Pietschmann, ed., *Atlantic History*, 91–92; Beerbühl, "German Merchants and the British Empire," 45–47.

158 Schivelbusch, *Tastes of Paradise*, 117.

159 On tobacco and chocolate, see Marcy Norton, *Sacred Gifts, Profane Pleasures* (Ithaca, N.Y., 2008).

160 Schivelbusch, *Tastes of Paradise*, 131–46.

161 Mustafa, "Arnold Delius and the Hanseatic 'Discovery' of America," 57–58; Schivelbusch, *Tastes of Paradise*, 111; Renate Pieper, "Der Einfluss lateinamerikanischer Erzeugnisse auf strukturelle Veränderungen in Europe," *JbLA* 35 (1998): 336–37.

162 I lean here on Kenneth Pomeranz and Steven Topik, *The World That Trade Made* (Armonk, N.Y., 2013), 99.

163 Schivelbusch, *Tastes of Paradise*, 103. Norton, *Sacred Gifts, Profane Pleasure*, qualifies the "medicinal" argument.

164 Sidney W. Mintz, *Sweetness and Power* (New York, 1985), 96–108.

165 Smith, "Curing the Body Politic," 207.

166 Ibid., 206; Stols, "Expansion of the Sugar Market," 251–53.

167 Mintz, *Sweetness and Power*, 95.

168 Mary Lindemann, *Patriots and Paupers* (New York, 1990), 3.

169 Schramm, *Hamburg: Ein Sonderfall*, 6.

170 Angus Calder, *Revolutionary Empire* (New York, 1981), 254.

171 Weber, "Deutschland, der atlantische Sklavenhandel und die Plantagenwirtschaft," 60–61.

172 Pieper, "Der Einfluss lateinamerikanischer Erzeugnisse," 328–29; Redcliffe Salaman, *The History and Social Influence of the Potato* (Cambridge, 1949), 115, 489.

173 Pieper, "Der Einfluss lateinamerikanischer Erzeugnisse," 330.

174 Gordon Uhlmann, "Hamburg," in van der Heyden and Zeller, eds., *Kolonialismus hierzulandee*, 349–50.

175 Schivelbusch, *Tastes of Paradise*, 15.

176 Pomeranz and Topik, *The World That Trade Created*, 91–94; Christine Fertig and Ulrich Pfister, "Coffee, Mind and Body," in *The Global Lives of Things*, ed. Anne Gerritsen and Giorgio Riello (New York, 2016), 221–40; North, *"Material Delight,"* 153.

177 North, *"Material Delight,"* 68–69, 163–64, using evidence from Frankfurt, Braunschweig, Hamburg, Stralsund, and Greifswald.

178 North, *"Material Delight,"* 159; Weber, "Deutschland, der atlantische Sklavenhandel und die Plantagenwirtschaft," 61; Jan de Vries, "The Industrial Revolution and the Industrious Revolution," *Journal of Economic History* 54 (1994): 240–70.

179 North, *"Material Delight,"* 166; Pomeranz and Topik, *The World That Trade Created*, 94–95.

180 Robert Liberles, *Jews Welcome Coffee* (Waltham, Mass., 2012).

181 Schivelbusch, *Tastes of Paradise*, 63, 69.

182 Bethany Wiggin, "The Geography of Fashionability," *Seminar: A Journal of Germanic Studies* 46, no. 1 (2010): 315–29, also discusses the Coffee Cantata (but uses a slightly different translation).

183 Uhlmann, "Hamburg," 349; North, *"Material Delight,"* 154–56.

184 Schivelbusch, *Tastes of Paradise*, 72.

185 Jürgen Habermas, *The Structural Transformation of the Public Sphere* (Cambridge, Mass., 1989).

186 See Blackbourn, *Long Nineteenth Century*, 40–44.

CHAPTER FOUR: REVOLUTIONS

1   John Darwin, *After Tamerlane* (New York, 2008), 162. See also David Armitage and Sanjay Subramanyam, eds., *The Age of Revolutions in Global Context, c. 1760–1840* (Basingstoke, Eng., 2010).

2   C. A. Bayly, *The Birth of the Modern World, 1780–1914* (Malden, Mass., 2004), 41.

3   Ibid., 27–48; Kevin O'Rourke and Jeffrey G. Williamson, *Globalization and History* (Cambridge, Mass., 1999), 109.

4   David Armitage, *The Declaration of Independence: A Global History* (Cambridge, Mass., 2007), 11.

5   Horst Dippel, *Germany and the American Revolution* (Chapel Hill, N.C., 1977), 194.

6   Reinhart Koselleck, "The Eighteenth Century and the Beginning of Modernity," in *The Practice of Conceptual History* (Stanford, Calif., 2002), 168.

7   Ernst Wolfgang Becker, *Zeit der Revolution!—Revolution der Zeit?* (Göttingen, 1999).

8   Writers Jean Paul and Germaine de Staël were among those who helped to establish the idea.

9   Ute Frevert, "Tatenarm und Gedankenvoll?," in *Deutschland und Frankreich im Zeitalter der Revolution*, ed. Helmut Berding et al. (Frankfurt/Main, 1989), 263–92.

10 Rolf Engelsing, *Der Bürger als Leser* (Stuttgart, 1974), 256–67.

11 The "century of words" was Klemens von Metternich's formulation in 1808, cited in Daniel Moran, *Toward the Century of Words* (Berkeley, Calif., 1989), 1.

12 Dror Wahrman, *The Making of the Modern Self* (New Haven, 2004).

13 Dippel, *Germany and the American Revolution*, 136–37.

14 Ibid., 12, 206.

15 Ibid., 101.

16 Dietrich Heinrich von Bülow, *Der Freistaat von Nordamerika in seinem neuesten Zustand*, 2 vols. (Berlin, 1797). Georg Friedrich Rebmann also called the United States a "free state" in *Hans Kiekindiewelts Reisen in alle vier Welttheile und den Mond* (Leipzig, 1794), 271.

17 Hans-Gerd Winter, "Klopstocks Revolutionsoden," in *"Sie, und nicht Wir": Die Französische Revolution und ihre Wirkung auf Norddeutschland und das Reich*, ed. Arno Herzig et al. (Hamburg, 1989), 1:135.

18 Dippel, *Germany and the American Revolution*, 213–23.

19 Janet Polasky, *Revolution Without Borders* (New Haven, 2015), 58.

20 Winter, "Klopstocks Revolutionsoden," 1:131–51.

21 Alain Ruiz, "Deutsche Augenzeugen," in *Revolution und Konservatives Beharren*, ed. Karl Otmar von Aretin and Karl Härter (Mainz, 1990), 203.

22 H.-J. Lüsebrink and Rolf Reichardt, *Die "Bastille"* (Frankfurt/Main, 1990).

23 Roger Paulin, *Ludwig Tieck* (New York, 1985), 11.

24 Germans constituted a fifth of foreign citizens in Paris: Oliver Faron and Cyril Grange, "Paris and Its Foreigners in the Late Eighteenth Century," in *Migration Control in the North Atlantic World*, ed. Andreas Fahrmeir et al. (New York, 2003), 39–54.

25 Ruiz, "Deutsche Augenzeugen," 198–99.

26 Erich Hinkel, *Johann Jakob Hauer* (Bruchsal, 2007).

27 Ruiz, "Deutsche Augenzeugen," 200–2; David A. Bell, *The First Total War* (Boston, 2007), 114–16.

28 Ruiz, "Deutsche Augenzeugen," 203–20; Heinrich Scheel, *Süddeutsche Jakobiner* (East Berlin, 1962); Walter Grab, *Norddeutsche Jakobiner* (Frankfurt/Main, 1967); Horst Günther, ed., *Die Französische Revolution: Berichte und Deutungen deutscher Schriftsteller und Historiker* (Frankfurt/Main, 1985); Karsten Witte, *Reise in die Revolution* (Stuttgart, 1971); Thomas P. Saine, *Black Bread—White Bread: German Intellectuals and the French Revolution* (Columbia, S.C., 1988); Anne Cottebrune, *"Deutsche Freiheitsfreunde" versus "deutsche Jakobiner"* (Bonn, 2002).

29 Jörn Garber, "Von der nützlichen zur harmonischen Gesellschaft," in Herzig et al., eds., *"Sie, und nicht Wir,"* 245–87; Saine, *Black Bread—White Bread*, 11–12, 22–26.

30 Ruiz, "Deutsche Augenzeugen," 206.

31 Daniel Schönpflug, *Der Weg in die Terreur* (Munich, 2002).

32 Susanne Lachenicht, *Information und Propaganda* (Berlin, 2004); Erich Pelzer, *Die Wiederkehr des girondistischen Helden* (Bonn, 1998), 86–106.

33 Helmut Berding, ed., *Soziale Unruhen in Deutschland während der Französischen Revolution* (Göttingen, 1988).

34 Ian McNeely, *The Emancipation of Writing* (Berkeley, Calif., 2003), 81–84.

35 For an example, see Claudia Ulrich, "Traditionale Bindung, revolutionäre Erfahrung und soziokultureller Wandel, Denting 1790–1796," in Aretin and Härter, eds., *Revolution und Konservatives Beharren*, 113–30.

36 Franz Dumont, *Die Mainzer Republik von 1792/93* (Alzey, 1982).

37 Cottebrune, *"Deutsche Freiheitsfreunde,"* 33.

38 Jürgen Goldstein, *Georg Forster* (Chicago, 2019), 142–43; Polasky, *Revolution Without Borders*, 111.

39 Goldstein, *Forster*, 151.

40 Saine, *Black Bread—White Bread*, 258–59, citing a writer in the *Schlesisches Journal*.

41 G. P. Gooch, *Germany and the French Revolution* (New York, 1920), 215–16.

42 Ruiz, "Deutsche Augenzeugen," 212–15.

43 Saine, *Black Bread—White Bread*, 30.

44 Franz Brümmer, "Rebmann, Georg Friedrich von," *ADB* 27, 483–85; Georg Seiderer, "Rebmann, Johann Andreas Georg Friedrich von," *NDB* 21, 226–28; Maria Anna Sossenheimer, *Georg Friedrich Rebmann und das Problem der Revolution* (Frankfurt/Main, 1988); Elmar Walde and Gerhard Sauder, eds., *Georg Friedrich Rebmann (1768–1824)* (Sigmaringen, 1997).

45 [Andreas] Georg Friedrich Rebmann, *Briefe von Erlangen* (Leipzig, 1792), 4.

46 *The New Gray Monster (Das neue Graue Ungeheuer)* has been digitized by the Bayerische Staatsbibliothek.

47 Cottebrune, *"Deutsche Freiheitsfreunde,"* 29–44; Becker, *Zeit der Revolution!—Revolution der Zeit?*, 77–88. Rebmann's *Hans Kiekindiewelts Reise*, 148–50, contains an extensive dialogue between the protagonist and his traveling companion, Herr Plitt, on the justifications, if any, for terror.

48 Georg Forster to Christian Wilhelm Dohm, Apr. 5, 1791, cited in Becker, *Zeit der Revolution!—Revolution der Zeit?*, 81.

49 Cottebrune, *"Deutsche Freiheitsfreunde,"* 29–31, 42–49; Saine, *Black Bread—White Bread*, 260–81; Becker, *Zeit der Revolution!—Revolution der Zeit?*, 78–81.

50 Timothy C. W. Blanning, *The French Revolution in Germany* (Cambridge, 1985), 9–15.

51 Karl Otmar von Aretin, "Deutschland und die Französische Revolution," in Aretin and Härter, eds., *Revolution und Konservatives Beharren*, 17.

52 Katrin Kohl, *Friedrich Gottlieb Klopstock* (Stuttgart, 2000), 35.

53 For "g——," see Klopstock to Johann Gleim, Nov. 9, 1795, cited in ibid., 25; on La Rochefoucauld, see Winter, "Klopstocks Revolutionsoden," 139–40.

54 "Das Neue" and Klopstock's other odes are available at Zeno.org. See also Winter, "Klopstocks Revolutionsoden," 140–46.

55 The poem about the sleep of reason is "An der Genius der Schönen Zeit. (Vor Ausbruch der Empörungen)," from 1793. An asterisk indicates that the word *Genius* signifies "reason" (*"die Vernunft"*): Johann Wilhelm Gleim, *Sämmtliche Werke* (Karlsruhe, 1820), 4:176.

56 Pelzer, *Die Wiederkehr des girondistischen Helden*, 173–80.

57 Zwi Batscha and Jörn Garber, eds., *Von der ständischen zur bürgerlichen Gesellschaft* (Frankfurt/Main, 1981), 373–90.

58 Volker Press, "Österreich, das Reich und die Eindämmung der Revolution in Deutschland," in Berding, ed., *Soziale Unruhen in Deutschland*, 237.

59 Leighton S. James, *Witnessing the Revolutionary and Napoleonic Wars in German Central Europe* (New York, 2013), 129–31; Saine, *Black Bread—White Bread*, 51–78.

60 Timothy C. W. Blanning, *The Origins of the French Revolutionary Wars* (London, 1986).

61 Nicholas Boyle, *Goethe: The Poet and the Age*, vol. 2, *Revolution and Renunciation (1790–1803)* (New York, 2000), 128. The consensus view is that Goethe never delivered his famous words around the campfire.

62 Carl von Clausewitz, *On War*, ed. Michael Howard and Peter Paret (Princeton, N.J., 1976), 591–92 (bk. 8, chap. 3). Klopstock referred to "the new shape of war": Winter, "Klopstocks Revolutionsoden," 139.

63 Bell, *First Total War*, 239.

64 On Westphalia and Berg, see Helmut Berding, *Napoleonische Herrschafts- und Gesellschaftspolitik im Königreich Westfalen (1807–1813)* (Göttingen, 1973); Bettina Severin-Barboutie, *Französische Herrschaftspolitik und Modernisierung* (Göttingen, 2008); Gerd Dethlefs et al., eds., *Modell und Wirklichkeit* (Paderborn, 2008); Sam A. Mustafa, *Napoleon's Paper Kingdom* (Lanham, Md., 2017).

65 George Rudé, *Revolutionary Europe 1783–1815* (London, 1964), 256.

66 Paul Nolte, *Staatsbildung und Gesellschaftsreform* (Frankfurt/Main, 1990), 118; Lloyd E. Lee, "Baden Between Revolutions," *CEH* 24 (1991): 248–67.

67 David Blackbourn, *The Conquest of Nature: Water, Landscape, and the Making of Modern Germany* (New York, 2006), 77–119.

68 Eberhard Weis, *Montgelas* (Munich, 2005).

69 Hans Rosenberg, *Bureaucracy, Aristocracy and Autocracy* (Cambridge, Mass., 1958), 161.

70 Hermann von Petersdorff, "Struensee, Karl August von," *ADB* 36 (1893): 661–65.

71 Matthew Levinger, *Enlightened Nationalism* (New York, 2000), 46. On the Prussian reformers, see Bernd Sösemann, ed., *Gemeingeist und Bürgersinn* (Berlin, 1993); Thomas Stamm-Kuhlmann, ed., *"Freier Gebrauch der Kräfte"* (Munich, 2001); Barbara Vogel, ed., *Preussische Reformen 1807–1820* (Königstein, 1980).

72 Levinger, *Enlightened Nationalism*, 27.

73 Bell, *First Total War*, 7.

74 Calculated from Alan Forrest, *Napoleon's Men* (New York, 2002), 18–19.

75 James, *Witnessing the Revolutionary and Napoleonic Wars*, 82–83; Julia Murken, *Bayerische Soldaten im Russlandfeldzug 1812* (Munich, 2006), 28, 38–40; Ute Planert, *Der Mythos vom Befreiungskrieg* (Paderborn, 2007), 414–17.

76 "Verlustliste: 1812—Württembergische Korps (Offiziere)," in K[arl] G[ottlieb] F[riedrich] Kurz, *Der Feldzug von 1812, Die Württemberger in Russland, Denkwürdigkeiten eines württembergischen Offiziers*, ed. Horst Kohl (Leipzig, 1912).

77 James, *Witnessing the Revolutionary and Napoleonic Wars*, 108.

78 Ibid., 75; Murken, *Bayerische Soldaten*, 62–77.

79 Heinrich August Vossler, *With Napoleon in Russia, 1812: The Diary of Lt. H. A. Vossler, a Soldier of the Grand Army, 1812–1813*, trans. Walter Wallich (1969; repr., London, 1998), 92–93. For another Swabian account, see Jakob Walter, *The Diary of a Napoleonic Foot Soldier*, ed. Mark Raeff (New York, 1993).

80 Vossler, *With Napoleon in Russia*, 95–122.

81 Murken, *Bayerische Soldaten*, 154.

82 Bell, *First Total War*, 11–12.

83 Peter Fritzsche, *Stranded in the Present* (Cambridge, Mass., 2004), 110–11.

84 Polasky, *Revolution Without Borders*, 243; Blanning, *French Revolution in Germany*, 87.

85 James, *Witnessing the Revolutionary and Napoleonic Wars*, 49.

86 Planert, *Mythos vom Befreiungskrieg*, 184–92; James, *Witnessing the Revolutionary and Napoleonic Wars*, 134. Forrest, *Napoleon's Men*, 140–41, discusses French soldiers' accounts, with their own euphemisms ("We seized hold of all the girls and made them dance").

87 John McNeill, *Mosquito Empires* (New York, 2010), 265–66; Johannes-Peter Rupp, *Gelb-fieberabwehr in Mitteleuropa* (Düsseldorf, 1981).

88 Karen Hagemann, "'Unimaginable Horror and Misery,'" in *Soldiers, Citizens, and Civilians*, ed. Alan Forrest et al. (New York, 2009), 170; Manfred Vasold, "Die Fleck-fieberepidemie von 1813/14 im mainfränkischen Raum," *Würzburger Medizinische Mitteilungen* 23 (2004): 217–32.

89 Carsten Küther, *Räuber und Gauner in Deutschland* (Göttingen, 1976).

90 Georg Mölich et al., eds., *Klosterkultur und Säkularisation im Rheinland* (Essen, 2002); Alois Schmid, ed., *Die Säkularisation in Bayern 1803* (Munich, 2003).

91 The German remnant of the collection is in the Wallraf-Richartz Museum, Cologne, the source for details of the cultural looting.

92 Wolfgang Burgdorf, *Ein Weltbild verliert seine Welt* (Munich, 2006).

93 Blanning, *French Revolution in Germany*.

94 Jeffry Diefendorf, *Businessmen and Politics in the Rhineland, 1789–1834* (Princeton, N.J., 1980).

95 David Sorkin, *The Transformation of German Jewry, 1780–1840* (New York, 1990), 21–33.

96 Werner Danckert, *Unehrliche Leute* (Berne, 1963).

97 Katherine Aaslestad, "Remembering and Forgetting," *CEH* 38 (2005): 384–416; Bernhard Mehnke, "Anpassung und Widerstand: Hamburg in der Franzosenzeit von 1806 bis 1814," in Herzig et al., eds., *"Sie, und nicht Wir,"* 333–49.

98 Jonathan Sperber, *Rhineland Radicals* (Princeton, N.J., 1991); James M. Brophy, *Popular Culture and the Public Sphere in the Rhineland, 1800–1850* (New York, 2007).

99 Burgdorf, *Ein Weltbild verliert seine Welt*; Fritzsche, *Stranded in the Present*.

100 Heribert Raab, *Joseph Görres* (Paderborn, 1978); Jon Vanden Heuvel, *A German Life in the Age of Revolution: Joseph Görres, 1776–1848* (Washington, D.C., 2001).

101 Levinger, *Enlightened Nationalism*, 63–64, 88–96.

102 Michael Jeismann, *Das Vaterland der Feinde* (Stuttgart, 1992).

103 Hans-Ulrich Wehler, *Deutsche Gesellschaftsgeschichte* (Munich, 1987), 1:523, 533. James H. Billington, *Fire in the Minds of Men* (New York, 1980) links the phrase "a great sea of fire in the mind" to Dostoyevsky's *The Possessed*, not to Arndt. Both no doubt borrowed it from the Book of Revelation.

104 Friedrich von Gentz, *The Origin and Principles of the American Revolution: Compared with the Origin and Principles of the French Revolution*, trans. John Quincy Adams (1800).

105 Volker Depkat, *Amerikabilder in politischen Diskursen* (Stuttgart, 1998), 268.

106 Ibid., 330.

107 Günter Kahle, *Simón Bolívar und die Deutschen* (Berlin, 1980), 12.

CHAPTER FIVE: KNOWLEDGE

1 J. Fred Rippy and E. R. Brann, "Alexander von Humboldt and Simón Bolívar," *AHR* 52, no. 4 (1947): 701. See also Manfred Kossok, "Alexander von Humboldt und der historische Ort der Unabhängigkeitsrevolution," in *Alexander von Humboldt* (Berlin, 1969), 1–26.

2 Richard Konetzke, "Alexander von Humboldt und Amerika," *JbLA* 1 (1964): 343.

3 Alexander von Humboldt, *Personal Narrative of a Journey to the Equinoctial Regions of the New Continent* (Harmondsworth, Eng., 1995).

4 Gabrielle Bersier, "Picturing the Physiognomy of the Equinoctial Landscape," in *Forster—Humboldt—Chamisso*, ed. Julian Drews et al. (Göttingen, 2017), 336.

5 Jason Wilson, "Introduction," in Humboldt, *Personal Narrative*, xxxvii.

6 Mary Louise Pratt, *Imperial Eyes* (New York, 1992), 111–43; Donald McCrory, *Nature's Interpreter* (Cambridge, 2010), 49–112; Andreas W. Daum, *Alexander von Humboldt* (Munich, 2019), 44–61.

7 Jorge Cañizares-Esguerra, "How Derivative Was Humboldt?," in *Colonial Botany*, ed. Londa Schiebinger and Claudia Swan (Philadelphia, 2005), 148–65.

8 Nicolaas A. Rupke, *Alexander von Humboldt* (Frankfurt/Main, 2005); Andreas W. Daum, "Die Ironie des Unzeitgemässen: Anmerkungen zu Alexander von Humboldt," *Zeitschrift für Ideengeschichte* 4 (2010): 5–23.

9 Daniel Kehlmann, *Measuring the World* (New York, 2006).

10 Anne Marie Claire Godlewska, "From Enlightenment Vision to Modern Science?," in *Geography and Enlightenment*, ed. David N. Livingston and Charles W. J. Withers (Chicago, 1999), 243.

11 Margaret Meredith, "Friendship and Knowledge," in *The Brokered World*, ed. Simon Schaffer et al. (Sagamore Beach, Mass., 2009), 151–91.

12 Andreas Daum, "German Naturalists in the Pacific Around 1800," in *Explorations and Entanglements*, ed. Hartmut Berghoff et al. (New York, 2018), 79–102.

13 Harry Liebersohn, *The Travelers' World* (Cambridge, Mass., 2006), 155–62; Chunjie Zhang, *Transculturality and German Discourse in the Age of Colonialism* (Evanston, Ill., 2017), 43–64; David Igler, "Indigenous Travelers and Knowledge Production in the Pacific," *History Compass* 15, no. 12 (2017), https://doi.org/10.1111/hic3.12431.

14 Daum, "German Naturalists," 92–95.

15 Hugh West, "Göttingen and Weimar," *CEH* 11, no. 2 (1978): 150–61; Justin Stagl, *A History of Curiosity* (Chur, 1995), 88–89.

16 Tim Fulford, Debbie Lee, and Peter J. Kitson, *Literature, Science and Exploration in the Romantic Era* (New York, 2004), 92; Liebersohn, *Travelers' World*, 127–29.

17 Daum, "Ironie des Unzeitgemässen," 16–17.

18 Daum, *Alexander von Humboldt*; Ottmar Ette, *Alexander von Humboldt und die Globalisierung* (Frankfurt/Main, 2009); Ottmar Ette, *Weltbewusstsein: Alexander von Humboldt und das unvollendete Projekt einer anderen Moderne* (Weilerswist, 2002).

19 Humboldt provided the first reliable estimate of bullion flows to Europe from the Americas: Ward Barrett, "World Bullion Flows, 1450–1800," in *The Rise of Merchant Empires*, ed. James D. Tracy (Cambridge, 1990), 230–32.

20 Ryan Tucker Jones, *Empire of Extinction* (New York, 2014), 119; Liebersohn, *Travelers' World*, 39.

21 Donald Worster, *Nature's Economy* (New York, 1994), 47; Clarence Glacken, *Traces on the Rhodian Shore* (Berkeley, Calif., 1967), 542.

22 Aaron Sachs, *The Humboldt Current* (New York, 2006).

23 Paul Warde, *The Invention of Sustainability* (New York, 2018), 322.

24 Jones, *Empire of Extinction*, 163–64, 198–203, 222.

25 Ibid., 203.

26 Martin Rudwick, *Bursting the Limits of Time* (Chicago, 2005), 243–61.

27 Jones, *Empire of Extinction*, 195.

28 Jones, *Empire of Extinction*, Liebersohn, *Travelers' World*, and Daum, "German Naturalists in the Pacific," all explore this question; so does Helmut Peitsch, *Georg Forster* (Berlin, 2017).

29 Glyndwr Williams and Peter J. Marshall, *The Great Map of Mankind* (Cambridge, Mass., 1982). Edmund Burke coined this term in 1777: Karl S. Guthke, *Exploring the Interior* (Cambridge, 2018), 3.

30 Liebersohn, *Travelers' World*, 33.

31 Hans Vermeulen, "The German Invention of Völkerkunde," in *The German Invention of Race*, ed. Sara Eigen and Mark Larrimore (Albany, N.Y., 2006), 123–45.

32 Jones, *Empire of Extinction*, 159–65, 198–203, 222.

33 Alan Bewell, "Romanticism and Colonial Natural History," *Studies in Romanticism* 43, no. 1 (2004): 20.

34 Liebersohn, *Travelers' World*, 50–53.

35 Harriet Guest, *Empire, Barbarism, and Civilisation* (New York, 2007), 55.

36 Fulford, Lee, and Kitson, *Literature, Science and Exploration*, 114.

37 Guest, *Empire, Barbarism, and Civilisation*, 54.

38 See Fulford, Lee, and Kitson, *Literature, Science and Exploration*, 135; David Bindman, *Ape to Apollo* (London, 2002), 123–50.

39 Guest, *Empire, Barbarism, and Civilisation*, 132.

40 On Forster's ambivalence, see Liebersohn, *Travelers' World*, 41–42; Jörg Esleben, "Georg Forster's Dialectic of Imperialism," *Seminar: A Journal of Germanic Studies* 37, no. 4 (2001): 305–22; Madhuvanti Karyekar, "Translating Observation into Narration" (PhD diss., University of Indiana, 2014).

41 Guest, *Empire, Barbarism, and Civilisation*, 49.

42 Susanne Zantop, *Colonial Fantasies* (Durham, N.C., 1997), 8, 38–42.

43 Michael E. Hoare, *The Tactless Philosopher* (Melbourne, 1976), 82.

44 Guest, *Empire, Barbarism, and Civilisation*, 137.

45 Robert Bernasconi, "Introduction" and "Who Invented the Concept of Race?," in *Race*, ed. Robert Bernasconi (Malden, Mass.,2001), 1, 11–36. Michael Banton, "The Vertical and Horizontal Dimensions of the Word *Race*," *Ethnicities* 10, no. 1 (2010): 127–49, argues that Kant's use of "race" has been misunderstood.

46 Bernasconi, "Who Invented the Concept of Race?," 14.

47 In addition to ibid., see John Zammito, "Policing Polygeneticism in Germany, 1775," and Susan Shell, "Kant's Concept of a Human Race," in Eigen and Larrimore, eds., *The German Invention of Race*, 35–54, 55–72; Zantop, *Colonial Fantasies*, 68–70.

48 Bernasconi, "Who Invented the Concept of Race?," 28.

49 Timothy Lenoir, "Kant, Blumenbach and Vital Materialism in German Biology," *Isis* 71 (1980): 77–108.

50 Zammito, "Policing Polygeneticism in Germany," 47; Londa Schiebinger, "The Anatomy of Difference," *Eighteenth-Century Studies* 23, no. 4 (1990): 389–99.

51 Zammito, "Policing Polygeneticism in Germany," 48.

52 J. F. Blumenbach, *On the Natural Variety of Mankind* (London, 1865), 265; Stephen Jay Gould, "The Geometer of Race," *Discover*, Nov. 1, 1994, 1–8.

53 Suzanne Marchand, *Down from Olympus* (New York, 1996). See Michael Chaouli, "Laocoön and the Hottentots," in Eigen and Larrimore, eds., *The German Invention of Race*, 29, on Wilhelm von Humboldt's view that white skin was preferable "because its clarity and transparency allows the subtlest expression and because it permits mixtures and nuances, for in black all color ceases to be."

54 Samuel Thomas Soemmering, *Über die körperliche Verschiedenheit des Mohren vom Europäer* (Mainz, 1784), 32. Soemmering's arguments were continued by his student Friedrich Tiedemann: see Jeannette Eileen Jones, "'On the Brain of the Negro,'" in *Germany and the Black Diaspora*, ed. Mischa Honeck et al. (New York, 2013), 134–52.

55 Frank Dougherty, "Johann Friedrich Blumenbach und Samuel Thomas Soemmering," in *Samuel Thomas Soemmering und die Gelehrten der Goethezeit*, ed. Günter Mann and Franz Dumont (Stuttgart, 1985), 35–36; Robert Bernasconi, "Kant's and Blumenbach's Polyps," in Eigen and Larrimore, eds., *The German Invention of Race*, 84; Zantop, *Colonial Fantasies*, 73. It complicates our picture to know that Soemmering and Georg Forster were close friends: Franz Dumont, "Das 'Seelenbündnis': Die Freundschaft zwischen Georg Forster und Samuel Thomas Soemmering," in *Der Weltumsegler und seine Freunde*, ed. Detlef Rasmussen (Tübingen, 1988), 70–100.

56 Christoph Meiners, "Ueber die Natur der afrikanischen Neger," *Göttingische Historisches Magazine* 6 (1790), 385–456.

57 Frank Dougherty, "Christoph Meiners und Johann Friedrich Blumenbach im Streit um den Begriff der Menschenrasse," in *Die Natur des Menschen*, ed. Günter Mann and Franz Dumont (Stuttgart, 1990), 89–111; Zantop, *Colonial Fantasies*, 79, 82–94; Uta Sadji, *Der Negermythos am Ende de 18. Jahrhunderts* (Frankfurt/Main, 1979), 222–27; Urs Bitterli, *Die Entdeckung des Schwarzen Afrikaners* (Zurich, 1970).

58 Walter Demel, "Trade Aspirations and China's Policy of Isolation," in *Maritime Asia: Profit Maximisation, Ethics and Trade Structure, c. 1300–1800*, ed. Karl Anton Sprengard and Roderich Ptak (Wiesbaden, 1994), 106, citing Johann Heinrich Justi, *Vergleichungen der Europäischen mit Asiatischen und anderen vermeintlich Barbarischen Regierungen* (Berlin, 1762).

59 *A Voyage Round the World . . . By Lewis de Bougainville . . . Translated by John Reinhold Forster* (London, 1772), 204, https://ia802800.us.archive.org/7/items/VoyageAroundTheWorldByLewisDeBougainville1766-9/Bougainville_Voyage_Eng_Transcr_JFF.pdf.

60 Dippel, *Germany and the American Revolution*, 52, citing Matthias Christian Sprengel, *Vom Ursprung des Negerhandels* (Halle, 1779).

61 Eric Weitz, "Self-Determination," *AHR* 120, no. 2 (2015): 465, citing Hannah Arendt, *The Origins of Totalitarianism* (1951; repr., Cleveland, 1958), 296.

62 See Susan Buck-Morss, "Hegel and Haiti," *Critical Inquiry* 26, no. 4 (2000): 837–38; Susan Buck-Morss, *Hegel, Haiti, and Universal History* (Pittsburgh, 2009).

63 Karin Schüller, *Die Deutsche Rezeption Haitianischer Geschichte in der Ersten Hälfte des 19. Jahrhunderts* (Cologne, 1992).

64 Andreas Gestrich, "The Abolition Act and the Development of Abolition Movements in 19th Century Europe," in *Humanitarian Intervention and Changing Labor Relations*, ed. Marcel van der Linden (Leiden, 2011), 247.

65 Ibid., 247–48. See also Rebekka Mallinckrodt, "There Are No Slaves in Prussia?," in *Slavery Hinterland: Transatlantic Slavery and Continental Europe, 1680–1850*, ed. Felix Brahm and Eve Rosenhaft (Rochester, N.Y., 2016), 109–31.

66 Zantop, *Colonial Fantasies*, 154.

67 Ibid., 148.

68 Buck-Morss, "Hegel and Haiti."

69 Ibid., 859*n*120; see also Peter K. J. Park, *Africa, Asia, and the Philosophy of History* (Albany, N.Y., 2013), 113–31.

70 Terry Pinkard, *Hegel* (New York, 2000), 203.

71 Georg Wilhelm Friedrich Hegel, *The Phenomenology of Spirit*, preface.

72 Pinkard, *Hegel*, 213, 228–29.

73 Terry Pinkard, *German Philosophy, 1760–1860* (New York, 2002), 218.

74 Nicholas Boyle, *Goethe: The Poet and the Age*, vol. 2, *Revolution and Renunciation (1790–1803)* (New York, 2000), 34.

75 William Clark, "The Death of Metaphysics in Enlightenment Prussia," in *The Sciences in Enlightened Europe*, ed. William Clark et al. (Chicago, 1999), 463–64, citing Heinrich Heine, in his 1834 "History of Religion and Philosophy in Germany."

76 Pinkard, *German Philosophy*, 15.

77 Weitz, "Self-Determination," 469.

78 Jerrold Seigel, *The Idea of the Self* (New York, 2005), 304.

79 Pinkard, *German Philosophy*, 36; see also Frederick Beiser, *The Fate of Reason* (Cambridge, Mass., 1987).

80 See James Turner, *Philology* (Princeton, N.J., 2014). Particular aspects of the centrality of language are examined by Jonathan Sheehan, *The Enlightenment Bible* (Princeton, N.J., 2005) and Suzanne Marchand, *German Orientalism in the Age of Empire* (New York, 2009).

81 Richard Konetzke, "Neue Veröffentlichungen über Alexander von Humboldt," *JbLA* 11 (1974): 347.

82 Ian McNeely, "Wilhelm von Humboldt and the World of Languages," *Ritsumeikan Studies in Language and Culture* 23, no. 2 (2011): 129–47; James Underhill, *Humboldt, Worldview and Language* (Edinburgh, 2009); Jürgen Trabant, "Linguistik und Philologie," in *Das Potential europäischer Philologen*, ed. Christoph König (Göttingen, 2009), 140–61.

83 Turner, *Philology*, 119, 136–40.

84 William Clark, *Academic Charisma and the Origins of the Research University* (Chicago, 2006), 377, citing Friedrich Gedike. Thomas H. Broman refers to Göttingen's "boundless capacity for self-promotion": *The Transformation of German Academic Medicine, 1750–1820* (New York, 1996), 49.

85 Clark, "The Death of Metaphysics," 424.

86 Clark, *Academic Charisma*, 443–44.

87 See Mitchell G. Asch, ed., *Mythos Humboldt* (Vienna, 1999); Manfred Eichler, "Die Wahrheit des Mythos Humboldt," *HZ* 294, no. 1 (2012): 59–78.

88 See Rainer Schwinges, ed., *Humboldt International* (Basel, 2001), and Asch, ed., *Mythos Humboldt*. See also Eichler, "Die Wahrheit des Mythos Humboldt," and compare Rüdiger vom Bruch, "Humboldt-Universität zu Berlin," in *Universitäten und Hochschulen in Deutschland, Österreich und der Schweiz*, ed. Laetitia Boehm and Rainer A. Müller (Düsseldorf, 1983), 50–68, with Rüdiger vom Bruch, "Langsamer Abschied von Humboldt," in Asch, ed., *Mythos Humboldt*, 29–57.

89 James Dennis Cobb, "The Forgotten Reforms" (PhD diss., University of Wisconsin, 1980); Peter Moraw, "Humboldt in Giessen," *Geschichte und Gesellschaft* 10 (1984): 47–71;

Wolfgang Hardtwig, "Wilhelm von Humboldt, Berlin und die dezentrierte Universitätsreform," in Schwinges, ed., *Humboldt International*, 151–62; R. Steven Turner, "Universitäten," in *Handbuch der deutschen Bildungsgeschichte*, ed. Karl-Ernst Jeismann and Peter Lundgren, vol. 3, *1800–1870* (Munich, 1987), 221–49.

90 Hanno Schmitt, *Visionäre Lebensklugkeit* (Wiesbaden, 1996); Friedrich Overhoff, "Ein Panorama des aufklärerischen Denkens," *HZ* 289, no. 2 (2009): 365–82.

91 Overhoff, "Ein Panorama," 374–75.

92 Clark, *Academic Charisma*, 379–80, quoting a 1782 tract, *Das Universitätswesen in Briefen*, on the "academic factory" and a former Göttingen student Wilhelm Mackensen, writing in 1791, on the "great merchant house of scholarship."

93 But see Frederic S. Steussy, *Eighteenth-Century German Autobiography* (New York, 1996).

94 Karl Philipp Moritz, *Anton Reiser*, vol. 1 (Berlin, 1785), second (unnumbered) page ("die innere Geschichte des Menschen schildern soll"), https://catalog.hathitrust.org/Search/SearchExport?handpicked=006057279&method=ris. On "Werther fever," see Nicholas Boyle, *Goethe: The Poet and the Age*, vol. 1, *The Poetry of Desire (1749–1790)* (New York, 2000), 168–78; T. J. Reed, *Goethe* (New York, 1984), 18–20.

95 Richard van Dülmen, *Die Entdeckung des Individuums 1500–1800* (Frankfurt/Main, 1997), 70–76.

96 Claire Gantet, *Der Traum in der Frühen Neuzeit* (Berlin, 2010), 344–460.

97 Van Dülmen, *Die Entdeckung des Individuums*, 76–79; Raimund Bezold, *Popularphilosophie und Erfahrungsseelenkunde im Werk von Karl Philipp Moritz* (Würzburg, 1984).

98 Matt ffytche, *The Foundation of the Unconscious* (New York, 2011). Henri F. Ellenberger, *The Discovery of the Unconscious* (New York, 1970), also emphasizes the nonphilosophical roots of the concept in Christian traditions and movements such as Mesmerism.

99 Fulford, Lee, and Kitson, *Literature, Science and Exploration*, 113, 143–45.

100 Seigel, *The Idea of the Self*, 327.

CHAPTER SIX: WORLD LITERATURE

1 Bernhard Fabian, "The Reception of British Writers on the Continent," *Hungarian Journal of English and American Studies* 13, no. 1–2 (2007): 15–16.

2 Martin Swales, *The German Bildungsroman from Wieland to Hesse* (Princeton, N.J., 1978); Franco Moretti, *The Way of the World: The Bildungsroman in European Culture* (New York, 2000).

3 Michael Kater, *Weimar* (New Haven, 2014), 1–38; Birgit Tautz, *Translating the World* (University Park, Pa., 2018), 162–79, 195.

4 Alexander von Humboldt, *Personal Narrative of a Journey to the Equinoctial Regions of the New Continent* (Harmondsworth, Eng., 1995), 15.

5 Debra Prager, *Orienting the Self* (Rochester, N.Y., 2014), 119.

6 James J. Sheehan, *German History 1770–1866* (New York, 1989), 332.

7 On the Romantics as avant-garde, see Renato Poggioli, *The Theory of the Avant-Garde* (Cambridge, Mass., 1968), 42–59. Other scholars have discussed the Romantics as "modernists"—see, for example, Karl Heinz Bohrer, *Der Romantische Brief* (Munich, 1987).

8 Roger Paulin, *Ludwig Tieck* (New York, 1985), 134.

9 *Germany by the Baroness Staël-Holstein* (London, 1813), xiv. See also Michel Espagne, "De l'Allemagne," in *Deutsche Erinnerungsorte*, ed. Étienne François and Hagen Schulze (Munich, 2001), 1:225–41.

10 Jeffrey L. High, ed., *Who Is This Schiller Now?* (Rochester, N.Y., 2011), 9.

11 Earl Leslie Grigg, "Ludwig Tieck and Samuel Taylor Coleridge," *The Journal of English and German Philology* 54, no. 2 (1955): 262–68.

12 James Turner, *Philology* (Princeton, N.J., 2014), 158–60.

13 F. W. Stokoe, *German Influence on the English Romantic Period, 1788–1818* (Cambridge, 1926).

14 Maggie Allen, "Emily Brontë and the Influence of the German Romantic Poets," *Brontë*

Studies 30, no. 1 (2005): 7–10; Paola Tonussi, "From Werther to Wuthering Heights," *Brontë Studies* 33, no. 1 (2008), 30–43.

15 Georg Brandes, *The Romantic School in Germany* (London, 1902), 328–29.

16 Candace Mary Beutell Gardner, "The Reception of Don Quixote in Seventeenth and Eighteenth Century Germany and Friedrich J. Bertuch's Pioneering Translation (1775–77) of It," *The Quiet Corner Interdisciplinary Journal* 1, no. 1 (2015): 17–43.

17 Bettina Brandt, "Taming Foreign Speech," *GSR* 41, no. 2 (2018): 355–72.

18 Maria Tatar, *The Hard Facts of the Grimms' Fairy Tales* (Princeton, N.J., 1987).

19 Howard Gaskill, ed., *The Reception of Ossian in Europe* (New York, 2004); Wolf Gerhard Schmidt, *"Homer des Nordens" und "Mutter der Romantik,"* 3 vols. (Berlin, 2003); Gerald Bär, "'What We Wish, We Easily Believe': Wolf Gerhard Schmidt's *Opus Magnum* on the Reception of Ossian in German-Speaking Literature," *Comparative Critical Studies* 3, no. 3 (2006): 405–9.

20 Gauti Kristmannsson, "The Nordic Turn in German Literature," in *Edinburgh German Yearbook*, vol. 1, *Cultural Exchange in German Literature*, ed. Eleoma Joshua and Robert Vilain (Rochester, N.Y., 2007), 63–72.

21 Eberhard Werner Happel's *Der insulanische Mandorell* (1682) was one possible inspiration for Defoe, although many sources have been identified. The name "Crusoe" is an Anglicized version of "Kreutznaer," readers learn.

22 Chunjie Zhang, *Transculturality and German Discourse in the Age of Colonialism* (Evanston, Ill., 2017), 65–67.

23 Susanne Zantop, *Colonial Fantasies* (Durham, N.C., 1997), 103.

24 William E. Stewart, *Die Reisebeschreibung und ihre Theorie in Deutschland des 18. Jahrhunderts* (Bonn, 1978), 188–90; Zantop, *Colonial Fantasies*, 32.

25 Adam Henss, *Wanderungen und Lebensansichten des Buchbinder-Meisters Adam Henss* (Jena, 1845), 4.

26 Karl S. Guthke, *Exploring the Interior* (Cambridge, 2018), 6.

27 Fritz Brüggemann, *Utopie und Robinsonade* (Hildesheim, 1978).

28 Zhang, *Transculturality and German Discourse*, 68–85; Zantop, *Colonial Fantasies*, 102–20.

29 Michelet made these comparisons in 1831 and 1841, respectively. See Gabriele Bleeke-Byrne, "French Perceptions of German Art (1800–1850)" (PhD diss., Brown University, 1989). I thank Annette Schlagenhauff for bringing this to my attention.

30 E[liza] M[arian] Butler, *The Tyranny of Greece over Germany* (Cambridge, 1935). See also Suzanne L. Marchand, *Down from Olympus* (Princeton, N.J., 1996); George S. Williamson, *The Longing for Myth in Germany* (Chicago, 2004), 35–41.

31 Sheehan, *German History*, 173.

32 Terry Pinkard, *Hegel* (New York, 2000), 212 (Hegel quoted *Rameau's Nephew* in his *Phenomenology of Spirit*). Goethe viewed Diderot as a "true German": Joseph Jurt, "Das Konzept der Weltliteratur: Ein erster Entwurf eines internationalen literarischen Feldes?," in *"Die Bienen fremder Literaturen,"* ed. Norbert Bachleitner (Wiesbaden, 2012), 28.

33 Steven G. Yao, *Translation and the Language of Modernism* (New York, 2002), 2; Tautz, *Translating the World*, 60–61, 85–86.

34 Suzanne Marchand, *German Orientalism in the Age of Empire* (New York, 2009), 63; Raymond Schwab, *The Oriental Renaissance* (New York, 1984).

35 E. T. A. Hoffmann, *E. T. A. Hoffmann's Musical Writings*, ed. David Charlton (Cambridge, 2003), 105.

36 Turner, *Philology*, 95.

37 Michael J. Franklin, *Orientalist Jones* (New York, 2011); Turner, *Philology*, 98.

38 Marchand, *German Orientalism*, 59–60.

39 Prager, *Orienting the Self*, 131.

40 Leon Poliakov, *The Aryan Myth* (New York, 1974); Douglas T. McGetchin et al., eds., *Sanskrit and "Orientalism"* (New Delhi, 2004); Stefan Arvidsson, *Indo-European Mythology as Ideology and Science* (Chicago, 2006); Chen Tzoref-Ashkenazi, *Der romantische Mythos vom Ursprung der Deutschen* (Göttingen, 2009); Douglas T. McGetchin, "'Orient' and 'Occident,' 'East' and 'West' in the Discourse of German Orientalists,

1790–1930," in *Germany and "the West,"* ed. Riccardo Bavaj and Martina Steber (New York, 2015), 111–23.

41 Dorothy Matilda Figueira, *Translating the Orient* (Albany, N.Y., 1991).

42 Jörg Esleben, "'Indisch lesen': Conceptions of Intercultural Communication in Georg Forster's and Johann Gottfried Herder's Reception of Kalidasa's Sakuntala," *Monatshefte für deutschen Unterricht, deutsche Sprache und Literatur* 95, no. 2 (2003): 217–29; Madhuvanti Karyekar, "Translating Observation into Narration" (PhD diss., University of Indiana, 2014), 157–201.

43 Schwab, *Oriental Renaissance*, 57–64.

44 Turner, *Philology*, 95; Franklin, *Orientalist Jones*, 251; Schwab, *Oriental Renaissance*, 66.

45 Prager, *Orienting the Self*, 120; Nicholas A. Germana, "The Orient of Europe" (PhD diss., Boston College, 2006), 108–18.

46 Edward Said, *Orientalism* (New York, 1978), remains fundamental, although his focus was on Britain and France, not Germany. That gap has been superbly filled by Marchand, *German Orientalism*. See also Jean W. Sedlar, *India in the Mind of Germany* (Washington, D.C., 1982); Todd Kontje, *German Orientalisms* (Ann Arbor, Mich., 2004); Douglas McGetchin, *Indology, Indomania and Orientalism* (Madison, Wisc., 2009).

47 Marchand, *German Orientalism*, 60, drawing on Bradley L. Herling, *The German Gita* (London, 2006).

48 Marchand, *German Orientalism*, 49.

49 Germana, "The Orient of Europe," 106.

50 Lionel Gossman, "History as Decipherment," *New Literary History* 18, no. 1 (1986): 29.

51 Prager, *Orienting the Self*, 119–78; Kontje, *German Orientalisms*, 93–99.

52 Marchand, *German Orientalism*, xxv. That Orientalism can take different forms is also central to the argument of Kontje, *German Orientalisms*. See also Russell A. Berman, *Enlightenment or Empire* (Lincoln, Neb., 1998); Chunjie Zhang, "German Indophilia, Femininity, and Transcultural Symbiosis Around 1800," in *Imagining Germany Imagining Asia*, ed. Veronika Fuechtner and Mary Rhiel (Rochester, N.Y., 2013), 204–19.

53 See "In the Time of Not Yet: Marina Warner on the Imaginary of Edward Said," *London Review of Books*, Dec. 16, 2010.

54 Marchand, *German Orientalism*, 87–88; Katharina Mommsen, *"Orient und Okzident sind nicht mehr zu trennen"* (Göttingen, 2012), 45–62.

55 Masoomeh Kalatehseifary, "Joseph v. Hammer Purgstall's German Translation of Hafez's *Divan* and Goethe's *West-östliche Divan*" (MA thesis, University of Waterloo, 2009).

56 Daniel Barenboim and Edward W. Said, *Parallels and Paradoxes*, ed. Ara Guzelimian (New York, 2002), 7, 11; Said, *Orientalism*, 167–68.

57 Hans Ruppert, *Goethes Bibliothek* (Weimar, 1958), 109–255.

58 Johann Peter Eckermann, *Gespräche mit Goethe in den letzten Jahren seines Lebens* (1836; repr., Wiesbaden, 1955), 196; Franco Moretti, *Distant Reading* (New York, 2013), 44–45.

59 John Pizer, "Goethe's 'World Literature' Paradigm and Contemporary Cultural Globalization," *Comparative Literature* 52, no. 3 (2000): 215.

60 Homi K. Bhabha, *The Location of Culture* (London, 1994); Pizer, "Goethe's 'World Literature' Paradigm," 213–27; David Damrosch, *What Is World Literature?* (Princeton, N.J., 2003); Pascale Casanova, *The World Republic of Letters* (Cambridge, Mass., 2004); John Pizer, *The Idea of World Literature* (Baton Rouge, 2006); Emily Apter, *The Translation Zone* (Princeton, N.J., 2006), 42; Moretti, *Distant Reading*, 43–62, 107–19; B. Venkat Mani, *Recoding World Literature* (New York, 2017).

61 Karl Marx and Friedrich Engels, *"The Communist Manifesto,"* in Karl Marx and Frederick Engels, *Selected Works in One Volume* (London, 1968), 39; S. S. Prawer, *Karl Marx and World Literature* (New York, 1978), 144; Moretti, *Distant Reading*, 44–45.

62 Isaac Nakhimovsky, *The Closed Commercial State* (Princeton, N.J., 2011), 69, 162.

63 Goethe referred to "world literature" on around twenty different occasions: Jurt, "Das Konzept der Weltliteratur," 28*n*32.

64 Casanova, *World Republic of Letters*, 14; Bethany Wiggin, "Monolinguism, World Literature, and the Return of History," *GSR* 41, no. 3 (2018): 494–95; Elizabeth Powers,

"Fritz Strich and the Dilemmas of World Literature Today," *Goethe Yearbook* 26 (2019): 244.

65 Kristmannsson, "The Nordic Turn in German Literature," 65.

66 Hans-J. Weitz. "'Weltliteratur' zuerst bei Wieland," *Arcasia* 22 (1987): 206–8. I owe this reference to a paper by Claire Baldwin at a German Studies Association seminar in 2013, "C. M. Wieland's Practices of World Literature." The full quotation is also given in Jurt, "Das Konzept der Weltliteratur," 29.

67 Baldwin, "C. M. Wieland's Practices of World Literature," 9–10.

68 Irmtraut Sahmland, *Christoph Martin Wieland und die deutsche Nation* (Tübingen, 1990).

69 Pizer, "Goethe's 'World Literature' Paradigm," 217–18.

70 Gail Finney, "Of Walls and Windows," *Comparative Literature* 49, no. 3 (1997): 261.

71 Fritz Strich, *Goethe und die Weltliteratur* (Berne, 1946); Jurt, "Das Konzept der Weltliteratur," 29–30.

72 Casanova, *World Republic of Letters*, 38, 75–79.

73 On translation as a weapon and the "translation zone" as a "war zone," see Apter, *Translation Zone*, xi.

74 Marchand, *German Orientalism*, 68.

75 Jurt, "Das Konzept der Weltliteratur," 33.

CHAPTER SEVEN: A NATION AMONG OTHERS

1 P[aul] A[chatius] Pfizer, *Briefwechsel zweier Deutschen* (Stuttgart, 1831), 160, 164–65.

2 Christian Kennert, *Die Gedankenwelt des Paul Achatius Pfizer* (Berlin, 1986); Theodor Schott, "Pfizer, Paul," *ADB* 25 (Leipzig, 1887): 668–77.

3 Pfizer, *Briefwechsel*, 167.

4 Anne-Marie Thiesse, *La Création des identités nationales* (Paris, 1999), 11.

5 Christian Jansen, "The Formation of German Nationalism, 1740–1850," in *The Oxford Handbook of Modern German History*, ed. Helmut Walser Smith (New York, 2011), 240, citing Friedrich Karl Moser, *Von dem Deutschen national-Geist* (Frankfurt/Main, 1765), 9.

6 Hagen Schulze, *The Course of German Nationalism* (New York, 1991), 46; Michael North, *"Material Delight and the Joy of Living"* (Burlington, Vt., 2008), 55–58, 60.

7 Klaus Bohnen, "Von den Anfängen des 'Nationalsinns,'" in *Dichter und ihre Nation*, ed. Helmut Scheuer (Frankfurt/Main, 1993), 121–37; Hans Peter Herrmann, Hans-Martin Blitz, and Susanna Mossmann, *Machtphantasie Deutschland* (Frankfurt/Main, 1996); Eckhart Hellmuth and Reinhard Stauder, eds., *Nationalismus vor dem Nationalismus?* (Hamburg, 1998); Hans-Martin Blitz, *Aus Liebe zum Vaterland* (Hamburg, 2000).

8 Ute Planert, "Wann begann der 'moderne' deutsche Nationalismus?," in *Die Politik der Nation*, ed. Jörg Echternkamp and Sven Oliver Müller (Munich, 2002), 25–59; Jörg Echternkamp, *Der Aufstieg des deutschen Nationalismus (1770–1840)* (Frankfurt/Main, 1998), 41–159.

9 Schulze, *Course of German Nationalism*, 52.

10 Echternkamp, *Aufstieg*, 292–98.

11 William Vaughan, *German Romantic Painting* (New Haven, 1982), 96 and pl. 61; Joseph Leo Kerner, *Caspar David Friedrich and the Subject of Landscape* (London, 1990), 190–94 and pl. 74.

12 Christopher B. Krebs, *A Most Dangerous Book* (New York, 2011).

13 Dieter Düding, *Organisierter gesellschaftlicher Nationalismus in Deutschland (1808–1847)* (Munich, 1984), 23*n*35.

14 Friedrich Jahn, *Deutsches Volksthum* (Lübeck, 1810), 199-200.

15 Echternkamp, *Aufstieg*, 356; Joachim Burkhard Richter, *Hans Ferdinand Massmann* (Berlin, 1992), 61–62.

16 Paul Wentzcke, *Geschichte der Deutschen Burschenschaft*, vol. 1, *Vor- und Frühzeit bis zu den Karlsbader Beschlüssen* (Heidelberg, 1965); Karin Luys, *Die Anfänge der deutschen Nationalbewegung von 1815 bis 1819* (Münster, 1992).

17 Echternkamp, *Aufstieg*, 386.

18 Schulze, *Course of German Nationalism*, 98, 124.

19 Günter Steiger, *Aufbruch Urburschenschaft und Wartburgfest* (Leipzig, 1967); P. Brandt, "Das studentische Wartburgfest vom 18./19. Oktober 1817," in *Öffentliche Festkultur*, ed. Dieter Düding et al. (Reinbek, 1988), 89–112; Gary D. Stark, "The Ideology of the German *Burschenschaft* Generation," *European Studies Review* 8 (1978): 323–48; Steven Press, "False Fire: The Wartburg Book-Burning of 1817," *CEH* 42, no. 4 (2009): 621–46; George S. Williamson, "Who Killed August von Kotzebue?," *JMH* 72, no. 4 (2000): 890–943.

20 Press, "False Fire."

21 Williamson, "Who Killed August von Kotzebue?," 936.

22 Mona Ozouf, *Festivals and the French Revolution* (Cambridge, Mass., 1991).

23 Williamson, "Who Killed August von Kotzebue?," 937.

24 Stark, "The Ideology of the German *Burschenschaft* Generation," 337.

25 Günter Steiger, "Die Teilnehmerliste des Wartburgfestes von 1817," in *Darstellungen und Quellen zur Geschichte der deutschen Einheitsbewegung*, ed. Paul Wentzcke et al. (Heidelberg, 1963), 4:65–113; Helge Dvorak, *Biographisches Lexikon der Deutschen Burschenschaft*, 9 vols. (Heidelberg, 1996–2018).

26 Carl Meltz, "Horn, Karl," *NDB* 9 (1972): 629–30; Friedrich Wilhelm Krummacher, *Eine Selbstbiographie* (Berlin, 1869), 202–4.

27 Hans Lülfing, "Frommann, Friedrich," *NDB* 5 (1961): 659–60.

28 Christoph Freiherr von Maltzahn, "Leo, Heinrich," *NDB* 14 (1985): 243–45.

29 Even his sympathetic biographer says Massmann lived in a "patriotic fantasy world" in the 1840s: Richter, *Massmann*, 309.

30 Dieter Langewiesche, *Reich, Nation, Föderation* (Munich, 2008), 137.

31 Echternkamp, *Aufstieg*, 342–43, 575n94.

32 Richter, *Massmann*, 218–24; Echternkamp, *Aufstieg*, 422.

33 Wilhelm Schulz, *Briefwechsel eines Staatsgefangenen und seiner Befreierin* (Mannheim, 1846), 2:122.

34 Krummacher, *Selbstbiographie*, 54.

35 See Steiger, "Die Teilnehmerliste des Wartburgfestes von 1817," and Dvorak, *Biographisches Lexikon der Deutschen Burschenschaft*.

36 Edmund Spevack, *Carl Follen's Search for Nationality and Freedom* (Cambridge, Mass., 1997).

37 Ernst Feise, "Heinrich Heine, Political Poet and Publicist," *Monatshefte* 40, no. 4 (1948): 214.

38 Jörg Ludwig, *Deutschland und die spanische Revolution von 1820–1823* (Leipzig, 2012), 43–46.

39 Rudolf Elvers, "Huber, Victor Aimé," *ADB* 13 (1881): 249–58.

40 Ludwig, *Deutschland und die spanische Revolution*, 113–206.

41 Depkat, *Amerikabilder*, 166, 180, 301–11, 326–31; Karin Schüller, "Das Urteil der deutschen Liberalen des Vormärz über Lateinamerika," *JbLA* 31 (1994): 189–207.

42 Günter Kahle, "Friedrich Rasch und Carl Sowersby," *JbLA* 27 (1990): 200–1, 216; Günter Kahle, *Simón Bolívar und die Deutschen* (Berlin, 1980).

43 Rafe Blaufarb, "The Western Question," *AHR* 112, no. 3 (June 2007): 743; Alfred Hasbrouck, *Foreign Legionaries in the Liberation of Spanish South America* (New York, 1928).

44 Robin Kiera, *Der grosse Sohn der Stadt Kassel?* (Marburg, 2009).

45 Kahle, "Friedrich Rasch und Carl Sowersby," 223.

46 Jan Rüger, *Heligoland* (New York, 2017), 35–36.

47 David Brewer, *The Greek War of Independence* (London, 2001), 144.

48 Echternkamp, *Aufstieg*, 411–14; Christoph Hauser, *Anfänge bürgerlicher Organisation* (Göttingen, 1990); James M. Brophy, *Popular Culture and the Public Sphere in the Rhineland, 1800–1850* (New York, 2007), 71–72, 120–21.

49 The newspaper editor was Johann Wirth, one of the two organizers of the Hambach festival in May 1832: J. G. A. Wirth, *Der Nationalfest der Deutschen zu Hambach*, no. 1 (Neustadt, 1832), 3.

50 Echternkamp, *Aufstieg*, 414–17; Brophy, *Popular Culture*, 79–83, 124–25.

51 Wirth, *Nationalfest der Deutschen*, 3–4, 24–25, 41–42.

52 Williamson, "Who Killed August von Kotzebue?," 925–26. However, the transcript of Hambach shows that no speech was given by a woman.

53 Wirth, *Nationalfest der Deutschen*, 20–24.
54 Paul Pfizer, *Gedanken über die Aufgaben und das Ziel des Deutschen Liberalismus* (1832; repr., Berlin, 1911), 341.
55 This democratic nationalist was Hermann Laube: Echternkamp, *Aufstieg*, 454.
56 Wirth, *Nationalfest der Deutschen*, 33–34.
57 Ibid., 41–54.
58 Schulze, *Course of German Nationalism*, 64–66; Cecilia Hopkins Porter, "The *Rheinlieder* Critics," *The Musical Quarterly* 63 (1977): 74–98; Lorie A. Vanchena, "The Rhine Crisis of 1840," in *Searching for Common Ground*, ed. Nicholas Vazsonyi (Cologne, 2000), 239–51; James M. Brophy, "The Rhine Crisis of 1840 and German Nationalism," *JMH* 85, no. 1 (2013): 1–35.
59 Brophy, "Rhine Crisis," 3–4, cites the many historians who argue along these lines.
60 Ibid., 9, 15. Brophy gives many other examples.
61 Jonathan Sperber, *Rhineland Radicals* (Princeton, N.J., 1991), 94–105; Brophy, *Popular Culture*, 54–63, 171–215; Rudolf Schenda, *Volk ohne Buch* (Munich, 1977), 334–44; Ute Planert, *Der Mythos vom Befreiungskrieg* (Paderborn, 2007), 630–61.
62 Charles McClelland, *The German Historians and England* (Cambridge, 1971), 64; Roland Ludwig, *Die Rezeption der Englischen Revolution im deutschen politischen Denken und in der Historiographie im. 18. und 19. Jahrhundert* (Leipzig, 2003), 257–65.
63 Thomas Nipperdey, "Nationalidee und Nationaldenkmal in Deutschland im 19. Jahrhundert," *HZ* 206 (1968): 529–85; Charlotte Tacke, *Denkmal im sozialen Raum* (Göttingen, 1995).
64 Andreas Etges, "Von der 'vorgestellten' zur 'realen' Gefühls- und Interessengemeinschaft?," in Echternkamp and Müller, eds., *Politik der Nation*, 66.
65 Echternkamp, *Aufstieg*, 342.
66 Ibid., 458.
67 Etges, "Von der 'vorgestellten' zur 'realen' Gefühls- und Interessengemeinschaft?," 73–75.
68 Ibid., 74.
69 Eckhart G. Franz, *Das Amerikabild der deutschen Revolution von 1848/49* (Heidelberg, 1958), 87.
70 Charlotte A. Lerg, *Amerika als Argument* (Bielefeld, 2011), xx.
71 Mark Hewitson, *Nationalism in Germany, 1848–1866* (New York, 2010), 38.
72 Brian E. Vick, *Defining Germany* (Cambridge, Mass., 2002), 114.
73 Monika Wegmann-Fetsch, *Die Revolution von 1848 im Grossherzogtum Oldenburg* (Oldenburg, 1974), 27.
74 Rosemary Ashton, *Little Germany* (New York, 1986), 30.
75 Hans Victor von Unruh, *Erfahrungen aus den letzten drei Jahren* (Magdeburg, 1851), 95.
76 Hans Boldt, "Federalism as an Issue in the German Constitutions of 1849 and 1871," in *German and American Constitutional Thought*, ed. Hermann Wellenreuther (New York, 1990), 272.
77 Sperber, *Rhineland Radicals*, 289–92.
78 Manfred Kittel, "Abschied vom Völkerfrühling?," *HZ* 275 (2002): 374–75.
79 An example is Gottlieb Christian Schüler. See his letters: Sibylle Schüler and Frank Möller, eds., *Als Demokrat in der Paulskirche* (Cologne, 2007).
80 Günter Moltmann, *Atlantische Blockpolitik im 19. Jahrhundert* (Düsseldorf, 1973), 211.
81 Lerg, *Amerika als Argument*; Boldt, "Federalism as an Issue," 260–78; Michael Dreyer, "American Federalism—Blueprint for Nineteenth-Century Germany?," in Wellenreuther, ed., *German and American Constitutional Thought*, 328–36.
82 Merle E. Curti, "John C. Calhoun and the Unification of Germany," *AHR* 40, no. 3 (1935): 476–78.
83 Vick, *Defining Germany*, 111–12, 119.
84 Ibid., 116.
85 Hewitson, *Nationalism in Germany*, 48–50; Vick, *Defining Germany*, 126–36.
86 Schulze, *Course of German Nationalism*, 30; Wilhelm Rüstow, *Stehendes Heer und Volkswehr* (Mannheim, 1848), 9, 51; Sperber, *Rhineland Radicals*, 268; Vick, *Defining Germany*, 76–77.

87 Gregor Thum, "Megalomania and Angst," in *Shatterzones of Empire*, ed. Omer Bartov and Eric D. Weitz (Bloomington, Ind., 2013), 49.

88 Alberto Mario Banti, "Sacrality and the Aesthetics of Politics," in *Giuseppe Mazzini and the Globalisation of Democratic Nationalism, 1830–1920*, ed. C. A. Bayly and Eugenio F. Biagini (New York, 2008), 68.

89 Vick, *Defining Germany*, 150.

90 Günter Wollstein, *Das "Grossdeutschland" der Paulskirche* (Düsseldorf, 1977), 146–50; Kittel, "Abschied vom Völkerfrühling?," 343; Vick, *Defining Germany*, 154–59; Thum, "Megalomania and Angst," 48.

91 Thum, "Megalomania and Angst," 47. I have made small stylistic changes to Thum's translations.

92 Kittel, "Abschied vom Völkerfrühling?," 352–54.

93 Wollstein, *Das "Grossdeutschland" der Paulskirche*, 243–54; Kittel, "Abschied vom Völkerfrühling?," 354–56.

94 Rüger, *Heligoland*, 49–50.

95 Kittel, "Abschied vom Völkerfrühling?," 370, citing the newspaper *Schwäbische Merkur*.

96 Vick, *Defining Germany*, 245n32.

97 Matthew Fitzpatrick, *Liberal Imperialism in Germany* (New York, 2008), 32 and 45n32.

98 Vick, *Defining Germany*, 73.

99 Moltmann, *Atlantische Blockpolitik*, 140–65.

100 The Russian anarchist Mikhail Bakunin and exiled Czech and Polish revolutionaries fought alongside Wagner: Rolf Weber, *Die Revolution in Sachsen 1848/49* (Berlin, 1970), 277–86, 326–48.

101 Wilhelm Ribhegge, *Das Parlament als Nation* (Düsseldorf, 1998); Wollstein, *Das "Grossdeutschland" der Paulskirche*; Hans Fenske, "Ungeduldige Zuschauer," in *Imperialistische Kontinuität und nationale Ungeduld im 19. Jahrhundert*, ed. Wolfgang Reinhard (Frankfurt/Main, 1991), 87–123; Manfred Meyer, *Freiheit und Macht* (Frankfurt/Main, 1994).

102 Helena Toth, *An Exiled Generation* (New York, 2014), 20–36.

103 Ashton, *Little Germany*, 34–55; Sabine Sundermann, *Deutscher Nationalismus im englischen Exil* (Paderborn, 1997).

104 Toth, *Exiled Generation*, 55–60.

105 Richard J. Evans, *Tales from the German Underworld* (New Haven, 1998), 147–78.

106 Stanley Nadel, *Little Germany* (Urbana, Ill., 1990); Stanley Nadel, "From the Barricades of Paris to the Sidewalks of New York," *Labor History* (1989): 47–75; Mischa Honeck, *We Are the Revolutionists: German-Speaking Immigrants and American Abolitionists After 1848* (Athens, Ga., 2011).

107 See "General Walker und die Filibusters in Central-Amerika," *Die Gartenlaube*, no. 31 (1856), 413–15. Christopher Mapes drew my attention to these movements.

108 Ashton, *Little Germany*, 139–50.

109 Kapp to Hartmann, July 24, 1860, in Christian Jansen, ed., *Nach der Revolution 1848/49 . . . Politische Briefe deutscher Liberaler und Demokraten, 1849–1861* (Düsseldorf, 2004), 692.

110 Wilhelm Schulz-Bodmer to Gottfried Keller, Mar. 31, 1851, in ibid., 199.

111 "Entwurf eines Rundschreibens an deutsche Demokraten, Anfang 1850," in ibid., 67–75.

112 Wolfram Siemann, *"Deutschlands Ruhe, Sicherheit und Ordnung"* (Tübingen, 1985).

113 David Blackbourn, *The Long Nineteenth Century* (New York, 1998), 270–83.

114 August Ludwig von Rochau, *Grundsätze der Realpolitik* (Stuttgart, 1853); Christian Jansen, *Einheit, Macht und Freiheit* (Düsseldorf, 2000), 255–65; James J. Sheehan, *German Liberalism in the Nineteenth Century* (Chicago, 1978), 104, 112–13; Andreas Biefang, *Politisches Bürgertum in Deutschland 1857-1868: Nationale Organisationen und Eliten* (Düsseldorf, 1994), 38–48.

115 Nikolaus Buschmann, *Einkreisung und Waffenbruderschaft* (Göttingen, 2003).

116 Jansen, *Einheit, Macht und Freiheit*.

117 Pius IX denounced "progress, liberalism and modern civilization" in the Syllabus of Errors (1864): Anne Freemantle, *The Papal Encyclicals in Their Historical Context* (New York, 1956), 143–52.

118 Paul Schroeder, *Austria, Great Britain and the Crimean War* (Ithaca, N.Y., 1972), 406–7, 418–19.
119 On Italy as a model, see Jansen, *Einheit, Macht und Freiheit*, 288–315.
120 Biefang, *Politisches Bürgertum*, 101–4.
121 Rainer Noltenius, "Schiller als Führer und Heiland," in Düding et al. eds., *Öffentliche Festkultur*, 237–58; Thorsten Gudewitz, "Die Nation vermitteln: Die Schillerfeiern von 1859," in *Das 19. Jahrhundert als Mediengesellschaft*, ed. Jörg Requate (Munich, 2009), 56–65.
122 Carl Vogt to the editors of the *National-Zeitung*, May 17, 1859, in Jansen, ed., *Nach der Revolution*, 504.
123 Karl Biedermann to Max Duncker, July 17–19, 1859, in ibid., 554.
124 Karl Heinz Börner, *Die Krise der preussischen Monarchie von 1858 bis 1862* (Berlin, 1976), 63.
125 Frank Lorenz Müller, "The Spectre of a People in Arms," *EHR* 122 (2007): 82–104.
126 Thomas Parent, "Die Kölner Abgeordnetenfeste im preussischen Verfassungskonflikt," in Düding et al., eds., *Öffentliche Festkultur*, 271; Dieter Langewiesche, *Liberalismus in Deutchland* (Frankfurt/Main, 1988), 96–100; Jansen, *Einheit, Macht und Freiheit*, 377–86; Biefang, *Politisches Bürgertum*, 191–206.
127 James Retallack, "'Something Magical in the Name of Prussia . . . ,'" in *Germany's Two Unifications*, ed. Ronald Speirs and John Breuilly (New York, 2005), 141; Frank Lorenz Müller, *Britain and the German Question* (New York, 2002), 191–92.
128 John Maynard Keynes, *The Economic Consequences of the Peace* (New York, 1920), 82.
129 Ludwig Simon used these terms ("from below to above, and not from above to below") in writing to Carl Mayer in 1853: see Jansen, ed., *Nach der Revolution*, 315. Simon also used the phrase "from below to above" in *Aus dem Exil* (Giessen, 1853), 1:121.
130 Belgium, created after the revolution of 1830, was an exception; so was Norway, which separated peacefully from Sweden in 1905: Siegfried Weichlein, "Nation State, Conflict Resolution, and the Culture War, 1850–1878," in Smith, ed., *Oxford Handbook of Modern German History*, 292.
131 Jonathan Steinberg, *Bismarck* (New York, 2011), 312–13.
132 Langewiesche, *Reich, Nation, Föderation*, 25–26; Buschmann, *Einkreisung und Waffenbruderschaft*, 219–40.
133 Heinrich Simon to Carl Mayer, Feb. 4, 1858, in Jansen, ed., *Nach der Revolution*, 459.
134 Lothar Gall, *Bismarck, the White Revolutionary*, 2 vols. (London, 1985).
135 Hans-Ulrich Wehler, *The German Empire, 1871–1918* (Leamington Spa, Eng., 1985), 55–62. More critical of "Bonapartism" as a concept: Lothar Gall, "Bismarck und der Bonapartismus," *HZ* 223 (1976): 618–37; Allan Mitchell, "Bonapartism as a Model for Bismarckian Politics," *JMH* 49 (1977): 181–99.
136 Charles Bright and Michael Geyer, "World History in a Global Age," *AHR* 100, no. 4 (1995): 1034–60; Charles S. Maier, *Leviathan 2.0* (Cambridge, Mass., 2012), 79–150.
137 Ralph Ketcham, "Discussion," in Wellenreuther, ed., *German and American Constitutional Thought*, 349.
138 Daniel Nagel, *Von republikanischen Deutschen zu deutsch-amerikanischen Republikanern* (St. Ingbert, 2012). However, Helena Toth (*Exiled Generation*, 156–57) notes that, for professional officers, the 1850s had often been a difficult time in the United States.
139 Messages from Chicago and Cincinnati gymnasts respectively, accompanying contributions to a Friedrich Jahn memorial in Berlin: Langewiesche, *Reich, Nation, Föderation*, 139.
140 See letter of the Italian Society, Dec. 1, 1859, and the reply of the Nationalverein, Dec. 12, 1859, both in Andreas Biefang, ed., *Der Deutsche Nationalverein 1859–1867: Vorstands- und Ausschussprotokolle* (Düsseldorf, 1995), 22–23. On the conflict of interest between the two organizations, see Feodor Streit to Theodor Müllesiefen, July 12, 1860, in Jansen, ed., *Nach der Revolution*, 681–82.
141 Wilhelm Rüstow, *Der italienische Krieg 1859*, 2 vols. (Zurich, 1860–1861).
142 Arnold Ruge to Max Duncker, May 26, 1859, in Jansen, ed., *Nach der Revolution*, 515.
143 Theodore Hamerow, *Social Foundations of German Unification, 1858–1871* (Princeton, N.J., 1972), 17.

144 British Ambassador Lord Loftus in Berlin to Foreign Secretary Clarendon, Apr. 17, 1869, in Veit Valentin, ed., *Bismarcks Reichsgründung im Urteil englischer Diplomaten* (Amsterdam, 1937), 542–43.

145 On the history of the phrase, see Stephanie Malia Hom, "On the Origins of Making Italy: Massimo D'Azeglio and 'Fatta l'Italia, bisogna fare gli Italiani,'" *Italian Culture* 31, no. 1 (2013): 1–16.

146 Matthew P. Fitzpatrick, *Purging the Empire* (New York, 2015), 143–76.

147 John J. Kulczycki, *School Strikes in Prussian Poland, 1901–1907* (Boulder, Colo., 1981).

148 George C. Windell, *The Catholics and German Unity, 1866–71* (Minneapolis, 1954); Hugo Lacher, "Das Jahr 1866," *Neue Politische Literatur* 14 (1969): 83–99, 214–31.

149 Christopher Clark and Wolfram Kaiser, eds., *Culture Wars* (New York, 2003). On Germany, see David Blackbourn, "Progress and Piety," *History Workshop Journal* 26 (1988): 57–78; Helmut Walser Smith, *German Nationalism and Religious Conflict* (Princeton, N.J., 1995); Michael Gross, *The War Against Catholicism* (Ann Arbor, Mich., 2004).

150 Blackbourn, "Progress and Piety," and David Blackbourn, *Marpingen* (New York, 1994), describe many violent incidents.

151 Julius Bachem, *Erinnerungen eines alten Publizisten und Politikers* (Cologne, 1913), 133.

152 On "composite monarchies" and the nonunitary state, see Dieter Langewiesche, "Monarchy—Global," *JMEH* 15, no. 2 (2017): 299–300.

153 Abigail Green, *Fatherlands* (New York, 2001).

154 The memoirs of the religious conservative and former Wartburg festival participant Friedrich Krummacher refer to the area around Anhalt (where he ogrew up) as a "second fatherland," alongside his original birthplace on the Lower Rhine, but he also describes Germany as his birthplace: Krummacher, *Selbstbiographie*, 35.

155 Celia Applegate, *A Nation of Provincials* (Berkeley, Calif., 1990).

156 Siegfried Weichlein, *Nation und Region* (Düsseldorf, 2004); Jean-Michel Johnston, *Networks of Modernity* (New York, 2021), 199–241.

157 Vanessa Ogle, *The Global Transformation of Time: 1870–1950* (Cambridge, Mass., 2015), 1–2, 32–54; Oliver Zimmer, "One Clock Fits All?," *CEH* 53, no. 1 (2020): 48–70.

158 Svenja Goltermann, *Körper der Nation* (Göttingen, 1998); Geoff Eley, *Reshaping the German Right* (New Haven, 1980); Roger Chickering, *"We Men Who Feel Most German"* (Boston, 1984).

CHAPTER EIGHT: ON THE MOVE

1 Aristide Zolberg, "The Exit Revolution," in *Citizenship and Those Who Leave*, ed. Nancy Green and François Weil (Urbana, Ill., 2007), 33–60.

2 Klaus J. Bade, *Vom Auswanderungsland zum Einwanderungsland?* (Berlin, 1983), 18; Mack Walker, *Germany and the Emigration, 1816–1885* (Cambridge, Mass., 1964); Peter Marschalck, *Deutsche Überseewanderung im 19. Jahrhundert* (Stuttgart, 1973).

3 Edith M. Burlage, *The Life of a Priest in Two Worlds* (Manitowoc County, Wisc., 1973).

4 *Utopia—Revisiting a German State in America*, ed. Traveling Summer Republic and City Archives of Giessen (Bremen, 2013).

5 Mischa Honeck, *We Are the Revolutionists: German-Speaking Immigrants and American Abolitionists After 1848* (Athens, Ga., 2011).

6 The classic account of emigration from Württemberg is Friedrich List, *Die Ackerverfassung, die Zwergwirtschaft und die Auswanderung* (Stuttgart, 1842). See also Wolfgang von Hippel, *Auswanderung aus Südwestdeutschland* (Stuttgart, 1984).

7 Klaus J. Bade, *Migration in European History* (Malden, Mass., 2003), 46–47.

8 Panikos Panayi, *German Immigrants in Britain During the 19th Century, 1815–1914* (London, 1995); Panikos Panayi, "Sausages, Waiters and Bakers," in *Migration and Transfer from Germany to Britain, 1660–1914*, ed. Stefan Manz et al. (Malden, Mass., 2009), 147–59; Horst Rössler, "Germans from Hanover in the British Sugar Industry," in Manz et al., eds., *Migration and Transfer from Germany to Britain*, 49–63.

9 Gregory Anderson, *Victorian Clerks* (Manchester, Eng., 1976), 60–64.

10 Günter Moltmann, "German-American Return Migration in the Nineteenth and Early

Twentieth Centuries," *CEH* 13, no. 4 (1980): 378–92; Karen Schniedewind, *Begrenzter Aufenthalt im Land der unbegrenzten Möglichkeiten* (Stuttgart, 1994).

11 Tanja Fittkau, *In die neue Welt—Von Bremerhaven nach Amerika* (Stuttgart, 2010), 39–43.

12 C. A. Bayly, *The Birth of the Modern World, 1780–1914* (Malden, Mass., 2004), 451–87, referring to the years 1890–1914.

13 Rudolf Reimer, *Süd-Australien* (Berlin, 1851), 31.

14 David Schubert, *Kavel's People* (Highgate, Aust., 1997).

15 Reimer, *Süd-Australien*, 25; Jürgen Tampke, *The Germans in Australia* (New York, 2006), 25–32.

16 Reimer, *Süd-Australien*, 9; James Jupp, ed., *The Australian People* (Cambridge, 2001), 363.

17 Tampke, *Germans in Australia*, 17.

18 Michael Bollen, "The Hospital That Never Was," in *Germans*, ed. Peter Monteath (Kent Town, Aust., 2011), 104.

19 Renata Vollmer, *Auswanderungspolitik und soziale Frage im 19. Jahrhundert* (Frankfurt/Main, 1995).

20 Josef Vondra, *German Speaking Settlers in Australia* (Melbourne, 1981), 31–32.

21 Tampke, *Germans in Australia*, 75–89.

22 Bollen, "The Hospital That Never Was," 111.

23 Pauline Payne, "Richard Schomburgk," in Monteath, ed., *Germans*, 126–43; Janice Lally and Peter Monteath, "'Essentially South Australian': The Artist Alexander Schramm," in ibid., 147–48; Tampke, *Germans in Australia*, 90–91.

24 Tampke, *Germans in Australia*, 72, 85, 106.

25 Brigitte Bönisch-Brednich, *Keeping a Low Profile* (Wellington, N.Z., 2002), 15–16.

26 Udo Sautter, "Deutsche in Kanada," in *Deutsche im Ausland—Fremde in Deutschland*, ed. Klaus J. Bade (Munich, 1992), 189.

27 Bollen, "The Hospital That Never Was," 114.

28 Michael Clyne, *Perspectives on Language Contact* (Melbourne, 1972); Janet M. Fuller, "Language and Identity in the German Diaspora," in *German Diasporic Experiences*, ed. Mathias Schulze et al. (Waterloo, Ont., 2008), 3–33.

29 Jürgen Tampke, ed., *Wunderbar Country* (Marrickville, Aust., 1982), 21–27, 56–65, 90–99.

30 These statistics are based on Hermann Kellenbenz and Jürgen Schneider, "La Emigración Alemana a América Latina desde 1821 hasta 1930," *JbLA* 13 (1976): 386–403.

31 Walter Ludwig, "Ein deutscher Kaufmann in Südamerika, 1905–1911," *JbLA* 27 (1990): 337–73.

32 Jürgen Buchenau, *Tools of Progress: A German Merchant Family in Mexico City, 1865–Present* (Albuquerque, 2004); Jürgen Buchenau, "The Life Cycle of a Trade Diaspora," *JbLA* 39 (2002): 275–97; Joachim Kühn, "Das Deutschtum in Mexico um 1850," *JbLA* 2 (1965): 335–72.

33 Ronald C. Newton, *German Buenos Aires, 1900–1933* (Austin, 1977); Anne Saint Saveur-Henn, "Die deutsche Migration nach Argentinien (1870–1945)," in *Die Beziehungen zwischen Deutschland und Argentinien*, ed. Peter Birle (Frankfurt/Main, 2010), 21–53; Isabelle Rispler, "Negotiating 'German-ness' Within the Transatlantic Space," *Revue Interdisciplinaire de Travaux sur les Amériques* 6 (2013), http://www.revue-rita.com/notes-de-recherche6/isabelle-rispler.html.

34 David Brandon Dennis, "Seduction on the Waterfront," *GH* 29, no. 2 (2011): 175–201.

35 Ibid., 198.

36 Sandra Carreras et al., eds., *Die deutschen Sozialisten und die Anfänge der argentinischen Arbeiterbewegung* (Buenos Aires, 2008).

37 Alfred Hasbrouck, "The Conquest of the Desert," *Hispanic American Historical Review* 15, no. 2 (1935): 195–228, is a triumphalist account. President Sarmiento's *Facundo* (1845) has "civilization" (associated with northern Europeans) and "barbarism" in its subtitle. On Volga German settlements in Argentina, see https://vgi.fairfield.edu/immigration/ar.

38 Percy Ernst Schramm, *Neun Generationen* (Göttingen, 1963), 2:202–3, 221–22.

39 Sebastian Conrad, *Globalisation and the Nation in Imperial Germany* (New York, 2010), 282–333.

40 Ibid., 284; Richard Graham, "Free African Brazilians and the State in Slavery Times,"

in *Racial Politics in Contemporary Brazil*, ed. Michael Hanchard (Durham, N.C., 1999), 48–49.

41 See Karl [Carlos] von Koseritz, "Jakobine Maurer, die deutsche 'Christusin' in Brasilien," *Die Gartenlaube* (1874), part 1 in no. 40, 643–45, and part 2 in no. 43, 696–98.

42 Dirk Hoerder, "The German-Language Diasporas," *Diaspora: A Journal of Transcultural Studies* 11, no. 1 (2002): 26.

43 Günter Moltmann, ed., *Deutsche Amerikaauswanderung im 19. Jahrhundert* (Stuttgart, 1976), 201.

44 Albert Bernhardt Faust, *The German Element in the United States*, 2 vols. (Boston, 1909).

45 Audrey L. Olson, *St. Louis Germans, 1850–1920* (Lawrence, Kans., 1970); James Bergquist, "German Communities in American Cities," *Journal of American Ethnic History* 4 (1981): 9–30; Guido Dobbert, *The Disintegration of an Immigrant Community* (New York, 1980); Stanley Nadel, *Little Germany* (Urbana, Ill., 1990); Russell A. Kazal, *Becoming Old Stock* (Princeton, N.J., 2004); Monika Kugemann, *Between Cultures* (Hamburg, 2009).

46 Barbara Lorenzkowski, *Sounds of Ethnicity: Listening to German North America, 1850–1914* (Winnipeg, Man., 2010), 81.

47 John Gurda, *The Making of Milwaukee* (Milwaukee, 1999), 170.

48 H. Glenn Penny, "Atlantic Transfers," *GH* 26, no. 4 (2008): 566, drawing on Katja Wüstenbecker, *Deutsch-Amerikaner im Ersten Weltkrieg* (Stuttgart, 2007).

49 John Koegel, *Music in German Immigrant Theater* (Rochester, N.Y., 2009), 485–86n21.

50 Kathleen N. Conzen, "Ethnicity as Festive Culture," in *The Invention of Ethnicity*, ed. Werner Sollors (New York, 1989), 53.

51 See Kathleen N. Conzen, "German-Americans and the Invention of Ethnicity," in *America and the Germans*, ed. Frank Trommler and Joseph McVeigh, vol. 1, *Immigration, Language, Ethnicity* (Philadelphia, 1985), 131–47; Kathleen N. Conzen, *Immigrant Milwaukee, 1836–1860* (Cambridge, Mass., 1976).

52 See the German Historical Institute's five-volume project *Immigrant Entrepreneurship: German-American Business Biographies, 1720 to the Present*, available online at https://www.immigrantentrepreneurship.org/about/.

53 Uwe Spiekermann, "Claus Spreckels, Robber Baron and Sugar King," in ibid., vol. 2, *The Emergence of an Industrial Nation, 1840–1893*, ed. William J. Hausman, http://www.immigrantentrepreneurship.org/entry.php?rec=5.

54 Tobias Brinkmann, "Jews, Germans, or Americans?," in *The Heimat Abroad*, ed. Krista O'Donnell et al. (Ann Arbor, Mich., 2005), 111–40; Cornelia Wilhelm, *Deutsche Juden in Amerika* (Stuttgart, 2007).

55 Hoerder, "The German-Language Diasporas," 24; Nadel, *Little Germany*; Hartmut Keil, *German Workers in Chicago* (Urbana, Ill., 1988); Hartmut Keil, ed., *German Workers' Culture in the United States 1850 to 1920* (Washington, D.C., 1988); Christiane Harzig, "The Role of German Women in the German-American Working-Class Movement in Late Nineteenth-Century New York," *Journal of American Ethnic History* 8 (1989): 87–107; Gurda, *The Making of Milwaukee*, 204–11.

56 Anke Ortlepp, *"Auf denn, Ihr Schwestern!"* (Stuttgart, 2004), 221–22.

57 Paul Avrich, *The Haymarket Tragedy* (Princeton, N.J., 1984); Bruce C. Nelson, *Beyond the Martyrs* (New Brunswick, N.J., 1988). Timothy Messer-Kruse, *The Haymarket Conspiracy* (Urbana, Ill., 2012), argues that the brother-in-law of one defendant threw the bomb.

58 Gurda, *The Making of Milwaukee*, 189.

59 Thanks to Eric Kurlander for bringing the origins of the Louisville Slugger to my attention.

60 "The Katzenjammer Kids," in *The Encyclopedia of American Comics*, ed. Ron Goulart (New York, 1990), 212–13.

61 Ortlepp, *"Auf denn, Ihr Schwestern!"*

62 Christiane Harzig, "Lebensformen im Einwanderungsprozess," in Bade, ed., *Deutsche im Ausland—Fremde in Deutschland*, 166.

63 Peter Connolly-Smith, *Translating America* (Washington, D.C., 2004).

64 Lorenzkowski, *Sounds of Ethnicity*, 83.

65 Glenn Gilbert, ed., *The German Language in America: A Symposium* (Austin, 1971).

66 John Nau, *The German People of New Orleans, 1850-1900* (Leiden, 1958).

67 Karen Schniedewind, "Fremde in der alten Welt," in Bade, ed., *Deutsche im Ausland—Fremde in Deutschland*, 181–82.

68 Ibid., 183.

69 Walter D. Kampfhoefner et al., eds., *News from the Land of Freedom* (Ithaca, N.Y., 1991).

70 In 1857 the German publisher and bookseller Wilhelm Engelmann listed two hundred handbooks, travel guides, and advice books under the heading "Writings on Emigration": Heinrich Krohn, *Und warum habt ihr denn Deutschland verlassen?* (Bergisch Gladbach, 1992), 128–29.

71 Friedrich Gerstäcker, *Nach Amerika!* (Jena, 1855).

72 Jeffrey Sammons, *Ideology, Nemesis, Fantasy* (Chapel Hill, N.C., 1998); A. J. Prahl, "Gerstäcker und die Probleme seiner Zeit" (PhD diss., Johns Hopkins University, 1933).

73 L[udwik] P[owidaj], "Polacy i Indianie," *Dzennik Literacki*, part 1 in no. 53 (Dec. 9, 1864), and part 2 in no. 56 (Dec. 30, 1864). Thanks to Patrice Dabrowski for bringing these articles to my attention and translating passages. See also David Blackbourn, *The Conquest of Nature: Water, Landscape, and the Making of Modern Germany* (New York, 2006), 303–4.

74 Harry Liebersohn, *Aristocratic Encounters* (New York, 1998); H. Glenn Penny, *Kindred by Choice* (Chapel Hill, N.C., 2013).

75 Christine Hansen, "Die deutsche Auswanderung im 19. Jahrhundert—Ein Mittel zur Lösung sozialer und sozialpolitischer Probleme?," in Moltmann, ed., *Deutsche Amerikaauswanderung*, 22, citing Hans von Gagern, *Über die Auswanderung der Deutschen*.

76 Harald Focke, "Friedrich List und die südwestdeutsche Amerikaauswanderung 1817–1846," in Moltmann, ed., *Deutsche Amerikaauswanderung*, 80.

77 Hans Fenske, "Imperialistische Tendenzen in Deutschland vor 1866," *Historisches Jahrbuch* (1978): 346.

78 Howard Sargent, "Diasporic Citizens," in O'Donnell et al., eds., *The Heimat Abroad*, 22–23; Eli Nathans, *The Politics of Citizenship in Germany* (New York, 2004); Dieter Gosewinkel, *Einbürgern und Ausschliessen* (Göttingen, 2001).

79 Bradley D. Naranch, "Inventing the *Auslandsdeutsche*," in *Germany's Colonial Pasts*, ed. Eric Ames et al. (Lincoln, Neb., 2005), 21–40.

80 Donna Gabaccia, "Juggling Jargons: 'Italians Everywhere,' Diaspora or Transnationalism?," *Traverse: Zeitschrift für Geschichte* 12, no. 1 (2005): 56.

81 Gerhard Weidenfeller, *VDA—Verein für das Deutschtum im Ausland* (Berne, 1976); H. Glenn Penny, "Material Connections," *Comparative Studies in Society and History* 59, no. 3 (2017): 519–49; Stefan Manz, *Constructing a German Diaspora* (New York, 2014), 227–60.

82 Fenske, "Imperialistische Tendenzen," 345; Jens-Uwe Guettel, *German Expansionism, Imperial Liberalism, and the United States, 1776–1945* (New York, 2012), 57–58.

83 Frank Lorenz Müller, "Imperialist Ambitions in *Vormärz* and Revolutionary Germany," *GH* 17, no. 3 (1999): 351 (I have slightly altered the wording for stylistic reasons).

84 Franz Löher, *Geschichte und Zustände der Deutschen in Amerika* (Cincinnati, 1848); P. Wittmann, "Löher, Franz von," *ADB* 52 (1906): 56–62.

85 Ernst Ludwig Brauns, *Neudeutschland in Westamerika* (Lemgo, 1847), 75.

86 Ibid., 77–78.

87 Fenske, "Imperialistische Tendenzen," 370–71; H. Winkel, "Der Texasverein," *VSWG* 55 (1968): 348–72; Walter Struve, *Germans and Texans* (Austin, 1996), 46–50.

88 Thomas R. Hietala, *Manifest Design* (Ithaca, N.Y., 1985); Brian DeLay, *War of a Thousand Deserts* (New Haven, 2008).

89 Guettel, *German Expansionism*, 72–73; Müller, "Imperialist Ambitions," 365; Matthew Fitzpatrick, *Liberal Imperialism in Germany* (New York, 2008), 41.

90 Müller, "Imperialist Ambitions," 357–66.

91 Examples in Fenske, "Imperialistische Tendenzen," 347.

92 Gavin Henderson, "German Colonial Projects on the Mosquito Coast, 1844–1848," *EHR* 59 (1944): 257–71; Thomas Schoonover, "Germany in Central America, 1820s to 1929," *JbLA* 25 (1988): 39–41; Fitzpatrick, *Liberal Imperialism*, 61–65.

93 Karl Gaillard, *Wie und Wohin?* (Berlin, 1849), 35.

94 Focke, "Friedrich List und die südwestdeutsche Amerikaauswanderung," 82; Müller, "Imperialist Ambitions," 355; Fenske, "Imperialistische Tendenzen," 348.

95 H. von der Oelsnitz, *Denkschrift über die Erhebung Preussens zu einer See-, Kolonial- und Weltmacht ersten Ranges* (Berlin, 1847), 9, 13, 19, 33–34.

96 Friedrich Fabri, *Bedarf Deutschland der Colonien?* (Gotha, 1879).

97 Sebastian Conrad, *German Colonialism* (New York, 2012), 21.

98 Sigmund Freud, *The Interpretation of Dreams* [1900], vol. 4 of *The Penguin Freud Library*, ed. Angela Richards (Harmondsworth, Eng., 1991), 388–89, 415–19.

99 Wilhelm Hübbe-Schleiden, *Deutsche Kolonisation* (Hamburg, 1881).

100 Ernst von Weber, *Die Erweiterung unseres deutschen Wirthschaftsgebiets und die Grundlegung zu überseeischen deutschen Staaten* (Leipzig, 1879), 1.

101 Klaus J. Bade, *Friedrich Fabri und der Imperialismus in der Bismarckzeit* (Erlangen, 1975), 157.

102 Eugen von Enzberg, *Heroen der Nordpolarforschung* (Leipzig, 1905), 128–75 (quotation at 175); Reinhard A. Krause, *Die Gründungsphase deutscher Polarforschung, 1865–1875* (Bremerhaven, 1992).

103 Horst Gnettner, *Der Bremer Afrikaforscher Gerhard Rohlfs* (Bremen, 2005).

104 Felix Lampe, *Grosse Geographen* (Leipzig, 1915), 245–51; Cornelia Essner, *Deutsche Afrikareisende im neunzehnten Jahrhundert* (Stuttgart, 1985); Ursula von den Driesch, "Schweinfurth, Georg August," in *NDB* 24 (2010): 50–51; Wolfgang Saida, ed., *150 Jahre Karl Mauch, Afrikaforscher, 1837–1987* (Kernen, 1987); Claus Priesner, "Nachtigal, Gustav," in *NDB* 18 (1997): 682–84; Wilhelm Obers Focke, "Mohr, Eduard," in *ADB* 22 (1885): 66–67.

105 Examples in Fabri, *Bedarf Deutschland der Colonien?*, 30, 39–40.

106 Arne Perras, *Carl Peters and German Imperialism, 1856–1918* (New York, 2004).

107 Steven Press, *Rogue Empires* (Cambridge, Mass., 2017), 131–65.

108 Hans-Ulrich Wehler, *Bismarck und der Imperialismus* (Cologne, 1969); Hans-Ulrich Wehler, "Bismarck's Imperialism, 1862–1890," *PP* 48 (1970): 119–55; Martin Werner, *Deutschlands Griff nach Übersee* (Hamburg, 2014).

109 Fabri, *Bedarf Deutschland der Colonien?*, 87–89.

110 Fitzpatrick, *Liberal Imperialism*; Geoff Eley, "Social Imperialism," *Social History* 1, no. 3 (1976): 265–90.

111 Alfred von Tirpitz, *My Memoirs* (New York, 1919), 1:80–81.

112 Rüdiger vom Bruch and Björn Hofmeister, eds., *Kaiserreich und Erster Weltkrieg, 1871–1918* (Stuttgart, 2000), 268–70.

113 Horst Gründer, *Geschichte der deutschen Kolonien* (Paderborn, 1985), 241–45; Klaus J. Bade, "Die deutsche Kolonialexpansion in Afrika," in *Afrika im Geschichtsunterricht europäischer Länder*, ed. W. Fürnrohr (Munich, 1982), 7–47.

114 George Steinmetz, *The Devil's Handwriting* (Chicago, 2007), 243–315.

115 Ibid., 317–58; Matthew P. Fitzpatrick, "Embodying Empire: European Tattooing and German Colonial Power," *PP* 234 (2017): 101–35.

116 Klaus J. Bade, "Culture, Cash, and Christianity," *Pacific Studies* 10, no. 3 (1987): 65–66.

117 Conrad, *Globalisation and the Nation*, 258–67.

118 Steinmetz, *Devil's Handwriting*, 15–16, 434–36. On Richthofen, see ibid., 405–14, and Shellen Xiao Wu, *Empires of Coal* (Stanford, Calif., 2015), 33–65.

119 Steinmetz, *Devil's Handwriting*, 436–507; Klaus Mühlhahn, *Herrschaft und Widerstand in der "Musterkolonie" Kiautchou* (Munich, 2000).

120 Andreas Eckert, *Kolonialismus* (Frankfurt/Main, 2006), 65–66.

121 Steinmetz, *Devil's Handwriting*, 185.

122 Ibid., 180.

123 Ibid., 6–12, 135–239; Helmut Bley, *Southwest Africa Under German Rule* (Evanston, Ill., 1971); Jon M. Bridgman, *The Revolt of the Herero* (Berkeley, Calif., 1981); Nils Ole Oermann, *Mission, Church and State Relations in South West Africa Under German Rule (1884–1915)* (Stuttgart, 1999); Jürgen Zimmerer, *Deutsche Herrschaft über Afrikaner* (Münster, 2001); Jakob Zollmann, *Koloniale Herrschaft und ihre Grenzen* (Göttingen, 2010); Isabel

V. Hull, *Absolute Destruction* (Ithaca, N.Y., 2005), 5–92; Susanna Kuss, *German Colonial Wars and the Context of Military Violence* (Cambridge, Mass., 2017).

124 Hull, *Absolute Destruction*, 145–47; Kuss, *German Colonial Wars*, 157–75. On colonial policies and famine in German East Africa, see Mike Davis, *Late Victorian Holocausts* (London, 2001), 204.

125 Steinmetz, *Devil's Handwriting*, 6.

126 Daniel R. Headrick, *The Tools of Empire* (New York, 1981), 102.

127 Woodruff Smith, *The German Colonial Empire* (Chapel Hill, N.C., 1978), 75–90.

128 Arthur J. Knoll, *Togo Under Imperial Germany, 1884–1914* (Stanford, Calif., 1970); Peter Sebald, *Togo, 1884–1914: Eine Geschichte der deutschen "Musterkolonie"* (Berlin, 1988); Dennis Laumann, "A Historiography of German Togoland, or the Rise and Fall of a 'Model Colony,'" *History in Africa* 30 (2003): 195–211; Andrew Zimmerman, *Alabama in Africa* (Princeton, N.J., 2011), 112–38; Smith, *German Colonial Empire*, 66–74.

129 Oermann, *Mission, Church and State Relations*, 83.

130 Michael Pesek, *Koloniale Herrschaft in Deutsch-Ostafrika* (Frankfurt/Main, 2005); Zollmann, *Koloniale Herrschaft und ihre Grenzen*.

131 Karl Liebknecht, *Militarismus und Antimilitarismus* (Leipzig, 1907).

132 David Schoenbaum, *Zabern* (Boston, 1982).

133 Jürgen Zimmerer, *Von Windhuk nach Auschwitz?* (Berlin, 2011); Jürgen Zimmerer, "Colonial Genocide and the Holocaust," in *Genocide and Settler Society*, ed. A. Dirk Moses (New York, 2004), 49–76.

134 That is the argument of Hull, *Absolute Destruction*.

135 Dieter Langewiesche, "Das Jahrhundert Europas," *HZ* 296 (2013): 30–31, citing Charles Edward Callwell, *Small Wars* (London, 1886).

136 See Dirk van Laak, "Kolonien als 'Laboratorien der Moderne'?," in *Das Kaiserreich transnational*, ed. Sebastian Conrad and Jürgen Osterhammel (Göttingen, 2004), 257–79; Conrad, *German Colonialism*, 142–49.

137 Zimmerman, *Alabama in Africa*.

138 James C. Scott, *Seeing Like a State* (New Haven, 1998), 21–22, 269–82, 294; John McNeill, *Something New Under the Sun* (New York, 2000), 218–24; Zimmerman, *Alabama in Africa*, 120–21.

139 Andreas Eckert, *Grundbesitz, Landkonflikte und kolonialer Wandel* (Stuttgart, 1999); Wilhelm Matzat, *Die Tsingtauer Landordnung des Chinesenkommissars Wilhelm Schrameier* (Bonn, 1985), 2–33; Klaus Mühlhahn, *Herrschaft und Widerstand in der "Musterkolonie" Kiautschou* (Munich, 2000).

140 Gwendolyn Wright, *The Politics of Design in French Colonial Urbanism* (Chicago, 1991); Robert G. Irving, *Indian Summer* (London, 1981).

141 van Laak, "Kolonien als 'Laboratorien der Moderne'?," 263.

142 Matthew P. Fitzpatrick, *Purging the Empire* (New York, 2015).

143 Florian Hoffmann, *Okkupation und Militärverwaltung in Kamerun* (Göttingen, 2007), pt. 2, 248–52; Pascal Grosse, *Kolonialismus, Eugenik und bürgerliche Gesellschaft in Deutschland 1850–1918* (Frankfurt/Main, 2000).

144 Jake W. Spidle, "Colonial Studies in Imperial Germany," *History of Education Quarterly* 13, no. 3 (1973): 237–41; Marianne Harries, "Fabarius, Ernst Albert," in *NDB* 4 (1959): 717–18.

145 On the complexities of racial line-drawing, see Robbie Aitken, *Exclusion and Inclusion* (New York, 2007).

146 Lora Wildenthal, *German Women for Empire, 1884–1945* (Durham, N.C., 2001), 134.

147 Ibid., 155.

148 Ibid., 134.

149 Ibid., 164–65.

150 Daniel J. Walther, "Racializing Sex," *Journal of the History of Sexuality* 17, no. 1 (2008): 11–24; Fitzpatrick, *Purging the Empire*, 229–30, 251–52.

151 Oermann, *Mission, Church and State Relations*, 69.

152 Fitzpatrick, *Purging the Empire*, 252.

153 Ibid.

154 Wildenthal, *German Women for Empire*, 54–78, 134.

155 Frieda von Bülow's fictionalized account is *Im Lande der Verheissung: Ein deutscher Kolonial-Roman* (Dresden, 1899).

156 van Laak, "Kolonien als 'Laboratorien der Moderne'?," 267; Birthe Kundrus, *Moderne Imperialisten* (Cologne, 2003), 29 and *n*77.

157 Thorsten Heese, "Das koloniale Osnabrück," in *Kolonialismus hierzulande: Eine Spurensuche*, ed. Ulrich van der Heyden and Joachim Zeller (Erfurt, 2007), 41.

158 Robbie Aitken and Eve Rosenhaft, *Black Germany* (New York, 2013), 9.

159 Ibid., 31, 33.

160 Ibid., 2.

161 Peter Fritzsche, *Reading Berlin 1900* (Cambridge, Mass., 1996).

162 David Ciarlo, *Advertising Empire* (Cambridge, Mass., 2011). Frank Trentmann, *Empire of Things* (New York, 2016), 172–73, reminds us that Black people appeared in just 3 percent of coffee advertisements.

163 Sierra Bruckner, "Spectacles of (Human) Nature," in *Worldly Provincialism*, ed. Matt Bunzl and H. Glenn Penny (Ann Arbor, Mich., 2003), 127–55; Alexander Honold, "Ausstellung des Fremden—Menschen- und Völkerschau um 1900," in Conrad and Osterhammel, eds., *Kaiserreich transnational*, 170–90; Anne Dreesbach, *Gezähmte Wilde* (Frankfurt/Main, 2005); Cordula Grewe, ed., *Die Schau des Fremden* (Stuttgart, 2006).

164 The phrase "commercial ethnography" comes from Bruckner, "Spectacles of (Human) Nature." See also Andrew Zimmerman, *Anthropology and Antihumanism* (Chicago, 2002), 16–20; Ciarlo, *Advertising Empire*, 81–84.

165 Hilke Thode-Aurora, *Für fünfzig Pfennig um die Welt* (Frankfurt/Main, 1989); Nigel Rothfels, *Savages and Beasts* (Baltimore, 2002), 44–142.

166 Jochen Lingelbach, "War da was? Spuren des Kolonialismus in Leipzig," in van der Heyden and Zeller, eds., *Kolonialismus hierzulande*, 53–55.

167 Anne Dreesbach and Michael Kamp, "Kolonialismus in München," in van der Heyden and Zeller, eds., *Kolonialismus hierzulande*, 72–73.

168 "Als auf der Wiesen noch fremde Völker zur Schau gestellt wurden," *Süddeutsche Zeitung*, Sept. 27, 2018.

169 Mamoun Fansa, ed., *Das Somali-Dorf in Oldenburg 1905* (Oldenburg, 2005).

170 Alf Rössner, "Das koloniale Weimar," in van der Heyden and Zeller, eds., *Kolonialismus hierzulande*, 27–33.

171 Wildenthal, *German Women for Empire*; John Philip Short, *Magic Lantern Empire* (Ithaca, N.Y., 2012).

172 Jeff Bowersox, *Raising Germans in the Age of Empire* (New York, 2013), 32, 42; Bryan Ganaway, *Toys, Consumption, and Middle-Class Childhood in Imperial Germany, 1871–1918* (Frankfurt/Main, 2009).

173 Jan Rüger and others in "Forum: The German Colonial Imagination," *GH* 26, no. 2 (2008): 251–71, question how pervasive the "culture of colonialism" was.

174 Oermann, *Mission, Church and State Relations*, 80.

175 Anne Dreesbach, "Colonial Exhibitions, 'Völkerschauen' and the Display of the 'Other,'" *EGO: European History Online*, March 5, 2012, paragraph 24, http://ieg-ego.eu/en/threads/backgrounds/european-encounters/anne-dreesbach-colonial-exhibitions-voelkerschauen-and-the-display-of-the-other?set_language=http://ieg-ego.eu/en/threads/backgrounds/european-encounters/anne-dreesbach-colonial-exhibitions-voelkerschauen-and-the-display-of-the-other; Dressbach, *Gezähmte Wilde*.

176 Langewiesche, "Das Jahrhundert Europas," 32–33, citing Ernst Troeltsch, "Das Neunzehnte Jahrhundert" (1913).

177 Kevin H. O'Rourke and Jeffrey G. Williamson, *Globalization and History* (Cambridge, Mass., 1999); Kevin H. O'Rourke and Jeffrey G. Williamson, "When Did Globalisation Begin?," *European Review of Economic History* 6 (2002): 23–50; Cornelius Torp, "Weltwirtschaft vor dem Weltkrieg," *HZ* 279 (2004): 561–609; Jürgen Osterhammel and Niels Petersson, *Globalization* (Princeton, N.J., 2005), 81–89.

178 Quinn Slobodian, "How to See the World Economy," *JGH* 20 (2015): 317, citing Adolph Wagner, *Grundlegung der politischen Ökonomie* (Leipzig, 1894).

179 Ibid., 308; Mark Hewitson, *Germany and the Modern World, 1880–1914* (New York, 2018), 215, 219.

180 David Blackbourn, *The Long Nineteenth Century* (New York, 1998), 330; Alan Milward and S. B. Saul, *The Economic Development of Continental Europe, 1780–1870* (London, 1973), 473.

181 Blackbourn, *Long Nineteenth Century*, 313.

182 Maiken Umbach, "Made in Germany," in *Deutsche Erinnerungsorte*, ed. Étienne François and Hagen Schulze (Munich, 2001), 2:405–18; Walter E. Minchinton, "E. E. Williams: 'Made in Germany' and After," *VSWG* 62, no. 2 (1975): 229–42.

183 Toni Pierenkemper and Richard Tilly, *The German Economy During the Nineteenth Century* (New York, 2004), 153–56.

184 Steven Press, *Blood and Diamonds* (Cambridge, Mass., 2021).

185 Andrew Zimmerman, "Race and World Politics," in *The Oxford Handbook of Modern German History*, ed. Helmut Walser Smith (New York, 2011), 362.

186 Sven Beckert, *Empire of Cotton* (New York, 2015), 357, citing the economist Karl Helfferich.

187 Gründer, *Geschichte der deutschen Kolonien*, 239; Conrad, *German Colonialism*, 97.

188 Adolph Wagner, *Agrar- und Industriestaat* (Jena, 1902), 192.

189 Conrad, *German Colonialism*, 62.

190 Cornelius Torp, *Die Herausforderung der Globalisierung* (Göttingen, 2005), 79.

191 Martin Kitchen, *The Political Economy of Germany, 1815–1914* (London, 1978), 193.

192 Blackbourn, *Long Nineteenth Century*, 335–36.

193 Werner Abelshauser, David Gilgen, and Andreas Leutsch, "Kultur, Wirtschaft, Kulturen der Weltwirtschaft," in *Kulturen der Weltwirtschaft*, ed. Werner Abelshauser et al. (Göttingen, 2012), 9–28.

194 James J. Sheehan, *The Career of Lujo Brentano* (Chicago, 1966).

195 Heinrich Dietzel, *Das neunzehnte Jahrhundert und das Programm des Liberalismus* (Bonn, 1900), 14.

196 Kenneth D. Barkin, *The Controversy over German Industrialization, 1890–1902* (Chicago, 1970).

197 Karl Polanyi, *The Great Transformation* (New York, 1944), 202.

198 The historian is Helmut Böhme. See Blackbourn, *Long Nineteenth Century*, 315–17.

199 Karl Hardach, *Die Bedeutung wirtschaftlicher Faktoren bei der Einführung der Eisen- und Getreidezölle in Deutschland 1879* (Berlin, 1967).

200 Geoff Eley, "*Sammlungspolitik*, Social Imperialism and the Navy Law of 1898," *Militärgeschichtliche Mitteilungen* 1 (1974): 29–63; Cornelius Torp, "The Coalition of 'Rye and Iron' Under the Pressure of Globalization," *CEH* 43, no. 3 (2010): 401–27.

201 David Blackbourn, *Populists and Patricians* (Boston, 1987), 122–26.

202 Ibid., 230.

203 James C. Hunt, "Peasants, Grain Tariffs, and Meat Quotas," *CEH* 7, no. 4 (1974): 311–31.

204 Ulrich Teichmann, *Die Politik der Agrarpreisstützung* (Cologne, 1955), 463–74; David Blackbourn, *Class, Religion and Local Politics in Wilhelmine Germany* (New Haven, 1980), 49–50.

205 Brett Fairbairn, *Democracy in the Undemocratic State* (Toronto, 1997).

206 Trentmann, *Empire of Things*, 159.

207 Uwe Spiekermann, "Dangerous Meat?," *BGHI* 46 (2010): 99–100, citing *New-York Tribune*, Mar. 21, 1883.

208 Teichmann, *Politik der Agrarpreisstützung*, 569–604; Hunt, "Peasants, Grain Tariffs, and Meat Quotas," 313–16; Cornelia Knab, "Infectious Rats and Dangerous Cows," *ConEH* 20, no. 3 (2011): 281–306.

209 Blackbourn, *Long Nineteenth Century*, 315.

210 Adolf Wermuth, *Ein Beamtenleben* (Berlin, 1922), 48–50.

211 James T. Cariton and Jonathan B. Geller, "Ecological Roulette," *Science* 261 (July 1993), 78–82.

212 Johannes Baptist Kissling, *Geschichte des Kulturkampfes im Deutschen Reiche* (Freiburg i. B., 1916), 3:58, citing a writer in *Im Neuen Reich*.

213 Sarah Jansen, *"Schädlinge"* (Frankfurt/Main, 2003).

214 Conrad, *Globalisation and the Nation*, 239, citing a 1906 issue of *Deutsche Volkszeitung*.

215 Bade, *Migration in European History*, 157–64; Hermann Schäfer, "Italienische 'Gastar-

beiter' im deutschen Kaiserreich, 1890–1914," *Zeitschrift für Unternehmensgeschichte* 27 (1982): 192–214.

216 Otto Uhlig, *Die Schwabenkinder aus Tirol und Vorarlberg* (Stuttgart, 1978). In 2021 Johnathon Speed completed a dissertation at Vanderbilt University on the Swabian children.

217 Blackbourn, *Conquest of Nature*, 237.

218 Jack Wertheimer, *Unwelcome Strangers* (New York, 1987). Just 75,000 of the 2 million remained in Germany.

219 Richard W. Tims, *Germanizing Prussian Poland* (New York, 1966); William W. Hagen, *Germans, Poles, and Jews* (Chicago, 1980).

220 Max Weber, "The Nation State and Economic Policy," in *Weber: Political Writings*, ed. Peter Lassman and Ronald Speirs (Cambridge, 1994), 1–28.

221 Roger Chickering, *"We Men Who Feel Most German"* (Boston, 1984), 104.

222 Conrad, *Globalisation and the Nation*, 250–51, drawing on Sibylle Küttner, *Farbige Seeleute* (Erfurt, 2000).

CHAPTER NINE: GLOBAL TRAFFIC AND THE CLAIMS OF GERMAN CULTURE

1 Mark Hewitson, *Germany and the Modern World, 1880–1914* (New York, 2018), 228; Joachim Radkau, "Technik im Temporausch der Jahrhundertwende," in *Moderne Zeiten*, ed. Michael Salewski and Ilona Stölken-Fitschen (Stuttgart, 1994), 61–76.

2 Hans-Otto Kleinmann, "Der atlantische Raum als Problem des europäischen Staatensystems," *JbLA* 38 (2001): 22.

3 Alexander Schmidt-Gernig, "The Philosophical World Journey in the Nineteenth Century," in *The Mechanics of Internationalism*, ed. Martin Geyer and Johannes Paulmann (New York, 2001), 405–33.

4 Regina Höfer, ed., *Die Indienreise von Erzherzog Franz-Ferdinand von Österreich-Este* (Vienna, 2010).

5 Horace Rumbold, *Recollections of a Diplomatist* (London, 1902), 2:228. See also David Blackbourn, " 'Taking the Waters,' " in Geyer and Paulmann, eds., *Mechanics of Internationalism*, 435–57.

6 Bonnie Anderson, *Joyous Greetings: The First International Women's Movement, 1830–1860* (New York, 2000), 99, 159.

7 Susan Zimmermann, "Frauenbewegungen, Transfer und Trans-Nationalität," in *Transnationale Öffentlichkeiten und Identitäten im. 20. Jahrhundert*, ed. Hartmut Kaelble et al. (Frankfurt/Main, 2002), 263–302.

8 Leila J. Rupp, "Constructing Internationalism," *AHR* 99, no. 5 (1994): 1571–1600; Jean H. Quataert, " 'Being Heard on Important Matters of International Life,' " in *Wilhelmine Germany and Edwardian Britain*, ed. Dominik Geppert and Robert Gerwarth (New York, 2008), 173–95.

9 Georges Haupt, *Socialism and the Great War* (New York, 1972).

10 Roger Chickering, *Imperial Germany and a World Without War* (Princeton, N.J., 1975).

11 Glenda Sluga, *Internationalism in the Age of Nationalism* (Philadelphia, 2013), 11–44.

12 Michael D. Gordin, *Scientific Babel* (Chicago, 2015), 105–58; Markus Krajewski, "Organizing a Global Idiom," in *Information Beyond Borders*, ed. W. Boyd Rayward (New York, 2014), 97–108.

13 Chris Leonards and Nico Randeraad, "Transnational Experts in Social Reform, 1840–1880," *International Review of Social History* 55, no. 2 (2010): 220, citing Christopher Lasch.

14 Dirk Hoerder, "Local, Continental, Global Migration Contexts," in *Beyond the Nation? Immigrants' Local Lives in Transational Cultures*, ed. Alexander Freund (Toronto, 2012), 21–22.

15 May Seikaly, "Haifa at the Crossroads," in *Modernity and Culture*, ed. Leila Tarazi Fawaz and C. A. Bayly (New York, 2002), 99–104.

16 Jeffrey Wasserstrom, *Global Shanghai, 1850–2010* (New York, 2008), 40.

17 Brian Letwin, "The Lost History of Germans in Saigon," *Saigoneer*, May 20, 2014.

18 Uwe Spiekermann, "Claus Spreckels," *Business and Economic History On-Line* 8 (2010): 19.

19 Jessie Gregory Lutz, *Opening China* (Grand Rapids, Mich., 2008); Albert Monshan Wu, *From Christ to Confucius* (New Haven, 2016), 19–20, 30, 44–46.

20 Wu, *From Christ to Confucius*, 62.

21 Ulrike Kirchberger, "'Fellow-Labourers in the Same Vineyard,'" in *Migration and Transfer from Germany to Britain, 1660–1914*, ed. Stefan Manz et al. (Malden, Mass., 2009), 81–92; Bill Edwards, "The Moravian Church in South Australia," in *Germans*, ed. Peter Monteath (Kent Town, Aust., 2011), 41–46.

22 Kirchberger, "'Fellow-Labourers in the Same Vineyard,'" 87–88.

23 Rebekka Habermas, "Mission im 19. Jahrhundert—Globale Netze des Religiösen," *HZ* 287 (2008): 652–60.

24 Kirchberger, "'Fellow-Labourers in the Same Vineyard,'" 84.

25 Wu, *From Christ to Confucius*, 63–65.

26 Ibid., 44–45.

27 Habermas, "Mission im 19. Jahrhundert," 643–44.

28 Robbie Aitken and Eve Rosenhaft, *Black Germany* (New York, 2012), 44–53.

29 Johannes Paulmann, "Regionen und Welten," *HZ* 296 (2013): 687–93.

30 Wolbert Smidt, "'Schwarze Missionare' in Deutschland des 19. Jahrhunderts," in *AfrikanerInnen in Deutschland und Schwarze Deutsche*, ed. Marianne Bechhaus-Gerst and Reinhard Klein-Arendt (Münster, 2004), 46.

31 Ibid., 44.

32 Eduard Hüsgen, *Ludwig Windthorst* (Cologne, 1911), 296.

33 Renate Hücking and Ekkehard Launer, *Aus Menschen Neger machen* (Hamburg, 1986), 94–95, 102–3; Hans Debrunner, *Presence and Prestige* (Basel, 1979), 363–64.

34 Paul Göhre, *Drei Monat Fabrikarbeiter und Handwerksbursche* (Leipzig, 1891).

35 Habermas, "Mission im 19. Jahrhundert," 654–56.

36 Thomas Hahn-Bruckart, *Friedrich von Schlümbach* (Göttingen, 2011).

37 Patrick Streiff, *Der Methodismus in Europa im 19. und 20. Jahrhundert* (Stuttgart, 2003).

38 Christoph Ribbat, *Religiöse Erregung* (Frankfurt/Main, 1996), 35–73, 120–31.

39 Shellen Xiao Wu, *Empires of Coal* (Stanford, Calif., 2015), 38–65; Paulmann, "Regionen und Welten," 684–87; Ulrike Kirchberger, "Deutsche Naturwissenschaftler im britischen Empire," *HZ* 271 (2000): 621–60.

40 H. Glenn Penny, "Latin American Connections: Recent Work on German Interactions with Latin America," *CEH* 46, no. 2 (2013): 373–74.

41 R. A. Swan, "Neumayer, Georg Balthasar von (1826–1909)," in *Australian Dictionary of Biography*, vol. 5 (Melbourne, 1974).

42 Darrell Lewis, *Where Is Dr. Leichhardt: The Greatest Mystery in Australian History* (Clayton, Aust., 2013).

43 Leichhardt to Friedrich August Schmalfuss, Oct. 21, 1847, and Feb. 22, 1848, both in "Ludwig Leichhardt: A German Explorer's Letters Home," www.environmentandsociety.org.

44 Wu, *Empires of Coal*, 38–46.

45 Cornelia Essner, *Deutsche Afrikareisende im neunzehnten Jahrhundert* (Wiesbaden, 1985).

46 Moritz von Brescius et al., eds., *Über den Himalya* (Vienna, 2015); Moritz von Brescius, *German Science in the Age of Empire* (New York, 2019).

47 Joachim Radkau, *Nature and Power* (New York, 2008), 174.

48 Indra Munshi Saldanha, "Colonialism and Professionalism," *Environment and History* 2, no. 2 (1996): 195–219; Ravi Rajan, "Imperial Environmentalism or Environmental Imperialism?," in *Nature and the Orient*, ed. Richard Grove et al. (New York, 1998), 324–71; Ulrike Kirchberger, "German Scientists in the Indian Forest Service," *Journal of Imperial and Commonwealth History* 29, no. 2 (2001): 1–26; Gregory Barton, *Empire Forestry and the Origins of Environmentalism* (New York, 2002).

49 Henry Gerhold, *A Century of Forest Resources Education at Penn State* (University Park, Pa., 2007), 15–17.

50 David Blackbourn, *The Long Nineteenth Century* (New York, 1998), 194; James Hodkin-

son, "Transnational Encounters in Algeria," *Studies in Travel Writing* 21, no. 3 (2017): 262–77.

51 Gerhard Brunn, "Deutscher Einfluss und Deutsche Interessen in der Professionalisierung einiger Lateinamerikanischer Armeen vor dem I. Weltkrieg," *JbLA* 6 (1969): 278–336; Frederick Nunn, "European Military Influence in South America," *JbLA* 12 (1975): 230–52.

52 Donald Stoker, *Clausewitz* (New York, 2014), 283.

53 Hoi-eun Kim, *Doctors of Empire* (Toronto, 2014).

54 Frank Trentmann, *Empire of Things* (New York, 2016), 358.

55 Steven Muller, "German Influences on the Development of German Higher Education," in *A Spirit of Reason*, ed. Jackson Janes (Washington, D.C., 2014), 15.

56 Donald Fleming, *William H. Welch and the Rise of Modern Medicine* (Baltimore, 1954); B. D. Silverman, "William Henry Welch (1850–1934)," *Baylor University Medical Center Proceedings* 24, no. 3 (2011): 236–42; Michael Bliss, *William Osler* (New York, 1999); Gerald Imber, *Genius on the Edge* (New York, 2010); Laurence D. Longo, "Kelly, Howard Atwood," *American National Biography* (2000); Charles S. Roberts, "H. L. Mencken and the Four Doctors," *Baylor University Medical Center Proceedings* 23, no. 4 (2010): 377–88.

57 Thomas N. Bonner, *American Doctors and German Universities* (Lincoln, Neb., 1987), 23.

58 Konrad H. Jarausch, *Students, Society, and Politics in Imperial Germany* (Princeton, N.J., 1982), 67.

59 Elizabeth Dale Ross, *The Kindergarten Crusade* (Athens, Ohio, 1976); Roberta Lyn Wollons, ed., *Kindergartens and Cultures* (New Haven, 2000); Charles J. Wallman, *The German-Speaking 48ers* (Madison, Wisc., 1992); Ann Taylor Allen, *The Transatlantic Kindergarten* (New York, 2017).

60 John R. Davis, "Friedrich Max Müller and the Migration of German Academics to Britain in the Nineteenth Century," in Manz et al., eds., *Migration and Transfer from Germany to Britain*, 96.

61 Mary Peabody Mann, *Life of Horace Mann* (Boston, 1865), 174.

62 Burke Hinsdale, *Horace Mann and the Common School Revival in the United States* (New York, 1898), 170–74.

63 Michael B. Katz, *The Irony of Early School Reform* (Cambridge, Mass,, 1968), 151.

64 Jarausch, *Students, Society, and Politics*, 38, 51, 64–65.

65 Adolf Birke, *Britain and Germany* (London, 1987), 19; Peter Alter, *The Reluctant Patron* (Oxford, 1987), 25.

66 Richard B. Haldane, *An Autobiography* (London, 1929), 11–21; Dudley Sommer, *Haldane of Cloan* (London, 1960), 44–46, 318–19.

67 Peter Alter, "Science and the Anglo-German Antagonism," in *Late Victorian Britain*, ed. T. R. Gourvish and Alan O'Day (Basingstoke, Eng., 1988), 277; Eugene Cittadino, *Nature as the Laboratory* (New York, 1990).

68 Anja Werner, *The Transatlantic World of Higher Education* (New York, 2013).

69 Michael O'Brien, *Intellectual Life and the American South, 1810–1860* (Chapel Hill, N.C., 2010), 36.

70 Fritz K. Ringer, *Education and Society in Modern Europe* (Bloomington, Ind., 1979), 247.

71 Andrew Dickson White, *Autobiography of Andrew Dickson White* (New York, 1905), vol. 1, chap. 15–17, https://www.gutenberg.org/ebooks/1340.html.images.

72 Henry Adams, *The Education of Henry Adams* (1907; repr., Harmondsworth, Eng., 1995), 57.

73 William Clark, *Academic Charisma and the Origins of the Research University* (Chicago, 2006), 435.

74 Rainer Schwinges, ed., *Humboldt International* (Basel, 2001).

75 Davis, "Friedrich Max Müller," 96.

76 Thomas Adam and Gisela Mettele, eds., *Two Boston Brahmins in Goethe's Germany* (Lanham, Md., 2009).

77 Bernard Bailyn, "Why Kirkland Failed," in *Glimpses of the Harvard Past*, ed. Bernard Bailyn et al. (Cambridge, Mass., 1986), 19–44.

78 Burke A. Hinsdale, *History of the University of Michigan* (Ann Arbor, Mich., 1906), 42.

79 *American Journal of Education*, n.s., no. 7 (Sept. 1863), 641. The editor was Henry Barnard.

80 Wolfgang J. M. Drechsler, *Andrew D. White in Deutschland* (Stuttgart, 1989).

81 White, *Autobiography of Andrew Dickson White*, vol. 1, chap. 2.

82 Ibid., chap. 18.

83 Ibid., chap. 17.

84 Ibid., chap. 19–20.

85 Andrew Dickson White to Daniel Coit Gilman, Mar. 26, 1874, in Fabian Franklin, *The Life of Daniel Coit Gilman* (New York, 1910), 342–43.

86 Ibid., 75.

87 Mame Warren, *Johns Hopkins* (Baltimore, 2000).

88 Hugh Hawkins, *Pioneer* (Baltimore, 1960), 37.

89 Franklin, *Life of Daniel Coit Gilman*, 229–30.

90 Ibid., 101.

91 Donald Fleming, "Eliot's New Broom," in Bailyn et al., eds., *Glimpses of the Harvard Past*, 64–65.

92 Eugen Kuehnemann, *Charles W. Eliot, President of Harvard University* (Boston, 1909), 1–2.

93 Ibid., 30.

94 "George Herbert Palmer," *Ithaca (N.Y.) Journal*, May 12, 1933, 4.

95 George Herbert Palmer and Alice Freeman Palmer, *The Teacher* (Boston, 1908), 264.

96 Ibid., 265.

97 Gabriele Lingelbach, "Cultural Borrowing or Autonomous Development," in *Traveling Between Worlds: German-American Encounters*, ed. Thomas Adam and Ruth Gross (College Station, Tex., 2006), 100–23.

98 Lenore O'Boyle, "Learning for Its Own Sake," *Comparative Studies in Society and History* 25, no. 1 (1983): 20–25.

99 Max Weber, "American and German Universities," in *Max Weber on Universities*, ed. Edward Shils (Chicago, 1974), 24–25. See also Max Weber, "Science as a Vocation," in H. H. Gerth and C. Wright Mills, *From Max Weber* (New York, 1946), 129–56.

100 Sven Oliver Müller, "'A Musical Clash of Civilisations?': Musical Transfers and Rivalries Around 1900," in Geppert and Gerwarth, eds., *Wilhelmine German and Edwardian Britain*, 309.

101 Jessica Gienow-Hecht, *Sound Diplomacy* (Chicago, 2009), 52.

102 Adams, *Education of Henry Adams*, 80–81, 84.

103 Celia Applegate, *Bach in Berlin* (Ithaca, N.Y., 2005), 80–124; Michael North, *"Material Delight and the Joy of Living"* (Burlington, Vt., 2008), 124.

104 On the concert hall, see William Weber, *Music and the Middle Class* (New York, 1975).

105 Müller, "'A Musical Clash of Civilisations'?," 308; Gienow-Hecht, *Sound Diplomacy*, 143; Axel Körner, "Music of the Future," *European History Quarterly* 41, no. 2 (2011): 189–212.

106 Stephen Walsh, *Debussy* (New York, 2018).

107 Jean Gribenski and Patrick Trieb, eds., *Mozart et la France* (Lyons, 2014); Aaron Singer Allen, "Beethoven's Music in Nineteenth-Century Italy" (PhD diss., Harvard University, 2006); George S. Bozarth, "'A Modern of the Moderns,'" in *Brahms and His World*, ed. Walter Frisch and Kevin C. Karnes (Princeton, N.J., 2009), 287–306; Hannu Salmi, *Wagner and Wagnerism in Nineteenth-Century Sweden, Finland, and the Baltic Provinces* (Rochester, N.Y., 2005); David C. Large and William Weber, eds., *Wagnerism in European Culture and Politics* (Ithaca, N.Y., 1984).

108 Margaret Mehl, *Not by Love Alone* (Copenhagen, 2014), 2.

109 David Gramit, "Constructing a Victorian Schubert," *19th-Century Music* 17, no. 1 (1993): 65–78.

110 Körner, "Music of the Future."

111 Ronald de Leeuw, ed., *The Letters of Vincent van Gogh* (London, 1996), 357.

112 Bozarth, "'A Modern of the Moderns,'" 291–99; Gienow-Hecht, *Sound Diplomacy*, 149, 156.

113 Daniel Gregory Mason, *Music as an International Language* (New York, 1913).

114 Celia Applegate, "How German Is It?," *19th-Century Music* 21, no. 3 (1998): 274–96.

115 Müller, "Musical Transfers and Rivalries," 313–19.
116 Fritz Weber, "Heroes, Meadows and Machinery," in *Fin de Siècle and Its Legacy*, ed. Mikulas Teich and Roy Porter (New York, 1990), 225.
117 https://de.wikipedia.org/wiki/Musikverlag_Zimmermann.
118 Cyril Ehrlich, *The Piano* (London, 1976), 47–87.
119 Henry Lee Higginson to Sir George Grove, Sept. 22, 1882, for the 1883 edition of *Grove's Dictionary of Music and Musicians*.
120 Ruth Berges, "The Damrosch Family," *The American-German Review* (Feb.–Mar. 1961): 28–30; Gienow-Hecht, *Sound Diplomacy*, 66–108, 225–26.
121 Yvonne Wasserloos, *Das Leipziger Konservatorium im 19. Jahrhundert* (Hildesheim, 2004).
122 Gienow-Hecht, *Sound Diplomacy*, 61.
123 Anderson, *Joyous Greetings*, 144–47.
124 Barbara Packer, "Signing Off," in *There Before Us*, ed. Roger Lundin (Grand Rapids, Mich., 2007), 19.
125 Adams, *Education of Henry Adams*, 63.
126 David Clay Large, *The Grand Spas of Central Europe* (Lanham, Md., 2015), 175.
127 Haldane, *Autobiography*, 85–86, 354; Trevor Wilson, *The Downfall of the Liberal Party, 1914–1935* (London, 1968), 60.
128 Jeffrey Sammons, *Kuno Francke's Edition of "The German Classics" (1913–15)* (Berne, 2009).
129 Bernd Martin, *Japan and Germany in the Modern World* (New York, 1995), 46–47.
130 Frank Trommler, *Kulturmacht ohne Kompass* (Cologne, 2014), 45; Barbara Gödde-Baumanns, "L'Idée des deux Allemagnes dans l'historiographie françaises des années 1871–1914," *Francia* 12 (1984): 609–20.
131 Pascale Casanova, *The World Republic of Letters* (Cambridge, Mass., 2004), 96–99, 158–59.
132 Beat A. Föllmi et al, eds., *Music and the Construction of National Identities in the 19th Century* (Baden-Baden, 2010).
133 Müller, "Musical Transfers and Rivalries," 326 and n35.
134 Terry Pinkard, *Hegel's Phenomenology: The Sociality of Reason* (New York, 1994), 2. James Stirling's *The Secret of Hegel* was published in 1865.
135 Max Nordau, *Degeneration*, introduction by George L. Mosse (New York, 1968); Steven E. Aschheim, "Max Nordau, Friedrich Nietzsche and Degeneration," *JCH* 28, no. 4 (1993): 643–57; Daniel Pick, *Faces of Degeneration* (New York, 1989).
136 Matthew Arnold, *Culture and Anarchy* (London, 1875), preface. This preface was added in the 1875 edition.
137 Franco Moretti, *Distant Reading* (New York, 2013), 33–34.
138 Carl Schorske, *Fin-de-Siècle Vienna: Politics and Culture* (New York, 1980).
139 Blackbourn, *Long Nineteenth Century*, 387.
140 Peter Fritzsche, *Reading Berlin 1900* (Cambridge, Mass., 1996), 17.
141 Julius Bab, *Die Berliner Bohème* (Berlin, 1904); Laird M. Easton, *The Red Count* (Berkeley, Calif., 2002), 65–68.
142 Robert Hughes, *The Shock of the New* (New York, 1981).
143 Max Dauthendey, *Geschichten aus den vier Winden* (Munich, 1913), 43.
144 Andreas Sattler, "Alles für eine Weltreise," *Die Zeit*, Mar. 13, 1958; Aleksandra Rduch, *Max Dauthendey, Gaugin der Literatur und Vagabund der Bohème* (Frankfurt/Main, 2013).
145 Rachel Esner, " 'Art Knows No Fatherland,' " in *The Mechanics of Internationalism*, ed. Martin Geyer and Johannes Paulmann (New York, 2001), 372.
146 Ibid., 364–65.
147 Peter Paret, *The Berlin Secession* (Cambridge, Mass., 1980).
148 Peter Gay, *Modernism* (New York, 2008), 123.
149 Christian Weikop, "Early Engagements," in *The Routledge Companion to Expressionism in a Transnational Context*, ed. Isabel Wünsche (New York, 2019), 275.
150 Ibid., 277.
151 Sarah M. Bryan, "African Imagery and Blacks in German Expressionist Art from the Early Twentieth Century" (MA thesis, Kent State University, 2012); Jost Hermand,

"Artificial Atavism," in *Blacks and German Culture*, ed. Reinhold Grimm and Jost Hermand (Madison, Wisc., 1986), 65–86.

152 Katharina Erling, "Der Almanach der Blaue Reiter," in *Der Blaue Reiter*, ed. Christine Hopfengart (Cologne, 2000), 188–239.

153 Peter Jelavich, *Munich and Theatrical Modernism* (Cambridge, Mass., 1985); Gernot Schley, *Die Freie Bühne in Berlin* (Berlin, 1967); Elisabeth Erdmann-Macke, *Erinnerung an August Macke* (Frankfurt/Main, 1987), 95.

154 Casanova, *World Republic of Letters*, 159–63.

155 Jürgen Schutte and Peter Sprengel, eds., *Die Berliner Moderne, 1885–1914* (Stuttgart, 1987), 396.

156 Jelavich, *Munich and Theatrical Modernism*, 74–99.

157 Ibid., 76.

158 Easton, *Red Count*, 13–39.

159 Jan Romein, *The Watershed of Two Eras* (Middletown, Conn., 1978), 517.

160 Karl Schlögel, *Das Russische Berlin* (Munich, 2007), 81–83; Easton, *Red Count*, 196–215.

161 Easton, *Red Count*, 197.

162 Ibid., 197–200, drawing on Ruth St. Denis's *An Unfinished Life* (New York, 1939); Elizabeth Kendall, *Where She Danced* (Berkeley, Calif., 1979), 11–69.

163 Kendall, *Where She Danced*, 201–4.

164 Martin Green, *Mountain of Truth* (Hanover, 1986).

165 Corinna Treitel, *A Science for the Soul* (Baltimore, 2004); Romein, *The Watershed of Two Eras*, 501–6; Edith Hanke, *Prophet des Unmodernen* (Tübingen, 1993).

166 Wolfgang R. Krabbe, *Gesellschaftsveränderung durch Lebensreform* (Göttingen, 1974).

167 Radkau, "Technik im Temporausch," 61–91.

168 Michael Hau, *The Cult of Health and Beauty in Germany* (Chicago, 2003); Avi Sharma, *We Lived for the Body* (DeKalb, Ill., 2014).

169 Ulrich Linse, "'Geschlechtsnot und Jugend,'" in *"Mit uns zieht die neue Zeit,"* ed. Thomas Koebner et al. (Frankfurt/Main, 1985), 245–309.

170 Edward Ross Dickinson, *Sex, Freedom, and Power in Imperial Germany, 1880–1914* (New York, 2014), 215–20.

171 Ibid., 152–76 (Ulrichs quotation at 153); Harry Oosterhuis, *Step-Children of Nature* (New York, 1991); Robert Beachy, "The German Invention of Homosexuality," *JMH* 82 (2010): 801–38; Robert Beachy, *Gay Berlin* (New York, 2014), 3–119; Marti M. Lybeck, *Desiring Emancipation* (Albany, N.Y., 2014).

172 Sigmund Freud and Josef Breuer, *Studies on Hysteria* [1895], vol. 3 of *The Penguin Freud Library*, ed. Angela Richards (Harmondsworth, Eng., 1991).

173 Max Weber, *The Protestant Ethic and the "Spirit" of Capitalism*, ed. and trans. by Peter Baehr and Gordon C. Wells (New York: Penguin, 2002), 121. Baehr and Wells translate the famous phrase (more accurately) as "steel-hard shell"; I have retained the more familiar "iron cage."

174 Weber, "Science as a Vocation," 155.

175 See *Art and Literature*, vol. 14 of *The Penguin Freud Library*, ed. Albert Dickson (London, 1990).

176 James Wierzbicki, "Max Weber and Musicology," *The Musical Quarterly* 93, no. 2 (2010), 263–96; Edith Weiller, *Max Weber und die Literarische Moderne* (Stuttgart, 1994).

177 Joachim Radkau, *Max Weber* (Malden, Mass., 2009), 219, 290–97, 346–83; Michael Löwy, *Georg Lukacs—From Romanticism to Bolshevism* (London, 1979), 38.

178 Kevin Repp, *Reformers, Critics, and the Paths of German Modernity* (Cambridge, Mass., 2000), 193–286; Bab, *Berliner Bohème*, 33–37; Beachy, *Gay Berlin*, 99–100.

179 Jelavich, *Munich and Theatrical Modernism*, 160.

180 Astrid Eichstedt and Bernd Polster, *Wie die Wilden* (Berlin, 1985); Fred Ritzel, "Synkopen-Tänze," in *Schund und Schönheit*, ed. Kaspar Maase and Wolfgang Kaschuba (Cologne, 2001), 61–83.

181 Patrick Brantlinger, "Mass Media and Culture in Fin-de-siècle Europe," in Teich and Porter, eds., *Fin de Siècle and Its Legacy*, 99; Lynn Abrams, "From Control to Commercialization," *GH* 8 (1990): 282.

182 Christiane Eisenberg, *"English sports" und deutsche Bürger* (Paderborn, 1999).

183 Stefan Manz, Margrit Schulte Beerbühl, and John R. Davis, "Introduction," in Manz et al., eds., *Migration and Transfer*, 13.

184 See Moretti, *Distant Reading*, 31–32; he is talking mainly about literature.

185 Jelavich, *Munich and Theatrical Modernism*, 188, 209; Brantlinger, "Mass Media and Culture," 106–7.

186 "Asphaltcowboys and Stadtindianer," in *Envisioning America*, ed. Beeke Sell Tower (Cambridge, Mass.: Busch-Reisinger Museum/Harvard University, 1990), 17–36.

187 Schutte and Sprengel, eds., *Die Berliner Moderne*, 571–74.

188 Wolfgang Leppmann, *Goethe und die Deutschen* (Stuttgart, 1962).

189 R. J. V. Lenman, "Art, Society and the Law in Wilhelmine Germany," *Oxford German Studies* 8 (1973–74): 86–113.

190 Gordon Craig, *The Politics of the Unpolitical* (New York, 1995), 125–42.

191 Jelavich, *Munich and Theatrical Modernism*, 118.

192 Easton, *Red Count*, 149–50.

193 Rolf-Peter Sieferle, *Fortschrittsfeinde?* (Munich, 1984), 166; see also Andrew Lees, *Cities Perceived* (New York, 1985), 182–84.

194 Corey Ross, *Media and the Making of Modern Germany* (New York, 2008), 56.

195 Blackbourn, *Long Nineteenth Century*, 389.

196 Maiken Umbach, "The Vernacular International," *National Identities* 4, no. 1 (2002): 45–68; Joy Campbell, *The German Werkbund* (Princeton, N.J., 1978); Easton, *Red Count*, 88–91, 104–6; Michael H. Kater, *Weimar* (New Haven, 2014), 100–34.

197 Trommler, *Kulturmacht ohne Kompass*, 99–100.

198 Paul Rohrbach, *Der deutsche Gedanke in der Welt* (Düsseldorf, 1912).

199 Guido Goldman, *A History of the Germanic Museum at Harvard University* (Cambridge, Mass., 1989); Franziska von Ungern-Sternberg, *Kulturpolitik zwischen den Kontinenten* (Cologne, 1994).

200 Trommler, *Kulturmacht ohne Kompass*, 68–116; Rüdiger vom Bruch, *Weltpolitik als Kulturmission* (Paderborn, 1982).

201 Easton, *Red Count*, 139–44.

202 Thomas Weber, *Our Friend "The Enemy"* (Stanford, Calif., 2007).

203 David Blackbourn, "'As Dependent on Each Other as Man and Wife,'" in Geppert and Gerwarth, eds., *Wilhelmine German and Edwardian Britain*, 35.

204 Jan Rüger, *Heligoland* (New York, 2017), 126.

205 Paul Kennedy, *The Rise of the Anglo-German Antagonism, 1860–1914* (London, 1980), 389–400.

206 Easton, *Red Count*, 212, 219–21.

207 Käthe Kollwitz, *Aus meinem Leben* (Munich, 1967).

208 Tim Cross, *The Lost Voices of World War I* (London, 1988), 126.

209 Vera Brittain, *Testament of Youth* (1933; repr., Harmondsworth, Eng., 1989), 12, 463.

CHAPTER TEN: WAR, REPUBLIC, THIRD REICH

1 Fritz Stern, *Einstein's German World* (Princeton, N.J., 1999), 3.

2 Frank Möller, "Aufbruch ins 20. Jahrhundert," *Geschichte in Wissenschaft und Unterricht* 50 (1999): 730–39.

3 Dieter Langewiesche, *Reich, Nation, Föderation* (Munich, 2008), 147.

4 Konrad H. Jarausch and Michael Geyer, *Shattered Past* (Princeton, N.J., 2003), 31.

5 George F. Kennan, *The Decline of Bismarck's European Order* (Princeton, N.J., 1979), 3.

6 Jörn Leonhard, *Pandora's Box* (Cambridge, Mass., 2018), 24; Erich Ludendorff, *Der totale Krieg* (Munich, 1935).

7 Thomas Mann, foreword to *The Magic Mountain* (Harmondsworth, Eng., 1960), first published as *Der Zauberberg* (1924).

8 Lawrence Sondhaus, *World War One: The Global Revolution* (Cambridge, 2011).

9 Caroline Ethel Cooper, *Behind the Lines: One Woman's War, 1914–18; The Letters of Caroline Ethel Cooper*, ed. Decie Denholm (London, 1982), 65–66.

10 Aaron Friedberg, *The Weary Titan* (Princeton, N.J., 1988).

11 Arden Buchholz, *Moltke, Schlieffen, and Prussian War Planning* (Providence, 1993).

12 Volker R. Berghahn, *Der Tirpitz-Plan* (Düsseldorf, 1971).

13 C. H. Fairbanks, "The Origins of the *Dreadnought* Revolution," *International History Review* 13 (1991): 246–72.

14 Niall Ferguson, "Public Finance and National Security," *PP* 142 (1994): 141–68; Niall Ferguson, *The Pity of War* (New York, 1998), 105–42.

15 Brendan Simms, *Europe* (New York, 2013), 281.

16 Christopher Clark, *The Sleepwalkers* (New York, 2012), 295.

17 Dieter Groh, "'Je eher, desto besser,'" *Politische Vierteljahresschrift* 13 (1972): 501–21; Fritz Fischer, *War of Illusions* (London, 1975), 161–464; J. C. G. Röhl, "Dress Rehearsal in December," in *The Kaiser and His Court* (New York, 1994), 162–89.

18 Margaret MacMillan, *The War That Ended Peace* (London, 2013), 538, 589–96.

19 Clark, *Sleepwalkers*, 414.

20 Ibid., 422.

21 Fischer, *War of Illusions*, 224.

22 Konrad H. Jarausch, "The Illusion of Limited War," *CEH* 2, no. 1 (1969), 48–76.

23 Clark, *Sleepwalkers*, 416–19.

24 Volker R. Berghahn, *Germany and the Approach of War in 1914* (New York, 1993), 191.

25 Ernst Schulin, "Der Erste Weltkrieg und das Ende des alten Europa," in *Jahrhundert-wende*, ed. August Nitschke et al. (Hamburg, 1990), 1:375–76.

26 Ferguson, *Pity of War*, 218.

27 Olivier Razac, *Barbed Wire* (New York, 2003), 38.

28 Stern, *Einstein's German World*, 120–21.

29 Leonhard, *Pandora's Box*, 175–76.

30 Kris Manjapra, "The Illusions of Encounter," *JGH* (2006): 375.

31 Ibid., 364; Simms, Europe, 297.

32 Stefan M. Kreutzer, "Wilhelm Waßmuß—Ein deutscher Lawrence," in *Erster Welt-krieg und Dschihad*, ed. Wilfried Loth and Marc Hanisch (Munich, 2014), 91–117. For another "Lawrence," see Hans-Ulrich Seidt, "From Palestine to the Caucasus," *GSR* 24, no. 1 (2001): 1–18.

33 Keith Jeffery, *1916: A Global History* (New York, 2015), 180–90.

34 Gerhard Höpp, *Muslime in der Mark* (Berlin 1997).

35 Tom Murray and Hilary Howes, "Douglas Grant and Rudolf Marcuse," *History and Anthropology* 32, no. 3 (2011): 351–80; Andrew D. Evans, *Anthropology at War* (Chicago, 2010).

36 Jeffery, *1916*, 99.

37 R. F. Foster, *Vivid Faces* (New York, 2015), 224.

38 Pieter Judson, *The Habsburg Empire* (Cambridge, Mass., 2016), 406–7.

39 Jeffery, *1916*, 216–27.

40 David Killingray, "The War in Africa," in *A Companion to World War I*, ed. John Horne (Chichester, Eng., 2010), 112–26; William Boyd, *An Ice Cream War* (London, 1982).

41 Sondhaus, *World War One*, 116–20; Leonhard, *Pandora's Box*, 178–82.

42 David Abernethy, *The Dynamics of Global Dominance* (New Haven, 2000), 112; C. A. Bayly, *Remaking the Modern World, 1900–2015* (Hoboken, N.J., 2018), 34, 39.

43 Ferguson, *Pity of War*, 185.

44 Golo Mann, *Reminiscences and Reflections* (New York, 1990), 33.

45 Cooper, *Behind the Lines*, 130, 136, 154–55, 189.

46 Jay Winter and Jean-Louis Robert, eds., *Capital Cities at War*, vol. 1 (New York, 1997) and *Capital Cities at War*, vol. 2, *A Cultural History* (New York, 2007).

47 C. Paul Vincent, *The Politics of Hunger* (Athens, Ohio, 1985); Avner Offer, *The First World War: An Agrarian Interpretation* (New York, 1989); Jarausch and Geyer, *Shattered Past*, 276–80.

48 N. P. Howard, "The Social and Political Consequences of the Allied Food Blockade of Germany, 1918–19," *GH* 11, no. 2 (1993): 164–68.

49 Roland Wenzlhuemer, *Connecting the Nineteenth-Century World* (Cambridge, 2013), 129–30.

50 Ferguson, *Pity of War*, 253–54.

51 Alexander Watson, *Ring of Steel* (New York, 2014), 396, 405.

52 Thaddeus Sunseri, "Exploiting the *Urwald*," *PP* 214 (2012): 305–42.

53 Vejas Liulevicius, *War Land on the Eastern Front* (New York, 2000); Jesse Kauffman, *Elusive Alliance* (Cambridge, Mass., 2015).

54 Cooper, *Behind the Lines*, 128.

55 Isabel V. Hull, *Absolute Destruction* (Ithaca, N.Y., 2005), 230, 242.

56 Watson, *Ring of Steel*, 386.

57 John Horne and Alan Kramer, *German Atrocities 1914* (New Haven, 2001); John Horne and Alan Kramer, "German 'Atrocities' and Franco-German Opinion, 1914," *JMH* 66, no. 1 (1994): 1–33; Alan Kramer, *Dynamic of Destruction* (New York, 2007), 6–30; Hull, *Absolute Destruction*, 230–42.

58 Peter Schöttler, "Geschichtsschreibung in einer Trümmerwelt," in *Plurale Deutschland— Allemagne Plurielle*, ed. Peter Schöttler et al. (Göttingen, 1999), 297–99.

59 Thomas Mann, *Betrachtungen eines Unpolitischen* (Berlin, 1918).

60 Kramer, *Dynamic of Destruction*, 19.

61 Howard, "Social and Political Consequences," 162–63; Kramer, *Dynamic of Destruction*, 141–43.

62 Donald Bloxham et al., "Europe in the World," in *Political Violence in Twentieth-Century Europe*, ed. Donald Bloxham and Robert Gerwarth (New York, 2011), 173–74, 183–84; Eric Lohr, *Nationalizing the Russian Empire* (Cambridge, Mass., 2003); Joshua Sanborn, "Unsettling the Empire," *JMH* 77, no. 2 (2005): 306–10.

63 Norman M. Naimark, *Fires of Hatred* (Cambridge, Mass., 2001), 17–56.

64 Donald Bloxham, *The Great Game of Genocide* (New York, 2005); Ulrich Trumpener, *Germany and the Ottoman Empire, 1914–1918* (Princeton, N.J., 2015); Hull, *Absolute Destruction*, 263–90; Margaret Lavinia Anderson, "Who Still Talked About the Extermination of the Armenians?," *BGHI* (Fall 2011): 9–29; Benny Morris and Dror Ze'evi, *The Thirty-Year Genocide* (Cambridge, Mass., 2019).

65 Hull, *Absolute Destruction*, 278.

66 For example, see "The Horrors of Aleppo . . . Seen by a German Eyewitness," http:// digital.library.wisc.edu/1711.dl/History.Niepage.

67 Anderson, "Who Still Talked?," 16.

68 "Letter, Dated Aleppo, 8th October, 1915, from Four Members of the German Missions Staff in Turkey to the Imperial German Ministry of Foreign Affairs at Berlin," in Viscount Bryce, *The Treatment of Armenians in the Ottoman Empire* (New York, 1916), xxxiii–xxxiv.

69 "Wholesale Massacres of Armenians by Turks: Lord Crewe Denounces Influence of the Germans as 'an Unmitigated Curse,'" *NYT*, July 29, 1915.

70 Watson, *Ring of Steel*, 416; Adam Tooze, *Deluge: The Great War, America and the Remaking of the Global Order, 1916–1931* (New York, 2015), 58.

71 Niall Ferguson, *The War of the World* (New York, 2006), 127.

72 Thomas Boghardt, *The Zimmermann Telegram* (Annapolis, Md., 2012).

73 Sondhaus, *World War One*, 308–11.

74 Panikos Panayi, *The Enemy in Our Midst* (Stuttgart, 2003); Stefan Manz, *Migranten und Internierte* (Stuttgart, 2003); Gerhard Fischer, *Enemy Aliens* (St. Lucia, Aust., 1989); Frederick C. Luebke, *Germans in Brazil* (Baton Rouge, 1987).

75 Jessica Gienow-Hecht, *Sound Diplomacy* (Chicago, 2009), 183.

76 Guido Goldman, *A History of the Germanic Museum at Harvard University* (Cambridge, Mass., 1989).

77 Katja Wüstenbecker, *Deutsch-Amerikaner im Ersten Weltkrieg* (Stuttgart, 2007), 247.

78 Tooze, *Deluge*, 12–13; Watson, *Ring of Steel*, 449.

79 Simms, *Europe*, 307.

80 Klaus Epstein, *Matthias Erzberger and the Dilemma of German Democracy* (Princeton, N.J., 1959), 166–78; David Stevenson, "The Failure of Peace by Negotiation in 1917," *The Historical Journal* 34, no. 1 (1991): 73–74.

81 Martin Kitchen, *The Silent Dictatorship* (New York, 1976), 103; Stevenson, "Failure of Peace by Negotiation," 71.

82 Max Weber, "Parliament and Government in Germany Under a New Political Order,"

in *Weber: Political Writings*, ed. Peter Lassman and Ronald Speirs (Cambridge, 1994), 130–271.

83 Kitchen, *Silent Dictatorship*, 145–46.

84 Simms, *Europe*, 313.

85 Douglas Newton, "The Lansdowne 'Peace Letter' of 1917 and the Prospect of Peace by Negotiation with Germany," *Australian Journal of Politics and History* 48, no. 1 (2002): 16–39.

86 Tooze, *Deluge*, 139–40.

87 Watson, *Ring of Steel*, 529–30.

88 Kitchen, *Silent Dictatorship*, 256–57.

89 Kater, *Weimar*, 189–91.

90 Tooze, *Deluge*, 54.

91 Ulrich Heinemann, *Die verdrängte Niederlage* (Göttingen, 1983); Wolfgang Schivelbusch, *The Culture of Defeat* (New York, 2003), 189–225.

92 Markus Payk, *Frieden durch Recht?* (Oldenburg, 2018).

93 Dirk van Laak, "Kolonien als 'Laboratorien der Moderne'?," in *Das Kaiserreich transnational*, ed. Sebastian Conrad and Jürgen Osterhammel (Göttingen, 2004), 274, citing Carl von Ossietzky writing in *Die Weltbühne* in 1928. Abernethy, *Global Dominance*, 210 makes the same point that the loss of colonies was also a blessing.

94 Omer Bartov and Eric D. Weitz, eds., *Shatterzones of Empires* (Bloomington, Ind., 2013); Robert Gerwarth, *The Vanquished* (New York, 2016); Robert Gerwarth and John Horne, "Veterans of Violence," *JMH* 83 (2011): 489–512.

95 Annemarie Sammartino, *The Impossible Border* (Ithaca, N.Y., 2010); Gerwarth, *The Vanquished*, 70–76.

96 Caitlin E. Murdock, *Changing Places* (Ann Arbor, Mich., 2010), 97–111.

97 James Bjork, *Neither German nor Pole* (Ann Arbor, Mich., 2008), 244–57.

98 Keith Nelson, "The 'Black Horror on the Rhine,'" *JMH* 42, no. 4 (1970): 606–27; Sally Marks, "Black Watch on the Rhine," *European Studies Review* 13, no. 3 (1983): 297–333; Gisela Lebzelter, "Die 'Schwarze Schmach,'" *Geschichte und Gesellschaft* 11, no. 1 (1985): 37–58; Sandra Mass, *Weisse Helden, Schwarze Krieger* (Cologne, 2006); Iris Wigger, *Die "schwarze Schmach am Rhein"* (Münster, 2007); Julia Roos, "Nationalism, Racism, and Propaganda in Early Weimar Germany," *GH* 30, no. 1 (2012): 45–74; Peter Collar, *The Propaganda War in the Rhineland* (London, 2013).

99 Robert Reinders, "Racialism on the Left," *International Review of Social History* 13 (1968): 1–28.

100 Walter McDougall, *France's Rhineland Policy* (Princeton, N.J., 1978), 157.

101 Ibid., 269–70.

102 Martin Geyer, *Verkehrte Welt* (Göttingen, 1998).

103 Celia Applegate, *A Nation of Provincials* (Berkeley, Calif., 1990), 145–47.

104 Cooper, *Behind the Lines*, 156.

105 Günter Minnerup, "Introduction," *Debatte*, 11, no. 2 (2003): 103.

106 Richard Bessel, *Germany After the First World War* (New York, 1993), 243.

107 Moritz Föllmer, "The Unscripted Revolution," *PP* 240 (2018): 189.

108 Ibid.; Keith Michael Baker and Dan Edelstein, eds., *Scripting Revolution* (Stanford, Calif., 2015).

109 Philipp Scheidemann, *Memoiren eines Sozialdemokraten* (Dresden, 1928), 310–11.

110 Julia Boyd, *Travellers in the Third Reich* (London, 2017), 22–23.

111 Eszter B. Gantner, *Budapest-Berlin* (Stuttgart, 2011).

112 Eric Hobsbawm, *Interesting Times* (New York, 2005), 132.

113 Karl Schlögel, *Das Russische Berlin* (Munich, 2007), 189.

114 David W. Morgan, *The Socialist Left and the German Revolution* (Ithaca, N.Y., 1975), 80–81.

115 Ibid., 99.

116 Schlögel, *Das Russische Berlin*, 55, 188.

117 Max Hoelz, *From White Cross to Red Flag* (New York, 1930), 42; John Ondrovcik, "All the Devils Are Loose" (PhD diss., Harvard University, 2008). See also Walter Tormin,

Zwischen Rätediktatur und sozialer Demokratie (Dusseldorf, 1954), 26–33; Eberhard Kolb, *Die Arbeiterräte in der deutschen Innenpolitik 1918–1919* (Frankfurt/Main, 1978), 56–62.

118 Tankred Dorst, ed., *Die Münchner Räterepublik: Zeugnisse und Kommentar* (Frankfurt/Main, 1966), 105.

119 Ibid., 92, 103.

120 George Eliasberg, *Der Ruhrkrieg von 1920* (Bonn, 1974); Erhard Lucas, *Zwei Formen von Radikalismus in der deutschen Arbeiterbewegung* (Frankfurt/Main, 1976).

121 Gerwarth, *The Vanquished*, 129.

122 Schlögel, *Das Russische Berlin*, 179–208.

123 Geoff Eley, *Forging Democracy* (New York, 2002), 152–74.

124 Sigrid Koch-Baumgarten, *Der Aufstand der Avantgarde* (Frankfurt/Main, 1986); Stefan Weber, *Ein kommunistischer Putsch?* (Berlin, 1991); Rosa Levine-Meyer, *Inside German Communism* (London, 1977), 17–20, 50–57; Larissa Reissner, *Hamburg at the Barricades* (London, 1977); Otto Wenzel, *1923: Die gescheiterte Deutsche Oktoberrevolution* (Münster, 2003).

125 Schlögel, *Das Russische Berlin*, 62, 278.

126 Robert Gerwarth, "Central European Counter-Revolution," *PP* 200 (2005): 421–39.

127 Trude Maurer, *Ostjuden in Deutschland, 1918–1933* (Hamburg, 1986); Sammartino, *Impossible Border*, 120–37; Joseph Roth, *What I Saw* (New York, 2004), 31–50.

128 Schlögel, *Das Russische Berlin*, 12, 103–45.

129 Klaus J. Bade, *Migration in European History* (Malden, Mass., 2003), 174, 177.

130 Cooper, *Behind the Lines*, 167.

131 Sammartino, *Impossible Border*, 71–95.

132 Stefan Rinke, "Deutsche Lateinamerikapolitik, 1918–1933," *JbLA* 34 (1997): 368–74; Bade, *Migration in European History*, 185–88.

133 Abernethy, *Global Dominance*, 117.

134 Carl-Ludwig Holtfrerich, *The German Inflation, 1914–1923* (New York, 1986).

135 Schoonover, "Germany in Central America," *JbLA* 25 (1988): 54.

136 Rinke, "Deutsche Lateinamerikapolitik," 360–68.

137 Detlev Peukert, *The Weimar Republic* (London, 1991), 116.

138 Robert Brady, *The Rationalization Movement in German Industry* (New York, 1974).

139 Mary Nolan, *Visions of Modernity* (New York, 1994).

140 Derek Aldcroft, *From Versailles to Wall Street* (Berkeley, Calif., 1977), 85.

141 McDougall, *France's Rhineland Policy*, 260.

142 *Menschen am Sonntag* (dir. Robert Siodmak and Edgar G. Ulmer, 1930). See also Eric Weitz, *Weimar Germany* (Princeton, N.J., 2007), 230–32.

143 Moritz Föllmer, "Unscripted Revolution," 176.

144 Peter Gay, *My German Question* (New Haven, 1998); Sebastian Haffner, *Defying Hitler* (New York, 2002).

145 Siegfried Kracauer, "The Little Shopgirls Go to the Movies," in *The Mass Ornament* (Cambridge, Mass., 1995).

146 Roth, *What I Saw*, 153–75 (quotation at 171).

147 Ibid., 113.

148 Christian Schär, *Der Schlager und seine Tänze in Deutschland der 20er Jahre* (Zurich, 1991); Michael J. Budds, ed., *Jazz and the Germans* (Hillsdale, N.Y., 2002), especially Frank Tirro's essay, "Jazz Leaves Home: The Dissemination of 'Hot' Music to Central Europe."

149 Mary Nolan, *The Transatlantic Century* (New York, 2012), 83; Victoria de Grazia, *Irresistible Empire* (Cambridge, Mass., 2005), 210.

150 De Grazia, *Irresistible Empire*, 231–32.

151 Siegfried Kracauer, *The Salaried Masses* (1930; repr., New York, 1998); Hans Speier, *German White-Collar Workers and the Rise of Hitler* (1977; repr., New Haven, 1986); Ursula Nienhaus, "Rationalisierung und 'Amerikanismus' in Büros der zwanziger Jahre," in *Amerikanisierung*, ed. Alf Lüdtke et al. (Stuttgart, 1996), 67–77.

152 Helmut Frei, *Tempel der Kauflust* (Leipzig, 1997); Paul Lerner, *The Consuming Temple* (Ithaca, N.Y., 2015).

153 De Grazia, *Irresistible Empire*, 164–69.

154 See Alys Eve Weinbaum et al., "The Modern Girl as Heuristic Device," and Uta G. Poiger, "Fantasies of Universality?," in *The Modern Girl Around the World*, ed. Alys Eve Weinbaum et al. (Durham, N.C., 2008), 1–24, 317–44.

155 Irene Gammel, "Lacing Up the Gloves," *Cultural and Social History* 9, no. 3 (2012): 369–90.

156 Linda Mizejewski, *Divine Decadence* (Princeton, N.J., 1992), 15–23, 139–40.

157 Marti M. Lybeck, *Desiring Emancipation* (Albany, N.Y., 2014), 153, 155.

158 Ibid., 155, citing the writer and director Mel Gordon.

159 Boyd, *Travellers*, 59, 61.

160 Peter Edgerley Firchow, *Strange Meetings* (Washington, D.C., 2008), 105.

161 Robert Beachy, *Gay Berlin* (New York, 2014), 197.

162 Ibid., 192

163 Ibid., x.

164 Boyd, *Travellers*, 54.

165 Beachy, *Gay Berlin*, xi–xii.

166 Alfred Döblin, *Berlin Alexanderplatz* (1929; repr., New York, 2018); David Blackbourn, "Where Weimar Germany Went Wrong: The Turbulent Politics of 'Berlin Alexanderplatz,'" *Foreign Affairs*, Feb. 28, 2019.

167 Peter Jelavich, *Berlin Alexanderplatz* (Berkeley, Calif., 2006).

168 Alan Lareau, "Jonny's Jazz," in Budds, ed., *Jazz and the Germans*, 19–60.

169 J. Bradford Robinson, "Jazz Reception in Weimar Germany," in *Music and Performance During the Weimar Republic*, ed. Bryan Gilliam (New York, 1994), 107–34.

170 Ivan Goll, "The Negroes Are Conquering Europe" [1926], in *The Weimar Republic Sourcebook*, ed. Anton Kaes et al. (Berkeley, Calif., 1994), 559–60.

171 Manjapra, "The Illusions of Encounter," 377.

172 Pascale Casanova, *The World Republic of Letters* (Cambridge, Mass., 2004), 138; Schlögel, *Das Russische Berlin*, 103–45.

173 Boyd, *Travellers*, 71, 100.

174 Jarausch and Geyer, *Shattered Past*, 290–92.

175 De Grazia, *Irresistible Empire*, 38.

176 Frank Trommler, *Kulturmacht ohne Kompass* (Cologne, 2014), 323–24.

177 Schöttler, "Geschichtsschreibung in einer Trümmerwelt," 304–6.

178 Hans Rollmann, "Die Beziehungen Ernst Troeltschs zu England und Schottland," in *Troeltsch-Studien*, ed. Horst Renz and Friedrich Wilhelm Graf (Gütersloh, 1984), 3:326–31.

179 Trommler, *Kulturmacht ohne Kompass*, 318–22.

180 Ibid., 300–11.

181 Kris Manjapra, "Stella Kramrisch and the Bauhaus in Calcutta," in *The Last Harvest*, ed. R. Sivakumar (Ahmedabad, 2011), 34–40.

182 Akira Iriye, *Cultural Internationalism and World Order* (Baltimore, 1997), 63–64.

183 Daniel Laqua, "Reconciliation and the Post-War Order," in *Internationalism Reconfigured*, ed. Daniel Laqua (London, 2011), 209–38.

184 Stefanie Hanke, "Vater des Jugendherbergswerks," *Preussische Allgemeine Zeitung*, Dec. 10, 2011.

185 John Willett, *The New Sobriety* (London, 1978), 156–57.

186 Kris Manjapra, *The Age of Entanglement* (Cambridge, Mass., 2014), 176–79.

187 Frithjof Benjamin Schenk, "Tannenberg/Grunwald," in *Deutsche Erinnerungsorte*, ed. Étienne François and Hagen Schulze (Munich, 2001), 1:438–54.

188 Marcia Klotz, "The Weimar Republic," in *Germany's Colonial Pasts*, ed. Eric Ames et al. (Lincoln, Neb., 2005), 135–47; Luke Springman, "Exotic Attractions and Imperialist Fantasies in Weimar Youth Literature," in *Weimar Culture Revisited*, ed. John Alexander Williams (New York, 2011), 100–15.

189 Rudy Koshar, *Social Life, Local Politics and Nazism* (Chapel Hill, N.C., 1986), on Marburg; David Imhoof, *Becoming a Nazi Town* (Ann Arbor, Mich., 2013), on Göttingen. See also Geoffrey Giles, *Students and National Socialism in Germany* (Princeton, N.J., 1985).

190 Kater, *Weimar*, 163–211; Stephen Brockmann, *Nuremberg* (Rochester, N.Y., 2006), 119–22.

191 Stephen Brockmann, *A Critical History of German Film* (Rochester, N.Y., 2010), 46.

192 Karl Mutschler, *Die Hitlerbewegung im Kreis Aalen* (Aalen, n.d), 130.

193 Robert O. Paxton, *The Anatomy of Fascism* (New York, 2004), 48.

194 Joseph Conrad, *Heart of Darkness* (1902; repr., New York, 2006), 49.

195 Stefan Ihrig, *Atatürk in the Nazi Imagination* (Cambridge, Mass., 2014), 105.

196 Timothy W. Ryback, *Hitler's Private Library* (New York, 2008), 50; Manuel Sarkisyanz, *Adolf Hitlers englische Vorbilder* (Ketsch am Rhein, 1997), 122–40.

197 Michael Kellogg, *The Russian Roots of Nazism* (New York, 2005); Paul Hanebrink, *A Specter Haunting Europe* (Cambridge, Mass., 2018), 29.

198 Ryback, *Hitler's Private Library*, 69–71; Stefan Link, "Rethinking the Ford-Nazi Connection," *BGHI* (Fall 2011): 135–50.

199 Stefan Kühl, *The Nazi Connection* (New York, 1994), 85; Ian Frazier, "Old Hatreds," *New Yorker*, Aug. 26, 2019, 37.

200 Wolfgang Schieder, *Mythos Mussolini* (Berlin, 2013).

201 Klaus-Peter Hoepke, *Die deutsche Rechte und der italienische Faschismus* (Düsseldorf, 1968); Karl-Egon Lönne, *Faschismus als Herausforderung* (Cologne, 1981); Wolfgang Schieder, "Das italienische Experiment," *HZ* 262 (1996): 73–125; Matthias Damm, *Die Rezeption des Italienischen Faschismus in der Weimarer Republik* (Baden-Baden, 2013).

202 Daniel Siemens, *Stormtroopers* (New Haven, 2017), 14.

203 Simonetta Falasca-Zamponi, *Fascist Spectacle* (Berkeley, Calif., 1997).

204 Walter Benjamin, "The Work of Art in the Age of Mechanical Reproduction" [1936], in *Illuminations* (London, 1973), 243; David Blackbourn, "Politics as Theatre," in *Populists and Patricians* (Boston, 1987), 258–61.

205 Marleen Rensen, "Fascist Poetry for Europe," in *Fascism Without Borders*, ed. Arnd Bauerkämper and Grzegorz Rossolinski-Liebe (New York, 2017), 202.

206 Martin Kitchen, *Fascism* (London, 1976); Roger Griffin, *The Nature of Fascism* (London, 1991); Philip Morgan, *Fascism in Europe, 1918–1945* (London, 2003); Michael Mann, *Fascists* (Cambridge, 2004); Paxton, *Anatomy of Fascism*; Arnd Bauerkämper, *Der Faschismus in Europa 1918–1945* (Stuttgart, 2006).

207 Paul Corner, *Fascism in Ferrara* (New York, 1975); Rudolf Heberle, *Landbevölkerung und Nationalsozialismus* (Stuttgart, 1963); Paxton, *Anatomy of Fascism*, 55–68.

208 Paxton, *Anatomy of Fascism*, 95.

209 Benjamin Carter Hett, *Burning the Reichstag* (New York, 2014).

210 Ian Kershaw, *Hitler*, vol. 1, *1889–1936: Hubris* (New York, 1999), 460, 463; Nikolaus Wachsmann, "The Dynamics of Destruction," in *Concentration Camps in Nazi Germany*, ed. Jane Caplan and Nikolaus Wachsmann (New York, 2010), 17–43.

211 Paul Preston, *The Spanish Holocaust* (New York, 2012).

212 Kitchen, *Fascism*, 7.

213 Johannes Bähr, "The Personal Factor in Business Under National Socialism," in *Business in the Age of Extremes*, ed. Hartmut Berghoff et al. (New York, 2013), 153–71.

214 Adelheid von Saldern, *Mittelstand im "Dritten Reich"* (Frankfurt/Main, 1979).

215 Richard Grunberger, *A Social History of the Third Reich* (Harmondsworth, Eng., 1974), 426.

216 Richard Overy, "Cars, Roads, and Economic Recovery in Germany, 1932–1938," *EHR* 28 (1975): 466–83.

217 Johan Schot and Vincent Lagendijk, "Technocratic Internationalism in the Interwar Years," *JMEH* 6, no. 2 (2008): 196–207.

218 Thomas Zeller, *Driving Germany* (New York, 2006); Thomas Zeller, "Molding the Landscape of Nazi Environmentalism," in *How Green Were the Nazis? Nature, Environment and Nation in the Third Reich*, ed. Franz-Josef Brüggemeier et al. (Athens, Ohio, 2005), 147–70; Rudy Koshar, "Driving Cultures and the Meaning of Roads," in *Beyond the Windshield*, ed. Christof Mauch and Thomas Zeller (Athens, Ohio, 2008), 14–34.

219 Wolfgang König, "Adolf Hitler vs. Henry Ford," *GSR* 27, no. 2 (2004): 249–68; Link, "Rethinking the Ford-Nazi Connection," 147–48; Nolan, *Transatlantic Century*, 143–44; Frank Trentmann, *Empire of Things* (New York, 2016), 290–91; Adam Tooze, *The Wages of Destruction* (New York, 2006), 154–56; Bernhard Rieger, *The People's Car* (Cambridge, Mass., 2013).

220 Victoria de Grazia, *The Culture of Consent* (New York, 1981). The Dopolavoro group was officially known as the National Recreation Club.
221 Shelley Baranowski, *Strength Through Joy* (New York, 2004).
222 Detlev Peukert, *Inside Nazi Germany* (New York, 1989), 195.
223 David Welch, *Propaganda and the German Cinema, 1933–45* (New York, 1983); Eric Rentschler, *The Ministry of Illusion* (Cambridge, Mass., 1996); Sabine Hake, *Popular Cinema of the Third Reich* (Austin, 2001).
224 Trentmann, *Empire of Things*, 291.
225 Corey Ross, "Visions of Prosperity," in *Selling Modernity*, ed. Pamela Swetts et al. (Durham, N.C., 2002), 52–77.
226 Pamela Swetts, *Selling Under the Swastika* (Stanford, Calif., 2014).
227 Jeff Shutts, "'Die erfrischende Pause,'" in Swetts et al., eds., *Selling Modernity*, 151–81.
228 Michael H. Kater, *Culture in Nazi Germany* (New Haven, 2019), 41–46.
229 Noël O'Sullivan, *Fascism* (London, 1983), 143.
230 Victoria de Grazia, *How Fascism Ruled Women* (Berkeley, Calif., 1992), 31.
231 Claudia Koonz, *Mothers in the Fatherland* (New York, 1987), 149, 177–87; de Grazia, *How Fascism Ruled Women*, 91–92.
232 Michelle Mouton, *From Nurturing the Nation to Purifying the Volk* (New York, 2007), 256–57.
233 De Grazia, *How Fascism Ruled Women*, 77–115.
234 Jeremy Noakes, "The Oldenburg Crucifix Struggle of November 1936," in *The Shaping of the Nazi State*, ed. Peter D. Stachura (New York, 1978), 201–33; Johann Neuhäusler, *Kreuz und Hakenkreuz* (Munich, 1946), 118–19.
235 Catrine Clay and Michael Leapman, *Master Race: The Lebensborn Experiment* (London, 1995); Volker Koop, *"Dem Führer ein Kind schenken"* (Cologne, 2007).
236 Atina Grossman, *Reforming Sex* (New York, 1995), 136–65.
237 Peukert, *Inside Nazi Germany*, 217.
238 Young-Sun Hong, "Neither Singular nor Alternative," *Social History* 30, no. 2 (2005): 148.
239 Marc B. Adams, ed., *The Wellborn Science* (New York, 1990).
240 Christian Geulen, "The Common Grounds of Conflict," in *Competing Visions of World Order*, ed. Sebastian Conrad and Dominic Sachsenmaier (New York, 2017), 89.
241 Koonz, *Mothers in the Fatherland*, 150–51.
242 Stefan Kühl, *The Nazi Connection* (New York, 1994).
243 Gisela Bock, *Zwangssterilisation im Nationalsozialismus* (Opladen, 1986); Christian Gansmüller, *Die Erbgesundheitspolitik des Dritten Reiches* (Cologne, 1987); Robert Proctor, *Racial Hygiene* (Cambridge, Mass., 1988); Peter Weingart, Jürgen Kroll, and Kurt Bayertz, *Rasse, Blut und Gene* (Frankfurt/Main, 1988); Paul Weindling, *Health, Race and German Politics Between Unification and National Socialism, 1870–1945* (New York, 1989).
244 Amir Teicher, "Why Did the Nazis Sterilize the Blind?," *CEH* 52, no. 2 (2019): 289–309.
245 Reiner Pommerin, *Sterilisierung der Rheinlandbastarde* (Düsseldorf, 1979); Clarence Lusane, *Hitler's Black Victims* (New York, 2002), 129–43; Robert Bernasconi, "After the German Invention of Race," in *Remapping Black Germany*, ed. Sara Lennox (Amherst, Mass., 2016), 97–100.
246 Robbie Aitken and Eve Rosenhaft, *Black Germany* (New York, 2012), 231–78; Maria I. Diedrich, "Black 'Others'?," in Lennox, ed., *Remapping Black Germany*, 135–48.
247 Tina Campt, "The Motion of Stillness," in Lennox, ed., *Remapping Black Germany*, 154–55; Aitken and Rosenhaft, *Black Germany*, 268.
248 Peukert, *Inside Nazi Germany*, 211.
249 Ute Bruckner-Boroujerdi and Wolfgang Wippermann, "Das 'Zigeunerlage' in Berlin-Marzahn," *Pogrom—Zeitschrift für bedrohte Völker* 130 (1987): 77–80; Wolfgang Benz, "Das Lager Marzahn," in *Die Normalität des Verbrechens*, ed. Helga Grabitz et al. (Berlin, 1994), 260–79.
250 Lisa Pine, *Hitler's "National Community"* (London, 2007), 164.
251 Marion Kaplan, *Between Dignity and Despair* (New York, 1998), 90.
252 David Clay Large, *Nazi Games* (New York, 2007), 76–83.

253 Kaplan, *Between Dignity and Despair*, 125.
254 Helmut Walser Smith, *The Butcher's Tale* (New York, 2002).
255 Hanebrink, *A Specter Haunting Europe*, 101.
256 Bloxham et al., "Europe and the World," 19–20.
257 Cooper, *Behind the Lines*, 43, 46.
258 George Steinmetz, *The Devil's Handwriting* (Chicago, 2007), 226–27, 335–37; Helmut Walser Smith, "The Talk of Genocide, the Rhetoric of Miscegenation," in *The Imperialist Imagination*, ed. Sara Friedrichsmeyer et al. (Ann Arbor, Mich., 1998), 107–23.
259 Steinmetz, *Devil's Handwriting*, 473.
260 Birthe Kundrus, "Von Windhoek nach Nürnberg?," in *Phantasiereiche*, ed. Birthe Kundrus (Frankfurt/Main, 2003), 110–34; Dieter Gosewinkel, "Rückwirkungen des kolonialen Rasserechts?," in Conrad and Osterhammel, eds., *Das Kaiserreich transnational*, 236–56.
261 Jonathan Wiesen, "American Lynching in the Nazi Imaginatiom," *GH* 36, no. 1 (2018): 38–59.
262 James Q. Whitman, *Hitler's American Model* (Princeton, N.J., 2017).
263 Large, *Nazi Games*, 84.
264 Maria Höhn and Martin Klimke, *The Breath of Freedom* (New York, 2010), 13–18.
265 Boyd, *Travellers*, 266. Both the common features and the differences are explored by the contributors to Norbert Finzsch and Dietmar Schirmer, eds., *Identity and Intolerance: Nationalism, Racism, and Xenophobia in Germany and the United States* (Cambridge, 1998). See also Jeffrey Herf, "Comparative Perspectives on Anti-Semitism, Radical Anti-Semitism in the Holocaust and American White Racism," *Journal of Genocide Research* 9, no. 4 (2007): 575–600.
266 Dietrich Orlow, *The Lure of Fascism in Western Europe* (New York, 2009); Bauerkämper and Rossolinski-Liebe, eds., *Fascism Without Borders*.
267 Aristotle Kallis, "Transnational Fascism," in Bauerkämper and Rossolinski-Liebe, eds., *Fascism Without Borders*, 50.
268 Paxton, *Anatomy of Fascism*, 9, 166.
269 Claudia Baldoli, *Exporting Fascism* (New York, 2003); Rinke, "Deutsche Lateinamerikapolitik," 373–74.
270 Monica Fioravanzo, "Italian Fascism from a Transnational Perspective," in Bauerkämper and Rossolinski-Liebe, eds., *Fascism Without Borders*, 245–47.
271 Benjamin G. Martin, *The Nazi-Fascist New Order for European Culture* (Cambridge, Mass., 2016).
272 Iriye, *Cultural Internationalism*, 122; Ricky W. Law, *Transnational Nazism* (Cambridge, 2019); Sarah Panzer, "Prussians of the East," in *Beyond Alterity*, ed. Qinna Shen and Martin Rosenstock (New York, 2014), 52–69.
273 Kallis, "Transnational Fascism," 39, citing the historian Federico Finchelstein.
274 Klas-Göran Karlsson, "The Evil Twins of Modern History?," in *Perspectives on the Entangled History of Communism and Nazism*, ed. Klas-Göran Karlsson et al. (Lanham, Md., 2015), 9–50.
275 Abbott Gleason, *Totalitarianism* (New York, 1995).
276 Ian Kershaw and Moshe Lewin, "Introduction," in *Stalinism and Nazism*, ed. Ian Kershaw and Moshe Lewin (Cambridge, 1997), 3–4.
277 Richard J. Evans, *In Hitler's Shadow* (New York, 1989).
278 Kitchen, *Fascism*, 71–82; Jost Dülffer, "Bonapartism, Fascism and National Socialism," *JCH* 11 (1976): 109–28.
279 Johan Dietsch, "Herbert Norkus and Pavel Morozov as Totalitarian Child Martyrs," in Karlsson et al., eds., *Perspectives on the Entangled History*, 103–18.
280 Sheila Fitzpatrick and Robert Gellately, "Introduction," in *Accusatory Practices*, ed. Sheila Fitzpatrick and Robert Gellately (Chicago, 1997), 11.
281 Emilio Gentile, "Political Religion: A Concept and Its Critics," *Totalitarian Movements and Political Religions* 6 (2005): 19–32; Klaus Vondung, *Deutsche Wege zur Erlösung* (Paderborn, 2013); Siemens, *Stormtroopers*, 104.
282 Ian Kershaw, "'Working Towards the Führer,'" *ConEH* 2, no. 2 (1993): 103–18.
283 Ian Kershaw, *Hitler, 1939–1945: Nemesis* (New York, 2000), 198–99.

284 Christian Gerlach and Nicolas Werth, "State Violence," in *Beyond Totalitarianism*, ed. Michael Geyer and Sheila Fitzpatrick (New York, 2009), 133–79.

285 Fitzpatrick and Gellately, "Introduction," 9; Kershaw and Lewin, eds., *Stalinism and Nazism*; Robert Gellately, *The Gestapo and German Society* (New York, 1990).

286 Anton Weiss-Wendt, "The Intertwined History of Political Violence in the Soviet Union and Nazi Germany," in Karlsson et al., eds., *Perspectives on the Entangled History*, 77–102.

287 Frank Caestecker and Bob Moore, eds., *Refugees from Nazi Germany and the Liberal European States* (New York, 2010).

288 Peter Hayes, *Why?* (New York, 2017), 273.

289 Ann Beaglehole, *Refuge New Zealand* (Dunedin, N.Z., 2013), 30–40.

290 Margit Franz, "Netzwerke der Zwischenkriegszeit als Fluchthilfen aus Zentraleuropa nach Britisch-Indien," in *Networks of Refugees from Nazi Germany*, 38–58 (quotation at 44), https://doi.org/10.1163/9789004322738_004; Margit Franz, *Gateway India* (Graz, Austria, 2015).

291 Steve Hochstadt, *Exodus to Shanghai* (New York, 2012).

292 Leo Spitzer, *Hotel Bolivia* (New York, 1998); Charles W. Arnade, "A German Mining Engineer in Bolivia," *JbLA* 40 (2003): 373–80.

293 Marion Kaplan, *Dominican Haven* (New York, 2008).

294 Hayes, *Why?*, 265–72.

295 Kater, *Culture in Nazi Germany*, 253.

296 Ibid., 256–57.

297 Helga Schreckenbeger, ed., *Die Alchemie des Exils* (Vienna, 2005).

298 Nigel Hamilton, *The Brothers Mann* (New Haven, 1978), 320–30.

299 Stephen Parker, *Bertolt Brecht* (New York, 2014), 305.

300 Ibid., 431–84.

301 Erhard Bahr, *Weimar on the Pacific* (Berkeley, Calif., 2007).

302 Parker, *Brecht*, 443.

303 Anthony Heilbut, *Exiled in Paradise* (Boston, 1984).

304 Laura Fermi, *Illustrious Immigrants* (Chicago, 1968); Lewis Coser, *Refugee Scholars in America* (New Haven, 1984); Corinna Unger, *Reise ohne Wiederkehr?* (Darmstadt, 2009); Axel Fair-Schulz and Mario Kessler, eds., *German Scholars in Exile* (Lanham, Md., 2011).

305 Graham Whitaker, "Philosophy in Exile," in *Ark of Civilization*, ed. Sally Crawford et al. (Oxford, 2017), 341–60.

306 Daniel Snowman, *The Hitler Emigrés* (London, 2002).

307 Andreas W. Daum et al., eds., *The Second Generation* (New York, 2016).

308 James Jupp, ed., *The Australian People* (Cambridge, 2001), 384.

309 Reinhold Andress, "Deutschsprachige Schriftsteller auf Mallorca (1931–6)," *GSR* 24, no. 1 (2001): 115–43.

310 Fritz Pohle, *Das mexikanische Exil* (Stuttgart, 1986).

311 Karin Bruns, "Pfemfert, Franz," in *NDB* 20 (2001): 330.

CHAPTER ELEVEN: THE PIVOTAL DECADE

1 Brendan Simms, *Europe* (New York, 2013), 381

2 Sven Lindqvist, *A History of Bombing* (New York, 2001), 81.

3 E. H. Carr, *The Twenty Years' Crisis* (New York, 1939).

4 Robert Gerwarth, *The Vanquished* (New York, 2016), 214–15.

5 Winson Chu, *The German Minority in Interwar Poland* (New York, 2012).

6 Ian Kershaw, *Hitler*, vol. 2, *1936–1945: Nemesis* (New York, 2000), 122–23.

7 Detlev Peukert, *Inside Nazi Germany* (New York, 1989), 191–92.

8 Claud Cockburn, *I, Claud* (Harmondsworth, Eng., 1967), 206.

9 Adam Tooze, *The Wages of Destruction* (New York, 2006), 65.

10 *Deutschland, Bleiche Mutter* (dir. Helma Sanders-Brahms, 1980).

11 Victor Klemperer, *I Will Bear Witness: A Diary of the Nazi Years, 1933–1941* (New York, 1998), 315. The book was *LTI—Lingua Tertii imperii*.

12 Gerhard Weinberg, *Germany, Hitler, and World War II* (New York, 1995), 2.

13 Jeremy Noakes and Geoffrey Pridham, eds., *Nazism 1919–1945*, vol. 3, *Foreign Policy, War and Racial Extermination* (Exeter, Eng., 1988), 680–87; Kershaw, *Hitler: 1936–1945*, 46–51.

14 On the American fixation, see Andreas Hillgruber, "Hitler und die USA," in *Europas Mitte*, ed. Otmar Franz (Göttingen, 1987), 125–44; Tooze, *Wages of Destruction*; Brendan Simms, *Hitler: A Global Biography* (New York, 2019).

15 Jochen Thies, *Hitler's Plans for Global Domination* (New York, 2012).

16 Helmuth James von Moltke, *Letters to Freya, 1939–1945* (New York, 1990), 45–79.

17 Raffael Scheck, *Hitler's African Victims* (New York, 2006).

18 Kershaw, *Hitler: 1936–1945*, 299.

19 Klemperer, *I Will Bear Witness*, 337.

20 Ulrich Raulff, *Farewell to the Horse* (New York, 2018), 109–10.

21 Moltke, *Letters to Freya*, 187.

22 David Stahel, *Operation Barbarossa and Germany's Defeat in the East* (New York, 2009).

23 Ian Kershaw, *Fateful Choices* (New York, 2007), 382–430.

24 Mark Mazower, *Hitler's Empire* (New York, 2008); Shelley Baranowski, *Nazi Empire* (New York, 2011).

25 David Blackbourn, *The Conquest of Nature: Water, Landscape, and the Making of Modern Germany* (New York, 2006), 298.

26 Daniel Siemens, *Stormtroopers* (New Haven, 2017), 238.

27 Gerhard Hirschfeld, *Nazi Rule and Dutch Collaboration* (New York, 1988); Philippe Burrin, *Living with Defeat* (London, 1996); Joachim Lund, ed., *Working for the New Order* (Copenhagen, 2006); Philip Morgan, *Hitler's Collaborators* (New York, 2018).

28 Benjamin G. Martin, *The Nazi-Fascist New Order for European Culture* (Cambridge, Mass., 2016), 184.

29 Madeleine Herren, "'Outwardly . . . an Innocuous Conference Authority,'" *GH* 20, no. 1 (2002): 67–92.

30 Martin, *The Nazi-Fascist New Order*; Johannes Dafinger, "The Nazi 'New Europe,'" in *Fascism Without Borders*, ed. Arnd Bauerkämper and Grzegorz Rossolinski-Liebe, 264–87; Philipp Gassert, "'No Place for the West,'" in *Germany and "the West,"* ed. Riccardo Bavaj and Martina Steber (New York, 2015), 216–29.

31 Rolf-Dieter Müller, *The Unknown Eastern Front* (New York, 2012).

32 Klaus-Michael Mallmann and Martin Cüppers, *Halbmond und Hakenkreuz* (Darmstadt, 2006); Jeffrey Herf, *Nazi Propaganda for the Arab World* (New Haven, 2009); Francis Nicosia, *Nazi Germany and the Arab World* (New York, 2014).

33 David Motadel, *Islam and Nazi Germany's War* (Cambridge, Mass., 2014), 217–322.

34 John Connelly, "Nazis and Slavs," *CEH* 32, no. 1 (1999): 1–33.

35 On Islam, see Motadel, *Islam and Nazi Germany's War*. On Japan, see Ricky W. Law, *Transnational Nazism* (Cambridge, 2019); Sarah Panzer, "Prussians of the East," in *Beyond Alterity*, ed. Qinna Shen and Martin Rosenstock (New York, 2014).

36 Birthe Kundrus, *"Dieser Krieg ist der grosse Rassenkrieg"* (Munich, 2018), 10.

37 Phillip T. Rutherford, *Prelude to the Final Solution* (Lawrence, Kans., 2007).

38 Winson Chu, Jesse Kauffman, and Michael Meng, "A *Sonderweg* Through Eastern Europe? The Varieties of German Rule in Poland During the Two World Wars," *GH* 31, no. 3 (2013): 318–44.

39 Berndt von Staden, "Erinnerung an die Umsiedlung," *Jahrbuch des baltischen Deutschtums* 41 (1994): 62–75; Robert L. Koehl, *RKFDV* (Cambridge, Mass., 1957), 53–75; Jürgen von Hehn, *Die Umsiedlung der baltischen Deutschen* (Marburg, 1982); Harry Stossun, *Die Umsiedlungen der Deutschen aus Litauen während des Zweiten Weltkrieges* (Marburg, 1993); Valdis O. Lumans, *Himmler's Auxiliaries* (Chapel Hill, N.C., 1993).

40 Chad Bryant, *Prague in Black* (Cambridge, Mass., 2007); Eric C. Steinhart, "Policing the Boundaries of 'Germandom' in the East," *CEH* 43, no. 1 (2010): 85–116; Connelly, "Nazis and Slavs."

41 Christian Ingrao, *The Promise of the East: Nazi Hopes and Genocide, 1939–43* (Medford, Mass., 2019).

42 "'Yes, the "Wild East" is Nerve-racking': The Posen Diaries of Anatomist Hermann Voss," in *Cleansing the Fatherland*, ed. Götz Aly et al. (Baltimore, 1994), 146.

43 Elizabeth Harvey, "Die deutsche Frau im Osten," *Archiv für Sozialgeschichte* 38 (1998): 191–214; Elizabeth Harvey, *Women and the Nazi East* (New Haven, 2003); Wendy Lower, *Hitler's Furies* (Boston, 2013).

44 Frank's report of Dec. 9, 1942, is in A. J. Kaminski, *Nationalsozialistische Besatzungspolitik in Polen und der Tschechoslowakei, 1939–1945: Dokumente* (Bremen, 1975), 89–90.

45 Ibid., 88.

46 Götz Aly and Susanne Heim, *Vordenker der Vernichtung* (Hamburg, 1991), 194; Blackbourn, *Conquest of Nature*, 270–71.

47 Gregor Thum, ed., *Traumland Osten* (Göttingen, 2006).

48 Hans-Dietrich Schultz, *Die deutschsprachige Geographie von 1800 bis 1970* (Berlin, 1980), 226–27.

49 Aly and Heim, *Vordenker der Vernichtung*, 198; Erhard Mäding, *Regeln für die Gestaltung der Landschaft* (Berlin, 1943), 55–62; Herbert Frank, "Dörfliche Planung im Osten," in *Neue Dorflandschaften: Gedanken und Pläne zum ländlichen Aufbau in den neuen Ostgebieten und im Altreich* (Berlin, 1943), 45.

50 Alan Steinweis, "Eastern Europe and the Notion of the 'Frontier' in Germany," *Yearbook of European Studies* 13 (1999): 56–57; Blackbourn, *Conquest of Nature*, 293; Kershaw, *Hitler: 1936–1945*, 434–35; Werner Jochmann, ed., *Monologe im Führer-Hauptquartier, 1941–1944* (Hamburg, 1980), 70, 78, 398–99.

51 Jochmann, ed., *Monologe*, 91.

52 Wolfgang Wippermann, "Das Slawenbild der Deutschen," in *Slawen und Deutsche zwischen Elbe und Oder* (Berlin, 1983), 70, quoting the writer Johann Friedrich Reitemeier.

53 Gert Gröning and Joachim Wolschke-Bulmahn, *Die Liebe zur Landschaft*, pt. 3, *Der Drang nach Osten* (Munich, 1987), 132, citing Himmler's *Der Untermensch* [1942].

54 Blackbourn, *Conquest of Nature*, 299.

55 See Koehl, *RKFDV*; Hans-Dieter Müller, *Hitlers Ostkrieg und die deustche Siedlunspolitik* (Frankfurt/Main, 1991); Bruno Wasser, *Himmlers Raumplanung im Osten* (Basel, 1993); Mechtild Rössler and Sabine Schleiermacher, eds., *Der Generalplan Ost* (Berlin, 1993); Uwe Mai, *"Rasse und Raum"* (Paderborn, 2002).

56 For one example, from hundreds, of the jargon in the General Plan for the East, see Artur von Machui, "Die Landgestaltung als Element der Volkspolitik," *Deutsche Arbeit* 42 (1942): 287–305.

57 Gröning and Wolschke-Bulmahn, *Die Liebe zur Landschaft*; Klaus Fehn, "'Lebensgemeinschaft von Volk und Raum,'" in *Naturschutz und Nationalsozialismus*, ed. Joachim Radkau and Frank Uekötter (Frankfurt/Main, 2003), 207–24; Aly and Heim, *Vordenker der Vernichtung*, 125–88.

58 Blackbourn, *Conquest of Nature*, 262–64, 299.

59 Friedrich Kann, "Die Neuordnung des deutschen Dorfes," in *Neue Dorflandschaften*, 100.

60 Patrick Bernhard, "Hitler's Africa in the East," *JCH* 51, no. 1 (2016): 73, quoting a settlement expert named H. Thierbach.

61 Richard Bergius, "Die Pripetsümpfe als Entwässerungsproblem," *Zeitschrift für Geopolitik* 18 (1941): 668.

62 Bernhard, "Hitler's Africa," 61–90.

63 Stephan Lehnstaedt, *Occupation in the East* (New York, 2017).

64 Lumans, *Himmler's Auxiliaries*, 140.

65 Wendy Lower, *Nazi Empire-Building and the Holocaust in Ukraine* (Chapel Hill, N.C., 2005); Lehnstaedt, *Occupation in the East*; Stephen A. Connor, "Golden Pheasants and Eastern Kings" (PhD diss., Wilfred Laurier University, 2007).

66 Timothy L. Schroer, "Civilization, Barbarism, and the Ethos of Self-Control Among the Perpetrators," *GSR* 35, no. 1 (2012): 39 (emphasis in original).

67 Nicholas Stargardt, *The German War* (New York, 2015), 289.

68 Manfred Weissbecker, "'Wenn hier Deutsche wohnten . . . ,'" in *Das Russlandbild im Dritten Reich*, ed. Hans-Erich Volkmann (Cologne, 1994), 37.

69 Mazower, *Hitler's Empire*, 286.

70 Olivia Manning, *The Balkan Trilogy* (Harmondsworth, Eng., 1981); it consists of *The Great Fortune* (1960), *The Spoilt City* (1962), and *Friends and Heroes* (1965).

71 Hans-Erich Volkmann, "Zur Ansiedlung der Deutsch-Balten," in Volkmann, ed., *Das Russlandbild im Dritten Reich*, 541–42.

72 Tooze, *Wages of Destruction*, 366.

73 Werner Präg and Wolfgang Jacobmeyer, eds., *Diensttagebuch des deutschen Generalgouverneurs in Polen, 1939–1945* (Stuttgart, 1975), 590–92.

74 Christian Gerlach, *Kalkulierte Morde* (Hamburg, 1998); Alex J. Kay, *Exploitation, Resettlement, Mass Murder* (New York, 2006); Gesine Gerhard, "Food and Genocide," *CEH* 18, no. 1 (2009): 45–65; Wigbert Benz, *Der Hungerplan im "Unternehmen Barbarossa" 1941* (Berlin, 2011).

75 Noakes and Pridham, eds., *Nazism 1919–1945*, 3:682–83.

76 Anand Toprani, *Oil and the Great Powers* (New York, 2019), 143.

77 Tooze, *Wages of Destruction*, 412.

78 Dietrich Eichholtz, *War for Oil* (Washington, D.C., 2012); Toprani, *Oil and the Great Powers*; "H-Diplo Roundtable XXI-48 on Anand Toprani, *Oil and the Great Powers: Britain and Germany, 1914–1945*," https://hdiplo.org/to/RT21-48.

79 Tooze, *Wages of Destruction*, 385.

80 Mazower, *Hitler's Empire*, 263, 307–8; Thad Allen, *The Business of Genocide* (Chapel Hill, N.C., 2002).

81 Marc Buggeln, *Arbeit und Gewalt* (Göttingen, 2009).

82 Hilke Günther-Arndt, "Leben ohne Spuren," in *Nationalsozialismus und Zwangsarbeit in der Region Oldenburg*, ed. Katharina Hoffmann and Andreas Lembeck (Oldenburg, 1999), 243.

83 Ulrich Herbert, *A History of Foreign Labor in Germany, 1880–1980* (Ann Arbor, Mich., 1990), 127–92; Mark Spoerer, *Zwangsarbeit unter dem Hakenkreuz* (Stuttgart, 2001).

84 Karl Schlögel, *Das Russische Berlin* (Munich, 2007), 43.

85 Katharina Hoffmann, "Lebensverhältnisse von ausländischen Zwangsarbeiterinnen und Zwangsarbeitern in der Stadt Oldenburg während des Zweiten Weltkrieges," in Hoffmann and Lembeck, eds., *Nationalsozialismus und Zwangsarbeit*, 84.

86 Joachim W. Ziegler, ed., *Die Sintflut im Ruhrtal* (Meinerzhagen, 1983).

87 Mazower, *Hitler's Empire*, 303.

88 Stargardt, *German War*, 293–94.

89 Jill Stephenson, *Hitler's Home Front* (New York, 2009).

90 Birthe Kundrus, "'Verbotener Umgang,'" in Hoffmann and Lembeck, eds., *Nationalsozialismus und Zwangsarbeit*, 155, 168.

91 Rolf Hochhuth, *A German Love Story* (London, 1980).

92 Herbert, *History of Foreign Labor*, 181–84.

93 Schlögel, *Das Russische Berlin*, 45.

94 Wolfram Wette, *The Wehrmacht* (Cambridge, Mass., 2006), 91.

95 Christian Streit, *Keine Kameraden* (Stuttgart, 1978), was the first to write about this.

96 David W. Wildermuth, "Widening the Circle," *CEH* 45, no. 2 (2012): 312.

97 Walter Manoschek, ed., *Die Wehrmacht im Rassenkrieg* (Vienna, 1996); Mark Mazower, *Inside Hitler's Greece* (New Haven, 1993); Lehnstaedt, *Occupation in the East*; Karel C. Berkhoff, *Harvest of Despair* (Cambridge, Mass., 2004); Christian Hartmann et al., eds., *Verbrechen der Wehrmacht* (Munich, 2005); Ben Shepherd, *Terror in the Balkans* (Cambridge, Mass., 2012); Waitman W. Beorn, *Marching into Darkness* (Cambridge, Mass., 2014).

98 Shepherd, *Terror in the Balkans*, 125–42.

99 Pascal Grosse, "What Does German Colonialism Have to Do with National Socialism?," in *Germany's Colonial Pasts*, ed. Eric Ames et al. (Lincoln, Neb., 2005), 115–34; Dirk Schumann, "Europa, der erste Weltkrieg und die Nachkriegszeit," *JMEH* 1 (2003): 23–43.

100 Bryce Sait, *The Indoctrination of the Wehrmacht* (New York, 2019).

101 Omer Bartov, *The Eastern Front, 1941–1945* (New York, 1986).

102 Johannes Hürter, *Hitlers Herrführer* (Berlin, 2006).

103 Moltke, *Letters to Freya*, 179.
104 On Ukraine, see Berkhoff, *Harvest of Despair*; Lower, *Nazi Empire-Building*. See also Baranowski, *Nazi Empire*, 286–89.
105 Mazower, *Hitler's Empire*, 152, 458.
106 Bernhard Chiari, *Alltag hinter der Front* (Düsseldorf, 1998), describes these "combing" operations in Belarus.
107 Rüdiger Overmans, *Deutsche militärische Verluste im Zweiten Weltkrieg* (Munich, 1999).
108 Olaf Groehler, *Bombenkrieg gegen Deutschland* (Berlin, 1990); Richard Overy, *The Bombers and the Bombed* (New York, 2013).
109 Katrin Schreiter, "Morale, Bombs, and the Gender of Affect, 1942–1945," *CEH* 50, no. 3 (2017): 347–74.
110 Kurt Vonnegut, *Slaughterhouse-Five* (New York, 1969); David Irving, *The Destruction of Dresden* (New York, 1963); Lindquist, *History of Bombing*, 5-6, 92-104, 183 (numbered sections 11, 200-18, 391); Igor Primoratz, ed., *Terror from the Sky* (New York, 2010).
111 *Die Grosse Liebe* (dir. Rolf Hansen, 1942).
112 Christian Goeschel, "Suicide at the End of the Third Reich," *JCH* 41, no. 1 (2006): 153–73; Christian Goeschel, *Suicide in Nazi Germany* (New York, 2009).
113 Marlis Steinert, *Hitlers Krieg und die Deutschen* (Düsseldorf, 1970); Stargardt, *German War*, 233–67.
114 Ursula von Kardorff, *Berliner Aufzeichnungen aus den Jahren 1942 bis 1945* (Munich, 1962), 274; Friedrich Reck-Malleczewen, *Diary of a Man in Despair* (London, 2000), 185; Albrecht Haushofer, *Moabit Sonnets* (New York, 1978), 78–79, 94–95; Moltke, *Letters to Freya*, 175, 252.
115 Moltke, *Letters to Freya*, 181; Haushofer, *Moabit Sonnets*, 92–93.
116 Ernst Klee et al., eds., *"The Good Old Days"* (New York, 1991), 43–44.
117 Stargardt, *German War*, 473.
118 Klemperer, *I Will Bear Witness*. The original German title is *Ich will Zeugnis ablegen bis zum letzten*.
119 Zoë Waxman, "Testimony and Representation," in *The Historiography of the Holocaust*, ed. Dan Stone (Basingstoke, Eng., 2004), 488–90.
120 Samuel D. Kassow, *Who Will Write Our History?* (Bloomington, Ind., 2007).
121 Bernard Mark, *The Scrolls of Auschwitz* (Tel Aviv, 1985).
122 Primo Levi, *The Drowned and the Saved* (New York, 1988), 31.
123 Dan Diner, "The Destruction of Narrativity," in *Catastrophe and Meaning*, ed. Moishe Postone and Eric Santner (Chicago, 2003), 67; Jan Surmann, "Restitution Policy and the Transformation of Holocaust Memory," *BGHI* (Fall 2011): 45; Alon Confino, *Foundational Pasts* (New York, 2011).
124 Sergio DellaPergola, "Reflections on the Multinational Geography of Jews After World War II," in *Displacement, Migration, and Integration*, ed. Françoise S. Ouzan and Manfred Gerstenfeld (Boston, 2014), 13–33
125 Kershaw, *Fateful Choices*, 443–44.
126 For Frank's report of Dec. 9, 1942, see Kaminski, *Nationalsozialistische Besatzungspolitik*, 89–90.
127 Christopher R. Browning, *The Origins of the Final Solution* (Jerusalem, 2004), 81–89; Saul Friedländer, *The Years of Extermination* (New York, 2007), 81–82.
128 Browning, *Origins of the Final Solution*, 111–68; Charles G. Roland, *Courage Under Siege* (New York, 1992).
129 Andrew Charlesworth, "The Topography of Genocide," in Stone, ed.., *Historiography of the Holocaust*, 241.
130 Noakes and Pridham, eds., *Nazism 1919–1945*, 3:1069.
131 Friedländer, *Years of Extermination*, 221–23.
132 Ibid., 197; Berkhoff, *Harvest of Despair*, 65–69, 75–77.
133 Peter Longerich, *Heinrich Himmler* (New York, 2012); Schroer, "Civilization, Barbarism, and the Ethos of Self-Control," 33–54.
134 Andrej Angrick, *Besatzungspolitik und Massenmord* (Hamburg, 2003), on *Einsatzgruppe* D.
135 Deborah Dwork and Robert Jan van Pelt, *Holocaust* (New York, 2002), 275–76.

136 Kershaw, *Fateful Choices*, 465.
137 Mark Roseman, *The Wannsee Conference and the Final Solution* (New York, 2002).
138 Simms, *Hitler*, 443.
139 Nikolaus Wachsmann, *KL* (New York, 2015), 288–337; Peter Hayes, *Why?* (New York, 2017), 125–31.
140 Levi, *The Drowned and the Saved*, 74; Tadeusz Borowski, *This Way for the Gas, Ladies and Gentlemen* (1959; repr., New York, 1976), 35.
141 David Rousset, *L'univers concentrationnaire* (Paris, 1946).
142 Inga Clendinnen, *Reading the Holocaust* (New York, 1999), 166.
143 Charlesworth, "Topography of Genocide," 227–28.
144 Hayes, *Why?*, 133.
145 Dwork and van Pelt, *Holocaust*, 285–86.
146 Eliyahu Yones and Susanne Heim, *Die Strasse nach Lemberg* (Frankfurt/Main, 1999); Thomas Sandkühler, "Anti-Jewish Policy and the Murder of the Jews in the District of Galicia, 1941/42," in *National Socialist Extermination Policies*, ed. Ulrich Herbert (New York, 2000), 111–12.
147 Omer Bartov, *Anatomy of a Genocide* (New York, 2018).
148 Friedländer, *Years of Extermination*, 649.
149 Andreas Kossert, "Endlösung on the 'Amber Shore,'" *Leo Baeck Institute Yearbook* 49, no. 1 (2004): 3–22.
150 Bartov, *Anatomy of a Genocide*, 177.
151 Ibid., 198, 208, 227–28.
152 Ulrich Herbert, "Extermination Policy," in Herbert, ed., *National Socialist Extermination Policies*, 32.
153 Christopher Browning, *Ordinary Men* (New York, 1992); Edward Westermann, *Hitler's Police Battalions* (Lawrence, Kans., 2005); Ian Rich, *Holocaust Perpetrators of the German Police Battalions* (New York, 2018).
154 Dieter Pohl, *Die Herrschaft der Wehrmacht* (Munich, 2008), 337.
155 Sönke Neitzel, *Tapping Hitler's Generals* (Barnsley, Eng., 2007), 130.
156 Manoschek, ed., *Die Wehrmacht im Rassenkrieg*; Shepherd, *Terror in the Balkans*; Gerlach, *Kalkulierte Morde*; Angrick, *Besatzungspolitik und Massenmord*.
157 Raul Hilberg, *The Destruction of the European Jews* (Chicago, 1961); Hannah Arendt, *Eichmann in Jerusalem* (New York, 1963).
158 Michael Marrus, *The Holocaust in History* (New York, 1989), 108.
159 Hayes, *Why?*, 178.
160 Primo Levi, *If Not Now, When?* (Harmondsworth, Eng., 1986).
161 Blackbourn, *Conquest of Nature*, 276–309.
162 Hayes, *Why?*, 178–79.
163 Carole Fink, *Marc Bloch* (New York, 1989), 295–321.
164 Renée Poznanski, *Jews in France During World War II* (New Haven, 2001), 421.
165 Sara Bender, *The Jews of Bialystok During World War II and the Holocaust* (Hanover, 2008).
166 Adam Czerniakow, *The Warsaw Diary of Adam Czerniakow*, ed. Raul Hilberg et al. (New York, 1979), 344.
167 Hayes, *Why?*, 187.
168 Friedländer, *Years of Extermination*, 434.
169 Lawrence Langer, "The Dilemma of Choice in the Deathcamps," *Centerpoint* 4, no. 1 (Fall 1980): 53–58.
170 Yehuda Bauer, *Rethinking the Holocaust* (New Haven, 2001), 131–32.
171 Levi, *The Drowned and the Saved*, 36–69.
172 Dan Michman, "Jewish Leadership *in Extremis*," and Robert Rozett, "Jewish Resistance," both in Stone, ed., *Historiography of the Holocaust*, 319–63.
173 For the text of the declaration, see https://www.holocaustremembrance.com/about-us/stockholm-declaration.
174 Dominik Schaller and Jürgen Zimmerer, eds., *The Origins of Genocide* (London, 2013); Douglas Irvin-Erickson, *Raphael Lemkin and the Concept of Genocide* (Philadelphia, 2017).

175 Kevork B. Bardakjian, *Hitler and the Armenian Genocide* (Cambridge, Mass., 1985); Stefan Ihrig, *Justifying Genocide* (Cambridge, Mass., 2016).

176 Margaret Anderson, "Who Still Talked About the Extermination of the Armenians?," *BGHI* (Fall 2011): 10.

177 Marrus, *Holocaust in History*, 22–24; Bauer, *Rethinking the Holocaust*, 45–49; Kershaw, *Fateful Choices*, 432–33.

178 Christopher Browning, *The Path to Genocide* (New York, 1992), ix.

179 Ian Hancock, "Romanies and the Holocaust," in Stone, ed., *Historiography of the Holocaust*, 383–96.

180 Bauer, *Rethinking the Holocaust*, 59–66; Michael Zimmermann, *Rassenutopie und Genozid* (Hamburg, 1996); Guenther Lewy, *The Nazi Persecution of the Gypsies* (New York, 2000).

181 Bauer, *Rethinking the Holocaust*, 39–67; Omer Bartov, *Germany's War and the Holocaust* (Ithaca, N.Y., 2003), 106–7.

182 Aristotle Kallis, "Transnational Fascism," in *Fascism Without Borders*, ed. Arnd Bauerkämper and Grzegorz Rossolinski-Liebe (New York, 2017), 55. See also Aristotle Kallis, *Genocide and Fascism* (New York, 2009).

183 Dwork and van Pelt, *Holocaust*, 177–80, 267–73; Friedländer, *Years of Extermination*, 166–69, 225–27; Radu Ioanid, *The Holocaust in Romania* (Chicago, 2000).

184 Friedländer, *Years of Extermination*, 228–30.

185 Randolph Braham, *The Politics of Genocide* (Detroit, 2000); Hayes, *Why?*, 231–34.

186 Baruch Tenembaum, "Perlasca, the Great Pretender," International Raoul Wallenberg Foundation, https://www.raoulwallenberg.net/saviors/others/perlasca-great-pretender/.

187 Susan Zuccotti, *The Italians and the Holocaust* (New York, 1987).

188 Klee et al., eds., *"The Good Old Days,"* 24–27.

189 Christoph Dieckmann, "The War and the Killing of the Lithuanian Jews," in Herbert, ed., *National Socialist Extermination Policies*, 240–51; Karl-Heinz Schoeps, "Holocaust and Resistance in Vilnius," *GSR* 31, no. 3 (2008): 489–512.

190 Andrew Ezergailis, *The Holocaust in Latvia, 1941–1944* (Washington, D.C., 1996); Anton Weiss-Wendt, *Murder Without Hatred* (Syracuse, 2009), on Estonia; Chiari, *Alltag hinter der Front*, and Gerlach, *Kalkulierte Morde*, on Belarus.

191 Shmuel Spector, *The Holocaust of Volhynian Jews, 1941–1944* (Jerusalem, 1990).

192 Jan T. Gross, *Neighbors* (Princeton, N.J., 2001).

193 Hayes, *Why?*, 249.

194 Bartov, *Anatomy of a Genocide*, 164–66.

195 Levi, *The Drowned and the Saved*, 43.

196 Omer Bartov, *Mirrors of Destruction* (New York, 2000), 65; Michael R. Marrus and Robert O. Paxton, *Vichy France and the Jews* (New York, 1981).

197 W. G. Sebald, *Austerlitz* (New York, 2001), 288–89.

198 Martin Dean, *Robbing the Jews* (New York, 2008).

199 Bob Moore, *Victims and Survivors* (London, 1997).

200 Dwork and van Pelt, *Holocaust*, 156.

201 Hayes, *Why?*, 256.

202 David Kertzer, *The Popes Against the Jews* (New York, 2001); Daniel J. Goldhagen, *A Moral Reckoning* (New York, 2003); Peter Godman, *Hitler and the Vatican* (New York, 2004); Hubert Wolf, *Pope and Devil* (Cambridge, Mass., 2010); Jacques Kornberg, *The Pope's Dilemma* (Toronto, 2015).

203 http://db.yadvashem.org/righteous/family.html?language=en&itemId=4017230.

204 Jean-Claude Favez, *The Red Cross and the Holocaust* (New York, 2000); Gerald Steinacher, *The Red Cross in the Shadow of the Holocaust* (New York, 2017).

205 Thomas Doherty, *Hollywood and Hitler, 1933–1939* (New York, 2013), 199.

206 Ben Urwand, *The Collaboration* (Cambridge, Mass., 2013).

207 Henry Gonshak, *Hollywood and the Holocaust* (Lanham, Md., 2015), 63–77.

208 "Allies Condemn Nazi War on Jews," *NYT*, Dec. 18, 1942.

209 125 Parl. Deb. Lords (5th ser.) (Dec. 17, 1942), col. 608.

210 Bernard Wasserstein, *Britain and the Jews of Europe, 1939–1945* (London, 1979), 259.

211 Marrus, *Holocaust in History*, 162; Yehuda Bauer, *American Jewry and the Holocaust* (Detroit, 1981), 39–40; Deborah Lipstadt, *Beyond Belief* (New York, 1986), 127.

212 Jorge Semprún, *Literature or Life* (New York, 1997), 60, 73, 122.

213 Borowski, *This Way for the Gas*, 164.

214 Schlögel, *Das Russische Berlin*, 38.

215 Wolfgang Jacobmeyer, "The 'Displaced Persons' in West Germany, 1945–1951," in *The Uprooted*, ed. Göran Rystad (Lund, Swe., 1990), 271–88; Mark Wyman, *DPs* (Ithaca, N.Y., 1998); Anna Holian, *Between National Socialism and Soviet Communism* (Ann Arbor, Mich., 2011).

216 Winson Chu, "Ethnic Cleansing and Nationalization on the German-Polish and German-Czech Borderlands," *GSR* 41, no. 1 (2018): 149.

217 Atina Grossmann, *Jews, Germans, and Allies* (Princeton, N.J., 2007).

218 Gerald Daniel Cohen, *In War's Wake* (New York, 2012).

219 Marion Dönhoff, *Namen, die keiner mehr nennt* (Düsseldorf, 1962); Neil MacGregor, *Germany: Memories of a Nation* (London, 2014), 476–91.

220 Wolfgang Benz, ed., *Die Vertreibung der Deutschen aus dem Osten* (Frankfurt/Main, 1985); Norman M. Naimark, *Fires of Hatred* (Cambridge, Mass., 2001), 108–38; Benjamin Frommer, *National Cleansing* (New York, 2005); R. M. Douglas, *Orderly and Humane* (New Haven, 2012); Hugo Service, *Germans to Poles* (New York, 2013); Eagle Glassheim, *Cleansing the Czechoslovak Borderlands* (Pittsburgh, 2016).

221 Peter Gatrell, *The Making of the Modern Refugee* (New York, 2013), 85–196; Philipp Ther and Ana Siljak, eds., *Redrawing Nations* (Lanham, Md., 2001); Pertti Ahonen et al., *People on the Move* (New York, 2008).

222 Manuel Borutta and Jan C. Jansen, eds., *Vetriebene und Pieds-Noirs in Postwar Germany and France* (New York, 2016).

223 Franz J. Bauer, "Aufname und Eingliederung der Flüchtlinge und Vertriebenen," in Benz, ed., *Die Vetreibung*, 207.

224 Meryn McLaren, "'Out of the Huts Emerged a Settled People,'" *GH* 28, no. 1 (2010): 26, 37–41.

225 Andreas Kossert, *Kalte Heimat* (Munich, 2008); Ian Connor, *Refugees and Expellees in Post-War Germany* (New York, 2007).

226 Leo Harting in *A Small Town in Germany* (London, 1968).

227 Helmut J. Schneider, ed., *Deutsche Landschaften* (Darmstadt, 1981), 625, citing Max Frisch, *Tagebuch, 1946–49*.

228 "Your Job in Germany" (dir. Frank Capra [uncredited], 1945), Military Film Unit of the U.S. War Department.

229 Florian Alix-Nicolai, "Ruins and Visions," *The Modern Language Review* 109, no. 1 (2014): 67–68.

230 Jeremy Treglown, "So Glad You Saw the King, Darling," *Times Literary Supplement*, Oct. 13, 1995.

231 Ulrike Weckel, *Beschämende Bilder* (Stuttgart, 2012).

232 Konrad H. Jarausch and Michael Geyer, *Shattered Past* (Princeton, N.J., 2003), 278–79; Tony Judt, *Postwar* (New York, 2005), 21.

233 Stargardt, *German War*, 577.

234 Norman M. Naimark, *The Russians in Germany* (Cambridge, Mass., 1995), 69–140.

235 Harald Jähner, *Wolfszeit* (Berlin, 2019).

236 Stig Dagerman, *German Autumn* (London, 1988), 27–28.

237 Nancy F. Cott, *Fighting Words* (New York, 2020), 195–96, 297–98.

238 Victor Gollancz, *In Darkest Germany* (London, 1947), 15.

239 Alix-Nicolai, "Ruins and Visions," 58.

240 Ibid., 68.

241 Michael R. Marrus, ed., *The Nuremberg War Crimes Trial, 1945–46* (Boston, 1997), 21.

242 Michael Biddiss, "Victor's Justice," *History Today* 45 (1995): 44.

243 Marrus, ed., *Nuremberg War Crimes Trial*, 28.

244 Levi, *The Drowned and the Saved*, 168.

245 Kevin John Heller, *The Nuremberg Military Tribunals and the Origins of International Criminal Law* (New York, 2011).

246 Hayes, *Why?*, 329.

247 Norbert Frei, *Adenauer's Germany and the Nazi Past* (New York, 2002), 94.

248 Clemens Vollnhals and Thomas Schlemmer, eds., *Entnazifizierung* (Munich, 1991), 13.

249 Lutz Niethammer, *Die Mitläuferfabrik* (Bonn, 1982).

250 Vollnhals and Schlemmer, eds., *Entnazifizierung*, 27.

251 Naimark, *Russians in Germany*, 172.

252 Sergej Mironenko et al., eds., *Sowjetische Speziallager in Deutschland 1945 bis 1950*, vol. 1, *Studien und Berichte* (Berlin, 1998).

253 See Wendell Wilkie, *One World* (New York, 1943).

254 https://avalon.law.yale.edu/20th_century/trudoc.asp.

255 Timothy Garton Ash, *In Europe's Name* (New York, 1993), 23–24, raises this issue in slightly different form.

256 Odd Arne Westad, *The Cold War* (New York, 2017), 108–9; W. R. Smyser, *From Yalta to Berlin* (New York, 1999), 32–42.

257 Brian Blouet, *Geopolitics and Globalization in the Twentieth Century* (London, 2001), 130–31.

258 Simms, *Europe*, 376.

259 Mazower, *Hitler's Empire*, 561.

260 Carolyn Eisenberg, *Drawing the Line* (New York, 1996), 172, 175.

261 Walter LaFeber, ed., *The Origins of the Cold War, 1941–1947* (New York, 1971), 131–34.

262 Eisenberg, *Drawing the Line*, 277–317.

263 Ibid., 305–13.

264 https://www.oecd.org/general/themarshallplanspeechatharvarduniversity5june1947 .htm.

265 For Ambassador Smith's letter to General Eisenhower of Dec. 10, 1947, see Eisenberg, *Drawing the Line*, 359.

266 Westad, *Cold War*, 115–16.

267 Eisenberg, *Drawing the Line*, 382.

268 Daniel F. Harrington, *Berlin on the Brink: The Blockade, the Airlift, and the Early Cold War* (Lexington, Ky., 2012).

269 Charles S. Maier, "Who Divided Germany?," *DH* 22, no. 3 (1998): 482–83.

270 Omer Bartov, "Germany's Unforgettable War," *DH* 25, no. 3 (2001): 407.

271 LaFeber, ed., *Origins of the Cold War*, 56–58.

272 Tony Smith, *America's Mission* (Princeton, N.J., 1994), 146–76.

273 Mary Fulbrook, *A History of Germany, 1918–2014* (Malden, Mass., 2015), 6.

274 Wilfried Loth, *Stalins ungeliebtes Kind* (Berlin, 1994). Naimark, *Russians in Germany*, sees Stalin as acting indecisively.

275 Smyser, *Yalta to Berlin* 97.

276 Lewis J. Edinger, *Kurt Schumacher* (Stanford, Calif., 1965), 135.

277 Gareth Pritchard, *Niemandsland* (New York, 2012).

CHAPTER TWELVE: THE GERMAN QUESTION ANSWERED

1 Holger Nehring, *Politics of Security* (New York, 2013), 54.

2 Christa Wolf, *Der geteilte Himmel* (1963; repr., Munich, 1973), 111.

3 Donna Harsch, "Footnote or Footprint? The German Democratic Republic in History," *BGHI* (Spring 2010): 13.

4 See Frank Biess, *Homecomings* (2006); Christiane Wienand, *Returning Memories* (Rochester, N.Y., 2015); Jörg Arnold, *The Allied Air War and Urban Memory* (New York, 2011); Jeanette Madarasz-Lebenhagen, "Perceptions of Health After World War II: Heart Disease and Risk Factors in East and West Germany," in *Becoming East German*, ed. Mary Fulbrook and Andrew I. Port (New York, 2013), 121–40.

5 Carlos Gaspar, "Aron and the Cold War: 'Brother Enemies,'" in *The Companion to Raymond Aron*, ed. José Colen and Elisabeth Dutartre-Michaut (New York, 2015), 45–57.

6 Hope Harrison, *Driving the Soviets Up the Wall* (Princeton, N.J., 2003).

7 The Rogers–Kissinger telephone conversation took place on Dec. 20, 1970: see William Glenn Gray, "Paradoxes of *Ostpolitik*," *CEH* 39, no. 3–4 (2016): 438.

8   William E. Griffith, *The Ostpolitik of the Federal Republic of Germany* (Cambridge, Mass., 1978), 127–28; Jeremi Suri, *Power and Protest* (Cambridge, Mass., 2003), 216–26; Holger Klitzing, "To Grin and Bear It: The Nixon Administration and Ostpolitik," in *Ostpolitik, 1969–1974*, ed. Carole Fink and Bernd Schaefer (New York, 2009), 80–110.

9   Hans Kundnani, *The Paradox of German Power* (New York, 2015), 33.

10 Frederic S. Pearson, *The Global Spread of Arms* (Boulder, Colo., 1994), 17 (table 1.1).

11 Marshall Michel, "F–104: Germany's Widow Maker," Spangdahlem Air Base, July 30, 2015, https://www.spangdahlem.af.mil/News/Commentaries/Display/Article/730527/f-104-germanys-widow-maker/.

12 Peter Speiser, "The British Army of the Rhine and the Germans (1945–1957)" (PhD diss., University of Westminster, 2012), 113.

13 Norman M. Naimark, *The Russians in Germany* (Cambridge, Mass., 1995), 506n267.

14 Maria Höhn, *GIs and Fräuleins* (Chapel Hill, N.C., 2002).

15 Speiser, "British Army of the Rhine," 172.

16 Ibid., 168.

17 Ibid., 141.

18 Eric Burton, "Decolonization, the Cold War, and Africans' Routes to Higher Education Overseas," *JGH* 15, no. 1 (2020): 186.

19 Heide Fehrenbach, *Race After Hitler: Black Occupation Children in Postwar Germany and America* (Princeton, N.J., 2005).

20 David E. Murphy et al., *Battleground Berlin* (New Haven, 1997), 113, 183–237, 261–63.

21 Christopher Andrew and Oleg Gordievsky, *KGB* (New York, 1991), 448–49.

22 Markus Wolf, *The Man Without a Face* (New York, 1997); Kristie Macrakis et al., eds., *East German Foreign Intelligence* (London, 2010).

23 Dean Vuletic, *Postwar Europe and the Eurovision Song Contest* (New York, 2018).

24 Colleen Elizabeth Anderson, "'Two Kinds of Infinity': East Germany, West Germany, and the Cold War Cosmos, 1945–1995" (PhD diss., Harvard University, 2017).

25 Lucie Filipova, *Erfüllte Hoffnung: Städtepartnerschaften als Instrument der deutsch-französischen Versöhnung 1950–2000* (Göttingen, 2015); Wilbur Zelinsky, "The Twinning of the World," *Annals of the Association of American Geographers* 81, no. 1 (1991): 1–31.

26 Johannes Dieter Steinert, "Drehscheibe Westdeutschland," in *Deutsche im Ausland—Fremde in Deutschland*, ed. Klaus Bade (Munich, 1992), 386–92; Alexander Freund, "Introduction," in *Beyond the Nation? Immigrants' Local Lives in Transational Cultures*, ed. Alexander Freund (Toronto, 2012), 4; Dirk Hoerder, *Geschichte der deutschen Migration* (Munich, 2010), 104–5; Josef Vondra, *German Speaking Settlers in Australia* (Melbourne, 1981), 14–15.

27 Rita Chin, "Guest Workers, Migration and the Unexpected Return of Race," in *After the Nazi Racial State*, ed. Rita Chin et al. (Ann Arbor, Mich., 2009), 83.

28 Rita Chin, *The Guest Worker Question in Postwar Germany* (New York, 2007), 1–7.

29 Klaus J. Bade, *Ausländer, Aussiedler, Asyl* (Munich, 1994), 41–54.

30 Stephen Castles and Mark J. Miller, *The Age of Migration* (New York, 2003), 73.

31 Frank Trentmann, *Empire of Things* (New York, 2016), 328.

32 John Gillingham, *European Integration, 1950–2003* (New York, 2003), 12.

33 Volker Berghahn, *The Americanization of West German Industry, 1945–1973* (New York, 1986).

34 Luuk van Middelaar, *The Passage to Europe* (New Haven, 2013), 49–54.

35 Bernhard Rieger, "From People's Car to New Beetle," *Journal of American History* 97, no. 1 (2010): 91, citing *Schwäbische Landeszeitung*, Apr. 6, 1957. See also Bernhard Rieger, *The People's Car* (Cambridge, Mass., 2013).

36 Michael Wildt, *Am Beginn der "Konsumgesellschaft"* (Hamburg, 1994); Axel Schildt, *Moderne Zeiten* (Hamburg, 1995); Jonathan Wiesen, "Miracles for Sale," in *Consuming Germany in the Cold War*, ed. David F. Crew (New York, 2003), 151–78.

37 Göran Therborn, *European Modernity and Beyond* (Newbury Park, Calif., 1995), 142 (table 7.7).

38 Axel Schildt et al., eds., *Dynamische Zeiten* (Hamburg, 2003).

39 Victoria de Grazia, *Irresistible Empire* (Cambridge, Mass., 2005), 359.

40 "Supermarkt," *Die Zeit*, June 20, 1957.

41 Joachim Scholtyseck, *Otto Beisheim* (Paderborn, 2020).

42 Jan Logemann, "European Imports?," *BGHI* 52 (Spring 2013): 113–33.

43 Joshua Derman, *Max Weber in Politics and Social Thought* (New York, 2012).

44 Mary Nolan, "Americanization? Europeanization? Globalization? The German Economy Since 1945," *BGHI* 54 (Spring 2014): 49–63.

45 De Grazia, *Irresistible Empire*, 367.

46 Christoph Klessmann, *Zwei Staaten, eine Nation* (Göttingen, 1988), 492–93.

47 Heide Fehrenbach, *Cinema in Democratizing Germany* (Chapel Hill, N.C., 1995).

48 Uta Poiger, "Rebels with a Cause?," in *The American Impact on Postwar Germany*, ed. Reiner Pommerin (Providence, 1995), 104; Uta Poiger, *Jazz, Rock, and Rebels* (Berkeley, Calif., 2000); Angelika Linke and Jakob Tanner, eds., *Attraktion und Abwehr* (Cologne, 2006); Petra Galle, *RIAS Berlin und Berliner Rundfunk, 1945–1949* (Münster, 2003).

49 Hanna Schissler, ed., *The Miracle Years* (Princeton, N.J., 2001), especially Uta Poiger, "A New 'Western' Hero? Reconstructing German Masculinity in the 1950s," and Kaspar Maase, "Establishing Cultural Democracy: Youth, 'Americanization,' and the Irresistible Rise of Popular Culture."

50 https://ghdi.ghi-dc.org/sub_document.cfm?document_id=833&language=english.

51 Julia Sneeringer, *A Social History of Early Rock 'n' Roll in Germany* (New York, 2018).

52 Michael J. Budds, "The New World Enriches the Old," in *Jazz and the Germans*, ed. Michael J. Budds (Hillsdale, N.Y., 2002), 16–17.

53 Poiger, *Jazz, Rock, and Rebels*, 137–67.

54 Kaspar Maase, "Amerikanisierung von Unten," in *Amerikanisierung*, ed. Alf Lüdtke et al. (Stuttgart, 1996), 301.

55 Nolan, "Americanization?," 55.

56 Fehrenbach, *Cinema in Democratizing Germany*, 159–61.

57 Jeff R. Schutts, "Born Again in the Gospel of Refreshment?," in Crew, ed., *Consuming Germany in the Cold War*, 121–50.

58 David Blackbourn, *The Conquest of Nature: Water, Landscape, and the Making of Modern Germany* (New York, 2006), 336.

59 Mark Landsman, *Dictatorship and Demand* (Cambridge, Mass., 2005).

60 Anne Kaminsky, "'True Advertising Means Promoting a Good Thing Through a Good Form,'" in *Selling Modernity*, ed. Pamela E. Swett et al. (Durham, N.C., 2007), 262–86.

61 Eli Rubin, *Synthetic Socialism* (Chapel Hill, N.C., 2008).

62 Jonathan R. Zatlin, "The Vehicle of Desire," *GH* 15, no. 3 (1997): 358–80.

63 Dieter Staritz, *Geschichte der DDR 1949–1985* (Frankfurt/Main, 1985), 157–62; Dieter Hoffmann and Kristie Macrakis, eds., *Naturwissenschaft und Techik in der DDR* (Berlin, 1997).

64 David Edgerton, "The 'White Heat' Revisited: The British Government and Technology in the 1960s," *Twentieth Century British History* 7, no. 1 (1996): 53–82.

65 Therborn, *European Modernity*, 143 (table 7.8).

66 Ina Merkel, ed., *Wunderwirtschaft* (Cologne, 1996); Ina Merkel, "Working People and Consumption Under Really-Existing Socialism," *International Labor and Working-Class History* 55 (Spring 1999): 92–111.

67 Judd Stitziel, "On the Seam Between Socialism and Capitalism," in Crew, ed., *Consuming Germany in the Cold War*, 51–85.

68 Katherine Pence, "'A World in Miniature,'" in Crew, ed., *Consuming Germany in the Cold War*, 37.

69 Ibid.

70 Andreas Daum, "America's Berlin 1945–2000," in *Berlin*, ed. Frank Trommler (Washington, D.C., 2000), 61.

71 Ibid., 49.

72 Andreas Daum, *Kennedy in Berlin* (New York, 2008).

73 Edith Sheffer, *Burned Bridge* (New York, 2011), 218–21; Astrid Eckert, *West Germany and the Iron Curtain* (New York, 2019), 85–123.

74 Greg Castillo, "Housing as Transnational Provocation in Cold War Berlin," in *Transnationalism and the German City*, ed. Jeffry Diefendorf and Janet Ward (New York,

2014), 125–26; Emily Pugh, *Architecture, Politics, and Identity in Divided Berlin* (Pittsburgh, 2014), 37–38.

75 Castillo, "Housing as Transnational Provocation," 133.

76 Arnd Bauerkämper et al., eds., *Demokratiewunder* (Göttingen, 2005).

77 David Childs, "East German Foreign Policy," *International Journal* 32, no. 2 (1977): 347–49; Stefan Berger and Norman LaPorte, *Friendly Enemies* (New York, 2010).

78 Barbara Keys, *Globalizing Sport* (Cambridge, Mass., 2006).

79 Molly W. Johnson, *Training Socialist Citizens* (Boston, 2008), 165–202.

80 Uta Balbier, *Kalter Krieg auf der Aschenbahn* (Paderborn, 2007), 74–87.

81 Alan McDougall, "Playing the Game," in Fulbrook and Port, eds., *Becoming East German*, 257–76.

82 Andrea Orzoff, "Citizen of the *Staatsoper*," *CEH* 54, no. 2 (2021): 343–48.

83 Stephen Parker, *Bertolt Brecht* (New York, 2014), 583.

84 Ibid., 594.

85 Paul Betts, "Die Bauhaus-Legende," in Lüdtke et al., eds., *Amerikanisierung*, 270–90.

86 Frank Trommler, *Kulturmacht ohne Kompass* (Cologne, 2014), 659–60 and illus. on 657.

87 Harald Kimpel, *Documenta, Mythos und Wirklichkeit* (Cologne, 1997).

88 Stephen Brockmann, *A Critical History of German Film* (Rochester, N.Y., 2010), 213–33.

89 Rosemary Wakeman, "Was There an Ideal Socialist City?," in Diefendorf and Ward, eds., *Transnationalism and the German City*, 111–12; Jon Maciuika, "Whose Schlossplatz?," *BGHI*, supp. 7 (2011): 15–18.

90 Jost Hermand, "Attempts to Establish a Socialist Musical Culture in the Soviet Occupation Zone and the Early German Democratic Republic," in *A Sound Legacy?*, ed. Edward Larkey (Washington, D.C., 2000), 13–14.

91 David G. Tompkins, *Composing the Party Line* (West Lafayette, Ind., 2013).

92 Poiger, *Jazz, Rock, and Rebels*, 158.

93 Trommler, *Kulturmacht ohne Kompass*, 660–72.

94 Ibid., 652.

95 Ibid., 684.

96 Johannes Lill, *Völkerfreundschaft im Kalten Krieg?* (Cologne, 2014); Karrin Hanshew, "Cohesive Difference: Germans and Italians in a Postwar Europe," *CEH* 52, no. 1 (2019): 67–69.

97 Sara Lorenzini, *Global Development: A Cold War History* (Princeton, N.J., 2019).

98 Wolf, *Man Without a Face*, 342–45.

99 William Glenn Gray, *Germany's Cold War* (Chapel Hill, N.C., 2003), 2.

100 Katherine Pence, "The East and West German Scramble for Africa," German Studies Association seminar paper (2013); Ulf Engel and Hans Georg Schleicher, *Die beiden deutschen Staaten in Afrika zwischen Konkurrenz und Koexistenz, 1945–1990* (Hamburg, 1998), 37.

101 Katherine Pence, "Showcasing Cold War Germany in Cairo," *JCH* 47, no. 1 (2012): 69–95.

102 Brendan Simms, *Europe* (New York, 2013), 443.

103 Tony Judt, *Postwar* (New York, 2005), 292.

104 Matthew Connelly, *A Diplomatic Revolution* (New York, 2002), 121, 134, 163, 202–3.

105 Timothy Scott Brown, *West Germany and the Global Sixties* (New York, 2013), 21–22.

106 Rui Lopes, *West Germany and the Portuguese Dictatorship* (New York, 2014), 145–46.

107 Susanna Schrafstetter, "A Nazi Diplomat Turned Apologist for Apartheid," *GH* 28, no. 1 (2010): 44–66.

108 Wolf, *Man Without a Face*, 290–93; Quinn Slobodian, *Foreign Front* (Durham, N.C., 2012), 63–64.

109 Bastian Hein, *Die Westdeutschen und die Dritte Welt* (Munich, 2006), 97–103.

110 Young-Sun Hong, *Cold War Germany, the Third World, and the Global Humanitarian Regime* (New York, 2015).

111 Jeremi Suri, *Power and Protest* (Cambridge, Mass., 2003).

112 Hans Kundnani, *Utopia or Auschwitz* (New York, 2009), 64.

113 Slobodian, *Foreign Front*, 9.

114 Nehring, *Politics of Security*, 184–85.

115 Martin Klimke, *The Other Alliance* (Princeton, N.J., 2011).

116 Simms, *Europe*, 446.

117 David Blackbourn, "In the Opposite Direction," *London Review of Books*, Mar. 25, 2010.

118 Dorothee Weitbrecht, *Aufbruch in die Dritte Welt* (Göttingen, 2012).

119 Slobodian, *Foreign Front*, 72–73; Brown, *West Germany and the Global Sixties*, 39.

120 Slobodian, *Foreign Front*, 101–34, 241n94.

121 Astrid Haas, "A Raisin in the East: African American Civil Rights Drama in GDR Scholarship and Theater Practice," in *Germans and African Americans*, ed. Larry A. Greene and Anke Ortlepp (Jackson, Miss., 2011), 166–84.

122 Katrina Hagen, "Ambivalence and Desire in the East German 'Free Angela Davis' Campaign," in *Comrades of Color*, ed. Quinn Slobodian (New York, 2015), 157–87.

123 H. Glenn Penny, *Kindred by Choice* (Chapel Hill, N.C., 2013), 183–86.

124 Jennifer Ruth Hosek, *Sun, Sex, and Socialism* (Toronto, 2012), 55–75.

125 Ibid., 151–72; Wolf, *Man Without a Face*, 345–46.

126 Gerd Horten, "Sailing in the Shadow of the Vietnam War," *GSR* 36, no. 3 (2013): 558.

127 Anne E. Gorsuch and Diane Koenker, eds., *The Socialist Sixties* (Bloomington, Ind., 2013).

128 Hong, *Cold War Germany*, 51–82.

129 Quinn Slobodian, "The Maoist Enemy," *JCH* 15, no. 3 (2016): 635–59.

130 Sarah Pugach, "African Students and the Politics of Race and Gender in the German Democratic Republic, 1957–1990," in Slobodian, ed., *Comrades of Color*, 131–56; Hong, *Cold War Germany*, 200–14.

131 Hagen, "Ambivalence and Desire," 171–72.

132 Mary Fulbrook, *Anatomy of a Dictatorship* (New York, 1995), 193–99; Timothy S. Brown, "'1968' East and West," *AHR* 114, no. 1 (2009): 84–96.

133 Katherine White, "East Germany's Red Woodstock," *CEH* 51, no. 4 (2018): 585–610.

134 Ibid., 600.

135 Inga Emmerling, *Die DDR und Chile (1961–1989)* (Berlin, 2013); Felix A. Jiménez Botta, "From Antifascism to Human Rights," Zeitgeschichte Digital, 2020, 63–90, https://doi.org/10.14765/zzf.dok-1770; Petra Vráblíková, "The Path of Solidarity," https://blog.hostwriter.org/the-path-of-solidarity/.

136 On similar tensions regarding Chile in the United Kingdom, see Christopher Moores, "Solidarity for Chile, Transnational Activism, and the Evolution of Human Rights," *Journal of Social History and the History of Social Movements* 57 (2017): 115–36.

137 Samuel Moyn, *The Last Utopia* (Cambridge, Mass., 2010); Akira Iriye et al., eds., *The Human Rights Revolution* (New York, 2012).

138 *Die Legende von Paul und Paula* (dir. Heiner Carow, 1973); Brockmann, *Critical History of German Film*, 258–73.

139 Stefan Aust, *Baader-Meinhof* (New York, 2009), 181–83, 199–200.

140 Klitzing, "To Grin and Bear It," 107.

141 Carole Fink and Bernd Schaefer, "Conclusion," in Fink and Schaefer, eds., *Ostpolitik*, 269.

142 See Amit das Gupta, "India and *Ostpolitik*," Milan Kosanovic, "'You Have the Political Prestige and We the Material Opportunity': Tito and Brandt and Toto Between *Ostpolitik* and Non-Alignment," and Meung-Hoan Noh, "West German *Ostpolitik* and Korean South-North Relations," all in Fink and Schaefer, eds., *Ostpolitik*.

143 Timothy Garton Ash, *In Europe's Name* (New York, 1993), makes the case eloquently.

144 Bernd Schaefer, "Ostpolitik, 'Fernostpolitik,' and Sino-Soviet Rivalry," in Fink and Schaefer, eds., *Ostpolitik*, 129–47.

145 Trommler, *Kulturmacht ohne Kompass*, 601, 708–9.

146 Simms, *Europe*, 480.

147 Federico Romero, "Cross-border Population Movements," in *The Dynamics of European Integration*, ed. William Wallace (London, 1990), 171–76.

148 Trommler, *Kulturmacht ohne Kompass*, 711.

149 Wolf, *Man Without a Face*, 293.

150 Ibid., 294–98.

151 Jason Verber, "True to the Politics of Frelimo?," in Slobodian, ed., *Comrades of Color*, 188–210.
152 Bernd Schaefer, "Socialist Modernization in Vietnam, in Slobodian, ed., Comrades of Color, 95-116."
153 Frank Bösch, *Zeitenwende 1979* (Munich, 2019), 187–228.
154 Andrew Port is completing a study of Germans and postwar genocides.
155 Ian Buruma, *The Wages of Guilt* (New York, 1994), 156.
156 Luc Boltanski, *Distant Suffering* (New York, 1999).
157 Lora Wildenthal, *The Language of Human Rights in West Germany* (Philadelphia, 2012), 101-31.
158 Erika Harzer, *Aufbruch nach Nicaragua* (Berlin, 2009).
159 Ned Richardson-Little, "Between Dictatorship and Dissent," *BGHI* 56 (Spring 2015): 69–82.
160 Odd Arne Westad, *The Cold War* (New York, 2017), 390–91; Oliver Bange and Gottfried Niedhart, eds., *Helsinki 1975 and the Transformation of Europe* (New York, 2008).
161 Simms, *Europe*, 464; Garton Ash, *In Europe's Name*, 259–67.
162 Sarah B. Snyder, *Human Rights Activism and the End of the Cold War* (Cambridge, 2011), 71–72; Garton Ash, *In Europe's Name*, 195, 260.
163 John Torpey, *Intellectuals, Socialism, and Dissent* (Minneapolis, 1995), 64–70; Eberhard Neubert, *Geschichte der Opposition in der DDR* (Berlin, 1997), 170–244.
164 *Deutschland im Herbst* (multiple directors, 1978).
165 Michael Müller, *Die RAF-Stasi-Connection* (Berlin, 1992); Wolf, *Man Without a Face*, 308–11.
166 Aust, *Baader-Meinhof*, 433; "34 jähriger Mann von Polizei erschossen," *Stuttgarter Nachrichten*, June 26, 1972.
167 Sonja Glaab, ed., *Medien und Terrorismus* (Berlin, 2007).
168 Heinrich Böll, *Die verlorene Ehre der Katharina Blum* (Cologne, 1974).
169 "Forum: 1977," *GH* 25, no. 3 (2007): 401–21.
170 Belinda Davis, "Activism from Starbuck to Starbucks, or Terror: What's in a Name," *Radical History Review* 85 (2003): 50.
171 Karrin Hanshew, *Terror and Democracy in West Germany* (New York, 2012).
172 Quinn Slobodian, "Guerrilla Mothers and Distant Doubles," Zeitgeschiche Digital, 2015, 39–65, https://doi.org/10.14765/zzf.dok-1461.
173 Yanara Schmacks, "'Motherhood Is Beautiful,'" *CEH* 53, no. 4 (2020): 823–25, 832.
174 Stephen Milder, *Greening Democracy* (New York, 2017).
175 Frank Uekötter, *The Greenest Nation?* (Cambridge, Mass., 2014), 95; Dolores L. Augustine, *Taking on Technocracy* (New York, 2018), 93–125.
176 Andrew S. Tompkins, *Better Active Than Radioactive!* (New York, 2016); Hanspeter Kriesi et al., *New Social Movements in Western Europe* (1995), 145–64.
177 Michael Bess, *The Light-Green Society* (Chicago, 2003), 102; Andrew S. Tompkins, "Transnationality as a Liability? The Anti-Nuclear Movement at Malville," *Revue Belge de Philologie et d'Histoire*, 89, no. 3–4 (2011): 1365–79.
178 Albrecht Lorenz and Ludwig Trepl, "Das Avocado-Syndrom," *Politische Ökologie* 11 (1993–1994): 17–24.
179 Rolf Zundel, "Anschlag auf die Parteien oder Ventil der Verdrossenheit?," *Die Zeit*, Aug. 5, 1977.
180 Blackbourn, *Conquest of Nature*, 332.
181 Uekötter, *Greenest Nation?*, 118.
182 Belinda Davis, "The Gender of War and Peace," *Mitteilungsblatt des Instituts für Soziale Bewegungen* (Fall 2004): 99–130.
183 Frank Zelko, *Make It a Green Peace* (New York, 2013).
184 Stephen Milder, "Thinking Globally, Acting (Trans)-Locally: Petra Kelly and the Transnational Roots of West German Green Politics," *CEH* 43, no. 2 (2010): 301–26.
185 Sidney Tarrow, *Strangers at the Gate* (New York, 2012), 181–99.
186 Blackbourn, *Conquest of Nature*, 342–43.
187 Ibid., 341–42.
188 Augustine, *Taking on Technocracy*, 185–211.

189 Merrill E. Jones, "Origins of the East German Environmental Movement," *GSR* 16, no. 2 (1993): 243.

190 Nathan Stolzfus, "Public Space and the Dynamics of Environmental Action," *Archiv für Sozialgeschichte* 43 (2003): 385–403.

191 For the Family Code of the German Democratic Republic (1965), see https://ghdi .ghi-dc.org/sub_document.cfm?document_id=1096.

192 Donna Harsch, *Revenge of the Domestic* (Princeton, N.J., 2007); Josie McLellan, *Love in the Time of Communism* (New York, 2011); Paul Betts, *Within Walls* (New York, 2010).

193 McLellan, *Love in the Time of Communism*, 129.

194 David Featherstone, *Solidarity* (London, 2012), 162–65.

195 John Sandford, *The Sword and the Ploughshare* (London, 1983); Brendan R. Ozawa-De Silva, "Peace, Pastors, and Politics," *Journal of Church and State* 47, no. 3 (2005): 503–29.

196 Fulbrook, *Anatomy of a Dictatorship*, 204.

197 Bärbel Bohley, *Englisches Tagebuch 1988*, ed. Irena Kukutz (Berlin, 2011), 89–90.

198 McLellan, *Love in the Time of Communism*, 107–12; Marianne Krüger-Potratz, *Anderssein gab es nicht* (Münster, 1991); Eva-Maria Elsner and Lothar Elsner, *Zwischen Nationalismus und Internationalismus* (Rostock, 1994).

199 Peggy Piesche, "Making African Diasporic Pasts Possible," in *Remapping Black Germany*, ed. Sara Lennox (Amherst, Mass., 2016), 229.

200 Bösch, *Zeitenwende 1979*, 225, citing Harry Waibel, *Der gescheiterte Antifaschismus der SED—Rassismus in der DDR* (Frankfurt/Main, 2014), 128–30.

201 Bade, *Ausländer, Aussiedler, Asyl*, 95–99.

202 Chin, "Guest Workers, Migration and the Unexpected Return of Race," 85–87.

203 Chin, *Guest Worker Question*, 147.

204 Bade, *Ausländer, Aussiedler, Asyl*, 100–1.

205 Jutta Roitsch, "Kühn warnt Deutsche vor einen neuen rassischen Hochmut," *Frankfurter Rundschau*, Dec. 17, 1979.

206 "Heidelberger Manifest," *Frankfurter Rundschau*, Mar. 4, 1982.

207 R. W. Apple Jr., "Mrs. Thatcher Touches a Nerve and British Racial Tension Is Suddenly a Political Issue," *NYT*, Feb. 22, 1978.

208 Chin, *Guest Worker Question*, 150–54.

209 Bade, *Ausländer, Aussiedler, Asyl*, 93.

210 Klaus J. Bade, ed., *Das Manifest der 60* (Munich, 1994).

211 Chin, *Guest Worker Question*, 191–216.

212 Dieter Oberndörfer, *Die offene Republik* (Freiburg i. B., 1991), 67.

213 Sarah Thomsen Vierra, *Turkish Germans in the Federal Republic of Germany* (New York, 2018).

214 Chin, *Guest Worker Question*, 140.

215 Ibid., 210–12.

216 Niall Ferguson et al., eds., *The Shock of the Global* (Cambridge, Mass., 2010).

217 Anselm Doering-Manteuffel and Lutz Raphael, *Nach dem Boom* (Göttingen, 2008).

218 Uekötter, *Greenest Nation?*, 90.

219 Sebastian Haffner, "Geht es nicht auch ohne Öl?," *Stern*, Nov. 15, 1973.

220 William G. Gray, "Floating the System," *DH* 31, no. 2 (2007): 295–323.

221 Daniel Bell, *The Coming of Post-Industrial Society* (New York, 1973).

222 Peter C. Caldwell and Karrin Hanshew, *Germany Since 1945* (London, 2018), 175; Daniel Sargent, "The United States and Globalization in the 1970s," in Ferguson et al., eds., *Shock of the Global*, 61.

223 Simon Donig, "'As for the East European Producers, East Germany Provided the Only Success Story,'" in *Historische Erinnerung im Wandel*, ed. Heiner Timmermann (Berlin, 2007), 164.

224 Jeffrey Kopstein, *The Politics of Economic Decline in East Germany, 1945–1989* (Chapel Hill, N.C., 1997), 93–94.

225 Jonathan R. Zatlin, *The Currency of Socialism* (New York, 2007), 127.

226 Charles S. Maier, *Dissolution* (Princeton, N.J., 1997), 77, 95.

227 Westad, *Cold War*, 515.

228 Donig, "'As for the East European Producers,'" 153.

229 Ibid., 135–66; Maier, *Dissolution*, 73–76; Zatlin, *Currency of Socialism*, 182–86; Kristie Makrakis, *Seduced by Secrets* (Cambridge, 2008).

230 Eli Rubin, *Amnesiopolis* (New York, 2016).

231 Zatlin, *Currency of Socialism*, 299.

232 Ibid., 244, 262–64.

233 Maier, *Dissolution*, 60.

234 Stephen Kotkin, "The Kiss of Debt," in Ferguson et al., eds., *Shock of the Global*, 80–93.

235 Zatlin, *Currency of Socialism*, 93.

236 Mary E. Sarotte, *The Collapse* (New York, 2014), 105–19.

237 Ibid., 127–53.

238 Thomas Lindenberger, "What's in This Footnote? World History!," *BGHI* (Spring 2010): 31, quoting Timothy Garton Ash.

239 Bohley, *Englisches Tagebuch*, 122.

240 David Turnock, "Environmental Problems and Policies in East Central Europe," *Geo-Journal* 55, no. 2 (2001): 489.

241 Susanne Buckley-Zistel and Daniel Stahl, "Ulrike Poppe," *Quellen zur Geschichte der Menschenrechte*, 2014, https://www.geschichte-menschenrechte.de/personen/ulrike-poppe.

242 Bohley, *Englisches Tagebuch*, 44, 49, 63, 100, 108.

243 Ibid., 17.

244 Seth Howes, "'Killersatellit' and *Randerscheinung: Punk and the Prenzlauer Berg*," *GSR* 36, no. 3 (2013): 588.

245 Dick Hebdige, *Subculture: The Meaning of Style* (New York, 2004), 106–7.

246 Jeff Hayton, "Crosstown Traffic," *ConEH* 26, no. 2 (2017): 353–77; Tim Mohr, *Burning Down the Haus* (Chapel Hill, N.C., 2018).

247 Hayton, "Crosstown Traffic," 365.

248 See, for example, the fake banknote reproduced in Neubert, *Geschichte der Opposition in der DDR*, 640–41.

249 Hayton, "Crosstown Traffic," 371; Edward Larkey, *Rotes Rockradio* (Münster, 2007).

250 Rory MacLean, *Berlin* (London, 2014), 329–47.

251 Simms, *Europe*, 486.

252 Garton Ash, *In Europe's Name*, 4.

253 Timothy Garton Ash, *The Magic Lantern* (New York, 1990), 47–60.

254 Garton Ash, *In Europe's Name*, 370–71; Sarotte, *Collapse*, 21–31.

255 Garton Ash, *In Europe's Name*, 108; *NYT*, June 21, 1989.

256 Christian Joppke, *East German Dissidents and the Revolution of 1989* (London, 1995), 138.

257 Albert O. Hirschman, *Exit, Voice, and Loyalty* (Cambridge, Mass., 1970).

258 Fulbrook, *Anatomy of a Dictatorship*, 251.

259 Albert O. Hirschman, "Exit, Voice, and the Fate of the German Democratic Republic," *World Politics* 45, no. 2 (1993): 173–202; Joppke, *East German Dissidents*, 139.

260 For the founding appeal of the New Forum, see Konrad H. Jarausch and Volker Gransow, eds., *Uniting Germany* (Providence, 1994), 39–41.

261 Joppke, *East German Dissidents*, 140–43; Neubert, *Geschichte der Opposition in der DDR*, 859–63.

262 Garton Ash, *Magic Lantern*, 67–69; Joppke, *East German Dissidents*, 144–59; Fulbrook, *Anatomy of a Dictatorship*, 253–57; Maier, *Dissolution*, 135–46; Sarotte, *Collapse*, 32–82.

263 Interview in Ernst Elitz, *Sie waren dabei* (Stuttgart, 1991), 40, 47–49.

264 Garton Ash, *In Europe's Name*, 344.

265 Mary Fulbrook, *A History of Germany, 1918–2014* (Malden, Mass., 2015), 271–76; Konrad H. Jarausch, *The Rush to German Unity* (New York, 1994).

266 Sarotte, *Collapse*, 162.

267 Ibid., 161.

268 Fulbrook, *Anatomy of a Dictatorship*, 262–63.

269 Elitz, *Sie waren dabei*, 45.

270 Garton Ash, *In Europe's Name*, 346.

271 Peter Schjeldahl, "Berlin, 1989," in *Hot, Cold, Heavy, Light* (New York, 2019), 182.

272 Eckert, *West Germany and the Iron Curtain*, 73.

273 Zatlin, *Currency of Socialism*, 338.

274 A. M. Rosenthal, "Germany: Hidden Words," *NYT*, Feb. 4, 1990; Charles Krautham-mer, "The German Revival," *New Republic*, Mar. 26, 1990.

275 Smyser, *Yalta to Berlin*, 358.

276 Westad, *Cold War*, 593–94.

277 Garton Ash, *In Europe's Name*, 348.

278 Smyser, *Yalta to Berlin*, 361.

279 Garton Ash, *In Europe's Name*, 348.

280 Frank Elbe, "The Diplomatic Path to German Unity," *BGHI* (Spring 2010): 35.

281 Martin Sabrow, "1990: An Epochal Break in German History," *BGHI* (Spring 2017): 31–42.

282 Jennifer L. Allen, "Against the 1989–1990 Ending Myth," *CEH* 52, no. 1 (2019): 127.

283 Axel Schildt, *Ankunft im Westen* (Frankfurt/Main, 1999); Heinrich August Winkler, *Germany: The Long Road West*, vol. 2 (New York, 2007).

284 Bohley, *Englisches Tagebuch*, 138–39.

285 Westad, *Cold War*, 618, 624.

286 Stephen F. Szabo, *Germany, Russia, and the Rise of Geo-economics* (New York, 2015), 61–82.

EPILOGUE

1 Melissa Eddy, "In Foreign Policy U-Turn, Germany Ups Military Spending and Arms Ukraine: In Turnaround, Germany Vows Military Boost," *NYT*, Feb. 28, 2022.

2 "Europe's Reluctant Hegemon," *Economist*, June 15, 2013.

3 David Childs, "Peter Struck," *Independent*, Jan. 2, 2013.

4 Martin Chulow and Helen Pidd, "Curveball: How US Was Duped by Iraqi Fantasist Looking to Topple Saddam," *Guardian*, Mar. 18, 2011.

5 "Germany Approves Deployment in Sudan," *DW*, Apr. 22, 2005; Steve Crawshaw, "Germany Finds Inner Peace at Last," *Financial Times*, May 4, 2005.

6 Jeffrey Herf, "Berlin Ghosts," *New Republic*, Mar. 23, 2011.

7 Jochen Bittner, "Germany's Path to Pacifism," *NYT*, July 25, 2019.

8 Omer Bartov, *Germany's War and the Holocaust* (Ithaca, N.Y., 2003), 218; Jeffrey Peck, *Being Jewish in the New Germany* (New Brunswick, N.J., 2006); Klaus J. Bade, *Aus-länder, Aussiedler, Asyl* (Munich, 1994), 98–102.

9 Tony Judt, *Postwar* (New York, 2005), 676.

10 "Europe's Reluctant Hegemon."

11 Hans Kundnani, "Germany as a Geo-economic Power," *Washington Quarterly* 34, no. 3 (2011): 31–45.

12 Georg Blume, "Deutschland hat nie bezahlt!" (interview with Thomas Piketty), *Zeit-Online*, June 25, 2015, https://www.zeit.de/zustimmung?url=https%3A%2F%2Fwww.zeit.de%2F2015%2F26%2Fthomas-piketty-schulden-griechenland.

13 Aditya Chakrabortty, "Which Is the No. 1 Problem Economy in Europe?," *Guardian*, Aug. 9, 2011.

14 Oliver Nachtwey, *Germany's Hidden Crisis* (London, 2018).

15 "Germany Home to Growing 'Super Rich' Class," *The Local.de*, June 1, 2011, https://www.thelocal.de/20110601/35407/.

16 Hans-Ulrich Wehler, *Land ohne Unterschichten?* (Munich, 2010); Hans-Ulrich Wehler, *Die Deutschen und der Kapitalismus* (Munich, 2014).

17 Keith Bradsher and Jack Ewing, "Biden's China Plans Run into Germany: The City of Taicang, with Its Sauerkraut and Pretzels, Illustrates Deep Ties That Merkel Is Loath to Disrupt," *NYT*, Mar. 23, 2021; "Dissecting the Miracle," *Economist*, June 15, 2013.

18 Anna Sauerbrey, "Germany's China Problem," *NYT*, Jan. 17, 2019.

19 Rob Edwards, "Dirty Tricks in a Dirty Business," *New Scientist*, Feb. 18, 1995: Jennifer Clapp, "The Toxic Waste Trade with Less-Industrialised Countries," *Third World Quar-terly*, 15, no. 3 (1994): 505–18.

20 "German Arms in the Yemen War," *DW*, Feb. 26, 2019, https://learngerman.dw.com/en/in-yemen-war-coalition-forces-rely-on-german-arms-and-technology/a-47684609.

21 Laura Gitschier and Alexander Neubacher, "Greenwashing After the Phase-

out," *Spiegel-Online*, Sept. 15, 2011, https://www.spiegel.de/international/business/greenwashing-after-the-phase-out-german-energy-revolution-depends-on-nuclear-imports-a-786048.html; David Blackbourn, "The Culture and Politics of Energy in Germany: A Historical Perspective," *Rachel Carson Center Perspectives* 2013, no. 4, https://doi.org/10.5282/rcc/5624.

22 Steve Fosdick and Peter Marsh, *Football Hooliganism* (Cullompton, Eng., 2013), 51–52, 183–84.

23 Karrin Hanshew, "Cohesive Difference: Germans and Italians in a Postwar Europe," *CEH* 52, no. 1 (2019): 77–84; Nina Berman, *Germans on the Kenyan Coast* (Indianapolis, 2017).

24 Rita Chin, *The Guest Worker Question in Postwar Germany* (New York, 2007), 254–58.

25 Antonia von der Behrens, "Lessons from Germany's NSU Case," *Race and Class* 59, no. 4 (2018): 84–91.

26 Jürgen Kocka, "A New Special Path for Germany," *Telos*, June 28, 2016.

27 https://borgenproject.org/human-trafficking-in-germany/.

28 https://www.dw.com/en/germanys-new-bundestag-who-is-who-in-parliament/a–41082379.

29 Chin, *Guest Worker Question*, 216–42.

30 https://heimatkunde.boell.de/de/2008/11/18/deutsch-tuerkisch-deutsch-tuerkisch-wie-tuerkisch-ist-die-deutsch-tuerkische-literatur.

31 *Gegen die Wand* (dir. Fatih Akin, 2004).

32 Peter Schjeldahl, *Hot, Cold, Heavy, Light* (New York, 2019), 106.

33 https://www.sadlerswells.com/pina-bausch/The-Singular-Art-of-Pina-Bausch/.

34 Ralf Niemczyk, "Crossover Diversity," *magazine-Deutschland.de*, Oct.–Nov. 2010, 62–64.

35 "Who the Fuck Is Franz Münterfering?," *Der Tagesspiegel*, July 7, 2002.

36 Quinn Slobodian and Michelle Sterling, "Sacking Berlin: How Hipsters, Expats, Yummies, and Smartphones Ruined a City," *The Baffler*, Aug. 23, 2013.

37 Brian Ladd, *Ghosts of Berlin* (Chicago, 1997), 175.

38 Nikolaus Wachsmann, *KL* (New York, 2015), 14.

ILLUSTRATION CREDITS

———

INDEX

Page numbers in *italics* indicate illustrations.